Countries, Peoples & Cultures

Western Europe

Countries, Peoples & Cultures

Western Europe

First Edition

Volume 3

Editor

Michael Shally-Jensen, PhD

SALEM PRESS
A Division of EBSCO Information Services, Inc.
Ipswich, Massachusetts

Grey House
Publishing

Publisher's Cataloging-In-Publication Data
(Prepared by The Donohue Group, Inc.)

Western Europe / editor, Michael Shally-Jensen, PhD. – First edition.
  edition.

    pages: illustrations; cm. – (Countries, peoples & cultures ; v. 3)

  Includes bibliographical references and index.
  ISBN: 978-1-61925-796-2 (v. 3)
  ISBN: 978-1-61925-800-6 (set)

    1. Europe, Western – History. 2. Europe, Western – Economic conditions. 3. Europe, Western – Social life and customs. 4. Europe, Western – Religion. I. Shally-Jensen, Michael.

D1053 .W47 2015
940

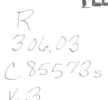
First Printing
PRINTED IN CANADA

Contents

Publisher's Note vii

Introduction ix

Western Europe 1
Andorra 3
Austria 21
Belgium 41
Denmark 61
England 81
Finland 103
France 123
Germany 141
Greece 161
Iceland 181
Ireland, Republic of 201
Italy 221
Liechtenstein 243
Luxembourg 255
Malta 273
Monaco 291
Netherlands 307
Northern Ireland 327
Norway 347
Portugal 367
San Marino 387
Scotland 405
Spain 425
Sweden 445
Switzerland 467
Vatican City 487
Wales 499

Appendix One: World Governments 519
Commonwealth 520
Communist 522
Confederation/Confederacy 524
Constitutional Monarchy 526
Constitutional Republic 528
Democracy 530

Dictatorship/Military Dictatorship..532
Ecclesiastical...534
Failed State...536
Federal Republic 538
Federation 540
Monarchy 542
Parliamentary Monarchy...544
Parliamentary Republic...546
Presidential...548
Republic 550
Socialist...552
Sultanate/Emirate...554
Theocratic Republic 556
Totalitarian 558
Treaty System 560

Appendix Two: World Religions..563
African Religious Traditions...564
Bahá'í Faith...570
Buddhism 576
Christianity..583
East Asian Religions 590
Hinduism..597
Islam...604
Jainism 611
Judaism 617
Sikhism 624

Index 631

Publisher's Note

Countries, Peoples & Cultures: Western Europe is the third volume of a new 9-volume series from Salem Press. *Central & South America* and *Central, South, and Southeast Asia* were published earlier this year. *Countries, Peoples & Cultures* offers valuable insight into the social, cultural, economic, historical and religious practices and beliefs of nearly every country around the globe.

Following the extensive introduction that summarizes this politically and physically complex part of the world, this volume provides 20-page profiles of the 27 countries that make up western Europe. Each includes colorful maps—one highlighting the country's location in the world, and one with its major cities and natural landmarks—and a country flag, plus 10 categories of information: General Information; Environment & Geography; Customs & Courtesies; Lifestyle; Cultural History; Culture, Society; Social Development; Government; and Economy. Each profile also includes full color photographs, valuable tables of information including fun "Do You Know?" facts, and a comprehensive Bibliography.

Each country profile combines must-have statistics, such as population, language, size, climate, and currency, with the flavor and feel of the land. You'll read about favorite foods, arts & entertainment, youth culture, women's rights, health care, and tourism, for a comprehensive picture of the country, its people, and their culture.

Appendix One: World Governments, focuses on 21 types of governments found around the world today, from Commonwealth and Communism to Treaty System and Failed State. Each government profile includes its Guiding Premise, Structure, Citizen's Role, and modern-day examples.

Appendix Two: World Religions, focuses on 10 of the world's major religions from African religious traditions to Sikhism. Each religion profile includes number of adherents, basic tenets, major figures and holy sites, and major rites and celebrations.

The nine volumes of *Countries, Peoples & Cultures* are: *Central & South America; Central, South & Southeast Asia; Western Europe; Eastern Europe; Middle East & North Africa; East & Southern Africa; West & Central Africa; North America & the Caribbean;* and *East Asia & the Pacific.*

Introduction

Geographically, Europe is the western extension of the earth's largest landmass, Eurasia. *Western* Europe, in turn, is simply the western portion of Europe, as distinguished from central and eastern Europe. There are, however, irregularities in this scheme. In particular, the Greek peninsula, extending into the Mediterranean Sea, is often considered part of western Europe (for historical reasons) despite the fact that Greece abuts Balkan states that traditionally are treated as lying outside the region. This fact underscores the cultural and historical connections among the countries of western Europe and how these countries contrast with those located in other parts of the continent. In the modern era, the western/non-western divide corresponds with the boundaries established during the Cold War, when the Soviet Union led a bloc of Soviet-influenced countries in the eastern and central regions and the non-communist countries of the western region stood in opposition to them. Thus, today's western Europe consists of Austria, Belgium, France, Germany, Lichtenstein, Luxembourg, Netherlands, and Switzerland in the center of the region; Denmark, Finland, Iceland, Sweden, Norway, the United Kingdom, and Ireland in the north; and Andorra, Greece, Italy (plus Vatican City), Malta, Monaco, San Marino, Spain, and Portugal in the south.

Geographical Features

The landforms of Europe present a wide diversity, from below-sea-level flatlands and steep fjords along the Atlantic to blocky plateaus and high, crested mountains farther inland. The Alps, near the center, form a curve running northward and eastward along the borders of Italy, France, Switzerland, Germany, Austria, and into eastern Europe. At Mont Blanc, near the junction of the French, Swiss, and Italian frontiers, the range reaches its highest point: 15,780 ft (4,810 m). Between France and Spain lie the Pyrenees, and

in southern Spain, the Sierra Nevada. Forming the spine of Italy are the Apennines, while in Greece the Pindus occupy much of the central area. There are only limited north-south openings through the high mountain barrier extending from Iberia (i.e., Spain and Portugal) to Greece, mainly in the Rhone River Valley in France and in a section northeast of the Pyrenees known as the Carcassonne. Besides these, mostly mountain passes allow movement between the north and south. Farther afield, in Scandinavia, the Kjölen range forms a backbone between Sweden and Norway, its glacier-carved valleys composing the famous fjords.

The remainder of western Europe is a collection of plains and low hills lying between the mountainous areas. In the Netherlands and Belgium, the western edge of the plain has been reclaimed from the sea by means of dikes and pumping stations. The North Sea, which is relatively shallow, fills the opening between the mainland and the British Isles, just as the English Channel divides northern France and southern Britain. In the south, the deep Mediterranean extends, via the Adriatic and Aegean seas, along the coasts of Italy and Greece, respectively. In northern Europe, the Norwegian and Baltic seas flank the Scandinavian Peninsula. Numerous rivers flow across the region and into these seas. Among the more notable are the Rhine and Elbe, in Germany; the Seine and Rhone, in France; the Po and Tiber, in Italy; the Tagus and Douro in Spain and Portugal; and the Thames in England. The lakes of western Europe, which have been carved out through glaciation, are concentrated in Scandinavia and at the edges of the Alps.

Languages

For all of its physical diversity, western Europe is in many ways just as diverse with respect to its people. Linguistically, for example, two main branches of the family of human languages are represented here: Germanic languages and Romance languages. However, numerous sub-branches, and sub-sub-branches, exist within these two broad groups; and a small number of languages from altogether different branches are present, as well. Throughout European history, linguistic differences have played a major role in the growth of nationalism and the development of distinct national cultures.

In the Germanic group fall the modern Scandinavian languages (Icelandic, Norwegian, Swedish, and Danish) along with German itself (which once was comprised of far more tongues and dialects than is the case today) and Dutch and English. The latter is a blending of the speech of Angles, Saxons, and Jutes, who invaded and settled Britain in the 5th century; a strain of French was added following the 11th-century Norman conquest of England. In even more ancient times, yet surviving to some extent today, an entirely separate Celtic group of languages was spoken both on the mainland (in Gaul, Iberia, and elsewhere) and in the British Isles. Today, members of this group—Irish, Welsh, and Breton (from Brittany, France)—survive mostly through concerted efforts at language preservation and revival. The language of Finland, Finnish, belongs to a separate family, Uralic, to which Estonian also belongs.

The Romance languages have their origins in the Latin of the Roman Empire, in particular the spoken variety known as Vulgar Latin. With the fall and breakup of the empire in the 5th and 6th centuries, language unity began to disintegrate and distinct languages, albeit with a common root, arose throughout southern Europe and France. Today the main Romance languages in western Europe are French, Italian, Spanish, and Portuguese. A variety of more localized Romance languages—Catalan and Galician, in Spain; Provençal, in France; Sicilian and Sardinian, in Italy—continue to survive, as does the entirely distinct Basque language of the Basque people inhabiting northeastern Spain. Greek, too, stems from a separate branch, the Hellenic languages, and has one of the longest documented histories (34 centuries) of any language. Maltese,

the language of Malta, is a Semitic language unrelated to the others noted here, yet modern Maltese does include many Italian, Sicilian, and English words.

History

By the 2nd millennium BCE, most of the population groups that would become the peoples and cultures of classical European history were in place. The Minoan and Mycenaean civilizations of the Bronze Age gave way to the city-states of ancient Greece, which formed a loose empire that reached its height in the 4th century BCE. Together with influences from the ancient Near East, Greek culture laid the foundation for European civilization. By the mid-2nd century BCE, the Greeks had come under the control of the Romans, who built a great empire and extended it into parts of Europe as far afield as the British Isles. During the 4th and 5th centuries CE, Germanic peoples from northern Europe repeatedly attacked the western half of the Roman Empire, leading to its collapse in 456. (The eastern empire, or Byzantine Empire, remained alive.) Filling the void, the Franks, a Germanic-speaking people of Gaul (France), asserted authority over much of continental Europe, particularly under the rule of Charlemagne (c. 745–814), who established the Holy Roman Empire. Farther north, in Scandinavia, the Viking Age was launched under various conquering chieftains and persisted into the mid-1000s; the Vikings would leave their mark in Britain and northern France as well as throughout the northern region. In an effort to expand the influence of Christianity, the Roman Catholic Church sanctioned a series of violent Crusades beginning in 1095 and lasting nearly 200 years. Although the Catholic faith was spread, no lasting unity was achieved; defeats outside of Europe (in Egypt and elsewhere) led to the end of the Crusades.

With the Renaissance of the 15th and 16th centuries, the fields of science, discovery, theology, and art were advanced. In this context, the Protestant Reformation under Martin Luther (1483–1586) got under way, producing a separation from the Roman Catholic Church in western and northern Europe. In England, King Henry VIII (1491–1547) proclaimed an independent Church of England and seized Papal lands and property. In Spain and Portugal, the Muslim Moors were expelled and investments were made in overseas exploration, including in the Americas. As European colonial powers arose, so too did wars at home over influence, authority, and control. A long series of wars and revolutions through most of the 17th century dovetailed with the beginning of the Enlightenment, an intellectual movement in which conceptions of God, nature, humanity, and the state were questioned and the power of reason was advanced; developments in science, mathematics, philosophy, art, and politics ensued. Enlightenment ideas contributed to the downfall of France's Ancient Régime during the French Revolution (1787–1789) and the spread of democratic principles. Given the progress witnessed in so many areas and the riches flowing in from colonial empires, a new world of innovation in industry emerged, dubbed the Industrial Revolution. Through it, machine manufacturing and the factory system began to displace traditional agrarianism and fostered European commercial and military dominance over much of the world in the 19th century.

Tensions among the European imperial powers grew, and by the early 20th century they were divided politically to the point of war, which came in July 1914. The Great War (World War I) pitted the United Kingdom, France, Russia, and, later, the United States as Allied Powers against Germany, Austria-Hungary, Italy, and, later, the Ottoman Empire as the Central Powers. The destruction and loss of lives was unprecedented. Among other things, the war, which the Allies succeeded in winning near the end of 1918, effectively ended monarchical rule in Europe and created a crop of new nations in central and eastern Europe. The terms of peace imposed a heavy burden on Germany, including the forfeiture of its overseas lands and the payment of reparations. With the onset of the Great Depression in 1929, conditions were ripe for the likes of Adolf Hitler (1889–1945) and his Nazi Party to take control of the German government in 1933. War mongering and aggressive moves ensued, leading to World War II in 1939. Again it was the British Commonwealth, France (in principle), the Soviet Union, and the United States allied against Germany, Italy, and, now, Japan. The devastation was even greater than that of World War I, and it included concentration camps in which millions of Jews and other targets of the Nazis were killed. By the end of the war, in 1945, the center of world power had passed from the nations of western Europe to the United States and the Soviet Union.

The period after the war saw the rise of communism in Eastern Europe under the Soviet Union and its satellite states. Most non-communist European countries aligned themselves with the United States under the North Atlantic Treaty Organization (NATO) and worked to develop the European Economic Community, a trade alliance which helped produce the broader European Union (EU) in 1993. By then, communism had collapsed in the Soviet Union and elsewhere, and Germany, which had been divided, was reunited. Immigration, both internally and abroad, became an issue throughout the region as populations adapted to the changed political economy. Although the EU emerged as a major force on the continent, it and its member nations were severely impacted by the worldwide recession beginning in 2008. Since then some states, notably Greece and the United Kingdom, have questioned the value of EU membership. Today, governance in Europe is a unique blend of state leadership and EU guidance and oversight.

Michael Shally-Jensen, PhD

Bibliography

Granata, Cora, and Cheryl A. Koos, eds. *The Human Tradition in Modern Europe: 1750 to the Present.* Lanham, MD: Rowman and Littlefield, 2008.

Innes, Matthew. *An Introduction to Early Medieval Western Europe, 300–900: The Sword, the Plow, and the Book.* London: Routledge, 2007.

Judt, Tony. *Postwar: A History of Europe since 1945.* New York: Penguin Press, 2005.

Kümin, Beat A. *The Communal Age in Western Europe, c. 1100–1800: Towns, Villages, and Parishes in Pre-Modern Society.* Basingstoke: Palgrave Macmillan, 2013.

Lacqueur, Walter. *After the Fall: The End of the European Dream and the Decline of a Continent.* New York: Thomas Dunne Books, 2012.

Lindemann, Albert S. *A History of Modern Europe: From 1815 to the Present.* Malden, MA: Wiley Blackwell, 2013.

Salmi, Hannu. *Nineteenth Century Europe: A Cultural History.* Cambridge, UK: Polity, 2008.

WESTERN EUROPE

An ancient chapel in Andorra/Stock photo © Bareta

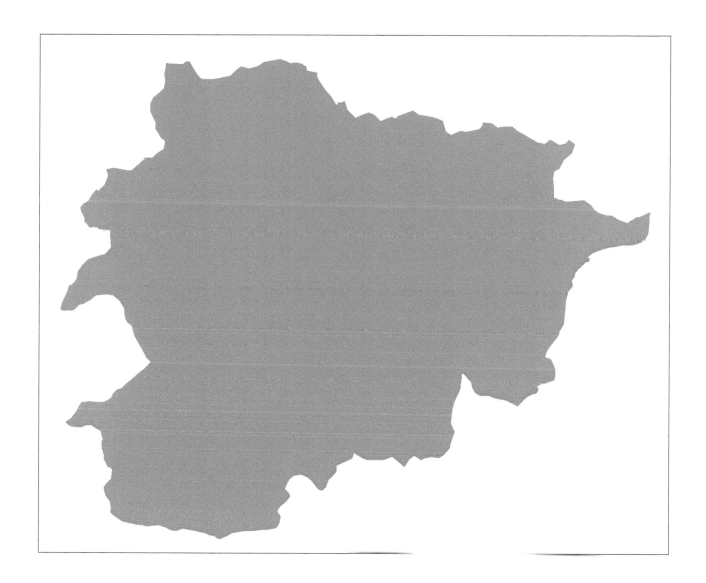

ANDORRA

Introduction

The Principality of Andorra is a tiny nation located in the Pyrenees Mountains, between France and Spain. It is part of the cultural region known as the "Catalan Countries" (Paisos Catalans), which includes parts of eastern Spain, southern France, and the Balearic Islands.

Established as a principality in the late 13th century, Andorra was ruled for centuries as a feudal domain. Since 1993, Andorra has been a parliamentary democracy, with the co-princes as heads of state. Andorra's modern prosperity has come through tourism and its status as a tax haven.

After centuries of isolation, Andorra has become increasingly involved in the world community. Though not a European Union (EU) member, it uses the Euro common currency. It joined the United Nations in 1993 and the Council of Europe in 1994.

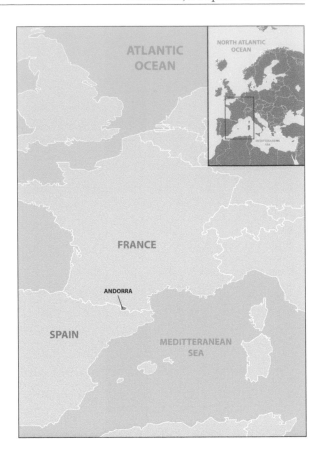

GENERAL INFORMATION

Official Language: Catalan (Català)
Population: 85,458 (2014 estimate)
Currency: Euro
Coins: The euro is available in 1, 2, 5, 10, 20 and 50 cent coins. A 1 and 2 euro coin is also available.
Land Area: 468 square kilometers (180 square miles)
National Motto: "Virtus unita fortior" (Latin, "Unity provides strength")

National Anthem: "El Gran Carlemany" ("The Great Charlemagne")
Capital: Andorra la Vella
Time Zone: GMT +1
Flag Description: Andorra's flag features three vertical stripes of blue, yellow, and red, with the Andorran coat of arms emblazoned in the center yellow stripe, which is slightly wider than the other stripes.

Population

As of 2014, Andorra's estimated population was 85,458, with foreign residents making up the majority of that number. Spaniards, Portuguese and French nationals were the largest groups, representing 24.6 percent, 14.3 percent, and 3.9 percent of the population respectively. The dominance of foreigners is due in part to the migration of many Andorran natives in search of work, as well as Andorra's popularity as a tourist center and tax haven. The median age is just over

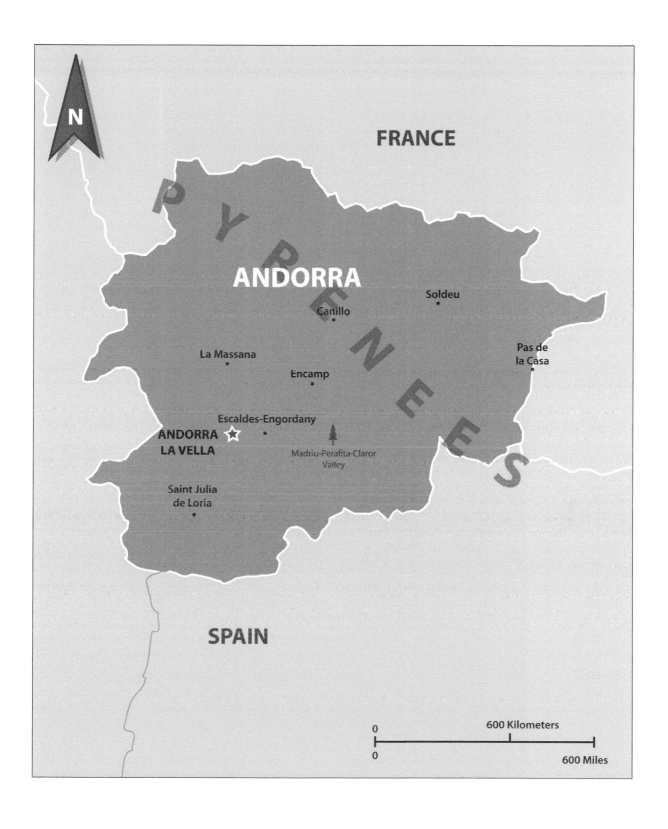

Principal Cities by Population (2008):

- Andorra la Vella 20,643 (2012 est.)
- Escaldes-Engordany 17,008
- Encamp 8,900
- Sant Julià de Lòria 8,012
- La Massana 5,192

42 years. As of 2009, population growth was estimated at .17 percent.

Languages

Catalan (Català), a Romance language, is Andorra's only official tongue. The languages of Andorra's foreign residents (particularly Castilian Spanish, Portuguese, and French) are also commonly used, however. The Catalan language is spoken by over 6 million people, in the Spanish regions of Catalonia, Valencia, and the Balearic Islands, as well as parts of southern France and Sardinia. As part of the "Ibero-Romance" language family, Catalan is closely related to Castilian Spanish, Portuguese, and the languages of southern France, such as Provençal.

Native People & Ethnic Groups

Andorra can date its ancestry at least to Roman times, as Catalan is directly descended from the Latin language. Improvements in transportation after World War II made Andorra more accessible to foreigners. Today, heavy immigration, particularly by French, Spanish, and Portuguese nationals, has made it largely a nation of foreigners.

Religions

Roman Catholicism is not the country's official religion, though the parish system of division in Andorra recalls the country's Catholic origins, and its historic status as a principality co-governed by the Roman Catholic Bishop of Urgel, in neighboring Spain. Approximately 90 percent of the population identifies as Roman Catholic, making Andorra one of the most Catholic countries in Europe. The rest of the population includes several thousand Muslims, Mormons, Jehovah's Witnesses, and various denominations of Protestants, including Anglican.

Climate

Andorra's climate is largely temperate, though it experiences cold and snowy winters, particularly up in the mountains, which helps the skiing industry. The average January temperature is between 2° and 4° Celsius (35° and 39° Fahrenheit). The influence of Mediterranean breezes also moderates the weather. Summers are warm and generally dry. The average temperature in July is around 20° Celsius (68° Fahrenheit). The average yearly precipitation is roughly 80 centimeters (around 30 inches) per year.

ENVIRONMENT & GEOGRAPHY

Topography

Located in the eastern Pyrenees, Andorra is a country comprised largely of mountain valleys. Tributaries of the Valira River (the country's longest river) flow down separate valleys, to meet at Escaldes. These formations mean that Andorra has a great deal of potential hydroelectric power.

In addition to the rivers, there are many lakes in Andorra; the largest is the Juclar. The country's highest mountain is the Alt de Coma Pedrosa, which rises 2,942 meters (9,652 feet).

Plants & Animals

Andorra's natural life is typical of the Pyrenees region, including alpine species such as the chamois (a large mammal similar to a goat). The forests are full of other large mammals such as wild boar, and smaller species such as foxes and hares. There are many bird species found in Andorra, including partridges, robins, and woodpeckers.

Common species of trees and wildflowers found in Andorra range from sub-alpine to alpine varieties. Typical tree species include pine, birch, and oak. One of the most common wildflowers is poet's narcissus.

CUSTOMS & COURTESIES

Greetings

In Andorra, most acquaintances and business associates greet each other with a firm handshake. Family members and close friends—especially woman—may instead kiss each other on the chcck. It is not uncommon for men to embrace friends and family mcmbers in welcome.

Common Catalan phrases of greeting include "Hola" ("Hello"), "Bon dia" ("Good morning"), and "Bona tarda" ("Good afternoon/evening"). Friends and family members may greet each another with an informal "Què hi ha de nou?" ("What's new?").

Although not as outgoing as other southern European cultures, the Catalan culture of Andorra and neighboring northeastern Spain is a friendly one. Andorrans commonly acknowledge strangers, and travelers are expected to return such greetings and farewells. Because of the great numbers of foreign residents in Andorra, customs native to other European countries can also be observed. Residents hailing from France may be seen exchanging a series of kisses on altcrnating cheeks in greeting. Spaniards are likely to shake hands, cmbracc, or kiss others depending on their level of intimacy. Spanish men may use both hands when shaking hands, placing the left atop the right.

Gestures & Etiquette

In Andorra, hody movements and hand gestures arc oftcn used emphatically during conversation. They can be used either to express complete thoughts or to support ideas stated in verbal conversation. For example, an Andorran may shrug his or her shoulders to indicate a lack of knowledge. In Catalan culture, personal space has smaller dimensions than in other Western cultures. As a result, Andorrans prefer to stand fairly close together when talking. Often, Catalans use physical contact as a part of conversation, lightly touching the shoulder, arm, or back of the person to whom they arc talking. Adults in the Catalan region may pat the heads or backs of children to show friendly approval or affection.

For centuries, Catalans have prided themselves on being dedicated, frugal individuals, and this mindset is exemplified in the way that Andorrans intcract with the world. Punctuality is important, as is personal appearance. Catalans are generally interested in fashion and are always well and neatly dressed, even when wearing casual clothes. In the business world, both men and women wear conservative business suits to the office. Relationship building is also an important part of Catalan etiquette, particularly in the business world. Andorrans take great pride in their Catalan culture, and using the Catalan tongue shows respect for their heritage.

Eating/Meals

Today's busy Andorran families rarely cat breakfast or lunch together, although leisurely family dinners are common. Breakfast may consist of light fare, such as cereal, fresh fruit, pastry or an egg accompanicd by cold meats (often varieties of ham such as bacon or prosciutto) and cheese. Bccause most Andorrans work outside the home, lunch is often eaten at neighborhood restaurants or sandwich shops. Typically, lunch is not eaten until the early afternoon. Like their Spanish and French neighbors, Andorrans typically dinc fairly late in the evening. Dinner is traditionally quite substantial and usually fcatures traditional Andorran cuisinc, which includes dishes cooked in the Catalan cassola, or casserole.

Andorrans cat in the continental style: fork in the left hand and the knife in the right hand. Many Andorrans maintain a less conservative attitude toward alcohol consumption and allow children to have wine with dinner. Picnic meals, while hiking or camping in Andorra's mountains, is a popular pastime for families and friends. Food festivals are also popular events throughout the nation, and traditional Andorran cuisine takes center stage at the annual Gastronomic Fair of Andorra. Specific dishes and ingredients, such as the Andorran meat and vegetable stew escudella and the truffle, a well-known delicacy of the mushroom family, also make up the basis for food festivals.

Visiting

Catalans tend to prefer entertaining in restaurants or other public places rather than at home, reserving home visits for especially close friends and family. Someone asked to a Catalan home for a meal or visit should recognize that invitation as a step toward a closer personal relationship with the host. This is particularly true if an acquaintanceship has been made through business. A Catalan host customarily pays when inviting guests to a meal or drinks at a restaurant or café.

In Andorra and throughout the greater Catalan region, visitors often present small gifts to their host or hostess as a token of appreciation. Chocolates, wine, and flowers are all popular choices. However, certain types of flowers should be avoided. These include roses, which are associated with romance in Andorran culture, and chrysanthemums, which are often displayed at funerals. European tradition generally dictates that multiples of an item should be presented in odd numbers, with the exception of the unlucky number thirteen.

LIFESTYLE

Family

For centuries, Andorra's agricultural economy heavily influenced familial structures. Large rural families were patriarchal in nature and children were expected to contribute to the family farm. The majority of the land passed through inheritance to the oldest son, or hereu, and many younger siblings left the country seeking better job opportunities.

In recent times, however, Andorra's shift from rural to urban life has greatly altered these traditional family relationships. Although family members still work together at a family enterprise, that business is much more likely to be a retail store or restaurant than a farm. Andorran women increasingly work outside the home, shifting the responsibilities of child-rearing to day cares and school programs. Women are also taking on equal positions with Andorran men as heads of families. Because modern businesses offer increased employment opportunities, fewer Andorrans are forced to leave the family fold to find work.

However, not all Andorrans welcome the changes associated with these increased economic opportunities. Familial bonds have decreased as parents and children spend more time apart, and some Andorrans believe that young people are less well adjusted than in the past.

Housing

Throughout Andorra, Romanesque buildings blend with modern construction, although few buildings stand from the intervening centuries. One type of traditional Andorran home, the borda, is a common feature in the rural landscape. These stone houses provided shelter and storage for traveling livestock herders during Andorra's agricultural past. As few people now participate in this traditional activity, many bordas are today being converted into popular and unique Andorran restaurants.

Andorra's growth in modern times has led to an explosion of new construction. Many urban Andorrans reside in apartment buildings in the early 21st century, because of the high costs of purchasing a single-family home. Wealthy Andorrans may live in luxury apartments or in comfortable homes located on the edges of urban areas, while those lower on the economic scale reside in smaller apartments. In the countryside, many newer homes are faced with the same mountain stone used to construct ancient homes. Because of the ready availability of this stone, it served as the primary construction material for centuries. In fact, some areas of the nation require its use—up to 30 percent—in new buildings to retain architectural ties to Andorra's past.

Food

Andorran cuisine reflects the geography and resources of the small, landlocked nation. For centuries, the sheep raised by Andorran herders, in addition to domesticated cattle, rabbit, pigs, and goats, made up a central part of Andorrans' diets. Meats are often roasted or grilled over a charcoal or wood fire using a technique called carn a la brasa. Lamb—called xai is Catalan—is sometimes traditionally grilled on a hot slab over a fire made from rhododendron shrubs and served alongside slow-roasted potatoes and dandelion greens. Wild mushrooms are extremely popular with Andorrans, who seek out the fungi on hiking expeditions in the mountains. This mushroom hunting is typical of Andorrans' great interest in food and eating.

Andorra's location between France and Spain is evident in its cuisine. For example, the popular Andorran dip and condiment allioli is a close cousin of the French olive oil and garlic mayonnaise known as aioli. This sauce appears in such Andorran dishes as conill amb all i oli, or grilled rabbit served with the garlicky allioli. A modified form of Spanish dish paella appears in Andorran cuisine, with freshwater fish, particularly trout raised in Andorra's mountain streams, replacing the saltwater fish and shellfish of the original. French and Spanish restaurants are common throughout the nation, and Andorrans enjoy such imported products as foie gras and wine.

Life's Milestones

For centuries, Andorrans routinely participated in Roman Catholic sacraments such as baptism, communion, marriage, and last rites. However, the increased secularism of the past few decades has contributed to rise of civil marriage ceremonies and an overall decrease in participation in the church. Despite this shift away from religious practice, many traditions and ceremonies relating to Roman Catholicism are still common throughout the country. This is especially true to in the more rural parts of Andorra, where the changes brought by urbanization have been less significant.

Andorran funerals typically occur within forty-eight hours of death, and consist of a religious service and a visit to the burial site or crematorium by close family and friends. Rather than burying the deceased in underground graves, Andorrans rent small niches called nínxols for a period of six to eight years. Because this is neither a permanent arrangement nor available to those who are not Andorran citizens or long-term residents, many choose cremation rather than interment.

CULTURAL HISTORY

Art

Andorra's early Romanesque churches became the showplaces for the nation's finest visual art form: the fresco. Painted on the interior walls of churches, these religious murals reflected the piety of early Andorran society and the pride the people had in their places of worship. Frescoes survived in some form at eleven Andorran churches. The unknown master artist of Santa Coloma produced some of the nation's finest frescoes for four churches—Andorra la Vella's Santa Coloma, Les Bons' Sant Romà, Engolasters' Sant Miquel, and Anyós' Sant Cristòfol. The master artist of La Cortinada is remembered for his work at Sant Martí. Andorra's close ties with the Spanish region of Catalonia can be seen in the similarities between these murals and those found in Catalonian Romanesque churches.

Another traditional Andorran art form is wood carving. Although Andorran artisans adorned the simple wooden furniture found in family homes, they are perhaps best known for their carved altars. A period of economic development throughout the Pyrenees region during the 17th century afforded Andorrans the opportunity to renovate existing Romanesque churches. These renovations often included the installation of grand wooden altars carved in the baroque style. The altar of the church at La Massana, featuring twelve distinct carved images, is considered the most impressive example of this style.

Architecture

Andorra remained an agrarian nation until well into the 20th century, a characteristic which shaped its national architecture. Scattered throughout the mountainous country are numerous simple rag-stone shelters used for centuries by wandering herders following flocks of livestock. These buildings silently attest to Andorra's traditional agricultural lifestyle. Family homes, built with stone masonry and furnished with goods made from native wood, exemplify the self-reliance and lack of interaction with other regions.

Another unique feature of Andorra's picturesque architectural heritage is the country's famed early Romanesque churches. (Romanesque is the predominant style of Andorran art.) These churches, made of local mountain stone, were the social, cultural, and defensive centers of Andorran life for many centuries. Church porches provided community gathering places, and bell towers were typically the tallest and most striking features of small communities. The oldest church is believed to be Església de Santa Coloma (Santa Coloma Church). It is mentioned in writing as early as the ninth century and which contained 12th century religious murals. Bridges built in the same style are functional reminders of Andorra's simple and rustic past.

Modern architecture has also taken firm root in the nation. In Andorra's cities, contemporary structures stand alongside ancient stone buildings, with little to represent the many centuries of rural Andorran life. The concrete and glass offices of Andorra's national government in Andorra la Vella stand in sharp contrast to the nearby Casa de la Vall. In Escaldes-Engordany, the peaks of the Caldea spa resort stretch toward the sky in a modern glass-and-steel vision reminiscent of the surrounding Pyrenees.

Dance

Andorrans celebrate their history through the performance of the folk dance la marraxta. In this traditional dance, two men wearing hats adorned with brightly colored ribbons each dance with three women. According to tradition, each dancer represents a person or place related to Andorran history—the men, the two co-princes of the country, and the women, the six original Andorran parishes. Today, the marraxta is performed as part of festivals, particularly around the town of Sant Julià de Lòria.

The sardana originated in the northern part of Catalonia sometime during the 19th century and soon spread throughout the region. To perform the sardana, dancers form a circle and join hands, then move left and right with alternating small and large steps while moving their arms up and down in a prescribed arrangement. The dance, with its circular form and group movement, represents Catalan unity and allows Andorrans to celebrate their shared cultural pride. The sardana is so closely identified with the Catalan identity that it was banned for a time during the 20th century by the Spanish dictator Francisco Franco (1892–1975) as part of an attempt to suppress the independent leanings of the Catalan region.

Music

Traditionally, Andorran music has served as accompaniment to religious services or to folk dances. The music of the sardana is closely tied to the dance and is performed by a traditional band called a cobla. Members of the cobla play instruments that include the trumpet, trombone, flute, bass, drum, English horn, and oboe. Because the oboe usually carries the melody, the music of a cobla has a distinctive, somber tone.

Andorrans use music to celebrate not only their traditional culture, but also their nation's history. According to legend, the Frankish king Charlemagne (742–814) established Andorra as a sovereign state in 788 in recognition of the nation's resistance to a Moorish invasion from Spain. No historical evidence supports this legend, but the story is heralded in the song "The Great Charlemagne." Written in the early 20th century by Andorran Enric Marfany Bons (1871–1942) and Spanish co-prince Joan Benlloch i Vivò (1864–1926), the song was formally adopted as the national anthem on September 8, 1914.

Literature

Although Andorra has only a limited literary tradition, writers have played a significant part in the nation's cultural, social, and political life in recent years. Award-winning novelist Juli Minoves Triquell (1969–) has served as both the Andorran minister of foreign affairs and the Andorran minister of culture, and the children's novelist and fiction writer Albert Salvadó

(1951–) has won many prizes for his work. His books have been translated from Catalan into several other languages, spreading Andorran ideas and culture around the world. Andorran native Michèle Gazier (1946–) has also achieved fame outside of Andorra as a respected writer and literary critic now based in France. Each year, Andorra awards the Fiter i Rossell literary prize in honor of the nation's first notable literary figure, the 18th century writer and lawyer Anton Fiter i Rossell.

CULTURE

Arts & Entertainment

Andorra has a diverse and thriving artistic community that belies the nation's small size and low population. The rise of this artistic community has largely accompanied Andorra's explosive development over the past several decades, as urbanization and modernization have provided fertile ground for the growth of a contemporary arts movement.

Jazz music is popular throughout the Catalan region, and one of the most widely known of Andorra's arts events today is the Escaldes-Engordany International Jazz Festival. For over twenty years, jazz acts from around the globe have gathered each July in the town of Escaldes-Engordany near Andorra la Vella to participate in the week-long festival. Escaldes-Engordany is also home to other, diverse music festivals throughout the year, which are known collectively as the Colors de Música Festival Season. In neighboring Andorra la Vella, the annual Season of Music and Dance, which lasts from November to May, celebrated its fifteenth anniversary in 2008–2009.

Classical music plays a prominent role in the modern Andorran arts community. The Orquestra Nacional Clàssica d'Andorra (National Classical Orchestra of Andorra, or ONCA) was first conceived as the Orquestra Nacional de Cambra d'Andorra, or National Chamber Orchestra of Andorra, in 1992. During its relatively brief existence, the orchestra has performed throughout Europe, including concerts in Spain, France, Germany, Italy, Belgium, and Portugal. It has also played numerous concerts at Andorran music halls and festivals. Andorra's Catalan heritage can be heard on ONCA's recordings of works by Catalan composers such as Pau Casals (1876–1973) and Eduard Toldrà (1895–1962). Opera is represented by the Montserrat Caballé International Singing Competition, co-founded by renowned soprano Montserrat Caballé (1933–) in 1997 and held annually in Sant Julià de Lòria.

Perhaps appropriately for a country catapulting into the future, Andorra has become a home for contemporary sculpture. In 1991, Andorra began a national program to sponsor and display modern sculpture, commissioning several pieces to be displayed throughout the country. Some of these can be seen along the road between Arans and Llorts, as a tribute to the iron industry that once existed in the area. Over 250 sculptures produced by the respected Spanish native Josep Viladomat (1899–1989) can be seen at the Viladomat Museum in Escaldes-Engordany, where the sculptor lived and worked.

Cultural Sites & Landmarks

With its mountainous climate and rustic landscapes dotted with picturesque villages and rural stone shelters, Andorra is one of Europe's most unique destinations. The country receives millions of visitors each year, many of whom come to enjoy its famed ski culture—five ski resorts dot Andorra's mountains, offering over 300 kilometers (186 miles) of trails. Andorra is also home to one World Heritage Site, as recognized by the United Nations Educational, Scientific and Cultural Organization (UNESCO). The Madriu-Perafita-Claror Valley, an isolated glacial valley, and its cultural landscape were recognized in 2004 for the area's mountain culture and rural stone refuges. According to UNESCO, the valley is a microcosm of how early inhabitants lived among the few resources of the Pyrenees.

Many of Andorra's cultural sites relate to the nation's religious history. Of the Romanesque churches dotting the mountain landscape, perhaps the best known is Sant Martí de la Cortinada near Ordino. This church contains many frescoes depicting St. Martin and other religious imagery, as well as four representative altars in the Andorran baroque style. Once the center of Andorra's iron industry, Ordino offers a glimpse of Andorra's traditional way of life. This village is populated with buildings in the mountain architectural style of the past. It also is home to a number of museums, including the Icon Museum dedicated to Christian and Orthodox religious icons, the Andorran Postal Museum, and the Miniature Museum, home to the world's largest collection of miniature paintings.

Located in the parish of Canillo, the Meritxell Sanctuary honors Our Lady of Meritxell, the patron saint of Andorra and namesake of the national holiday. According to Andorran legend, a statue of the Virgin Mary and Jesus was found alongside a wild rose bush one winter in the late 12th century. Despite moving the statue repeatedly into the local church, villagers continued to find it returned to its original spot near the bush. Soon, the people of Meritxell decided to build a chapel on the site, where it stood until damaged by a fire in 1972. In 1976, the Meritxell Sanctuary opened on the same site. The modern Meritxell Sanctuary now stands alongside the refurbished original chapel, an example of the juxtaposition of ancient and contemporary architecture that has become commonplace in Andorra .

As the nation's capital and largest city, Andorra la Vella is home to sites of political and historic significance. Among these is the Casa de la Vall (House of the Valley), built in 1580 in what is now the Barri Antic, Andorra la Vella's small historic district. This area dates from the city's earliest years and offers visitors a vision of a bygone Andorra. In 1702, the Casa de la Vall became the home of the Andorran parliament, which still meets there today. The building also houses a museum.

Libraries & Museums

There are numerous unique museums in the Principality of Andorra, such as the National Automobile Museum. The oldest item in the museum, a steam machine named the *Pinette*,

dates back to 1885. Other museums include a perfume museum and a museum dedicated to the work of sculptor Josep Viladomat (1899–1989). The town of Ordino is home to a number of museums, including the Icon Museum dedicated to Christian and Orthodox religious icons, the Andorran Postal Museum, and the Miniature Museum, or Nicolaï Siadristy's (1937–) micro-miniature museum, home to the world's largest collection of miniature paintings.

Andorra's national repository is the Biblioteca Nacional d'Andorra (National Library of Andorra). It was established in 1930.

Holidays

Andorra's major holidays are Roman Catholic saints' days. The national holiday is Our Lady of Meritxell Day (September 8), which honors the Virgin Mary. Other popular saints are Saint Jordi (George), the patron saint of Catalonia; and Saint Stephen, whose feast day is observed on December 26.

In the country's capital of Andorra la Vella, summer festivals are often three-day celebrations, reflecting Spain's cultural influence. They feature traditional music, dance, and food. Andorra la Vella also enjoys a specific music and dance season, which lasts from November to May. The city's theater season, known for its quality and innovation, runs from October to February.

Youth Culture

Andorran youth generally resemble their counterparts throughout Western Europe, a trend that has become more prevalent due to increased urbanization and a decreased focus on traditional agricultural practices. Winter sports remain the most popular sports, and dancing and attending nightclubs is a popular activity for older youth. Music by Andorran bands is popular among young people, as is music imported from the US, Great Britain, and the rest of Europe. Technology is also becoming an everyday part of youth culture, and Andorran youth are enjoying increased opportunities; both represent hallmarks of the new Andorra.

Since the establishment of the University of Andorra, fewer young people are leaving the country to pursue higher education. Today, the university attracts more than one-quarter of Andorra's college students, mostly to distance learning and graduate programs. Other young Andorrans attend foreign universities, typically in France or Spain. Regardless of their educational status, Andorran youth often live with their families well into their twenties due to the steep costs of renting an apartment or purchasing a home.

SOCIETY

Transportation

Drivers in Andorra drive on the right hand side of the road. Four major roads crisscross Andorra, following the paths of rivers and connecting the nation to neighboring France and Spain. There is one road that runs from Spain to France through Saint Julià, Andorra laVella, Escaldes-Engordany, Encamp, Canillo, and Soldeu. Cars are required to carry spare bulbs, a warning triangle, and a yellow reflective jacket. Because Andorra is nestled in the Pyrenees, it is recommended that cars be outfitted with snow tires or chains when necessary.

Transportation Infrastructure

The country's transportation infrastructure is limited, despite economic growth since World War II. The nation's roadways total about 167 miles (270 kilometers). Buses are a common and efficient means of transport, particularly since Andorra has no railroad or other mass transportation. Parking is a challenge in Andorra's cities, and residents control many of the available parking spots.

The closest airports are in Barcelona, Spain, and Toulouse, France, both located nearly two and a half hours from Andorra. However, in 2007, Spain announced plans to build an airport in Seu d'Urgell, only 15 minutes from the border. This city—long a point of entry to Andorra—should see commercial and private air traffic beginning in 2010 or 2011.

Media & Communications

Prior to the creation of the public broadcaster Ràdio i Televisió d'Andorra (RTVA) in 1997, which broadcasts entirely in Catalan from its studios in Andorra la Vella, Andorrans relied exclusively on television broadcasts from Spain and France. Although many French and Spanish radio stations can be easily heard in Andorra, Andorra itself has few local stations. These include the public Radio Andorra and Andorra Musica, as well as commercial station Radio Valira, Andorra 1, and Andorra 7. Andorra is also home to four daily newspapers, all of which publish in Catalan. The largest of these papers are *Diari d'Andorra* and *El Periodic*.

Andorrans have embraced the cell phone, with an estimated 68,500 mobile units vastly outnumbering an estimated 37,200 landlines in 2007. Internet access in widely available to both residents and visitors, and Internet cafés are a common sight in tourist districts. As of 2014, an estimated 94 percent of the population were Internet users

SOCIAL DEVELOPMENT

Standard of Living

According to the US Department of State, Andorra's gross domestic product (GDP) was USD $3.163 billion in 2012; the GDP per capita was USD $37,200 as of 2011. According to the United Nations Human Development Report, Andorra ranks number thirty-seven in the world, meriting a high human development rating.

The average life expectancy for an Andorran citizen is just over eight-two years. Women have a longer life expectancy, at almost eighty-five years, while men have a life expectancy of about eighty years.

Water Consumption

Due to its location, water resources are plentiful in Andorra. Mountain rivers and streams provide clean water and hydropower. Sanitation is also well addressed.

Education

School attendance in Andorra is mandatory up to the age of sixteen, and the literacy rate is 100 percent. The country's unique geographical position has led to the development of three parallel educational systems: French, Spanish, and Andorran. Approximately one-third of all students attend French schools; one-third attend Spanish schools; and one-third attend Andorran schools.

In the 1990s, Andorra began developing a system of higher education. The University of Andorra has established in 1997, and is comprised of the University School of Nursing, the Advanced Computer School, the Centre for Virtual Study, and a continuing-education program.

Women's Rights

Although women have historically played a subservient role to men in Andorran society, Andorra has witnessed a change to traditional gender roles in recent years. Increasing urbanization and modernization have brought women new status within the family, the workforce, and the political arena. Contemporary Andorran society generally views woman as equals to men. In 1997, Andorra ratified the UN Convention on the Elimination of All Forms of Discrimination against Women (CEDAW), a testament to its commitment to women's rights. However, in day-to-day life, Andorran women do not enjoy complete equality with men, despite laws prohibiting gender-based discrimination. Two national organizations, the Andorran International Women's Association (AIWA) and the Andorran Women's Association (AWA), work to both support existing rights and campaign for further improvements.

In a nation already slow to develop a political identity, Andorran women continue to achieve advancements in politics. Women obtained suffrage in 1970, and the first woman to serve on Andorra's parliament took her seat in 1984, two years after the creation of that legislative body. By 2011, that number had grown to fifteen, making Andorra the first European country to elect a majority female legislature, and the second globally, after Rwanda. Despite these advances, the traditional familial authority of men in Andorran society has caused continuing challenges for women, who continue to experience professional discrimination. While women make up a significant proportion of the Andorran workforce and Andorran women enrolled at universities outnumber their male counterparts, women fill only one-third of top level positions and generally earn about one-third less than men performing similar jobs. Some women also reported losing their jobs as a result of pregnancy.

Andorra is one of only a few European countries with a longstanding and near-complete ban on abortion. Procedures may be legally performed within the nation in order to save the life of the mother, causing some Andorran women to leave the country seeking treatment. In 2008, the Council of Europe issued a resolution urging Andorra to change this policy.

A significant issue facing Andorran women is domestic abuse. No Andorran law prohibits domestic violence, and physical abuse is not uncommon. Reports of physical abuse have grown steadily over the past several years, from only four in 1999 to nearly 162 in 2009 (a forty percent increase from 2008). According to the Ministry of Health, Welfare and Family, authorities prosecuted approximately 50 persons for violence against women. Andorra lacks shelters for victims of domestic violence; however, the government has worked with the AIWA to find safe havens for abused women and children. Andorran law does not prohibit sexual harassment and human trafficking, though both abuses were not considered to be societal problems.

Health Care

Andorra has a nationalized health-care system, though private medical care is also available. All employed persons must belong to the system, which is funded by payroll taxes. The system is administered by the Andorran Health Care Service. Life expectancy is high, at just over 82 years for the total population.

GOVERNMENT

Structure

Andorra was founded as a principality in 1278, when the Count of Foix (in France) and the Bishop of Urgel, Spain agreed to settle their territorial dispute by ruling the land jointly as "co-princes." The rights of the Counts of Foix passed in 1589 to the French Crown and from there to the French president.

Andorra gained its current parliamentary government in 1993, as the result of a referendum. The co-princes remain as titular heads of state, but executive power is held by the prime minister. A delegate of the co-princes represents them in Andorra.

Even before the referendum, however, Andorra had made some moves in the direction of greater popular government. In 1981, the country established a prime minister and cabinet. Previously, the rule of the co-princes had been exercised by an executive officer known as the "Syndic" and the 28-member General Council of the Valleys.

The executive branch is known as the Executive Council, headed by a president elected from its own membership for a term of four years. The co-princes formally appoint the president, who serves as head of government.

The Andorran legislature is the General Council of the Valleys (Consell General de las Valls), a single-house body with 28 members (councils). Elections are by direct popular vote, for four-year terms. The legislature mimics the action of a two-house legislature by having 14 members represent the entire nation, while the other 14 members represent the country's seven parishes. The leadership is known as the Sindicatura, or Speaker's Office.

Andorra's highest court is the Supreme Court of Justice. There are a number of inferior courts, including the Constitutional Tribunal, which handles cases involving constitutional law. The legal system is based on the civil law of France and Spain.

Political Parties

Andorra's last election was held on March 31, 2015. Parliamentary democracies often have a large number of political parties, which have a tendency to shift in terms of political platform and their alliance with other parties sharing common interests. Often, parliamentary systems are ruled by coalitions of two or more parties that unite to form a majority coalition. These coalitions differ in nature, with some coalitions having a lasting strength and others failing to govern at all. Additionally, it's not unusual for parties to dissolve because of personality conflicts within the organization.

In 2015, Antoni Marti Petit was elected Head of government with 68 percent of the General Council vote. The Democrats hold 15 of the 28 seats with the opposition parties holding the remaining 13 seats. There has been talk during this Parliament of a referendum to determine the future relationship with the European Union (EU).

Local Government

Local government is handled by the country's seven parishes. Andorra la Vella, the capital, forms one parish. The others are Canillo, Encamp, Ordino, La Massana, Sant Julià de Lòria, and Escaldes-Engordany. Each parish is led by an elected mayor.

Judicial System

Andorra's judicial system finds its roots in Roman and Catalan law. Civil cases are heard by a group of four judges (appointed by the co-princes), called the Tribunal de Batlles. There is a Court of Appeals. Criminal cases are heard before the Tribunal of Courts. The highest court is the Superior Council of Justice.

Taxation

Andorra has long been known as a tax haven, or a place where taxes might be avoided. It enjoys a special relationship with the European Union, as it uses that currency and is treated as a member for trade of manufactured goods but not of agricultural products.

Local taxes involving services, fees, and real property are levied, but there is no system of direct taxation of people, profits, or assets. The Andorran government has indicated, though, that an inheritance tax, a tax on services, and an eco-tax are planned.

Indirect taxation in Andorra is comprised of a tax on the production, development and import of goods; an excise tax on the importation of agricultural products; and taxes on electric and telephone, vehicles, and brand registration. There is also a flat tax on businesses.

Armed Forces

Andorra has no military forces, only police. The country's national defense is shared by France and Spain.

Foreign Policy

Because of Andorra's longstanding relationship with Spain and France, the small country itself has had little direct involvement with foreign policy and political affairs. Throughout its history, the nation has participated in practically no international conflicts. Although Andorra declared war on Germany during World War I, it did not actively field any troops in the conflict. During negotiations for the Treaty of Versailles, which ended the war, Andorra was, in fact, forgotten and remained officially at war with Germany until the 1950s, despite declaring its neutrality during World War II. The nation established limited international diplomatic relations only in 1952.

Modern Andorra maintains a position of neutrality in international conflict, and has little need for external security. Officially, Spain and France share responsibility for protection of Andorra, and the nation itself has no military forces and defense budget. Internal security remains the duty of the Andorran government, which maintains a small police force. As another reflection of Andorra's relationship with the two larger nations, each year either Spanish or French police aids the Andorran force.

Following increased political autonomy in 1993, Andorra began participating more actively on an international level. The nation's membership in the United Nations (UN) that same year preceded new formal diplomatic relations with countries throughout the world, including China in 1994 and the United States in 1995. Today, Andorra holds membership in numerous international bodies. These include the International Monetary Fund (IMF), the Organization for Security and Cooperation in Europe (OSCE), Council of Europe, and Interpol, among others. However, the nation's international interests often continue to be represented by Spain or France.

Although Andorra has consistently declined to pursue membership in the European Union (EU), the nation has worked to bring itself into alignment with many of that body's standards. Since 1991, Andorra and the EU have maintained economic relations. In 2005, the two entered in a cooperation agreement affirming these existing trade and customs relations and declaring their intentions to work together on issues including the environment, culture and communication, education, health care, and transportation. Under the agreement, Andorra also committed to participating in regional affairs.

Andorra's relations with the outside world are primarily commercial rather than diplomatic. The nation's duty-free shopping and tourism activities in many ways define its image within neighboring countries. Andorra is well known for its lack of both personal and corporate income taxes, which attract wealthy retirees and corporations to the nation. Continuing international complaints about the country's tax laws led to its being declared an uncooperative tax haven by the Organization for Economic Cooperation and Development (OECD) in 2002. However, Andorran leaders continue to reject this assertion. Because Andorra's laws forbid foreign interests from controlling more than one-third of a company, Andorra argues that using the nation as a tax shelter is an unworkable scheme.

In 2009, Andorra agreed to lift its banking secrecy laws.

Human Rights Profile

International human rights law insists that states respect civil and political rights, and also promote an individual's economic, social and cultural rights. The United Nations Universal Declaration on Human Rights (UDHR) is recognized as the standard for international human rights. Its authors sought the counsel of the world's great thinkers, philosophers, and religious leaders, and were careful to create a document that reflects the core values shared by every world culture. (To read this document or view the articles relating to cultural human rights, go to: http://www.udhr.org/UDHR/default.htm.)

Andorra's contemporary human rights record is generally a strong one. The nation has ratified a number of UN human rights agreements, including those forbidding torture and supporting the rights of children. In 1998, the nation furthered its human efforts by creating the position of ombudsman within the national government. This person oversees the implementation of human rights policy throughout the country and deals with complaints from Andorrans regarding public institutions. In April 2001, Andorra further demonstrated its commitment to international human rights enforcement by signing the Rome Statute. This document supported the creation of an international court responsible for prosecuting war crimes, genocide, and mass human rights violations.

Nonetheless, Andorra continues to face certain human rights challenges. Despite—or perhaps because of—the high number of foreign residents within the nation, a number of rights and privileges are exclusive to Andorran citizens. These rights primarily relate to land and business ownership. Foreigners resident in Andorra, particularly those who are not married to Andorran citizens, face significant barriers to full citizenship. Andorra's longstanding close ties with the Roman Catholic Church prevented the practice of divorce for many years, but today, rights of both marriage and divorce are guaranteed. However, at least one partner in a union must be an Andorran citizen in order for a couple to marry within the country. Although marriage rights are not extended to same-sex couples, Andorra does perform and recognize same-sex civil unions, which carry legal rights and protections equal to those of traditional marriage.

Although Andorra's constitution recognizes in theory the rights of workers to organize labor unions, in practice no law guarantees these rights. Workers find it difficult to effectively form collective bargaining associations and can face negative consequences as a result of union membership. In 2007, a number of Andorrans publicly demonstrated in favor of the creation of law that would adequately protect workers' rights. Another reported human rights shortfall is the sometimes lengthy holding of an accused criminal before trial. This generally results from a lack of staff needed to adequately process detainees. As of 2008, nearly one-third of Andorra's overall prison population was composed of these pretrial detainees. About three-quarters of those subject to extended detentions were foreigners.

ECONOMY

Overview of the Economy

Andorra was a relatively poor country well into the 20th century, because of its geographical remoteness and lack of resources. For many years, Andorra was seen as a place where tourists from France and Spain could buy duty-free goods, particularly items such as alcohol and cigarettes. The country also had a reputation as a transit point for smuggled goods.

The nation's relationship with the European Union has changed Andorra's economy somewhat, although the principality still retains its special duty-free status in many cases. In addition, Andorra is cracking down on smuggling in order to comply with EU regulations.

In 2012, the gross domestic product (GDP) was estimated at $3.163 billion (USD), with a growth rate of around -1.6 percent. Per capita GDP was $37,200 (USD) in 2012. Almost 95 percent of the workforce was employed in the services industry, with most of the rest engaged in industry. Less than one percent worked in agriculture.

Industry

Andorra is now promoting itself as winter sport resort. Another main business sector is serving as a tax haven. Many banks have relocated to Andorra, in order to take advantage of Andorra's low tax rates. Other light industries include the manufacture of furniture and consumer goods such as brandy. The country's main trading partners are neighboring Spain and France.

Labor

As of 2012, Andorra has a four percent unemployment rate. The majority of the workforce (94.9 percent) works in the service sector, while those in manufacturing number 4.7 percent of the workforce and less than one percent engage in agriculture.

Energy/Power/Natural Resources

Andorra is historically poor in natural resources, other than timber and hydroelectric power. Andorra's rivers produce substantial quantities of hydroelectric power, about 40 percent, and the rest is imported from Spain. Energy agreements are handled by the state-run energy company, Forces Electriques d'Andorra. The electric grid was first constructed during the 1930s.

There are some minerals deposits, mostly iron ore and lead. Agriculture is minimal, due to the lack of arable land (slightly more than two percent of the total land area). Andorra's natural environment has been hurt through pollution and waste treatment. Other problems include erosion due to overgrazing, and deforestation due to excessive timbering.

In 2004, Andorra's Madriu-Claror-Perafita Valley was designated a World Heritage Site by the United Nations Educational, Scientific, and Cultural Organization (UNESCO). The site was added because it demonstrates how the mountain peoples of the Pyrenees have sustained themselves with limited resources over the centuries.

Fishing

Andorra imports its fish and seafood products for domestic use from Spain.

Forestry

Twenty-two percent of the total land area of Andorra is forested. Although forestry is not a major industry, different areas of forest are cut each year in order to rotate harvesting and supply national construction needs. Reforestation efforts are largely comprised of pine.

Mining/Metals

Andorra's mining industry is not a major economic contributor. While iron ore deposits exist, access is difficult given the terrain; lead and alum are also mined.

Agriculture

Due to lack of arable land, Andorra has a very small agricultural sector. The major crops are rye, wheat, barley, and oats.

Animal Husbandry

Many farmers raise sheep or cattle, though this has contributed to erosion on the mountain meadows.

Tourism

Tourism is the main economic sector, Andorra receives over 10 million visitors each year; many of them come to the principality to enjoy mountain sports such as skiing and hiking. Most tourists come from the neighboring countries of France and Spain, and the remainder largely from other Western European countries.

In addition to mountain sports and shopping, tourist attractions include picturesque medieval churches in the Romanesque style, and the National Automobile Museum in Ordino.

Vanessa Vaughn, Ann Parrish, Alex K. Rich

DO YOU KNOW?

- Andorra's name derives from the Navarrese dialect, probably meaning "land covered with shrubs."

Bibliography

"Andorra." Encyclopedia Britannica. *Encyclopedia Britannica Online.* <http://scarch.eb.com.ezproxy. libraries.wright.edu:2048/eb/article-9007461>.

"Andorra." *World Data Analyst.* Encyclopedia Britannica. <http://www.world.eb.com.ezproxy.libraries.wright. edu:2048/wdpdf/Andorra.pdf>.

"Andorra." The World Factbook. *Central Intelligence Agency.* <https://www.cia.gov/library/publications/the-world-factbook/geos/an.html>.

"Andorra." U.S. Department of State: Diplomacy in Action. *United States Department of State.* <http://www.state. gov/r/pa/ei/bgn/3164.htm>.

Augustin, Byron D. *Andorra.* New York: Marshall Cavendish Benchmark, 2009.

Claverol, Valenti. *Andorran Memories.* New York: Turtle Point Press, 2000.

Eaude, Michael. *Catalonia: A Cultural History.* New York: Oxford University Press, 2008.

Eccardt, Thomas M., *Secrets of the Seven Smallest States of Europe.* New York: Hippocrene Books, 2005.

"Portal Turistic d'Andorra." Ministry of Tourism. Government of Andorra. < http://www.Andorra.ad/en-US/Pages/default.aspx>

Works Cited

"2008 Human Rights Report: Andorra." U.S. Department of State: Diplomacy in Action. *United States Department of State.* <http://www.state.gov/g/drl/rls/hrrpt/2008/ eur/119065.htm>

"Andorra." Encyclopedia Britannica. *Encyclopedia Britannica Online.* <http://search.eb.com.ezproxy. libraries.wright.edu:2048/eb/article-9007461>

"Andorra." World Data Analyst. *Encyclopedia Britannica.* <http://www.world.eb.com.ezproxy.libraries.wright. edu:2048/wdpdf/Andorra .pdf>

"Andorra." The World Factbook. *Central Intelligence Agency.* <https://www.cia.gov/library/publications/the-world-factbook/geos/an.html>

"Andorra." U.S. Department of State: Diplomacy in Action. *United States Department of State.* < http://www.state. gov/r/pa/ei/bgn/3164.htm>

"Andorra." U.S. Department of State: Diplomacy in Action. United States Department of State. <http://www.state. gov/g/drl/rls/hrrpt/2000/eur/670.htm>

"Andorra: 30th country to ratify the Rome Statute-Halfway towards the International Criminal Court." *Amnesty International* 1 May 2001. <http://www. amnesty.org/en/library/asset/EUR12/002/2001/en/dom-EUR120022001en.html>

"Andorra Abortion Policy." *United Nations.* <www.un.org/ esa/population/publications/abortion/doc/andorra1.doc>

"Andorra Business Travel Guide." *World Travel Guide.* <http://www.worldtravelguide.net/country/9/business/ Europe/Andorra .html>

Augustin, Byron D., *Andorra.* New York: Marshall Cavendish Benchmark, 2009.

"Barcelona Business Profile." *World Travel Guide.* <http:// www.worldtravelguide.net/city/11/business/Europe/ Barcelona.html>

"Barcelona: Getting to Know: Fast Facts." *Frommers. com.* <http://www.frommers.com/destinations/ barcelona/0045020016.html>

"Cadena Pirenaica de Ràdio I Televisió." *Radio Valira.* <http://www.radiovalira.com/index2.php?q=en>

"China and Andorra." Ministry of Foreign Affairs of the People's Republic of China. *Government of the People's Republic of China.* <http://www.fmprc.gov.cn/eng/wjb/ zzjg/xos/gjlb/3266/t16858.htm>

"Cooperation Agreement between the European Community and the Principality of Andorra." *Official Journal of the European Union.* <http:// eur-lex.europa.eu/LexUriServ/site/en/oj/2005/l_135/ l_13520050528en00140018.pdf>

"Country Report on Human Rights Practices in Andorra." U.S. Department of State: Diplomacy in Action. *United States Department of State.* <http://www.state.gov/g/drl/ rls/hrrpt/2005/61634.htm>

"Country Report on Human Rights Practices in Andorra." U.S. Department of State: Diplomacy in Action. *United States Department of State.* <http://www.state.gov/g/drl/ rls/hrrpt/2007/100545.htm>

Cramer, Mark. *Culture Shock! Barcelona at Your Door.* Singapore: *Times Media Private Limited*, 2001.

"Cultural Routes." *European Institute of Cultural Routes.* <http://www.culture-routes.lu/php/to_do_downld. php?ref=00002993/00002993.pdf&saveas=romanic_ang. pdf&PHPSESSID=1084e3b293>

Darmanin, David. "Abortion should be legal and available—Council of Europe." *Malta Today.*<http:// www.maltatoday.com.mt/2008/03/23/n13.html>

"Departament d'Estudis i Estadistica." *Government of Andorra.* <http://www.estadistica.ad/serveiestudis/web/ index.asp?lang=4>

Eccardt, Thomas M., *Secrets of the Seven Smallest States of Europe.* New York: Hippocrene Books, 2005.

"Etiquette—Barcelona Safety and Travel Security Guide." *Professional Travel Guide.* <http://www. professionaltravelguide.com/Destinations/Barcelona/ Safety/Etiquette>

"First Woman Takes Her Seat in the Parliament of Andorra." *New York Times* 28 Oct. 1984. <http://query. nytimes.com/gst/fullpage.html?res=9E06E2DE1239 F93BA15753C1A962948260&scp=31&sq=Andorra &st=cse>

Foster, Dean. *The Global Etiquette Guide to Europe.* New York: John Wiley and Sons, 2000.

"ICC—Frequently Asked Questions." *International Criminal Court.* http://www.icc-cpi.int/NetApp/App/ MCMSTemplates/Index.aspx?NRMODE=Published

&NRNODEGUID={D788E44D-E292-46A1-89CC-D03637A52766}&NRORIGINALURL=/Menus/ICC/About+the+Court/Frequently+asked+Questions/&NRCACHEHINT=Guest#id_1

"La Massana." *Cyber Andorra.* <http://www.cyberAndorra.com/wiki/en/Andorra-la-massana>

"Local Etiquette: Barcelona." *Geobeats.* <http://www.geobeats.com/videoclips/spain/barcelona/local-etiquette>

"ONCA—National Classic Orchestra of Andorra." *National Classic Orchestra of Andorra.* <http://www.onca.ad/eng/descobriu.htm>

"Phrases English Catalan Spanish." *Project BABEL.* <http://projetbabel.org/catala_espanol_english.htm>

"Portal Turistic d'Andorra." Ministry of Tourism. *Government of Andorra.* <http://www.Andorra.ad/en-US/Pages/default.aspx>

"Principality of Andorra." European Union and Principality of Andorra (EU). *European Union.* <http://ec.europa.eu/external_relations/Andorra /index_en.htm>

"Ratifications and Reservations." Office of the United Nations High Commissioner for Human Rights. *United Nations.* <http://www2.ohchr.org/english/bodies/ratification/index.htm>

"Romanesque and Baroque Art in Andorra." *Hola Andorra!* <http://www.hola-Andorra .com/arinsal/english/romanicgb.html>

"Sardana." Encyclopedia Britannica. *Encyclopedia Britannica Online.* <http://search.eb.com.ezproxy.libraries.wright.edu:2048/eb/article-9065756>.

"Sardana: Catalan Dancing in Barcelona." *Tourist Guide Barcelona.* < http://www.barcelona-tourist-guide.com/en/general/catalan-dancing-sardana.html>

Tagliabue, John. "Hard Times Hit a Postage-Stamp Land." *New York Times* 25 Mar. 2008. <http://www.nytimes.com/2008/03/25/world/europe/25Andorra .html?_r=2>

"UNTC." United Nations Treaty Collection. United Nations. <http://treaties.un.org/Pages/ViewDetails.aspx?src=TREATY&id=326&chapter=4&lang=en>

"Visiting Escaldes-Engordany, Andorra." *TripAdvisor.* <http://www.tripadvisor.com/Tourism-g190397-Escaldes_Engordany-Vacations.html>

"What to do when someone dies in Andorra." *Andorran English-Speaking Church.* <http://www.Andorranchurchenglishspeaking.com/special/WHAT%20TO%20DO%20WHEN%20SOMEBODY%20DIES%20IN%20ANDORRA .pdf>

Williams, Roger. *Eyewitness Travel: Barcelona and Catalonia.* London: Dorling Kindersley Limited, 2006.

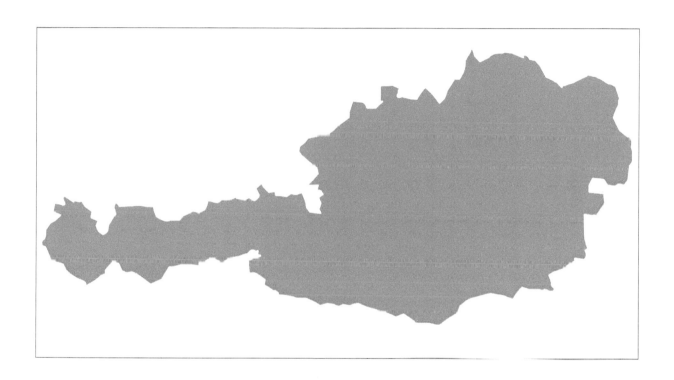

AUSTRIA

Introduction

Located in Central Europe, Austria (German: Österreich, or "eastern realm") is both one of the oldest and youngest European countries. Austria was originally established in the Middle Ages as a "march" or border province of the Holy Roman Empire. The modern Republic of Austria, a land-locked nation, was established following World War I after the breakup of the Austro-Hungarian Empire, which had included the now-independent countries of Slovenia, the Czech Republic, Slovakia, and Hungary.

Austria's neighbors include Italy, Switzerland, Liechtenstein, and Germany. Austria was part of Nazi Germany during World War II, but regained independence and democratic government after the war. The economy is diverse and well developed. Major industries include manufacturing, financial services, and tourism.

Vienna, the capital, has been a major political and cultural center for centuries, and is known for its music and theater. The Vienna Philharmonic Orchestra, founded 1842, remains one of the world's most respected orchestras. Traditional Austrian culture also includes folk dancing. Among the most popular dances are the polka, waltz, and landler, often done in traditional costume. Yodeling, which originated in the Alps, is also highly popular in Austria.

GENERAL INFORMATION

Official Language: German
Population: 8,223,062 (2014 estimate)
Currency: Euro
Coins: The euro is available in 1, 2, 5, 10, 20 and 50 cent coins. A 1 and 2 Euro coin is also available.
Land Area: 83,871 square kilometers (32,382 square miles)
Water Area: 1,426 square kilometers (550 square miles)
National Anthem: "Land der Berge, Land am Strome" ("Land of Mountains, Land of Rivers")
Capital: Vienna
Time Zone: GMT +1
Flag Description: The flag of Austria features three horizontal bands of red (top), white (middle), and red (bottom). This tri-colored flag is among the oldest national symbols, dating back to the 13th century.

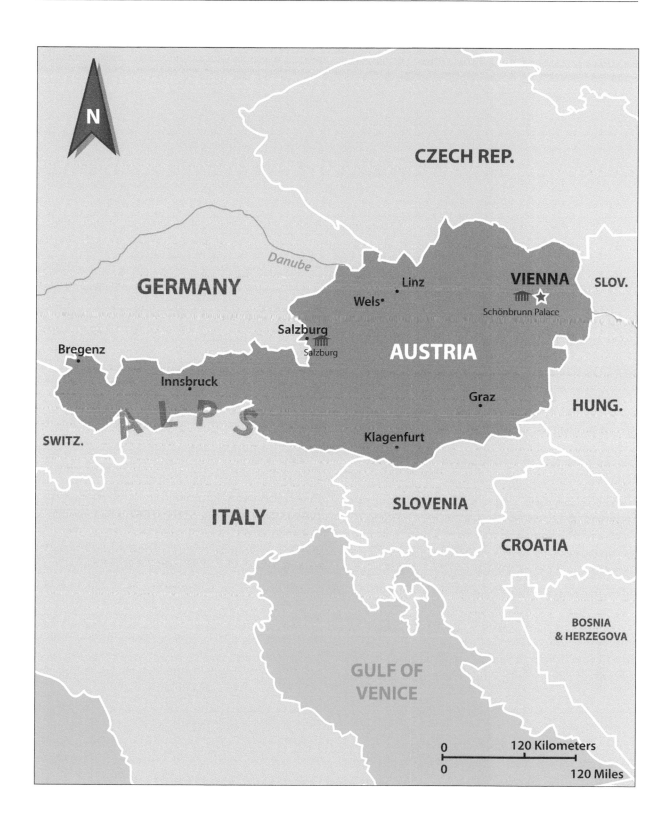

Principal Cities by Population (2012):

- Vienna (1,700,000)
- Graz (261,836)
- Linz (188,599)
- Salzburg (149,218)
- Innsbruck (119,524)
- Klagenfurt (93,383)
- Villach (59,383)
- Wels (58,430)
- Sankt Pölton (52,430)
- Dornbirn (45,474)

Population

Austria's population is almost entirely Germanic: approximately 90 percent is of German origin. There are six officially recognized minorities: the Croats, Czechs, Hungarians, Roma/Sinti (Gypsies), Slovaks, and Slovenes. Austria also has many "guest workers" ("gastarbeiter") from Turkey and the former Eastern Bloc.

Approximately 66 percent of the population lives in urban areas. Vienna is by far the largest and most important city, with a population of around 1.7 million. It serves as the country's political, cultural, and economic heart. Other major cities with populations over 100,000 include Graz, Linz, Salzburg, and Innsbruck.

Languages

German is Austria's official language, based largely on the southern Germanic dialects known as Austro-Bavarian; the one exception is the Alemannic dialect known as "Vorarlbergerisch," spoken in the western state of Vorarlberg and related to Swiss German. Vienna has its own unique dialect, with many words derived from Old High German and Middle High German, as well as Italian, Hungarian, and Czech.

Native People & Ethnic Groups

The territory now belonging to Austria has been settled for at least 3,000 years. The region was first inhabited by Celts, including the La Tène and Hallstatt cultures. The ancient Kingdom of Noricum had a mixed population of Celts and Illyrians (related to modern Albanians).

Rome annexed Noricum in 16BCE, introducing a Latin element. The Alemanni and the Bavarians, both Germanic tribes, began arriving several centuries later. They settled in western Austria and eventually dominated the entire region. The Slavs arrived in the 600s, moving westward to escape the Avars.

Ethnic divisions have long troubled Austria. During the 19th century, many people sought independence from the empire. The Hungarians achieved the most success, gaining equal status with the German-speaking regions in 1867.

Austria's once-large Jewish population was essentially destroyed during World War II, and now numbers only around 7,000.

In 2010, it was estimated that some 90 percent of the country's population are Austrian (or of German origin). Minority groups that comprise the remaining 10 percent include Serbians, Croatians, Bosnians, and Turks.

Religions

Roman Catholicism dominates, though today the Church no longer takes part in politics. Christian feasts are celebrated as official holidays. Around 74 percent of Austrians consider themselves Catholics. Other Christians include Lutherans and members of the Eastern Orthodox Church. There is also a substantial Muslim community, accounting for about 4 percent of the population.

Climate

Austria's climate is generally "continental" and temperate. Except in the mountains, where snow is frequent, winters and summers both tend to be cool. There are three main climate regions: Continental Pannonian, Central European, and Alpine. The first tends toward cool winters, warm summers and relatively little rainfall, usually less than 800 millimeters (31 inches). The Central European climate has moderate seasons and relatively high rainfall, usually between 700–2,000 millimeters (28–79 inches). The Alpine climate has substantial snowfall, long winters, and short summers.

ENVIRONMENT & GEOGRAPHY

Topography
Austria lies largely within the Alps mountain chain, running from east to west. The highest mountain is the Grossglockner, located in the High Tauern range and rising to a height of 3,798 meters (12,460 feet). The main river is the Danube, which runs from east to west. Vienna is located in the Danube River Valley, in the region known as the "Vienna Basin."

Another low-lying region is the Pannonian Lowlands. The Bohemian Massif is a mountainous region of forests near the Czech border. Around 45 percent of the country is forested, with firs in higher regions and deciduous species such as oak and beech in the lower regions.

Plants & Animals
Around half of Austria is covered with forests, mostly beech and oak, although the forests at higher elevations are mostly fir, larch, and pine. The northern Alpine foothills are covered with grassland. The region known as Pannonia is low-lying heath, covered with scrub vegetation. Austria is renowned for its alpine wildflowers, particularly the edelweiss, the national flower made famous by the musical *The Sound of Music.* Other common species include gentian (Enzian).

Austria is full of wildlife. Game animals include bear, deer (red and roe), and smaller mammals such as badgers, foxes, and squirrels.

The edelweiss is Austria's national flower.

The chamois (horned antelope) and ibex (a type of mountain goat) are found in the Alpine regions.

Austria is home to many game birds, including the partridge and the pheasant. The Pannonia region is home to many bird species, including wild geese, the heron, and the spoonbill, which live near Lake Neusiedel. Austria has established nature parks and preserves around the country to protect its forests.

CUSTOMS & COURTESIES

Greetings
Methods of greeting in Austria vary according to age and the level of formality. The handshake is still commonly used among older people and in formal or business settings. Additionally, it is often used when two people are first introduced to one another, and may also be used at the end of a meeting as a means of taking one's leave. The right hand is typically used, and to refuse a handshake may be considered insulting. Also, it is not entirely uncommon for an older Austrian man to greet a woman by kissing her hand. However, it should be noted that intimate contact such as kissing and embracing are not widely practiced in public.

In Austrian culture, it is important to use the appropriate title and greeting when addressing someone. For example, all women over the age of eighteen are referred to by the honorific "Frau" ("Mrs." or "Madam"), regardless of marital status. Thus, when addressing someone for the first time, it is common to use the titles of "Herr" ("Mr.") or "Frau," followed by their title and surname. At the same time, titles and surnames are used much more commonly than first names, which tend to be reserved for close friends and family.

German is the official language of Austria. The most common greeting, particularly in informal situations, is "Guten tag" ("Good day"). A more informal greeting is "Grüß Gott" ("May God greet you"). In addition, there are many informal ways of saying "Goodbye," including "Servus," "Ciao," and "Ba-Ba."

Gestures & Etiquette

On the whole, Austrian culture is quite conservative, and behavior in public reflects this. Business communication tends to be very formal and protocol is followed quite closely. In addition, it is considered appropriate for a business card to have one side translated into German. (German is the official language of Austria and the two nations share a close relationship.) However, Austrians are proud of their nationality and are likely to be offended if assumed to be German.

Punctuality is held in very high regard and is considered a sign of respect. To arrive late for an appointment is typically seen as an indicator of rudeness. Also, directness or confrontational behavior tends to be seen as aggressive. Additionally, the person who invites people to a meal at a restaurant usually pays the bill. Rather than offering to pay one's share of the bill, the guest should invite the host out to dinner in order to reciprocate the gesture. Business should not be discussed during a meal, unless the host initiates it.

Regarding gestures, the thumbs up signal commonly used in the U.S. and other Western cultures to indicate "that's good" refers to the numeral one in Austria.

Eating/Meals

Austrians typically eat three meals per day. Breakfast usually includes light fare such as bread and jam with hot chocolate or coffee. This may be followed by a heartier breakfast of sausage later in the morning. Depending upon when the main meal is served, the lighter meal of the day will often consist of bread, cheese, and cold meats. There may also be a mid-afternoon or late night pastry.

Traditionally, the midday meal was the largest daily meal in Austria, but work schedules in recent years have dictated that, for most families, the evening meal is now the largest. The evening meal is also the time when the family comes together, and is therefore considered an important part of family life.

Commonly, meals are eaten according to the continental style, with the fork in the left hand and the knife in the right. After sitting, it is also customary for the napkin to be placed in one's lap. It is customary to begin meals by saying the colloquial phrases "Mahlzeit" or "Guten appétit," both loosely meaning "Enjoy your meal," with the former traditionally used for lunchtime meals.

Visiting

Receiving an invitation to another's home in Austrian culture is a great honor. As such, punctuality should be observed, as lateness is considered very rude. If a guest is to be delayed for any reason, they should be sure to call their host immediately. Although gifts are typically not expected, a small gesture such as flowers, wine or chocolate will most certainly be appreciated. However, flowers should be given in odd numbers only (even numbers being considered bad luck). Further, certain flowers carry particular connotations and should therefore be avoided. For example, red roses symbolize passion and romance while red carnations are linked to a political party. Lilies and chrysanthemums are used at funerals. Perfume or clothing is considered very personal gifts, and are reserved for very close friends or family members.

When invited to a meal, the guest should not sit until the host has shown them to their seat. Often the host may assign seating and to sit elsewhere may cause offense. The host should always offer the first toast, whereupon the guests look the host in the eye and say "Prost." One way to compliment the chef in Austria is to not use a knife when cutting meat. Instead, the side of the fork should be used, signifying that the meat is incredibly tender. One should also always use the side of the fork when cutting a dumpling. At the end of the meal, the knife and fork should be placed side by side on the plate. Leaving food uneaten on the plate is considered impolite.

If invited for dinner, one should take a gift and send a thank you note afterward. It is not considered impolite to decline an invitation or to decline the offer of refreshments, but it would be considered rude to accept and then to not attend or to be late. It is wise to call ahead before visiting someone without an invitation. Lastly, when entering someone's home, a guest should remove their hat if they are wearing one. In some Austrian households, it is still customary to remove one's shoes when entering someone's house. It is also customary to wait to be invited inside by the host.

LIFESTYLE

Family

Historically, Austrian culture has been influenced by Catholicism. At the turn of the 21st century, the majority of Austria's population—an estimated 74 percent—was of Roman Catholic heritage. A 1999 survey reported that traditional gender roles were very much embraced in Austrian society. The overwhelming majority wanted to marry, two children was the ideal family size, and divorce was frowned upon, particularly if the marriage had produced children. However, 2007 brought about a marked difference in terms of family life and ideals. According to 2007 statistics, the nation has an overall divorce rate of 49 percent and women are delaying childbearing. In addition, the average family had decreased to 1.38 children.

However, while other family trends have emerged in the 21st century, certain traditions have remained. For example, the majority of young adults continue to live with their parents until they have completed school or until they marry, especially in rural areas. Afterward, it is common for them to move into their own housing. Austrians tend to remain very close to their hometown and there is less migration within the country than elsewhere in Europe.

Housing

Urban housing in Austria often consists of long rows of terraced houses (where the houses are joined together) or condominiums and apartments. Houses in more rural areas tend to be freestanding, and are more often built of wood and locally available materials. Many rural homes have been owned within the same family

for generations, and are traditionally passed on to the next generation.

Homeownership figures in Austria have remained stable for several decades. As of 2001, 58 percent owned their own home. The remainder typically rent, most likely from a private landlord or from a local municipal housing authority. Home ownership rates are higher in rural areas than in urban areas, where people are more likely to rent.

Food

The cuisine of Austria is multicultural and often characterized by region. For example, Austrian cuisine in certain regions reflects the country's neighboring cultures, most notably Italy, Hungary, and Germany. Viennese cuisine is often distinctly different from Austrian food, and often considered a national cuisine unto itself. Austrian cuisine is also based upon historical influences from elsewhere in Europe, both east and west, including Jewish, Turkish, Bavarian, and Croatian influences.

In general, most Austrian meals are centered on meat, often pork or veal. A full meal may have as many as seven courses, depending upon the occasion and the importance of any guests who are invited. Soup (a beef broth) may precede a meal and dessert may include both a pastry and a lighter "after-dessert." Popular Austrian dishes include wiener schnitzel, veal cutlets that have been breaded and fried (also a famous dish of Viennese cuisine); goulash, a stew of Hungarian heritage typically made with beef, onions, and paprika; goose liver and onions; speck, a spiced ham; and noodles and dumplings.

Austria is also known for its sweets and pastries. Two examples of Austrian pastries that are known outside of Austria are apple strudel and linzertorte. Apple strudel is made from slices of spiced apples wrapped within very thin layers of pastry. Linzertorte is a flaky cake filled with raspberry jam and covered with cake dough. Coffee—and the coffeehouses where it is famously served, often with their own special blends—has become an important part of Austrian social life, and people frequently socialize over a cup of coffee and a pastry. Schnapps and cherry liqueur are popular aperitifs, and wine or beer is typically served with meals.

Life's Milestones

The majority of the population of Austria—approximately 74 percent—is Roman Catholic. Many of life's milestones are therefore still observed in accordance with church tradition.

Marriages in Austria are customarily lively occasions, bound by many traditions that are still honored. For example, it is considered bad luck for the bride to wear her entire outfit before the actual day of the wedding. As a result, a stitch is left undone and is not finished until the very last minute before the bride leaves for her wedding. In addition, the bride will often wear myrtle (a flowering plant) in her veil to symbolize life.

The groom traditionally wears a shirt either bought or made for him by the bride. The shirt is then stored and kept for his funeral.

In many rural areas, the bride is still accompanied to the church by a procession of musicians. After the ceremony, a man assigned to the role of wedding director is responsible for overseeing the reception, which typically includes music and dancing.

CULTURAL HISTORY

Art

The history of art in Austria goes back to prehistoric times. In the early 20th century, one of the earliest specimens of human art, a sculpture known as the *Venus of Willendorf*, was found in Lower Austria. The sculpture, which depicts a female figure with exaggerated physical features, is said to date back to 22000 BCE. The *Venus* has become one of the most widely recognized specimens of prehistoric art in modern times.

Due to its association with the Catholic Church and the Habsburg House (a noble family that ruled from the 14th to the 18th centuries), the arts were historically well supported in Austria. During the Middle Ages, much gothic religious art was produced. Some of the best surviving examples of gothic art include carved wooden altars such as the one in St. Wolfgang's, which was carved by Michael Pacher (1440–1498). During the Renaissance, art in Austria shifted from a predominantly religious focus to one that included the natural world. The Danube School, for example, was a 16th-century Renaissance art movement in Austria (as well as Bavaria) whose members were known for their innovative depiction of landscape in their works.

Baroque art flourished in Austria in the 17th and 18th centuries, exemplified in the work of painters such as Johann Michael Rottmayr (1656–1730), known for his church frescoes, and Paul Troger (1698–1762). Notable baroque sculptors include Georg Rafael Donner (1693–1741), known for his fountain (known as the Donner Fountain) in Vienna's Neuer Markt.

At the turn of the 20th century, the Vienna Secession (1897–1905) movement began. The progressive art movement featured many notable artists, such as Gustav Klimt (1862–1918) and Koloman Moser (1868–1918). Klimt, a painter, garnered international fame for his painting *The Kiss* (1907–1908), while Moser worked in an array of mediums, including printmaking, painting, ceramics, and stained glass. By the mid 20th century, the Vienna Group (Wiener Gruppe) had become established; its aesthetic was modern, a fusion of surrealism and Dadaism.

Architecture

Austria has a rich and varied architectural history, perhaps best exemplified by the capital of Vienna. The city is renowned for its blend of traditional and modern architecture, and for its representation of several different eras and styles of architectural history in Europe. The construction of the Hofburg, or Imperial Palace, spanned seven centuries. The original medieval fortress was built in the 13th century, while additional residences, chapels, museums, libraries, and other buildings were built over the years. As a result of the continued expansion, the building now embodies a range of styles from gothic to art nouveau, and even an art-deco glass butterfly house.

One of Austria's finest examples of baroque architecture is the Karlskirche, or St. Charles Church, built after the last great plague swept through Vienna in 1713—one of many since the Great Plague of Vienna occurred in 1679. The church was built to honor Saint Charles Borromeo, the patron saint of plague sufferers. The columned entrance of the church is reminiscent of ancient Greece, while the huge dome reflects the contemporary baroque style of Rome. Complementing these historic traditions are the modern elements of Austrian architecture that have also come to define the country and its capital. During the early 20th century, an Austrian form of art nouveau, known as Jugendstil, was popular. One example of this style is the Goldman and Splotch Building, which signaled a transition from the elaborate and decorative styles of the Viennese Secession to the simplicity of modernism.

Austria, and Vienna in particular, is also home to some of history's most significant architects, beginning in the 17th century with Josef Emanuel Fischer von Erlach (1693–1742), and Johann Bernhard Fischer von Erlach (1656–1723). These four designed a number of the city's court buildings and churches, mostly in the baroque style. At the turn of the 20th century, the art nouveau movement was pioneered in Vienna by famed architects such as Otto Wagner (1841–1918) and Adolf Loos (1870–1933). Wagner was one of the founders of an influential group of Austrian artists and architects known as the Vienna Secession (1897–1905), while Loos is considered the father of modern architecture in Austria.

Dance

Austrian dance ranges from traditional folk forms to widely known standards such as polka and the waltz. The polka became popular throughout central Europe and much of the United States. It is a very fast, lively dance and many tunes were written for it by famed Austrian composer Johann Sebastian Strauss (1835–1899). The waltz was considered quite shocking when it was first introduced, largely due to the physical closeness of

the two dance partners, though it soon became quite fashionable. In general, the polka and the waltz became two standards that most Viennese composers included in their repertoire.

Austria is also home to the schuhplattler, a traditional folk dance that involves a large amount of foot stamping and slapping of feet and thighs, coupled with jumping. A similar dance is mentioned in medieval literature as a form of courtship, with the men dancing to display their prowess. By the 18th century, women began to join in the dance, spinning while the men engaged in the more boisterous parts of the dance. The schuhplattler continues to be a very popular Austrian dance and is practiced by traditional dance groups in Austria, Bavaria and the US. Additionally, it is perhaps one of Europe's oldest dances. Some historians believe that a precursor to schuhplattler was practiced as far back as Neolithic times (3000 BCE) as a type of war dance, while other historians argue that it originated in the 18th century.

Music

During the 18th and 19th centuries, the Austrian royal family—known as the House of Habsburg—encouraged classical music. Their patronage made Vienna a center for the development of European classical music. It was during this period that world-renowned composers such as Wolfgang Amadeus Mozart (1756–1791) and Ludwig van Beethoven (1770–1827) flourished. Mozart's genius was recognizable form an early age, and he was soon playing in both Salzburg and Vienna, as well as in neighboring Germany. A large number of his works, including *The Marriage of Figaro*, *Cosi fan Tutte*, and *Don Giovanni*, were composed and first performed in Vienna.

Beethoven, although German by birth, spent much of his career in Austria and studied in Vienna under both Mozart and another famous Austrian composer, Joseph Haydn (1732–1809). All three composers are associated with the classical period (1750–1820) of Western music, characterized as lighter and less complex than its predecessor, baroque music. Other native

Austrian composers of note include Johann Sebastian Strauss (1825–1899) and Gustav Mahler (1860–1911). Strauss is credited with developing the famous Viennese waltz dance through his compositions—*The Blue Danube* being perhaps the most famous example—as well as a number of other widely practiced dances of the era. Mahler is associated with the late-romantic period, following the Industrial Revolution.

Austria also has a rich body of traditional folk music. The elegant waltz is believed to have evolved from a more vigorous dance known as the ländler, which consisted of a great deal of stomping, often in heavy work boots. The accompanying music, later played on the harpsichord or string section, would often have been played on the accordion. Also, the yodel, a type of throat singing, is also associated with Austrian culture. It was believed to have originated in the Swiss Alps as a means of communicating across the mountains, and remains a melodious type of folk music specific to the Alpine regions.

Literature

Austria's oft-changing geographical and political boundaries have made it difficult to pinpoint a body of literature as specifically Austrian until the 18th and 19th centuries. Generally, 18th-century literature in Austria was distinctly romantic in nature, with links to the nobility, royalty, and accompanying themes. However, a key change in the body of Austrian literature can be traced to the early 19th century, when the end of the Napoleonic wars in 1815 marked a new trend in literature known as the Biedermeier movement (1815–1848).

The Biedermeier movement in the arts was very much connected to the industrial changes that were occurring in Europe at the time. Society was transitioning from the rural, agrarian model to a more urbanized, industrial model. This led to the development of an urban middle class that gave birth to the Biedermeier movement (the prior Romantic authors having been born mainly to the noble classes). The movement was also a response to the growing censorship and political oppression that was sweeping through Europe. Writers belonging to the Biedermeier movement include poet and playwright Franz Grillparzer (1791–1872) and Adalbert Stifter (1805–1868), whose work marked the end of the movement and the transition toward realism.

Other notable Austrian writers include Felix Salten (1869–1945), Thomas Bernhard (1931–1989) and Franz Kafka (1883–1924). Salten is known for two major works that are at opposite ends of the literary spectrum: *Bambi, A Life in the Woods* (1923), which was famously adapted into a Disney movie, and the anonymously published erotic novel *Josephine Mutzenbacher* (1906), banned as pornographic until the 1960s. Bernhard rose to prominence abroad following World War II, and his works are known for their themes of isolation and abandonment. Kafka is best known for his existential works, such as *The Metamorphosis* (1915) and *The Trial* (1925), and is considered one of the most influential writers of the 20th century. More recently, the playwright and novelist Elfriede Jelinek was awarded the Nobel Prize in Literature in 2004.

CULTURE

Arts & Entertainment

Given the cultural and linguistic variety that has been part of Austria's history, cultural preservation plays an important part in Austrian society. Although not specifically mentioned in the national constitution, the arts are supported financially at the national, provincial, and municipal levels.

As a result of the 2006 elections, arts and education were combined under the umbrella of the Federal Ministry for Education, Arts and Culture. The ministry announced a number of plans to be enacted between 2007 and 2010, including greater support for cultural education within schools, free entry to museums on certain days of the year, greater support for young artists in order to create a presence on the international art scene, improved financing for the Austrian film industry, and an expansion of library resources.

However, specific cultural minorities in Austria may or may not be entitled to funding, depending upon their cultural origin. For example, Hungarians, Czechs, Slovenes, and Croats—all ethnic groups whose borders have overlapped at various points in history—may apply for funding to support their cultural heritage and diversity. Other more recent migrant groups, though, are not legally recognized as minority groups, and are therefore not eligible for such funding. Moreover, the budget that has been allotted to support such cultural diversity has remained unchanged since the early 1990s.

In recent years, policies regarding the distribution of funding for the arts have come under some criticism. It is often argued, for example, that those on low incomes are excluded from participation due to a lack of financial support for the poor. This resulted in a major project from 2002 to 2005, intended to bring discussion of poverty, gender, health care, and immigration into the artistic arena. Since the participants were primarily women, it appeared to reinforce the social divisions that it was attempting to highlight. Following this was the "Hunger for Arts and Culture" project, which provides free admission to cultural events and institutions for the unemployed and those with low incomes.

Generally, Austria has a very lively festival calendar with a variety of festivals, from the internationally renowned Salzburg Festival to the lesser known, but no less elaborate, World Bodypainting Festival. In Vienna, carnival season spans several weeks of opera performances and elegant balls, of which the most famous is the Viennese Opera Ball. Vienna also plays host to several film festivals through the year. However, only three percent of box office income in Austria is from domestic films. There is a small independent film community within Austria which has achieved more critical acclaim in the early 21st century, though the cinema's focus on social realism has led to its being dubbed "depressing" by many audiences. Nonetheless, the 2006 film *Die Fälscher* (The Counterfeiters) won the Academy Award for Best Foreign Film in 2007.

Sports are popular in Austria, especially Alpine sports such as skiing. Austrians have played a major role in the development of skiing, and have produced many Olympic champions. Football (soccer) is also popular, run by the Austrian Football Federation. Other popular sports include motor sports, cycling, and tennis.

Cultural Sites & Landmarks

Austria's wealth of culture and history is perhaps best defined by its eight World Heritage Sites as designated by the United Nations Educational, Scientific and Cultural Organization (UNESCO). For Austria, they include the historic centers of the towns of Graz, Salzburg and Vienna; the Palace and Gardens of Schönbrunn, in Vienna; the cultural and natural landscapes of Hallstatt–Dachstein/Salzkammergut and Wachau; Lake Neusiedl; and the Semmering railway, considered the oldest mountain railway in Europe.

In 2003, Graz was named the 2003 European City of Culture. It offers a labyrinth of well-preserved medieval streets and alleyways. Additionally, the Old Town of Salzburg, famous for its baroque architecture, was inscribed as one of Austria's first World Heritage Sites in 1996. The city is primarily known as the birthplace of Mozart, and the location for the film musical *The Sound of Music* (1965). The city is also noted for its Italian-influenced gothic and baroque architecture, and is home to Salzburg castle (Festung Hohensalzburg), one of the largest medieval fortresses in Europe.

Vienna, Austria's capital, is considered one of the cultural capitals of Europe. In fact, the city boasts the world's largest collection of historic architecture, and is home to numerous renowned museums and galleries of fine art. The National Theater, or Burgtheater, one of the first German-language theaters in Europe, is located in Vienna's first district. Its white marble façade features statues of Teutonic (German) literary and allegorical figures. Other landmarks in the city include the St. Stephen's Cathedral, built in 1147; the Vienna Opera House, home to the renowned Vienna Philharmonic Orchestra; and the art nouveau Anchor Clock, constructed between 1911 and 1917, located in Vienna's oldest square. The clock is decorated with mechanical figures depicting famous personalities from Vienna's past, including composers, empresses, and princes. The city is also home to the Schönbrunn Palace, once the magnificent summer residence of the Hapsburg emperors. The palace is renowned for its baroque architecture and well-preserved gardens, and was the site of the world's first zoo in 1752. The palace and its gardens, along with the Historic Centre of Vienna, are inscribed as a World Heritage Site.

In addition to the mountainous Alps in the west, the eastern part of the country offers rolling farmlands, lakes, forests and the wine-growing region within the Danube basin. The Wachau Cultural Landscape, designated a World Heritage Site in 2000, is famous for its architecture and agricultural importance. In addition, the Venus of Willendorf, an ancient statuette dating back to 24000 BCE, was unearthed there, and the remains of medieval monasteries and Roman settlements still lie beneath the region's small towns and villages. Likewise, the cultural landscapes of both the alpine regions of Hallstatt—Dachstein and Salzkammergut—are famous for their prehistoric human activity and fine architecture.

Connecting Lower Austria with Styria is the Semmering Railway. The railway line was completed in the mid-19th century, and its bridges, tunnels and curves are a monument to the beginnings of the industrial age in Austria. It was inscribed as a World Heritage Site in 1998. In addition, Austria's Lake Neusiedl region was designated a World Heritage Site in 2001 as the Fertő/Neusiedlersee Cultural Landscape. It was recognized primarily for the region's diffusion of cultures, environmental importance, and rural architecture. The lake itself is known as the "Sea of the Viennese."

Additionally, the mountainous landscape of Austria is a popular destination of outdoor recreationists such as skiers and hikers. In fact, the medieval town of Innsbruck hosted the Winter Olympics in both 1964 and 1976, and the surrounding area of the Tyrol region has a variety of ski resorts. The Vorarlberg region, located west of the Tyrol region bordering Germany and Switzerland, also offers an impressive selection of skiing and other outdoor activities.

Libraries & Museums

Vienna is home to numerous museums, including the Albertina Graphic Arts Collection, home to works of European masters from the Renaissance through the 20th century; the MUMOK Museum of Modern Art; the Mozart House museum, located in a former home of the great composer and dedicated to his life and work; and the Museum of Young Art, dedicated to European art produced since 2000. Other cultural institutions in Vienna include the museums at the Belvedere Palaces, which display three centuries of Austrian painting; the Museum of Fine Arts, which houses paintings by masters such as Peter Paul Rubens, Rembrandt Harmenszoon van Rijn, Johannes Vermeer, Albrecht Dürer, Raphael, Titian, and Pieter Bruegel; the Secession Museum, which specializes is contemporary art and whose façade is frequently altered by artists house many famous artworks; and the Sigmund Freud Museum, housed in the famous psychoanalyst's former home and office.

The Austrian National Library, home to over 7 million items in its collection, is located in Vienna, in the Hofburg Palace. (The Hofburg Palace, or Imperial Palace, also houses museum collections of musical instruments, weapons, and exotic butterflies.) As of the early 21st century, there were more than 1,560 public libraries throughout the country.

Holidays

Austria's public holidays are largely Christian feast days; in addition to Christmas and Easter, Austrian Catholics celebrate feasts including the Immaculate Conception (Mariä Empfängnis) and Corpus Christi (Fronleichnam). December 26 is St. Stephen's Day (Stefanitag).

Secular holidays include the State Holiday (Staatsfeiertag), and National Day (Nationalfeiertag), October 26, which commemorates the 1955 passage of the law confirming Austria's neutrality.

Youth Culture

In 2008, Austrian youth became the first in Europe to be allowed to vote in national elections at sixteen years. Intended to balance the increasing senior population in Austria, the law granted suffrage to those who are not yet legal adults. Eighteen also remains the age when one can legally marry, consume alcohol, and obtain a driver's license.

Austrian television and radio are subject to a heavy influx of American programming, and Americanized culture is often widespread. Nevertheless, certain other musical influences remain popular. Electronic music and acid-house (dance music) have retained their popularity in Austria, and much of continental Europe in general. Prominent Austrian musicians include DJ Ötzi, who has achieved success both within and outside of his homeland. Youth culture in Austria is also influenced by neighboring cultures. For example, German punk bands such as Die Ärzte also have a strong following in Austria.

SOCIETY

Transportation

Despite its mountainous geography, Austria has an extensive and widely used public transportation system. Local buses provide routes between small towns and villages, as well as within cities. The railway system is largely considered clean and efficient, providing connections with the rest of Europe. In addition to local trains, several high-speed trains pass through the country from Germany to Italy and Eastern Europe. According to a 2008 European transportation report, Austrians travel more by train per year than other Europeans, an average of 195 kilometers (121 miles) per person each year.

Traffic moves on the right-hand side of the road in Austria.

Transportation Infrastructure

The majority of railway services in Austria are owned and operated by the state, with a few privately-owned services operating in more remote areas. The Austrian National Railway comprises 5,800 kilometers (3,543 miles) of track. The Federal Road network comprises around 2,000 kilometers (1,242 miles) of motorways and express roads. Road traffic remains the most commonly used method of transportation for freight, although the waterways, particularly the Danube, also play an important role.

Media & Communications

Until the very end of the 20th century, the public broadcast station Oesterreichischer Rundfunk (ORF) was the principal source of television and radio output. In the 1990s, local commercial radio stations were permitted and they soon began to spring up across the country. The major commercial stations are Krone Hit Radio, and the Vienna-based Energy 104.2 and Radio Arabella. Commercial television station ATV began in 2000 and since then, local commercial television stations have also begun to appear.

A wide range of newspapers, both national and regional, are published in Austria. The largest newspapers in terms of circulation are *Neue Kronen-Zeitung* and *Kurier*. Of the broadsheet newspapers, *Die Presse* and *Der Standard* both have the highest circulation. In addition, Internet usage—as well as mobile phone usage—is high in Austria, with an estimated 74 percent of the population classified as Internet users in 2010.

SOCIAL DEVELOPMENT

Standard of Living

Austria ranked 21st out of 187 countries on the 2014 United Nations Human Development Index, which measures quality of life and standard of living indicators.

Water Consumption

Access to water and sanitation services is very high in Austria, with 100 percent of the population having access to these resources. Most water (around two-thirds of the 84 billion cubic meters used annually) is used by the industrial sector while around 35 percent is used for drinking and 5 percent is used in the agricultural sector.

Education

Schooling in Austria is compulsory for nine years, and most children attend public schools. Private schools are generally religious, run by the Catholic Church. Historically, Austria has had a "two-track" system of upper secondary education: vocational and academic. Before 1962, a student was forced to choose a track by the age of ten. The School Law of 1962 did away with this requirement, and also made higher education more accessible to the general public.

The Volksschule, or primary school, covers grades one through four. Besides the Volksschule, students can attend the Hauptschule, which provides general secondary education; or the Gymnasium, which focuses on academic studies. After the age of fourteen, students must decide between vocational education, which lasts for five years, and university. In order to receive higher education, a student must receive a certificate known as the Reifeprüfung or Matura.

Austria has many universities, some of which date back centuries. The University of Vienna, founded in 1365, is one of the oldest in Europe. Other public universities include Graz, Salzburg, Innsbruck, and Krems on the Danube. Private universities include the Catholic-Theological Private University in Linz.

The national literacy rate of Austria is around 98 percent, and the average number of years a student spends in school is fifteen. The gender gap in education favors women in the early 21st century, with 59 percent of women enrolled in tertiary education compared to 50 percent of men.

Women's Rights

Austrian policy regarding women is based upon the concept of equal treatment as opposed to equal rights. It is accepted that certain spheres of work will be gender specific and therefore unequal, so it attempts to compensate for that inequality. For example, mothers are paid

allowances to compensate them for raising children. Meanwhile, in terms of employment, measures are taken to ensure equal pay and equal treatment. Sixty-eight percent of Austrian women participate in the labor force, compared to 81 percent of men. Kindergartens, although free, are difficult to find, making it hard for mothers of young children to work outside the home. According to the 2010 Gender Gap Index, women comprised just over one quarter (28 percent) of the national parliament.

Pregnant women are not allowed to work eight weeks before their due date and for at least eight weeks after the birth. This leave is paid at the full salary rate. Parents are also entitled to take two years of parental leave. This may be used entirely by one parent (as maternity or paternity leave), or it may be split between the two. During that time, they will receive benefits and their employer must rehire them at the same rate of pay and status once the leave is completed. Mothers also receive a monthly allowance for each child until the age of 21 if the child is still at home and either unemployed or in school, and up to the age of 27 if the child is attending university.

The 1998 amendment to the Austrian constitution ensured that Austrian law met the requirements of the UN Convention on the Elimination of all forms of Discrimination Against Women (CEDAW). In 2007, additional European directives were added to further anti-discrimination legislation. In a 2005 UN report, Austria ranked 28th among 50 countries on a Gender Empowerment Measure (GEM) that looked at political participation, economic power and availability of education and healthcare. Although Austrian women rank fairly well in healthcare, their levels of economic participation and educational attainment are lower than in the majority of European nations.

Health Care

Austria has a nationalized system of health care comparable to that in other Western European nations. People are required to pay into state-operated health-insurance programs. Life expectancy is generally high: 77 years for men, and 83 years for women (2014 estimate).

Austrians typically have many health problems, in part due to a rich diet heavy in carbohydrates, sugar, and fat. Other problems are related to high rates of smoking and alcohol abuse. In 2002, Austria had one of the highest suicide rates in Europe.

GOVERNMENT

Structure

Until 1920, with the establishment of the Republic of Austria, the country had been ruled by monarchs. For centuries, the ruling Habsburg (or Hapsburg) family also held the title of Holy Roman Emperor. The Hapsburg hereditary lands expanded over the years until they covered much of southeastern Europe. In 1867, the Austrian Empire reorganized itself as the Austro-Hungarian Empire, reflecting 19th-century nationalism.

After World War I, the victorious Allies broke up the Austro-Hungarian Empire into many national states, with the German-speaking parts comprising the landlocked Republic of Austria. The republic was dissolved in 1938, when Nazi Germany swallowed up Austria in an event known as the Anschluss ("annexation"), but was reestablished after World War II. The modern republic uses the Constitution of 1929.

Austria is a federal republic, with a parliamentary system of government. The president, who is elected to a six-year term, serves as head of state but has largely ceremonial powers. The prime minister (chancellor) is nominated by the president from the party with the most seats in parliament. The chancellor then chooses a Cabinet.

The parliament has two houses. The popularly-elected lower house, or National Council (Nationalrat), is the main law-making body. The upper house, or Federal Council (Bundesrat), has limited powers to veto bills from the lower house. Its members represent the provinces, and are chosen by the state assembles rather than the public.

Political Parties

The main political parties are the Social Democratic Party of Austria (Sozial Demokratische Partei Österreichs) and the conservative Austrian People's Party (Österreichs Volkspartei). The far-right Freedom Party of Austria (Freiheitliche Partei Österreichs) raised fears throughout Europe about a resurgence of neo-Nazism, due to the party's strong showing in recent elections, making large strides in the 2013 election. For a time, Austria was shunned by other nations because of the prospect that the Freedom Party might form a coalition government with the People's Party.

Local Government

Austria has nine provinces or federal states (Bundesländer; singular Bundesland), each of which has its own popularly-elected assembly. These include the cities of Vienna and Salzburg, as well as the states of Lower Austria, Upper Austria, Carinthia, Tyrol, Vorarlberg, Styria, and Burgenland.

Judicial System

The judiciary is independent. The Supreme Court has final jurisdiction over civil and criminal cases. The Administrative Court handles administrative law, involving government agencies. The Constitutional Court handles cases involving constitutional law. The federal states have their own provincial and district courts. There are also many local courts, for handling lesser offenses.

Taxation

In Austria, a high income tax is levied, with the top income tax rate being 50 percent, as well as a corporate tax, with the top rate being 25 percent (2010). Other taxes levied include a real estate transfer tax and a value-added tax (VAT).

Armed Forces

The Austrian Armed Forces consist of two major service branches: Land Forces and Air Forces. Conscription lasts six months and 18 is the minimum age for service. The active personnel number 35,000, while reserves total 72,000 strong. The armed forces have contributed to and participated in more than fifty international humanitarian and peace missions since 1960.

Foreign Policy

Following the Second World War, Austria was governed by the Allied Commission (composed of France, the United Kingdom, the United States, and the Soviet Union). Upon gaining independence in 1955, the nation adopted a policy of political neutrality. Technically, the policy remains in place although the concept of neutrality has undergone some redefinition in the new millennium. Although not a member of the North Atlantic Treaty Organization (NATO), Austria joined the Partnership for Peace (PFP) in 1995, and has since participated in peacekeeping missions in Bosnia and elsewhere. In 2002, the nation became part of the International Security Assistance Force (ISAF) in Afghanistan, providing troops to help oversee elections, protect women's rights, and fight drug trafficking.

Regionally, Austria became a member of the European Union (EU) in 1995, but had been actively involved in European trade relations before then. Austria was one of the founding members of the European Free Trade Association (EFTA) in 1960, a trade bloc that acted as the precursor to the European Economic Community (ECC). Austria adopted the common currency of the EU, the euro, in 2002. Austria also maintains an active role in the Organization for Security and Co-operation in Europe (OSCE). In addition, Austria was instrumental in helping the Czech Republic, Poland, Slovakia, Slovenia, and Hungary gain admittance to the EU with the establishment of a Regional Partnership in 2001.

Due to its geographic location, Austria frequently serves as a gateway between Western and Eastern Europe. This is reflected in the number of organizations that have their headquarters in Vienna. The OSCE, the International Atomic Energy Agency, the UN Industrial Development Organization, and the UN Drug Control Program all have main offices in the city. In 2008, Austria completed a three-year term on the UN Economic and Social Council. Additionally, Austria is a member of the Organization for Economic Co-cooperation and Development (OECD), a collective of 30 countries that works to support sustainable economic growth and assist the economic development of other nations.

In 1999, the EU imposed sanctions against Austria in response to growing right-wing political extremism in the country's government and the entry of the far-right Freedom Party into the country's ruling coalition. These sanctions were later dropped. However, the EU, the US, and Israel continue to keep a close eye on the country's anti-immigrant groups, particularly after right-wing parties scored large victories in the 2008 and 2013 elections, ostensibly due to its stance on limited immigration, which has been criticized as xenophobic, particularly toward Muslim and Jewish populations.

Human Rights Profile

International human rights law insists that states respect civil and political rights, and also promote an individual's economic, social and cultural rights. The United Nations Universal Declaration of Human Rights (UDHR) is recognized as the standard for international human rights. Its authors sought the counsel of the world's great thinkers, philosophers, and religious leaders, and were careful to create a document that reflects the core values shared by every world culture. (To read this document or view the articles relating to cultural human rights, go to: http://www.udhr.org/UDHR/default.htm.)

The Austrian constitution, in accordance with Article 2 of the UDHR, provides equal rights for its citizens, regardless of race, religion or gender. The media faces little censorship from the government, and the law is very strict regarding the denial or belittlement of crimes against humanity or against any racial group. As such, denial of the Holocaust is illegal and several scholars (most notably British historian David Irving) have been subject to jail sentences for the crime of Holocaust denial.

Freedom to marry, as outlined in Article 16, is protected. The legal age for marriage is 1 for both men and women, although court permission may be sought for an 18-year-old to marry someone as young as sixteen years. Gay marriage or civil partnerships are not legally recognized. Legislation was due to be enacted in 2008, but the dissolution of the parliament meant plans were placed on hold. Further attempts to legalize same-sex marriage stalled again in 2013.

Freedom of religion, outlined in Article 18 of the declaration, is protected by the constitution, although there are some societal prejudices against certain religious sects such as the Jehovah's Witnesses and Scientologists. Attacks against Muslims have also increased in recent years. Additionally, the rights to freedom of expression and freedom of assembly, as defined by Articles 19 and 20 of the declaration, are protected and generally observed. However, freedom of expression has been contested, particularly in cases involving Holocaust denial.

On the whole, Austria has a good record for protecting human rights. However, there has been a rise in anti-Semitic attacks and attacks against Muslims and immigrants in the new millennium. In 2006, an Islamic cemetery in Vienna was subjected to an arson attack, and attempts to ban headscarves in public were struck down as unconstitutional. Reports of police violence, particularly racially motivated violence, increased in 2006. Overcrowding of prisons and detainment centers was also raised as a problem, as in many parts of Europe.

Lastly, Austria's position as a geographic bridge between Eastern and Western Europe has also made it a hub for the trafficking of both women and children. Human rights activists have repeatedly exposed cases of women being brought into the country and then forced into prostitution, as well as those who are then transported elsewhere.

ECONOMY

Overview of the Economy

Austria has one of the most developed economies in Europe. The economy is largely focused on services and industry. In 2014, the country's gross domestic product (GDP) was $386.9 billion (USD), and its estimated per capita GDP was $45,400 (USD). Austria's main industries include iron and steel, chemicals, industrial equipment, and consumer goods. The remainder of the country's GDP is generated by agriculture.

Vienna is the linchpin of the Austrian economy, generating around a third of the nation's gross domestic product (GDP) and employing about a quarter of the national workforce. The Austrian federal government and the various international organizations headquartered in Vienna are some of the capital's largest employers. The city is the center of Austria's banking and insurance sector.

Austria has been a member of the European Union (EU) since 1995, and uses the euro as its national currency. The EU (especially neighboring Germany) and the United States are major trading partners, as are Hungary and Switzerland.

Like other European nations, Austria is seeking to improve productivity through lower taxes and privatization of state-run industries. Its GDP has grown substantially in the late 20th and early 21st centuries, represented substantial growth in GDP, which was $174.8 billion (USD) in 1992, compared to $386.9 billion (USD in 2009).

Industry

Austria's economy is based primarily on services, particularly finance and tourism. Industry is also important, representing about 30 percent of the GDP. The major manufacturing sectors include industrial equipment, textiles, paper, chemicals, iron, and steel. Besides Vienna, the most important centers of manufacturing include Linz, Innsbruck, and Graz.

Austria nationalized many industries after World War II, though the government is now moving toward privatization. International investment is important, and Austria is trying to build up its high-technology sector (including electronics and telecommunications).

The Danube, which flows into the Black Sea, is a major inland waterway for cargo and passenger traffic. The major port is Vienna, considered

Europe's largest inland container port. The country has dozens of airports, with international flights out Vienna, Graz, and other cities.

Labor

The labor force comprised 3.77 million workers in 2014, with the majority (68 percent) being employed in the services industry. The unemployment rate in 2014 was 4.5 percent.

Energy/Power/Natural Resources

Austria possesses a variety of mineral resources, including iron ore, tungsten, lignite, and cement. Energy resources include petroleum and natural gas. Timber is abundant, as almost half the country is covered with deciduous and coniferous forests.

Hydro power remains a major provider of electricity production. It is estimated that only 20 percent of Austria's power production is from gas or oil.

Fishing

A landlocked country, Austria must import its seafood, and fish and seafood consumption is low. The fishing industry is small, employing fewer than 250 workers.

Forestry

Approximately 47 percent of Austria is forested. The forestry industry employs approximately 300,000 workers, and the timber industry brings in an estimated $1 billion (USD) annually.

Mining/Metals

In the early 21st century, commonly mined metals in Austria include aluminum, copper, lead, iron ore, and tungsten. Commonly mined industrial materials include gravel and sand, salt, limestone, marble, talc, and soapstone.

Agriculture

Agriculture represents only about 2 percent of Austria's gross domestic product and employs around six percent of its labor force. While a relatively small economic sector, the agricultural industry meets a significant portion of domestic consumption. The main crops include grain (barley, oats, and rye), potatoes, and sugar beets.

Animal Husbandry

Livestock farming includes cattle, pigs, and chickens. In 2009, there were an estimated 2 million head of (bovine) cattle, 3.1 million swine, and 350,000 sheep in Austria.

Tourism

Tourism is a major industry in Austria. In 2004, there were around 19.4 million foreign visitors, many of them from neighboring Germany and Switzerland as well as from the United States and Britain. Many tourists visit Austria for the country's great natural beauty, particularly in the Alpine regions, where one can enjoy winter sports and the quaint mountain villages.

Tourism is an important and growing component of the Viennese economy, and Vienna is a premier location for international trade shows and political summits due to its state-of-the-art infrastructure and accommodations (as well as Austria's general location). The city's numerous historical and cultural attractions also draw millions of foreign visitors each year. In 2009, tourism was valued at around 10 percent of Austria's GDP.

Austria has also been recognized as one of the premier destinations for sustainable tourism by the World Economic Forum's Travel & Tourism Competitiveness Report.

Fiona Young-Brown, Eric Badertscher,
Beverly Ballaro

DO YOU KNOW?

- Captain Georg Von Trapp, depicted in the musical *The Sound of Music*, was a hero during World War I. He served as a submarine commander in the Austro-Hungarian Navy.

- The favorite Christmas song "Silent Night" ("Stille Nacht") was written in 1818, with words by parish priest Joseph Mohr and composer Franz Gruber, in the Austrian village of Oberndorf.

Bibliography

Beller, Steven. *A Concise History of Austria.* Cambridge: Cambridge University Press, 2007.

Brook-Shepherd, Gordon. *The Austrians: A Thousand-Year Odyssey.* New York: Basic Books, 2002.

Gieler, Peter. *Austria – Culture Smart!* London: Kuperard, 2007.

Haywood, Anthony. *Austria.* Oakland, CA: Lonely Planet, 2014.

Hobelt, Luther. *Defiant Populist: Jorg Haider and the Politics of Austria.* Lafayette, IN: Purdue University Press, 2003.

Humphreys, Rob, and Jonathan Bousfield. *Rough Guide to Austria.* London: Rough Guides, 2008.

Kristan, Markus. *Austrian Architecture in Europe.* Berlin: Springer Press, 2003.

Krzyzanowski, Michal and Ruth Wodak. *The Politics of Exclusion: Debating Migration in Austria.* Piscataway, NJ: Transaction Publishers, 2008.

Mayer-Brown, Elisabeth. *Best of Austrian Cuisine.* New York: Hippocrene Books, 2001.

Works Cited

"Austria: Principal Cities." http://www.citypopulation.de/Oesterreich-Cities.html

"Austria Transportation and Telecommunications." http://www.photius.com/countries/austria/economy/austria_economy_transportation_and t~164.html

"Country Profile: Austria." http://news.bbc.co.uk/2/hi/europe/country_profiles/1032215.stm#media

"Country Reports on Human Rights Practices 2007: Austria." *U.S. Department of State.* http://www.state.gov/g/drl/rls/hrrpt/2007/100547.htm

"Cultural Policies and Trends in Austria." http://www.culturalpolicies.net/web/austria.php?aid=41&cid=1040&lid=en&curl=1.

"Cultural Policy in Austria." http://www.wwcd.org/policy/clink/Austria.html.

"Demographic Indicators." http://www.statistik.at/web_en/statistics/population/demographic_indices/demographic_indicators/index.html.

"European Database: Women in Decision-Making." http://www.db-decision.de/CoRe/Austria.htm

"European Union. Europe in Figures – Eurostat Yearbook 2008". Available for download from http://europa.eu

"Family Benefits." http://countrystudies.us/austria/81.htm

"Family Values in Austria." http://family.jrank.org/pages/141/Austria-Family-Values.html.

"OECD Country Statistical Profile." http://stats.oecd.org/wbos/viewhtml.aspx?queryname=457&querytype=view&lang=en

"Overview of Gender Equality Issues in Austria." http://www.gender-equality.webinfo.lt/results/austria.htm

"Social Housing in Austria." http://www.cecodhas.org/index.php?option=com_content&task=view&id=75&Itemid=117

"The Austrian Foreign Ministry." http://www.bmeia.gv.at/en/foreign-ministry/foreign-policy/europe.html

"The History of the Vienna Hofburg." http://www.hofburg-wien.at/en/things-to-know/history-of-vienna-hofburg.html

"The Mozart Project." http://www.mozartproject.org/biography/index.html

"The Johann Strauss Society." http://www.johann-strauss.org.uk/composers/index.php3?content=johann2

"Women's Empowerment: Measuring the Global Gender Gap." *World Economic Forum.* http://www.unece.org/stats/gender/publications/Multi-Country/WomenEmpowerment.pdf

The top of the Royal Flemish Theater /Stock photo © Michael Luhrenberg

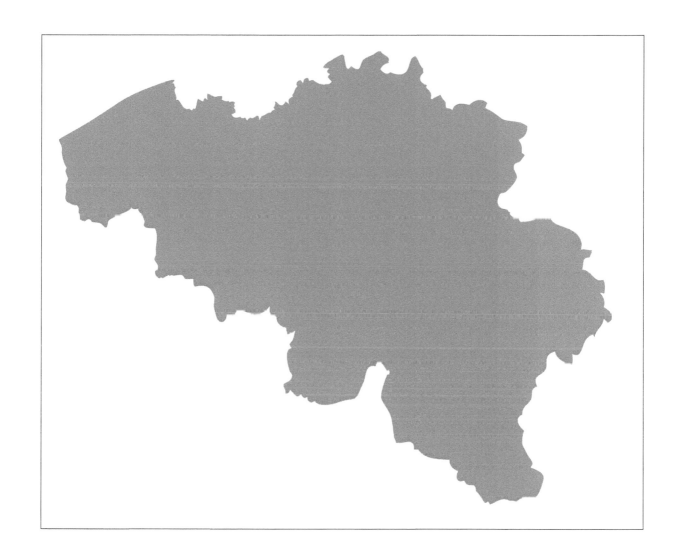

BELGIUM

Introduction

A small country in northwestern Europe, Belgium has been a cultural and economic crossroads since ancient times. It was ruled successively by ancient Rome, Spain, Austria, France, and the Netherlands until 1830, and some of the fiercest battles of both World War I and World War II were fought on Belgian soil.

Following the end of World War II, Belgium has vigorously promoted international cooperation. It is a founding member of the United Nations, the North Atlantic Treaty Organization (NATO), and the European Union. Belgium was also one of the first European countries to recover economically after World War II. Today, Belgium is a technologically developed nation whose economy depends largely on trade and on the presence of international organizations and businesses.

GENERAL INFORMATION

Official Language: Dutch (Flemish), French, and German
Population: 10,449,361 (2014 estimate)
Currency: Euro
Coins: The Euro is available in 1, 2, 5, 10, 20 and 50 cent coins. A 1 and 2 Euro coin is also available.
Land Area: 30,278 square kilometers (11,690 square miles)

Water Area: 250 square kilometers (97 square miles)
National Motto: "L'Union fait la force/ Eendracht maakt macht" (French/Dutch, "Unity Makes Strength")
National Anthem: "The Brabançonne" ("Song of Brabant")
Capital: Brussels
Time Zone: GMT +1
Flag Description: The flag of Belgium features three vertical bands of color: one black, one yellow, and one red. The black represents determination, the red represents bravery and strength, and the yellow represents generosity.

Population

With 354 people per square kilometer (919 people per square mile), Belgium is one of the world's most densely populated countries. A total of 97 percent of the population lives in cities and

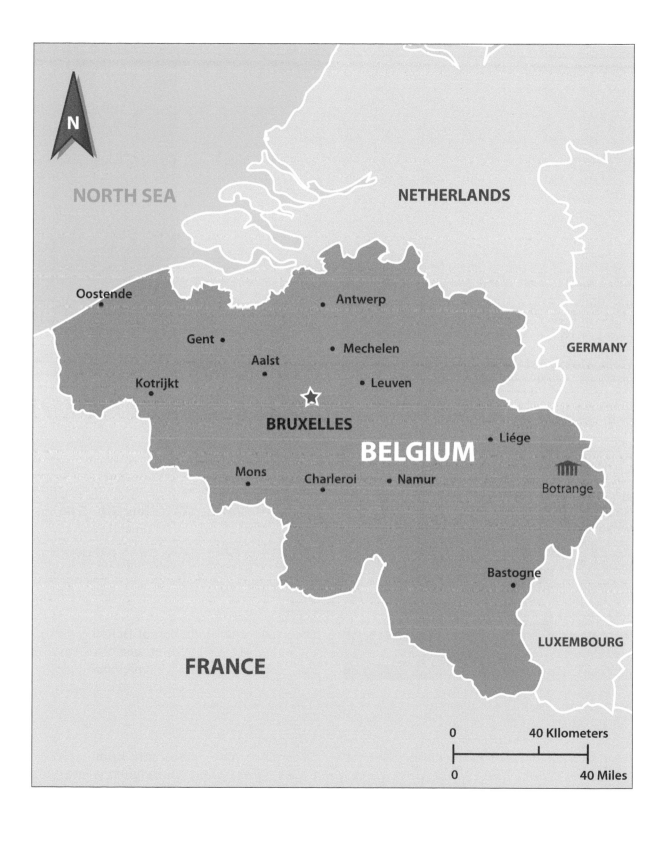

Principal Cities by Population (2012):

- Bruxelles (1,100,000)
- Antwerp (493,920)
- Ghent (248,285)
- Charleroi (202,981)
- Liège (195,076)
- Schaerbeek (123,537) (2009 estimate)
- Brugge (116,342)
- Namur (109,686)
- Anderlecht (105,492) (2009 estimate)
- Leuven (95,060) (2009 estimate)

towns, and only a small percentage live in rural areas. The Brussels-Capital Region is the country's largest urban area, and has a population of 1.1 million (2012). Antwerp, the major seaport, has a population of approximately 493,920 people.

Those who live in Flanders, in the northern part of the country, are called Flemings. Residents of the Wallonia region are called Walloons.

Languages

The Flemings, who make up roughly 60 percent of the population, speak a dialect that used to be called Flemish, but is now called Dutch. The Walloons speak French, one of the country's two official languages. Both Flemings and Walloons live in Brussels, which is officially bilingual. German is the official language for the small community of German-speakers on Wallonia's border with Germany.

Native People & Ethnic Groups

There is evidence of habitation since prehistoric times in what is now Belgium. The country's name comes from the Belgae, a group of Celtic tribes that arrived from Britain after 100 BCE. During the first century, Julius Caesar defeated the Belgae and incorporated their territory into Gaul. The Romans developed cities, industries, and a system of roads.

When the Franks, a Germanic tribe, were pushed west by Attila the Hun, they settled in what is now Belgium. Those who settled in the south, where Roman influence was strong, were absorbed into the population.

The Franks who settled in the north developed a separate culture and language. These became the Flemings. They drove the Romans out of what is now Flanders in the fifth century. Charlemagne (768–814) is the best-known Frankish king. Under his rule, Belgium developed an empire that incorporated much of Western Europe. In 1302, armored French knights invaded Flanders. Peasants and artisans repelled them in a victory that is commemorated each July 11 in Flanders.

As a result of political marriages, Belgium was ruled by the Spanish (1519–1713) and then the Austrians (1713–1794). Napoleon conquered Belgium in 1795. After his defeat at the Battle of Waterloo (just south of Brussels) in 1815, the Congress of Vienna awarded Belgium to the Netherlands. Belgium gained its independence in 1830.

Today, Dutch speaking Flemish people make up the majority ethnic group in Belgium, numbering approximately six million people. There are approximately 3.5 million French-speaking Walloons. Minority ethnic groups in Belgium include Italians, Moroccans, Algerians, Indians, and Congolese.

Religions

While about 5 percent of Belgians claim no religion, most are Christians. Roman Catholics constitute 85 percent of the population, but fewer than 30 percent of those are regular churchgoers. Freedom of worship is guaranteed in the constitution, and the government gives money to all "recognized religions."

Climate

Belgium's climate is temperate. Temperatures in Brussels, in the center of the country, usually range from 0° Celsius (32° Fahrenheit) in the winter to 22° Celsius (72° Fahrenheit) in the summer. The average temperature on the coast ranges from 1° Celsius (34° Fahrenheit) in January to 14° Celsius (69° Fahrenheit) in July.

The elevated Ardennes experiences temperature variations from −1° Celsius (28° Fahrenheit) in winter to 16° Celsius (61° Fahrenheit) in summer.

Belgium is wet, and experiences a great deal of rain and mist. Rainfall on the coast averages between 58 to 71 centimeters (23 to 28 inches) a year. Brussels receives an average of 82 centimeters (32 inches) of rain a year. In the Ardennes, precipitation averages one meter (40 inches) annually. While all parts of the country receive snow, it melts quickly everywhere but the Ardennes.

ENVIRONMENT & GEOGRAPHY

Topography

Belgium is a small country, about the size of the American state of Maryland, in northwest Europe. It is bounded on the north by the Netherlands, on the east by Germany and Luxembourg, on the south by France, and on the west by the English Channel of the North Sea.

Belgium has four main topographical regions: the coastal and interior lowlands, the Kempenland (the Campine), the central low plateaus, and the Ardennes.

The treeless lowlands stretch across the north of the country. Polders (lowlands) near the sandy coast are protected from the sea by dykes (barriers), and are crossed by drainage canals. The Kempenland, just to the south of the lowlands, lost most of its birch forests with the discovery of coal in the early 20th century. Quick-growing evergreens have been planted to replace the missing birches. The land has been drained and planted with cereal crops.

The central low plateaus lie south of the Kempenland. The southern part of this area contains the best farmland, watered by the Sambre and Meuse Rivers. It is also the site of the country's largest cities.

The Ardennes is the least-populous part of the country, with sandstone ridges, limestone valleys, rugged mountains, and woodlands with winding rivers and numerous river-carved caves. The highest point in Belgium is the 694-meter

(2,777-foot) Signal Botrange Mountain in the Ardennes.

Most West European capitals are within 1,000 kilometers (621 miles) of Belgium. Its central location and large navigable rivers are important for trade. Belgium has no large natural lakes, but the damming of southern rivers has created some artificial lakes. The largest is Lac de la Plate-Taille, 374 hectares (924 acres), in Ardennes.

The 901-kilometer (560-mile) Meuse River rises in northeast France and flows through Belgium into the Netherlands, where it becomes the Maas. At the North Sea, it forms a delta with the Rhine. The Meuse is linked to Antwerp by the Albert Canal. Other important rivers include the Sambre and the Schelde.

Plants & Animals

Many species of plants and animals in Belgium have become extinct. Up to one-half of the remaining wildlife is threatened. One in ten bird species and half of the freshwater fish species are threatened. Recent efforts have helped, though, and some species are increasing in numbers.

Common wildlife includes wild boars, deer, and wildcats in the Ardennes forests. Other animals include pheasants, foxes, weasels, martens, badgers, hedgehogs, and squirrels.

Plants that flourish in Belgium include strawberries, goldenrod, periwinkles, hyacinths, wild arum, foxglove, and lilies-of-the-valley. Pine, elm, beech, and oak trees have been planted throughout the country.

CUSTOMS & COURTESIES

Greetings

The two major languages of Belgium are French and Flemish, with a small pocket of the country speaking German. However, speaking the wrong language can cause great offense. As such, English is particularly advised, and widely used for business purposes in Brussels.

In French speaking parts of Belgium, a customary greeting involves saying "Bon jour" ("Hello"). Common farewell phrases include "Àtoute à l'heure," ("See you later"), "Àdemain," ("See you tomorrow") or "Au revoir" ("Goodbye"). A casual Flemish greeting is "Hallo" ("Hello"). In a more formal setting, or if speaking to an elder, "Goeiemorgen" ("Good morning") is common. Additionally, "Ik zie je later" ("See you later") or "Vaarwel" ("Goodbye") would be used as common farewell phrases.

Shaking hands is the most common way of greeting someone, particularly in a business or formal setting. In more casual situations, men still continue to shake hands, while women may exchange three kisses on the cheek with their friends, be they male or female. Taking the form of an air kiss rather than an actual kiss on the cheek, it should begin on the left side and then alternate. This series of kisses may be repeated upon departure.

Gestures & Etiquette

Belgian people tend to dress quite conservatively. Although this will vary in degree depending upon the age of the person, it should be noted that dark colors, suits, and dresses for women are appropriate in most business and formal situations. With regard to conversation, certain topics are typically not raised except among very close friends. This is particularly true when discussing the relationship between Wallonia and Flanders, a very sensitive and politically tense topic, or the subject of the monarchy.

Gestures are not widely used in conversation. In fact, speaking loudly, making large or exaggerated gestures, or pointing at someone, are all considered rude behavior. Additionally, snapping one's fingers to attract someone's attention is considered impolite, while the causal slapping of the back, intended as a friendly greeting, is likely to cause offense. Furthermore, eye contact is usually considered important. To avoid eye contact may raise suspicions about one's level of honesty or motives. As in other Western cultures, a comfortable level of eye contact should always be maintained, especially in business situations.

Punctuality is important to most Belgians, particularly in the business world. If an individual is likely to be late, every effort should be made to let the other person know. Business meetings tend to be quite formal and business cards are usually exchanged.

Given the risk of causing offense by using the wrong language, it is not uncommon for English to be used for business transactions; since Belgians are taught several languages in school, they tend to be quite comfortable using English.

Eating/Meals:

The typical Belgian breakfast follows the continental style of bread, jam, cheese, and coffee. Lunch is traditionally the main, or largest, meal of the day, while dinner is typically lighter. Many businesses and schools will close, allowing employees and children to return home for a typical two-hour lunch break. Supper may consist of leftovers or a light meal of eggs, fish or cheese. However, as cities have become more industrialized, the long midday break is becoming more difficult to maintain. As such, the Sunday noon meal is increasingly becoming all the more important and extravagant.

Meal etiquette is still rather formal when compared to habits in other Western cultures. Guests should wait until their host tells them where to sit, and toasts are commonly made during a meal. Typically, no one will take a drink until the host or guest of honor has offered a toast. Glasses are raised twice in the toast, at the beginning and again at the end.

Table manners and the use of utensils in Belgium follow the continental style. While eating, the fork should be held in the left hand, and the knife in the right hand. Wrists should be kept above the table during the meal. When the meal is finished, the knife and fork should be placed side by side on the plate with the handles pointing to the right. Guests should also note that leaving food is considered rude and wasteful, and all food on the plate should be eaten.

Visiting

Belgians take great care to maintain their privacy, and it is widely considered rude to call unannounced at someone's home. It is quite common for close friends and family to meet publically, often at a local restaurant, bar or coffee shop. Because socializing in Belgium is typically done outside the home, to be invited to someone's home is considered an indicator of trust and friendship. Invitations, if written, should be responded to with an equally polite written notice.

When visiting, punctuality is considered important. Since privacy is highly respected in Belgium, it is not common for guests to ask for a tour of the house. Additionally, a gift for the hostess is considered appropriate, and may include candy for any children or flowers (chrysanthemums are often used to symbolize death and therefore are not suitable as a gift). Gifts that are overly extravagant are typically avoided, as this may cause the host to feel uncomfortable. Gifts are commonly opened during the visit.

LIFESTYLE

Family

Families typically live within the nuclear family unit—traditionally, two married parents with children—with the exception of those living on farms in very rural areas. As of 2006, 37 percent of Belgian households were comprised of the nuclear family unit, while an additional 31 percent of households were single-parent families. The average family size is one or two children, and it is common for both parents to work.

Additionally, the majority of Belgians remain loyal to both family and community. They tend to live within a close distance of family and where they grew up and it is not common to move far from home. As a result, grandparents and other family members usually live close by.

Housing

Homeownership is common in Belgium, with ownership rates in the country among the highest in Western Europe. Most Belgians live in single-family homes. In fact, only 10 percent of the population lives in apartments, a testament to the importance of privacy in Belgium. In addition, the government assists in offering low interest mortgages to encourage home ownership.

Generally, Belgium consists mainly of small towns and villages where terraced houses (each joined to the next) are the norm. Typically, these houses are built among the narrow streets, churches, and marketplaces. Farms are more common in the north.

Food

Belgium is world-renowned for its cuisine, which has French, German and, to a lesser extent, Dutch influences. In fact, Belgian food is commonly referred to as having the quality of French cuisine, and the quantity, or sizeable portions, of German cuisine. Herbs, spices, vinegars, mustards, and beer are widely used ingredients, with herbs such as tarragon, thyme, chives, and parsley and spices such as saffron, ginger, and nutmeg often featured prominently. The use of vegetables is important to most dishes, with potatoes and endives (a leafy vegetable) heavily used. Game meat and seafood, especially mussels, are popular, and often form the staple of most meals.

Two popular dishes that are generally internationally associated with Belgium are frites (fried potatoes) and waffles. Frites are considered an important part of Belgian culture—they are often referred to as the national food—and the twice-fried potatoes are typically served with mayonnaise. Belgium waffles have gained international fame, and are typically served with powdered sugar, strawberries, ice cream, or chocolate. Both waffles and frites are commonly consumed as street snacks.

Mussels and frites, and waterzooi, a stew consisting of fish or chicken, vegetables, eggs, cream, and butter, are popular dishes commonly found in the north. Throughout the country, raw minced meat or steak is customarily eaten with frites as a staple meal. Other traditional dishes include carbonnades, a Flemish beef stew cooked in beer; anguille au vert, which is eel prepared in a green herb sauce; and rabbit, often stewed in sour beer. Generally, traditional Belgian cuisine has changed relatively little since the medieval era, and Belgians typically prefer to stick with their home cuisine rather than adopt fast food.

Belgian is also renowned for its gourmet chocolate and beer. Roughly 172,000 tons of Belgian chocolate are produced each year, and traditional chocolatiers are common even in the smallest villages. Belgian chocolate pralines, a confectionary food typically consisting of nuts in a chocolate shell, are particularly popular. Traditionally, pralines can be made with a variety of ingredients, including coffee, fruit, or nougats. Belgium's chocolate shops operate on the same level of prestige as a French winery, and typically offer tours and tastings.

Brewing in Belgium dates back to the 12th and 13th centuries, when monasteries brewed Trappist ale (beer brewed under the strict control of Trappist monks, a religious order of the Roman Catholic Church). In addition to the complex Trappist style, other popular styles include lambic, kriek, and white (wheat). The lambic style has a distinctive sour taste, while kriek beer is the lambic style further fermented with fruit. Additionally, some of the popular ingredients used in Belgian cooking—such as dried fruits, chocolate, and spices including saffron, cinnamon, and ginger—are commonly used in beer brewing. Overall, there are over 450 varieties of beer brewed in Belgium.

Life's Milestones
Religious traditions continue to play an important role in the celebration of major milestones in Belgian culture. Statistics from a 2000 survey show that 64 percent of babies are baptized as Catholic, while 76 percent of funerals are carried out in the Catholic tradition. In addition, the rites of first communion are still widely celebrated when a child reaches the age of eleven years.

Traditionally, Belgian marriage invitations are sent out on two pieces of paper, one from each family. By sending them out together, the union of two families into one is symbolized. As in many parts of the Western world, the bride customarily wears white. She often carries a handkerchief on which the names of other brides

and grooms in the family have been embroidered, along with the appropriate wedding dates. Additionally, while civil marriages are required for a union to be recognized by the government, many couples will also hold a Catholic ceremony after their civil ceremony.

CULTURAL HISTORY

Art
Belgium's contributions to the art world have been substantial. In fact, some of the leading names in the art history hailed from the northern Flanders region, one of the three official regions of Belgium. Historically, this region has also included parts of France and the Netherlands. The Dutch-speaking inhabitants of Flanders are often referred to as Flemish.

In the 15th and early 16th centuries, early Netherlandish painting—a combination of Renaissance and Gothic styles—emerged in Flanders and other parts of the Low Countries. (The Low Countries are a historical region, associated with early modern Europe in the 1400–1600s. They encompass present-day Belgium, Luxembourg, and the Netherlands.) Early Netherlandish art is distinguished from the Italian Renaissance style by a preference for portraits and religious icons rather than mythology. Important artists of this early style included Hubert van Eyck (c. 1366–1426) and his brother Jan van Eyck (c. 1385–1441). As the movement adapted more Italianate influences, it eventually evolved into the Flemish Renaissance. This period also marked the development of the landscape genre in Belgium. Artists from this era include Pieter Brueghel the Elder (c. 1525–1569), who specialized in landscapes, and his son Pieter Brueghel the Younger (1564–1636), known for his depictions of the grotesque.

Peter Paul Rubens (1577–1640), an artist and diplomat, painted in the Flemish baroque style. This style, which emerged in the late 16th century and remained popular until 1700, was largely produced in the southern Netherlands. Flemish baroque painting is characterized by wealth, intense light and dark dynamics, rich use of color, and the use of the female form. His work, like that of many Flemish baroque artists, featured mostly religious subjects. Anthony van Dyck (1599–1641), born in Antwerp, studied under Rubens and went on to become a painter in the royal court in England. He is particularly known for his portraits, notably of English royalty such as King Charles I (1600–1649). Later, in the 19th and 20th centuries, Belgian painters achieved success in more modern schools of art. Most notably, surrealist René Magritte (1898–1967) had a strong influence on the conceptual pop art movement.

Architecture

Historically, Belgium's architecture has been influenced by the country's location—it is bordered by the Netherlands and Germany to the north, and France to the south. As a result, architecture in Belgium features a range of architectural styles.

Brugge was a thriving seaport during the Middle Ages (roughly 400 BCE–1500 CE) and has retained much of its medieval style and layout. The city provides an excellent example of early architectural style in Belgium. In fact, the city's historic center was designated as a World Heritage Site by the United Nations Educational, Scientific and Cultural Organization (UNESCO) for its medieval architecture. The Gothic architectural style is particularly evident in the Stadhuis (town hall). This style is typified by pointed arches, large windows, and towering spires. Gothic architecture was also popular in the construction of religious buildings, such as the Church of St. Bavo in Ghent. Additionally, many guild houses throughout the country were built in the Gothic style, illustrating the importance of commerce in the medieval period.

Baroque architecture emerged in Belgium in the 17th century. This style is generally characterized by rich ornamentation, often in the form of frescoes (a type of painting typically done on plastered walls or ceilings). In addition, the baroque style is considered a rounded style, as opposed to the sharp and pointed Gothic style.

One of the finest examples of baroque architecture in Belgium is the former Jesuit Church in Antwerp (now known as the Church of St. Carrolus-Borromeus). This particular style developed somewhat differently in the Catholic south, which was ruled by Spain, then in the Protestant north, which was a part of the United Provinces with the Netherlands, and featured Italian-trained architects.

By the beginning of the 20th century, Belgian architecture featured the highly stylized plant-like designs of the art nouveau movement. This is particularly true in Brussels, Belgium's largest urban area and the capital of the European Union (EU). In addition to floral and plant-inspired designs, the art nouveau architectural style is characterized by curved lines and forms, and is based on the principle that art should exist in harmony with life. Belgian architects Victor Horta (1861–1947) and Henry van de Velde (1863–1957) are considered the two leading figures in Belgian art nouveau architecture. Horta's work includes many of the leading hotels in Brussels, as well as the Brussels railway station. Van de Velde designed a number of private residences in both Belgium and Germany, as well as the library at Ghent University.

Drama

Belgian cinema witnessed a recent international surge of popularity and acclaim, beginning in the late 20th century with such films as *Man Bites Dog* (1992) and *Rosetta* (1999). This success continued with *The Alzheimer Case* (2003) and *Ben X* (2007). While Belgian cinema is often considered a blend of Dutch and French cinematic styles, it has gained recognition for its own unique, nationalistic characteristics. A number of prominent film festivals are now held throughout the year in Belgium, including the Flanders International Film Festival, the Brussels International Festival of Fantastic Film (BIFFF), and the Brussels International Independent Film Festival.

Music

The region encompassing present-day Belgium has a long and rich tradition in classical music.

Before the nation of Belgium existed, a number of classical composers came from the Flemish region, including Guillaume Dufay (c. 1397–1474). Dufay was considered one of Europe's most noted and influential composers of the early Renaissance. Notably, Ludwig van Beethoven (1770–1827) was also of Flemish descent.

Historically, Belgium music has traditionally combined its French and Dutch heritages with influences from Germany. As such, traditional music varies by region, with French-speaking regions playing music from various parts of France, while maintaining a certain amount of Celtic influence. Folk music, in particular, has undergone a vibrant revival in Flanders, and Flemish folk music has been revived at a time when many other forms of folk music are declining in practice. Generally, modern Flemish folk music has taken traditional styles and combined it with modern ideas and gypsy, or Romani, music.

Perhaps Belgium's proudest addition to the musical world is the saxophone, invented by Adolphe Sax (1814–1894) in the 19th century. The son of an instrument maker, Sax combined the body of a brass instrument with the mouth of a woodwind instrument, thus creating the saxophone. The instrument would later prove integral in the development of jazz and blues music in America.

More recently, traditional Belgium music has blended with musical styles from the country's African immigrant populations. Generally, contemporary musical tastes run a broad spectrum from electronic and hip-hop to indie-punk to African-European fusion.

Literature

Because of the regional cultural and linguistic differences, Belgian literature followed two distinct paths. Flemish literature was once part of the same body as Dutch literature. Following Belgium's independence in 1830, the Flanders region saw a literary revival that aimed to distinguish itself from its Dutch neighbors. At first, Dutch was suppressed in favor of French, but a movement for the use of Dutch/Flemish soon gained support in the northern parts of the country. Henri "Hendrik" Conscience (1812–1883) was one of the foremost pioneers of Flemish literature. His works include *The Lion of Flanders, The Decayed Gentleman*, and *The Miser.*

To the south, the French-speaking Walloons (inhabitants of the Walloon region, one of the three main regions of Belgium) followed the literary trends of the Parisians. The poet Emile Verhaeren (1855–1916) was one of the founders of symbolism, a French and Belgian artistic movement that sought to move away from realism. He nearly won the Nobel Prize in Literature in 1911, but was beaten by fellow countryman Maurice Maeterlinck (1862–1949). Maeterlinck was a poet, playwright, and essayist. Fascinated by death and mysticism, some of his key works include *The Intruder* and *The Blind.* Later works such as *The Intelligence of Flowers* championed socialist causes.

However, the body of Belgian literature to receive greatest fame has been comic strips. Georges Prosper Remi (1907–1983), known better through his pen name Hergé, authored the internationally famed *The Adventures of Tintin*, while Pierre Culliford (1928–1992), better known as Peyo, is known for creating the beloved children's comic strip, *The Smurfs.*

CULTURE

Arts & Entertainment

In general, the Belgian government is very supportive of the contemporary arts. A great deal of pride is placed in the nation's heritage of art, architecture, literature, and folk arts. This support is typically carried out in the form of grants, scholarships, and subsidies. Both French and Flemish opera companies, orchestras, and ballet companies enjoy high levels of patronage, as well as support from community subsidies. In addition, the Royal Academies for Science and the Arts of Belgium (RASAB), an umbrella organization comprised of the Royal Flemish Academy of Belgium for Science and the Arts and the Royal Academy for Sciences, has been instrumental in promoting contemporary Belgium art on the international stage.

Traditional folk arts are revered in Belgium as an important part of the nation's cultural and economic heritage. Lace making, in particular, has a rich history in Belgium. It was taught by royal decree in schools and convents as far back as the 15th century. Today, Belgian lace is considered to be some of the finest in the world, with different towns or regions featuring their own unique styles. A high concentration of lace museums and shops are found in Flanders.

In some of the larger towns, particularly Brussels, there has been an influx of African immigrants. Many of these immigrants have emigrated from regions of Africa formerly under Belgian rule, such as the Congo. As a result, the contemporary arts scene in Belgium has witnessed a recent fusion of European and African styles. Belgium's hip-hop music scene, for example, developed largely around the talents of African immigrants. This scene has now expanded to encompass both white and black multilingual rappers.

The two most popular sports in Belgium are soccer and race cycling. On weekends, cycling clubs with members of all ages cover the countryside. For vacations, many Belgians travel to the seacoast or to the Ardennes area.

Cultural Sites & Landmarks

Brussels is an important European cultural site. The small municipality, the City of Brussels, serves as the country's capital. The larger urban area is the administrative center of the EU, and thus considered the de facto capital of Europe. Largely considered a lively city with a strong international flavor, Brussels combines Flemish and Walloon (or French) influences, and features a variety of medieval architectural styles. In addition, the city has an impressive collection of baroque and Gothic guild houses, and several hotels are representative of Victor Horta's art nouveau style. The city also features a series of town houses designed by Horta, all of which have been were inscribed as World Heritage Sites by the United Nations Educational, Scientific and Cultural Organization (UNESCO).

The Grand Place, the central market square in Brussels, is largely considered the city's most important landmark. The square is surrounded by many guild houses. Seasonally, the square is famously illuminated at night while classical music plays. The square was designated as a World Heritage Site in 1998. Also located in Brussels is the Belgian Center for Comic Strip Art, a museum dedicated to the art of the cartoon. The center, designed in the art nouveau style, focuses on the many famed artists from Belgium. Brussels is also home to the world-renowned Mannekin Pis statue. The statue, one of Belgium's most famous landmarks, is a fountain sculpture famously depicting a little boy urinating into the lower basin.

The medieval town of Brugge, or Bruges, is largely considered one of the best-known World Heritage Sites due to the preservation of the city's medieval architecture and layout. Often referred to as "Venice of the North," Brugge is home to a number of notable buildings, including the Basilica of the Holy Blood and the famous Belfry of Bruges, a medieval bell tower which offers magnificent views of the surroundings. In addition, the lace center offers frequent demonstrations of one of Belgium's finest exports. The city is also known for its extensive museums and festivals.

Other culturally relevant cities in Belgium include Antwerp and Ghent. In addition to several museums, Antwerp is home to the Rubens house, the historic home of Flemish artist Peter Paul Rubens, as well as the Royal Museum of Fine Arts, which boasts more than 1,500 paintings by the Old Masters (European painters prior to the 19th century). The city of Ghent offers walks along historic canals and Gravensteen Castle, built in the 12th century. It is the only castle in Belgium to have remained virtually intact. Originally built as a fortress, the castle was later used as a mint, a prison, and then a cotton plant.

In 1998, UNESCO designated the Flemish Béguinages as a World Heritage Site. Located in Flanders, is the site is a series of houses, known as a béguinage, used by the sisterhood of the Roman Catholic Church. During the Crusades, a series of military campaigns waged mainly against Muslims during the Middle Ages, many women saw their husbands go off to war, never to return. Rather than close themselves away in nunneries, they chose to devote themselves to God while still remaining active in the world. The béguinages were enclosed communities that met all of their needs, both secular and spiritual.

Adding to Belgium's long list of significant religious buildings is the Cathedral of Notre Dame in Tournai. The cathedral was built in the 12th century and is a striking combination of Romanesque and Gothic architecture. In addition, historical belfries are a particularly important feature of Belgium's cultural landscape. Belfries once served as evidence of a town's power and wealth, and functioned as storage space for the merchants. Both the Cathedral of Notre Dame in Tournai and a collection of fifty-six belfries—shared with France—are listed as World Heritage Sites.

Libraries & Museums

Approximately 80 museums are located within the Brussels-Capital Region, including the Museum of Ancient Art and the Museum of Modern Art (both part of the Royal Museums of Fine Arts), as well as the Belgian Brewers Museum, the Belgian Comic Strip Center, the Natural Science Museum of Belgium, and the Museum of Musical Instruments (part of the Royal Museums of Art and History).

The Plantin-Moretus Museum in Antwerp, listed as a World Heritage Site, documents the history of the printing industry. Similarly, the Diamond Museum, the largest of its kind in the world, and also in Antwerp, traces the entire history and manufacturing processes of the precious stone

The Royal Library of Belgium is the country's national library. The national depository is located in Brussels, and the library dates back to the 15th century. The National Archives of Belgium are also located in the capital of Brussels.

Holidays

Belgium's official holidays include Labor Day (May 1), Independence Day (July 21), and Armistice Day (November 11). Several regional holidays are also celebrated, one for each linguistic group. Flemish Community Day is held on July 11, commemorating the 1302 defeat of armored French knights by peasants. French Community Day is celebrated on September 27, and German Community Day on November 15.

Youth Culture

Belgium's youth are often faced with a huge influx of cultural influences. For example, many youth are faced with reconciling their strong Flemish or Walloon heritages with a larger national culture. At the same time, as Europeans, these youth are also heavily influenced by American culture. As a result, they are typically very open to a wide variety of influences.

Musical tastes vary widely, but one fusion style that has become immensely popular is tecktonik. Originally developed in French nightclubs, tecktonik blends hip-hop and techno dance styles of the late 20th century with cyberpunk, resulting in high-energy beats, elaborate arm movements, and futuristic fashions. Techtonik has spread widely, thanks in large part to the Internet.

Recurring political and cultural tensions between the two primary segments of the country's population mean that Belgian youth tend to be more concerned with issues of identity that other European youth might be. Regional identity often trumps national identity, since there is an underlying sense of uncertainty about the future of Belgium.

SOCIETY

Transportation

Belgium has a highly regarded and well-maintained public transportation system. Trains or buses are the most efficient means of transportation. Local trains conveniently connect most small towns and villages, while the Eurostar train runs from Brussels to both London and Paris. Buses offer service both between and within the towns. Ferry service also connects Belgium with England, and there are a number of airports throughout the country. Automobile traffic in Belgium travels on the right-hand side of the road.

Since most towns are quite old in their origins, they tend to have defined town centers and local neighborhoods. As such, it is common to see people walking to work or to the grocery store. Bicycling is also very popular, both as a form of daily transport, and as a leisure activity.

Transportation Infrastructure

Belgium's road network is considered one of the more efficient European road systems. In addition, high-speed trains connect to other major European cities, including London, Frankfurt, Amsterdam, and Paris. The country has five international airports. The country's major shipping ports are Antwerp, Ghent, Liege, and Zeebrugge.

Brussels' public transit system is operated by four independent companies, which manage the city's buses, metro, trains, and extensive tram system. Brussels also offers car- and bicycle-sharing services. Two airports serve Brussels, although neither is in the city proper. Brussels's Central Station, with six underground tracks, often has 100 trains passing through each hour during busy times of day.

Media & Communications

Due to the bilingual nature of Belgium, the media does not have a single public broadcasting organization. Instead, there are a number of linguistically and culturally separate entities, primarily French, Dutch, and German. For example, *Le Soir* and *La Libre Belgique* are the nation's leading French language dailies, while *Grenz Echo* is the German language daily; Dutch newspapers include *Het Nieuwsblad, De Standaard,* and several others. The press is self-regulated by the Federation of Editors. Belgium also has one of the highest rates of cable television subscribers in the world: 95 percent as of 2008. A number of channels are available in both French and Dutch.

Although Belgium was considered to be relatively late in adopting Internet use (in comparison to other European countries), access to services is growing rapidly. In 2010 77 percent of the Belgian population used the Internet, a significant increase since 2000.

SOCIAL DEVELOPMENT

Standard of Living

Belgium ranked 21st out of 187 countries on the 2014 United Nations Human Development Index, which measures quality of life and standard of living indicators.

Water Consumption

Fresh water is widely available in Belgium. Surface waters constitute the country's main water sources, including the Albert canal and the Maas River. The city of Brussels is dependent on the Wallonia region for water. Developments in the county's water and sanitation infrastructure resulted in an 80 percent increase in water tariffs between 2003 and 2008.

Education

About 90 percent of Belgian children between the ages of two and three attend state-funded preschools. Education is compulsory for children between the ages of six and eighteen years. The government supports all schools, whether public or private, religious or secular.

Elementary education is provided in three two-year cycles. Comprehensive high schools provide instruction in basic subjects plus specialized technical, vocational or college-preparatory courses. After age 1, students may opt to attend school only part time until age eighteen.

The oldest university in the country is the Catholic University in Louvain, founded in 1425. The Free University in Brussels was founded by Freemasons in 1834. In the early 19th century, the state founded universities in Ghent and Liège. Several more universities were founded in the latter 20th century, including Antwerp University for Dutch speakers and Mons University for French speakers.

The government pays 95 percent of university costs. In addition, nearly 20 percent of university students receive government scholarships. The literacy rate in Belgium, among both males and females, is estimated at 99 percent.

Women's Rights

The rights of women in Belgium are protected by both national and European legislation designed to prevent gender discrimination. In 1919, suffrage was granted to the mothers and widows of soldiers killed during World War I. Women could not vote at the national or provincial level, but could be elected. Voting rights were extended to all women in 1948. Voting is compulsory for all Belgian citizens over the age of 18 years.

In general, the rights and legal protections available to women in Belgium are average when compared with much of Europe, although their economic opportunities and participation tend to rank fairly low. In a 2005 UN report, Belgium ranked 20th among 50 countries on a Gender Empowerment Measure that measured political participation, economic power, and availability of education and healthcare.

Eighty percent of all part-time employees and 33 percent of all full-time employees in Belgium are women. Seventy percent of women with pre-school age children are employed outside the home. The retirement age for women has increased from 60 to 65, equal to that for men. Both Belgian and European Law promise equal pay for equal work, although gender inequity remains a problem. Although girls typically outperform boys throughout school and university, they often face more discrimination when transitioning to the workforce.

Politically, women continue to be underrepresented. In 2000, women formed 24 percent of the lower house and 29 percent of the upper house in parliament, as well as 17 percent of the government. Historically, the first woman to gain a seat in Belgian parliament was Marie-Anne Spaak Johnson in 1921. The first woman minister in government was Maguriete de Reimacker-Ligot, the minister of family and housing from 1965–1969.

Women are entitled to maternity leave and benefits in Belgium. Currently, women are entitled to 82 percent of their salary for the first thirty days of maternity leave, and 75 percent of their salary for the time following (up to fifteen weeks is permitted for maternity leave). One week must be taken before the baby is due and at least eight weeks must be taken after the birth. Paternity leave of up to 10 days is allowed, with 82 percent of the man's salary being paid for seven days.

A number of women's groups and movements rose up in the latter half of the 20th century to focus on the issues of abortion, contraception, and family planning. Until 1973, contraception and information regarding its use was illegal in Belgium. Abortion remained illegal until 1990, when the Belgian parliament liberalized the nation's abortion laws. Abortion is now permitted during the first twelve weeks of pregnancy, and after 12 weeks if two physicians agree that it will not endanger the mother's life.

Health Care

While health care is provided mostly by private concerns, it is funded by the government through compulsory health care insurance. Both employers and employees contribute to the insurance.

A new and growing health concern is obesity, especially among children. According to recent studies, one-half of all Belgians, and more than 10 percent of children, are clinically obese. Health officials blame this on a diet high in sugar. Measures have been proposed to ban junk-food vending machines from schools.

Life expectancy is seventy-nine years overall—seventy-six years for men and eighty-three years for women (2014 estimate). The per capita expenditure on health is approximately $2,481 (USD) per year.

GOVERNMENT

Structure

Belgium is a constitutional monarchy. Suffrage is universal and mandatory at 18 years. Non-voters are fined.

The monarch is the head of state. The monarch appoints the prime minister, who is the head of government. The prime minister advises the monarch in appointing the other ministers of the Council of Ministers (cabinet). The council in fact exercises the executive authority. The ministers have no set terms, and serve at the pleasure of the monarch. The council is responsible to the Chamber of Representatives.

The bicameral Parliament consists of the 150-member Chamber of Representatives and the 71-member Senate. Forty of the senators are elected directly, another 21 are elected by provincial councils, and the final 10 are elected by the other senators. The members of Parliament serve four-year terms unless, at the prime minister's request, the monarch dissolves Parliament. At that time, new elections are held.

Political Parties

Political parties in Belgium cover a wide spectrum of philosophies, though none operate on a national level. The country's vast multi-party system is organized along linguistic, regional, and religious lines. Major political coalitions include Christian Democrats, Social Democrats, and Liberal Democrats. Communist, nationalist, and Green party organizations also exist.

Local Government

Administratively, Belgium is divided into 10 provinces, three regions (Flanders, Wallonia, and Brussels), and three language communities (French, Dutch, and German), as well as 589 municipalities. The regions and the language communities are largely autonomous, each with its own prime minister, council of ministers, and parliament. Provinces are overseen by an appointed governor, who is supported by a provincial council. Provincial council members are elected to six-year terms in office. The number of members on each council is proportionate to the region it represents.

Judicial System

Belgium's judicial system is based on the Napoleonic code of law and is similar in structure and organization to the judicial system of France. The Supreme Court of Justice ("Hof van Cassatie" in Dutch or "Cour de Cassation" in French) is the highest court in the land. Members of the Supreme Court are appointed for life by the Belgian monarchy. The Court of Appeals ("Cour d'Appel") presides as the last option of appeal prior to the Supreme Court. The first level of the Belgian judicial system is comprised of four courts: the "Tribunal de Police," the "Tribunal des Juges de Paix," the "Tribunal de Premiere Instance," and a labor and taxation court.

Taxation

Belgium has one of the highest taxation rates in Europe. Income tax rates can range as high as 50 percent. Other taxes include property taxes, municipal taxes, fuel taxes, and capital gains taxes. Citizens of Belgium pay a variable rate of their income into the country's social security system. In addition to federal taxes, communal and region taxes are collected.

Armed Forces

The Belgium Armed Forces consist of an army, air force, and navy, as well as a medical component. Belgium troops are part of the International Security Assistance Force in Afghanistan; the United Mission in Sudan; the Mission of the United Nations Stabilization Mission in Democratic Republic of Congo; and the Belgian Luxemburg Force in Lebanon. As of 2010, the military numbers 47,000 strong (and in active duty); the Belgian military has reduced its total personnel to 39,500 by 2015.

Foreign Policy

Belgium continues to maintain an important presence on the global political stage. The country sat on the United Nations Security Council for the 2007–2008 session, and was also elected to serve on the UN Commission on the Status of Women for four years, beginning 2007. In addition, the North Atlantic Treaty Organization (NATO – of which Belgium is a founding member) and the EU both have their headquarters in Brussels.

Historically, Belgium has maintained a strong relationship with the United States. Recently, Belgium celebrated the 175th anniversary of its friendly relationship with the US in 2007. While Belgium has been critical of U.S. foreign policies in the 21st century, it has offered a great deal of assistance during military campaigns in Afghanistan, Iraq, and the Balkans. Brussels is also home to the European headquarters of a number of American companies, further strengthening U.S.-Belgium ties.

Generally, Belgium has been a strong advocate of European Union (EU) political and economic integration. For example, Belgium supported the adoption of a single currency, the euro. The country has also been keen to welcome new member states from central and Eastern Europe. Since Belgium views itself as a successful federation of several nationalities, it views its participation in the EU along similar lines.

Belgium enjoys a close relationship with its neighboring countries. In particular, Belgium shares a common cultural and historical background with Luxembourg and the Netherlands, as they are all constitutional monarchies. The three are commonly referred to as Benelux. Belgium also enjoys close trade ties with France and Germany. In fact, Belgium was one of the first nations to rebuild diplomatic ties with Germany following First World War. Furthermore, until the early 21st century, Belgian troops trained in German garrisons, and troops from both nations continue to be jointly deployed in a number of UN peacekeeping missions. In addition, Germany is Belgium's principal trading partner, ahead of even France or the Netherlands, and each nation has made considerable economic investments in the other.

Beyond cultural and linguistic ties, Belgium and France share many common interests and issues. One notable issue involves African immigration, as both countries have experienced a recent influx of immigrants from their former colonies on the African continent. In addition, France and Belgium continue to establish significant economic ties. In September 2008, for example, French and Belgian power grid operators announced plans to establish a joint power coordination center. Both nations expressed hopes that other European neighbors would join the collaboration. The center is part of a plan to eventually create an integrated single market for European electricity.

Human Rights Profile

International human rights law insists that states respect civil and political rights, and also promote an individual's economic, social, and cultural rights. The United Nations (UN) Universal Declaration of Human Rights (UDHR) is recognized as the standard for international human rights. Its authors sought the counsel of the world's great thinkers, philosophers, and religious leaders, and were careful to create a document that reflects the core values shared by every world culture. (To read this document or view the articles relating to cultural human rights, go to: http://www.udhr.org/UDHR/default.htm.)

Belgium regards human rights as a key component of its foreign policy, and it works within the EU and the UN to ensure that human rights are upheld. For the most part, Belgium has a positive history of human rights, although several areas of concern exist.

In accordance with Article 2 of the Universal Declaration of Human Rights, Belgian law prohibits discrimination on the basis of race, religion, or gender. However, domestic violence remains a problem. Belgium also has difficulties with human trafficking. The country often serves as a pass-through point for many trafficking victims. The government has addressed this issue by establishing and maintaining several shelters for trafficking victims.

Freedom to marry, as outlined in Article 16, is provided to all men and women over the age of eighteen in Belgium. Those younger than eighteen who wish to marry must obtain permission from juvenile court, and can only do so "on serious grounds." In 2003, Belgium passed a law recognizing same-sex marriage. Freedom of religion, outlined in Article 18 of the declaration, is protected in Belgium. The law offers "recognized" status to six major religions, including Catholicism, Protestantism, Judaism, Anglicanism, Islam, and Orthodox. However, others are generally free to practice.

Belgian law protects the rights to freedom of expression and freedom of assembly, as defined by Articles 19 and 20 of the declaration. However, there are some exceptions. Any public statements that may incite national, racial or religious hatred are outlawed. This includes denial of the Holocaust. The press is largely self-governing, and speaking out against the government does not bring any threat of legal reprisals.

Although prisons meet international standards of quality, they are often overcrowded, with foreign nationals accounting for nearly half of all inmates as of 2007. Furthermore, in 2006 the Council of Europe's Committee for the Prevention of Torture expressed concerns about reports of police brutality and mistreatment of prisoners while in custody.

ECONOMY

Overview of the Economy
Belgium has a free market economy, importing raw materials and exporting manufactures. This means that its economy is very dependent on world market conditions. Economic development has been slowed by the lack of cooperation among the language communities, resulting in high unemployment (12 percent) and low economic growth. In 2014, the per capita GDP was an estimated $41,700 (USD).

Industry
Products manufactured in Belgium include engineering and metal products (particularly steel), cement, chemicals and chemical products, paper, textiles, glass, leather goods, and processed foods. In the capital, Brussels, the most important industrial center is in the Senne Valley, concentrated around the city's port and rail lines. Textiles are still an important part of the city's manufacturing industry.

Annual export revenues were an estimated $373 billion (USD) in 2008. Major exports include iron and steel, automobiles, food and live animals, chemicals and related products, textiles (including the world-famous Belgian lace), food products (including chocolate), and mineral lubricants and fuels.

Labor
Over 50 percent of Belgium's workforce is unionized. The three main trade unions in the country are the Confederation of Catholic Labor Unions, the Belgian Socialist Confederation of Labor, and the Confederation of Liberal Labor Unions. Belgian labor unions are politically dynamic institutions that take public stances on issues ranging from abortion and women's rights to defense spending and education. In addition, labor unions in Belgium provide unemployment benefits and health insurance programs to their members.

Energy/Power/Natural Resources
Belgium's coal deposits have been depleted, and the last coal mines were closed in the 1990s. Its few remaining natural resources include natural gas, silica sand, and carbonates.

Industrialization, intensive farming and husbandry (raising livestock), urbanization, and dense transportation facilities have polluted Belgium's air and water. Environmental improvement plans have been delayed by the debate between the federal government and regional administrations over responsibility for the damage.

Fishing
Belgian marine fisheries catch cod, plaice, sole, line, and shrimp. Plaice and sole were the most prominent catches in terms of tonnage in 2009. Belgian marine fisheries adhere to the catch regulations established by the European Union. In 2003, there were 125 trawler vessels in Belgian's commercial fishing fleet. Important regional fishing grounds include the English Channel, the Irish Sea, and the North Sea. Shellfish, particularly mussels, are widely consumed in Belgium. The country also exports fisheries products to the Netherlands, France, Denmark, and Germany.

However, agriculture as a whole represents only about one percent of the country's GDP. There is no significant in-land, freshwater fishing industry in Belgium.

Forestry

The majority of Belgium's forests are located in the south eastern region of the country. Forest products manufactured in the country include paper (newsprint and cardboard) and wood furniture. However, Belgium is a net importer of timber and forestry does not represent a significant portion of the country's economic output. Antwerp is Europe's largest forest product terminal. The city is the base of export operations to Germany and France.

Mining/Metals

Mining and metals make up a significant part of the Belgian economy and the production of metal products is one of the country's main industries. Belgium exports base metals, including copper, aluminum, and steel, in addition to precious metals such as gold and silver. There are approximately 1,500 diamond companies located in the diamond district of Antwerp. Belgium is also a well-known producer of marble.

Agriculture

Small farms, often rented by families, produce barley, flax, cattle, milk, hops, sugar beets, potatoes, rye, and wheat. A total of 45 percent of Belgium's land is used for farms, half of this in pasture. The average farm size is 18 hectares (44 acres).

Agriculture accounts for less than two percent of the country's GDP. Dairy and livestock farming account for roughly two-thirds of Belgium's agricultural income. In 2009, an estimated 83,900 were employed in the agricultural sector.

Animal Husbandry

Common livestock in Belgium include cattle, poultry, and pigs, as well as goats, sheep, and horses. Over half of the farms in Belgium specialized in livestock cultivation, particularly laying hens and dairy cows.

Tourism

Belgium welcomes more than 7.6 million tourists a year, earning revenues of over $7 billion (USD).

Brussels is known for its beer and good cuisine. It has excellent examples of architecture of the baroque and Gothic periods. Medieval castles and modern bars and cafés mark Antwerp. The entire medieval center of Bruges is on the United Nations Educational, Scientific and Cultural Organization's (UNESCO) list of World Heritage Sites. Bruges has the best-preserved medieval architecture in Europe.

The Ardennes is the site of the Battle of the Bulge, a wintery offensive carried out in the latter stages of the Second World War. Today it is serene and beautiful, with ancient citadels, riverside villages, and mineral springs.

Fiona Young-Brown, Ellen Bailey, Alex K. Rich

DO YOU KNOW?

- Brussels is well-known for its cartoon culture. In addition to the murals and the Cartoon Museum, Brussels is the birthplace of cartoonists Hergé and Peyo, who created "Tintin" and "The Smurfs," respectively, and hosts Anima, an annual cartoon and animated film festival. In fact, Belgium has more cartoonists per square kilometer than any other country.

- Brussel sprouts are so named because they were originally cultivated in Brussels.

Bibliography

Blom, J.C.H., ed. *History of the Low Countries*. Oxford: Berghahn Books, 2006.

Deschouwer, Kris. *The Politics of Belgium*. Basingstoke: Palgrave Macmillan, 2012.

Elliott, Mark. *Belgium and Luxembourg*. Oakland, CA: Lonely Planet, 2013.

Elliott, Mark. *Culture Shock! Belgium: A Quick Guide to Customs and Etiquette*. London: Graphic Arts Center Publishing Company, 2013.

Humes, Samuel. *Belgium: Long United, Long Divided*. London: Hurst & Co., 2014.

Mosley, Philip. *Split Screen: Belgian Cinema and Cultural Identity*. New York: State University of New York Press, 2000.

Noltze, Kathy. *Flanders: Bits of Belgium*. London: Magnum Travel, 2008.

Rough Guide. *Rough Guide to Belgium and Luxembourg*. London: Rough Guides, 2015.

Scholliers, Peter. *Food Culture in Belgium*. Westport, CT: Greenwood Press, 2008.

Shawe-Taylor, Desmond. *Bruegel to Rubens: Masters of Flemish Painting*. London: Royal Collection Enterprises, 2007.

Works Cited

"A Digital Archive of Architecture: Architecture in Belgium." http://www.bc.edu/bc_org/avp/cas/fnart/arch/brussels.html

"Abortion Policy." www.un.org/esa/population/publications/abortion/doc/belgiu1.doc

"At What Age?" http://www.right-to-education.org/content/age/belgium.html

"Belgium." http://www.amnesty.org/en/region/europe-and-central-asia/western-europe/belgium

"Belgium." http://www.ediplomat.com/np/cultural_etiquette/ce_be.htm

"Belgium Profile." http://www.state.gov/r/pa/ei/bgn/2874.htm

"Belgium: Internet Usage Stats and Market Report." http://www.internetworldstats.com/eu/be.htm

"Belgium: Housing." http://original.britannica.com/eb/article-25000/Belgium

"Belgium: Intercultural Issues." http://www.intercultures.ca/cil-cai/intercultural_issues_print-en.asp?lvl=0&ISO=BE

"Belgium: Principal Cities." http://www.citypopulation.de/Belgium-Mun.html

"Belgium: Social Security." http://www.diplomatie.be/EN/belgium/belgiumdetail.asp?TEXTID=49097

"Belgium, the Netherlands and Luxembourg." http://www.civitas.org.uk/eufacts/FSMS/MS6.htm

"Compendium: Cultural Policies and Trends in Europe." http://www.culturalpolicies.net/web/belgium.php?aid=72

"Council of Europe Demographic Yearbook."

"Countries of the World and Their Leaders Yearbook 2009 Vol. 1"

"Country Profile: Belgium." http://news.bbc.co.uk/2/hi/europe/country_profiles/999709.stm#media

"Country Reports on Human Rights Practices 2006: Belgium." *U.S. Department of State*. http://www.state.gov/g/drl/rls/hrrpt/2006/78803.htm

"Country Reports on Human Rights Practices 2007: Belgium." *U.S. Department of State*. http://www.state.gov/g/drl/rls/hrrpt/2007/100550.htm

"Etiquette and Protocol Guidelines for Belgium." http://www.kwintessential.co.uk/resources/global-etiquette/belgium-country-profile.html

"Flemish Phrases and Sentences." http://www.linguanaut.com/english_flemish.htm

"France and Belgium to Strengthen Electricity Connection." http://www.euractiv.com/en/energy/france-belgium-strengthen-electricity-interconnection/article-175171

"Foreign Policy: Human Rights." http://www.diplomatie.be/en/policy/policynotedetail.asp?TEXTID=2069

"Het Katholicisme in België." http://www.kuleuven.be/icrid/religies/christ_nl_katholiek.htm

"International Religious Freedom Report 2007: Belgium." *U.S. Department of State*. http://www.state.gov/g/drl/rls/irf/2007/90166.htm

Martin Hickman. The Big Question: How Does Michelin Award its Stars–and Do They Still Matter? *The Independent*, January 25, 2008. http://www.independent.co.uk/extras/big-question/the-big-question-how-does-the-michelin-guide-award-its-stars-ndash-and-do-they-still-matter-773848.html

"Public Transportation in Brussels." http://www.stib.be/index.htm?l=fr

"The Belgian Tourist Office." http://www.visitbelgium.com/food.htm

"United Nations Economic Commission for Europe." http://w3.unece.org

"Women in Decision Making." http://www.db-decision.de/CoRe/Belgien.htm

"Women's Empowerment: Measuring the Global Gender Gap." http://www.unece.org/stats/gender/publications/Multi-Country/WomenEmpowerment.pdf

Botanical Garden glass house at the University of Copenhagen in Denmark /Stock photo © fotoVoyager

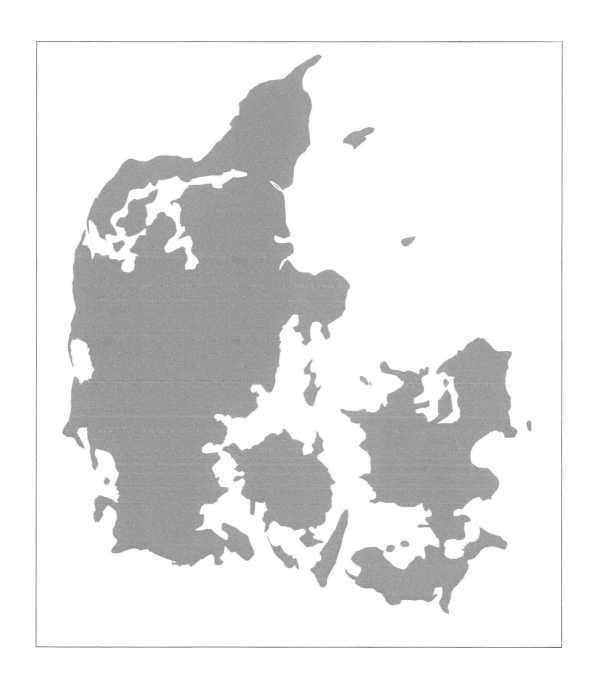

DENMARK

Introduction

The Kongeriget Danmark (Kingdom of Denmark) is the oldest monarchy in Europe. A small country in the North Sea, Denmark once ruled most of England and all of Scandinavia and Finland. Denmark is a welfare state and a constitutional monarchy, and is known for its agricultural products, and its achievements in science and the arts.

GENERAL INFORMATION

Official Language: Danish
Population: 5,569,077 (2014 estimate)
Currency: Danish krone
Coins: The Danish krone is divided into 100 øre, and coins are available in denominations of 50 øre, and 1, 2, 5, 10, and 20 kroner.
Land Area: 42,434 square kilometers (16,383 square miles)
Water Area: 660 square kilometers (254 square miles)
National Motto: (Queen's motto) "God's help, the Love of the People, Denmark's Strength"
National Anthem: "Kong Christian" ("King Christian"), used on special days of the Royal House; and "Der er et Yndigt Land" ("There is a Lovely Country"), for national events.
Capital: Copenhagen
Time Zone: GMT +2

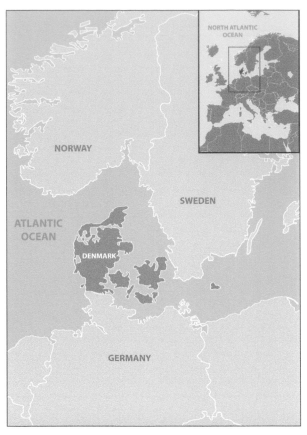

Flag Description: The flag of Denmark features a red background with a white cross. The horizontal line of the cross extends the width of the flag, as does the vertical its height; however, the vertical line is shifted off-center, positioned more toward the hoist (left) side of the flag.

Population

About one-fifth (1.2 million) of Danes live in greater Copenhagen, which lies mostly on the island of Sjaelland (Zealand), and partly on the smaller adjacent island of Amager. Other large cities include Arhus (population 256,292), Odense (168, 906), and Alborg (104,771). In 2010, the municipality of Copenhagen had an estimated population of 678,873 people with a population density of 3,769 people per square kilometer. Almost 87 percent of the people live in urban areas.

Principal Cities by Population (2012):

- Copenhagen (1,200,000)
- Århus (256,292)
- Odense (168, 906)
- Ålborg (104,771)
- Esbjerg (71,686)
- Randers (61,078)
- Kolding (55,596) (2008 estimate)
- Horsens (51,670) (2008 estimate)
- Vejle (50,213) (2008 estimate)
- Roskilde (45,824) (2008 estimate)

Languages

The official language is Danish. Faroese and Greenlandic (East Inuit dialect) are spoken in the Faroe Islands and Greenland, respectively (two constituent countries under the Danish realm). German is widely spoken along the German border.

Native People & Ethnic Groups

The Danes, a Gothic-German people, are the native inhabitants of Denmark. Ethnic groups in Denmark include Scandinavians, Inuit (Greenland), Faroese (Faroe Islands), and Germans (along the border with Schleswig-Holstein in Germany).

By the early 21st century, Denmark was home to a diverse group of ethnic minorities, including those who emigrated from Turkey, Iraq, Lebanon, Bosnia, Pakistan, Somalia, Sri Lanka, Vietnam, and Iran. This influx of diversity resulting from immigration has challenged Denmark's reputation as a tolerant, inclusive society. Difficulties faced by ethnic minorities in Denmark include disproportionately low unemployment (some claim unemployment among ethnic minorities is as high as 50 percent, much higher than that of "ethnic Danes"), as well as police discrimination and decreased access to quality housing, particularly for elderly ethnic minorities.

Religions

Lutheranism is the state religion, and 95 percent of Danes are Lutherans. Another 3 percent are Protestant or Roman Catholic, and 2 percent are Muslim.

Climate

Denmark's climate is classified as temperate marine. The North Atlantic Drift, part of the Gulf Stream, gives Denmark a milder climate than other places at the same latitude. The weather tends to be humid and overcast, with cool summers. Winters, though mild, can be windy.

There is little variation in weather throughout the country. Frequent fogs and mists occur in winter, especially on the west coast. In winter, the sea warms the land, and in summer, it cools the air. Winter temperatures average 0° Celsius (32° Fahrenheit). Sometimes the eastern water freezes over, and the resultant bitter temperatures can drop as low as –9° to –7° Celsius (15° to 20° Fahrenheit). Snow falls 20 to 30 days a year, but melts quickly.

Summer temperatures average 17° Celsius (63° Fahrenheit). Some summers, warm winds from the east raise the temperature as high as 24° 28° Celsius (72° to 82° Fahrenheit).

Most rainfall occurs in August and October, with a yearly average of 6 centimeters (24 inches). The spring months are the driest.

ENVIRONMENT & GEOGRAPHY

Topography

Denmark consists of the peninsula of Jutland on the North Sea coast of Germany, plus many islands. The major ones are Sjaelland (Zealand), Fyn (Funen) Lolland, Fallster, and Bornholm in the Baltic Sea to the east of the peninsula.

Denmark is separated from Norway by the Skagerrak, a gulf of the North Sea, and from Sweden by the Kattegat, a strait in the Baltic. Denmark controls both the Skagerrak and the Kattegat. The country shares its 68-kilometer (42-mile) southern border with Germany.

There are no large rivers or lakes in Denmark. The longest river is the 157-kilometer (98-mile) Gudena in north-central Jutland. The river rises in Viborg County, flows northeast through Aarhus County and empties into Randers Fjord at Randers on the east coast. Many small lakes dot the country. The largest, Arreso, covers 41 square kilometers (16 square miles).

Formed by glaciers, Denmark is low, with 75 percent of the land lying below 100 meters (373 feet). The highest point is Yding Skovhoej, in east-central Jutland, at 173 meters (568 feet). The lowest point, Lammefjord, is 7 meters (23 feet) below sea level. In areas where flooding is an ever-present threat, dikes are constructed to keep flood waters at bay.

The country has five distinct land regions: the sandy beaches of the Western Dune Coast, the flat Western Sand Plains, the East-Central Hills (the largest region), the Northern Flat Plain, and the granite island of Bornholm.

The capital, Copenhagen, is located in eastern Denmark and is spread over two islands in Denmark's eastern archipelagos, occupying the east coast of the island of Sjaelland and the northwest coast of the island of Amager. Part of the Øresund Region, the area split by the Øresund strait separating Denmark from Sweden, Copenhagen is partially surrounded by canals and waterways fed by the Øresund.

Plants & Animals

Deciduous forest, especially beech, is the natural vegetation in Denmark. Today, however, there is no natural forest. All of the country's timber has been planted. Conifers have done well in parts of western Jutland, and spruce and pine thrive in the dune areas.

Other flora includes old-time medicinal plants such as calamus, motherwort, lovage, ground elder, water thyme, rice grass and giant hogweed. Hundreds of species of algae, mosses, lichen and fungi are also found.

Because of long-term intense cultivation, most large mammals are domesticated farm animals. Animals needing protection include the pine marten and 14 other mammal species, 74 bird species, five amphibian species, two reptile species, 15 freshwater fish species and 964 beetle species.

The surprisingly low number of marine species is partially attributed to the muddy sea bottom and shallowness of the waters around Denmark. The Skagerrak is the only place where the depth is more than 100 meters (328 feet). Over-fishing has led to restrictions on the catch.

CUSTOMS & COURTESIES

Greetings

Typically, when greeting, handshakes are firm and eye contact is considered important. Often, the host is not expected to introduce guests within a group, as the responsibility of that formality is placed upon the individual. In addition, there is a tendency toward bluntness in Danish culture, expressed by both adults and children. This is largely a result of upbringing, since Danish parents generally cite honesty as the top-ranked value they wish to instill in their children.

Gestures & Etiquette

Danes are known for their modest social attitude. This ethos, or fundamental cultural spirit or belief, is derived from the Jante Law, a set of laws ascribed to Danish/Norwegian author Aksel Sandemose (1899–1965). Essentially, the law—which Danes apply to themselves as much as to others—focuses on a single theme: you're no better than anyone else. This school of thought is typically expressed throughout Danish culture, particularly in general social interactions, gestures and etiquette. For example, Danes shake hands with everyone, children included, and use first names when meeting people. In addition, modesty is emphasized; most Danes are modest about their wealth.

Eating/Meals

Danes typically eat three main meals a day. Breakfast, though considered an important meal, is usually rushed. Though some families try to have a group breakfast, the responsibilities of work and school generally have gradually changed many breakfast traditions. For example, most Danes regularly skip breakfast, often opting instead for a quick, nutrition-free snack. Lunch, likewise, is also rushed. Typical lunch fare in

Denmark is sandwiches, known as smørrebrød. Dinners in Denmark are largely more relaxed. Similar to evening meals in the U.S. and other Western cultures, Danish dinner meals typically feature meat (usually pork) or fish. In addition, dinner is typically served early (a usual work day in Denmark ends between four and five o'clock).

Additionally, there are general, outlined rules for toasting in Danish culture. Generally, the ritual of toasting is as follows: a glass is raised to all assembled no higher than eye level, with eye contact typically established with everyone. The toast then commonly concludes in a chorus of "Skål" ("Cheers"). Following the spoken portion of a toast, beer and wine are typically sipped.

Visiting

Dining out is typically very expensive in Denmark. As such, invitations to eat a host's home rather than a restaurant are common. In addition, it is not uncommon for dinner parties to last four hours or longer. When visiting, it is customary for a guest to remove their shoes before entering (many Danes even bring "inside-only shoes" for social calls). Small gifts such as wine, or flowers are considered appropriate and appreciated. More importantly, punctuality is generally essential, and it is important for guests to be on time.

One particularly important element of Danish culture and etiquette is summarized by the Danish word "hygge." Roughly translated as a cozy and inviting feeling or mood, hygge often expresses the pleasure a host takes in entertaining their guests. In addition, the idea of hygge can involve taking an ordinary situation and applying extraordinary attention. Often hygge is associated with family and fellowship, as well as simplicity and living well. For example, elements of hygge include good food (often home-baked), a candle, and friends.

LIFESTYLE

Family

The traditional nuclear family, typically consisting of two parents and their children, is in the norm in Danish society. However, Denmark has low marriage rates: about one-fifth of all couples who live together are unmarried. In addition, Denmark reported 35,000 marriages and 15,000 divorces in 2006 alone, making the rate of failed marriages about 40 percent for that year. Denmark legalized same-sex marriage in 1989, the first country in the world to do so.

Danish parents are entitled to approximately 52 weeks of partially-paid maternity or paternity leave (adoptive parents are granted 48 weeks). This generous leave program is one of the four main components of Denmark's lifetime health coverage for its citizens. The other three areas are education, retirement benefits and elderly care. Thus, the financial burdens that so many other families around the world face are typically diminished in Denmark. In addition, most Danes average a 37-hour work week.

Housing

Approximately 85 percent of Danes live in cities and towns. In addition, over half of Danes own their own homes, a statistic unusually high for Europe, where renting is typically the norm, especially in urban areas. The predominant housing style in Denmark is the bungalow style (generally, a single-story residence), typically with a backyard garden. For those in apartments, many maintain small gardens at the edge of town. These allotment gardens usually have room for a shed with a stove, where families can camp out overnight. Many urban residents also own tax-free seaside cottages, typically known as summerhouses.

Danish homes generally have small bedrooms, with the majority of the square footage designated as communal living space. Bathrooms also tend to be small.

Generally, it is rare for an extended family to live in a single home. Most elderly Danish live on their own, or in assisted living facilities. Young people typically leave home in their mid-twenties, often living alone or with friends. As such, many towns have apartments built particularly for young people. In addition, nearly half of the population lives in one- or two-person households.

Food

Denmark's cuisine shares many similarities with the national cuisines of its Scandinavian neighbors, largely because these countries share the same climate and a similar agricultural heritage. Traditionally, meat and seafood—in particular, smoked or marinated herring and pork—are staples of the Danish diet. In addition, because Denmark has historically been an agricultural country, dairy and cereal products have played a large role in defining the national cuisine. Other locally grown items that figure prominently in the traditional diet include potatoes, rye, mushrooms, apples, carrots and onions.

There are numerous signature dishes that define the national cuisine of Denmark, the centerpiece of which is the small, open-faced sandwich known as smørrebrød. The smørrebrød is typically composed of a thin slice of buttered rye bread, on top of which is piled meat (such as liver or pork), fish (perhaps shrimp or plaice, a flatfish), sauce (commonly, horseradish or mayonnaise) and fresh or pickled vegetables (such as dill, onions or cabbage). Smørrebrød is typically the second course in a three-course meal, and most often served at lunch. Herring usually precedes the sandwich course, and an array of cheeses concludes the meal. The sandwich is generally eaten with knife and fork, and not with the hands. Typically, fish and meat are not mixed within the same sandwich.

Frikadeller, meatballs served with cabbage and white sauce, is considered the Danish national dish. Other traditional and popular Danish dishes include lever med løg, which is liver and fried onion; flæskesteg med rødkål, or roast pork and red cabbage; and biksemad, which is beef hash traditionally served with fried egg and sauce, either béarnaise or ketchup. Another singularly Danish food is the two-ingredient dish of stegt flæsk med persille sovs, or pork fat in parsley sauce. In addition to herring, other seafood and fish commonly consumed includes cod, eel, mackerel, salmon and Norway lobster. In more recent years, Danish cuisine has become a fusion of foreign influences, most notably French, Asian and American.

The Danish are also known for their pastries, which are characteristically flaky and airy. A popular Danish pastry is wienerbrød, meaning "Vienna bread." In fact, during a 19th century labor strike involving Danish bakers, backers from Vienna, Austria, were brought in. Danish bakers then incorporated the multiple layering techniques used by Vienna bakers to develop Denmark's characteristic puff pastries.

Beer is popular, and Danish beers are internationally renowned, especially Tuborg and Carlsberg. On special days, many Danes drink aquavit, a strong, caraway-flavored liquor. Coffee is another very popular drink.

Life's Milestones

Religion typically plays a central role in Danish celebrations. More than 90 percent of Danes belong to the state-supported Evangelical Lutheran Church. As such, events such as weddings and funerals are observed in a traditional or religious context. In addition, many observed and practiced ceremonies are religious in nature, such as baptism or confirmation.

Outside of religious events, secular observances such as birthdays are also traditionally regarded as important milestones. Additionally, it is not uncommon for Danes to celebrate American independence on the Fourth of July. In fact, thousands of Danes typically congregate in a park in the northern city of Ålborg to eat American food and to listen to speeches by well-known Americans. However, the most important holiday of the year for Danes is Christmas. One particularly unique Christmas Eve tradition involves the secret placement of an almond in a serving of rice pudding. In addition to receiving a prize, it is believed that the person who discovers the almond will also have good luck in the following year.

CULTURAL HISTORY

Art

The arts in Denmark have their roots in the ancient civilizations of Scandinavia, a geographical and historic region that typically encompasses Denmark, Norway, and Sweden. During the Viking Age (c. 700–1066 CE), a period of Viking expansion in medieval Scandinavia, many traditional arts developed. These included jewelry-making, woodcarving, sculpture and metalworking (wrought gold and silver personal ornamentations that featured interlaced designs). In addition, the artistic styles developed by the Norsemen of this era are similar to the complex styles and themes of Celtic art. The art developed during this period is often referred to as Norse art, or Viking art, both umbrella terms used to describe ancient art in Scandinavia.

During the Middle Ages (roughly 400 BCE– 1500 CE) and the European Renaissance of the 14th through the 17th centuries, art in Denmark was created by religious and royal decree, mainly by foreign artists. However, following the founding of the Royal Danish Academy of Fine Arts in 1754—then called the Royal Danish Painting, Sculpture and Building Academy, Denmark began to focus on educating and producing national artists and craftsmen. This led to the first fruitful period of nationally defined art in Denmark. This period, in the early-to-mid 19th century, is known as the Golden Age of Danish art.

This particular period in Danish art history is characterized by a movement of national romanticism, and artists focused on themes of mythology, Danish history, and beauty, often romanticizing the Danish landscape. Sculptor Bertel Thorvaldsen (1770–1844) was renowned for his Romanesque statues. His most famous piece is a marble depiction of the myth of Jason and the Golden Fleece. Painter Christoffer Wilhelm Eckersberg (1783–1853), considered the father of Dutch painting, created detailed scenes of everyday Danish life. Other important artists during this period include Christen Købke (1810–1848), who painted portraitures and landscapes, and Johan Thomas Lundbye (1818–1848), also known for his landscape paintings and depictions of rural Denmark. This was followed by a period of significant French and other foreign influences, as exemplified in

the symbolism in the works of Laurits Andersen Ring (1854–1933), and in the more realistic and poetic depictions of life in the portraitures of Vilhelm Hammershøi (1864–1916).

The 20th century saw the emergence of the avant-garde art movement known as CoBrA—so named because its artists came from Copenhagen, Brussels, and Amsterdam, This experimental movement featured painting, etchings and sculpture in an abstract, modern style. Some of the famous artists from this period include Asger Jorn (1914–1973), Karel Appel (1921–2006) and Constant Nieuwenhuys (1920–2005).

Architecture

Denmark is a country rich in architectural heritage, from its numerous ancient castles to the ornate residences of the royal family. As such, various architectural styles such as Gothic, Renaissance or other architectural traditions are widespread. However, it is the sleek, functional, and spare style first displayed in the mid-20th century for which Denmark is famous. This emergence of modern design is often credited to Denmark's late shift from a largely agricultural economy toward an industrialized one. This late transition allowed Danes to keep a sense of care and craftsmanship well into the 20th century. Additionally, Denmark was largely spared the bombings inflicted on other countries during World War II, allowing designers to focus on crafting the future, and not rebuilding the past.

The 20th century was also a time of innovation for interior and industrial design. In 1949 architect Karre Klint (1888–1954) created the Round Chair, a chair designed with the then-revolutionary idea that seating should be comfortable, classic and durable. Arne Jacobsen (1902–1971) also became synonymous with the "Danish Modern" aesthetic. An architect and industrial designer, Jacobsen was known for his attention to detail and his classic furniture designs. Danish architect Jørn Utzøn (1918–2008) is famous for the futuristic design of the Sydney Opera House in Australia. Completed in 1973, the opera house—a blend of forward-thinking architectural and engineering design—is recognized as one of the most important architectural contributions of the 20th century. It was named a United Nations Educational, Scientific and Cultural Organization (UNESCO) World Heritage Site in 2007.

Drama

Denmark experienced its "golden age" of cinema in the early 20th century. During this period, the first Danish film company was established and Danish films began to gradually increase in length. During the 1920s, Danish cinema achieved international acclaim through the works of director Carl Theodor Dreyer (1889–1968). Dreyer directed nine silent and six sound films. His most famous work is *The Passion of Joan of Arc*, a 1928 silent film about the French heroine that is viewed as an enduring cinematic classic.

Danish cinema was again dominant in the 1930s, during which light comedies were the popular genre. Following World War II, Danish films developed more cynical and artistic themes, and by the 1960s, Danish cinema had gradually become more erotic. The Danish Film Institute (DFI) was established in the mid-1970s, providing funds for would-be Danish film makers. Since its founding, the institute has funded a part of nearly all Danish films made. In fact, during the early 21st century, Danish filmmaking remains almost entirely run through the state-controlled DFI.

Music

Performance arts have a long history of popularity and sponsorship in Denmark, beginning with the founding of the Royal Danish Theater in 1748. First established as a theater only for royalty, the Royal Danish Theater has been a staple of the Danish cultural scene for centuries, and is home to the world-famous Danish Royal Ballet. Ballet master August Bournonville (1805–1879), famed for establishing a distinctive style of ballet known as the Bournonville School, served as the choreographer for the royal ballet from 1830–1877. The Royal Danish Orchestra, which dates back to 1448, also performs there.

Many Danish composers have also achieved international recognition, most notably conductor and violinist Carl August Nielsen (1865–1931), considered Denmark's greatest composer. Nielsen has recently received attention in the United States, where numerous rising conductors have focused on his symphonies. Additionally, Danish-born performer Victor Borge (1909–2000), a classical musician known for his humor, became a prominent figure in popular culture. The popular humorist is often affectionately referred to as the "Clown Prince of Denmark" and "The Great Dane."

Literature

Literature in Denmark dates back to the Middle Ages, when Scandinavian myths and ballads were first transcribed. Prominent 16th- and 17th-century writers included humanist Christiern Pedersen (c. 1480–1554) and poet Thomas Hansen Kingo (1634–1703), known for his baroque poetry (characterized by grandeur). In addition, the works and comedies of playwright Ludvig Holberg (1684–1754) are still performed in Denmark today. Influential philosopher and writer Søren Kierkegaard (1813–1855) emerged following this period. Kierkegaard was part of the existentialist movement, a 20th-century school of philosophy defined by the individual creation of meaning and essence in life.

Danish literature began to achieve international acclaim during the 19th and 20th centuries. This was due in large part to the works of Hans Christian Andersen (1805–1875) and Karen Blixen (1885–1962), who wrote under the pen name Isak Dinesen. Andersen's most famous works include his fairy tales, most notably *The Little Mermaid*, *The Emperor's New Clothes*, and *The Ugly Duckling*. Andersen's influential fairy tales have been translated into over 150 languages worldwide. Blixen is best known for her autobiography *Out of Africa* (1937), an account of her life on a Kenyan coffee plantation.

Although Andersen, Kierkegaard, and Blixen achieved international fame, it is Nikolai Frederik Severin Grundtvig (1783–1872) who had the most profound effect on Danish life and culture.

A minister, philosopher and scholar, he penned some 1,500 hymns and remains the most prolific Danish writer in history. N.F.S. Grundtvig's most enduring contribution to Danish culture was the establishment of folk schools. At these boarding schools, adults can take classes in any number of courses, including such areas as art, writing and organic farming.

CULTURE

Arts & Entertainment

Though Denmark has been a constitutional monarchy since 1849, it became a parliamentary democracy in 1901, Danes exhibit a very strong sense of egalitarianism (a political philosophy in which equality is favored). This ethic is woven into all aspects of Danish life, from the state funding of health care and education to the government's generous support of art and culture. Generally, these funds come from Denmark's high taxes, considered some of the highest in the world, the aim of which is to distribute wealth evenly. In 2003, in particular, parliament established the Danish Arts Council, or Kunstrådet. This government organization provides support, both national and internationally, for the contemporary arts in Denmark.

There are over 200 music festivals held each year throughout Denmark. Since 1971, Denmark has held a large music festival in the town of Roskilde. It is the largest outdoor music event in Europe, typically lasting four days and attracting various international acts. The proceeds of the event are donated to charity. In addition, the Copenhagen Jazz Festival takes place every July and lasts ten days. As apart of the festival, Danish and international jazz musicians perform at hundreds of music venues.

Contemporary Danish cinema has achieved international status with the emergence of Dogme (or Dogma) 95. This experimental film movement universally rejects the over-the-top production values associated with the Hollywood film industry. Dogme 95 consists of a group of Danish filmmakers who focus on a realistic,

documentary-style aesthetic. For example, these films typically forego additional lighting, special wardrobes more technical cameras and large budgets, resulting in a stripped-down style of filmmaking.

Hundreds of "associations," or clubs, are devoted to chess, which Danes have enjoyed since the days of the Vikings. Dane Jorgen Moller is still honored for inventing the "Moller variation" on the Italian opening. Danes have participated in every chess tournament sponsored by the Federation Internationale des Eches (International Chess Federation).

Bridge is also popular, and the Danish Bridge Federation is affiliated with the European Bridge League and the World Bridge Federation. In addition, many Danes participate in amateur sports, including rifle marksmanship, swimming and polo.

Cultural Sites & Landmarks

As the oldest monarchy in Europe, Denmark has many landmarks that provide a window to its past. Perhaps the country's most significant landmarks are its World Heritage Sites, chosen by the United Nations (UN) for their contribution to international culture. These include the strategically-placed Kronborg Castle, the Roskilde Cathedral and the Jelling Runic Stones. In addition, Denmark is credited with a fourth World Heritage Site, Ilulissat Icefjord, a glacier located on Greenland. (Greenland is a part of the Kingdom of Denmark.)

Kronborg Castle, added as a World Heritage Site in 2000, is a 15th-century fortress that was vital to northern Europe's history in the Middle Ages. A model of Renaissance design, it is probably best known as the setting for William Shakespeare's famous tragedy *Hamlet*. The Roskilde Cathedral, located on the island of Zealand, Denmark's largest island, was designated as a World Heritage Site in 1995. It is considered the first cathedral built in the Gothic style to be constructed of brick, and dates back to the 12th and 13th centuries. Jelling, a small town in Central Jutland, is home to the Jelling Runic Stones. The site consists of carved rune stones and burial mounds built during the Viking Age.

The statue of the Little Mermaid, based on the Hans Christian Andersen tale, is perhaps Denmark's best-known cultural landmark. The sculpture, located in the harbor of Copenhagen, Denmark's capital, is considered a Danish icon, and is perhaps the most photographed site in Denmark. Created by sculptor Edvard Eriksen (1876–1959), the melancholy, lifelike sculpture was commissioned in 1909 by the head of Carlsberg Beer. Nearly 100 years later, the brewery commissioned yet another Little Mermaid to be sculpted. Copies of the statue are located in various towns of significant Danish heritage throughout North America.

Tivoli Gardens, which first opened in 1843, is an eight-hectare (20-acre) amusement park and garden oasis in the center of Copenhagen. Roughly four million people visit annually, drawn by the amusements as well as theaters, restaurants, concert halls, marching bands and a museum. Two nights a week, the gardens put on a midnight fireworks show.

Libraries & Museums

The Royal Library, founded in 1648, is the national library of Denmark and also the library of the University of Copenhagen. Its collections include historical manuscripts (such as the Old Royal Collection) that date back to the Middle Ages, as well as comprehensive collections of Danish newspapers (dating as early as 1634) and a collection of over 100,000 digitized historical images.

Museums in the capital of Copenhagen include the Post & Tele Museum, Dansk Design Center, and Museum Erotica. Various art collections are on display at the Louisiana Museum, north of Copenhagen; the Arken, south of Copenhagen; the North Jutland Art Museum in Aalborg; and the National Museum in Copenhagen. Danish design is exhibited in the Museum of Applied Art and Industrial Design in Copenhagen. The National Museum also displays Viking artifacts, as does the Viking Ship Museum in Roskilde. The Frilandsmuseet (Open Air Museum) is a reconstructed village in Lyngby, a northern suburb of Copenhagen.

Holidays

June 5 is Constitution Day, and Olaifest is celebrated in the Faroe Islands on July 29. Denmark has celebrated American Independence Day on July 4 since 1912. In that year, Danish immigrants to the United States purchased land near Alborg and donated Rebild Park to the people, on the condition that American Independence Day is celebrated annually. The tradition has been followed every year except during the Nazi occupation of Denmark during World War II.

Youth Culture

Life for most youth in Denmark is typically routine and structured. Since most parents work, children are often enrolled in daycare at an early age. In addition, most young children stay in day care after school, allowing their parents to have full-time jobs. Education, mandatory from age seven through 16, is free, even at the university level. In fact, full-time university students can be paid as much as $400 (USD) per month to help cover the cost of food and rent. In addition, school attendance at the primary and secondary levels is typically 100 percent.

While education is considered well-structured in Denmark, it also has a very lax culture. For example, there is no hierarchy of names: even from the earliest grades, teachers and students refer to each other by first name. Furthermore, all schools are co-ed and do not require uniforms. Typically, students stay with the same teacher and classmates in the same building for their first 10 years of schooling.

Dental care is free for all children, and dentists usually establish their offices on school grounds. Lunch is typically fast—about ten minutes long—and the school day ends at noon for those ten and under. For school children between the ages of eleven and sixteen, school typically ends at two o'clock in the afternoon. In addition, sixth- and seventh-grade students, both boys and girls, typically receive in-school housekeeping and cooking instruction.

Thirteen is the earliest age that children are allowed to work, while 18 is the legal voting age. Eighteen is also the age at which drivers' licenses are issued. However, few Danish teens own a vehicle. The legal age for tobacco and alcohol consumption is 15 years. Overall, more teens have cell phones than have Internet access. As such, text messaging is popular. Generally, sexual attitudes in Denmark are relaxed. However, despite a certain amount of permissiveness among youth, teen pregnancies and abortions are rare. (Abortion has been legal in Denmark since 1973.)

SOCIETY

Transportation

The geography of Denmark largely consists of one large peninsula extending from northern Europe (often referred to as Jutland) and over 400 islands, nearly 80 of which are inhabited. As such, two of the most popular modes of public transportation in the country are trains and ferries.

The car remains the primary mode of transportation in Denmark, with one in three Danes owning a car. However, a 200 percent tax on new automobile purchases was recently enacted. For example, a car that costs $20,000 (USD) in the U.S. costs $60,000 (USD) in Denmark. The high tax is part of Danish lawmakers' plans to curb pollution.

Bicycles are also a popular form of transportation in Denmark. In Copenhagen, Denmark's largest city, bicycles typically outnumber automobiles more than two to one. The city also sponsors a promotion in which approximately 2,000 bikes are available to the public for free.

In addition, Denmark's entire coastline is considered public land—a 1937 law prohibits private construction within 100 meters (328 feet) of the sea—making the coast fully accessible to bicyclists and hikers. Traffic moves on the right-hand side of the road in Denmark.

Transportation Infrastructure

The infrastructure in Denmark is highly developed, and the public transportation system is highly efficient. In addition, all major cities in the country can be reached in roughly half an hour by air; as of 2009, the country had 92 airports, as well as rail infrastructure totaling 2,667 kilometers (1,657 miles). The capital of Copenhagen, in particular, benefits from its infrastructure, as its carefully designed system of roads, waterways, railways, and airports permit easy transport of goods to and from the rest of Scandinavia.

Media & Communications

Denmark boasts a nearly 100 percent literacy rate nationwide. The Danish population borrows more library books—nearly 20 per capita annually—than any other country. Denmark has roughly 50 daily newspapers, with the *Jyllands Posten* of western Denmark maintaining the largest circulation. The *Jyllands Posten*, in fact, was involved in an international controversy in 2006 when it published what was largely perceived as derogatory cartoon renderings of the Prophet Mohammed. Islamic law forbids the visual representation of Mohammed in any form. *The Copenhagen Post* is the only English-language newspaper published in Denmark.

There are several television stations in Denmark, from government-sponsored commercial-free channels to TV2 Zulu, which features sports and comedy targeted for younger viewers. Prior to the 1980s, television in Denmark was run as a monopoly, with only a single channel. Television and radio broadcasting in Denmark is now generally divided into three categories: national, regional and local. With the exception of cartoons and films for children, television programs from abroad are never dubbed, but rather subtitled. In addition, the Internet is widespread in Denmark, with over 4.7 million Internet users in 2010, representing nearly 87 percent of the population. This was a large increase from 1997, when only 16 percent of households had access. As such, the number and diversity of electronic media in the country is steadily increasing.

SOCIAL DEVELOPMENT

Standard of Living

Denmark ranked 10th on the 2014 United Nations Human Development Index, which measures quality of life indicators (based on 2007 data). As of 2007, an estimated 12 percent of the population lived below the poverty line.

Water Consumption

Access to improved drinking water sources and sanitation services is very high in Denmark, with approximately 100 percent of the urban and rural populations having access to them.

Education

The Danes value education. Education is compulsory for nine years (ages seven to 16), and both state and private schools at that level are supported by state funds. Students who complete their 10th year of school may go on to general education or choose one of two types of vocational training.

Higher education offers three types of programs, lasting from three years to four-plus years. The short programs train students for such careers as lab technician, computer specialist and business manager. The medium-length courses lead to a bachelor's degree, and the long courses lead to the degree of kandidat, which is roughly equivalent to the master's degree. An additional three-year research program has recently been added, which leads to the Ph.D. degree.

The University of Copenhagen was established in 1479. There are also universities at Alborg, Arhus, Odense, and Roskilde. Numerous business and technical institutions are available, and many Danes also study in adult education programs that have no exams and grant no degrees.

Denmark's literacy rate is 100 percent. Approximately 60 percent of students in higher education are women; however, in 2005, there were almost twice as many male students than female at the University of Arhus' Faculty of Science. So while the gender gap has in some ways closed, certain subjects (such as mathematics and science) attract a disproportionate number of male students.

Women's Rights

Generally, women's rights have not been an issue in Denmark, and women are well represented politically and in the workforce. For example, over one-third of the members of parliament (MPs) are women, while half the Danish workforce is female. Overall, Denmark also has Europe's highest percentage of working women, and it is a country that prides itself on gender equality. Furthermore, government-funded day care makes finding and keeping meaningful employment a reality for Danish women. A 2006 study revealed that Denmark and Norway have the highest level of maternity benefits in Europe. However, Danish women tend to earn 10 percent less than their male colleagues, and are not as well represented in levels of upper management.

Most notably, Denmark's Queen Margrethe II (b. 1940–) is female. (Although Queen Margrethe I ruled from 1375 until her death in 1412, she was not considered an official monarch of Denmark.) In 1953, voters overturned the "kings only" law, thereby allowing Margrethe II to take the throne in 1972. Although the role is largely ceremonial—much like Queen Elizabeth in Great Britain—Denmark's queen remains an empowering figure for women.

In addition, Denmark is also home to one of the world's few museums devoted to the history of women. Known as the Kvindemuseet, the museum was established in 1984, and receives over 40,000 visitors annually.

Health Care

Denmark is one of the world's oldest welfare states. Health care is free to all residents and is paid for by tax revenues. Dental care is provided free to all children up to age fifteen; thereafter, the cost is shared by the state and the patient. Per capita expenditure on health is $2,503 (USD).

Life expectancy is 79 years overall, 76 for men and 81 for women (2014 estimate). In the

Faroes, it is even higher: 79 overall, 76 for men, and 83 for women. Greenland does not fare as well. Life expectancy there is just 69 years overall, 66 for men, and 73 for women.

GOVERNMENT

Structure
Denmark is a constitutional monarchy, with universal suffrage for adults 18 years of age and older. The constitutional monarchy was established in 1849, and in 1953, the constitution was revised to permit a woman to become monarch. In 1972, Margrethe, daughter of Frederick IX, became the first reigning queen. She chose the name Margrethe II to honor her ancestor, the medieval Margrethe.

The prime minister is appointed by the monarch and is usually the leader of the majority party or of the majority coalition. The prime minister then appoints the Cabinet, which is approved by Parliament. The Folketing (Parliament) has 179 seats, including two each from Greenland and the Faroes. Members are elected by popular vote and serve for four years. The monarch appoints Supreme Court judges for life. In addition, citizens have the right to question government actions through an ombudsman, who oversees the conduct of the cabinet and decisions of the administration.

Greenland and the Faroe Islands are self-governing overseas administrative divisions of Denmark.

Political Parties
Political parties include the Liberal Party, Social Democrats, Danish People's Party, Conservative People's Party, Socialist People's Party, Social Liberal Party, and the Christian Democrats. The Social Democratic Party helped revitalize Copenhagen in the postwar years, establishing extensive welfare programs, many of which still remain in place.

In the 2011 parliamentary elections, the Liberal Party won 47 seats, the Social Democrats won 44 seats, the Danish People's Part won 22 seats, the Social Liberal party won 17 seats, the Social People's party won 16 seats, the Red-Green Alliance won 12 seats, while several other parties won under 10 seats each.

Local Government
Denmark is divided into five regions and 98 municipalities. Each region and municipality is governed by an elected council that appoints a mayor.

Judicial System
The judicial system in Denmark comprises a Supreme Court, High Courts (one in Eastern Denmark and the other in Western Denmark), County Courts, the Court of Impeachment of the Realm, and the Special Court of Indictment and Revision.

Taxation
Denmark levies an income tax, corporate tax, country municipal taxes, state taxes, a vehicle tax, a health tax, and a value-added tax (VAT). Income taxes tend to be high (59 percent in 2009), and the top corporate tax rate is, as of 2010, 25 percent. Tax revenues accounted for 49.5 percent of the country's GDP in 2009.

Armed Forces
The armed forces of Denmark consist of the Royal Danish Army (Hæren, or HRN), Royal Danish Navy (Søværnet, or SVN), Royal Danish Air Force (Flyvevåbnet, or FLV), and the Danish Home Guard (Hjemmeværnet, or HJV). The primary focus of the armed forces is national defense and conflict prevention. Since 2003, the Danish government reports that more than 64,000 Danish troops have participated in UN, NATO, and OSCE missions. In 2009, the Danish government announced plans to establish an Arctic military command and task force.

Foreign Policy
Historically, Denmark's foreign relations have been defined by the country's longstanding policy of neutrality. However, Denmark ended its neutral stance when it joined the North Atlantic

Treaty Organization (NATO) in 1949. In recent years, Denmark has been supportive of international military campaigns, such as the U.S.-led military operations in Afghanistan. In addition to NATO, Denmark is a member of the United Nations (UN), and also holds membership in the World Bank, the International Monetary Fund (IMF), and the Organization for Economic Co-operation and Development (OECD).

A member of the European Union (EU) since 1973, Denmark has played a prominent role in policies and issues affecting Europe, and has developed a reputation as a nation that seeks equality and cohesion with others. However, Denmark was one of three EU countries—Great Britain and Sweden being the others—to reject the adoption of the euro as its currency (Denmark voted to retain the Danish Krone, or DKK). Nonetheless, Denmark has actively supported the integration of Eastern and Central European nations into the EU. The country maintains membership on several European councils, including the Council of Europe, the Baltic Council and the Nordic Council.

Denmark is widely perceived as a conscientious and generous country. In fact, Denmark gives more aid per capita to overseas countries in need than any other nation in the world. The country contributes nearly one percent of its gross national product (GNP) to foreign aid and development programs. In addition, Denmark was the first country to create a Ministry of the Environment, doing so in 1971. Denmark also became one of the first countries to enact strong environmental protection laws in the 1980s. Today, two-thirds of all Danish waste is recycled, and the country is considered a leader in windmill technology (55 percent of the world's wind turbines were Danish-made). Additionally, 17 percent of Denmark's own electricity is wind-powered, and there are no nuclear generators in the country.

Generally, Denmark maintains strong relations with its neighbors, particularly Germany, the only nation with which Denmark shares a land border. However, the flying of the German flag in Denmark is illegal. In addition, the relationship between Sweden and Denmark was particularly strengthened in 2000 when a bridge project linking the two Scandinavian countries—the Øresund Bridge and Tunnel—was completed. Denmark also maintains a strong relationship with Greenland. The world's largest island is, in fact, a part of the Kingdom of Denmark, though the country was granted self-government in 1979 (Denmark still maintains a degree of control over foreign affairs). Iceland, a former Danish possession, declared its complete independence in 1944.

In addition, Denmark is involved in several territorial disputes, most notably a sovereign dispute with Canada over Hans Island (an uninhabited island in the Arctic Ocean); a territorial dispute with Ireland, the United Kingdom (UK) and Iceland over the Faroe Islands; and territorial claims with several countries in the North Pole.

Dependencies

Denmark's two dependencies are the Faroe Islands and Greenland. The Faroe Islands attained self-government under Denmark in 1948; since then, the islands have been largely autonomous, with Denmark assisting in matters of defense, foreign affairs, and justice. Greenland became an official part of Denmark in 1953, but the country had a presence on the island as early as the 18th century. In 1979, Greenland was granted a degree of autonomy, but Denmark still intervenes in matters of foreign affairs, security, and financial policy.

Human Rights Profile

International human rights law insists that states respect civil and political rights, and also promote an individual's economic, social and cultural rights. The United Nations Universal Declaration on Human Rights (UDHR) is recognized as the standard for international human rights. Its authors sought the counsel of the world's great thinkers, philosophers, and religious leaders, and were careful to create a document that reflects the core values shared by every world culture. (To read this document or view the articles relating to cultural human rights, go to: http://www.udhr.org/UDHR/default.htm.)

Generally, Denmark maintains an excellent reputation in regards to human rights. Denmark was chosen as the world's least-corrupt nation in a 1998 analysis of 99 countries. A similar global study in 2008 named Denmark as the world's happiest country. In addition, Denmark is consistently rated as having one of the world's highest standards of living, with a more-equalized distribution of wealth than most industrialized nations.

However, some issues continue to generate controversy, most notably immigration. In the late 1960s, Denmark's formerly restrictive laws on immigration were opened to address a national labor shortage. As a result, many immigrant workers—from Turkey, Pakistan, Somalia, and Ethiopia—arrived in Denmark. Many of these immigrants settled as permanent residents, resulting in a population surge in the country's Muslim community. In 2000 and 2002, however, the Danish parliament passed certain restrictive immigration laws, including a law limiting marriages between Danes and foreigners. Such legislation contradicts Article 16 of the UDHR, which ensures marital freedom without any distinction of race, nationality or religion. In addition, international bodies have also questioned Denmark's adherence to Article 21—which grants all people the right to governmental involvement—stating that immigrants and other groups are underrepresented politically.

In regard to Article 3, which states that citizens have the right to life, liberty, and security, Denmark is widely perceived as being one of the safest countries in Europe. However, there have been instances where Denmark's adherence to this principle has been questioned. For example, in the early 21st century, police began been positioning themselves outside Christiana, a countercultural commune begun in 1970 in Copenhagen on the grounds of a defunct army base, in what its residents considered a threatening way. Police have also raided the commune, leading to arrests. While many Danes view Christiana as a harmless experiment in non-traditional living, others feel less kindly toward the non-tax paying residents. Recently, lawmakers have proposed certain property laws and have tried to prove that

the residents of the commune have no claim or ownership over the land. Further complicating the matter is the fact that Christiana sits on potentially valuable waterfront property.

ECONOMY

Overview of the Economy
The 2014 estimate of Denmark's gross domestic product (GDP) is $248 billion (USD). Exports of meat, meat products, machinery, instruments, dairy products, fish, chemicals, furniture, ships and windmills bring in 361.2 billion DKK ($64.16 billion USD).

Reflective of Denmark's overall economic climate, Copenhagen enjoys a strong free-market economy. Copenhagen is Denmark's industrial center, manufacturing a good portion of its ships, ship engines, textiles, porcelain, and packaged foodstuffs for both domestic use and export, and almost all of its information technology (IT), biotechnology, and pharmaceutical products.

Industry
Denmark's major industries include food processing, machinery and equipment, textiles and clothing, chemical products, electronics, construction, furniture and other wood products, shipbuilding and windmills. Food processing is the leading industry, producing bacon, butter, cheese, eggs, meat, and beer. Most manufacturing takes place in and around the country's large cities.

Labor
In 2014, the labor force was estimated at about 2.8 million. The unemployment rate is 5.2 percent. Increasing numbers of the labor force are employed in service occupations—an estimated 77 percent as of 2014. Similarly, in Copenhagen, approximately two-thirds of the area's workforce is employed in the services sector.

Energy/Power/Natural Resources
The Danfield (the Danish sector of the North Sea) produces petroleum, natural gas, and fish. Air and water pollution, though of some concern,

are not extreme. In recent years, the Danes have minimized the use of fertilizer and pesticide, and have shifted to perennial crops to reduce the run-off of nitrogen and phosphorus into the North Sea. Air pollution comes mainly from vehicle emissions and power plants. Drinking water is sometimes polluted by animal waste and pesticides. Approximately one-fifth of electricity in Denmark is generated through wind power.

Fishing

Denmark is the largest exporter of fish to the 27 countries of the European Union, and is the fourth largest exporter of fish globally. The industry employs approximately 6,500 people. Prawns are an important species in the industry.

Forestry

Approximately 12 percent of Denmark is forested. Common tree species include Norway spruce, beech, pine, and oak. Forestry contributes 0.24 percent to the country's GDP. Forestry-related industries, such as paper and furniture, contribute approximately four percent to the GDP.

Mining/Metals

Denmark is not rich in mineral resources. However, limestone, clay and gravel, salt, chalk and sand are mined in several areas. In addition, granite and kaolin are mined on the Baltic island of Bornholm.

Agriculture

About 70 percent of the land in Denmark is used for farming, yet agriculture employs only about two percent of the labor force; as of 2010, there were an estimated 17,000 farmers. Barley is the principal crop, followed by grass and green fodder, and root crops (potatoes and sugar beets). Most of these crops are used for livestock feed.

Some farms are small, averaging about 21 hectares (52 acres) and are generally family owned. Most farmers, however, are affiliated with cooperatives, which process and market the farm produce.

Denmark is world famous for its bacon and dairy products. Agriculture is worth 71.6 billion DKK ($12.7 billion USD) annually.

Animal Husbandry

In 2009, there were approximately 24,000 livestock farms in Denmark, including 8,000 cattle farms, 3,000 pig farms, and 330 poultry farms. There are approximately 900,000 head of cattle, 980,000 pigs, and 67,800 poultry. In the 1990s, the use of antibiotics to promote growth in hogs was restricted.

Tourism

Denmark's fourth largest industry is tourism. Each year, approximately two million tourists visit the country, generating more than 22 million DKK ($3.9 million USD) in revenue.

Popular tourist sites include Denmark's historic cities, such as Copenhagen with its six-story buildings and church steeples; Ribe, the country's oldest town, founded as a market town in the eighth century; and Aarhus, the country's commercial and cultural center. Bicycle routes crisscross the country and swimming beaches abound. For scenery lovers, the Island of Mon, south of Zealand, sports the Mons Klint, white chalk cliffs rising 128 meters (420 feet).

Viking history is a big draw, and the sixth-century rune stones at Jelling, marking the burial mounds of King Gorm the Old and Queen Thyra, are on the list of United Nations World Heritage sites.

Many historic castles have been converted to museums. Some famous castles in Denmark include Frederiksborg Castle, on a man-made island north of Copenhagen; Elsinore; Kronborg (Hamlet's Castle), whose owners once demanded tribute from passing ships; Rosenborg Castle in Copenhagen, where the crown jewels are stored; and Egeskov Castle, built on a small lake during the Renaissance, its foundation supported by thousands of upright oak trunks.

Hope L. Killcoyne, Ellen Bailey, &
Jamie Aronson

DO YOU KNOW?

- The Øresundsfordindelsen bridge/tunnel combination, opened in 2000, is the first piece of land infrastructure to link Denmark and Sweden. It stretches 15.5 kilometers (9.6 miles) across the Øresund between its end points in Copenhagen, Denmark and Malmö, Sweden.

- The Copenhagen Jazz Festival is an annual ten-day music festival that attracts musicians and music fans from all over the world.

- Legoland, near Billund, is a 10-hectare (25-acre) amusement park built entirely from plastic Lego blocks.

Bibliography

Bain, Carolyn. *Denmark.* Oakland, CA: Lonely Planet, 2012.

Britannica Educational. *Denmark, Finland, and Sweden.* Perth, WA: Britannica Educational, 2013.

Dyrbye, Helen, Steven Harris, and Thomas Golzen. *The Xenophobe's Guide to the Danes.* 2nd ed. London: Oval Books, 2008.

Jespersen, Knud J.V. *A History of Denmark.* New York: Palgrave Macmillan, 2011.

Mouritsen, Lone, and Roger E. Norum, and Caroline Osborne. *The Rough Guide to Denmark.* London: Rough Guides, 2010.

Randsborg, Klavs. *Anatomy of Denmark: Archaeology and History from the Ice Age to the Present.* London: Duckworth, 2009.

Steinberg, Shirley R. *Teen Life in Europe.* Westport, CT: Greenwood Press, 2005.

Strange, Morten. *Culture Shock! Denmark: A Survival Guide to Customs and Etiquette.* Tarrytown, NY: Marshall Cavendish, 2009.

Works Cited

"Arne Jacobsen 1902–1971)," *Fritz Hansen Furniture,* Allerød, Denmark. http://www.fritzhansen.com/composite-229.htm

Deedy, Carmen Agra. *The Yellow Star.* 1st. Atlanta: Peachtree Publishers, Ltd., 2000.

"Background Note: Denmark," Bureau of European and Eurasian Affairs. *U.S. Department of State.* http://www.state.gov/r/pa/ei/bgn/3167.htm

Conaway, Laura. "Those Happy, Happy Danes," The Bryant Park Project from NPR News. *National Public Radio,* Washington, DC. http://www.npr.org/blogs/bryantpark/2008/07/those_happy_happy_danes.html

"Copenhagen and Ærø." Rick Steves' Europe. Rick Steves. *Oregon Public Broadcasting,* Edmonds, WA. 2005.

"Denmark." CIA – The World Factbook. *Central Intelligence Agency.* https://www.cia.gov/library/publications/the-world-factbook/geos/da.html

"Denmark.dk, the Official Website of Denmark," *Ministry of Foreign Affairs of Denmark.* Copenhagen, Denmark. http://www.denmark.dk/en/Denmark.htm

"Denmark 'happiest' country in the world," CNN.com/health. 02 Jul 2008. *Turner Broadcasting Corp.* http://www.cnn.com/2008/HEALTH/07/02/nations.happiness/index.html

"Denmark Undergoes a Musical Makeover." *All Things Considered.* Chris Nickson. National Public Radio, Washington, DC. http://www.npr.org/templates/story/story.php?storyId=16846072

Diaz, Jesus, "Everything You Always Wanted to Know About Lego," The Lego Mega-Guide. *Gizmodo, the Gadget Guide.* http://gizmodo.com/5019797/everything-you-always-wanted-to-know-about-lego

Finfacts: Ireland's Business and Financial Portal. From World Bank Development Indicators 2007 Feb 2008: *International Comparison Program.* http://www.finfacts.ie/biz10/globalworldincomepercapita.htm

Hansen, Ole Steen. *Country Insights, Denmark, City and Village Life.* Austin: Steck-Vaughn Company, 1998.

Ikea Store Catalog. http://www.ikea.com/us/en/catalog/allproducts/

'Is IKEA Giving Danes the Doormat Treatment?' *Retraction,* 6 Mar 2008. http://www.spiegel.de/international/business/0,1518,539709,00.html

"Jacob Riis: Shedding Light On NYC's 'Other Half'." *All Things Considered.* Robert Siegel. National Public Radio, Washington, DC. http://www.npr.org/templates/story/story.php?storyId=91981589

Jan Besson, photographer, "The Little Mermaid, A Publication of the Northwest Danish Foundation." Seattle, Washington. http://www.northwestdanishfoundation.org/about-our-foundation/little-mermaid-archive/jan-feb-2007-little-mermaid.pdf

Jones, W. Glyn. *Nations of the Modern World, Denmark.* New York: Praeger Publishers, Inc., 1970.

"Legoland, Billund," *Lego, Billund, Denmark.* http://www.legoland.dk/?lc=en

Mark Sullivan. "Maternity Benefits—European Study Shows Wide Variations," Mercer, London, United Kingdom. http://www.mercer.com/summary.htm?siteLanguage=104&idContent=1221340

"Ministry of Foreign Affairs of Denmark," Copenhagen, Denmark. http://www.um.dk/en

Murphy, Patricia J. *Countries of the World, Denmark*. Mankato, MN: Bridgestone Books, Capstone Press, 2003.

"Music at Roskilde," *Roskilde Festival English 2008: Programme,* Roskilde, Denmark.

O'Mahony, Paul. "Ikea Guilty of 'Cultural Imperialism': Danes," *The Local, Sweden's News in English*. http://www.thelocal.se/10054/20080220/

"Provisional Lineup," *Roskilde Festival English 2008: Schedule,* Roskilde, Denmark. http://www.roskilde-festival.dk/fileadmin/user_upload/documents/Spilleplan_2008.pdf

Ross, Alex, "Inextinguishable: The Fiery Rhythms of Carl Nielsen," *The New Yorker*. http://www.newyorker.com/arts/critics/musical/2008/02/25/080225crmu_music_ross

"Seeds of Ethnic Cleansing Sprout in Europe." *Talk of the Nation*. World. Guy Raz, Sylvia Poggioli. National Public Radio, Washington, DC. http://www.npr.org/templates/story/story.php?storyId=92421149

"Smart Travels Europe with Rudy Maxa: Belgium, Amsterdam & the Netherlands, Denmark." *American Public Television, Small World Productions*. 2003.

Soares, Claire. "Ikea and loathing: What's in a product name?" *The Independent*. 7 Mar 2008. http://www.independent.co.uk/news/world/europe/ikea-and-loathing-whats-in-a-product-name-792774.html

"Teitur: Pride of the Faroe Islands." *Day to Day*. Christian Bordel. NPR Music, Washington, DC. http://www.npr.org/templates/story/story.php?storyId=90944181 http://www.roskilde-festival.dk/2008/frontpage/programme/

"University of Leicester Produces the First Ever World Map of Happiness," *University of Leicester Press Release*. http://www2.le.ac.uk/ebulletin/news/press-releases/2000-2009/2006/07/nparticle.2006-07-28.2448323827

"Vayama" (travel web site), *Danish Etiquette Tips*. http://www.vayama.com/denmark-etiquette

Witkowska, Monika, and Joanna Hald. *Eyewitness Travel Guides, Denmark*. 1st American Edition. New York: Dorling Kindersley Publishing, Inc., 2005.

Weir, Bill and Sylvia Johnson "Denmark: The Happiest Place on Earth; Despite High Taxes, Danes Rank Themselves as Happy and Content," *20/20*, ABC News. http://abcnews.go.com/2020/story?id=4086092&page=1

"World Heritage List: Denmark," World Heritage Centre, United Nations. *UNESCO.org*. http://whc.unesco.org/en/statesparties/dk

"World Heritage List: Australia," World Heritage Centre, United Nations. *UNESCO.org*. http://whc.unesco.org/en/statesparties/au

Queen Elizabeth II has reigned over England for more than 60 years. /Stock photo © EdStock

ENGLAND

Introduction

England is a country in northwestern Europe, located in the southern part of the island of Great Britain, with coastlines on the English Channel, the North Sea, and the Irish Sea. Together with Scotland, Wales, and Northern Ireland, England makes up the United Kingdom. Indeed, England is the home of the former British Empire, which controlled colonies all over the world from the 17th century until the mid 20th century. English dominance over Great Britain has been so strong throughout history that many people consider the terms synonymous.

England's capital city, London, is a major cultural, economic, and travel hub. From it, England has made major contributions to world culture, particularly in literature, drama, and language. English has become a global language, and authors such as William Shakespeare are read around the world.

GENERAL INFORMATION

Official Language: None (English is the only language generally used for official business.)
Population: 64,510,000 (2014 estimate)
Currency: Pound Sterling (GBP)
Coins: The pound sterling is available in 1, 2, 5, 10, 20 and 25 pence denominations. A 1 and 2 pound coin is also available.
Land Area: 130,395 square kilometers (50,346 square miles)

National Anthem: None (Unofficial anthems include "God Save the Queen" and "Rule Britannia")
Capital: London
Time Zone: GMT (Summer: GMT +1)
Flag: The flag of England is the St. George's Cross.

Population

Most English people are of Anglo-Saxon descent, though there are also many immigrant Irish and Scots as well as large ethnic minorities from the countries of the Commonwealth of Nations. The largest minority groups in England are from Asia and the Caribbean, including about 1.4 million Indians, 706,000 Pakistanis, and 590,000 black West Indians.

Most people live in the southeast of England, but there are many large urban areas in the north,

Principal Cities by Population (2011 census):

- Copenhagen (1,200,000)
- London (8,250,205)
- Birmingham (1,085,810)
- Liverpool (552,267)
- Sheffield (518,090)
- Bristol (535,907)
- Manchester (510,746)
- Leeds (474,632)
- Leicester (443,760)
- Coventry (325,949)
- Kingston upon Hull (284,321)

including the industrial cities of Birmingham and Manchester. London, with around 8.2 million people, is Europe's largest city.

Languages

English is the major language not only in England, but also in the Commonwealth countries and in former colonial territories such as the United States. English is one of the world's most widely-used languages, with approximately 400 million native speakers and hundreds of millions who speak English as a second language.

English derives mainly from Anglo-Saxon, but with heavy influences from France and Scandinavia. Many regional variations exist in pronunciation and vocabulary, often making it hard for one region to understand another. The major distinctions are among Northern England, the Midlands, East Anglia, and South East England. The most prestigious variety is "Received Pronunciation," also known as the "Queen's (or King's) English," based on upper and middle-class speech.

Native People & Ethnic Groups

England's modern population is comprised largely of native "English" (Anglo-Saxon); the country's name means "land of the English." There are also large populations of Celtic and Scandinavian heritage. The earliest inhabitants were the Britons, a Celtic people who dominated southern Britain until the Roman conquest in 43 CE.

Beginning in the fifth century, Britain was settled by Germanic peoples known as the Angles, Saxons, and Jutes, who eventually combined as the "Anglo-Saxons." The Vikings arrived from Scandinavia in the ninth century and established a realm in eastern England known as the "Danelaw." The Norman Conquest in the 11th century added a strong French element. In recent times, racial violence has broken out between the "native" English and immigrants from the Commonwealth countries.

Native British people make up the large majority of England's population. Africans and Asians make up the largest minority groups.

Religions

The Church of England is the official church. The most senior bishop is the Archbishop of Canterbury, who heads the Church's southern province. The second most senior bishop is the Archbishop of York, based in Northern England. The Archbishop of Canterbury also presides over the "Anglican Communion," a worldwide confederation of 38 national churches derived from the Church of England. England's non-Christian populations include Buddhists, Muslims, Hindus, Sikhs, and Jews.

London is one of the least religious cities in the world, with over 20 percent of the population claiming to have no religion at all. This percentage accounts is the same as the combined percentages of all the Muslims, Hindus, Jews, and Sikhs in the city. In fact, those with no religion are the second most numerous group by religion, after Christians, who account for 48 percent of the population.

Climate

England's climate is mild, even though the country is located far north of the equator. Much of the mildness is due to warm sea currents. England has a reputation for wet weather. Southern England tends to receive less than 700 millimeters of rainfall per year, while northern regions can receive as much as 2,000 millimeters of precipitation annually. Snow is relatively rare except in the mountains. The southern coastal regions are quite sunny, while the mountains are usually cloudy.

Temperatures are relatively mild throughout the year in the southern and coastal areas, though winters can sometimes be quite cold. The mean annual temperature in low-lying areas is around 10° Celsius (50° Fahrenheit), while in the mountains it can drop to around 4° Celsius (39° Fahrenheit).

ENVIRONMENT & GEOGRAPHY

Topography

England covers 130,365 square kilometers (50,334 square miles), approximately half of Britain's total 243,000 square kilometers (93,000 square miles). Much of the country is surrounded by water, but there is relatively little inland water. There are, however, many rivers. The longest are the 236 mile long Thames (which runs through London) and the 220 mile long Severn, in southwestern England. Other important rivers are the Avon, which runs through Shakespeare's hometown of Stratford, and the Trent, the Humber, and the Mersey.

Much of Southern England is covered with rolling hills, though there are also several large plains. The east and southeast are low and often marshy. The central Midlands are a large plain. Northern England is covered with mountains and moors.

There are two main mountain ranges in England. The Pennines run north to south in north central England. The Cumbrian Mountains, in the northwest, are home to the Lake District. Among the hilly regions are the Chiltern Hills and Cotswold Hills, in Southern England.

Several islands off the British coast are within English jurisdiction: the Isle of Wight in the English Channel, and the Scilly Islands off the coast of Cornwall.

The city of London grew from a Roman fort called Londinium, the remains of which are roughly in the center of the modern county known as the City of London ("The City," or "The Square Mile," colloquially). Piccadilly Circus is generally regarded as London's center, and is a landmark in its own right, particularly because of the renowned lighted signs.

The Greater London area, consisting of the city and 32 boroughs, spans 1,610 square kilometers (620 square miles) and is one of the world's largest cities by area. London straddles the Thames River, which has been significantly embanked during the city's development. Because the Thames is a tidal river, and because London has been slowly "tilting," the risk of flooding in parts of the city has remained a constant concern.

Plants & Animals

England is noted for the rich variety of its plant and animal life. There is relatively little large game, due to hunting and human settlement, but there are still large populations of various wild animals. Large mammals include deer; the red and roe species are native; others, such as the fallow deer, were introduced from elsewhere. Smaller mammals include badgers, foxes, and rabbits. Fox hunting, long popular with the English upper class, has come under attack in recent years as being cruel to animals. Common game birds include grouse, woodcocks, and pheasants.

CUSTOMS & COURTESIES

Greetings

Methods of greeting vary in England and are largely dependent upon age and the level of formality. The traditional handshake is commonly used among older people and in formal or business settings. It is also often used when two people are first introduced to one another. One should always be sure to use the right hand, and to refuse a handshake may be considered insulting. It is also important not to grip the other person's hand too tightly, or to offer a limp, or weak, grasp.

On the whole, the English are quite reserved. As such, physical forms of contact, such as hugs or kisses, tend to be used only with more intimate friends or relatives, particularly when they have not seen each other for some time. If a kiss on the cheek is appropriate, one kiss is usually sufficient. This form of greeting tends to be more popular among close female friends.

Common verbal greetings include "Hello," or the more casual "Hi," or "Morning" (note that the "good" is dropped in informal situations). A greeting commonly used at a formal introduction is "How do you do?" This is not intended as a question, and the correct response is "How do you do?" Farewells such as "Goodbye" or simply "Bye" are the most common expressions used when parting. Other informal expressions include "Cheers" and "Ta-ra."

Gestures & Etiquette

It is often claimed that English people are very reserved in terms of manners and speech. While this is true to a certain degree, it also will vary according to age and social class. On the whole, teenagers and young adults will be far less concerned with etiquette than their elders.

The English tend not to use a large number of gestures while speaking, but it may be considered rude to stand with your arms folded while talking to someone. To do so is often interpreted as a sign of either hostility or boredom. Men should also be careful not to put both hands in their trouser pockets in formal situations as this is sometimes considered impolite. If someone taps the side of their nose with their index finger while talking, it implies that what they are telling you is confidential.

Timekeeping is important to most English people, and to be late for an appointment is a sign of rudeness. If an individual is likely to be late, every effort should be made to let the other person know. Queuing (standing in line) is very much expected when waiting for a bus or for entry somewhere. As such, queue jumping is highly frowned upon.

With regards to conversation, certain topics should not be raised except among very close friends. These taboo topics may include money and personal information such as age, weight,

or marital status. The British also commonly show respect for personal space when engaged in conversation.

Eating/Meals

The evening meal is typically the largest daily meal in England, and is usually eaten in the early evening. The exception to this is Sunday, when the midday meal is typically the largest. On this occasion, the evening meal may just consist of sandwiches and cake. The evening meal, regardless of what is served, is commonly referred to as dinner, tea, or supper.

In most English homes, dinners are served either family-style, with everyone serving themselves from large bowls on the table, or ready-plated. Knives, forks, and spoons are used for most foods, although it is acceptable to eat with one's hands in an informal situation, such as a barbecue or picnic. It is also typically considered impolite have your elbows on the table while eating or to put your knife in your mouth. Talking with a mouth full of food or eating noisily is also frowned upon.

Although dining etiquette has become less formal, there may still be occasions when for a formal meal, proper use of silverware is thus important. When confronted with more than one knife and fork, the diner should remember to start at the outside and work their way in choosing the proper utensil. Rather than slicing a bread roll, it is more proper to place a little butter on a plate, and to break off pieces of the roll and butter them individually. It is also considered proper to refrain from eating until everyone has been served and the host indicates that the meal may begin.

Visiting

If invited to an English person's house, visitors should be sure to be punctual and to not arrive late. This is in keeping with the British etiquette of properly observing time. Although gifts are typically not expected, a small gesture such as flowers, wine or chocolate will most certainly be appreciated. If invited for dinner, one should take a gift and send a thank you note afterwards.

Furthermore, it is not considered impolite to decline an invitation or to decline the offer of refreshments, but it would be considered rude to accept and then to not attend or to be late. It is wise to call ahead before visiting someone without an invitation.

In addition, when entering someone's home, a guest should remove their hat if they are wearing one. English people do not typically expect guests to remove their shoes and may be surprised if you do so. It is also customary to wait to be invited inside by the host, and to wait until you are invited to sit down. Overall, British etiquette is very much in line with Western standards.

LIFESTYLE

Family

As of 2013, 29 percent of English households were comprised of one person, 7 percent were single parent families and 46 percent were married couples with or without children. The proportion of children born outside of marriage had risen to 47.5 percent that same year. Birth rates have been relatively stable for the last thirty years and are expected to remain so. At the same time, the population is aging, and the 2011 census revealed that there were more people over the age of sixty than there are under sixteen.

The majority of young adults in England live with their parents until they have completed school or university. Afterwards, it is common for them to move into their own housing. Grandparents usually live separately, as it is not customary in England for children to take care of their elderly parents in such a manner.

Housing

Homeownership is typical in English society, although it has been dropping since 2003. In 2014, roughly 63 percent of people in England own their own home, down 7 percent from its peak. The remainder usually rent from a private landlord or from a local council housing authority. Houses tend to be built from brick or stone,

as they have traditionally been the most readily available materials.

In crowded urban areas, houses are often joined to one another. These long rows are called terraces. Also common in both urban and more rural areas are semi-detached (two houses joined together) and detached (freestanding) properties. The population is fairly evenly distributed, with approximately 25 percent living in each type of house. Others may live in apartments, known in England as "flats," or in "maisonettes," which are apartment-type dwellings within an individual house.

Food

Typically, traditional English meals revolve around a large cooked breakfast and a Sunday roast dinner, which usually consists of a roasted meat, vegetables and pudding (dessert), which is made from batter, but English eating habits have changed according to work patterns. Many people no longer have time to prepare a large breakfast—often consisting of sausage, bacon, eggs, and toast—before going to work. In addition, while customary British cuisine has often centered on a meat dish accompanied by two vegetables, England has also taken on a number of influences from its growing immigrant populations. As a result, Indian and Chinese foods have become as popular as fish and chips, a well-known British dish. Tea remains the beverage of choice, and has long been seen as a symbol of Englishness due to its important trade status during England's colonial period.

The British diet has changed somewhat due to overfishing, which has led to a shortage of cod and some other fish that once formed dietary staples. Fish and chips, consisting of fish (often cod) that is battered and deep fried and served with deep fried potatoes, has suffered as a result, but remains popular and has adapted when necessary by using other, less endangered fish.

Many of the English dishes that have retained their popularity require a lot of preparation. The availability of prepared foods means that they can still be enjoyed without people spending long hours in the kitchen. For example, steak and kidney pudding, a typical British dish that consists of a meat baked in a pastry shell, would once have taken most of a day to prepare. The steak and kidney mixture would have been stuffed inside a suet pastry, widely used in British cooking for various dishes, and steamed for up to six hours (suet is fat from raw beef or mutton). Today, canned and frozen versions of the dish can be found in the grocery store.

During World War II, and in the years following, the reputation of British cuisine suffered greatly. Rationing and overcooking led to many jokes and stereotypes that continue to this day. In the last decade or so, English cooking has undergone something of a renaissance. Today, one can find a huge array of international foods. In addition, highly respected English chefs, such as Gordon Ramsey and Nigella Lawson, have become popular television personalities.

Londoners have adopted many foreign foods, such as tea and curry, as their own, a result of the country's colonial pursuits. London is home to cuisine from more than seventy different countries and has many stores where a wide variety of ingredients can be purchased.

Life's Milestones

Since the population of modern England has much greater racial and cultural diversity than in the past, weddings and special occasions are often celebrated in a variety of ways.

The Church of England is the official religion, and many people celebrate milestones in accordance with church tradition, even if they are not particularly religious. It is still a common practice for infants to be christened in the church while they are babies. Many schools are linked with local churches and admission may be based upon whether one has been christened. Therefore, it remains a popular tradition, even if not always for religious reasons.

Marriages in England may be either religious or civil. Civil ceremonies must be held at either a register office or at a location approved for civil marriages. Notice of intent to marry must be declared in one of three ways: by the banns of marriage, which is a public announcement in the church where the ceremony will take place, by certificate, or by license. As with marriages, funerals may or may not be a religious ceremony, according to the wishes of the deceased. Both burial and cremation are commonly practiced in England, and it is customary to be attired in black when in attendance.

CULTURAL HISTORY

Art & Architecture

English art during the Middle Ages was largely religious in nature. Unfortunately, since much was destroyed during the Reformation, few examples remain. Not until the 18th century did English art really develop as a tradition or style distinct from the rest of Europe. Pastoral, or country, landscapes and portraits formed the primary subject matter of the day. This style of painting was popularized by Thomas Gainsborough (1727–1788), and other artists such as Sir Joshua Reynolds (1723–1792) and Sir James Thornhill (1675–1734). Historical painting was also very popular during this period.

Landscapes continued to be the principal theme in the English school of painting throughout the first half of the 19th century. John Constable (1776–1837) and J.M.W. Turner (1775–1851) are two of the most recognizable names during this period, with the latter widely regarded as the most celebrated painter of his era. At the same time, William Hogarth (1697–1764) was gaining a reputation as the first "proper" English artist with his paintings that offered a satirical view of the world around him.

The 19th century saw the emergence of the Pre-Raphaelite Brotherhood, a group of English artists founded in 1848 who rejected the artistic style of their contemporaries. This group of painters and poets felt English art had become too materialistic and influenced by industrialization. In particular, they resented the influence of Sir Joshua Reynolds, whose portraiture painting was criticized as being too academic and imperfect. Instead, they advocated a return to the rich colors and simplicity of medieval and Renaissance art and culture.

The result was a series of paintings by Dante Gabriel Rossetti (1828–1882), John Everett Millais (1829–1896), William Holman Hunt (1827–1910) and others. Their paintings often reflected the literary themes of Shakespeare and Keats. In particular, the quantity of symbolic detail in each painting is considered impressive. Although the Pre-Raphaelite movement was short-lived, its influence was profound, and there was a resurgence of interest in the later 20th century.

England also has a rich architectural history. It begins in the pre-Roman age, when the prehistoric monument of Stonehenge was built. It continues into the modern day, with the construction of 30 St. Mary Axe, a rounded energy-efficient tower nicknamed "The Gherkin." Many of England's architectural masterpieces can be attributed to foreign influence, religious differences and the rise of industry and artistic movements.

During England's medieval period (roughly 1000 to 1600 CE), art and religion were almost inseparable. Churches were typically adorned with both Christian and pagan symbols. In the early years of the Middle Ages, churches were built in the Romanesque style. This meant that they were very similar to Roman architecture, and featured rounded arches and decorative columns and stonework. This was followed by the Gothic style, which became popular around 1200 CE. This style featured pointed rather than rounded arches, and included larger windows and towering spires and columns. The latter were largely influenced by the minarets, or tall spires, used in Islamic architecture. The English were exposed to these elements while overseas during the Crusades.

The Georgian era (1714–1811) in England's architectural history was largely inspired by Palladian architecture. This style comes from Italian architect Andrea Palladio, who was heavily influenced by ancient Roman buildings. His style was widely imitated throughout England. Thus, Georgian architecture was very much influenced by the classical designs of ancient Rome, and many buildings from the Georgian era are adorned with marble columns. One century later, the Victorians would rebel against the classic symmetry of the Georgian era with a Gothic revival. Under this style, extravagant buildings incorporated glass and iron, products of the industrial age, which took place during the late eighteenth and early nineteenth centuries.

Music

Although England's contributions to classical music have often been overshadowed by other European composers, the nation has a long history of folk music. Much of this music survives in the form of religious hymns or folk ballads. From the medieval period, when music was first recorded, or written down, it became evident that musical forms were influenced by class. During this period Italian-inspired madrigals, or unaccompanied vocal compositions, gained popularity among the nobility.

Meanwhile, pipes, bagpipes and fiddles were the instruments of the peasant or working classes. Folk music developed distinct regional sounds and styles. Morris dance, a form of English folk dance, became popular throughout England, and followed different patterns of movement depending upon where it was performed. The northern part of the country adopted Scottish influences from its Scottish neighbors, and coastal areas were heavily influenced by the sea. This included the singing of sea shanties, so named because they were work songs typically sung by sailors.

The advent of rock and roll in the 1950s marked the dawning of another era of English music. English musicians adapted American styles, adding traditional folk, blues and gospel influences, and developed a distinctly British sound. Skiffle, a type of folk music incorporating country, jazz and blues from the United States, became a major musical style in England in the 1940s and 1950s. This was followed by what is often referred to as the "British Invasion," with British rock and roll groups such as the Beatles, the Who, the Kinks, the Rolling Stones and many others achieving worldwide success.

From this major music movement emerged a folk music revival in the 1970s. A hard rock sound eventually led to the emergence of the punk rock movement, largely popularized by the Sex Pistols. Each movement spawned its own sub-movements, and out of punk came new wave music, often called "post-punk." The emergence of indie, or alternative, artists in the 1990s and beyond has helped maintain England's status in the musical world.

Literature

England's extensive literary heritage dates back to early medieval England with the epic poem *Beowulf*. It is one of the most important works of Anglo-Saxon literature, and is considered a national epic, or a work which is characteristic of a particular nation. After the Norman conquest of England in 1066, a decidedly French influence could be seen in which the theme of courtly love was prominent. This theme is evident in segments of *The Canterbury Tales* and other contemporary pieces.

It was during the Elizabethan era (1558–1603) that England entered what is considered its golden age, during which English poetry and literature flourished. The writings of William Shakespeare, still regarded for their depth and variety, had an enormous impact on the English language during this period. It is estimated that he introduced nearly 3,000 commonly used words into the English language. Until the 16th century, French and Latin were the primary languages for literature in England. However, Shakespeare's command of the English language helped it become more standardized.

The 17th and 18th centuries witnessed several new movements, including the metaphysical poetry movement. This group of philosophical poets, which featured John Donne, Samuel Johnson and George Herbert, focused on the experience and nature of mankind. The Romantic (1793–1815) poets, such as William Blake, William Wordsworth, Samuel Tyler Coleridge and Lord Byron, became more emotionalized and introspective in their work, and focused heavily on themes of war. England is also known for its neoclassical period, in which satire was popularized as a genre by writers such as Jonathan Swift and Alexander Pope.

As the Industrial Revolution swept England in the late eighteenth and early nineteenth centuries, literature embraced more industrial themes and writers adopted a collective social conscience. Writers such as Thomas Hardy, D.H. Lawrence and Elizabeth Gaskell explored the changing economic and social situations of England, particularly the clash of urban industry with pastoral settings and life. During this period, known as the Victorian era (roughly 1837–1901), the novel became the popular form of literature in England. This was followed by modernist literature, which grew from the disillusionment of the Victorian era. England continued to produce noteworthy writings throughout the 20th century, and in 2007 Doris Lessing became the latest English writer to be awarded the Nobel Prize.

Film

Even though the first British film was made in 1895, British cinema wasn't particularly prominent until the 1930s and 1940s. During this period, World War II helped bolster the film industry in England, as documentary techniques became popular. More realistic films were also being produced, though British films would typically have decreasing worldwide success in the post-war era. British cinema experienced a boom in the 1960s, particularly due to its liberal treatment of taboo subjects such as sex, but the industry declined again in the following decade.

British cinema enjoyed a resurgence in popularity and success during the 1980s. Channel Four Films, a subdivision of the Channel Four television network, funded independent film productions, many of which received critical acclaim. Regional, race and gender issues often featured prominently. Early films included *Letter to Brezhnev*, about two Russian soldiers on shore leave in Liverpool, *My Beautiful Launderette*, looking at interracial and gay relationships in 1980s London, and *Sammy and Rosie Get Laid*, which explores issues of race and class in the inner-city. During the 1990s, commercial success equaled critical acclaim for many English films.

In the 21st century, British cinema was typically regarded with acclaim. Encouraged by this success, the BBC and the Arts Council have also given financial support to English cinema. Much of this success is attributed to Channel Four Films, which, as the newly renamed Film4, was behind 2006's Academy Award winning *The Last King of Scotland*. Other notable British films in the new millennium include *Billy Elliot*, which explored gender, sexuality and class through the story of a northern working class boy who becomes a ballet dancer; and *The Queen*, which details the events following the death of Princess Diana. Also, the international success of romantic comedies such as *Bridget Jones's Diary* helped bolster England's film industry

CULTURE

Arts & Entertainment

England's cultural life focuses on London, a cosmopolitan city with many theaters and arts festivals, as well as numerous symphony orchestras, opera companies, and dance companies. Cultural institutions include hundreds of museums, art galleries, and libraries, many of which are found in London. Among the most famous are the British Museum, the National Gallery, and the British Library.

England is famous as a center for the dramatic and musical arts, especially in London. The city's rich theatrical history has survived into the modern era, with more than 100 theater groups currently active in the city, including the world-famous Royal Shakespeare Company,

The United Kingdom has around 300 theaters, a third of which are in London. Among the most famous is the Royal National Theatre. London has three main opera companies: the Royal Opera, the English National Opera, and Covent Garden. Dance companies include the English National Ballet, the Northern Ballet Theatre, and the Birmingham Royal Ballet.

England maintains a very lively festival calendar with a variety of internationally renowned festivals, from the Hay Festival of Literature and Arts to Glyndebourne Opera Festival

and Glastonbury Festival of Contemporary Performing Arts. In addition, the BBC Proms is an eight-week series of classical concerts at the Royal Albert Hall in London, and has been called the world's greatest classical music festival. This festival features live classical music that culminates in the nationally televised Last Night of the Proms, where audience members are dressed in formal attire and patriotic themes are typically performed.

If the Proms are the archetypal celebration of traditional England, the Notting Hill Carnival represents modern, multicultural England. The annual two-day event was first organized by Caribbean immigrants in the 1960s as a response to racial attacks and poor living conditions. Since then it has grown into an enormous celebration of racial diversity featuring elaborate costumes and steel band music. Calypso, a form of political and social commentary set to music, is prominently played during the carnival.

The arts in England have received greater funding in recent years following the establishment of a National Lottery. As part of this program, the Arts Council of England, formerly part of the Arts Council of Great Britain, distributed roughly $2.2 billion (USD) between 2006 and 2008. The secretary of state for culture, media, and sport appoints the 15-person national council which then decides how the money is to be disbursed. Large grants such as this have continued since that time.

The English are noted sports fans, and have exported their national games of cricket and football (soccer) around the world. Rugby is also popular. English teams play several different tournaments against the Scottish, Welsh, and Northern Irish national teams, as well as teams from other countries.

Cultural Sites & Landmarks

London, the capital of England, is home to many cultural attractions, including Buckingham Palace, the official London residence of the British monarchy; Westminster Abbey, a large Gothic-style church; Hampton Court Palace, the former palace of the monarchy; and the Royal

Botanical Gardens. The capital is also host to several museums. England's royal history is evident throughout the country as 101 castles still remain standing.

Perhaps England's most famous historic monument, outside of Stonehenge, is the Tower of London, built by Normandy's William the Conqueror in the 11th century. During this time it served as a fortress, and later a prison. Anne Boleyn and Lady Jane Grey, both former queens of England, were beheaded there. It was used again as a prison during the First and Second World Wars. The last execution in the tower was held in 1941, and the last prisoners were held in 1952. Today, the tower is a popular attraction because it features the Crown Jewels of the United Kingdom. This refers to the various coronation objects, such as crowns and scepters, and other ceremonious regalia, held at the tower since 1303.

One of the most popular tourist attractions in London is an aluminum statue in Piccadilly Circus known as Eros. The statue is in fact a depiction of the Angel of Christian Charity, in honor of the Earl of Shaftesbury, who was an active social reformer.

Stonehenge, believed to have been erected between 3000 and 1600 BCE, is one of England's most popular and mysterious cultural attractions. The original purpose of the large stone circle remains unknown, and historians have been unable to explain how the five ton rocks were brought to the site from the Welsh mountains, more than 200 miles away. It has been recently speculated that the large standing rocks served as a type of burial ground in it earliest stages of use. Stonehenge is listed as a United Nations Educational, Scientific and Cultural Organization (UNESCO) World Heritage Site.

In Canterbury, southeast of London, stands St. Martin's Church, the oldest church in England. The church also houses the remains of St. Augustine's Abbey, built to commemorate the saint's landing on the Kent Coast and his introduction of Christianity to England. Canterbury is also home to Canterbury Cathedral, seat of the archbishop of Canterbury, who is the spiritual head of the Church of England. A World Heritage Site, it is considered the most famous Christian building in England.

In northern England stands Hadrian's Wall. Built by the Roman Emperor Hadrian, the wall was constructed across the entire width of England between 122 CE and 128 CE to repel the Barbarian Picts who lived in Scotland. For more than 250 years, it fulfilled its job as a boundary against invasion. Much of the stone wall remains today and it is one of the most visible reminders of England's Roman history.

The Devon and Dorset coastlines in the southwest of England are notable for their geological significance. In the early 19th century, amateur geologist Mary Anning uncovered a number of fossils, including the first full plesiosaur skeleton. Since then, landslides in the area have continued to expose more than 185 million years of history.

In addition, England is home to nine National Parks. The parks cover more than 10,360 square kilometers (4,000 square miles). The Peak District is the oldest National Park, officially created in 1951, while the aptly named New Forest, established in 2005, is the newest. The parks are key wildlife conservation areas and indicate the varied nature of the English landscape.

Libraries & Museums

The British Museum is one of the largest museums in the world and houses more than 13 million objects from every single continent. Established in 1753, the museum has since expanded, with the Natural History Museum located in Kensington, and the British Library now in a separate building. The vast collection of antiquities stored in the British Museum includes the Rosetta Stone, an artifact of ancient Egypt; and the Elgin Marbles.

London is home to the Tate Modern Gallery, often referred to as "The Tate," the world's largest modern art gallery. Founded in 1897 by a grant from Henry Tate, the inventor of the sugar cube, the Tate London contains British art from 1500 to the present, and sponsors the Turner Prize, a prestigious modern art award. The gallery changes its displays semiannually, but important works from Monet, Picasso, Warhol, Dalí, and other major artists are usually on display.

The British Library holds 170 million items, including about 15 million books, over 900,000 journal and newspaper titles, 58 million patents, and about 6 million sound recordings, among other archived items.

Holidays

England's public holidays are known as "bank holidays," referring to the fact that on these days banks are closed and no other business is done. Most employees have the day off, while essential public workers, such as policemen, receive additional pay. "Boxing Day" (or "St. Stephen's Day") is celebrated December 26, the day after Christmas.

Guy Fawkes Day, November 5, commemorates the failed "Gunpowder Plot" of 1605, in which a band of conspirators tried to blow up the Houses of Parliament.

Youth Culture

England's youth are very much members of the modern Internet era. Cell phone technology and social networking sites (SNS) are a widely used and ingrained part of British youth culture. The consumer power of British youth has also become increasingly significant. Youth make up a large segment of England's population, and television, music and pop culture are all marketed toward their age group. Musical tastes vary widely, with American and European influences merging with styles that have become distinctly British.

The school leaving age has recently been set at eighteen. Previously it had been sixteen, but was changed due to the decreasing demand for unskilled labor and the increasing need for more training to prepare for skilled employment. However, the law does allow those under eighteen to leave full time studies to enter an apprenticeship program or part time studies and 20 hours of work a week. These options often create separate groups within English culture, and those with less formal education tending to come from poorer families. It is hoped that raising the school leaving age will help deter youth violence, which has become a growing problem in English society. Substance abuse and teen pregnancies also occur at a much higher rate in England than elsewhere in Europe.

SOCIETY

Transportation

A highway system enables easy driving of long distances in England, and there are roughly 362,000 kilometers (225,000 miles) of road in the country. Cars remain the most popular form of transportation, and three quarters of all households in England own at least one car.

Unlike America or the rest of Europe, vehicles in England travel on the left side of the road, a practice that dates to the days of travel on horseback, when riders kept swords or sidearm at their right hip. Since most people were and are right-handed, access to weapons required freedom of space on the right.

Traditionally, most English towns have grown with defined town centers and local neighborhoods. As a result, it is common to see people walking to work or to the grocery store. As towns have grown and more housing developments are built in the suburbs, the need for transportation has become more noticeable.

Transportation Infrastructure

England has an extensive public transportation network, with buses and trains readily available even in rural areas. Public transportation is a popular choice among those who commute long distances to work. Since traffic congestion is a serious problem in the central London area, those who wish to drive must pay a daily congestion charge. This is designed to encourage people to make more use of the bus and underground railway system, locally referred to as the "tube." England is also connected by Euro trains which travel under the English Channel through the Channel Tunnel, which connects England to mainland Europe.

The London Underground, commonly referred to as "The Tube," is the city's major transportation system, connecting sixteen rail lines serving central London and the northern suburbs. The Underground is the oldest and largest subway system in the world, with Londoners making approximately three million journeys each day, and approximately 1.265 billion in 2014.

Although nearly 100 livery companies, descended from London's 14th century trade guilds, still exist in the city, they retain relatively little political and economic influence. The liverymen now elect the lord mayor of London, but this position is purely ceremonial.

Media & Communications

The BBC is the largest broadcasting corporation in the world and has provided radio (and later television) service since the 1920s. Households in England pay a license fee which provides funding for the BBC. In 2015, service included eight national television stations, as well as regional service; ten national radio stations; and forty local radio stations and the World Service. There are also stations which do not broadcast in English, for many of the immigrants. There are also several independently owned television stations, including Channel 4 and regional ITV (independent television) affiliates. In recent years, satellite television has grown in popularity, and an estimated 55 percent of homes have access to satellite broadcasts in 2014, a decline from its peak in the previous decade. In addition, the overwhelming majority (84 percent in 2014) of homes also have Internet access, with 90 percent of the homes receiving broadband access.

Since 2003, the Office of Communications (OfCom) has been the independent authority responsible for regulating television, radio and communications. Prior to this, there were five separate agencies in place. In response to complaints from viewers, OfCom has adopted such measures as restricting the advertising of junk food to ensure that it is not aimed at children. Certain forms of advertising, as well as sexual content and violence, are only allowed to be shown after 9:00 pm.

England has thriving mass media. Newspapers include "The Times" of London, and tabloids such as "The Daily Mail." The British Broadcasting Company (BBC), the state-funded broadcaster, operates television, radio, film and internet divisions and runs a global news organization known as the BBC World Service. Privately owned networks include SkyTV, owned by Rupert Murdoch's News Corp.

SOCIAL DEVELOPMENT

Standard of Living

In 2013, the United Kingdom ranked 14th on the Human Development Index, which included 187 nations.

Water Consumption

The average household England uses about 150 liters (about 40 gallons) of water per day. In recent years, efforts have been made to curb water consumption in the country and to increase awareness of water as a valuable resource. Generally speaking, England faces few issues related to the availability of clean drinking water. Water pollution was at one time a serious problem in London but increased regulations and widespread clean-up efforts have helped improve the conditions of the city's rivers and waterways.

Education

England has an extensive public education system, with nearly 100 percent school attendance and 99+ percent literacy. Children must attend twelve years of school, from ages five through eighteen. The educational system is under the UK Department for Education and Skills (DfES), headed by the Secretary of State for Education. Primary education goes from ages five to 11, and secondary education from ages twelve to eighteen. State-run secondary schools include community schools, foundation schools, and religious schools. "Public schools" are actually private schools; the name refers to the fact that they are open to any member of the public who can pay the fees.

England has many notable institutions of higher learning. The oldest and most prestigious are the University of Oxford and the University of Cambridge, founded in the Middle Ages. They are often seen as the training ground for the upper classes. Other important universities include the University of London, founded in the 19th century. England provides compulsory universal public education. The overall literacy rate is an estimated 99 percent.

Women's Rights

The rights of English women are protected by British and European legislation designed to prevent gender discrimination. Suffrage was granted to single women over the age of 30 in 1918, and was extended to all adults over 21 in 1928. In 1970, the voting age was lowered again to eighteen. In recent general elections, women have turned out to vote in the same numbers as men.

Seventy percent of English women are employed outside of the home, and more than 50 percent of women with pre-school aged children are employed. Women are also more likely than men to work beyond the retirement age, which has long been set at 60 for women and 65 for men. In 2020, 65 will be the retirement age for women. The Equal Pay Act of 1970, the Employment Rights Act of 1996 and European Law all promise equal pay for equal work, although gender inequity remains a nationwide problem.

Women first became eligible to stand for Parliament in 1918. Since then, there have been only 291 women elected, a mere six percent of the total. In June 2008, one in five members of the House of Commons was female. This was a significant growth since the 1980s, when women had never held more than five percent of the positions available. In 2005, the Labour Party introduced a series of women-only shortlists as a way to increase the proportion of female candidates. The 2015 election brought a record number of women into Parliament, 29 percent of the total. In England, the Conservatives and Labour parties (and elsewhere the Scottish Nationalist Party) increased the percentage of women serving in Parliament. England had a female prime minister from 1979 to 1990, and as of 2008, five of 23 cabinet posts were held by women. As of May, 2015, the initial cabinet members in the new government (for all of the United Kingdom) included seven women and fifteen men, with another two women and six men eligible to sit with the cabinet. Women are represented at the local council level, with 29 percent of the seats.

During the prime ministry of Tony Blair, a number of new laws were enacted to bring England in line with much of continental Europe and to benefit working mothers.

Paid paternity leave was introduced as a companion to the already existing maternity leave, and vouchers for daycare enabled women to continue working. Men may take up to two weeks paternity leave while women are allowed up to fifty-two weeks. Women also have the right to request flexible maternity leave and their jobs are protected until they return. In 2015, the law was changed giving both parents the right to participate in shared parental leave. The amount available for either parent is calculated by subtracting the amount of maternity leave taken from 52 weeks, with the balance becoming shared parental leave.

In general, the rights and legal protections available to women in England are on par with, or better than, much of Europe. In a 2013 UN report, England ranked fourteenth best among one hundred eighty-seven countries on the Gender Inequality Index that looked at political participation, economic power, and availability of education and healthcare.

Health Care

England is part of the United Kingdom's nationalized health care system, the National Health Service (NHS). The NHS is responsible to the British Department of Health and has a separate organizational structure for each country within the UK. Reforms have decentralized NHS responsibilities to give more authority to local doctors and the local health authorities (Primary Care Trusts). As of 2012, life expectancy was 79.5 years for men and 83.25 years for women.

GOVERNMENT

Structure

In 1801, the kingdoms of England and Scotland became the United Kingdom of Great Britain and Ireland. Since then, England has been ruled by the British Parliament at Westminster.

The 20th century has seen a move toward "devolution," or giving more power to the United Kingdom's constituent countries. In 1999, the UK Parliament reinstituted the Scottish Parliament (which had not met since 1707) and established a National Assembly for Wales, to have authority over many local issues. There is, however, no purely "English Parliament," something which some groups would like to re-establish. Others think this is not necessary, since England 533 of the 650 seats in the United Kingdom's parliament are English.

England and Wales share a legal system, based on "common law," a system of precedents built up over the years rather than a single, systematic code. Scotland and Northern Ireland each have their own laws and courts, but the British House of Lords serves as the ultimate court of appeal in all three countries, except for criminal cases in Scotland. Local courts known as magistrates' courts can try less serious offenses such as theft and burglary. Crown Courts handle more serious cases, such as murder, manslaughter, and robbery.

The Lord Chancellor (also titled the Secretary of State for Constitutional Affairs) heads the English judicial system, assisted by the Lord Chief Justice of England and Wales. The UK Home Secretary has day-to-day responsibility for police, prisons, and criminal law in England.

Political Parties

The main political parties in England are the Labour Party, the Conservative Party, and the Liberal Democratic Party. As of 2015, the Conservative Party is the ruling party, having won two consecutive elections. Labour is the Official Opposition, or largest minority party.

Local Government

The UK Deputy Prime Minister has overall responsibility for local government in England. The highest level is the nine regions, including Greater London (which has an elected mayor rather than an appointed council). Beneath the regions are unitary authorities or "two-tier" authorities (county council and district council). The unitaries were established in the 1990s to replace the traditional county system. These counties were historically known as shires (such as Gloucestershire), but these jurisdictions now have only historical significance.

In the capital, London's central district is uniquely governed, thanks to centuries-old decrees by William the Conqueror. Despite being the home of both the local and national democratic government, London is also the site of a de facto oligarchy called the Corporation, which runs the city, and owns most of it.

Judicial System

England's highest court is the Supreme Court of the United Kingdom—which is also the highest court of Wales, Northern Ireland, and Scotland (with the exception of Scottish criminal cases). Members of the court are chosen by the prime minister but officially appointed by the monarchy. In addition to the Supreme Court, there is also the Judicial Committee of the Privy Council, which is the highest court of appeals in England. Members of the Supreme Court are also members of the council.

The Court of Appeal makes up the second level of England's judicial system. It is organized into a criminal and civil division. This civil court sector is subdivided into the High Court of Justice, which consists of the Queen's Bench Division, the Family Division, and the Chancery Division. Lower courts in England include the Crown Court, the Magistrates' Courts, and County Courts.

Taxation

In England and in the United Kingdom at-large, taxes are collected by the central government and by local government. Corporations pay a chargeable gains or income tax, in 2015, of 20 or 21 percent. Personal income tax is established through a "personal allowance" system. After an individual has surpassed an allowance (10,600 GBP in 2015) their income becomes taxable. The rate of this tax is based on how much revenue is earned, beginning at 20 percent and going as high as 45 percent. Other taxes including "motoring taxes" for automobiles, excise duties, and value-added taxes (VAT).

Both individuals and corporations in England contribute to the National Insurance system. Tax revenue collected by this system covers nationalized health care and unemployment monies.

Armed Forces

England's army is jointly referred to as Her Majesty's Armed Forces and the British Armed Forces. It consists of the Royal Navy and the British Army. In 2012, England had 162,550 active military personnel. Officially, the army is commanded by the British monarch. In practice, the political power of Britain lies with the prime minister, who also controls the kingdom's armed forces.

The annual budget for the British Armed Forces was an estimated 37.4 billion GBP in 2015. This ranked the UK fourth in the world in over all military expenditures.

Foreign Policy

As a member of the constitutional monarchy of the United Kingdom (UK), England's foreign policy is linked with that of Northern Ireland, Scotland, and Wales. The term "British foreign policy" refers to the collective diplomacy and foreign relations of the UK. The term UK is synonymous with the term Britain.

Despite its small size, Britain plays a major role in the global stage. Through its history in the Commonwealth of Nations, it maintains a close connection with countries on all continents. Britain holds a permanent seat on the United Nations (UN) Security Council. A member of the European Union (EU) since 1973, the nation is actively involved in all areas of EU government, including agriculture and trade policy, but has

chosen not to adopt the common currency, the euro. Although active within Europe, England (in fact, Britain as a whole) has clashed with other member states on quite a few occasions. The products of an island nation, the British have shown an eagerness to protect their national identity and are reluctant to adopt too many measures that may endanger this.

Britain has frequently clashed with other EU member states, particularly France and Germany, in recent years. The source of the conflict has been Britain's support of America in the 2003 Iraq War. Popular opinion has often conflicted with government policies regarding the Middle East. The British government has committed significant aid to developing Afghani democracy and is the largest bilateral donor to the Afghanistan Reconstruction Trust Fund. In addition to close ties within Europe, Britain has long enjoyed a close relationship with the US, which also maintains multiple military bases in England.

Queen Elizabeth II is the head of the commonwealth, and the head of state of sixteen of the commonwealth's 53 member nations, including Canada. When conflicts arise between the commonwealth and EU states, Britain tends to take the side of Europe. Nevertheless, Britain has an especially close relationship with India and has upheld a cordial relationship with Pakistan, despite disagreements between the two Asian nations and Britain's suspension of Pakistan from the commonwealth between 1999 and 2004. Pakistan was suspended again in 2007 in response to President Pervez Musharraf's refusal to lift a state of emergency and restore an independent judiciary. Following general elections in Pakistan in February 2008, the country was readmitted.

Dependencies

The Isle of Man and the bailiwicks of Jersey and Guernsey are Crown Dependencies. Although they are not a part of the United Kingdom, they are not sovereign territories.

Human Rights Profile

International human rights law insists that states respect civil and political rights, and also promote an individual's economic, social and cultural rights. The United Nations (UN) Universal Declaration of Human Rights (UDHR) is recognized as the standard for international human rights. Its authors sought the counsel of the world's great thinkers, philosophers, and religious leaders, and were careful to create a document that reflects the core values shared by every world culture. (To read this document or view the articles relating to cultural human rights, go to: http://www.udhr.org/UDHR/default.htm.)

Overall, England has a positive history of human rights. Britain is an elected member of the UN Human Rights Council. However, some individual rights have become increasingly restricted following the terrorist attacks of September 11, 2001 and in London in 2005. The European Court of Human Rights has voiced concern about these restrictions and has cited numerous violations of the European Convention of Human Rights and the United Kingdom (UK)'s Human Rights Act of 1998.

English law provides its subjects with equal rights, regardless of race, religion, or gender, in accordance with Article 2 of the Universal Declaration of Human Rights. There are some gender distinctions, for example, retirement age, but these differences are being phased out in order to meet the standards set forth by the European Court of Human Rights. Legislation also ensures equal rights for gay, lesbian and transgendered people.

Freedom to marry, as outlined in Article 16, is provided to all men and women over the age of eighteen. Those aged between sixteen and eighteen wishing to marry must provide written parental consent. The Civil Partnership Act of 2004 allowed same-sex couples to enter into legally binding arrangements, which offer most of the same benefits as marriage. However, in 2014, the legal definition of marriage was changed in England and Wales to allow same-sex couples to marry. Freedom of religion, outlined in Article 18 of the declaration, is protected in England, but there is evidence of increasing discrimination against Muslims following the 2001 terrorist attacks in New York.

The rights to freedom of expression and freedom of assembly, as defined by Articles 19 and 20 of the declaration, are also becoming increasingly threatened as a result of the terrorist attacks. The Terrorism Act of 2006 has made it illegal to glorify terrorism and allows the government to disband any groups thought to be doing so. Critics say that the law is too broad and stifles freedom of expression and debate within Islamic communities, which they contend may be helpful in overcoming extremism.

Furthermore, Britain has been repeatedly criticized for its laws that increase the amount of time a terror suspect may be detained without charge. As of 2015, the current maximum period is twenty-eight days (considered excessive and in violation of Article 10 according to Human Rights Watch). This has been in place for almost a decade, and during this time several unsuccessful attempts have been made to extend it.

ECONOMY

Overview of the Economy
England is the largest constituent part of the United Kingdom, which has the world's sixth largest economy (2013). London is one of the world's oldest and most important financial centers, helping to make English companies world leaders in direct foreign investment.

Industry
England is a highly industrialized nation, with a mature economy. The major industries include manufacturing (including aerospace and automotive), electronics, finance, chemicals, electronics, mass media, and tourism. As the largest economy within the UK, England provides the major share of Britain's exports.

Long a major world port, London exports clothing, precision instruments, jewelry, and stationery, and imports petroleum, tea, wool, raw sugar, timber, butter, metals, and meat. The city is responsible for about twenty-two percent of the United Kingdom's gross domestic product (GDP).

Labor

As a result of the 2008 global financial crisis, unemployment numbers in England have increased. Jobs in manufacturing and construction saw the largest decreases. In addition, earnings growth for England's employed population remained stagnant during the recession. Individuals between the ages of 16 and 24 represent the largest unemployed demographic, with the rate of about 22 percent in early 2015. The government introduced a 20 billion (GBP) stimulus package in response to the country's economic recession. By early 2015, the labor market had rebounded. Unemployment was at 5.5 percent (lowest since 2008) and average wages (excluding bonuses) had risen by 2.2 percent over the previous year.

Energy/Power/Natural Resources

The United Kingdom generates the majority of its energy through oil and natural gas. In 2012, it was estimated that 37 percent of the UK's energy came from oil and another 33 percent came from natural gas. Another 16 percent of energy was produced from coal. Approximately 6 percent of energy in the UK is from nuclear power sources. Renewable energy makes up about 8 percent of energy use. The UK has recently established new goals for renewable energy use; it hopes that 20 percent of the kingdom's electricity will come from such sources by 2020 (generation was 19 percent in the fourth quarter of 2014).

Although the UK continues to obtain natural gas from reserves in the North Sea and holds a large domestic supply of coal, it became a net energy importer in 2013.

Fishing

The UK's fishing industry has contended with substantial challenges in recent years. Overfishing has depleted stocks of cod in the North Sea. However, EU fishing regulations have helped improve stocks of monk fish. Sole and herring are also harvested by UK fisherman. Critics of the EU's Common Fisheries Policy say it unfairly restricts the number of fish that can be caught by UK-based fisheries.

Forestry

Most of England was covered by forests in ancient times. By the Middle Ages, human settlement had reduced the forests to about 15 percent of the land. Britain's remaining forests cover about 8 percent of the country. Most of the country's wooded lands are in private hands. The remaining 25 percent are managed by Britain's Forestry Commission. Estimates are that deforestation has stopped in England, and since 2010 there has been a slight increase in the size of its forests.

Mining/Metals

Coal is the most important industrial mineral, and has been mined since the 1700s. It was the main power source during the Industrial Revolution of the eighteenth and nineteenth centuries. Other industrial minerals include sand, limestone, gravel, and gypsum. In ancient times, Britain was an important source of minerals such as iron ore, tin, and copper, but these are produced only in relatively small quantities today.

Agriculture

Only a small percentage of England's economy (less than 1 percent in 2012) is dedicated to agriculture, though the rural-urban distinction remains an important part of English life. Major crops include wheat, barley, potatoes, and vegetables.

Animal Husbandry

Livestock farming focuses on cattle, sheep, pigs, and poultry. In the past decade, the UK has seen a decrease in overall live stock numbers. Approximately 10 million cattle were produced in 2014 for domestic use and exports, as well as 2 million dairy cows, 4 million pigs, and 23 million sheep.

Tourism

In 2003, tourism was responsible for 9 percent (2013) of the total British economy, and valued at around £127 billion ($210 billion USD). Around 33 billion people from overseas, most of them from the United States or Western Europe, visited Britain in 2014, spending £24 billion ($40 billion USD).

Visitors from former colonies such as the United States look upon England as the "Mother Country," and travel there in order to gain a sense of their own heritage. Others visit England for its natural beauty and to visit quaint towns and villages. Some of the most popular attractions in London are Buckingham Palace, the Tower of London, and Kew Gardens.

Fiona Young-Brown, Eric Badertscher,
Alex K. Rich

DO YOU KNOW?

- The dish known as "Beef Wellington" was named for the Duke of Wellington, who defeated Napoleon's army at the Battle of Waterloo in 1815.

- The world owes the sandwich to an 18th century English nobleman, the Earl of Sandwich. A famous gambler, the Earl reputedly refused to leave the gaming table in order to eat, so he had a servant bring him meat placed between two pieces of bread.

- London hosted the 1908, 1948, and 2012 summer Olympic Games.

- A popular tourist activity in London is watching the Changing of the Guard, a ceremony performed by the Queen's regiments. The ceremony occurs daily as part of the duties first established in the 17th century.

- Despite their extravagant uniforms and ceremonial duties, the Queen's seven Household Regiments are still active members of England's official army.

Bibliography

Corthorn, Paul and Jonathan Davis. *The British Labour Party and the Wider World: Domestic Politics, Internationalism and Foreign Policy*. London: Tauris Academic, 2008.

Coxall, Bill, Lynton Robins and Robert Leach. *Contemporary British Politics*. London: Palgrave Macmillan, 2003.

DK Publishing. *History of Britain and Ireland*. London: DK Publishing, 2013.

Fox, Kate. *Watching the English: The Hidden Rules of English Behaviour.* (Rev. Ed.) London: Nicholas Brealey Publishing, 2014.

Lonely Planet and Neil Wilson. *Lonely Planet England*. 8th ed. London: Lonely Planet, 2015.

Mason, Laura. *Food Culture in Great Britain*. Westport, CT: Greenwood Press, 2004.

Matera, Marc. *Black London: The Imperial Metropolis and Decolonization in the Twentieth Century.* (California World History Library) Berkeley, University of California Press, 2015.

Norbury, Paul. *Britain – Culture Smart!: The Essential Guide to Customs & Culture*. London: Kuperard, 2010.

Norwich, John Julius, ed. *Treasures of Britain: The Architectural, Cultural, Historical and Natural Heritage of Britain*. London: Automobile Association Guides, 2002.

Stacey, Gill. *London*. Milwaukee, WI: World Almanac Library, 2003.

Steves, Rick. *Rick Steves' England.* 6th ed. Berkeley: Avalon Travel Publishing, 2013.

Watts, Duncan and Colin Pilkington. *Britain in the European Union Today.* Manchester: Manchester University Press, 2005.

Wright, Tony. *British Politics: A Very Short Introduction.* 2nd ed. Oxford: Oxford University Press, 2013.

Works Cited

Arts Council of England Key Facts. http://artscouncil.org. uk/aboutus/sr2007_key_facts.php

British Foreign Policy. http://www.britainusa.com/sections/ index_nt1.asp?i=41021&d=10

Catherine Mayer. "Britain's Mean Streets." *Time*, March 26, 2008. http://www.time.com/time/magazine/ article/0,9171,1725547,00.html

"Country Reports on Human Rights Practices 2005: United Kingdom." *U.S. Department of State.* http://www.state. gov/g/drl/rls/hrrpt/2005/61683.htm

"Country Reports on Human Rights Practices 2006: United Kingdom." *U.S. Department of State.* http://www.state. gov/g/drl/rls/hrrpt/2006/78847.htm "United Kingdom Foreign and Commonwealth Office."

"Demographics and the Workforce in England and Wales: Trends and Projections." *Employers' Organization.* http://www.idea.gov.uk/idk/aio/5689207

Duncan Robertson. "Artists Ordered to Reveal if They are Gay When Applying for Grants." The Daily Mail, April 2, 2008. http://www.dailymail.co.uk/news/article-553630/Artists-ordered-reveal-gay-applying-grants.html

"Great Britain: Principal Cities." http://www.citypopulation.de/UK-England.html

Mark Brown. "England's Arts Face Bloodiest Cull in Half a Century as Finds Are Cut for 200 Groups." The Guardian, December 17, 2007. http://www.guardian.co.uk/uk/2007/dec/17/theatrenews.artsfunding

"Human Rights Annual Report 2007." www.fco.gov.uk/resources/en/pdf/human-rights-report-2007

"Medieval Architecture." *Human Rights Watch.* http://www.britainexpress.com/History/Medieval_art_and_architecture.htm

Richard Cracknell. "Women in Parliament and Government." *House of Commons Library Social and General Statistics Section.* http://www.parliament.uk/commons/lib/research/notes/snsg-01250.pdf

Robert Verkaik. "Britain in the Dock for Human Rights Failures After More Than 100 'Guilty' Judgements Filed." *The Independent*, October 3, 2005. http://www.independent.co.uk/news/uk/crime/britain-in-the-dock-for-human-rights-failures-after-more-than-100-guilty-judgements-filed-509348.html

"The Electoral Commission." http://www.electoralcommission.org.uk/elections/results

"The Fall and Rise of British Cinema." http://www.britishfilm.org.uk/article.php?art=filmfour

William Horsley. "Polls Find Europeans Oppose Iraq War." *BBC News*, February 11, 2003. http://news.bbc.co.uk/1/hi/world/europe/2747175.stm

"Women's Empowerment: Measuring the Global Gender Gap." *World Economic Forum.* http://www.unece.org/stats/gender/publications/Multi-Country/WomenEmpowerment.pdf

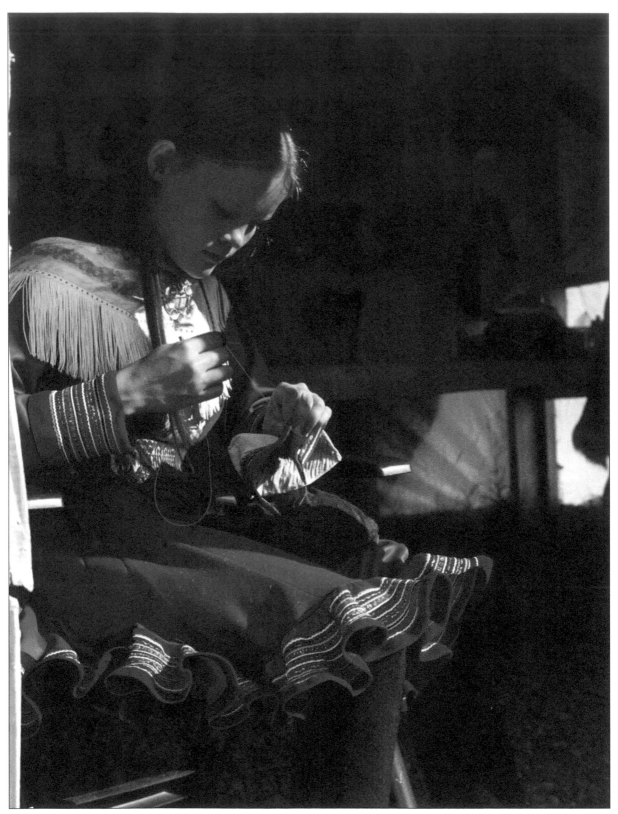

The Sami, also known as Lapps, are the native people of Finland. /Stock photo © Paolo Cipriani

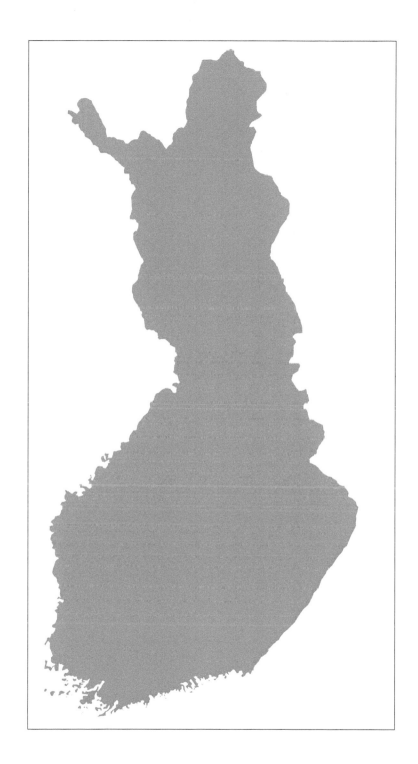

FINLAND

Introduction

Finland is a country in northeastern Europe. It is bordered by Russia to the east, Sweden to the west, and Norway to the northwest. Most of Finland is covered by forests, and the country is a leading producer of paper and wood products. The nation has a very high standard of living and its welfare system is one of the best in the world.

Helsinki, located on the Gulf of Finland, is the capital of Finland. It includes at least 315 islands, and is often called the "City of the Sea." It is also known for being one of the northernmost capitals in the world, with long, dark winter days and midnight sun in summer. The Gulf of Finland is the northeastern arm of the Baltic Sea and separates Finland from Estonia.

Throughout Finland's history, the sea has been both beneficial and harmful. It has fostered trade, but has also provided a means for invading armies to attack. The unpolluted sea around Helsinki, as well as the nature reserves and wooded areas, provide Finns and visitors alike with opportunities to experience unspoiled nature.

GENERAL INFORMATION

Official Language: Finnish and Swedish
Population: 5,268,799 (2014 estimate)
Currency: Euro
Coins: The Euro is available in 1, 2, 5, 10, 20 and 50 cent coins. A 1 and 2 Euro coin is also available.

Land Area: 303,815 square kilometers (117,303 square miles)
Water Area: 34,330 square kilometers (13,254 square miles)
National Anthem: "Maamme" ("Our Land")
Capital: Helsinki
Time Zone: GMT +2
Flag Description: The flag of Finland is white and features a blue Nordic cross.

Population

Finland has a population of over 5.2 million, with the most densely populated areas found along the southern and western coasts. About one million people live in the greater Helsinki area, which includes the cities of Espoo, Vantaa, and Kauniainen.

Helsinki is the largest city in Finland, with 583,331 inhabitants (and a metropolitan urban area with a population of over one million), and

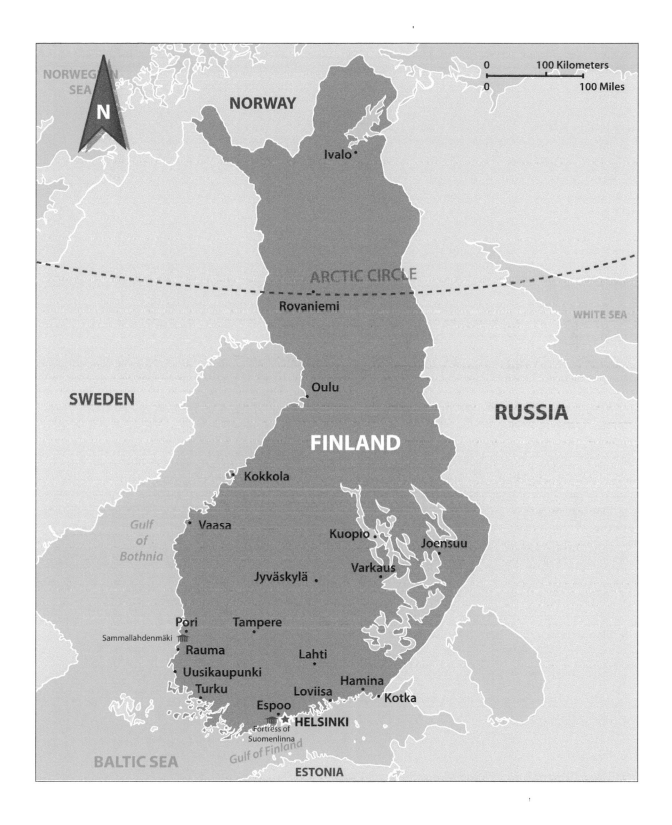

Principal Cities by Population (2012):

- Helsinki (583,331)
- Espoo (251,896)
- Tampere (216,486)
- Vantaa (202,125)
- Abo (175,965)
- Oulu (136,292)
- Lahti (100,530)
- Koupio (92,093)
- Lappeenranta (71,913) (2008 estimate)
- Hämeenlinna (66,504) (2008 estimate)
- Kotka (54,769) (2008 estimate)
- Porvoo (47,832) (2008 estimate)

Espoo is the second largest with 251,896 people. Other major cities include Tampere, about 175 kilometers (109 miles) north of Helsinki; Turku, in southwestern Finland; and Oulu, in the north. Rovaniemi is the major city in Lapland, the northernmost province of Finland.

Approximately 84 percent of the population resides in urban areas, while about 16 percent lives in rural areas. According to 2004 estimates, the population density is 15 persons per square kilometer (40 per square mile). Lapland, with a population of approximately 200,000, has the sparsest population density of Finland's six provinces.

Finland's population is fairly homogenous, with 93 percent of the people being of Finnish descent. Swedish-speaking Finns, accounting for about six percent of the population, are concentrated in the areas to the south around Helsinki and the Åland Islands. Russians, Sami, and other minority groups represent less than two percent of the population. Since the collapse of the Soviet Union, Finland has seen a wave of immigration from Russia, Vietnam, Somalia, and the former Yugoslavia.

Languages

Finnish, spoken by 93 percent of the population, belongs to the Finno-Ugric group of languages. It bears more similarities to Hungarian, Estonian, and some Siberian languages than it does to other Scandinavian languages. Finnish words that have made their way into the English language include "sauna," a steam bath, and "tundra," a flat or slightly hilly treeless plain. Swedish, also an official language, is spoken by about six percent of the population. The Sami speak a variety of dialects that are collectively referred to as Lappish, spoken by less than ONE percent of the total population.

Native People & Ethnic Groups

The Sami, also known as Lapps, are the native people of Finland, numbering around 6,500 or slightly over one-tenth of a percent of the total current population. Traditionally reindeer herders, they migrated north to Lapland as other ethnic groups began to arrive. Some Sami continue to raise reindeer in huge cooperatives, using modern farming techniques.

Gypsies, who are also known as Kale and Roma, have lived in Finland since the mid 1500s. Their unique culture and dress caused them to be subjected to centuries of prejudice and mistreatment. Government aid programs in the modern era have improved literacy and living standards among Finland's Roma population.

Finland has one of the lowest rates of foreign citizens in the European Union. An estimated 2.5 percent of the population is foreign citizens, mostly from Russia, Estonia, and Sweden.

Religions

Finland has two official state churches: the Finnish Evangelical Lutheran Church and the Finnish Orthodox Church. The vast majority of the population belongs to the former, with only about one percent identifying as Finnish Orthodox. Roman Catholics, Jews, Muslims, and members of other Protestant faiths account for less than one percent of the population.

Climate

Finland's climate is warmer than might be expected, due to the moderating influences of warm Gulf Stream breezes and the Baltic Sea. The weather is more extreme in the area above the Arctic Circle, where temperatures can reach

-30° Celsius (-22° Fahrenheit) in the winter and 27° Celsius (80° Fahrenheit) in the summer. In the central and southern regions, winters are milder and shorter. Precipitation averages about 65 centimeters (25 inches) per year in the south, with slightly less in the north.

From mid-May to mid-July, the sun never sets in northern Lapland. Summer days are long in central and southern Finland, where twilight lasts until about midnight. The situation reverses during the winter, when days are very short. At the southern tip of Finland, Helsinki has less than seven hours of daylight in January and February. The sun never rises above the horizon at all in northern Finland from early December to early January, creating an eerie bluish glow called polar night, or kaamos (Finnish for "darkness").

ENVIRONMENT & GEOGRAPHY

Topography
Finland is bordered by Russia to the east, Sweden to the northwest, and Norway to the north. To the south, the Gulf of Finland separates the country from Estonia. The Åland Islands, a 6,500-island archipelago to the south in the Gulf of Bothnia, cover 1,528 square kilometers (590 square miles). About one-third of Finland lies above the Arctic Circle.

There are three major regions in Finland. The coastal plain is relatively narrow in the south and southwest, becoming wider in the western region near the Gulf of Bothnia (a northern arm of the Baltic Sea). This is where the largest urban centers are found. The interior plateau, which includes the Lake District, forms the central part of the country. Lapland forms the northern region, one-third of which is covered by marshes and bogs. The most mountainous areas are in northwestern Finland, near the borders with Norway and Sweden. Finland's highest point is Mount Haltia, at 1,328 meters (4,357 feet) above sea level.

Finland's coastline is about 4,442 kilometers (2,760 miles) long. Thousands of islands are found off the coast, mostly in the southwest.

Winding ridges called eskers were formed by retreating glaciers that left deposits of sand and gravel in their wake. Three parallel ridges known as the Salpausselkä ridges form an arc along the southern coast. After the glaciers melted, the land began rising, and is still doing so at a rate of six to nine millimeters (less than 1 inch) per year.

Inland waters cover nearly 10 percent of Finland's area. The largest of the country's tens of thousands of lakes is Lake Saimaa, in the southeast. Other major lakes include the Päijänne, Pielinen, Oulu in central Finland, and Inari in the far north. Finland's longest river is the 552-kilometer (343-mile) long Kemi.

Helsinki is located in southern Finland and is surrounded by forest on the Vironiemi Headland, a peninsula on the southern tip of the Gulf of Finland. There are many wooded areas within the city. As the capital has grown, it has fanned out to include many of the islands around the peninsula. These islands, composed of granite boulders, sparsely support pine trees. They are otherwise devoid of plant life.

Plants & Animals
More than 70 percent of Finland is covered by forests, mainly spruce, pine, and birch. Cloudberries grow in the swamps and bogs in the northern tundra.

Over 300 species of birds are found in Finland, including seabirds and waterfowl. Woodland animals that are native to Finland include brown bears, moose, elk, wolves, wolverines, and lynx. Reindeer are still found in Lapland, but they are semi-domesticated.

Fish such as salmon, trout, and siika (common whitefish) are plentiful in northern rivers, while Baltic herring is the most abundant sea fish.

CUSTOMS & COURTESIES

Greetings
Finns typically greet one another with a handshake or nod, and place particular emphasis on eye contact. This formal and friendly manner is

even extended to children. It is also not unusual for a man to tip his hat when greeting another person. Finns will usually introduce themselves with their first names, followed by their surnames, placing importance on professional titles. This is a common practice even in casual settings. The most common greeting among Finns is "Hei" ("Hello"), though younger people might use the equivalent of "Moi." The greeting "Terve" ("Healthy") may also be used. Many Finns also speak English.

Gestures & Etiquette
A word that could describe Finnish character is "sisu," which means "courageous, independent, and strong." Generally, Finns are a friendly and courteous people, but are often private as well. This privacy also extends to the Finnish home, which a person typically does not visit without first calling.

Maintaining a certain level of social etiquette is important in Finnish culture. For example, it is considered extremely rude to interrupt another person when he or she is talking. Likewise, though cell-phone use is widespread in the country, Finns consider talking on a cell phone in public places inconsiderate. A person's word, as much as the written word, is also important to Finns, who expect a person to follow through. This value placed on words also extends to conversation, where Finns typically refrain from "small talk."

Eating/Meals
Finns typically eat three meals per day. Breakfast usually consists of pulla, a braided dessert bread, and coffee or the more traditional kahvi, which is egg-cleared coffee. Meats and cheese eaten as open-faced sandwiches may also be part of breakfast. Rural Finns might eat an even heartier breakfast, consisting of a larger meat portion or fish, along with potatoes and cheese.

The traditional full Finnish lunch is called the "sandwich table," or voioleipapoyta. Bread and butter are the basis of the meal, along with various fish (fresh and salted), stuffed pastries, cured meats, fresh fruit or compotes, and cheese.

Cakes or cookies might then be served with coffee. If there is occasion for a mid-day break at home or otherwise, a traditional "coffee table" is set with good-quality coffee and bread and pastries. This occasion might also call for more elaborate layered cakes that are filled with jams or creams. Coffee and pulla (or other desserts) is also traditionally served after a meal, prior to guests leaving.

Table manners include using the continental style of holding the knife and fork. In this manner, the fork is in the left hand and turned upside down, so that the knife can scoop or slide food onto the back of the fork. Finns also eat only bread, or sometimes shrimp, with their hands. When finished eating, it is customary to place the knife and fork, with the prongs facing down, across the plate. It is also customary for guests to wait to begin eating until the hostess invites everyone to begin eating.

Visiting
Etiquette when visiting a Finn at his or her home involves such formalities as bringing a bouquet of flowers or quality chocolates as a token of appreciation. One rule to follow with flowers, though, is that white and yellow flowers are often used at funerals, and are inappropriate for other uses. The home environment is fairly informal, though Finns and their visitors typically remove shoes before entering the home. When visiting Finns at their home, coffee and buns (kahvi and pulla) are often served before the evening is over. Finns are also known for entertaining business associates at home with the family, instead of eating in a restaurant.

It is estimated that Finland is home to nearly two million saunas, an astounding number that conveys the importance of this tradition, especially considering that the population is about 5.3 million people in the early 21st century. The sauna is considered a rejuvenating experience that cleanses the body, and the Finns enjoy saunas on a regular basis, having done so for thousands of years. Many Finns have saunas in their homes or apartment complexes, and friends and family use them together regularly. The country's cold winter climate makes saunas especially inviting.

LIFESTYLE

Family

Family life in Finland focuses mostly on the nuclear family unit, which includes an average of two children. Extended families rarely live together, and young couples typically do not live in close proximity to their parents or grandparents. While both parents in the average Finnish family work, the culture continues to emphasize the importance of child rearing. In fact, Finland is consistently given a high international ranking for child well-being. Additionally, fathers also receive paid family leave, and males have been increasingly taking advantage of the opportunity to raise their children in recent years.

Finland's old nickname is the "Land of the Thousand Lakes," and the landscape is famous for its hiking. For Finns, spending time outdoors is paramount when spending time with the family. Many families own or rent summer cottages, typically along lakes or the coast. This cottage life has become an important aspect of Finnish culture.

Housing

In the years following World War II, the Finnish government oversaw the construction of homes and other buildings to help protect the environment. Finland also saw increased population numbers in the latter half of the 20th century, resulting in greater numbers of apartments. Thus, the majority of buildings constructed in Finland are reasonably modern. However, a great deal of these postwar homes offered little aesthetic value, and frequently were built far from necessary services.

More recently, Finnish homes are equipped with modern amenities and often feature European minimalist design, including different types of natural wood and shades of white. Ecologically minded and energy efficient home design has particularly taken root in Finland in the early 21st century. Often, these newly designed homes require no extra heating devices, are well insulated, and utilize the extra heat from lighting, appliances and its occupants.

Food

With long coastal areas and thousands of lakes, fish and seafood feature prominently in Finnish cuisine. Finns try to eat fish seasonally, when it is freshest, but they have various methods for preserving it, such as salting or pickling. Traditionally, pike and perch were eaten in the spring, and herring in the autumn. Fried perch might be served with a beet sauce, and fried Baltic herring steaks might be served with a butter sauce. Grilled salmon is also a popular food. Finnish cuisine is also known for its herring caviar. One of the more common fish delicacies is blini (crepes) served with caviar, onion, and smetana (sour cream). A winter burbot soup is made with fish, potato, onion, and often milk.

In the winter, Finns eat a lot of casseroles, soups, and cabbage dishes. Pea soup, made with dried peas, onion, and pork shoulder, is common. Other popular dishes include cabbage rolls, called kaalikääryleet, which are made by wrapping cooked cabbage leaves around fillings such as ground meat (lamb, pork), onions, and spices. Roasted lamb, sausages, and salted meats are especially common in the colder months. During late spring and summer, Finns eat a wide variety of fruits and vegetables, including cucumber, strawberries, and bilberries, which they are able to grow in the southern areas. Potatoes are also harvested in the summer. Additionally, while Finns in the western parts of the country tend to eat more fish and meat, eastern Finns tend to eat more vegetables.

Like many European countries, grains are a staple in Finland, and breads and other baked goods are eaten regularly. Rye, oats, and barley are used in many different types of recipes. Rye bread and ginger snaps, and traditional Finnish buns, which are made with cardamom spice and almond slivers, are a festive addition to a Finnish meal. Because milk is also consumed throughout Finland, cheese and butter are included in many recipes, spread on breads and muffins, and often added to soups.

Life's Milestones

Nearly 80 percent of Finns belong to the Lutheran Church, specifically the Evangelical Lutheran

Church of Finland. Thus, many milestones and rites of passage are rooted in the Christian faith. This includes baptism, marriage, and funerary practices.

The most important milestone in adulthood is marked by the wedding. Finnish wedding ceremonies often take place in a Lutheran church, but some opt for a civil ceremony. The couple usually bears the burden of costs for the ceremony, and Finns often try to marry on a warm, sunny day near a lake. Many wedding traditions bear resemblance to Anglo-American weddings, such as the designation of bridesmaids and groomsmen, and customs such as throwing rice and cutting the wedding cake. One Finnish tradition involves the bride wearing a golden crown, and is similar to the throwing of a bride's bouquet. At the celebration, the bride is then blindfolded, and must place the crown on a guest's head, designating that person the next to be wed.

There are also certain milestones that are not religious in nature, but still unique to Finland. For example, Finns mark the transition to adulthood when they graduate, at age 18, from high school. All graduates traditionally wear a white captain's cap and girls carry red roses to signify their entrance into a new life. Students first take an exam to graduate, and then celebrate their graduation on the last Saturday in May.

CULTURAL HISTORY

Art

For most of its history, the visual arts in Finland followed European artistic styles. During Finland's golden age, however, Finnish artists, many of whom trained in Paris, were determined to bring a sense of national character and heritage to their art. The Finnish landscape became a particularly important theme, and many Finnish musicians and writers, such as painter Akseli Gallen-Kallela (1865–1931), were inspired by the Kalevala and Karelian folklore (a phenomenon described as Karelianism). Equally important were Finnish sculptors, who created monuments and busts that celebrated the country's newfound

nationalism. Eila Hiltunen (1922–2003) sculpted a famous monument to honor composer Jean Sibelius in 1967, and Wäinö Aaltonen (1894–1966) created a sculpture of a famous Finnish Olympic runner, Paavo Nurmi, in 1952.

By the turn of the 20th century, art nouveau, a highly stylized and organic international art movement, encompassed most areas of art, including architecture. During the mid-20th century, the Finnish modern art movement took hold, specifically in abstract painting and sculpture. Finnish artists then began working in the "informalism" movement, which was similar to expressionism, the artistic style that combined abstract forms with a spontaneous method of expression. Laila Pullinen (1933–) created abstract informalist sculptures in the 1960s, particularly by blasting copper into contorted shapes. Video art and photography became important artistic mediums in the late decades of the 20th century. The Kiasma, a contemporary art museum located in the capital of Helsinki, opened in 1998, giving Finnish and international artists an important venue for people of all social classes to view the changing art world.

Outside of the fine arts, Finland has a long tradition of handicrafts and traditional arts, including woodworking, textile arts, and ceramics. The Sámi people were known for a type of traditional handicraft called duodji. Considered a collective term, duodji refers to "homecrafts" that fuse functionality with aesthetics. Mostly apparent in clothing and tools, and typically using the traditional colors of blue, yellow, green, and red, this native handicraft made use of antlers, wood, bone, leather or pewter. The majority of these traditional arts have maintained their popularity and practice as a contemporary art. For example, during the mid-20th century, Finnish ceramists garnered international acclaim for their work, and Finnish designers in other mediums such as glass and textiles also gained international recognition.

Architecture

Early Finnish architecture was rooted in the traditions of Europe and classical antiquity, and included timber construction such as log-building and medieval castle architecture. During the 19th century, German architect Carl Ludvig Engel (1778–1840) brought the neoclassical style to Finland. This style included elements of ancient Greek and Roman architecture. Engel essentially designed most of the capital of Helsinki himself in the early 19th century, adopting the neoclassical style from St. Petersburg, in Russia.

Most of Finland's architectural achievements occurred in the modern era. In fact, the majority of Finland's famous architecture—an estimated 87 percent—was created during the 20th century. During this century Finland's architecture became modernist, with architects simultaneously designing functionality into aesthetic arrangements. For example, architects often took into account the lack of sunlight in the winter and its abundance in summer, designing structures that utilized light efficiently. The textures of surfaces, color, sparseness, and simplicity of design were woven throughout 20th-century Finnish architecture.

Following the Second World War, the need for functional housing led architects to make the most of materials. Finnish architect Alvar Aalto (1898–1976) became known throughout the world for his simple lines that blend into the landscape, according to tradition. Also a designer of furniture, Aalto is celebrated for designing such buildings as Finlandia Hall in Helsinki, and numerous civic and commercial buildings, including universities, opera houses, and hospitals. At the end of the 20th century, Finland's contribution to architecture and design continued to expand in the modernist vein.

Drama

Finnish drama originated as folk rituals about hunting and fishing, with performances as early as the mid-17th century. In 1650, the first known Finnish-language theatrical event, *Tuhlaajapoika* ("The Prodigal Son"), was performed in Finland. It was not until the 19th century that theater became a widespread, popular art form. In 1827, the first theater in Helsinki opened with a seating capacity of 393 seats. In 1872, Suomalainen Teatteri (The Finnish Theatre) was founded.

Nationalism helped fuel the spread of drama by staging Aleksis Kivi's tragedy *Kullervo,* (1859) based on *Kalevala.* By the 1930s, after Finnish independence, an influx of influences from Europe and Russia made their way to Finland.

Twentieth-century Finnish theater experienced a surge in popularity, particularly considering the size of the country's population at the time. The famous Finnish architect Alvar Aalto designed several theater houses, and drama created by Finns figured prominently throughout the century. During the 1960s, theater changed focus and became more ideological. By the 1990s, experimental theater became popular, though traditional theater was still performed.

Finland has a small government-subsidized film industry that produces about twelve movies per year. *Mies Vailla Menneisyyttä* (*The Man without a Past*), a film by Aki Kaurismaki, won the Grand Prix at the Cannes Film Festival in 2002 and was nominated for an Academy Award for Best Foreign Film.

Music

Finland's location just west of Russia has historically positioned the northern European country as a cultural bridge between East and West. Thus, like its national literature, the history of Finnish music has its roots in both Eastern and Western traditions. One of the earliest music forms in Finland was the sung metre expressed in folk tales such as those in *Kalevala,* which derived from Karelia (now divided between Finland and Russia). The metre consisted of either two- or four-line tunes, each with five beats, called trochaic tetrameter, and was typically chanted by a soloist. Karelian traditional music also expressed Finnish myths, a prevalent theme in Finland's national epic, the *Kalevala.*

Another type of Finnish folk music is a tonal, Nordic music called pelimanni. This dance music originated in central Europe, and arrived in Finland through Sweden in the 17th century. Pelimanni instruments include the clarinet, fiddle, and accordion, which accompany such dances as the polka, waltz, and mazurka. Western forms of early Finnish music include Christian polyphony chant from continental Europe, which originated in the 12th century. Music during the subsequent Middle Ages was mostly religious in nature, until the 18th century, when classically composed music began to emerge.

Finland's first composer is considered to be Erik Tulindberg (1761–1814), who wrote famous music for string quartets. Russia's annexation of Finland in 1809 and the growth of opera in Europe also greatly influenced Finnish music. By the middle of the nineteenth century, German composer Fredrik Pacius (1809–1891) had written Finland's first opera, and by the end of the century, Finland saw the creation of Kansanvalistusseura (the Society for Culture and Education). The composer Jean Sibelius (1865–1957) wrote the vocal symphony *Kullervo* in 1892, and Sibelius's patriotic *Finlandia* (1899) is credited with ushering in Finnish independence.

During the "golden age" of Finnish art, which occurred from the 1980s to the 1920s, opera grew in Finland, with the founding of the Domestic Opera and opera festivals. After independence, Finnish music developed along more conservative lines, but by the mid-20th century, European classical music had influenced innovative Finnish composers, who experimented with new music.

The music of the native Sámi people, who are indigenous to northern Europe, has been compared to traditional Native American chanting. The joik, a type of spiritual song, is sung a cappella and considered a personal, spiritual attempt to invoke a person or place, most often in Northern Sámi (the region of northern Finland, Sweden, and Norway).

Literature

Finnish literature has its roots in the ancient folk tales and oral traditions of the region, as well as in the writings of the Roman Catholic Church. A national literature did not emerge until the 16th century, when Finnish clergyman Mikael Agricola (c. 1510–1557) developed the Finnish language into a writing system and translated the New Testament. Prior to this, important literary works, mostly religious in nature,

were written in other European languages. The next greatest achievement in Finnish literature occurred in the 19th century, with the publication of the epic poem *Kalevala*, considered to be the national epic.

The *Kalevala* reflects Finland's cultural history and is perhaps Finnish culture's best-known work of literature. During the early decades of the 19th century, Elias Lönnrot (1802–1884) compiled the huge collection of Finnish and Karelian folklore into what would become the *Kalevala* after collecting and analyzing hundreds of thousands of verses throughout Finland and the Republic of Karelia, in Russia. The poems represent a powerful collection of stories, such as how people confront uncertainties and protect their families, to people trying to control their destiny. This national epic is credited with awakening a nationalistic conscience during the 19th century and helped Finnish become a national language.

The first novel in the Finnish language was *Seven Brothers* (1870), written by Aleksis Kivi (1834–1872). The novel relates the ways in which 19th-century middle-class and peasant cultures confront industrialization. Written during a period in which most novels were penned in the Swedish language, *Seven Brothers* marked the turn toward realistic depictions of Finns and Finnish concerns. Other notable Finnish writers include Väinö Linna (1920–1992), who offered a realistic Finnish view of war with the Soviet Union in *The Unknown Soldier* (1954), and Frans Eemil Sillanpää (1888–1964), who wrote about rural life in Finland and won the Nobel Prize in Literature in 1939.

CULTURE

Arts & Entertainment

The contemporary arts in Finland include many elements of traditional culture. In particular, Finland became internationally renowned for what was called the modern Finnish design. This was carried across multiple materials, including furniture, jewelry, glass, and textiles, and is characterized by practical and streamlined designs and themes. However, *Kalevala* animal motifs, such as reindeer and bears, are also designed onto textiles and jewelry.

Both furniture and interior design have developed a wide following in Finland. Known for designing a multi-sensory experience that includes streamlined shapes that are highly functional and engaging, furniture and interior designers are now frequently showcased in museums and known throughout the world. Designers incorporate the busy Finnish lifestyle and surrounding environment into their designs, often working closely with architects. Leading contemporary designers include interior architect Pentti Hakala (1949–), ceramic artists Kristina Riska (1960–), and architect Mikko Heikkinen (1949–). Contemporary Finnish visual arts have also flourished. Finland's joining of the European Union (EU) in 1995, and the subsequent influx of immigrants, has begun to alter the previously homogeneous culture, much of which photographers are capturing. The indigenous Sámi are also a popular photography subject.

Finns enjoy a range of music, from classical to rock and roll. Important compositions from the 20th century are still performed, and the country is home to many well-known conductors. Finnish folk music continues to influence young musicians in different genres, often including socially engaged lyrics. Popular music in Finland includes a wide mix of genres, such as retro-funk, rock, hip-hop, and jazz. The increasingly popular metal music includes many popular bands, including Apocalyptica and Lordi. The latter won the 2006 Eurovision Song Contest, an annual competition among certain European states.

Some 70 musical festivals are held in Finland each year, mainly during the summer months. The most famous is the Savonlinna Opera Festival, a month-long event that takes place at Olavinlinna Castle in the Lake Region. Internationally renowned jazz musicians perform at the Espoo Jazz Festival in April and the Pori Jazz Festival in July.

Outdoor sports, especially ice hockey, are popular in Finland. During the colder months, people like to ski or go snowmobiling or snowshoeing. Ice fishing and dog sled and reindeer safaris are other common winter activities. During the summer, Finns enjoy watching soccer and a form of baseball called pesäpallo. Finland has many lakes and rivers, so fishing, swimming, and river rafting are common outdoor activities during the warmer months. There are more hunters per capita in Finland than in any other European nation.

Saunas or steam baths are part of the cultural tradition, although they did not originate in Finland. Many apartment and office buildings have their own saunas. There are nearly two million saunas in Finland, so they are almost universally accessible.

Cultural Sites & Landmarks

Finland's earliest cultural and historic site, the burial site of Sammallahdenmäki, dates back to the Bronze Age (roughly 2300–600 BCE), more than three millennia ago. It includes over thirty granite cairns (stones piled as a marking or memorial) and provides insight into the funerary practices of Bronze Age northern Europeans, who created the site near Lake Saarnijärvi. The cairns are organized in a variety of ways, such as a long structure that resembles a wall or in concentric circles. The site was inscribed as a World Heritage Site in 1999 by the United Nation's Educational Scientific and Cultural Organization (UNESCO).

Finland's landscape is dotted with well-preserved medieval castles, which also represent some of Finland's oldest structures. Mainly built for defensive purposes during Swedish occupation—which lasted from the 13th through the 19th centuries—they were largely reconverted as prisons or storehouses in the 17th century after the advent of firearms. The largest medieval castle is Turku Castle in Turku, which was originally the capital of Finland. Built in 1280, the castle served as a fortress and withstood a total of nine sieges before 1600. Häme Castle, built in the 1290s near Helsinki, is another important Finnish landmark which was built to defend the land and its inhabitants from Russia. It then became a prison and granary, and now operates as an exhibition hall of the Finnish National Museum. Olavinlinna Castle in Savonlinna, built in 1475, is on the Finnish-Russian border and today houses the Savonlinna Opera Festival.

In addition to the burial site of Sammallahdenmäki, Finland is home to six other World Heritage Sites, including two transboundary sites (shared with other countries). The Fortress of Suomenlinna near Helsinki, inscribed by UNESCO in 1991, was considered one of the world's largest dry docks when it was constructed in the mid-18th century. Built atop six islands, the fortified complex remains one of the most popular attractions in the capital. Another site on UNESCO's World Heritage List is one of the oldest harbors in Finland, built around a Franciscan monastery. On the Gulf of Bothnia, Rauma (or Old Rauma) is a wooden, Nordic town. Today Old Rauma consists of about 600 buildings with about 800 people currently living there. Other World Heritage Sites include the Verla Groundwood and Board Mill, a 19th- and early 20th-century settlement that is representative of the rural industrial settlements common during that period in northern Europe, and the Petäjävesi Old Church, a wooden Lutheran church constructed in the 18th century.

Helsinki is also recognized for its cultural heritage, particularly its neoclassical architecture. The city's greatest landmark is perhaps the Uspenski Cathedral, which was built in the Byzantine design to honor Nicholas I of Russia (the tsar of Russia from 1825–1855). It was built from redbrick and contains thirteen gold cupolas (dome-like structures). Inside the cathedral are many icons of the Russian Orthodox Church. For a more typical experience in Helsinki, the Market Square is where people shop for fresh fish and food and other items. The capital is also home to the national museum and theater, and the Helsinki Olympic Stadium, which served as the primary venue during the 1952 Summer Olympics.

Libraries & Museums

The National Library of Finland is overseen by the University of Helsinki. The library was originally built in 1844. Finish law requires that five copies of everything printed in Finland be given to the library. The library also plays host to lectures, exhibitions, and concerts throughout the year.

Finland is home to a variety of art museums, including the Museum of Contemporary Art, the Gallen-Kallela Museum, and the Gosta Serlachius Museum of Fine Arts. In addition, the Finnish National Gallery has several venues throughout Helsinki.

Holidays

National holidays celebrated in Finland include May Day or Vappu (May 1), an occasion that marks the beginning of spring. Midsummer's Day, held on the first Saturday between June 20 and June 26, celebrates the summer solstice. Independence Day (December 6) commemorates Finland's declaration of independence from Russia in 1917.

Youth Culture

As with most cultures, music is an important aspect of youth culture in Finland. Hip-hop and metal are two increasingly popular genres, and popular music in general is similar to other European countries. Finnish youth are also becoming increasingly technology-savvy and typically use the Internet and electronic music-sharing devices on a daily basis.

Finnish youth have also become more career focused in the early 21st century. The economic challenges of the 1990s and the ensuing high unemployment rate revealed the importance of focusing on education to increase the chances of a good job. Young Finns also are increasingly interested in pursuing work that they consider meaningful. However, the desire for high-status work is a developing trend. In general, young Finnish professionals are considered independent-minded, and often move to the southern areas of the country for work and education, as there is typically better access to wider opportunities.

SOCIETY

Transportation

Coaches and buses operate throughout the country, and are typically administered privately or regionally. Helsinki, Viipuri, and Turku are the three Finnish cities that have tram service. The capital also has a subway system, the Helsinki Metro, the only subway service in Finland. Traffic in the country moves on the right-hand side of the road.

Transportation Infrastructure

Finland has an extensive transportation system, with a road network covering an estimated 78,821 kilometers (48,977 miles). Railway lines also run to all of Finland's major cities and various rural towns, totaling 5,741 kilometers (3,567 miles).

Though Finland is home to 148 airports, large and small, the primary international airport is Helsinki-Vantaa Airport, through which more than 13 million travelers passed in 2007. This one airport is a primary stop for international travelers between the Far East and Western Europe.

Ports are extremely important for Finland's economy. The country's nine major ports are Helsinki, Hamina, Kokkola, Kotka, Naantalii, Ppori, Raahe, Rauma, and Turku. Many port towns in Finland also have ferry service.

Media & Communications

Finland is home to roughly 200 newspapers, more than 2,000 professional journals, and more than 300 magazines. The newspaper with the widest circulation in Finland is *Helsingin Sanomat,* produced by the most powerful media organization in all the Nordic countries, Sanoma Oyj. Sanoma Oyj also produces a business-focused newspaper, a tabloid, and a television news channel. Finland is also home to five national public service radio channels and nearly seventy commercial radio stations. In addition, all television channels operate digitally. Finland's National Broadcasting Company, Yleisradio Oy (YLE), is similar to the British Broadcasting Company (BBC) in form, and maintains thirteen radio and five television channels.

As a highly industrialized economy that supports private business enterprise, Finland supports some of the most advanced communications infrastructures in the world. High-speed internet and broadband connections exist throughout the country's cities, and nearly 86 percent of the population uses the Internet (2010).

SOCIAL DEVELOPMENT

Standard of Living

Finland ranked 24th out of 187 countries on the 2014 United Nations Human Development Index, which measures quality of life and standard of living indicators.

Finland has one of the world's lowest infant mortality rates. The average life expectancy is about 79 years (2014 estimate).

Water Consumption

Throughout the 1980s, Finland faced significant problems related to water pollution. The country's paper factories regularly polluted its waterways with carcinogens and chemicals. The phenomenon became known among Finns as "ugly water."

Improvements in pollution regulations and water treatment infrastructure resulted in vast improvements in Finland's water quality. The nation's drinking water is now some of the highest rated in the world by the United Nations.

Education

Finland has a high literacy rate, nearly 100 percent. Education is compulsory and free for children between seven and 16 years of age. Finnish students attend primary schools for six years and lower secondary schools for three years. Secondary schools are either vocational or academic institutions. Students who plan to go on to college must attend academic secondary schools for three years. Students who attend vocational schools may spend one or two years in school to prepare for entry-level jobs, or three-to-four years for managerial or supervisory positions.

There are 13 universities in Finland, the largest being the University of Helsinki with an enrollment of about 26,000. Other notable institutions of higher learning include the University of Turku, the University of Tampere, the University of Oulu, and the Helsinki School of Economics and Business Administration. Students who plan to attend a university must pass a national examination before they are accepted. About 58 percent of Finnish secondary school students enroll in college, and about 10 percent of college students earn degrees.

Women's Rights

Women in Finland receive fairly strong equal treatment and are legally provided equal status in the home, as well as in the workplace. (Women, in fact, are the recipients of family benefits in Finnish households). After independence, Finland industrialized later than most other Western countries, requiring the labor of both women and men. Thus, men were not the sole money earners from early on. Finnish women also were the first European women to attain suffrage—in 1906—the same year as all men. In 1919, under the new constitution, they gained legal equality, and the subsequent Marriage Act, passed in 1930, granted both spouses legal equality. The 1921 Comprehensive Education Act then required equal rights to education beginning at the elementary level. However, equal education levels have not translated into equal pay.

As is typically the case in Nordic countries, equal treatment and rights are considered not just a legal aspect of society, but inherent in a just system of government. Finland's social democratic political system is one that is often called a "welfare state," as the government provides many social services not ordinarily provided in liberal democracies. Also referred to as "state-ensured welfare," Finland's means of government support helps ensure families receive the support they need, such as extended leaves of absence for infant care, allowance for childcare leave, and insurance. The Council for Equality, established in 1972, has advised Finland's lawmakers on how to establish women's complete legal equality. Then in 1987, legislation called the Equality Law was passed to prohibit gender discrimination in the work place.

However, in recent years, social and gender inequality have increased in Finland. For example, women earn about 20 percent less pay than men do, and it is rarer for women to attain high-level positions in business or public administration. Recent negative trends in gender equality have been partially attributed to the recession during the 1990s, when job competition increased. Also, one-fifth of Finnish working women have reported experiencing sexual harassment, and until 1985, it was illegal for married women to keep their own last names. Minority women groups face more discrimination than those in the majority. Roma women face discrimination at work, with unemployment higher among the Roma than among the majority. They typically face discrimination in housing, putting mothers and their children in jeopardy.

Finland was one of the first countries to sign and ratify the optional protocol to the United Nations Convention on the Elimination of All Forms of Discrimination against Women (CEDAW) in 1999. The committee continues to monitor women's rights in Finland, making suggestions for improvement, such as with violence toward women, workplace and pay discrimination, and the need for more women in more powerful roles in the country.

Health Care

Finland's national health care system provides medical care at little or no cost. Health care centers are located throughout the country. The government operates most of the nation's hospitals, where patients have to pay only 13 percent of the cost of services. Children are provided with free medical and dental care up to age 17.

GOVERNMENT

Structure

Finland is a sovereign parliamentary republic. It has been an independent nation since

December 6, 1917. The president, elected to a six-year term of office by popular vote, is the head of state, and may serve two consecutive terms in office. Finland also has a prime minister, who is appointed by the president and approved by the parliament. Between 12 and 18 cabinet ministers are also appointed by the president.

The legislative branch, known as the Eduskunta, is a unicameral parliament with 200 members who are elected by popular vote. Members of parliament serve four-year terms, with no limit on the number of terms they may serve. The judicial branch is headed by the Supreme Court, or Korkein Oikeus, whose judges are appointed by the president.

Political Parties

Finland has a multi-party political system. Its political parties form coalition governments. Major political parties in Finland include the Center Party (Kesk), the Christian Democrats (KD), the Green League (VIHR), the Social Democratic Party (SDP), and the Swedish People's Party. Other parties include the Left Alliance, the Freedom Party, and Workers Party of Finland.

Local Government

Finland's six provinces are divided into 444 self-governing municipalities. Primary municipalities are elected by popular vote. They oversee tax collection, public service, health services, and social welfare.

Judicial System

Finnish law has its roots in Roman law and Swedish law. Finland's courts are divided into two units: civil and criminal courts and administrative courts. Civil and criminal courts include the Supreme Court, appellate courts, and local courts. Finland's Supreme Administrative Court hears cases involving legal conflicts between citizens and the country's public administration. The High Court of Impeachment hears criminal cases for government officers.

Taxation

Finns pay a progressive personal income tax—those with higher incomes pay more taxes. Individual income taxes range from 6.5 to 30 percent. Other individual taxes include a municipal tax, capital gains tax, and a church tax. Individuals in Finland also pay into a pension program and a social security program. There is a standard corporate income tax rate of 26 percent.

Armed Forces

The Finnish Defence Forces consist of an army, navy, and air force. Conscription exists, and consists of six-, nine-, or 12-month service terms. Eighteen is the minimum military age. The philosophy of the armed forces is based upon national defense and military non-alliance, and the country has participated in a range of global peacekeeping operations, including in Afghanistan and Kosovo.

Foreign Policy

Finland's foreign policy in the early 21st century is based upon national interests and security. The country has become more aligned with other Western nations, and has become increasingly involved in global governance and economics. Finland is also an advocate of regional cooperation, and joined the EU in 1995, signaling its membership in the wider European community. Finland's foreign policy is also influenced by neighboring Russia, and the Finnish government views relations with the neighboring superpower as a matter of balance.

Since declaring independence in 1917, Finland has had an often tense relationship with the now defunct Soviet Union and a stronger one with Western nations, particularly as it developed into a market economy. Finland fought the Soviet Union twice—during World War II and the Continuation War in 1944—and sought to establish peaceful relations. The February 1947 treaty that Finland signed with the Soviet Union limited Finland's defense capabilities, ceded Finnish territory to the Soviets, and provided for the leasing of specific territory to the Soviets for a naval base. Finland's prior experiences with

Soviet aggression have since become influential in the country establishing national security as a foreign policy priority.

The foreign policy that Finland's presidents J.K. Paasikivi and Urho Kekkonen followed between 1946 and 1981—called the "Paasikivi-Kekkonen Line"—involved the survival of Finland's independent status as a sovereign nation. To protect its sovereign status, the new country's leaders believed that maintaining peaceful cooperation with the Soviet Union was crucial. Finland formally signed the Agreement of Friendship, Cooperation, and Mutual Assistance with the Soviet Union in 1948. The agreement was designed specifically to deter attacks from Germany or countries that belonged to the North Atlantic Treaty Organization (NATO), but it also formally recognized Finland's larger foreign-policy goals of avoiding large-scale conflicts with powerful nations.

The critical term, "Finlandization," was used during this period, primarily by the German press, to refer to the restrictions that the Soviet Union placed on Finland, which in turn restricted certain freedoms of its country's citizens so as not to incite a Soviet backlash. The Finnish press adapted pro-Soviet perspectives and censored attitudes that could be perceived as more democratic or intolerant of Soviet power. However, the 1991 disbanding of the Soviet Union allowed Finland much greater freedom to participate in economic and political alliances with Western countries. Since then, Finland has become more involved in purchasing Western military support, such as F-18 fighter planes from the United States in 1994. Because of its history as Russia's neighbor, The U.S. has been particularly interested in developing and maintaining a close relationship with Finland.

To build cooperative economic and cultures ties with other northern European nations, Finland joined the Nordic Council in 1955. The council has also focused on building a labor market among members. Also in 1955, Finland joined the UN, and in 1956 began assisting the UN in peacekeeping missions around the world. In 1994, Finland joined the NATO Partnership for Peace. The 23-member Partnership for Peace aims to develop trust among NATO members and the other European nations, and the former Soviet Union. As such, Finland has supported NATO efforts in Afghanistan.

Human Rights Profile

International human rights law insists that states respect civil and political rights, and also promote an individual's economic, social and cultural rights. The United Nations Universal Declaration on Human Rights (UDHR) is recognized as the standard for international human rights. Its authors sought the counsel of the world's great thinkers, philosophers, and religious leaders, and were careful to create a document that reflects the core values shared by every world culture. (To read this document or view the articles relating to cultural human rights, go to: http://www.udhr.org/UDHR/default.htm.)

Finland is a constitutional republic, whose laws to protect basic human rights are in accord with the UDHR. Finnish legislation provides freedom for its citizens and allows for many basic rights that are common to democracies. Its law stipulates the prohibition of discrimination according to race, gender, ethnic background, political opinion, disability, or national or social origin. Finland's constitution even stipulates the equality of sexes, including pay. Finnish law also recognizes the right to assemble and own property, the right to privacy, the right of expression and to access information, the right to hold a religious belief, and the right to vote. Finnish men and women can marry, regardless of race, religion, nationality, and the government provides for parental leave and family care. Finnish citizens are also protected by law from arbitrary arrest and detention.

While Finnish and Swedish are the official languages, Finland's indigenous people, the Sámi, have the right to develop their own language and culture, and can even use their language officially. The Roma and other peoples, though discriminated against in some cases, have the right to practice their own languages and cultures under the Finland constitution.

Violence against women is considered the most severe human rights violation in Finland. It is currently increasing, especially violence that is committed by someone outside the family. However, violence against women inside the family also occurs, and only in 1994 was rape that occurs in a marriage criminalized. Finland has also come under criticism for its treatment of those who opt for civilian service alternatives instead of military service. Those who are conscientious objectors, or refuse to perform military service, must fulfill 395 days' worth of civilian service, whereas military service requires only 180 days' worth of service.

ECONOMY

Overview of the Economy

In 2014, Finland's gross domestic product (GDP) was estimated at $221.5 billion (USD), or $40,500 (USD) per capita. Over the past few decades, Finland has undergone a transition from a resource-based economy to a knowledge-based economy. The majority of the work force is employed in the public services sector. The services industry accounted for an estimated 70 percent of the GDP in 2014.

Finland's major trading partners are Germany, Sweden, Great Britain, and other members of the European Union. Finland also has substantial trade with the United States, Russia, and Norway. Finland became a member of the European Union in January 1995.

Industry

Manufacturing is the primary sector of the economy, with production of paper, pulp, wood and chemical byproducts, metals, engineering and electronic products, and telecommunications equipment being the major activities. Other manufactured products include computerized mechanical systems, snowmobiles, icebreaker ships, furniture, ceramics, textiles, and home accessories.

Helsinki is home to the economic powerhouse Nokia, and supports a stock exchange.

Cell phones, in fact, are a primary source of employment in the capital. Nokia, which at one point held a 30 percent market share of all cell phones produced in the world, has transformed the city's economy. The biggest company in Finland, Nokia produces more than 4 percent of the GDP for the entire country and brings in at least one of every five dollars Finland receives from abroad.

Shipbuilding is an industry which has been pursued for centuries in Finland, specifically Helsinki. Also, fresh fish are sold directly from red and blue fishing boats in the harbor. A world-famous Helsinki product is Fiskars scissors, the most-imitated brand on earth. Other industries include printing, sugar refining, textiles, and porcelain. The Arabia porcelain factory, founded in the late 19th century, is Europe's largest ceramics maker.

Labor

In 2014, Finland had an estimated labor force of 2.66 million. Over 60 percent of Finns are employed by private business. However, over 23 percent of Finns are employed by either the central government or by local government. Entrepreneurs make up approximately 13 percent of the country's labor force. Finland's private sector includes industry, construction, finance, and communications.

Energy/Power/Natural Resources

Forests are Finland's most abundant natural resource. The country also has significant copper and zinc reserves, and other minerals such as chromite, lead, nickel, silver, and gold are mined commercially. Because it lacks natural energy sources, except for wood and hydroelectric power, Finland must import oil, with Russia being the largest supplier.

Fishing

There are approximately 3,500 professional fishing vessels in Finland. Fishing contributes an estimated 0.2 percent to the country's overall GDP. Common fish species caught include cod, salmon, herring, and sprat. An estimated 270,000 tons of herring are caught annually in the waters off Finland, particularly in the Gulf of Bothnia. Stocking programs and catch quotas have been put in place in order to manage the country's fish supplies. Recreational fishing is popular throughout the country, given the country's many lakes and rivers. Perch and pike are commonly caught by recreational fisherman. The value of the countries fish production in 2003 was estimated at $36 million.

Forestry

Finland's forest industry makes up approximately 5 percent of its gross domestic product (GDP). Forest products make up 18 percent of the country's exports. An estimated 24,000 people are employed in Finland's forest industry. About 60 percent of paper and other forest products produced in Finland are exported to countries in the European Union.

Mining/Metals

Finland's mining industry produces copper, nickel, and zinc. Australian and Canadian mining outfits are active in the country's mining industry. Finland has some diamond mines, which continue to be explored. The nation's gold deposits also continue to be explored.

Agriculture

Agriculture currently accounts for about 4 percent of Finland's GDP. Major cash crops include barley, wheat, potatoes, and sugar beets. Other major agricultural products are dairy cattle and fish. The majority of Finnish farms are small and family-operated. In the 1990s, the Finnish government initiated began subsidizing farmers in order to aid their conversion to organic farming.

Animal Husbandry

Livestock include poultry, cattle, pigs, reindeer, horses, and sheep. Reindeer breeding is concentrated in Lapland. Approximately 25 percent of Finland's farms are dairy farms.

Tourism

Due to its remote location, Finland attracts fewer foreign tourists compared to Denmark, Sweden or Norway. Most of its foreign tourists come from Russia, with the next largest number coming from Sweden. Tourism, both domestic and international, is a growing sector of Helsinki's economy. Vantaa is the main international airport. Over 9.7 million passengers pass through the airport each year. More than seven million passengers take international flights to or from Vantaa.

Some of the country's notable tourist attractions include Olavinlinna Castle, built as a fortress in the 15th century at Savonlinna; Ainola, a museum that was once the home of composer Jean Sibelius; the Kiasma modern art museum in Helsinki; and Gallen-Kallela Museum, dedicated to Finnish artist Akseli Gallen-Kallela.

Kathryn Bundy, Patricia Martin, Ellen Bailey

DO YOU KNOW?

- Finland became the first nation to give women the right to vote in 1906.
- The world's northernmost film festival, the Midnight Sun Film Festival, is held in Lapland in June.
- Because of the numerous islands and forested mainland, it is fairly easy for Helsinki families to have simple summer cottages on the water.

Bibliography

Britannica Educational. *Denmark, Finland, and Sweden.* Perth, WA: Britannica Educational, 2013.

Connah, Roger. *Finland: Modern Architectures in History.* London: Reaktion Books, 2006.

Hill, Anja. *The Food and Cooking of Finland.* Chicago: Aquamarine, 2008.

Lavery, Jason. *The History of Finland.* Westport, Connecticut: Greenwood Press, 2006.

Leney, Terttu. *Finland—Culture Smart!: The Essential Guide to Customs and Etiquette.* London: Kuperard, 2006.

Lonnrot, Elias. *The Kalevala: The Epic Poem of Finland.* Charleston, SC: Forgotten Books, 2008.

Meinander, Henrik. *A History of Finland.* New York: Oxford University Press, 2014.

Norum, Roger. *Rough Guide to Finland.* London: Rough Guides, 2010.

Swallow, Deborah. *Culture Shock! Finland: A Survival Guide to Customs and Etiquette.* Tarrytown, NY: Marshall Cavendish, 2011.

Symington, Andy. *Finland.* Oakland, CA: Lonely Planet, 2012.

Valkonen, Markku. *Finnish Art Over the Centuries.* Trans. M.G. Abrahamsen. Finland: Otava Publishing, 1999.

Works Cited

"Background Note: Finland." http://www.state.gov/r/pa/ei/bgn/3238.htm.

Botticelli, Peter. "Finland's Relations with the Soviet Union, 1940–1986." http://www.loyno.edu/history/journal/1985-6/botticelli.htm. Loyola University Student Historical Journal; Loyola University.

"Finland." https://www.cia.gov/library/publications/the-world-factbook/geos/fi.html.

"Finland." http://www.europe-cities.com/en/657/finland/history/chronology/. Europe-cities.com

"Finish Youth in a Global Context." http://www.kairosfuture.com/en/news/finnishyouth. Kairos Future.

"Finland: Language, Culture, Customs, and Etiquette." http://www.kwintessential.co.uk/resources/global-etiquette/finland-country-profile.html. Kwintessential Cross Cultural Solutions.

"Food from Finland." http://www.foodfromfinland.com/.

Kruhse, Pauli. "History of Finland: A Selection of Events and Documents." http://www.histdoc.net/history/history.html.

Paul Gazzola (AU/DE). http://antifestival.com/anti-2008/program/teokset/paul-gazzola-de/.

Population Register Center of Finland. http://www.vrk.fi/vrk/files.nsf/files/54A237331305AC01C225751900325A7C/$file/081130.html.

"Sammallahdenmäki, Lappi." http://www.nba.fi/en/sammallahdenmakieng. National Board of Antiquities.

Solsten, Eric, and Sandra W. Meditz, Ed. *Finland: a country study.* Washington D.C.: Federal Research Division Library of Congress, 1988.

Smith-Spark, Laura. "Finland's Trailblazing Path for Women." *BBC News.* http://news.bbc.co.uk/2/hi/europe/5036602.stm.

"Submission to the United Nation's Committee on the convention on the Elimination of All Forms of Discrimination against Women." *Office of the United Nations High Commissioner for Human Rights, 41st Session (30 June–18 July 2008).* http://www2.ohchr.org/english/bodies/cedaw/cedaws41.htm..

"Theatre in Finland." http://www.teatteri.org/english/theatre-finland/index.html.

"Virtual Finland: Your Window on Finland." Ministry for Foreign Affairs of Finland, Department for Communication and Culture/Unit for Public Diplomacy. http://virtual.finland.fi/History/.

Women's rights: http://virtual.finland.fi/netcomm/news/showarticle.asp?intNWSAID=25731; http://virtual.finland.fi/netcomm/news/showarticle.asp?intNWSAID=25777.

*France is noted for its many rivers. The Rhone, shown here, drains into the Mediterranean Sea. /Stock photo ©
Frederic Prochasson*

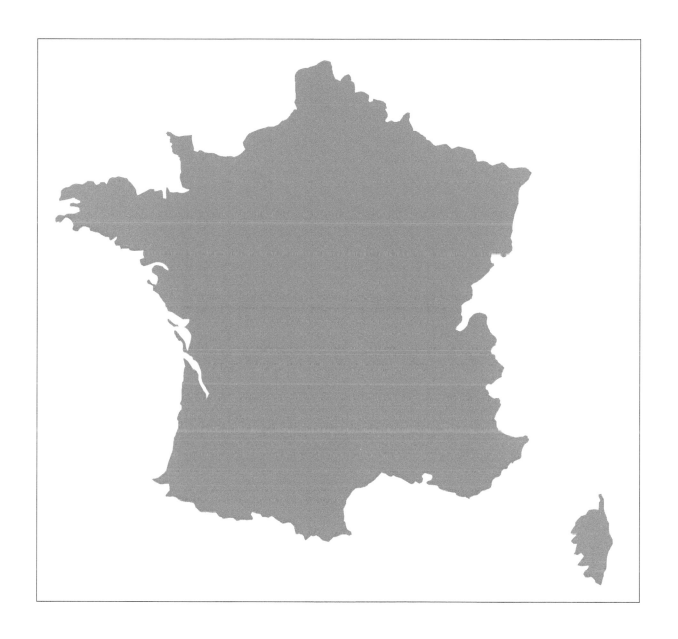

FRANCE

Introduction

Throughout history, France has played a leading role in the evolution of government and world politics. Located in Western Europe, it has also been an international cultural center throughout the modern era. The country's capital of Paris is known as the "City of Light," and has for centuries served as the center of French life and one of the world's most renowned tourist destinations.

GENERAL INFORMATION

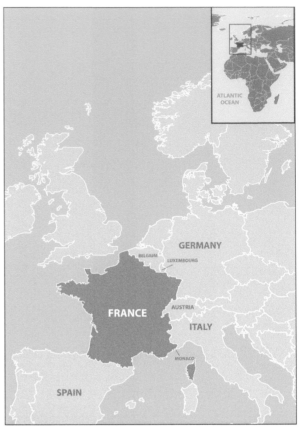

Official Language: French
Population: 66,259,012 (2014 estimate)
Currency: Euro
Coins: The Euro is available in 1, 2, 5, 10, 20 and 50 cent coins. A 1 and 2 Euro coin is also available.
Land Area: 674,843 square kilometers (260,558 square miles)
National Motto: "Liberté, Egalité, Fraternité" ("Liberty, Equality, Brotherhood")
National Anthem: "La Marseillaise"
Capital: Paris
Time Zone: GMT +1 (Summer: GMT +2)
Flag Description: The flag of France depicts three vertical color bands; one blue, one white and one red. It is known as "Le drepeau tricolore" (French Tricolor). The blue and red represents Paris while the white represents the Bourbon Dynasty. The colors have also been associated with the national motto.

Population

France is one of the most populous countries in Europe, following Russia and Germany, with an estimated population of around 66.2 million as of 2014. About 79 percent of the population is urban; 52 urban areas have over 150,000 inhabitants, and five have over a million. Paris is the country's most populated city; the city and its environs is the home of over 10 million people. Other large cities are Lyon, Marseille, and Toulouse.

Languages

French is the official language of France. It is a Romance language, descended from Latin. French is a language of global commerce, diplomacy, and sports, and the language is spoken in fifty-three countries besides France. In fact, an estimated 51 million have learned French as a second language.

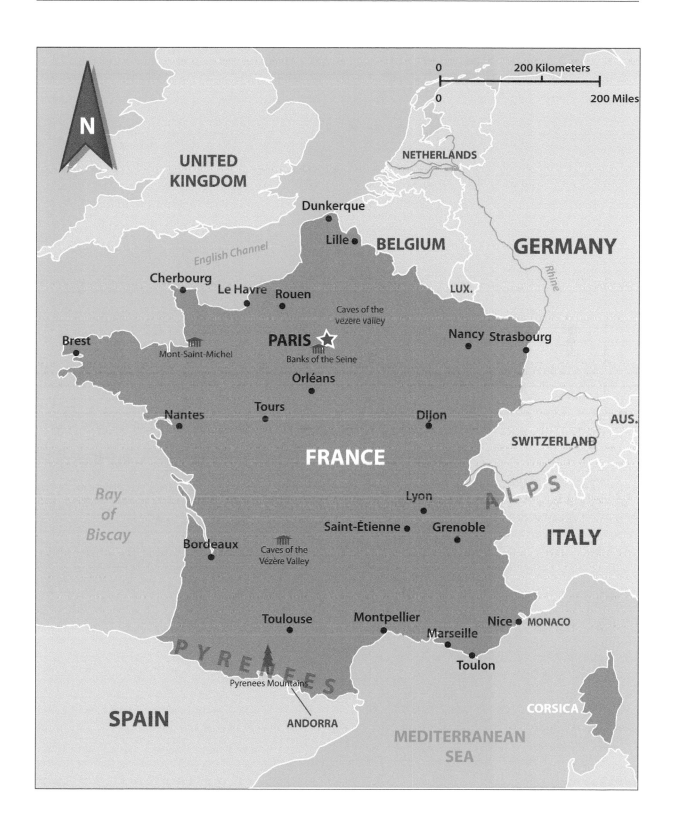

N

UNITED KINGDOM

NETHERLANDS

200 Kilometers

200 Miles

Dunkerque

Lille

BELGIUM

GERMANY

Rhine

English Channel

Cherbourg

Le Havre

Rouen

LUX.

Caves of the
Vézère Valley

Brest

Mont-Saint-Michel

PARIS

Banks of the Seine

Nancy Strasbourg

Orléans

AUS.

Nantes

Tours

Dijon

SWITZERLAND

FRANCE

Bay
of
Biscay

Lyon

ALPS

Saint-Étienne

Grenoble

ITALY

Bordeaux

Caves of the
Vézère Valley

Toulouse

Montpellier

Nice MONACO

Marseille

PYRENEES

Toulon

Pyrenees Mountains

CORSICA

SPAIN

ANDORRA

MEDITERRANEAN
SEA

**Principal Cities by Population
(2012 estimate, unless noted):**

- Paris (2,000,000)
- Marseille (795,600)
- Lyon (495,840)
- Toulouse (469,854)
- Nice (329,311)
- Nantes (283,226)
- Strasbourg (282,496)
- Lille (273,168)
- Montpellier (266,654)
- Bordeaux (229,500)
- Rennes (209,375) (2006 estimate)

The oldest French academic society is the forty-member French Academy (Académie française), founded in 1635 to protect the purity of the French language. However, after centuries of a French-only policy, the national government is beginning to express greater support for regional languages. These include Alsatian, a Germanic tongue spoken in the province of Alsace; Flemish, a Dutch dialect spoken in Flanders; and Catalan and Franco-Provençal, which are spoken in the southern regions of the country.

To promote French language and culture, France has established an international community of French-speaking, or "Francophone," nations, similar in concept to the British Commonwealth of Nations.

Native People & Ethnic Groups
France's native population is largely of mixed Celtic, Latin, and Germanic ancestry. The original inhabitants were Celts known collectively as the "Gauls," who were conquered by the Romans in the first century BCE and adopted their language. As Rome declined, the Germanic Franks conquered Gaul, renaming it "Frankland" (the origin of the name "France").

Today, France has large minorities from its former colonies in North Africa and Indochina. There is also a large Basque minority in the Pyrenees Mountains separating France and Spain.

Religion
France is highly secularized, though the constitution protects freedom of religion. Since 1905, politics have been governed by the principle of laïcité (lay control) or strict separation between church and state, partly as a reaction against the Catholic Church's political activity. Over 80 percent is nominally Catholic, but only around 5 percent attend church regularly. Up to one-third of all French people consider themselves atheists. There is a large Muslim population (around 8 percent of the total population) of immigrants from North Africa, Turkey, and Asia. This influx has created cultural conflict and a nativist backlash.

Climate
Metropolitan France has a generally temperate climate, with pleasant summers and cool winters. Because of the country's size and location, however, there are four regional climates: "Atlantic" along the northern and western coasts, "Mediterranean" along the southern coast, "continental" in the main inland region, and "alpine" in the mountains of the Alps. The Mediterranean climate, with its hot summers, is marked by a strong wind known as the mistral which blows from north to northwest.

ENVIRONMENT & GEOGRAPHY

Topography
Mainland ("metropolitan") France is the largest nation in Western Europe. In addition to the mainland, France possesses numerous overseas departments and territories that are considered part of France proper. These include territories in the Americas, the Caribbean, the Indian and Pacific Oceans, as well as territory claimed in Antarctica. France also claims a large region of coastal waters as an "exclusive economic zone" (EEZ); this zone covers just over 11 million square kilometers (around 4.26 million square miles).

France is bordered on several sides by water, with nearly 5,500 kilometers (3,418 miles) of coastline facing the Mediterranean Sea, the Atlantic Ocean, the English Channel and the North Sea. Land borders include Spain and Andorra (southwest), Switzerland and Italy (southeast), Germany (east), and Luxembourg and Belgium (northeast).

The country is noted for its many rivers. The most important include are the Seine, which flows through Paris; the Rhône, which drains into the Mediterranean; and the Garonne and Dordogne, which drain into the Bay of Biscay on the Atlantic Coast.

Much of northern and western France is covered by plains or low hills. The south and east are mountainous, except for the southern plain near the Mediterranean. The major ranges are the Pyrenees in the south, on the Spanish border, and the Alps in the East. Mont Blanc, part of the Alps, is Western Europe's highest mountain, rising 4,807 meters (15,771 feet). Other mountain ranges are the Massif Central and the Vosges.

Plants & Animals

France's wild animal population has largely vanished, except in forested regions and national parks, due to centuries of agricultural cultivation. The major wildlife species include deer and wild boar, as well as small mammals such as rabbits, beavers, and foxes. Endangered species include the brown bear and Atlantic salmon.

There are seven national parks and over 100 nature reserves, as well as thirty regional nature parks throughout France. Although much of the country is covered with farmland, there are still many forested regions.

CUSTOMS & COURTESIES

Greetings

Shaking hands upon greeting and parting is customary in France among acquaintances and business associates. The handshake should be firm, but an overly aggressive handshake is considered impolite. Greetings among family and friends, as well as those introduced by them, are often accompanied by kisses on both cheeks, beginning on the left side. However, different regions of France, from Paris to Provence, vary the practice, and up to three or even four kisses may be exchanged.

A general expression of greeting is "Bonjour" ("Hello"). It is customary to greet everyone at the first encounter of the day. For example, in an office, a colleague need not be acknowledged at every chance meeting, but a greeting should be offered the first time. When greeting anyone, it is important to make eye contact rather than to avoid it, which would be considered dismissive.

Gestures & Etiquette

Generally, it is important to address someone properly when speaking or writing in French culture. Informal language, or slang, is commonly used only in conversation between close friends. Especially significant is the form of the word "you." In French, one uses the formal "vous" for those one does not know well and in business situations, while the more familiar "tu" is used for friends, family and children. It is also proper to address new acquaintances, even peers, in the more formal style.

Many gestures, such as pressing the forefinger and thumb together and the classic French pout, are used to emphasize meaning, but these are usually reserved for conversations between friends and family. One uniquely French gesture is the "Gallic shrug." This raising of the shoulders with palms open may convey a number of meanings, ranging from the expressions "I don't know" to "It can't be helped" to "It's not my fault"—or even a combination of all three.

Eating/Meals

Food is often perceived as an art in France, and the country has a proud history surrounding the preparation and consumption of their meals. In fact, it is believed that the first French cookbook was produced in the Middle Ages (not long after the advent of the printing press). The oldest restaurant in France, Le Tour D'Argent in Paris, claims to have invented the fork. The ritual of leisurely meals is also important in France. Formal lunches and dinners, both in restaurants and at people's homes, include many courses and may last several hours.

A typical French breakfast usually consists of a croissant, pain au chocolat (croissant-type pastry with chocolate inside) or bread, with coffee or hot chocolate, sometimes drunk from a large bowl. Lunch was once the traditional main meal of the day, but it has been replaced by dinner in recent times, especially among the urban population (people tend to eat earlier in rural areas). Many French people also continue to purchase fresh meat and produce at the market daily. Fresh bread, usually the long, thin baguette, is a staple of the French diet, and it is common to see business men and women on their way home from work carrying a loaf under their arms.

The entrée, meaning "entry," corresponds to what Americans know as the appetizer. A typical entrée might be a liver pate served with bread, a bowl of soup, a plate of mixed charcuterie (smoked or dried meats and sausages) or escargot (snails cooked in butter and garlic). The main course, or plat principal, is usually meat or fish, served with vegetables. A simple green salad comes after the main course, and cheese may be traditionally served after the meal. France, in fact, produces hundreds of different cheese varieties, and many fine dining establishments use a wheeled cheese cart to present their selections after dinner. Hosts serving dinner in their homes may typically offer their guests between three and five cheeses. Dessert such as cake or fruit will commonly follow, with coffee traditionally served after, rather than with, dessert.

Meals in France can be long, and the dining table is often considered an extended meeting place to linger over good food and lively conversation. Even business lunches are considered a time to build relationships, rather than to conduct business. Fast food, however, has made inroads in France in recent years, and, with the advent of globalization, some of the old traditions surrounding food have begun to fade. For example, long lunches and leisurely trips to open markets are becoming less common as people adopt time-saving measures.

Visiting

When invited for dinner, it is customary for guests to bring a small gift or flowers. Some still follow the custom of sending flowers ahead of time. Wine is typically not appropriate as a gift, as the wine for dinner will already have been carefully selected by the host. French people value privacy, and doors to bedrooms and other parts of the house will probably be closed and off-limits to visitors. Guests should also not expect to be given a tour of the household. Dinner guests should expect to eat at least an hour later than the invitation time, as there will probably be a long period of drinks and conversation before being called to the table.

Traditionally, intimacy in France is earned over time, so receiving an invitation to someone's home is a privilege. When the invitation arrives, it is an honor that signals that the invitee is now considered a member of the host's circle of friends and acquaintances.

LIFESTYLE

Family

Close family relations are highly valued in France. Children generally move out of their parents' homes later than in other Western cultures, and will usually maintain close ties with their parents throughout their adult lives. Additionally, the rebellion often associated with adolescence in other cultures is largely absent. In the south of France, large extended families spanning several generations still live in the same neighbourhoods.

While women still bear most of the responsibility of child rearing, the men of the house have been more involved in parenting in recent years, especially as more women work outside the home. Family pets, especially dogs, are very popular in France, with one recent study showing one dog for every two people in the population. Well-behaved dogs are even allowed in some restaurants.

Housing

In France, less than half the population lives in apartments, while the rest reside in homes that they either rent or own. Buildings constructed before the 1960s were usually made of stone, while more modern structures have been built with more easily-produced concrete, cinderblock and brick. Wood is not often used as a building material in France.

In Paris, many stone apartment buildings still in use were built in the 19th century, giving the capital its distinctive "Old-World" appeal. In other, newer cities, and especially in the suburbs of Paris, modern concrete and brick buildings are more common. In the early 21st century, following widespread urban migration, an estimated 25 percent of population still lives in small villages in the country.

Food

France's varied climate—allowing for the production of a wide variety of agricultural products—and reputation for haute cuisine (high or grand cooking) may have something to do with the country's talent for innovation in food preparation. The word "cuisine" is, in fact, French for both "kitchen" and "cooking," and is used around the world to refer to cooking at its best. Famous cooking schools such as the Ritz cooking school in Paris teach the techniques and ingredients used in the art of fine French cooking, which has traditionally involved complex sauces. Typical French dishes include coq au vin (poultry in wine sauce) and blanquette de veau (veal in a creamy sauce). In recent years, nouvelle cuisine, or "new cuisine," has favored a lighter style of cooking with less heavy sauces.

French wines are renowned the world over, and viniculture (winemaking) is considered both an art and science in French culture. Many wineries around the world have modelled their winemaking methods on those first developed in France centuries ago, and many common styles of wines such as Bordeaux, Chablis and burgundy are derived from the specific regions in France in which the grapes are grown. The use of these names is very strictly regulated, and a wine produced from grapes just outside the Chablis region, for example, will not be allowed to use the name Chablis on its label. However,

for wines produced in other countries, the same names refer to the species of grape, rather than to the region.

Cheese, bread, and pastries also figure prominently into French cuisine. Many French cheeses (there are over 400) such as Roquefort, Münster and Beaufort, are protected under European Union (EU) law with a Protected Designation of Origin (PDO) status. French pastries, especially the flaky, buttery croissant, are commonly served at breakfast. Other popular French pastries include the éclair, an oblong cousin to the cream-filled donut, and the Napoléon, a many-layered flaky dessert named for the famous general and political leader.

Life's Milestones

France is considered a widely diverse nation—half the country (an estimated 51 percent in 2007) identifies as Roman Catholic. France is also the leading refugee destination in Western Europe. In fact, as recently as 2005, France was home to nearly 5 million foreign-born immigrants, and recent legislation has been enacted to limit Eastern European immigration. Thus, there is much ethnic and religious variation concerning traditions and milestones within the country. However, certain milestones still adhere to strict rules. Marriage is one example, and couples who wish to marry in France must all first have a civil marriage ceremony, most likely in the city hall of their town, before any wedding in any place of worship. Therefore, all couples who choose marry in a religious ceremony in France are already legally married before their wedding when this ceremony takes place.

Another unique milestone in France is a required—and often described as gruelling—three-week examination called the baccalauréate, which typically occurs at 17 years of age. The subjects covered on the baccalauréate exam depend on whether the student attended an academic, vocational or technical high school. Passing this series of tests is equivalent to graduation from high school in the United States. The exam is essential for students who want to continue their education, so passing one's "bac" is considered a major life milestone.

CULTURAL HISTORY

Art

French art has its origins in prehistoric times, and Palaeolithic cave paintings can still be found at the prehistoric sites of Lascaux and Chauvet, among others. A predominant art during the medieval period was manuscript illumination, in which books were decorated with intricate hand-painted images, often in tempera and gold leaf. This was followed by the Romanesque period, which developed in Western Europe around 1000 CE, and included art such as enamelwork and sculpture. This evolved into the Gothic period, which emerged in France in the mid-12th century.

The Italian Renaissance significantly influenced the French arts beginning in the 15th century. This period witnessed the development of French painting and printing, which continued into the 17th century. Notable painters include Charles Le Brun (1619–1690), who produced large-scale works for the "Sun King" Louis XIV (1638–1715); François Boucher (1703–1770), who worked with numerous media, including porcelain, tapestry and manuscript illustrations, and is known for his pastoral paintings and portraitures; Jean-Honoré Fragonard (1732–1806), who is associated with the 18th century rococo style; Eugène Delacroix (1798–1863), considered France's most important Romantic painter, and whose *Liberty Leading the People* (1830) is France's most famous patriotic image.

Several famous innovations in painting also originated in France. Artists such as Claude Monet (1840–1926), Camille Pissarro (1830–1903) and Edgar Degas (1834–1917) were leaders of a movement called Impressionism, considered radical at the time. Impressionism favored the unique point of view of the individual painter over the strict realism of merely copying a landscape or object. Later on, French painters such as Georges Braque (1882–1963) and Pablo Picasso (1881–1973) would take this idea a step further in cubism. Surrealism would follow, cementing the ideal of the artist as creator of his or her own unique universe.

France has made its mark on other fine arts besides painting. The art of sculpture dates back to prehistoric clay engravings, and developed throughout several classical periods. French sculptor Auguste Rodin (1840–1917) is considered one of the fathers of modern sculpture, and his most famous sculptures, such as *The Thinker* (1902), are on display outside the Musée Rodin (a hotel that was once the sculptor's residence). Modern movements such as cubism, futurism and abstract art heavily influenced French sculpture in the 20th century.

Architecture

Gothic architecture, as exemplified by the Notre-Dame de Reims, the Notre Dame de Paris, and Chartres cathedrals, evolved from the Romanesque style beginning in the 12th century. During the thirteenth and sixteenth centuries, when this style of architecture was widespread throughout Europe, it was commonly known as "the French style." A key innovation of Gothic architecture was the flying buttress, a structure outside a building that bears some of the weight of the walls. This allowed buildings to have larger windows, particularly those made of stained glass. Ornamental and grand architecture, characteristic of both the Renaissance and baroque architectural styles, followed.

Beginning in the 18th century, French architecture became more refined and reserved, adopting classical styles and motifs. In the mid-19th century, tall, stately stone buildings with ornate decoration became the norm in the capital of Paris. In the 20th century, French architects embraced more innovative and modern styles. This is evident in some of the more controversial structures in Paris such as the glass Louvre Pyramid addition to the Musée du Louvre (Louvre Museum) and the François Mitterrand Library (which featured so many windows that books needed to be stored underground to protect them from the light).

In 2008, French architect Jean Nouvel (1945–) won the prestigious Pritzker Prize, often considered equivalent to a Nobel Prize in architecture. He has designed ultra-modern museums and other buildings in France and around the world.

Music

The history of music in France dates back to the medieval period, with most early music sacred in nature and associated with Christianity. While regional folk music has its place in France's musical history, French classical music and opera were predominant, beginning with the baroque period (roughly 1600–1750) and famous French composers such as Jean-Philippe Rameau (1683–1784) and François Couperin (1668–1773). French music achieved greater prominence in the nineteenth and early 20th centuries. Some of the most notable modern French composers include the Romantic composers Georges Bizet (1838–1875), best known for his opera *Carmen*, and Hector Berlioz (1803–1869), who composed the *Symphonie fantastique* (*Fantasy Symphony*); impressionists Maurice Ravel (1875–1937), known for his piano compositions and famous orchestral piece *Boléro*, and Claude Debussy (1862–1918); and Camille Saint-Saëns (1835–1921), who is perhaps best known for *The Carnival of the Animals*, an orchestral composition also for the piano, harmonica, and xylophone.

It is believed that the traditional "love song" originated in France in the 13th century, when French troubadours (poet-musicians) performed their songs at various royal courts. France has continued this tradition of solo vocal artists with personalities as distinctive as their voices. Édith Piaf (1915–1963) began her singing career as a poor girl on the streets of Montmartre and became an international star. Singer Maurice Chevalier (1888–1972) brought his musical talents to Hollywood and popularized the image of the debonair French crooner in America.

Film

The Lumière brothers—Louis (1864–1948) and Auguste (1862–1954)—are considered to be among the first filmmakers. They held their first motion picture screening in 1895, including a demonstration of their first film, entitled *La Sortie des usines Lumière* (*Workers Leaving the Lumière Factory*). Since that time, the French word "cinema" is now synonymous with quality film the world over. France has given the world many famous directors, such as Jean-Luc Godard (1930–), François Truffaut (1932–1984), and Jean Renoir (1894–1979). France is perhaps best known for hosting the prestigious Cannes Film Festival, an internationally influential film exhibition which was established in the 1930s.

Literature

France's rich tradition of storytelling dates back to the Middle Ages, when French medieval poetry and prose (which developed in the late Middle Ages) were influenced by the romantic and epic narrative traditions of the troubadour (such as the Arthurian legends). Early French literature also consisted of chronicles (historical accounts) and texts associated with the church. As French literature developed, it has given the world such memorable novels as *The Three Musketeers* (1844) and *The Count of Monte Cristo* (1845) by Alexandre Dumas (1802–1870), and *Les Miserables* (1862) and *The Hunchback of Notre Dame* (1831) by Victor Hugo (1802–1885). Other famous French writers include novelist Honoré de Balzac (1799–1850), considered one of the founders of the European realism movement, and Guy de Maupassant (1850–1893), who helped popularize the modern short story.

The canon of French literature was also heavily influenced by intellectualism. During the French Renaissance, scholar Michel de Montaigne (1533–1592) introduced the essay as a literary genre. François-Marie Arouet (1694–1778), better known as Voltaire, and Charles de Secondat (1689–1755), known as the Baron de Montesquieu, both were highly influential writers who wrote during the Enlightenment. This period was characterized by philosophical works about equality in society that first expressed the democratic ideas that would form the core of American society years later. Commentary on society and the human condition thus became a common feature in French literature.

French philosophy continued into the 20th century with writers such as Albert Camus (1913–1960) and Jean-Paul Sartre (1905–1980), both part of a French-born school of thought called existentialism. Their point of view was that life is absurd, a series of random events with no meaning. Additionally, playwrights such as Eugene Ionesco (1909–1994) developed the theatre of the absurd, which was commonly associated with existentialism. In 2008, French author J.M.G. Le Clézio (1940–) was awarded the Nobel Prize in Literature. Though France has a long history of literary Nobel Prize winners, Le Clézio was the first French-language writer since 1985 to win the award. In 2014 another French writer, Patrick Modiano (1945–), won the award.

CULTURE

Arts & Entertainment

The fine arts are a part of everyday life in France, with most major cities having at least one fine art museum. The famous School of Beaux-Arts in Paris has educated art students for centuries. Many of France's most famous painters, including Delacroix, Monet and fellow impressionist Pierre-Auguste Renoir (1841–1919), were trained there. The Centre Georges Pompidou in Paris, also known as the Beaubourg Museum, is a huge structure dedicated to contemporary art. The museum itself was controversial when it was built in the 1970s; its colourful tubes, vents, escalators and other inner workings were placed on the outside of the building. Additionally, Paris's urban landscape is dotted with small art galleries, and informal showings by local artists held in unexpected places such as wine cellars and cafés are common.

Fashion is another art in which France has always been a major player on the international stage and is seen as an important industry and source of national pride. Paris is often called the "fashion capital of the world," and high fashion is commonly known by its French name, haute coûture. France's fashion week, held twice a year in Paris, is one of the city's top social, business and cultural events.

Opera and ballet also remain popular—French ballet gave the dance tradition certain vocabulary such as plié (bending at the knees) grande jetée (a leap through the air) and pas de deux (a dance performed by a duo)—and the government has recently subsidized ambitious architectural projects to build new halls to accommodate them.

Festivals dedicated to the arts are held annually throughout France, often as the cultural event of the year for the cities and towns that host them. One of the best known is the Festival of Avignon, in Provence, which showcases various performing arts such as dance, opera and theatre. Opera festivals are typically held in summer, when the regular opera seasons of the major cities are on hiatus. Comic book art is celebrated in Angouleme at the Festival de la Bande Dessinee (comic strip festival), held annually since the 1970s and attracting up to 250,000 attendees. The Fete de la Musique, which takes place on June 21, the first day of summer and the longest day of the year, involves numerous cities and towns, and consists of free concerts featuring music of all styles.

In general, contemporary art in France receives substantial government funding and encouragement, with many festivals subsidized or state-run, as are most museums. The minister of culture, a government post established in 1959, oversees the arts in France, and is charged with fostering the "democratization" of the French arts. Under President Mitterand, politician Jack Lang (1939–), then the minister of culture, made efforts to promote hip-hop and comic book art in order to make the arts more inclusive and accessible. The government further recognized the importance of art in society by giving the unemployed free admission to all museums run by the state, helping to ensure that income is not a factor in the ability of any French citizen to enjoy and participate in the culture of the country.

There is some conflict, however, in recent years regarding the role of the minister of culture as both protector of the arts in France and the person charged with making the arts more democratic. A recent influx of immigrants, in addition to foreign language and cultural products, has led many to question whether traditional French culture was being diluted by outside influences. This has prompted numerous ministers and government officials to propose and enact various related laws, including requiring the translation into French of advertisements in foreign languages, to established quotas dictating the French-language content of songs played on radio stations.

Cultural Sites & Landmarks

France is home to one of the greatest number of World Heritage Sites—thirty-three sites as of 2008—a list of culturally and naturally significant sites maintained by the United Nations Educational, Scientific and Cultural Organization (UNESCO). Some of the earliest inclusions include the Chartres Cathedral, famed for its Gothic architecture, the prehistoric sites and caves of the Vézère Valley, and the Palace of Versailles. Some of the newest additions—added in 2008—include the fortifications of Vauban, a series of historic, fortified structures, and the New Caledonia Barrier Reef (listed as the Lagoons of New Caledonia and its associated ecosystems), the world's second-longest coral reef.

Paris is often considered one of the leading cultural cities in the world, and is home to a wealth of France's cultural sites and landmarks. Cathédrale Notre Dame de Paris (Notre Dame Cathedral), built during the 12th century, is considered to be the very center of Paris, and, therefore, of France. (Road markers all over France tell the precise distance from a marker located at Notre Dame.) The cathedral is famous for its huge, stained-glass "rose windows," named for their shape, and for its gargoyles and Gothic architecture.

France's most well-known landmark is perhaps the Tour Eiffel, or the Eiffel Tower, in Paris. The iron tower was built by Gustave Eiffel in 1889 for the Expo in Paris exhibition. At the time it was the tallest structure ever built (a record it would hold until construction finished on New York City's skyscrapers in the 1930s). The tower

was intended to be only a temporary structure, and many at the time considered it an architectural eyesore. Nonetheless, it has become an enduring symbol of France, and is used today as a radio tower.

Napoleon Bonaparte (1769–1821), emperor of the first French Empire (1804–1814), is largely responsible for some of the other most prominent Parisian landmarks. "The Arc de Triomphe," or "grand triumphal arch," crowns the wide boulevard of the Champs-Elysees. It was commissioned by Napoleon to celebrate his victories on the battlefield. Under Napoleon, Paris also witnessed the construction of the golden-domed military hospital Les Invalides (which now holds his tomb) and the massive church Église de la Madeleine, built in the neoclassical style.

Paris is well-known for its many beautiful churches. In addition to Cathédrale Notre Dame de Paris, the Basilica of the Sacré-Cœur overlooks the city from atop Montmartre. It was built in memory of the fallen French soldiers of the Franco-Prussian War. Construction on Sacré-Cœur began in 1875 and was completed in 1914. A few miles north of the center of Paris is the hill of Montmartre. In addition to Sacré-Cœur, the hill is also famous for the artist's square and the Moulin Rouge night club.

The most famous shopping district of Paris is the Champs-Élysées Avenue, which stretches from the Place de la Concorde—the former location of the guillotine—to the Arc de Triomphe.. Many of the worlds most noted designers have boutiques along the Champs-Élysées. The traffic circle around the Arc at the end of the avenue connects all of the main streets of the Champs-Élysées Quarter and is itself a local landmark.

The educational hub of Paris is the Latin Quarter, which includes the University of Paris, also known as the Sorbonne. This quarter is known for its bookstores, cafes and public gardens.

More recently, former French President François Mitterrand (1916–1996) commissioned modern Paris landmarks during his time in office. These include the Louvre Pyramid, located in the plaza of the Louvre, and a new opera house and a massive arch in the La Défense area (the city's major business district). The latter resembles Napoleons' Arc de Triomphe. Like the Eiffel Tower in its day, Mitterrand's modern landmarks have had their detractors, but over time his contributions to the Paris landscape have become more accepted.

Outside of Paris, the Palais des Papes, or the old papal palace, can be found in the city of Avignon (once the home of the papacy) in the Provence region in the south for France. The historic center of Avignon, which includes the papal palace and a historic 12th-century bridge, was named a World Heritage Site in 1995. Provence is also home to some ancient stone amphitheatres from the days of the Roman Empire. In Normandy, the most famous landmarks include the Mont Saint-Michel monastery, an original World Heritage Site that is built on a mountain off the coast (and accessible only at low tide), the natural limestone arches along the coast at Etretat, and the famous "D-Day" beaches where Allied forces landed during World War II. France is also famous for its Loire Valley, a river valley and World Heritage Site that contains numerous historic towns and castles; it is known as the "garden of France."

Libraries & Museums

The French capital is home to the Musée d'Orsay and to the famed Louvre Museum, once a royal palace. It houses one of the largest art museums in the world and contains some of the world's most well-known pieces of art in its collection, including Leonardo Da Vinci's *Mona Lisa*, and the armless Roman marble statue *Venus de Milo*.

The National Library of France (Bibliothèque nationale de France), located in Paris, houses nearly 31 million documents. The origins of this national repository can be traced back to the 14th century.

Holidays

France's national holiday is the Fête Nationale (National Day), celebrated on July 14 in honor of the storming of the Bastille (July 14, 1789) during the French Revolution, and the Fête de

la Fédération (July 14, 1790), a day of national reconciliation.

Youth Culture

Young people in France are considered academically active, and rigorous study and hours of homework often preclude participation in sports and other activities outside school. University students in France have also developed a reputation for spearheading social movements and protests, dating back to the protests of 1968, in which students demonstrated against the rigidity of traditional French social and educational systems. The student protests spread to the French labor force and resulted in massive strikes that brought the country to a standstill, eventually leading to certain reforms.

In more recent years, the tradition of outdoor student-led demonstrations has evolved into more peaceful music festivals and concerts. Since the mid-1980s, June 21 is not only the official start of summer, but the official Fête de la Musique (festival of music) in France, with free concerts organized all over the country. Due to France's status as a premiere asylum destination, a significant percentage of French youth in the early 21st century is made up different ethnicities, largely from North Africa, the Caribbean and Arab nations. This multi-cultural mix is reflected in popular music, especially French rap and hip-hop music, as well as in popular slang.

SOCIETY

Transportation

France is considered a world leader in transport by rail. Its status was cemented in 1981 with the launch of the Train à Grande Vitesse (TGV, or High-Speed Train) that linked Paris and Lyon in only two hours. The immediate success of the project led to its rapid expansion all over France and eventual export of its technology to other countries. Today, an estimated 45,000 people use the TGV daily to commute from home to work, and the high-speed rail technology of the TGV also helped to bring European capitals closer: travel between London and Paris has been reduced to nearly two and a half hours. An estimated 20 million people travelled across Europe by TGV trains in 2005.

In addition to being a popular sport within the country—evidenced by the Tour de France, the world's biggest bicycle race—cycling also remains a popular mode of transportation in France. In Paris, an hourly rental system for public bicycles, called vélib (a combination of the words for "bicycle" and "freedom"), was created in 2004, and is a popular and environmentally friendly way of getting around town.

French drivers operate their vehicles on the right side of the road. The country has an extensive system of highways and roadways, and a large segment of the population owns automobiles for personal use.

Transportation Infrastructure

France has one of the world's densest transportation networks, with 146 kilometers (91 miles) of road and nearly six kilometers (four miles) of railway for every 160 square kilometers (62 square miles). Paris is the major hub of travel in and out of France, with two international airports, Orly and Roissy-Charles-de-Gaulle. Air France is one the leading European airlines and was ranked third worldwide in terms of international passenger transport since following its merger with KLM Royal Dutch Airlines in 2003.

Media & Communications

Only a handful of French companies work with several different types of media and entertainment, such as television, radio, daily newspapers, magazines and video games. These companies include Hachette-Lagardère (magazines, radio, satellite television,), Bertelsmann (magazines, radio and television), Bouygues (satellite and traditional broadcast television and telephony), and Vivendi Universal (broadcast, satellite and cable television and video games).

Radio France is the umbrella company for the France's public service radio stations and there are five national TV channels. All television and radio stations in France were once entirely state-owned. Since a loosening of this in the 1970s, however, non-government private TV and radio stations have outnumbered state-run stations, leading to more choice in programming. Television shows are regularly imported from other countries, especially the US, and played either with the sound dubbed (re-recorded) in French or in the original language with French subtitles. A law adopted in April 2008 states that all TV commercials on French state-owned stations was phased out by 2011, to coincide with the final switch from analog to digital broadcasting. Commercial television stations in France are still able to run advertising.

Internet and wireless cellular communications have broad penetration in France, with even public parks and Paris cafés providing offering free wireless Internet connections. However, computers in France are still considered to be primarily for work, and only around 55 percent of French households have a personal computer. As of 2008, and estimated 58.1 percent of the population nearly 36 million were Internet users.

SOCIAL DEVELOPMENT

Standard of Living

The majority of French people enjoy a high standard of living. The country ranked 20th overall in the 2014 Human Development Index, which is compiled by the United Nations.

Water Consumption

France faces few issues with the availability of clean water. In addition, water pollution is not a major problem. The country's water infrastructure and water quality laws are overseen by the Ministry of Interior, the Ministry of Ecology, Energy, Sustainable Development and Territorial Planning, and the Ministry of Health.

Education

French public education extends from kindergarten (école maternelle or maternal school) through university, and has produced a literacy rate of around 99 percent. Children, from ages six to 11, attend elementary school (école élémentaire).

The first level of secondary education, or collège, has students ages 11 to 15 and is equivalent to junior high or middle school in the United States. The second level of secondary education, the lycée, is equivalent to a U.S. high school and has three main tracks: general, technological, and professional.

Études supérieures ("superior studies") refers to post-secondary education, including vocational/technical training, university education, and studies to prepare for the elite Grandes Écoles (literally, "great schools") which produce most of France's top government and business leaders. In 2014, France had an estimated literacy rate of 99 percent.

Women's Rights

The failure to include women in France's Declaration of the Rights of Man was objected to as early as 1791, when activist Olympe de Gouges (1748–1793), also known as Marie Gouze, proposed her Declaration of the Rights of Woman and the Female Citizen. However, French women have been struggling to achieve equal rights ever since.

In the 19th century, French law recognized the family as the basic social unit, with the man as undisputed head of the household and legal authority over all family property (even property brought into the marriage by the wife). There was very little education available for girls; the first secondary schools for girls did not open until the 1860s, and many towns had to wait almost until the turn of the century for such a school. Higher education remained off limits to women until the late 19th century, but by 1914, around 10 percent of university students were women. Women finally won the right to vote in 1945, and it was not until the 1946 Constitution of the French Fourth Republic that women were finally granted the rights of equal opportunity and status.

While rights for women have substantially improved, women remain far from achieving true equality in contemporary French society. While 56 percent of civil servants in France are women,

they hold only an estimated 10 percent of the top civil service positions. Further, only 10 percent of chief executive officers (CEO) and 12 percent of parliament members in France are women. Inequalities in the workplace and the balancing of motherhood and career are factors. France maintains a generous maternity leave policy: new mothers are allowed to remain home with their newborns for several months, and are guaranteed to have the same job when they return to work. Domestic abuse also remains an issue, and forced marriages and female genital mutilation (FGM) has increased among immigrant populations in recent years.

Health Care

France has nationalized health care, but is establishing "Primary Care Trusts" to give responsibility back to local and regional authorities. Medical care is essentially free, paid by social security or medical insurance. Many private clinics and non-profit health organizations also exist.

GOVERNMENT

Structure

France's government is a democracy, operating on a mixed presidential system, in which a strong president serves as head of state but delegates much authority to a prime minister and cabinet whom he appoints. The president is elected by popular vote, and serves a five-year term. Duties include serving as commander-in-chief of the armed forces and appointing high officials including judges and senior civil servants.

France's parliament is made up of the National Assembly (Assemblée Nationale) and the Senate, and is responsible for all legislation. National Assembly members, known as deputies, are elected to five-year terms by popular vote in their individual districts. Senators serve for nine-year terms, and are elected by the local administrative units known as departments, by means of an electoral college.

France's judicial system is based on Roman law. Civil courts include ordinary courts for general cases, as well as specialized courts for handling matters such as commercial law. Criminal courts are divided among petty offences, misdemeanors, and serious crimes. The Assize Court is the only criminal court with trial by jury. The Supreme Court of Appeal is the highest court, but the Council of State serves as highest administrative court.

The nine-member Constitutional Council rules on the constitutionality of legislation and oversees elections.

Political Parties:

France's politics are strongly divided along left-right lines. Leftist parties include the Socialists, Communists, and Greens. Rightist parties include the neo-Gaullist Rally for the Republic (Rassemblement pour la République) and the hard-right National Front.

Local Government

Metropolitan France is organized into departments, which are grouped into twenty-two regions. Each region and department has its own council, elected by popular vote. Each department is further divided into districts (arrondisements), cantons, and communes. The mayors of the communes are in charge of municipal services and serve in parliament.

Judicial System

The French Supreme Court is known as the Court of Cassation. The court resides in Paris at the Hall of Justice. Lower courts are organized into two sections; civil courts and criminal courts. Civil courts oversee cases involving land disputes, employment disputes and social security. The Criminal Court is comprised of the Police Court for minor offenses and the Court of Sessions for felonies.

Taxation

Taxes in France are collected by the central government, local governments, and the social security association. Most corporations pay a standard tax rate of 33.1 percent. Individuals pay an income tax (impôt sur le revenu) which is determined annually and organized into seven categories. Local government's collect housing taxes and land taxes. The total number and variety of taxes imposed on French citizens has been a controversial political issue in recent years. France has one of the highest overall tax rates in Europe.

Armed Forces

The military of France, known as the French Armed Forces, is commanded by the president. It is comprised of the French army, navy, air force and gendarmerie. France possesses nuclear weapons and is estimated to have the third largest military budget in the world. Total annual military expenditures were an estimated €42.5 billion in 2010. The total number of active enlisted members in the French army is approximately 360,000.

Foreign Policy

Since 1945, France has been instrumental in promoting the vision of a united Europe, with its countries cooperating as member states within the EU, similar to the relationship among the states in the US. Once comprised only of countries in Western Europe, the EU has twenty-seven member states as of 2008, some of which are Eastern and Central European countries. The presidency of the EU is rotated among the member states every six months, and France held the presidency of the EU council in 2008.

France is one of five nuclear powers that include the United Kingdom (UK), the U.S., Russia and China, and sees its nuclear arsenal as a necessary deterrent to outside aggression, while working toward the eventual goals of disarmament and a ban on all nuclear testing. France maintains stable relations with all these countries, though relations with the US were somewhat strained following the 2003 Iraq War (France opposed the invasion and certain "war on terror" policies, such as extradition). As a permanent member of the UN Security Council (UNSC), France has participated directly in many UN peacekeeping operations. France is also one of the founding members of the North Atlantic Treaty Organization (NATO), which was formed after World War II in 1949 to preserve peace and security in the North Atlantic region.

France remains a global leader in humanitarian and foreign aid, especially regarding the development of Africa. In recent years, there has been an increase in Eastern European immigration—and subsequent rise in ethnic tension—and the French government has enacted laws to curb this influx. France is also involved in several international disputes, though the majority are territorial in nature, and of lesser status. They include disputes involving the territories of Mayotte, an overseas collectivity (claimed by the island nation of Comoros), and French Guinea, an overseas region of France in South America (disputed by Suriname), as well as various other islands and territorial claims in Antarctica.

Dependencies

The former colonies of Guadeloupe, Martinique, French Guiana (Guyana), and Reunion are considered overseas departments and are part of France proper.

Human Rights Profile

International human rights law insists that states respect civil and political rights, and also promote an individual's economic, social and cultural rights. The United Nations Universal Declaration on Human Rights (UDHR) is recognized as the standard for international human rights. Its authors sought the counsel of the world's great thinkers, philosophers, and religious leaders, and were careful to create a document that reflects the core values shared by every world culture. (To read this document or view the articles relating to cultural human rights, go to: http://www.udhr.org/UDHR/default.htm.)

France has always held human rights as a core value of its society. The equality of all people is an idea expressed by a number of French thinkers through the ages, one of the most famous being Voltaire. France was one of the first nations to draft a declaration proclaiming human rights. The Declaration of the Rights of Man was one of the results of the French Revolution of 1789, and is considered a template for other documents declaring international human rights, despite having addressed neither the rights of women nor the question of slavery. The declaration also made the people sovereign, ending once and for all the divine right of kings, so it is a key document in the history of democracy.

However, many human rights issues remain prevalent in modern day France. Foremost are the issues of police abuse and ethnic and religious discrimination, particularly involving the treatment of migrants and refugees. France's immigration policy has also been criticized by human rights groups for establishing an immigration quota, and certain religions such as the Church of Scientology and Jehovah's Witnesses are listed as cults by the French government. Non-governmental organizations (NGOs) have also raised the issue of detention center and prison conditions, as well as human trafficking, largely for the purposes of prostitution and domestic slavery.

ECONOMY

Overview of the Economy

France has one of the world's largest and most diversified economies, with strong agricultural, manufacturing, and service sectors. In 2014, the estimated gross domestic product (GDP) was €2 trillion ($2.6 trillion USD).

A leading exporter, France exports many durable goods. France is Europe's leading agricultural exporter, with products focusing many on grains and other foodstuffs. Other important market sectors are transportation, telecommunications, and financial services.

France is a leading member of the European Union. Over half its trade is with EU partners, though the United States, China, and Japan is also important. The economy has become increasingly market-driven, as governments have privatized state-run industries and allowed greater competition.

Yet, France has many serious economic problems, including slow growth. This is related to over-regulation, including labor laws that require a 35-hour work week. The unemployment rate is relatively high, at 9.7 percent in 2014.

Industry

Major industries in France include agribusiness, financial services, heavy manufacturing, automotive, aerospace, and tourism. France is home to many World-famous brands. Peugeot-Citroën and Renault are among the World's best-known car makers. In aerospace, France is a major player in Europe's Airbus Industrie consortium of aircraft manufacturers.

France has a large railroad system, operated by the National Society of French Railways (Société Nationale des Chemins de Fer Français). Many people own cars, but gasoline taxes are high in order to promote mass transit.

The country is a major maritime nation, with ports on the Atlantic and Mediterranean coasts. Among the largest are Marseilles on the Mediterranean, and Brest and Bordeaux on the Atlantic.

Labor

In 2014, France's unemployment rate was an estimated 9.7 percent. Widespread issues with unemployment among young people and minority groups were exacerbated by the impact of the 2008 global financial crisis. In 2009, the government unveiled a €26 billion stimulus package to spur economic growth in France.

Energy/Power/Natural Resources

France's greatest natural resources are agricultural fertility and extensive forests. Over half of the country is covered with rich farmland, and around 26 percent is forested. There is very little oil or natural gas in France and the country relies mostly on nuclear energy for its power.

Fishing

France's fishing industry makes up only a small part of its overall economy as it relates to agriculture. Nonetheless, the government has supported fuel subsidies and grants for fisherman, as well as negotiated to prevent the imposition of harsher catch limits on species such as tuna.

Forestry

France is the third most forested country in the European Union. A government operated forest management system has allowed for an increase in forest growth in recent decades. Although not a major contributor to the country's agricultural economy, France does export wood products, including hard woods such as oak, which is used in construction.

Mining/Metals

In recent years, the French mining industry has undergone a shift from being an industry existing under government regulation to one that is more influenced by private ownership and market forces. France's mineral reserves have decreased in recent decades, which has increased mineral imports and resulted in the closing of several mines. As an example, lead and zinc are no longer mined in France, and the country's industrial sector instead relies on imports from China and elsewhere.

Agriculture

France is one of the world's largest agricultural exporters, with around 680,000 farms that cover over half the country's area. Major crops include grains (wheat, corn, and barley), potatoes, and sugar beets. France is also a leading produce of wine, from regions such as Burgundy, Bordeaux, and Champagne.

Animal Husbandry

Livestock such as cattle, pigs, sheep, and goats are important contributors to France's agricultural economy.

Tourism

France is one of the world's leading tourist nations, with around 80 million foreign visitors annually. Tourism provides around 3.9 percent of France's GDP, creating around 2.8 million jobs directly. Tourism policy is handled by the Ministry of Tourism. In 2003, foreign tourists and visitors spent €32.3 billion ($42.8 billion USD) in France; approximately 83 million international travelers visited France in 2012. Visitors come to enjoy the high cultural life in cities such as Paris, as well as the nation's great natural beauty.

Lisa Rothstein, Eric Badertscher,
Lynn-nore Chittom

DO YOU KNOW?

- The national anthem is "La Marseillaise," a marching song composed during the French Revolution in 1792. It has been the national anthem since 1795.

- In addition to the Eiffel Tower, Gustave Eiffel also designed the interior structure of the Statue of Liberty. An exact replica of the statue sits on a bank of the Seine facing west toward New York City.

- There is a small lake beneath the Opéra de Paris Garnier, which was the inspiration for the underground waterways in Gaston Leroux's novel "The Phantom of the Opera" (1909).

Bibliography

Abram, David, and Greg Ward. *Rough Guide to France.* London: Rough Guides, 2013.

Asselin, Gilles, and Ruth Mastron. *Au Contraire! Figuring Out the French.* Boston: Intercultural Press, 2010.

Darnton, Robert. *The Great Cat Massacre: And Other Episodes in French Cultural History.* New York: Basic Books, 2009.

Downs, Laura Lee and Stéphane Gerson. *Why France? American Historians Reflect on an Enduring Fascination.* Ithaca, NY: Cornell University Press, 2007.

Fenby, Jonathan. *France on the Brink: A Great Civilization in a New Century.* New York: Arcade, 2014.

Haine, W. Scott. *Culture and Customs of France.* Portsmouth, NH: Greenwood Publishing Group, 2006.

Hewitt, Nicholas, Ed. *The Cambridge Companion to Modern French Culture.* New York: Cambridge University Press, 2003.

Jenkins, Cecil. *A Brief History of France.* Philadelphia: Running Press, 2011.

Price, Roger. *A Concise History of France.* Cambridge, UK: Cambridge University Press, 2005.

Robb, Graham. *The Discovery of France: A Historical Geography from the Revolution to the First World War.* New York: W. W. Norton & Company, 2007.

Williams, Nicola. *France.* Oakland, CA: Lonely Planet, 2015.

Works Cited

"The U.S. and NATO: Frequently Asked Questions." *U.S. Department of State.* http://www.state.gov/p/eur/rls/fs/14626.htm

"Profile of France," *Republique Francaise Ministerie des Affaires Europeens et Etrangeres.* http://www.diplomatie.gouv.fr/en/france_159/discovering-france_2005/profile-of-france_1977/france-foreign-policy_1403.html

"European Union Profile," *U.S. Department of State,* http://www.state.gov/p/eur/rls/fs/104648.htm

"Economy: Major Industries." *Republique Francaise Ministerie des Affaires Europeens et Etrangeres.* http://www.diplomatie.gouv.fr/en/france_159/discovering-france_2005/france-from-to-z_1978/economy_1981/major-industries_1424.html#sommaire_7

"Museums," *Republique Francaise Ministerie des Affaires Europeens et Etrangeres,* http://www.diplomatie.gouv.fr/en/france_159/discovering-france_2005/france-from-to-z_1978/culture_1979/museums_4412/the-world-most-famous-painting-has-the-louvre-all-aflutter_6824.html

"Economy of France, Its People, Culture and Flag." *Maps of the World.* http://www.mapsofworld.com/country-profile/france1.html

"The 50 largest French Cities." *Guy Kervella, European Editor, City Mayor Statistics,* http://www.citymayors.com/gratis/french_cities.html

"French Art History," *The University of North Carolina at Greensboro,* http://www.uncg.edu/rom/courses/dafein/civ/art.htm

http://minerals.usgs.gov/minerals/pubs/country/2001/frmyb01.pdf

http://en.wikipedia.org/wiki/Taxation_in_France

http://www.olis.oecd.org/olis/2005doc.nsf/LinkTo/NT00002E0A/$FILE/JT00187984.PDF

GERMANY

Introduction

Located in the heart of Europe, Germany has had a profound impact on the history, cultures, and economy of the region. Today, Germany boasts some of the highest levels of education, artistic exploration, economic productivity, and technological development in the world.

GENERAL INFORMATION

Official Language: German
Population: 80,996,685 (2014 estimate)
Currency: Euro
Coins: German currency has eight denominations: 1, 2, 5, 10, 20, and 50, as well as 1 Euro and 2 Euro coins.
Land Area: 137,847 square miles (357,021 square kilometers)
National Anthem: "Das Lied der Deutschen" ("Song of Germany")
Capital: Berlin
Time Zone: Central European Time Zone (GMT +1)
Flag Description: The German flag features three equally sized horizontal stripes of black, red, and yellow. The colors are significant in that they were featured on the flag of the Holy Roman Emperor in the 14th century that depicted a black eagle with a red beak and claws set against a yellow background.

Population

Germany is the second most populous country in Europe, after Russia. It was estimated in 2014 that 75 percent of the country's population was situated in urban areas. The country features many medium-sized cities. The North Rhine-Westphalia concentration of cities has created the Rurhstadt (Rurh City), with a population of about 5 million.

The cities of Berlin, Hamburg, and Bremen are the most densely populated "Länder" or states. The least densely populated are Mecklenburg-Vorpommern and Brandenburg.

North Rhine-Westphalia contains about one-fifth of the country's total population. About 100,000 Sorbs, a Slavic group (also known as Wends), live in the Brandenburg and Saxony area in the east. The Sorbs speak Lusatian, also called

Principal Cities by Population (2012 estimate):

- Berlin (3,500,000)
- Hamburg (1,800,000)
- Munich (1,400,000)
- Cologne (1,000,000)
- Frankfurt (687,107)
- Stuttgart (611,342)
- Düsseldorf (591,122)
- Dortmund (591,122)
- Essen (572,962)
- Bremen (546,952)

Wendish or Lusatian Sorbic. Many Germans also speak English as a second language.

Languages

The country's official language is German. Many Germans also speak English as a second language.

Native People & Ethnic Groups

Ethnic Germans are the native people of Germany. Ethnic Germans compose 91.5 percent of the population. Another 2.4 percent are Turkish, while Greek, Italian, Polish, Russian, Serbo-Croatian and Spanish ethnic groups account for approximately 6 percent of the population. In addition, a small Danish population lives near the northern border.

About 100,000 Sorbs, a Slavic group (also known as Wends), live in the Brandenburg and Saxony area in the east. The Sorbs speak Lusatian, also called Wendish or Lusatian Sorbic.

Religions

Approximately 35 percent of the population is Protestant, 34 percent is Roman Catholic, and roughly four percent is Muslim. In addition, up to 28 percent of the population is unaffiliated with any religion.

Climate

The northwestern coastal area has a marine climate, with warmer, moist air from the North Sea that brings warm summers and mild but cloudy winters. Most of Germany has a continental climate, with more variations in weather, but with generally warmer summers and colder winters. The Alpine region has a mountain climate, with lower temperatures and higher precipitation.

January is the coldest month, with an average temperature of 1.6° Celsius (35° Fahrenheit) in the north and -2° Celsius (28° Fahrenheit) in the south. In July, the northern temperature averages 16° to 18° Celsius (61° to 64° Fahrenheit) and the southern temperature averages 19.4° Celsius (67° Fahrenheit).

Most of the country receives 60 to 80 centimeters (24 to 31 inches) of precipitation annually. The greatest variation is in the north, where 2 meters (79 inches) is normal; and the area around Mainz, where only about 40 centimeters (16 inches) falls annually.

ENVIRONMENT & GEOGRAPHY

Topography

About the size of the American state of Montana, Germany is situated in the middle of central Europe. It is bounded on the west by the Netherlands, Belgium, Luxembourg, and France; on the north by Denmark; on the east by the Czech Republic and Poland; and on the south by Switzerland and Austria.

Helgoland, Germany's only large island, lies 43.5 miles (70 kilometers) offshore in the North Sea. There are also numerous small islands, including the Frisian Islands.

The northern part of the mainland is flat, the central and southern regions are hilly, and the southern border with Austria is formed by the German Alps. The highest point is the Zugspitze in the Alps, at 9,721 feet (2,963 meters). The lowest point is Neuendorf bei Wilster, at 11.61 feet (3.54 meters) below sea level in Schleswig-Holstein, on the border with Denmark.

The Danube, rising in the Black Forest and emptying into the Black Sea in Romania 1,770 miles (2,848 kilometers) away, is the second-longest river in Europe (the Volga is the longest).

Canals link the Danube to the Main, the Oder, and the Rhine. The Danube, the Rhine-Main-Danube canal and the Danube-Black Sea Canal constitute the Trans-Europe Waterway.

The Rhine, at 820 miles (1,319 kilometers), is much shorter than the Danube. It rises in southeast Switzerland, flows west to form part of the border with Germany, and then turns north through western Germany and the Netherlands to empty into the North Sea.

Other major rivers include the Elbe, which rises in the Czech Republic and flows north through Germany, emptying into the Baltic Sea at Cuxhaven; and the Oder, which rises in the Czech Republic, flows north through Poland, forms part of the northern German-Polish border and empties into the Baltic Sea.

Der Bodensee, or Lake Constance, is formed where the Rhine descends from the Alps and broadens before continuing north. The lake is bordered by Germany, Austria, and Switzerland. With an area of 220 square miles (570 square kilometers), it is the second-largest freshwater lake in Europe (after Lake Ladoga).

The Kiel Canal, nearly 62 miles (100 kilometers) long, is the world's busiest artificial waterway. The canal joins the North and Baltic seas.

Berlin is by far the largest city in Germany. Other major cities include Hamburg, Munchen (Munich), Cologne, Frankfurt, and Essen.

Plants & Animals

Like much of Europe, Germany has few remaining wild species and a long list of endangered animals, including the lynx and the wolf, which has been reintroduced. The problem is especially bad in Germany because of its many roads, lack of a speed limit and high noise pollution. To protect its remaining wildlife, Germany has instituted a vigorous program of protection.

One of the most innovative programs is the construction of "green bridges" over roadways. These structures, planted with grasses, shrubs and trees, provide a safe way for animals to cross busy highways. In addition, amphibians are protected by the construction of culvert-like (but noise-reduced) underpasses. Roadside fences also provide protection for animals.

CUSTOMS & COURTESIES

Greetings

A typical greeting in Germany is the phrase "Guten tag," meaning "Good day." It is commonly used to address all individuals encountered during the course of the day. In the evening, "Guten abend," or "Good evening," may be used. The formal greeting for goodbye is "Auf wiedersehn;" while the casual parting is "Tschuss." An extremely useful word is "Bitte" which functions not only as "Please," but also as "You're welcome" or "Can I help you?"

Respect is a matter of principle in Germany. With the exception of the younger generation, surnames should be used when addressing strangers until an invitation is extended to use a first name. There are two forms of address, the formal greeting being "Sie," or "You," which should be used with virtually everyone. Close friends and children may be referred to as "Du," which is the familiar form of "Sie." In Germany, it may take years to shift from "Sie" to "Du" while addressing colleagues or acquaintances. In addition, the equivalent of the formal title of "Mr." in German is "Herr," whereas "Mrs." is translated as "Frau." If an individual is a doctor, then that formal phrasing precedes that acknowledgment, such as "Herr Dr."

Gestures & Etiquette

Germans traditionally greet others with handshakes. It is also common to shake hands as a farewell gesture. Refusing to shake hands would be considered quite rude. Also, it is considered to be polite if the man waits for the woman to extend her hand first before shaking it. Often, if there are men and women present, the men will acknowledge the women first out of respect. Reaching over or under another's handshake is considered impolite in Germany.

Other commonly used hand signals include pointing the index finger at one's own head, which indicates an insult being directed at another person. In Germany, the hand sign for wishing good luck is to squeeze the thumb in between the index and middle fingers, rather than crossing fingers as is customary in American culture. Among younger people, these rules are not strictly observed.

Eating/Meals

Unlike the majority of Western Europe, Germany's traditional main meal has always been lunch, even during the week. For decades, German children and working parents typically came home for a full cooked lunch, and then returned to school and work. This practice has been changing in recent years. Lunch and dinner traditions have also been switched, given the changing schedules of the modern workforce. Hence, dinner is now usually a cooked meal, whereas lunch is a simpler meal similar to breakfast.

Typically, meals can be two to seven courses, including a vorspeise (appetizer), suppe (soup), hauptspeise (main dish), beilagen (side dishes) and nachspeise (desserts). Germans frequently drink wine, beer or champagne with their meals, depending on the style of the meal. In addition, families might organize afternoon parties with pastries and coffee for friends and families during the weekends. German hosts always offer coffee to guests, as it is a very common beverage. Saying "Guten appetit" or "Good appetite," is a polite way to start the meal when eating with others.

Another German tradition is the beer garden, or Hofbräu. The Hofbräu shaus in Munich is one of the oldest and most famous breweries and beer gardens in the world. it serves thousands of tourists every year. In addition to the original Hofbräu beer, the restaurant serves regional Bavarian specialties and German pretzels. The convivial atmosphere also comes from the folk musicians who perform there every day.

Whereas Germans used to be very traditional in consuming sit-down meals, there are now numerous "der schnellimbiss," or fast food stalls found throughout urban areas. A typical meal served at these stalls includes bratwurst and other sausages. The most popular fast food in Germany is the kebab, or pita filled with spicy lamb, vegetables and yogurt sauces, found at the Turkish "schnellimbiss" stands. The popularity of these stands has increased in recent years; there are roughly 1,500 Turkish stands in Berlin. Given the influx of Turkish residents, Turkish restaurants are widespread in Germany. These restaurants specialize in serving Mediterranean meat and vegetable dishes, such as feta artichoke casserole, braised lamb cooked in a clay pot, and Turkish pastries.

Visiting

When visiting a German home, whether for a dinner party or other special events, guests typically bring flowers or wine. Often, they unwrap these gifts for the hosts, who might be occupied with other preparations. Gift giving is an integral part of German culture, and friends frequently present small gifts when meeting for coffee or when coming back from a trip abroad.

During the winter holidays, families typically visit each branch of the family and share meals and gifts together. However, unannounced visits between neighbors are not customary, except for among college students in dormitory housing. Generally, Germans pride themselves on punctuality, so guests should arrive as close to the set time as possible. In addition, it is considered proper etiquette for men to always stand when a woman enters the room.

LIFESTYLE

Family

Germany families tend to be close, and parents emphasize orderliness, responsibility, and a strong work ethic. Large families have not been common in Germany for quite some time, and the average family has no more than two children. The average age for marriage is the late twenties. It is common practice for German couples to reside together before marriage, and even to live together permanently without marrying. Typical wedding ceremonies are civil and are performed at the town hall rather than at church. Some couples prefer to have both a secular and religious ceremony. Wedding rings are worn on the right hand in Germany, rather than the American style of wearing them on the left.

Housing

Only 40 percent of Germans own their own homes, and the majority of Germans in urban areas live in apartments. As such, high-rise apartment buildings are common in large cities. In rural areas there is a much wider range of housing, from historic country estates, mansions and castles to farmhouses.

Traditionally, many Germans in rural villages and towns lived above their own stores, though this practice is much less common today. Overall, most Germans live in single-family houses or apartments.

Although the federal government provides subsidies for housing, Germany has developed a small homeless population. In the 1990s, approximately three million families received federal housing aid for rent or mortgages that were disproportionate in relation to household salaries. In the years before and after unification between East and West Germany, there was also a housing crisis in urban areas such as Berlin, owing to the influx of refugees. The German government responded by building hundreds of thousands of apartments. The government is also responsible for upgrading and maintaining apartment complexes.

Generally, German families are known for their close attention to hygiene and cleanliness, which is particularly apparent in personal homes and in the general maintenance of apartment complexes. This also extends to recycling, which is highly sophisticated in Germany, and color-coded containers are found on the streets and in apartment complexes for separating colored glass, clear glass, plastics, paper and miscellaneous other items.

Food

Although German cuisine has traditionally been heavily meat-based, modern cuisine has become increasingly lighter and more international. German cuisine also varies by region, with some local dishes heavily influenced by other European cultures, particularly Austria and Switzerland. For breakfast, or frühstück, fresh whole-grain rolls, often purchased daily from the artisan bakers that are found throughout Germany, are commonly eaten. These rolls are accompanied by spreads such as marmalade, butter and fruit preserves. In addition, sliced cold meats such as ham and salami are served along with cheese. Muesli, a breakfast cereal of rolled oats, nuts and fruits, is also a popular breakfast item.

Pork is the most popular meat consumed in Germany, followed by beef and chicken. Many meats are served pot-roasted or in sausage form. In fact, Germany is a major producer of sausage, which is a main ingredient for lunches and dinners. Trout, perch and herring often form the basis for popular seafood dishes. Winter vegetables, such as cabbages, carrots and peas, are common ingredients in German cuisine. Sauerkraut, or fermented cabbage, is a popular side dish served with meats. Healthy whole grain breads are also very popular, and are most often made from a variety of flours and seeds.

In Bavaria, spannferkel, or roasted baby pig, is a popular dish, as is handkaes, a cheese and sour cream mixture served with meat. In sauerbraten, a major German dish originating in the Black Forest region, beef is left marinating for two days in red wine vinegar. After being dried and salted, it is prepared with carrots, onions, and potatoes, then topped with a sauce made of sour cream. It is served with potato dumplings.

German desserts are also prepared by artisan bakers, who often study for many years in order to become master bakers and pastry chefs. Fruit cakes are popular, such as the Black Forest cake, which is a dark chocolate cake filled with pitted cherries, whipped cream and kirschwasser liqueur (fruit brandy). The cake is then topped with shaved bittersweet chocolate. The Dresdner stöllen is a popular holiday cake that is shaped like a swaddled baby and sprinkled with confectioner's sugar.

Life's Milestones

As with many Western cultures and societies, milestones and celebrations in Germany can vary depending on religion. For example, baptisms and confirmations are common practices in Germany for the Catholic and Protestant populations. Also, baby showers and wedding showers, largely based on American traditions, are becoming more popular even though they are not traditionally part of German culture. Overall, marriage ceremonies are mostly civil, as opposed to religious, in contemporary German society.

The German Humanist Association promotes a secular rite of passage known as Jugendweihe. Once widely practiced in the former East Germany, Jugendweihe is considered an alternative to confirmation, and celebrates a child's fourteenth birthday. Also known as Jugendfeier (youth ceremony), it is now mostly celebrated with parties and presents. Generally, education is considered a privilege in Germany, and the successful completion of the challenging German abitur, or high school examination, is considered a significant achievement.

CULTURAL HISTORY

Art & Architecture

German architecture was influenced by other European cultures, and was first developed during the rule of Charlemagne (742–814), who eventually controlled all of Western Europe. The first notable instance of German architecture appears around 800 CE with the construction of the Aachen Cathedral. The architectural style of the church closely resembles a Roman church in Ravenna, showing how early German architecture imitated Roman architecture.

Beginning in the 13th century, German architecture was influenced by the Gothic style, also known as the "French style" at the time. Characteristics of this style include vaulted ceilings supported by arches and the use of flying buttresses, a support structure that commonly projects from a wall. This style is evident in many of Germany's historical churches and cathedrals. One of the most famous examples of this architectural style is Cologne Cathedral—once considered the tallest structure in the world—which was based on the Amiens Cathedral in France.

The Italian Renaissance brought a new style of humanist influence to German art and architecture. The artist Albrecht Dürer (1471–1528), influenced by the Italian painters, became a leading artist in northern Europe. He incorporated Italian techniques of color and the minute details of landscape painting into his art. Dürer also created countless engravings, drawings and woodcuts during his lifetime. In fact, his numerous woodblock prints were some of the first works of art to be created in mass production, a result of the innovations in printing in Germany during the 15th century.

The Protestant Reformation in Germany coincided with a decline in the arts. During this time, promising portraiture artists such as Hans Holbein (c. 1497–1543) left Germany to seek employment in England. Following this period, Germany was once again influenced by French art and architecture during the Baroque period, popularized in 17th and early 18th centuries. St. Michael's Cathedral in Munich is an example of the influence of Baroque architecture in Germany. In addition, many German aristocrats modeled their castles on the architectural style of the French Palace of Versailles. For example, the Pommersfelden castle in Germany, constructed in 1715, features elaborate ornamentation in the Baroque style.

In the late 19th and early 20th centuries, artists and architects broke with tradition and developed simple lines that demonstrated functionality. This included the emergence of the German Romanticism movement. Artists of this movement found greater value in beauty, intellect and humor in art and society, and also appreciated simplicity in art. Landscape artist Casper David Friedrich (1774–1840) is often considered the leading figure of German Romanticism. His painting *Landscape in the Silesian Mountains* captures the melancholic mood typical of the movement.

The Bauhaus school was developed by Walter Gropius (1883–1969) in Germany in the early 20th century. The school, particularly influential in architecture, demonstrated the close relation between art and engineering. Ultimately, the students of Bauhaus were taught that beauty derives from function. German architect Ludwig Mies van der Rohe (1886–1969) helped pioneer the Bauhaus style in modern architecture. In addition, abstract expressionism also took hold in Germany, challenging classical rules of art. Auguste Macke (1887–1914), Max Beckmann (1884–1950), and Franz Marc (1880–1916) were prominent painters in this style.

An explosion of modern cutting-edge architecture and design took place in Germany in the late 20th century, particularly after the fall of the Berlin Wall. Architects were faced with the dilemma of constructing new buildings or renovating existing cultural landmarks that had decayed during communist rule.

This is particularly true of Berlin. The eastern and western halves of the city maintain distinctive architecture, reflecting the differing ambitions of East and West Germany during the division of the country. Even prior to the division, the eastern boroughs of Berlin tended to be home to more working class residents, and were eventually associated with slums. The Prenzlauer Berg in East Germany had a negative reputation; however, the area has become more developed since reunification. The western boroughs of the city, on the other hand, tended to house wealthy Berliners in upscale residential developments.

In addition, the Sony Center complex was a famous building that was redeveloped. The new design combines older stone architecture with contemporary additions, such as a glass roof and walls that have sails arranged in an intricate design throughout the roof structure. As exemplified by the Sony complex, Berlin is now a city where steel structures, glass walls and baroque exteriors can be found in the same building.

Music

Germany has a significant role in the history of classical music, thanks to the major composers the nation has produced since the late Renaissance. German music was also influenced by Martin Luther's Protestant reforms, which included a revision of music's role in church. Among his numerous contributions, he incorporated the Lutheran chorale into the service in 1524. This chorale is commonly known as the congregational hymn today. Luther's followers also introduced the cantata, a vocal composition accompanied by instruments, into religious services.

Baroque composer Johann Sebastian Bach (1685–1750) was one of Germany's most renowned composers in the early 18th century. In particular, he perfected the cantata style introduced by the followers of Lutheranism. Some of his best pieces include the *Well-Tempered Clavier, Goldberg Variations, Brandenburg Concertos, Cantata No. 4, St. Matthew's Passion* and the *Mass in B Minor.* In talent and fame, Bach's counterpart in German musical history is Ludwig van Beethoven (1770–1827), although their styles are quite different. In spite of his progressive deafness, Beethoven composed nine major symphonies, five piano concertos, 16 string quartets, 30 piano sonatas, and numerous important compositions in other forms. Among his best-known works are the *Ninth Symphony, Emperor Concerto, Fidelio,* and the *Moonlight Sonata.*

German 19th century opera is best exemplified in the works of Carl Maria von Weber (1786–1826) and Richard Wagner (1813–1883). Weber's *Der Freishütz* established Germany's reputation for Romantic opera, which is characterized by a plot drawn from medieval history with supernatural happenings that affect the fate of human protagonists. Wagner created musical dramas that also bore weight on contemporary politics and thought. His best-known operas are the epic *Ring of the Nibelung, The Valkyrie,* and *Tristan and Isolde.* His revolutionary departure from classical styles influenced many 20th century composers, and impacted the rise of late 19th century German nationalist politics.

Drama & Dance

By the 19th century, German drama held a central position in European culture. Prominent playwrights of the period include Johann Wolfgang von Goethe (1749–1832) and Friedrich Schiller (1759–1805). Schiller was influenced by Greek tragedy and by Shakespearean drama. Goethe's *Faust* represents the idealism and skepticism of the 18th century. German expressionism emerged in the 20th century and focused on the essence of humanity, often outside of organized society. For example, expressionist playwright Georg Kaiser's (1878–1945) *From Morning to Midnight* removes a man from his bourgeois daily life in order to focus on his thoughts and feelings.

Bertolt Brecht (1898–1956) was the most prominent playwright in 20th century German drama. Brecht thought that diminishing focus on plot would encourage the audience to think carefully about the ideas presented in the play. In the 1930s, Brecht adopted communism and wrote politically controversial plays throughout the rest of his career.

Modern dance in Germany has its roots in the performances of American dancer Isadora Duncan (1877–1927), who performed in Germany in the 1920s. During that decade, modern dance in Germany was known as "dance of expression." Dance theorist Rudolf Laban (1879–1958) directed dance theatre in Berlin in the 1930s. He argued that society had corrupted man's sense of self, and that only through dance could man regain a kinship with the cosmos. In particular, Laban formed the movement of "free dance" that was performed without music. Modern dance gained popularity until the rise of Nazi Germany, only to experience a resurgence in the 1960s.

Literature

Germany has a rich literary history. The Old High German (500–1050 CE) and Middle High German (1050–1300 CE) periods of the German language produced translations of the Bible into the German vernacular. Courtly and romantic epics and poetry also characterized the latter period, including the *Nibelungenlied* ("Song of the Nibelungen"), a national epic of narrative poetry, and Gottfried von Strassburg's *Tristan*, a retelling of the Arthurian legend of Tristan and Isolde.

The Early New High German (1350–1650 CE) period witnessed a transformation in the production and dissemination of literature through the invention of moveable type printing by Johannes Gutenberg (c. 1400–1468). During this period, Martin Luther's religious reforms were extended to literature. He printed the Bible in a vernacular form that was accessible for the most ordinary citizen in 1534. Luther's translation is considered a significant landmark in German literature. This era also included German poet Ulrich von Hutton (1488–1523) and Conradus Celtes (1459–1508), the country's first poet laureate.

Romanticism, or the focus on the individual, had a strong movement on German literature in the late 18th and early 19th centuries. Often, Romanticism incorporated themes of travel and nature, along with the adaptation of mythology. Famous writers during this period include Ludwig Tieck (1773–1853), Friedrich Hölderlin (1770–1843) and E.T.A. Hoffmann (1776–1822), as well as famous Romantic poet Heinrich Heine (1797–1856). In the late 19th century, German poets and novelists were influenced by French symbolist poets Charles Baudelaire (1821–1867) and Stéphane Mallarmé. German philosopher Friedrich Nietzsche (1844–1900) in particular had a profound impact on 20th-century German literature with his secular philosophy.

Perhaps the most exemplary German novelist of the early 20th century is Thomas Mann (1875–1955). His novel *The Magic Mountain* demonstrates the angst and identity crises that Europe experienced before the onset of the First World War. In addition, the German novelist Franz Kafka (1883–1924) continues to be widely read. The term "Kafkaesque" derives from the themes in his work, which often depicts the irrational element in society stemming from the complications of bureaucracy. Since the mid 20th century, modern German authors have been recognized worldwide, particularly Günter Grass (1927–2015), who received the Nobel Prize in Literature in 1999.

CULTURE

Arts & Entertainment

The arts are prevalent in contemporary German society, and the performing arts and museums are subsidized at the federal and local level throughout Germany. Arts festivals are widespread. Many of the 100-plus yearly music festivals are held in honor of musicians such as Bach (Thuringia, in March) and Richard Wagner (Bayreuth, July). Other festivals showcase a specific music genre, such as the Stuttgart (April) and Berlin (July) jazz festivals.

In addition, nearly 120,000 performances take place in Germany annually, drawing approximately 35 million attendees. Collectively, the sixteen federal states in Germany contribute approximately $2 billion (USD) annually to ensure successful operations of theaters, opera houses and symphonies. The arts in Germany are considered progressive and highly attuned with current trends, particularly in Berlin.

Contemporary German theater is generally regarded as intellectual. Often, directors and playwrights aim to engage the viewer in cutting-edge political and social issues. The Volksbühne Berlin Theater stages productions of contemporary playwrights such as Thomas Ostermeier and Frank Castorf. These productions typically attract both younger and older audiences. Also, German theater professionals usually undergo extensive apprenticeships, education and training.

German music aficionados have many opportunities to attend concerts throughout the country. In fact, the active presence of roughly 140 orchestras points to the continued demand for music performances and the popularity of classical music. In Berlin, in particular, the impressive Berliner Philharmoniker plays in the Philharmonic concert hall in the Kulturforum, a collection of cultural buildings and venues. Berlin is also home to three major opera houses: the German Opera, the Berlin State Opera and the Comic Opera. In addition, Germany sponsors radio orchestras that perform live for stations that commission works regularly throughout the year. Contemporary classical music is also well received in Germany.

German cinema in the 21st century has been attributed with healing the scars left by the division of East and West Germany. The film *Good Bye Lenin!* won the prize for best film in Germany in 2003. It reveals both the comedy and tragedy of transitioning from life in East Berlin to life in a united Berlin. Another film that works to reconcile the wounds inflicted by the censorship of the arts under communist rule in East Berlin is *Das Leben der Anderen.* The film, which tells the story of a secret policeman and a playwright and an actress who are under surveillance for possible subversive art in the 1980s, received an Oscar in 2006.

Fasching ("Winter Carnival") occurs just before Lent. Fall festivals include the Rhineland's Rhine in Flames, with fireworks displays from barges on the river. Oktoberfest, Munich's lager festival, is chaotic. Families prefer the Christmas fairs held in many places, including Berlin, Munich, Lübeck, Münster, Nuremberg, and Heidelberg.

Sports

Sports are also an important entertainment. Germany leads the world in track and field, tennis, cycling and Formula One auto racing. Nearly every community offers a schwimmbad (swimming pool), and the Deutscher Sportbund (German Sports Federation) sponsors physical fitness programs.

Football (soccer) is the national sport, with thousands of amateur clubs and numerous professional teams playing heavily attended matches every week. The German national team has won the World Cup three times. Bayern Munich is one of the world's top football clubs.

Other popular sports include tennis; skiing in the German Alps; winter sports such as luge, bobsledding, and figure skating; hiking in the mountains; and windsurfing and sailing on Germany's many lakes and rivers.

Cultural Sites & Landmarks

Despite extensive reconstruction after two world wars, Germany maintains numerous landmarks and cultural sites. The country is home to 33 United Nations Educational, Scientific and Cultural Organization (UNESCO) World Heritage Sites. The Cologne and Aachen Cathedrals are listed for their architecture as well as interior art, as is the Bauhaus, or "building school," in which the famed Bauhaus style was developed and taught.

Other World Heritage Sites include the frontiers of the Roman Empire, which are marked and preserved in Germany, and the city of Trier. Founded in 16 BCE, Trier is Germany's oldest city and home to numerous monuments. In fact, Trier is believed the longest-established city in the world. Famous castles designated as World Heritage Sites include Wartburg Castle, constructed in central Europe's feudal period, and the castles of Augustusburg and Falkenlust, located in Brühl.

Although there are other historically significant castles in Germany, the most famous may be the Neuschwanstein Castle, built in the 19th century. Commissioned by Ludwig II (1845–1886), then king of Bavaria, it is located near the Austrian border in the German state of Bavaria. It is known for its picturesque setting, as the castle is surrounded by Alpine lakes and mountains.

Germany's role in the Protestant Reformation is celebrated by memorials to Martin Luther in Eisleben and Wittenburg, both considered World Heritage Sites. Its deacute;cor demonstrates the affluence of 18th-century Germany. In addition, several town centers are listed as World Heritage Sites, such as the Old Town of Quedlinburg, Stralund, Wismar, Regensburg, Bremen and Bamberg.

Berlin's tumultuous 20th century history as a wartime capital, then a divided city inside the former East Germany, and now the capital of a reunified country makes it an important cultural study in contrasts. There is a dense cluster of landmarks there, including the Brandenburg Gate and a remnant of the Berlin Wall.

A fragment of the Berlin Wall remains as one last symbol of communism, the Cold War, and the forced division of the city and its people. The wall was torn down in 1989 and 1990.

The reunified German government reconstructed a 70-meter (230-foot) portion of the wall, using steel and fragments from the original wall. Today, the Berlin Wall Memorial allows visitors to peer through slits to experience the feeling of separation felt by Germans for almost 30 years.

There are also many famous natural landmarks in Germany. These include the Black Forest in southern Germany. The Garden Kingdom of Dessau-Wörlitz is a celebrated monument from the Enlightenment that features landscape design with manicured English gardens as well as land preserves.

Libraries & Museums
Germany is home to hundreds of cultural institutions. The Deutsches Museum (German Museum), located in Munich, is regarded as the largest museum of technology and science in the world, while the Senckenberg Natural History Museum, located in Frankfurt am Main, is considered to be the largest natural history in the country.

The most frequented museum in Germany is the Jewish Museum in Berlin that traces the history of Judaism in Germany and documents life for Jews in Nazi Germany through the Holocaust. It has extensive genealogical collections, a library, art galleries and visiting exhibitions. At the Pergamonmuseum, also in Berlin, visitors can see the entire reconstructed Pergomon Altar and Ishtar's Gate as it was reconstructed from its original site in Babylon.

The German National Library, the national repository, will release the German Digital Library in 2011. The inventory of the library itself includes over 24 million items.

Holidays
The Day of Unity, observed on October 3, commemorates the reunification of East and West Germany in 1990.

Youth Culture
Berlin is arguably the most progressive German city in terms of underground youth culture, with trends continually evolving in music, design and

art. German youth music is often attributed with setting the worldwide scene for trance music, a movement spearheaded by prominent artist Paul van Dyk. Berlin is also known for its punk bands, such as Chicks on Speed. In addition, the most famous techno party in the world takes place in Berlin—the Love Parade typically draws over one million ravers. Berlin is also known throughout Europe for its underground clubs and bars.

Although Berlin is the center of the cutting-edge club scene, other German cities have a vibrant youth culture, particularly Hamburg, Cologne and Munich. In Cologne, the "Belgian Quarter" neighborhood is famous for its retro bars and international cafés. In Munich, there are underground art groups that organize ongoing exhibits as well as innovative film houses that produce independent avant-garde films.

Overall, German youth culture is very much influenced by American youth culture and other European nations. For example, German rap or hip-hop, popularized since the 1990s by bands such as Die Fantasischen Vier, has been influenced by American rap. In addition, Germany has numerous music video television stations, including German MTV and VIVA, with programming comparable to popular American networks.

SOCIETY

Transportation

Germany has the highest traffic volume on its roadways of any other European country. Although there is no legal speed limit on the Autobahn, German authorities suggest 130 kilometers per hour (80 miles per hour) as a good standard; however, vehicles may travel at speeds between 160–180 km/h (90 to 110 mph). Seat belts are required by law, both in the front and back seats of vehicles. In cities and towns, the speed limit is usually around 50 km/h (around 30 mph), and on highways other than the autobahn, the limit is usually 100 km/h (around 60 mph). Cell phone use while driving is prohibited; it is also illegal to pass another vehicle on the right.

Many streets in Germany feature bike lanes to accommodate bicyclists, who generally have the right of way. Bike lanes are also featured on many of the country's sidewalks.

Public transportation is considered extremely efficient in Germany. The Duetsche Bahn railway system has an extensive timetable for express trains from domestic cities to destinations throughout Europe and beyond. The InterCity Express (ICE) and InterCity (IC) and EuroCity (EC) operate multiple travel routes within and outside of Germany. The ICE charges extra for its premier fast-train service.

In cities, the bus and metro systems are also considered efficient. In Berlin, the U-Bahn and S-Bahn service the city and its environs with closely spaced inner-city stations, as well as stations that extend to immediate areas such as Potsdam and Oranienburg. In addition, the bus system in Berlin is considered relatively safe and clean, and is widely used by the public and tourists.

Transportation Infrastructure

The highway system in Germany is a sophisticated network of roads known as the autobahn. In Germany, speed limits are flexible and generally not enforced. City driving is complicated in urban centers because of traffic jams and lack of adequate parking. Bicycles are another common form of transportation, and cycle lanes are found throughout urban centers.

In 2009, there were 550 airports in Germany. As of 2008, the country's busiest airport, Frankfurt, was the third most-used airport in Europe. The next-largest airport in Germany is in Munich. An early 21st-century goal in Germany is to increase links between the airports and rail systems. The Frankfurt, Cologne-Bonn, and Dusseldorf airports are connected to the high-speed rail system. In 2008–2009, there were over 24,000 kilometers (nearly 15,000 miles) of railway track in Germany.

Media & Communications

Germany has a reputation for having a sophisticated media network, and freedom of the press is taken very seriously. As a country that reads extensively, Germany takes interest in current events and quality reporting. There are dozens of newspapers published daily in Germany. *Die Zeit*, published in Hamburg, and *Die Welt*, published in Berlin, are two well-known examples. Most newspapers in Germany are also published on the Internet daily, although daily circulation is still quite high. The weekly news magazine *Der Spiegel* offers translations of headline articles in English.

Germany's public and private television networks are highly acclaimed in Europe. There are two national channels, ARD and ZDF, three international channels, and multiple special interest channels. Cologne is considered a media hub, and numerous television stations are located there. WDR, RTL, VIVA and VOX all have headquarters in Cologne. Overall, Germany's television market is considered the largest in Europe, with nearly 35 million households. Radio continues to be popular in Germany. In fact, there are approximately 360 radio stations in the country. In addition, there were over 65 million Internet users as of 2009.

SOCIAL DEVELOPMENT

Standard of Living
In 2014, the Human Index Ranking of Germany was 6th (out of 187 countries).

Water Consumption
The quality of drinking water in Germany between the years 2005 and 2007 was rated as "good" to "very good" by the Federal Environment Agency (UBA) and the Federal Minister for Health (BMG). In 2007, the average annual cost of drinking water supplies per household was approximately €190. In 2004, the average daily amount of water used per individual was around 127 liters, representing a 14 percent decline from the daily average usage in 1990. Annually, the country uses approximately 21 percent of its renewable freshwater supply (2004). In 2000, 96 percent of wastewater in Germany was treated with the highest European Union (EU) purification standard.

Education
According to research from 2009, German males and females spend an average of 16 years in school, from primary to tertiary education. As of 2003, the literacy rate for both men and women was 99 percent. In 2009, education expenditures accounted for 4.9 percent of the country's GDP.

Education is compulsory for children between the ages of six and 15 (or 16 in some Länder). This covers primary education for four to six years, and lower secondary school.

After lower secondary school, a student must be enrolled in a full-time school, a full-time vocational school, or in a program of part-time school and part-time vocational training until 18 years of age.

The August–to-July school year lasts from 188 to 206 days. Schools operate mostly in the mornings, and in some Länder, school is in session six days a week.

German students wishing to attend university take either the Arbitur, a final exam, or an aptitude test known as Begabtenprüfung. In 2007, approximately 432,500 qualified for entrance into higher education institutions, representing a 4.6 percent increase from the number who qualified in 2006.

The nation boasts numerous universities. The oldest university in Germany is Ruprecht Karls Universität in Heidelberg, founded in 1386. It has produced several Nobel Prize winners, the most recent being Bert Sakmann, who received the prize for medicine in 1991. Karlsruhe University is a center of technological research. It was here that Heinrich Hertz developed radio technology and Ferdinand Redtenbacher founded the field of mechanical engineering.

Historic figures who have taught at German universities include Jacob and Wilhelm Grimm, Wilhelm Conrad Roentgen, Robert Koch, Immanuel Kant, and Martin Luther.

Women's Rights
Women are guaranteed full and equal rights and protection by law in Germany, beginning with the granting of suffrage in 1919. Germany also has a designated federal ministry that works to

maintain and supervise equal rights for women. German federal law also requires that women and men receive equal compensation for equal work. However, following German unification, women were particularly affected by rising unemployment rates, and women's salaries remain approximately 30 percent lower than their male counterparts.

Germany is sensitive to creating opportunities for women in both the humanities and the sciences. The federal ministry that oversees women's rights awards the Gabriele Müntzer Prize annually to women artists. In addition, the Frauenkulturbüro NRW, or the Women's Culture Bureau, helps fund the work of women in the arts. The German Research Foundation (DFG) is committed to the advancement of women in the sciences, in particular. The DFG promotes equal opportunity for hiring women researchers and professors in the sciences at the university level and in scientific management.

Domestic abuse continues to be an issue, and it is reported that one out of five women are abused each year. German law provides for restraining orders against those who inflict violence on women. The government also sponsors medical aid and social services for women who are victims of violence. In addition, German law protects women from sexual harassment at the workplace, although incidents are frequently reported and punished. Women who are not protected by their employers after reporting harassment are entitled to leave with full pay and benefits until the offender has been dismissed or reprimanded.

Forced marriages are illegal in Germany. However this has been an issue in the German Muslim community, and Germany has taken measures to study the problem, although specific goals have not yet been reached. Prostitution is legal in Germany, although it is prohibited in certain residential areas.

Health Care

Germany's per capita expenditure on health amounts to €2,138 ($2,820 USD) annually. For every 1,000 people, there are 3.6 doctors.

Under Germany's health care system, workers make mandatory contributions to the health insurance fund up to a certain income level, and then private insurance takes over. About 88 percent of Germans are covered by the national health fund, 9 percent by private health insurance, and two percent (police, soldiers, etc.) by free government care. Less than one percent of Germans are uninsured.

One unique German service is care for parents and children. Mothers (97 percent of parents using the service are mothers) who are tired and depressed can check into a health resort for three weeks with their children. Mental and physical problems are addressed for both the mother and the children, as needed. If the children are in school, they can continue their studies at the health resort.

GOVERNMENT

Structure

Germany is a federal republic, founded in 1949. The Federal Republic of Germany (formerly West Germany) and the German Democratic Republic (formerly East Germany) reunited in 1990. The country has universal adult suffrage for citizens 18 and older.

While the president is titular head of state, the chancellor is the actual head of the government. The Bundestag (lower chamber of parliament) elects the chancellor for a four-year term, and the Federal Assembly elects the president for a five-year term. The Federal Assembly is composed of the Bundestag members and an equal number of state delegates, and meets only for this purpose.

The Bundestag consists of at least two representatives for every electoral district in the country. If a party's elected representatives are more than its proportional representation, the party may receive more seats. The Bundesrat, the upper chamber, has 69 members elected from the 16 Länder (states).

The independent Bundesverfaussungsgenicht (Federal Constitutional Court) is the nation's highest court. Of the sixteen Länder (states), three—Berlin, Bremen and Hamburg—are cities.

Political Parties

Major German political parties include the Christian Democratic Union (CDU), the Social Democratic Party (SPD), and the Free Democratic Party (FDP). Minor political parties include the Alliance 90/Greens, and The Left.

The Christian Democratic Union (CDU) is a center-right, conservative party that was established after World War II. In the 2013 general elections, the CDU earned 40 percent of the vote and 255 seats in the Bundestag.

The Social Democratic Party was established in 1875 and represented socialist ideals. In 1933, the SDP was the only political party vote against the Enabling Act, one of the major routes through which Adolf Hitler obtained dictatorial powers. The Nazi party banned the SDP that same year. In 1959, the SDP shifted from its socialist foundations and began to favor a social market economy while maintaining certain centre-left ideals in social policy. In the 2013 general elections, the SDP earned 30 percent of the vote and 192 seats in the Bundestag, making it the largest opposition party.

The Free Democratic Party (FDP) was established in 1948 and represented the ideals of social liberalism until the 1980s, when its politics became more pro-business. In 2005, the FDP earned around 10 percent of the vote, but in 2013, earned only 4.8 percent of the vote (and zero in the Bundestag). In the early 21st century, the FDP has stated goals including tax reduction for small and medium-sized business, a simplified tax structure, and increased civil liberties and rights for citizens.

The Left Party won 10.2 percent of the vote and 64 seats in the 2013 elections, while the Alliance 90/Greens won 10 percent and 63 seats.

Local Government

Germany is divided into 16 states, or Länder, 13 of which are area states and three of which are city states. The structure of the local (or municipal) governments varies by state, but there are some general similarities. For instance, in fifteen of the sixteen states, there exists a council system through which municipal councils (or local governments) are elected to terms ranging from four to six years. Each municipal council is headed by a mayor, who is elected to serve a term ranging from four to nine years. Municipal governments deal with issues such as water management and social assistance programs. There are roughly 14,000 municipal governments in the 16 Länder.

Judicial System

The German judicial system is based on Roman law principles and consists of three levels of courts: ordinary, specialized, and constitutional. The highest court is the Federal Constitutional Court, to which sixteen judges are appointed for 12-year terms.

Taxation

Germans are taxed by the Federation (Bund), the State (Länder), and the Municipalities (Gemeinden). The country has an income tax, a value-added tax (VAT), a corporation tax, a trade tax, a property tax, an inheritance tax, and a capital gains tax.

Armed Forces

The German armed forces are known as the Bundeswehr, and is made up of the navy (Marine), army (Heer), air force (Luftwaffe), central medical services (Zentraler Sanitätsdienst), and the joint support service (Streitkräftebasis).

Foreign Policy

Germany has a strong network of international relations, and strives to maintain its status as a peacekeeping nation. As such, it maintains membership in several key international organizations. Germany is a founding member of the European Union (EU), a conglomeration of 27 states that are politically and economically linked. Germany has also been a member of the North Atlantic Treaty Organization (NATO). Germany is also a founding member of the

Group of 8 (G8). This international organization formed 1973 as an informal discussion between world leaders in order to address economic concerns. In addition, Germany is closely involved with the United Nations (UN), which it first joined in 1973 as two separate countries, East Germany and West Germany. In 1990, Germany maintained membership as the Federal Republic of Germany. Germany is considered the third largest economic supporter of the UN. However, as a result of its role in the Second World War, Germany does not have a seat on the UN Security Council.

Germany is a key member in European affairs and has strong diplomatic and economic relations with its neighbors, all of which belong to the EU, with the exception of Switzerland. In addition, Germany has made progress in integrating Eastern Europe into the EU. It served as a peacekeeping force in the Balkans during the ethnic conflicts between Yugoslavia, Bosnia and Serbia. Following German reunification, Germany and Poland agreed on a treaty that would establish the border between the Oder and Neisse rivers, known as the Oder-Neisse line. Germany also supports economic development in Central and Eastern Europe.

From 1989–1990, Germany witnessed one of the most monumental political transformations in the 20th century, stemming from the dismantlement of the Soviet Union and its conglomerate of Soviet bloc countries. The loosening of the borders between Hungary and Austria in 1989 ignited a movement of East Germans into the West at a rate that was difficult for foreign governments to accommodate. The further collapse of the Soviet Union instigated the revolution in Germany that resulted in tearing down the wall that divided East and West Berlin.

On November 9, 1990, the East German government announced that the lifting of travel restrictions in other Soviet bloc countries meant that the Berlin Wall would no longer prove effective in separating the two countries. This resulted in a mass exodus from East to West Germany. In July 1990, the two parts of Germany were united with a single currency, the German deutschmark,

which symbolized the end of the two separate states. (Today, the euro is the common currency in Germany.) However, this transition was not smooth. As unemployment rose in the East, demand for East German commodities dropped sharply. In October 1990, the first elections were held in the Federal Republic of Germany.

The U.S. and Germany share close economic and political ties. Following the Second World War, the US established military bases throughout West Germany. These bases were downsized following the fall of the Berlin Wall. In addition, Germany has shown solidarity with the U.S. during the turbulent early years of the 21st century. For example, Germany supported the American-led invasion of Afghanistan in 2001.

Human Rights Profile

International human rights law insists that states respect civil and political rights, and also promote an individual's economic, social and cultural rights. The United Nations Universal Declaration on Human Rights (UDHR) is recognized as the standard for international human rights. Its authors sought the counsel of the world's great thinkers, philosophers, and religious leaders, and were careful to create a document that reflects the core values shared by every world culture. (To read this document or view the articles relating to cultural human rights, go to: http://www.udhr.org/UDHR/default.htm.)

Germany's government is respectful of the human rights laws dictated by the UN and the European Court of Human Rights (ECHR). In keeping with Article 2 of the UDHR, freedom of speech and freedom of the press are granted liberally in Germany, with the exception of publications by extremist nationalist groups. Article 19, which entitles freedom of expression and opinion, is also observed in Germany. However, any instances of neo-Nazism are addressed and severely punished. For example, in 2007 Germar Rudolf was sentenced to nearly three years in prison for denying the Holocaust. In addition, his book on the subject of the Holocaust was censured.

German police have been accused of abusing prisoners and detainees. In 2006, the Council of Europe's Committee for the Prevention of Torture (CPT) noted that prison conditions were not meeting the CPT's standards. There have also been instances of racial violence against Muslims and Jews by right-wing extremists.

Germany's treatment of refugee cases has been brought into question in several instances. Human Rights Watch indicated in July 2007 that Germany's federal agency for migration and refugees was violating human rights policies by revoking the refugee status of Iraqis. In July 2008, Amnesty International reported that Germany was forcibly returning a refugee to Eritrea. Amnesty International also reported that Germany's proposed revisions to its national refugee laws did not adhere to international refugee law standards. Such criticisms persist today.

Germany's human rights policies have been questionable in regards to gastarbeiter, or foreign guest workers who are mostly migrant workers from Turkey. The gastarbeiter were hired as unskilled laborers who were expected to return home after a certain period of time. However, many of these migrant workers from Turkey settled in Germany and raised families. This unforeseen problem of integration generated human rights issues, such as racial hostility, access to political citizenship, and cultural and social integration.

In the decade after German unification, racial violence, and attacks on foreigners increased significantly, although the government and public firmly opposed these incidents. Furthermore, EU policy allows nationalization by forfeiting citizenship in countries of origin, and children of immigrants who have been legally residing in Germany for eight years or more are given German citizenship.

Germany does not entirely adhere to Article 18's provision for freedom of religion. There are some minority religious groups in Germany that are carefully watched. The government has banned Scientology, citing the religion as a threat to democratic order and classifying it as a cult.

In addition, the government has banned Muslim girls from wearing headscarves in schools and has had instances of employee discrimination based on wearing headscarves.

Migration

Violence against foreign workers, particularly those of Turkish descent, has been an issue in Germany, particularly the eastern areas. In 2009, both unemployment and poverty rates in eastern Germany were approximately seven percent higher than in the rest of the country. Turks began immigrating to Germany in the 1950s and continued through the 1970s. In the decades following the 1990 reunification of East and West Germany, anti-ethnic violence has occurred intermittently. In Cologne in 2004, a bomb was detonated in a commercial area known as "Little Istanbul" that housed many Turkish-owned businesses.

ECONOMY

Overview of the Economy

Germany has the fifth-largest economy in the world and the largest in Europe. Reunification, however, has caused strains as the country tries to integrate the former East German and West German economies. The process has taken longer than expected, although the country has made a significant improvement in the standard of living in the east. In 2014, the gross national product (GDP) of Germany was $3.621 trillion (USD), and its per capita GDP was $44,700 (USD).

Industry

Iron and steel, coal, chemicals, electrical products, ships, vehicles and construction account for 34 percent of the GDP. Exports of machinery, transport equipment, chemicals, iron and steel products, manufactured goods and electrical products add €470 billion ($628 billion) to the economy.

Labor

In 2014, Germany had a labor force of 44.76 million people. As of 2011, almost three-quarters of the labor force was employed in the services industry, while 24 percent and 1.6 percent worked in industry and agriculture, respectively. In 2014, the unemployment rate was five percent, but it tends to be higher in the eastern part of the country.

Energy/Power/Natural Resources

Germany's major natural resources are iron, potash, lignite (brown coal), hard coal and natural gas. The nation's intense industrialization has led to serious pollution problems. Automobiles and factories using outdated technology and burning sulfurous coal are the main causes of air pollution.

About one-quarter of the trees in the country have been damaged by acid rain, caused by sulfur dioxide emissions. Water is polluted by industrial waste, oil from ships, fertilizers, herbicides and pesticides. In the east, out-of-date sewage treatment facilities also contribute to water pollution.

Radioactive waste is another concern. Spent fuel rods are stored in an old salt mine at Morsleben in Saxony-Anhalt. Other underground sites are in the planning stages. Government-mandated intensive recycling has reduced the amount of solid waste, but it is still high. Waste is burned at 52 plants.

Fishing

In 2000, there were approximately 2,300 fishing vessels in Germany. The country is known for its mackerel, herring, sardines, and cod. Inland fisheries in Germany accounted for around 26 percent of the total European Union's inland production in 2000.

Forestry

Around 30 percent of Germany is covered by forests. Dominant species include pine, spruce, and European beech. In 2014, forestry accounted for less than one percent of the national GDP.

Mining/Metals

Germany's major resources are iron, potash, lignite (brown coal), and hard coal.

Agriculture

Because of Germany's poor soil, agriculture accounts for less than one percent of the GDP (2014). Farms are small, and the principal crops are corn, wheat, potatoes, cabbages, fruit, sugar beets, barley, hops and wine grapes.

Animal Husbandry

The animal husbandry industry contributed less than one percent to the country's GDP in 2014. In the early 21st century, there were approximately 14 million head of cattle in Germany, over four million of which were used for dairy purposes.

Tourism

In 2008, over 133 million tourists visited Germany, bringing in over €27.2 billion. It is the seventh most popular travel destination in the world, and the city of Berlin is the eighth most-visited city in the world.

From May to October there is abundant sunshine, and popular tourist attractions include beer gardens, cafes, outdoor events, festivals, cycling, swimming, hiking, and beach and mountain resorts.

Other attractions include the Alps, especially the Zugspitze and the resort town of Garmisch-Partenkirchen; the Thuringian Forest in central Germany, noted for good hiking; the Black Forest, with the spa of Baden-Baden; the wooded Harz Mountains, source of many legends and folktales; the many resorts of the Baltic coast; Lake Constance, a resort area and one of Germany's warmest spots; the Frisian Islands in the North Sea; cruises on the Rhine; and numerous historic cities from Wittenberg to Aachen, Nuremberg, Heidelberg, Berlin, and Cologne.

Michelle Slater, Ellen Bailey, Alex K. Rich

DO YOU KNOW?

- The North Sea island of Helgoland is officially designated as a health resort because of its clean water and unpolluted, pollen-free air.

- In 1995, Bulgarian artist Christo wrapped the Reichstag in silver fabric. The wrappings stayed on for two weeks, after which the newly renovated building was unveiled.

- The Brothers Grimm fairytale characters Hansel and Gretel were lost in Germany's Black Forest.

Bibliography

Coles. Waltraud and Uwe Koreik. *Customs and Etiquette of Germany*. London: Global Books, 2006.

Fulbrook. Mary. *A Concise History of Germany*. Cambridge: Cambridge University Press, 2007.

Kettenacker, Lothar. *Germany 1989: In the Aftermath of the Cold War*. New York: Routledge, 2009.

MacGregor, Neil. *Germany: Memories of a Nation*. New York: Viking, 2014.

Nees, Greg. *Germany: Unraveling an Enigma*. Boston: Intercultural Press, 2011.

Reimer, Robert, et al. *German Culture through Film: An Introduction to German Cinema*. Newburyport, MA: Focus Press, 2005.

Rough Guides. *Rough Guide to Germany*. London: Rough Guides, 2015.

Sanders, Ruth. *German: Biography of a Language*. New York: Oxford University Press, 2012.

Schulte-Peevers, Andrea. *Germany*. Oakland, CA: Lonely Planet, 2013.

Tomalin, Barry. *Germany – Culture Smart! The Essential Guide to Customs and Culture*. London: Kuperard, 2010.

Wellbery, David, and Judith Ryan, Eds. *A New History of German Literature*. Cambridge, MA: Belknap Press, 2005.

Works Cited

"Tables: Water Supply Industry." *Statistisches Bundesamt Deutchland*. http://www.destatis.de/jetspeed/portal/cms/Sites/destatis/Internet/EN/Navigation/Statistics/Environment/EnvironmentalSurveys/WaterSupplyIndustry/Tables.psml

http://www.scientificblogging.com/news_releases/

http://www.diplo.de/diplo/en/Aussenpolitik/Themen/Menschenrechte/uebersicht.html

http://www.state.gov/g/drl/rls/hrrpt/2006/78814.htm

http://hrw.org/english/docs/2007/07/10/german16369.htm

http://www.culturalpolicies.net/web/germany.php?aid=4210

https://www.cia.gov/library/publications/the-world-factbook/geos/gm.html

http://www.foodnetwork.com/food/ck_gc_germany/

http://www2.amnesty.de/

http://www.germany.info/relaunch/politics/foreign/foreign.html

http://whc.unesco.org/en/search/?criteria=germany&x=0&y=0

http://www.germanmedia.com/

http://www.countryreports.org

http:/www./countrystudies.us/germany

http://www.nationsencyclopedia.com/Europe/Germany-transportation.html

GREECE

Introduction

Greece is located on the Balkan Peninsula of southern Europe. It also contains two large groups of islands. In the west, the Ionian Islands include seven principal islands, as well as many smaller ones. In the east and south, the Aegean Islands include Euboea, Samos, Chios, Lesbos, and Crete. Greece borders Albania, Bulgaria, Turkey, and Macedonia. Citizens of Greece are known as Greeks. However, some Greeks prefer to be called Hellenes, and refer to their country as the Hellenic Republic (or "Hellas"), after the mythological figure Hellen, considered the patriarch of the Hellenes.

Greece has a rich cultural legacy that spans thousands of years, particularly in art, literature, architecture, drama, politics, and philosophy. Classical Greek culture has had such a profound influence on the rest of the world, in fact, that Greece is widely considered one of the cradles of Western civilization. The country is also home to many important archeological sites, including the Agora, an ancient marketplace where it is said Socrates used to teach, the Acropolis of Athens, and the ruins of the Temple of Olympian Zeus. These sites and many others are cherished in Greece, as they preserve the country's classical culture.

Greece's economy was negatively affected by the global economic downturn that began in 2007. This economic instability grew, resulting in the country's monetary crisis in 2010, when the prime minister requested emergency economic assistance from neighboring countries and the International Monetary Fund. Today the Greek economy remains relatively unstable.

GENERAL INFORMATION

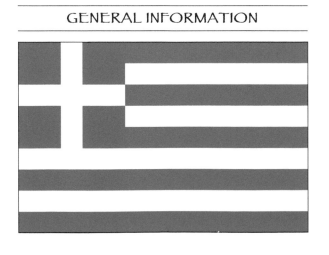

Official Language: Greek
Population: 10,775,557 (2014 estimate)
Currency: Euro
Coins: The Euro is available in 1, 2, 5, 10, 20 and 50 cent coins. A 1 and 2 Euro coin is also available.
Land Area: 130,647 square kilometers (50,443 square miles)
Water Area: 1,310 square kilometers (505 square miles)
National Motto: "Eleftheria i Thanatos" ("Freedom or Death")
National Anthem: "Imnos eis tin Eleftherian" ("Hymn to Liberty")
Capital: Athens
Time Zone: GMT +2
Flag Description: The flag of Greece features nine horizontal stripes of equal size that alternate between blue and white, with the top and bottom stripes being blue. In the upper-hoist (upper-left) side is a white cross set against a blue square. Although there is no official significance to the nine stripes, some think they represent the nine

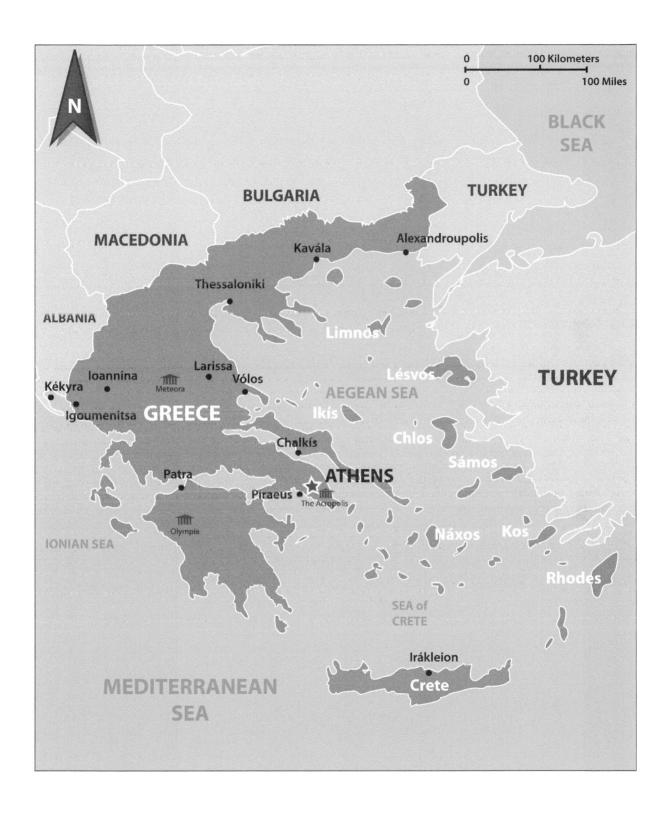

Principal Cities by Population (2012):

- Athens (762,698)
- Thessaloniki (363,987)
- Piraeus (179,479)
- Patras (168,906)
- Peristeri (147,598)
- Larissa (138,264)
- Heraklion (130,914) (2001 estimate)
- Kallithea (111,714)
- Nikaia (95,403) (2001 estimate)
- Kalamaria (87,255) (2001 estimate)

letters that make up the Greek word for "freedom," and others contend they represent the Nine Muses from Greek mythology. The cross represents the Greek Orthodox Church.

Population

The population in Greece is largely homogenous—over 98 percent of the population is of Greek descent. Ethnic minorities include Turks, Bulgarians, Macedonian Slavs, Albanians, Armenians, Jews, Roma, and Vlachs. There are approximately 11 million Albanians in Greece, though many do not hold official Greek citizenship. (In the early 1990s, after the collapse of the Soviet Union, many Albanians moved into Greece looking for work.)

Most Greeks (77 percent) live in urban areas. Athens, the capital, has a metropolitan population of approximately 4 million and is the cultural and political center of Greece. Thessaloniki (metropolitan population nearly 1 million) is another densely populated city, located in the northern part of the country. Other important cities in Greece include Patras, Kalamaria, Volos, Ioannina, Kavala, Sparta, and Alexandroupoulis. As of 2014, the country had a population growth rate of 0.1 percent.

The majority of Greece's population lives on or near coastal areas.

Languages

Modern Greek, a language thousands of years old, is the official language in Greece, and is spoken by 99 percent of the population. The modern spoken language is called dimotiki. In total, there are fourteen living languages in the country, including Albanian, Bulgarian, Pontic, Romani (Balkan), Romani (Vlax), Romanian, Slavic, Tsakonian, and Turkish. English and French are also spoken.

Native People & Ethnic Groups

Archeologists speculate that people from Asia Minor began settling in Greece around 2000 BCE. Greek culture grew remarkably sophisticated, and reached a high point in the fifth century BCE. During this period, ancient Greeks became internationally famous for their prominent poets, philosophers, and historians, and made important contributions to science. They were also the first group of people to experiment with democracy. Many different ethnic groups, including the Minoans, Mycenaeans, Macedonians, and Phoenicians, have influenced Greece during its long history.

In the early 21st century, the largest minority group in Greece is the Albanians, of which there are an estimated 500,000. Another major ethnic group is the Turks.

Religions

The primary and official religion in Greece is the Eastern Orthodox Church. However, the country promises religious liberty to its citizens, and proselytizing is forbidden by the constitution. The majority of Greeks (98 percent) are Greek Orthodox. Approximately 1.3 percent of the Greek population is Muslim.

Climate

The climate varies in Greece, but in general the country experiences mild winters and hot, dry summers. Weather is subject to rapid changes, and people have been known to experience several different seasons in one day in the mountainous regions.

The greatest amount of rainfall occurs in the Ionian Islands. Snow falls primarily in the mountains during the winter, but rarely in the maritime regions.

The capital, Athens, has a Mediterranean climate. Summers are hot and dry, with an average daytime temperature of about 33° Celsius (91° Fahrenheit), and winters are cool, with temperatures around 13° Celsius (55° Fahrenheit). The temperature rarely falls below freezing, and snow is rare. Most of the rainfall occurs between October and May. This mild climate allows for year-round outdoor activity.

ENVIRONMENT & GEOGRAPHY

Topography

Greece is situated on the southern Balkan Peninsula in southern Europe. It is located between the continents of Europe, Asia, and Africa. The mainland is dominated by the peripheries (administrative regions) of Thrace and Macedonia in the north; Epirus and Thessaly and Central Greece in the center of the country; and the Peloponnesus peninsula in the south.

One-fifth of Greece is made up of islands, and almost all parts of Greece are close to the sea. Greece includes more than 1,400 islands, the largest of which are Crete, Euboea, Lesbos, Rhodes, Khios, Kefallonia, Corfu, Limnos, Samos, and Naxos. Greece has 13,676 kilometers (8,498 miles) of coastline.

The vast majority of Greece is mountainous. The famous Mount Olympus is the highest point of elevation in the country, at 2,917 meters (9570 feet). Prominent mountain ranges include the Pindus; the Leflka Ori (or White Mountains), located in Crete; the Taiyetos, in the south; and Parnon in the east.

Greece has 1,140 square kilometers (440 square miles) of water area. Major rivers include the Mesta, Strimon, Arakhthos, Akheloos, Aliakmon, Pinios, and Alfios. Greece also borders several different seas including the Aegean Sea, the Ionian Sea, and the Mediterranean Sea.

Athens, the capital, is located on the Attic Peninsula, in a plain surrounded by mountains and the sea to the west. The city itself, which comprises about 38 square kilometers (14.7 square miles), is about 8 kilometers (5 miles) from the ocean. The greater metropolitan area covers 427 square kilometers (165 square miles) and stretches from the seaside to the slopes of the surrounding mountains. Within the city there are a number of prominent hills, the most striking being Lykabettos (227 meters/745 feet) and the Acropolis (156 meters/512 feet).

Plants & Animals

Many different plants can be found in Greece. At lower elevation are oranges, olives, dates, almonds, pomegranates, figs, cotton, and tobacco. Common trees include myrtle, oleander, lenstisk, plane, and white poplar, as well as the famous Greek cypress trees. Oak, chestnut, and beech trees are also found at the country's higher elevations.

Bears, wolves, jackals, foxes and polecats may be found in the mountains of Greece. In the north, there are populations of wild boar.

There are more than 350 species of birds in Greece, two-thirds of which are migratory. These include golden and imperial eagles, yellow vultures, falcons, owls, bustards, partridges, wood cocks, snipes, wood pigeons, and turtle doves. There are sixty-one species of reptiles, five types of tortoise, and nine species of amphibians. In terms of marine life, there are dolphins and whales and 246 species of fish.

CUSTOMS & COURTESIES

Greetings

Greeks use a variety of greetings depending on the social situation and their association with the person they are greeting. Generally, handshakes are common and used as both a greeting and at parting. Among friends and acquaintances, an embrace, kiss or a combination of both may be used. A more commonly used greeting, however, is a hug accompanied by a kiss on both cheeks. Older people are greatly respected in Greece, and youth are instructed to address them first in a formal and respectful manner, which often involves the use of titles.

The Greek greeting is often elaborate. Often, inquiries about one's family and health are expected and taken seriously. Common expressions include "Kherete" ("Greetings"), "Yasas" ("Your health") or "Kalos orisate" ("Welcome"). A common reply is "Kalos sas vrikame" ("Glad to see you"). Though mostly prevalent in rural areas, it is still customary to greet others with "Kalimera" ("Good day") or "Kalispera" ("Good evening").

Gestures & Etiquette

The Greeks are a very friendly people and may ask very personal questions of a stranger, especially foreigners. For instance, inquiries about family, occupation, salary, and political views are very common, as Greeks generally believe relationships are built over small-talk and arguments. In addition, body language and non-verbal communication are an important part of conversing. Arguments, for example, are often accompanied by expressive gestures.

The Greeks have specific gestures for many things. For instance, crossing the first two fingers is a sign of two people in a romantic relationship, while a pursed hand is a sign of excellence. Pulling on one's lower eyelid may be a sign for disbelief or suggestive of superiority.

Jerking the head upward in a backward motion typically means "No," while tilting the head to the side typically means "Yes." Additionally, waving with an open palm is commonly considered to be an insult, and waving is done with the palm closed. In recent years, however, many Greeks have begun to adopt gestures common in Western cultures such as the United States.

In general, traditional Greek etiquette requires that the elderly are treated with respect. Often, they are given seats and helped whenever the need arises, such as assistance in crossing the street. When eating, they are always served first. Another aspect of Greek etiquette involves women. Traditionally, they are expected to behave conservatively and demurely in public.

Eating/Meals

Greeks are passionate about their food and consider eating not only to be a family custom, but a traditional part of their culture. They customarily eat three meals per day, with breakfast usually the smallest and most insignificant meal. Lunch is typically the heaviest meal, and is traditionally followed by a siesta, or afternoon nap. Dinner is also an important meal, but is typically smaller than lunch. Traditionally, dinner was taken between eight and eleven o'clock at night in winter, and between nine and one in the morning in summer. In rural areas, meal times tend to be earlier.

Greeks also tend to dine out frequently, regardless of socioeconomic status, and generally prefer local cuisine. There are a variety of different types of restaurants, ranging from the proper restaurant (estiatoria) and tavern (taverna), to the dairy (galaktopoleion) and the pâtisserie (zakhar oplasteion), or bakery. In taverns, it is customary to visit the kitchen to choose one's food. Communal dining is also popular when eating out, and the pouring of wine is often an elaborate ritual.

Visiting

Greeks are known for their hospitality, and will typically not hesitate to invite a stranger to their home. Upon entering a Greek house, the visitor may be given a traditional offering of preserves with coffee and water. Refusing food is often perceived as a slight, and it is customary to drink the water first, then eat the preserves and place the spoon in the glass. The coffee is then drunk at leisure.

When visiting someone's house, it is customary to bring a gift for the hostess, such as flowers, chocolates or cake. Gifts for the children of the house are also acceptable. It is also considered polite to compliment the children of the host. If one is invited to dine at a Greek home, the guest is usually offered second and third helpings. It is not polite to refuse these, as accepting more food is a means of paying a compliment to the host. Greeks are also casual about keeping appointments, and those which are to be kept at the exact time stated are often referred to as "English rendezvous."

LIFESTYLE

Family

Greek society has historically been structured around the family unit and the institution of marriage. However, faced with increasing modernization and urbanization, traditional family patterns have begun to disappear in the late 20th and early 21st centuries.

Traditionally, Greek families were large in size and lived in extended, close-knit family systems. Even after marriage, children lived close, if not with, their parents, and it was not uncommon for three generations to reside in the same household. In the early 21st century, however, many couples have no more than two children, and the Greek government offers economic assistance to couples with more children. In addition, because of external migration and urbanization, the Greek family unit has become nuclear, and married couples are less likely to live close to their parents.

Greece has traditionally been a patriarchal society, but gender roles have also changed, and have become increasingly egalitarian. Beginning with the enactment of the Family Law in 1983, both husband and wife now have equal rights and obligations, bringing about a decline in traditional male authority. Marriage, once perceived to be the union of two families and traditionally arranged, is now a decision made by the couple. In addition, the dowry system, in which a bride's family offers a payment of goods, property or money to the bridegroom's family, has been legally abolished. Greece also maintains a low divorce rate, the second lowest in Europe in the early 21st century.

Housing

Many houses in Greece are built of stone or stucco, with red tiled roofs. Due to Greece's Mediterranean climate, most houses are painted white to reflect the sunlight and keep the interior cool. Because of this warm weather, Greeks spend most of their time outdoors and use their houses mainly for eating and sleeping. Even in their houses, they have patios and courtyards, or in the case of apartments, balconies. Many houses have traditionally included the eikonostasi, a place for Orthodox Greek icons. The kitchen is usually the center of household activity and sometimes includes an informal sitting area. The formal parlor, used to receive guests, is called the saloni. Traditionally, there was no concept of children having their own bedrooms, although this is now changing.

Urban housing has been dominated in the last century by a few characteristic styles. The first has a marked Turkish influence, and consists of a largely enclosed house with a tiled roof. Often, the ground floor will have only a few windows, the upper story juts out over the street, and the house will contain small courtyards and gardens. The second major style is the rectilinear multi-story house with a flat roof, balconies, and symmetrical windows on all floors. The third is often referred to as the island home, and is typically rectangular with an interior whitewashed courtyard and balconies on the upper floor. Another style, the long-house, is a single-story rectangular building traditionally constructed in the mountains. In recent years, high-rise apartment buildings have also become common.

Food

Greek cuisine is rich in flavor and varies seasonally and from region to region. It is similar to Mediterranean cuisine, while also sharing distinct characteristics with the cuisines of neighboring cultures and regions such as Italy, the Balkans, and the Middle East. In general, Greek food is characterized by the use of olive oil and fresh seasonal produce, cooked in its natural flavor. Mayirefta are oven-baked dishes which are prepared early in the morning and left to cool all day to enhance the flavor. Examples of such dishes include yemista, which are stuffed vegetables, and moussaka, which is a baked dish of sliced eggplant or aubergines, mince meat, and cheese arranged in layers with butter and spices.

A Greek meal typically begins with a course of rice, such as pilafi saltsa, pasta or pies. Pies come in many varieties, such as tiropita, or cheese pie, and spanakopita, or spinach pie. Vegetables, especially horta (or wild greens), fruits, and beans are also an important part of the meal. Bread is usually taken with the meal and comes in many varieties. Horiatiko is a country bread made in a wood oven, while paximadia are rusks made from barley-flour or whole wheat and double-baked to produce a hard loaf. Cheese is another important ingredient in Greek cuisine. In addition to the popular feta cheese, there are many other varieties, usually made of goat or sheep milk. These include kasseri, kefalotiri, the ricotta-like myzithra, and manouri. Cheeses are a common part of the orektika, or appetizers, which are served on meze tables and include kalamata olives, spicy meatballs, crunchy almonds, and crispy fried squid.

Fish is a popular part of traditional Greek cuisine, and is often grilled whole and flavored with ladholemono, which is a lemon and oil dressing. Kalamaria, or squid, is eaten in a variety of ways, grilled or fried, and ohtapudi, or octopus, is a delicacy. Common meats include pork, lamb, kid goat, and chicken. They may be grilled or baked with potatoes and a lemon and oregano dressing. They may also be cooked as a stew, such as the kokkinisto, a tomato-based casserole. Traditionally, every part of the animal was consumed; for example, "ameletita," or "unspeakables," are fried sheep's testicles, while kokoretsi is a spicy, spit-roasted offal wrapped in intestines. Souvlakia, pieces of meat grilled on a skewer, is another popular food.

Desserts are an important part of Greek cuisine, and include koulouria, a round, sesame-covered fresh pretzel-like bread, and baklava, a layered pastry filled with honey and nuts. Ouzo is a strong licorice-flavored Greek spirit made from grape stems and flavored with aniseed. Usually served before dinner or with meze, it is added to a glass of water to create a whitish mixture. Many varieties of wine and beer are produced locally, and Turkish coffee is another popular drink.

Life's Milestones

The Greek Orthodox faith is the predominant religion, and an estimated 98 percent of the population identifies as Greek Orthodox. It is a part of the large Eastern Orthodox Christian Church, and many Greek milestones and observances are rooted in this faith. One of the most famous celebrations associated with the Orthodox faith is Greek Orthodox Easter, a festive and religious season that has a carnival atmosphere and is a traditional time for family to gather. Another unique celebration, the name day, is based on the feast day of a particular saint, which in the Greek Orthodox calendar occurs every day of the year. Many people in Greece are named after Greek Orthodox saints, and name days are celebrated by children and adults alike. Birthdays are typically only celebrated for children.

Greek weddings are elaborate affairs, and traditionally held on Sundays. The ceremony is both secular and religious, and involves customs such as the showing of the dowry, the exchanging of the rings, and the crowning of the bride and groom with garlands of flowers. Traditionally, the ceremony is followed by the public procession of the bride, along with her possessions, to the groom's house. Once there, elaborate threshold-crossing ritual ceremonies are performed, followed by feasting and dancing.

Greek funerals are equally elaborate. After the death, the body of the deceased is washed and dressed and laid out in the house by distant relatives. Within twenty-four hours, the body is brought to the church in a procession for the funeral. Traditionally, relatives may kiss the deceased, whose hands, feet, and jaw are now untied, and the priest empties a bottle of wine over the body in the shape of a cross before it is buried. Once returning home, it is customary to touch burning charcoal before entering the house, as it is believed to clear away the pollution of death. Following the funeral, memorial services are held on the third, the ninth, and the fortieth days, after six months, and after a year. After two or three years, the body is exhumed. If the bones are clean and white, the body is deposited in a metal ossuary and buried again. If not, it is reburied as it is and exhumed later.

CULTURAL HISTORY

Art

Often regarded as the cradle of Western civilization, Greece boasts a rich tradition of art which dates back several millennia, and which influenced the art of modern Europe. Ancient Greek art can be broadly divided into three periods: the Minoan and Mycenaean period (c. 2700–1100 BCE), the Hellenistic period (323 BCE–146 CE), and the Byzantine period (c. 300–1453 CE).

The Minoans used fresco painting to decorate their palaces. This style is characterized by small brushstrokes, with details added in tempera. Popular themes included landscapes, scenes depicting crowds, and life-size portraitures. The Mycenaean civilization developed fresco painting in the 13th and 14th centuries BCE. Mycenaean frescoes usually depicted scenes of violence, such as war or hunting, and are characterized by firm outlines, stylized figures, and a formal composition. Painting was not particularly developed during the Hellenistic period, and survived mainly as mural painting in the fourth and third centuries BCE. In the Byzantine period, the focus of art shifted to religion. Mosaic art became prominent while painting became iconic, depicting Christian religious figures, and both were used primarily in the decoration of churches. There was little artistic output during the Ottoman period of Greek history (1458–1821 CE), and modern art and painting reemerged after Greece gained independence in 1821. Nineteenth-century Greek painting was largely secular in nature and followed European trends.

Sculpture has a long history in the Greek islands, dating back to the Neolithic period. The Minoans developed monumental sculpture, and terracotta and ivory figures characterize the Mycenaean period. Kouros and kourai, male and female votive statues, had been made in Attica (in southern Greece) since c. 600 BCE. The greatest achievements in sculpture occurred in the Hellenistic period, when sculptors decorated temples and treasuries with narrative scenes from popular myths. Early Classical sculpture (c. 480–450 BCE) was characterized by a realistic depiction of the human form. In the fourth century, sculpture became naturalistic, depicting figures in relaxed poses with softer outlines. As sculpture further developed, it became animated and vivacious, but declined as an art form after the Hellenic age.

Like sculpture, the tradition of ceramics in Greece dates back to the Stone Age. Around 2000 BCE, the technique of using the pottery wheel was introduced. Minoan pottery was characterized by beak-like spouts and red or white decoration on a dark background. The designs varied from spiraling plant motifs to curvilinear abstracts. Mycenaean pottery was influenced by the Minoans, and included long-stemmed goblets and globular vases. After c. 1550 BCE, motifs were applied in dark colors on a light background, and included flowers, plants, and marine subjects, particularly the octopus. Pottery began to diminish after c. 475 BCE.

Architecture

Minoan architecture is characterized by royal tombs and palaces. Minoan palaces, such as the palace at Knossos, were labyrinthine, and groups of rooms were designed around a central court. The Mycenaeans modified the Minoan plan, and established the center of the palace as a suite of state rooms which formed a rectangular megaron (great hall). The palaces had a small court, an aithousa (pillared porch), a prodomos (anteroom), and a domos (throne room). Examples include the 13th and 14th-century palaces at Mycenae, Tiryns, and Pylos.

The Hellenic period saw tremendous advancement in temple architecture, of which the greatest is perhaps the Doric order. The Doric order of classical temple architecture included a columnar porch which led into a great hall. The columns were placed directly on the upper foundations without a base, and the fluted shafts of the columns tapered upwards with a convex curve; they eventually became taller, thinner, and spaced farther apart. The columns and the superstructure were initially made of wood and limestone, but after the sixth century BCE, all buildings were made of marble. The Parthenon in Athens (438 BCE) is the finest example of the Doric order.

In the sixth century BCE, the Ionic order was developed. It was characterized by the columns having tiered bases, slimmer shafts, and deeper fluting. The architrave, an ornamental door frame, consisted of three slabs with sculptured decoration. The most famous examples of this style include the Erechtheion and the Temple of Nike in Athens. The Corinthian order was used in many fourth-century buildings, such as the Temple of Olympian Zeus at Athens. This was characterized by the columns bearing a single or double row of ornate, leafy scrolls.

Byzantine architecture focused on the construction of churches. These churches were characterized by a central dome, which was supported by four arches on piers. The churches were made either of stone or brick, and the exterior was sometimes inlaid with designs. The monasteries at Mount Athos and churches in central Greece are examples of this style. In the 19th century, the predominant architectural style was the neoclassical, used in various public and civic buildings. There was little development of innovative architecture in the 20th century.

Drama

Theatre began to develop in Greece during the sixth century BCE, and an annual playwriting contest was held at the Theatre of Dionysus in Athens. Aeschylus (c. 525–456 BCE) is known as the "father of tragedy," and his most famous work is the *Oresteia* trilogy. Sophocles (c. 496–406 BCE) is known as the greatest of Greek tragedians and produced over a hundred plays, including *Antigone*, *Electra*, and the famous *Oedipus Rex*. His plays were characterized by themes from Greek myths and had complex plots.

Euripides (c. 485–406 BCE) wrote over eighty plays which were characterized by exciting plots, and include *Medea*, *Andromache*, *Orestes*, and *Bacchae*. Aristophanes (c. 427–387 BCE) was considered the master of comedy, producing works which were often indecent in their humor and dealt with topical issues.

Theatre continued to develop into an important socio-cultural activity and remained a prestigious and well-organized art for centuries after the Romans conquered Greece. Under Ottoman rule, Greek theatre adopted a Turkish shadow puppet theatre called "Karagiozis." Initially, the themes and characters used were Turkish, but by the 19th century, this form of shadow theatre began to portray everyday Greek life. The golden period of Karagiozis occurred in the early 20th century, when it transcended social classes and featured social and political themes.

Drama declined during the Byzantine and Ottoman periods until the emergence of a national theatre in 1930. Modern Greek theatre became preoccupied with preserving the romanticized ideal of its classical past. After the devastation of the Second World War, Greek theatre undertook a quest to regain national pride. Theatre had always been a means of didactic entertainment in Greece, and after the 1950s, it began to explore and criticize concepts such as authority, ignorance, lost ideals, alienation, and dehumanization. Karolos Koun (1909–1987), Katrina Paxinou (1900–1978), and Alexis Minotis (1904–1990) were important practitioners of Modern Greek theatre.

Music & Dance

Music remains an important part of Greek life from ancient times. Ancient Greek musical instruments included the lyre, the lute, piktis (pipes), kroupeza (percussion instrument), kithara (string instrument), aulos (wind instrument), barbitos (similar to a cello), and the magadio (harp-like instrument). In Modern Greek music, the bouzouki is commonly used; long-necked, it resembles a lute, and may have six or eight strings. In addition, the baglamas, a smaller version of the bouzouki, is used widely in rembetika music, while the outi, a bulbous stringed instrument, and the toumberleki, a lap drum that makes a staccato rap sound, also feature prominently. Other common traditional instruments include the Cretan lyra (lyre), the mandolin, and the gaida (bagpipes).

Modern Greek music can be classified into five main types: the demotika, laika, mirolayia, rembetika, and the Greek Orthodox hymnology. The demotika style was developed during the Ottoman period, and includes appropriate songs for occasions such as death, marriage, feasting, and dancing. Demotika songs often deal with epic themes such as freedom, death, love, parting, pain, and justice. A lighter and more upbeat variant of demotika is nisiotika, and in both, the clarinet is commonly used. The rembetika is largely considered the music of the underclass, and is sometimes known as the Greek version of blues music. Rembetika emerged in the late 19th century, but has declined as a modern form of music.

The laika is the most popular form of Greek music, and is an offshoot of the rembetika. It also deals with themes like love, hate, death, parting, and migration. Mirolayia are the laments of mourning sung at funerals by women, and vary regionally. The songs focus on themes of separation and loneliness. Greek Orthodox hymns are a result of the Byzantine influence in Greece. They are typically chanted, with different hymns for every occasion. In the 20th century, entehno, or artistic music, became a popular genre. It drew on folk music and instruments, but was more symphonic. It created popular music out of poetry, and became a form of social commentary during the junta years (1967–1974).

Dance has also been an important aspect of Greek culture since the Hellenic age, when it was a part of military education and ritualistically performed in temples. In modern times, dance remains an important social function and follows tradition strictly. There are believed to be over 4,000 modern Greek folk dances, with most dances performed in an open circle formation with the dancers moving left to right. These dances vary from region to region and often reflect the temperament of the people. For example, the epiros, from the mountainous regions, is a stately, slow, and dignified dance, while the kotsari is a rigorous, war-like dance of the Pontic Greeks (Greeks of Pontus, in modern-day Turkey). The zorba, or syrtaki, is a famous stylized dance in which two or three people link arms on each other's shoulders and dance in a long circle to a quickening beat.

Literature

The Greek literary tradition dates back several millennia, with poetry being the most significant genre. Although a tradition of oral poetry already existed, the roots of Greek poetry extend as far back as Homer's epic poems *The Iliad* and *The Odyssey*, written in the eighth or ninth century BCE. The poet Hesiod (c. 700 BCE) wrote didactic and pastoral poems in epic verse. The sixth-century poets Alcaeus, Sappho, and Anacreon wrote emotional poems about love, war, and death. Cretan poetry flourished in the 16th and 17th centuries, the same time in which Vitsenzos Kornaros (1553–1617), one of the most important Greek poets, wrote *Erotokritos*, a romance in heroic verse that became a landmark in Greek literature.

As Greek poetry progressed into the modern age, poets began to deal with themes such as war and conflict, liberty, and national identity. Poets often referred to old Homeric and classical myths and motifs. One important school of poetry was the Old School of Athens (1830–1880), a literary movement which characterized post-independence Greek literature. These poets were strongly influenced by English Romanticism and their work often drew on classical motifs. Other important movements included the School of the Ionian Islands (also called the Heptanese School), which produced patriotic poetry, and the

New School of Athens, which greatly influenced modern Greek symbolic poetry. Kostis Palamas (1859–1943), a prominent member of this latter group, had a profound effect on modern Greek poetry.

Twentieth-century Greek poetry was dominated by symbolism, and speaks of the search for identity, isolation, and nostalgia for past glory. Important modern poets include George Seferis (1900–1971) and Odysseus Elytis (1911–1996), who both won the Nobel Prize in Literature in 1963 and 1979, respectively, and Constantine Cavafy (1863–1933), often regarded as the father of modern Greek poetry. His works, such as "Waiting for the Barbarians," are realist commentaries on human nature.

Greek prose has been slow to develop, and early novels told tales of old traditions and rural life. In the 20th century, city life, especially that of Athens, became a prominent subject matter, as did themes like the meaning of man's destiny, sacrifice, and death. Important novelists include Theotokas (1906–1966), Vassilikos (1934–), and Kazantzakis (1883–1957).

CULTURE

Arts & Entertainment

One of the prevailing concerns of contemporary Greek art is the preservation of the nation's classical cultural heritage, and this is especially true for theatre. Greece's official theatre season lasts from October until the week prior to Easter, though some theatres remain open until May. However, many prestigious theatre festivals continue to occur, the most renowned of these being the Epidaurus Festival. The festival, which begins at the end of June and lasts until the end of August, is devoted exclusively to staging the works of classical playwrights and takes place in the preserved Theatre of Dionysus, located at the foot of the Acropolis in Athens. The Greek Ministry of Culture also actively supports contemporary drama, and has established an annual Playwright's Award for new and established playwrights.

Contemporary Greek cinema is a burgeoning institution, and film festivals, such as the Thessaloniki Film Festival, are held each year in order to promote the national film industry. Greece also has a growing arts scene, and there are regular exhibitions of local and international artists at the various galleries in Athens. Greece also boasts a number of museums that support both the contemporary and classical Greek visual and plastic arts. Athens itself contains the National Museum of Athens and the new Museum of Contemporary Art. In addition, the National Art Gallery, also in Athens, and the Rhodes Art Gallery carry the largest collections of modern Greek art.

Cultural Sites & Landmarks

Greece has a large number of historical sites and monuments from each of the major periods of its long history, including seventeen sites recognized by the United Nations Educational, Scientific and Cultural Organization (UNESCO). These include the famed Acropolis of Athens, the Temple of Apollo at Bassae, the Eastern Orthodox monastery complexes of Meteora and Mount Athos, and the preserved medieval town of Rhodes. Significant archaeological sites include Olympia, home to the Ancient Olympic Games, and the ruins at Delphi, home to the most important oracle in ancient Greece.

The Acropolis of Athens, dedicated to the goddess Athena, is perhaps the finest archeological site from Ancient Greece. Although inhabited much earlier, many of the monuments of the Acropolis were constructed in the fifth century BCE under Pericles (c. 495–429), and reveal the glory and might of ancient Athens. The Parthenon, a double peripheral Doric temple with sculptural decoration, is perhaps the most impressive building on the Acropolis. Other archeological remains on site include the Temple of Athena Nike and the Erechtheum, an ancient temple renowned for its unique architectural features. The Temple of Apollo at Bassae, inscribed as Greece's first World Heritage Site in 1986, is famous for its well-preserved temple architecture that dates back to the fifth century BCE.

The site of Delphi was an important religious center of ancient Greece. Dating from the sixth century BCE, Delphi was the site of the famous oracle of the god Apollo. The Peloponnesian site of Olympus is another important historical site. Inhabited since prehistoric times, it is the birthplace of the Ancient Olympic Games, which were held at Olympia every four years beginning in 776 BCE. Olympia was also a religious center from the 10th century BCE, and the site has many temples. Another important historical site is the ancient city of Aigai, near Vergina in northern Greece. Listed as a World Heritage Site in 1996, the ruins include a palace, decorated with elaborate painted mosaics and stuccoes, and a burial ground, which has over 300 tumuli (burial mounds), some of which date from the 11th century BCE. One of the royal tombs in the Great Tumulus is believed to belong to Philip II of Macedonia (382–336 BCE), the father of Alexander the Great (356–323 BCE).

The Minoan Palace at Knossos in Crete is the largest such building discovered and is considered a masterpiece of Minoan architecture. Covering an estimated area of 22,000 square meters (236,808 square feet), it is believed to have been the seat of the mythical King Minos. The palace was an important social, political, and economic center of Minoan civilization. The port city of Thessaloniki was settled in 315 BCE, and later became an important center of Christianity. There were numerous churches constructed in the city from the fourth until the 15th century, all of which are fine examples of early Christian art. Mount Athos is another important Christian center. First inhabited in 1054 CE, this "Holy Mountain" has a number of monasteries, of which twenty are still inhabited by more than 1,400 monks.

Libraries & Museums

Athens has many museums. The National Archaeological Museum houses a magnificent collection of ancient Greek art. There are also museums on the Acropolis and in the Agora, which house works of art that were found at those sites. The Benaki Museum, which began as a private collection, has an eclectic mix of ancient and modern art as well as some Islamic, Chinese, and Coptic art. There are also a number of museums dedicated to later Greek periods, including the Byzantine Museum, National Historical Museum, the Jewish Museum of Greece, and the National Gallery and Soutzos Museum.

The National Library of Greece, located in Athens, was established in the early 19th century and houses many significant religious and historical manuscripts, such as a codex of four Gospels and the first published edition of the works of Homer, an ancient Greek poet. There are over 500 public libraries in Greece in the early 21st century, as well as forty university research libraries and 500 school libraries.

Holidays

There are many festivals held throughout the year in Greece, including the Athens Festival (June to October), the Lycabettus Festival (May to September), and the Nauplia International Music Festival (June).

Public holidays include the Feast of the Assumption (August 15), St. Stephen's Day (January 6), Ohi Day (May 1), Spring Festival/Labour Day (February), New Year's Day (January 1), Greek Independence Day (March 15), and Orthodox Easter Sunday, in March or April.

Youth Culture

The youth culture of modern-day Greece is a blend of tradition and Western influence. Pubs, video arcades, and modern-style cafés, often equipped with Internet, are the most popular destinations for young people. Generally, these places allow both sexes to socialize freely, in sharp contradiction to the barriers which had traditionally been imposed. At night, socialization may also take place in town squares or parking lots. Smoking is common, and although alcohol use also occurs regularly, it is much less than that in other European countries. At home, television and the mass media, including the Internet and computer gaming, are popular pastimes.

As with many cultures, Greek youth place great emphasis on physical appearance. International fashion trends and Western ideals of beauty are commonly followed, and there is a pronounced preoccupation with being slim.

SOCIETY

Transportation

Road travel is the main form of transportation in Greece. However, Greek cities are notorious for their traffic and Greece has maintained one of the worst accident rates in Europe. One mode of transportation that is popular is bus services, common between main urban centers. In the cities, there is an extensive network of city buses; these are often over-crowded and stopped by raising a hand. Metered taxi cabs are also common in the cities and are relatively inexpensive. Due to increasing traffic, bus and taxi lanes have been introduced to encourage the use of public transportation. Cars are also readily available for hire, as are motorbikes and even bicycles. In the rural areas, walking is often the most common form of travel and pathways and paved tracks are common. Traffic moves on the right-hand side of the road.

Transportation Infrastructure

Because Greece is an island nation, maritime transportation plays a large role, with the main ports being Piraeus, Thessaloniki, Kavalla, Patras, Rhodes, and Crete. The port city of Piraeus in the greater metropolitan area is the busiest port in Greece, and offers ferry service to the Greek islands and other destinations.

Rail service plays a minor role, and Greece was, in fact, the last country in Europe to develop a railway network, beginning as late as 1881. This is largely due to the country's difficult terrain, which consists of mountains and islands. Air travel is also a common form of transportation, and the national airline, Olympic Airways, has an extensive internal network.

In Athens, because of the Olympic Games in 2004, a new international airport was built and the metro system was improved and greatly expanded, with further expansion planned.

Media & Communications

There are over 30 national dailies in Greece, including leading newspapers such as the *Kathimerini* ("Daily"), *Eleftherotypia* ("Free Press"), *Ethnos* ("Nation"), and *The Athens News*, an English-language weekly newspaper. Most Greek newspapers are openly partisan in their political affiliations, while many are tabloids. In 1989, government monopoly of television and radio broadcasting ended, allowing the private ownership of media for the first time; as of 2009, there were over 1,700 private radio and television stations, many of which are unlicensed. However, the majority of newspapers and television and radio stations are owned by a few major entrepreneurial groups.

Greece has an extensive network of communications in all parts of the country. In 2009, there were three main cellular phone companies: Vodafone, WIND, and Cosmote. In 2006, there were an estimated 3.8 million Internet users, representing over 33 percent of the population. Greece also operates a telecommunications satellite, Hellasat, which provides services in a large part of Eastern Europe and Western Asia.

The Greek constitution provides for an independent and uncensored media and recognizes the social role of media in providing objective information. However, political parties continue to use broadcast media as a propaganda tool, and the media was heavily censored as recently as the Greek military junta of 1967–1974. Even in the post-junta period, communist publications such as *Rizospastis* and *Odigitis* were censored. The media is also prohibited from criticizing the president and religious authorities of the Greek Orthodox Church, and obscenity laws influenced by the Orthodox religion are strictly implemented. Additionally, the anti-terrorist laws of Greece prohibit the publication of terrorist statements.

SOCIAL DEVELOPMENT

Standard of Living

Greece ranked 29th out of 187 countries on the 2014 United Nations Human Development Index, which measures quality of life and standard of living indicators.

Water Consumption

In their 2014 World Health Statistics publication, the World Health Organization estimated that 99 percent of the population of Greece has access to improved drinking water sources and 98 percent had access to improved sanitation.

Education

Most Greek children begin their formal schooling at the age of six. The first nine years of public education is funded by the central government. According to the 2012 census, the literacy rate is 96 percent.

Primary education (dimotiko) lasts for six years. At this point, students move onto secondary schools. Secondary education includes two stages of training. The first three years consist of the lower secondary stage of study (gymnasio) when students are 12 to 15 years old. The second three years prepare students for college or other technical vocations. These programs are called lykeios and tees.

Students usually begin university study at the age of eighteen. University attendance, including books, is publicly funded, but students must meet strict standards and other criteria. A student's scores on state-administered tests, as well as his or her grade-point average and choice of major, are all considered when applying for university study. Universities are therefore very competitive, and only one-quarter of applicants are admitted. There are approximately 100,000 students enrolled in Greek universities. The country's major universities are in Athens, Salonika, Thrace, Ioannina, Crete, and Patrai.

The gender gap in education has largely closed in Greece in the early twenty-first century, with roughly the same percentages of female and male adolescents attending lower and upper secondary school.

Women's Rights

Throughout Greece's history, women have played an important, although somewhat subdued, role in society. Though women were more liberated in ancient Greece than other cultures of the time, their status was greatly reduced under the influence of Christianity and Islam. The social status of women remained poor until the beginning of the 20th century, and improved dramatically after the Second World War, largely because of female participation in the National Resistance (1941–1944). Women also factored in the organized resistance to the Greek military junta of 1967–1974, which helped provide the impetus for the women's movement in Greece. Following the adoption of the Constitution of Greece in 1975, women were granted equal rights and obligations. Further legislation, such as the Family Law Bill (1983), was passed to improve the conditions of women, and the Greek legal system is often regarded as the most feminist in early 21st-century Europe.

However, gender inequality is still present in all spheres of Greek society. In terms of political representation, there were only 31 women members of parliament—out of 300 total—that were elected in 2000. Women also continue to be underrepresented in the work force, and recent surveys indicate women's salaries continue to be less than their male counterparts, even though women are required to be paid on par with male colleagues under Greek law. Domestic violence against women continues to be an issue. According to a 1999 survey of European Union (EU) member states, Greece had the highest level of domestic abuse. Rape within marriage is not considered a crime, and only a small percentage of men convicted for rape are actually convicted, and typically given lenient sentences. Furthermore, the legal system and pervading social stigma discourages victims from reporting rape and domestic abuse.

Health Care

The government devotes approximately 8 percent of Greece's gross domestic product (GDP) to health care. Since the 1990s, the government has attempted to build more hospitals and in general improve all medical facilities and provide advanced training for medical workers.

The National Health System was introduced in 1983, and provides medical coverage including hospitalization, maternity care, dental coverage, and other medical benefits for Greek citizens. However, the system has suffered from lack of funds and resources.

In Greece, children under one year of age are immunized against measles, diphtheria, pertussis, and tetanus. Life expectancy in Greece is eighty years (2014). Air quality has been a major problem in Greece, and has been known to cause health problems.

GOVERNMENT

Structure

Greece became a parliamentary republic when the monarchy was removed in 1974. There is a constitution and the president is elected by parliament for a maximum of two five-year terms. However, if the candidate does not win a majority in parliament, a general election is called. The president chooses the prime minister, who then serves as the head of parliament. Parliament (Vouli) is made up of 300 deputies who are directly elected to four year terms.

Political Parties

The two major political parties in Greece are the Panhellenic Socialist Movement (PASOK) and New Democracy (ND). Other parties include the Communist Party of Greece (KKE), the Coalition of the Left (SYN), and the Democratic Social Movement (DIKKI).

In the 2010 parliamentary elections, the coalition led by New Democracy won 129 seats and the Coalition of the Left won 71 seats. The former party in power, the Panhellenic Socialist Movement, was reduced to only 33 seats.

Local Government

On the local level, the country is divided into thirteen administrative regions (peripheries).

These are broken up into fifty-one prefectures (nomos). They include Agion Oros, Achaia, Aitolia kai Akarnania, Argolis, Arkadia, Arta, Attiki, Chalkidiki, Chania, Chios, Dodekanisos, Drama, Evros, Evrytania, Evvoia, Florina, Fokidos, Fthiotis, Grevena, Ileia, Imathia, Ioannina, Irakleion, Karditsa, Kastoria, Kavala, Kefallinia, Kerkyra, Kilkis, Korinthia, Kozani, Kyklades, Lakonia, Larisa, Lasithi, Lefkada, Lesvos, Magnisia, Messinia, Pella, Pieria, Preveza, Rethymnis, Rodopi, Samos, Serres, Thesprotia, Thessaloniki, Trikala, Voiotia, Xanthi, and Zakynthos. This decentralization of power provides districts with more direct control over local issues.

Judicial System

The court system of Greece comprises a Supreme Court (Aeropagus) of appeal, the Council of State, the Audit Office, and the Special Supreme Court.

Taxation

Taxes levied include an income tax and corporate tax. As of 2010, the top income tax rate was 40 percent, while the top corporate rate was 25 percent. Other taxes levied include a value-added tax (VAT), a tax on interest, and an inheritance tax.

Armed Forces

The armed forces of Greece consist of several service branches, including the Hellenic Army, Hellenic Navy, and Hellenic Air Force. There is conscription, between the ages of 18 and 45, which consists of a nine-month service obligation. As a European Union and NATO member, Greece soldiers have participated in various international peacekeeping missions, including in Afghanistan, Bosnia and Herzegovina, Chad, and Kosovo. Greek military spending is high, and the United States has been a primary exporter of weaponry and military supplies to Greece.

Foreign Policy

Greece's foreign policy is largely determined by three factors: full membership in the European

Union (EU), which it joined in 1981; the country's unique geographical location in the regional sub-system of southeastern Europe; and Greece's position in the wider international political arena, where it participates actively in various international forums such as the UN, which it joined in 1945. Also, the particular cultural and religious history of Greece has had a formative effect on Greek politics and foreign relations. For instance, Greece is the only EU state that observes the Eastern Orthodox tradition, as well as the Western liberal one, a co-existence of traditions that is often reflected in its foreign relations.

Greece holds membership in several global and regional alliances, including the North Atlantic Treaty Organization (NATO) and the Mediterranean Member States group. The latter seeks to achieve a common EU foreign and defense policy, which will ensure the inviolability of EU borders. Also, Greece has attempted to further the economic relations of the EU with developing nations. During its 1994 presidency of the EU, Greece successfully enlarged the union, and continues to favor the acceptance of Turkey. It also favors the development of an independent government capable of handling the union's increasing economic and political responsibilities, as well as the strengthening of the EU's institutions and military capabilities. Greece has also strived to create bilateral relations of economic and technical cooperation with the Balkan region, as well as with other nations belonging to Eastern Europe, and is a founding member of the Organization of the Black Sea Economic Cooperation (BSEC).

One particular dispute that has sometimes overshadowed Greece's foreign relations is the dispute over Cyprus, an island in the eastern Mediterranean. Essentially, the Republic of Cyprus has been divided by the Turks and Greeks, with the Turkish community establishing the Turkish Republic of Northern Cyprus (TRNC). However, the TRNC is only recognized by Turkey, and Greece maintains a strong military presence on the island. This dispute has strained relations between Turkey and Greece, and has even prompted U.S. and UN mediation.

Relations between both countries are further strained by a sovereignty dispute involving the Aegean Sea. Greece also refuses to recognize the Republic of Macedonia, due to the existence of a province named Macedonia in Greece.

Human Rights Profile

International human rights law insists that states respect civil and political rights, and also promote an individual's economic, social and cultural rights. The United Nations (UN) Universal Declaration of Human Rights (UDHR) is recognized as the standard for international human rights. Its authors sought the counsel of the world's great thinkers, philosophers, and religious leaders, and were careful to create a document that reflects the core values shared by every world culture. (To read this document or view the articles relating to cultural human rights, go to: http://www.udhr.org/UDHR/default.htm.)

Since gaining independence, Greece has legally provided for the safeguarding of the rights and liberties of its citizens. In particular, the constitution of 1975 safeguards the human rights of Greek citizens in compliance with the UDHR. Thus, with the exception of brief periods of military rule, Greece has maintained a relatively decent human rights record; however, lapses in the protection of rights occur regularly.

The year 1967 marked the beginning of a period of military dictatorship in Greece after the monarchy was overthrown in a coup. At this time, many articles of the previous constitution, drafted in 1952, were suspended, especially those guaranteeing human rights, leading to numerous violations. First and foremost, the regime suspended the parliament and replaced the constitution, while also setting up special courts and dissolving political parties. Arbitrary arrest and detention was widespread, with the regime even establishing exile camps on remote islands for those who maintained left-wing political affiliations, particularly journalists. Often, these political prisoners were held in inhumane conditions and subjected to torture and degrading treatment. The prisoners were also not provided free and fair trials.

Though the military regime ended in 1974, several major human rights concerns still exist in Greece. In violation of Article 18, freedom of religion is still not fully granted, with the Greek constitution only allowing for "known religions." The constitution also prohibits proselytism (the practice of converting others) and appointed the Greek Orthodox Church as the predominant church to which all religious appeals must be directed. Minority and ethnic groups in Greece also face several problems. For example, the Greek state does not recognize the existence of minorities such as the Macedonian minority in northern Greece. Furthermore, the Macedonians have been subjected to a symbolic ethnic cleansing in the last fifty years as their right to their own culture has been abolished. In particular, they have been stripped of their Greek citizenship and subjected to persecution and harassment. Similarly, the small Turkish minority in Thrace was also persecuted and stripped of Greek citizenship.

ECONOMY

Overview of the Economy

Greece's public sector provides about half of the country's gross domestic product (GDP). In 2014, the GDP was $284.3 billion (USD), and the per capita GDP was $25,800 (USD), a considerable decline over previous years.

Services such as tourism and hospitality dominate the economy, contributing 79.9 percent to the GDP, while industry and agriculture supply 16 percent and 3.8 percent, respectively. The labor force is made up of 4.98 million people, 65 percent of whom work in the services sector and 22 percent of whom work in industry, while the remaining 12 percent work in agriculture.

In 2013, Greek exports totaled $36.6 billion (USD). Leading exports were food and beverages, manufactured goods, petroleum products, chemicals, and textiles. Greece's major trading partners include Germany, Italy, Bulgaria, Cyprus, France, Turkey, and the United States.

In April 2010, Greece faced a national economic emergency related to its high level of national debt. After regulatory agencies downgraded the status of the country's debt rating to "junk," meaning that it was unlikely Greece could pay back it back, Greek leaders and economic analysts feared a nationwide economic collapse. The Greek government began to negotiate for a bailout package, stating that a collapse of the Greek economy would have serious consequences for the European Union (EU) and the global economy. Later in the month, the International Monetary Fund (IMF) and the EU agreed to a financial bailout for Greece, valued at over $60 billion USD. Unfortunately, Greece was unable to meet the criteria for the bailout and austerity measures were introduced.

A second round of bailouts amounting to about $169 billion was provided to Greece in 2011. More austerity measures followed, further crippling the Greek economy. Although some gains were made in 2013, as the decline in the GDP slowed, a new round of stock crises resulted in further bailout negotiations as recently as February 2015.

Industry

Greece's major industries include the production of textiles, chemicals, and metal products. The petroleum industry is also very important to the economy. Technology and telecommunications are two of the country's newer, expanding industries. Due to its geographic location, shipping has always been an important industrial sector in Greece.

Half of the country's industrial and manufacturing jobs are located in the greater metropolitan area of Athens. Athenian businesses make a variety of products, from pottery and carpets to books, alcohol, soap, and chemicals. Businesses that cater to tourism are also among the chief sources of income.

Labor

The labor force was estimated at nearly 3.9 million in 2013. Over two-thirds of the work force is employed in the services industry. The unemployment rate was recorded as an astounding 26.8 percent in 2014.

Energy/Power/Natural Resources

Greece has many natural resources, including petroleum and natural gas. Other natural resources are bauxite, iron ore, marble, and hydropower. Most of Greece's resources, however, are not very valuable to the economy.

Approximately 20 percent of Greece's land is arable. About 28 percent of Greece is forested. Air and water pollution are the most serious environmental (and health) threats, especially in Athens, though in the years leading up to the 2004 Olympics, Athens made great strides in reducing this problem. The city is prone to temperature inversion, in which a mass of warmer air becomes stationary over a layer of cooler air. This prevents the normal flow of air and traps pollution near ground level.

Fishing

An estimated 40,000 people are employed in the fishing industry in the early 21st century. Common catches include brown shrimp, cuttlefish, octopus, sardine, anchovy, red mullet, hake, and prawn. The bluefin tuna is a significant species to the fishing industry; however, in 2007, the European Union placed a ban on catching bluefin tuna as their numbers have been depleted by overfishing. In the early 21st century, the EU promised funds to improve the infrastructure of the fishing industry.

Forestry

Approximately one-fifth of the land in Greece is covered by forest. Deforestation is a significant issue in Greece and has led to soil erosion, as well as desertification. Clear cutting, forest fires, overgrazing, and population growth have contributed to the country's deforestation problems.

Mining/Metals

Metals significant to Greece's mining industry include aluminum, steel, perlite, clays, marble, and coal.

Agriculture

Agriculture comprises 3.5 percent of Greece's GDP, and is an important resource for the country. Greek crops feed over half the population and supply many important exports.

Wheat is the primary crop. Major crops produced for export include sugar beets, tomatoes, corn, oranges, peaches, nectarines, olive oil, cotton, barley, apples, and tobacco. Greece is also one of the world's major sources of olive oil and raisins.

Greek agriculture faces several natural, environmental, and financial challenges, including drought, soil erosion, and lack of investment. Its contribution to the GDP has been steadily declining since the 1950s. The federal government has sought to address these issues by providing tax exemption for some agricultural income as well as generous tax credits to farmers.

Animal Husbandry

In the early 21st century, there were approximately 8 million dairy sheep and 5.5 million goats in Greece—these two species are the most significant livestock animals in the country. The country meets almost all of its domestic demand for sheep and goat milk, eggs, and honey.

Tourism

Tourism is a major source of revenue for Greece, accounting for as much as 15 percent of the national GDP. More than 12 million international tourists visited Greece in 1999. In that same year, tourism receipts were $8.7 billion (USD). In the early 21st century, however, the Greek tourist industry was negatively affected by the global economic downturn that began around 2007.

As of 2013, an estimated 657,000 people are employed in the tourism sector, and tourism revenue accounts for approximately 16 percent of the country's gross domestic product.

Visitors are welcomed in Greece, though passports are required for most travelers. Some of the major tourist sites include the Parthenon, the site of the ancient oracle at Delphi, the Agora at Corinth, and the Minoan ruins on Crete.

Izza Tahir, Kim Nagy, Jennifer Eastman

DO YOU KNOW?

- In 2004, Greece spent $10 billion to hold the Olympic Games in Athens.

- Greece joined the European Union as its tenth member in 1981.

- Until 1687, the Parthenon on the Acropolis was one of the best-preserved temples from ancient Greece, because it had been in continual use since the time it was built around 440 BCE. In 1687, however, Venetian forces fighting the Turks bombed the Parthenon, where there was a large store of ammunition. The explosion shattered the building.

Bibliography

Korina Miller. *Greece.* Oakland, CA: Lonely Planet, 2014.

James Pettifer. *The Greeks.* London: Penguin Group, 1993.

Rough Guides. *Rough Guide to Greece.* London: Rough Guides, 2015.

Robin Sowerby. *The Greeks: An Introduction to Their Culture.* New York: Routledge, 2015.

Thomas, Carol G. *Greece: A Short History of a Long Story, 7,000 BCE to the Present.* Malden, MA: Wiley Blackwell, 2014.

Stathis Kalyvas. *Modern Greece: What Everyone Needs to Know.* New York: Oxford University Press, 2015.

Works Cited

Amnesty International. *Amnesty International. Report on Torture.* London: Duckworth & Co. Ltd., 1973.

"Country Profile: Greece," *BBC Country Profiles.* <http://news.bbc.co.uk/2/hi/europe/country_profiles/1009249.stm>

Donna Birdwell-Pheasant and Denise Lawrence-Zuniga, Eds. *House Life: Space, Place and Family in Europe.* Oxford: Berg, 1999.

George Mongor. *Marriage Customs of the World.* Santa Barbara (CA): ABC-CLIO, 2004.

"Greece." Encyclopædia Britannica. *Encyclopædia Britannica Online* <http://www.britannica.com/EBchecked/topic/244154/Greece>.

"Greece." *World Heritage.* <http://whc.unesco.org/en/statesparties/gr>

"Greece Communications." *The CIA World Factbook.* <http://www.theodora.com/wfbcurrent/greece/greece_communications.html>

"Greece Cultural Events." *Greece.* <http://www.greeka.com/greece-cultural-events.htm>

"Hellenic World Heritage Monuments". *Odysseus.* <http://odysseus.culture.gr/h/2/eh20.jsp>

"Human Rights Watch World Report 1997: Events of 1996." New York: *Human Rights Watch, 1996.*

Jean S. Forward, *Endangered Peoples of Europe.* London: Greenwood Press, 2001.

Kathleen Malley-Morrison. *International Perspectives on Family Violence and Abuse.* New Jersey: Lawrence Erlbaum Associates Inc., 2004.

"List of Cities in Greece." *Wikipedia.*

Mike-Frank G. Epitropolous. and Victor Roudomelof. *American Culture in Europe.* Westport (CT): Greenwood Publishing Group, 1998.

Paul Hellander, et al. *Greece.* London: Lonely Planet, 2006.

Robin Barber. *Greece.* New York: WW Norton & Company, Incorporated, 1988.

Terri Morrison, et al. *Kiss, Bow or Shake Hands.* Holbrook (MA): B. Adams, 1994.

Theresa M. Beatty, *Food and Recipes of Greece.* New York: Power Kids Press, 1999. <http://en.wikipedia.org/wiki/List_of_cities_in_Greece>

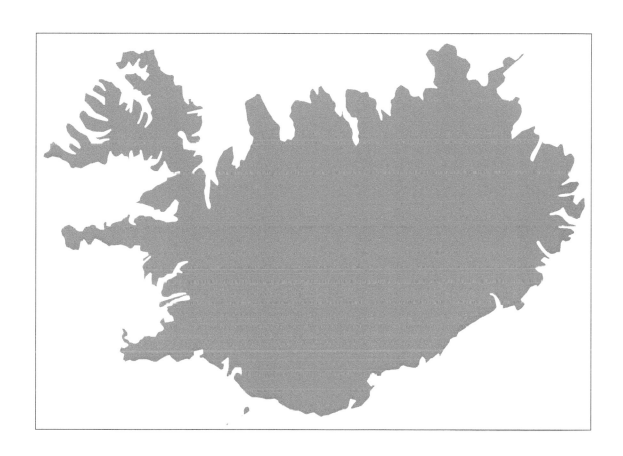

ICELAND

Introduction

Iceland is the northernmost country in Europe, a Nordic island in the Atlantic Ocean that borders the Arctic Circle. It is one of the most geologically active places in the world, containing numerous volcanoes, geysers, and hot springs.

Iceland is heralded worldwide for its pristine and extensive environment. The country is also recognized for the stringent government policy and cultural outlook that have partnered to preserve its land. The island is treasured by its citizens and government alike, who have deliberately placed nature conservation at the forefront of the nation's environmental policy.

An established arts scene in the larger cities provides Icelanders with many cultural activities to enjoy. Reykjavík has numerous museums, art galleries, theaters, and concert venues, earning it the title "European City of Culture" in 2000.

Iceland's banking industry was devastated by the global financial crisis of 2008, which had disastrous effects on the country's economy. Unemployment numbers remain high as the country tries to reestablish its financial base by focusing on agriculture and fishing.

GENERAL INFORMATION

Official Language: Icelandic
Population: 317,351 (2014 estimate)
Currency: Icelandic króna

Coins: The króna exists in coin denominations of 1, 5, 10, 50, and 100 krónur
Land Area: 103,000 square kilometers (39,770 square miles)
Water Area: 2,796 square kilometers (1,079 square miles)
National Anthem: "Lofsöngur" ("Song of Praise")
Capital: Reykjavík
Time Zone: Greenwich Mean Time (GMT)
Flag Description: The flag of Iceland is blue. It features a red cross, laid horizontally toward the hoist side of the flag, outlined in white. The color blue represents the waters surrounding Iceland, while red represents volcanoes and white represents the country's snow and ice.

Population

Iceland is partitioned into eight geographic regions, which are further divided into counties,

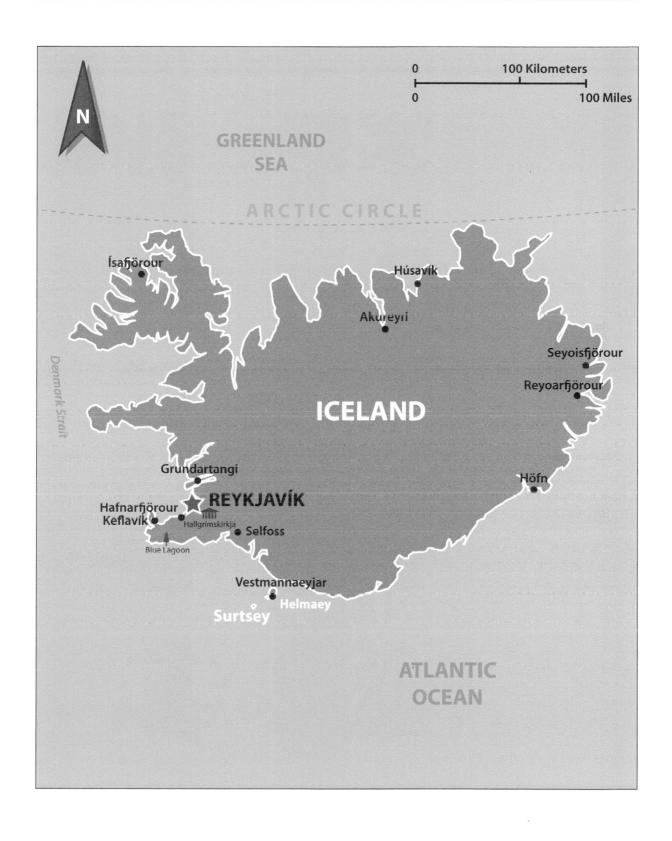

**Principal Cities by Population
(2012 estimate):**

- Reykjavík (119,474)
- Kópavogur (33,045)
- Hafnarfjörður (28,085)
- Akureyri (17,770)
- Keflavik (14,000)
- Garðabær (11,420)

municipalities, and other localities. The vast majority (99 percent) of Icelanders live in cities or towns of more than 200 residents, while the other 1 percent lives in rural areas.

Reykjavík is Iceland's capital and largest city in terms of area (274.5 square kilometers/106 square miles) and population (approximately 120,000). It is located on the southwestern coast inside the Flaxaflói Bay. The greater Reykjavík area, in which 60 percent of Icelanders live, consists of seven municipalities. Two of these, Kópavogur and Hafnarfjörður, are Iceland's second and third most-populous cities.

Languages

Icelandic is the official language of Iceland. Many Icelanders speak English as well. Icelandic in its current form is very similar to its progenitor, Old Norse, spoken by Iceland's Norwegian settlers over a thousand years ago. To keep the language pure, foreign words are rarely incorporated into the Icelandic lexicon.

Iceland is an ethnically homogenous nation, due to its geographical isolation and strict immigration policies. Its population is comprised mainly of descendants of its original Norwegian and Celtic settlers. Immigration policies have relaxed in recent years allowing an influx of different cultures, but ethnic diversity is still negligible.

Native People & Ethnic Groups

Iceland was uninhabited until the ninth century, when Vikings began settling the island. They were followed by other Scandinavian and Celtic settlers. Today, the majority of the island's

population, or 93.2 percent, are native Icelandic. However, some 5,000 Polish immigrants also live and work on the island. Smaller demographic groups include people from Lithuania, Germany and Denmark.

Religions

A mass conversion from paganism to Christianity occurred in Iceland in 1000 AD. Today, most Icelanders belong to the Evangelical Lutheran Church (the state church). Approximately 75 percent of the population is Lutheran (although church attendance is extremely low), 3.5 percent is Roman Catholic, and 6 percent are nonreligious. The remainder belong to other denominations including Ásatrú, a modern pagan religion based on the ancient religions of the Germanic people. Religious freedom is constitutionally guaranteed.

Climate

Due to its close proximity to the Gulf Stream, Iceland has a relatively mild climate. Reykjavík enjoys a coastal climate, but the Gulf Stream's proximity to Iceland's cold northern seas also produces a fair amount of rain, fog, and wind, as well as fierce storms. The southern and western parts of the country are wetter than the eastern and northern parts, and experience less snow and temperature variation as well. During the hottest part of summer, temperatures average around 11.8° Celsius (53° Fahrenheit) while during the coldest days of winter they average around -0.2° Celsius (32° Fahrenheit). Thanks to its location just below the Arctic Circle, from the middle of May through August, the capital experiences the phenomenon of the midnight sun. During this period, the sun remains, to some degree, visible round the clock. By the end of December, though, the city enjoys only two hours of twilight and twenty-two hours of darkness.

In fact, Iceland offers a dramatic view of the polar northern lights, also known as the aurora borealis. Once thought by the Inuit to be the souls of the dead, the pulsating streaks of natural light can be seen on clear nights in Iceland from September through May.

ENVIRONMENT & GEOGRAPHY

Iceland is heralded worldwide for its pristine and extensive environment—less than 1 percent of Iceland is covered with trees. The country is also recognized for the stringent government policy and cultural outlook that have partnered to preserve it. The island is treasured by its citizens and government alike, who have deliberately placed nature conservation at the forefront of the nation's environmental policy. Accordingly, the unspoiled scenery draws visitors from all corners of the world. From waterfalls to volcanoes to glaciers, Iceland's pristine landscape and one-of-a-kind geological landmarks make it a premier ecotourism destination.

Topography

Iceland is a geologically young volcanic island that is situated on the Mid-Atlantic Ridge, a fault line where the North Atlantic and European continental plates converge. The ridge runs from the southeast to the northwest through the middle of Iceland, dividing the country via a line of volcanoes and fissures and causing tremendous geological activity.

Iceland has about 30 active volcanic systems (mostly fissure volcanoes that have accounted for a majority of the Earth's lava output over the past 500 years), 780 hot springs, and 250 geothermal hotspots comprised of geysers and mud pits.

Only 21 percent of Iceland is arable, mostly along the coast. More than 50 percent of Iceland is desert plateau, 12 percent is covered by icecaps, 11 percent is lava field, and 4 percent is sand delta. Fjords are found along the coast as well as in the northern and eastern areas of the country. Mountains and desert plateaus are present in the interior. The highest point in Iceland is Hvannadalshnúkur, a mountain with an elevation of 2,119 meters (6,952 feet). The largest icecap is Vatnajökull with an area of 8,400 square kilometers (5,219 square miles); a volcanic eruption occurred under the glacier there in 2011, causing disruptions. This followed a 2010 eruption at Eyjafjalljökull in the south of Iceland. The longest river is Þjorsá, which is 230 kilometers (143 miles) long.

Plants & Animals

Geographic isolation, deforestation, and the sub-arctic climate have restricted the variety of plants that grow in Iceland. Along the coast are low grasses and plants common to marshes and bogs. The interior is mostly grassland and tundra that contain shrubs, lichens, mosses, and dwarf willow trees. Birch and other large trees exist in limited amounts thanks to reforestation efforts.

The arctic fox is Iceland's only native land mammal. However, the original settlers introduced reindeer and mink, which have built up considerable populations and continue to thrive, along with the arctic fox, in unpopulated areas.

Domesticated animals include cows, sheep, and horses. The Icelandic horse is an interesting breed: it has five gaits instead of four, is as small as a pony, and is of pure genetic stock. Its bloodline has not been compromised by other breeds since the original settlers brought it to Iceland.

Over 350 species of birds, including auks, puffins, gannets, guillemots, kittiwakes, fulmars, shags, and razorbills, among others, may be spotted in Iceland. Most are migratory, but some breed among the steep cliffs on the coast. Waterfowl and marsh birds inhabit both coastal waters and inland lakes.

Whales, seals, dolphins, porpoises, and numerous species of fish flourish in the ocean surrounding Iceland, thanks to the temperature-moderating Gulf Stream.

CUSTOMS & COURTESIES

Greetings

Iceland's unique combination of small size, folkloric culture, and relatively un-commercialized geography has rendered a proud, close-knit and welcoming people. In keeping with this strong sense of community, communication and exchange is friendly and informal. For example, because Icelanders do not have typical surnames, greetings typically occur on a first name basis, despite socioeconomic status.

A typically greeting may be "Góðan daginn," which means "good morning," or "Gott kvöld," which means "good evening." A more casual "Saell" (which roughly translates to "happiness") is a colloquial pleasantry meaning "Hello, how are you?" A typical response is "Allt gott" ("Good/ All is well"). When parting, an informal "Takk" ("Thanks") is common, as is the expression "Bless" ("Bye-bye"). "Skall" ("Cheers") is another popular expression, and commonly used when congratulating someone, wishing them good health, or simply as a toast.

Gestures & Etiquette

In general, Icelanders are considered very friendly and free-spirited, but also quite straightforward. They typically do not mince words, and often speak with directness and eye contact. Handshakes are a common form of greeting, and Icelandic conduct is very sedate. For example, upon meeting, Icelanders do not engage in a lengthy series of pleasantries; rather, they discuss the matter at hand. Icelanders also tend to avoid loud speech and abrupt gestures.

Similarly, Icelanders are meticulously hygienic and they expect the same of visitors. One particular gripe is visitors' neglect to wash thoroughly before swimming (whether this be in a private swimming pool or public spring), as this contaminates water which is otherwise not treated with chemical cleaners. Interestingly, Icelanders, for the most part, have adopted a very open-minded and easy-going philosophy of life. Relative to other countries with a strong corporate culture, Iceland's workplace operations are very relaxed and liberal. Attire is comfortable and business transactions are often incorporated into a leisurely meal or other activity. In contrast, much attention may be given to appearances during seemingly casual and recreational circumstances—such as a meeting of friends—and Icelanders tend to dress up for these occasions.

Eating/Meals

Traditional Icelandic food is simple and rustic fare that centers on lamb or fish. It is generally only prepared in the deep rural areas or in celebration of national holidays. On a typical day-to-day basis, the diet of the average Icelander is similar to what is eaten in most modern urban societies.

Icelanders eat three standard meals per day and, since much of the population resides in and around Reykjavik, quick meals are the default choice for breakfast and lunch. Cereal or skyr (soured curds often served with berries) are common breakfast selections. A café meal of soup and a sandwich makes a typical lunch, but fast food is also popular. The cheap and ubiquitous pylsur (a hotdog made of lamb) is served with toppings of ketchup, mustard, relish and deep-fried onions.

Icelanders typically dine late in the evening, beginning well after eight o'clock. Fusion cuisine (hybrid meals that borrow from Icelandic food and other ethnic cuisines) is the focus of urban contemporary menus. For a sweet or savory snack, Icelanders frequent the many food stands, bakeries (a legacy of Danish occupation), and even gas stations that offer favorites like harofiskur (strips of wind-dried haddock), pönnukökur (cinnamon pancakes) or kleinur (donuts).

Visiting

There is a very informal approach to visiting in Icelandic culture, and it is not uncommon for guests to drop in unannounced. However if an invitation is extended, it is expected that a guest will arrive on time. A gift of flowers or a bottle of wine is commonly appreciated, and it is customary to remove one's shoes upon entering the house. It is not necessary to address someone as "Fru" (Mrs.) or "Herra" (Mr.) when meeting for the first time. Greeting each other by first name is standard, and is not interpreted as too familiar or disrespectful. After a meal is enjoyed, it is polite to say "Takk fyrir mig" as a thank you before leaving the table, and again at the end of the stay.

LIFESTYLE

Family

Iceland has a close-knit population of roughly 300,000 people, and family values are relatively traditional. However, Iceland also has a high divorce rate; in fact, Icelanders view divorce as healthy and the arrangements are generally quite amicable. There has historically been little foreign influence in Iceland, and Icelanders also mostly marry other Icelanders. In this way, the population has managed to stay more or less contained. These generations of isolation have resulted in a uniquely homogenous population that is highly valuable to scientists conducting genetic study.

In the 12th century, Icelandic historian Ari Thorgilsson (known as Ari the Learned) compiled very detailed history accounts of Iceland—*Landnámabók* (*The Book of Settlements*) and *Íslendingabók* (*The Book of the Icelanders*)—which allow Icelanders to trace their family history back to the ninth century. This, in addition to a government-created database of each citizen's genetic and medical records, provides a historical goldmine for researchers. The release of this information has been hotly contested, although the findings have helped to discover origins of heart disease, stroke and asthma.

As years go by, however, the Icelandic family unit will no longer be such a novelty. Recent development and construction has attracted a surge of immigrant laborers and the population is set to diversify.

Housing

Before the Industrial Revolution of the late 19th century, Icelandic homes were typically constructed out of sod. Because there is very little forestation on the island, wood could not be counted on for construction, so Icelanders improvised with stone, whalebone and earth. Many of these homes still exist in the countryside, although most are not in use.

Today, the average home is completely modernized. There is widespread availability of geothermal power and hydroelectricity as the country's many geysers, waterfalls and rivers are harnessed for use. As a result of this plentiful natural power source, the average resident not only enjoys a consistently heated home, but exceptionally low utility costs as well.

One notable feature of Icelandic interiors is the presence of "blackout curtains," which are heavyweight black drapes that are drawn to darken a room during the summer months. Because of Iceland's northern exposure, the country experiences almost complete sunlight during the summer months of July through September. The curtains are drawn at night to simulate darkness and encourage sleep.

Food

Icelandic cuisine is characterized mainly by uncomplicated preparations of fish and meat that hail from an industrious time in the country's history when significant efforts were made to ensure that food was not wasted. The cuisine incorporates the limited variety of food resources available to early Icelanders. Some of the most classic celebratory meals include rotten shark meat (buried in the ground to ferment for several months); lundi, cooked puffin; svið, boiled sheep's head; slátur, sheep's blood (served in sheep's diaphragm); skyr, a yogurt-type dairy product; pressed loaves of head cheese (traditionally, the prepared meat portions of a pig's head); and Brennivín, an alcoholic drink made from potatoes and caraway seeds. Today these delicacies are typically served only during the ancient winter festival of Thorri.

Traditional Icelandic food still has a place at the contemporary table, however. Modern cuisine still draws heavily from local resources. Roasted lamb and sheep are popular dishes, while another standard meal is plokkfiskur (fish in white sauce); and harðfiskur, or dried haddock. Of the three meals that Icelanders eat each day, dinner is the most elaborate. Seafood, lamb, or beef is usually an ingredient in the main course.

Since three-quarters of the island are barren of vegetation, produce is harvested in geothermal greenhouses and is quite expensive. One common side dish, however, is caramel potatoes. This dish is prepared by melting and mixing sugar and butter in a frying pan to form caramel, then adding small potatoes that are then coated with candy.

Lastly, kleinur is a beloved dessert and snack. This dish is prepared by rubbing butter into two pounds of flour and adding hartshorn, baking powder and baking soda. This creates a dough that is then added to buttermilk, one egg and cardamom extract. The dough is then rolled, cut into diamonds, with a diagonal slit in each so that one end is pulled through each slit. It is then deep-fried until golden brown.

Life's Milestones

The Icelandic naming tradition is uniquely simple in that the last name does not reflect the family lineage, as it does in most cultures. The father's first name (often in the possessive form) serves as the root, and is followed by a qualifier of -sson (son) or -dóttir (daughter). Therefore, Svana Hinriksdóttir declares Svana to be "Hinrik's daughter." Last names must be changed legally in order to be derived from the mother, and women do not commonly take their husbands' last name upon marrying.

The selection of first names is equally as traditional, if not strict, as preservation of the Icelandic culture is highly valued. The country has established the Icelandic Naming Committee, and a child's name is chosen from a government list approved by the committee. Anyone who would like to use a name outside of the list must seek approval from the national naming committee.

Marriage is taken rather seriously in Iceland. It is customary for a couple to remain engaged for up to five years so as to sincerely evaluate their commitment and establish financial security. There was a time when an Icelandic wedding celebration would last as long as a week. Today, a typical ceremony is modeled after the American tradition of bachelor and bachelorette parties, ring bearers, flower girls, and the throwing of rice.

CULTURAL HISTORY

Art

Because Iceland's population was historically small and spread out, there were sparse resources for artistic study and practice. As a result, the fine arts did not flourish until the 19th century. In the beginning, the country's most successful artists would study abroad and return to fuse European styles with Icelandic subject matter. Idealistic renditions of landscape were especially popular, serving as expressions of nationalism during a time when Icelanders were craving independence from Danish rule.

Thorarinn Thorlaksson (1867–1924) painted landscapes almost exclusively. He is commonly thought of as the father of Iceland's visual arts scene, mostly for having paved the way for future artists. For the most part, Thorlaksson was a student of the realist school of painting, though he also experimented with dramatic light and shadow. Asgrimur Jonsson (1876–1958), considered Iceland's first truly great landscape painter, was a disciple of impressionism. He garnered international fame for his sweeping, emotional interpretations of Iceland's countryside. Einar Jonsson (1874–1954) is considered responsible for introducing sculpture to Iceland. Though he studied in Europe and his practice took him to America for several years, the dark and mystical themes of Jonsson's works were distinctly Icelandic.

Music

Icelandic music is relatively new in comparison to other European countries. This is due to the lack of forestation and austere standard of living which dominated the culture until the Industrial Revolution of the late eighteenth and early 19th century. Musical instruments were considered a great luxury, and were all but non-existent until the 20th century. However, two Viking creations were brought over from Scandinavia: the fiola and the langspil. Each instrument was a variation of the dulcimer, having two to six strings and played with a horsehair bow.

For most of Iceland's musical history, singing was the primary form of expression. Icelandic song was rooted mainly in Norse styles, and consisted primarily of Protestant hymns until the country's own rimur emerged in the 19th century. Considered the hallmark of Icelandic musical tradition, rimur is an elaborate rhyming and alliterative chant, performed a capella. Rimur recounts Icelandic poetry and the ancient sagas. The form involves highly complex rhyme schemes and sometimes similarly challenging harmonies, when performed as a duet. Sigurdur Breidfjord (1798–1846) is the most famous of the rimur poets.

More recently, the eclectic singer-songwriter Björk (1965–), has become a renowned international artist in the popular music genre.

Literature

Iceland's literary history begins with the epic Icelandic Sagas. Written between 1180 and 1300 CE, the Sagas are Iceland's best-known literary accomplishment, and are internationally renowned as the country's greatest cultural achievement. Tasked with reporting on the country's history and genealogy, the Saga writers (who remain unknown) depicted Iceland's greatest heroes with dark, romantic, larger-than-life accounts of vanquishing evil and defending virtue. The most famous among these is the Neal's Saga, an epic tale of infidelity, thieving, and bitter blood feuds that is a perfect example of the writers' intention to glorify themes such as courage, honor and pride. Although originally a source of entertainment, the Sagas quickly became a revered piece of cultural heritage. For hundreds of years, they have been re-interpreted through painting and song. Because the language has remained virtually unchanged, they continue to be read and upheld as the cornerstone of Icelandic writing.

During this same Saga Age, poetry surfaced as an alternative literary expression. The two main forms are Eddic poetry and Skaldic poetry. The Eddic poems follow Germanic poetry of that time and are categorized in three ways: Mythical Eddic poetry, which glorifies the adventures of the Norse gods and was likely intended as an affront to the growth of Christianity; Gnomic Eddic poetry, which centers on common life; and Heroic Eddic poetry, which tells of mortal heroes such as kings and other military figures. The construction of the Eddic poems is fairly simple and uncomplicated

as compared to the Skaldic tradition. Skaldic poetry mainly praises the Scandinavian kings. Its tightly structured syllables and alliterative phrases are highly descriptive, and the form is acknowledged for later serving as the basis for 19th century rimur chant.

In the 20th century, modern literature flourished in Iceland. Halldór Laxness (1902–1998) won the Nobel Prize in 1955 for his brilliant novels and other writings. Other modernist Icelandic writers have met with modest success outside of Iceland as well.

CULTURE

Arts & Entertainment

Outdoor activities such as hiking, fishing, bird watching, skiing (downhill and cross-country), camping, and bathing in hot springs are favorite pastimes in Iceland. Colder regions permit winter sports year-round. An established arts scene in the larger cities provides Icelanders with many cultural activities to enjoy. Reykjavík has numerous museums, art galleries, theaters, and concert venues, earning it the title "European City of Culture" in 2000.

Iceland's contemporary arts are characterized by political expression and national pride. As international recognition of Iceland's government and policy achievements increases, Icelandic artists waver between retrospective pieces that cling to the purity of the "olden days" and cutting-edge, innovative pieces that exploit the country's technological prowess.

Iceland's film industry is a mere thirty years old, but it is making a name for itself in spite of its youth. With the help of government support, the industry is accessible to domestic filmmakers while also attracting Hollywood types who want dramatic scenery on a tight budget. Domestic films are seldom feature length; shorts are more common and, like popular TV programs, tend to possess a dark and eccentric aesthetic that appeals to Icelanders' wry humor and objectivity. The most popular Icelandic filmmaker to date is Fridrik Thor Fridriksson (1954–), who directed

Children of Nature (1991), nominated for an Oscar in 1992 in the category of best foreign language film.

The country's music scene has become increasingly popular, and has been recently spotlighted by the international success of Icelandic musicians such as singer Björk (1965–) and minimalist rock band Sigur Rós. Music is fast becoming the primary mode of expression for Icelanders under age 35, and the result is a flood of soloists and bands in and around Reykjavik. The growth of Iceland's music industry has also made way for the annual Iceland Airwaves festival in Reykjavik, which features performances by emerging independent artists and is gaining an international following.

Icelanders are also considered avid readers, and the most digested genres are poetry and fiction. Icelandic writing employs black humor and is sardonic in tone. For example, *101 Reykjavik* by Hallgrimur Helgason (1959–) is a hugely popular dark comedy that spawned a film (by the same name) with a cult following. Perhaps the best-known representative of contemporary Icelandic writing is Halldor Laxness (1902–1998), who won the Nobel Prize in Literature in 1955. Rich with ironic plot twists, black humor, and sympathetic characters, his deeply sensitive novels (most notable among them is *Independent People*) offer a window into the Icelandic heart and mind. Somewhat autobiographical, his works address living conditions in the early 20th century and themes like justice and revenge. His writings depict Icelanders as a quirky and flawed people. When his books were first released, audiences hesitated to support his exposé of Icelandic culture.

Although there are still pockets of artists producing variations on traditional handicrafts, this tends only to be a draw for tourists. These days Icelandic art is almost exclusively abstract. The pop art icon, Erro (1932–), is praised for making a name of contemporary Icelandic art after working extensively in Paris and other European markets. He donated the majority of his collection to the Reykjavik Art Museum in 1989, and his graphic pieces are now a part of the permanent collection there.

Aside from painting, sculpture is the most popular visual medium. Asmunder Sveinsson (1893–1982) is the most prominent sculptor, and helped further the development of abstract art through figurative sculpture that depicts Icelandic folklore. Perhaps most importantly, Sveinsson is also recognized for his determination to push the visual arts beyond elite status, and make it accessible to the general public. His work can still be seen in and around Reykjavik, whether in front of the University of Iceland or in a roadside field.

Cultural Sites & Landmarks

Reykjavík is Iceland's capital and political, economic, and cultural center. It is the *world* northernmost national capital. Located on the edge of the Arctic Circle, Reykjavík blends natural beauty and urban sophistication. It is a city where flocks of geese regularly migrate overhead and through which a salmon-filled river flows—but it is also a city renowned for its cutting edge use of information and eco-friendly technologies.

Formally established as Iceland's capital in the late 19th century, Reykjavík has evolved, especially during the decades encompassing the late nineteenth and early twenty-first centuries, from an obscure town into an increasingly popular international business and tourist destination.

The capital's name, which translates to "Smoky Bay," stems from its founder, Ingolfur Arnarson, who noted the columns of steam rising out the geothermal springs on the small farm he had established on the site of present-day Reykjavík. The area remained a farm until the mid-18th century when a small town sprang up around it. Hoping to modernize Iceland's economy and traditional way of life, Skuli Magnusson, sometimes called "the Father of Reykjavik," set up wool processing workshops in the area.

Modest urban development followed, leading to the formal chartering of Reykjavík as a town in 1786. In 1845 Iceland's government reestablished itself in Reykjavík, which became the national capital after Iceland gained independence from Denmark in 1944.

The Reykjavík Capital Area consists of seven municipalities scattered across a peninsula jutting into the Atlantic Ocean. Its southern shore is situated on Faxafloi Bay while its northern limit is defined by Mt. Esja, which looms 914 meters (just under 3,000 feet) over the capital. On a clear day, Reykjavík also affords views of the Snaefellsjokull glacier, even though it lies some 97 kilometers (60 miles) west of the city. The glacier was made famous by Jules Verne's decision to make its topmost crater the entry point for the characters in his famous novel "Journey to the Center of the Earth." Reykjavík is noted for its hot springs. In the past, people used these springs to wash clothes and bathe. Today, the geothermal fields in the capital and its vicinity provide a source of renewable energy. This rich resource has helped drive Reykjavík's surging economy.

Reykjavík is both considerably smaller and newer than its neighboring Scandinavian and European capitals. End to end, its downtown can be traversed on foot in less than half an hour. Construction on its most famous landmark, the Hallgrímskirkja church, began in the late 1940s and didn't open until 1986.

The city's Old Quarter, which is the site of both Town Hall and Iceland's National Assembly building, is centered on the geothermally heated Lake Tjornin, where the first recorded settlement in the area was established in 874. During the winter when the small lake freezes over, it becomes a popular venue for ice skating and hockey. The lake's waters run underground and empty into Reykjavík's harbor. The modern portion of the capital branches out east of this lake district.

Although the main thoroughfare, Laugavegur, is home to many elegant shops, Reykjavík does not possess many ancient monuments or examples of stately architecture. The side streets of the city's center are largely residential in character. The houses, some of white-washed wood but mostly made of concrete and corrugated iron to protect against the Atlantic storms that regularly batter the area, tend to be painted in bright shades of red, yellow, blue, and green. Nearly every neighborhood in Reykjavík boasts its own geothermally heated pool.

One of Reykjavík's two most notable landmarks is the Hallgrímskirkja, an imposing white concrete church; its 75-meters-tall (246-foot) tower resembles a spire of volcanic basalt. The tower, whose top is accessible by elevator, offers panoramic views of Reykjavík. At the base of the church, on its front lawn, stands a statue of Leifur Eríksson, described as the "Son of Iceland, Discoverer of Vinland."

Reykjavík's other distinguished landmark is the so-called Pearl, a glass-domed, revolving restaurant, complete with an outside viewing platform, perched on Oskjuhlid Hill overlooking the capital and the surrounding Atlantic. Built in 1988 atop the city's enormous hot water storage tanks, the Pearl also features a large exhibition atrium and an artificial geyser.

One of Reykjavík's most renowned buildings is Hofdi House, built in 1909 as the residence of the French consul. Though it is now owned by the City of Reykjavík, Hofdi House is used to host official meetings, the most famous of which was the 1986 Russian-American summit effectively ending the Cold War. Hofdi House's other claim to fame is the ghostly presence alleged to inhabit it. The so-called White Lady spirit reportedly so unnerved a British ambassador who once lived in the house that the British Foreign Office ended up selling it.

The Icelandic countryside is a world apart from the metropolitan flavor of Reykjavik. Although the cultural heritage is valued equally in the urban areas, the countryside has a certain quietness to it that is difficult to find in an increasingly commercialized world. Visitors who travel Iceland's Ring Road outside the capital will observe a landscape virtually free of modern influences — hardly even a municipal trash bin for collecting litter.

Iceland is home to two World Heritage Sites, as designated by the United Nations Educational, Scientific and Cultural Organization (UNESCO). These two sites were both recognized for their natural and scientific importance to humanity, and include the Þingvellir National Park

(Thingvellir National Park) and the volcanic island of Surtsey. Thingvellir National Park marks the place where the Althing assembly—the world's oldest democracy and the first functioning parliament—met from 930 to 1798. Existing remnants include portions of booths built from sod and stone. The surrounding land still holds evidence of medieval Germanic and Norse agricultural practices. The volcanic island of Surtsey is a fascinating source of scientific study. A new island, it was formed by volcanic eruptions that occurred between 1963 and 1967. Since its formation Surtsey has been legally protected from human interaction, and is highly valued as a resource for the study of ecological evolution.

The Vatnajokull glacier, located in the southeastern portion of the island, covers 10 percent of the country, making it Iceland's largest glacier, as well as the largest in all of Europe. The country's most famous waterfall is Gullfoss, located in the southwestern Hvita River. Boasting a roaring 36-meter (120-foot) double fall, it is the most popular tourist attraction in the country. Geysir (from which the English word in derived), is found in the Haukadalur Valley. It is the oldest known geyser and arguably the most impressive, though eruptions are infrequent. Iceland is also renowned for its geothermal spas, including the Blue Lagoon. One of Iceland's most spectacular environmental treasures, the glowing waters of the lagoon are warmed by a nearby lava formation. The lagoon is rich in minerals such as silica and sulfur that are said to have extreme health benefits.

Libraries & Museums

Reykjavík's most noteworthy museums include the National Museum, whose collections of religious relics, farming implements, nautical equipment, and early fishing boats reflect Norse and Icelandic culture from its beginnings; the Árni Magnússon Institute, an organization housing medieval Icelandic manuscripts; the Saga Museum, where waxwork figures are used to depict major figures and events in Icelandic history; the Reykjavík Art Museum, devoted to both Icelandic and international modern art; the

Arbaejarsafn, an open-air museum featuring historically preserved selected old houses; and the Reykjavík Settlement Exhibition in the city's center, which allows access to the recently discovered, oldest settlement ruins in *Iceland*, possibly dating to the time of the city's founder, Ingolfur Arnarson, or his descendants.

Holidays

Public holidays unique to Iceland include the First Day of Summer, which falls on the third Thursday in April and symbolizes the end of Iceland's long winter. National Day, on June 17, honors Iceland's independence from Denmark on June 17, 1944. Commerce Day, on the first Monday in August, pays tribute to shop keepers and office workers by closing businesses for the day and giving them a three-day weekend. The First Day of Summer and National Day are both celebrated with outdoor festivities such as picnics, parades, and street entertainment. People take advantage of Commerce Day by using the long weekend to travel.

The year is filled with other festivals, from the biannual Arts Festival in Reykjavík to religious-themed festivals on Christmas and Easter. Some other interesting festivals are Þorrablót, or Midwinter Feast, in January or February; Beer Day, on March 1; and Sjómannadagurinn, or Sailor's Day, on the first Sunday in June.

Youth Culture

The majority of college students in Iceland study locally in Reykjavik. Fashion is an important aspect of youth culture in Iceland, and downtown Reykjavik has become a fashion hub, with numerous one-of-a kind designer boutiques. (Reykjavik is also renowned for its music and arts scene, and has become an important center for youth culture in the country.) Outdoor sports are also extremely popular—the unspoiled Icelandic Highlands cover roughly 60 percent of the country's interior. The youth population is very active, enjoying the country's excellent conditions for rock climbing, hiking, horseback riding and other recreational activities. Handball is also very popular, and is considered the unofficial national sport. In fact, the national team is consistently one of the top-ranked teams worldwide.

Though the youth culture in Iceland is sometimes characterized as trendy, politics and the environment have begun to influence the leisure choices and buying habits of Icelandic youth in recent years. For example, the Icelandic youth population has demonstrated increasing loyalty to environmentalism through purchase of organic clothing or the patronage of eco-friendly establishments. However, these behaviors and attitudes have also earned them the moniker "Krutt-kynslotin," or the "Cuddly Generation," from older Icelanders who sometimes view their youth population as pampered but well intentioned.

SOCIETY

Transportation

Like drivers in the United States, Icelanders drive on the right-hand side of the road, with the steering wheel on the left hand side of the car. They are also very dependent on their personal cars. There is an average of one car per person over 17 years of age—one of the highest levels of private automobile ownership worldwide. This results in more greenhouse gas emissions than nations such as France or Spain (although Iceland is the only country that offers hydrogen filling stations for cars that run on fuel cells). Contributing to this statistic is the absence of a railway system and inconsistent public transit. According to the U.S. Department of State, less than a third of the roads in Iceland are paved. Driving conditions in the country can also be hampered by snowy and icy weather conditions. Keflavik International Airport is located just outside the capital, and offers easy access to Europe.

Transportation Infrastructure

As nearly half of the population resides in and around Reykjavik, there are some freeways present in that region, and little need for further development. Beyond that, only a small percentage of the country's roadways are paved, and

the icy interior of the country is mostly uninhabitable. Even Ring Road, a main artery that circles the island, is only one lane in each direction. However, it is a refreshing dichotomy for many, for as cutting-edge and techno-savvy as Icelanders are, the pristine countryside remains largely unblemished by infrastructure.

Media & Communications

Iceland's small population enjoys several national daily newspapers, including *Morgunblaðið* (*The Morning Paper*), *DV* (*Dagblaðið Vísir*) and *Fréttablaðið* (*The Newspaper*), and over 100 other periodicals. *The Reykjavík Grapevine,* based out of Reykjavik, is an English language casual alternative to traditional news sources, and is especially enjoyed for its reviews of cultural interests and nightlife. In addition to these, news websites are increasingly popular (including the English news source, Icelandreview.com), and many choose to have headlines delivered directly to their email.

Iceland had only one television station until 1988, and it did not broadcast on Thursdays, so as to promote healthier leisure activities. Although it is not omnipresent, as in other developed nations, television is nonetheless a source of entertainment for Icelanders. As with their print publications, the top-ranking shows are consistently news programs and satire.

Iceland prides itself on being one of the world's most technologically advanced countries. The nation has more cell phones than it does people, and boasts the highest rate of computer usage per capita: over 90 percent of Icelanders own a personal computer or smart phone and use the Internet regularly.

SOCIAL DEVELOPMENT

Standard of Living

In the 2014 Human Development Index (HDI), an indicator of standard of living published by the United Nations Development Programme (UNDP), Iceland ranked 21st out of 198 nations. Icelanders have an estimated life expectancy of about 80 years, and an infant mortality rate of three out of every 1,000 births.

Water Consumption

Iceland has some of the cleanest water in the world. Its water supply is not treated with chemicals and has very few issues with pollution. The country's water infrastructure is well developed and the tap water is safe to drink. There are few if any issues related to availability of clean water in Iceland.

Education

Icelanders place great importance on education, as evidenced by the country's average literacy rate of 99.9 percent among both men and women, which is among the highest in the world.

Icelanders attend primary and lower secondary school from ages 6 to 16 (attendance at these levels is mandatory). Students go on to upper-secondary school for four years, followed by university. Public universities do not charge tuition.

Women's Rights

According to the traditional Icelandic sagas, if a woman is slapped in the face, retribution surely will follow. This formula is repeated even in contemporary art and pop culture; heroines are typically stricken at the beginning of a story, and then spend the remainder of the plot seeking—and finding—revenge. As exaggerated as this seems, it is a philosophy that appears to weave through the Icelandic women's movement: where there is a perceived wrong, they work relentlessly to make it right.

Suffrage was a particular milestone for women's rights; after a nearly 50-year movement toward representation, the women of Iceland won the right to vote in 1915. However, the right was restricted to women of a certain social status aged 40 and over, as there was concern that granting suffrage for too many would result in a complete gender overhaul in parliament, and thus shed too much attention on women's issues. In 1922, seven more years of perseverance were rewarded by the election of the first woman in parliament, Ingibjorg Bjarnason (1867–1941).

This same fiery activism was revisited decades later on October 24, 1975, when an estimated 90 percent of Iceland's women went on strike for a day, refusing to work, cook, or take care of their children. It began when a women's movement group called the Red Stockings wanted to call attention to gender-based wage discrepancies. The strike, initially organized as a "day off," served as a reminder of women's many contributions to daily life. The effect was extreme: public institutions and businesses such as schools, banks, factories and newspapers ran at barely half capacity, or had to shut down altogether. (The men of Iceland refer to that day as "The Long Friday"). Although the strike did not produce immediate pay increases—wage discrimination remains an issue—the event helped plant the seeds for future reform, particularly in politics. Just five years later, in 1980, Vigdis Finnbogadottir (1930–) became the world's first elected female president.

Today the status of Iceland's men and women is praised throughout the world as a model of egalitarianism. The country is increasingly supportive of single mothers and working women. National policy makes generous accommodations for subsidized day care and socialized health care. Working women are allowed three months paid maternity leave, with the option to extend for three months at 80 percent pay. National law mandates that, in sectors that are underrepresented by women, employers give preference to hiring and promoting them. Iceland also leads the world as one of the few nations to have 30 percent representation of women in government.

In spite of the momentous track record of the country's feminist movement, the fight against wage discrimination continues. A rise in violence against women, particularly rape and domestic violence, has emerged as a perplexing side effect of their elevated status.

Health Care

Icelanders benefit from very good health that is attributable not only to a high standard of living, but also to free and easily accessible quality health care.

A universal health care system that is publicly funded and administered by the Minister of Health and Social Security provides Icelanders with free, nearly comprehensive health care. This includes hospitals, rehabilitation institutions, nursing homes, care homes, health care centers, specialists, and preventative services. A drawback to Iceland's universal health care system is the financial burden it places on taxpayers.

GOVERNMENT

Structure

Iceland is a constitutional republic. Its government is run according to a set of principles outlined in its constitution, which requires that the president and the parliament be elected by the people. The constitution also guarantees equality under the law regardless of sex, race, and religion. Iceland became a republic on June 17, 1944, when it declared total independence from Denmark, under whose control it languished in various degrees since the 14th century.

The central Icelandic government has an executive branch, a legislative branch, and a judicial branch. The executive branch consists of the president, who does not have much executive power; the head of government, or prime minister, who, along with the cabinet has the most executive power; and the cabinet, a body selected from the parliament either by the president or political party leaders within the parliament. The cabinet minister is chosen by the president, and the Supreme Court and district court judges are appointed by the Minister of Justice, who is a member of the cabinet.

The legislative branch is comprised of the parliament, or Althing, an assembly of 63 elected officials of various political affiliations. The Althing has existed in some form since 930 CE.

The judicial branch consists of a Supreme Court and eight district courts.

Universal suffrage permits all residents 18 years old and over to vote for the president and the Althingi (the president and Althingi members serve four-year terms).

Political Parties

Iceland has many political parties, and the country's smaller population often results in the need to form alliances among differing groups. Parties include the Social Democratic Alliance, the Left-Green Movement, the Independence Party and the Progressive Party.

Local Government

The constitution provides municipalities with the right to manage their own affairs, in the form of a local council. Local councils are supervised by the central government, and members are elected to four-year terms by residents of the municipalities they represent. Elections are held via secret ballot.

Judicial System

Iceland's judicial system is made up of the Supreme Court of Iceland and eight lower district courts. The Supreme Court, which held its first case in 1920, is comprised of nine judges.

Taxation

The corporate income tax in Iceland applies to 15 percent of a corporation's income. There is no wealth tax or municipal corporate tax. Individuals pay a national income tax and a municipal income tax. The government imposes a 10 percent capital income tax. Fishermen in the country qualify for several tax breaks.

Armed Forces

Iceland does not maintain an army, navy or air force. The country hosted a U.S. Navy base until 2006. Iceland's government does not have a formal defense department. The Icelandic Coast Guard, which was founded in 1918, patrols the waters surrounding the country and assists when needed with emergency and peacekeeping operations.

Foreign Policy

Iceland is consistently ranked as one of the most developed countries in the world, particularly in recognition of its high levels of economic and civil freedoms. The country shares close ties with other Nordic countries, as well as the U.S. (Iceland supported the U.S. invasions of Afghanistan in 2001 and Iraq in 2003). It holds membership in the UN, the European Free Trade Association (EFTA), the European Environment Agency (EEA), and the Organization for Economic Cooperation and Development (OECD). Iceland, however, is not a member of the European Union (EU), primarily because of concern for loss of fishing resources. In a move to secure broad economic stability, Iceland formally applied to the EU in July of 2009. However, a turnaround occurred in 2013, when opinion polls led government leaders to state that they would postpone joining. Iceland is also a part of the European Economic Area and a founding member of the North Atlantic Treaty Organization (NATO), although the country has no armed forces.

Human Rights Profile

"International human rights law insists that states respect civil and political rights, and also promote an individual's economic, social and cultural rights. The United Nations Universal Declaration on Human Rights (UDHR) is recognized as the standard for international human rights. Its authors sought the counsel of the world's great thinkers, philosophers, and religious leaders, and were careful to create a document that reflects the core values shared by every world culture. (To read this document or view the articles relating to cultural human rights, go to: http://www.udhr.org/UDHR/default.htm).

International watch groups who are tasked with detecting and monitoring human rights violations have rightfully paid little attention to Iceland. In a remarkable feat of government efficacy, reports on Iceland's human rights record indicate virtually no violations. Some speculate that this is attributed to the small population (which is presumably more easily managed). However, even on a percentage basis, Iceland's inhabitants are generally considered to be content and happy, and its government is viewed as a true advocate for its citizens. The United Nations Development Program's (UNDP)

Human Development Index (HDI) consistently ranks Iceland as first. (The index, established to measure human development, takes into account concerns such as life expectancy, literacy and the level of education achieved).

Compared to other developed countries, Iceland maintains a considerably high standard of living (due mostly to its open economy). In fact, reports regularly indicate that a mere one-tenth of one percent of the population is homeless—which accounts for a scant 40 people. Unemployment is hardly discernible and the national literacy rate is an impeccable 100 percent. The country has no reported incidences of police mistreatment or arbitrary arrest and there is no record of torture, cruel or degrading treatment, politically motivated disappearances, or unlawful deprivation of life. Freedom of speech is not compromised, freedom of the press is not threatened, and freedom of assembly is not prohibited. In fact, the only recent hints of human rights infringement were the observation that juvenile offenders are housed in adult facilities instead of a separate juvenile facility (although prison conditions were noted as superior).

The task then, for a country all but devoid of mistreatment, is to continue working to encourage healthy practices nationally, and to spread this action abroad. On the domestic front this is evidenced in a variety of ways. The Icelandic government bans the production, exhibition, distribution, and/or sale of motion pictures depicting violence or brutality against people and animals. The government also partners with the Icelandic Association of University Women to improve the status of women and children and protect families. This partnership recently resulted in legislation that improved living conditions for refugees; they are now entitled to free housing and utilities for a year, in addition to full health care and social benefits.

Internationally, the Icelandic government is an outspoken member of the UN, the UN Security Council (UNSC), and the United Nations Development Fund for Women (UNIFEM), with particular attention given to initiatives that support gender equality, fight global violence against women, ban landmines, combat global terrorism, and protect children from involvement in armed forces.

Migration

Iceland has seen an increase in the number of immigrants in recent years. In 2014, it was estimated that approximately six percent of the island's population was foreign born. This figure was just over one percent in 1985. Residents of the European Union are allowed to travel to Iceland for work without a work permit. However, the global economic crisis of 2008 resulted in a severe decline in available employment in Iceland.

ECONOMY

Overview of the Economy

Iceland was devastated economically by the 2008–09 worldwide financial crisis. In an emergency maneuver, the country arranged a loan of billions of dollars from the International Monetary Fund.

Iceland's economy is based mainly on the service industry, tourism, and the export of marine products. In 2014, Iceland earned an estimated $5 billion (USD) in exports. Marine products, mostly fish, account for 40 percent of all exports; aluminum, ferrosilicon, diatomite (skeletal algae), and woolen goods mostly account for the rest. Iceland is considering exporting hydroelectric power in the future. Imports include oil, food, textiles, and machinery.

The gross domestic product (GDP) was an estimated $16.2 billion (USD) in 2014. The per capita GDP was $42,600 (USD). The unemployment rate was an estimated 4.5 percent.

Industry

Sectors in the technology industry include biotechnology and information technology, while sectors in the service industry include health care, education, public administration, communication, and real estate. The financial industry in Iceland was severely impacted by the 2008–09 global financial crisis. Manufacturing produces equipment used in fishing and fish processing, aluminum goods, and mineral wool.

Labor

In 2014, the service industry employed the largest amount of the workforce (70.7 percent), while industry employed the second largest number (22.4 percent) and agriculture the third (six percent).

The rapid development of the capital's modern industrial base has attracted a sizeable migration of people from more rural areas of Iceland to Reykjavík and its vicinity. This population boom has, in turn, fueled the growth of the construction industry and the services sectors.

Energy/Power/Natural Resources

Renewable energy is the pride of Iceland's industry. Geothermal power and hydroelectric power are Iceland's most abundant natural resources. Geothermal power (water from hot springs) is used to heat over 80 percent of homes in Reykjavík. It is also used to heat businesses, swimming pools, and greenhouses, and is pumped underneath sidewalks to keep ice from accumulating.

Iceland contains many fast-flowing rivers that have been dammed to produce hydroelectric power. Hydroelectric power plants around the country harness this energy and distribute it as an alternative fuel source. The combined use of geothermal and hydroelectric power keeps Iceland nearly pollution-free.

Its mastery of hydroelectricity and geothermal power has garnered international acclaim. Iceland has even consulted India and China to advise them on harnessing clean energy sources.

Fishing

Fishing has traditionally been the driving force of the country's economy, accounting for nearly half of all exports and employing nearly 10 percent of the workforce. In recent years, however, declining fish stock and a drop in world fish prices have made the trade vulnerable. To temper this, Iceland has hinted at extending its fishing zone. Disputes over fishing rights have historically created a rift between Iceland and Britain (the famous "Cod Wars" of the 1950s ended in Iceland's favor).

The country is also being scrutinized by environmentalists. Despite its tremendous success with domestic nature preservation, Iceland has been criticized for its whaling practices. The practice was abandoned in 1989 as part of an international moratorium. Years later, Iceland instituted scientific whaling, with the stated intention of investigating the impact on fish stock. In 2006, it resumed commercial hunts, and within one week three endangered fin whales had been killed. The government maintains that it is immune to the criticism of environmentalists, as there has been no discernable negative impact on tourism.

Forestry

Forestry is not a viable industry in Iceland, as less than one percent of its territory is covered by trees.

Mining/Metals

The production of aluminum, which currently represents about 13 percent of the nation's exports, is steadily increasing. Aluminum smelting is a thriving industry. The availability of sustainable geothermal energy to power the aluminum industry has led many to predict that aluminum will play a key role in Reykjavík's financial future.

However, because it uses vast amounts of energy (and Iceland's hydroelectricity is plentiful and inexpensive), it is most cost effective for a country to have the aluminum smelted in Iceland and then shipped back. This is booming in Iceland, despite criticism that the practice–both aluminum smelting and hydropower—threatens fragile wildlife. The most hotly debated example of this is Iceland's Karahnjukar hydroelectric project that dams two rivers, floods a 147-square kilometer (57 square mile) area of wilderness, and creates a giant aluminum smelter in the Eastfjords. It was hailed at first as a source of jobs and a boost to the economy, but it has since come to be seen as a devastating blow to the environment, both internationally and domestically.

Agriculture

Because such a small area of Iceland is suitable for farming, and an even smaller area (one percent of the total) is actually cultivated, agricultural products are sold primarily on the domestic market.

Sheep and cattle comprise the majority of Iceland's agricultural yield, and much of Iceland's cultivated land is used to grow hay and grasses for livestock feed instead of grain for human consumption.

Cash crops grown without the aid of greenhouses include potatoes, turnips, and carrots. Greenhouses allow Iceland to grow fruit and vegetables, such as tomatoes and cucumbers, which would not survive its climate otherwise. In 2014, revenue generated from agriculture accounted for six percent of the GDP.

Animal Husbandry

Large numbers of sheep are raised in Iceland. They are used for mutton and lamb meat as well as for wool products. Cattle are raised in large numbers for dairy production purposes. In recent years, breeding of the Iceland horse has grown in popularity.

Tourism

Tourism now represents one of Reykjavik's fastest-growing sectors. Today more than five percent of the Icelandic gross domestic product (GDP) is based on tourism revenues, which also represents the third largest source of foreign trade earnings after marine products and aluminum.

Natural landmarks are popular tourist attractions. Some frequently visited natural landmarks are Dettifoss, a large waterfall located in Jökulsárgljúfur National Park on the north coast; and Geysir, the original geyser that lent its name to the English word "geyser," near Reykjavík. Other attractions include lava fields, glaciers, lakes, and geothermal hotspots. Eco-tourism, specifically whale watching, is one of Iceland's most popular tourist activities.

Jamie Aronson, Heidi Edsall, Beverly Ballaro

DO YOU KNOW?

- A popular myth in Iceland is that the territory is home to trolls, elves, fairies, and other types of "wee folk."

- Reykjavík occupies a place in Icelandic folklore as a gathering place for the rock-dwelling supernatural beings known locally as "huldufólk" ("Hidden People"). Tales of the huldufólk date to the 15th century but widespread belief in them—and their penchant for bedeviling humans who intrude on them—persists to this day.

- The planned construction of roads, housing developments, and shopping malls in and around Reykjavík has occasionally been modified so as not to disturb boulders with spirits allegedly in residence.

- By law, Icelanders must use a patronymic or matronymic naming system, one that is based on the first names of their fathers or mothers with the added suffix "son" for boys and "dottír" for girls. For example, the last name of Erik Stefansson's sons must be "Eriksson," and the last name of his daughters must be "Eriksdottír."

Bibliography

Brandon Presser. *Iceland*. Footscray, Vic: Lonely Planet, 2013.

David Leffman. *Rough Guide to Iceland*. London: Rough Guides, 2013.

Gunnar Karlsson. *The History of Iceland*. Minneapolis, MN: University of Minnesota Press, 2000.

Halldor Laxness. *Independent People*. New York: Vintage International, 1997.

Jon Hjalmarsson. *History of Iceland*. Reykjavik, Iceland: Iceland Review, 1993.

Jon Krakauer and David Roberts. *Iceland: Land of the Sagas*. New York: Villard, 1998.

Karen Oslund. *Iceland Imagined: Nature, Culture, and Storytelling in the North Atlantic*. Seattle: Vidar Hreinsson. *The Complete Sagas of Icelanders Including 49 Tales (English translation)*.

Nan Rognvaldardottir. *Icelandic Food and Cookery*. New York, New York: Hippocrene Books. Reykjavík, Iceland: Leifur Eriksson Publishing, LTD, 1997.

Sarah Moss. *Names for the Sea: Strangers in Iceland*. Berkeley, CA: Counterpoint, 2013.

Sigurdur G. Magnusson. *Wasteland with Words: A Social History of Iceland*. London: Reaktion Books, 2010. University of Washington Press, 2011.

Works Cited

"Amnesty." *Amnesty International*. http://www.amnesty.org.

"BBC." *British Broadcasting Corporation*. http://www.bbc.co.uk.

Aslaug Benediktsdottir. *An Icelandic Cookbook*. Reykjavik, Iceland: Iceland Review, 1993.

"City Population." *City Population*. http://www.citypopulation.de

"Council on Foreign Relations." *World Trade Organization*. http://www.cfr.org.

"Explore Iceland." *Explore Iceland*. http://www.exploreiceland.is>.

"The Guardian." *The Guardian*. http://www.guardian.co.uk

"HRW." *Human Rights Watch*. http://www.hrw.org.

"Iceland Review." *The Iceland Review*. http://www.icelandreview.com

"Ministry of Foreign Affairs." *Icelandic Ministry of Foreign Affairs*. http://www.mfa.is

"Rykjavik Art Museum." *Reykjavik Art Museum*. http://www.artmuseum.is

"UN." *United Nations*. http://www.un.org/.

"UNICEF." *UNICEF*. http://www.unicef.org.

"UNIFEM News." *UNIFEM*. http://www.unifem.org.

"UNOG." *United Nations Office at Geneva*. http://www.unog.ch.

"USAID." *USAID*. http://www.usaid.gov/.

"U.S. Department of State." *U.S. Government*. http://www.state.gov.

"Visit Iceland." *Icelandic Tourist Board*. http://www.icetourist.is.

"World Heritage." *UNESCO*. http://whc.unesco.org.

Ireland's traditional individual dance is called sean-nos ("old style") dancing. /Stock photo © darkbird77

IRELAND,
Republic of

Introduction

Nicknamed the "Emerald Isle" for of its lush, green landscape, the Republic of Ireland (Ireland) is known for its significant impact on Western literature, folk music and dance.

GENERAL INFORMATION

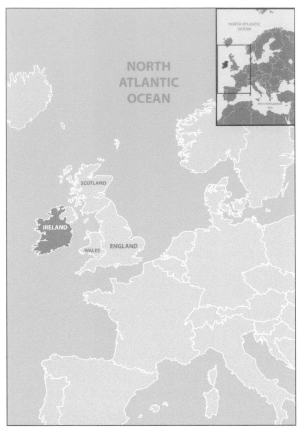

Official Languages: Irish, English
Population: 4,798,339 (2015 estimate)
Currency: Euro, which Ireland began using in January 2002.
Coins: The Euro has eight coin denominations: 1, 2, 5, 10, 20, and 50, as well as a 1 Euro coin and a 2 Euro coin. While the denomination side of a Euro coin remains the same throughout all countries that have adopted the Euro as currency, the image on the coin's face side varies according to the country that released the coin into circulation.
Land Area: 27,133 square miles (70,273 square kilometers)
Water Area: 1,390 square miles (3,600 square kilometers)
National Anthem: "Amhrán na bhFiann" ("The Soldier's Song")
Capital: Dublin
Time Zone: Western European Time, GMT +0
Flag Description: The Irish flag is a tricolored flag with equal-sized vertical stripes of green, white and orange. The green in the flag is thought to symbolize the older Roman Catholic population that inhabited the island prior to the invasion of William of Orange, who firmly established the Anglo-Irish population, largely Protestant

(and represented by the color orange), following the Battle of the Boyne in 1690. The white stripe between the green and orange stands for the peace between the two religious populations within the Republic.

Population

Historically, Ireland has experienced dramatic reductions in population in certain decades, such as in the 1840s during the Great Irish Famine. In 2006, it was estimated that the population level was more than 2 million below that of 1841. In recent years, the Republic of Ireland has seen the population number increase—the April 2011 census revealed a population swell of over 341,000 in a five-year span. In 2011, it was estimated that Ireland had the youngest population of any European Union member country.

Though most of Ireland's people live in urban areas, a large percentage (37 percent, as

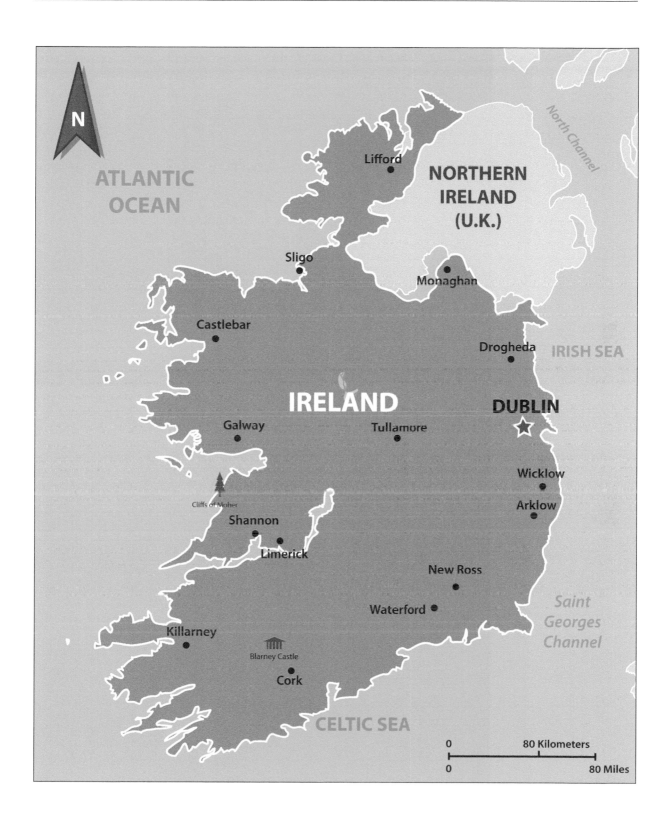

Principal Cities by Population (2011 census):

- Dublin (527,612)
- Cork (119,230)
- Galway (75,529)
- Blanchardstown (68,156)
- Tallaght (64,282)
- Limerick (57,106)
- Waterford (46,723)
- Clondalkin (45,165)
- Lucan (45,861)
- Swords (36,924)

of 2014) still lives in rural settings. The people of Ireland are predominantly white Europeans. In 2007, it was reported that the biggest increases in immigration, at least since 2002, have been from Lithuania, Poland, and Nigeria. However, in terms of the number of immigrants, most are from the United Kingdom, with the other European Union countries as the second largest group.

Languages

Both Irish and English are considered official languages. English is most frequently used, and is spoken with a unique intonation and pronunciation (called a "brogue"). Irish is rarely spoken in conversation, but it is taught in schools and is used in governmental affairs. The Irish language is a dialect of ancient Gaelic, which was the language of the native Celtic people. Many of Ireland's popular sayings are written in Irish, such as "Cead mile failte," ("One hundred-thousand welcomes"), and "Erin go bragh," ("Ireland forever").

Native People & Ethnic Groups

The first civilized settlers of Ireland were the Celts, who came to the island around the year 400 BCE. There are several other native peoples from which the modern population of Ireland has descended. These include the Vikings, the Normans, and the British.

Despite the successive invasions of these other tribes, the Celts remain the most important to the modern population, which continues to observe Celtic traditions and folklore. Imagery such as Celtic crosses and Celtic knots are abundant in Irish craftwork.

Religions

Roman Catholicism is the dominant religion in Ireland. Nearly 85 percent of all residents of Ireland reported themselves as Catholic in the 2011 Census, while the second largest group is Protestant, belonging to the Church of Ireland. However, for the first time in 2011, more selected "no religion" than any grouping except Catholic. Citizens of Ireland are granted freedom of religious belief and practice.

Climate

Ireland's climate is generally categorized as wet, though mild. The island is not subjected to many harsh storms, but its rainy weather comes in long, drizzly spell. Annual rainfall is around 150 centimeters (60 inches). Because of the abundance of rain and the lack of a harsh cold season, Ireland's agriculture remains active throughout most of the year.

The temperature is generally cool and comfortable throughout the year, with an average of 5° Celsius (41° Fahrenheit) in the winter, and 15° Celsius (59° Fahrenheit) during the summer.

ENVIRONMENT & GEOGRAPHY

Topography

The Republic of Ireland occupies most of the island of Ireland, which lies to the west of England, Scotland, and Wales. Dublin is located midway along the eastern coast of Ireland at the mouth of the River Liffey.

Central Ireland, in the agricultural lowlands, is characterized by rolling fields and peat bogs. The mountainous areas in Ireland exist mainly in the west. These include the Connemara, Kerry, and Donegal Mountains. Ireland's highest point is atop Carrauntoohil, in Kerry. Carrauntoohil's peak is 1,041 meters (3,141 feet) high.

Despite Ireland's small size, it is home to many notable geographical features. The west coast is dotted with bays that support industry along the shore. Some of the more notable bays are the central Galway Bay, Dingle Bay in the south, and Donegal Bay in the north. In the east, there are two major bodies of water that separate Ireland from England and the rest of Great Britain. These are the Irish Sea, to the east of Dublin, and St. George's Channel, which lies off the southeastern coast.

Ireland is home to many rivers and lakes, including the River Liffey, which runs through the center of Dublin, and the River Shannon, which at 370 kilometers (230 miles) is the Republic's longest. The River Shannon feeds three major lakes, or loughs. These are the Lough Allen, Lough Lee, and Lough Derg.

The Aran Islands lie to the west of Galway Bay, and are a popular tourist attraction. The islands feature expansive fields with ancient stonewall structures dividing pastures and retaining flocks of sheep. The famous Aran wool sweaters are handmade and sold on the islands. At the end of the main island is a large cliff with castle ruins at its peak.

Plants & Animals

Because of the wet climate, plant life is lush and green, and thick moss grows rampantly. Ireland is considered the only island without native snakes. Though legend attributes the ridding of snakes from Ireland to Saint Patrick (c. 387–493), evidence suggests that the island never had snakes in its history.

CUSTOMS & COURTESIES

Greetings

English is the main language spoken in Ireland. The Irish language is also used, but more often in combination with English. Therefore, while Irish people most often use common English greetings, such as "Hi," and "How are you," they may also say "Dia dhuit," which means "God be with you." The proper reply to this greeting would be "Dia's Mhuire dhuit," or "God and Mary be with you." If one is addressing a group of people, the Irish greeting would be "Dia dhaobh," or "God be with all of you." Handshakes are also common, but embracing is not, despite Ireland's informal social atmosphere.

There are a number of phrases associated with the Irish, such as "Begorrah" and "Top o' the morning to you." However, despite their stereotypical popularity elsewhere, these phrases are not, and typically have never been, used in everyday Irish speech. Often, such phrases are referred to as "stage Irish," and considered condescending or rude.

Gestures & Etiquette

In Ireland, social interactions are marked by informality and a willingness or expectation to engage in casual conversation in almost any social situation. This is particularly true in the countryside and other rural areas. In the cities, life might move at a faster pace, but there is still an emphasis on sociability and leisure. As such, social hierarchies are less pronounced than they might be in other cultures. For example, political leaders are commonly referred to by their first names.

Additionally, the Irish workplace often functions without an overt or specific observation of a hierarchical organization. Also, a foreign businessperson or visitor might spend more time exchanging pleasantries before attending to any particular matter at hand. This is also a routine interaction in other social settings, including at the shop or in a restaurant.

In conversation, the Irish tend to avoid directness in favor of subtlety, irony, and understatement. For example, in the Irish language there is no direct translation for the words "Yes" and "No." This may be reflective of the Irish tendency to talk around a subject in either language, English or Irish. Also, as a mark of social informality, the habit of "slagging," or teasing, is common, and is accepted in most situations.

Eating/Meal

Meal traditions vary in Ireland, typically depending on whether one is in the city or the country and according to different work schedules. In urban areas, eating schedules are more likely to be dictated by working hours. For example, breakfast may consist of a light meal of tea and scones, and lunch might be taken in one of the plentiful small sandwich shops. Additionally, any newsagent (convenience store) is likely to have a sandwich bar in the back, and pubs usually serve light meals at midday. The main meal is usually taken in the evening, and often represents the first time that the family is gathered together that day.

In rural areas, the more traditional full Irish breakfasts are common. These heavier meals typically consist of several types of sausages, bacon, potatoes, and a tomato, often all fried in grease. The midday meal is the main meal of the day, and usually includes meat, potatoes and a vegetable. Supper would then be a lighter meal. Generally, the continental European custom of eating supper late at night is rare in Ireland.

Tea-time is generally observed throughout Ireland, regardless of economic status or location. Employees usually receive a tea break in the middle of the afternoon. Similar to a coffee break, this short time includes tea and biscuits (cookies) and socializing. The food rarely extends beyond biscuits; however, in some cases small sandwiches may be provided.

The Irish pub traditionally functions as a social hub in Irish culture, and there are patterns of etiquette here as with meals. For example, it is common for groups of people to buy drinks in rounds, with each member of the group taking their turn purchasing the drinks. It is also important to refrain from overspending, as this can be perceived as showing off. In addition to drinks, pubs usually offer food, ranging from snacks such as cocktail sausages or bags of crisps (potato chips) to meals such as beef stew or fish and chips. Visitors may be surprised to see that chicken or chips (French fries) with curry sauce is a common staple in Irish pubs. However, this is not so much a sign of a more cosmopolitan culture, but rather more of a residual effect of the long-held popularity of Indian food in England.

Visiting

Ireland is particularly known for its tradition of hospitality. Generally, Irish people have a well-earned reputation for being especially welcoming to visitors. When visiting an Irish home, for example, one can expect to be offered a cup of tea, with the offering of a meal likely to follow. When staying for an extended visit, it is always a good idea to bring a gift for the hosts. In addition, the common etiquette for house guests dictates that the comfort of both guest and host should be observed. As such, a guest should remember to thank the host, accommodate the host's schedule by not overstaying, and accept what is given to them with sincere appreciation.

The tradition of hospitality extends into the public sphere as well. For example, traditional pubs (short for "public house") in small towns often function as a public living room rather than a drinking establishment. Irish people are more likely to gather at the local pub than at a private home, with the clientele a mixture of people of all ages and social classes. Typically, the social atmosphere is outgoing, and visitors can expect to be regularly engaged in conversation with strangers.

LIFESTYLE

Family

Family life in Ireland has changed considerably since the country achieved statehood in 1922. At that time, came late in life. According to the 1926 census, Ireland had a larger percentage of unmarried people than in any other country that kept such records. The high number of unmarried people in Ireland can be linked to the economic hardships endured by the Irish in the early 20th century. Because there was such little opportunity, most marriageable people had left. Additionally, when people did get married, they tended to have very large families. Thus, the low marriage rate in the early 20th century can also be attributed to the fact that marriage carried with it the responsibility to raise many children, which most people could not afford at the time.

In the 1970s, Irish society began to go through dramatic changes. In 1971, more than half of Ireland's population lived in cities, with over a third of the population residing in the greater Dublin area alone. Higher education became more accessible to middle and lower classes, and there were more white-collar job opportunities in the cities. At the same time, there was a significant rise in the number of young people getting married. Family size dropped off at the same time, with more couples having first and second children, but fewer having four or more. More—and younger—married couples were living in urban or suburban neighborhoods, subsisting on a fixed middle-class income, and having a smaller number of children. Ireland's families began to fall into the "nuclear family" pattern prevalent in other modern Western countries (typically consisting of a mother, father and two children).

Family life changed again in the 1990s, when women's social roles saw some important changes. As careers became as important to women as marriage, the age at which people got married increased. Also, the traditional family pattern of a working father and stay-at-home mother with a house in the suburbs diminished as rising housing prices demanded that mothers go to work. In the 21st century, Irish families have begun to experience significant generational differences between family members who grew up in any of these three periods. For example, young people tend to get married later in life and have fewer children, and their attitudes toward marriage and sexuality are likely to be very different from those of their parents.

Housing

In both rural and urban areas, Ireland has undergone dramatic changes in housing styles since the early 20th century. In Dublin, the Georgian style is the most characteristic architecture style. Brick townhouse buildings built in this style are commonplace, though the majority have now been converted into apartment or office space. These houses are typically four stories tall, often with a parlor on the first floor, a ballroom

on the second, and servants' quarters on the top floor. The facades, or exteriors, of these houses are usually without any elaborate architectural embellishment other than an ornately sculpted doorway (it is said that no two Georgian style doors in Dublin are exactly alike). It was not unusual for entire streets to be composed only of these houses, creating a picturesque effect.

In the 1950s, with more people moving to the cities in search of opportunity and modern amenities, the urban population began to shift out to adjacent suburbs and housing developments. These new developments, often built over farmland, featured detached or semi-detached houses with driveways, yards and garages.

In rural areas, the traditional and iconic home is the tiny thatched-roof cottage. However, though these cottages have a charming appeal and appear on countless postcards, they are not considered practical for modern families. Typically, they are constructed of stone and usually whitewashed, with the roof covered with thatch or tightly packed straw. These cottages traditionally have two rooms, the larger one having a hearth that warms the building and serves as the center for family life. A smaller bedroom is usually in the back. Today, more modern two-story houses built of concrete are much more common in rural areas.

Food

The national cuisine of Ireland has long had a reputation of being bland, simple and unpalatable, consisting of flavorless boiled meat and potatoes. In reality, traditional Irish food can be much more diverse, and rich in natural and locally-grown meats, seafood, and produce. In addition, the prevalence of small, family-owned farms ensures that food is very likely to be fresh and of good quality. More recently, French and other European culinary influences have blended with traditional Irish cooking, resulting in traditional Irish dishes that have been reinvented in new ways.

Meat and dairy remain at the heart of traditional Irish cuisine, and lamb, pork, rabbit and pheasant feature prominently in traditional Irish recipes. Historically, beef was not readily available in Ireland, and corned beef is an Irish tradition rooted solely in Irish-American households. As such, Ireland is renowned for its cheeses and meat dishes, specifically the traditional Irish stew. This renowned Irish staple is made with lamb, potatoes, and vegetables. A similar dish, Guinness beef stew, contains beef, potatoes and vegetables stewed in a sauce flavored with Guinness stout (a dark, malty-tasting beer). Coddle, which is potatoes cooked with sausages and bacon, and colcannon, which is mashed potatoes and kale (a form of cabbage), are two other traditional Irish dishes. Commonly used vegetables in Irish cuisine include carrots, parsnips, cabbage, scallions and onions.

Seafood is also plentiful and very popular in Ireland. As an island nation, Ireland has an active and productive fishing industry and cod, salmon, mackerel, trout, sole, mussels, lobster, oysters, and cockles (a type of shellfish similar to clams) are common. Traditional Irish seafood dishes include scallop pie, a seafood variation of the traditional meat pie made with mashed potatoes, and Dublin lawyer, which is lobster in a whiskey cream sauce.

One of the more well-known Irish dishes is the full Irish breakfast, also sometimes called a "fry-up." It consists of several different kinds of meat, including rashers (a thick type of bacon, similar to ham), sausage links, and pudding, which is a kind of sausage. Traditionally, there are two types of pudding: black pudding, also called blood pudding, which is made from pigs' blood and grains, and white pudding, which is also pork-based, and made from fat. An egg and a tomato half are typically added to the meats. Traditionally, this entire platter is fried in plenty of grease, and the full fry is usually served with Irish soda bread, a dense, grainy type of bread ideal for soaking up juices.

Ireland is famous for its alcoholic beverages, particularly whiskey and Guinness, a type of stout first brewed in Dublin. More than 500 pubs are located in the city, and those in the Temple Bar area are among the most popular with tourists.

Life's Milestones

Despite Ireland's recent transition from an insular, Catholic society, to a more worldly and secular one, the observation of weddings and funerals has remained an important facet of Irish life.

Wedding celebrations tend to last longer than in other Western cultures, with very large families often celebrating through the night and into the next day. Traditionally, Irish funerals begin with a wake at the deceased's home. There, the body is typically displayed so that family and friends may pay their respects. However, rather than the somber occasion that funerals tend to be in other Western cultures, Irish funerals or wakes commonly involve a festive atmosphere of food and drink. This is so mourners can celebrate the transition of the deceased from this world into the next. Recently, though, wakes are shifting to funeral homes, where they are more formal and quiet in tone.

CULTURAL HISTORY

Music

Ireland has a long, diverse musical tradition. Despite the idea of the native authenticity of Irish or Gaelic music, Ireland's musical traditions have always been influenced by other cultures. For example, the music of 18th-century Irish composer and harpist Turlough O'Carolan (1670–1738), largely considered Ireland's national composer, bears a resemblance to the Italian works that were popular in his day. In fact, throughout O'Carolan's lifetime Ireland nurtured an enthusiastic and active audience for English and continental music. The famous English composer George Frederic Handel (1685–1759) even spent time in Dublin. He wrote and premiered the renowned "Messiah" oratorio there in 1742 (an oratorio is an extended musical composition featuring vocal and orchestra music).

In the 19th century, traditional Irish music was largely influenced by cultural nationalism. This was the idea that a nation could define itself through a shared cultural independence and distinctiveness, as opposed to a shared national identity through religion, ethnicity or civics. Certain characteristics began to define Irish music and culture, such as the harp, which even appears on the national currency. Furthermore, in the interest of preserving a native culture, the collection and publishing of Irish tunes in book form became more prevalent. Famous collections of folksongs and ancient Irish music by both Edward Bunting (1773–1843) and George Petrie (1790–1866) helped introduce the genre to new audiences.

Generally, traditional Irish music, or Irish folk music, is an umbrella term used to cover the various genres of regional music played throughout Ireland. Historically, traditional Irish music consisted of folk songs or ballads, often accompanied by the fiddle, flutes, harp, bodhrán (hand-held drum), banjo and uilleann pipes, or Irish bagpipes. The accordion was added in the late 19th and early 20th centuries. Much of this music derived from the 18th and 19th centuries, when many traditional compositions were first recorded. Prior to that, traditional music was largely transmitted from musician to musician through an oral tradition. Another important aspect of traditional Irish music is its community spirit. This sense of community is stressed over the spotlighting of any one performer. Lastly, traditional Irish music is often categorized according to the type of dance that accompanies it, with reels, jigs, hornpipes and polkas among the most popular.

Dance

Traditional Irish dance is generally divided into two categories: individual dances meant for performance and competition, and group dances meant for social gatherings. In individual dance, the oldest form is called sean-nos ("old-style") dancing. This type of dancing is characterized by percussive footwork, often referred to as "battering," and a loose, relaxed torso and arms. This style of dance also allows for improvisation. Conversely, step dancing is a type of Irish dance that is seen more often in competitions and in popular contemporary international stage shows

such as *Riverdance*. Generally, step dancing is much more regulated, calls for a rigid torso and arms, and involves intricate footwork with either soft or hard shoes.

Group dances such as céilí dancing can involve a large number of people. Often, group dances take the form of couples dancing in a long line or around a circle. Set dancing is another popular group dance. Similar to American square dancing, it typically involves a "square" set of four couples.

Literature

Irish literature has an extensive history, having been developed through two distinct languages, English and Irish Gaelic. Generally, the history of literature in Ireland is often divided between an "Anglo-Irish" (referring to the 17th and 18th century English settlers and their descendants) Protestant English-speaking upper class, and a Catholic Gaelic-speaking lower class. While this perception is certainly popular, it is also misleading since writers in each language were not only aware of, but influenced by their contemporaries.

Among the best-known Anglo-Irish writers are Jonathan Swift (1667–1745), author of *Gulliver's Travels* (1726); Edmund Burke (1729–1797), a famous conservative political philosopher; and Bram Stoker (1847–1912), the renowned author of *Dracula* (1897). Other notable Anglo-Irish writers include Edith Somerville (1858–1949) and Violet Martin (1862–1915), co-authors of *The Real Charlotte* (1894), and Elizabeth Bowen (1899–1973), author of *The Last September* (1929).

The latter authors are significant in that they represent a sub-genre of Anglo-Irish literature known as the "Big House novel." This is, typically, a type of novel that chronicles the lives of families of the estate houses of the Anglo-Irish upper class. These novels often explore themes of clashes between the Protestant upper class and the Catholic lower class. The novel *Castle Rackrent* (1800) by Maria Edgeworth (1767–1849) is considered one of the earliest and most exemplary examples of this, an almost entirely female-written genre.

In the early 20th century, Anglo-Irish writers dominated what is called the "Irish literary revival" period. During this period of heightened nationalism, revolution and independence—the Irish Free State came into being in 1922—Irish writers and scholars believed that a native and national literary culture needed to be established. Active writers during this time included William Butler Yeats (1865–1939), Lady Augusta Gregory (1852–1932), John Millington Synge (1871–1909) and Douglas Hyde (1860–1949), who consequently served as president of Ireland from 1938–1945. They believed that the establishment and institutionalization of a literary culture would give Ireland a unique national identity. As a result, Yeats and Gregory established the Irish Literary Theatre in an effort to make audiences aware of Ireland's literary traditions and to help elevate Irish culture beyond the stereotypes prevalent in Victorian drama. Often, these stereotypes included the drunken Irishman, a popular theatrical standby at the time.

In the middle of the 20th century, a new generation of writers reacted against the tendency of the so-called "revivalists" to idealize Irish culture. Instead, this new generation exposed the realities of life in a country marked by economic hardship and dominated by the powerful and conservative Catholic Church. Writers such as Seán Ó Faoláin (1900–1991), Liam O'Flaherty (1896–1984) and Frank O'Connor (1903–1966) turned to realism as a genre that could represent rural life as one without meaning or hope. Additionally, a significant number of Irish writers have established their careers outside of Ireland, among them the famous and influential novelist James Joyce (1882–1941). Joyce's landmark novel, *Ulysses* (1922), is largely recognized as one of the most important, and most difficult, novels of the 20th century. Another expatriate writer, Samuel Beckett (1906–1989), is known for his experimental plays and novels. The poet Seamus Heaney (1939–2013) won the Nobel Prize in Literature in 1995. The novelist and short-story writer Colm Tóibín (1955–) is widely acclaimed.

The lineage of today's Irish language poets dates back centuries to the bardic tradition. As part of this tradition, poets were held in high esteem and sponsored by wealthy families. The 18th-century poet Aodhagán Ó Rathaille (c.1670– c.1726) was especially well-known and influential. Raised in a privileged family and educated in both Latin and English, Ó Rathaille witnessed the decline of the native Irish nobility class and the rise of the English settlers to power. His poetry often grieves the old Irish nobility on which his family depended for subsistence, while looking forward to a future national liberation.

In the 20th century, Irish language poets showed both commitment to the Irish language tradition and openness to innovation. The novelist Mairtín Ó Cadhain's (1906–1970) work *Cré na Cille* is influenced by European modernism. In addition, the poet Séan Ó Ríordáin (1917–1977) took his influence from the major English language poets such as Yeats, T.S. Eliot (1888–1965) and Gerard Manley Hopkins (1844–1899).

CULTURE

Arts & Entertainment

Ireland has enjoyed a boom in the arts in the 21st century. The new generation of musicians, composers, artists, poets, novelists, memoirists and playwrights is characterized by diversity. This broad overview points to a nation that is breaking from its stereotypical image as a quiet, rural and homogeneous Catholic country.

Irish traditional music has enjoyed a resurgence since the mid-1990s, a time when Ireland enjoyed new economic prosperity and Irish culture enjoyed a new popularity worldwide. This popularity can also be traced to the folk music revival of the 1960s, which inspired Irish bands such as Planxty who brought traditional Irish music to the small, intimate venues in which folk singers usually performed. A new and younger generation of Irish musicians, including groups such as Lunasa, Altan, and Solas, and individual musicians such as Kevin Burke, Liz Carroll, Sharon Shannon and Eileen Ivers, are hugely popular in Ireland and abroad. Irish traditional music is now promoted in Ireland as a major tourist attraction.

Traditional dance in Ireland has also experienced a resurgence. With music by the Irish composer Bill Whelan (1950–), the *Riverdance* stage show began as a short interlude during the 1994 Eurovision Song Contest, an annual music competition in Europe, and quickly expanded into a full-length Irish dance presentation. The show played to sold-out audiences in Ireland, England, the United States, Australia, and other venues around the world. However, the effect of the show's success in the Irish dance community is mixed. Though Irish dancing is now known throughout the world at an unprecedented level, many Irish dancers and choreographers now feel it is difficult to develop the art beyond what is represented in the show.

Ireland has long held an established presence in the rock and roll music scene, beginning with the emergence and success of Van Morrison, who became known for his blues/folk sound. Musical groups such as Thin Lizzy, the Waterboys, the Pogues, and the Chieftains, who have maintained a traditional sound, have followed Morrison to international success. Regardless, no Irish musical group has achieved the international fame and success of U2. Though the band remains very influential in Ireland today, the most popular new band out of Ireland is the Frames. The group's singer and songwriter, Glen Hansard, is known for his style of earnest, heartfelt music (Hansard won a 2008 Academy Award for his contributions to the soundtrack of *Once*). Generally, Ireland has an active music scene that is influenced by the "indie rock" sound popular throughout the U.S. and England.

Ireland is also home to a new generation of poets, novelists and playwrights, including novelists Roddy Doyle (1958–), Anne Enright (1962–) and Patrick McCabe (1955–) and Irish language poets Nuala ni Dhomhnaill (1952–) and Louis de Paor (1961–). This new generation of literary artists has gained recognition for their tendency to portray Ireland as significantly different from the stereotypical impoverished and rain-soaked

country. Ireland has also recently witnessed a resurgence of interest in Irish language poetry. Ni Dhomhnaill's poetry is especially interesting in that she uses the Irish language to write about contemporary life in Ireland, particularly when Irish language literature often focuses on traditional ways of life.

Theater is also especially vibrant in Ireland. Dublin boasts a large number of theatres and theatre companies, with many independent and experimental theater companies focusing on young, emerging playwrights. The Project Arts Centre in Dublin is another venue that emphasizes the work of new artists. Ireland also has produced a high number of young playwrights that have become successful outside of Ireland, including Martin McDonagh (b. 1970–), who achieved success with his Tony-award winning *The Beauty Queen of Leenane*. In fact, the noticeably high number of young Irish playwrights to make an impact on the international theater scene has led to events such as the 2008 Irish Theater Festival in New York. This international event gives special recognition to the number of Irish productions that have already made their way into the spotlight, and also exemplifies the new global appeal of Irish arts and culture.

Perhaps the most popular form of entertainment in Ireland is football, or "soccer," as it is known in the United States. The Irish have a number of professional football clubs that compete against each other and other European teams. Gaelic football is another popular sport. Ireland is the only country that professionally plays this unique blend of football and rugby. Also unique to Ireland is a ball game called hurling. Hurling is a high contact field sport that uses a long stick and a thick canvas ball. In addition to these team sports, horse racing is a popular form of recreation that has existed on the island for centuries.

Cultural Sites & Landmarks
Ireland is home to a wealth of cultural sites and landmarks. Most notably, Ireland is famous for its numerous ancient and medieval archaeological sites and landmarks. These include medieval

castles and monasteries and ancient stone circles and cairns (piles of stones marking burial sites or tombs). Ireland is also famous for another type of ancient tomb: dolmens. These simple stone structures usually consist of three or more large upright stones or boulders. One particularly well-known example is the Poulnabrone dolmen in western Ireland, dating back to the Neolithic era, a New Stone Age period that spread through Europe roughly between 6000 and 2000 BCE.

The Hill of Tara, located in the County Meath, carries symbolic and historical significance for Ireland. The former seat of the Irish kings, it is also the location of a number of archaeological finds. The area consists of a number of different forts and mounds, one of which is a passage grave dating from about 2500 BCE. Within sight of the Hill of Tara is the Boyne Valley (Brú na Bóinne), which contains three major archaeological sites: the burial mounds Newgrange, Knowth, and Dowth. Newgrange is the most visited of the three, and dates back to around 3200 BCE. It contains a long passage toward a central burial chamber, with the mound and passageway supported by large boulders decorated with spiral motifs. Because the passage was believed to have been constructed in a manner to trap sunlight only on the winter solstice, many archeologists speculate that Newgrange served as a calendar, as well as a burial site.

Due to the archeological significance of the Boyne Valley, it was designated as a World Heritage Site by the United Nations Educational, Scientific and Cultural Organization (UNESCO) in 1993. It is one of two sites in Ireland with that particular distinction, the other being Skellig Michael, the larger of two islands that form the Skellig Islands. Skellig Michael is a small island 12 kilometers (seven miles) off the rocky southwest coast of County Kerry. On this steep, high rock—approximately 230 meters (754 feet) high—a monastery was maintained from the sixth to the 12th or 13th centuries. Though the buildings remain, visitors must climb a set of 600 steps cut into the rock face to reach them. In addition, both islands, Little Skellig and Great Skellig, are also important nature reserves, and feature a diverse population of seabirds.

A more accessible monastery site is Glendalough, situated in the Wicklow Mountains just south of Dublin. The monastery was at its height in the ninth century, when thousands of monks and students lived there. However, various Viking attacks between 775 and 1071 and an attack from English invaders in 1398 decimated the population until it was abandoned in the 17th century. Today, Glendalough is one of the most popular tourist attractions in Ireland because of its proximity to Dublin and its scenic location by a lake in a lush mountain valley. The monastery itself is expansive and well-preserved, and includes an exemplary round tower, a unique Irish structure. This particular tower stands 33 meters (108 feet) tall and 16 meters (52 feet) in circumference, and served as protection during raids.

There are numerous castles and medieval sites open to visitors throughout Ireland. Of particular importance is the historic Rock of Cashel. This site is a collection of medieval buildings set on a limestone rock formation that overlook the quiet, scenic town of Cashel in the southeast county of Tipperary. Believed to be originally used as a base by the Eóghanachta clan, the site mostly likely changed hands and was used as a seat of power. Though the origins of the site date back to the fifth century CE, most of the existing buildings are from the 12th and 13th centuries. One of the central attractions to the site, the Romanesque Cormac's Chapel, dates back to 1127 and boasts well-preserved medieval architectural features such as intricate carvings on the arched doorway.

Trinity College, also known as the University of Dublin, is located in the city center. Established in 1320, it is Ireland's oldest institute of higher education and has evolved into one of its most prestigious. The campus contains notable 18th-century architecture, and its library serves as a repository for a copy of every book published in Ireland and Great Britain. It is also home to illuminated manuscripts from the seventh and eighth centuries, such as the Book of Kells.

Libraries & Museums
The National Gallery and the National Museum are two of Dublin's preeminent museums. Highlights

of the National Gallery include paintings by Dutch and Italian masters as well as contemporary displays of Irish art. Exhibits in the National Museum trace the history of the country from ancient times, and many important archaeological artifacts of high craftsmanship are on display. In all, there are nearly 150 museums in Ireland. The National Library of Ireland dates back to 1877.

Holidays

On February 1, the Irish honor one of their patron saints as they celebrate Saint Brigid's Day. The other patron saint of Ireland, Saint Patrick, is celebrated on March 17 in Ireland as a day of feasting.

Youth Culture

A generation gap exists today in Ireland between those who grew up before the economic boom of the late 20th century, in the 1990s, and those who mainly know the more secular, capitalist and urban society that Ireland has become in the 21st century. Young people tend to live in or close to the cities of Dublin, Galway, Limerick or Cork. The pub scene has perhaps seen the most impact from this generational gap. In the cities, for example, the small, traditional Irish pubs that have long defined Irish society have given way to trendy bars and dance clubs. As such, the quiet social atmosphere that is the norm in traditional, older pubs has given way to the more fast-paced and loud atmosphere of these new venues. The legal drinking age in Ireland is eighteen.

In fact, this social shift is indicative of a wider cultural shift. In the traditional Irish pub, drinks are taken slowly and with food, people of all ages drink together, and the pub functions as a social hub, so that a person is likely to know—or be related to—many of the pub's patrons. However, the new urban bar is oriented solely to young people, often promoting heavy drinking. This is particularly evident in the decreasing consumption of heavy stouts among youth. Instead of heavy stout, such as those brewed by Guinness and Murphy's, which tends to be taken in sips, the popular drinks have become light beer, often imported, and cocktails and shots.

Additionally, the 1990s saw the emergence of the so-called "super-pub." These pubs are typically enormous places where intimacy of setting is given over to a massive party atmosphere and anonymity. Also, as drinking patterns have changed, alcoholism and binge drinking have been on the rise in Ireland, and alcoholics now tend to be younger. Furthermore, a possible residual effect of this cultural shift has been an increase in random violence in larger cities such as Dublin. The capital, in particular, witnessed a 160 percent increase in public order offenses between 1996 and 2002. After peaking in 2008, these, and other, similar criminal offenses declined by 13 percent between 2008 and 2012.

SOCIETY

Transportation

Ireland has a fairly efficient and affordable bus and rail system connecting the cities and larger towns. In the Dublin area especially, there is an extensive commuter system of light rail (the DART, or Dublin Area Rapid Transit) and streetcars connecting the city center to the suburbs. As such, most residents do not need a car for most of their transportation needs.

Travelers on a budget can rely on the bus system, However, they are typically limited in the number of places they can visit, as some villages are visited by buses only once every two days.

In the country, cars are a necessity for transportation. Hitchhiking, while frowned upon, is still frequently done in the countryside (but not near the cities). Vehicles in Ireland drive on the left side of the road. Seat belt use is compulsory in both the rear and front seats, and the use of a handheld mobile phone, while driving, is illegal.

Transportation Infrastructure

It has become increasingly difficult to navigate major routes through the cities. Since roads were largely designed before most people owned personal cars, traffic is often backed up, making it faster to travel on foot.

In November 2005, the Irish government announced an infrastructure plan called Transport 21, aimed to improve and expand the Republic of Ireland's transportation infrastructure. The development plan included extensions to highways and rail lines, plans for a rural railway system, and infrastructure upgrades to major roads out of Dublin, as well as plans for an integrated rail system in the city. The plan also included the expansion of the Dublin Bus public transport system. However, economic and political changes doomed Transport 21 by 2010. In 2012 another transportation plan was unveiled, with a longer timetable and less ambitious goals.

Media & Communications

Ireland enjoys relative freedom of expression today. There are several Irish newspapers and television and radio stations that give a variety of perspectives on Irish news and culture. The two major Irish newspapers are the *Irish Times*, which is largely considered to be a Protestant or pro-British publication, and the *Irish Independent*, which leans towards a Catholic or republican perspective. Recently, the *Times* has become more nonpartisan in politics and religion and is more respected for its writing and reporting, while the typically conservative *Independent* has a wider readership. There are also a number of smaller local dailies such as Dublin's *Evening Herald*, which carries local news and listings.

Irish television and radio is dominated by the Radio Teilifís Éireann (RTÉ) network, which produces three television channels, RTÉ 1, Network 2, and TG4. RTÉ1 and Network 2 are English language channels that broadcast Irish-produced programs as well as popular American shows. TG4 is an Irish language channel and produces news programs, sports coverage, soap operas and other programs entirely in Irish Gaelic. RTÉ also has three English language radio stations as well as the Irish language Radio na Gaeltachta. In addition, the British Broadcasting Corporation (BBC) television network, the Northern Irish Ulster Television, the independent TV3, and a number of local radio stations are available throughout Ireland.

Irish people are well connected through mobile networks and Internet technologies. Mobile phones are as common as they are in America. In addition, cyber cafés are more plentiful in Ireland than they are in most other Western societies, ensuring that anyone who does not own a computer still has access to the Internet.

SOCIAL DEVELOPMENT

Standard of Living

In 2013, Ireland had a Human Development Index (HDI) ranking of 11th out of 187 countries.

Water Consumption

Generally, Ireland has good water quality, and does not charge households for water usage. According to a 2013 OECD Environmental Performance Review of Ireland, more than 99 percent of public drinking water meets health standards.

In January 2010, the Irish government announced an increase in their investment into water infrastructure. The lack of household water charges has been cited as an impediment in Ireland's water services sector.

Education

Ireland is known for its universities, which include the National University of Ireland, which has campuses in Dublin, Galway, and Cork; the University of Limerick; and Ireland's most famous university, Trinity College in Dublin. Alumni of Trinity College include Irish writers Oscar Wilde and George Bernard Shaw.

Irish youth are required to attend school between six and 15 years of age. Most of these students attend schools that are privately owned by the Roman Catholic Church and the Church of Ireland. Students wear uniforms and usually attend same-sex schools at the secondary level.

Secondary schools are largely divided into two groups. Some schools are traditional secondary academies, while others are vocational schools that specialize in technical skills. A smaller group includes comprehensive schools, which offer both secondary and vocational programs. As of 2014, the literacy rate is Ireland was 99 percent.

Women's Rights

The social position of Irish women in the 20th century has been closely intertwined with the influence of the Catholic Church on the Irish government and on daily life in Ireland. The 1937 constitution of the new Irish Republic gave primacy to "the family" as a fundamental cornerstone of Irish society. The constitution also stated that the state "would endeavor to ensure that mothers shall not be obliged by economic necessity to engage in labor to the neglect of their duties at home." In this aspect, Article 41 bears a strong resemblance to Article 16 of the UDHR, which similarly privileges the family as the fundamental unit of society. The article was widely interpreted as a state-endorsed push to limit women to the roles of mothers and homemakers. Further, the 1932 public service marriage bar prevented married women from employment as civil servants or as national school teachers. This remained in effect until 1973.

The 1970s saw a number of other advances for women's rights in Ireland. The 1972 Commission on the Status of Women initiated a government-appointed study into the social position and status of women. Among its recommendations were the removal of the public service marriage bar, wage equity legislation, and the implementation of paid maternity leave for female employees. This report was followed by legislation on equal pay (1974) and employment equality (1977).

In more recent years, much attention has been paid to the history of the "Magdalen laundries," institutions that effectively imprisoned an estimated 30,000 unmarried women, denied them access to the outside world, and forced them into labor in institutional laundries. Typically, the women were poor, or pregnant, or both. Children born to the women were taken from their mothers. Shockingly, the last Magdalen laundry in Drumcondra, County Dublin, did not close until 1996.

The issues of divorce, contraception and abortion have also figured prominently into women's rights in Ireland. Divorce only became available in Ireland recently, through a narrowly won (50.28 percent) referendum in 1995. Contraception and literature about birth control was banned until 1979. In 1985, condoms became available without a prescription to those aged 18 or older. Abortion remains illegal in Ireland today, except for cases in which the mother's life is at stake. This includes cases in which the mother is at risk for suicide. While a 1983 constitutional amendment explicitly protects the right to life of an unborn child, only in 2013 did the government enact a statute to clarify what it meant to have the "mother's life at stake," slightly broadening the definition of this condition.

Mary Robinson broke ground for Irish women when she became the first woman elected to the presidency of the republic. She served from 1990–1997, leaving office to become the United Nations' High Commissioner for Human Rights.

Health Care

In 2005, the Irish government began issuing medical cards to eligible residents. These cards entitle a holder to limited medical services free of charge. Senior citizens and students are automatically qualified for cards. In addition to these cards, Irish residents may enroll for health care through an employer or through a medical institution, in a system similar to that used in the United States.

GOVERNMENT

Structure

The Irish Constitution was drafted in 1937. In 1949, Ireland's status as a commonwealth of Great Britain officially ended, making it an independent free state. The Republic of Ireland is now a member of the European Union.

Like the United States, Ireland is a democracy with a President as the head of state. The people of Ireland elect their president to a seven-year term. People who are at least eighteen years old and have lived in the Republic for a minimum of five years are eligible to vote.

Like Great Britain, Ireland has a parliament, which in Irish is called the Oireachtas, and a prime minister, called the Taoiseach. The Taoiseach is nominated by the Oireachtas and is appointed by the President.

The Oireachtas' legislative branch is the House of Representatives, or Dáil Éireann. The executive branch is the Senate, or Seanad Éireann.

Political Parties

Ireland is a parliamentary democracy where coalitions have become the norm. In fact, no one party has ruled the government since the late 1980s. Often, within parliamentary systems, coalitions unite to form a majority coalition. These coalitions differ in nature, with some coalitions having a lasting strength and others failing to govern at all. Additionally, it's not unusual for parties to dissolve because of personality conflicts within the organization.

There are several active political parties in Ireland, and the party holding the majority in the Oireachtas (parliament) is led by the Taoiseach, or prime minister. Active political parties include the Republican Party (Fianna Fáil), the Labour Party, Sinn Féin, the Fine Gael, the United Left Alliance, Progressive Democrats, and the Green Party. The biggest political parties are Fianna Fáil and Fine Gael, neither of which identifies itself as center-right or center-left. (Each represented different sides in the 1922–23 civil war.) As of the 2011 elections, Fine Gael and Labour created a governing coalition, with Fianna Fail and Sinn Féin forming the official opposition coalition.

Local Government

Local governance in the Republic of Ireland is divided among twenty-nine administrative counties, 24 of which have an elected county council. (The county of Tipperary is subdivided by two, while Dublin is subdivided by three.) In addition, the five city councils of Dublin, Cork, Galway, Limerick, and Waterford have equal administrative status as counties. Town and borough councils make up the administrative sub-tier below counties. Generally, councils are locally elected, maintain a council manager, and have limited administrative power regarding areas such as health and sanitation, housing, education, agriculture, local planning, and sports.

Judicial System

In Ireland, as in other countries, the Supreme Court is the court of final appeal. Courts of first instance, or trial courts, include a High Court, which has full jurisdiction in civil and criminal matters, and the Circuit Court and District Court, which are organized and operate regionally, and have limited jurisdiction. The Supreme Court and High Court are considered the superior courts.

Taxation

For citizens, the main tax in the Republic of Ireland is income tax. Ireland is believed to have some of the lowest income taxes in the world. In 2015, the standard rate of the income tax in Ireland was 20 percent, with a 40 percent rate for high income individuals. Other levied taxes include the capital gains tax, inheritance tax, value-added tax (VAT), and property taxes. Additionally, at 12.5 percent, the rate of corporation tax is also considered among the lowest globally.

Armed Forces

The armed forces of Ireland, referred to as the Irish Defence Forces (Óglaigh na hÉireann), consist of an army, navy, and air corps. As of 2014, there are approximately 8,500 women and men in the army, and 1,144 personnel serving in Ireland's naval service, and 800 in its air corps. Ireland also maintains a Reserve Defence Force.

Foreign Policy

Since gaining its independence from the United Kingdom (UK) in 1921, Ireland's foreign policy stance has been largely defined by its commitment to neutrality. Ireland, in fact, remained neutral through World War II, refusing to assist

England or the Allied forces in the war effort. However, Ireland did declare an official state of emergency during World War II, allowing the Irish government more authority and control over the economy. During this time, Northern Ireland, as a part of the United Kingdom, was at war.

Following the conclusion of the Second World War, Ireland refused to join the North Atlantic Treaty Organization (NATO), an international military and defense alliance, in 1949. Though Ireland has still not officially joined, it did join the NATO-affiliated Partnership for Peace (PfP) in 1999. This organizational body is a loose partnership of neutral nations that align their foreign policy to NATO guidelines, often participating selectively in peacekeeping missions. Additionally, Ireland has been a member of the United Nations (UN) since 1955, and has participated in over 50,000 peacekeeping missions. Recently, Ireland was involved in UN peacekeeping missions in Lebanon, East Timor, Kosovo, Cyprus, Iraq and Kuwait, Bosnia-Herzegovina, the Democratic Republic of the Congo, and Ethiopia and Eritrea.

Ireland has been a member of the European Union (EU) since 1973. That affiliation has largely been beneficial for Ireland, and has opened up the Irish economy by allowing it to use the Euro, the single currency used by most EU countries. In addition, Ireland has received funds and aid from the EU for improvements to the national infrastructure. Membership in the EU has also allowed Ireland a greater degree of cultural and economic independence from the UK (which is not a member of the EU).

However, partly in the interest of Ireland's commitment to neutrality, many people in Ireland distrust the EU when it comes to local autonomy. For example, Ireland made international headlines in June 2008 when it was the only member of the EU to reject the Lisbon Treaty, a document that would have consolidated and streamlined the EU government. This stance reflects a suspicion prevalent among the population that Ireland, as one of the smallest members of the EU, will not receive adequate representation and influence in a strong, central European government.

Ireland's foreign policy is also marked by its strong ties to the United States. With over 30.5 million Americans who claim Irish descent—representing nearly 11 percent of the total US population—Irish-American relations have historically been very close. The two countries enjoyed a friendly relationship in the 1990s when the administration of former US President Bill Clinton (1993–2001) took an active role in brokering the 1998 Good Friday Agreement. This peace agreement, between the political leaders of Ireland, England and Northern Ireland, made significant progress in bringing peace to Northern Ireland.

However, Irish attitudes toward the administration of US President George W. Bush were not positive. The Irish people were largely opposed to the US-led invasion of Iraq in 2003. Furthermore, even though there are Irish personnel among the UN peacekeeping forces stationed in the Middle East, Ireland was not a member of the multinational force that invaded and occupied Iraq and Afghanistan. Nonetheless, Ireland's role in the Iraq War and the "war on terror" has been a contentious issue because American military aircraft have been allowed to land at Shannon Airport (located at the western tip of Ireland) to refuel.

The election of Barack Obama brought relations between the United States and Ireland back to a more positive footing. His policies have been more in line with Ireland's and it hasn't hurt that he can trace some of his ancestors to Ireland. The focus has mainly been economic issues, rather than the conflict in the Middle East.

Human Rights Profile

International human rights law insists that states respect civil and political rights, and also promote an individual's economic, social and cultural rights. The United Nations Universal Declaration on Human Rights (UDHR) is recognized as the standard for international human rights. Its authors sought the counsel of the world's great thinkers, philosophers, and religious leaders, and were careful to create a document that reflects the core values shared by every world culture.

(To read this document or view the articles relating to cultural human rights, visit: http://www.udhr.org/UDHR/default.htm.)

Article 2 of the UDHR concerns discrimination on the basis of "race, colour, sex, language, religion, political or other opinion, national or social origin, property, birth, or other status." The Irish constitution carries no such discrimination on the level of public policy, but several instances and patterns of such discriminations have recently become an issue.

Since the economic boom of the 1990s, Ireland has for the first time experienced more immigration than emigration, with large numbers of asylum seekers, refugees, and economic migrants entering the country. For example, there are now large communities of people from Nigeria, China, Romania, and Poland. In addition, there is also a large Muslim community drawn from several different countries. As is the case in other European countries experiencing large influxes of immigrants, racism and hate crimes have been on the rise.

The immigration issue also touches upon marriage rights, which are the focus of Article 16 of the UDHR. The proposed Immigration Residence and Protection Bill contains a broad array of reforms in immigration law, including tighter restrictions on the right of non-nationals to marry. In order for a marriage between two non-citizens or between a non-citizen and an Irish citizen to be legal, an application will need to be made to the minister for justice, equality and law reform. The applications can then be refused for a very broad variety of reasons. This restriction is considered indicative of a broad suspicion that immigrants exploit marriage in order to gain citizenship.

Articles 18 and 19 of the UDHR, concerning freedom of religion and of speech, are generally widely respected in Ireland. There is a vibrant and healthy national press and the current generation in particular has produced innovated and challenging artists in a number of different media. Although censorship was common in the early years of the Irish republic, it is rarely practiced today.

Migration

Due to a financial boom in the 1990s, Ireland, a country traditionally characterized by emigration, saw its immigration rate increase. In fact, from the year 1980 to 2006, immigration per year increased from below 20,000 to over 100,000. Ireland attempted to curb this increased migration flow by altering its asylum determination process and citizenship policy. Economic issues, particularly an increased unemployment rate, have further complicated the migration issue in recent years. In early 2009, the unemployment rate for migrants was nearly 15 percent, five percentage points higher than nationals. After a sharp decline in 2010, by 2014 immigration had climbed back to about 60,000. However, as has been the case since 2010, more people have been leaving Ireland, with about 80,000 emigrating to other nations.

ECONOMY

Overview of the Economy

Ireland has a trade-dependent economy, and the export sector remains a key economic sector. The industry and service sectors are also important economic sectors (the agriculture sector lags far behind). The Irish economy experienced a boom beginning in the 1990s, and at one point, the country was considered the fourth most affluent nation in the Organization for Economic Cooperation and Development. Between 1995 and 2007, Ireland experienced GDP growth—averaged at 6 percent—with house prices rising rapidly.

However, as with numerous countries, Ireland's economy has been severely troubled by the 2008–09 global financial crisis which, combined with falling property prices (housing prices fell as much as 50 percent) led to the 2008–10 Irish banking crisis, in which government assistance was required to bail out financial institutions. According to the Irish Central Statistics Office, Ireland was the first European Union member country to officially enter a recession. By 2014, Ireland was once again growing, but at a more restrained 3.6 percent.

Industry

The significance of industry to the economy of Ireland has increased in the past century. While agriculture remains important, high technology companies have created most of modern Ireland's job market. The manufacturing industry is not as prevalent as service industries, which include sectors such as trade, construction, and communication.

Ireland's major exports include meat and dairy, textiles such as wool, and manufactured products. Great Britain is its largest trading partner, and nearly 75 percent of Ireland's exported goods are sent to countries within the European Union.

Labor

As of 2014, Ireland's unemployment rate is high at 11.3 percent, despite a recent history of growth. For migrant workers, the unemployment rate in 2014 was about 5 percent higher than for Irish citizens.

Energy/Power/Natural Resources

Peat is widely used as a fossil fuel in the absence of coal. Heavy industrial growth has caused water pollution in many freshwater habitats, prompting the European Union to write laws for the protection of Ireland's peat bogs.

Fishing

Fishing, as an industry, is considered to be underdeveloped in Ireland. It is estimated that only a low percentage of fish caught in Irish waters is from Irish fishing vessels.

Forestry

There are few trees on the island due to a history of heavy logging, and Ireland's forest cover is below that of the European Union average.

Mining/Metals

Ireland's chief natural resources are mainly geological. The land is rich with minerals that are valuable as building stones. Zinc and lead are heavily mined in the lowland areas.

Agriculture

The export economy of Ireland relies on the agricultural sector. Ireland does not import much food, mostly because of its abundant pastures and ideal climate for year-round farming. Inland pastures cover two-thirds of the country. Cattle and vegetables, especially potatoes, are particularly important as both food and commodities, as are wheat and barley. Ireland's agriculture sector remains one of the major beneficiaries of the European Union's farm subsidies.

Animal Husbandry

Cattle are particularly important as both food and commodities. In 2005, Ireland achieved record exports in the dairy and meat industry. That year, beef accounted for nearly 20 percent of total food exports. In 2014, dairy products accounted for about 29 percent of the exports, while beef was at 22 percent.

Tourism

Tourists are a large part of the Irish economy. During 2013, nearly 6.7 million people visit Ireland, generating almost $4.5 billion USD in revenue. Popular tourist attractions include Ireland's many castles, such as Bunratty Castle, Ashford Castle and Blarney Castle. Visitors to Blarney are given the chance to kiss the Blarney Stone for good luck.

Tourists often visit the Aran Islands and the Cliffs of Moher. Popular tourist attractions in Dublin include the Guinness Brewery and the trendy Temple Bar area.

Because of the great number of Irish descendants living in the United States, many Americans visit Ireland in an attempt to trace their lineage. There is a large market for heritage-based products, such as family crests and information about the origins and meaning of Irish surnames.

Many tourists are particularly interested in buying the famous Waterford Crystal products, such as stemware and vases, made in the southern city of Waterford. Souvenirs such as Claddagh rings and Celtic crosses are also popular among visitors to Ireland.

Rebecca Troeger, Richard Means,
Michael Aliprandi

DO YOU KNOW?

- One-third of all American presidents have been Irish descendants. In Galway, Ireland, there is a famous park named after John F. Kennedy, the 35th President of the United States.

- The popular style of rhymed-verse poem known as "limerick" gets its name from the city of Limerick, Ireland, where the style was originated.

- The horse race known as the steeplechase was invented in 1752 when two Irish men engaged in an off-course countryside race from the steeple of one church to the steeple of another.

- Dublin means "Dark Pool" in the Irish language. Its official Irish name is Baile Átha Cliath ("Town of the Ford of the Hurdles").

Bibliography

Brown, Terence. *Ireland: A Social and Cultural History 1922–2002*. London: Harper Perennial, 2004.

Carson, Ciaran. *Irish Traditional Music*. Belfast: Appletree Press, 1986.

Cleary, Joe, and Claire Connolly, Eds. *The Cambridge Companion to Modern Irish Culture*. Cambridge: Cambridge University Press, 2005.

Coughlan, Gerry. *Irish Language and Culture (Lonely Planet Language & Culture: Irish)*. 2nd ed. Oakland: Lonely Planet, 2013.

Ferriter, Diarmaid. *The Transformation of Ireland*. Woodstock and New York: The Overlook Press, 2005.

Goodby, John, ed. *Irish Studies: The Essential Glossary*. London: Arnold Publishers, 2003.

Jewers, Jack. *Frommer's Ireland 2015*. 23rd ed. New York: FrommerMedia, 2014.

Kiberd, Declan. *Inventing Ireland*. London: Jonathan Cape, 1995.

Killeen, Richard. *A Brief History of Ireland*. London: Constable & Robinson Ltd., 2012.

Levy, Patricia. *Ireland: Culture Shock! A Guide to Customs and Etiquette*. Rev. Ed. Portland, OR: Graphic Arts Center Publishing Company, 2006.

McCormack, W. J., Ed. *The Blackwell Companion to Modern Irish Culture*. Oxford: Blackwell Publishers Ltd., 2001.

Scotney, John. *Culture Smart! Ireland*. New Ed. London: Kuperard, 2006.

Works Cited

Catriona Beaumont. "Gender, Citizenship and the State in Ireland, 1922–1990." In Brewster, Scott, Crossman, Virginia, Becket, Fiona and Alderson, David (eds.). "Ireland in Proximity: History, Gender, Space." London and New York: Routledge, 1999. 94–108. p. 97–98.

Diarmaid Ferriter. "The Transformation of Ireland." Woodstock and New York: The Overlook Press, 2005. p. 538.

Deirdre Mulrooney. *Interview with Colin Dunne*. In Mulrooney, Ed. p. 237.

Deirdre Mulrooney, Ed. *Irish Moves: An Illustrated History of Dance and Physical Theatre in Ireland*. Dublin: The Liffey Press, 2006.

Gwen Orel. *Theater Festival Presents New Voices From A New Ireland*. New York Times. August 31, 2008. <http://www.nytimes.com/2008/09/01/theater/01walsh.html.

"Information Leaflet on the Immigration, Residence and Protection Bill." Dublin: *Integrating Ireland, Immigrant Council of Ireland, Refugee Information Service, Migrant Rights Centre Ireland, Irish Refugee Council and NASC, 2007*.

Kevin Whalen. *Lecture: "Society and Culture in Contemporary Ireland."* July 7, 2004

"Reproductive Rights." *Irish Council for Civil Liberties*. <http://iccl.ie/DB_Data/issues/ReproductiveRights_10015_General.htm>

ITALY

Introduction

Italy is located in south central Europe, occupying a long narrow peninsula that extends into the Mediterranean Sea, as well as several islands. The country's official name is La Repubblica Italiana, or in English, the Italian Republic.

From the reign of the Roman Empire to the artistic and architectural innovations of the Renaissance, Italy's long history and cultural achievements have exerted an almost unparalleled influence on Western culture. Italian cuisine is celebrated all over the world and the country's artistic influence, particularly in architecture and fashion design, continues today.

Italy's masterworks of art and architecture, as well as its reputation for being the home of some of the world's finest foods and wines, have made the country one of the most popular travel destinations on the globe. As a political entity, Italy is one of the most active and productive members of the European Union, although recent years have been marked by lingering economic problems.

GENERAL INFORMATION

Official Language: Italian
Population: 61,680,122 (2014 estimate)
Currency: Euro
Coins: The Euro is available in 1, 2, 5, 10, 20, and 50 cent coins. A 1 and 2 Euro coin is also available.

Land Area: 301,338 square kilometers (116,346 square miles)
Water Area: 7,210 square kilometers (2,784 square miles)
National Anthem: "Fratelli d'Italia" ("Brothers of Italy")
Capital: Roma (Rome)
Time Zone: GMT + 1
Flag Description: The flag of Italy features three vertical bands of color—one red, one white, and one green. It was formally adopted as the country's flag in 1948. The green represents the Italian countryside, the white represents the Alps, and the red represents the blood of Italians killed during the country's wars for independence.

Population

Over 65 percent of the population of Italy is between 15 and 64 years of age. As of 2014, the country had an almost even population growth rate. However, in the past decade it has

Principal Cities by Population (2012):

- Roma (2,400,000)
- Milano (1,300,000)
- Napoli (937,501)
- Torino (854,299)
- Palermo (633,182)
- Genoa (575,087)
- Bologna (371,088)
- Firenze (380,802)
- Bari (301,521)
- Venice (261,532)

experienced a slight increase in the overall birth rate. Life expectancy at birth is an estimated 84 years for women and 79 years for men.

There has been significant internal migration in Italy over the past half century from rural to urban areas. Rome, with an estimated population of over 2.4 million, is the country's largest city. Approximately one-third of the Italian population lives south of Rome, a predominantly rural region. The larger proportion occupies the more urbanized northern region of the country. Population density is 200.5 people per square kilometer (519 per square mile), making Italy one of the most densely populated countries in Europe.

Ethnically, the Italian population is largely homogenous, but culturally, it is diverse. Exceptions to this general picture include small minority groups that inhabit border areas as well as immigrants from developing countries. Only about 100,000 of Europe's largest minority group, the Roma, or Gypsies, live in Italy.

Languages

Italian is a Romance language spoken by the vast majority of the population of Italy, though often not solely. Modern Italian derives from the dialect of Tuscany, particularly as it evolved in the city of Florence in medieval times. Regional dialects became less common following the advent of uniform education standards and improved

communication between disparate regions of the country. However, some dialects are still spoken alongside Italian, some by only a handful of people. A few larger groups, such as Fruilian and Napoletano, continue to maintain their unique dialect.

Minority languages or dialects not related to Italian include Occitan, spoken in the Piedmont region; Slovenian, spoken in areas bordering Slovenia; Tosca, an Albanian dialect spoken in the southeast; French in the Valle d'Aosta; German in the region of Trentino Alto Adige; Greek in the southern provinces of Lecce and Reggio Calabria; and Sardinian, spoken on the island of Sardinia.

Native People & Ethnic Groups

The Italian peninsula has been home to a pageant of peoples dating back to antiquity. It is from these that the common Italian stock derives. Following unification in 1861, a national identity began to be forged, though regional identities still remain important to this day. Historically, it has been economic disparities rather than ethnic differences which have challenged the Italian identity: the richer, urbanized north versus the less developed south.

Religions

Italy is steeped in the traditions of the Roman Catholic Church, and 98 percent of the population considers itself Roman Catholic. It is no longer the official state religion, however, and the percentage of practicing Catholics in the country continues to decrease. Religious minorities include Jews and Protestants. Over the last several decades, the Muslim population has grown through immigration.

Climate

Italy's average annual temperature falls between 11° and 19° Celsius (52° to 66° Fahrenheit). A Mediterranean climate prevails throughout much of the peninsula, with sea breezes moderating both summer and winter temperatures. The south, including the islands of Sicily and Sardinia, has a much hotter and drier climate. Rainfall, which is heaviest during the winter and spring, is much lower in the southern regions than in the central and northern regions.

In the north, away from the seas, summers and winters are cooler, the climate being more continental. In the mountains of the far north, the summers are cool and the winters are freezing, with heavy snowfall.

Climate is adversely affecting culture in one particularly pressing case: that of the northeastern city of Venezia (Venice), which was built on a lagoon and encompasses numerous canals. The city is prone to seasonal flooding from high tides. The higher levels and increasing salinity of the water have damaged many of its buildings, causing concern about whether the city can be preserved. An ambitious project is currently being undertaken to put movable dams in the lagoon. These dams will be submerged unless they are needed to prevent high tides from flooding the city.

ENVIRONMENT & GEOGRAPHY

Topography

Italy is composed of the mainland, over half of which is the long, narrow boot-shaped peninsula, and several islands. Sardinia and Sicily are the largest of these. The Adriatic Sea is to the east of the peninsula, the Ionian Sea is to the south, and the Tyrrhenian Sea is to the west, giving Italy 7,600 kilometers (4,631 miles) of coastline. Major indentations along the coast include the Gulf of Taranto and the Gulf of Salerno. The terrain is generally hilly and mountainous except on coastal lowlands and the Plain of Lombardy in the north.

There are two major mountain ranges in Italy: the Alps, which dominate the northern portion of the country, and the Appenines, which rise along the peninsula in several ridges. The approach to Monte Bianco is the highest point in Italy. The mountain's summit, at 4,810 meters (15,782 feet) lies in France. Monte Corno is the highest peak of the Appenines at 2,912 meters (9,554 feet).

There are several active volcanoes in Italy. Mount Vesuvius, towering over the Bay of Naples, is historically the most famous. The largest and most active, Mount Etna, is found on the island of Sicily. It rises approximately 3,323 meters (10,902 feet), but its elevation is altered by frequent volcanic activity.

The Po and the Adige are Italy's two most significant rivers. The Po, the longest, flows 652 kilometers (405 miles) and feeds the Plain of Lombardy. Like the Adige, it flows into the Adriatic Sea. Other noteworthy rivers are the Tevere (Tiber), which runs through Rome, and the Arno, which flows through Firenze (Florence). The largest lakes are Garda, Como, Maggiore and Lugano, all in northern Italy.

Plants & Animals

Italy is home to about 90 species of animals, 14 of them threatened. The Mediterranean Monk Seal is listed as critically endangered, and the brown bear is on the verge of extinction. Common mountain animals include the wolf, boar, and fox. Small scorpions and several types of viper are the only poisonous animals.

With 84 percent of the land listed as being highly disturbed by human activity, it is not surprising that Italy has fewer animal species than other European countries. Marine animals include a wide variety of fish as well as shrimp, octopus, and mussels.

In the mountains, forests of oak, chestnut, and pine trees are prevalent. The lower lands are dominated by Mediterranean shrubs and trees, olive, citrus and other fruit-bearing trees among them.

CUSTOMS & COURTESIES

Greetings

Italians often judge others by first impressions, so proper etiquette when meeting for the first time is important in Italian culture. Thus, "Fare la bella figura" is a motto that figures prominently, but quietly, in Italian life. While difficult to translate, its essential meaning is "to make a good impression." This includes the capacity to make something pleasing from even the simplest of resources. The motto is particularly evidenced in Italian fashion and cuisine.

One customary greeting is a handshake (not too firm), often used when meeting strangers or in business settings. Friends or acquaintances commonly greet with two light kisses, first on the right cheek and then the left. Upon meeting someone for the first time, it is polite to say "Piacere," which means "Pleased to meet you." When departing, the greeting kiss would be repeated. This is sometimes accompanied by a casual saying, such as "Ciao," "a presto," "a domani," or "arrivederci." The latter is used to say farewell in more formal situations, while "Ciao" is a greeting that can be given either in meeting or departing, but is only spoken to a friend or acquaintance.

Gestures & Etiquette

Gesturing with the hands while speaking is common in everyday communication among Italians. Italians offer supporting emphasis to words and thoughts through gestures and give visual impact to expressions of thought. In the proper context, many gestures need no translation. However, the complexities in meaning and context of Italian gestures reveal intricate and important layers of the Italian culture. These can be as compelling as the verbal language itself. In fact, many books have been written on the subject.

When entering a shop, it is polite to greet the salesperson with "Buon giorno" in the morning or "Buona sera" in the later afternoon and evening. These greetings are friendly, and the shopkeeper will appreciate the manners of the greeter. When paying, the money is often placed on a surface or in a dish, and the change is also placed there.

When visiting a basilica, duomo, or other religious site, proper dress is important. Short skirts and shorts are usually frowned upon, and women should cover up exposed arms, back, chests, and shoulders. Some sites will prohibit entrance to those not considered properly clothed, while others may provide cover-ups.

Eating/Meals

Many Italians consider themselves gourmets, and great care is taken in the preparation, consumption, and discussion of food. In addition, both professional Italian cooks and everyday people pride themselves on using the freshest and ripest ingredients.

For breakfast, called colazione, Italians most commonly eat bread with butter and jam, or a light pastry. This is accompanied by a café acute; latte, which is warm milk mixed with espresso. Often the beverage is served in a small bowl, and is sipped from the rim of the bowl. Cappuccino, a drink of espresso with hot milk topped with a layer of foamed steamed milk might also be taken in the morning, though rarely after 10:30 a.m.

Lunch, called pranzo, is usually served around 1:00 p.m. It is the largest and most important meal of the day. It typically consists of three courses: a pasta or rice dish, or soup; a meat or fish dish accompanied by a vegetable; and a third course consisting of fruit or dessert served with coffee. Also, many restaurants offer antipasti, an appetizer or first dish that offers small portions of salami, cooked vegetables, olives, and raw ham, or ham treated with salt and cured.

As recently as the 1980s, it was often customary in the warmer parts of Europe for businesses to shut down in the early afternoon so that the entire family could gather for the meal. In smaller towns, shops and offices often close, giving the impression that the city is asleep until mid-afternoon. The impact of technology and globalization is such that businesses in many larger cities no longer adhere to this custom; however, it is still very common throughout Italy.

Dinner, called cena, is usually eaten at 8:00 pm or later. In fact, many restaurants don't open until later in the evening. The same type of food served at lunch is also served in the evening, but it is usually lighter and does not include pasta. Soup is common.

There are several types of restaurants in Italy. A ristorante is more elaborate, with seating at one's own table, and waitstaff service. A trattoria or osteria is more informal, and is more like eating at home. It is not uncommon for osteria diners to sit at long tables with benches, although individual tables are also common.

Throughout Rome and the country's other urban areas, Western foods and restaurants serving foreign foods are available.

Visiting

Part of "la bella figura" or a good impression, of visiting in Italy is the "passeggiata," which means "the stroll." This custom follows lunch and precedes dinner, and allows Italians to be social as they speak and visit with people they know, often in formal attire. During the long summer hours, this custom might be repeated after dinner with a short stop for gelato, which is Italian ice cream.

In Italy, hosts often invite guests to tour their home with them, room by room. Houseguests in particular are often welcomed in this manner. When invited to share a meal, it is customary to bring a gift, such as a dessert, chocolates, or wine. Certain flowers, however, should not be brought as gifts. For example, large yellow or white chrysanthemums are associated with decorations found in cemeteries. In addition, red flowers have negative connotations. Italians also refrain from using the color purple or black, especially as a gift wrap, as they are symbols of mourning and bad luck.

If invited to a meal in an Italian home, it is usually customary to wear stylish clothes. Even if the mood is informal, women should wear a dress, skirt, or tailored outfit, and men should wear a jacket. Punctuality is not mandatory, and arriving 15 minutes late is acceptable. Keeping your hands in your lap at a meal is considered bad manners. It is considered polite to keep your hands on the table, but not your elbows.

LIFESTYLE

Family

Family values are considered the backbone of Italian society, and most Italian families are closely tied together emotionally and financially. Some Italian families live together in one house,

and in others the extended family might share a home. The elderly are treated with respect, and often live with their children. In this relationship, the grandparents often care for the grandchildren when the parents are working. In return, the children take care of parents after they retire. Most notably, the mother is the center of the family.

In many towns and villages, Sundays are considered family days. The family eats together and then spends the day together taking walks or just visiting one another. In the smaller towns, most shops and businesses are closed on Sunday, and this time is devoted to the family.

Housing

Homes in Italy are commonly built of stone, brick, or concrete. In the mountainous regions of the north, some houses, called chalets, are built with wood. Inside homes, it is common to see tiles cover the floors, with wooden floors being the exception. Few homes have screens on windows. Instead of screens for doors, Italians use glass or plastic "curtains" which cover the doors during the day. These curtains are actually tiny beads strung on hanging threads, which are easily moved when entering or exiting. The glass or plastic beads move slightly in the breeze, thus discouraging insects from entering.

Thousands of residential homes in Italy were destroyed during World War II. Gradually, more modern homes and apartment buildings replaced the original stone buildings. As such, ancient buildings sometimes stand next to more contemporary structures. In addition, many Italians have restored old stone farmhouses and use them as homes or villas. Laws require these homes to be constructed with the integrity of the original in mind.

Food

Italian food varies from region to region. Almost every province typically includes pasta, risotto (a creamy rice dish), and olive oil as main ingredients. In the northwest regions near France, the food is influenced by French cuisine. In the areas bordering Austria, chefs are fond of heavier soups and smoked meats.

In the northern and central part of Italy, olive groves are prolific and cuisine often centers on olive oil and olives. In addition, because Italy has an extensive coastline, seafood is readily available. In the more forested regions such as Abruzzo and Umbria, cinghiale (wild boar) is hunted and made into sausages. The northern and central parts of Italy also are known for a delicacy known as truffles, which are red or black nuggets of funghi that sell for as high as $500 (USD) a pound. Truffles are commonly made into sauces and sometimes served over pasta. As one travels south through Basilicata, Campania, Calabria, and on to the islands of Sicily and Sardinia, sauces become more dominated by tomatoes and spicier chili peppers, and flavors are influenced by the spices of Greece and the southern Mediterranean. Where southern Italy meets the coast, seafood is highlighted.

Italy is also renowned for its cheeses, of which there as many as 450 types. Caprese salad is a popular dish made with slices of fresh mozzarella (a soft white cheese made from the milk of cows or buffalo), fresh leaves of basil, and slices of ripe red tomatoes, all drizzled with virgin olive oil. Tuscany is known for its pecorino cheese (made from sheep's milk), which can be eaten alone or with crackers, or spread with honey and freshly ground pepper. Parmigiano Reggiano cheese (Parmesan) is made in the Parma region of Emilia-Romagna. Parmigiano is a hard, strong cheese, which Italians typically use as a garnish in pasta or soups. Ricotta, which likely originated in Sicily, can be creamy, soft and textured, a consistency smoother than cottage cheese, or firm and sliceable. Technically, it isn't a cheese at all, but a curd, make from whey proteins in cow or sheep milk. It is a staple in Italian cooking.

Two well-known Italian food products are prosciutto and bruschetta. Prosciutto is a type of ham rubbed with salt and cured (by either drying or smoking) for anywhere from two months to two years. Like Parmigiano cheese, it is another culinary star from the region of Parma. It is typically eaten raw alone or with

melon, but can also be lightly cooked in soups or pastas, or served in antipasto. Bruschetta, an appetizer served in all parts of Italy, is made from grilled or toasted bread covered with tomatoes, beans, cheese, or proscuiutto. An easy way to prepare bruschetta is to toast small round slices of bread drizzled with olive oil. A mixture of chopped basil and chopped tomatoes is then spread on top.

Cappuccino is a signature Italian coffee beverage consisting of espresso and hot milk, topped with a layer of steamed and foamed milk. In Italy, one customarily drinks cappuccino only in the morning. The drink takes its name from the brown hooded habit worn by the Capuchin Franciscan friars, which originated in medieval Italy. The Italian word for "hood" is "cappuccio." Cappuccino literally means "little hood."

Life's Milestones

Weddings are a particularly important part of Italian culture. They incorporate family and cultural traditions that date back to ancient Roman customs. The bride carries a bouquet to represent fidelity and fertility. The bride's veil is worn to protect her from evil spirits, and the ring symbolizes the marriage bond. After the marriage, the groom carries his bride over the threshold, just as ancient Romans did with the Sabine women they kidnapped for marriage. In fact, the kidnapping of Sabine woman, who are an Italic tribe from ancient Italy, was a popular theme in the history of Italian art, particularly during the Renaissance period.

In addition, before the wedding the couple is honored with several parties to celebrate the wedding. On the night before the wedding, the bride wears green, which encourages abundance and wealth for their future. Because most of Italian citizens are Roman Catholic, many of their other traditions and customs are religious. Funerals in Italy are also well-attended affairs that honor the death of a loved one. Cemeteries are treated more like parks, and family members visit to tend the graves and have picnics nearby.

CULTURAL HISTORY

Art

Perhaps no other artists and architects have wielded more historical influence than those from Italy. Italian art dates back to the Etruscans, an ancient civilization (900–100 BCE) that pre-dated the Roman Empire in Italy. They espoused Greek influences and an appreciation of art and sculpture. The impact of their artistic skills extended to the beginning of Roman rule.

By 1000 CE, art and architecture had become a prominent part of Italian society. Elaborate public buildings were erected, and tower-fortresses were characteristic of the wealthiest and most influential cities. By the early 15th century the Italian Renaissance was beginning to take root. During the next two centuries, affluent city-states such as Florence, considered the birthplace of the Renaissance, and Sienna competed with each other to create the most elaborate sculptures, paintings, cathedrals, and other works. This period of cultural rebirth and achievement continues to influence modern art.

During this period, wealthy families and church officials strove to communicate their prosperity and power through art. They commissioned artists and architects to create decorative buildings. This patronage, or financial support, gave rise to a multitude of artists, sculptors, and architects – a veritable who's who of masters in the art world. Michelangelo Buonarotti (1475–1564), a triple power as painter, sculptor, and architect painted the Sistine Chapel in Rome and sculpted the statue *David*. Leonardo da Vinci (1452–1519) was his contemporary and sometimes rival, as sculptor, inventor, and painter, most notably of *The Last Supper* and *La Giaconda* (also known as the *Mona Lisa*). Filippo Brunelleschi (1377–1446) was commissioned to design an innovative dome atop the major cathedral in Florence. Donatello (1386–1466) was considered the greatest sculptor of the Renaissance, with many of his masterpieces on display in Florence. Other artists such as Raphael (1483–1520), Sandro Botticelli (c. 1445–1510),

Titian (c. 1488–1576), and Tintoretto (1518–1584) were also prominent.

Another of Italy's great art forms is fashion. The history of Italian fashion dates back to the Middle Ages and the Italian Renaissance. Even though political instability made it difficult to export Italian goods during these periods, Italy became well known for its fashions. For example, leather goods were known for their high quality and modern style. Fashionable eyeglasses were crafted in the 14th century, and the 15th century saw the design and production of more complicated and ornate textiles.

Years of foreign occupation, division and war cloaked this rich and prolific creative heritage through the end of World War II. However, after World War II, Italy's art scene reawakened, and modern sculptors, architects, artists and fashion designers have found new success. Government sponsorship of the restoration and exhibition of classical and ancient art has helped conservation efforts, but much still needs to be done. There is less state funding for modern art. Private galleries and foundations are thus left to sponsor exhibitions and encourage innovation.

During the 20eth century, artists and designers created new fashion designs based on the traditions and artistry in the preceding 800 years. At the beginning of the century, leather goods and fashion accessories were exported throughout the world. Italian-made goods began to be synonymous with the highest quality. In 1920, a renowned fabric company in Venice called Fortuny began exporting rich fabrics that married the artistry of the past with modern styles.

In the middle of the 20th century, American buyers sent representatives to the fashion centers in Milan, Florence, and Rome to find products for high-end, or luxury, stores. Finally, the Italians began their own marketing program and established labels and iconic design houses such as Armani, Valentino, Dolce & Gabbana, Ferragamo, Ferré; Prada, Gucci, Trussardi, and Versace. These design houses and their fashions had their roots in the rich cultural heritage of the Italian Renaissance, and are synonymous with quality and innovation.

Architecture

Architecture is at the forefront of Italy's rich and historic artistic heritage, ranging from the country's Roman era in ancient times, to the development of architectural order and the use of classical ornamentation during the Renaissance, as well as the dynamic style of the Baroque movement, which emerged in Italy in the 1600s.

Much of Italian architecture has been influenced by classical antiquity. Cornerstones of Italy's architectural heritage include the Coliseum, considered a classical example of Roman architecture. This oval-shaped ancient amphitheater is known for its range of styles in its tiered columns, including both the Doric and Ionic orders of classical architecture. (The Romans absorbed much of the ancient Greek style of architecture). Another cornerstone of Roman classical architecture is the Roman Forum, characterized by Corinthian columns and use of mosaics. As evidenced by these two structures, Roman architecture, which is also characterized by the use of arches, is known particularly for its public structures.

Several architectural movements would follow, from early Byzantine architecture, characterized by the use of mosaics and iconic elements, to Romanesque and Gothic architecture, the latter prominently highlighted by the Milan Cathedral. Considered the fourth-largest church in the world, and needing five centuries to complete, the Milan Cathedral is characterized by its pinnacled roofline, Gothic-inspired façade, and the five naves (church's central area) of its interior.

Structures that typify the highest expressions of the Renaissance period include Brunelleschi's Dome in Florence, a masonry dome that dominates Florence's skyline; the Church of San Lorenzo, the arches and columns of which harken back to Rome's classical years; and the Medici-Riccardi Palace, the design of which also used Roman principles of architecture.

In general, the architecture of the Renaissance era is characterized by geometric proportions and harmonious elements and forms, and punctuated by arches, columns, and domes, among other architectural elements.

The Italian Baroque period brought with it an invigoration of the classical style, highlighted by the almost theatrical and lavish Baroque churches of Rome, with elements such as ceiling frescoes and sculptural interiors, and the innovative use of light and color. Many other architectural styles would follow, from neoclassical, again using Greek and Roman themes, to modern styles such as art nouveau (an organic, curvilinear style) and fascist architecture, an overpowering style that emerged in the 1920s. Present-day architecture in Italy is largely defined by the global work of Renzo Piano (1937–), an award-winning architect whose body of international work includes museums, national art centers, skyscrapers, and airports, buildings that purportedly embody a vision of the future while looking back towards the past.

Drama

The first important film genre in Italian cinema was the historical film. Prior to and during World War II, propaganda films became popular. During the fascist regime of Benito Mussolini, a town was even commissioned, named Cinecittà in which everything was built exclusively around filmmaking. After the end of World War II, Italy emerged from the authoritarian rule of Mussolini and into a period of more stylized cinema.

Industrial expansion and economic prosperity pushed the country forward, and the phrase "la dolce vita," which means "the sweet life," has become synonymous with Italy and its culture. For example, Italian filmmakers such as Roberto Rossellini (1906–1977) began making important films that exposed realistic life situations in postwar Italy. This style became known as Italian neorealism. Federico Fellini, who made some of the most respected post-war films, including *La Dolce Vita* (1960) and *8½* (1963), and Michelangelo Antonioni became masters in Italian cinema in the 1950s and 1960s, and students of filmmaking continue to study their techniques. Other directors of international repute include Vittorio de Sica (1901–1974), Pier Palo Pasolini (1922–1975), and Lina Wertmuller (1926–).

Sergio Leone (1929–1989), another Italian filmmaker, also became synonymous with Italian cinema, as did his popular genre of westerns dubbed "spaghetti westerns." Incorporating quality cinematography on a smaller budget, the films became widely popular around the world. During the late decades of the twentieth century, however, Italian cinema declined, and was characterized as having little artistic value. Though comedies remained the popular genre, art films were becoming few and far between in the mainstream.

Italian cinema has since undergone a revival heading into the 21st century. Acclaimed directors include Giuseppe Tornatore (1956–), who won the Academy Award for Best Foreign Language Film in 1989 for *Nuovo Cinema Paradiso* (1988), Gabriele Salvatores (1950–), who won the Best Foreign Language Film Oscar in 1991 for *Mediterraneo*, and actor and director Roberto Benigni (1952–), who also won the Oscar for best foreign language film for 1997's *Life is Beautiful*. Benigni also won the Best Actor Oscar for his performance in the film.

Music

Like its art and fashion, Italy's music is derived from its cultural heritage. Just as dialects were sprinkled all over the country, so were different kinds of music. In Naples, the "canzone napoletana" ("Neapolitan songs") developed. *Il Solo Mio* is one of the more popular Neapolitan songs associated with this genre. In addition, bagpipes were popular in southern Italy in the more rural areas. In the northern regions, Celtic music was very influential.

Historically, Italian music has its origins in the Catholic Church, which influenced many musicians. In the fourth century, religious chants were sung a cappella (without accompaniment) to accompany formal worship. These chants are still popular and are sold commercially.

In the 17th century, Italians began staging operatic performances of Greek plays. They believed that the Greeks sang their plays instead of speaking, so all the dialogue was sung. Venice became the city where most opera was

performed, but later Milan took over the opera scene. Opera writers like Puccini, Verdi, Rossini, Donizetti, and Bellini were the most famous, and their operas are still performed today. The famed opera house in Milan, La Scala ("the steps"), is one of the country's premier opera houses. Italian audiences there are known for their high level of appreciation, and have been known to boo performers off the stage.

Instrumental and classical music also has a rich heritage in Italy. Composers such as Antonio Vivaldi, Donizetti, and Verdi crafted sacred music, concertos and orchestral music. "The Four Seasons" by Vivaldi is one of the most popular and well-known concertos in the world. In the 20th and 21st centuries, Italy's acclaimed musical heritage has been enriched by the careers of operatic tenors Enrico Caruso (1873–1921) and Luciano Pavarotti (1935–2007), as well as legendary film composer Ennio Morricone (1928–), considered one of the most acclaimed and influential film score composers of the modern era, and who received an Academy Honorary Award in 2007 for his extensive body of work.

Dance

The saltarello is a popular traditional dance of Northern Italy, which dates back to the 13th century. The quintessential dance of Italy's southern regions is known as the tarantella, which is still performed. Theaters and opera houses throughout Italy continue to present dance performance. These include the Teatro Dell'Opera Di Roma in Rome and the Teatro Verdi in Busseto. The Piccolo Teatro Arsenale in Venice holds a Contemporary Dance Festival each year. The festival features contemporary dance and performances from foreign dance companies.

Literature

Much of Italy's classical literature derives from the Roman period, when famous orators such as Cicero (106–43 BCE) wrote about politics and philosophy. He wrote about events that occurred during the rise and fall of the Roman Empire, including the reign of Julius Caesar. Virgil was a classical Roman poet influenced by Hellenistic, or Greek, culture. He lived from 50 to 19 BCE and wrote the *Aeneid*. This epic poem tells a mythical story in which Aeneas, a Trojan, founds the Roman Empire. Twelve centuries later, troubadours, or poet-musicians, travelled throughout Italy, performing their lyric poetry and songs for the wealthy.

During the 14th century, three great writers and poets emerged during the Renaissance. They, in turn, created a rich cultural revolution in literature. Dante Alighieri (c. 1265–1321) wrote the *Divine Comedy* between 1314 and 1321. This poem chronicled the spiritual progress of Italians since the fall of the Roman Empire. Francesco Petrarca (also known as Petrarch) perfected the sonnet in poems about love, patriotism, and religion. Giovanni Boccaccio (1313–1375) introduced the first short story form in *The Decameron*. These one hundred stories described life in the 14th century.

During the Renaissance, many dialects were spoken in Italy, with Latinthe the prominent language. Dante lived in Florence and spoke the Florentine dialect. This dialect would help formalize the modern Italian language. Other luminary Italian authors are Luigi Pirandello (1867–1936) and Italo Calvino (1923–1985). Major thinkers include Nicolo Machiavelli (1469–1527), whose treatise on statecraft, *The Prince*, is still widely discussed today, and 20th-century philosopher writers such as Antonio Gramsci (1891–1937) and Benedetto Croce (1866–1952).

Italian literature is further distinguished by the works of Carlo Collodi (1826–1890), who penned *The Adventures of Pinocchio*, a classic work of children's literature. Other internationally renowned Italian writers include Umberto Eco (1932–), author of *The Name of the Rose* (*Il nome della rosa*, 1980); dramatist Luigi Pirandello (1867–1936), who won the Nobel Prize in Literature in 1934; and poet Filippo Tommaso Marinetti (1876–1944), founder of the Futurist movement, which embraces technology. Italians have been awarded the Nobel Prize in Literature five times, most recently in 1997.

CULTURE

Arts & Entertainment

Contemporary and traditional Italian culture and art stand side by side. In a country rich with artistic treasures, the standards for quality are high and tastes are sophisticated.

Modern Italian filmmakers are especially known for the genres of drama and comedy. American films are also popular in Italy, but English subtitles are not. American films are dubbed with the voices of Italian actors. In addition, once an actor assumes an English or American actor's voice, he or she assumes that actor's roles in all subsequent films.

In the 21st century, the thriller detective story, or "giallo," became immensely popular in Italy. Niccolo Ammaniti's *I'm Not Scared* (2001) is a story about a child who loses his innocence in the adult world of violence. This book was made into a movie in 2003 that enjoyed success in Italy and abroad. Daniele Bonati, Stefano Benni, and Aldo Busi are a few of Italy's prominent modern writers.

Music in Italy is also culturally important. Italians enjoy all types, including classical, jazz, folk, and pop. American musicians have influenced their Italian counterparts since the latter half of the 20th century, but Italian performers have their own distinctive styles. Pop music is celebrated at a popular festival in San Remo each year, and the Italian television station, RAI, boasts four orchestras. Orchestras all over the world seek violinists Uto Ughi and Salvatore Accardo as well as Maurizio Pollini, the world-renowned pianist. Composers Luciano Berio, Luigi Dallapiccola, and Luigi Nono are famous Italian classical composers. Guiseppe Verdi and Giacomo Puccini are two of the foremost composers, while the tenor Luciano Pavarotti had a long, successful career as a performer and recording artist.

The popularity of Italian pop stars rivals that of American and British performers. The melodic musician Luccio Battisti is one of the most popular, as is Adriano Celentano, who has sold over 70 million records and whose style ranges from melodic to rock to rap. In the 1950s, Italians developed their own styles of folk music. Fabrizio De André was one of the first singer-songwriters who wrote politically influenced songs like those of Bob Dylan. Rock singer Zucchero, Laura Pausini, Eros Ramazzotti, and Andrea Bocelli are some of the other Italian singers and musicians popular on the international stage.

In 1958, the Festival dei Due Mondi ("Festival of Two Worlds") was established in Spoleto, Italy. Its founder, Gian Carlo Menotti, conceived an arts festival that would celebrate concerts, opera, dance, visual arts, drama, and science in the small town of Spoleto in Umbria. It has become one of the most important cultural events in Italy. Menotti partnered with American organizers in an attempt to showcase both European and American art, side by side, and a sister show was organized in Charleston, South Carolina. The Italian festival is held in June and July, and the American festival is celebrated in May and June. Several of Italy's other major festivals take place in the city of Venice. These include Carnival, the Venice Film Festival, and the Venice Biennale, which has long attracted artists of the highest caliber in every field.

Football (soccer) is by far the most popular sport in Italy. The Italian Football Federation oversees a variety of national tournaments and national football leagues. Leagues include the Lega Nazionale Professionisti Serie A and B, the Lega Italiana Calcio Professionistico, and the Lega Nazionale Dilettanti. Some of the most popular clubs in the country include Juventus, Internazionale, Milan, Genoa, and Torino. Football Club Internazionale Milano has been competing professionally since 1908. Italy played host to the 2006 FIFA World Cup. The Italian national team, winner of four FIFA World Cups, is the second most successful team in tournament history. Other popular sports in Italy include cycling and basketball. Volleyball, cricket, and rugby are also played.

Cultural Sites & Landmarks

Rome, the capital of Italy, was the birthplace of the Roman Empire. According to legend, the city was founded by the two brothers, Remus and Romulus, in 753 BCE. The many ruins of the ancient sites where the inhabitants of the Roman Empire once lived and worked are famous landmarks, such as the Forum. At this site, people came to socialize or discuss politics in ancient Rome. Another famous Roman landmark is the Colosseum (or Coliseum), an amphitheater commissioned by Emperor Vespasian (9–79 CE) for the purpose of circus-like entertainment, including gladiator fights. Completed in 72 CE, the Colosseum was designed with archways, interior corridors and multiple exits to assist with the seating and movement of over 55,000 spectators.

Close to Rome, Hadrian's Villa is an excellent example of second century art and architecture. Hadrian, a Roman emperor, built a complex of buildings in the styles of Greek and Egyptian architecture. Near Hadrian's Villa is the Villa d'Este, a 16th century garden that serves as an example of Renaissance-era landscape architecture.

Two important landmarks are the preserved sites of Pompeii and Herculeum. In 79 CE, Mount Vesuvius erupted and covered these two seaside resort cities in ash. People were buried alive, and seventeen centuries later these cities were excavated. The ash preserved the buildings and bodies of some residents, and modern visitors can view glimpses everyday life two millennia ago.

Another important cultural site is San Gimignano, in the province of Tuscany. The town once boasted seventy-two towers, some as high as 50 meters (164 feet). During the Middle Ages, such towers signified power and wealth. Fourteen of these towers still stand.

Assisi, a small hill town in the region of Umbria, is the birthplace of St. Francis of Assisi. St. Francis founded the Franciscan order of monks and is considered the patron saint of animals and nature. After the death of St. Francis, the Basilica of San Francesco was built to honor the saint. The basilica houses great works of medieval art by Pietro Lorenzetti, Simone Martini and Giotto. St. Francis is buried in the crypt below the basilica, and visitors travel from all over the world to sit and pray in the presence of his earthly remains.

Italian cities are themselves works of art, from the small village of Todi to the remarkable industrial city of Milan. Venice, for example, is a city surrounded by the sea and interconnected with famous canals. The Piazzo San Marco, Venice's main square, is a central gathering place for locals and visitors alike, complete with serenading musicians. In addition, Perugia in Umbria, a university town, contains passageways that serve as a reminder of life during Etruscan rule to the Renaissance eras.

Florence itself, once the capital of the Italian Renaissance, is rich in cultural sites and landmarks, including the Baptistry, the Gates of Paradise, and the Duomo. They are all spiritual monuments reminiscent of the art and architecture of medieval Florence.

Libraries & Museums

Florence also has some of the most renowned art museums in the world. The Uffizi Gallery is perhaps the most impressive in the country, with masterpieces by Michelangelo, Leonardo da Vinci, Botticelli, and Caravaggio. The National Museum of Rome, renowned for its archeological collection, is a series of different museums set out across the city, while other prominent museums in the country include Venice's Peggy Guggenheim Collection, devoted to modern art; the National Archeological Museum in Naples, known for both its Roman and Greek antiquities; as well as Rome's National Etruscan Museum, the Museum of the Roman Civilization, and the National Museum of Oriental Art.

Italy has two central libraries, the Italian National Central Library in Florence and the National Central Library in Rome, the latter of which contains over 7 million volumes of books.

Holidays

National holidays in Italy include the Anniversary of the Republic (June 2) and Liberation Day, celebrating the defeat of the German army in Italy (April 25). In addition to the standard religious holidays of the church calendar, numerous feast days are celebrated throughout the country in honor of saints associated with particular villages, towns or cities.

Youth Culture

Italian teens take pride in the way they dress, and keep track of the latest fashions and trends. Like teenagers all over the world, they are fond of casual dress, such as jeans and t-shirts. Trends vary from season to season, and Italian teens are often at the forefront. One recent fad consisted of couples writing their names on padlocks, attaching them to lampposts or other public places, and throwing the keys into public fountains or nearby rivers. This trend caught on after two romantic characters in a movie entitled *Three Metres above the Sky* had done the same thing.

About 97 percent of youth in Italy own a cell phone, and they are adept at using cell phone technology, such as texting. Although Internet use is pervasive, Italian teens are also reading books and newspapers in increasing numbers and surveys show that 78 percent read a newspaper at least once or twice a week. In addition, reportedly over 60 percent of young Italians read at least three fiction or nonfiction books a year.

Italian teens also tend to socialize in groups, and they often hang out and talk in small bars and cafes that commonly serve coffee, gelato, and soft drinks. Italian teens usually stay out later than American teens on weekends, and enjoy dancing in discos that remain open until the early hours of morning. Also, since operating smaller vehicles such as scooters or subcompact cars like the Smart Car do not require a license, these modes of transportation are popular among Italian youth.

Many young Italians live at home until they marry. Some 80 percent of Italian men aged 18 to 30 still live with their parents. Consequently, getting married and having children is often delayed until a career has been firmly established.

SOCIETY

Transportation

Italy has a modern, extensive transportation system. International airports serve most major airlines, and railway system is efficient. In addition, the high-speed Eurostar train connects major cities, while local trains connect the smaller towns and rural areas. Local bus services are prevalent. The "autostrade," or motorways similar to the interstate system in the United States, run through the major regions of Italy, but levy expensive tolls. Contrary to common belief, Italian autostrade do post speed limits (though they are generally a bit higher than those in the U.S.). They are also regularly patrolled and monitored. Automobile traffic in Italy travels on the right hand side of the road. Travel by train, bus and car is common. In the major cities, it is also common to see people navigating narrow streets by motorscooter.

In the northeastern Italian city of Venezia (Venice), all motorized vehicles and also bicycles are prohibited, and in fact, impractical. The island city is criss-crossed and surrounded by water – lagoons, bays, canals – and its streets and bridges are too narrow for motorized traffic. Venezia's residents, economy and culture are literally buoyed up by the barges, motorboats, water taxis, and gondolas that ply the waterways.

Transportation Infrastructure

There are 19,460 kilometers (12,092 miles) of railways in Italy, and roughly 484,688 kilometers (300,171 miles) of paved roads.

Media & Communications

Italian law allows freedom of speech, and the government and courts are responsible for upholding these rights. Two Italian newspapers, the *Corriere della Sera* and the *La Stampa*, are internationally known. The *International Herald Tribune* is the standard English newspaper in Italy. A government corporation runs RAI (Radiotelevisione Italiana), which broadcasts on radio and television. Italian media freely offers a broad spectrum of political opinions and viewpoints, although it should be noted that Italian politician and industry magnate Silvio Berluscone does maintain dominant financial control or outright ownership of several important private Italian media outlets.

Telephone service is available through multiple providers, and cell phone service is generally available, even in remote areas. In 2009, there were more than 30 million Internet users in Italy, representing just over half of the population. In 2012, there were 97.2 million cellular phones, averaging out to more than one cell phone for each citizen. High speed Internet and broadband access is available in most cities and towns.

SOCIAL DEVELOPMENT

Standard of Living

Italy ranked 26th on the 2014 United Nations Human Development Index, which measures quality of life and standard of living indicators.

Water Consumption

Drinking water is widely available in Italy and tap water is considered safe to drink. However, Italy faces significant challenges related to the age of its water infrastructure. A September 2010 study by the Italian research group Utilitatis estimated that over 60 billion EUR will be needed for the repair and modernization of the country's water systems. According to the study, up to 40 percent of the nation's available water supply is being lost by leaks. In addition, 30 percent of Italian territories remain without wastewater treatment facilities.

Education

Education in Italy is universal and compulsory for children between the ages of six and 14 years. Elementary school is divided into five levels. Students may then complete secondary school, during which time they prepare for university or receive technical training.

Some of the oldest European universities are found in Italy, such as the University of Bologna. The University of Rome has the most students, but there are large institutions spread throughout the country, offering programs in every field. Around two million students matriculate at this level.

The literacy rate among people in Italy, both male and female, was an estimate 99 percent in 2012. School enrollment rates are high throughout the country.

Women's Rights

Traditionally, Italian women were raised to be wives and mothers, and the patriarchs made major decisions and ensured the financial well-being of the family. Women in Italy did not secure the right to vote until 1946. Even though the roles have been slowly changing since the 20th century, many Italian males still feel the woman's role is mostly domestic, and women still do not enjoy the same salaries or positions as men. Italian women in the 21st century are more educated and hold jobs outside the home. For example, about 60 percent of university students are female.

According to Italian law, men and women share the same rights in marriage, property, and in matters of inheritance. Italian legislation protects women from abuse, and in recent years, there has been an increase in the reporting of psychological and physical abuse. Public awareness of the problem has resulted in more women receiving help. In the event of an attack, Italian law also shields female victims from publicity.

In 2003, the Italian government passed legislation to protect women in the workplace from sexual harassment. In addition, government offices have been established to protect women's rights. Women have also taken leadership roles in the government, most notably in the Ministry for Equal Opportunity. In addition, the office of the prime minister and the labor ministry both employ an equal opportunity commission that works to ensure that women's rights are upheld and discrimination is prevented in the workplace.

However, women remain underrepresented in government positions. As of 2014, less than a third of the seats in the two chambers of parliament were held by women. Women also serve in a few cabinet positions. In the business arena, women are also underrepresented in management positions and earn about 26 percent less than their male counterparts. In addition, more women are employed in northern Italy than in southern Italy. Organizations such as Arcidonna still push for women's rights in Italy by sponsoring initiatives, educating the public, training women for jobs, providing help and advice for entrepreneurs, and encouraging women to publish.

Health Care

Italy has a national health care system that treats the medical needs of the population for free or at low cost. It is the third largest health care system in Europe and is rated highly by international standards, though there is some regional disparity between north and south as regards the quality of the care.

GOVERNMENT

Structure

Italy is a democratic republic and one of the founding members of the European Union. The executive branch of the government consists of a president, who can serve a single seven-year term, and a prime minister. Though some powers are vested in the president, it is the prime minister who has the responsibility for running the government. The prime minister is appointed by the president and approved by the legislature.

The legislature is bicameral. The Chamber of Deputies consists of 630 members serving five-year terms. The Senate of the Republic consists of 326 members, and they too are elected for five-year terms, with the exception of 11 senators, who are elected for life. Three-quarters of the members in each house are elected by direct vote; the others are assigned seats by proportional representation.

The highest judicial powers are divided between the Supreme Court of Cassation and a constitutional court, whose fifteen judges are solely responsible for interpreting the constitution. The president, the legislature, and the Supreme Court each appoint five of the judges.

Political Parties

Italy's numerous political parties cross the spectrum from right-wing to left-wing, and sometimes form alliances. Chief among the parties are Italia, Bene Comune (Italy, Common Good), Partito Democratico (Democratic Party), Casa delle Liberta (House of Liberty), Ulivo (Olive Tree), Alleanza Nazionale (National Alliance), Lega Nord (Northern League), Democrazia Cristiana

(Christian Democrats), and Federazione dei Verdi (The Green Federation).

There is also a plethora of region political parties throughout Italy. For example, the Province of Trento boasts eight different regional political alliances. The autonomous region of Sardinia has seven political parties focused on issues related solely to that island.

Local Government

Local government is concentrated at the regional level. Each of the fifteen regions has a directly elected council and an executive. Italy's ninety-four provinces are presided over by appointed prefects. The commune is the form of local government below the provinces and is presided over by a directly elected council and an appointed mayor.

Judicial System

The Italian legal system is notoriously slow, complex, and fragmented. The country's laws are based on Roman law and French Napoleonic laws and include numerous laws that are centuries old, obscure and no longer enforced. Italy's administrative ties to the Europe Union ad another layer to an already complicated legal bureaucracy.

There are three types of courts in Italy; civil courts, administrative courts, and criminal courts. Each of these courts are further subdivided into courts overseen by either individual judges or panels of judges. Individual rights regarding legal representation are different than most Western countries. The majority of criminal proceedings in Italy and civil complaints against corporate or government entities tend to take place over a prolonged period. Widespread incidents of corruption and misuse of influence further impact judicial expediency.

Taxation

Italy's taxation system, like its judicial system, is complex. Taxes for Italians remain high compared to most Western countries, with some Italians contributing some 45 percent of their income to the government. The Italian tax system operates on three levels; local, regional and national.

Italian citizens pay taxes on their personal income, property, trash collection and bank accounts. Income tax rates vary from region to region. Italian employers and employees contribute are required to contribute to the country's social security system, are self-employed individuals. Italy also has a VAT (value-added tax) and inheritance tax.

In recent decades, the Italian government has made efforts to streamline and modernize its tax system. Nonetheless, the tax rates in Italy remain some of the highest in Europe and the rest of the world.

Foreign Policy

Since the height of the Roman Empire, Italy has had a history of democratic ideals. In 1861, the nation was ruled by King Victor Emmanuel II and a parliamentary government. In the 1920s, Benito Mussolini stripped many freedoms through his fascist dictatorship, and the country allied with Nazi Germany in World War II. Following the war, Italy joined the Atlantic Alliance for security purposes. Italy became a democratic republic and is still governed by judicial, executive, and legislative branches.

Economic recovery followed, and Italy became a charter member of the North Atlantic Treaty Organization (NATO) and the European Economic Community (EEC). Italy is also a long-standing member and supporter of the United Nations (UN). In 1999, it joined the Economic and Monetary Union and unified with other European countries in the use of the euro currency. At the same time, Italy employed a tight fiscal policy, and has enjoyed lower interest rates and lower inflation as a result. Italy also supports a European Security and Defence Policy (EDSP) and considers it a companion to the protection that NATO provides. Italy also believes that NATO should intervene when necessary in humanitarian circumstances, but only with the sanctioning of the UN.

Significant foreign trading partners with Italy include Germany, France, the U.S., Spain, and the United Kingdom (UK), particularly in regards to exports. Italy mainly imports from Germany, France, Netherlands, China, Spain, and Belgium.

Since the conclusion of World War II and the collapse of the Soviet Union in the 1990s, the Italian government has fostered a special relationship with the U.S. For example, Italy reinforced this partnership when it agreed to send troops to Afghanistan in 2001. This action, resulting in the taking of Italian hostages taken in Iraq, was criticized as taking attention away from important domestic issues, such as the cost of living and constitutional reforms.

Possibly as a result, Italian society and its political leaders have increasingly become more autonomous and less dependent on foreign influence. The Italian government continues to be pro-European, but is not shy of disagreeing or asserting its own stances. American influence has been waning for the past twenty years, with many Italians disagreeing with American policies. In particular, the U.S.-led conflict in Iraq has become increasingly unpopular in Italy. In 2008, Italy voted not to maintain 2,000 troops in Afghanistan, and denied the US rights to expand a military base near Vicenza, a city in northern Italy. However, in recent years, perhaps owing to Italy's unstable economy, the country has increasingly begun to take part in international peacekeeping efforts, including participating in a no-fly zone over Libya.

Human Rights Profile

International human rights law insists that states respect civil and political rights, and also promote an individual's economic, social and cultural rights. The United Nations Universal Declaration on Human Rights (UDHR) is recognized as the standard for international human rights. Its authors sought the counsel of the world's great thinkers, philosophers, and religious leaders, and were careful to create a document that reflects the core values shared by every world culture. (To read this document or view the articles relating to cultural human rights, visit: http://www. udhr.org/UDHR/default.htm.)

Italy is a parliamentary democracy, and its laws and efforts to protect essential human rights are in sync with international human rights laws. Italian law provides freedom for its citizens and respect for human rights. Italian legislation prohibits discrimination according to race, gender, ethnic background, or political opinion. Furthermore, Italian law stipulates that citizens have the right to gather and associate with whomever they please.

There is also some protection against discrimination for those with disabilities and language issues. However, in 2004, there were several instances of abuse of the law for discrimination against women and those with disabilities.

As a parliamentary democracy, Italy's system of government allows its citizens to change its government through free elections. It is against the law to bribe or pay any public official to do his or her job. When reports of such misconduct occur, the accused are required to stand trial.

The Italian government is also committed to providing an education for its youth. Italian children from the ages of seven to eighteen are given the right to attend school free of charge, and attendance is compulsory. Children under the age of 15 cannot work, and it is against the law to force any child to work. These laws have been enforced, even within immigrant communities where child labor is sometimes condoned.

While the Catholic Church retains much influence in Italian culture and education, Italian law assures its citizens of the freedom of religion. Religious icons and symbols are common in public buildings, and the government pays teachers to teach Catholicism. Muslim women are allowed to wear veils in public offices and schools, but some complaints and fines have been made against women who wear burqahs, or large cloths designed to cover the body and face.

In addition, government surveys show that there is some prejudice against immigrants, many of whom are from Muslim countries.

Many Moroccan immigrants believe they are discriminated against when they apply for jobs. Waves of refugees recently arrived from North Africa have strained immigrant relations further. The government has also been proactive in educating the public about Judaism and preventing anti-Semitism by organizing educational meetings.

Italian law also prohibits arbitrary arrest and detention, and these laws are upheld. Warrants are required for searches except in the case of immediate danger. The law requires each detainee the right to a fair trial, and a defendant is presumed innocent until proven guilty. The Italian government allows independent human rights organizations to assess inmates' quality of life in the prison systems, and there have been some reports of overcrowding and antiquated, or outdated, prison facilities.

ECONOMY

Overview of the Economy

Italy compensates for its relative dearth of natural resources with a robust industrial sector. It is the fifth largest economy in the world and is a member of the Group of Eight. Gross domestic product (GDP) per capita is around $34,500 (USD) (2014 estimate). Inflation, which has long plagued Italy, has been decreasing, though foreign debt is still an outstanding problem. In fact the country's credit rating has been downgraded, and fear of continued economic hardship is a concern across the Euro Zone.

Industry

Unemployment, estimated at 12.5 percent in 2014 of a workforce numbering 2.5 million, is a greater problem in the agricultural south and explains the internal migration to the north, where industry is concentrated. Italy's main trading partners are other European countries.

Small- and medium-sized businesses, privately owned, make up 94 percent of all Italian businesses. Thirty-three percent of the GDP is generated by the manufacturing industry.

Italian automobiles and clothing labels are two of the largest industries. Fiat and Alfa Romeo are the most famous automobile makers, and Italian fashion, centered in Milan, is respected the world over for labels such as Gucci, Benetton, and Versace. These two industries alone make up a major portion of the country's exports.

Labor

In 2014, Italy's unemployment rate was an estimated 12.5 percent. The automobile industry is the country's largest employer. The largest automobile company in Italy is Fiat, which has been expanding aggressively into foreign markets. Tourism, telecommunications, and agriculture also make up significant sections of the labor market. There are higher unemployment rates among women and young people in Italy in comparison to men. Approximately 40 percent of the Italian work force is unionized.

Energy/Power/Natural Resources

Italy does not have a wealth of natural resources, and many of the resources that once existed have been successfully exploited and exhausted. Sulfur, lignite, pumice, mercury, zinc, bauxite and lead are among the most prevalent minerals.

Environmental problems confronting Italy include water pollution of rivers and seas, both by industrial effluent and poor wastewater treatment, leading to deadly algae blooms among other problems. Major urban centers are also afflicted by poor air quality as a result of emissions from industry and transportation.

Fishing

Italians operate approximately 16 percent of the total European fishing fleet. Popular fish in Italy include salt cod ("baccala") and tuna. Shrimp, anchovies and sardines are also widely used in Italian dishes. The country's fishing industry also harvest shell fish such as mussels, oysters and clams.

Forestry

Forestry is an important part of the Italian economy. Italy exports a range of forest products to

Europe and the United States. The country's varied geography present a range of forest types. The most common trees in Italy are evergreen oaks, poplar trees and chestnut trees.

Mining/Metals
Stone is one of the most important mined substances in Italy. Its quarries in such areas as Carrara are legendary for having provided stone from some of the greatest structures and sculptures in the western hemisphere. Marble, travertine, and granite are all mined and processed in Italy.

Agriculture
Thirty-one percent of the total land is given over to permanent crops, with agricultural production being concentrated in the south. Less than five percent of the labor force is employed in agriculture, and though it only contributes two percent to the GDP, it is important for both domestic consumption and export to other European countries.

Among the important crops cultivated in Italy are tomatoes, apples, pears, and citrus fruits. In the north and center of the country, wheat is dominant, while in the Po Valley, potatoes, corn and sugar beets are the major crops. Grape and olive cultivation, and their subsequent processing into wine and olive oil, makes Italy a leader in these industries.

Animal Husbandry
Sheep are the most common type of large livestock, at 10.9 million head, followed by pigs, cattle, and goats. Poultry is also numerous.

Tourism
Italy is the fourth most-visited country in the world, and both foreign and domestic tourists are vital to the Italian economy. It has a highly developed infrastructure and a variety of attractions, both natural and cultural. Tourism generated over $40 billion (USD) in 2012, a decrease from a high of $46 billion in 2008. The summer months see the most visitors. The service industry, of which tourism is a part, accounts for nearly 64 percent of the total GDP.

There is no shortage of tourist sites in Italy, which boasts an estimated 95,000 churches and 20,000 cities or towns with historic and cultural value. Major archaeological sites include the Roman ruins scattered throughout the country and particularly in Rome, and the lava-preserved cities of Pompeii and Herculaneum. Other attractions are the sculpted fountains of Rome, the squares and canals of Venice, and the well preserved hilltop town of Siena.

Claire Daniel and Michael Aliprandi

DO YOU KNOW?

- An estimated 7 million Italians immigrated to the United States between the late 19th and early 20th centuries.
- Italy has two independent countries within its borders: San Marino and Vatican City.

Bibliography

Barzini, Luigi. *The Italians*. New York: Touchstone, 1964.

Costantino, Mario and Gambella, Lawrence R. *The Italian Way*. Chicago: McGraw-Hill, 1996.

Duggan, Christopher. *The Force of Destiny: A History of Italy since 1796*. Boston: Houghton Mifflin, 2007.

Hendrix, John. *History and Culture in Italy*. Lanham, MD: University Press of America, 2003.

Hofmann, Paul. *That Fine Italian Hand*. New York: Henry Holt and Company, 1990.

Jones, Tobias. *The Dark Heart of Italy*. New York: North Point Press 2003.

Killinger, Charles L. *Culture and Customs of Italy*. Westport, CT: Greenwood Press, 2005.

La Rocca, Cristina. *Italy in the Early Middle Ages*. New York: Oxford University Press, 2002.

Lazzarin, Paola. *One Hundred and One Beautiful Small Towns of Italy*. New York: Rizzoli, 2004.

Newell, James L. *The Politics of Italy*. New York. Cambridge University Press, 2010.

Nickels, Greg. *Italy: The People*. New York: Crabtree Publishing, 2001.

Parks, Tim. *Italian Ways: On and Off the Rails from Milan to Palermo*. New York: Norton, 2014.

Powers, Alice Leccese (Ed.). *Italy in Mind: An Anthology*. New York: Random House, 1997.

Works Cited

"A New School of Fashion," *Metropolitan Museum of Art*. http://www.metmuseum.org/TOAH/hd/itfa/hd_itfa.htm

"Best Italian Popular Music." Life in Italy. http://www.lifeinitaly.com/music/

"Cicero's Life," *Internet Encyclopedia of Philosophy*. http://www.iep.utm.edu/c/cicero.htm

"Cicero." *Plutarch*. http://classics.mit.edu/Plutarch/cicero.html

"Cicero Texts." http://www.utexas.edu/depts/classics/documents/Cic.html#Texts

Dana Faaros, and Michael Pauls. *Tuscany Umbria and the Marches. Cadogan*, 1999.

Diedre Strahan. "How Italians Live." *Beginning with Italy*. http://www.beginningwithi.com/italy/living/housing.htm

Douglas Faherty. "Italian Foreign Policy." *Naval Postgraduate School Monterey CA*. http://www.stormingmedia.us/29/2947/A294714.html

Graziana Lazzarino, Maria Cristina Peccianti, Janice Aski, and Andrea Dini. "La Moda Italiana," *Prego!* 6th Edition. McGraw-Hill, 2004.

"High School in Italy," *Center For Cultural Exchange*. http://www.cci-exchange.com/countries/italy.sht

"Holy See, Italy." http://whc.unesco.org/en/list/91

Hooker, Richard. "Italian Renaissance." http://www.wsu.edu:8080/~dee/REN/BACK.HTM

http://news.bbc.co.uk/2/hi/europe/3034600.stm
http://www.food.com/library/ricotta-cheese
291http://www.worlddiscoveries.net/Europe/Italian%20Music%20History.htm
http://www.state.gov/g/drl/rls/hrrpt/2004/41688.htm

"Human Rights Practices in Italy." *U. S. Department of State*.

"Italian Cars." *Life in Italy*. http://www.lifeinitaly.com/italian-cars/

"Italian Customs," *Passion for Italy*. http://www.passionforitaly.com/43-Italian_Customs/Default.html

"Italian Food Guide." *Kwintessential*. http://www.kwintessential.co.uk/articles/article/Italy/Italian-Food-Guide:-Regional-Food-in-Italy/291

"Italian Foreign Policy." *Encyclopedia of the Nations, 2003*. http://www.nationsencyclopedia.com/World-Leaders-2003/Italy-FOREIGN-POLICY.html

"Italian Literature," *Encyclopedia Britannica*.

"Italian Literature." *Italy 1*. http://italy1.com/literature/

"Italian Music History," *World Discoveries*. "Italian Foreign Policy." *Encyclopedia of the Nations*, 2003. http://www.nationsencyclopedia.com/World-Leaders-2003/Italy-FOREIGN-POLICY.html

"Italian Opera." *Italian Culture*. http://www.italianculture.net/english/opera.html

"Italian Society and Culture." *Italian Family and Culture*. http://www.syr.it/img/PDF/Student-Life/Housing/Homestays/3%20Italian%20Family%20&%20Culture.pdf

"Italian Youth Culture." *School Journals*. http://www.schooljournals.net/eline3/index.php?action%5B%5D=IArticleShow::showArticle ('1830')

"Italian Wedding Customs." *Essortment*. http://www.essortment.com/lifestyle/worldetiquette_sgde.htm

"Italy Artists." *National Geographic*. http://www.worldmusic.nationalgeographic.com/worldmusic/view/page.basic/country/content.country/italy_346?fs=www3.nationalgeographic.com&fs=plasma.nationalgeographic.com

"Italy Language, Culture, Customs and Etiquette." *Kwintessential*. http://www.kwintessential.co.uk/resources/global-etiquette/italy-country-profile.html

"Italy's Contemporary Art Scene." *New York Times*. http://www.nytimes.com/slideshow/2008/03/13/arts/20080316_KIMM_SLIDESHOW_2.html

"Italy." *Britannica Book of the Year*. <http://www.britannica.com/eb/article-9437868>

"Italy." *City Population*. http://www.citypopulation.de/Italy-Cities.html

"Italy." *City Population. Online*. Accessed June 20, 2008. http://www.citypopulation.de/Italy-Cities.html

"Italy." *Encyclopedia Britannica*. <http://www.britannica.com/EBchecked/topic/297474/Italy>.

"Italy Media." Nations Encyclopedia. http://www.nationsencyclopedia.com/Europe/Italy-MEDIA.html

Jeff Israly. "The Fading Future of Italy's Young," *Time Europe* http://www.time.com/time/europe/html/060410/story.html

"Life of Virgil." http://virgil.org/vitae/

"Made in Italy." *Metropolitan Museum*. http://www.metmuseum.org/TOAH/hd/itfa/hd_itfa.htm

Michael Kimmelman. "From Postwar Italy, with Style." *New York Times*. http://query.nytimes.com/gst/fullpage.html?res=9D03E0DF103DF934A35753C1A962958260&scp=1&sq=Italy%20culture%20post%20war&st=cse

Osvaldo Croci. "The Second Berlusconi Government and Italian Foreign Policy." http://www.iai.it/pdf/articles/Croci.pdf

Richard Hooker. "Italian Renaissance." http://www.wsu.edu:8080/~dee/REN/BACK.HTM

"The Aenid," *Online Literature*. http://www.online-literature.com/virgil/aeneid/

"The Definitive Guide to Relocating to Italy." *Living in Italy*. http://www.escapeartist.com/e_Books/Living_In_Italy/Living_In_Italy.html

"The Italian Mother"

"The Ultimate Treasure Hunt: Finding Truffles." *Herbarium*. http://herbarium.usu.edu/fungi/funfacts/Truffind.htm

"The Roman Forum," *Italy Guides*. http://www.italyguides.it/us/roma/rome/ancient_roman_empire/roman_forum.htm

"The Sistine Chapel." *Vatican Museum*. http://mv.vatican.va/3_EN/pages/CSN/CSN_Storia.html

"When in Rome." *Italy Heaven*. http://www.italyheaven.co.uk/manners.html

"Young Italians Reading More." *Life in Italy*. http://www.lifeinitaly.com/news/news detailed.asp?newsid=9841

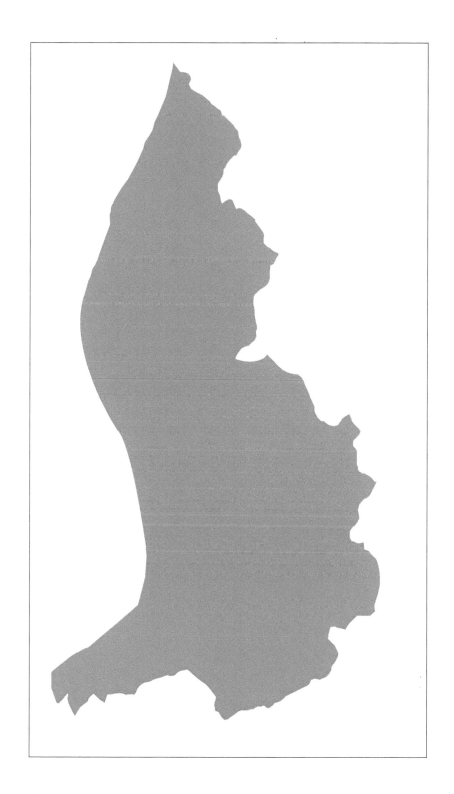

LIECHTENSTEIN

Introduction

A diminutive country sandwiched between Switzerland and Austria, Liechtenstein is a tourist center and also a center of banking because of its privacy laws. It arose as a principality in 1719, following the merger of two lordships under the Holy Roman Empire. A German-speaking country, it was part of the German Confederation (1815–1866) before becoming fully independent. Liechtenstein adopted the Swiss currency in 1921 and two years later joined the Swiss customs union. A nearly 60-year ruling coalition broke up in 1997, and in 2003, at the urging of Prince Hans-Adam II, the nation adopted a new constitution.

Liechtenstein has virtually no natural resources of commercial value, and most of its raw materials have to be imported. At the same time, Liechtenstein is one of the richest countries in the world, on a per capita basis, and it has one of the world's lowest unemployment rates (1.5 percent). Although not a member of the European Union, it belongs to the European Free Trade Association and other regional common markets.

GENERAL INFORMATION

Official Language(s): German
Population: 37,313 (2014 estimate)
Currency: Swiss franc
Coins: Swiss coins come in denominations of 5, 10, and 20 rappen (a rappen is equal to one hundredth of a franc), and 0.5, 1, 2, and 5 francs. While older coins of varying denominations are still in circulation, the aforementioned are the only coins now minted.

Area: 160.4 square kilometers (62 square miles)
National Motto: (Für Gott, Fürst und Vaterland" ("For God, Prince and Fatherland")
National Anthem: "Oben am jungen Rhein" ("Up on the Young Rhine")
Capital: Vaduz

PEOPLE & CULTURE

Population

The landlocked microstate of Liechtenstein is called a principality because the head of state is a prince. Only about two-thirds of the people living in the principality—nearly an estimated 66 percent—are native Liechtensteiners. Most of the roughly 12,000 foreigners come from the neighboring and nearby countries of Switzerland, Austria, Italy, and Germany. Even though the principality is highly industrialized, its population is far more rural than urban, with only about 14 percent living in urban areas (2012 estimate).

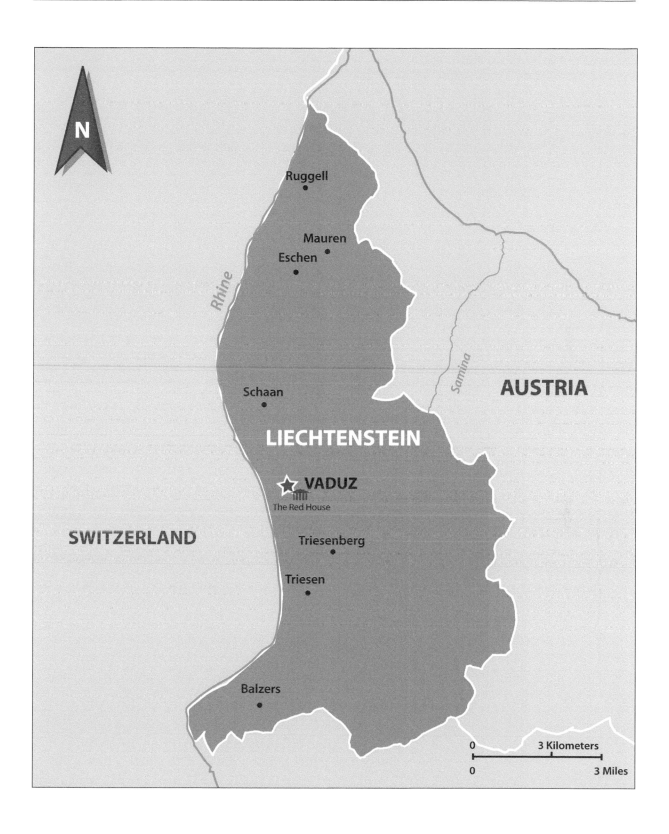

Principal Cities by Population (2012 census):

- Schaan (5,829)
- Vaduz (5,161)
- Triesen (4,738)
- Balzers (4,528).

The country is divided into eleven regions, called communes. As of 2014, the population growth rate in the microstate was 0.82 percent.

Languages

The official language of the principality is German, but many people speak the Alemannic dialect, which is derived from High German (so called because it developed in the geographically higher areas of the Germanic regions, and now serves as the more formal form of the language).

Native People & Ethnic Groups

Most Liechtensteiners are originally descended from the Alemanni (or Alamanni) tribe. This confederacy or allegiance of Germanic tribes arose in the third century CE between the Main and Danube Rivers. Early in the fifth century, the Alemanni invaded and conquered what is today Liechtenstein and much of the surrounding area. Some native Liechtensteiners are known as Walsers, and are descended from peoples who came from what is today the Swiss canton (federal state) of Valais. They often speak their own Walser dialect, also derived from High German.

The high percentage of non-Liechtensteiners living in the principality has led to a mild feeling of "überfremdung," or foreign infiltration or influence. At the same time, the cultural similarities between many of the country's native and non-native citizens, and the high rate of inter-marriage, has meant that these concerns rarely lead to social tension.

Religions

Nearly 80 percent of the general population, and about 95 percent of native Liechtensteiners, are Roman Catholic. Civil marriage has only been allowed since 1974, and in national parades, priests can be seen walking behind the prince. As of 2010, the largest religious minority was Protestantism, practiced among an estimated 6.5 percent of the population.

Climate

In spite of its mountains and landlocked location in the heart of Europe, Liechtenstein has a mild climate. Average temperatures range from −1 to 21° Celsius (30 to 70° Fahrenheit), with an average 40 inches of rain and snow annually, though precipitation in the mountains is near double that. The foehn, a regular warm wind, blows in from the south and serves to moderate the weather, allowing crops such as grapes and corn to flourish.

The plain in what is now known as the Unterland once flooded periodically, posing a regular danger to people living there. However, it plays an important role in the region's ecosystem. Dams built along the Rhine in the 19th century acted to limit the flooding, and the Binnenkanal has controlled the flow of water between the Unterland and the river since 1943.

ENVIRONMENT & GEOGRAPHY

Topography

Liechtenstein is only about 26 kilometers (16 miles) long from north to south, and less than 6.5 kilometers (about four miles) across. Geographically, Liechtenstein is split into two regions: the Oberland (Upper Country) in the south and the Unterland (Lower Country) in the north. Both parts of the country feature mountains—in the Oberland, these are the Western and Eastern Alps—but the Unterland is also characterized by the Rhine River floodplain. The Rhine River provides its western border, and the river's floodplain is the principality's agricultural region. The country's highest mountain is the Grauspitz, at 2,599 meters (8,526 feet); the Eschnerberg, standing in Unterland, measures 730 meters (2,395 feet). Another major waterway in the country is the Samina River, which originates in Liechtenstein's south, and feeds into Austria's Ill River. The Samina is used to produce electricity and to provide drinking water.

Liechtenstein is often referred to as a doubly landlocked country, due to the fact that the microstate itself is landlocked, and the countries surrounding it are all landlocked as well.

Plants & Animals

The plant and animal life in Liechtenstein is surprisingly varied for the principality's small size. This is a result of the three different terrains that characterize the country: the Rhine Valley, the Rhine Valley slopes, and the Alps. The valley is known for its wildflower meadows, which host up to 100 different plant species. The slope areas (and a total of nearly 45 percent of the territory in Liechtenstein) are forested, and the Alps feature some 800 species of mountain flora. In 1989, the government declared the Alpine region a preservation area, separating out special pasture areas for livestock farmers. Forty-eight orchid species grow throughout the principality, including the one-leaved bog orchid, the rare ghost orchid, and the Alpine orchid.

Liechtenstein's fauna are equally varied, with 55 different mammal species, seventeen

The Alpine salamander, is the only amphibian in the country that gives birth to live young (rather than laying eggs).

different kinds of bats, and an estimated 120 butterfly species. The mountains are home to red deer, chamois, ibex, and golden eagles, as well as the Alpine salamander, the only amphibian in the country that gives birth to live young (rather than laying eggs). However, the animal life in Liechtenstein's Unterland is threatened by the environmental damage already done to the marshes, as well as growing urbanization, but wetlands preservation projects aim to diminish these losses.

CULTURAL HISTORY

History

Liechtenstein was founded in 1719, but its history is rooted in the Thirty Years' War (1618–1648), which ended more than 60 years earlier. In broad terms, the Thirty Years' War was a struggle between Protestant principalities and the Roman Catholic Holy Roman Empire (962–1806). The war ended with the Peace of Westphalia, and the empire became a loose federation of sovereign states. The emperor granted the aristocratic Liechtenstein family of Austria princely status in 1608, but because the family's land holdings were not under his direct rule, the new princes were not given a seat on the Council of Princes.

In 1699, Johann Adam Andreas (or Hans-Adam I, 1657–1712) purchased the territory of Schellenberg; thirteen years later, he obtained Vaduz, both of which were considered immediate to the empire. These were consolidated in 1719 and given the status of imperial principality. It was considered unusual that the young state was given the name of its ruling family, and the princes did not actually live in Liechtenstein until 1938, ruling until then from Austria.

Napoleon Bonaparte (1769–1821), who later became emperor of France, briefly occupied the principality after the Holy Roman Empire's collapse in 1806. However, with Napoleon's defeat at the Battle of Waterloo in 1815, Liechtenstein became a member of the German Confederation. Each member of the confederation was required to provide its people with a constitution (though these were not necessarily democratic). In 1862, Prince Johann II (1840–1929), only twenty-two at the time, signed a new constitution. This balanced the monarchy's powers with those of a parliament, though most of the power still rested with the prince. Parliament could make laws, but the prince had the right to summon or disband parliament. The confederation dissolved in 1866, a result of the Seven Weeks War between Prussia and Austria. Two years later, the Liechtenstein parliament voted to disband its 80-man military, and the country has since maintained strict neutrality in all international conflicts.

A new constitution, negotiated between prince and parliament in 1921, leaned on the political system of dualism, or the separation of powers. The royal house had significant political powers, but the country also enjoyed direct democracy. The 1862 constitution allowed the prince to name three of the 15 members of parliament. (In modern-day Liechtenstein, all are elected). In the past, the prince also appointed the head of Liechtenstein's government, always an Austrian who served as the prince's deputy, though the prime minister is now required to be a Liechtensteiner by birth. The people could also vote to call or dismiss parliament, and all judges were to be elected, rather than named or dismissed by the prince.

Following the Seven Weeks' War, Liechtenstein's foreign relations were handled by the Hapsburg dynasty in Austria. When that monarchy was abolished after World War I, the principality turned to Switzerland. In the early 1920s, Liechtenstein began to use Swiss currency, and the two countries formed a customs union in 1924. The relationship became especially important when Liechtenstein had to defend its neutrality during World War II.

The late 1920s and early 1930s proved a very difficult time for the small country. A dike on the Rhine River burst in 1927, flooding the Rhine valley in the Unterland and some of the surrounding area and causing massive damage. In addition, a 1928 banking scandal almost bankrupted the principality, and Liechtenstein was also affected by the economic devastation of the Great Depression. Furthermore, Liechtenstein's leader for seventy-one years, Prince Johann II, died in 1929. He was replaced by his son, Prince Franz I, who served until his own death in 1938.

The government responded to Liechtenstein's crises with a large public works program, including the construction of the Binnenkanal. The canal was dug from Liechtenstein's southern border to the north, along the Rhine, to control the flow of water between river and floodplain. Much of the construction was done with manual labor. The environmental impact of the canal led to a restructuring project in the 21st century. However, at the time of its construction, the canal was a source of great national pride.

In 1939, Liechtenstein weathered a failed coup attempt by a pro-Nazi group. The incident led to an outburst of Liechtensteiner patriotism, and the principality was able to remain neutral throughout World War II. (Liechtenstein was later suspected of allowing Nazis to protect stolen assets in its banks, but an independent commission of historians found in 2001 that this was not the case). Following World War II, Liechtenstein developed quite rapidly from an agricultural economy to one of the most industrialized countries in the world, known best for its powerful financial sector. In 1984, Prince Franz Joseph II (1906–1989) gave executive authority to his son, Hans Adam II (1945–).

Today, the principality has the highest per capita income in the world, and also features a wide variety of small businesses. However, the principality's small size is a source of some anxiety, and Liechtenstein has consistently sought strong international ties, in addition to its close relationship with Switzerland. The country joined the International Court of Justice (ICJ) in 1950, the Conference on Security and Co-operation in Europe (later the Organization for Security and Co-operation in Europe, or OSCE) in 1975, and the Council of Europe in 1978. It joined the United Nations (UN) in 1990 and the World Trade Organization (WTO) in 1995.

In 2003, the country's citizens voted decisively to change their constitution to grant the prince more executive power. As a result, the prince may now dissolve parliament or dismiss the government unilaterally, and veto any legislation without explanation, simply by leaving it unsigned it for six months. He also regained final say on all judicial appointments. These changes were proposed by the prince himself, who threatened to move to Austria if they were not adopted by popular vote. The Council of Europe expressed concern that the modifications to the constitution would effectively return Liechtenstein to the status of an absolute monarchy, the only such country in Europe. The vote may seem surprising to those outside Liechtenstein, but for many Liechtensteiners, the country is truly synonymous with the royal house.

Cultural Sites & Landmarks

Liechtenstein's low urban concentration makes the country a good destination for outdoor enthusiasts. Many hiking trails can be found in the mountains, as well as botany walks in the valley area. The Ruggeller Riet, a moor just outside the town of Ruggell, is the lowest point in the principality and one of Liechtenstein's most bio logically diverse nature preserves. The moor was formed some 10,000 years ago, when streams flowing through the valley and feeding into the Rhine dried up. The variety of flora and fauna includes the Siberian Iris and the Crested Shield Fern, as well as roughly 146 bird species and 534 different species of butterfly. Alpine skiing also draws tourists to the resort at Malbun, though the skiing season is short, with snows lasting only from early January into April.

The Vaduz Castle (Schloss Vaduz) stands above the capital of Vaduz against a striking Alpine backdrop, visible from anywhere in the city. Built as a fortress in the 12th century, the prominent landmark was expanded in the 16th and 17th centuries. The princes of Liechtenstein have owned the castle since 1712, but it has only served as the royal family's primary residence since 1938. The interior of the castle is not accessible to visitors. Another important landmark in Vaduz is the Red House, located on Prince Franz Joseph Street. It features a late-medieval gabled

stairs construction—the roof resembles two staircases meeting at the top—and a massive tower was added onto the original house in 1904. The Red House stands in a vineyard and once housed a wine press, a reflection of Liechtenstein's tradition of vinification (winemaking).

To the north, in Schellenberg, stands the Biedermann House. Originally built in 1518, it is the oldest wooden dwelling in Liechtenstein, but it has been taken apart and moved several times, most recently in 1993. The latest move included a renovation that repurposed the house into a living history museum, reproducing the lifestyle of peasants in the 18th century. Also in the Unterland is the town of Eschen, where archeologists have discovered signs of human settlement from the Neolithic Age (or New Stone Age, beginning about 9500 BCE), as well as the foundation walls of a Roman villa (country house). At the heart of Eschen stands a parish church (as is true in all towns in Liechtenstein), as well as two semi-detached homes dating to the Middle Ages and the 14th-century Pfrundhaus, used for municipal business, concerts, and art exhibits.

Arts & Entertainment

The culture of Liechtenstein is heavily influenced by the principality's Catholic heritage, as well as its central location and tiny size. The prince maintains extensive art collections, and Vaduz is home to the imposing Kunstmuseum

Liechtenstein stamps are prized around the world

Liechtenstein (Fine Arts Museum). The principality is naturally part of a larger and regional culture as well.

The royal house maintains several art collections, dating back 500 years. The custom of princely art collection reflects a tradition of royal patronage of the arts. It was considered the duty of a monarch to encourage artistic pursuits in the land he governed. The collections are diverse, including paintings, sculpture, furniture, and decorative household items, many of which are considered masterpieces. In 1945, Prince Franz Joseph II began to sell off significant parts of the collections, but his son launched efforts to re-purchase many of these in the late 20th century. The collections are on display in Vaduz, and Vienna, Austria.

In the late 20th century, both the private and public sectors of Liechtenstein began to actively support the arts as a national endeavor, a result of the country's growing economy. Today, all 11 communes maintain separate, local cultural initiatives, and the tourism industry plays an important role in promoting Liechtenstein's culture. In 2007, the Ministry of Foreign Affairs announced that cultural promotion would become a key element in Liechtenstein's foreign policy. This is considered an important factor in the principality's integration in Europe.

The principality maintains many public cultural institutions, including the Museum of Fine Arts, the Music School, the National Library, and the National Museum. It also funds individual artists, cooperative projects, and cultural events. The National Museum is the country's oldest cultural facility, established in 1954 by the Historical Society (founded in 1901). The 2008 Cultural Promotion Act specifically states the government's respect for the independence and freedom of the country's artists.

A surprising aspect of Lichtenstein's national artistic expression is the design of postage stamps. One of the country's best-known exports, Liechtenstein's stamps are prized around the world. The Postage Stamp Museum in Vaduz details the history of Liechtenstein's stamp production, and a free stamp is given away as a souvenir at the capital's post office.

ECONOMY

Overview of the Economy

The principality's per capita gross domestic product (GDP) is the highest in the world, standing at $89,400 (USD). The work force numbers some 35,830, and close to 16,000 of these workers commute from Germany, Austria, and Switzerland. Only 0.8 percent of Liechtenstein's labor force work in agriculture (producing 8 percent of the GDP), with 39.4 percent in industry and 59.9 percent working in the service sector (2012 estimates).

Industry

Liechtenstein has undergone rapid industrialization since the end of World War II, when the country was poor and the economy was primarily agricultural. The principality's lack of commercially useful natural resources, however, has meant that it has no heavy industry, such as mining or steel production. Instead, the economy is lead by financial services and a variety of small businesses. Liechtenstein's chief exports include prepared foodstuffs, small specialty machinery, dental products, and stamps.

The bulk of the services that Liechtenstein provides are in banking. Because of its low business taxes and easy rules of incorporation, many international firms open what are called "letter-box" offices in the principality. These are offices at which little is done, but which allow corporations to claim Liechtenstein's financial advantages. Liechtenstein has also occasionally become a haven for illegal money laundering. There has been growing international pressure on the principality in the 21st century to improve the transparency of its tax and banking laws.

Energy/Power/Natural Resources

Liechtenstein's natural resources have little commercial value, and the principality must import most of its raw materials, including wood. More than 90 percent of its energy sources come from elsewhere, and the principality has no heavy industry. The Samina and Lawena rivers provide some hydroelectric power, and the Unterland contains arable land.

Though the country remains largely rural, growing urbanization has damaged Liechtenstein's natural environment somewhat. Efforts are being made to preserve and restore open spaces and wetlands. Eight large nature reserves now make up 1.5 percent of all of Liechtenstein's land. Liechtenstein is known, however, for its environmentally friendly industry, which pollutes little and is constructed to fit into the natural environment.

The Rhine Valley's natural habitat was badly disrupted by the construction (1931–1943) of the Binnenkanal (Inland or Inner Canal), built to control the flow of water through the Unterland to the Rhine River. The removal of gravel from the Rhine's floor (1950–1970) was also damaging to the Rhine's ecosystem. However, the canal was redesigned and restructured in 2003, allowing for an increase in biodiversity and the return of species that had been missing for decades.

Agriculture

Until the mid-20th century, Liechtenstein's economy was based on farming. In the early 21st century, not quite two percent of the work force is employed in agriculture. Farms have gotten bigger and more efficient, and the main crops include dairy, corn, and grapes for wine production. Dairy production makes up more than half of Liechtenstein's gross agricultural return, and prepared foodstuffs are among Liechtenstein's primary exports. Yet, the principality must import most of the food its citizens consume.

Liechtenstein has long been known for its wine production. In the late 19th century, wine was the principality's main export. New rail lines increased competition throughout Europe, however, and after several bad harvests in the early 20th century, the local wine industry collapsed. Efforts to revive the industry have been somewhat successful in recent decades, and some 100 grape growers produce both white and red varieties.

Tourism

Tourism plays an important role in the public relations of Liechtenstein, though it does not bring in nearly as much money as the financial sector or manufacturing. Because of Liechtenstein's size and proximity to other tourism centers, overnight stays are not common. This makes it difficult to arrive at a precise figure for the number of tourists arriving every year and the revenues they generate. However, the principality does report that some more than 77,000 tourists stay overnight annually, renting rooms for a total of more than 183,000 nights each year. Most visitors head to the mountainous regions, particularly the ski resort in Malbun. Hiking and other outdoor pursuits are considered the backbone of Liechtenstein's tourism business. The capital of Vaduz and surrounding region is another popular destination.

SOCIETY

Transportation

Liechtenstein's primary form of transportation is the privately owned passenger car. According to 2002 estimates by the UN, the principality is home to approximately 23,000 cars, along with about 350 mopeds and motorcycles. There is also a small railroad network, and the country is notably proud of its public bus system. Most of Liechtenstein's buses run on low-emission natural gas, but specially adapted diesel engine vehicles are used in the mountainous regions. Ground transportation is available to the nearby countries, as well, but Liechtenstein does not have its own airport. The nearest airport is in Zurich, Switzerland, a little more than an hour's drive northwest of Vaduz. The country does have a heliport.

Media & Communications

The tiny population of such a small country does not allow for the development of an extensive local media. Two newspapers, *Liechtensteiner Vaterland* and *Liechtensteiner Volksblatt*, are produced six days a week, and another paper, *Liewo*, produced by the same media company as *Liechtensteiner Vaterland*, appears only on Sundays. *Liechtensteiner Vaterland* has the country's largest circulation, followed by

Liechtensteiner Volksblatt, which, founded in 1878, is Liechtenstein's oldest paper. The principality is dependent on neighboring countries and satellite broadcasts for radio and television. As of 2010, there were an estimated 23,000 Internet users.

GOVERNMENT

Structure

Lichtenstein is a hereditary constitutional monarchy. The head of state is a prince, whose royal stature and position is inherited. The royal house shares power with a democratically elected parliament, based on the provisions of the country's 1921 constitution. Liechtenstein's Landtag (parliament) is unicameral (has only one house), and the 25 members are elected to four-year terms. The government is made up of four ministers and a prime minister, all of whom are appointed by the prince on the recommendation of the Landtag. Adults may vote from their 20th birthday, though women have enjoyed this right only since 1984. (Three of the country's 11 communes did not allow women to vote in local elections until 1986.)

The Progressive People's Party and the Patriotic Union (or Fatherland Union) are the principality's two leading political parties; one minor party exists, Free List, but it maintains only three parliament seats as of 2013. For most of the state's modern history, the two have formed a "grand coalition," together holding the vast majority of the 25 seats in parliament. After the 2001 elections, the Progressive People's Party was able to form a government on its own, but the results of the 2005 elections resulted in the reforming of a coalition. As of 2013, the Progressive People's Party held 10seats in the Landtag of Liechtenstein, while the Fatherland Union held eight seats.

In most other constitutional monarchies, such as Great Britain or Sweden, the monarch serves either a very limited role in the actual governing of the country, or an entirely ceremonial role. This is not the case in Liechtenstein. In 2003, the citizens of Liechtenstein voted to allow their prince extensive new powers, essentially returning the country to the days of absolute monarchy. Attempts to return some of that power to the legislature as recently as 2014, have failed.

Foreign Policy

The primary focus of Liechtenstein's foreign policy is the maintenance of its independence. The country's tiny size and lack of a military mean that this can only be accomplished diplomatically. The heart of Liechtenstein's foreign relations is in bilateral diplomatic ties and its membership in international organizations. The principality is a member of several international bodies, including the UN, the OSCE, the ICJ, the International Atomic Energy Agency (IAEA), the European Free Trade Association (EFTA), the European Economic Area (EEA), and the Council of Europe, among other regional and international institutions.

Liechtenstein's closest relationship, however, is with Switzerland, which is responsible for Liechtenstein's defense in case of war. The two countries enjoy an open border and a customs union, and Swiss custom officials secure Liechtenstein's Austrian border. In addition, more than 40 percent of the principality's workforce is made up of foreign workers who commute across the border. Liechtenstein's biggest trade partners include Germany, Austria, and the United States. Trade with Switzerland is significant as well, but the customs union means that statistics are unavailable.

Long represented by Switzerland in the US, Liechtenstein has had its own representative in America since 2000. An embassy was built in Washington, DC, in 2002. One of the main areas of cooperation between Liechtenstein and the US is the issue of money laundering, particularly with regard to the funding of terrorism. The royal house of Liechtenstein also funds the Liechtenstein Institute, at Princeton University's Woodrow Wilson School of Public and International Affairs. The institute promotes research, publishing, teaching, and private diplomacy.

The changes made to Liechtenstein's constitution in 2003 were not welcomed by the countries of Europe. Prior to the vote, the Parliamentary Assembly of the Council of Europe convened a special commission to study the issue. The Venice Commission found that the changes would "constitute a serious step backward" for Liechtenstein and "could lead to an isolation of Liechtenstein within the European community of states."

Human Rights Profile

International human rights law insists that states respect civil and political rights, and also promote an individual's economic, social and cultural rights. The United Nations Universal Declaration on Human Rights (UDHR) is recognized as the standard for international human rights. Its authors sought the counsel of the world's great thinkers, philosophers, and religious leaders, and were careful to create a document that reflects the core values shared by every world culture. (To read this document or view the articles relating to cultural human rights, visit: http://www.udhr.org/UDHR/default.htm).

The human rights record of Liechtenstein is generally good, but there are areas in which the small country has been called upon to make important improvements. For example, the Economics and Social Council (ECOSOC) of the UN has urged the principality to improve its treatment of minorities, particularly expressing concern about discrimination against Muslims and persons of Turkish origin. One specific issue regards hiring practices. Liechtenstein law forbids firing a worker on the basis of race, color, descent, nationality or ethnic origin, but there is no such protection regarding recruitment, pay, or promotion.

Another issue for foreigners surrounds language use. Amnesty International (AI) has expressed concern over the fact that Liechtenstein requires foreigners to have a certain level of fluency in German before they can join family in the principality. AI has also found that people who seek political asylum in Liechtenstein are interrogated with little concern for their health. Asylum seekers who suffer psychological problems have faced special difficulties, and AI has called on Liechtenstein to provide public servants with systematic human rights training.

Another issue concerns the rights of women, whether they are foreign-born or native. Liechtenstein did not grant women the vote in national elections until 1984, and in some communes, women weren't allowed to vote in local elections until 1986. This was in clear violation of Article 2 of the UDHR. However, the principality became one of 181 countries that ratified the UN Convention of the Elimination of All Forms of Discrimination against Women (CEDAW) in 1996. The UN has pointed out, however, that the problem of domestic violence persists in the principality. Liechtenstein engaged in a campaign (2001–2004) to raise public awareness of abuse, but it has no overall national plan to combat the problem.

Emily L. Hauser

DO YOU KNOW?

- The first known reference to the House of Liechtenstein comes from a document dating to 1136, mentioning "Hugo of Liechtenstein." Hugo named himself after Liechtenstein Castle, outside of Vienna, Austria. The castle was named after the chalk cliff – the "light stone," or liecht stein – on which it stands.

- The royal family of Liechtenstein is closely related to the royal family of Luxembourg.

- Liechtenstein has nine Olympic medals: two gold, two silver, and five bronze. All were won at the Winter Olympics, and most are held by the same family. Four medals—both gold medals, a silver and a bronze—were won by skier Hanni Wenzel (1956–), while her younger brother Andreas (1958–) won silver and bronze.

Bibliography

Beattie, David. *Liechtenstein: A Modern History*. London: I.B. Tauris, 2004.

Eccardt, Thomas M. *Secrets of the Seven Smallest States of Europe: Andorra, Liechtenstein, Luxembourg, Malta, Monaco, San Marino, and Vatican City*. New York: Hippocrene Books. 2005.

Ostergren, Robert. "Defining Liechtenstein: Sovereign Borders, Offshore Banking, and National Identity," in A.C. Diener and J. Hagen, eds., *Borderlines and Borderlands: Political Oddities at the Edge of the Nation-State*. Lanham, MD: Rowman and Littlefield, 2010.

Works Cited

http://www.about-liechtenstein.co.uk/

http://www.amnestyusa.org/document. php?lang=e&id=ENGIOR410442008

http://news.bbc.co.uk/2/hi/europe/country_ profiles/1066002.stm

http://www.britannica.com/EBchecked/topic/13769/ Alemanni/13769rellinks/Related-Links

http://www.citypopulation.de/explanation.html

https://www.cia.gov/library/publications/the-world-factbook/print/ls.html

http://www.culturalpolicies.net/web/liechtenstein. php?aid=1

http://encarta.msn.com/encnet/refpages/RefArticle. aspx?refid=761571552

http://www.fco.gov.uk/en/about-the-fco/country-profiles/ europe/liechtenstein?profile=all

http://www.forbes.com/2004/06/02/cx_0602hot.html

http://www.fuerstenhaus.li/en/fuerstenhaus/

http://www.google.com/url?sa=t&source=web&ct=re s&cd=4&url=http%3A%2F%2Fwww.liechtenstein. li%2Fen%2Fpdf-fl-historikerkommission-pressemitteilung.pdf&ei=WnGDScvuIYjKNLem4PoD& usg=AFQjCNE31nhXC7FCG285TT41OlUX9tpkjw&si g2=9h6PdIiXvrUOng6FVUSj6g

http://www.google.com/url?sa=t&source=web&ct=res& cd=2&url=http%3A%2F%2Fwww.unece.org%2Ftran

s%2Fmain%2Fwp6%2Fpdfdocs%2FABTS2005.pdf& ei=btCRSbH4Cpr0sAOmytS9Cw&usg=AFQjCNHo6 bhsKYlFJudTwb577rsOskkhiQ&sig2=u78H8fXT80-Sfon9683CQA

http://www.google.com/url?sa=t&source=web&ct=re s&cd=2&url=http%3A%2F%2Fwww.liechtenstein. li%2Fen%2Fpdf-fl-staat-verfassung-sept2003.pdf&ei=s BqTSYexCoKOsQP8uZyoCw&usg=AFQjCNHHymib qii_ADAVnk616BYMWuxhXQ&sig2=LHuUjJSrIzMr7 QkLnUmcxw

http://www.google.com/url?sa=t&source=web&c t=res&cd=8&url=http%3A%2F%2Fwww.llv. li%2Fpdf-llv-avw-statistik-fliz-2006-complete_ brochure&ei=ZSKLSbaANJC4MveN_NYH&usg=AFQj CNHf1tCn1LcDETrEoAmzIKQupXChag&sig2=owptIO 4Sl__DlIp-_JDS4Qhttp://www.liechtenstein.li/en

http://www.internetworldstats.com/euro/li.htm

http://www.lrz-muenchen.de/~hr/lang/dt-dial.html#hoch

http://www.mongabay.com/igapo/2005_world_city_ populations/Liechtenstein.html http://encarta.msn.com/ encnet/refpages/RefFAF.aspx?refid=631504803

http://query.nytimes.com/gst/fullpage.html?res=9800E0 DE1E3EF936A25750C0A9659C8B63&n=Top/News/ World/Countries%20and%20Territories/Liechtenstein&s cp=4&sq=liechtenstein%202003&st=cse

http://www.skiliechtenstein.com/skiing.php

http://www.state.gov/r/pa/ei/bgn/9403.htm

http://www.tageo.com/index-e-ls-cities-LI.htm

http://www.un.org/members/list.shtml

http://www.walser-alps.eu/dialect/from-valais-german-to-walser-german/view?set_language=en

http://www.nationmaster.com/country/ls-liechtenstein/int-internet

http://www.unhchr.ch/tbs/doc.nsf/898586b1dc7b4043c1256 a450044f331/b3699dcecff3c2c8c1257198007290f1/$FI LE/G0642548.pdf

Tamar Büchel-Brunhart, Assistant to the Ambassador of Liechtenstein. Email: tamara.brunhart@was.rep.llv.li

Wilfried Marxer, researcher and political scientist with the Liechtenstein Institute in Bendern, Liechtenstein. Email: wm@liechtenstein-institut.li

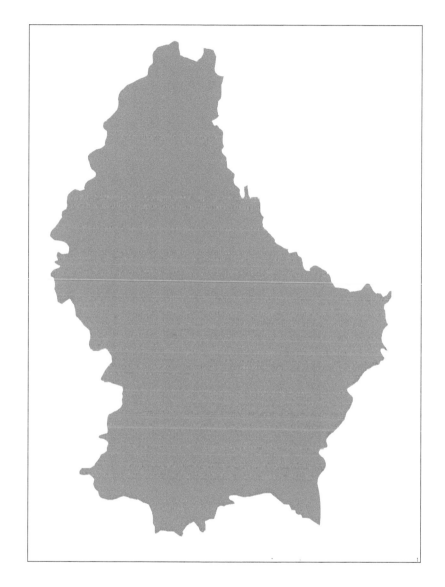

LUXEMBOURG

Introduction

Established as a political state in 963, the Grand Duchy of Luxembourg is a tiny nation nestled between Germany and Belgium, with France to the south. It is only 82 kilometers (51 miles) long and 58 kilometers (36 miles) wide, slightly larger than metropolitan London. Because of its location between France, Germany, and Belgium, Luxembourg's history is a turbulent one, highlighted by a host of takeovers, diplomatic deals, and struggles to gain its independence from its larger neighbors. Much of Luxembourg's history is the history of central Europe, particularly the Netherlands, Belgium, and Germany.

In spite of its size, Luxembourg has a cosmopolitan mix of European residents and a standard of living to be envied by most nations of the world. In 1951, Luxembourg was one of the six founding states of the European Coal and Steel Community (ECSC), an organization that eventually grew to become the European Union. Today, Luxembourg continues to play an important role in the dynamic political and economic decisions of the EU.

GENERAL INFORMATION

Official Language: Luxembourgish
Population: 520,672 (2014 estimate)
Currency: Euro

Coins: The Euro is available in 1, 2, 5, 10, 20 and 50 cent coins. A 1 and 2 Euro coin is also available.
Land Area: 2,586 square kilometers (998.6 square miles)
National Motto: "Mir wëlle bleiwe wat mir sin" ("We want to remain what we are")
National Anthem: "Ons Heemecht" ("Our Motherland")
Capital: Luxembourg
Time Zone: GMT +1
Flag Description: The flag of Luxembourg features a tricolor design composed of three equal horizontal bands of red (top), white (middle), and light blue (bottom). The colors are derived from the Luxembourg coat of arms.

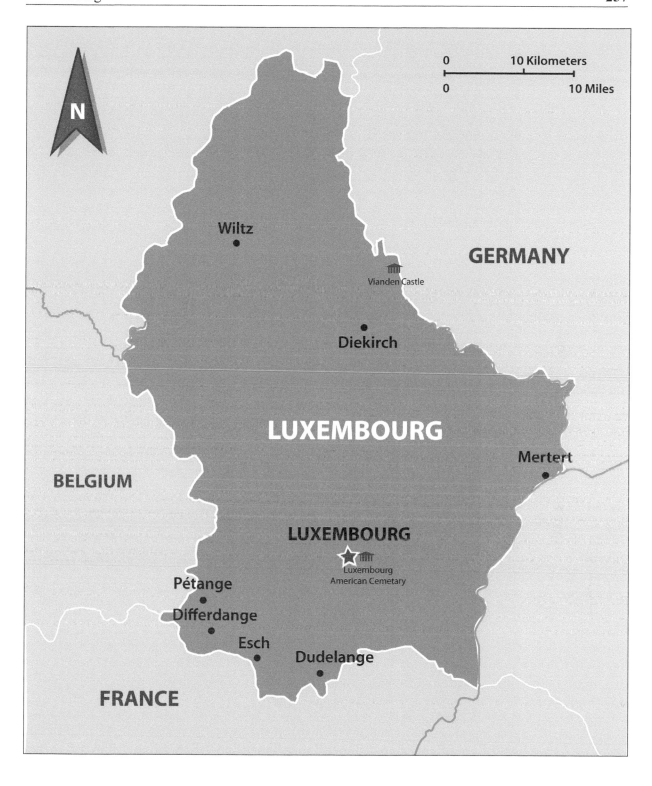

Principal Cities by Population (2012):

- Luxembourg City (74,738)
- Esch-sur-Alzette (29,616)
- Differedange (20,979) (2009 estimate)
- Dudelange (18,898)
- Pétange (15,398) (2009 estimate)
- Sanem (14,255) (2009 estimate)
- Hesperange (12,786) (2009 estimate)
- Bettembourg (9,722) (2009 estimate)
- Schifflange (8,556)
- Ettelbruck (7,714) (2009 estimate)

Population

Befitting the country's central location in Western Europe, Luxembourgers are a thorough mix of European ethnicities. The region has a strong Celtic base that has become mixed with French and German influences. Significant populations of French, German, Portuguese, Italian, and Slavs from Montenegro, Albania, and Kosovo have made their home in the duchy. Other Europeans live in Luxembourg as guests or resident workers.

According to a 2006 census, 32 percent of Luxembourg City's estimated 90,000 residents are foreign nationals, mostly from Western Europe. Many work in the city's thriving banking and finance industry, are employees of the EU administration, or are employed in the electronics sector. An estimated 89.9 percent of the population is urban. As of 2014, the population growth rate was 1.12 percent.

Languages

Luxembourg is known for having a complex of languages: most of the population is at least tri-lingual, speaking French, German, and Lëtzebuergesch (Luxembourgish), a dialect of Frankish. Although Luxembourgish is the national language and has been taught in schools since 1984, only a few hundred native speakers of the language remain. German and French are spoken with equal fluency in the city, and most residents also speak some English, as it is compulsory in the city's middle and high school grades.

Native People & Ethnic Groups

The area that is now Luxembourg was once inhabited by Magdalenian, Neolithic, and finally, Celtic tribes. During the first century, the area was swallowed up by the expanding Roman Empire, but not until local Treviri Celts had fought a number of successful battles of resistance. The hostility of the Celtic and later Frankish inhabitants prevented Rome from ever holding the region securely.

During the eighth century, the Frankish King Charlemagne settled the region with Saxons, who mixed with the Celtic and Frankish populations. Over the subsequent centuries, Luxembourg developed some of Europe's oldest and most influential aristocratic lines. From its location among French and German powerhouses, the House of Luxembourg became a European power base, producing four emperors of the Holy Roman Empire and intermarrying with aristocracy across Europe.

The lack of natural boundaries around Luxembourg encouraged a general mixture of ethnicities and cultures in the state, even among the peasant classes. This tendency toward cultural blending continues in modern Luxembourg, where up to 35 percent of the duchy's residents are from outside the country.

Minority ethnic groups in Luxembourg include an estimated 162,000 immigrants from Bosnia and Herzegovina, Montenegro, and Serbia.

Religions

Luxembourg's population is largely Roman Catholic (87 percent). The remaining 13 percent of religiously active Luxembourgers are generally Protestant, Muslim, or Jewish.

Climate

Luxembourg has a temperate climate with seasonal, and some regional, variation. In the capital, temperatures drop to –1° Celsius (30° Fahrenheit) in the winter and ranges from 13° to 23° Celsius (55° to 73° Fahrenheit) in the summer months. Temperatures are often significantly cooler in the Ardennes.

ENVIRONMENT & GEOGRAPHY

Topography

Luxembourg consists of two separate regions. In the northern two-thirds of the country, the land rises to a plateau where the Ardennes Forest begins (the forest flows into Belgium and France). The Ardennes uplands consist of rugged but fertile woods that become mountainous farther north.

Luxembourg's lowlands make up only 32 percent of the country's landmass, but this region is the most heavily populated portion of the duchy. These fertile, hilly lowlands are known as the Bon Pays ("good country") and are carved with deep, broad river valleys and the Moselle flood plain to the east.

Most of Luxembourg's rivers drain into the Sauer that flows east toward the southeastern border with Germany, where it merges with the Moselle. The country's lowest point is in the Moselle floodplain, where elevation is 133 meters (463 feet). The highest point of elevation is Buurgplaatz in the Ardennes at 559 meters (1,834 feet).

Luxembourg City is a commune situated on the southern half of the Luxembourg Plateau, a lowlands area of grassy plains that is cut by the Alzette and Pétrusse Rivers. Its traditional center, Luxembourg Castle, sits on a rocky outcropping called the Bock that overlooks the junction between the two rivers, and is the highest point of the city at 443 meters (1,319 feet.) The total area of the city is 51.46 square kilometers (19.87 square miles). Luxembourg lies at the direct center of Western Europe, thus making it an important area for commerce.

Plants & Animals

Freshwater fish like pike, trout, eel, carp, and pikeperch swim in Luxembourg's plentiful rivers, lakes, and streams.

The Ardennes is a habitat for wild boar, deer, and hare, as well as a variety of bird life. The industrialized and heavily populated lands to the south are no longer home to as many native plant or animal species, although birds like warblers, osprey, heron, and egret live in the area around the Moselle River.

CUSTOMS & COURTESIES

Greetings

Greetings in Luxembourg typically begin with a brief, firm handshake, even when greeting children. Greetings among acquaintances and strangers are formal, while close friends might greet each other with a kiss on the cheek—three times, beginning on the left cheek, then the right, then the left again. Men, however, always only shake hands with other men, even though women kiss women and men. Depending on the language—French and German, along with Luxembourgish, are the official languages—honorific titles are customarily used before the surname. For example, when speaking in French, the formal titles of "Madame" or "Monsieur" (equivalent to "Mrs." and "Mister") come before the surname. When using French, it is also considered polite and customary to use the formal use of "you," which is "vous," instead of the familiar "tu."

Generally, Luxembourgers are reserved and exert patience when getting to know somebody. Small talk is a customary formality while getting acquainted, with subtlety often emphasized over directness. However, Luxembourgers are not shy about expressing what they really think, though it is typically done politely.

Gestures & Etiquette

As Luxembourgers are fairly private people and not emotionally demonstrative, they are customarily reserved with strangers. They are also conscious of subtle body language that may convey casualness or informality, and thus rarely place their hands in their pockets or chew gum in public. They tend to separate business from their personal lives, such as friendships that develop outside of the working environment, and are generally less rushed in their endeavors as compared to other European cultures. In formal settings, such as in business, punctuality is important and particular respect is paid to those in higher positions.

Eating/Meals

Luxembourgers typically eat three meals per day, starting with breakfast. This usually includes light fare such as coffee or tea with bread and preserves (called a continental breakfast). Traditionally the main meal, lunch is now a fairly light meal that might include a soup appetizer with a main course of meat or fish, or a salad or sandwich. Though some schools are beginning to build cafeterias, schoolchildren typically go home for lunch. Dinner is the main meal in Luxembourg, and is usually served in communal fashion. However, it is also common for plated meals to be served when guests are being entertained. As in other European countries, cheese often follows a more formal meal in Luxembourg.

Eating out in Luxembourg cities is increasingly common, especially in Luxembourg City, which houses a number of international organizations. Dining out is also reserved for special occasions such as birthdays, anniversaries or other celebrations, and on Sundays, families enjoy going out for brunch. Most food in Luxembourg is eaten with utensils, which are used in the continental style: holding the fork in the left hand and the knife in the right.

Visiting

Etiquette when visiting a Luxembourger's home involves being punctual, though it is also customary to arrive 15 minutes late. It is considered proper etiquette to bring a gift, such as flowers or good chocolates, for both formal and casual dining. (In Luxembourg, chrysanthemums are used for funerals, and so are not considered a thoughtful gift for the dinner host or hostess.) Even a small gift for the children is considered highly thoughtful and appreciated.

As with greetings and general etiquette, dining is a formal event that requires good manners, such as not sitting at the dinner table until invited. Guests should also wait to eat until the hostess begins. When finished eating, guests should

place the fork and knife across the right side of the plate. It is considered good manners for guests to eat all the food on their plate. Should a toast be in order, it is typically up to the hostess to give the first toast. Guests are encouraged to return a toast at another point in the meal.

LIFESTYLE

Family

Family life is important in Luxembourg. Extended families keep in close contact, and Luxembourgers feel a strong obligation to their relatives. Within the family, each member has specific responsibilities, which are often gender-oriented, such as women and mothers handling the child rearing and certain domestic responsibilities. Families traditionally spend time together on holidays, many of which are religious in nature.

In Luxembourg, couples often wait to get married until they have developed some financial security. In a country in which religion figures fairly prominently—though a secular state, an estimated 87 percent of the population identifies as Catholic—only a civil authority can legally marry a man and a woman. Couples can get married in a church, but they must first be married by a civil authority and present a certificate. Even in the early 21st century, parents continue to play an important role in their children's choices of spouse and career.

Housing

The majority of Luxembourg's citizens live in urban areas, where services and infrastructure are readily available. Housing in Luxembourg is fairly comfortable, partly owing to the country's high standard of living, the highest in the European Union (EU). The most common homes have two or three bedrooms, are heated by oil, and have wood floors. In addition, amenities such as marble countertops and parquet floors are not uncommon. Luxembourgers also take great pleasure in their gardens, which most houses have. City dwellings, whether houses or apartments, might have window boxes instead, due to lack of yard space.

Traditional structures are made of stone, a technique developed in antiquity, and stone houses, barns, and smokehouses covered in stucco still exist throughout the country. Other characteristics of older homes include wood ceilings and stairways, and windows constructed of stone beams and wooden shutters; roofs are typically black slate, but red cylindrical half-tiles are used in the Moselle valley region. A design that resembles a wheel can still be found on many entrances to these older buildings.

Food

The cuisine of Luxembourg has been heavily influenced by the neighboring cultures of both France and Germany—it is often said that food in Luxembourg is served with a French style, but in German quantity—as well as a long history of immigration. Fish and meat dishes are fairly common, and Luxembourgers tend to prepare these staples in traditional dishes with sauces or according to French tradition. Additionally, because of their good soil and decent growing conditions, Luxembourgers eat a great deal of fruits and vegetables, much of which is grown in their region or in neighboring European countries.

The range of appetizers and light fare found in Luxembourg shows the national cuisine's diverse influences. Popular appetizers include bounenschlupp, a bean soup made with fava beans; a boiled cheese dish called kachkéis, which resembles the French cheese camembert; and quenelles, which are tiny dumplings that are most often stuffed with ground fish and topped with a cream sauce. A lighter appetizer might be made with Luxembourg ham, which resembles the smoke-cured, thinly sliced, Italian prosciutto. A major French influence includes pâté, which is a spread typically made from chicken or calf liver, and German foods include potato pancakes and buckwheat dumplings. Salads are also popular, and include staple salads made from fresh greens, a boiled egg, and an oil and vinegar dressing, or feierstengszalot, made with sliced cold meat and cream sauce.

Potatoes are common in traditional Luxembourg meals. For example, if meat quenelles are eaten for a main course, they are frequently accompanied by boiled potatoes and sauerkraut. Sausages with black pudding, called tréipen (an English delicacy of blood sausage), and potatoes are a favorite throughout Luxembourg. Hunting season adds a variety of game, such as rabbit and wild boar, to the cuisine. Small river fish are often fried, such as in friture de la Moselle, often served in the Moselle wine country; tiny freshwater fish are dipped in an egg and flour batter and deep-fried in pork fat and traditionally eaten with the fingers. French dishes are served throughout Luxembourg, from omelets to numerous meat and vegetable dishes, sometimes with the French béchamel sauce made from milk, flour, and butter.

Traditional desserts include cheesecake or apple cake, known as kéiskuch and äpplekuch respectively, and plum tart, called quetschentaart, made from fresh plums in September. In Luxembourg, people drink coffee (kaffi) with dessert, which might include cheese for a more formal meal. White wine of the Moselle River region often accompanies meals, and Luxembourgers have a fondness for good beer, especially from neighboring Belgium.

Life's Milestones

Because the major religion in Luxembourg is Roman Catholicism, the religious rituals of baptism, first communion, and confirmation are common rites of passage. As in other countries around the world in which Catholicism is a major religion, Luxembourgers also celebrate Carnival Week before Lent with parades and celebrations. Students are off from school, and families get to enjoy the many pageants and costume balls.

For an even larger majority of people, a student's graduation from secondary or technical school is considered an extremely important event. By the age of 12, students are slated either for secondary or technical school. Families mark a student's graduation with parties and other celebrations.

CULTURAL HISTORY

Art

The fine arts did not fully develop in Luxembourg until the turn of the 20th century. In fact, one characteristic of Luxembourg art is that it is an imitation of earlier artistic styles. One of the earliest known artists in Luxembourg was expressionist Joseph Kutter (1894–1941), who was known for his portraitures and landscapes. Considered Luxembourg's most important artist, he trained in Munich, Germany, and is known as one of the more prominent European expressionists. Another expressionist, Nico Klopp (1894–1930), painted works that challenged the reigning academic perspective. He led the country's first secessionist exhibition in 1927. Artists from the postwar period include Émile Kirscht (1913–1994), considered a pioneer of contemporary art in the grand duchy, and renowned sculptor Lucien Wercollier (1908–2002). Her famous work, *Political Prisoner*, was created after World War II, during which she was detained in a Nazi concentration camp as a political prisoner.

Architecture

Early architecture in Luxembourg includes timbered and stone structures, and is often militaristic in nature. Notable buildings built before the 17th century include fortified châteaux (manor houses), fortresses and classic stone churches. The old town of Luxembourg City is particularly known for its fortifications and historical architecture, and represents the grand duchy's only contribution to the World Heritage List, as maintained by the United Nations Education, Scientific, and Cultural Organization (UNESCO). The town was built beginning in the 14th century and was considered one of the most fortified cities in Europe from the sixteenth until the late 19th century.

Much like Luxembourg art, the architecture of Luxembourg began to imitate other classical, European styles, such as rococo and baroque. A distinct Austrian influence can be seen in some 18th-century churches and public buildings. After Luxembourg gained independence, its architecture mimicked the art nouveau and art deco styles that were common in cultural capitals such as Berlin and Paris. During the early- and mid-20th century, Bauhaus design was popular, and the construction of modern apartment flats and office buildings changed the face of urban architecture in the industrial south. By the end of the 20th century, architecture was expressed in contemporary terms, with minimal lines and shapes.

Drama & Dance

The concerted development of drama in Luxembourg occurred in the 20th century with the building of the Grand Theater of the City of Luxembourg in 1964. Known mostly for amateur theater, Luxembourg productions have helped launch the international careers of numerous Luxembourgers. Beginning in 1985, Luxembourg City created the Théâtre des Capucins de la Ville de Luxembourg as a venue for semiprofessional theater companies to stage their productions. The grand duchy continues to host various theatrical festivals, including the open-air festival in Wiltz, in the Ardennes, and other open-air theaters in Bourscheid and Kehlen, popular in the summer months.

Though Luxembourg does not boast a distinctly developed tradition of dance, the small country is home to a unique folk dance tradition that can be traced back to the eighth century. The Dancing Procession of Echternach, which takes place annually in June in the town of Echternach, honors Saint Willibrord (658–739), the patron saint of Luxembourg. (St. Willibrord founded the famous Abbey of Echternach in the seventh century, which attracts pilgrims and tourists alike.) The procession, considered the last traditional dance procession in Europe, is done as an act of penance (repentance of sins), a transformation which many believe occurred during the Middle Ages.

Literature

Luxembourgian literature arose to new heights after the country achieved independence in 1839. Drawing on nationalism and political themes of a new nation, writers such as Edmond de la Fontaine (1823–1891), who wrote under a pen name, began to write in the Luxembourgish language. Considered Luxembourg's national poet, Fontaine became one of the most significant literary figures, and also wrote the famous ethnographic work *Luxemburger Sitten und Bräuche* ("Luxembourg Customs and Traditions," 1883). Other important literary figures from this period include writer and poet Michel Rodange (1827–1876), whose national epic, *Rénert the Fox* (1872), is a satirical adaptation of medieval tales, and poet Michel Lentz (1820–1893), who penned the country's national anthem. Literature prior to World War I also took on a decisively German tone (as Germany was Luxembourg's economic ally), and works published in the German language were popular.

During the mid-20th-century authors wrote in both French and German, and genres such as Romanesque literature (characterized by romance and fanciful language) emerged. Fiction writing was firmly established by the 1970s, and Luxembourgian literature has remained multilingual. In 1995, the government of Luxembourg organized a national literature archive, called the National Literature Centre (CNL), which is located in Mersch, near Luxembourg City. The centre opened as a research library and today includes more than 40,000 volumes of books written by those living in Luxembourg or those of Luxembourgish descent.

CULTURE

Arts & Entertainment

Twenty-first century art in Luxembourg represents a diverse range of European cultures. For example, the country has hosted the annual European Cities of Culture festival, which is held in a different European Union (EU) city each year. The organizers of this particular festival aimed to draw all types of artists from around Europe, so as to encourage the arts within the country, as well as in the city of Luxembourg. The festival indeed encouraged local artists, and

the city earned the title of European Capital of Culture in 2007, drawing an estimated 3.3 million visitors to more than 5,000 cultural events that year.

The chamber orchestra European Soloists Luxembourg pulls together soloists from numerous European countries. The Luxembourg-based orchestra plays in such European cities as Paris, Frankfurt, and Budapest. Folk music is also popular in Luxembourg, where the group Dullemajik performs classic folk music on accordions, flutes, bagpipes, and even the hurdy-gurdy, a hand-cranked stringed instrument that is sometimes called a wheel fiddle. The instrument is believed to have originated during the Middle Ages in Western Europe or possibly the Middle East. In the spring and summer, Luxembourgers enjoy music festivals that include the large Echternach Festival, Jazz in the City, the Printemps musical de Luxembourg, and smaller ones in other cities.

Luxembourg's display of contemporary architecture is visible in its European banking institutions, which feature functional designs of steel, copper, and glass in forms that range from cylindrical to cubic. The design of the well-known Hypobank contains both cylindrical and cubic forms, while another structure features a glass roof. Office buildings, especially, in recent years have been designed in this manner. In addition, the steel building which houses the court of justice for the EU was designed to corrode just enough to the point of stabilization, but also to develop an aesthetically pleasing bronze surface.

Contemporary visual arts in Luxembourg are on display at the Grand Duke Jean Museum of Modern Art (MUDAM). The MUDAM features world-renowned artists from around the world. Casino Luxembourg—Forum of Contemporary Art is a showcase for contemporary visual artists, many from around Europe and the rest of world. Exhibitions include artistic examinations of financial crises and the role of morality. Other exhibits, permanent and temporary, explore the range of human perspectives in the creation of art as well as the variety of methods for understanding the modern world. The Slovakia-based organization KulturFabrik has transformed a former Luxembourg slaughterhouse into a building that now exhibits young film, performance, and other visual artists, as well as writers. The environment is intended for community artists to develop installations and exhibits that draw attention to urban, social, and civic issues, opening up opportunities for young artists to participate in cultural events.

Like many other Europeans, Luxembourgers enjoy biking, hiking, and skiing when they are not at work or school. The favorite local spot for weekend getaways is Müllerthal (Miller's Valley) surrounding the town of Echternach northeast of Luxembourg City. The area is full of scenic woodland and gentle hiking trails. Like their counterparts across the French border, Luxembourgers also have a passion for cooking. Restaurants are easy to find in the capital or in small villages, but most Luxembourgers have their own well-guarded recipes and food-centered traditions.

Cultural Sites & Landmarks

Though it is one of the smallest states in Europe, Luxembourg is home to a wealth of cultural and historic sites. These range from Celtic tombs and funerary chambers that date back to the Late Iron Age (500–100 BCE), to remnants of the once great Roman Empire, including the ruins of a 3,500-spectator Roman theater that can only be viewed only during specific times of the year. Another important historic site is the Abbaye Neumünster, built by Benedictine monks near Luxembourg City in 1606. Throughout its long life the abbey has burned down and been rebuilt (1688), served as a prison, and was the locale for deportees during the Nazi occupation in World War II. It has since become a cultural center for the city.

Once a fortified state without comparison throughout medieval Europe, the grand duchy is now home to a large number of castles. One of the best-preserved castles in Luxembourg is in Vianden and dates to the early Middle Ages, and was built during the Romanesque and Gothic

periods of construction. The complex history of the castle begins when the counts of Luxembourg abandoned it when they went to the Netherlands. After fire and an earthquake damaged the structure, it was sold to a local businessman who then resold its masonry and all of its contents. Then, in 1871, the French author Victor Hugo (1802–1885) lived at Vianden for three months. By 1977, little effort had been made to restore the castle, until the grand duke of Luxembourg turned it over to the state to refurbish it. In the Eisch valley in central Luxembourg, seven castles stretch from the border of Belgium and head northeast along a stream. Each castle is about 10 kilometers (six miles) apart and varies according to their degree of ruin. The last castle on this journey ends at Mersch, where the remains of a Roman villa still showcase mosaics, sculptures, and a large bathing pool.

The destructive force of World War II took its toll on Luxembourg at the Battle of the Bulge. American troops helped liberate Luxembourg during the war, and more than 5,000 are buried at the Luxembourg American Cemetery and Memorial at Hamm. The memorial is maintained by the American Battle Monuments Commission (ABMC). All except one of the graves, that of General George Patton (1885–1945), are identical. The small country's World War II heritage also includes the National Museum of Military History in Diekirch. Near the Ardennes, the site of a major German offensive during the Second World War's latter stages, are several areas and sites renowned for their natural beauty. The Upper-Sûre Nature Park includes a lake for swimming and sailing, and the surrounding region has trails for horseback riding, bicycling, and walking. Cultural sites include pottery studios at Lueresmillen and a cloth factory in Esch-sur-Sûre, where demonstrations are given on traditional cloth-making practices.

Libraries & Museums

Luxembourg has a number of museums, the most famous of which is the Musée d'Art Moderne Grand-Duc Jean (MUDAM). Designed by the famous architect I.M. Pei, the museum houses the collections of many famous modern artists. The former Neumünster Abbey is not only a historical site, but an exhibition space for contemporary artists. There are also museums of natural history, military history, regional culture, as well as three museums focused on the history of transportation. Luxembourg's National Art and History Museum houses a large number of Roman sculptural, artistic, and architectural remnants, along with archaeological finds from the Neolithic and Bronze Age.

The origins of the National Library of Luxembourg can be traced back to the late 18th century. The library, officially established in 1899 in name, serves as the country's legal depository and houses over one million items. The country is also home to 18 public libraries and 36 school libraries (2010 estimate).

Holidays

Public holidays include the Catholic standards like Christmas, Carnival, Easter, Ascension Day, Assumption Day, White Monday, All Saint's Day, and St. Stephen's Day. In addition, Luxembourg recognizes May Day, and National Day on June 23. Luxembourg City Fete takes place in early September.

Luxembourgers celebrate with zeal. Christmas begins with a children's parade in early December when St. Nicholas (Klees'chen) and Black Peter (Hoùseker) first appear in town. Every night afterward, children leave their shoes out on windowsills or in front of bedroom doors to collect the chocolates and other small treats that Klees'chen leaves while performing his pre-Christmas Day rounds. On Christmas Eve, the shoes are traded in for a plate to catch Christmas toys.

National Day Eve and National Day begin with the changing of the guard outside the grand duchy palace. A torch-lit parade through town ends with fireworks. In Luxembourg City, National Day morning is ushered in with a 100-gun salute and a special mass at the Notre Dame cathedral for Luxembourg notables. Similar ceremonies take place in towns all over the country.

Echternach is known for its White Tuesday (also Pentecost Tuesday) dance procession through the historic town.

Youth Culture

Youth culture in Luxembourg is similar to that of other countries in the EU. Music is often a central aspect, and youth have become more Internet and technologically-savvy since the turn of the 21st century. Because of Luxembourg's central location in Europe, it is a frequent tour destination for many popular musical groups. Often, large venues attract audiences from neighboring countries. Though Luxembourg youth do not play organized sports in large numbers, they are getting more involved. While there is no national sport, football (soccer), tennis, and cycling are popular.

The law also provides for free primary and secondary, compulsory education, from the age of six to 15 years of age. As part of the Council of Europe, Luxembourg is one of many European countries that are in the beginning phases of implementing community living education in their curriculums. The goal is to educate students on the ideas behind interpersonal relationships, social cohesion, and the many other aspects involved in living in a community. As recently as 2004, Luxembourg has also participated in an EU initiative to increase youth-exchange programs with other member countries. The initiative was launched as a reaction to what many European communities felt was a noticeable decline in interest by youth to participate in public life.

Luxembourg's declining numbers of adolescent teens and young adults are entering the workforce later than in previous years, as they focus on extending their education. There has also been a downturn in terms of work opportunities and wages for Luxembourgian teens—similar to other European countries—with about 32 percent of 12- to 25-year olds employed in the early 21st century.

SOCIETY

Transportation

The national railway, the Chemins de Fer Luxembourgeois (CFL), runs Luxembourg's extensive railway network. Because the railway is the easiest way to travel, visitors often purchase tickets that allow them to ride a certain distance within a certain amount of time, perhaps for two or three days. Family passes are also available. In urban areas, people often walk because of the cities' compact and accessible nature. In Luxembourg City, the only public transportation is the bus, and people take buses to travel throughout the country. Traffic travels on the right-hand side of the road.

Transportation Infrastructure

The national railway, the Chemins de Fer Luxembourgeois (CFL), runs Luxembourg's extensive railway network. It carries millions of passengers a year, as well as goods. Considering the small size of the country, the 275-kilometer (170-mile) track is considerable. The CFL also hooks into other cross-border railway systems that run into Germany, France, and Belgium, making the railway an easy mode of travel either within Luxembourg or to a neighboring country. The less-extensive highway system is still an important mode of travel. Luxembourg has one major airport, and the national airline is Luxair.

Media & Communications

Media and communications companies are fairly concentrated in Luxembourg, and the country has traditionally operated media services that reach a wide European audience. The country is home to Europe's largest television, radio, and production company, RTL Group, which operates television and radio stations throughout Europe. In addition to RTL, Der Neue Radio (DNR) is another broadcast radio station, and Radio Latina broadcasts in Portuguese. The satellite transmission company Société Européenne des Satellites (SES), which is Europe's largest satellite operator, is also headquartered in Luxembourg, and transmits nearly 2,300 digital and analogue television and radio channels throughout Europe. The government also runs a communications development agency whose goal is to support new media through start-up assistance. As of 2009, the country was home to an estimated 424,000 Internet users.

Diversity and firm readership are said to be hallmarks of the print media in Luxembourg, which is mostly privately owned. About 2e local newspapers exist in the country, written in French, German, English, and two national newspapers, one in French and one in German. Daily newspapers include *Tageblatt, Luxemburger Wort,* and *Lëtzebuerger Journal.* This multilingual diversity is important as nearly two-thirds of the working population in Luxembourg consists of foreigners. Freedom of speech and freedom of the press are guaranteed in the Luxembourg constitution.

SOCIAL DEVELOPMENT

Standard of Living

Luxembourg ranked 21st out of 187 countries on the 2014 United Nations Human Development Index, which measures quality of life and standard of living indicators.

The quality of life enjoyed by Luxembourgers is among the highest in Europe. Average life expectancy is 76 years for men and 83 years for women (2014 estimate). The birth rate is nearly 12 births per 1,000 people, but the death rate is an equally modest 8.53 deaths per 1,000 (2014 estimates).

Water Consumption

Luxembourgers enjoy universal access to both improved sanitation and clean sources of drinking water. Recent reports have suggested that Luxembourg's current water supply will not be sufficient to meet the country's growing population, which is expected to reach approximately 700,000 by the mid-21st century. Water consumption in 2009 is estimated at roughly 200 liters daily per inhabitant.

Education

Primary education in Luxembourg is compulsory from six through 15 years of age. The first six years of schooling are provided by primary schools, after which students may attend a secondary lycée or lycée technique (high school or technical high school).

Those who complete four years of lycée receive a Secondary School Leaving Certificate. Students may alternatively complete a seven-year program (beginning at age 12) at a technical secondary school and earn a Technical Secondary School Diploma in marketing, international trade, secretarial studies, accounting and management, or motion pictures. The University of Luxembourg opened in 2003, and is the grand duchy's only university. Luxembourg's literacy rate was estimated at 100 percent in 2010.

Women's Rights

Women's suffrage has existed in Luxembourg since 1919. Under the law, women and men share the same rights regarding property and family, and are considered equal by the judicial system. In 1995, the government instituted the Ministère de la Promotion Feminine (Ministry for the Advancement of Women) as an independent organization whose goal is the promotion of equal opportunities for women in Luxembourg. Initially, the ministry focused on developing campaigns about violence against women and children and conducting studies on the participation of women in Luxembourg politics.

Regardless of the rights and status of women under the Luxembourgian constitution, there are notable disparities. Though women are legally required to receive the same pay as men, it is estimated that they average about 20 to 30 percent less pay than their male counterparts do for performing the same job. In addition, though women make up about 40 percent of the national workforce, they are mostly concentrated in the health and educational sectors or in the social assistance and domestic service industries. Child-care facilities are also limited in Luxembourg, making it harder for women to work. Luxembourg's government has recently been criticized for continuing the stereotypes of men and women in the educational system. In particular, discriminatory attitudes and images tend to persist regarding a women's traditional role as a caretaker in society. Even though the government supports parental leave for both genders, women are still considered the primary caretaker of the family.

While Luxembourg law prohibits domestic violence against women, such abuse does occur. Over 300 cases were reported of violence against women in 2007. Domestic violence is gender neutral in the country, however, and police are legally responsible for pursuing cases to prevent victims from dropping charges in instances of intimidation.

Though divorce is legal, Luxembourgers must wait a set period of time before remarrying, creating inequalities in the institution of marriage. The trafficking of women and girls into Luxembourg from Romania and Bulgaria has also been reported in recent years, with up to eleven people convicted in 2007. The United Nations Convention on the Elimination of All Forms of Discrimination against Women (CEDAW) in 2008 recommended that Luxembourg pass an all-inclusive anti-trafficking bill to help identify and investigate such matters, as the current law excludes some aspects of human trafficking.

After parliamentary elections were held in 2013, women only held 28 percent of the seats in the national parliaments. Additionally, as of 2009, of the 15 cabinet members, only three are women, though nearly half of the Supreme Court's 32 members are women. Colette Flesch (1937–) became the first female mayor of Luxembourg in 1970, and she held that office until 1980. In the 1980s, Flesch served in national positions as minister of foreign affairs, minister of economy, and minister of justice. Lydie Polfer (1952–) served as deputy prime minister from 1999 to 2004, and has served as a member of the EP.

Health Care

Luxembourg's health care system begins with compulsory health insurance. Based on rates set by the Union of Sickness Funds, Luxembourgers pay premiums into insurance funds managed by the USC and nine other professionally-based funds.

The statutory insurance plan pays for "essential" medical care, and is subsidized by taxes collected by the government. Approximately three-quarters of Luxembourgers buy an additional private health insurance policy to pay for medical services not covered under the public insurance plan. About one percent of Luxembourg's residents are exempted from the public insurance plan. Most of these residents are civil servants or citizens of other European countries who receive health care under different plans.

Luxembourg has fourteen acute care hospitals, including one for-profit maternity care center. Half of the remaining hospitals are run by non-government, not-for-profit organizations like churches. Luxembourg's Ministry of Health provides preventative and acute care through a network of public services, private health care providers, and not-for-profit organizations. Patients are eligible for payment of medical fees regardless of provider or level of care. Although hospitals negotiate individually with the Ministry of Health for fee schedules, individual care providers are paid according to a comprehensive schedule of fees published by the Ministry.

GOVERNMENT

Structure

Luxembourg lost half of its territory to Belgium in 1830, when Belgium broke from the Netherlands, splitting Luxembourg in the process. In response, the grand duchy demanded its autonomy from the Netherlands, gaining official recognition in the 1867 Treaty of London.

The country was occupied by Nazi Germany during World War II, but reemerged as an independent nation in 1948. Surrendering its pre-war neutral nation status, Luxembourg became a central force in the creation of new political and economic alliances, including NATO, the United Nations, and Benelux (an economic union with Belgium and the Netherlands).

Since helping to found the predecessor organization to the European Commonwealth (now the European Union), Luxembourg has served as a driving force in EU governing organizations and policy decisions.

Luxembourg is a constitutional monarchy. Divided into the three administrative districts of Diekirch, Grevenmacher, and Luxembourg, the country recognizes the hereditary Grand Duke as its chief of state.

Legislative functions are performed by the Chambre des Deputes (Chamber of Deputies), which has 60 members chosen by popular election to five-year terms. The Grand Duke customarily appoints the leader of the majority political party in the Chamber of Deputies, or the coalition leader in certain instances, to the post of Prime Minister. In turn, the Prime Minister selects a cabinet of ministers, who are formally appointed by the Grand Duke.

The Chamber of Deputies is also served by a Council of State, whose twenty-one members are chosen by the Prime Minister and appointed by the Grand Duke.

Political Parties

Luxembourg has a multi-party system of government. The country's three major parties are the Christian Social People's Party (CSV), the Luxembourg Socialist Workers' Party (LSAP), and the Democratic Party. Other parties include The Greens, the Alternative Democratic Reform Party (ADR), and the Communist Party (KPL).

Local Government

Local government in Luxembourg is organized into 118 communes. Members of communal councils are elected to six-year terms by popular vote. Each commune is administered by a mayor or municipal council that is appointed by the communal council.

Judicial System

Luxembourg's court system is divided into two separate systems: the judicial order and the administrative order. The judicial order is organized into magistrate courts, district courts, and the Supreme Court of Justice. The country's Supreme Court is not a single entity, but is organized into two courts: the Court of Cassation and the Court of Appeals. The administrative order is comprised of the administrative tribunal and the administrative courts. The highest court in Luxembourg is the Constitutional Court, which is comprised of nine judges.

Taxation

Citizens of Luxembourg are charged an income tax on their worldwide income, while non-citizens are charged an income tax on the income they earn in the country. Income tax rates are organized into different classes related to the amount on income earned. Employees and employers in Luxembourg contribute to the country's social security system. Corporations operating in the country pay an income tax, municipal business tax on profits, a value-added tax (VAT), inheritance tax, and a wealth tax. As of 2010, the top income tax rate is 39 percent, while the top corporate rate is approximately 22 percent.

Armed Forces

Luxembourg maintains an all-voluntary army, the Luxembourg Army, with no naval—the country is landlocked—or air force branches. As of 2010, ongoing missions include participation in KFOR (Kosovo Force), ISAF (International Security Assistance Force in Afghanistan), Operation Althea (a European Union mission in Bosnia and Herzegovina), and EUSEC CONGO (Mission of the European Union in reforming the security sector in Democratic Republic of Congo). Seventeen is the minimum age for voluntary military service, though soldiers under the age of eighteen are not deployed.

Foreign Policy

Because of Luxembourg's strategic location in Western Europe, it has historically been of great interest to foreign powers, and its political history has been characterized and shaped by cooperation. In particular, Luxembourg has been integral in the movement toward European integration, and began this process in 1921 when the grand duchy formed the Belgium-Luxembourg Economic Union (BLEU). The goal of BLEU was the development of a currency that could be used in both countries along with common business customs. Since that time, Luxembourg has been a founding member of both the EU and the European Economic Community (EEC), the latter transformed into one of the three pillars of the EU in 1993.

As a centrally located country within the EU, Luxembourg is the seat of some prominent EU organizations, including the European Court of Justice (ECJ), the European Investment Bank (EIB), the secretariat, or administrative body, of the European Parliament (EP), and the European Court of Auditors. Luxembourg has also been a member of the Benelux Economic Union. Since 1958, this economic union—which includes the neighboring countries of Belgium, the Netherlands, and Luxembourg—has supported the free exchange of goods, services, workers, and capital among their countries. Luxembourg also holds membership in the Organization for Security and Cooperation in Europe (OSCE) and the Organization for Economic Cooperation and Development (OECD).

The foreign policy of Luxembourg is also pro-Western, and the small country is a strong ally of the United States. As a member of the North Atlantic Treaty Organization (NATO), which was formed following World War II to provide military assistance to member countries in need of collective defense, Luxembourg has participated in missions throughout Africa and in the war in Afghanistan that began in 2001. In addition to its involvement with NATO, Luxembourg has also contributed financial support for the Gulf War in 1991 and humanitarian support during the 2003 U.S.'s invasion of Iraq. In Eastern Europe, Luxembourg sent civilian troops to the war in Kosovo, supplies to Albania, and participated in international peacekeeping efforts in Rwanda.

As a member of both the EU and NATO, Luxembourg also participates in Eurocorps, the army corps consisting of individuals from several EU and NATO member countries.

Human Rights Profile

International human rights law insists that states respect civil and political rights, and also promote an individual's economic, social and cultural rights. The United Nations Universal Declaration on Human Rights (UDHR) is recognized as the standard for international human rights. Its authors sought the counsel of the world's great thinkers, philosophers, and religious leaders, and were careful to create a document that reflects the core values shared by every world culture. (To read this document or view the articles relating to cultural human rights, visit: http://www.udhr.org/UDHR/default.htm.)

Luxembourg is a constitutional monarchy, whose laws to protect basic human rights are in accord with international human rights laws. As set in their constitution, all Luxembourgers are entitled to basic rights regardless of race, ethnicity, language, religion, gender, or birth status. However, at least fourteen incidents of racial discrimination, some including violence, occurred against people in Luxembourg in 2008. Based on an earlier review and recommendation by the European Commission against Racism and Intolerance (ECRI), Luxembourg has yet to implement a provision that makes hate crime a criminal offense. However, though the law prohibits human trafficking, it has been known to exist in Luxembourg in recent years, especially with women and young girls, many of whom are brought from Bulgaria and Romania.

Luxembourgers are guaranteed the right to freedom of speech and the press, including the Internet. The independent press in Luxembourg is unrestricted and shares a fairly expansive array of views. Censorship is prohibited, and writers and publishers are free to write and publish without fear of persecution. People in Luxembourg also enjoy the right to peaceful assembly and association. While they enjoy freedom of religion, the government does financially support some churches and religious facilities that are sectarian in nature.

The Luxembourg constitution prohibits arbitrary arrest and detention, as well as torture and cruel punishment, exile, and detention. According to the constitution, suspects have the right to an attorney, provided by the government if necessary. People within the country also are afforded numerous additional protections that help ensure a safe and fair work and living environment. For example, Luxembourgers have the freedom to join and form trade unions, and the law provides for social security and government healthcare. Luxembourg law also prohibits discrimination against persons with disabilities, and the government is actively engaged in helping persons with disabilities find employment. In fact, businesses that employ at least twenty-five people must also hire persons with disabilities to fulfill a legal quota. However, there have been occasions when the law has not been well enforced.

ECONOMY

Overview of the Economy

Luxembourg boasts one of the world's highest per capita gross domestic product (GDP); estimated at more than $92,400 (USD) in 2014. The duchy also enjoys low inflation and a low unemployment rate. Luxembourg has also greatly benefited from its status as an EU administrative center. Several major offices of the EU are headquartered there, including the European Investment Bank (EIB) and the European Court of Justice (ECJ).

Industry

Agriculture and iron and steel remain important industries in Luxembourg, though the country no longer extracts iron ore. In addition, Luxembourg manufactures plastic and rubber, chemicals, and mechanical and electrical equipment.

Banking and insurance have become modern-day mainstays of Luxembourg's national economy. Relaxed banking and tax regulations lure investors from throughout Europe, including those for whom financial transactions are kept secretive. Tourism is also an important industry for the scenic, centrally located duchy.

Labor

According to 2009 estimates, over half of Luxembourg's work force is cross-border foreign workers, mainly from Germany, France, and Belgium. In all, the labor force numbers just over 200,000, with the bulk—an estimated 80 percent—concentrated in the services sector. The unemployment rate was reported as 7.1 percent in 2014.

Energy/Power/Natural Resources

Historically, Luxembourg's most important natural resources are its iron ore deposits and its arable land. For most of its history as a modern nation, the duchy's primary source of revenue was iron ore and the industries that came with it. Today, the iron mines are closed and the metal is no longer being extracted.

The vast majority of Luxembourg's arable land is in the southern third of the country. Although only about six percent of Luxembourgers are employed in agriculture, farms still account for almost 24 percent of the country's territory.

Fishing

Fishing in Luxembourg is mostly recreational, and restricted to the landlocked nation's estuaries and rivers (and along the border, where a separate fishing license is required), though some limited species, such as eel, are caught for commercial purposes. Commercial fishing is mainly for domestic consumption.

Forestry

Forestry accounts for a miniscule percentage of Luxembourg's gross domestic product (GDP).

Mining/Metals

Luxembourg processes a small amount of industrial minerals for domestic use. In addition, it is a significant processing center and information hub of the Belgian mining industry, which exports iron and steel.

Agriculture

Luxembourg's chief agricultural products include barley, oats, potatoes, wheat, fruits, and cheeses. The country also produces livestock. Wine and wine grape crops are central to the economy of the Moselle region.

Animal Husbandry

Luxembourg is not a major agricultural producer. Approximately 3 percent of the country's work force are employed in agriculture and they majority of that number are involved in livestock harvesting and dairy farming for domestic consumption.

Tourism

Luxembourg has a thriving tourist industry based on its picturesque landscapes, easy accessibility, multilingual population, and medieval architectural treasures. Known as the "Green Heart of Europe," the duchy boasts more than 100 medieval castles throughout the countryside, and an extensive railway and highway network. Only a short high-speed ride from Paris, Brussels, Trier, and Antwerp, it has become a favorite weekend getaway destination for many Western European tourists.

Kathryn Bundy, Amy Witherbee, Pilar Quezzaire

DO YOU KNOW?

- Local legend holds that a mermaid named Mélusina lives in the river Alzette. According to myth, Mélusina was the wife of Count Seigfried, the founder of Luxembourg.

- One of Luxembourg City's historical nicknames is the "Gibraltar of the North" because of the strength of its fortress. Gibraltar was considered the strongest fortress in Europe; Luxembourg's fortress was considered to be a close second.

Bibliography

Andrew Reid. *Luxembourg: The Clog-Shaped Duchy: A Chronological History of Luxembourg from the Celts to the Present Day.* Bloomington, IN: Authorhouse, 2005.

Herman Van Berjeijk and Otakar Macel. *Architectural Guide: Netherlands, Belgium, Luxembourg.* New York: Birkhäuser, 1998.

Jul Christopher. *Luxembourg.* Santa Barbara, CA: Clio Press, 1997.

Mark Elliot. *Belgium and Luxembourg.* Oakland, CA: Lonely Planet, 2013.

Patricia Sheehan and Sakina Dhilawala. *Luxembourg (Cultures of the World).* New York: Benchmark, 2007.

Peter Clark. *Luxembourg.* New York: Routledge, 1994.

Pit Peporte, et al. *Inventing Luxembourg: Representations of the Past, Space, and Language from the Nineteenth to the Twenty-First Century.* Boston: Brill, 2010.

Thomas M. Eccardt. *Secrets of the Seven Smallest States of Europe: Andorra, Liechtenstein, Luxembourg, Malta, Monaco, San Marino, and Vatican City.* New York: Hippocrene Books, 2005. London: Survival Books, 2001.

Works Cited

"Art and Culture in Luxembourg." *Luxembourg Presidency of the Council of the European Union.* http://www.eu2005.lu/en/savoir_lux/culture/culture_mouvement/index.php#5.

"A Short History of the Hurdy-Gurdy." http://www.hurdy-gurdy.org.uk/history.htm.

"Background Note: Luxembourg." http://www.state.gov/r/pa/ei/bgn/3182.htm.

"Centre national de litérature Mersch." http://www.cnl.public.lu/.

"Cities and Agglomerations in Luxembourg." http://www.citypopulation.de/Luxemburg.html.

"Customs of Luxembourg." http://encarta.msn.com/sidebar_631522225/customs_of_luxembourg.html.

"Hate Crime Report Card—Luxembourg." http://www.humanrightsfirst.org/discrimination/pages.aspx?id=123.

"KulturFabrik." http://www.kulturfabrik.sk/en_KF.htm.

"Luxembourg: Country Reports on Human Rights Practices–2006." http://www.state.gov/g/drl/rls/hrrpt/2006/78825.htm.

"Luxembourg in a Nutshell." http://www.luxembourg.co.uk/nutshell.html.

"Luxembourg and Greater Region, European Capital of Culture 2007—Final Report." http://www.eukn.org/luxembourg/themes/Urban_Policy/Economy_knowledge_and_employment/Urban_economy/Specific_sectors/Tourism__recreation_and_culture/European-Capital-of-Culture-2007_1154.html.

"Luxembourg." *Council of Europe: Education.* http://www.coe.int/t/dg4/education/edc/Country_profiles/Profile_LUXEMBOURG270508_en.asp.

"Luxembourg—Language, Culture, Customs and Etiquette." *Kwintessential Cross Cultural Solutions.* http://www.kwintessential.co.uk/resources/global-etiquette/luxembourg.html.

"Luxembourg Traditional Architecture in the United States." http://www.institutgrandducal.lu/Joomla/index.php?option=com_content&task=view&id=129&Itemid=240. Institut Grand-Ducal.

"Nature Parks of Luxembourg." http://www.walkingworld.com/home/index.asp?id=37&nid=321.

"2008 Country Reports on Human Rights Practices—Luxembourg." *UNHCR: The UN Refugee Agency.* http://www.unhcr.org/refworld/country,LUX,4562d8b62,47d92c43c,0.html.

"Population par subdivision territoriale au 1ᵉʳ janvier 2001–2008." STATEC Luxembourg. http://www.statistiques.public.lu/stat/TableViewer/tableView.aspx?ReportId=470&IF_Language=fra&MainTheme=2&FldrName=1.

"Vianden Castle." http://www.castle-vianden.lu/english/index.html.

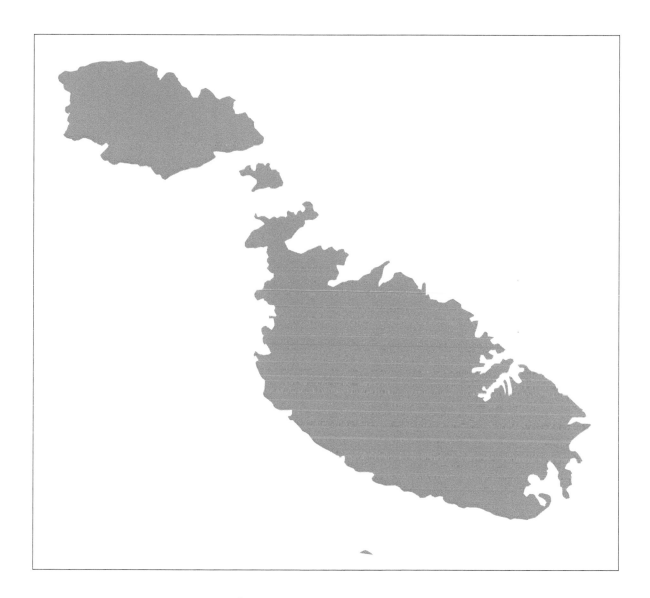

MALTA

Introduction

The Republic of Malta is an archipelago of five islands located in the southern Mediterranean Sea. Malta has experienced a dynamic history of invasions and influences, from the ancient Phoenicians and Romans to the Normans, French, and British. As a result, it carries a rich cultural heritage. This is especially evident in the islands' architecture, built from the native stone.

During the Second World War, the islands were the center of a battle for North Africa. A crippling siege, worse than London' Blitz, devastated the cities and the population, and left them in the grip of starvation, but not defeated. For its heroism, the entire population of Malta was decorated with Britain's highest civilian honor, the George Cross.

Malta was granted full independence from Britain in 1974. The republic has established itself as a center for shipping, and in recent decades tourism has become its most important mainstay.

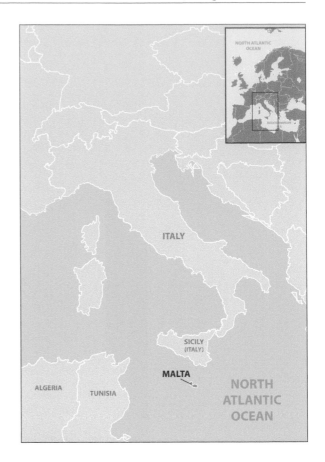

GENERAL INFORMATION

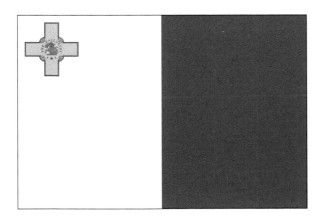

Official Language: Maltese and English
Population: 412,655 (2014 estimate)
Currency: Euro

Coins: The Euro is available in 1, 2, 5, 10, 20 and 50 cent coins, with a 1 and 2 Euro coin also available.
Land Area: 316 square kilometers (122 square miles)
Water Area: 2,796 square kilometers (1,079 square miles)
National Anthem: "L-Innu Malti" ("Maltese Hymn")
Capital: Valletta
Time Zone: GMT +1 (Summer: GMT +2)
Flag Description: The flag of Malta is half white, half red. There is a George Cross in the flag's upper right-hand corner

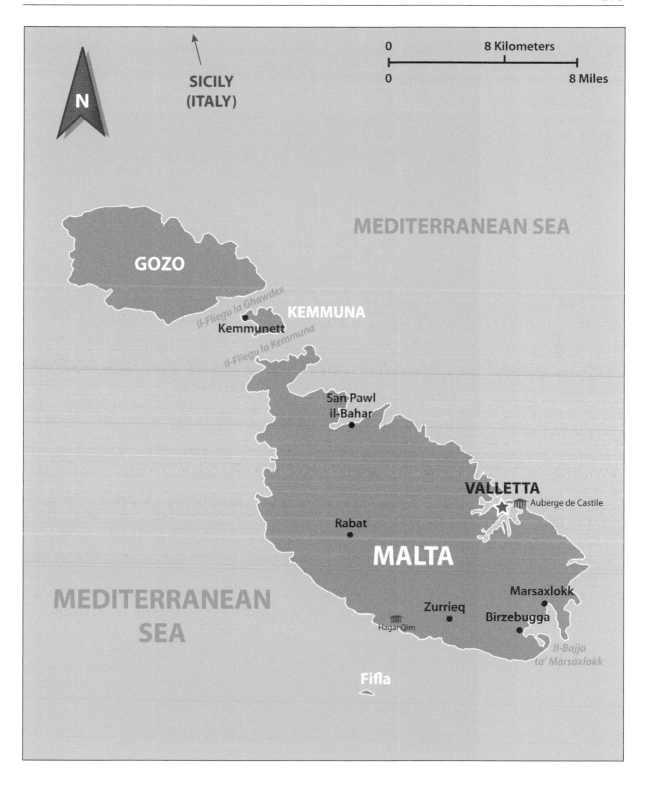

Principal Cities by Population (2012):

- Birkirkara (20,552)
- Mosta (19,644)
- Qormi (15,300)
- Zabbar (14,546)
- Sliema (13,733) (2009 estimate)
- San Pawl Il-Bahar (13,412) (2007 estimate)
- San Gwann [Msierah] (12,737) (2007 estimate)
- Naxxar (13,405)
- Rabat (11,473) (2007 estimate)
- Fgura (11,429) (2007 estimate)
- Valletta (5,465)

Population

Malta's population is showing only slight growth and has a median age of 42 years. Life expectancy is comparable to other European countries: 77 years for men and 82 years for women.

Since the German siege by sea and aerial bombings of Valletta during World War II, the population of the city has decreased to about a third of its peak numbers. However, the city remains the political and commercial hub of the island.

Population density is 1,282 persons per square kilometer (3,339 per square mile), but 95 percent of the population is concentrated in urban centers. The largest city, located on the island of Malta, is Birkirkara, with a population of 20,552. The capital and shipping center of Valletta has a population of only 5,465, but this figure does not include the city's suburbs. Marsaxlokk is also a major port. Rabat is the only sizable settlement on the island of Gozo.

The population of Malta is almost totally homogenous. Maltese people are a mixture of several ethnic groups from the Mediterranean region.

Languages

Both Standard Maltese and English are the country's official languages: the former being used in daily life, government, and the media, the latter often being the language of instruction. Italian is also widely spoken.

Maltese is a Semitic language, written in a modified Latin alphabet, and derived from Maghrebi Arabic. Over the centuries, colonizers also added to this many loanwords from Romance languages and the Sicilian dialect. Consequently, Standard Maltese has several dialects, most significantly the dialect spoken on the island of Gozo.

Native People & Ethnic Groups

Malta's position strategic position has attracted settlers and invaders from throughout the Mediterranean region. The archipelago was first settled by immigrants from Sicily around 4000 BCE. As Phoenicians, Greeks, Romans, and Arabs arrived, the typical character was gradually modified. The modern Maltese people and their culture reflect these many historical influences.

Religions

The majority (98 percent) of the population professes Roman Catholicism. The Maltese trace their conversion to Christianity to the first century, when Saint Paul was shipwrecked on the main island. Scholars, however, have not been able to substantiate the widely accepted version of events. In any case, Catholic traditions permeate the culture and have withstood periods of Byzantine and Muslim conquest.

Climate

Malta experiences a typical Mediterranean climate, with warm summers and temperate winters. Hot sirocco winds from Africa prevail throughout the summer, with temperatures averaging 32° Celsius (90° Fahrenheit). July and August are the hottest months, and January is the coldest. In the winter, the average temperature is 14° Celsius (57° Fahrenheit).

Precipitation occurs in the form of rain. It falls most heavily between November and February and averages 56 centimeters (22 inches) annually, though some years are considerably drier. Malta experiences at least 300 days of sunshine a year.

The city of Valletta has a Mediterranean climate that consistently ranks it as one of the best retirement locations in European travel magazines. Winters are usually mild, with temperatures rarely falling below 10° Celsius (50° Fahrenheit). Summers are sunny and hot, with temperatures rising to an average of 30° Celsius (86° Fahrenheit), but daily highs often climb higher. Average annual rainfall is only 600 millimeters (24 inches). A dry season usually occurs in the summer months.

ENVIRONMENT & GEOGRAPHY

The Maltese archipelago is located in the deep southern Mediterranean Sea. It's an isolated location of stark beauty and blue-green waters, approximately 100 kilometers (62 miles) from Sicily and 290 kilometers (180 miles) from the coasts of Tunisia and Libya in North Africa. The limestone islands are not lush, and have a flat, rugged terrain, and low elevations. Deep, narrow straits separate the three main islands, and the main island of Malta offers naturally deep water harbors that lend themselves to shipping, cruise ship tourism, and yachting.

Topography
Malta consists of a string of five islands; only three of them (Malta, Comino, and Gozo) are inhabited; the other two, Kemmunett and Filfa, are uninhabited.

Malta is the largest island, covering 246 square kilometers (95 square miles). Its coastline measures 197 kilometers (122 miles) and has many natural harbors. Some stretches are characterized by high cliffs, others by stony beaches. Ta'Dmejrek is the country's highest point at 239 meters (784 feet). It rises in the southwestern portion of the island in the Bingemma Hills. Gozo, the second largest island, has fewer natural harbors but otherwise resembles the island of Malta.

The country's capital, Valletta, is situated at the end of the long narrow Scibberas peninsula, flanked on either side by the two natural deep-water harbors of Marsamxett and the Grand Harbour. Valletta is one of the smallest capitals in the World in terms of land area, with the entire city compromising no more than .55 square kilometers (.31 square miles). The city is built on the side of Mount Scibberas, which rises up from the harbor at sea level to a height of 17 meters (51 feet).

Plants & Animals
Malta's dry, relatively barren landscape does not provide habitats for extensive plant and animal life. It is thought that the islands were, for the most part, deforested in ancient times. Today, there are small stands of Aleppo pine, buskett, holm oak, olive, willow, poplar, elm, laurel, and carob trees. Shrubs and grasses are predominant as undergrowth and in areas where the land has been degraded by overgrazing or the topsoil is of poor quality.

Insects, reptiles, a few migrating birds, and several types of shrew live on the islands. In addition, the waters surrounding the islands are rich in marine life.

CUSTOMS & COURTESIES

Greetings
The Maltese language is Semitic, chiefly Arabic. It is written in the Roman alphabet, with words and phrases taken from Italian, Spanish, English, Greek, and some French. The official languages in Malta are Maltese and English, and many also speak Italian. Customary greeting phrases include "Merhba" ("Hello") and "Bongiu" ("Good morning").

Kisses may be exchanged upon greeting and saying goodbye between women, and sometimes between women and men, by touching cheek to cheek. Strangers might kiss if they're being introduced by a mutual friend; in large groups an extended hand will suffice as a greeting. Maltese men usually greet with a hug or a handshake. The use of honorific titles is customary, followed by the last name. Maltese may give a warm, friendly smile at an initial interaction; however, both personal and professional relationships may come across to them as a hustle if proper acquaintance has not developed over time.

Gestures & Etiquette

In Malta, etiquette can depend on class, age, and social associations. Those of higher social rank tend to be more aloof and proper, where as those of the middle and lower classes can be dramatically more affectionate and expressive. The Maltese are usually helpful and hospitable, but can be wary of strangers and closed off to anything more than superficial relations with foreigners. Religion and superstition are important components to traditional society. This includes superstitions linked to the "evil eye," a curse, and many traditional Maltese still practice certain sacraments to ward off bad luck.

Upholding one's family name and maintaining or saving face is important in Maltese society. One famous Maltese proverb states "Who I see you with is who I see you as." Dress is reserved, less so with the young, but with the exception of a beach holiday, they generally refrain from very short skirts and shorts. Revealing styles of clothing are forbidden in churches.

Eating/Meals

Malta's cuisine is a rich blend of fresh, local ingredients influenced by its Greek, Roman, Arab, French, Spanish, Jewish, and English past, and its location in the Mediterranean Sea. Maltese cooking involves a great deal of fish, vegetables, and pork, as well as garlic and olive oil to add flavor to its signature dishes.

There are three traditional meals a day in Malta. Breakfast is simple and may consist of fresh fruits, juices, breads, and coffee or cappuccino. Large pasta dishes prepared with unique twists on signature Italian and Sicilian recipes, accompanied with a green salad and fresh-baked bread, are usually enjoyed during lunch. The Maltese traditionally practice afternoon breaks after their meal. Shop owners will close their stores and the island people rest until later in the day when the sun is less penetrating (though this practice is waning in recent years). Dinner in Malta is often eaten late in the evening as in the classic Mediterranean tradition, and may include pasta, meat, fish, salad, soup, and a desert.

Wine is a very important component of every Maltese meal. Due to Malta's year round sunny climate and warm weather, several varieties of wine grapes are grown in abundance. Community farmers bottle and sell a variety of homemade wines to locals, tourists, and international distributors alike.

Visiting

In Malta, friends and family enjoy socializing in bars or outdoor cafés in the early evening. These types of gatherings are often spontaneous, and generally preferred to being inside the family home. Maltese can also be noticeably reserved in their initial taking to strangers. Thus, home dinner parties are considered special, non-routine occasions that are usually reserved for holidays, the birth of a child, or weddings.

If an invitation is extended to visit a Maltese home, it is important visitors dress modestly and have a well-groomed appearance. They should also bring a gift of wine, some chocolates, or fresh picked flowers as a token of appreciation for the host or hostess.

Like most Mediterranean cultures, food and drink are an essential aspect of social situations. The typical Maltese home does not have a separate dining area for entertaining guests, and for that reason food is customarily enjoyed around a table set inside the kitchen where it was prepared. The Maltese take pride in their hearty portions, and it is typical for hosts to gossip about their guests' appetite. Conversations around a dinning table, formal or informal, can last long hours into the night, and are often accompanied with a bottle of local wine and talk of politics.

LIFESTYLE

Family

Marriage is an opportunity for two families to establish ties, strengthen economic status, and provide a support network for offspring. Traditionally, Maltese men play the dominant role within the family unit while women are expected to be good housewives and devoted mothers. It is because of this that many Maltese tend to foster closer relationships with the maternal side of the family. Although it is preferred to establish a separate living situation all together, when necessary it is more common for a husband, wife, and newborn to live with the woman's side of the family. A wife's mother, sisters, and nieces often provide additional support in caring for children and tending to household responsibilities.

Housing

Most Maltese homes are constructed out of large limestone rock drawn from plentiful quarries found on the island. Because they weather rapidly in Malta's salty air, most modern buildings are coated by protective plasters which give a rustic appearance to the exteriors. Often, Maltese homes are attached to each other in rows situated close to sidewalks or streets, and are not identified by number, but by family name. This close proximity causes many homeowners to install only a few windows and doors, and to enclose balconies with metal shutters to facilitate privacy and security.

Because water is scarce, Maltese homes are flat-roofed to collect rainwater. This water may be later distilled and used for drinking or bathing. Lack of water also inhibits the amount of green space residents have available for gardens and recreation. In both urban and rural areas, people tend to live in neighborhoods surrounding a church where manicured lawns are preserved for public use. Exposed wooden beams, colored floor tiles, and high ceilings are common and decorative interior fixtures in many homes.

Food

Primarily Italian in nature, Maltese cuisine also borrows from the culinary traditions of North Africa and the Eastern Mediterranean. Over the centuries, all of these distinctive flavors have merged into a unique national cuisine. Pasta features prominently, and is used with vegetables, meat, cheese, and rice. Fish is also a staple in the Maltese diet. Bass, stone fish, groupers, red mullet, swordfish, tuna, and lampuka (dolphin fish) are commonly fried, marinated, baked, or grilled in many traditional dishes. Dishes that are stewed and stuffed are also common, and fresh foods are primary ingredients.

Soppa ta'l-armla (widow's soup), made from fresh vegetables set in a thick tomato stock, and minestra (thick vegetable soup), made from various types of greens and meats, are traditional starters to most meals. It is also customary to have a loaf of bread set on the table. Hobz bizzejt are round crusty hunks of bread dipped in olive oil, onto which sun-dried tomatoes, capers, olives, garlic, and basil are added as garnish. Pastitsi is one of the most popular dishes, and is prepared with flaky dough similar to Greek filo. A ricotta cheese or meat mixture seasoned with onion, tomato paste, and peas is wrapped inside the dough and baked in an oven with a tomato sauce and mozzarella. Imquarrun fil forn (baked macaroni) is another popular meal smothered with a sauce of ground beef, tomato, and garlic. Stuffed artichoke and eggplant are also common meals.

Foods for holidays or festivals are prepared with great time and attention to flavor. The fenkata is a feast made of rabbit marinated for twelve hours in bay leaves and wine. It's usually accompanied by fresh pasta, potatoes, and salad. Tenderized lamb is eaten at Easter and lampuki pie is a pastry covered fish casserole containing spinach, cauliflower, chestnuts, and sultanas (seedless grapes) eaten only when in season. For dessert, tat-tork are delicious deep-fried pastries stuffed with dates, anisette, chopped nuts, orange rind, and lemon rind. These are traditionally found in most Maltese homes during wedding or baptism celebrations. Cylinder-shaped cannoli shells stuffed with sweet cream, ricotta cheese, pieces of chocolate, and fruit preserves are also popular.

Life's Milestones

Malta is mostly (98 percent) Roman Catholic, and social traditions are largely rooted in the Catholic faith. As such, baptism remains an important milestone. At this time close family members are chosen to act as parrina (godmother) and parrinu (godfather) to ensure the child is raised in the Catholic faith. First communions occur at age six and confirmations at 10 years. At this time, a third parrina or parrinu, always the same gender as the child, is appointed to serve as a life long mentor and confidant. Godparents may also be responsible for financially supporting educational costs or marriage celebrations.

For women, a Maltese bridal shower is a sophisticated affair held inside a hall or banquet room with a multi-course meal and desert table. The typical Roman Catholic wedding follows a mass sermon. The bride is accompanied by several bridesmaids while the groom has one best man at his side.

By Maltese law, a woman is legally obligated to obey her husband, occupy residency where he wishes or where his profession requires, and take his last name. Children also inherit the father's surname, and in many cases the oldest male child will receive his first name as well. Until 2011, when a referendum led to the law being changed, Malta was the only European nation where divorce was not legally recognized.

Purchasing graves is an important decision many Maltese make in old age, or upon the death of a family member. Though common graves are widespread, a family grave, with space to fit four or five coffins, is considered more honorable.

CULTURAL HISTORY

Art
In the 17th century, European painters, sculptors, and architects sought to portray intensity, texture, sensory images, detail, and individualism in the innovative baroque style. Michelangelo Merisi da Caravaggio (1571–1610), popularly known as Caravaggio, was an Italian painter whose shadow techniques became characteristic of baroque painting throughout Rome. Impulsive acts of violence, including murder, eventually made him flee Italy for Malta in 1607, where he was received as a renowned artist. There he was able to complete several important works, the most significant

being *The Beheading of Saint John the Baptist* (1608) for the cathedral in Valletta, considered one of the masterpieces of baroque painting.

Caravaggio's influence on Maltese art was substantial, though brief. Among his Maltese followers, Giulio Cassarino (1588–1637) and Stefano Erardi (1620–1716) are the most noteworthy. The work of these two artists may be seen in numerous parish churches throughout Malta today. Baroque did not have a substantial impact in Malta until the later half of the 17th century, when Italian artist Mattia Preti (1613–1699) settled on the island. He was made a Knight of Grace in The Order of St. John and granted permission to alter the interior of St. John's Co-Cathedral in Valletta with a series of huge religious baroque-style paintings.

The archipelago's limestone megalithic temples are considered some of the oldest standing stone structures in the world, dating from 4000 to 2500 BCE. Little is known about the culture that built them except that it was probably agrarian in nature and most likely derived from Sicily. The buildings were rediscovered and restored by archaeologists in the nineteenth century. Typical architectural elements of these unearthed buildings include five semicircular rooms that connect at the center, an open dome, and horizontal arches. Some of the oldest examples of Maltese pottery can be found in these ancient chambers as well.

Centuries after Malta's first inhabitants arrived, the Roman occupation introduced more advanced architectural structures, as well as architectural elements such as decorative mosaic floors, marble columns, and classic statues. After the Romans, Malta was occupied by Sicilian Arabs then living in Tunisia. The city of Mdina, reconstructed during this period, architecturally resembles towns found in North Africa. Similar to other European cultures, Malta featured a range of architectural influences throughout the medieval and modern age, ranging from Romanesque and Gothic, to rococo and neoclassical. Under the Knights of St. John (the Order of St. John of Jerusalem, or Knights Hospitaller), Malta witnessed the building of churches, palaces, and fortifications in the baroque style.

Malta is also known for its military architecture. As evident from its multicultural past, the Maltese islands are situated in a position of vulnerability in the Mediterranean, and various conquerors have had to erect systems of fortification to protect their cities. Numerous fortresses that remain today were built by the Order of St. John of Jerusalem in the sixteenth century, who used the island's natural stone to extend the surrounding cliffs to create a barrier of defense. The Fortress of St. Elmo, in particular, was built to protect against the Ottoman Empire (1299–1923 CE).

Dance

Malta's traditional dances are performed by women wearing what is considered the country's national costume—a headdress 122 centimeters (four feet wide) known as the ghonella. The ghonella covers the head and body, but displays the face prominently. Introduced to Malta in 1227 by Sicilian nuns, country and noble women alike adopted the ghonella, varying only in the material used (cotton or silk, black or white). The black cotton costume was used for everyday wear, while the white silk costume was typically worn by noble women for their weddings.

One lively Maltese dance, presented by women to welcome autumn and the coming of the rains to the island, is named and performed in honor of the ghonella. Another folkdance performed by men and women wearing the ghonella is an interpretive routine called miltija, which describes the victory of the Maltese over the Turks in 1565. In addition, many traditional dances are carried out with props that have derived from various cultures that once resided on the islands. One in particular uses a lit candle or a lantern in commemoration of the Christian holiday Good Friday. Another, which is usually performed at the grand baroque palaces in Valletta, implements Spain's use of the fan.

Music

Ghana (għannej) is a form of traditional Maltese folk music played on acoustic guitar, sometimes a bagpipe and drum, with singers known as ghannejja. There are three main types of Ghana music: fil-għoli, tal-fatt, and spirtu pront. In fil-għoli, men sing in extremely high vocal registers mimicking the singing style of Maltese women. Tal-fatt ballads recount well-known legends, community events, or humorous folktales. Spirtu pront, the most common form of Ghana, involves two or more singers debating a topic in friendly, melodious tones.

Ghana has been with the Maltese nation for centuries, but it was initially shunned by the upper classes for its association with peasant culture. Today, Ghana has progressed from being music of the poor to a more universal form of entertainment. The top Ghana singers in Malta are celebrities regularly heard on the radio and seen on television programs. They also visit countries like Canada, England, France, and Australia to perform in concert halls and special events. Two of the most popular singers of Maltese folk music were Fredu Abela (1944–2003) and Frans Baldacchino (1943–2006), known as il-Budaj.

CULTURE

Arts & Entertainment

Though it is a small country, Malta offers an array of sites and activities and a sunny, mild climate. The historic megalithic structures and ruins as well as numerous well preserved towns and villages dating from the medieval era abound. Popular activities on and around the islands include scuba diving, hiking, and yachting.

Malta has a rich cultural heritage; this is especially evident in the islands' architecture. Secular and sacred structures, ancient and medieval, were constructed from the native stone, giving the towns and villages of the island a unified look, and demonstrating considerable skill in stone dressing.

Malta has developed a formidable literary canon, though Maltese did not become a widespread literary language until the 19th century. It is based on European literary forms and strongly influenced by Italian literature. Novelists and playwrights are popular, but poets are considered to have created the purest expressions of Maltese language and culture. Francis Ebejer (1925–1993) and poets Victor Fenech and Achille Mizzi are just a few of the country's well respected authors.

Folk music has a long history in Malta. The most popular traditional form is l-ghana, which was influenced by both European and Arabic music. Lyrically, l-ghana can entail carefully crafted poetic verses or a call and response format, in which two singers "duel" as they make up the song in an impromptu fashion. Nowadays, the music is accompanied by acoustic guitar.

The Manoel Theater is in the center of Valletta. The theater was built in 1772 and still operates as the national theater of Malta. The ornate interior is considered an architectural treasure and the theater is the third-oldest surviving public theater in all of Europe.

As in most European countries, Western sports, especially football (soccer), are popular in Malta.

Cultural Sites & Landmarks

Malta's small size masks a heritage that is rich in history and culture. The island nation boasts three World Heritage Sites, as recognized by the United Nations Educational, Scientific and Cultural Organization (UNESCO). They include the capital of Valleta; the Hal Saflieni Hypogeum, an excavated prehistoric subterranean structure; and the island's seven megalithic temples. In addition, the island is known for its architectural heritage, as it has come under the control and influence of numerous civilizations, including the Greek, Romans, Phoenicians, Byzantine, Arabs, and British.

Valletta, known for its old world traditions, refined culture, Grand Port, and elaborate architecture, is recognized as the best example of successive rule in Malta. It is particularly known for the military and baroque architecture of the Order of St. John of Jerusalem.

The city also contains approximately 320 landmarks, a testament to the rich concentration of historic and cultural sites in the capital. Some

notable landmarks include the Cathedral of St. John, and Auberge de Castile, an 18th-century palace. In front of the palace are auberges, or inns, that were constructed for the Knights of St. John, a charitable-turned-military order that cared for the injured crusaders in Jerusalem and assumed control of Malta. The knights built the Sacra Infermeria in 1574, once considered one of finest hospitals in all of Europe. Apart from its rich architecture and historical sites, Valletta has beautiful floral gardens, outdoor markets, and museums.

The Hal Saflieni Hypogeum is a large-scale underground structure that dates back to prehistoric times. Believed to be originally constructed as a sanctuary, it later was used as a necropolis, or burial grounds. It is considered the only prehistoric subterranean temple in existence. On the southern tip of Malta, the megalithic temple sites of Ġgantija, Ħaġar Qim, Mnajdra, Tarxien, Ta' Ħaġrat, and Skorba are considered architectural works of genius, given the limited accessible resources available to their prehistoric builders.

In the fishing village of Marsaxlokk (pronounced Mar-sa-SHLOK), visitors can see the traditional "Luzzu" fishing boats, painted in bold primary colors and decorated with Phoenician symbols warding off the evil eye. Remnants of the grand temple of the fertility goddess Juno are also in Marsaxlokk, echoing the days of Malta's occupation by Rome.

Mdina is an ancient city with an unusual mix of medieval and baroque architecture, built when Arabs controlled the archipelago. Mdina, along with Birgu (a.k.a. Vittoriosa), are stunning walled cities, renowned for their narrow streets built so that no enemy could out-maneuver the arrows slung from defenders' bows.

While steeped in history, Malta is also known for its natural attractions. North of the island of Malta is the small island of Comino. Its main attraction is known as the Blue Lagoon, a secluded cove of iridescent aquamarine water and white sand ideal for snorkeling. Further north, Gozo Island is known for its natural sights and prehistoric structures. Ramla Bay, on the east coast of Gozo, is the alleged location of the cave where Odysseus was said to be a prisoner of love to the witch Calypso. The Blue Grotto is an enormous cave located near the town of Wied iz-Zurrieq accessible only by boat. From Wied iz-Zurrieq, the uninhabited lizard island of Filfla is visible. When Malta was a British colony, Filfla was used for target practice by the British military.

Libraries & Museums

The National Museum of Fine Art, housed in an eighteenth-century palace, and the National Museum of Archaeology, which contains important finds from prehistoric sites, are both situated in the city center. The fortified walls of Fort St. Elmo, built in 1565 by the Order of St. John to guard Grand Harbor and Marsamxett Harbor, today stands as the backdrop for historical reenactments of full-scale military spectacles performed in period costume. The islands' other museums include the Malta at War Museum; Toy Museum; Museum of Natural History; Malta Classic Car Museum; Maritime Museum; Folklore Museum; and Aviation Museum.

Malta's public libraries consist of the main Central Public Library, seven regional libraries, and 38 branch libraries. The National Library of Malta originates in 1555, and the country also maintains a national archives.

Holidays

A strong tradition of Roman Catholicism provides the context for Malta's major celebrations. In addition to the numerous feast days of the Catholic calendar, the Maltese celebrate the Feast of St. Paul's Shipwreck (February 10), which commemorates St. Paul's accidental visit to the island, and Imnarja (June 29), which marks the beginning of the harvest season and the time of year when villages throughout the islands commemorate their patron saints. Feast days in Malta are characterized by parades, folk music, processions with statues, and church services. The beginning of the Lenten fasting season is preceded by Carnival. Revelers wear masks and join processions in the streets.

Secular holidays include the Commemoration of the 1919 Uprising (June 7), Independence Day (September 21), and Republic Day (December 13). The Regatta (September 8) commemorates the Great Siege of 1565, when the population repelled an attack by the Turks, as well as the siege and bombing of the islands during War World II.

Youth Culture

During adolescence, Maltese parents are customarily strict with their children in regard to studying and maintaining a decent reputation. Sex has traditionally been a forbidden subject, puberty not generally discussed in detail, and dating until age eighteen is unacceptable. However, as Malta is a popular tourist destination, Maltese youth have increasing adopted foreign culture and trends in recent years.

Nightclubs and discotheques are popular among older youth, and European music often dominates the music scene. Football (soccer) remains the most popular sport, and foreign teams often train on the island nation due to the mild climate in winter months. The Malta Football Association is considered the oldest such association in Europe.

The Maltese culture places a high priority on formal education, and school attendance is mandatory from five through 16 years of age. The University of Malta, founded in 1592, offers classes from architecture and engineering to arts and theology, and has fourteen specialized research institutes. All university students receive free tuition and a monthly stipend. One institute focuses its investigations on youth affairs and the range of problems they face in contemporary society. A recent report stated that Maltese youth engage in higher rates of voluntary work than other European youth. Similar to their European counterparts, membership in traditional associations, such as political and religious groups, has declined.

Malta is home to numerous government-sponsored youth organizations and non-governmental organizations (NGOs) committed to increasing employment opportunities for Maltese youth and engaging them in activities to better their future and society. These include the Malta National Youth Council (KNZ) the Malta Girl Guides, the Scout Association of Malta (Boy Scouts), the Malta Gay Rights Movement (MGRM), and the Maltese Association of Youth Workers (MAY), as well as the Ministry of Education and the Ministry of the Family and Social Solidarity.

SOCIETY

Transportation

Bus services are the main mode of public transportation in Malta, with the main terminal in Valletta. Public buses reach the larger towns and fares tend to be inexpensive and can be purchased per ride, or on a three-day, five-day, or seven-day pass with unrestricted travel. However, Maltese public buses are characterized by being behind schedule, and overcrowded, and newer buses are gradually being introduced. These new buses typically provide air conditioning, comfortable seating, and keep to more reliable time tables. Unmetered taxis are also frequent means of transportation.

Vehicles in Malta travel on the left-hand side of the road. The majority of the country's roadways are paved.

Transportation Infrastructure

Bus services are the main mode of public transportation in Malta. Regular ferry service connects the three major islands. There are two ferry terminals on Malta, but the most commonly used is Cirkewwa, located at the northern most point of the island. Malta International Airport is the only airport in the archipelago.

Media & Communications

There are several main daily newspapers in Malta, including *The Times, In-Nazzjon Taghna*, and *L-Orizzont*, and numerous weekly newspapers, including *It-Torca* and *Mument*. Accordingly, bilingualism has resulted in half of the newspapers published in English and the other half in Maltese.

The most widely read newspapers are *The Times* and *The Sunday Times*, publishes weekly. Nevertheless, subscription rates have decreased in recent years due to increasing popularity of radio, television, and other mediums as news sources.

There are a dozen or more national radio stations, and several community radio stations, with permanent licenses to broadcast throughout Malta. Political parties, the church, and the university all maintain privately-run radio and television stations. The public broadcaster is Television Malta (TVM) and almost every home has at least one television set with cable or satellite reception.

Internet subscriptions are on a rapid increase, and almost all broadcasting and print media is available on the Web. As of 2009, there were an estimated 240,600 Internet users. Malta is also considered one of the preeminent countries offering government services online.

SOCIAL DEVELOPMENT

Standard of Living

Malta ranked thirty-ninth on the 2014 United Nations Human Development Index.

There is a marked lack of fresh water sources on the islands, and residents must depend on desalinization (the removal of salt from seawater) programs for potable water. Approximately 70 percent of the country's water supply is now desalinated.

Education

Malta's educational system is highly developed and reflects British influence. Education is free and compulsory between the ages of five and sixteen; kindergarten and the upper levels of secondary school are also free, and enrollment after the age of sixteen is high.

Students sit a national exam after the fifth year of secondary school as well as at its end. Students who choose to continue their education are then streamlined into academic and vocational programs. Private schools, many of which are Catholic, follow a similar educational structure and are also free. The literacy rate is 92 percent. English is commonly the language of instruction.

The University of Malta, founded in 1592 by the Jesuits, is the country's most prestigious institute of higher education. It offers a wide range of degrees and has several institutes operating under its auspices. In 2009, Malta's literacy rate was an estimated 92.8 percent.

Women's Rights

Maltese women have the same legal rights as men under family, property, and judicial law. In spite of existing legislation which bans gender discrimination, statistics reveal that women receive lower pay than male counterparts and are underrepresented in the workforce. Violence against women and prostitution also hinders women on the island from achieving equal status.

Women are represented in a variety of distinguished professions, including in the legal, science, and health sectors. Females serve on the sixty-five-seat parliament and the 14-member cabinet of ministers, and are represented through ambassadorships and in the high judicial courts and the police force. However, involvement in executive bodies is lacking and women are underrepresented in management positions.

Malta has also begun introducing measures aimed to combat violence against women. The law prohibits domestic violence and rape; however, the police receive more reported cases each year. Penalties range from three months to 20 years imprisonment. A special police unit and several voluntary organizations provide support to victims of domestic violence, and there is a hotline to assist victims of abuse. Women's advocacy groups stress that domestic violence often goes underreported, primarily because of cultural attitudes and the attitudes of law enforcement and medical service providers.

Malta is a country where women from North Africa, Russia, Ukraine, Romania, and other Eastern European countries are trafficked for commercial sexual exploitation and forced prostitution. Trafficking is prohibited by law and perpetrators face two to nine years in prison if convicted. The government has begun to take initial steps toward providing victims with counseling referrals and specialized training for law enforcement officials. Nevertheless, many victims report being treated more like an accomplice in the crime than a casualty of it, and the government has been deficient in implementing trafficking prevention actions.

The status of women in Malta has advanced considerably in the last twenty years. Many believe that more needs to be done before women in Malta assume major roles in decision making positions and are afforded adequate protection. The Ministry for the Family and Social Solidarity and the National Commission for the Promotion of Equality for Men and Women promote the integration of women into Maltese society and advocate for more effective government policies in favor of sexual equality. The country has introduced several measures to encourage women to work such as paid maternity leave, career breaks for public workers, the creation of state kindergartens, and summer school programs for primary school students

Health Care

Malta's national health care system is highly developed and free. It covers every citizen of Malta under the National Insurance Scheme, which receives funds from the government, employers, and general taxation. The comprehensive system covers the full range of patient needs, including pharmaceuticals.

As part of the European Union, Malta has reciprocal agreements with other EU countries to provided health care to all EU citizens. In addition to the national health care system, there are private hospitals which patients pay for either out-of-pocket or through private insurance policies. The Ministry of Health oversees both public and private health systems.

GOVERNMENT

Structure

Malta was under the jurisdiction of Great Britain from 1814 until 1964, when it became independent but remained within the Commonwealth. Ten years later, Malta became a republic. Since 1974, Malta has been a parliamentary republic. According to the amended constitution, the executive branch consists of a president who acts as head of state and a prime minister who acts as head of government. The president is appointed by the parliament to a five-year term. The prime minister is the leader of the party which wins the majority in parliamentary elections. He or she is assisted by a cabinet which is chosen by the president on the recommendation of the prime minister. The parliament can withdraw support from the prime minister and the cabinet, thereby ending their term.

The unicameral legislature is overseen by the House of Representatives, a body consisting of 65 members who are elected to five-year terms by popular vote. In order to guarantee a majority, seats are allotted proportionally along party lines.

The judicial branch is overseen by a chief justice and sixteen judges. They are appointed by the president, upon the recommendation of the prime minister, and cannot serve past 65 years of age. The highest court is the Constitutional Court. There is also a criminal court, a civil court, a commercial court, and lower courts.

Political Parties

Two parties dominate the political scene in Malta: the Nationalist Party, which has a conservative ideology, and the Malta Labor Party, which has a democratic socialist ideology.

Malta's two main political parties are the Nationalist Party (Partit Nazzjonalista) and the Labour Party (Partit Laburista). The Nationalist Party is a conservative party that supports a Christian democratic political philosophy. The Labour Party operates on a social democratic platform. Other parties include the Democratic Alternative Party, the National Action Party, and

the Imperium Europa. In the 2013 general elections, the Labour Party became the majority party with 39 seats in the parliament, compared with the Nationalist Party's 26 parliament seats.

Local Government

Malta is divided into 58 units (54 in Malta proper and 14 on the island of Gozo), which are overseen by a local council. A mayor heads each council, which is elected by popular vote every three years. The local councils work closely with the central government.

Judicial System

The judicial system of Malta consists of a Court of First Instance and a Court of Appeal. The country's legal system is based on English common law and Roman law.

Taxation

The government of Malta collects a progressive income tax based on wages. Income tax ranges from zero to 35 percent. A base corporate tax of 35 percent is imposed on businesses. The country's tax collection and tax law is the responsibility of the Ministry of Finance, Economy and Investment.

Armed Forces

The Armed Forces of Malta consists of three infantry battalions and a Marine Squadron. Service in the Maltese military is voluntary. The force had an estimated 2,100 active members in 2002. In 2000, the country's annually military budget was 60 million (USD). Malta's armed forces are commanded by the president.

Foreign Policy

Since its appointment into the European Union (EU) in May 2004, Malta has been developing relationships with other EU members and increasing its voice in international affairs. As of 2009, there are Maltese embassies and consulates in 152 foreign countries, with 122 nations holding diplomatic representation on the island. Malta supports organizations that promote multilateral partnership, particularly the United Nations (UN), the Commonwealth (made up of former British colonies), the Council of Europe, and the Organization for Security and Co-operation in Europe (OSCE).

Malta has a reputation for frequently voicing its concern for peace and economic development in the Mediterranean region. The nation is an active member in the Euro-Mediterranean Partnership, formed in Spain in 1995 to promote regional policy development. Under this umbrella partnership, EU member states and Mediterranean countries work together to develop relationships aimed at achieving peace, stability, and growth in the region. Its central location in the Mediterranean also makes Malta a cultural and geographic bridge between Europe and North Africa.

In addition to its functioning role in developing Mediterranean foreign policy, Malta is also working toward improving European-North African relations. Malta enjoys particularly friendly diplomatic and commercial ties with Libya and Tunisia, and they hosted the first EU-Arab League ministerial meeting in 2008. The Ministry for Justice and Home Affairs has reported that illegal refugees seeking asylum from North Africa and Iraq has been increasing at detrimental rates. Many Maltese feel that Malta is not getting enough support from the EU to curb this problem. Legal foreigners who reside in Malta are primarily retired British nationals.

Australia and Malta have a strong bond due to their memberships in the Commonwealth. More importantly, the Maltese migrant community in Australia represents the largest Maltese community outside of Malta with a population of close to half a million people.

The government also desires closer relations with the United States, particularly in trade and private investment. The U.S. has been supportive of Malta's campaign, and several U.S. businesses have set up operations in Malta.

Human Rights Profile

"International human rights law insists that states respect civil and political rights, and also promote an individual's economic, social, and cultural rights. The United Nations Universal Declaration on Human Rights (UDHR) is recognized as the standard for international human rights. Its authors sought the counsel of the world's great thinkers, philosophers, and religious leaders, and were careful to create a document that reflects the core values shared by every world culture. (To read this document or view the articles relating to cultural human rights, visit: http://www.udhr.org/UDHR/default.htm).

Malta's government generally respects the rights of its citizens. In 2014, for instance, the parliament passed a Civil Unions Act, granting same-sex couples the same rights as heterosexual couples in civil marriage. Discrimination on grounds of sexual orientation was also prohibited. The constitution provides freedom of speech and press, and independent and international media frequently express diverse views without restriction, particularly concerning human rights. Nonetheless, there have been situations where journalists' homes have been vandalized after publishing articles advocating human rights for migrants and refugees. Other challenges that the Maltese government faces in regard to human rights include child abuse, trafficking in women, and inhumane conditions in refuge detainment facilities.

The government puts great effort into protecting the rights of children. The law prohibits employment of anyone under age sixteen and government provides free, mandatory education through the secondary level. Health care is free to all citizens and clinics that specialize in childhood illnesses and disorders can be found in cities as well as small villages. On the other hand, National Social Welfare Services deals with hundreds of cases of child abuse each year including several allegations of sexual molestation of minors filed against the Catholic Church. There are also frequent reports that women and young children are being trafficked into Malta from Eastern Europe.

The law prohibits arbitrary seizure, and a warrant is required before police can detain suspects. The police have 48 hours to inform detainees on the grounds for their arrest, file formal charges, or release them. If charged, a person has the right to a lawyer and a public jury trial, access to government held evidence pertinent to their case, and the right to question witnesses and present evidence in their defense. Suspects are presumed innocent until guilty and have the right to an appeal. Prison conditions meet international regulations, and to guarantee this, the government permits visits by human rights observers such as the Council of Europe's Committee for the Prevention of Torture (CPT).

Malta receives a high number of North African and Middle Eastern refugees each year. The law provides asylum to these people in accordance with the 1951 UN Convention Relating to the Status of Refugees and its 1967 protocol. The government also provides temporary protection to hundreds of migrant workers who do not qualify as refugees under international law. Asylum seekers may stay up to 18 months while their cases are processed. Authorities place men, women, children, the disabled, and elderly in detention centers where they are free to move about upon arrival into the country. There have been numerous reports issued by the EU and the UN criticizing the length of time illegal immigrants are confined in these centers and their conditions. Reported problems include crowded facilities, lack of activities within the centers, and lack of access to legal aid. Maltese armed forces have also subjected asylum seekers and migrants to physical assaults resulting in serious injuries.

ECONOMY

Overview of the Economy

Malta has a strong, diverse economy which is somewhat curtailed by its reliance on imports, since it lacks its own energy resources and produces only 20 percent of its own food.

World War II decimated the Maltese economy. Post-war, the government crafted an economic policy that shifted the island into new industries. While the harbor in Valletta was repaired and modernized to attract foreign trade, especially in ship refit and repair, it was the government-directed investment into the textile and electronic industries that helped transform the economy. A highly educated workforce allowed these two trades to flourish and soon created an export market. Most importantly, the government began to promote Malta as a tourist destination, and tourism began to slowly and steadily grow.

Now that Malta is a member of the European Union, investments are expected to increase. Membership also means that the local economy must meet stringent EU standards.

Industry

The industrial sector accounts for 12.9 percent of the GDP and employs 22 percent of the labor force.

The most important industry is shipping, with Malta's ports offering extensive dry-dock facilities, ship construction, and ship repair. Each year, over 20 million tons of cargo passes through its ports, making the country one of the largest registers in the World. In addition, the port of Valletta is a common stop for cruise ships, and has ferry links with other Mediterranean ports.

Textiles, electronic goods, pharmaceuticals, food, beverages and clothing are all produced in Malta.

Labor

The labor force numbers approximately 190,500, of which 5.9 percent is unemployed. In 2008, the gross domestic product (GDP) per capita was estimated at $31,700 (USD).

Energy/Power/Natural Resources

Malta is seriously limited in terms of natural resources, of which salt and limestone are its two most prevalent. Given the generally poor conditions of the soil, arable land is minimal, though some areas are highly cultivated with typical Mediterranean crops.

In the future, exploration for oil on the continental shelf between Malta and Tunisia might occur.

Fishing

Fishing does not represent a significant sector of the country's economy. The industry contributes less than one percent to Malta's GDP. However, the cultural relevance of regional fish species and fisherman is significant. Fisherman in Malta catch lampuka or dolphin fish.

Forestry

Forestry in Malta is negligible.

Mining/Metals

Mining is restricted to limestone, which is an important source of building material for the islands, and also an important labor industry.

Agriculture

Agriculture accounts for only three percent of the GDP and employs only five percent of the labor force. Despite poor soil conditions, a variety of agricultural products are grown, often on terraced fields. They include wheat, barley, citrus fruits, tomatoes, and cauliflower as well as seeds and flowers.

Animal Husbandry

Poultry, swine, cattle, goats, and sheep are raised in small numbers.

Tourism

Over the last several decades, tourism has become Malta's most dynamic sector. Services, of which tourism is a major part, account for 74 percent of the GDP and employ 71 percent of the labor force. Over 1.5 million tourists visited Malta in 2013, many arriving by cruise ship. During the onset of the 2008–09 global financial crisis, the Maltese travel and tourism industry remained mostly stable. The country, like most Mediterranean states, suffered a decline in 2009.

Jennifer O'Donnell, Michael Aliprandi,
Jeffrey Bowman

DO YOU KNOW?

- The entire population of Malta received the George Cross from Great Britain in recognition of its heroic resistance to German siege during World War II.

- Valletta has been the location for many famous films, including *Midnight Express* (1978), *Munich* (2005), *Gladiator* (2000), and *Troy* (2004).

- Valletta has one the highest population densities in Europe, with an astounding 13,909 people per square kilometer.

Bibliography

Abigail Blasi. *Malta and Gozo.* Oakland, CA: Lonely Planet, 2013.

Britannica Educational. *Cyprus, Greece, and Malta.* Perth, WA: EB Books, 2013.

Marquis De Sain and Shirley Johnson. *Splendor of Malta.* New York: Rizzoli, 2001.

Mary-Ann Gallagher. *Top 10 Malta and Gozo.* New York: DK Publishing, 2013.

Stefan Goodwin. *Malta, Mediterranean Bridge.* Westport, CT: Greenwood Press, 2002.

Quentin Hughes. *Malta: The Baroque Island.* Malta (Mont.): Midsea Books, 2003.

Deborah Manley. *Malta: A Traveller's Anthology.* Oxford: Signal, 2010.

Works Cited

Amnesty International. "Malta: Alleged ill-treatment of asylum-seekers must be investigated." January 2005. http://www.amnesty.org/en/library/asset/EUR33/001/2005/en/dom-EUR330012005en.html.

Andreassi, Diane. "Maltese Americans." *Countries and their Culture.* http://www.everyculture.com/multi/Le-Pa/Maltese-Americans.html.

"Architecture." *Government of Malta Superintendence of Cultural Heritage.* http://www.culturalheritage.gov.mt/page.asp?p=3103&l=1.

Brinkhoff, Thomas. "Malta." *City Population.* http://www.citypopulation.de/Malta.html.

"Caravaggio." Web Gallery of Art. http://www.wga.hu/frames-e.html?/bio/c/caravagg/biograph.html.

"Country Reports on Human Rights Practices Malta." *U.S. Department of State*. http://www.state.gov/g/drl/rls/hrrpt/2006/78827.htm.

"Cuisine and Dining." *Travel Guides*. http://www.aboutmalta.net/6048cuisineanddining.asp.

"Culture of Malta." *Countries and their Culture*. http://www.everyculture.com/Ma-Ni/Malta.html.

Dominic Cutajar. "An Overview of the Art of Malta." http://www.hopeandoptimism.com/essay.htm.

Judicial System. http://www.mjha.gov.mt/justice/judicialsystem.html

"Malta Country Brief." *Australian Government Department of Foreign Affairs and Trade*. http://www.dfat.gov.au/geo/malta/malta_brief.html.

"The Euro-Mediterranean Partnership." *European Commission External Relations*. http://ec.europa.eu/external_relations/euromed/index_en.htm.

Robert Galea and Michelle Galea. "The Nude in Maltese Art." http://www.timesofmalta.com/articles/view/20081026/letters/the-nude-in-maltese-art.

"Valletta - Malta's Capital City." *Guide to Malta*. http://www.guidetomalta.net/Places-in-Malta/valletta.

"Malta." Ministry of Foreign Affairs. http://www.esteri.it/MAE/EN/Politica_Europea/AffariGen_RelazEst/UE_allargamento/paesimembri/Malta.htm.

"Malta." UNESCO World Heritage. http://whc.unesco.org/en/statesparties/mt/?ordre=&region=&.

"Malta Council for Culture and the Arts Act." *Malta Council for Culture and the Arts. Malta Parliamentary Act*. http://www.maltaculture.com/filebank/docs/chapter444.pdf.

"Malta." *U.S. Department of State*. http://www.state.gov/r/pa/ei/bgn/5382.htm.

"Maltese Phrases and Expressions." *Linguanaut*. http://www.linguanaut.com/english_maltese.htm.

Ministry of Foreign Affairs. "Strategic Objectives of Malta's Foreign Policy." http://www.doi.gov.mt/en/press_releases/2006/02/pr0184a.doc.

"Trafficking in Persons Report 2008 - Malta, 4 June 2008." *U.S. Department of State*. http://www.unhcr.org/refworld/docid/484f9a2a32.html.

"The Daphne Lungaro Folklore Group." *Inside Malta*. http://inside-malta.com/folklore.html.

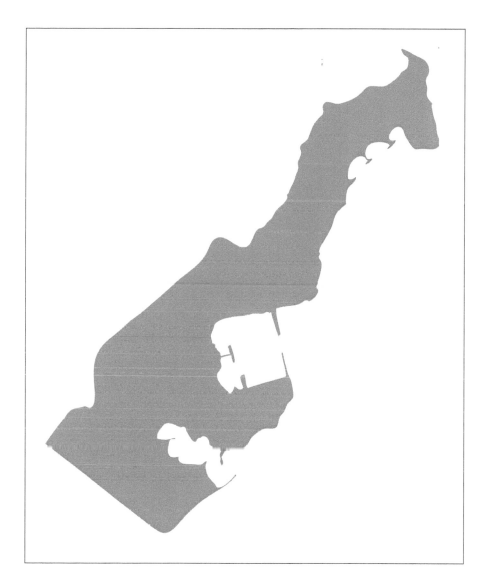

MONACO

Introduction

The Principality of Monaco is the world's second-smallest independent and sovereign state, and has been presided over by the Grimaldi royal dynasty for over 700 years. It lies on the east coast of France, along the Mediterranean Sea and close to the Italian border, in a region known as the Riviera. Monaco is a member of the United Nations but not of the European Union.

One of the French Riviera's premier resort destinations, the principality of Monaco has famously served as a favorite getaway for some of the world's most affluent people. It is also renowned for its uncanny success in preserving its political autonomy and cultural identity amid centuries of European conflict.

Monaco is the home of the world famous Monte Carlo resort and casino, but the Theater of Monte Carlo is almost as important to the culture as the casino. In fact, Monaco's arts and entertainment are at the center of the country's way of life, perhaps more than in any European nation. Monaco's residents, known as Monégasques, stress the role of the arts in everyday life.

The capital of this tiny nation—which measures 5 kilometers long by less than 1 kilometer wide (3 miles long by 5 miles wide)—is located in Monaco-Ville, or the Old City section, which sits atop a rocky land formation jutting into the Mediterranean.

GENERAL INFORMATION

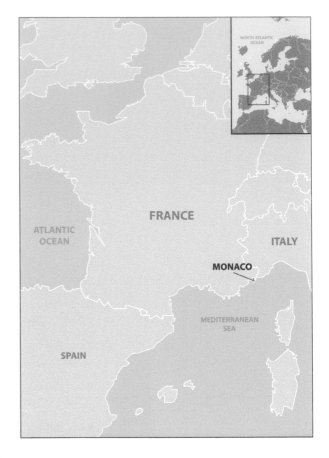

Official Language: French
Population: 30,508 (2014 estimate)
Currency: Euro
Coins: The Euro is available in 1, 2, 5, 10, 20 and 50 cent coins. A 1 and 2 Euro coin is also available.
Land Area: 1.95 square kilometers (0.76 square miles)
National Motto: "Deo Juvante" (Latin, "With God's Help")
National Anthem: "Hymne Monégasque"
Capital: Monaco (Monaco Ville)
Time Zone: GMT + 1
Flag Description: The flag of Monaco consists of two equally-sized horizontal bands of red (top) and white (bottom). Red and white represent the heraldic colors of the royal Grimaldi family.

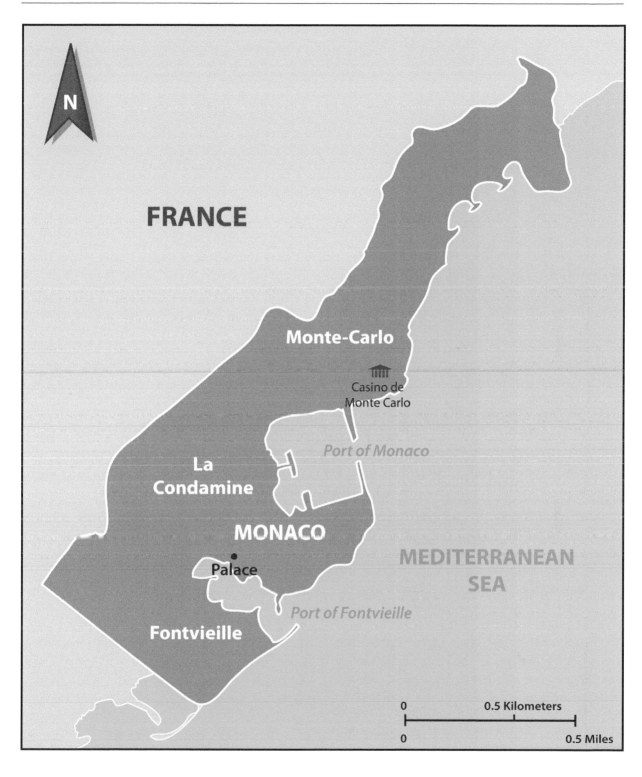

Principal Wards by Population (2000):

- Larvotto/Bas Moulins (5,443)
- La Condamine (3,847)
- Saint Michel (3,807)
- Fontvielle (3,292)
- La Rousse/Saint Roman (3,223)
- Monte Carlo/Spélugues (3,034)
- Moneghetti/ Bd de Belgique (3,003)
- La Colle (2,822)
- Les Révoires (2,515)
- Monaco-Ville (1,034)

Population

Monaco has few official citizens, and most of its inhabitants are either visiting or vacationing. About 5,000 of the residents are Monégasque. Another 5,000 are Italian, and the remaining majority is French. Wealthy residents live extravagant lifestyles in the small, prosperous nation.

The town of Monte Carlo, established in 1866, is home to a resort and casino. However, official citizens of the country are strictly prohibited from entering the casinos of Monte Carlo.

Due to the small land area and the relatively large amount of people, Monaco is very densely populated. Population density is calculated on the basis of number of people per square mile. Since Monaco is less than 2 square miles in area, it has the world's highest population density, and it is one of the only nations whose population density per square mile is greater than its population.

Languages

The people of Monaco primarily speak French, the official language, but Italian and English are also spoken throughout the country. In addition, some of Monaco's residents speak le monégu, a Monegasque language that is a blend of French Provençal and Italian. In general, the language is rarely spoken outside of primary schools, where it is a compulsory part of the curriculum.

Native People & Ethnic Groups

Thanks to its strategic coastal location and natural harbor, Monaco has been a site of human settlement since ancient times. Prime location on the Mediterranean Sea made it an attractive trading port for Romans and those traveling to African countries. It fell under the sway of a succession of powerful civilizations, including the Phoenicians, Romans, and Saracens. In 1215, Monaco was colonized by the Genoese, who built a fortress and a city encircled by defensive walls on the territory.

Because of its small size and high rate of tourism, only about one-fifth of the people living in Monaco are permanent citizens. Minority populations include people from the United States, Belgium, and Great Britain.

Religions

The official state religion of Monaco is Roman Catholicism. The importance of this religion to the nation is a product of French and Italian influence throughout Monaco's history. Many of Monaco's cultural traditions and practices are based in Christianity. Despite the strong presence of Catholicism, absolute freedom of worship is a right of Monégasques as described in Monaco's constitution.

Climate

Monaco's climate is dry, fair, and warm. The winter is comfortable with an average temperature of 8.2° Celsius (47° Fahrenheit), and the Mediterranean summer is generally hot with temperatures averaging at 25.5° Celsius (78° Fahrenheit).

Monaco is a rather dry country, with infrequent rain. During the spring, Monaco generally experiences cool temperatures and clear skies thanks to the effects of the mistral, a cold, dry wind that blows in from the north. The average annual temperature is a mild 16° Celsius (60° Fahrenheit).

ENVIRONMENT & GEOGRAPHY

Topography

Monaco is a coastal nation built mainly on cliffs and beaches. France's Mont Agel lies along the northwestern border. The country is bordered on the east by the Mediterranean Sea. The capital is set on a cliff 61 meters (200 feet) high, and is the location of the principality's royal palace and ancient fortress.

There are no significant bodies of water in Monaco. Although it is situated on the Mediterranean coast and there are several major ports and harbors, there are no lakes or rivers within the boundaries of the small nation.

Monaco consists of four main, traditional sections, or quarters: Monaco-Ville, which is the Old Town and seat of the government, sits atop a rocky land formation jutting into the Mediterranean; La Condamine, Monaco's commercial district, located along the principality's port; Monte-Carlo, a major residential area and a haven for the casino gambling industry; and Fontvieille, a light industrial and recreational zone built on land reclaimed from the sea during the past two decades. (Formerly made up of municipalities, Monaco is now subdivided into 10 wards, with an expected 11th ward, Le Portier).

Plants & Animals

Monaco's location on the shore of the Mediterranean Sea, as well as its high cliffs, creates a friendly environment for many species of birds and rare plants. However, since most of contemporary Monaco is urbanized, many of these native plants and animals can no longer live and grow in their original habitats. Instead, they can mostly be found in artificial environments throughout Monaco.

The Exotic Garden is a popular destination for tourists, and contains many varieties of desert plants from the Mediterranean region. Similarly, most of Monaco's animal population may be found in the Zoological Gardens. The zoo also has many foreign reptiles, monkeys, birds, and rodents.

CUSTOMS & COURTESIES

Greetings

The official language of Monaco is French, though many of its residents also speak English, Italian, and Monégasque. Monégasque is a

Romance language dating from the Middle Ages, combining French, Italian, and various other Provencal dialects. After nearly disappearing by the 1970s, Monégasque was revived in the 1980s to raise national pride in the country's culture. Though it is only used by a small percentage of residents, it is now taught in Monaco's schools. Most Monégasques speak French at home.

Monégasque greetings are similar to those of southern France. For example, two Monégasques might typically kiss each other on the cheek between one and three times, alternating between cheeks, and the process is usually repeated when they part company. Typical greetings include "Bonjour" (French) or "Salve" (Monégasque), both of which translate as "Hello."

Gestures & Etiquette

Similar to French and Italian custom, Monégasques typically use their hands to gesture emphatically while talking. These gestures are used for emphasis and help the speaker to communicate a range of emotions.

The cultural etiquette of Monaco can perhaps be described as polished. Formal attire is generally required for all religious buildings and the casino, and revealing attire such as swimsuits is confined to beaches and pool areas. Honorific titles are the norm, as it is considered too familiar to introduce a Monégasque using a first name. Instead, titles such as "Monsieur" for males, "Madame" for older or married women, and "Mademoiselle" for younger women are typically used.

A main point of etiquette in speaking French revolves around a particular word choice. The French language has two words for "you": the more formal "vous" and the informal "tu." The former is used for most adult acquaintances or strangers, while the latter is typically used more casually among friends, young people of the same age, and families. It can seem overly familiar, and thus offensive, to use "tu" rather than "vous" in certain situations.

Eating/Meals

Monaco shares many of its eating customs and cuisine with the neighboring French region of

Provence, as well as the adjacent nation of Italy. A typical Monégasque breakfast is simple and might consist of light fare, such as a baguette or croissant with orange juice and coffee, usually eaten at home. Most working adults eat lunch at restaurants, while young children eat their midday meal at school. The family will typically return home for dinner, which is the most substantial meal of the day. Traditionally, Monégasques have eaten their main meal at midday, a practice common in neighboring European countries such as France and Italy. Dinner might then consist of a salad or other light dish. However, many residents of Monaco have started making dinner their primary meal in the evening.

Monégasque Christmas is a traditional family celebration that features several eating customs. Traditional dishes served at the evening meal include brandaminciún (salt cod dish), friscioei (apple fritters), and fougasse (cake sprinkled with black and red sugared aniseed), as well as round-shaped Christmas bread. Children also traditionally received pastry shaped as dolls. Easter, Ash Wednesday, and Lent are other holidays that have their own traditional eating customs.

Visiting

Monégasques frequently celebrate holidays with their friends and extended family. Elaborate dinners marking these and other celebrations are frequently eaten at home and might last for two or three hours. Monaco also holds a variety of religious festivals throughout the year. For example, just before Ash Wednesday, a huge celebration called Carnivale takes place for two days. Similar to the Caribbean or Latin American tradition, this festivity includes various parties and parades of children dressed in traditional costumes. In June, Saint John's Day is celebrated with a large bonfire accompanied by folk musicians in traditional garb and a procession through the city. Monaco's National Day (or Feast of the Prince) takes place on November 19; festivities include a parade to the palace, traditional folk dances, and a public appearance and greeting by the prince.

LIFESTYLE

Family

Traditionally, family continues to act as the most important social adhesive, the average family in Monaco typically falls in the mid- to high-income brackets, as housing in Monaco itself is relatively expensive. The most common family structure is the nuclear family, which consists of two parents and two children.

Housing

Due to Monaco's dense population—as of 2009, Monaco is the world's most densely populated sovereign state—urban housing is predominant throughout the principality. Most middle-income families live in relatively modern high-rise apartment buildings built into the hillside overlooking Monaco's harbor. Wealthier residents might live in larger apartments, villas, or multi-bedroom homes. A common feature of these villas and homes are façades of pastel-colored stucco. Modern high-rise apartment buildings are increasingly replacing 19th-century villas in order to accommodate greater numbers of residents. However, the city retains a variety of architectural styles dating back to the Renaissance.

Food

Monégasque cuisine draws from the availability of local ingredients. Many traditional dishes feature olive oil, garlic, and herbs, as well as an abundance of fresh ingredients. For example, fresh fruit (such as oranges, lemons, melons, apricots, cherries, grapes, and figs) is a staple of Monégasque dishes because it is readily available from the surrounding region. Monaco's geographic location on the coast means that seafood is also quite popular, in particular sea bass, tuna, red snapper, anchovy, and cod. The most common meat in Monégasque cooking is lamb, frequently roasted with herbs for flavor. Beef is more commonly served in a daube, or slow-cooked stew, rather than as a roast or steak.

Monaco's food is also strongly influenced by the culinary traditions of its neighbors, namely southern France and Italy, as well as Mediterranean cooking. The influence of nearby Provence is particularly apparent in dishes such as pissaladière, a savory tart topped with onions, anchovies, and olives; and salade niçoise (niçoise means "from Nice"), a salad topped with tuna, hard-boiled eggs, anchovies, and olives. In Monaco, salade niçoise is often served in a roll and called pan-bagnat. Other popular French dishes include ratatouille, a stew of onions, eggplant, zucchini, green peppers, and artichokes cooked with tomatoes, garlic, and herbs; soupe au pistou, a thick vegetable soup similar to minestrone and topped with pistou (a pesto-like sauce made from garlic, fresh basil, and olive oil); and soupe de poisson (a fish soup) served with rouille (a spicy mayonnaise made from crushed chili peppers) and toasted bread.

Monégasque cuisine also includes several dishes specific to Monaco. These include fougasse, a sweet flat bread made with orange flower water and topped with nuts and aniseed; barbagiuan, a fried dough fritter filled with rice and zucchini or pumpkin; and soccas, pancakes made from chickpea flour. Other Monégasque specialties consist of entrées like stocafi, which is cod cooked in white wine, cognac, and tomato sauce; and tourte de blette, a pie filled with Swiss chard, Parmesan cheese, rice, onions, eggs, and herbs. Traditional desserts include navette, which are cookies flavored with orange blossom and anise; and fraises de bois au vin rouge, or wild strawberries in red wine.

Life's Milestones

Monaco's official religion is Roman Catholicism—an estimated 95 percent of the population identifies as Roman Catholic—and many milestones are observed or celebrated in accordance with the Catholic faith. Ceremonies associated with the church remain an important part of the culture, and include baptism, marriage, and feast days. Roman Catholic families frequently celebrate the days of individual saints for whom family members are named.

Families also usually observe Epiphany, on January 6, by buying a galette des rois, a cake made of puff pastry with cream filling. Inside the cake is embedded a feve (traditionally a bean but now more often a plastic or porcelain trinket), and the person who finds the feve in their slice is crowned king for the day. At Christmas, many Monégasque families observe a longstanding tradition in which the youngest child dips an olive branch into a glass of wine and then recites a poem honoring the olive tree. The rest of the family then drinks from the wine before eating a meal of traditional dishes that typically includes fougasse.

CULTURAL HISTORY

Architecture

Monaco's fine arts have historically remained linked with that of Paris, France, particularly its architecture. Monaco is known for its Belle Époque (1890–1914) architecture and style, a period known for its opulence. The architecture of this affluent period is often characterized by artistic creativity and exaggeration, organic features, and decorative, if not frivolous, elements such as mosaic paintings and ornate plasterwork. Buildings built in this style include the Place d'Armes, the famed Casino de Monte Carlo, and Monaco's Opera House (Salle Garnier), a replica of the Paris Opera House. The latter two were designed by French architect Charles Garnier (1825–1898). The architecture of Monaco also has a distinct Mediterranean influence, such as terra-cotta tiles roofs and porticoes (porches). The principality's small size and urban planning have also resulted in numerous high-rise structures.

Literature

In 1927, Louis Notari (1879–1961) published *A leganda de Santa Devota*, or *Santa Devota*, widely considered the first piece of Monégasque literature. Prior to Notari's poem, the Monégasque language was exclusively expressed through oral literature. The poem retold the story of Saint

Devota, Monaco's patron saint, who was martyred after the turn of the fourth century CE. According to Monégasque legend, although her body was placed by fellow Christians in a boat bound for Africa, winds forced the boat ashore at Monaco, and her body was buried there. Notari also wrote the lyrics to Monaco's national anthem, "Hymne Monégasque," in 1931. (The first version of the anthem dates to 1841, when Théophile Bellando de Castro wrote the music.) Other notable writers and literary figures that have contributed to the development of Monégasque literature and language include Georges Franzi (1914–1997) and lexicographer Louis Barral (1910–1999).

CULTURE

Arts & Entertainment

Perhaps more than any European nation, Monaco's arts and entertainment are at the center of the country's way of life. In fact, despite its small size, Monaco has developed a significant reputation in the world of the arts, particularly in dance and music.

The ruling Grimaldi family has long maintained a tradition of art patronage. The late Prince Rainier III (1923–2005) and Princess Grace (1929–1982)—who, as Grace Kelly, had an established career as an actress prior to retirement in 1956—both had a profound effect on Monaco's arts. In 1961, Prince Rainier initiated the first Monte-Carlo Television Festival, which would become an internationally acclaimed gathering by the end of the century. It is held annually in July. In 1964, the princess founded the Princess Grace Foundation in order to provide financial aid to the arts, as well as to medical and social institutions. The foundation funds, among other programs, the Princess Grace Dance Academy, and the Princess Grace Irish Library. Prior to her death in September 1982, Princess Grace also created the Monte-Carlo Ballet and the Monaco Garden Club, in addition to pursuing a wide range of charity work.

In 1996, Prince Rainier established the Prince Pierre Foundation in honor of his father, Prince Pierre, Duke of Valentinois (1895–1964). The foundation awards several prizes each year, including the Grand Literary Prize, the Prince Rainier III Prize for Musical Composition, and the International Contemporary Art Prize.

Monaco boasts numerous annual arts festivals and welcomes performances by renowned international artists and groups from a wide range of artistic genres. The Monaco International Circus Festival, held in winter, is one held dear to the Grimaldi family. Another festival, the Monte-Carlo Spring Arts Festival, is held each April. It encompasses concerts, recitals, and both classical and modern dance performances that are held throughout the city's public squares.

The Monte-Carlo International Sculpture Festival is a biennial event that runs from June to October. Sculptors submit works fitting a festival theme, and in a variety of media. Many of the prizewinning works are displayed in Monaco's public gardens.

Other annual concerts and events include Jazz on the Rock, which takes place each September; the Monaco International Film Festival; the World Music Awards, Monte Carlo International Fireworks Festival, held in the summer; and Imagina, a festival dedicated to computer graphics.

In addition to the Monte-Carlo Philharmonic Orchestra, Opera, and Ballet, the country boasts several smaller musical groups. Les Petits Chanteurs de Monaco (The Little Singers of Monaco) is a choir comprised of approximately thirty boys from Monaco, France, and Italy. Originally formed by Prince Antoine I (1661–1731) in the early 18th century in order to provide liturgical music for the palace's Palatine Chapel, the group was revived in the early 1970s. In addition to performing each day at the Palatine cathedral, the choir also embarks upon an international tour twice a year.

Monaco is also world-renowned for its place in world of auto racing. Since 1929, the Monaco Grand Prix has taken place on a Sunday in late May. Along with the Indianapolis 500 and the 24

Hours of Le Mans, the Grand Prix is one of the most famous car races in the world. The racecourse, which drivers must complete seventy-seven times, covers many steep hills and extremely tight turns. It passes directly through the heart of the city and provides a striking spectacle for those who assemble on rooftops and balconies to watch the race. Another race, the Monte Carlo Rally, takes place each January. The course of this three-day race runs through Provence and begins and ends in Monaco. January and February also witness the Monte Carlo Historic Car Rally, in which historic sports cars race from Valence, France, to the finish line in Monaco.

Cultural Sites & Landmarks

The small principality contains a wealth of exuberant architecture, both palatial and religious. The Cathedral of the Immaculate Conception, constructed between 1875 and 1885, is the largest church in Monaco. Built from cream-colored Italian marble, the cathedral houses the remains of several members of the royal family, including Princess Grace. The considerably smaller Palatine Chapel contains remarkable stained glass windows and ceiling paintings. Elsewhere, the Church of Saint Devota, Monaco's patron saint, dates to the 15th century and contains various paintings and sculptures dedicated to the patron saint of Monaco.

The Palais Princier (Prince's Palace) is the official residence of Monaco's prince.

The palace dates to 1215. Once the site of a medieval fortress, it now houses the royal family's state apartments. The palace is notable for several design features, including lavish frescoes, and a central courtyard paved with three million white and colored stones laid out in intricate geometric patterns. Originally pale yellow, the exterior was renovated in a salmon pink hue, at the request of the late Princess Grace.

Carrying on a tradition that is more than 100 years old, carabiniers (guards) in full dress uniform perform a daily changing of the guard ceremony at the palace's main entrance. Interestingly, in order to safeguard the palace and Monaco's

royalty from revolt, none of the guards are Monégasque citizens.

The palace might also be a destination for car enthusiasts. One hundred historic cars, from race cars to a Rolls Royce, make up Prince Rainier III's Collection de Voitures Anciennes (Collection of Classic Cars). The collection is open to the public.

Monaco's most famed landmark is perhaps the Casino de Monte Carlo. The sumptuous marble building contains gaming rooms ornately decorated with stained glass windows and allegorical statues and paintings. Designed by architect Charles Garnier, whose work also includes the Paris Opera House, the casino represents more than just a luxury gaming enterprise. Garnier created within it a significant cultural space, the Salle Garnier. It is the home of the Monte Carlo Opera, the Monte Carlo Philharmonic Orchestra, and the Ballets de Monte Carlo. In the mid-20th century, well-known artists such as Jean Cocteau (1889–1963) and Pablo Picasso (1881–1973) designed sets for their performances, and the Salle Garnier has witnessed performances by some of the past two centuries' most renowned artists.

Though most of Monaco's space is occupied by buildings, the principality is known for its exquisitely beautiful gardens. One of the more notable gardens is the Jardin Exotique (Exotic Garden), which originated in 1933 after thousands of cacti were planted into cracks in the cliff wall. The botanical garden has since been expanded to include over 2,000 more species of exotic plants. The garden is also known for its landscaping, as its various sections are connected with footbridges and winding paths. Another notable garden, the Jardins du Casino (Casino Gardens), is comprised of striking floral gardens planted around Monaco's famed casino, the Monte Carlo Casino. Its grounds include rotating art exhibits displayed along the central path. Overlooking the sea, the Jardins Saint Martin (Saint Martin Gardens) are composed of an array of pine trees interspersed among the ruins of medieval fortifications and 18th-century turrets. These gardens are believed to have inspired the

French poet Guillaume Apollinaire (1880–1918). One of Monaco's newer gardens, the Princess Grace Rose Garden in Fontvieille, displays over 150 varieties of roses in a large park.

Libraries & Museums

Monaco's many cultural sites include numerous museums. The Musée Océanographique (Oceanographic Museum & Aquarium) was built in 1910 by Prince Albert I (1848–1922). Set into a cliff wall and characterized by sea-themed décor, the museum features a world-renowned aquarium with a vast coral reef, as well as many varieties of sharks, fish, and other marine life. Famous marine explorer Jacques-Yves Cousteau (1910–1997) directed the museum for 30 years, until 1988.

Other museums include the Museum of Napoleonic Souvenirs et Archives Historiques du Palais (the Historic Archives of the Palace); the Naval Museum, containing over 200 model ships; Villa Sauber, the National Museum of Monaco; and the Wax Museum of the Princes of Monaco, which displays historic wax representations of important moments in the Grimaldi family history.

The Louis Notari Library serves as Monaco's legal depository. The library houses 450,000 volumes. The library observed its one-hundredth anniversary in 2009. The Princess Grace Irish Library, opened in 1984, honor's Princess Grace's Irish heritage. The library houses Princess Grace's personal collection of Irish books.

Holidays

As a Roman Catholic nation, Christian holidays and traditions such as Christmas and Lent are observed. In addition to these, Monaco has many holidays and festivals that honor individual saints. The patron Saint of Monaco is Saint Dévote, who was martyred for her Christianity. On February 6 of each year, Monégasques lead a series of processions and ceremonies in honor of Dévote, followed by nighttime fireworks and a large pyre that is burned and sent in a boat into the Mediterranean.

Saint John the Baptist is commemorated with festivities that include folk dance, mandolin music, costumes, and a large feast in Monte Carlo. Saint Roman's Day, on August 9, commemorates another patron saint of Monaco.

One of the biggest celebrations held each year in Monaco is the Monégasque National Holiday, which is also called Saint Rainier's Day. This occurs every year on November 19, and involves a religious mass followed by fireworks and a large formal function at the Monte Carlo Opera House.

Youth Culture

Education in Monaco is compulsory from the ages of six through sixteen, and the curriculum mirrors that of the French educational system, including diplomas earned. It is estimated that a quarter of Monégasque children attend private school. Many youth attend college in France, while some remain in Monaco to attend specialized schools. These include the Technical Lycée of Monte-Carlo, which focuses on hotel and restaurant management; the Princess Grace Academy of Classical Dance; the Municipal School of Plastic Arts; and the Prince Rainier III Academy of Music.

The minimum employment age is sixteen, and special restrictions govern the hiring, work hours, and other conditions of workers between sixteen and eighteen years old. Young people also enjoy the variety of sports that Monaco's warm climate and coastal location permit. Tennis, golf, and boating are all popular, and Monaco has both national football (soccer) and rugby teams.

SOCIETY

Transportation

Generally, Monaco's small size means that walking is the preferred mode of transportation. Urban bus lines, of which there are six, offer one mode of public transportation in and around Monaco, and taxis are also common. The small country is also served by several high-speed train lines, such as the TGV Méditerranée that runs between Paris and Monaco, and various regional trains that run along the Côte d'Azur. As of 2009, Monaco has one heliport, but no regional airport. Traffic moves on the right-hand side of the road.

Transportation Infrastructure

As of 2007, Monaco had an estimated 50 kilometers (31 miles) of paved roads. Monaco is readily accessible by boat and boasts a massive port. The original Port of Monaco was built between 1901 and 1926, before a floating dike doubled its capacity in 2002. An environmentally friendly electric boat has served as a shuttle in Monaco's Harbor since 2007.

Media & Communications

Monaco does not publish any daily newspapers, and instead relies on French media for coverage. The main regional daily, *Nice-Matin*, publishes two pages on Monaco. Within Monaco, several weekly publications circulate, including *Monaco Hebdo*, which covers current affairs, and *Journal de Monaco*, which is a government journal. Other papers include *Monaco Actualité*, *Gazette Monaco-Côte d'Azur*, and *Monte Carlo Méditerranée*. The *Riviera Reporter*, which comes out every two months and is targeted at residents of the French Riviera, is Monaco's only English-language publication.

Monaco's broadcast media features Radio Monte-Carlo, which reaches beyond Monaco's borders into France and Italy. Radio France Internationale (RFA) also operates Monte-Carlo Doualiya, described as a pan-Arab station. Monaco's general entertainment television network is Télé Monte Carlo (TMC), considered the oldest private channel in Europe; it is partially owned by the principality. Monaco's constitution and laws provide for the freedom of speech and the press, which has been largely respected by the government. Monaco's independent media are not typically restricted from expressing a wide range of views. In one exception, the law does prohibit any public criticism of the royal family.

The state previously held a monopoly on Monaco's telephone system, which is connected via underground cables into the French communications network. As of 2008, the state owns 45 percent of the telephone network, while Cable and Wireless Communications and the Compagnie Monégasque de Banque hold the remaining 49 and six percent, respectively. The state retains its monopoly on the postal service. In 2010, there were an estimated 23,000 Internet users, representing just over 75 percent of the population.

SOCIAL DEVELOPMENT

Water Consumption

Monaco's drinking water supply is primary sourced from the Vésubie canal, a hydraulic structure in France, and from Italy. A small percentage—approximately 30 percent—comes from a catchment area and local springs. The entire population has access to clean and safe drinking water and sanitation and waste collection. The principality has reduced water consumption by 10 percent since 2000.

Education

Monaco's citizens are highly literate, and are typically educated in the fine arts, service learning, and traditional academics. School attendance is mandatory for residents between six and sixteen years of age. Education is one part of Monaco's culture that ties the native Monégasques to the French, since schools in Monaco use the same course materials and lesson guidelines as schools in France.

There are many specialized public and private secondary schools in Monaco. The three main secondary schools specialize in financial studies and commercial career preparation. These schools are the Lycée Albert I, Charles III College, and the Technical Lycée of Monte Carlo. Schools specializing in the arts include the Rainer III Academy of Music and the Princess Grace Academy of Classical Dance.

The English-language International University of Monaco specializes in providing a business-oriented education—for example, the institute offers a Master's in Luxury Retail Management—and is the only institute of higher learning in the principality. As of 2010, the literary rate is an estimated 99 percent.

Women's Rights

Monaco's civil code mandates the equality of men and women, though no official institution exists that monitors gender inequalities. Various surveys suggest that women have fairly good representation in many professions, but are less present in business roles. In general, women received pay comparable to male counterparts, but a small and slowly decreasing discrepancy in pay between genders has been reported by unofficial sources. Women are also less represented than men politically. For instance, in 2013 only fifteen women, out of seventy-two candidates, ran for a seat in the national council. Five women won election.

Rape, including spousal rape, is classified as a criminal offense. Monaco's laws also prohibit spousal abuse and make provisions for victims to bring criminal charges against their spouse. Overall, domestic abuse is rare, and there have been few reported cases of violence against women in recent years. Sexual harassment is also illegal, and there have been scarce reports of such occurrences.

Health Care

Monaco's government spends about $2,016 USD per capita on health care for its residents each year. Health care provisions include workplace injury compensation and care for the disabled.

GOVERNMENT

Structure

As a principality, Monaco has a prince as its reigning leader and a minister of state in charge of directing governmental affairs. The prince appoints the minister of state, while the citizens democratically elect the National Council of 18 legislators. Monaco's government is closely related to the government of France. Several political parties vie for control of the National Council. The National and Democratic Union is the party that has historically controlled the council.

Although Monaco is a principality, the prince's actual power is limited, since most of the government's activities are conducted democratically. The prince oversees councilors of the interior, finance, and public works, in addition to the Council of the Crown, which reviews procedures within the principality.

In many ways, the principality remains under France's partial guardianship. Monaco is reliant on France for trade and resources, and shares its neighbor's systems of education and governance. If at any point there is no male heir to the throne, France will gain full rule of Monaco. Some public services, such as Monaco's television transmitters on Mont Agel, also remain under the dominion of France.

Historically, Monaco fell under French rule for an extended period of time during the French Revolution. The principality regained independent status in 1861, but remained a French territory. In 1911, Monaco's constitution was written, and the nation became independent and self-governing in 1918, with the signing of the Treaty of Versailles.

Political Parties

Historically, Monaco was dominated by one political party, the conservative National and Democratic Union (Rally for Monaco), but this changed as of the 2003 elections, when the coalition party Union for Monaco gained twenty-one of twenty-four seats. Representing three parties (Union for the Principality, National Union for the Future of Monaco, and Promotion of the Monegasque Family), the Union for Monaco retained its seat majority in the 2008 elections. In 2013, the coalition split into Union for Monaco and Monaco Horizon, resulting in a substantial victory by Monaco Horizon.

Local Government

The Communal Council of Monaco, which consists of fifteen members elected to four-year terms, oversees the principality's four quarters. The council is presided over by a member-selected mayor.

Judicial System

Monaco's judicial system is based on France's Napoleonic Code. The Supreme Court acts as the principality's highest court and is charged with the interpretation of the constitution. Other courts include Court of First Instance, Court of Appeal, High Court of Appeal, and Criminal Court.

Taxation

Due in large part to its resorts, tourism is a large economic and social force in Monaco. Monaco's citizens enjoy full tax exemption, because taxes are drawn from gaming facilities and retail sales. Profit taxes are high at a minimum of 25 percent, and apply to all forms of sales.

Armed Forces

Monaco has no standing army, and its palace guards comprise a small and primarily ceremonial force. France is responsible for Monaco's national defense.

Foreign Policy

Monaco's foreign policy is closely aligned with the policies of France, which is officially responsible for Monaco's national defense. A 2002 treaty between France and Monaco allowed the principality more sovereignty and to expand its foreign relations. The treaty also declared that if no heirs should be born to continue the Grimaldi dynasty, Monaco would remain an independent country rather than reverting to France. The treaty also maintained France's role in Monaco's defense.

Monaco joined the United Nations (UN) in 1993 and is economically associated with the European Union (UN), but not a member state. However, the euro is Monaco's official currency. Monaco is a member of the Council of Europe, joining in 2004, and also maintains membership in specialized agencies of the UN, such as the World Health Organization (WHO) and the World Intellectual Property Organization (WIPO), as well as the International Agency for Atomic Energy (IAEA), which reports to the UN. Monaco also holds membership in the International Whaling Commission (IWC).

Because Monaco has no personal income tax and is known for the discretion of its banks, it attracts extremely wealthy residents from all over the world. Many of these people do not in fact spend the majority of their time in Monaco or have businesses there, instead claiming residency in order to avoid paying income taxes elsewhere. This practice has caused friction in the past between Monaco and other European countries in particular. The International Monetary Fund (IMF) and the Council of Europe have both identified Monaco as a tax haven, while the Organization for Economic Cooperation and Development (OECD) has named Monaco as one of several countries that have not adequately addressed problems with money-laundering and multi-national fraud.

Human Rights Profile

International human rights law insists that states respect civil and political rights, and also promote an individual's economic, social and cultural rights. The United Nations Universal Declaration on Human Rights (UDHR) is recognized as the standard for international human rights. Its authors sought the counsel of the world's great thinkers, philosophers, and religious leaders, and were careful to create a document that reflects the core values shared by every world culture. (To read this document or view the articles relating to cultural human rights, visit: http://www.udhr.org/UDHR/default.htm).

Monaco is governed by a constitutional monarchy, which is hereditary. The monarch appoints the minister of state from a list of three French citizens presented by the French government who serves as head of government. The national council is made up of twenty-four popularly elected representatives and shares legislative authority with the prince. Most of these elections have been considered free and fair, and the government largely respects its citizens' human rights. However, citizens do not hold the right to change their government, as the prince retains sole authority to change the government. The prince can also revise the constitution in agreement with the national council.

Monaco's constitution ensures the equality of its citizens. While Monégasque citizens are given hiring preferences, free education, unemployment assistance, and other benefits, all residents are accorded certain rights, such as the inviolability of the home. The law also prohibits discrimination based on race, gender, disability, language, or social status. In addition, freedom of assembly and association are protected by Monaco's constitution and laws. Outdoor meetings must be authorized by the police, while formal associations require registration with and authorization by the government. None of these permissions have been denied for political or other reasons in recent years, according to reports.

While Roman Catholicism is Monaco's state religion, and approximately 90 percent of Monaco's citizens are Roman Catholic, the government has generally respected the freedom of the country's other religious groups. Religious organizations are registered with the state and given permission to operate. However, Monaco does not extend these privileges to organizations listed on the French Interministerial Mission for Monitoring and Combating Cultic Deviances (MIVILUDES), a database of "cult" groups. There have been no recent reports of religious discrimination or harassment, as well as no reports of anti-Semitic acts against Monaco's extremely small Jewish denomination.

Monaco's legal system is based on French law, and although it is a member of the UN, Monaco has not accepted compulsory jurisdiction of the International Court of Justice (ICJ), the judicial body of the UN. Regardless, Monaco's constitution and law prohibit arbitrary arrest and detention and require arrest warrants. Detainees must be brought before a judge within twenty-four hours of the arrest in order to be informed of their lawful rights and the charges against them. The constitution and law also

mandate an independent judiciary. In criminal cases, a three-judge tribunal considers evidence and hears arguments. The defendant has the right to counsel, at public expense if necessary, and to be present at the trial, as well as the right to question and present witnesses. If convicted, prisoners are transported to a French prison for the duration of their sentence.

ECONOMY

Overview of the Economy

Monaco's economy revolves around tourism, finance, and commerce. The services sector employs nearly half of Monaco's total labor force. The tourist industry and its related components account for about a quarter of Monaco's estimated gross national product (GNP). Each year more than half a million visitors spend time in Monaco. Monaco's gross domestic product was an estimated $78,700 (USD) per capita in 2013.

Industry

Many visitors are drawn to Monaco by its gaming industry. Since Monaco's storied casino first opened in 1863, wealthy gamblers have flocked to the principality. Casino gambling accounts for about 5 percent of the government's revenues. The banking and investment industries make up another important sector of Monaco's economy.

Long regarded as a tax haven, Monaco has historically drawn many rich foreign individuals and companies eager to take advantage of Monaco's generous corporate tax incentives. There is no personal income tax in Monaco. Monaco derives a significant portion of its revenues (around 40 percent) from value-added taxes imposed on hotels, banks, and the industrial sector.

While it has no commercial-scale agriculture, Monaco does feature a small and increasingly eco-friendly industrial base. The principality's exports include chemicals, cosmetics, pharmaceuticals, glassware, ceramics, plastics, precision instruments, processed foods, postal stamps, and milled flour. These are primarily shipped to Monaco's trading partners, the largest of which is France.

Many of Monaco's residents work in sales, manufacturing, or other sectors that involve the tourism industry. Industrial workers account for roughly 16 percent of Monaco's residents. The service industry, including jobs in entertainment, resorts, and hotels, employs approximately half of Monaco's working residents, and generates the majority of the nation's revenue. Monaco's industrial district is kept separate from the other areas of the principality.

Labor

Monaco's workforce totaled nearly 52,000 in 2014. The private sector was the leading employer, with an estimated 44,736 workers. Industry accounted for about 16 percent of the labor force.

Energy/Power/Natural Resources

Monaco has no natural resources of its own, mostly due to the fact that it is entirely urban. Residents rely on resources that are imported, mainly from France.

Agriculture

Agriculture is essentially nonexistent in Monaco. Because the nation is so densely populated and is 100 percent urban, there is no substantial farming or internal sources of produce. Any agricultural goods are either imported or grown in France. Tomatoes, grapes, and other vine fruits are widely consumed in Monaco, but are not widely grown there. Monaco does have an active fishing industry, but it is not an important part of trade.

Tourism

Revenue generated by tourism is usually around $530 million USD annually. The Monte Carlo Resort and Casino, and other attractions in Monaco draw over 600,000 visitors each year.

Tourists are anxious to gamble at the casinos, watch the Monte Carlo Rally and the Monaco Grand Prix auto races, and visit the palace of the Prince. Shopping, relaxing at the beaches, going to nightclubs, and attending theater performances are among the most popular activities for visitors. Tourists also collect Monaco's unique postage stamps as souvenirs.

Alyssa Connell and Richard Means

DO YOU KNOW?

- Monaco's Prince Rainier III was married to American film star Grace Kelly until her accidental death in 1982.

- The entire country of Monaco is smaller in area than New York City's Central Park.

- The study of le monegú in the principality's schools was introduced in 1976. Each year, the Monaco City Council sponsors a le monegú language competition, which is open to secondary school students. The students must take translation, reading comprehension, and vocabulary, grammar, and oral language tests. The winners are awarded prizes by Monaco's prince in a ceremony conducted at the City Hall courtyard.

Bibliography

Anne Edwards. *The Grimaldis of Monaco*. New York: William Morrow and Company, 1992.

David C. King, David C. *Cultures of the World: Monaco*. New York: Marshall Cavendish, 2008.

Emily Filou, Emily, et al. *Provence and the Côte d'Azur*. Oakland, CA: Lonely Planet, 2013.

Martin Hintz. *Monaco (Enchantment of the World Series)*. New York: Children's Press, 2004.

Michael Hewett. *Monaco Grand Prix: A Photographic Portrait of the World's Most Prestigious Motor Race.* Somerset: Haynes Publishing, 2007.

Thomas Eccardt. *Secrets of the Seven Smallest States of Europe: Andorra, Liechtenstein, Luxembourg, Malta, Monaco, San Marino and Vatican City.* New York: Hippocrene Books, 2005.

Williams, Roger. *Provence and the Côte d'Azur.* New York: DK Publishing Co., 2004.

Works Cited

Glanville Price. "Monégasque." *Encyclopedia of the Languages of Europe.* Blackwell Publishing, 2000. 325–326

"Hymne Monégasque." *Wikipedia* <http://en.wikipedia.org/wiki/Hymne_Mon%C3%A9gasque>

"Important Dates." *Monte-Carlo.mc: Le Guide de la Principauté.* <http://www.monte-carlo.mc/index-important_dates-en.html>

Jennifer B. Petersen, "Grace Kelly." *History Reference Center.* 2005. EBSCO. <http://search.ebscohost.com/login.aspx?direct=true&db=khh&AN=18055831&site=ehost-live>

"Louis Notari." *Wikipedia.* <http://en.wikipedia.org/wiki/Louis_Notari>

"Monaco." *Encyclopaedia Britannia.* 2009 <http://proxy.library.upenn.edu:3225/eb/article-9053301>

"Monaco." *Wikipedia.* <http://en.wikipedia.org/wiki/Monaco>

"Monaco Overview." *iExplore.* 2009. Adventure Travel. <http://www.iexplore.com/dmap/Monaco/Overview>

"Monégasque Language." *Wikipedia.* <http://en.wikipedia.org/wiki/Mon%C3%A9gasque_language>

"The Church of St Devote of Monaco." *Principauté de Monaco: Ministère d'Etat.* <http://www.gouv.mc/devwww/wwwnew.nsf/1909$/7F82F4DC1F0415D9C125706F00468819GB?OpenDocument&2GB>

NETHERLANDS

Introduction

The Netherlands is known officially as the Kingdom of the Netherlands. It is also unofficially known as Holland, which means "land in a hollow." Its overseas territories include the Netherlands Antilles, located off the coast of Venezuela, and Aruba, an island in the Caribbean Sea.

The Netherlands has made valuable contributions to Western culture, sports and the sciences, and has produced such famous artists as Rembrandt, Vermeer, and van Gogh.

GENERAL INFORMATION

Official Language: Dutch
Population: 16,877,351 (2014 estimate)
Currency: Euro, which the Netherlands began using in January 2002.
Coins: The Euro has eight coin denominations: 1, 2, 5, 10, 20, and 50, as well as a 1 Euro coin and a 2 Euro coin. While the denomination side of a Euro coin remains the same throughout all countries that have adopted the Euro as currency, the image on the coin's face side varies according to the country that released the coin into circulation.

Land Area: 13,086 square miles (33,893 square kilometers)
Water Area: 2,953 square miles (7,650 square kilometers)
National Anthem: "Wilhelmus van Nassouwe" (William of Nassau)
Capital: The constitutional capital of the Netherlands is Amsterdam; the seat of government is The Hague.
Time Zone: Central European Standard Time, GMT +1
Flag Description: The tricolor flag of the Kingdom of the Netherlands consists of three equal and horizontal stripes of red (top), white (middle) and blue (bottom). It is considered the first and oldest tricolor flag in use today.

Principal Cities by Population (2012):

- Amsterdam (776,226)
- Rotterdam (576,302)
- Den Haag (490,282)
- Utrecht (311,171)
- Eindhoven (225,421)
- Almere (216,369)
- Tilburg (209,542)
- Groningen (183,147)
- Breda (181,887)
- Nijmegen (158,347) (2008 estimate)
- Apeldoorn (157,217) (2008 estimate)

Population

The Netherlands is a densely populated country, with most of its people living in the provinces of North Holland and South Holland (Noord/Zuid-Holland). No cities in the Netherlands have a population exceeding 1 million. It is estimated that over 80 percent of the population is Caucasian Dutch, mainly of German and Gallo-Celtic ancestry. In recent years, the population of the Netherlands has been classified as ageing; it is estimated that by 2030, 4 million citizens will be over the age of 65, representing roughly a quarter of the population.

Languages

The most commonly spoken language in the Netherlands is Dutch, a Germanic language. In the bilingual province of Friesland, Frisian is also spoken. Most Dutch people also speak English.

Native People & Ethnic Groups

The Dutch are primarily of Germanic heritage, although the Netherlands is also home to a number of minority groups, including Moroccans, Turks, Indonesians, and Surinamese. In the 1970s, many non-white immigrants came to live in the country, most from the Netherlands Antilles, Java, Molucca, and Suriname. This wave of immigration caused racial tensions to rise.

One result of large-scale immigration has been policy reform, which placed more restrictions on residence permits and the granting of asylum. In spite of the liberal atmosphere in the Netherlands, non-whites continue to confront economic and social discrimination.

The Netherlands has an international reputation as open and tolerant society, but it lives with painful memories of recent oppression. The country was occupied by Nazi Germany from 1940 to 1945. The Dutch government went into exile during the occupation and the country's Jewish population faced deportation and certain death at concentration camps. All told, three-quarters of the Netherlands' Jewish population was killed.

Religions

Although around 40 percent of the Dutch population does not belong to any organized religion, the Roman Catholic Church and the Dutch Reformed Church are the major religious institutions. Only about one percent of the current population is Jewish.

The Dutch enjoy religious freedom and tolerance; however, society in the Netherlands is divided along religious lines. Catholics live primarily in the south, while Protestants are concentrated in the southeast and northwest.

Climate

The Netherlands has a temperate climate. Winters are typically mild, with temperatures around 2° Celsius (35° Fahrenheit), and summer temperatures averaging 17° Celsius (63° Fahrenheit). The cool summers and mild winters are a result of the country's location near the North Sea, which keeps temperatures in the moderate range. Coastal areas tend to be cooler than inland regions.

ENVIRONMENT & GEOGRAPHY

Topography

The Netherlands is located in northwestern Europe. The country is bounded by Germany to the east, Belgium to the south, and to the north and west by the North Sea.

More than half of the population lives on land that is below sea level (around 27 percent of the total land area). To the southeast, the elevation rises to about 321 meters (1,053 feet) above sea level. The lowest part of the Netherlands, located northeast of Rotterdam, is 6.7 meters (22 feet) below sea level.

Three major rivers (the Rhine, the Meuse, and the Scheldt) form a delta that has created the country's lowlands. Another notable body of water is the Zuiderzee, or "south sea." The Zuiderzee is an example of the constant battle for the Dutch to reclaim dry land that has been repeatedly flooded. A major flood in 1953, in which over a 1,000 people were killed, prompted the government to develop a system of floodgates and dams to control the water.

Amsterdam has a metropolitan area of 219 square kilometers (84.56 square miles). It is located in the northwestern region of the country, in the province of North Holland. The city is about 24 kilometers (15 miles) inland from the North Sea.

Amsterdam originally developed around the seaport region of the IJ Bay and the Amstel River. The city's name was originally Amstellerdam, derived from the two Dutch words meaning "dam on the Amstel River." As the city grew, a network of over forty canals was established, radiating outward from the heart of the city. The streets of Amsterdam are joined by over 400 bridges, which cross the canals. The many canals of Amsterdam have earned the city the nickname "Venice of the North."

The canals are functional as well as beautiful. They are one of many solutions the Dutch have found to keep their land from flooding, along with a network of dikes and drainage ditches. The first dikes were constructed over 2,000 years ago. Windmills and electric pumps are also used to keep the water at bay and to reclaim land, known as "polder," from the sea. The extensive series of canals in the Netherlands are used for trade, travel, and recreation.

Plants & Animals

Although the Netherlands has over 100 native species of trees and shrubs, only around 8 percent of the country is covered with woodland. Rare species of trees include crab apple (Malus sylvestris), barberry (Berberis vulgaris), and red honeysuckle (Lonicera xylosteum). Most existing forest consists of pine trees.

The Netherlands is rich in bird life, especially migratory waterfowl. Common species include the black-winged stilt, the Terek sandpiper, and Heuglin's gull.

Grasslands are used to graze dairy cattle and other livestock. The Dutch have developed several notable breeds of domestic animals. The Dutch warmblood horse is a popular sport horse, used in events such as jumping and dressage. There are two breeds of Dutch warmblood: the Gelderlander and the Groningen. The Keeshond and the Dutch Shepherd are breeds of dog developed for guard duty and herding.

CUSTOMS & COURTESIES

Greetings

The Dutch customarily greet one another with a strong handshake, smile and exchange of names, and traditionally offer greetings to all the people in a gathering, including children. The Dutch use formal titles and last names for all people except intimate friends and family. Good friends or family may kiss one another on the cheek two or three times. Common Dutch greetings include "Hallo" ("Hello"), "Goedemorgen" ("Good day"), "Goedenavond" ("Good evening"), "Goedenacht" ("Goodnight"), "Dag" (loosely meaning "hi" or "goodbye"), "Gauw tot ziens" ("See you soon"), "Hoe gaat het?" ("How are you?"), and "Alles goed?" ("Is everything good?").

The Dutch are generally characterized as private and reserved in all areas except conversation. The Dutch respect people who are direct and avoid extra conversational filler. Subtlety is not considered to be a strength or virtue in the Netherlands. The Dutch limit praise and compliments, and excessive praise is often considered to be insincere or self-interested. For example, parents or bosses tend not to use superlatives when speaking to children or employees.

Gestures & Etiquette

Proper etiquette requires that people maintain physical space and not move toward someone when they are speaking. (The desire for physical or social space may be linked to how densely-populated the Netherlands has become.) Eye contact and friendly expressions are important, and the Dutch may wave a finger in the air to make their point during conversation.

The Dutch do not invite acquaintances or new friends to their homes as homes are private and reserved for intimate friends and family. Also, the Dutch do not traditionally equate food or drink with friendship or hospitality, and food is almost exclusively shared between family members or extremely close friends. The Dutch value punctuality or even arriving early, and lateness may be considered rude and lazy. As such, written schedules at work and at home are followed strictly, and work activities, events, chores, socializing and leisure are commonly scheduled in advance.

While Dutch etiquette follows the norms of most Western nations, the Dutch do have some unique ways. For instance, the Dutch people do not form lines when waiting for events or to purchase tickets. In public settings, such as elevators or trains, the Dutch do not generally speak with strangers. The Dutch culture is also very egalitarian. For example, all Dutch, regardless of age or status, refer to one another with the informal "jij" (you) rather than the formal "u" (you). As a result of this equality, no person, regardless of social status, gender and age, is given any extra consideration (such as a seat on the bus) when out in public.

Taboo gestures or acts include pointing a finger to the forehead to suggest that someone is crazy, chewing gum while talking, and pushing between people who are engaged in conversation.

Eating/Meals

The Dutch eat three meals a day including breakfast, lunch and dinner. For urban people, dinner is the main meal of the day, while for rural people, the midday lunch is the largest meal of the day. Traditionally, meals are eaten at home with family. Dinner invitations are rarely extended to anyone except the closest of friends and family. Friends and neighbors often share coffee and cookies rather than meals. The Dutch, at work and at home, take a break from their activities and socialize during their coffee breaks.

Table manners and meals tend to be formal in the Netherlands. The Dutch eat nearly all food, including sandwiches, with utensils, and generally make it a habit to wash their hands scrupulously before eating. Per proper etiquette, hands are kept above the table throughout the meal. The Dutch also hold their utensils in the continental style: fork in the left hand and the knife in the right.

Family members arrive at meals on time and begin eating simultaneously and will stay seated until everyone is done eating. The Dutch consider it rude to raise one's fork before others have begun to eat, and it may not be uncommon to hear "eet smakelijk" ("eat deliciously") proclaimed by the host prior to eating. Leaving food on one's plate is considered rude and wasteful, and it is customary to rest any utensils in parallel positions on the plate when finished.

Visiting

For the Dutch, the home is very private and usually considered the exclusive domain of family and intimate friends. As such, casual visiting is traditionally uncommon, and the Dutch customarily refrain from visiting unannounced or uninvited. When the Dutch invite good friends and family over for a visit, social custom dictates that the visitor or guest bring a wrapped gift of flowers, chocolate or wine. When giving flowers, odd numbers are preferred (though the number thirteen is considered to be unlucky). When guests arrive, they should wait be invited in before entering the home. Despite the formality and structure of visiting in the Netherlands, Dutch families are generous hosts and work to make guests feel welcome.

Family and intimate friends customarily visit one another on holidays, including New Year's Eve and Christmas. Christmas breakfast includes kerststol (fruit and almond bread) or krentebolletjes (current buns). Christmas dinner may include fondue, roast pork or kroketten (fried breaded ragout). Families attend church together on Christmas Eve and Christmas Day. The Dutch invite neighbors over for coffee and dessert on Christmas and 2de Kerstdag (Second Christmas Day).

LIFESTYLE

Family

Families in the Netherlands are strong and enduring. The nuclear family unit remains common and extended family is important, though multi-generational households are not the norm. Extended families also tend to live close to one another.

Women are increasingly choosing to work outside the home, and grandparents and other older relatives often help with the childcare responsibilities of working parents. Additionally, women generally keep their maiden names when they marry.

Dutch couples are encouraged to live together before they marry and the government recognizes and endorses three types of unions: traditional marriage, registered partnership, and a cohabitation agreement. In 2001, the Netherlands became the first country in the world to legalize gay marriage.

Housing

The majority of Dutch housing and urban areas are practical, ordered, uniform, compact and well-planned. Dutch housing must meet the government's technical and aesthetic requirements as specified in the government's Building Decree (called Bouwbesluit). Dutch municipalities must approve the addition of roof dormers, bay windows, colors, gutters and new materials to new construction. Housing in the Netherlands is also strongly associated with the gracious canal houses built as early as the 17th century. Dutch homes generally have front gardens with flowers and kitchen herbs.

The Netherlands struggles to provide affordable housing for the population at large. Following World War II, the Netherlands experienced a building boom to rebuild the housing destroyed during the war. Despite the building boom, affordable housing tends to be hard to find in the Netherlands. Overcrowding and housing shortages remain national problems. The government subsidizes the building of lower income housing, and apartment buildings and houseboats (anchored on canals) are common in urban areas. Single-family homes are the norm in the countryside.

Food

Traditional Dutch cuisine, the cuisine of the Netherlands, is similar to neighboring Northern European cuisines and is often characterized by simplicity (boiled vegetables and potatoes and pan-fried meat) and hearty and ungarnished meals. A historically seafaring nation, fish and seafood are prominent staples, and the Dutch are known for their cheeses. Beef, chicken and pork are commonly eaten meats. Dutch cuisine has also been influenced by the nation's colonial experiences in Southeast Asia.

The Dutch breakfast may commonly include sandwiches of cheese, peanut butter or chocolate spread. Lunch tends to include a sandwich of cold cuts and small salad. Dinner, most often eaten in the early evening, includes many courses of meat, fish, chicken and potatoes. Immigrants from the former Dutch colonies of Suriname and Indonesia, as well as foreign workers from Turkey, are increasingly influencing the local flavors and foods of the Netherlands.

Traditional Dutch foods include stamppot, pea soup, patat, herring and stroopwafel. Stamppot is a traditional Dutch meal of rookworst (smoked sausage) served with a combination of mashed potatoes, carrot, kale and endive. The Dutch adore a very thick pea soup with bits of bacon and root vegetables. Patat are French fries, which are commonly sold be snackbars in many forms including patat met (French fries with mayonnaise) and patat speciaal (French fries with mayonnaise, ketchup, and raw onions).

The Dutch enjoy eating herring fish raw with chopped white onion. In the Netherlands, stroopwafel is a favorite dessert. Stroopwaffel is a sandwich cookie with a caramel syrup filling. The cookies are prepared with a special waffle iron, and Dutch families often pass down their stroopwaffel iron from generation to generation.

Life's Milestones

For most Dutch people, the most important life milestones are the religious rituals of baptism, first communion, confirmation and marriage—Roman Catholicism is the largest religion at nearly 30 percent of the population—while the most important secular milestones are annual birthdays. In fact, it is not uncommon for Dutch households to prominently display calendars with the birthdays of friends and families clearly marked.

The Dutch enthusiastically and traditionally celebrate their own birthdays, and those of friends and family (even distant family), with a party. Dutch birthday parties, called birthday circles, tend to be ritualized. To prepare for the party, the hosts will clean the house, prepare a cake, brew coffee, and arrange all available chairs in a circle in the largest room in the house. Guests bring gifts of wine, flowers, pastries, candy or gift certificates to the guest of honor. Etiquette requires that guests greet each person in the birthday circle with a congratulatory birthday greeting. After the guest has greeted each person, he or she takes a seat in the circle. Birthdays are also celebrated in the workplace. For the Dutch, the birthday ritual unites and reinforces the bonds of families and support networks.

CULTURAL HISTORY

Art

The Netherlands is known for its famous painters and history of art patronage. Dutch (the Netherlands' main ethnic group) painters have directed and inspired the international art scene since the 15th century. For instance, Dutch painter Hieronymus Bosch (1450–1516) painted fantastical and detailed narrative paintings which influenced painting styles for hundred of years.

In the 17th century, the Netherlands was the site of a rich and prolific "Golden Age" in painting. (The Netherlands' Golden Age was a time in which Dutch culture, art, architecture and science was internationally known and appreciated.) Dutch painters focused on particular genre and styles of painting such as portraitures, landscapes, still life and historical or epic paintings. Famous Dutch painters of the time include Rembrandt Harmenszoon van Rijn (1606–1669) and Jan Vermeer (1632–1675). Rembrandt is celebrated as a master portrait artist, while Vermeer painted domestic scenes and is considered a master of contrasting light and dark.

In the 19th and 20th centuries, Dutch painters continued to influence and direct international painting styles and movements. Dutch painter Vincent van Gogh (1853–1890) painted dramatic, emotional and colorful paintings while Pieter Cornelis Mondriaan (1872–1944) painted stark modern paintings of color grids. Willem de Kooning (1904–1997) painted abstract expressionist paintings in which the painter's marks and emotions are seen and felt.

The Dutch government, as part of its larger cultural policy, supports contemporary Dutch artists (specifically art academy graduates) through grants, programs, commissions and stipends. The Dutch people appreciate and support the arts, and culture in general, as demonstrated by the existence of more than 600 museums in the Netherlands.

Music

Dutch music includes a wide range of styles and genres such as folk, classical, jazz, pop, rock, hip-hop and electronic. Levenslied (life songs) is the main genre of Dutch folk music. Levenslied became newly popular in the 1970s. Song themes include death, birth, romantic love, and loss. The levenslied folk songs tend to be simple, sentimental and easy for large numbers of people to remember. Levenslied are traditionally performed along with accordion and barrel organ music.

Classical music is part of Dutch culture and identity. Dutch classical composers tend to be very experimental and forward thinking in their work. Over the past few hundred years, the Dutch people have recognized and celebrated numerous internationally known Dutch classical composers including Alphons Diepenbrock (1862–1921), Willem Pijper (1894–1947) and Jan Pieterszoon Swelinck (1562–1621).

Jazz music became popular in the Netherlands in the early 20th century. Dutch jazz music includes internationally celebrated musicians and composers. The Netherlands' annual jazz festivals bring international visitors to hear new and established jazz duos and trios. Dutch pop, rock, hip-hop and electronic also continue to be popular in the Netherlands. African and Middle Eastern immigrants to the Netherlands have shaped the pop, rock and hip-hop sounds over the past few decades. Dutch pop music, which is called nederpop, is generally sung in both Dutch and English.

American and British music, as well as the African inspired musical sounds and styles of former Dutch colonies such as the Netherlands Antilles, influence all types of contemporary Dutch music.

Dance

Traditional Dutch folk dances are referred to as folkloristisch, boerendansen (farmer-dancing) or klompendans (clog dancing). Folk dances are performed throughout the Netherlands. Traditional Dutch folk dances, such as the baanopstekker, riepe riepe garste, burenploff, ijs polka, slaapmuts, swart, vleegerd and zeeuwse rei, tend to be danced by couples. Many of these dances have their origins in rural life, farm chores and celebrations.

In the baanopstekker, couples dance together in a circle by hooking elbows and performing a gallop step. In the riepe riepe garste, couples form a double circle with men on the inside facing their female partners. The steps of the riepe riepe garste dance reference the physical act of harvesting barley. In the ijs polka, couples perform a hop step together in a circle, while in the

slaapmuts, couples dance in a circle facing the center.

Traditional Dutch folk dances are performed at festivals, parties and schools. Traditional dress is worn during dance performance and varies within the Netherlands' twelve provinces. Examples of traditional dress or costume for women include brightly colored wooden clogs, multilayered dark skirts, shawl or apron, lace cap or casque (helmet-shaped head covering), small purse and pendant or broach. The traditional Dutch dress or costume for men includes a vest or jacket, pants, hat, and brightly colored wooden clogs.

Literature

The Netherlands' literary tradition of religious writings, plays, satire and poetry began in the 16th century. Dutch writer Desiderius Erasmus (1466–1536) was an expert in Catholic theology and humanistic thought. Erasmus translated the New Testament into Latin and Greek. His work was considered controversial during the tumult of the Protestant Reformation, a religious reform movement of the early 16th and 17th centuries.

In the 17th century, during the Netherlands' Golden Age, Dutch writers Joost van den Vondel (1587–1679) and Pieter Corneliszoon Hooft (1581–1647) wrote plays, poems and historical accounts. In the 19th century, Dutch writers used their writing to challenge the practice of Dutch colonialism ad the established social order. For instance, Eduard Douwes Dekker (1820–1887) wrote a well-known novel entitled *Max Havelaar* (1860) which satirized the Dutch colonial presence in the Dutch East Indies colony.

Today, Dutch literature is read in countries around the world. Literary works, written in Dutch, are translated into a wide range of languages including English, Spanish, German and French. Well-known contemporary Dutch writers include Cees Nooteboom (1933–), Willem Frederik Hermans (1921–1995) and Jan Hendrik Wolkers (1925–2007). These prominent writers, along with many contemporary Dutch authors, write in multiple genres including essays, plays, poetry, novels, short stories and philosophical treatises.

CULTURE

Arts & Entertainment

In the Netherlands, the arts preserve and promote the country's cultural traditions and collective identity, and are a point of pride for the Dutch. The Dutch people work to preserve and support their national arts which they believe illustrates their unique skills, techniques, and traditions. In particular, the Dutch are particularly proud of their traditional crafts, Golden Age painters and performance arts.

Traditional Dutch crafts include blue-and-white Delft ceramics, rope making, wooden shoe (klompen) carving and knitting. Delft pottery, which is strongly associated with the Netherlands, was first produced in the city of Delft in 1653. The Dutch government has worked to subsidize an apprentice system that allows apprentices to enter the Delft pottery making trade at 16 and train with master potters for eight years. The designs on Delft plates, vases and pitchers were originally based on 17th-century Chinese porcelain. The techniques and skills of rope making (originally used on ships), wooden shoe (klompen) carving and knitting (traditional fisherman's sweaters, shawls and caps) are primarily passed down within families. The Dutch people admire people with traditional handiwork skills.

The performance arts are supported and promoted through performances and festivals. The Dutch appreciate ballet and classical music, and the Concertgebouw Orchestra, the National Ballet and the Netherlands Dance Theater are popular performance art venues.

The Dutch celebrate medieval and Renaissance music at the annual Early Music Festival of Utrecht. Other important performance art festivals include the North Sea Jazz Festival in The Hague, the Pinkpop Festival (rock festival), the Lowlands festival (popular music) and the Holland Festival (performance arts) in Amsterdam.

For recreation and leisure, the Dutch enjoy skating on frozen lakes and canals during the winter. Dutch speed skaters are consistently the worldwide leaders in their sport. Cycling is a popular mode of transportation in the Netherlands, and there are many scenic cycling tours for visitors. The national sport is football (soccer), and the Dutch Football Association is the country's largest sporting organization.

Cultural Sites & Landmarks

Landmarks that are often associated with the Netherlands include art museums, tulip gardens, windmills (called polder mills) and historical architecture.

Those searching for the Netherlands' famous tulip fields and windmills must travel outside of the major cities to the countryside. The Holland Tulip Garden, located in Vogelenzang, is open annually from March to May. The famed garden, which grows over 1,000 kinds of flowering bulbs and 700 types of tulips, showcases hundreds of thousands of flowers for visitors in its greenhouses, gardens and fields. As of 2009, there were fewer than 1,000 intact windmills (traditionally used in the Netherlands to harness the power of the wind for sawmills, farming and grain production) remaining in the Netherlands. Many of these preserved windmills are located in the Kinderdijk-Elshout region.

The United Nations Educational, Scientific and Cultural Organization (UNESCO) recognizes seven historical sites in the Netherlands as requiring international recognition and preservation efforts. They include the Defense Line of Amsterdam; Droogmakerij de Beemster (Beemster Polder or Low-Lying Land); Historic Area of Willemstad, Inner City and Harbour, Netherlands Antilles; Ir.D.F. Woudagemaal (D.F. Wouda Steam Pumping Station); Mill Network at Kinderdijk-Elshout; Rietveld Schröderhuis (Rietveld Schröder House); and the Schokland Peninsula. Many of these sites demonstrate the Dutch people's historic ability to harness the power of water through engineering and design.

The Defense Line of Amsterdam is the only remaining example of a city fortification that is based on the control of water (temporary flooding) through hydraulic engineering. Droogmakerij de Beemster (Beemster Polder), which dates to the 17th century, is a network of preserved fields, roads, canals, dykes and settlements. The Ir.D.F. Woudagemaal (D.F. Wouda Steam Pumping Station) is the largest steam-pumping station in the world, and the Mill Network at Kinderdijk-Elshout is a protected network of dykes, reservoirs, pumping stations, administrative buildings and preserved windmills. The Rietveld Schröderhuis (Rietveld Schröder House) is considered to be an icon of modern architecture. The Schokland Peninsula and surrounding area has evidence of human settlement from prehistoric times.

The Dam Square Royal Palace of the Netherlands is located in the oldest part of Amsterdam and sits atop the dam for which the city was named. The palace was built between 1648 and 1665 and has been used both as a royal palace and as a city hall. The royal family often receives international guests at the palace rather than at their residence in The Hague.

Libraries & Museums

The Van Gogh Museum in Amsterdam contains the world's largest collection of Vincent van Gogh paintings. The Rembrandt House Museum in Amsterdam is the actual house where Rembrandt lived between 1639 and 1658. The Rijksmuseum in Amsterdam houses a huge collection of Golden Age Dutch master paintings, etchings and drawings.

The Netherlands' folk museums, including the Enkhuizen Zuiderzee Museum, the Zaanse Schans Open-Air Museum and the Arnhem Open-Air Folk Museum, all which house examples of traditional Dutch crafts.

One of the most noted landmarks in Amsterdam is the Anne Frank House. Located in the region of Amsterdam known as the Western Ring of Canals, the attic annex of the row-house and factory shop at 263 Prinsengracht served as the hiding place for two Jewish families during the Nazi occupation of Amsterdam in World War II. The secret annex was raided on August 4, 1944, and Anne and the other occupants were immediately deported to concentration camps. The story of the secret annex was made public with the publication of Anne's diary, which she kept during her time in hiding. "The Diary of a Young Girl" was first published in 1947 and became a World-renowned record of Jewish persecution by the Nazis.

The National Library of the Netherlands was established in 1798. It houses over six million items. The institution completed a large-scale digital library in 2013.

Holidays

The national holiday of the Netherlands is Queen's Day (April 30). This holiday honors Princess Juliana, a member of the royal family who died on March 20, 2004. Queen's Day features celebrations in the streets that last all night, as well as eating and drinking, and sidewalk vendors selling various items.

Youth Culture

Youth culture in the Netherlands is focused on sports, education and family. Popular sports include football (soccer), tennis, and sailing, ice skating, field hockey, basketball, badminton, pole vaulting, and cycling. Bicycling is particularly popular among Dutch teenagers and adults, alike, and there are bike paths, called fietspaden, in every Dutch town and city.

The Dutch value education and youth must attend school from four to 18 years of age. Teachers encourage Dutch youth to develop their scientific thinking as well as artistic expression. Dutch youth tend to be close to their families and are typically reserved in public. Teenagers are given a lot of freedom to come and go as they please, but the majority of teens socialize with family and friends within their own homes.

SOCIETY

Transportation

The Dutch people prefer to travel between cities by car or train. Trains are either stoptreinen (local trains) or intercities (long distance trains). Metros, trams and busses run throughout the day in the major cities and on a reduced schedule at night. Whenever possible, the Dutch travel by bike. The Dutch, who value physical health, stamina, and self-sufficiency, attach big buckets with wheels on the front of their bikes to hold cargo or kids. Well-maintained and much used bike paths are a ubiquitous part of Dutch towns and cities. The Dutch drive on the right side of the road. Seat belts, both for front and rear occupants, are compulsory.

Transportation Infrastructure

Transportation in the Netherlands, a country the size of the state of Maryland, is generally characterized as well-planned, well-maintained, punctual and inexpensive. More than 12,000 companies are in service in the Dutch transportation sector. As of 2010, there were 28 airports, approximately 2,800 kilometers (1,745 miles) of railways, and nearly 125,575 kilometers (78,029 miles) of roadways, as well as an extensive waterway system. (There are no toll roads in the Netherlands).

The cities of Amsterdam, Ijmuiden, Rotterdam, Terneuzen and Vlissingen have major ports and terminals, and the transportation network connects all the major cities and towns.

Media & Communications

The Netherlands Broadcasting Foundation and the Netherlands World Broadcasting Service broadcast within the Netherlands and abroad. The television broadcasting market has been characterized as competitive and public programming is allocated to interest groups depending on their membership. The Dutch are highly literate people and value daily newspapers. In fact, the Dutch claim one of the oldest newspapers, *Oprechte Haarlemsche Courant*, first published in 1656, and still published today (merged with the *Haarlems Dagblad*). The Dutch constitution guarantees completed freedom of speech. As a result, media censorship is extremely rare in the Netherlands.

The Netherlands has a highly developed and well-maintained media and communications system. In 2012, there were over seven million landline telephone users, 19 million mobile phone users, and 15 million Internet users. The Dutch government oversees and operates the postal, telegraph and telephone systems. Radio and television stations are plentiful and reception is strong throughout the country.

SOCIAL DEVELOPMENT

Standard of Living

In 2009, the Netherlands were ranked fourth out of 187 countries on the Human Development Index (HDI).

Water Consumption

Water quality and sanitation in the Netherlands is generally regarded as good. The private provisioning of water supply is banned, and ten regional companies are responsible for providing drinking water. Water boards, considered one of the oldest forms of governance in the Netherlands (they date to the 13th century), oversee regional water quality.

Among developed countries, the Netherlands maintains one of the lowest rates of water consumption. Between 2003 and 2006, the consumption of tap water decreased slightly.

Education

The Dutch are a well-educated people, with almost universal literacy. The education system is decentralized, with students attending either public, Roman Catholic, or private schools. Both public and private schools are eligible for government funding. Primary education occurs between five and twelve years of age. Secondary education is compulsory for children between 12 and 15 years. Starting in the fifth grade, students must study the English language.

Major universities in the Netherlands include the Delft University of Technology, the Erasmus University of Rotterdam, and Utrecht University. The University of Amsterdam is the largest in the country. There are also adult education and vocational training centers throughout the country, which combine study with practical experience.

The Netherlands has a literacy rate of 99 percent, and primary and secondary school enrollment rates are higher for females than males.

Women's Rights

Since the early 20th century, when women in the Netherlands won the right to vote in 1917, Dutch women have gained the same legal rights as Dutch men, particularly as specified in Dutch family and property laws and in the judicial system. With the turn of the 21st century, the role and treatment of women in Dutch society and culture is changing as more women enter the workforce and hold elected office.

While more Dutch women are entering the workforce in the early 21st century, their participation remains limited due to a specific lack of affordable day care options. As a result, the majority of Dutch women, particularly mothers, tend to work part time, and unemployment is higher for women than men. In addition, Dutch women generally earn less money than their male counterparts. To combat the inferior placement of women in the workforce, the Dutch government has instituted affirmative action programs and collective labor agreements for women. For example, the Equal Treatment Commission investigates discrimination claims, and there are government programs in place to educate businesses and civil servants about the problem and consequences of sexual harassment and discriminatory hiring practices.

Violence against women (particularly domestic abuse, rape and honor-related violence) is considered to be a national problem. Domestic violence against women is common and frequently underreported, and Dutch law punishes spousal abuse with a greater penalty than regular assault and battery. However, an estimated three percent of spousal abuse allegations result in police arrest. Rape is a criminal offense, typically punishable by an eight- to 15-year prison sentence; between 1,000 and 2,000 rapes are reported

annually. In 2006, there were nearly 300 reported cases of honor-related violence against young women. The government's National Public Health Council is working to end the practice of female genital mutilation (FGM) among immigrant populations. In the Netherlands, the penalty for FGM is six to nine years in prison.

The government-subsidized TransAct Organization offers support for victims of domestic abuse, rape, and honor-related violence. The TransAct Organization has established national networks of support professionals and runs shelters for battered women throughout the Netherlands.

Prostitution is legal in the Netherlands. Prostitutes must be 18 years or older and engaged in the work of their own free will. The government monitors and licenses approximately 30,000 prostitutes. Regulations specify appropriate working conditions and required healthcare for all prostitutes. Despite government oversight of prostitution, coercion and violence are common problems in the sex trade. In addition, the trafficking of women for sexual exploitation is a growing problem in the Netherlands.

Health Care

The Netherlands is a welfare state, or verzorgingsstaat, which means "caretaking state" in Dutch. Tax revenues support health care services. Health insurance is available through the government's insurance program or through private medical insurers, which are organized under Zorgverzekeraars Nederland (ZN).

The state insurance program serves lower-income citizens with limited health benefits and basic care. In an effort to reduce costs for the state, some benefits have been eliminated and co-payments have been introduced.

The Dutch health care system is controversial due to its policy on euthanasia, or assisted suicide. Since 1997, euthanasia conducted under specific conditions and meeting certain criteria has been decriminalized. Some of these conditions include that the patient makes a voluntary and persistent request for euthanasia, and that the patient's suffering is considered unbearable, enduring, and hopeless. Policies and legal decisions regarding euthanasia continue to be publicly debated in the Netherlands.

The government of the Netherlands is known for its relaxed drug policy, which allows the use of cannabis, or marijuana. Using cannabis is not considered a criminal act. Sales of cannabis are strictly monitored and regulated by the government, which considers drug use a health problem rather than a crime. The government spends around $200 million per year to care for drug addicts.

GOVERNMENT

Structure

The Netherlands is a parliamentary democracy under a constitutional monarch. There are 12 provinces in the country: Drenthe, Flevoland, Friesland, Gelderland, Groningen, Limburg, Overijssel, Noord-Brabant, Noord/Zuid-Holland, Utrecht, and Zeeland. The twelve provinces do not have separate systems of government.

The constitution of the Netherlands protects freedom of speech, religion, and political freedom. It also ensures the separation of church and state. There are three major branches of government: the crown, the States General, and the courts.

Although the monarchy's role in government is for the most part ceremonial, the crown does have the power to appoint the "formateur," who organizes the Council of Ministers. This council is responsible for carrying out government policy. Another group, the Council of State, advises the government. The monarchy is also responsible for appointing judges.

There are two houses in the Dutch parliament (the States General): the First Chamber and the Second Chamber. The Second Chamber can initiate legislation and amend bills. Both houses can question ministers and other officials. Members of both houses are elected to four-year terms.

Political Parties

The Netherlands has a multi-party system and coalition governments, in which parties often govern together, can be commonplace. (For example, in February 2007, a coalition agreement was reached by the Christian Democratic Alliance, the Labour Party, and the Christian Union party). Political parties in the country include the centre Christian sDemocratic Alliance (CDA), the liberal People's Party for Freedom and Democracy (VVD), the social democratic Dutch Labour Party (PvdA), and the Socialist Party (SP)—all of which represent the four largest political parties in Dutch government. In the 2012 general elections, 11 political parties gained at least one seat in the House of Representatives; as of 2012, the VVD maintained the most seats.

Local Government

There are three levels of government in the Netherlands, with local governance operating on the provincial and municipal level. The country is divided into twelve provinces, and the governance of each is overseen by an elected provincial council. A provincial executive is then responsible for the day-to-day administration. The Netherlands is further subdivided by 458 municipalities, with each governed by a municipal council. Similar to the provincial executive, a municipal executive oversees the day-to-day management of the municipality. Members of both the municipal and provincial council are elected every four years.

Judicial System

The court system of the Netherlands consists of 62 cantonal courts, 19 district courts, five courts of appeal, and a Supreme Court that is made up of 24 justices.

Taxation

In the Netherlands, the three types of taxable income are income from work and home, income from savings and investments, and income from substantial interest. The tax rate is based on a rising scale, with four different tax brackets as of 2008. Other taxes include the value-added tax (VAT) and a corporate tax, determined at 25.5 percent in December 2008. Tax administration is overseen by the Dutch Tax and Customs Administration.

Armed Forces

The armed forces of the Netherlands is made up of four branches: the Royal Netherlands Army, the Royal Netherlands Navy (including the Marine Corps), the Royal Netherlands Air Force, and the Royal Military Police. Seventeen is the minimum age for voluntary recruitment. In 2008, there was an estimated 53,100 government armed forces personnel.

Foreign Policy

The Netherlands, while not a super power among nations, maintains an internationally active profile and has positive relations with most foreign countries. The Netherlands was a founding member of the North Atlantic Treaty Organization (NATO) and a member nation of the European Union (EU) and the United Nations (UN). The Netherlands is also active with the Organization for Security and Cooperation in Europe (OSCE), the Council of Europe (CoE), the International Monetary Fund (IMF), the International Court of Justice (ICJ), the Yugoslavia and Rwanda War Crimes Tribunals, Eurojust and Europol (European judicial and police organizations), the Organization for the Prohibition of Chemical Weapons (OPCW), and International Criminal Court (ICC). The government does not necessarily maintain neutrality, and the Netherlands takes an active role in international peacekeeping, conflict resolution, human rights, democracy building and Europe's economic stability. (For instance, the Netherlands' Customs Union with Belgium and Luxembourg—the Benelux group—was a precursor to the European Community, itself a precursor to the EU).

Despite the country's small size, the Dutch are the sixth largest provider of foreign aid in the world. For instance, in 2007 the Dutch gave over $6 billion (USD) in foreign aid, which is approximately 0.7 percent of the country's gross domestic product (GDP). The majority of foreign aid is given through the UN Development Programme (UNDP), international financial institutions and EU programs. In fact, as of 2008, the Netherlands provides more money to the general fund of the UN humanitarian program than any other country. The Netherlands also has twenty-nine partner countries that receive aid in a strategic effort to improve women's rights, conflict areas, climate change, private sector development and economic growth. Specific examples of Dutch foreign aid include $60 million (USD) for Afghanistan's reconstruction effort and the canceling of $300 million (USD) of Iraq's debt.

The Netherlands, while considered a friend and ally of nations around the world, struggles to control its international drug problem. The Netherlands is one of the world's biggest producers of synthetic drugs as well as a gateway for the European drug trade. The Dutch are working with the United States to increase the Netherlands international drug trafficking laws. In addition to the U.S.-Netherlands partnership on international drug trafficking laws, the two nations are strong supporters of one another. Both nations aggressively promote free trade and democracy, and are working together to build an open and market-led economy. The Netherlands' main trading partners include the U.S., Germany, Belgium, the United Kingdom (UK), France and Italy.

The Netherlands, which faces environmental problems such as water pollution, air pollution and acid rain, is an active participant in international environmental agreements. For instance the Netherlands is a member of the Antarctic-Environmental Protocol, the Antarctic Treaty and the Kyoto Protocol.

Dependencies

Netherlands' overseas territories include Curaçao, Sint Maarten, and the Caribbean Netherlands, located off the coast of Venezuela, and Aruba, an island in the Caribbean Sea. Curaçao, Sint Maarten, and Aruba are considered constituent countries, while the Caribbean Netherlands are considered special municipalities.

Human Rights Profile

International human rights law insists that states respect civil and political rights, and also promote an individual's economic, social and cultural rights. The United Nations Universal Declaration on Human Rights (UDHR) is recognized as the standard for international human rights. Its authors sought the counsel of the world's great thinkers, philosophers, and religious leaders, and were careful to create a document that reflects the core values shared by every world culture. (To read this document or view the articles relating to cultural human rights, visit: http://www.udhr.org/UDHR/default.htm.)

The Dutch human rights policy is based on the notion that social, moral, economic and cultural rights are interrelated and equally important, and the Netherlands encourages the protection of human rights for its own citizens (in the Netherlands as well as in the former Dutch colonies of Aruba and the Netherlands Antilles) and abroad. In fact, the nation's strong human rights profile is illustrated by an analysis of the ways in which the Dutch meet or exceed the human rights protections specified in the UDHR. Examples of this include recognition and endorsement of three types of marriage (traditional, registered partnership, and cohabitation agreement) by the Dutch government, the banning of capital punishment, and the country's status as a host nation for numerous human rights organizations and institutions.

Article 2 of the UDHR, which states that everyone is entitled to legal rights and freedoms without distinction of race, color, sex, language, religion, political, or other opinion, national or social origin, property, birth or other status, is supported by the Dutch constitution. While Dutch law promotes equality for all, Muslims in the Netherlands do experience extra scrutiny by the government and police. In 2005, a law was put in place that required everyone over the age of fourteen to carry identification. As recently as 2014, human rights groups have found that Muslims are asked to show identification more often than native Dutch citizens.

Article 18 of the UDHR, which supports the right to freedom of thought, conscience and religion, so long as the practice of religion does not violate public morality, decency, or the public order, is supported by Dutch law. Despite the guarantee of religious freedom, the Dutch do struggle with issues related to religious dress. Burqas (robes worn by Muslim females that cover the body from head to toe) are discouraged in school, but headscarves are allowed in Dutch schools. The government is working to ensure the security of its citizens without compromising religious freedoms.

There are some other areas of concern, including the trafficking of women, particularly for the purpose of sexual exploitation. Human rights organizations have also focused on the Netherlands for their treatment of terrorists and those seeking asylum. Lastly, while the Dutch press enjoys great freedom, Dutch law forbids the broadcasting of programs that incite hate.

Migration

In recent years, it is estimated that approximately 20 percent of the Dutch population are children of immigrants or immigrants themselves. Family migration is the primary source of migration in the Netherlands. Since 1998, immigration policies in the Netherlands have become stricter, with recent emphasis on restricting low-skilled migration. Emigration actually exceeded immigration in 2003, the first time since 1984. Restrictions on dual citizenship continue to be a debated issue.

ECONOMY

Overview of the Economy

Private enterprise supports much of the Dutch economy, with a high rate of corporate investment. Shipping and trade form an important part of the economy; exports are responsible for over half of the gross national product. The harbors of Rotterdam and Amsterdam, as well as the extensive system of canals, are vital to the shipping industry. The gross domestic product (GDP) was an estimated $798 billion (USD) in 2014. The GDP real growth rate is around 0.6 percent, and the GDP per capita around $47,400 (USD).

Industry

The service industry is important to the Dutch economy, especially in transportation, trade, and in financial industries like banking and insurance. In the industrial and manufacturing sectors, leading industries include metalworking, oil refining, chemical, and food processing. Traditional occupations such as agriculture and fishing have only a slight impact on the economy.

The Netherlands participates in the European Union (EU), the Benelux Economic Union, the European Monetary System, and the World Trade Organization (WTO).

Labor

According to the CIA World Factbook, as of 2014, the national labor force was estimated at 7.89 million. The services industry accounts for the majority of the Netherlands' labor force. Among member countries of the OECD, the Netherlands has a high labor force participation rate and low unemployment. During the global financial crisis, the unemployment rate increased slightly, to five percent in 2009. This increase, beginning in 2008, ended a three-year decline in unemployment. In 2014, the unemployment rate was 7.2 percent.

Energy/Power/Natural Resources

Natural gas fields near Slochteren in Groningen are an important energy source, and more affordable than coal. While the Netherlands has offshore oil fields, most of the country's oil supply must be imported.

Wind power is another energy resource. The largest wind power plant in Europe is located in the Netherlands, and produces 73 million kilowatt-hours per year. The country also has substantial salt and clay deposits. Salt benefits the chemical industries, while clay is used in the pottery and ceramic industries.

The Netherlands is working toward becoming a more environmentally friendly country in its agricultural and industrial practices. The National Ecological Network works to protect plants and animals that are threatened. The country has 19 national parks, including the Hoge Veluwe and the Veluwezoom.

Fishing

The Netherlands is one Europe's top exporters in the fishing industry, and approximately 80 percent of its catch (fish and shellfish) is sold internationally. As of 2009, most exports, which generate over €2 billion annually, go to European nations. There are over 400 companies in the Netherlands involved in the processing of fish.

Forestry

Forests occupy approximately 10 percent of the Netherlands' land area. Nearly 75 percent is available for recreational purposes as opposed to wood production. On the whole, forest management in the country is not profitable. Most timber and timber products are imported.

Mining/Metals

The southeastern region of the Netherlands has many coal deposits, although most of the coal mines have closed.

Agriculture

Agricultural products account for approximately 20 percent of exports from the Netherlands. Since most of the agricultural land is suitable for grazing cattle, dairy products like cheese are important. Famous cheeses like Gouda and Edam are produced in the towns of the same names. Cheese, butter, and powdered milk are exported in large amounts.

Wheat is an important field crop, and special greenhouses are used to grow vegetables and flowers. Unfortunately, although farming practices are advanced and efficient, they often cause pollution because of the large amounts of fertilizer and other chemicals used.

Flower bulbs are perhaps the most famous and important agricultural product of the Netherlands. Daffodils, hyacinths, irises, and tulips are grown in greenhouses and large fields, with around seven billion bulbs exported each year. The tulip is also the country's national symbol.

Animal Husbandry

Since most of the agricultural land is suitable for grazing cattle, dairy products like cheese are important in the agricultural sector.

Tourism

The tourism industry employs around 300,000 people in the Netherlands. Among the many tourist attractions in the country are the many windmills that were once used to pump water and mill grain. Cycling tours and the tulip fields near Lisse are also popular among tourists.

The long coastline provides many sandy beaches to visit, and many tourists enjoy hiking and walking tours. Other visitors are drawn to the Netherlands for the country's liberal policies on drug use and prostitution.

Simone Flynn, Christina Healey,
Lynn-nore Chittom

DO YOU KNOW?

- In the Netherlands, swimming lessons for children are supported by the government.

- The oldest known boat, the Pesse canoe, was found in Drenthe. This boat was constructed around 6000 BCE.

- The Eleven-City Tour, a long-distance race on ice skates, follows a 200-kilometer (124-mile) course across lakes and canals in Friesland. It was only held 15 times in the 20th century.

- The coastal city of Rotterdam is one of the largest ports in the world.

- According to the Guinness Book of World Records, Amsterdam is home to the narrowest house in the world. The street-side façade of the home measures a mere 101 centimeters (39.76 inches) across.

Bibliography

Colin White and Laurie Boucke. *The UnDutchables: An Observation of the Netherlands, Its Culture and Its Inhabitants.* Oakhurst, CA: White Boucke Publishing, 2013.

Geert Mak. *Amsterdam.* Cambridge, MA: Harvard University Press, 1999.

Martin Dunford and Phil Lee. *Rough Guide to the Netherlands.* London: Rough Guides, 2012.

Paul Arblaster. *A History of the Low Countries.* New York: Palgrave Macmillan, 2012.

Rudy B. Andeweg and Galen A. Irwin. *Governance and Politics of the Netherlands.* Houndsmills, UK: Palgrave Macmillan, 2014.

Ryan Ver Berkmoes. *The Netherlands.* Oakland, CA: Lonely Planet, 2013.

Sean Condon. *My 'Dam Life: Three Years in Holland.* Oakland, CA: Lonely Planet, 2003.

Sheryl Buckland. *Netherlands – Culture Smart!* New York: Kuperard, 2008.

Works Cited

"A Brief Description." *World Atlas.* http://www.worldatlas.com/webimage/countrys/europe/nl.htm.

"Art Museums in the Netherlands." *Artcyclopedia.* http://www.artcyclopedia.com/museums/art-museums-in-the-netherlands.html.

"Background Note: The Netherlands." *U.S. Department of State.* http://www.state.gov/r/pa/ei/bgn/3204.htm.

"Country Reports on Human Rights Practices." *U.S. Department of State.* http://www.state.gov/g/drl/rls/hrrpt/2006/78830.htm.

"Dutch Culture." *The Holland Ring.* http://www.thehollandring.com/dutchculture.shtml.

"Dutch Food and Eating Habits." *The Holland Ring.* http://www.thehollandring.com/food.shtml

"Folk Dancing in the Netherlands." *Volksdansverenigingen.* http://www.euronet.nl/~trio/

"Holland Tulip Garden." *What's On When?* http://www.whatsonwhen.com/sisp/index.htm?fx=event.detail&event_id=26404.

"Netherlands." *CIA World Fact Book.* https://www.cia.gov/library/publications/the-world-factbook/print/nl.html.

"Netherlands." *UNESCO World Heritage List.* http://whc.unesco.org/en/statesparties/nl.

"Netherlands: Language, Culture, Customs and Etiquette." *Kwintessentials.* http://www.kwintessential.co.uk/resources/global-etiquette/netherlands.html.

"Population Estimates for Cities in the Netherlands." *Mongabay.* http://www.mongabay.com/igapo/2005_world_city_populations/Netherlands.html.

"Universal Declaration of Human Rights." *United Nations.* <http://www.udhr.org/UDHR/default.htm>.

"Van Gogh Museum." *The Van Gogh Museum.* http://www3.vangoghmuseum.nl/vgm/index.jsp?lang=en.

Giant's Causeway, the result of an ancient volcanic eruption in Northern Ireland, comprises thousands of inter-locking rock formations (basalt columns). /Stock photo © LanceB

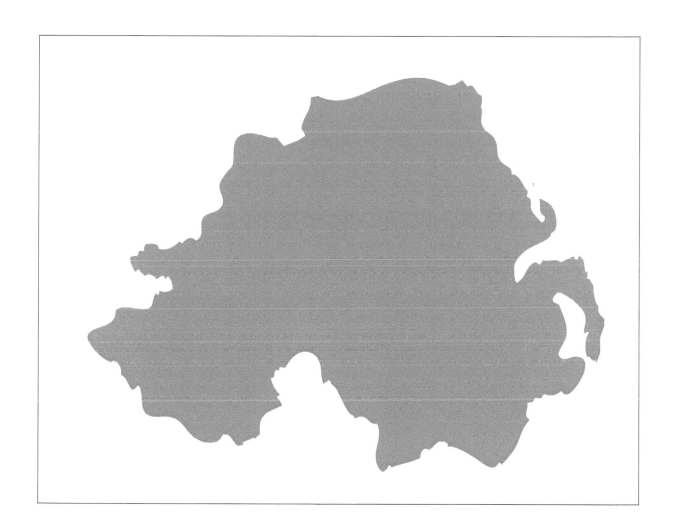

NORTHERN IRELAND

Introduction

Northern Ireland is a province of the United Kingdom of Great Britain (UK). Located in the northeastern portion of the island of Ireland, Northern Ireland consists of six counties: Antrim, Armagh, Down, Fermanagh, Londonderry (Derry), and Tyrone. While it is the most industrialized part of Ireland, Northern Ireland is also known for its scenic countryside and beautiful coastline.

Religious difference between Roman Catholics and Protestants has defined Northern Ireland's politics and culture throughout the 20th and into the 21st century. A majority of Northern Ireland's Catholics (also called republicans or nationalists) have sought independent, home rule for the province (or a reunification with the Republic of Ireland), while most Protestants (referred to as unionists or loyalists) have fought to retain ties to the United Kingdom. The conflict between the two positions resulted in unrest and civil war, referred to as "The Troubles," which lasted from the 1960s to the 1990s. In 1994, a ceasefire was declared between the Catholic-supported Provisional Irish Republican Army (IRA or PIRA) and Protestant loyalist paramilitaries.

The peace of the 1990s has been tenuous, and devolution efforts in the United Kingdom that created the Northern Ireland Assembly in 1999 met roadblocks, as the stalled peace process delayed the actions of a devolved government. Although politicians are working together, violence related to the future of Northern Ireland persists. However, the level of political violence is small compared to previous decades.

Northern Ireland is a traditional and resilient society. Life revolves around community, family and home. Although some family and religious traditions are declining in the early 21st century, attendance at Catholic and Protestant churches is still significant. Many social and community events are still based on religious institutions. In both city neighborhoods and country villages, communities are tight-knit, and family life is of central importance.

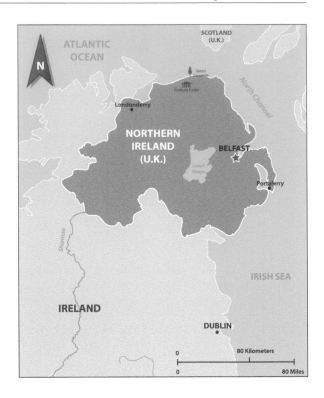

GENERAL INFORMATION

Official Language: English (government also recognizes Irish and Ulster Scots)
Population: 1,847,600 (2015 estimate)
Currency: British Pound Sterling
Coins: One hundred pennies (plural, pence) equal one pound sterling. Coins are issued in denominations of 1 and 2 pounds sterling and 1, 2, 5, 10, 20, and 50 pence.
Land Area: 13,360 square kilometers (5,158 square miles)
Water Area: 511 square kilometers (197 square miles)

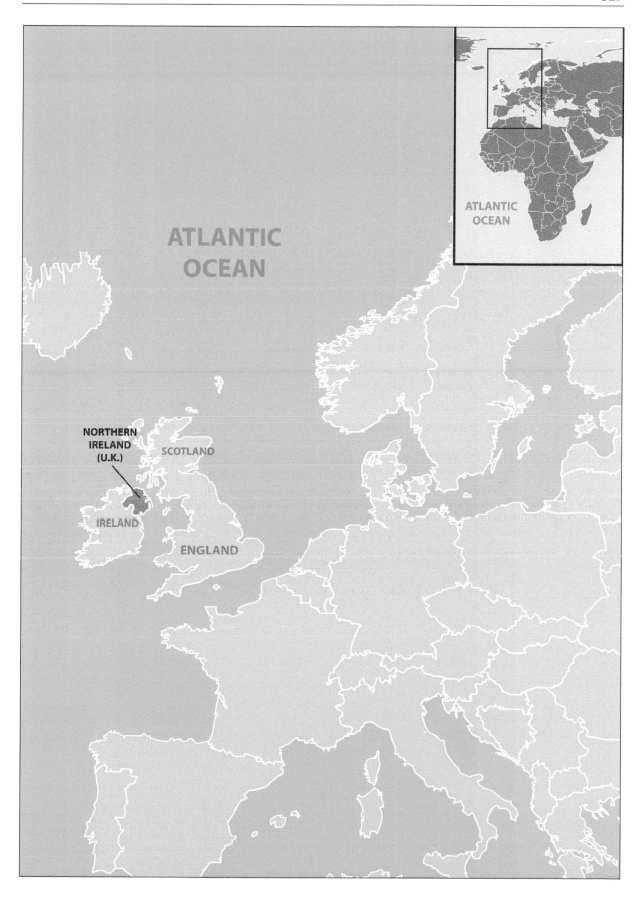

National Anthem: Because it is part of the UK, Northern Ireland shares the anthem "God Save the Queen," although the traditional Irish tune "A Londonderry Air" is also used at official functions.

Capital: Belfast

Time Zone: GMT

Flag Description: The government of Northern Ireland uses the Union flag (or Union Jack). The Union flag consists of a blue background with a white St. George's Cross, a red St. Andrew's Cross, and a red St. Patrick's Cross.

Principal Cities by Population (2011 census):

- Belfast (280,211)
- Londonderry (83,125)
- Lisburn (76,613)
- Newtonabbey (65,555)
- Craigavon (64,193)
- Bangor (61,401)
- Castlereagh (54,990)
- Ballymena (29,467)
- Newtownards (28,039)
- Newry (26,893)

Population

The population of Northern Ireland is largely urban, with about a third of the population settled in Belfast's metropolitan area. Farming remains an important part of life for many families.

Most of the people are white Europeans of English, Irish, or Scottish heritage, and are of either Catholic or Protestant religious background. These religious differences reflect the social and political divisions in the country. One of the problems resulting from these divisions is inequality between Protestants and Catholics; historically, government policy has favored Protestants over Catholics.

Londonderry, which is the second-largest city, is home to a majority of Catholics. Traditionally, the Catholic population of Northern Ireland has preferred the union of the province with the Republic of Ireland.

Languages

English is the official language, but the Irish language, or Gaelic, is sometimes taught in Catholic schools. Ulster Scots, a dialect of Scots, is also recognized by the government.

Native People & Ethnic Groups

Since the third millennium BCE, humans have settled in Northern Ireland. The first Neolithic people farmed the land with flint tools; later, during the Bronze Age (c. 1700 BCE), the area was mined for metals such as copper and tin, which were used to make more sophisticated implements. During the last millennium BCE, Celtic tribes invaded the island, bringing with them the Celtic culture that would become firmly established by the fifth century CE, when Christian culture began to be established there.

During the 17th century, England established control of the island. Colonial activity brought the English and Irish cultures into contact with each other. As a result, changes began to occur in both the agricultural and political way of life. One of the most important agricultural changes occurred in the 18th century, when the potato was introduced.

By the 19th century, the potato had become the most important crop in the Northern counties. As the linen industry declined and competition for agricultural land increased, the north relied more on the potato. This crop changed the relationship between tenant farmers and their landlords, and it helped to sustain the country's population increase. However, between 1845 and 1849, the failure of the potato crop caused widespread famine.

By 1849, the population in the north had dropped by about 20 percent. County Fermanagh suffered the most, losing 26 percent of its population to the famine. During this time, many Irish were forced to leave and immigrated to other countries. Belfast and Londonderry became major ports of departure for these immigrants. It was not until the 1990s that the population returned to the level recorded in the 1841 census.

Other ethnic communities living in Northern Ireland include Polish, Chinese, Indian, Pakistani, and Arab peoples.

Religions

The majority of Northern Irish citizens are Christian, either Protestant or Catholic. The Protestant population, estimated at more than 48 percent of the population in the 2011 census, consists of a number of different denominations, including Presbyterians, Anglicans, and Methodists. Catholics accounted for about 45 percent of the population in 2011.

Climate

A temperate province, Northern Ireland tends to receive less rainfall than the southern and western areas of Ireland. It has a high atmospheric humidity, little sunshine, and 200–225 days of rainfall throughout the year.

Due to the North Atlantic Drift current, winters are mild, and summer temperatures rarely rise above 15° Celsius (59° Fahrenheit). The Atlantic Ocean also produces depressions that make the weather changeable. Although Northern Ireland tends to be cooler than the southern portion of the island, snowfall is rare.

ENVIRONMENT & GEOGRAPHY

Topography

Northern Ireland is bordered by the Republic of Ireland to the west and the south, and by the Irish Sea to the north and east. Its central lowlands are surrounded by hills. Common physical features include mountains, cliffs, grasslands, heaths, moors, and bogs.

Glacial activity during the Ice Age caused the boulder clay soil to form into small hills known as drumlins and ridges called moraines, which dot the landscape.

Notable features include the Antrim Plateau, which is an area of upland 80 kilometers (50 miles)

long and from 16 to 26 kilometers (10 to 16 miles) wide. The Sperrin Mountains in County Londonderry include Keady Mountain (335 meters/1,100 feet), Donald's Hill (402 meters/1,318 feet), and Benbradagh (468 meters/1,535 feet).

Lough Neagh, located in the central part of Northern Ireland, is the largest lake in Ireland. Five counties (Antrim, Londonderry, Tyrone, Armagh, and Down) border the lake in the Lough Neagh basin.

The province's natural features are often connected with Irish legends. One of the most famous geological formations in Northern Ireland is the Giant's Causeway. Located on the north Antrim coast, these cliffs extend to the island of Skye and are made up of basalt columns, which are rock formations that were most likely formed by cooling lava. According to legend, a giant named Fionn mac Cumhaill (pronounced "Finn mac Cool") created the cliffs when he tried to build a road to Scotland.

Plants & Animals

During the first periods of human settlement, Northern Ireland was thickly forested with both coniferous and deciduous trees, such as oak, alder, arctic willow, hazel, pine, birch, and elm. Today, the land is nearly entirely deforested due to centuries of farming. According to tradition, native plants like hazel, rowan, primrose, and yarrow are endowed with magical properties; whitethorn is also thought to be a lucky plant.

Among the animal species native to Ireland are the Irish stoat and the Irish hare. Most animal species in Northern Ireland are similar to those found in the rest of the UK. Common fish species include pike, perch, trout, and salmon. Livestock such as sheep, cattle, and horses are also common.

CUSTOMS & COURTESIES

Greetings

A typical casual greeting in Northern Ireland could be "How's you?" "What about ye?" or "How's about you?" Likewise, saying "All right?" to someone is not viewed as a question into their well-being, but simply another courteous way to acknowledge their presence and to say "Hello." Additionally, "All right, mate," or "All right, fellas," is another general greeting used in a casual situation. "What's the craic?" is another informal expression using the Irish word craic (pronounced "crack"), which means "fun." The phrase itself means "What's happening?" or "What's going on?"

When saying farewell, the phrase "All the best" (short for "Wishing you all the best") is a commonly used expression. "Cheerio" is used as well, but more often in formal situations. Someone in a more casual setting may say "I'm away" or "That's me," to indicate they are leaving. Generally, Northern Ireland residents shake hands when meeting for the first time. Male friends will shake hands, and female friends will hug, while male-female friends may hug with one kiss on the cheek.

Gestures & Etiquette

The cultural divide in Northern Ireland is often apparent in the language. An awareness of subtle meanings conveyed by different words or terms can be crucial to avoiding offensive or tense situations. Certain terms will indicate whether a person's loyalties lie on the Catholic or Protestant side, and an innocent question asked by an outsider could convey more than intended. For example, Catholics living in Northern Ireland may refer to their home as "Ireland" or "The north of Ireland," while Protestants may say "Ulster," "Great Britain," or "the UK" (United Kingdom). Furthermore, the city of Derry is known as Londonderry among Protestants, and the pronunciation of the letter "H" also signifies one's background, as Catholics pronounce it "haitch" and Protestants pronounce it "aitch."

Certain topics are considered cultural taboos. These topics mainly reference religion or politics, or any other hint about someone's background. It's considered inappropriate to ask someone his or her religion, what church they go to, or anything else along those lines. Likewise, it's taboo to mention politics or any historical or

present-day conflict. It may also be considered intrusive to ask people where they are from or what neighborhood they live in. This is often used to determine one's religion. Directly asking "What are you?" is considered socially inappropriate.

Generally, people in Northern Ireland are very friendly and emphasize the importance of good conversation, banter and humorous comments. Despite this friendliness, visitors should not be surprised if people seem personally reserved or reluctant to bring up information about their background. Personal information is usually not volunteered.

While English is the main language spoken in Northern Ireland, the Irish language and Ulster Scots language are still culturally recognized. Government signs typically feature all three languages. Irish is spoken by a small but significant portion of the population, and considered an important part of cultural identity for Catholics/ nationalists. There are also Irish-language schools established for children.

Eating/Meals

In Northern Ireland, breakfast can range from a quick bowl of Weetabix cereal (a wheat-based cereal popular in the UK) on a weekday morning to an elaborate "Ulster fry" on a Sunday morning. An Ulster fry is the North's version of a traditional Irish breakfast, and commonly consists of sausage, rashers (thick portions of bacon), eggs, beans (straight out of the tin), potato farl (potato bread fried on the stovetop), soda bread, and a black or white pudding. During the week, a typical breakfast of just eggs, bacon or toast is also common. A cup of tea is standard fare for all breakfasts (fully caffeinated, "black" or with milk and sugar).

Lunches usually consist of a variety of sandwiches, prepared either cold (prepackaged sandwiches are available in most shops) or hot ("cheese toasties" or "bacon sarnies"). Dinner, sometimes called "tea," will generally involve the entire family, and "Sunday dinner," a cultural tradition, involves everyone gathering at the family house for a hearty late afternoon meal.

Typically, this meal includes "a meat and two veg" and dessert such as apple or rhubarb crumble or banana-toffee pie, which are local favorites. At family meals, food is served on individual plates as opposed to family style (where people serve themselves from large, communal dishes). Rather than putting the knife down in between use, utensils are commonly held in both hands while eating.

Fast food has also risen to its own cultural status in Northern Ireland, with "takeaway" or "carryout" meals of fish and chips, Chinese food or hamburgers often serving as a Friday night tradition to kick off the weekend. In addition, a "cup of tea" carries significant meaning in Northern Ireland. A proper workplace meeting will usually include tea and employees will drink tea or take "tea breaks" during the day. Stopping by someone's house for "a cuppa" is a tradition that has lasted in both urban and rural areas.

Visiting

A visitor to a home in Northern Ireland will commonly be invited to sit down and have a cup of tea, as well something to eat. It is considered polite to accept the tea and food and to eat in order to show the host you appreciate what they've prepared. Bringing a gift to someone's home is considered good manners, especially if a dinner or social event is being held. A bottle of drink (wine or whiskey) is considered an appropriate gift, as are desserts or other such treats.

LIFESTYLE

Family

Northern Ireland is a traditional society where life revolves around community, family and home. Although some family and religious traditions are declining in the early 21st century, attendance at Catholic and Protestant churches is still significant. Many social and community events are still based on religious institutions. In both city neighborhoods and country villages, communities are tight-knit, and family life is of central importance. Many young people live at

home while attending university or until they marry. Furthermore, it is common for young people who move into the city for school or work to frequently return to the family home on weekends.

Housing

Houses in Northern Ireland are characterized by timber frames, brick walls, and clay tile roofing. In urban areas, rows of connected houses known as "terraced houses" are typical, as well as "semi-detached" houses (two houses sharing one connecting wall). In urban areas, "estates" are terms for small housing developments, often bordered by brick walls and an entry gate. Rural areas tend to have more "detached" or single houses, which are typically larger and more cottage-style, often with sprawling land surrounding them.

Substandard housing in urban Northern Ireland has long been an issue. This dates back to when Catholics claimed unfair treatment from Protestant-dominated local borough councils that controlled public housing allocation. Since then, many measures have been taken against housing inequity, and overall housing quality in urban areas has greatly improved. In addition, recent changes in laws regarding home ownership have resulted in a significant rise in home ownership.

Food

Northern Irish cuisine is largely influenced by the country's farming culture, and Northern Ireland is renowned for its fresh dairy, meat, and bread products. Because of this agricultural abundance, meat is still typically bought at butcher shops, milk and other dairy products can still be delivered, and bakeries have remained popular for the purchase of breads and other ingredients for traditional dishes. Generally, staple foods and ingredients include fresh meat from local farms, including sausage, bacon (cut into thick "rashers"), ham, beef, and lamb (used in traditional Irish stew). Fish are abundant in local waters, and fresh catches of mussels, prawns, lobsters, cod, plaice, salmon and trout are commonly available.

Potatoes are another staple, with thick-cut chips (heartier than American-style French fries) a standard dish at most eateries. Potatoes are also prepared mashed, baked, as colcannon (mixed with cabbage), champ (mixed with spring onions), with garlic or in a variety of other forms.

Fresh bread products are an important part of the Northern Ireland diet, with a variety of bread products a key ingredient of meals: sliced bread (for toast), wheat or "brown" bread, soda bread, scones and buns. Fresh cheese, butter and eggs from local dairy farms are also commonly eaten.

A traditional meal of fish and chips (fresh plaice or cod is battered, fried, and served with thick-cut chips and malt vinegar) can be enjoyed at a fine restaurant, from a takeaway box, or prepared at home. Another local dish is champ, which combines mashed potatoes, butter, milk, salt and pepper and spring onions. In addition, dulse is a Northern delicacy sold along the coastline or available for collecting from the shore. It is a reddish seaweed that is dried, then eaten by itself or added to potato dishes. Carrageen, another Irish moss, can also be gathered from the sea and can be eaten fresh or dried. One of the most popular drinks in the province is Old Bushmills Irish whiskey, distilled in County Antrim.

International trends and influences have resulted in the popularity of curry dishes, both home and restaurant prepared. A growing Chinese immigrant population has also contributed to an increase in Chinese cuisine throughout the North.

Life's Milestones

Most milestones in Northern Ireland are celebrated in connection to one's church or cultural background. For Catholics (about half the population), births, marriages and other religious sacraments are all based on church ceremonies. For the Protestant population, births and marriages are also generally connected to a church service. Baby showers are given before a baby is born, and after the birth, families celebrate with a christening (name-giving religious ceremony) and gifts. The sacraments of first communion and confirmation for children are also celebrated in Catholic families with parties and gift giving.

In both Catholic and Protestant cultures, marriage brings with it the tradition of a "stag party" for men, or "hen party" for women, prior to the ceremony. This often consists of a weekend-long trip to another city for celebrating. "Leaving do" parties are thrown if a young family member is going away to university or traveling on a "gap year" before continuing with schooling.

In small villages, funeral processions may take place with the coffin being carried through the main street to the church. Poitin (illegal homemade liquor, pronounced "potcheen") was traditionally consumed at both weddings and funerals. For Catholics, dancing, music, and cultural and community festivals are part of yearly rituals to celebrate St. Patrick's Day, Easter and Halloween. In the Protestant community, the Marching Season (culminating on July 12) commemorating the Battle of the Boyne—symbolically, a British victory over a Catholic king—is an annual event often viewed as a coming-of-age ceremony. Once children have become old enough, they are then allowed to participate in the parades.

CULTURAL HISTORY

Art

Traditional Irish handicrafts such as linen and lace making, along with pottery production, have evolved over time to become hallmarks of Northern Ireland arts. Linen making even holds a place in mythology. Legends tell how foreigners from a distant land settled on the mountains of the North and taught the natives how to cultivate flax plants. The lengthy process of linen making involves cultivating the flax, separating and combing fibers from the plant, and spinning them into yarn. This became the basis for a fast-growing industry encouraged by the English government, which could import linen without taxes. Irish linen is still woven today in a smaller industry that focuses on quality and tradition of the work.

Lace-making is another traditional craft based in Northern Ireland. An Irish Lace Museum even pays homage to the art form with displays of five distinct types of lace (most named from their region of origin): Irish Crochet Lace, Youghal Needlelace, Inishmacsaint Needlelace, Carrickmacross Lace, and Limerick Lace. In addition, Irish ceramics have a rich history. In fact, pottery in Ireland dates back roughly 6,000 years; the potting wheel was most likely introduced to Northern Ireland in the 13th century. This decorative art still maintains a place in contemporary Irish culture.

Public art in Northern Ireland has been intertwined with the region's history of religious and political conflict. For example, mural painting in Northern Ireland, which dates back to the 19th century, was a way for artists to commemorate political activists or make political statements. Often, these murals, painted on thousands of gable walls (walls between the triangular edges of a roof), are by both amateur and professional artists.

For the established visual arts scene, landscape art developed as a popular painting style in the 19th and early 20th centuries. Famous landscape painters included Paul Henry (1876–1958), who painted western Irish landscapes, and Augustus Joseph Nicholas Burke (1838–1891). Surrealism, expressionism and other modern painting styles became popular in the 20th century, as evidenced by the work of artist Colin Middleton (1910–1983). However, Northern Ireland's political conflict spurred new trends in the 1980s toward painting around conflict, place and identity themes. Installation, video and digital art forms also became popular, but many artists left for Dublin to take advantage of a wider artists' network.

Architecture

Beyond crafts, Northern Ireland's architecture reflects largely upon the history of the region. The Irish countryside features castles with 11th- and 12th-century Norman architecture as well as thatched-roof cottages, all styles popular in early northern Europe. In addition, architecture in Ireland was largely influenced by the English. Many urban centers feature Gregorian architecture, a style popularized between 1720 and 1840, and Victorian architecture, which was dominant during the Victorian era, roughly 1837–1902. The city of Belfast, for example, has many Victorian commercial buildings due to a population boom in the 19th century, when Victorian-style architecture was predominant. Despite these European and British influences, the authenticity of Irish culture is commonly present in the modern Irish architecture of the 20th century.

Drama

Northern Ireland's dramatic arts are essentially tied to the theatrical past of the Republic of Ireland and Great Britain. Ireland had no formal theater until the 20th century; prior to that, theatrical productions were British imports that were performed in Dublin and larger cities. Irish writers, such as William Congreve (1670–1729), Oliver Goldsmith (1728–1774), Richard Sheridan (1751–1816), Oscar Wilde (1854–1900), and George Bernard Shaw (1856–1950), traveled to and settled in London in order to see their work produced.

Dublin's first theater, the Werburgh Street Theatre, was established in Dublin in 1637; it fell victim to the Puritans five years later. During the Restoration, another theater was established, the Smock Alley Theatre, which featured English plays of the period as well as English classics. The 18th century saw much of the same—English plays by Irish actors who, if they were good enough, moved to London to further their careers. Ireland stood as a regional theater, a step on the way to London (and later, New York) for playwrights and actors.

While travelling troupes sprung up during the 18th and 19th centuries, theater was still an English construct. It wasn't until 1899 that Ireland established its own distinctly Irish theater group, the Irish Literary Theatre, which performed in various venues within Dublin. Later, the group took up residence in a building on Marlborough Street, which came to be known as the Abbey Theatre. The theater featured the productions of those members of the

Irish Literary Revival: William Butler Yeats (1865–1939), John Millington Synge (1871–1909), Sean O'Casey (1880–1964), and Isabella Augusta, Lady Gregory (1852–1932). The theater immediately found itself in the center of Ireland's nationalist movement when nationalists criticized the theater for being apolitical.

In the 1920s, Yeats and Lady Gregory offered the Abbey as a gift to Ireland. While the state turned down the offer, it did begin to support the theater annually, making the Abbey Theater the first government-sponsored theater in the world.

By this time, Northern Ireland had been established (in 1921). The Ulster Literary Theatre was established in 1902, staging productions of Irish playwrights such as Yeats, James Cousins (1873–1956), George Russell (1867–1935), and Lewis Purcell (writing as David Parkhill). The Ulster Literary Theater (shortened to Ulster Theater in 1915) helped develop a distinctly Northern Irish dramatic community, with local writers and actors. In spite of its literary success, though, the theater closed its doors in 1934 due to financial difficulties.

The Lyric Theatre in Belfast was established in 1951, in the stable loft of its founders Mary and Pearse O'Malley. It moved to a building on Ridgeway Street in 1968, where it is being reconstructed (with completion in 2011). The Lyric boasts the patronage of Northern Ireland-born actor Liam Neeson (1952–), and stages works by Irish dramatists such as Brian Friel (1929–).

Music

Traditional Irish music, or Irish folk music, is an umbrella term used to cover the various genres of regional music played throughout Ireland. Historically, traditional Irish music consisted of folk songs or ballads, often accompanied by the fiddle, flutes, harp and uilleann pipes, or Irish bagpipes, with the accordion added in the late 19th and early 20th centuries. Much of this music derived from the 18th and 19th centuries, when many traditional compositions were first recorded.

Traditional music in Northern Ireland has long been influenced by the political divide in the region. Traditional Irish music is an important part of the nationalist or Catholic community, and a feature of musical gatherings or dance festivals, called ceílís. Protestant or loyalist music is centered on the marching band tradition, particularly the Lambeg drum, which is made of goatskin stretched over an oak shell.

Dance

Traditional Irish dancing evolved alongside traditional Irish music in the 18th and 19th centuries. Important Irish folk dances include reels and jigs, which are also names for the accompanying dance tunes. Irish step dancing, characterized by holding a still upper body while maintaining quick leg and feet movements, and set dancing, which developed in rural areas and is similar to square dancing, also grew alongside traditional Irish music.

In Northern Ireland, traditional Irish dancing has remained a large part of Catholic culture, particularly in the most sectarian and traditional neighborhoods. Many children, both boys and girls, begin taking Irish dancing lessons at an early age and perform in both competitions and ceílís. The 2008 World Irish Dancing competition was held in Belfast, symbolic of the importance of this tradition in the North.

Literature

Northern Irish literature can be traced back to ancient times with the Ulster Cycle, or Uliad Cycle, a group of heroic tales and legends derived from Celtic mythology. The tales originated during the first century CE, and were passed on orally, until recorded in manuscripts beginning in the 12th century. This rich tradition of storytelling was later manifested in poetry, such as the tradition of Ulster-Scots poetry and prose. (Ulster-Scots refer to the vernacular, or language, spoken in the northern province of Ulster where many Scottish settled.) A famous Irish poet in this tradition was James Orr (1770–1816), who followed the model of Scottish rhyming weavers. Poetry in Northern Ireland continued to flourish in the 20th century with the "Belfast Poets"—Seamus Heaney, Paul Muldoon, and Derek Mahon being the most noteworthy. Nobel Prize-winner Heaney is credited with pioneering the way for a new poetry revival in the North.

In step with the rich literary tradition of Ireland, the North has contributed its share of influential and internationally renowned writers of plays and novels. Belfast-raised C.S. Lewis (1898–1963), author of the popular children's classics *The Chronicles of Narnia*, is remembered by residents with a yearly parade and light festival. Playwright Brian Friel, who penned *Translations*, incorporated historical themes into his famous play. Other writers, such as Brian Moore (1921–1999), Bernard McLaverty, and Robert MacLiam Wilson, often showed the influence of sectarian issues and violence in their work.

In addition, the Gaelic Revival (c. 1890–1921), which renewed national interest in the Gaelic language and Celtic and Irish folklore, helped influence national sentiment in Northern Ireland. This literary renaissance continued to influence writers throughout the early 20th century. Other important writers of the 20th and early 21st century include Flann O'Brien (1911–1946) and poets Frank Ormsby (1947–) and Gerard McKeown (1980–).

CULTURE

Arts & Entertainment

The Arts Council of Northern Ireland is the lead development agency for the arts; it supports artists and art organizations with funding from the Treasury and the National Lottery. The council maintains a collection of art, including works by Colin Middleton, Henry Moore, John Luke, and William Scott.

There is relatively little public art and sculpture; however, works by artists such as Oisin Kelly and Caroline Mulholland are on display in different parts of the province. The Grand Opera House in Belfast provides a venue for the performing arts. Belfast also maintains a symphony orchestra.

Musicians James Galway and Van Morrison are originally from Northern Ireland, as are actors Liam Neeson, Kenneth Branagh, and Stephen Rea. Famous writers from Northern Ireland include C.S. Lewis, the Brontë family, poets Seamus Heaney, and Paul Muldoon, playwright Brian Friel, and novelist Brian Moore.

Popular sports in Northern Ireland include football (soccer) and Rugby Union football, as well as traditional activities like Gaelic football, hurling, and handball. Outdoor activities such as fishing and hiking are also popular pastimes.

Cultural Sites & Landmarks

Northern Ireland has a wealth of cultural sites and natural wonders, beginning with the Giant's Causeway. A stunning rock formation of roughly 40,000 black basalt columns on the northeast coast of Northern Ireland, the Giant's Causeway stretches out into the sea toward Scotland. It is believed that the formation is a result of volcanic activity over 50 million years ago. However, ancient legend says the causeway was built by the Irish giant Fionn mac Cumhaill (Finn McCool). The causeway, in the shadow of the cliffs of Antrim, was designated a United Nations Educational, Scientific and Cultural Organization (UNESCO) World Heritage Site in 1986.

In addition, the route up the northern coast leading to the causeway is dotted with a number of other landmarks, including the Carrick-A-Rede rope bridge. There, the brave of heart can walk across a wobbly bridge suspended between two cliffs jutting up 23 meters (75 feet) from the sea. The bridge was originally strung up by fishermen to check their salmon nets, and now offers tourists stunning views of Rathlin Island. Carrick-A-Rede has also been noted as an area of scientific interest for its geology, flora and fauna. Another attraction along the coastal route is the ruins of the medieval Dunluce Castle. The structure, still extensively intact, was built around steep drops and atop an ancient Irish fort.

Along the banks of the River Foyle in northwestern Ireland is the old walled city of Derry, or

Londonderry. Its medieval walls date back to the city's history as a planned settlement that sought to defend British interests from the surrounding Irish clans. After years of sieges, historical battles and conflict during the Troubles, the walls now provide a historic walk along the city's ancient perimeter. Important cultural sites such as Saint Augustine's Church and the Tower Museum can be viewed along the way.

St. Patrick's Centre in the town of Downpatrick honors Saint Patrick, the patron saint of Ireland, with an annual feast held on March 17. Saint Patrick was a Christian missionary who traveled across the island, using the shamrock—a three-leaf clover that has come to symbolize Ireland—to illustrate the Christian concept of the Trinity. Saint Patrick's remains are also buried in Downpatrick.

The town of Downpatrick is located in County Down, one of the nine counties of the province of Ulster. Another landmark in County Down is Strangford Lough, the largest sea lough (body of water) in the British Isles. The Strangford Lough features a huge array of wildlife, including Brent Geese, Knot, Bar-tailed Godwit and Terns, as well as a wide variety of plant and marine life. The Strangford Lough Wildlife Information Centre is a resource for visitors who can also enjoy walks, ferry rides and bird watching.

The city of Belfast, Northern Ireland's seat of government, is rich in cultural and political history. The city offers a number of tours that give visitors a firsthand account of its history. Belfast's "black cab" mural tours take visitors through the historically segregated Catholic and Protestant neighborhoods along the Shankill and Falls Roads, relaying the story of political violence in the city's past days. Taxicabs make frequent stops along the way to see the city's various political murals, and may also stop at the "peace wall" and memorial gardens.

The historic Belfast Castle was built in 1870, replacing a series of structures that had stood on the spot, including a castle built by the Normans in the late 12th century. Cave Hill, known to Belfast residents as "Napoleon's nose" for its shape, looks down on the stately Belfast Castle, which is nestled in a beautiful park with views of MacArt's Fort and the Lagan River.

In addition, the silhouette of Queen's University is often used as a symbol of Belfast city. The university is widely regarded as the North's top educational institution, and is situated next to the beautiful Botanic Gardens. The gardens feature artistically laid floral arrangements, a rose garden and the Palm House, a cast iron glasshouse.

Libraries & Museums

The Ulster Museum, part of the National Museums Northern Ireland system, is also located at the entrance of the Botanic Gardens, and features an array of art and historical artifacts from Northern Ireland and as far away as the South Pacific. Other museums in that system include the Ulster Folk and Transport Museum, the Ulster American Folk Park (featuring displays and artifacts from Irish emigrants to the US), the Armagh County Museum (a museum of that county), and the W5, a science center.

Ireland's repositories for national archives include the National Archives of Ireland and the National Library of Ireland, which houses a collection of drawings, prints, photographs, and historic papers from the country's past.

Holidays

Public holidays in Northern Ireland include New Year's Day (January), St. Patrick's Day (March 17), Good Friday and Easter Monday (March or April), Early May Bank Holiday and Spring Bank Holiday (May), Battle of the Boyne (or Orangemen's Day, July 12), Summer Bank Holiday (August), Christmas Day (December 25), and Boxing Day (December 26).

Youth Culture

Because of the emphasis on human rights in Northern Ireland following the Troubles, the rights of young people are protected through youth boards, forums, policy consultations, and more. Funding streams support youth centers and youth workers to counter "antisocial" behaviors and occupy young people. Despite concerns about crime and youth offenders, the Northern Ireland government offers many community and sport programs for youth, and has the second lowest crime rate in the world.

With a drinking age of eighteen, most young people go to dance clubs, pubs and bars to socialize. Young people go out in groups and rarely leave their mobile phones behind, as text messaging has become the primary means of communication. Social networking sites (SNS) like bebo.com are also popular among young Northern Irish. Modern dating trends like "speed dating" or online matchmaking occur along with traditional ways of meeting at bars or university. In addition, Northern Ireland's cities support vibrant music scenes, incorporating punk, alternative rock, and pop music.

Clothing styles in Northern Ireland generally follow in the fashion trends of London, with large pockets of counterculture teens sporting gothic and punk-style hair, outfits and attitude. Wearing clothing supporting sports teams is also a popular trend, but one that is divided along sectarian lines (Catholics and Protestants traditionally support different football teams, and jerseys indicate this preference).

SOCIETY

Transportation

Public transportation is considered an important common good, and Northern Ireland's transit companies typically involve the consumers in consultation and development. Most students take public transportation to get to school and senior citizens are offered free travel on all bus and rail systems throughout Northern Ireland. Many commuters use the train and bus system for getting to work and weekend journeying. However, the convenience and efficiency of a car is necessary for anyone wanting to drive beyond the city, since bus systems can be less frequent in rural areas.

Roads in Northern Ireland link together all major towns and are well maintained, but hilly

and narrow spots in the countryside can intimidate a city driver. It is common for teens in some small farming towns to get around by tractor. Cars typically have manual transmissions, and are driven on the left side of the road, with the driver's seat on the right side of the car.

Transportation Infrastructure

Bus and rail systems operate across Northern Ireland, linking major towns and providing connections to the UK and Ireland. Northern Ireland also has a nationalized public road transport system, separate from Belfast's municipal service. Since the 1960s, the Northern Ireland Transport Holding Company (NITHCo) has controlled railways, bus companies and the Belfast airport. In rural areas, the transportation can be infrequent and less convenient, although all train systems have refurbished or replaced their cars, adding automatic doors (previously manual) and other digitized features.

Transportation by sea is common in Northern Ireland as well, with commercial ports in Belfast, Coleraine, and Derry, and passenger ferries operating from Larne and Belfast to mainland UK. Belfast International Airport is the main point of air service for Northern Ireland, with flights to major cities in Britain, Europe and North America.

Media & Communications

State and commercial broadcasting both operate in Northern Ireland. The British Broadcasting Corporation (BBC) runs both Radio Foyle and Radio Ulster programming, along with national BBC services, and operates a BBC television studio in Belfast. Ulster Television PLC is an independent television service. There are also many independent radio stations in operation.

Belfast produces several daily newspapers, including the *Belfast Telegraph* and the *Irish News*, as well as numerous smaller community papers published regionally. Northern Ireland news is included in British newspapers as well. The media is certainly not free from the political divide: the *Irish News* holds a primarily Catholic readership, while the *News Letter* is favored by Protestants.

As Northern Ireland moves forward alongside Britain and Ireland in the information age, Internet cafés are becoming increasingly popular and more people are using the Internet in their homes. However, as of 2013, Northern Ireland's Internet access was measured at 80 percent, behind many other Western countries. In fact, Internet connectivity in Northern Ireland remains the lowest in all of the UK.

SOCIAL DEVELOPMENT

Standard of Living
Northern Ireland shares the United Nations Human Development Index (HDI) rating with the United Kingdom, which is ranked 14th of 187 countries. The UK's HDI measures quality of life and standard of living indicators.

Water Consumption
According to the World Health Organization, Northern Ireland's residents have 100 percent access to clean water. Correspondingly, access to improved sanitation is also at 100 percent. Threats to water resources in Northern Ireland include development, pollution, and climate change.

Education
Between the ages of five and 16, children in Northern Ireland attend primary and secondary schools. Education is compulsory, with most Catholic students attending Catholic schools and Protestant students attending state-run schools. These include grammar schools, secondary schools, and technical schools. Children must pass examinations to determine their placement.

Northern Ireland's major universities are the Queen's University at Belfast and the University of Ulster at Coleraine, which was created in 1984 by the merger of the New University of Ulster and Ulster Polytechnic.

Women's Rights
Like most Western cultures, Northern Ireland is a society in which women are proclaimed as equal, and are represented in the workplace and government. However, traditional gender roles are often adhered to, with many women acting as the chief caretaker of children and center of family life.

In Northern Ireland, the lack of right or access to abortions is a topic of contention amongst advocates for women's rights. The 1967 Abortion Act permitting abortions in Britain was never extended to Northern Ireland due to influence from the rest of Catholic-majority Ireland. As such, abortion is not readily available, and only in exceptional circumstances. Women in Northern Ireland seeking an abortion, which does not fall within categories established under Irish law, must travel to England and cover all costs personally. In 2013 alone, there were 802 women who traveled from Northern Ireland to have an abortion in England, while 56 had medical abortions within Northern Ireland. The Family Planning Association (FPA) of Northern Ireland has officially launched a campaign to secure abortion rights in Northern Ireland, supporting a cross-party group of MPs working to extend abortion rights. It also offers financial support to some women without funds to travel to England.

The UN has examined women's rights in regards to participation in the peace process and in policing in Northern Ireland, and has also looked at domestic violence and trafficking issues in the North. The Northern Ireland Assembly put the UN Security Council Resolution 1325, an international law that calls for participation of women in peace processes and policing, on trial for its effectiveness. Evidence supported the presence of women in decision-making levels in peacekeeping institutions.

The UN Committee for the Convention on the Elimination of Discrimination against Women, working with the Northern Ireland Human Rights Commission, examined the UK's progress in women's rights concerning domestic violence. The committee called for a strategy to prevent violence against women. The committee has also examined the issue of trafficking, and the Northern Ireland Human Rights Commission has called on the UK government to ratify the

Council of Europe Convention against the Trafficking of Human Beings.

Health Care

Because it is part of the UK, Northern Ireland is served by the National Health Service of Great Britain. Health care is state-subsidized, and is one of the government's chief expenditures. The Department of Health and Social Services directs provincial spending on health care. The Queen's University is one of the largest institutions in the province committed to health care and research.

GOVERNMENT

Structure

Northern Ireland became a province of the UK in 1921, and is governed by the United Kingdom of Great Britain (UK). The head of government is the British Prime Minister, and the head of state is the reigning British monarch. Social services such as health care, the military, and law enforcement are managed by the British government.

The country's government has long been entangled with politics and religion, and it will serve the reader to be acquainted with the history. Before its union with Britain, the north of Ireland saw hundreds of years of religious conflict between Protestants and Catholics. Urban riots also occurred throughout the 19th century over the question of home rule and other political and economic issues. During this time, nationalist political organizations demanded the overthrow of the British authority in the north.

In 1905, the Ulster Unionist Council (UUC) was organized to resist Home Rule (government independent of Britain) and to maintain the political power of Anglo-Irish leaders and the British government. While the Ulster Unionists attempted to preserve political union with Britain, the Sinn Féin (Ourselves Alone) party rejected the British Parliament and formed their own political leadership, the Dáil Éireann, in 1919.

The Government of Ireland Act of 1920 partitioned Ireland. In the north, Antrim, Down,

Armagh, Fermanagh, Derry, and Tyrone formed a parliament in Belfast under the UK Parliament (the rest of the island formed an independent republic in 1949). Militant resistance and guerilla violence followed throughout the early 1920s in Northern Ireland.

In 1966, the Ulster Volunteer Force (loyal to the British Union), a paramilitary group, committed acts of violence to inflame relations between Protestants and Catholics. Their goal was to demonstrate that Catholics were not loyal to the state. Tension increased in 1968 and 1969, as bombings, violent political demonstrations, and riots occurred more frequently in urban centers like Belfast. Nationalists were responding in kind, led by the Provisional Irish Republican Army (IRA), which split from the official IRA over ideological issues. The Provisional IRA launched an armed campaign targeted at British officials in both Northern Ireland and in England. By the end of the conflict, many on both sides had been killed.

During the 1990s, efforts were made to decommission paramilitary arms and to carry on peaceful negotiations, but continued violence prevented significant success. On April 10, 1998, the Belfast Agreement (also known as the Good Friday Agreement) was reached. It attempted to balance power between the separate communities while allowing Great Britain control over law enforcement in the province. Disarmament negotiations with the Provisional IRA were resumed in 2000. In 2005, the Provisional IRA announced that it would become committed to politics (at the prompting of its political arm, Sinn Féin) and end its armed aggression. An unprecedented agreement followed between Unionist and Loyalist leaders, who announced they would form a multi-party government in North Ireland. However, some car bombings and other violent incidents have occurred in the years following the agreement.

In 1998, a devolved assembly was created with the signing of the Belfast Agreement. Under devolution, Northern Ireland's assembly is granted power by the central government (in the UK). The assembly can make legislation, but the central government (in the UK), can overturn these actions if they wish. While the assembly suspended its actions in 2002 because of a breakdown in the peace process, the assembly was reconvened in 2007 under a power-sharing agreement between Sinn Féin and the Democratic Unionist Party.

In addition to the Northern Ireland Assembly (with 108 members), Northern Ireland also has 18 elected members of the British Parliament. Not all elected officials take their seats, as members of Sinn Féin refuse to take an oath to serve the British monarch.

Political Parties

Beginning in 2010, Northern Ireland's politics are drifting from political parties affiliated solely with either Catholicism or Protestantism, and according to some polling data, are moving away, somewhat, from the nationalist and unionist divide. The question about Northern Ireland's future, whether it remains a part of the UK, joins the Republic of Ireland, or becomes an independent state has become more complex than just a Protestant vs. Catholic question. Polls indicate that Northern Ireland's future is becoming more a political and economic question for its residents.

Four parties dominate Northern Ireland's politics. The Democratic Unionist Party (DUP) is a protestant unionist party. The DUP garnered over 30 percent of the vote in 2011 and holds 36 seats in the assembly. The Ulster Unionist Party (UUP) is also a unionist party, but is viewed as more moderate than the DUP. The UUP took almost 15 percent of the vote in 2011 and holds 18 seats in the assembly. Sinn Féin is a leftist republican party which received 26 percent of the vote and holds 28 seats in the assembly. The Social Democratic and Labour Party (SDLP) of Northern Ireland is also a nationalist party, and they earned 15 percent of the vote in 2011, taking 16 seats. The remaining seats were taken by the Alliance Party of Northern Ireland (eight seats) and two smaller parties.

Local Government

Northern Ireland is divided into 26 districts. Local government is run under a single-tier system, in which each district has an elected council. These councils are responsible for a number of local services, such as waste collection and economic development.

Judicial System

Northern Ireland has a common law system similar to English common law. Magistrates' courts hear minor criminal cases, county courts handle civil matters, and crown courts hear more serious criminal cases. The Court of Adjudicature of Northern Ireland is made up of three of the country's highest courts: the High Court, the Crown Court, and the Court of Appeal. The Supreme Court of the United Kingdom is the highest court of appeal in the UK (except for Scotland).

Taxation

Northern Ireland is known as being the most business-friendly country in Europe. Tax policy for businesses in Northern Ireland is geared towards creating jobs. To that end, a new corporate tax rate of 12.5 percent was passed in 2015, with a proposed start date of 2017. (Previously, the corporate tax was 30 percent.) Companies with fewer than 250 employees can take a 150 percent tax deduction on research and development expenditures. Northern Ireland levies a personal income tax, a capital gains tax, inheritance tax, stamp duty, a value added tax (VAT), as well as taxes on investments and savings.

Armed Forces

As part of the United Kingdom, Northern Ireland is protected under the British Armed Forces. The armed forces are comprised of the Royal Navy, the British Army, and the Royal Air Force. As of 2014, about 18,300 service members were stationed in Northern Ireland, the fewest since the Troubles began in 1969.

Foreign Policy

Northern Ireland's most significant foreign policies typically involve its immediate neighbors. Furthermore, because Northern Ireland is a constituent element of the UK, a position that has caused conflict over the past century, its foreign policy generally reflects that of the UK. As part of the UK, the British prime minister is Northern Ireland's head of government, and the monarch is its head of state.

Sectarian violence has occurred in Northern Ireland since the province was officially separated from Ireland in 1921. The last 30 years of the 20th century saw the worst of the violence between Catholic nationalists and Protestant loyalists, a period known as the Troubles. With influence from United States President Bill Clinton and British Prime Minister Tony Blair, the historic Good Friday Agreement was signed in April 1998. Under the terms of this agreement, Catholics and Protestants agreed to undergo a "power sharing" government. This coincided with the British government agreeing to end direct rule from London, reduce troop presence in the North, and recognize the nationalist Sinn Féin group as a legitimate political party. The agreement also promoted developing further relations with Ireland, including fostering cross-border initiatives. Furthermore, the Good Friday agreement has been hailed as a model for other similar global conflicts, such as the Palestinian-Israeli conflict and issues between the Basques and Spain.

Human Rights Profile

International human rights law insists that states respect civil and political rights, and also promote an individual's economic, social and cultural rights. The United Nations Universal Declaration on Human Rights (UDHR) is recognized as the standard for international human rights. Its authors sought the counsel of the world's great thinkers, philosophers, and religious leaders, and were careful to create a document that reflects the core values shared by every world culture. (To read this document or view the articles relating to cultural human rights, go to: http://www.udhr.org/UDHR/default.htm).

Northern Ireland bears a difficult history of human rights violations. Among the most significant are the attacks and discrimination based on religion that took place over the course of a

century, particularly in the 1970s and 1980s, during the worst years of civil violence.

In the wake of that turmoil and the lengthy peace process that followed, Northern Ireland has placed strong emphasis on human rights legislation. The Northern Ireland Human Rights Commission was formed as a requirement of the Good Friday Agreement in April 1998. It was established to promote human rights awareness in Northern Ireland and examine current laws, while consulting with government on necessary changes to protect human rights in the country. The commission conducts investigations and assists individuals going through the court system, as well as providing information and training on human rights issues.

Northern Ireland, under UK legislation, declares all citizens equal before the law. In 2001, legislation was passed declaring a commitment to eliminating race hate crime and sectarian hate crime, as well as incorporating the Human Rights Act of 1998, which made the European Convention of Human Rights part of the law in Northern Ireland. Despite these official declarations, race hate crime and sectarian hate crime still occurs in Northern Ireland, violating Article 2 of the UDHR. Chinese, African, and Eastern European groups in Northern Ireland have experienced racist attacks and discrimination, and homosexual groups have also been victims of discrimination and attacks.

Freedom of religion guaranteed in Article 18 has been violated over the course of Northern Ireland's history, although current legislation declares sectarian attacks to be criminal. The Troubles claimed over 3,600 lives and maimed 40,000 as nationalist Catholic groups battled loyalist Protestant forces. A great number of victims of violence and deaths based on religion have been amassed in Northern Ireland, and despite the official declaration of peace and legislation criminalizing sectarian attacks, sectarian violence, harassment and deaths still occur in violation of Article 18. During the Troubles, the inhumane treatment of many political prisoners violated Article 5, which guarantees protection from cruel, inhuman or degrading treatment or punishment.

Article 20, which declares the freedom of peaceful public assembly and association, is often contested in Northern Ireland when the Protestant Orange Order parades are restricted from marching through Catholic areas, due to claims of intimidation and harassment. In addition, the Northern Ireland Human Rights Commission claims that the Inquiries Act 2005 violates the independence of inquiries into investigations regarding deaths from the Troubles. Such independence would be protected under Article 19 of the UDHR, which declares freedom of seeking, receiving and imparting information.

Lastly, asylum seekers who are detained in the UK are often transported from Northern Ireland without official statistics being kept by the government. This raises concern over the rights of immigrants, asylum seekers and children, and the protection guaranteed by Articles 9, 13, and 14, which declare freedom from arbitrary detention, the right to seek asylum, and the right to move and reside within state borders and to leave any country to return to one's own country.

Migration

According to the Northern Ireland Statistics and Research Agency, 27,500 immigrants entered Northern Ireland between 2008 and 2009, and 21,700 left the country. This notes a decline in immigrants in the country, most likely due to a shift in immigration policy, called "managed migration," based on a points system (focused on skills, student education, and employment opportunity) for those immigrants from countries outside of the European Union. As of 2015, the current estimate is that about 725 more people left Northern Ireland than migrated into the area, during the past year.

ECONOMY

Overview of the Economy

Belfast's economy has been in a state of recovery since the signing of the Good Friday Agreement in 1998. Peace and economic incentives are attracting Northern Irish and international investors who had previously shied away from the city. This has resulted in more job opportunities, and in 2013, the Belfast area was employing 33 percent of Northern Ireland's population. In September, 2014, Northern Ireland's unemployment rate was 5.9 percent, the highest in the UK, although lower than the Republic of Ireland. Northern Ireland suffered in the global economic crisis that began in 2008, and as of the end of 2014 is getting back to the previous economic level.

Belfast's financial services, business services, information technology (IT) development, IT research, biotechnology, and tourism sectors, all traditionally underdeveloped, have experienced considerable growth in the 21st century. Belfast is currently Northern Ireland's commercial and financial hub, employing half of Northern Ireland's workforce in financial and business services, one third in transportation, communications, and entertainment services, and one quarter in retail, restaurant, hotel, and medical services.

The manufacturing sector, once the backbone of the Belfast economy, is still in decline. Service-oriented companies are replacing manufacturing companies as major employers. The factories that do remain manufacture ships, aircraft, textiles, carpet, tobacco goods, and packaged food products for export. Trade between Belfast and the rest of Europe is facilitated by Belfast's large port in Belfast Harbor and its two airports.

A huge redevelopment effort is taking place in Belfast to further stimulate the economy. The Titanic Quarter is being turned into a suburban waterfront community interspersed with office buildings. The Cathedral Quarter and the City Centre are home to many new restaurants, bars, apartments, and hotels.

Industry

Northern Ireland remains the poorest and most underdeveloped part of the UK. According to the Labour Force Survey, the country's rate of economic inactivity (those who are not employed and are not seeking employment) is the highest in the UK.

Historically, its economy depended upon industries such as linen and cotton production. By the 19th century, these industries became mechanized and factories began producing textile products. Shipbuilding was also a historically important industry, due to the province's strategic ports and its trade relationship with the British Empire.

Today, the port cities of Belfast and Larne are the province's most important industrial centers. Major manufacturing sectors include food processing, electronics, textiles, and aerospace. While manufacturing activity has declined, the service industries have become more important sources of employment.

Labor

Northern Ireland has the UK's highest rate of economic inactivity, standing at 26.8 percent. The unemployment rate, as of January, 2015, was 6.0 percent.

Energy/Power/Natural Resources

Peat, which is found throughout Northern Ireland, is an important domestic source of fuel. Northern Ireland must import most of its energy resources; for example, natural gas is imported from Scotland. The province is also connected to electric power grids in the Republic of Ireland and Europe.

Fishing

Northern Ireland's fishing fleet is feeling the impact of European Union (EU) catch quotas as well as limitations to the number of days at sea. Concerns have been raised in Northern Ireland that the cod (white fish) fishing fleet could be decimated by the limitations imposed by the EU.

Forestry

Northern Ireland's Forest Service manages 124 state forests. There are about 61,000 forested hectares (150,734 acres) in Northern Ireland, consisting of mostly conifers. Lumber is not a major industry in Northern Ireland.

Mining/Metals

Valuable mineral resources are scarce, and less than one percent of the population is employed in the mining industry. Among the minerals found in Northern Ireland are iron ore, bauxite, lead, and copper. Limestone, sand, and gravel are quarried there, and granite can be found in the Mourne Mountains.

Agriculture

Agriculture occupies 70 percent of the land in Northern Ireland, although only 1.5 percent of its GDP was from agriculture in 2013, and 3.6 percent of the jobs. The most successful farms are large and highly mechanized, however the average farm size is just above 100 acres. The major agricultural products include beef, bacon, eggs, milk, oats, seed potatoes, and barley.

The Lough Neagh basin provides the greatest area of arable soil in the province, and the lake is part of a soil drainage system that is valuable to farmers. Because of poorer soil, a more problematic climate, and steep slopes, land at higher elevations (above 180 meters/600 feet) is less conducive to farming. These areas are primarily used for grazing livestock, especially in County Fermanagh and in the west of County Tyro.

Tourism

In spite of a history of sectarian violence, the Northern Ireland Tourist Board maintains that the province is a safe and enjoyable place to visit. The tourism sector is seen as an important area for economic growth; it accounts for 5.1 percent of employment, and over two million tourists visited in 2014. Popular attractions include the Giant's Causeway, country house gardens, boating and fishing, and golfing.

Martha Cooney, Christina Healey

DO YOU KNOW?

- According to tradition, St. Patrick founded his church in Armagh, a place of ancient religious significance for both Catholics and Protestants.

- The earliest map of the island of Ireland was drawn by Ptolemy, a second-century Egyptian astronomer, around the year 150. This remained the best available map of Ireland for 13 centuries.

- The famous ocean liner "Titanic" began its doomed voyage across the Atlantic Ocean from the city of Belfast.

Bibliography

Alf McCreary. *101 Days Out in Northern Ireland*. Belfast: Lagan Books, 2006.

Brendan O'Leary and John McGarry. *The Politics of Antagonism: Understanding Northern Ireland*, 2nd ed. Athlone Press, 1996.

Doreen McBride. *Speakin' Norn Iron as She Shud be Spoke*. Banbridge, N. Ireland:

Adare Press, 1993.Feargal Cochrane. *Northern Ireland: The Reluctant Peace*. New Haven: Yale University Press, 2013.

John Conroy. *Belfast Diary: War as a Way of Life*. Boston: Beacon Press, 1987.

John Sugden and Alan Bairner. *Sport, Sectarianism, and Society in a Divided Ireland*. Leicester University Press, 1993.

Joseph Ruane and Jennifer Todd. *The Dynamics of Conflict in Northern Ireland: Power, Conflict and Emancipation*. Cambridge: University Press, 1996.

Lonely Planet and Fionn Davenport. *Lonely Planet Ireland*. 11th ed. Oakland: Lonely Planet, 2014.

Maria Power. *Building Peace in Northern Ireland*. Liverpool: Liverpool University Press, 2014.

Roisin Bonner. "Coming Home to a new Northern Ireland." *Citizen: The Definitive Guide to Northern Ireland*. April/May 2007.

Seamus Heaney. *North*. London: Faber and Faber, 1996.

Tim Pat Coogan. *The Troubles*. New York: Palgrave, 1995.

Works Cited

Alf McCreary. *101 Days Out in Northern Ireland*. Belfast: Lagan Books, 2006.

Craig Morgan Teicher. "Lyrical Latitudes." *Poets & Writers*. Nov/Dec 2006. http://www.britannica.com/EBchecked/topic/419739/Northern-Ireland

Doreen McBride. *Speakin' Norn Iron as She Shud be Spoke*. Banbridge, N. Ireland: Adare Press, 1993.

http://en.wikipedia.org/wiki/Irish_dance
http://en.wikipedia.org/wiki/Lambeg_drum
http://en.wikipedia.org/wiki/Northern_ireland
http://www.artscouncil-ni.org/artforms/TroublesArchive.htm
http://www.bbc.co.uk/food/tv_and_radio/food_heroes/directory_northernireland.shtml#ulster_fry
http://www.britannica.com/EBchecked/topic/419739/Northern-Ireland
http://www.cfr.org/
http://www.cfr.org/publication/15889/good_friday_agreement_has_lessons_for_mideast html?breadcrumb=%2Fregion%2F369%2Fireland
http://www.fergusonsirishlinen.com/aboutlinen/
http://www.foreignpolicy.com
http://www.irishlacemuseum.com/Museum/Museumpg.html
http://www.irish-architecture.com/buildings_ireland/antrim/belfast/index.html
http://www.lisburncity.gov.uk/irish-linen-centre-and-lisburn-museum/
http://www.medicalnewstoday.com/articles/116191.php
http://www.nihrc.org/index.php?option=com_content&task=view&id=4&Itemid=1
http://www.nio.gov.uk/race_crime_and_sectarian_crime_legislation_in_ni_-http://www.niwep.org.uk/summaryUNSCR1325.htm
http://www.udhr.org/UDHR/default.htm
http://www.un.org/Overview/rights.html
http://www.un.org/Overview/rights.html _a_summary_paper.pdf
www.belfasttours.com
www.discovernorthernireland.com
www.giantscausewaycentre.com
www.saintpatrickcentre.com
www.translink.co.uk

NORWAY

Introduction

More than a thousand years ago, Norwegian Vikings established colonies in Iceland and Greenland. During the early years of the 11th century, Norse explorer Leif Ericson became the first European to sail to North America. Norwegians are still seafarers, with some of the largest fishing and shipping concerns in the world.

Norway's arts, its music, dance, art, architecture and literature, tend to reflect Norway's fascination with the unspoiled rural countryside and lifestyle. The Kingdom of Norway is lauded for its high human development ranking, which reflects its high standards of education, health, and per capita income.

GENERAL INFORMATION

Official Language: Norwegian
Population: 5,147,792 (2014 estimate)
Currency: Norwegian krone
Coins: 100 øre equal one krone. Coins in Norway are issued in denominations of 50 øre and 1, 5, 10, and 20 krone.

Land Area: 304,282 square kilometers (117,483 square miles)
Water Area: 19,520 square kilometers (7,536 square miles)
National Motto: The King's Motto is "Alt for Norge" (Norwegian, "All for Norway")
National Anthem: "Ja vi elsker dette landet" ("Yes, We Love This Land")
Capital: Oslo
Time Zone: GMT +1
Flag Description: Norway's flag is solid red with a blue Scandinavian cross (outlined in white) set off-center, with the vertical cross placed to the hoist side. The red, white, and blue colors are thought to have been borrowed from the French tri-color.

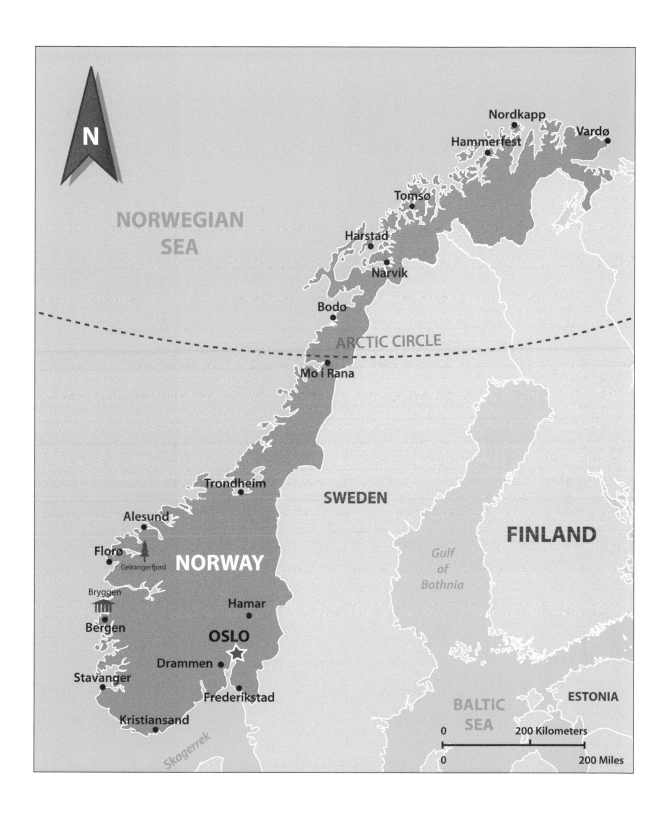

Principal Cities by Population (2012):

- Oslo (932,533)
- Bergen (239,249)
- Stavanger (206,309)
- Trondheim (170,851)
- Bærum (111,213)
- Fredrikstad (100,458)
- Drammen (94,901)
- Kristiansand (81,295) (2010 estimate)
- Tromsø (67,305) (2010 estimate)
- Sandnes (64,671) (2010 estimate)

Population

Norway's population density is roughly 15 persons per square kilometer (38 per square mile). About 75 percent of the people live in coastal cities. The main towns are Oslo, with a population of 932,533; Bergen, population 239,249; Stavanger/Sandnest, population 206,309; and Trondheim, population 170,851. All of these cities are on the coast or on fjords. Trondheim, established in 998, was the original capital of Norway.

The Svalbard Archipelago, north of the mainland, has a mostly-Norwegian population of 2,573.

Approximately 20,000 indigenous Sami, or Laps, live across the northern parts of Norway and Sweden, in an area known as Lapland. The Sami culture is one of the world's oldest.

Languages

The Norwegian language occurs in two forms, which are mutually intelligible and are considered equal. Bokmal is the form used most in cities and schools. Nynorsk (Neo-Norwegian) was developed deliberately in the mid-1800s to protest Danish influence. It is based on several different local village dialects. The Sami speak Lappish (Sami), and some Norwegians speak Finnish.

Native People & Ethnic Groups

Norwegians are Scandinavians and are close relatives of the Danes and Swedes. However, these people did not arrive in what is now Norway until the eighth century. While records are scarce, it is believed that the Sami, one of Europe's largest groups of indigenous people, have lived in the area for centuries.

The Sami territory, known as Lapland, extends through northern Norway, Sweden, Finland, and Russia. Although the Sami traditionally worked as reindeer herders, few continue in this profession today. In addition to their representation in Norway's government, the Sami are represented by a local authority known as the Sami Parliament.

Religions

The Evangelical Lutheran Church is the established church of Norway, but the constitution guarantees freedom of worship to all religions. About 85 percent of the population identifies as Christian (82 percent Lutheran; one percent Roman Catholic and the remainder a mix of Protestant religions); less than two percent of the population identifies as Muslim; and about 12 percent claims no religious faith at all. Non-Christian religions include Islam, Buddhism and Orthodox Judaism.

Climate

The Atlantic currents moderate the climate on the west coast and in the islands. For instance, the January temperatures near the Lofoten Islands are 25° Celsius (45° Fahrenheit) warmer than the average for other places at the same latitude. Any snow that falls melts quickly, and most harbors, even above the Arctic Circle, remain ice-free.

Inland, the winter temperatures average from −2° to 8° Celsius (28° to 46° Fahrenheit), and snow lies on the ground for at least three months. During summer, conditions are reversed. Ocean winds cool the western coast, and the inland areas are warmer, especially in the southeastern valleys.

From November through February, it is sometimes possible to see the Aurora Borealis, or the Northern Lights. This giant display of colorful light across the night sky occurs when the earth's magnetic field catches charged particles from the sun. The lights are not seen every night, and meteorological conditions must be just right for the display to occur.

Some areas of the west coast receive up to three meters (118 inches) of rain annually. The mountains in the center of the country prevent much rain from reaching the eastern inland regions, which receive as little as 30 centimeters (less than 12 inches) of rainfall annually.

ENVIRONMENT & GEOGRAPHY

Topography

Norway is a long, narrow country, with the northernmost strip bending to the east, over the top of Sweden, Finland, and the northwestern part of Russia. Sweden and Norway also share a long north-south border.

One-third of Norway is above the Arctic Circle, so for ten weeks each summer, the sun shines 24 hours a day. During a corresponding period in the winter, the days remain dark.

Deep fjords all along the coast create good harbors. They also create a jagged coastline that measures 21,351 kilometers (13,267 miles). If stretched out straight, the coastline of Norway would extend halfway around the globe. The longest fjord is Songe Fjord, which stretches inland for 204 kilometers (127 miles).

Norway's mountainous plateau consists of bare rock smoothed by glaciers. Many glacier lakes and valleys also occur in this area. The Hardanger Plateau, Europe's largest highland plain, rises in this region. The country's highest point is at the top of Galdhoppigen, with an elevation of 2,469 meters (8,100 feet).

The southeastern lowlands consist mainly of river valleys, particularly those of the 598-kilometer (327-mile) Glama (or Glomma), the country's longest river. The region's numerous waterfalls are used in producing hydroelectric power. Most of Norway's farming and forestry take place in the southeastern lowlands. The Trondheim lowlands consist of several flat, wide valleys that come together near the coast.

The largest of Norway's 150,000 lakes is Lake Mjosa in the southeastern part of the country, with an area of 365 square kilometers (141 square miles).

There are approximately 150,000 islands, some merely rocky reefs (skerries), off the coast of Norway. The Lofoten and Vesteralen Islands, the largest groups, are known for their cod fisheries. Between the two outermost Lofotens runs the strongest tidal current in the world, the Maelstrom, which creates dangerous whirlpools.

Plants & Animals

Norway has been working to preserve its dwindling wildlife. In recent years, the numbers of walruses, seals, polar bears, wolves, Arctic char (a salmon-like fish) and reindeer have been increasing as a result of conservation efforts. Wild reindeer herds have increased to the point that the government has reinstated seasonal reindeer hunting.

Moose are found in the southeastern part of the country. Other common animals include lynx, otters and game birds. Lakes and rivers are filled with fish, especially trout. Some rivers have been stocked with salmon.

Cliffs, on the west and north coasts, host numerous nesting seabirds, which in turn attract tourists. The sea eagle is Norway's largest bird of prey, and at least one has been reported to have carried off a bear cub. Next in size is the kongeorn (king, or bald eagle). Other Norwegian birds include kittiwakes and puffins.

Of the 19 tree species native to Norway, the most common are birch, and the Norway spruce and Scots pine (both conifers). Most native trees are broadleafs. The only other conifers native to Norway are yew and juniper.

Because of the warm trade winds and Atlantic currents, Norway has more than 30 indigenous species of small, low-growing orchids.

CUSTOMS & COURTESIES

Greetings

In Norway, people greet one another with a handshake and smile. An arm's length or more is generally maintained between people. In casual situations, first names are exchanged, while in more formal situations, titles of respect, such as "Herr" ("Mr.") or "Fru" ("Ms."), are exchanged along with last names. Norwegians tend to be physically reserved in their greetings. Thus, hugs and pats on the back are uncommon greetings. Norwegians exchange handshakes when leaving a person or group.

Common Norwegian greetings and phrases include the following: "Hei" ("Hi"), "God Morgen" ("Good morning"), "God kveld" ("Good evening"), "Velkommen" ("Welcome"), "Hvordan har du det?" ("How are you?"), "Vær så god" ("Hey friend"), "Jeg savnet deg så mye" ("What's new?"), and "Hadet bra" ("Goodbye"). Norwegians speak quietly and are comfortable with pauses or moments of silence in conversation.

In Norway, business associates tend to greet one another in a formal way by exchanging firm handshakes, direct eye contact and business titles. Norwegians expect business appointments to be made far in advance and for all parties to arrive punctually. Informal chatting about family, hobbies or current events tends to be very limited. Norwegians value politeness, trustworthiness and credibility. Business associates do not generally interrupt one another or raise their voices when speaking.

Gestures & Etiquette

Gesturing, a movement of the body made to communicate without speaking, is common in Norway. Norwegian culture includes many gestures that are familiar in Western culture. For instance, Norwegians convey non-verbal agreement through nodding head forward or making a thumbs-up sign. However, Norwegians have subtle variations to their gesturing that characterizes their own special form of non-verbal communication. For example, Norwegians tend to stand far apart when speaking to one another. Norwegians also have culturally-specific taboo gestures, and consider a raised fist with pinky and pointer finger extended to be a diabolical symbol or salute.

In Norway, proper etiquette dictates the exchange of handshakes when meeting a friend or business associate. A hug or pat on the back will be considered forward and presumptuous in business settings. In business situations, proper dress tends to be conservative. Norwegians do not usually bring attention to themselves through creative or provocative dress.

Gift giving in Norway is ritualized. Guests are expected to bring a small gift of flowers, wine, chocolate or bakery treats. Hosts will thank the gift giver and display or consume the gift at the event. When guests bring plants or flowers, etiquette dictates that no carnations, white flowers or even number of flowers should be given. This is because carnations, white flowers and even number of flowers are associated with illness, death, and funerals.

Eating/Meals

Norwegians eat three meals a day: breakfast (frokost), a noon meal (lunsj) and a late afternoon meal (middag). Breakfast and the late afternoon meal are the most substantial meals. Common breakfast food and drink include coffee, bread, smoked fish, sliced meat, hard-boiled eggs, yogurt, cheese , and milk. The noon meal, which may be eaten at work, school, home, or in a café, usually consists of a piece of fruit and a small open-faced sandwich of cheese and sliced meat. The late afternoon, which is generally eaten at home with family, includes fish or meat, boiled potato or root vegetable, and gravy.

Norwegians often invite friends and family over to share the late afternoon meal. Dinner guests are most often invited verbally. Guests arrive on time and usually offer to help the hosts with the meal. Mealtime conversations tend to focus on non-work or business topics. The host signals that it is time to eat by picking up his or her fork. Norwegians have formal table manners, and will hold the fork in their left hand and the knife in their right hand. Norwegians eat the majority of food, even sandwiches, with fork and knife. When dinner is over, Norwegians place their utensils gently on their plates.

Norwegians like to make toasts during the meal. "Skoal" ("To your health") is the most common toast. Toasts may be made by hosts and guests and men and women alike. Dinner parties tend to last late into the night. Guests stay hours after dinner is complete socializing and drinking alcohol or coffee. Norwegians tend to be polite and reciprocate dinner invitations promptly.

Visiting

In Norway, friends and families socialize often and traditionally gather to celebrate religious and national holidays. Important visiting days include New Year's Day, Labor Day, Christmas Day, Boxing Day, and Constitution Day. On Labor Day, families and friends get together to participate in and enjoy parades. On Christmas Day and Boxing Day (considered to be second day of Christmas), family and friends visit one another, exchange gifts, ski, attend church, and enjoy feast meals. Formal or ceremonial meals are eaten on Constitution Day and Christmas Day. On Constitution Day, Norwegians eat a typical Norwegian meal of milk porridge and flat bread with sliced meat. On Christmas Day, Norwegians eat roast pork, lutefisk, and kaldt bord.

When visiting a home in Norway, visitors are expected to take off their shoes and leave them inside the entranceway. Visitors may bring slippers to wear during their stay. Visitors are expected to bring a small gift for their hosts, and may be offered coffee and a small snack. Norwegians generally do not visit one another's houses on Sundays. Sundays are commonly a time in which friends and families (particularly those living in urban areas) travel to the countryside to picnic and hike. This is because Norwegians of all classes generally value Norway's rural culture and natural environment.

LIFESTYLE

Family

Norwegian families typically include parents and their young children. Adult children generally live in households apart from their parents. In rural areas, children, parents, grandparents, and other extended family members have historically chosen to live close to one another to offer help when needed. Many Norwegians live together and begin to have children before marriage. In Norway, there is no taboo over having children before marriage or even never marrying. In 2006, more than 50 percent of Norwegian children were born out of wedlock.

Marriage is considered to be a romantic and sacred event in Norway. Norwegians do not generally marry for practical reasons related to money and children. For the most part, families tend to be egalitarian; adults in the households share work, parenting, chores and decision-making responsibilities. Inheritance rights are also equal between men and women. The Norwegian government also recognizes registered partnerships for heterosexual and homosexual couples.

Housing

Following World War II, Norway had a housing shortage due to an increase in its population. The Norwegian government subsidized the building of homes and home payments throughout the 20th century, and the government built over 30,000 homes between 1967 and 1981. Today, housing in Norway is plentiful but tends to be expensive for both Norwegians and foreigners. Norwegian builders must meet strict requirements and codes for quality and safety. Single-family homes are more common than apartments and rentals.

Houses in Norway tend to be built in a Scandinavian design with simple and clean lines. Norwegian culture tends to value the natural environment over the built or urban environment. As a result, Norwegian housing, as well as its cities and towns, incorporate natural areas and elements. Houses, which are often built of wood and other natural materials, are constructed on a modest and human scale. Cities have paths for cross-country skiing and plentiful public spaces. Houses commonly have indoor-outdoor areas such as porches and decks.

Food

Norway's national motto, "food and joy equal health," reflects Norway's concern with healthful and happy living. The Norwegian diet reflects the available resources of the area. Common Norwegian foods include seafood, dairy, meat, root vegetables and grains. Norwegians like flat bread rather than highly leavened bread. Seafood includes fish (salmon, herring, and cod) as well as whale meat. Norwegians are well-known throughout Scandinavia for their hearty buffets (koldtbord) of cold dried meat, smoked or pickled fish, boiled eggs, yogurt, cheese, salad, and flat breads. Norwegians prefer open-face sandwiches, such as flat bread with thinly sliced brown cheese (brunost), rather than closed-face sandwiches. Popular Norwegian foods include lutefisk (dried cod in sauce), minke whale steaks or stew, brown cheese, and wild cloudberry and lingonberry jams.

Lutefisk is an ancient Norwegian delicacy of dried cod historically treated or preserved with lye. Lutefisk may be boiled or baked. After cooking, lutefisk should be sprinkled with salt and served hot with meat drippings, mustard, or butter. Side dishes include boiled potatoes, green peas and flatbread. Lutefisk is most commonly eaten in November and December. A meal of whale steak will be cooked with whale meat, salt, pepper, sliced onion, diced green pepper, chopped parsley and chopped gherkins. Whale steaks are commonly eaten with boiled potato and lettuce salad.

Norwegians have been enjoying brown cheese for over 300 years. The brown cheese, eaten with bread and meat, is always sliced very thinly with a cheese slicer rather than cut with a knife. The brown color of the cheese occurs during the cheese-making process when the milk, cream, and whey are combined.

Norwegians buy or gather wild cloudberries (also known as Arctic mulberries) and lingonberries (also known as lowbush cranberries or partridge berries) to make jams, preserves, syrups and juices. Cloudberries and lingonberries, which grow in mountainous areas, are combined with various amounts of sugar and other fruits such as orange and raspberry to make the sweet jams, preserves, syrups, and juices. Cloudberry and lingonberry jams, preserves and syrups are eaten with flatbreads and pancakes.

Norwegians drink coffee all day long, especially at meals. They also drink beer, sometimes with aquavit, a strong and colorless liquor.

Life's Milestones

In Norway, important life milestones include baptism, confirmation, and death. The majority of Norwegians belong to the Church of Norway (Lutheran faith), and Norwegians celebrate baptism, confirmation, and death through Christian traditions and rituals.

The sacrament of baptism represents the beginning of an infant's life in the church. The baptism ritual involves the priest pouring water over an infant's head three times. Families host a party to celebrate infant baptism. Children are confirmed between eight and 12 years of age. During the confirmation ritual, the child acknowledges and confirms the vows made on his or her behalf during baptism. Confirmation involves a religious ritual and a family party. A family may give their young girl a bunad (folk costume) at the time of her confirmation as way of recognizing that she is becoming a young woman.

In Norway, death is considered by many to be a blessing or release of sorts as the soul of the deceased is believed to ascent to heaven. When a person dies in Norway, a funeral service will be held and the body will either be cremated or buried in a church graveyard. Friends and families gather together after the funeral to remember and mourn the deceased.

CULTURAL HISTORY

Art

Norway has a majority culture (Norwegian) and minority culture (Sami) that have distinct artistic histories, sensibilities and aesthetics. The Sami, an indigenous group historically known as the Lapps, are a small racial and cultural minority of 40,000 people. They have their own arts, language and culture and have historically relied on reindeer as their main source of food, carving material and fur. In particular, they created an artistic tradition called duodji, which refers to

Sami handicraft. The Duodji style of artistic and functional production has historically been used to make knives, wooden carving, silverwork, textiles, sleds, pouches and other functional objects. Duodji are made with a wide variety of materials and processes, and Sami aesthetics and history influence the lines, shapes, colors and details of its arts. Duojar is the name for a duodji craftsperson.

In the 19th century, Norwegian artists shaped Norway's romantic vision of its national culture, history and environment. Dominant painting styles that emerged during this period of national romanticism include landscape painting, impressionism and realism. At the turn of the 20th century, Norway's most significant contributions to art came through the heavily symbolic work of Norwegian artist Edvard Munch (1863–1944), as well as the prolific work of Norwegian sculptor Gustav Vigeland (1869–1943). Many of Vigeland's 192 sculptures, primarily of human figures, are on permanent display at Oslo's Frogner Park. The 20th century also brought more modern artistic movements such as surrealism and abstract expressionism.

Contemporary Norwegian artists produce painting, sculpture, pottery, glass, jewelry, metalwork, and textiles influenced by Scandinavian design. (Scandinavia is the cultural and geographic region of Northern Europe including Norway, Denmark, Sweden, Finland and Iceland.) Simple and streamlined lines, forms and shapes characterize contemporary Norwegian art and design.

Architecture

Norwegians value the natural world, and that appreciation for nature is reflected in their architecture, which relies on natural materials such as wood and stone and a respect for natural settings. Economics also has had an impact, as Norway has not historically been a wealthy nation and, for many years, was territory of another country; thus, it lacks some of the more historical institutional landmarks, such as numerous and older palaces and vast cathedrals, that characterize many other European countries.

One of the oldest construction techniques in Scandinavian was timber frame "stave" construction, where load-bearing wooden staves or posts were attached to wooden sills using mortise and tendon or tongue and groove joints. Stave construction is most notable among the nation's oldest churches, of which about twenty remain. Stone construction was adopted from Anglo-Saxon cultures, and can be seen in several Romanesque structures from the 12th and 13th century.

As a Danish territory, 16th and 17th century construction reflected that country's style, introducing Renaissance and Baroque styles to Norway. When much of Oslo was consumed by fire, its reconstruction was characterized by brick. In the 18th century, the development of the gang saw led the way for panel siding on log houses, which helped tighten up houses, making them warmer and better able to withstand the elements, Vertical panels also provided a canvas for unique design elements.

In 1814, when Norway and Sweden were joined in a union, government buildings had to be constructed in Christiana to accommodate public services, many of which were constructed in the neo-classical style. The Royal Palace is an example of this wave of construction that also was included in the homes of wealthy merchants. In the mid-19th century, a romantic nationalistic movement sought to capture classical Romanesque and Gothic styles in brick in some major cities. Additionally, wooden structures began to reflect a Swiss style, evident in some of the country's remaining train stations from that period. Overall, Norwegian architecture was influenced by what was happening in Europe, including the construction of brick apartment houses and granite institutional structures in Art Nouveau (Jugend) style.

Modern Norwegian architecture is characterized by functionalism, featuring open design. Norway's influence on this movement has much to do with its fundamental use of those natural materials such as stone and wood.

Drama

Norway's theatrical history has its roots in the Danish theater, which dominated until Norwegian autonomy in the mid-19th century, when a nationalistic movement demanded that Norwegian dramatic works be both written and performed in Norwegian. Prior to this, Norwegians experienced, almost exclusively, Danish productions performed by Danish-speaking actors. Bergen's playhouse was the home to the Det Norske Teatret from 1849 to 1863, and this is where Norway's most famous playwright, Henrik Ibsen (1828–1906), began his career. Ibsen was said to be influenced by both Norwegian folk tales, the Norwegian author Henrik Wergeland, and the Danish philosopher Søren Kierkegaard. In 1858, Ibsen left Bergen for the capital, Christiana, where he became the creative director at the Christiana Theatre. He stayed in Christiana until 1864, when he moved to Italy and then Germany. While away from Norway for many years, his work was still written in his native language and set in his homeland.

Following Ibsen's departure, the Christiana Theater was led by Bjørnstjerne Bjørnson (1832–1910), who provided a diverse offering of both Norwegian works, as well as works from other classical and modern European playwrights. Bjørnson was also a playwright, and gained respect for his work that examined the real lives of Norwegians, providing a perspective on modern life and individual character that often proved as controversial as Ibsen's work. In 1877, the Christiana Theatre sustained heavy damage from a fire.

In 1899, Norway opened its National Theater in Oslo, led by Bjørn Bjørnson (son of the Christiana Theatre creative director and playwright). Vilhelm Krag, who took the reins of the National Theater in 1911, was said to have led the theater into its "golden age." Norway's National Theater, and the many theaters that sprang up in cities throughout the country, saw productions from playwrights such as psychological realist Helge Krog (1889–1962), communist Nordahl Grieg (1902–1943), absurdist Johan Borgen (1902–1977) and Tormod Skagestad (1920–1997).

Post-war Norway saw the development of popular theaters, the Oslo New Theatre and the Norwegian Theatre (focused on New Norse language productions), as well as concerted efforts to reach populations in far-reaching parts of the country. To that end, more regional theater groups arose. The 1960s saw the rise of psychological realism and anti-naturalism, led by writers such as Jens Bjørneboe (1920–1977) and Finn Carling (1925–2004), and the 1970s saw more political works.

In 2010, Norway's thriving dramatic arts community boasts more than twenty theaters, including the Sámi National Theatre Company in Kautokeino.

Music

Norway has strong classical and folk music traditions. Norwegian folk music generally belongs to either Nordic or Sami musical traditions and includes improvised songs, ballads, hymns and work songs. Common folk instruments include the hardingfele (fiddle), violin, harp, lur (trumpet), bukkehorn (horn), langeleik (zither) and seljerfloyte (flute). Sami folk music is characterized by a singing or chanting style called joik. Joiks may be descriptions of people or places, personal stories, folk tales, or epic stories. In some cases, joiks are tone-based and have no words at all. Sami singers are known to improvise joiks during performances.

Norway's classical tradition began in the 18th-century royal courts. Norway's most well-known musicians, composer Edvard Grieg (1843–1907) and violinist Ole Bull (1810–1880), were influenced by Norway's folk traditions. In the 19th century, musicians in Norway composed and performed music that furthered Norwegian nationalism and the romantic vision of Norway's culture, history and countryside. Following World War II, Norwegian composers and musicians adopted a more international style.

Dance

Norway has a strong tradition of folk dance and performance (which it shares with neighboring Sweden) that dates back to the 17th century. Norway's folk dances are strongly associated with rural Norway and the farming life. In

Norway, folk dances are most often performed to the accompaniment of hardanger fiddle music. Norway's traditional folk dances are referred to as courting dances or bygdedans (village or country dances). These dances were historically performed in rural areas during specific events such as courting, weddings, funerals, Christmas and New Year's Day. Popular folk dances include springar, springleik, halling, pols, rull, and gangar. Pols feature couples in a promenade, with a series of turns. The springdans (running dance) or springleik is a male-led dance, mostly practiced in western Norway, that can be more free-form, but is characterized by numerous holds and underarm passes and turns.

In the 19th century, Norway incorporated new European ballroom dance styles, such as the fandango, waltz, polka, and mazurka, into its dance tradition. These dance styles, commonly performed by couples, are referred to as either runddans (round dances) or gammeldans (old dances). Norwegians made the ballroom style dances their own by changing the ballroom style dances to match Norway's own rhythms and instruments.

Norway enjoys and supports its performing arts culture through its thriving performing arts festivals such as the Bergen International Festival and the Molde Jazz Festival. While there are many dance troupes in Norway, only two receive government funding: Den Norske Opera and Carte Blanche. Den Norske Opera, which offers both classical and modern pieces, receives 90 percent of its funding from the government and Carte Blanche, which receives 70 percent of its funding from the Norwegian government, is a contemporary dance troupe which performs at least three new pieces each year.

Literature

Since 12th century, Norwegian writers have contributed to the genres of poetry, epic sagas, mysteries, nature accounts, folk tale and psychological dramas. In the 19th century, Norwegian literature plated an integral role in building Norway's national culture. For instance, writers such as Peter Asbjørnsen (1812–1885) and Jørgen Moe (1813–1882) collected and retold classic Norwegian folktales. Norway's best-known writer, Henrik Ibsen, wrote influential psychological dramas. Other influential writers include Knut Hamsun (1860–1952), Sigurd Hoel (1890–1960), and Sigrid Undset (1882–1949). Norwegian writers Knut Hamsun and Sigrid Undset were each awarded the Nobel Prize in Literature.

Countries such as Norway that have a national language not commonly spoken worldwide often have trouble popularizing their nation's literature. Norwegian authors, with the exceptions of Ibsen, Hamsun and Undset, were relatively unknown to much of the world for most of the 20th century. Norway has addressed this problem through the establishment of a government-funded organization called Norwegian Literature Abroad (NORLA) in 1978. NORLA provides translation subsidies to foreign publishers, as well as grants for Norwegian authors to promote their books in foreign countries.

CULTURE

Arts & Entertainment

The contemporary Norwegian arts reflect and promote the nation's 21st century culture, traditions, collective experience and social consciousness. The arts are used to create and maintain continuity in Norway's national culture and self-identity. Since its independence in 1905, Norwegians have worked hard to shape their national identity and national culture. The arts allow Norwegians to tell their stories and history, represent their viewpoint and share their aesthetics, values and natural resources. The Norwegian government also subsidizes the incomes of Norwegian artists as a means of encouraging Norway's artistic community. Over 30 government-funded artists' organizations work to sponsor art exhibitions and shows, as well as provide grants to artists. The Norwegian government also provides Norwegian artists with a minimum income through retirement.

In the 19th and early 20th century, Norwegians began to construct a national history and identity that focused on carefully chosen elements such as the early Viking period, the Sami people, rural culture, folktales, wooden architecture, customs, traditional clothing, Nordic mythology, folk music, and peasant dialects. Norwegians crafted a bucolic rural national identity. Norwegians consider the country life, like their country.

Norway's arts, its music, dance, art, architecture and literature, tend to reflect Norway's fascination with the unspoiled rural countryside and lifestyle. Historically, Norwegian writers, painters, dramatists and musicians focused their artistic pursuits and productions on the culture of the rural peasants. For instance, folk or national costumes (bunad), a symbol of national identity, are worn in performances, seen in paintings, and described in books. Most Norwegians, old and young and rich and poor alike, own folk costumes which are modeled on peasant dress. The women's costumes include layered skirts, ruffled blouses, jackets, tights, and decorated shoes. Regional variations in color and adornment are common.

While Norway is proud of its internationally celebrated Norwegian design, as well as authors such as Henrik Ibsen, composers such as Edvarg Grieg, and painter Edvard Munch (*The Scream*). Norway most appreciates the arts for the way in which the arts promote and maintain the nation's rural identity and culture.

Outside of the arts, Norway's boasts a variety of entertainment. Skiing is the national sport, and may well have originated in Norway. Children learn to ski before they start school. Nearly every town has a ski jump, and Norwegians often take cross-country ski trips to nearby mountains and forests.

Other outdoor sports are also popular, and recreation areas are found throughout the country. Bandy, a game similar to hockey, is played in large rinks. The favorite summer sport is soccer.

Weekend hikes in the hills, mountains, and forests are common, and many Norwegians have mountain cabins for summer vacations. Hunting, sailing along the coast, swimming, and fishing are other popular activities.

Cultural Sites & Landmarks

Norway is a country rich with important historical and natural sites. The United Nations Educational, Scientific and Cultural Organization (UNESCO) recognizes six sites in Norway as requiring international recognition and preservation efforts. They include the old wharf of Bergen; the rock art of Alta; the wooden church of Urnes; Røros Mining Town; the Vegaøyan (Vega) Archipelago; and Geirangerfjord and Nærøyfjord (West Norwegian Fjords).

The bryggen (wharf) in the town of Bergen dates back to the 14th century. The old wharf is associated with Norway's growth as a 15th- and 16th-century trading empire. Despite fire damage, visitors to the wharf will see Norway's traditional wood houses. Historical restoration projects have preserved and maintained 62 structures in the old wharf of Bergen.

The rock art of Alta is of interest to scientists and tourists alike. The Alta Fjord, located near the Arctic Circle, was inhabited from 4200–500 BCE. Prehistoric inhabitants created thousands of paintings and petroglyphs (rock wall engravings). The images of hunter-gatherer life show herds of reindeers, boats, fish and hunters with bow and arrow.

The wooden church of Urnes is located in the rural county of Sogn og Fjordane. The church, which dates to the 12th century, joins together Norway's wooden architecture, Celtic artistic traditions, Viking sensibilities and Roman design. The town of Røros was a 17th-century copper mining town. The historic town, rebuilt after its destruction by Swedish soldiers, includes 80 wooden houses and buildings that have a medieval appearance.

The Vegaøyan (or Vega) Archipelago is a chain of islands South of the Arctic Circle. The islands have been inhabited since the Stone Age. Archaeological evidence of early human settlement includes fishing villages, lighthouses and farmsteads. The islands have historically been known as a nesting location of eider ducks and a source of down taken from eider ducks. Visitors to the islands often seek out demonstrations of the rarely seen eiderdown harvesting. Norwegians consider the Vega Archipelago to represent the ability of Norwegians to thrive in an inhospitable landscape.

The Geirangerfjord and Nærøyfjord Fjords, located in Western Norway, are considered by naturalists and artists to be some of the most scenic natural landscape in the entire world. Fjords are long narrow sea passages between steep cliffs. The Geirangerfjord and Nærøyfjord Fjords are two of the longest and deepest fjords in the world. Artists, scientists and tourists alike visit the Geirangerfjord and Nærøyfjord Fjords to see the majestic natural landscape. Ice crystal walls rise out of the sea creating icy caverns, while waterfalls, mountains, forests and glaciers also abound.

Libraries & Museums

Norway has no shortage of museums. Among the most visited include the Viking Ship Museum in Oslo, which features three recovered Viking ships, the Oseberg, Gokstad, and Tune, discovered in royal burial sites. Artifacts found at these sites include textiles, wagons, beds, and wood carvings from the age of the Vikings. The National Museum of Art, Architecture and Design is also in Oslo and encompasses the national gallery, as well as architecture, decorative art and design, and contemporary art museums in four different venues. Other museums of note include the Natural History Museum, the Bergen City Museum, and the Norsk Folkemuseum. Norway's National Library boasts a collection of 8.5 million, with a new feature of 50,000 Norwegian books accessible on the Internet.

Holidays

Norway's most prominent national holiday is Constitution Day, which is celebrated each year on May 17 with local parades. Labour Day, or International Workers' Day, is celebrated on May 1. Many Christian holidays, including Easter and Christmas, are also widely observed.

Youth Culture

Norwegians value and enjoy children and childhood. Norwegian youth are typically afforded a greater amount of freedom by adults, and are expected to be cooperative and independent. Teens are given the freedom and resources to plan parties, attend films and concerts, arrange lessons and extracurricular activities, and socialize with friends. In many instances, Norwegian youth are even allowed to set their own boundaries. Norwegian youth also accept certain responsibilities such as helping with younger siblings when their parents are working.

Norwegian teenagers tend to be very liberal in their worldview and will talk openly about most any topics. Teenagers tend to dress in a way that combines Norwegian traditional dress and personal style. Most teens own a bunda (national costume) and are expected to wear it at formal occasions. Generally, Norwegian youth culture is similar to the youth cultures of other European and Western countries, albeit with a distinct Nordic influence and a more liberal upbringing. Like most young people, Norwegian youth are also becoming increasing technology-savvy in the early 21st century.

Education is free and compulsory between the ages of six and sixteen. Norwegian youth are expected to attend 10 years of compulsory education followed by upper secondary—for youth aged 16 through 19—and then higher (university) or vocational training. With the exception of privatized and specialized schools, higher education is free, and none of the Norwegian universities charge tuition.

SOCIETY

Transportation

Norway is the longest country in Europe and stretches 1,770 kilometers (1,100 miles) from north to south. The width of the country is 435 kilometers (270 miles) across at its widest, and 6.4 kilometers (four miles) across at its narrowest. Despite long distances between cities and challenging terrain, Norway has built a safe, affordable and effective transportation system that is subsidized by the Norwegian government.

Norwegians average 70 minutes of travel each day, with road transportation the most common means of travel. Drivers in Norway travel on the right and seatbelt and 24-hour headlight use is required by law.

Transportation Infrastructure

Norway has nearly 100 airports and nearly 100,000 kilometers (over 62,000 miles) of roadway, the majority of which are paved. Scandinavian Airlines System (SAS) is the main international air carrier, while the Norwegian State Railway (NSB) is the main provider of rail transportation. Tram or streetcar travel is common within Norway's larger cities of Oslo, Trondheim and Bergen, and busses and ferries service Norway's most remote areas. Maritime ports and terminals include Bergen, Borg Havn, Haugesund, Maaloy, Mongstad, Narvik, Oslo, and Sture.

Media & Communications

Norway's communications system is one of the most developed in all of Europe. In 2007, Norway had approximately two million landline telephone users and five million mobile phone users. Norway shares submarine cable systems with Denmark, Finland, Iceland and Sweden. These cable systems allow for communication between the countries.

In the late 1990s, there were approximately four million radios and two million televisions. In 2012, 95 percent of the population claimed to have used the Internet. This statistic suggests that the majority of Norwegians have access to and use the Internet for work or leisure. Norway is also a highly literate country and media censorship is uncommon. Popular newspapers include *Aftenposten, Bondebladet, Dagbladet, Dagsavisen,* and *Verdens Gang.*

SOCIAL DEVELOPMENT

Standard of Living

In 2014, Norway ranked first overall out of 187 countries on the United Nations Human Development Index, which measures quality of life and standard of living indicators.

Water Consumption

Norway (along with New Zealand) has the second most secure water supply in the world. Access to clean water and sanitation is not an issue for Norwegians. According to the Norwegian government, challenges to the water supply include pollution from the petroleum industry, eutrophication (chemical runoff in agricultural and populations centers), and acidification of rivers and streams in the south.

Education

Virtually all Norwegians are literate. Education, for children from six to 16, is compulsory. Elementary and lower-secondary education is divided into three stages: the four-year barnetrinnet, three-year mellotrinnet and three-year ungdomstrinnet (lower-secondary). Students may then attend upper-secondary school for three years of vocational education or preparation for college.

The cities of Bergen, Oslo, Tromso and Trondheim all have universities. In addition, the country supports numerous technical schools. The University of Oslo boasts the biggest library in Norway. All cities and towns are required to have free public libraries, which are supported in part by government grants.

Women's Rights

The women's rights movement has a long history in Norway. In 1884, the Norwegian Association for Women's Rights (NAWR) formed to promote equality between men and women. The NAWR worked to help Norwegian women get the right to vote in 1913, worked to achieve access to equal education for boys and girls, and worked to abolish unequal taxes for men and women. The NAWR also formed the Norwegian Women's Public Health Association to provide education and social services to women and families. In 1978, the Equal Rights Law guaranteed equal pay, and Norway's Equal Rights Council was established to oversee the monitoring and enforcement of the law. The 1995 Working Environment Act was passed to protect employees from harassment or unseemly behavior.

Norwegian society and government are in constant discussion and negotiation over gender equality. For instance, Norwegians debated the effect that the 1998 Cash Benefit Act, which provides cash benefits for parents staying at home to care for small children, would have on women's role in the workplace. Opponents of the Act argued that the cash benefit would entice women to leave professional jobs. Due to the opposition and the large majority of women rather than men that have left the workforce, the Norwegian government has plans to phase out the Cash Benefit Act.

The Norwegian government and society is also concerned about women's rights on the international stage. The Norwegian government promotes women's rights in developing countries by making women's rights initiatives a condition of development aid. Norway requires its development partners, such as foreign governments and non-government organizations (NGOs), to develop a plan for women's rights and gender equality in their country. Particular areas of concern include women's political participation, economic participation, and sexual and reproductive health. Under Norway's funding system, development projects with women and gender equality as their main focus received priority funding.

Despite the equal rights women have achieved in Norway, violence against women remains a problem in Norway. Crisis telephone lines and shelters for battered women are common, and educational campaigns promote reporting of crimes. This outreach and educational efforts are working, as women are increasingly reporting incidents of rape and domestic violence. Lastly, prostitution remains legal in Norway, but organized prostitution is not.

Health Care

Norway's National Insurance Scheme, a mandatory-participation national health insurance program provides free medical and hospital care as well as sick pay for all Norwegians. The cost of the insurance is shared by the individual, the employer, local governments and the national government. Norwegians can choose to opt out of the government health care system, and some do, as wait times for some procedures have prompted some Norwegians to travel elsewhere for medical services paid out-of-pocket.

Average life expectancy is 81 years overall—79 for men and 83 for women (2014 estimate).

GOVERNMENT

Structure

Norway is a constitutional monarchy, with universal adult suffrage for citizens 18 years and older. The head of state is the monarch, who appoints the prime minister (usually the leader of the majority party) and is commander–in–chief of the military.

With the approval of the Storting, or parliament, the monarch also appoints the Statsrad (Council of State). The Statsrad is responsible to the Storting. In 2010, the Storting was comprised of 150 members elected by popular vote, based on proportional representation, with an additional 19 leveling seats elected nationally, for a total of 169 members. When the Storting is considering a bill, it divides into two chambers. About one-fourth of the members become the Lagting (upper house), and the remaining members form the Odelsting (lower house).

Political Parties

Norway's largest political party is the Labour Party, a social democratic party. In the 2013 election, the Labour Party took fifty-five seats in the Storting. However, the Conservative Party (Right), which took 48 seats, formed a ruling coalition with the Progress Party, the Christian Democrats, and Liberal party for a total of 96 seats in the Storting.

Local Government

The country is organized into nineteen fylker (counties) and 430 municipalities. The county electorate elects an assembly, which in turn elects a county governor. The king also appoints a governor or fylkesmannen for each county. County government is responsible for upper secondary education and transportation infrastructure, regional planning, and business and cultural development.

Municipalities have directly elected assemblies, a mayor, and a cabinet. They are responsible for pre-kindergarten, kindergarten, primary, and lower secondary education; medical and social services; land-use (including agricultural, environmental impact, local roads and harbors); and water and sewer. Oslo is considered both a county and a municipality.

Judicial System

Norway is a civil system. The highest court is the Supreme Court of Justice, whose 19 judges are appointed by the monarch. Lower courts include conciliation, district, city, and appellate courts. Norway has the lowest homicide rate in the world. The country abolished the death penalty in the late 20th century.

Taxation

Norway is known for its progressive tax system, the revenue from which supports the country's many social services, but which some claim discourages personal savings. Norway levies an income tax at 28 percent, taxes wealth (property), and requires social security contributions. Corporate taxes are levied at 28 percent of profit and capital gains.

Indirect taxes include a value-added tax (VAT), which can range between 12 and 25 percent of price.

Armed Forces

Norway has a mandatory 12-month military service obligation for men. The armed forces of Norway include an army, a navy, an air force, and a home guard.

Foreign Policy

Norway's foreign policy is shaped by the country's support of international peace and mediation, international strategic alliances such as the North Atlantic Treaty Organization (NATO), and its relationship with the rest of Europe. In fact, Norway's foreign policy model is often referred to as the Norwegian model due to the country's emphasis on conflict resolution and its international aid system. In addition, Norway's national defense plan is based on the idea of collective security, and the country maintains a collective agreement with other Nordic countries such as Denmark, Sweden, and Iceland, as well as the Nordic Council, to guarantee economic, social and cultural protection. Norway is a founding member of the United Nations (UN).

Though Norway shares a common foreign policy with the European Union (EU), it is not a member state. However, under a separate trade agreement called the European Economic Area (EEA), Norway trades freely with all of Europe. Thus, without being a member of the EU, Norway still has the freedoms of movements of goods, persons, services and capital guaranteed to all EU nations. In exchange for the friendly and reciprocal trade environment between Norway and the EU, Norway supports the EU's plans and directives and contributes to the organization's budget.

Norway is a country rich in natural resources. It has great quantities of petroleum, minerals, hydropower, timber and fish. Norway is also one of the largest producers of oil and gas in the world. Its main trading partners are the United Kingdom (UK), Germany, Netherlands, France, Sweden and Denmark. Norway also has small trade relations with the United States, China, and Canada. More importantly, Norway, one of the richest per capita countries in the world, lends and gives generously to developing countries. For example, Norway gave $2.954 billion (USD) in foreign aid in 2006, and has humanitarian programs in Africa and Asia that work to aid refugees, research the effect of climate change on poor farming communities, protect human rights and promote democratic governments and elections.

While Norway enjoys peaceful and mutually beneficial relations with most countries worldwide, Norway is involved in a few international disputes. For instance, Norway and Russia disagree about Russia's right to fish outside of the Svalbard territory (an arctic archipelago). Norway also disputes Russia's claim to territorial control over areas of the Barents Sea and claims disputed territory in Antarctica. However, relations have improved since the signing of a comprehensive maritime boundary agreement in 2010.

Dependencies

Norway has the following dependencies: Bouvet Island (an uninhabited volcanic island in the South Atlantic), Peter I Island (an uninhabited volcanic island in the Antarctic), and Queen Maud Land (6.475 million square kilometers, or 2.5 million square miles, of the Antarctic ice sheet between the British and Australian claims). The claim to Queen Maud Land has been contested.

Human Rights Profile

International human rights law insists that states respect civil and political rights, and also promote an individual's economic, social and cultural rights. The United Nations Universal Declaration on Human Rights (UDHR) is recognized as the standard for international human rights. Its authors sought the counsel of the world's great thinkers, philosophers, and religious leaders, and were careful to create a document that reflects the core values shared by every world culture. (To read this document or view the articles relating to cultural human rights, go to: http://www.udhr.org/UDHR/default.htm).

Norway has a strong human rights record and Norway's constitution and laws generally guarantee and protect the same rights stated in the UDHR. The government, which consists of a parliamentary democracy and constitutional monarchy, respects its citizens and has laws in place to prevent and address human rights injustices or abuses. Two current issues that are being addressed include anti-Semitism and violence against women.

Article 2 of the UDHR, which states that everyone is entitled to legal rights and freedoms without distinction of race, color, sex, language, religion, political or other opinion, national or social origin, property, birth or other status, is supported by the Norwegian Constitution and enforced by the government. For example, government buildings are accessible to all regardless of physical limitation or disability; numerous government subsidized programs and schools protect and teach indigenous Sami language and culture; and boys and girls receive equal access to education and health care.

Article 16 of the UDHR, which states that men and women of any race, nationality or religion have the right to marry and to found a family, is supported by Norway's constitution and culture. While the population tends to be homogeneous, Norwegians generally accept unions between Norwegians and immigrants or Norwegians and the indigenous Sami (largest indigenous group in Norway).

Article 18 of the UDHR, which supports the right to freedom of thought, conscience and religion, so long as the practice of religion does not violate public morality, decency, or the public order, is protected by the Norwegian constitution. That said, there is no separation between church and state, and the government provides financial support to the state church, the Evangelical Lutheran Church of Norway, and other registered religious communities in proportion to overall membership. The constitution also states that the king and a majority of the cabinet must belong to the Evangelical Lutheran Church of Norway. In addition, public schools are permitted to teach a Christian-based religious knowledge and ethics, and employers are allowed to ask job applicants about their religious views during interviews and reject applicants based on their answers.

Human rights abuses that do occur in Norway typically do so on a small scale, and are mostly associated with anti-Semitism and domestic violence against women. The small Jewish population (made up of an estimated 1,000 members) in Norway continues to report incidents of anti-Semitism, most notably an armed attack on a synagogue in Oslo in 2006. The government has programs in place to educate Norway's youth about the Holocaust and fight religious discrimination and intolerance.

Migration

Norway's migration rate is 7.9 migrants per 1,000 inhabitants. Between 2004 and 2009, Norway's immigrant population has increased by 41 percent. The majority of the immigrants are from Poland, Sweden, Pakistan, Iraq, and Somalia.

ECONOMY

Overview of the Economy

Norwegians have a high standard of living and a strong system of welfare capitalism. By law, every employee must receive four weeks of paid vacation each year. The National Insurance Act combines retirement pensions, job retraining, and aid to mothers, orphans, widows, widowers, and the handicapped. Participation in the insurance plan is mandatory. Local and national government and employers also contribute to the plan.

Any family with more than one child gets a yearly allowance for each child under 16, and may also get help paying rent. Large families with medium or low incomes receive tax reductions, as well.

Norway's gross domestic product (GDP) was estimated at $ 339.5 billion (USD) in 2014. The per capita GDP for the same year was approximately $65,900 (USD). The unemployment rate is roughly 3.4 percent in 2014.

Industry

Norway has some of the world's largest fishing and shipping interests. In addition, the country's chief manufactured products include ships, aluminum, wood pulp and paper, chemicals, processed foods, cement and refined petroleum. The mining industry produces natural gas, crude petroleum, iron ore, coal, ilmenite, lead, molybdenum, pyrites, and zinc.

Exports of mineral fuels, lubricants, petroleum and petroleum products, natural and manufactured gas, transport equipment, fish and basic manufactures result in receipts of more than $122.8 (2009) billion (USD) annually.

Labor

Norway's labor force numbers 2.72 million people. In 2012, 77 percent of the labor force worked in the service sector; 20 percent worked in industry; and almost two percent worked in agriculture. The unemployment rate in 2014 was 3.4 percent.

Energy/Power/Natural Resources

Norway's natural resources are almost all in the water. The sea yields an abundance of fish, as well as large off-shore deposits of petroleum and natural gas. Inland, swift mountain rivers produce hydroelectric power, providing Norway with extremely inexpensive electricity. Only three percent of Norway's land is arable, and there is little in the way of mineral deposits. Environmental concerns include water pollution, air pollution caused by vehicle emissions, and damage to forests, lakes and fish from acid rain.

Fishing

The country's largest fishing port is in Alesund, the "herring capital of the world." Despite international protests, Norway legalized whaling in the early 1990s. Among those fish caught off of Norway's coast are cod, mackerel, haddock, and saithe. Greenland halibut, blue whiting, redfish, eel, and sandeel. Aquaculture, particularly in salmon, is also a thriving industry. In 2008, the aquaculture industry produced 850,000 tons of fish.

Forestry

Forests cover about 38 percent of Norway and most are privately owned (88 percent). The forests are comprised primarily of spruce, Scots pine, and birch. Because harvests have come in under annual limits, the stock is growing and is in line with sustainable levels. Norway's government is committed to sustainable forests in order to mitigate in the impact of climate change.

Mining/Metals

Mining is a major employer in some areas of Norway. With rising demand for minerals in the developing world, a consideration to re-open old mines is proving controversial in some areas.

Agriculture

Only three percent of the land in Norway is arable. Farming is pursued mostly in the lowland regions. Principal agricultural products include barley, wheat, potatoes, pork, beef, veal and milk.

Animal Husbandry

Horses, pigs, sheep, goats, chickens, and rabbits are raised on Norwegian farms.

Tourism

More than 4.2 million tourists visit Norway annually, generating revenues of over $2 billion (USD).

Arctic tours are popular. Some include opportunities for birding, dog-sledding, riding a rubber dingy through the Maelstrom, snowmobiling, and practicing lasso-throwing on a wooden reindeer. Fishing tours are available in the country's coastal waters, fjords, lakes and streams. Cruises along the coast are another popular tourist attraction.

Visitors enjoy Norway's many museums, historic towns and buildings dating back to the Viking era. Among the attractions in the capital city of Oslo are the Royal Palace and the Storing (parliament), as well as the Lutheran Cathedral and the medieval Akershus Castle.

Simone Flynn, Ellen Bailey

DO YOU KNOW?

- In 1905 Norway declared its independence from Sweden and elected Prince Karl of Denmark as King Haakon VII.

- When King Harald V was the crown prince, he refused to marry until his father finally allowed him to wed "commoner" Sonja Haraldsen. Harald's son, Crown Prince Haakon, married a single mother, Mette-Marit Tjessem Hoiby, in 2001.

Bibliography

Anthony Ham. *Norway.* Oakland, CA: Lonely Planet, 2015.

Francis Sejerstad. *The Age of Social Democracy: Norway and Sweden in the Twentieth Century.* Phil Lee and Roger Norum. *Rough Guide to Norway.* London: Rough Guides, 2013.

James Larry Taulbee, et al. *Norway's Peace Policy: Soft Power in a Turbulent World.* New York: Palgrave Macmillan, 2014.

Linda March. *Norway – Culture Smart! The Essential Guide to Customs and Culture.* London: Kuperard, 2006.

Margaret Hayford O'Leary. *Culture and Customs of Norway.* Santa Barbara, CA: Greenwood Press, 2010.

Princeton, NJ: Princeton University Press, 2011.

Rolf Danielsen, et al. *Norway: A History from the Vikings to Our Own Times.* Oslo: Scandinavian University Press, 1995.

Works Cited

"Background Note: Norway." *U.S. Department of State.* http://www.state.gov/r/pa/ei/bgn/3421.htm.

"Lending a Helping Hand." *Publishers Weekly* 253.37 (18 Sep. 2006): S8-S8. Academic Search Complete. EBSCO. <http://search.ebscohost.com/login.aspx?direct=true&db=a9h&AN=22451958&site=ehost-live>.

"Norway: A Brief Description." *World Atlas* (n.d.). http://www.worldatlas.com/webimage/countrys/europe/no.htm.

"Norway." CIA World Fact Book. *U.S. Central Intelligence Agency.* Retrieved 4 Jan. 2009 https://www.cia.gov/library/publications/the-world-factbook/print/no.html

"Norway." *Encyclopedia of the Nations.* http://www.nationsencyclopedia.com/Europe/Norway.html.

"Norway." *UNESCO World Heritage List*. http://whc. unesco.org/en/statesparties/no.

"Norway." *U.S. Department of State Country Reports on Human Rights Practices*. http://www.state.gov/g/drl/rls/ hrrpt/2006/78831.htm.

"Norwegian Culture and Etiquette." *Kwintessential* (n.d.). http://www.kwintessential.co.uk/resources/global-etiquette/norway-country-profile.html.

"Norwegian Phrases." *Linguanaut*. http://www.linguanaut. com/english_norwegian.

Sami Siiddat (n.d.). "Sami Art and Duodji." http://home. earthlink.net/~arran4/siida/sami-duodji.htm.

Sundt, Magnar. "Norwegian folk music and folk dancing." *Olavsrosa* (n.d.). http://www.olavsrosa.no/en/ redaksjonelt.aspx?id=146103.

"The Kingdom of Norway." Background Notes on Countries of the World: 1. Academic Search Complete. EBSCO. <http://search.ebscohost.com/ login.aspx?direct=true&db=a9h&AN=7194471&site= ehost-live>.

"Universal Declaration of Human Rights." *United Nations* (1948). <http://www.udhr.org/UDHR/default.htm>.

"Velkommen til Bords." *Everything Norway*. http://library. thinkquest.org/C005340/culture.php3?id=food/.

PORTUGAL

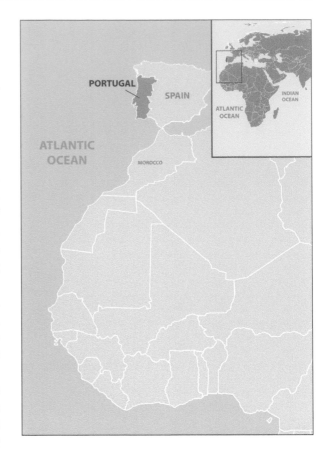

Introduction

Portugal, known officially as the Portuguese Republic (República Portuguesa), is a Western European nation located on the Atlantic coast of the Iberian Peninsula. Its only land neighbor is Spain. Portugal borders the Atlantic Ocean, where several of its island territories are located, including the Azores.

Portugal is noted for its rich and lengthy cultural history, especially global exploration, ceramics, textiles, and lace, and for its tradition of hospitality. Its Algarve coast attracts tourists worldwide. Portugal's name is thought to derive from the Latin phrase "Beautiful Port," dating from its days as a Roman province.

During the Age of Exploration, Portugal established a global colonial empire in such regions as Africa, Brazil, and the Indian subcontinent. Today, the country is a member of the European Union,

Lisbon is the capital of Portugal Lisbon's name in Portuguese is Lisboa, and is derived from the ancient word Olisipo, which is thought to be a reference to either the Homeric hero Odysseus or Elisha, the grandson of the biblical figure Abraham. Both Odysseus and Elisha have been credited as founders of the city, but modern scholars believe Lisbon was more likely founded by Phoenician colonists. Although the city has experienced political and natural turmoil throughout its history, it has recently grown to become one of the most important economic and cultural centers in the Iberian Peninsula, and in Europe as a whole.

GENERAL INFORMATION

Official Language: Portuguese
Population: 10,813,834 (2014 estimate)
Currency: Euro
Coins: Portuguese euro coins come in denominations of .01, .05, .10, .20, .50, 1, and 2 euros.
Land Area: 91,470 square kilometers (35,316 square miles)
Water Area: 620 square kilometers (239 square miles)
National Anthem: "A Portuguesa" (English, "The Portuguese Song")
Capital: Lisbon
Time Zone: GMT
Flag Description: The flag of Portugal features two horizontal bands of color, with a smaller green band on the left (or hoist) side that takes up roughly one-third of the flag, and red band on the right side. The national coat of arms of Portugal is featured along the colors' demarcation point and centered horizontally.

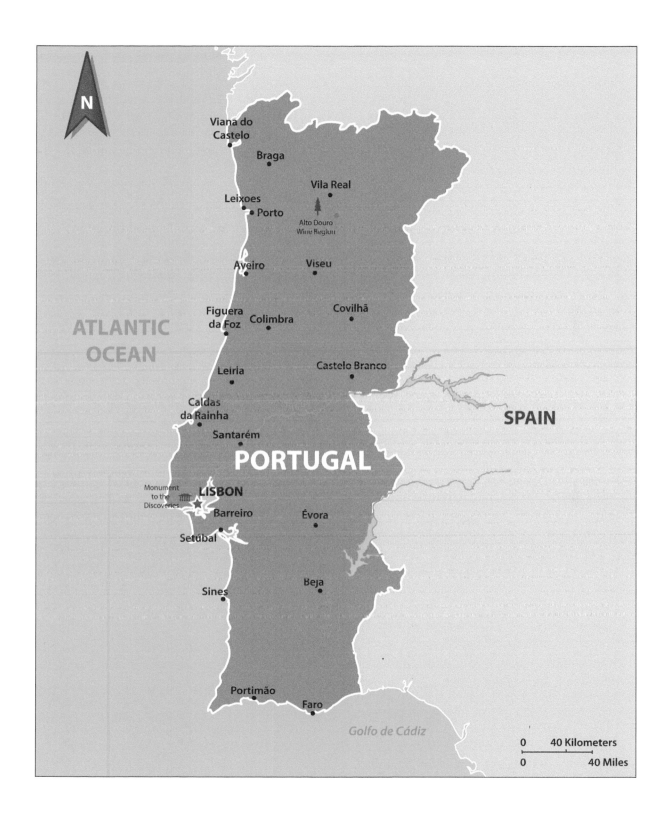

Principal Cities by Population (2012):

- Lisbon (475,353)
- Porto (219,099)
- Amadora (165,875)
- Braga (132,823)
- Queluz (130,895)
- Setabúl (121,506)
- Agualva-Cacém (115,577)
- Coimbra (106,824)
- Algueirao-Mem Martins (98,563)

Population

Portugal has a small but growing population of immigrants, especially Brazilians, Cape Verdeans, and Angolans, many of them from the former colonies. There is also a sizeable population of Ukrainians. Fifty-nine percent of the country's population lives in or near urban areas, while an estimated two-thirds of the population lives on or near the coast.

The largest city is Lisbon, the capital, with a metropolitan population of around 2.4 million people. Portugal's population declined during the 1960s and 1970s, due to economic stagnation and the country's colonial wars. The population has begun growing again, in part due to immigration from the former African colonies including Cape Verde and Angola. Lisbon has been a popular city for immigrants, particularly from Africa, since the 1960s. During the 1970s, many exiles from Angola and Mozambique immigrated to Lisbon, as well. This has all resulted in a vibrant, diverse population.

Despite the city's exploding prosperity and culture, there is significant poverty in Lisbon, and even a community of shantytowns at the edges of the city. Most of these towns are populated by immigrants. Beyond the shantytowns, Lisbon enjoys a high quality of life, ranking thirteenth in the European Union, and 57th in the world, according to a report based on 39 criteria, including personal safety, health, education, and transportation. Lisbon has one of the lowest crime rates among Organisation for Economic Co-operation and Development (OCED) member countries.

In 1996, Portugal formed a global community similar to the British Commonwealth of Nations, intended to link it more closely with its former colonies. Known as the Community of Portuguese Language Countries (Comunidade dos Países de Língua Portuguesa, or CPLP), its membership includes Angola, Brazil, Cape Verde, China, East Timor, Guinea-Bissau, Mozambique, Portugal and São Tomé and Príncipe.

Languages

Most inhabitants speak the Portuguese language. Thanks to Portugal's voyages of discovery and colonial expansion, Portuguese has also become a major world language, spoken by around 200 million people around the globe. Like Spanish, Portuguese is a Romance language, but it differs markedly from its neighbor in vocabulary and pronunciation.

The Mirandese language is a protected minority language spoken by up to 7,000 people in the Miranda de Douro region of northeastern Portugal, near the Douro River. This tongue is part of the family of Astur-Leonese Romance dialects also spoken in the northwestern part of Spain.

Native People & Ethnic Groups

Portugal's modern population is largely homogeneous. Historically, most Portuguese are the descendents of the Iberian tribes who intermarried with the country's various conquerors, including the Romans, the Germanic tribes, and Arabs. Portugal has relatively small populations of ethnic minorities. In the late 1980s, less than one percent of the population was foreign. This has changed somewhat, with Portugal's increasing connection to its former colonies and Europe.

Ethnic minorities in Portugal today include many natives of the former Asian and African colonies, such as Hindus from Goa and Chinese from Macao. There are also numerous Eastern Europeans, including many Ukrainians. Many minorities have not assimilated into the Portuguese culture, and face varying amounts of racial prejudice.

Religions

Most Portuguese are Roman Catholics, though not all are active churchgoers. Roman Catholicism is a strong influence in Portuguese culture, despite the official separation of church and state. There are also small populations of Muslims and Hindus, largely from the former Portuguese colony of Goa, India. The Jewish population is very small, around 1,000, due to expulsions led by the Spanish Inquisition.

The shrine at Fatima is a major site of international religious pilgrimage, where several children claimed to have seen visions of the Virgin Mary in the early 20th century.

Climate

Portugal's climate is a mix of Mediterranean and Atlantic. Temperatures tend to be cooler to the north and inland, though sea breezes serve as a moderating influence over most of the country. Portugal's average annual temperature is between 13° and 18° Celsius (55° and 64° Fahrenheit). The higher mountains of the Serra de Estrela chain often receive snow, but the overall climate is mild. Summer temperatures are hot, and winters are mild. The Azores and Madeira Archipelago also have generally mild climates, thanks to the sea winds and the flow of the Gulf Stream.

ENVIRONMENT & GEOGRAPHY

Topography

The Portuguese mainland is known as the "continente," reflecting its location on Continental Europe. Most of Portugal lies along the Atlantic coast, a fact which has dramatically shaped Portuguese history and culture.

North of the River Douro, the country is hilly or mountainous, with rugged river valleys. The country's highest point, Serra da Estrela (1,993 meters/6,539 feet), is located between the Douro and Tagus. Southern Portugal, lying south of the River Tagus (Tajo), is covered with plains and has a more Mediterranean climate. Central Portugal, lying between these two rivers, is the most heavily urbanized region. The Algarve, at the extreme southern end of the country, is Mediterranean in landscape and climate, with a strong Moorish influence.

Portugal's rivers play an important role in navigation and commerce. There are ten main rivers, five of which begin in Spain and flow west to the Atlantic. Besides the Douro and Tagus, these include the Sado, Guadiana, and Mondego.

Plants & Animals

Portugal's plant life reflects the country's unique geographic position as part of Western Europe, the Mediterranean world, and a neighbor of North Africa. Much of the country is forested, though the species differ depending on whether one is in the north or south. Common species in the north include pines and chestnuts. In the south, Mediterranean species are common, including oaks, olive trees, fig trees, and cork trees. A variety of wildlife may be found in the rural regions and mountainous areas of Portugal. In rural regions, one can find deer, foxes, rabbits, and hares, as well as wild goats and pigs. Wolves and lynx can be found in particularly remote mountain regions.

As befits a maritime country, Portugal is particularly blessed with fish and shellfish. Portugal has several national parks and wildlife conservation areas. These include the Peneda-Gerês National Park in northwestern Portugal and the Tapada Nacional de Mafra, a former royal park and hunting area.

CUSTOMS & COURTESIES

Greetings

The customary greeting between two men in Portugal is a firm handshake. Among close friends, pats on the back and firm embraces are common. People often greet those of the opposite sex with a kiss on each cheek, starting with the right cheek. This is also a common greeting between two women. Children are expected to kiss adults in their extended families when greeting them.

Generally, touching those with whom they are communicating is quite common among the

Portuguese. They tend to stand close to the people with whom they are talking, and it is natural to touch the other person when they are speaking. Common greetings include "Bom dia" ("Good day") and "Boa noite" ("Good evening").

In general, Portugal is a hierarchical society, and this formality carries over into face-to-face communication. Titles command great respect and should always be used when addressing someone with a title. Advanced college and technical degrees are commonly used to address those in professional positions. For example, when addressing a doctor, one would say "Senhor doutora."

Gestures & Etiquette

The Portuguese are usually reserved and formal in public and with those with whom they are not well acquainted. Once a friendship is established, however, the Portuguese can be very expressive and animated. Conversations become lively, with participants using facial expressions and physical gestures to emphasize what is said. In addition, the Portuguese have a variety of gestures that enhance or emphasize communication. For example, when someone wants to show a lack of interest or indifference, he or she places the hands out with the palms facing the body and rubs one hand across the other. When a person suspects that someone is exaggerating, the person pulls a lower eyelid down to expose the eyeball.

The "OK" sign used in the United States and other cultures around the world is not used in Portugal. Using the forefinger and the thumb to form an "O" is considered an insult in Portugal. To show appreciation or to signal approval, the Portuguese use the thumbs-up sign. After a particularly good meal or dining experience, many Portuguese pinch an earlobe with their index finger and thumb.

Humor plays a significant role in Portuguese culture. Much of this humor is often slapstick comedy or situational comedy. However, the Portuguese tend to avoid teasing or humiliating family members and women. In addition, the Portuguese tend to not use coarse or profane language in many social situations, particularly when women are present.

Eating/Meals

Breakfast, or pequeno almoço, is generally a light meal for most Portuguese. A cup of warm milk or coffee with buttered toast is a common meal. Almoço, or lunch, is generally eaten around 1:00 pm and is a much more substantial meal. Meat and seafood are both common lunch dishes, often served with potatoes, vegetables, bread, cheese, and olives. Dinner, called jantar, features dishes that are similar to those eaten for lunch. The Portuguese tend to eat dinner late.

Mealtimes are considered important social occasions and quality time for Portuguese families. Consequently, proper manners and some sense of formality are displayed so as not to disturb the meal. Making noises while eating, such as lip smacking, slurping, and burping, is frowned upon. Hands are kept above the table and elbows off the table when eating. Portuguese table manners follow the continental style: diners hold forks in their left hands and knives in their right. Cutting food first and using only a fork to eat are considered bad manners. When finished with a meal, it is customary to lay the knife and fork parallel on the plate, fork tines pointing up, and the handles facing to the right.

Visiting

The Portuguese are generally very sociable. Among relatives and friends, uninvited visits are common. Once a friendship is established, invitations to visit usually follow. It is customary that an invitation be reciprocated. First-time guests to a Portuguese home should present the host or hostess with a gift. Common gifts include pastries, wine, chocolates, or flowers. Guests should not bring red carnations, however. Red carnations are a symbol of the 1974 coup and carry significant political connotations.

Dinner guests are often served traditional family or local foods. The Portuguese take great pride in their culinary heritage, so it is considered impolite to refuse a taste. Following a dinner, it is customary for guests to remain and visit with the hosts and other guests.

LIFESTYLE

Family

Portuguese families have experienced rapid political, economic and social changes since the 1974 revolution. The birth rate in Portugal is about half the world average and population growth is slow. The family unit remains the most important aspect of Portuguese society. The traditional Portuguese family not only includes the immediate family, but also grandparents, aunts, uncles, cousins, and often godparents, as well.

The idea of the extended family is still important, but the family structure is changing. Economic conditions and evolving views of traditional roles of women in Portugal have led to more women entering the workforce. More women are also attending college, delaying starting families and entering careers. Although Portuguese parents are having fewer children, childcare is becoming increasingly difficult. Large numbers of families are migrating to urban areas, leaving behind their extended family members who often helped with child rearing. The traditional practice of children remaining at home until they marry, however, is still strong. In the early years of the 21st century, about 40 percent of children between the ages of nineteen and twenty-four lived with their parents. Although about half of these young adults are working, they usually are not expected to contribute to household expenses.

Housing

Modern Portugal has struggled to correct its housing shortage and substandard housing conditions. The constitution guarantees the right of all citizens to occupy a dwelling of adequate size, hygiene and comfort levels. However, in practice, this constitutional right has been difficult to protect. By European standards, the typical Portuguese dwelling is small. In addition, the Lisbon and Porto metropolitan areas saw a drastic increase in the construction of unsafe shanty-towns (informal settlements) during the 1980s. In rural areas, many homes were not equipped with electricity until the 1990s.

The type of housing structure is generally determined by location. Most people in large urban areas live in apartments. These range from smaller units in large complexes to luxurious multi-room condominiums. Amenities usually depend on the age of the building. Many older apartments are quite large and have wood floors and high ceilings and lack central heating. These occupants use electric or gas heaters along with fireplaces to stay warm.

In smaller or more rural communities, traditional homes, townhouses or villas (vivendas) are more common. Home ownership rates are also quite high. Homes are constructed with materials found locally. Stone and wood homes are common in northern Portugal, and are typically angular or square in shape. The architecture in the south is influenced by the Moors, who built round buildings that are often whitewashed. Homes throughout Portugal contain traditional blue and white tile that is commonly used in bathrooms and kitchens. Modern home construction is now on par with other countries around the world. New homes are better insulated and contain central heating as well as modern amenities.

Food

Portuguese cuisine has been shaped not only by its geographic location, but also by its historical role as a nation of explorers. Discoveries of maritime routes to the Far East, Africa and South America led to the use of spices such as coriander, pepper and paprika. Once-foreign fruits, vegetables and coffee were introduced to Portugal and have become staples in the Portuguese diet. The culinary scenes of Lisbon, Porto, and other larger urban areas have been influenced by Portugal's large immigrant populations. Dishes from North Africa, Brazil and the Far East are common and popular.

In addition, Portugal's long coastline provides an abundant source of fresh seafood. Prawns, squid, clams, crayfish and octopus are all common dishes in towns and communities along the coast. Some of the most popular fish used in Portuguese dishes include red snapper, sea bass, salmon, swordfish, tuna and sea bream. Bacalhau (salted cod) is perhaps one of the most common seafood items eaten in Portugal. Bacalhau pieces are soaked in water before they are cooked with other ingredients. Bacalhau com natal is shredded cod with cream and potatoes. Bacalhau is also combined with potatoes and scrambled eggs to make bacalhau a brás. Grilled sardines (sardinaha) are another extremely popular food in Portugal. Sardinaha in Portugal are usually served without being cleaned first, and include the guts.

Meat dishes vary according to regional traditions and availability. Presunto (smoked ham) and chouriço (spicy sausage) are popular in the north. Alheira is a smoked sausage fried in oil or baked and served with leafy greens, homemade fries and fried eggs. Feijoada is a traditional stew made of beans and a mixture of smoked meats. In addition, soups are an integral course of most meals. Stone soup (sopa da pedra) is a thick soup made from beans, pork, chouriço, vegetables, and a variety of spices.

Port is a fortified wine that originated in the Douro valley. Roman soldiers planted the first grape plants in Portugal. However, it was the British who added brandy to the local wine to balance out the taste of the harsh local wines and to aid in transport back to England. Port is classified according the quality of the grapes used and the amount of time the wine is aged.

Life's Milestones

Roughly 87 percent of Portugal's citizens are Christian, with the vast majority (81 percent in 2011) being Roman Catholic. Consequently, the majority of key milestones revolve around religious events. Baptisms are not only important family affairs, but also significant community events. A baptism welcomes the child into the religious community, so it is usually performed following weekly Sunday services. Parents invite relatives and close friends to share a large meal after the service. It is customary for guests to present gifts to the baptized child, such as silver crosses or medallions of saints.

College students celebrate their graduations during one week in May with the ribbon-burning (queima das fitas) tradition. The tradition started in the mid-19th century when students and faculty would gather and march from the university to the town's main square. There they would burn the ribbons they used to tie their books together. In modern Portugal, the event has taken on greater significance. The celebrations are stretched over an entire week and there are often organized activities and other festivities. The celebration typically kicks off with a group fado performance and the singing of other types of songs. Students display their ribbons and book bags and have their professors, families and friends sign their ribbons. Often the ribbons and book bags are blessed at a religious ceremony. The week continues with concerts, parties, and short skits in which students satirize professors and university life.

For many Portuguese, the act of marriage represents the most important milestone. Reverence for tradition plays an integral role in modern Portuguese weddings. In traditional weddings, on the day of the ceremony, the bride and groom and their respective bridal parties spend the day separated with their families and close friends, eating breakfast and preparing for the ceremony. Most Portuguese couples are married in a church, which is decorated with white flowers. Upon leaving the church following the ceremony, the newlyweds are showered with flower petals and rice. Most couples have a reception after the ceremony where a meal is served. After eating and dancing, guests visit the newlyweds' home for a brief visit before returning home for a siesta. After the siesta, guests gather once again with the newlyweds for another meal in the late evening.

CULTURAL HISTORY

Art

Portugal is an ancient country that for more than 1,000 years has maintained its unique culture while being influenced by various others. The Iberian Peninsula, which includes modern-day Portugal, has seen a constant influx of different cultures during the past 3,100 years. Iberian, Celtic, Phoenician, Carthaginian, Greek, Roman, Germanic, and Moorish peoples have all made an imprint on the region and the Portuguese people. Traditional Portuguese crafts include ceramics, basket making, embroidery, weaving, and lace-making.

Ceramics have been a part of the Portuguese culture since the seventeenth century. Over the centuries, influences from Asia, the Middle East, and Italy have transformed Portuguese ceramics into an exceptionally diverse craft. The various types and colors of clay found within in the region, along with the distinct traditions of the people, also contribute to this diversity. Artisans in Barcelos, in northern Portugal, are masters of small painted clay figurines. Many of their works use a red glaze speckled with white dots. Louça de Coimbra is perhaps the most famous type of Portuguese pottery. Potters in Coimbra work with a distinct blue porcelain that they decorate with flower and animal motifs. Colorful glazed tiles called azulejos are a uniquely Portuguese decorative art. Azulejos decorate the façades (exteriors) of churches, monasteries, palaces, and many of the older apartment and commercial buildings. Of particular note are the blue tiles that Portuguese artisans adopted from early Dutch styles.

In addition, Portuguese artisans have a rich tradition of crafting very fine works of embroidery, lacework and weaving. The bobbin lace of Vila do Conde is handmade by using threads wound on bobbins following a pattern laid out on a pillow. A museum in Vila do Conde promotes programs to keep this unique craft alive. Portuguese weavers use wool, silk, cotton and linen to create unique clothes and household items. Among the most popular clothing items are wool capes, called capas de honra, from Trás-os-Montes, and the capote Alentejano, which is made in the Alentejano region. The Alentejano is also home to some of the most sought-after rugs and carpets in Portugal. The finest rugs are called tapete bordado, which are hand-stitched and contain embroidered cross stitches.

Visual arts and artists were censored during the 20th century decades of the dictatorial Salazar government. It was not until after the 1974 revolution that the prevailing styles and trends in the international art world were freely accepted and explored by the Portuguese art community.

Architecture

Portuguese architecture owes much to the influence of the various peoples who settled the region. Much of Portugal's early architecture derives from antiquity, and examples of Paleolithic, Roman, and Moorish architecture are scattered throughout the country. In addition, Portuguese and foreign architects designed structures in the major European architectural styles, such as Romanesque, Gothic, Renaissance, baroque and neoclassicism. The Portuguese, however, did develop two styles of architecture that were unique: the Manueline style, an extravagant Portuguese version of late Gothic style; and the Pombaline style, a combination of late baroque and neoclassicism that developed after the great Lisbon earthquake of 1755.

Manueline architecture is named in honor of King Manuel I (1469–1521), during whose reign (1495–1521) most buildings of this style were built. Manueline mixes aspects of late Gothic styles with Renaissance architecture and decoration. Manueline buildings are noted for incorporating highly decorative carvings into the structures. Many of these decorative flourishes were inspired by Portugal's maritime successes and discoveries. Common motifs included twisting ropes, coral, ship anchors, armillary spheres and sea monsters. The most prominent Manueline structures are Mosteiro dos Jerónimos monastery (1501), the Tower of Belém (1515) in Lisbon, and the incomplete chapels at the Batalha Cathedral.

Many of Lisbon's buildings were destroyed by the 1755 earthquake. Marquês de Pombal (1699–1782), a powerful politician of the time, hired architects and engineers to rebuild damaged areas of the city. The new Pombaline style areas of Lisbon are known as much for their urban planning features as they are for their architecture. Pombaline style featured a grid pattern and wide streets. Buildings and homes were plain and undecorated, and the designs could be built easily and copied. The Praça do Comércio, Lisbon's most famous square, is an example of Pombaline architecture. Porto's Hospital de Santo Antonio and Feitoria Inglesa (Factory House) are other notable Pombaline structures.

Drama

The Portuguese film industry has largely been ignored by audiences outside of Portugal, largely due to inadequate distribution. However, Portuguese films and directors are usually well represented at the annual European film festivals and are often highly acclaimed. Manoel de Oliveira (1908–2015) is Portugal's most famous filmmaker. Oliveira's films include *The Convent* (1995), *Viagem ao Princípio do Mundo* (*Voyage to the Beginning of the World*, 1997) and *O Quinto Império* (*The Fifth Empire*, 2004). Current filmmakers are exploring the tragic and dark aspects of Portuguese society. Pedro Costa (1959–) and Teresa Villaverde (1966–) are two of Portugal's acclaimed directors.

Music

Portuguese music is represented by a wide variety of forms. The foundation of traditional Portuguese music, however, is its folk music, which originated with medieval troubadours. They accompanied their singing with guitars, violins, clarinets, wood percussion instruments, and even harmonicas. The most famous Portuguese music is fado, a form of melancholic music. Fado is closely associated with the Portuguese expression "saudade." Saudade refers to the emotions a person feels when they are in love with someone or something from which they've been parted. It conveys a distinct mixture of sadness, pain, nostalgia, happiness and love. Fado is accompanied by the Portuguese guitar and is performed as a set of three songs, each lasting three minutes.

Fado developed in the working class neighborhoods in Lisbon in the 18th century and soon caught on nationally. Its musical origins are probably a mixture of African rhythms with traditional music of Portuguese sailors, with Arabic influences. Two styles of fado developed in Portugal, one from Lisbon, and the other from the town of Coimbra. Lisbon fado is considered the most traditional and is often performed by women. Coimbra fado is performed by men and often is about women. Amália Rodrigues (1920–1999), Mariza (1973–), Ana Moura (1980–), Mísia (1955–), Dulce Pontes (1969–), and Cristina Branco (1972–) are some of Portugal's most famous fado performers.

Immigrants from former Portuguese colonies, particularly the African colonies, have settled in Portugal and have greatly influenced the contemporary music scene. Performers from Cape Verde, Mozambique and Angola, in particular, are injecting new sounds and styles into the already vibrant and unique Portuguese musical tradition. Mornas is a haunting and melodic musical style from Cape Verde that is similar to Portuguese fado. Cesária Évora (1941–2011) is the most famous mornas artist. Merengue and kizomba are Angolan dance music genres that are played at clubs in many of Portugal's larger cities. Marrabenta music originates in Mozambique, and is a fast-paced style that gets its name from the many guitar strings that are broken during a typical frenetic performance.

Dance

The Portuguese still perform traditional folk dances, especially in the north. Many dances are important aspects of festivals, pilgrimages, and the celebrations of the santos populares (popular saints). The bailarico, chula, vira and fandango are some of the most popular traditional dances. The dança dos pauliteiros from the Miranda do Douro region is one of the unique traditional Portuguese dances. Male dancers dress in kilts, smocks, black waistcoats, shawls, and hats covered with flowers and ribbons. The dance is notable for its rhythmic style accompanied by the cracking of the pauliteiros (sticks).

Literature

Lyrical poetry and realistic fiction have dominated the Portuguese literary scene. Luís Vaz de

Camões, also known as Camoens (1524–1580) is considered the country's greatest poet. His masterpiece is "Os Lusiadas," an epic poem which retells his country's history up through the 16th-century voyages of discovery.

For most of the 20th century, the arts were suppressed by the dictatorship of António de Oliveira Salazar (1889–1970). Many artists left Portugal to practice their crafts while some remained to document the repressive era. Poetry, like much of the fiction written during the dictatorship, was heavily censored. The 1960s in particular saw an increase in revolt against the stifling atmosphere of the Portuguese government. Poets pushed the limits by exploring political themes and expanding the traditional artistic norms of Portuguese society.

José Cardoso Pires (1925–1998) was a popular novelist who often wrote about life in the repressive Salazar era. *Balada da Praia dos Cães* (*Ballad of Dog's Beach*, 1892) is perhaps his most famous work, and recounts an actual 1960 political assassination during the Salazar era.

José Saramago (1922–2010) and António Lobo Antunes (1942–) are two of the most famous contemporary Portuguese writers. Saramago won the Nobel Prize in Literature in 1998 for his body of humorous and politically charged works. *O Evangelho Segundo Jesus Cristo* (*The Gospel According to Jesus Christ*, 1991) and *Cegueira* (*Blindess*, 1995) are two of his more popular books. Antunes's works are often historical in nature and contain elements of the supernatural. His 2002 novel *O Regresso das Caravelas* (*The Return of the Caravels*) describes a meeting between 15th-century sailors and soldiers and citizens of 1970s Lisbon.

CULTURE

Arts & Entertainment

Football (soccer) is the country's most popular sport, and Portuguese teams regularly rank among the top ten in the world. Jogo do Pau, or stick combat, is a Portuguese sport that originated in medieval times.

Porto hosts the annual Fantasporto-Oporto International Film Festival in February. This festival and competition is known most for its focus on fantasy and science fiction entries, but has included films from all genres. Film festivals are also held in Algarve, Viana do Castelo, Tróia, and Figueira da Foz each year.

The contemporary art scene in Portugal is centered in Lisbon and Porto. The Gulbenkian Foundation, Culturgest and the Museu do Chiado are organizations in Lisbon that host popular art exhibitions for contemporary artists. In addition, LisboArte Contemporânea is a collection of fifteen art galleries that organize a simultaneous bimonthly exhibition throughout Lisbon. The most popular trend in Portuguese contemporary art is in experimental media. Artists are working in—and often combining—video, multimedia, photography and installations to express their ideas.

Cultural Sites & Landmarks

Many of Portugal's significant landmarks are located in and around the capital of Lisbon. Among Lisbon's most popular attractions is Alfama, which is one of Lisbon's oldest neighborhoods and was once the center of the fado music scene. Located on the tallest hill in Lisbon, the neighborhood was greatly influenced by the Moors. The district is known for its maze of narrow streets, steep steps and dimly lit taverns and stores. Located within Alfama are the Castelo de São Jorge and the original buildings of the capital, as well as Igreja de São Vicente de Fora monastery, built in 1147.

Another major attraction in Lisbon is the Monument to the Discoveries, also in Belém. The centerpiece of the monument is a statue of Henry the Navigator, the prince who was responsible for beginning the expansion that became the Portuguese Empire, with sculptures of several other people behind him on a structure designed to look like the bow of a ship. The monument also includes a mosaic map showing the discoveries made by Henry and other explorers.

Lisbon is also home to two of Portugal's thirteen World Heritage Sites, as designated by the

United Nations Educational, Scientific and Cultural Organization (UNESCO). They are the Jerónimos Monastery (also called the Monastery of the Hieronymites) and the Tower of Belém, both examples of the Manueline style of architecture.

Porto's historic district, Ribeira, located on the banks of the River Douro, also contains many significant cultural sites, including ancient Roman ruins. In particular, it is home to the Casa do Infante, reputedly the birthplace of Henry the Navigator (1394–1460). The structure later served as the customs house of the city. The former stock exchange (Palácio da Bolsa) is a neo-classical exterior design with an extravagant baroque interior. Built between 1842 and 1910, the building's showcase is a ballroom called the Salao Arabe (Arabian Hall). This room is decorated with intricate Moorish designs on gilded walls. A cathedral that dates to the 12th century sits atop a hill overlooking the Ribeira. The cathedral was rebuilt in the 13th century and greatly altered in the 18th century, but its Romanesque and Gothic remains are still visible. Porto's historic center was named a World Heritage Site in 1996.

East of Porto is the Alto Douro Wine Region of Portugal. Inhabitants of the region have been making wine for more than 2,000 years. Beginning in the 18th century, winemakers in the region began making port, a fortified wine that has become one of Portugal's chief exports. The region was designated a World Heritage Site in 2001 because it is an example of traditional European winemaking, and it reflects the way humans have altered the landscape over time. Scattered throughout the Alto Douro landscape are elements of the winemaking trade, such as terraces, quintas (wine-producing farm complexes), villages, chapels, and roads. Similarly, the Landscape of the Pico Island Vineyard Culture was added to the World Heritage list in 2004 for its viticulture and history.

Other significant cultural sites include several monasteries, such as the Batalha Monastery and the Alcobaça Monastery, both noted for their historical and artistic importance; the historical center of Évora, which includes numerous historical monuments such as a Roman temple; the Cultural Landscape of Sintra, renowned for its 19th-century Romantic architecture; the Convent of Christ of Tomar, a religious stronghold built in the 12th century; Fatima, a site of religious pilgrimage honoring the Virgin Mary; and the Prehistoric Rock-Art Sites in the Côa Valley, which date from 22,000 to 10,000 BCE.

Libraries & Museums

The National Library of Portugal is located in Lisbon and serves as the country's legal deposit. The library has been amassing its collection since 1976, and as of 2010, houses approximately 2.5 million books, including printed works and manuscripts, some of which date as far back as the 15th century. The Calouste Gulbenkian Foundation and Museum in Lisbon is one of Portugal's most popular and important museums. The museum holds more than 6,000 pieces from the Greek, Roman, Egyptian, Islamic, Chinese, and Japanese traditions. Connected to the Calouste Gulbenkian Foundation and Museum is the Centro de Arte Moderna (Modern Art Center). The National Museum of Ancient Art is also located in Lisbon.

Holidays

Political holidays in Portugal include Freedom Day (April 25), celebrating the end of the Salazar dictatorship in 1974. The Implantation of the Republic (October 5) celebrates the founding of the Republic in 1910. The Restoration of Independence (December 1) commemorates Portugal's independence from Spain.

Many major holidays are connected with saints' days in the Roman Catholic Church. The most popular saints' days take place in June: Saint Anthony's Day (June 13), Saint John's Day (June 24), and Saint Peter's Day (June 29). As in other parts of Europe, Epiphany (January 6) is a major holiday, celebrating the arrival of the Magi to visit the baby Jesus. Carnival, the holiday which precedes the end of Lent, is also very popular.

Youth Culture

Before the 1974 democratic revolution, the majority of Portuguese citizens did not have more than a fourth grade level of education. A 1980s study further revealed that one-fifth of the population over the age of 15 was illiterate. Government emphasis on education has brought the literacy rate close to 90 percent in the early years of the 21st century. Almost all Portuguese children attend school, but dropout rates are still higher than in other European countries.

As in many other cultures, Portuguese youth have embraced the digital age, with telecommunications and computer technologies playing a significant role in their lives. Cell phones and text messaging are both popular forms of communication for Portugal's teenagers. A recent government initiative lowered the student-to-computer ratio in its schools to as low as two to one by the year 2010; the ratio prior to this goal was roughly five computers to each student.

Music is an important aspect of the Portuguese youth culture. Portuguese pop-rock and hip-hop tuga (a mixture of hip-hop, African music, and reggae, primarily performed by African-Portuguese) are popular in Portugal's urban areas. Dance culture, which includes genres such as psytrance (or psychedelic trance), has also become increasingly popular. Football (soccer) remains the most popular and practiced sport.

SOCIETY

Transportation

Portugal's road networks were seriously neglected under the authoritarian Salazar government. With a new democratic government in place, Portugal joined the European Union (EU) in 1986 and has received massive funding to rebuild its infrastructure. (Portugal is one of the largest beneficiaries of EU aid and assistance). A four-lane superhighway (auto-estrada) connects Lisbon to Porto, and similar systems are currently under construction to connect these two cities with major metropolitan areas in Spain. Smaller expressways and secondary roads connect most towns throughout Portugal.

Portugal's two largest metropolitan areas, Lisbon and Porto, have subway systems. The Lisbon Metro is one of the largest and most reliable in Europe, mainly connecting the city center with the northern and western districts. The Metro has seen significant improvement in recent years, which, along with highway expansion and construction of the Vasco de Gama Bridge, has reduced traffic congestion in the city, particularly in the city's center. As of 2009, it has four lines that serve most of the city's center and the outlying areas.

One of the other major forms of public transit in Lisbon is the tram, which was an idea imported from America. In fact, the trams were once called americanos. There are four major tram lines connecting Lisbon and the surrounding suburbs.

A light rail network, parts of which operate underground, serves Porto. Trams were once a very popular and important means of transportation in Porto. Only three lines remain in operation, however. A rebuilt funicular railroad shuttles passengers up Porto's steep hills from the riverfront to the city center.

The Portuguese rail system is state-owned. In 2009, the Portuguese government, along with the EU, began the planning and early construction stages of a high-speed TGV line (France's high-speed rail service) connecting Porto with Lisbon; Lisbon with Madrid, Spain; and Porto with Vigo, Spain. Construction is expected to conclude in 2015. Buses, taxis and regional trains remain the common modes of public transportation in urban areas.

Portela International Airport, located just seven kilometers (four miles) from the center of Lisbon, handles about 9.4 million passengers every year, a number that continues to grow at the highest rate in the world. Plans are in development for expansion, as well as for a second airport in the Ota district, to the north of Lisbon. Traffic in Portugal moves on the right-hand side of the road.

Transportation Infrastructure

The road system of Portugal comprises several types of roads, such as the auto-estradas, which are similar to freeways and motorways, as well as itinerários principais, or major routes; itinerários complementares, or secondary routes; regional roads; and national roads. In 2010, a plan to construct an additional five highways was postponed due to national budget issues.

Major airports include the Portela Airport in Lisbon; the Francisco de Sá Carneiro Airport in Porto; and the Faro International Airport (in Faro). Lisbon's port, the largest in Portugal, handles many different types of cargo, including cars, grain, iron ore, and fruit.

Media & Communications

Prior to the 1974 revolution that ousted the corporate-state government, all newspapers in Portugal were nationalized and heavily censored. Privatization of Portugal's print media began in 1979, three years after the 1976 constitution guaranteed freedom of the press. Today, most district capitals and many small towns have daily or weekly newspapers. The most influential papers in Portugal are *Diário Notícias* in Lisbon, Porto's *Jornal de Notícias*, and *O Público*. However, Portugal's illiteracy rate in the early years of the 21st century is around 10 percent. As a result, the daily newspaper circulation rate is one of the lowest in Western Europe. Consequently, Portuguese newspapers have seen a decline in readership as people seek their news from alternative sources, such as television and the Internet.

The development of Portugal's fixed line telephone networks was very limited in the 20th century. Consequently, the Portuguese have transitioned to cellular phone systems at a rapid pace. Portugal has one of the highest mobile phone penetration rates in the world. Government-driven reforms have liberalized and privatized the telecommunications industry, making it very competitive. In addition, Internet usage among Portuguese citizens has grown steadily in the early 21st century. As of 2012, roughly 95 percent of the population had access to the Internet. Computer usage and ownership is not as high as in other European countries, but the numbers are increasing. Paid Internet connections are available at many cafés, as well as many post offices. Free Internet access is also available to Portuguese citizens through the Espaço de Internet program.

SOCIAL DEVELOPMENT

Standard of Living

In 2014, Portugal was ranked 41st out of 187 countries on the United Nations Human Development Index, which measures quality of life indicators.

Water Consumption

In 2012, approximately 99 percent of the country's population had access to improved drinking water sources; that same year, it was estimated that 100 percent of the population was using improved sanitation facilities.

Education

Portugal has greatly improved public education since the fall of the military dictatorship. There has been a major effort to reduce illiteracy, which largely affects the elderly. In the early 1990s, literacy was still as low as 80 percent. The country's literacy rate was estimated at 94.5 percent in 2011.

Nine years of schooling, for students between the ages of six and 15, are compulsory. Following primary education, secondary students can prepare for university studies or take vocational courses. In addition to the public schools, a number of private schools exist.

Historically, only the political and economic elites had access to higher education. Since the establishment of the Republic in 1974, the government has sought to make higher education more accessible. Portugal has several distinguished universities, including those at Lisbon, Oporto, and Coimbra. The University of Coimbra, founded in 1290, is one of the world's oldest. There are also several private universities in Lisbon, including the Portuguese Catholic University, sponsored by the Vatican, and the Free University.

After completing the bachelor's (Bacharel) or licenciate (Licenciado) degree, students may seek a master's degree (Mestre), a doctorate (Doutor), and a post-doctoral level known as the Agregação.

In 2003, 76 percent of the working-age population had nine or fewer years of education. Women, however, fare well in the country's educational system; for example, out of the country's population aged 15 through 64, 10.6 percent of women had college degrees, compared to 6.9 percent of men (2003). Gender-based wage discrepancies, however, continue to be an issue in the 21st century.

Women's Rights

Since the 1974 democratic revolution, the role of women in Portuguese society has undergone a transformation. In 1975, Portugal granted women the same voting rights as men, one of the last developed countries to do so. In addition, the Portuguese civil code establishes equality for women, and the government has implemented a range of initiatives to protect women and to help them move into more prominent roles in society. For example, the government created the Portuguese Structure against Domestic Violence in 2005 to promote awareness of domestic violence. The program offers legal and personal help to women, trains health professionals, proposes legislation to improve legal representation for victims, and works with local authorities to help victims.

The Portuguese legal system protects women against rape, domestic violence and sexual harassment. Although fairly strict penalties exist for those found guilty of these offenses, traditional societal attitudes discouraged many women from using the legal system. Consequently, violence against women is still a problem. Recent statistics show that the majority of domestic violence charges were resolved by mediators working outside the court system. In addition, statistics from 2005 report that only half of all legal proceedings involving domestic violence resulted in prosecutions. Prostitution and human trafficking remain serious issues, as

well, and only the registration of prostitutes, and not prostitution itself, remains illegal.

The deep-seated traditional views of gender roles in Portugal limit women's move into careers in the workforce. Women are still viewed by most men and a large number of women as the primary caretakers of children and the household. These attitudes are changing, but the transformation is slow. Even with government initiatives and support, women are still struggling to gain a foothold in business and government power positions. Maria de Lourdes Pintasilgo (1930–2004) became the first female prime minister in 1979, but her accomplishment has had limited influence in changing traditional gender roles.

In 2005, only 19 percent of Portugal's parliament members were women. By 2014, the percentage had climbed to 31 percent. Women make up roughly 62 percent of the workforce in Portugal, yet earn less than 25 percent of their male coworkers. However, women have made progress in several professions. Recent statistics report that women make up around 40 percent of all Portuguese doctors and roughly the same percentage of lawyers. As of the 2014, women also comprised over half of the student population at Portuguese universities.

Sexual harassment is still prevalent in Portugal. According to Portugal's Commission on Equality in the Workplace and in Employment (CITE), a third of all women in the workforce claimed to be victims of sexual harassment. Pregnant mothers and new mothers were also victims of discrimination by their employers.

Health Care

Public health in Portugal was extremely poor until the late 20th century. In 1970, toward the end of the Salazar dictatorship, the infant mortality rate was over 50 deaths per 1,000. The situation has improved dramatically since then, with greater numbers of medical personnel and health facilities. Many improvements, however, have not affected rural areas, where folk remedies are still prevalent. Private medical care has become increasingly available as an alternative to the poor quality of the public system.

GOVERNMENT

Structure
Portugal is one of Europe's oldest nations, dating its independence to the early 12th century with the reign of King Afonso I (Afonso Henriques). Today, Portugal is a parliamentary republic. It is governed according to a constitution ratified in S1976 after overthrowing decades of fascist dictatorship.

The president, elected by popular vote to a five-year term, serves as the head of state. The prime minister, appointed by the president from the majority party in parliament, serves as head of government and governs with the aid of the Council of Ministers or cabinet. The president's Council of State is composed of leading political figures, all former Portuguese presidents, and other individuals appointed by the president and the parliament.

Portugal's parliament is a single-house body known as the Assembly of the Republic. The 230 members serve four-year terms, and are elected by proportional representation.

Political Parties
The main parties tend to be centrist: the Social Democratic Party (Partido Social Democratica) is center-right and the Socialist Party (Partido Socialista) is center-left. Other parties include the Democratic and Social Centre People's Party, the Popular Party (Partido Popular), the Left Bloc (Bloco de Esquerda), and the Democratic Unity Coalition.

In the 2011 legislative elections, the Social Democratic party won 108 seats; the Socialist Party won 79 seats; the Democratic and Social Centre People Party won 24 seats; and the Democratic Unity Coalition won 16 seats.

Local Government
Local government is highly centralized. Mainland Portugal has 18 administrative districts, each with a governor appointed by the central government. The minister of internal administration oversees local government. The Azores and the Madeira Islands are autonomous regions, and enjoy extensive self-government.

Judicial System
Law in Portugal is based on the civil law system. Portugal's judicial system has several levels. The Supreme Court is the nation's highest court. The Constitutional Tribunal, which has nine members, considers constitutional issues.

Taxation
The top income tax levied in Portugal is 42 percent, and the top corporate tax rate is 26.5 percent (2010). Other taxes levied include a value-added tax (VAT) and property taxes.

Armed Forces
The Armed Forces of Portugal comprise an army, navy, and air force. In the early 21st century, there were approximately 44,900 active military personnel.

Foreign Policy
Portugal's foreign policies are primarily shaped by its membership in the European Union. Portugal became a member of the European Communities (EC) in 1986, and was one of the original countries that established the EU in 1994. Years of neglect during dictatorship and military rule left Portugal's infrastructure in dire need of improvement. Funding for many of the projects has come from the EU. Consequently, Portugal is a very strong supporter of European integration. Portugal held the presidency of the EU Council during the final six months of 2007. The major accomplishment was the signing of the EU Reform Treaty by all 27 member countries. Also known as the Lisbon Treaty, the Reform Treaty is supposed to enhance the efficiency and democratic legitimacy of the EU.

In addition, Portugal participates in the EU foreign policy agenda, particularly in promoting the interests of its former colonies in Africa, Latin America and Asia. The former Portuguese colony of East Timor (Timor-Leste) is an important foreign policy issue for Portugal. Indonesia annexed East Timor in 1975, but Portugal did not recognize the action. Portugal has since worked to promote East Timorese independence. The Portuguese government has helped East Timor in its transition to independence and Portuguese forces have participated in UN missions in the country.

Portugal is a founding member of the North Atlantic Treaty Organization (NATO) and values its strong transatlantic relationships. In particular, Portugal has a long history of bilateral relations with the United States, dating back to the 1790s. Portugal calls itself an Atlanticist nation (promoting cooperation between North American and Western Europe) in terms of its defense and security relationship with the U.S. The Portuguese government has also promoted strong ties between its European neighbors and the U.S., and recent cooperative operations have centered on counterterrorism efforts and humanitarian missions. In addition, the U.S Air Force maintains a base at Terceira in the Azores islands. NATO also operates a command center near Lisbon, and Portugal continues to provide military troops to NATO's presence in the Balkans, Afghanistan and Africa. In addition, Portuguese soldiers are a part of the UN force in Lebanon. In per capita terms, Portugal is one of the most significant European contributors to international peacekeeping operations around the world.

In 1996, Portugal helped in the formation of the Community of Portuguese Language Countries (CPLP) to improve its relations with other Portuguese-speaking countries. Based in Lisbon, The CPLP has a legal personality and is financially autonomous. The chief goals of the CPLP include political and diplomatic consultation between its member states to strengthen their international presence; cooperation in areas such as education, health, science and technology, defense, agriculture, public administration, communications, justice, public security, culture, sports and media; and the promotion and dissemination of the Portuguese language.

Human Rights Profile

International human rights law insists that states respect civil and political rights, and also promote an individual's economic, social and cultural rights. The United Nations Universal Declaration on Human Rights (UDHR) is recognized as the standard for international human rights. Its authors sought the counsel of the world's great thinkers, philosophers, and religious leaders, and were careful to create a document that reflects the core values shared by every world culture. (To read this document or view the articles relating to cultural human rights, go to: http://www.udhr.org/UDHR/default.htm).

Generally, Portugal's human rights record is positive. The country has made great strides in the decades following the dictatorship of Salazar and his successors, and the Portuguese constitution provides for a wide range of internationally recognized human rights. Portugal is a member of the Council of Europe and has signed and ratified the European Convention on Human Rights (ECHR). It is also a member of the Organization for Economic Cooperation and Development (OECD) and has adopted the OECD guidelines for governing the protection of privacy and the transnational flow of personal information.

Portugal's constitution is generally in line with Article 2 of the UDHR. It guarantees the equality of all Portuguese citizens before the law, regardless of race, religion or gender. Portuguese of all races and religions receive equal benefits from the government. The rights of marriage outlined in Article 16 of the declaration are protected in Portugal. Currently, a government-recognized marriage in Portugal is between a man and a woman. Men and women share full equity in marriage and divorce under Portuguese law. In October 2008, the Portuguese parliament rejected a bill that would have legitimized same-sex marriages.

Religious freedoms, as outlined in Article 18 of the UDHR, are fully protected in Portugal. The 2001 Religious Freedom Act created a legislative framework for religions established in Portugal for at least thirty years, or those recognized internationally for at least sixty years. The Catholic Church, with counts roughly 80 percent of Portugal's citizens as members, does receive preferential treatment from the Portuguese government. For example, under an agreement with the government, the Catholic Church receives 0.5 percent of the income tax that citizens can allocate to various institutions in their annual tax returns. In addition, major Catholic holy days also are official holidays, and chaplaincies for the military, prisons and hospitals remain state-funded positions for Catholics only. A bill proposal that would grant all non-Catholic hospital patients equal access to religious services was presented to the government in 2007.

The Portuguese constitution outlaws torture and other cruel, inhuman, or degrading treatment or punishment. However, investigators from the government and non-governmental organizations (NGOS) have found credible evidence that mistreatment of prisoners is a problem. Issues include overcrowded or inadequate prison facilities, poor prisoner health conditions, and violence within the inmate community. Roughly 35 percent of the Portuguese inmate population was infected with HIV/AIDS or hepatitis B or C. In addition, there has been evidence of inappropriate use of force and abuse by police or prison guards.

ECONOMY

Overview of the Economy

For much of the 20th century, Portugal was one of the poorest countries in Western Europe. This has changed, however, since the end of the dictatorship and Portugal's entry into the European Union (EU) in 1986. Within the EU, Portugal once enjoyed a competitive advantage due to low labor costs; this has changed, however, since the addition of Eastern European members. Thanks to its economic reform efforts, Portugal became a founding member of the EU's single currency zone in 1999.

The economy shrank slightly in the first years of the 21st century, with an annual growth rate of −1.3 percent. Portugal's gross domestic product (GDP) in 2014 was $276 billion (USD), with a per capita GDP of $26,300 (USD). Approximately 66 percent of the workforce is employed by the government or in the services sector, another 23 percent works in industry, while the remaining 10 percent works in agriculture.

Industry

During the early 20th century dictatorship, Portugal became increasingly industrialized, but the economy remains heavily dependent on agriculture. Since the 1990s, governments have worked to privatize many industries and modernize the country's transportation and communications infrastructure.

Portugal's industry is mostly light, though there are some heavy industries such as mining, automobile manufacturing, and chemicals. Light industries include textile, clothing, and cork production.

Labor

The labor force comprised 5.271 million workers in 2014; that same year, the unemployment rate was 14.2 percent.

Energy/Power/Natural Resources

Portugal has numerous plant and mineral resources. Trees cover about one-third of the country, particularly pine, oak, olive, and eucalyptus. Mineral resources include tungsten, tin, and uranium. Portugal is a major producer of cork, accounting for about 50 percent of the world's production.

Fishing

Fishing remains an important industry in Portugal, with fishing ports found up and down the coast. Common catches include cod, tuna, sardine and mackerel.

Forestry

Almost 40 percent of Portugal is forested, so the wood-related industries such as paper and pulp production are important economic sectors. Other important forest products include cork, paper board, and eucalyptus.

Mining/Metals

Commonly mined minerals include copper, beryl, tin, and tungsten.

Agriculture

Much of mainland Portugal focuses on farming, though agriculture accounts for only about three percent of Portugal's gross domestic product. Major crops include cereals such as wheat and corn, as well as barley and rice. Olive plantations produce large quantities of olive oil. Fruit and nut production is also important.

Animal Husbandry

Many farmers raise livestock, particularly sheep, cattle, and goats.

Tourism

Portugal has become an increasingly popular tourist destination, thanks in part to improved transportation and the country's membership in the European Union. Favorite destinations include large cities such as Lisbon, the capital, with its cosmopolitan culture, as well as seaside and mountain resorts. Tourists also flock to the beaches of the Algarve region, on the country's southern coast. Portugal faces increasing competition from Eastern Europe as a low-cost tourist destination.

Michael Carpenter, Eric Badertscher,
Alex K. Rich

DO YOU KNOW?

- Portugal has been allied with England since the Middle Ages. This relationship is governed by the terms of the Treaty of Windsor (1386).

- Portugal is famous for its wines, particularly Madeira and port (the latter actually takes its name from the city of Porto or Oporto).

- On April 25, 1974, revolutionaries demonstrated their desire for a peaceful revolution by waving carnations. Eventually, the soldiers who were running the fascist government at the time responded by placing carnations in their rifles. This event became known as the Carnation Revolution.

- Lisbon's Twenty-Fifth of April Bridge (so named after the Carnation Revolution) was designed and built by the same engineers who built the Golden Gate Bridge in San Francisco. It is the longest suspension bridge in Europe.

Bibliography

Anne De Stoop. *Living in Portugal*. Milan: Flammarion, 2007.

Harvey Holtom. *Working and Living: Portugal*. London: Cadogan Guides, 2005.

James M. Anderson. *The History of Portugal: The Greenwood Histories of the Modern Nations*. Westport, CT: Greenwood Press, 2000.

Marion Kaplan. *The Portuguese: The Land and Its People*. Manchester, UK: Carcenet Press, 2006.

Miguel De Castro e Silva. *The Food and Cooking of Portugal*. London: Aquamarine, 2008.

Rough Guides. *Rough Guide to Portugal*. London: Rough Guides, 2013.

Regis St. Louis. *Portugal*. Oakland, CA: Lonely Planet, 2014.

Jose Saramago, (translated by Amanda Hopkinson, and Nick Caistor). *Journey to Portugal: In Pursuit of Portugal's History and Culture*. San Diego: Harvest Books, 2002.

Works Cited

"Alfama." Travel in Portugal website. http://www.travel-in portugal.com/Lisbon/alfama.htm

"Alto Douro Wine Region." UNESCO World Heritage website. http://whc.unesco.org/en/list/1046

Bobbin Lace European Network website. http://www.blen. net/blen_08/0803.htm

Brian Amble. "Women Still Rare in Europe's Boardrooms." *Management-Issues website*. June 20, 2006. http://www. management-issues.com/2006/8/24/research/women-still-rare-in-europes-boardrooms.asp

"Country Reports on Human Rights Practices—2007, released by the Bureau of Democracy, Human Rights, and Labor." *U.S. Department of State*. March 11, 2008. http://www.state.gov/g/drl/rls/hrrpt/2007/100579.htm

Geoff Duncan. "Microsoft Sends Suite Magellan to Portugal." *Digital Trends website*.

EQUAL website. http://ec.europa.eu/employment_social/ equal/practical-examples/opport-life-line-sandwich_ en.cfm October 3, 2008. http://news.digitaltrends.com/

news-article/18049/microsof sends-suite-magellan-to-portugal

Joni Hubrid. "World Press Encyclopedia: Portugal." *BNet website*. http://findarticles.com/p/articles/mi_gx5223/is_/ai_n19143196

"Leading Europe: Portugal Goes Global." *Foreign Affairs Magazine*, Sponsored Section, March/April, 2008.

Metropolitano de Lisboa website. http://www.metrolisboa.pt/Default.aspx?tabid=261

"Porto." *PortugalVisitor* website. http://www.portugalvisitor.com/index.php?cID=442&pID=1

"Portugal: Bills to Legalize Same-Sex Marriages Fail." New York Times website. October 10, 2008. http://www.nytimes.com/2008/10/11/world/europe/11briefs-BILLSTOLEGAL_BRF.html?_r=1&fta=y

"Portugal." *CIA World Factbook*. https://www.cia.gov/library/publications/the-world-factbook/geos/po.html

"Portugal Country Brief." *Australian Government Department of Foreign Affairs and Trade, March 2008*. http://www.dfat.gov.au/geo/portugal/portugal_brief.html

"Portugal." *Encyclopedia Britannica*. 2008. Encyclopedia Britannica http://www.britannica.com/EBchecked/topic/471439/Portugal

"Portugal: Language, Culture, Customs and Etiquette." *Kwintessential website*. http://www.kwintessential.co.uk/resources/global-etiquette/portugal.html

"Portugal: Usage and Population Statistics." *Internet World States website*. http://www.internetworldstats.com/eu/pt.htm

Portugal-Live website. http://www.portugal-live.net/UK/essential/economy-transportation.html

Regis St. Louis and Robert Landon. Portugal. London: *Lonely Planet*, 2007.

"Republic of Portugal." Privacy International website. http://www.privacyinternational.org/survey/phr2003/countries/portugal.htm?hl=en&tab=wl

Sandy Guedes de Queiroz. *Culture Smart! Portugal*. London: Kuperard, 2006.

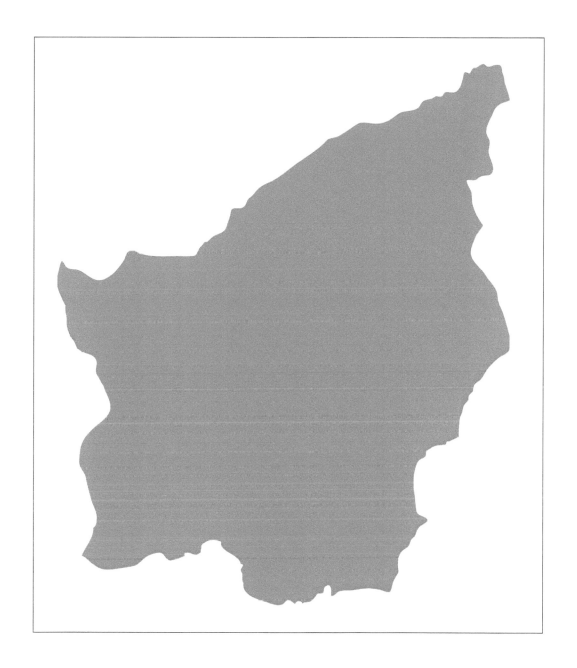

SAN MARINO

Introduction

San Marino is a European "microstate" located entirely inside Italy, in the Apennine Mountains, and is one of the world's smallest nations. Formally known as "The Most Serene Republic of San Marino" (Italian: "La Serenissima Repubblica di San Marino"), the nation considers itself the world's oldest republic, dating back to the early fourth century. Historically, it is a survivor of the medieval and Renaissance period, when Italy was divided into hundreds of city-states.

Located near Rimini in north-central Italy, San Marino has a population of around 28,000. The Sammarinese economy is based largely on tourism; other important activities are banking and the sale of postage stamps. San Marino relies on Italy for defense, and has a closely related foreign policy. Though not a member of the European Union (EU), San Marino is part of the Euro economic zone.

GENERAL INFORMATION

Official Language: Italian
Population: 32,742 (2014 estimate)
Currency: Euro
Coins: The Euro is available in 1, 2, 5, 10, 20 and 50 cent coins, with a 1 and 2 Euro coin also available. The Sammarinese euro coins have different designs for each coin.
Land Area: 61.2 square kilometers (23.5 square miles)
National Motto: "Libertas" (Latin, "Liberty")
National Anthem: "Inno Nazionale" ("National Hymn")
Capital: San Marino
Time Zone: GMT +2
Flag Description: The flag of San Marino is a bicolor flag that consists of two equal horizontal bands—a white stripe on top and a light blue stripe on the bottom. Centered in the flag is the country's national coat of arms, which features the three plumed towers of the citadel of San Marino (Guaita, Cesta and Montale) atop three mountain peaks, all below a crown and bordered in wreath-flanked gold. The motto "Libertas" rests on a ribbon situated below the wreath's branches.

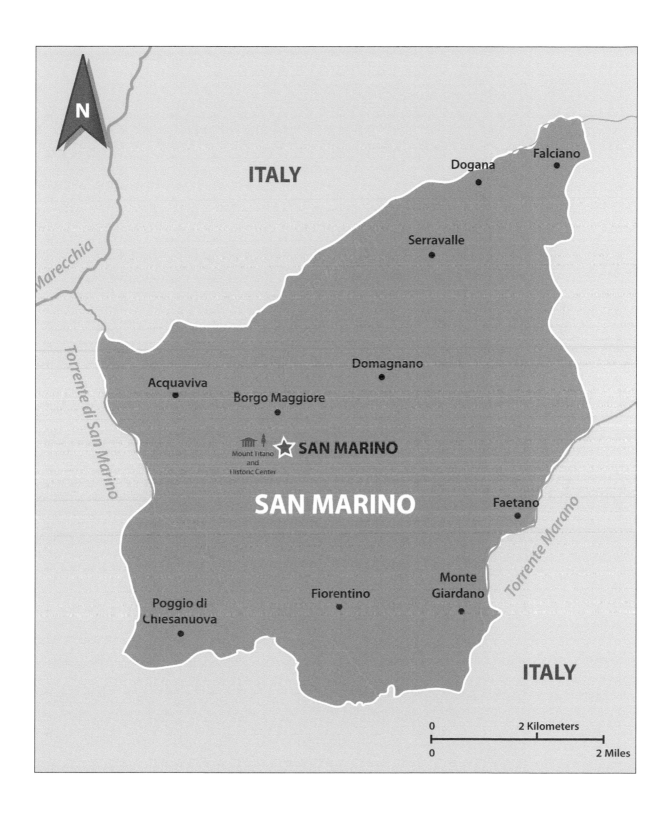

Principal Castles (Municipalities) by Population (2012):

- Serravalle/Dogano (9,936)
- Borgo Maggiore (6,054)
- Città (4,350) (2009 estimate)
- Domagnano (2,890)
- Fiorentino (2,525)

Population

The Sammarinese population is just over 32,742 as of 2014. The Sammarinese are similar to their Italian neighbors, in that they speak the same language and profess the same faith (Roman Catholicism). In addition, many Italian citizens live in the City of San Marino, the microstate's capital, which has a population of approximately 5,000. As of the early 21st century, the population of the microstate was roughly 85 percent Sammarinese, and 13 percent Italian. Many Sammarinese live in neighboring Italy and France, as well as in the United States. As of 2014, the microstate has an estimated population growth rate of 0.87 percent.

Languages

Although nearly everyone speaks the official language, Italian, many residents also speak Emiliano-Romagnolo, a local Italian dialect.

Native People & Ethnic Groups

The territory of present-day San Marino has been inhabited since prehistoric times, but the current population of native Sammarinese has been basically Italian since the Roman era (preceding the Middle Ages).

Religions

Roman Catholicism is the dominant religion in San Marino, practiced by an estimated 95 percent of the population. It is, however, not the established religion of the microstate. San Marino also has a small Jewish population.

Climate

San Marino has a Mediterranean climate typical of northern Italy, with temperate seasons. Winters are mild or even cool, while summers are generally warm and sunny. The average winter temperature is −7° Celsius (19° Fahrenheit), while the average summer temperature is 27° Celsius (80° Fahrenheit).

ENVIRONMENT & GEOGRAPHY

Topography

San Marino was originally established on Mount Titano, a limestone mountain in the Apennine range in north-central Italy. The difficult terrain helped the Sammarinese preserve their independence over the centuries, from the time of the city's founding.

The highest point is Mount Titano itself, which rising 755 meters (2,477 feet) above sea level. The lowest point is Torrente Ausa, 55 meters (180 feet) above sea level. The Marano and Ausa flow through the republic and into the Adriatic Sea.

Only a small portion of San Marino's land (about 16.5 percent) is suited for agriculture, and San Marino must obtain most of its food from Italy. An enclave inside Italy, San Marino shares a land border of 39 kilometers (24.2 miles) with its larger neighbor.

Plants & Animals

Most of San Marino's land is forested, with a mix of coniferous and deciduous species typical of the Mediterranean climate. Common species include oak and maple. The Apennine Mountains in general are home to some of Italy's remaining wild species, including the Italian wolf (gray wolf), the brown bear, and various deer species including the roe deer and red deer. Common bird species in the region include the golden eagle.

CUSTOMS & COURTESIES

Greetings

The language and customs of San Marino, including greetings, are largely imported from Italy. Friends and family members, particularly women, may press their cheeks together and kiss the air, while men often briefly embrace. Handshakes are common, and may be accompanied by "Piacere" ("Pleased to meet you"). Other formal greetings include "Buongiornio" ("Good day") and "Buonasera" ("Good evening"). A casual phrase of both greeting and parting is "Ciao," while "Arrivederci" ("Goodbye") is a more formal goodbye.

Honorific titles hold great importance in Italian cultures. Casual acquaintances and business associates may call one another by their title and surname. Men are addressed as signore (sir) and married women as signora (ma'am), and an unmarried woman uses the title signorina. Those who hold a professional title often use these designations socially as a reflection of their respected status. Young people are more likely to be informal than their elders, and may immediately use first names among peers.

Gestures & Etiquette

Physical movement plays a significant role in how the Sammarinese communicate with one another. Gestures commonly add emphasis to verbalized thoughts, and a rich vocabulary of gestures allows the Sammarinese and other Italian speakers to communicate without talking. Common gestures include pointing at one's eyes with the index and middle fingers and then sweeping the hand out, which loosely asks "did you see that," while cupping a hand behind the ear means signifies "come again." Some gestures are familiar to English speakers. For example, a Sammarinese shrug maintains the same meaning in other Western cultures, with the addition of hands spread and turned upward to reveal the palms. Similar to Italian speakers, the Sammarinese generally make eye contact and may stand quite close when having a conversation. Often, verbal speech is rapid and loud, with many friendly interruptions and exclamations.

Like the Italians, the Sammarinese place great importance on personal appearance. Although casual clothes may be worn at home, public attire typically reflects a simple elegance.

Muted colors and clean shapes contribute to an overall image of style and respectability. The people of San Marino are equally proud of their heritage of freedom and democracy. This pride contributes to the great value placed on hard work in Sammarinese culture, and success is largely defined through accomplishments, social status, and personal connections throughout the Italian peninsula.

Eating/Meals

San Marino shares its eating habits with the surrounding Italian countryside. Breakfast is usually light and may consist of cappuccino (a combination of coffee and frothy milk) alongside a pastry or roll. Traditionally, lunch was a substantial affair and served as the main meal of the day. However, this tradition has declined in recent years with the increasing importance of dinner, usually served fairly late in the evening. Regardless of the time, the largest meal of the day may comprise several courses.

To begin a meal, an antipasto, or appetizer, perhaps composed of cold fruits, meats, olives, or bread might be served. Next is the first course or primo piatto, normally a pasta or rice-based dish. The secondo piatto, traditionally some kind of seafood or meat, is the primary dish and may be accompanied by vegetable side dishes known as contorno. A salad course follows the secondo to clear the palate in preparation for a dolce, or sweet. This dessert may be as simple as a piece of fresh fruit or as complex as a multi-layered cake. Usually, the entire family gathers for at least one meal a day, and dining out at restaurants and cafés is a popular activity among friends.

San Marino adheres to the continental style: holding the fork in the left hand and knife in the right throughout the meal. Different sets of utensils may be provided for each course, and the size and shape of plates and bowls may vary depending on the food served. Lastly, when eating pasta, the Sammarinese do not cut long pieces or rely on a helper spoon; rather, they customarily twirl long pieces on a fork against the sides or bottom of their plates.

Visiting

Sammarinese culture is known for its emphasis on hospitality and Sammarinese hosts generally strive to make guests feel welcome. In fact, the Sammarinese consider spending time with family and friends to be one of the life's greatest pleasures. Entertaining at home is a frequent occurrence, and these visits often last well into the night. Those who stop by the home of a friend or family member are likely to be offered food or drink, regardless of the time of day or duration of the visit. Guests at an evening meal usually enjoy traditional foods accompanied by wine.

It is considered a polite offering for guests to bring a small gift, particularly when arriving for dinner. Popular choices include a bottle of good quality wine, flowers, or chocolates. Certain varieties of flowers, such as chrysanthemums, are often displayed at funerals throughout the Italian peninsula and should be avoided.

LIFESTYLE

Family

In San Marino, the pleasures and obligations of family are very important. Families strive to maintain close relationships, respecting elder generations and nurturing younger ones. Many Sammarinese continue to live with their parents until well into their twenties, and visit as often as time and distance allows upon moving out of the family home.

As more women enter the workforce in the early 21st century, traditional family structures are shifting, and men have a larger role in childrearing and housekeeping than in the past. However, these changes have not lessened the strong bonds connecting families across generations. Such institutions as the traditional family dinner and the celebration of holidays helps keep modern Sammarinese families closely allied.

Housing

Over the centuries, San Marino's mountainous location has influenced its building styles. Many older Sammarinese homes are constructed of locally-mined sandstone, while concrete and stucco are commonly found in more modern construction. Rooms are often decorated in warm colors and feature tile floors, and blinds and shutters are used to block out the strong summer sun and brisk winter winds.

Home ownership is an important measure of success in Sammarinese culture, and many houses have remained in the same family for generations. Parents often help children purchase homes after they complete their education or get married. However, due to the rising expense of purchasing and maintaining a home, young people may instead reside in apartments until marrying and starting a family. Most family homes are relatively small.

Food

Like much of the republic's culture, the cuisine of San Marino is heavily influenced by its connections with Italy, However, a number of dishes provide a local spin on shared regional cuisine. Pasta is frequently homemade, and may be stuffed with minced meat, as in the dish cappelletti in brodo. Beans are a popular ingredient in a variety of dishes, and when accompanied with bits of meat or fat, beans can form the basis of hearty, warming entrees and soups. Chickpeas served with pasta are part of the traditional Christmas Eve meal.

Perhaps the most famous Sammarinese delicacies are the titano and tre monti cakes. The torta titano combines the flavors of almond, honey, meringue, and chocolate in a light, fluffy cake. Inspired by the three castles overlooking the city of San Marino, the torta tre monti is multi-layered confection packed with a creamy mixture of chocolate and hazelnut. A third dessert, the ciambella paesana, is a popular local sponge cake.

San Marino produces a handful of respected culinary staples in addition to its well-known wines varietals such as moscato and sangiovese. Olive trees nurtured on the sides of Mount Titano bear fruit pressed into extra-virgin olive oil, and local beekeepers support the production of honey. Bakers use Sammarinese grains to make a thin flatbread called a piadina. Locally produced foodstuffs may bear an official designation of origin and typicality to signify their place in traditional Sammarinese culture.

Life's Milestones

The majority of people in San Marino follow the Roman Catholic faith—an estimated 95 percent—and traditional Roman Catholic sacraments accordingly hold great significance in Sammarinese life. The birth and subsequent baptism of a child is an exciting event for parents and their extended families and friends. Many children later affirm their faith by participating in the sacrament of confirmation.

Marriage may take place within the Roman Catholic Church or as a civil ceremony. Weddings are normally followed by receptions attended by friends and family of the couple. At the reception, the bride may toss her bouquet to a group of unmarried women. Deaths are usually marked with a special funeral mass before burial. Traditionally, family and friends visit the grave sites of deceased loved ones on All Saints' Day.

CULTURAL HISTORY

Art

Though ceramics as an art form in the San Marino region date back to Roman times, this traditional art truly flourished in the 20th century. Modern ceramics production began in earnest with the establishment of Marmaca in 1938, one of the republic's best-known ceramic makers. Many other artisans followed suit, clustering operations primarily around the village of Gualdicciolo. This rapid growth led to the production of sundry ceramic and pottery items, including bottles, decorative plates and tiles, and vases. Characterized by bold colors, the pieces often depicted notable Sammarinese sights such as the Three Towers of San Marino, located on Mount Titano, the republic's highest peak. In 1996, the republic mounted an exhibition covering the 20th-century development of its ceramic arts. Artisans continue to produce wares that have achieved both commercial and artistic recognition.

Architecture

San Marino's churches stand as striking examples of the architectural styles of their respective periods. The oldest of these is the Chiesa di San Francesco (Church of St. Francis). It mixes the Gothic-influenced Franciscan simplicity of wide spaces and religious ornamentation typical of its initial 14th-century construction, with neoclassical elements of later 17th- and 18th-century restorations. The interior of the church is home to Franciscan artifacts and an important 15th-century fresco, *Adoration of the Three Kings*, by early Renaissance Italian artist Antonio Alberti (1390–1449). A 20th-century monument to St. Francis designed by prominent Italian architect Edoardo Collamarini (1863–1928), stands in front the 16th-century Church of San Quirino. This building, with clean lines and a multi-arched portico, also exemplifies the Franciscan architectural style. A painting of St. Marinus decorates the church's simple wooden interior. Another famous church is the Basilica of San Marino, an imposing neoclassical building featuring a portico of eight Corinthian columns and a historic bell tower that dates back several centuries prior to the church's construction in the early 1800s.

Currency

San Marino gained the right to mint its own currency in 1862 after forming a monetary union with the newly consolidated Kingdom of Italy (1861–1946). This agreement also established Sammarinese currency as legal tender throughout Italy, with the stipulation that San Marino's money must follow the same weight, division, and naming conventions as Italian currency. The republic struck its first coin—a five-cent copper piece inscribed with an image of the Tre Monti (three peaks of Mount Titano)—in October 1864. With a limited production run of only 280, this coin set the path for all later Sammarinese currency, known primarily for its rarity and, thus, collectability. Sammarinese coins typically depict significant figures and places from the republic and its history. An important 1898 coin showed the republic's namesake, while many from later periods depicted Italian refugee and national hero Giuseppe Giribaldi (1807–1882). The themes of freedom and liberty are also popular choices.

Literature

Although famed poet Dante Alighieri (1265–1321) hailed from Florence, Italy, the people and history of San Marino are featured in his most famous work, the epic *Divine Comedy*. Because San Marino lay near the edges of the Papal States, a collection of Italian regions directly controlled by the pope, those who supported the secular rule of the Holy Roman Emperor (962–1806) wished to absorb the territory during the Middle Ages. Two influential families—the Malatestas on the papal side and the Montefeltros on the secular side—played starring roles in this dispute.

Sammarinese support for secular rule had earned its people a brief spell of formal expulsion from the Roman Catholic Church from 1247–1249. After this excommunication was lifted, the undeterred Sammarinese declared their support for Guido da Montefeltro (1223–1298). A proponent of papal rule, Dante immortalized da Montefeltro in the *Inferno,* the first book of the *Divine Comedy,* as a person eternally damned for giving advice that encouraged the use of deceit. In 1295, the nearby town of Rimini and surrounding areas came under the control of the Malatestas. The story of Francesca da Rimini (1255–1285), who became romantically entwined with her brother-in-law Paolo, is also recounted in Dante's *Inferno*. She further served as inspiration for numerous works of art, including paintings and operas. In 1463, much of the area controlled by the Malatesta family, including the towns of Fiorentino, Serravalle, and Faetano, became a part of San Marino in the final expansion of the tiny state.

CULTURE

Arts & Entertainment

San Marino's cultural life is characterized by a diversity and depth that may seem remarkable for a microstate. The Sammarinese actively and enthusiastically support numerous artistic and cultural endeavors, including music, visual arts, heritage festivals, and theater productions. The late 20th and early 21st century have witnessed an explosion of art and cultural offerings, and this trend shows practically no signs of slowing.

Contemporary choral music in the republic dates back to the creation of the San Marino Choir in 1960. This 35 person chorus has performed not only in its native land, but also throughout Europe and the world. The Istituto Musicale Sammarinese (San Marino Musical Institute) offers lessons in classical instruments to residents of the republic, and stages a number of classical music performances each year. Founded in 2002, the Allegro Vivo Association is a group of Sammarinese classical musicians who sponsor classical music concerts and series throughout the year. The association also hosts an annual juried piano competition for young pianists from around the world. The music of many nations can also be heard at the annual Ethnologic Festival. This event, held in San Marino's city center, celebrates the traditional music of cultures ranging from African to Eastern Europe to the Americas.

In 2008, San Marino made its debut at the wildly popular Eurovision song contest, with the band Miodio representing their nation with the Italian-language song "Complice." However, the act failed to advance to the Eurovision finals. Citing financial constraints, San Marino's public broadcaster and Eurovision sponsor, RTV, withdrew the nation from the competition the following year. Although the republic's brief period of participation and lackluster performance make the possibility of a quick re-entry into the competition seem questionable at best, the republic has expressed interest in returning to Eurovision in the future.

However, 2008 also saw a decision to return to the renowned biannual Venice International Arts Exhibition after a 15-year absence. The republic also regularly sends representative artists to the Biannual Exhibition of Young Artists from Europe and the Mediterranean. From 2004 to 2006, the nation hosted ARTMIX, a multimedia contemporary art workshop encouraging creative interaction among those working in music, dance, visual arts, and film. A similar blend of styles can be found at Centrarti, a creative center founded in 2005 that offers multidisciplinary performances and workshops.

In San Marino, support for local artists comes from a mixture of public and private sources. The Council of Cultural Associations, established in 1991, is a coalition of social and cultural non-profit institutions aimed at supporting member organizations and promoting cooperation within San Marino's arts community. Membership spans the visual and performance arts, and literature. A planned government-sponsored International Center for Contemporary Art is anticipated to provide limited funding and additional artistic development opportunities. Art lovers and historical aficionados throughout the republic may visit any of the government-owned museums, such as those at Rocca Guaita and the Cesta, free of charge. The republic also features four theaters, including the historic Titano Theater.

One popular Sammarinese cultural festival, Medieval Days, has taken place each July since 1997 in the historic center of the city of San Marino. During the five-day festival, local artisans and performers don medieval costumes and recreate life in the republic five centuries previously. A spectacular display comes from the well-known Sammarinese Crossbow Corps, who display their skill in archery to the accompaniment of period musicians and flag corps. Others participate in traditional arts and crafts or depict members of the medieval nobility. An opportunity to get a taste of traditional Sammarinese life, the festival attracts crowds from both the surrounding area and distant locales. Other festivals include the San Marino Jazz Festival, held for the first time in July 2010, and the San Marino Etnofestival, celebrating its 13th year in July 2010.

Sports in San Marino reflect both the country's present and its past. The most popular sport is football (soccer), which is run mainly through the San Marino Football Federation. The national team has played in international competition since the early 1990s, though with relatively little success. Crossbow competitions are also highly popular, reflecting the country's medieval heritage; competitions are a regular feature of National Day on September 3, as well as during a week-long crossbow festival in July.

San Marino has also given its name to a Formula One auto race; the San Marino Grand Prix has been held since 1981. Ironically, the race does not take place in San Marino itself, but in nearby Imola, Italy, about 100 kilometers (62 miles) northwest of the republic.

Cultural Sites & Landmarks

The antiquity of San Marino's city center earned the district a designation as a United Nations Educational, Scientific and Cultural Organization (UNESCO) World Heritage Site in 2008. Within this area is the Piazza della Libertà (Liberty Square), known locally as Pianello, which features a 19th-century marble statue depicting the ancient goddess Liberty. Ringing the square are a mix of historic buildings, such as the Casa dell'Arcipretura Vecchia, and later reconstructions of ancient structures. During the summers, the ceremonial changing of the guards occurs at the Palazzo Publico (Public Palace) on the square's western edge. This building, home of the republic's government for centuries, features a double throne for the use of the two captain regents of the country and sixty others for the council members. Medieval walls and towers enclose the old city, and the ancient main gate, known as the Porta di San Francesco (Gate of San Francesco), still serves as the primary entrance to the city. The capital is also the site of two unusual museums: the Museum of Curiosities, dedicated to depicting the strange-but-true, and the Museum of Torture, home to a large collection of historic instruments of torture.

The three fortresses—the 10th-century Rocca Guaita (a working prison until 1970) and the Cesta and Montale, both of which date to the 13th century—located on Mount Titano's rugged peaks are San Marino's most popular tourist attractions. Visitors can take advantage of panoramic views of the Adriatic as well as the opportunity to scramble along cliff-edge parapets once patrolled by medieval guards. The interior of the Cesta has been converted into a museum, which displays collections of antique weapons, such as crossbows. During medieval-themed festivals held each July in the capital, costumed performers engage in crossbow competitions to demonstrate how medieval archers used these powerful weapons.

Outside of the capital are numerous cultural sites that have developed around the republic's eight historic castles. The rarity of San Marino's stamps and currency are on display at the Museo Filatelico e Numismatico, or Stamp and Coin Museum, in Borgo Maggiore. This town is also home to the Centro Naturalistico Sammarinese (San Marino Nature Center), which contains exhibits on the republic's natural scientific history. The Santuario della Beata Vergine della Consolazione (Sanctuary of Blessed Virgin of Consolation) in Borgo Maggiore, built in the 1960s, is considered the premier example of 20th-century architecture in the republic.

The town of Serravalle dates from the Roman era and is home to one of the republic's ancient castles, the Rocca Malatestiana. The Maranello Rosso Collezione in Falciano, near Serravalle, features an impressive collection of red Ferrari sports cars among other vehicles. The area surrounding the town of Fiorentino also contains the ruins of three ancient castles dating from as early as the 11th century. Near one of these castles, the Castrum Pennarossa, lies a wooded nature preserve.

Libraries & Museums

The National Museum of San Marino, located in the Palazzo Pergami, includes extensive art and archeological collections dating back to the Stone Age. The Palazzo Valloni is home to the nation's library and official archives. The Basilica del Santo, largely rebuilt in the 19th century, is particularly notable because it is one of the few remaining churches in Italy built in the "pre-Romanesque" style. Private museums throughout the microstate include the Reptile Museum and Aquarium, the Ferrari Museum, the Museum of Modern Weaponry, the Waxworks Museum, and the Museum of Torture.

The National Library of San Marino, or the National Library and Book Patrimony (Biblioteca di Stato e Beni Librari), is home to over 107,000 volumes of books and 1,150 manuscripts, some dating back to the 15th and 16th centuries.

Holidays

San Marino's national holiday, which commemorates the establishment of the republic by Saint Marinus in the year 301, is observed on September 3. Saint Agatha's Day (February 5) celebrates San Marino's liberation from the 1739 invasion led by Cardinal Alberoni, papal legate of Ravenna. Other important holidays include many Roman Catholic feast days, such as the Feast of Corpus Christi (May 31).

Youth Culture

Sammarinese youth have plenty of opportunities for socializing. Groups of friends may gather at cafés or bars before attending the cinema, dancing at nightclubs, or engaging in other social activities. Sports such as volleyball and football (soccer) are popular, as is visiting the nearby coastal beaches of Italy. Young people enjoy listening to Sammarinese and Italian pop and rock music, as well as that of American and British artists. Other common recreational activities include watching television and playing video games. Dating is common, and cohabitation before marriage is socially acceptable for young couples. Increased educational and professional opportunities have encouraged the youth of San Marino to pursue a university education or begin a career before marrying and beginning families.

SOCIETY

Transportation

Some consider part of San Marino's charm to be its relative inaccessibility. The closest railway station to the republic is 27 kilometers (17 miles) away in Rimini, Italy, and air connections are limited to seasonal helicopter transports connecting San Marino to Rimini, the site of Federico Fellini International Airport. Several roads link San Marino with Italian cities and points beyond, with both taxis and buses running frequently between the republic and Rimini's mass transit stops. From Rimini, visitors enter the country at Serravalle; many continue to Borgo Maggiore, where a cable car travels up to the city of San Marino. Over 290 kilometers (180 miles) of roadways within the republic make intra-country travel convenient. Traffic moves on the right-hand side of the road.

Transportation Infrastructure

San Marino has a relatively small and undeveloped transportation network due in part to its small size. The country only has road connections with Italy, and there are 220 kilometers (137 miles) of highways with limited connections by bus. In addition, the microstate is located nearby one international airport, the Federico Fellini Airport (or Rimini-Miramare Airport), as well as three regional airports (Ancona Falconara Airport, Luigi Ridolfi Airport, and the Guglielmo Marconi Airport). The microstate does not have any airports or an operational railway.

Media & Communications

Because of a long-standing Italian ban on Sammarinese mass media, the republic has developed its own outlets only since 1987. Today, San Marino's public television broadcaster, RTV, provides sports, news, and local programming. In recent years, the country's two radio stations have expanded their offerings to include podcast programming in addition to over-the-air news and music. Two newspapers, *La Tribuna Sammarinese* (*The Sammarinese Tribune*) and *San Marino Oggi* (*San Marino Today*), are published daily.

Internet access is widely available; by 2009 the number of Internet users had grown to 17,000. Cell phone usage is prevalent, with nearly three mobile phones for every five people in the country. Sammarinese communications systems are also well connected with those of Italy, allowing the residents of the small republic access to the telecommunications resources and mass media outlets of its larger neighbor.

SOCIAL DEVELOPMENT

Standard of Living

San Marino is excluded from the United Nations Development Programme's 2014 list of all countries by Human Development Index (HDI), which measures quality of life indicators. Nonetheless, the country has a very high human development score. The country's estimated life expectancy in 2014 was 83 years—80.6 for males and 85.94 for females.

Water Consumption

Each household has access to clean drinking water and adequate sanitation.

Education

San Marino has an extensive system of public education, and a high literacy rate (above 95 percent). Education is free until the last grade of secondary school, and between the ages of six and 16, it is compulsory. Education is administered by the Secretary of State for Public Instruction, University, Cultural Institutions, Information and Research.

The University of San Marino (Università degli Studi) offers degrees in a wide variety of subjects, including communications, economics, technology, education, biomedicine, law, and history. The country's literacy rate is approximately 96 percent.

Women's Rights

In addition to its commitment to general human rights, San Marino holds a noticeable regard for the rights of women, both in theory and in practice. Sammarinese women largely enjoy the same rights and freedoms as their male counterparts and legislation offers many official protections. Overall, women face relatively few threats of physical or emotional harm. Although the Sammarinese government has no office specifically dedicated to women's affairs, the combination of effective legislation and few reports of women's rights violations demonstrate the government's widespread actions on behalf of its female citizens.

Sammarinese law prohibits violence against women, including instances of domestic and spousal abuse. These laws are well-enforced and carry stiff penalties. For example, a conviction of spousal abuse warrants two to 10 years of imprisonment depending on the circumstances. In 2008, the republic mounted a public campaign to further deter the already limited acts of violence against women. In October 2008, year-to-date, there were 60 reports of violence against women. Both rape and spousal rape are legally barred and carry punishments equal to those of spousal and domestic abuse. Furthermore, rape is rare in San Marino, with no reports of the crime in either 2007 or 2008.

Women in San Marino receive equal pay for equal work, and generally report no discriminatory workplace practices. Sexual harassment is a crime in the republic, and in 2007 and 2008, no instances of sexual harassment were reported. Equally rare is prostitution, which is also prohibited under Sammarinese law.

San Marino has a generally strong record on women's rights, and in 2003 ratified the UN Convention on the Elimination of All Forms of Discrimination against Women (CEDAW).

The long influence of the Roman Catholic Church can be seen in the republic's legal ban on abortion, except in cases that threaten the life of the mother. However, abortion services are legal and accessible in Italy. Another spot of potential improvement for the republic's women lies in their relative underrepresentation in San Marino's government. Latecomers to the republic's political life, women did not receive suffrage until 1959, and were not granted the right to stand for election to public office until 1973. As of 2008, only eight of the 60 seats of the Sammarinese Great and General Council were held by women, and two women out of a total of 10 members served in the Sammarinese Congress of State.

Health Care

San Marino has an excellent public-health system, and average life expectancy is around 83 years for the total population (2014 estimate). The infant mortality rate is low: less than 4.52 deaths per 1,000 live births. The public-health authority, or Salute, is under the jurisdiction of San Marino's Secretary for Health and Social Security.

GOVERNMENT

Structure

According to legend, San Marino was founded on Mount Titano in 301 by a Christian stonemason, Saint Marinus (Marino), who fled from Dalmatia to escape Roman persecution of Christians. The city was eventually named in his honor, as the "Land of San Marino."

In the following centuries, San Marino came under the control of the Dukes of Spoleto, but achieved independence by the 10th century. The tiny state's independence has been recognized multiple times over the centuries, though usually as the protectorate of a more powerful neighbor. There have also been occasional periods of foreign occupation, particularly during the Renaissance and World War II.

San Marino has becoming increasingly involved in world affairs since the late 20th century. It joined the Council of Europe in 1988 and the United Nations in 1992. It also belongs to a number of other international organizations, including the World Health Organization and the International Court of Justice.

San Marino's government is basically parliamentary, with the unique feature of dual heads of state: the co-equal Captains-Regent (Capitani Reggenti). The country adopted its first constitution on October 8, 1600. This has been expanded upon by the electoral law of 1926, as well as the 1974 declaration of rights (updated in 2002).

Like other European nations, large and small, San Marino is run by a coalition government. The main parties are the Democratic Christian Party, the Socialist Party, and the Progressive Democratic Party.

The two co-equal heads of state, or Captains-Regent, are elected every six months by the Sammarinese legislature. The practice is derived from the ancient Roman Republic, in which the Senate elected co-equal heads of state known as consuls. In San Marino, the office dates back to 1243. Their role is to preside over the legislature and the ten-member Congress of State (the cabinet). The cabinet, whose members are elected to a five year term by the legislature, handles the actual business of government. The Secretary of State for Foreign and Political Affairs serves as "prime minister," though Sammarinese law makes no official provision for a head of government.

The Grand and General Council (Consiglio Grande e Generale) is a single-house legislature with 60 members, who are elected to five-year terms through direct popular vote. This body is the descendent of the republic's medieval council, the Arengo.

The Grand and General Council is also responsible for electing the judicial branch, known as the Council of Twelve (Consiglio dei XII). The judges' term of appointment lasts only for the legislative session. Civil cases are handled by Justices of the Peace.

San Marino is noted for the liveliness of its political culture, with almost total voter turnout in the frequent elections. The country has universal suffrage, for citizens ages eighteen and older. One of the main political issues facing San Marino is whether to seek full membership in the European Union.

Political Parties

San Marino has a large number of political parties, and the Sammarinese government is traditionally ruled by coalitions of two or more parties that unite to form a majority coalition. The 2012 general elections were contested by several coalitions: the San Marino Common Good, winning 35 seats; the Agreement for the Country coalition, winning 12 seats; Active Citizenship, winning nine seats; and Civic Movement, winning four seats.

Local Government

The republic has nine municipalities or castelli (singular: castello). The word is derived from the Latin "castellum," or "fortress," recalling the days of medieval walled towns. These communities are all quite small, and retain many of their medieval customs and traditions, including markets and festivals.

Judicial System

The Sammarinese judicial system is based on civil law and influenced by the Italian legal system. There are four levels of courts, including general courts of first instance and second instance (appeal); the highest courts are presided over by foreign judges. All courts have a single judge and no jury. The Council of Twelve (Consiglio dei XII) serves as the appeals court in the third instance, or the Supreme Court.

Taxation

San Marino has a progressive taxation rate for personal income, between 12 and 50 percent, and a 17 percent corporate tax rate. Other levied taxes include a value-added tax (VAT), stamp duty, mortgage tax, and other small assorted taxes.

Armed Forces

The armed forces of San Marino represent one of the smallest armies in the world, and are mostly ceremonial. It consist of six branches: the Crossbow Corps (ceremonial); the Guard of the Rock (front-line unit that assists law enforcement); the Army Militia (largely ceremonial fighting force); the Military Ensemble (ceremonial military band); and the Corps of Gendarmerie of San Marino (military police service). Italy's armed forces are responsible for the microstate's national defense.

Foreign Policy

Despite its small size, the republic of San Marino participates actively in broader European and worldwide affairs. Since becoming the twenty-second nation to join the Council of Europe in 1988, San Marino has held the presidency of the Committee of Ministers of that organization twice, first in 1990 and again in 2006–2007. The republic is also a member of numerous international organizations, including the United Nations (UN), International Monetary Fund (IMF), and World Tourism Organization (WTO), and maintains official relations with the European Union (EU). The republic remains reluctant to fully join the EU, citing concerns over the difficulties of remaining cultural and politically independent within the context of the broader organization. San Marino has used its position in international bodies, particularly the UN, to support measures that it believes would most benefit the global community as a whole.

As of 2009, the republic had independently established official diplomatic relations with 114 states, including both European neighbors and far-flung countries. The most important of these relationships is unquestionably that between San Marino and Italy. Official agreements between the two nations cover topics ranging from labor to postal services. Although San Marino itself maintains limited consular services throughout the world due to financial and labor constraints, Sammarinese citizens abroad can use the services of Italian consulates, and the republic's defenses are primarily handled by the Italian military. Italy is also the only nation to maintain an ambassador in the republic. In 2006, the United States appointed an ambassador to San Marino, and the following year the republic appointed its own representative to the U.S. in return.

Unlike most of its fellow European microstates, San Marino has been the recipient of few accusations of unethical financial practices and has demonstrated a commitment to keeping such activities in check. In recent years, San Marino has increased efforts to battle foreign money laundering. Limited instances of foreign nationals bringing money obtained through criminal activities outside of San Marino and attempting to pass it through the Sammarinese banking system have occurred in the past. The republic responded in the mid-2000s by passing a number of laws aimed at halting money laundering, strengthening its own financial and banking structures, and increasing government oversight of financial activities. San Marino maintains official neutrality in all conflicts and international disputes.

Human Rights Profile

International human rights law insists that states respect civil and political rights, and also promote an individual's economic, social and cultural rights. The United Nations Universal Declaration on Human Rights (UDHR) is recognized as the standard for international human rights. Its authors sought the counsel of the world's great thinkers, philosophers, and religious leaders, and were careful to create a document that reflects the core values shared by every world culture. (To read this document or view the articles relating to cultural human rights, go to: http://www.udhr.org/UDHR/default.htm).

San Marino has a commendable human rights record. Its 1974 Declaration on Citizens' Rights, also known as the Fundamental Law, protects a number of basic personal rights and serves as a basis for much of the republic's modern legal practices. Articles 5 and 6 of this legislation strongly assert the sanctity of human rights and guarantee civil and political rights to all people in the republic, while Article 6 protects intellectual and religious freedoms. The republic has protected the rights of civil marriage and divorce since 1949—a period much longer than that its Italian neighbor—bringing it into agreement with the provisions of the UDHR. Political and judicial processes are both free and fair, allowing individual citizens the rights to full participation in society and to personal development. The Sammarinese also routinely exercise political rights, with near total voter turnout common in regular council elections.

In 2004, San Marino extended citizenship and its accompanying protections to any children born to either a Sammarinese father or mother. Prior to that, citizenship passed exclusively through the paternal line. Those born to Sammarinese citizens outside of the republic may also claim citizenship after 10 years of continuous residence within the republic. However, foreign nationals with no Sammarinese citizen parent must reside in the country for at least 30 continuous years, making naturalization practically unheard of within the republic.

San Marino has also demonstrated its commitment to the protection of human rights through the ratification of numerous treaties and conventions supporting human development. In 1989, the republic ratified the European Convention on Human Rights. It recognizes the authority of the European Court of Human Rights (ECtHR), as well as the European Commission to oversee and enforce any possible human rights violations within the republic. Further, San Marino is party to the UN Convention on the Rights of the Child, as well as to the International Covenant on Economic, Social, and Cultural Rights and the International Covenant on Civil and Political Rights.

ECONOMY

Overview of the Economy

San Marino is a small but prosperous nation, with tourism accounting for around half of the government's revenues. The government is fiscally frugal, refusing to maintain a national debt.

For the past several decades, tourism has been the mainstay of the capital's economy, generating more than half of the republic's gross domestic product (GDP). Another key source of revenue comes from the sale of specialty stamps and commemorative coins, which are highly sought after by collectors.

The banking industry has also played a significant role in San Marino, which has long served as a tax haven for wealthy investors. Banking is the second most important economic sector. Although the sale of duty-free consumer goods continues to generate revenues, the advent of the European Union (EU)—which has ushered in lower corporate tax rates in Italy and other EU nations—has significantly decreased the tax advantages enjoyed in the past in San Marino.

The country also receives an annual subsidy from Italy, under a treaty arrangement. As of 2014, the gross domestic product (GDP) was the equivalent of $2 billion (USD), with an estimated per capita income of $55,000 (USD). The euro is the official currency, under a special agreement with the European Union, although San Marino is not an official EU member.

Industry

San Marino generates much of its revenue from the sale of commemorative postage stamps and gold coins. This industry is handled by the State Philatelic and Numismatic Office. Stamps have been sold since the 1890s, and are very popular among collectors throughout the world. Under the terms of the postal agreement with Italy, Sammarinese stamps are valid only within the republic. San Marino also has an extensive manufacturing sector, producing consumer goods such as furniture, clothing, and ceramics.

As one might expect, San Marino's major trading partner is Italy. San Marino also trades extensively with the rest of Europe, as well as with South America and East Asia. Exports and imports were nearly equal in 2004, valued at $1.3 billion (USD) and $2 billion (USD), respectively.

Labor

As of 2012, the country's unemployment rate stood at seven percent, and the labor force was estimated at 21,960. That same year, the services sector accounted for 66.3 percent of the workforce, industry accounted for 33.5 percent, and the agricultural sector accounted for less than one percent.

Energy/Power/Natural Resources

San Marino has no mineral resources, other than stone for building. Much of the land is forested. Though only a small percentage of the land is arable, the Sammarinese have turned many acres into rich vineyards. Much of the wine produced in the country is exported.

Agriculture

Less than 17 percent of San Marino's land is arable, and the Sammarinese must import much of their food. There is, however, a fair amount of agricultural activity, including crop farming, and cattle and dairy farming. The main crops are wheat, grapes, corn, and olives. Though not much of the land is suitable for farming, San Marino has well-developed wine and cheese industries.

Tourism

Tourism is the mainstay of San Marino's economy, contributing more than half of the gross domestic product. Several million people visit San Marino each year. The major attractions are the spectacular mountain landscapes and the country's medieval heritage.

Popular tourist sites include the Palazzo Pubblico (town hall) in San Marino City's historic downtown plaza, the Piazza della libertà. During the summer months, the honor guard of the Guardia di Rocca, San Marino's police force, performs a changing of the guard ceremony in front of the Palazzo.

Vanessa Vaughn, Eric Badertscher,
Beverly Ballaro

DO YOU KNOW?

- San Marino is the third smallest country in Europe. The other two are Vatican City and Monaco.

- According to legend, before Saint Marinus could establish his new community on the slopes of Mount Titano, he first had to drive out the bears that lived on the mountain. The angry animals, the story goes, chose an enormous black bear to lead an attempt to reclaim their mountain home. But Saint Marinus, it is said, brandished a wooden cross in the animal's face. The bear, which was, according to the legend, not really a bear at all but the devil in disguise, disappeared in a cloud of sulfur and smoke.

- The city-state greatly expanded its territory in 1463, thanks to a successful war in which it was allied with Pope Pius II. As thanks for aiding him against Sigismondo Malatesta of Rimini, the pope gave San Marino the communities of Domagnano, Fiorentino, and Montegiardino, and Serraville.

- Napoleon Bonaparte, who invaded Italy in 1796, is said to have offered to increase the size of San Marino. The Sammarinese, fearful that adding territory to their republic by force would inevitably lead to conflict, turned down his proposition.

- San Marino has enjoyed diplomatic relations with Italy since 1862, when the Kingdom of Italy recognized the republic's independence. The two countries signed a postal agreement in 1877, which allowed San Marino to print its own stamps.

Bibliography

Christian Bonneto. "Emilia-Romagna and San Marino," in *Italy*. Oakland, CA: Lonely Planet, 2014.

Thomas M. Eccardt. *Secrets of the Seven Smallest States of Europe*. New York: Hippocrene Books, 2005.

Ellen Grady. *Blue Guide: The Marche and San Marino*. New York: Norton, 2015.

"Repubblica de San Marino." State Board of Tourism, Government of San Marino. http://www.visitsanmarino.com/on-line/en/home.html

"U.S. Relations with San Marino." *U.S. Department of State: Diplomacy in Action. United States Department of State.* http://www.state.gov/r/pa/ei/bgn/5387.htm

Veenendaal, Wouter. *Politics and Democracy in Microstates*. New York: Routledge, 2014.

Works Cited

"Aide Memoire." European Union. <http://ec.europa.eu/external_relations/sanmarino/docs/aidememoire_en.pdf>

"Allegro Vivo." Allegro Vivo Association. <http://www.pianocompetitionsanmarino.com/default.asp?id=2>

Barry Viniker. "San Marino leaves Eurovision Song Contest." ESCToday.com. 18 Dec. 2008. < http://www.esctoday.com/news/read/12736>

Thomas M. Eccardt. Secrets of the Seven Smallest States of Europe. New York: Hippocrene Books, 2005.

Ellen Grady. Blue Guide: The Marche and San Marino. New York: Norton, 2006.

"EU's relations with San Marino." European Commission External Relations. European Union. < http://ec.europa.eu/external_relations/sanmarino/index_en.htm>

"Human Rights Report: San Marino." U.S. Department of State: Diplomacy in Action. United States Department of State. <http://www.state.gov/g/drl/rls/hrrpt/2007/100582.htm>

"Gastronomy of San Marino." Delicious Italy. <http://www.deliciousitaly.com/prodotto.php?id=203&regione_id=5>

"Il Portale della Repubblica de San Marino." Sanmarinosite.com. <http://www.sanmarinosite.com/eng/index.php>

"Istituto Musicale Sammarinese." San Marino Musical Institute. <http://www.ims.sm/>

"La Serenissima: Ancient Cake Factory since 1942." La Serenissima. <http://www.laserenissima.sm/eng/index.asp>

"News on the Council of Europe." Council of Europe. <http://ifuw.org/uwe/docs/2008-coe-news-may.pdf>

"Radio e Televisione della Repubblica de San Marino." San Marino RTV. <http://www.sanmarinortv.sm/>

"Repubblica de San Marino: A Completely Different World." Ministry of Tourism, Sports, Telecommunications and Economic Cooperation. Government of San Marino. <http://www.visitsanmarino.com/default.asp?id=297>

"San Marino." Encyclopædia Britannica. Encyclopedia Britannica Online. <http://search.eb.com.ezproxy.libraries.wright.edu:2048/eb/article-9065362>.

"San Marino." World Data Analyst. Encyclopedia Britannica. <http://www.world.eb.com.ezproxy.libraries.wright.edu:2048/wdpdf/SanMarino.pdf>.

"San Marino." The World Factbook. Central Intelligence Agency. <https://www.cia.gov/library/publications/the-world-factbook/geos/sm.html>.

"San Marino." CultureGrams World Edition. ProQuest. <http://online.culturegrams.com/world/world_country.php?contid=5&wmn=Europe&cid=226&cn=San_Marino>

"San Marino: 1. Historical perspective: cultural policies and instruments." Compendium: Cultural Policies and Trends in Europe. <http://www.culturalpolicies.net/web/sanmarino.php>

"San Marino." U.S. Department of State: Diplomacy in Action. United States Department of State. <http://www.state.gov/r/pa/ei/bgn/5387.htm>

"San Marino and the Council of Europe." Council of Europe. <http://www.coe.int/T/E/Com/About_Coe/Member_states/e_sa.asp#TopOfPage>

"San Marino Historical Centre and Mount Titano." UNESCO World Heritage Centre. <http://whc.unesco.org/en/list/1245>

"Third Round Detailed Assessment Report on San Marino." European Committee on Crime Problems. Council of Europe. <http://www.coe.int/t/dghl/monitoring/moneyval/Evaluations/round3/MONEYVAL(2008)4Summ-SMR3_en.pdf>

Scottish currency /Stock photo © Briansc

SCOTLAND

Introduction

Scotland is a country in northwestern Europe, located in the northern part of Great Britain. It also includes islands such as the Hebrides, Orkneys, and Shetlands. Traditionally, Scotland was considered a highly industrialized nation, with a strong manufacturing economy. That has changed in the early 21st century as the economy has diversified. The country is famous for its writers, such as the poet Robert Burns, poet/novelist Sir Walter Scott, and novelist Robert Louis Stevenson. Tourists come to Scotland to enjoy the rich cultural life of cities such as Edinburgh, as well as the country's natural beauty.

For centuries, Scotland's capital has been an important cultural center not only for the British Isles but also for Europe as a whole. The University of Edinburgh produced such notable figures as philosopher David Hume and economist Adam Smith. In summer, tourists flock to Edinburgh to attend the many events which make up the Edinburgh Festival. Established in 1947, the festival has given rise to events such as the Edinburgh Fringe Festival, which promotes alternative art forms and is one of the world's largest festivals of its kind.

GENERAL INFORMATION

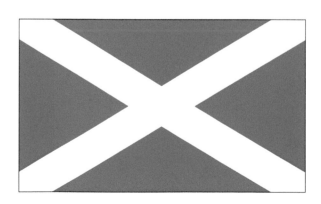

Official Language: English (de facto); Scottish Gaelic, Scots (recognized)

Population: 5,347,600 (2014 estimate)

Currency: Pound Sterling

Coins: One hundred pence equal one pound. Coins are issued in denominations of 1, 2, 5, 10, 20, 25, 50 pence and 1, 2, and 5 pounds.

Land Area: 76,409 square kilometers (29,501 square miles)

Water Area: 2,363 square kilometers (912 square miles)

National Anthem: "Flower of Scotland" (unofficial)

Capital: Edinburgh

Time Zone: GMT +0

Flag Description: Scotland's flag is known by two names: The Saltire and the Saint Andrew's Cross. It has a blue background with a white saltire or diagonal cross.

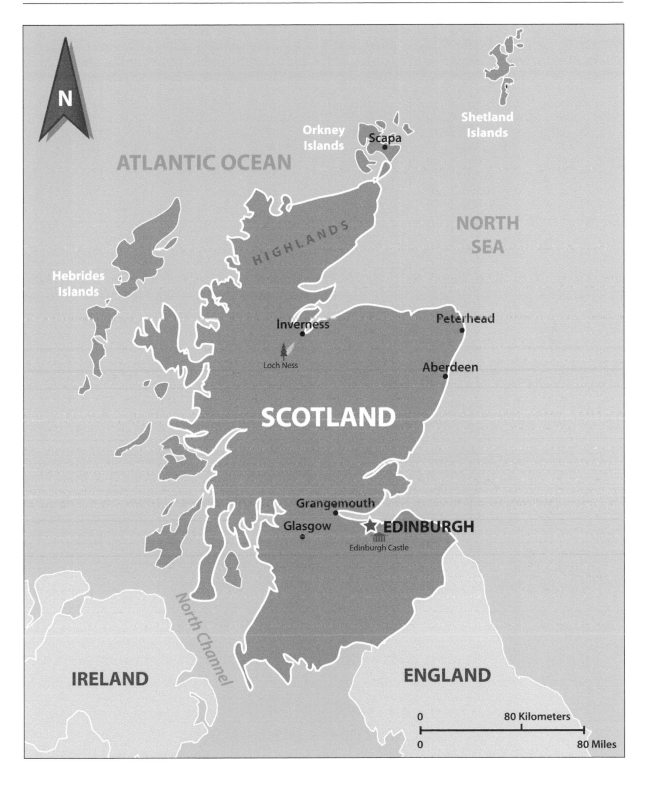

Principal Cities by Population (mid-2012 estimates):

- Glasgow (591,6200)
- Edinburgh (464,990)
- Aberdeen (196,670)
- Dundee (147,710)
- East Kilbride (74,740)
- Paisley (76,220)
- Livingston (56,570)
- Hamilton (53,200)
- Cumbernauld (51,610)
- Kirkcaldy (49,460)

Population

The population of Scotland is largely a mixture of Celtic and Anglo-Saxon, though there are some small minorities from Asia and elsewhere. Scotland's population is largely urban, with Glasgow as its largest city. The population is more concentrated in the Central Lowlands between Edinburgh and Glasgow. The northeast coast near Aberdeen and Inverness is also more densely populated. The Highlands have traditionally been thinly populated but have experienced some increased settlement from other areas of Great Britain, particularly those seeking respite from cities.

Languages

English and Scottish Gaelic are the official languages of Scotland, and both are used in official business. The English language predominates, as only about 1 percent of the population speaks Gaelic. The Scots language, also known as Lowland Scots or "Lallans," is derived from northern dialects of Anglo-Saxon. Until the union with England, Lallans was the official language of Scotland. Scottish Gaelic is spoken mostly in the Highlands and the Western Isles, but Gaelic speakers are almost always also fluent in English.

Native People & Ethnic Groups

Scotland was originally settled by Celtic tribes. The country takes its name from the Scots, a tribe from Ireland, but the Picts were actually the first people to settle the country. The Anglo-Saxons arrived in the fifth century, and established kingdoms in the Scottish Lowlands. The "Lallans" dialect is derived from a northern variety of Anglo-Saxon.

The Norse arrived later, in the Viking raids. There has been a sizeable Jewish population since the 19th century. More recent minority populations include immigrants from Eastern Europe, India and China.

Religions

The Church of Scotland, known in Scots as "The Kirk," is the official or established church, as of 2013, had approximately 398,389 members (7.5 percent of the population). Although established by law, the Church of Scotland rules itself and is not run by the government. A much smaller Presbyterian denomination is the Free Church of Scotland.

Other Protestant groups include the Methodists, Pentecostals, Salvation Army, Seventh-Day Adventists, and Quakers. Roman Catholicism is regaining strength in Scotland, after centuries of repression; about 13 percent of the population claims to be Roman Catholic. There are also small numbers of Jews and Muslims. Thirty-eight percent of the population, in 2011, claimed no religious affiliation.

Climate

Scotland has a generally mild climate, thanks to the Gulf Stream, although parts of the country (particularly the mountains) can be quite cold. The climate is also quite damp, with average rainfall of over 1,000 millimeters (39 inches) per year in most of the country. Despite this, parts of the country receive a great deal of sunshine, particularly parts of the Hebrides.

ENVIRONMENT & GEOGRAPHY

Topography

Mainland Scotland has three main regions: the southern uplands, the northern highlands, and the "central belt." The southern uplands are located along the Anglo-Scottish border and in southwestern Scotland, a hilly region covered by moors. The Highlands, as befits their name, are a mountainous region, home to the Celtic, Gaelic-speaking tribes known as clans. One of the major mountain chains is the Grampians, which include Ben Nevis (1,343meters/4,406 feet) the highest mountain in Scotland and the entire United Kingdom. The "central belt" or the lowlands is generally much lower and flatter than the rest of the country and runs from the Firth of Forth, in east of the country, to the Firth of Clyde in the west. Most of the population lives there and it is where most of Scotland's industrialization took hold.

The Scottish islands are comprised of three main chains: the Orkneys, the Shetlands, and the Hebrides. The first two chains are located off Scotland's northern coast, while the Hebrides are known as the "Western Isles."

Many of Scotland's lakes, or lochs, are actually inlets of the sea; some are salty, and some are fresh. The most famous is probably Loch Ness, allegedly the home of the aquatic Loch Ness Monster. Loch Lomond is the largest freshwater loch. Many lochs are linked by the Caledonian Canal, a 96-kilometer ( ) inland waterway.

Firths are estuaries, but much broader; among the most well-known are the Solway Firth, the Moray Firth, and the Firth of Forth. Scotland has many large rivers, among them the Clyde, the Forth, and the Tweed.

Plants & Animals

Scotland is home to many plant and animal species, including many endangered varieties. The Hebrides, for example, are particularly known as a home for wildlife, such as seals. Larger land mammals found in the wild include the red deer and roe deer, the wild goat, and the wildcat. Aquatic mammals include the basking shark, the harbor porpoise, the bottlenose dolphin, and the killer whale. Bird species include numerous kinds of birds of prey including the osprey and the peregrine falcon, as well as migratory birds such as pink-footed geese.

Dog breeding is popular in Scotland, and has given rise to notable national varieties such as the Border collie and Scottish ("Scottie") terriers.

CUSTOMS & COURTESIES

Greetings

For the most part, Scotland follows the greeting conventions of the other countries in the United Kingdom (UK). However, the Scots are generally regarded as warmer and friendlier than the rest of Great Britain (although the Scottish Highlanders have a reputation for being extremely reserved). In business and formal social situations, people generally prefer a third-party introduction rather than introducing themselves. When greeting, a handshake may be typically followed by "Hello" or the rhetorical "How do you do?" The phrase "Pleased to meet you" is also considered courteous. In general, social relationships are somewhat more formal in Scotland than in the United States, and adults usually initially address each other with a title and last name.

Among friends and younger people, a common greeting is "Alright?" or in Scottish dialect "Awright?" Hugging is not customary, even among those who are close.

Gestures & Etiquette

The Scots are not very physically expressive or dramatic in their language. They tend not to call attention to themselves with loud speech or hand gestures, and typically find those who do overbearing. If engaged in private conversations in public places, Scots tend to speak in quiet tones. It is also uncommon for strangers to strike up conversations with each other in public places (such as on the street or on public transportation), and such an approach would likely be considered uncomfortable.

Because Scots are generally reserved, they also maintain a good deal of personal space while speaking. Additionally, they appreciate orderly conduct in public—standing patiently and quietly in line—and expect courtesies such as "Please," "Thank you," and "Excuse me" in superficial public exchanges.

Eating/Meals

Traditionally, Scots ate a savory porridge for breakfast, but it has become more common to have a bowl of granola (called muesli in Europe). Another popular breakfast custom is the "Scottish breakfast," which includes bacon, sausage, eggs, grilled tomatoes or mushrooms, a tattie (potato scone), and black pudding (seasoned sausage stuffed with blood), or kippers (smoked herring) served with tea and orange juice.

A traditional Scottish lunch (often called dinner) often consists of a ploughman's lunch (a hunk of cheese, a roll, and a piece of ham), or a hot lunch served at a pub. In urban areas, people are more likely to grab a sandwich or take-away (take out meal) from a "chipper" (fish and chip shop) or other restaurant. The Scots also commonly follow the British tradition of afternoon tea, typically served around four o'clock in the afternoon. This usually consists of a pot of tea with shortbread (a sweet, crumbly type of cookie), Dundee cake (an almond-topped fruitcake), or Scottish pancakes (similar to an English muffin) served with jam. This custom is different than "high tea," which is more formal and now served mostly in hotels or other tourist locations, and which typically consists of sandwiches, scones, and a hot dish served in place of dinner.

Dinner (often called supper or tea) is typically served sometime between six and nine o'clock, and may include a soup such as cock-a-leekie soup (which includes chicken, leeks, and rice), a fish dish, and a potato side dish such as stovies (a potato and onion mixture). Scots also traditionally have a large Sunday dinner (typically served at lunchtime) with a roast and several side dishes.

Visiting

Because they are generally private people, it has traditionally not been common for Scots to arrive at another home unannounced or without an invitation (although this has become a more common practice among young people). Traditionally, in a middle and upper-class Scottish home, there was a lounge or sitting area at the front of the house reserved primarily for visitors. This room typically had the finest furniture and was rarely used by the family. If a meal were to be served, guests would also be invited into a formal dining room. Only family or very close friends would be invited into the kitchen or other family rooms. However, younger generations have largely abandoned this formality, too.

An invitation for tea (the meal in the late afternoon) is a common social tradition in Scotland. Guests traditionally wait for their host to pour the tea rather than do it themselves, and wait until the host begins eating before starting in their own food. If invited for dinner, it's customary to bring a small gift such as wine, chocolate or flowers. However, it's not expected that the host will open the gift in the guest's presence.

LIFESTYLE

Family

Although Scotland is historically known for its clans (extended families of the same name that maintained a strong kinship, or bond), the family unit in Scotland has adopted many different forms in the early 21st century. Over 10 percent of Scottish families are led by single parents, and it is rare for multiple generations of a family to live in the same home (although this practice is more common with members of Scotland's new immigrant communities). However, Scottish parents still often rely on extended family for childcare. The Scottish divorce rate has also gone up in recent years, while the marriage rate has gone down, and the number of unmarried couples living together has also increased.

Housing

The majority of the Scottish population in the early 21st century resides in urban or suburban areas, typically near major cities. Housing styles range from the terraced or row house (which shares common walls with other homes) and the semi-detached home or duplex (which shares one common wall and has symmetrical construction with its neighbor), to the single-family detached home and the modern medium or high-rise apartment building. Tenement blocks—low to medium-rise brick or sandstone apartment houses—have been common in Scottish cities since the Industrial Revolution of the late 18th and early 19th centuries. While tenement housing came to be often associated with poverty and harsh living, especially in the US, in Scotland these buildings were home to people of varying social classes, and many of these tenements have been renovated and modernized.

Detached, single-family homes are more common in the suburbs and in small towns and villages. In the Highlands and coastal areas, it's still possible to a come across a traditional crofter's cottage—a stone and thatched roof cottage originally built as the residence for a family running a small sheep farm. The grand Scottish sporting estates of the 19th century survive today not as private homes, but typically as hotels or attractions.

Food

While Scottish cuisine is in many ways similar to British cuisine, and has distinct Scandinavian and French influences, it maintains its own unique traditions. Perhaps the most famous Scottish culinary tradition is the national dish of Scotland, haggis. The dish is made from a sheep's stomach stuffed with oatmeal and spiced lamb, as well as cow lungs, liver and heart. The casing is then boiled, and split open with a special knife. However, haggis is no longer commonly eaten. Scotland is also known for its beef, particularly the Aberdeen Angus breed of beef cattle.

Increasingly, Scots eat more of the types of food found in other parts of the UK, and those influenced by new immigrant groups. In fact, national or international fast-food chains or "take away" restaurants which typically serve Indian food, Chinese food or the traditional British dish of fish and chips can be found in almost every Scottish town. However, pubs and finer restaurants still serve Scottish specialties

such as Angus steak, poached salmon, wood-smoked haddock (traditionally called Arbroath Smokie), neeps (mashed turnips) and tatties (mashed potatoes). In addition, while shortbread is a world-renowned traditional Scottish cookie, Scots are more likely to prepare and consume cranachan, a dessert made with toasted oats, cream and fresh fruit.

Lastly, Scotland is known around the world for the quality of its whiskey, an alcoholic beverage made from distilled barley and aged in oak casks. Different types of whiskey are made through different processes and in different parts of Scotland, but the highest quality type of scotch (as Scottish whiskey is commonly known) is the single malt type, which is made from only one kind of barley, rather than from a blend of grains and a blend of single malts.

Life's Milestones

In the Orkney Islands, located off the northern coast, newborns are welcomed by a tradition called "weein' the heed," or the wetting of the head. The tradition involves the consumption of a bottle of whiskey by male relatives and friends of the new baby. The newborn is then fed a drop of the whiskey by spoon (silver if possible) to protect it against illness (whiskey was and still is used as a cure for various ailments).

Scottish wedding traditions vary based on the area of the country, but it was once common to give the bride a silver sixpence on the day of her wedding, which she would then put in her shoe. At funerals, women traditionally did not accompany the casket to the gravesite, but stayed behind at the cemetery gates, then left to prepare the post-funeral meal. This tradition is still observed in some areas.

CULTURAL HISTORY

Traditionally, Highland culture varied from that of the Lowlands. Highlanders saw themselves as a warrior people, constantly at odds with the English and those who sided with the English kings in the Lowlands. Highlanders tended to be

Roman Catholic, seeing the conversion to Protestantism in the Lowlands as a concession to English culture. Highlanders also resisted Scotland's unification with England in a Kingdom of Great Britain.

In modern times, the distinction of the Highlands and Lowlands has much less weight, as the Highlands are revered for their natural beauty and for their retention of Scottish culture. The Lowlands, where the majority of the population lives, is the country's economic ballast, and both are appreciated for their contributions to a vibrant culture.

Art

Carved stone balls (called petrospheres) and embossed metal objects, both believed to be of religious or ceremonial significance, represent the earliest forms of Scottish art. Medieval art was religious in nature, and influenced by Celtic Christianity. This included manuscript art and ornate carvings and metalwork, much of which was concentrated in monasteries. With increasing English influence and the advent of the Protestant Reformation during the 16th century—a political and religious movement to reform the Roman Catholic Church—the arts in Scotland were undeveloped and then repressed. It wasn't until the Scottish Enlightenment in the 18th century that Scotland began to experience true native cultural development. The Royal Scottish Academy of Arts had been established by 1826, and by the late 19th century, portraiture and romantic landscape painting had emerged.

Architecture

Scottish architecture immediately evokes images of castle walls and turrets. From the earliest times up until the 18th century, Scotland's architectural development was indeed driven by the need for defense. The ancient prototypes for the castle were the crannog (a fortified artificial island with a house on top), the broch (an early stone tower) and the motte and bailey castle, which consisted of a chief's tower built on a raised mound with a walled-in living area for commoners. Beginning in the High Middle Ages (spanning between the 11th and 13th centuries)—and after

the Norman conquest of England in 1066—the large stone-built walled castle became the dominant building of Scottish medieval architecture.

From the early Middle Ages, Scottish architecture developed alongside that of England, from Gothic and Romanesque churches and abbeys to Renaissance-style elaborate palaces and mansions. In the 18th and 19th centuries, Scotland began to develop a more distinct and national style. Older, grand residences were converted into sporting estates for nobles, and new country houses were built in the Scottish baronial style. This new style was a revival of the Gothic style, and incorporated elements from Scotland's Renaissance-era castles and mansions. Scotland's most famous national architect is perhaps Charles Rennie Mackintosh (1868–1928), who often combined traditional Scottish architecture with contemporary ideals, and worked in the art nouveau style (popular from 1890 to 1905).

Drama

For a large part of Scotland's history, theatrical performances were banned. This dates back to the medieval period, and during the Reformation of the 16th century, theater was suppressed along with visual arts. Theater returned to Scotland in the 18th century, but most of the plays were derived from the English stage. Scotland didn't develop its own distinct playwriting tradition until the 20th century. Today, the country is considered to be at the forefront of modern theater in Europe.

Music

Scottish music is perhaps the best-known of the Scottish arts. It developed after Norse and Celtic settlers brought their tradition of musical storytelling to Scotland. Through the years, a strong Scottish ballad tradition developed, which helped preserve the country's history and folklore. Although ballads were originally sung at court, they soon became popular throughout the countryside, as well. Often accompanied by harp or flute, ballads represent one side of the spectrum of Scottish music, and the regimental marching music of the great Highland bagpipe represents the other. Starting around the 16th century, the bagpipe (which is made in many forms, including a smaller, quieter lowlands variety) came to be one of the most widely recognized symbols of Scotland. From the 19th century onward, bagpipe music has been used to express Scottish national pride and to distinguish Scottish from English culture.

Scottish folk music usually features the fiddle, tin whistle, and the accordion. It is strongly influenced by Scotland's Gaelic roots, and has similarities to Irish, French Breton and Spanish Galician music. Scottish folk music features both instrumental and vocal performances, and is often played at ceilidhs or in pubs. Scottish folk music also had a strong impact on the development of American country and folk music.

Dance

One of the oldest forms of folk dance in Scotland is Scottish Highland dancing, which include such athletic dances as the Sword Dance and the Highland fling. The tradition is believed to date back to the 11th or 12th century, and is performed in celebration or as feats of strength. Many believe that traditional Highland dancing was also largely based on medieval and Renaissance court dances. The steps became formalized when dance was incorporated into the Highland games competitions held by Scots beginning in the late 19th century.

Scottish country dancing and ceilidh dancing, the types of dance performed at ceilidhs (community gatherings held in homes and villages), were more common dances. Scottish country dancing is a type of folk dance involving arranged steps and sets of couples. It is considered a social dance, and similar to ballroom dancing. Ceilidh dancing is more informal, and often involves couples dancing on their own.

Literature

The Norse, Vikings, and Celts all brought a strong oral tradition to Scotland. Storytelling was a common activity at the courts of early chiefs and kings. Perhaps the earliest form of written literature in Scotland was poetry, beginning with

The Bruce (1376) by John Barbour (c. 1320–1395). This epic poem is considered Scotland's first literary work. During the 15th and 16th centuries, prior to the Reformation, many courts appointed poets, and these royal courtiers were generally referred to as makars (literally meaning "makers"). Through the years, popular folk ballads also developed, and these led to romantic poetry and Gothic revival movements in Scottish literature in the 18th and 19th century.

Among the best-known of the romantic poets are Sir Walter Scott (1771–1832), whose works on Scottish history and legend include *The Lady of the Lake* (1810), *Rob Roy* (1817) and *Ivanhoe* (1819). Scotland's national poet, Robert Burns (1759–1796), wrote in Scottish dialect, and his poems and songs came to symbolize Scottish identity. In fact, Burns's works, including the folk songs "Auld Lange Syne" and "A Red, Red Rose," are so beloved by those of Scottish ancestry that international Burns societies have become central to the promotion and preservation of Scottish culture. Later Scottish writers, such as Robert Louis Stevenson (1850–1894), author of *Treasure Island* (1883) and *Kidnapped* (1886), and J.M Barrie (1860–1937), author of *Peter Pan* (1911) made enduring contributions to children's literature. In addition, Scottish writer Sir Arthur Conan Doyle (1859–1930), creator of the Sherlock Holmes stories, is considered one of the originators of the genre of crime fiction.

CULTURE

Arts & Entertainment

Throughout centuries of British rule, the Scots have kept their distinctive cultural identity alive through dance, music, literature and other forms of art. Being part of Great Britain but outside the mainstream of English culture allowed Scottish arts to grow independently, and this fostered creativity. Today Scotland is considered to be at the forefront of many artistic disciplines in the UK.

Scotland is the only nation in the world that boasts two UNESCO "Creative Cities," a distinction given to cities with a strong and contemporary artistic environment. Edinburgh was named a "City of Literature" in 2006, and in 2008, Glasgow became a "World Centre of Music." Both cities reflect a Scottish arts renaissance that sprang up after decades of economic decline and depression during the mid-to-late 20th century.

Since the turn of the 20th century, Scottish artists and architects have risen to international prominence. During the era of art nouveau (which peaked from 1890 to 1905) and the arts and crafts movement (an international aesthetic movement that also peaked at roughly the same time as art nouveau), the Glasgow School of Art came to be known as one of Europe's finest art schools. Its most famous student, the architect Charles Rennie Mackintosh, designed groundbreaking buildings and furniture that helped usher in an era of modern architecture and design. Today, the Glasgow School of Art still attracts students from all over the world, and many credit the school and its students for maintaining Glasgow's status as a capital of the arts in the early 21st century.

The Edinburgh International Festival, which began as a theater, opera and dance festival in 1947, has also been a leading force in the country's artistic life. Now a three-week-long event featuring performers from all over the world, the festival has spawned additional cultural arts festivals, including the Edinburgh Fringe Festival, for the performing arts. Other festivals include the Edinburgh International Book Festival, the Edinburgh Film Festival, the Edinburgh Jazz and Blues Festival, and the Edinburgh Military Tattoo—an international celebration featuring Scottish regimental music and dance, held on the Edinburgh Castle Esplanade.

While the British once considered the Scottish "burr" inferior to the typical English accent, Scottish writers, starting with famed 18th-century poet Robert Burns, have always celebrated their unique speech patterns. Groundbreaking contemporary Scottish authors such as Irvine Welsh (1958–) and Suhayl Saadi (1961–) have taken this tradition a step further, capturing "the language of the streets" as it is spoken by modern working-class Scots and the new immigrant community. In addition to their innovative use of dialect, these writers are known for their accurate portrayal of the harsh economic and cultural realities faced by these segments of urban Scottish society.

While the bagpipe typically epitomizes Scottish music, Celtic and classical music thrive in Scotland as well. Since the 1980s, Scotland has also become a hotspot on the alternative rock scene, and home to bands such as Franz Ferdinand and Belle and Sebastian. In fact, Glasgow is largely considered second only to London as a house music center in the United Kingdom.

The most popular sports in Scotland include football (soccer), rugby, golf, and curling. Golf, which originated in Scotland, has been played since the Middle Ages, and one of the world's most famous courses is at St. Andrews. Highland Games are dedicated to traditional athletic events found in the Scottish Highlands. Events include hurling the Scottish hammer or "tossing the caber" (a long pole) end over end.

Cultural Sites & Landmarks

It is estimated that there have been over 2,000 historic castles in Scotland throughout the years (though it should be noted that the definition of what a castle is varies). Perhaps the best known and certainly most visited is Edinburgh Castle, which sits atop Castle Rock on the base of a long-extinct volcano in the city of Edinburgh. This spot, the highest in the area, was used as a defensive position for inhabitants of Scotland dating back to the Iron Age (which roughly lasted from around 800 BCE until the fifth century CE in the British Isles). Around 600 CE, a Celtic fortress there was taken by invading Angles (Germanic-speaking peoples) and given the name Edinburgh.

While the oldest part of the existing castle dates to the late 11th or early 12th century, buildings were added on through the years. The palace dates to the early 15th century, and the old Parliament Hall dates from around the same time. Surrounding the castle is the Royal Mile, a historic district that includes St. Giles, a 16th century cathedral; Holyrood House Palace, a former abbey which was converted into a palace; and the Parliament House, which was home to the first Scottish Parliament before it was dissolved by the English in 1707.

Scotland's historical and cultural heritage also includes five World Heritage Sites, as designated by the United Nations Educational, Scientific and Cultural Organization (UNESCO). They include St. Kilda, a grouping of remote islands which holds dual status as a cultural and natural site; the Old and New Towns of Edinburgh, recognized for their medieval and neoclassical architecture and planning, respectively; New Lanark, an 18th-century cotton mill village; and the Heart of Neolithic Orkney, a grouping of Neolithic monuments, including ceremonial and burial sites, that dates back five thousand years. The Antonine Wall, a fortification which is part of the border line of the ancient Roman Empire, was added in 2008 to the transnational World Heritage Site known as Frontiers of the Roman Empire.

Scotland is also a nation of renowned beauty, particularly evidenced by the glacial valley of Glencoe in the Scottish Highlands. The glacial valley is said to be among the most beautiful places in Scotland. It is also the site of the 1692 Glencoe Massacre, which increased tensions between the Scots and British and helped spur a series of rebellions and uprisings a generation later. Now a popular spot with hikers and walkers, its rugged beauty has also made it an ideal film location. Movies that have been filmed in Glencoe include *The Highlander* (1986), *Rob Roy* (1995) and *Harry Potter and the Prisoner of Azkaban* (2004).

Another natural site which has brought Scotland international fame is Loch Ness in the Scottish Highlands. While the body of water has the distinction of being Scotland's second deepest loch (and second largest by surface area, as well), most visitors are enamored with the loch's supposed resident, the Loch Ness Monster. Stories about a type of prehistoric water creature living in the lake have persisted for centuries, but

the mythical beast became famous after the release of a disputed photograph of the creature in 1934 (allegedly revealed to be a hoax in 1994). Since then, the lake has become one of Scotland's most popular tourist attractions and the site of numerous scientific studies.

Golf has incorporated itself into Scotland's rich cultural heritage, mainly because the Scots are credited with turning it into a sport. In fact, golf has been played in Europe in some form since the 14th century—some say as far back as Roman times. In 1744, the world's first golf organization, the Honorable Company of Edinburgh Golfers, was formed in Leith and established the first written rules for the game. In 1754, the Royal and Ancient Golf Club of St. Andrews (R&A) was established in the seaside town of St. Andrews, which contains the famed Old Course on St. Andrews, the oldest golf course in the world. As of 2010, there were over 550 other golf courses in Scotland.

Libraries & Museums

The National Museums Scotland is a family of six institutions: the National Museum of Scotland (consisting of the Museum of Scotland and the Royal Museum), the National Museum of Costume, the National Museum of Flight, the National War Museum, and the National Museum of Rural Life. The repository for all of these museums is the National Museums Collection Centre. Along with the country's extensive national museum system, the country also boasts organizations such as the National Trust for Scotland, which is the steward of many historical properties throughout the country.

Scotland's National Library has a collection of about 15 million printed items, more than 100,000 manuscripts, and about two million maps. Their online database catalogs their collection, as well as those in other libraries.

Holidays

In Scotland, as in England, public holidays are often known as "bank holidays," because banks are closed and many people have the day off from work. Like the English, Scots celebrate December

26 as Boxing Day (St. Stephens Day); historically, a day on which employers gave "Christmas boxes" or presents to their employees. New Year's Eve is celebrated as "Hogmanay," with bonfires, torch parades, gift-giving, and drinking. New Year's extends through January 2.

The birthday of Robert Burns (January 25) is celebrated as an unofficial holiday. On this and other occasions, "Burns Nicht" ("Burns Night") suppers are held in Scotland and around the world to honor the poet's memory.

Youth Culture

As in many parts of Europe, football (soccer) is very popular in Scotland. Thus, it is customary among youth to follow their favorite professional teams, often fanatically. Additionally, football is played both on school teams and in local leagues. Rugby is the second most popular sport, followed by shinty, a game similar to lacrosse that is played with a ball and stick. Curling, a winter sport which typically involves moving a granite stone across an ice surface with brooms to reach a target, is also popular. Equestrian sports and hunting are also common, especially in the Highlands and rural areas, and sailing and wind-surfing have become more popular in coastal areas in recent years.

As in other parts of the UK and Ireland, the local pub (formally known as a public house) is often the center of social life in neighborhoods or villages. Unlike drinking establishments such as bars in the U.S., pubs are considered to be suitable gathering places for families, and youth will often congregate at pubs to play darts or video games, or to listen to music. In urban areas, youth over the age of eighteen typically frequent clubs to hear live music. While traditional Scottish music remains popular, Scotland's growing pop and alternative rock scene is drawing larger and younger crowds.

SOCIETY

Transportation

Scotland's major cities are connected to each other, and to major cities in England and Wales,

with regular rail and bus service. Glasgow has a small underground train (subway) system. Commuter rail is available in and around major cities, although many prefer to use buses, which are inexpensive and typically offer more frequent service. Taxis (which are moderately expensive) are easy to find in the larger cities, but may only be available on call elsewhere. Bus service (called coach service for longer journeys) is available in both rural and urban areas, and other transportation hubs. In rural areas, private car ownership is often considered necessary.

Drivers in Scotland travel on the left hand side of the road, with the driver's seat on the right side of the car. Seat belts are required by law and cell phone use while driving is prohibited.

Transportation Infrastructure

Scotland's Trunk Road Network has over 3,400 kilometers (2,115 miles) of paved road which falls under the jurisdiction of the Scottish Ministers and the Transport Scotland team.

International flight service is available in Glasgow, Edinburgh, Aberdeen and Inverness, and international ferry service connects Scotland to Belgium, Northern Ireland and Norway. Additionally, there are many national and private ferry services available for reaching over 100 of Scotland's islands. Small, charter plane services also offer service to some islands.

While the major cities and towns are accessible by major roadways (called trunk roads), roads in the rural areas are generally small and often winding. In addition, travel to outlying areas can take a long time because of the slow speeds necessary to drive safely on these roads.

Media & Communications

Although the UK broadcasting system is nationalized, the media in Scotland and other parts of Great Britain are generally thought to maintain their objectivity, and do not suffer from government censorship.

BBC Scotland, the national television and radio broadcasting system for Scotland, is essentially an independent unit of the British Broadcasting Corporation (BBC), which is based in London. BBC Scotland operates the channels BBC Scotland One and BBC Scotland Two (two of the five television channels available without satellite or cable television service), and produces content specific to Scotland. It also runs two Scottish radio stations (one that broadcasts in English and one in Gaelic). BBC television and radio networks from London area available in Scotland, and Scots can get channels from Europe and elsewhere via satellite broadcasters or from cable services. Public access TV has also been introduced in recent years.

The Scotsman, published in Edinburgh, *The Herald*, from Glasgow, and *The Courier*, from Dundee, have the largest circulation for Scottish newspapers. Major British newspapers, such as *The Times* and *The Daily Mail* (based in London), publish limited editions (often called "tartan" editions, presumably referring to the tartan pattern found in weaving that is associated with Scottish culture) in Scotland.

Affordable access to wireless service, especially in rural areas, has become an issue in recent years. The government, non governmental organizations (NGOs), and private companies have made efforts to bring wireless to more remote locations in Scotland, but is smaller towns or rural villages, there may still only be a few paid public access points. However, it is estimated that Internet usage in Scotland stands at 80 percent of households in 2013.

SOCIAL DEVELOPMENT

Standard of Living

Scotland, as part of the United Kingdom, ranks 14th on the United Nations Human Development Index of 187 nations, as of 2013.

Water Consumption

Scotland, like other countries in the UK, abides by the EU Drinking Water Directive, which is based on World Health Organization standards for water quality. According to Water UK, Scotland's water supply is 99.89 percent in compliance with the EU Drinking Water Directive, according to the 2013 tests.

Access to adequate sanitation in Scotland is at the same high level as water access. According to an OECD (Organisation for Economic Co-operation and Development) publication, households in Scotland pay more for water usage than do many in countries such as Mexico because the government is pricing water in such a way that it accounts for the cost of supply as well as the cost of wastewater treatment.

Education

Scotland's educational system is separate from that of England. Since 1999, education has been controlled by the devolved Scottish Parliament, and is administered by the Scottish Executive's Education Department (SEED).

Scotland has a long history of support for public education, due in part to the Scottish Reformation, which emphasized that every Christian should be able to read and interpret the Bible. The Scottish Parliament established a system of general public education in 1696, making it the oldest such system in modern Europe.

There are preschools for three- and four-year-olds. Primary schools are for ages four through 12; these include "Gaelic Medium Schools" which teach all subjects in Gaelic. Secondary schools are for ages thirteen through sixteen. Specialized schools include religious schools run by the Roman Catholic Church, and independent schools ("private schools"), which provide either primary or early secondary education. After completing secondary schools, students must pass an examination (the Scottish Certificate of Education) in order to qualify to attend university.

Scotland has about a dozen universities, many of which date from the Middle Ages. The oldest is the University of St. Andrews, founded in 1413. It is the third oldest in the United Kingdom, after the Universities of Oxford and Cambridge. Other major university towns are Edinburgh, Glasgow, Aberdeen, and Dundee.

Women's Rights

Scottish women initially took part in the suffrage movement that gained momentum in England in the late 19th and early 20th century. By 1918, Scottish women over the age of thirty gained the right to vote. However, it was not until 1928 that all women over the age of 21 gained the right to vote, affording them equal voting rights to men. Despite having earned this right, Scottish women still lag behind their male counterparts in terms of political representation. As of the 2011 elections, about 35 percent of the members of Scottish Parliament are women, and as a result of the 2015 elections, 20 of Scotland's 59 members in British Parliament are women.

Pay inequality and equal access to advancement remain major issues for women in the Scottish workplace. As of 2014, Scottish men continue to earn an average of nine percent more than women in most professions, and female immigrants are routinely paid less than women native to Scotland. In addition, women are much less likely than men to hold executive positions, and more likely to hold secretarial or clerical posts. Furthermore, according to recent studies, sexual harassment is common in the Scottish workplace, but only a small percentage of women report harassment for fear of losing their jobs.

In the home, recent statistics show that nearly three-quarters of Scottish women have assumed most primary domestic responsibilities. In fact, faced with low wages and expensive or inaccessible childcare, many women chose not to enter or return to the workforce after childbirth. Women who do return to the workforce often leave children with family members, but are unable to earn enough money to pay them. As such, it is reported that nearly 500,000 women in Scotland work for free as caregivers.

Additionally, one in five Scottish women face domestic violence, according to Equal Opportunities Scotland. Women's rights advocates say that because of the stigma associated with domestic violence, there has been a definite lack of public education about the issue in Scotland.

The Scottish government has taken steps in recent years to address gender inequality in Scotland, including the passage of the Gender Equality Duty, which is part of the Equality Act in 2007. This legislation requires the government to set and meet goals for increasing equality in the workplace and in other aspects of public life. These include closing the earnings gap between men and women, and assessing how public policies can adversely affect women. The government has also invested in a campaign to end violence against women, and instituted a new maternity leave policy which ensures women a full year of leave without losing their jobs.

The new policy also designates that women receive a percentage of their regular pay rate for the first nine months of maternity leave. In addition, there are new laws in the works to ease the childcare burdens of working mothers, allowing them to request flexible work hours until their children reach 16 years of age. However, some critics contend that these benefits will discourage employers from hiring women, and instead advocate a more equal distribution concerning childcare between women and men, rather than continuing to assume that the caregiving will be done by women.

Health Care

Scotland is part of the UK National Health Service, the British nationalized system of health care. NHS Scotland is administered by the Scottish Executive Health Department (SEHD). Medical personnel either work directly for the NHS, or as independent contractors. The country is divided into fifteen area health boards. The country has 28 self-governing NHS Trusts, which provide medical services.

GOVERNMENT

Structure

In 1707, Scotland and England formally unified by signing the Acts of Union and establishing the United Kingdom. The Scottish and English Parliaments were dissolved, and a new United

Kingdom Parliament established. Scottish matters were then handled by an England-based Cabinet official.

When the Scottish Parliament was reestablished in 1999, the Scotland Executive (formerly called the Scottish Office) was established to represent Scotland at the UK level. This office is now part of the UK Department of Constitutional Affairs. Within the UK Parliament in Westminster, Scotland is represented by fifty-nine representatives. The UK Parliament continues to legislate matters related to taxes, social security, (UK) national defense and military, international relations, and broadcasting.

The Scottish Parliament is a unicameral body of 129 members. The queen appoints a first minister and an executive committee, known as the Scottish Government, who are recommended or nominated by the Parliament. The Scottish Government and Parliament are responsible for health care, education, the judiciary, laws, and local government. The Scottish Parliament may refer matters back to the UK Parliament should they feel that that body is better able to address it. Discussions continue within Scotland and the UK as to the future nature of the Scotland/UK relationship, with consideration of even further distance—running the spectrum from full independence on one side to simply increased fiscal control on the other. In 2014, a referendum was held in Scotland regarding separating from the United Kingdom, with just under 45 percent voting to become independent.

Political Parties

Scotland's main political parties are similar to those of the United Kingdom, with the Scottish Labour (center-left), Scottish Conservative (center-right), and Scottish Liberal Democrat (center-left, and federalist) Parties. Parties unique to Scotland include the Scottish National Party (SNP), which wants Scottish independence from Great Britain. In the 2011 Scottish Parliamentary election, the SNP prevailed, taking 64 seats. The Scottish Labour Party followed with 38 seats, the Scottish Conservatives won 15 seats, the Scottish Liberal Democrats took five seats, and the

Scottish Green Party won two seats, with three independents and one with no affiliation. In the 2015 election for the United Kingdom Parliament, the SNP took 56, with Labour taking one, the Conservatives winning one, and the Liberal Democrats winning the other seat.

Local Government

Scotland's local government is handled by 32 unitary local authorities, known as councils. Prior to reorganization in the late 20th century, local government was handled by 33 traditional counties. There are six cities in Scotland: Glasgow, Edinburgh, Aberdeen, Dundee, Inverness, and Stirling. Cities are designated as such by the government under a process known as letters patent.

Judicial System

Scotland has its own legal system, known as "Scots law," which is based on Roman law rather than on English-style common law. Three types of courts characterize the Scottish legal system: civil, criminal, and heraldic. Civil and criminal cases are heard in district and sheriff courts. The nation's supreme courts vary, with the Court of Session acting as the Supreme Court for civil appeals, the High Court of the Justiciary hearing criminal appeals, and cases related to heraldry are heard in the Court of the Lord Lyon.

Scotland's legal system is unique in its choice of verdicts, which may be "guilty," "not guilty," and "not proven." For the latter two verdicts, there is no possibility of retrial. Jury trials feature juries of 15 people as opposed to the common 12 seen in other countries.

Taxation

The government of the UK levies an income tax, a social security or national insurance tax, a value-added tax (VAT), and stamp tax. A council tax is levied by the local government. Corporations are also taxed.

As part of the discussions regarding Scotland's future relationship with the United Kingdom, taxation concerns have been raised. In 2010, further steps towards "fiscal autonomy" for Scotland were discussed.

Armed Forces

Scotland's national defense is part of the greater UK defense structure. The British Armed Forces are made up of the British Army, the Royal Navy, and the Royal Air Force.

Foreign Policy

While Scotland's Parliament (established in 1999) is responsible for virtually all of Scotland's domestic affairs, foreign policy is still determined by the British Parliament in London, at which Scotland has 59 elected representatives. Queen Elizabeth II (1926–) remains Scotland's head of state, and the country has no national prime or foreign minister, but rather is represented by a first minister, which is the leader of Scotland's ruling party. The first minister represents and promotes Scottish interests abroad in matters that are diplomatic or commercial. However, the first minister cannot represent the UK in political matters.

As part of the UK, Scotland does not have its own representatives at the European Union (EU), the UN, or other international governing bodies, nor does it have separate membership in treaties or pacts such as the North Atlantic Treaty Organization (NATO), or trade organizations such as the Organization for Economic Co-operation and Development (OECD). Additionally, Scottish troops are enlisted in the British military, and have served in every major British military engagement, including, most recently, the conflicts in Iraq and Afghanistan.

Scotland's independence movement, which has existed in some form or other as long as Scotland has been part of the UK, has gained support since the Scottish National Party (SNP) won a majority in Parliament in 2007. While the SNP has won all elections since then, it did lose the push for independence in the 2014 referendum. However, the push by the SNP for Scotland to be a completely independent country remains a part of its platform. Those opposed to Scottish independence argue that, in international policy issues, a united Great Britain has more power and can use resources more wisely. They also contend that Scotland as a separate nation would

be weaker, and that its monetary resources would be stretched too thin.

However, several foreign policy issues in recent years have shown how Scotland's foreign policy interests are often at odds with those of the greater UK, and these issues have helped the independence movement gain support. For example, there was widespread Scottish disapproval of the UK's participation in the U.S.-led invasions of Afghanistan and Iraq in 2001 and 2003, respectively. A majority of Scots are also at odds with the UK's plans to build nuclear weapons. Additionally, many Scots feel that when there are military base closings, they disproportionately affect areas of Scotland, and that Scottish interests are not being served in issues such as fishing rights off coastal waters or international environmental protection pacts.

Human Rights Profile

International human rights law insists that states respect civil and political rights, and also promote an individual's economic, social and cultural rights. The United Nations Universal Declaration on Human Rights (UDHR) is recognized as the standard for international human rights. Its authors sought the counsel of the world's great thinkers, philosophers, and religious leaders, and were careful to create a document that reflects the core values shared by every world culture. (To read this document or view the articles relating to cultural human rights, go to: http://www.udhr.org/UDHR/default.htm).

In Scotland, the adoption of the European Convention on Human Rights (which has been ratified by all member states of the EU) was technically passed by the newly revived Scottish Parliament even before the act that created the Parliament took effect. Human rights are therefore one of the central principles of the new Scottish-run government, but the enforcement of the convention has proved tricky.

Scotland has maintained its own legal system since becoming part of the UK in 1707. Based on Roman law, the Scottish legal system has unique features which distinguish it from the legal systems of other parts of the UK and other countries in the EU. However, lawyers and judges found that it was difficult to carry out the provisions of the convention under existing Scottish law. For example, the system through which people could file complaints according to the convention didn't match up with the Scottish system, and Scottish judges found themselves having to make difficult decisions about how to route human rights complaints. While the UK Equality and Human Rights Commission maintain a branch in Scotland, it was decided that, due to the legal particularities, Scotland should have its own authority. Thus, the Scottish Commission for Human Rights was established by law in 2006, and began operating in 2008.

While the goal of the UK Equality and Human Rights Commission is to protect human rights, the commission cannot give individuals legal assistance. Instead, it helps educate individuals about their rights under the law and institutions about how the law applies to their operation. The goal of the Scottish Commission for Human Rights is similar, and includes consulting and educational training. The commission is also charged with reviewing laws and monitoring the implementation of any recommendations made by the UN. Critics of both organizations say that neither can be effective because they cannot provide direct advice or assistance for those filing human rights claims.

In general, most human rights violation claims in Scotland have to do with equal pay or protection under the law, discrimination based on ethnicity or national origin, religion, gender, disability, age, sexual orientation, health status, or other issues of identity. The death penalty has been outlawed in the UK since 1969.

Migration

According to the government of Scotland, its migration rate fluctuates but has seen an increased number of immigrants in the early 21st century. In 2013, the net gain of immigrants from other UK countries and overseas was 10,000 people.

Overview of the Economy

Reestablishment of the Scottish Parliament has given Scotland far more control over its own economy. Scotland's economy is largely based on service industries (including tourism) and high technology. Scotland's economy improved dramatically in the late 1970s with the discovery of petroleum and natural gas in the North Sea. In the 1990s, Scotland developed its high technology industries, such as electronics and biotechnology.

The banking system in Scotland is different from that in the rest of the United Kingdom. There is no central bank, and several private banks (the Royal Bank of Scotland, the Bank of Scotland, and the Clydesdale Bank) are allowed to print their own bank notes. These are legal currency along with UK banknotes, but are not "legal tender" (that is, no one is required by law to accept them as payment). Edinburgh has become a center for financial services, and is one of the largest financial centers in Europe. In 2014, the financial services sector was responsible for 7.1 percent of the country's gross domestic product (GDP).

Industry

Scotland's industry is primarily based on service industries such as tourism and finance. Manufacturing and heavy industries such as shipbuilding, mining, and steel have declined sharply since the early 20th century (although Scotland retains a significant shipbuilding industry). Their place has been taken by high technology sectors, such as electronics and biotechnology. As of 2014, the gross domestic product per capita was an estimated $37,280 (USD).

Labor

According to the government statistics office, the employment rate in the first quarter of 2015 was 73.4 percent of the population, with an unemployment rate of 5.6 percent.

Energy/Power/Natural Resources

Scotland has large energy resources in the form of North Sea oil and natural gas, discovered in the late 1970s. Coal production has dropped sharply, from its peak during the 19th century.

Fishing

According to the Scottish Government, Scotland is responsible for netting over 60 percent of the UK's volume of fish. Fishing grounds are highly concentrated on the west coast and in the North Sea. Fuel costs are a constant concern in the fishing community, as are declines in fish stock, particularly haddock and cod. Commercial fish farms raise salmon and trout, but catches there are also declining.

Forestry

Just under 18 percent of Scotland's land area is covered in forest. The industry generates 42 percent of the UK's lumber production. Softwoods dominate the industry, but according to the Scottish Forest Industries Cluster, hardwood production is steady and should grow. The industry also predicts that the softwood sector harvest will increase by 25 percent during the next decade, offsetting the need for imports within the UK, which imports 90 percent of its paper and 80 percent of its lumber.

The Forestry Commission Scotland manages the country's 660,000 hectares (1,630,895 acres) of forest. The agency has plans to invest £15 million annually in new plantings in order to mitigate climate change, while still meeting the country's timber needs.

Mining/Metals

While mining in Scotland was critical to its economy in the 19th century, the last deep coal mine in operation in Scotland closed in 2002.

Agriculture

Agriculture is a fairly small sector of Scotland's economy. As of 2013, the agricultural sector (including forestry and fisheries) accounted for about 15 percent of GDP. Traditional farms had declined in profitability for several years, only significant government subsidies have allowed many to be profitable. However, heavy investment in aquaculture led to an increase in that portion by over 30 percent from 2012 to 2013, triggering the recent growth in the sector as a whole.

The main crops include wheat, barley, oats, and potatoes. Scotland is also noted for its production of whiskey.

Animal Husbandry

Livestock include dairy and beef cows, sheep, pigs, and poultry.

Tourism

The tourist trade is a major sector of the Scottish economy. In 2013, just under 11 percent of Scotland's jobs were tourism related. 2.4 million foreign visitors traveled to Scotland, as did 12 million from other parts of the United Kingdom, and spent £4.6 billion ($7.8 billion USD). The most popular destinations include the cities of Edinburgh and Glasgow, with their vibrant cultural attractions, and the Scottish Highlands, rich in natural beauty and history.

Joanne O'Sullivan, Eric Badertscher

DO YOU KNOW?

- The 18th century poet Robert Burns is the author of the famous poem "Auld Lang Syne," sung at New Year's Eve celebrations.

- Hugh MacDiarmid (Christopher Murray Grieve) was a poet who helped start Scotland's 20th century literary renaissance. He wrote many of his works in "Lallans" or Lowland Scots.

- Harris Tweed, a popular Scottish textile, is woven in the Outer Hebrides.

Bibliography

Anne-Valérie Cadoret, ed. *Scotland*. 1st American Ed. New York: Knopf, 2001.

Caroline Bingham. *Land of the Scots*. Glasgow: William Collins Sons & Co, 1983.

Christopher Harvie. *Scotland: A Short History* (new edition). Oxford: Oxford University Press, 2014.

Dominic Casciani. "Human Rights: The Scottish Experience." *BBC News*. October 3, 2000.

Fitzroy MacLean and Magnus Linklater. *Scotland: A Concise History*. (Illustrated National Histories) New York: Thames & Hudson, 2012.

John Abernathy. *Collins Little Book of Scottish History: From Bannockburn to Holyrood*. New York: HarperCollins, 2014.

Josephine Buchanan and Roger Smith, eds. *Insight Guides: Scotland*. 6th ed. London: Insight Guides (Apa Publications UK Ltd), 2014.

John Scotney. *Scotland – Culture Smart!: The Essential Guide to Customs & Culture*. London: Kuperard, 2009.

Lonely Planet, Neil Wilson and Andy Symington. *Lonely Planet: Scotland*. 8th ed. Oakland: Lonely Planet, Publication 2015.

Works Cited

Aidan Jones. "Equality Chief Warns of Maternity Law Backlash." *The Guardian*. 14 July 2008.

Angus Robertson. "It's Time for an Independent Foreign Policy." *Web Site of the Scottish National Party at Westminster*, 16 January 2007. http://westminster.snp.org/

Chitra Ramaswamy. "All Hands on Deck, Clubbers." *The Scotsman*. 18 March 2007.

"Customs of Scotland." *Encarta Encyclopedia Online*. http://cncarta.msn.com

David Batty. "Divorce Total Lowest For 29 Years." *The Guardian*. 30 August 2007.

David Maddox. "Baby Boom Helps Boost Scotland's Population." *The Scotsman*. 25 July 2006.

"Doing Business in the United Kingdom." *Communicaid*. http://www.communicaid.com/cross-cultural-training

"Dos and Don'ts: Scotland." *Career Mosaic India*. http://www.careermosaicindia.com.

Douglas Fraser. "Scotland Demands More of a Say in EU Affairs. " *The Sunday Herald*. 23 September 2001.

Fiona Shepard. "Glasgow Music and Club Scene." *See Glasgow*, www.seeglasgow.com

Graeme Murray. "Travel Guide proves it's No Rough Guide to City; Lonely Planet Insists Glasgow Is Alive and Kicking for Tourists." *Evening Times*. (Glasgow) 23 May 2007.

"His Life and Work." *Charles Rennie Mackintosh Society*. http://www.crmsociety.com/hislifeandwork.aspx

Marianne Taylor. "Arts Bible Devotes An Entire Issue To City Creative Scene." *Evening Times* (Glasgow) 9 November 2007.

Nick James, "Edinburgh in June." *Sight and Sound International*. August 2008.

Phil Miller. "Why Glasgow Really is The City of Music: U. N. Accolade Means Scotland Has Two Creative Cities." *The Herald* (Glasgow) 20 August 2008.

"Population Highest in 25 Years." *BBC News*. 24 July 2008. http://news.bbc.co.uk

Rosalyn Thiro, Ed. *Eyewitness Travel Guides: Scotland*. 1st American Ed. New York: DK Publishing, 1999.

"Scotland's Place in the United Kingdom (UK) and Ireland – Lone Parent Households." *General Register Office for Scotland* http://www.gro-scotland.gov.uk/statistics/publications-and-data/occpapers/

"Scotland's Population 2007 - The Registrar General's Annual Review of Demographic Trends." *General Register Office of Scotland*, 15 August 2008. http://www.gro-scotland.gov.uk/statistics

"Scottish English." *Learning and Teaching in Scotland*, http://www.ltscotland.org.uk

Shan Ross. "Don't Talk with Your Mouth Full, Scottish Slobs Are Told." *The Scotsman* 15 November 2005.

"Scotland's Languages: The Words We Use." Writing Scotland, Learning Journeys. *BBC Scotland and Creative Context*, http://www.bbc.co.uk/scotland/arts/writingscotland

"The Gender Agenda." *Equal Opportunities Commission Scotland*, July 2007

Sagrada Familia Cathedral in Barcelona, Spain /Stock photo © narvikk

SPAIN

Introduction

Through the centuries, the kingdom of Spain has had a profound influence on politics, music, art, and literature. It is a country with a widely diverse terrain and a highly homogeneous population, and the combination of history, natural beauty, and seasonable climate makes it a popular destination for tourists.

GENERAL INFORMATION

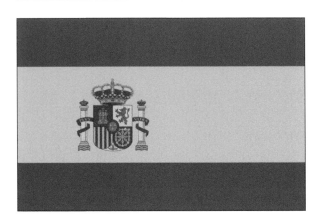

Official Language: Spanish
Population: 47,737,941 (2014 estimate)
Currency: Euro, which Spain began using in January 2002.
Coins: The Euro has eight coin denominations: 1, 2, 5, 10, 20, and 50, as well as a 1 Euro coin and a 2 Euro coin. While the denomination side of a Euro coin remains the same throughout all countries that have adopted the Euro as currency, the image on the coin's face side varies according to the country that released the coin into circulation.
Land Area: 192,278 square miles (498,980 square kilometers)
Water Area: 2,467 square miles (6,390 square kilometers)

National Motto: "Plus ultra" (Latin, "Further beyond")
National Anthem: "Marcha Real" ("Royal March")
Capital: Madrid
Time Zone: Central European Time (GMT +1)
Flag Description: The Spanish flag is composed of three horizontal stripes, with a large yellow stripe and the middle, bordered by two smaller red stripes. The yellow stripe is twice the size of each red stripe. In the left-hand side of the yellow band is a version of Spain's coat of arms, which generally consists of a crown atop a shield that is flanked by two columns.

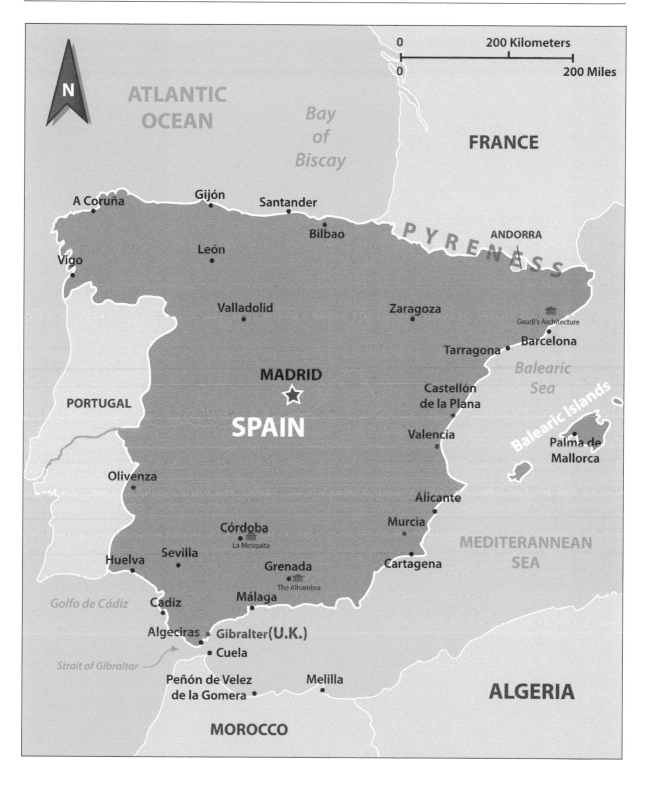

Principal Cities by Population (2012):

- Madrid (3,300,00)
- Barcelona (1,600,000)
- Valencia (831,598)
- Seville (703,029)
- Zaragoza (685,963)
- Maálaga (571,731)
- Murcia (453,985)
- Palma de Mallorca (419,285)
- Las Palmas (385,973)
- Bilbao (351,864)

Population

Spain has a lower population density than most European countries. As is the case throughout Europe, much of Spain's rural population is moving into the cities. Currently, the majority of the population—79 percent—reside in the urban areas, which are densely populated.

Immigrants have also recently begun to arrive, and while some non-Europeans have had trouble integrating into Spanish society, the resistance to immigrants appears to be lower in Spain than in many other European countries. According to the National Institute of Statistics (INE), the number of immigrants living in Spain in 2009 was 5.5 million, accounting for roughly 12 percent of the population.

As of 2014, roughly 55 percent of the population is between 15 and 54 years old. The average life expectancy in Spain is around 81 years; it is estimated that women in Spain have the highest life expectancy in Europe.

Languages

The official language, Spanish, is spoken by 74 percent of the population. Another 17 percent, in the northeast, around Barcelona, speak Catalan. Galician is spoken in the northwest of the country, and Basque is spoken by approximately two percent of the population in the north. In Spanish North Africa, Spanish and Arabic are spoken.

Native People & Ethnic Groups:

Most Spaniards are composites of Mediterranean and Nordic ethnicity. However, distinct ethnic groups include the Basques, Catalans, Galicians, and Gypsies.

There are 17 autonomous communities in Spain, including País Vasco (English, Basque Country; Basque, Euskal Herriko), in the northern part of the country. With a population of approximately two million, Basque Country is comprised of the Spanish provinces of Álava, Vizcaya, and Guipúzcoa. In recent years, the Basque government has declared its intention to secede from Spain, and a radical separatist movement known as ETA (Euskadi ta Askatasuna, or Basque Homeland and Liberty) has launched a violent campaign toward that end.

Gypsies have remained separate for centuries, but are now beginning to move into cities and integrate with Spanish society. As a result, conflicts sometimes arise in schools and neighborhoods.

Religions

Spain is predominantly a Roman Catholic nation, with a large percentage of the population consistently identified as such. According to a 2009 report from the Spanish Center of Sociological Research, an estimated 76 percent of Spaniards identify as Catholic. The constitution also recognizes the importance of the Catholic Church in Spain. Other religions include Anglican, Baptist, Spanish Evangelical, Greek Orthodox, Islam, and Judaism. In Spanish North Africa, most of the European population is Roman Catholic, while most of the North African Spaniards are Muslim.

Climate

In general, Spain's climate is temperate, with hot summers and cold winters (particularly in the interior hills). The coastal areas are more moderate, with cool, cloudy days.

The temperature varies widely. Along the northern coast, the average winter temperature is 9° Celsius (48° Fahrenheit), and the average summer temperature is 18° Celsius (64° Fahrenheit). The central plateau has an average winter temperature of 4° Celsius (39° Fahrenheit), and an average summer temperature of 24° Celsius (75° Fahrenheit).

The rest of mainland Spain has an average winter temperature of 11° Celsius (52° Fahrenheit) and an average summer temperature of 23° Celsius (73° Fahrenheit). The Canary Islands, Balearics and Spanish North Africa average more than 14° Celsius (57° Fahrenheit) in the winter and about 22° Celsius (72° Fahrenheit) in the summer.

Madrid has some of the most extreme weather in Spain, with average temperatures of 9° Celsius (48° Fahrenheit) in the winter, and 31° Celsius (88° Fahrenheit) in the summer. The city gets very little rain between June and October.

About three-quarters of Spain is dry, receiving less than 50 centimeters (20 inches) of rain annually, and experiencing frequent droughts. The northern coast receives more rainfall, approximately 97 centimeters (38 inches) each year. The central plateau receives less than 38 centimeters (15 inches). The rainfall in the rest of mainland Spain ranges from 25 to 60 centimeters (10 to 24 inches).

ENVIRONMENT & GEOGRAPHY

Topography

Spain is about the size of the American states Arizona and Utah combined. Geographically, Spain accounts for more than four-fifths of the Iberian Peninsula. There it is bordered on the north by the Bay of Biscay, France and Andorra, on the west by Portugal, on the east by the Mediterranean, and on the south by the Mediterranean Sea, Gibraltar and the Atlantic Ocean. Other Spanish territories include some small areas in Morocco, plus the Balearic Islands, and the Canary Islands.

Morocco is 30 kilometers (19 miles) to the south, across the Straits of Gibraltar. Along the coast are the Spanish regions of Melilla, a peninsula, and Ceuta, which includes Pennon de Velez

de la Gomera and two island groups. Together, these are known as Spanish North Africa.

The Canary Islands reveal a diverse landscape that includes volcanoes, forest and desert. The best-known Balearic Islands are Ibiza, Mallorca and Menorca. The islands are especially known for their beautiful beaches.

The central region of the country is a high plateau called the meseta. This plateau is really two plains areas nearly surrounded by mountain ranges. The most prominent and important of these are the Pyrenees, along the border with France. Other mountains include the Cantabrian Range in the north, the Iberian Mountains in the north and east, and the Sierra Morena in the south. Pasturelands are a main feature of the southern part of the country.

Most Spanish rivers are not navigable. The major rivers are the Tajo (Tagus), Duero (Douro), Guadiana and Guadalquivir. These rivers all run east to west and flow into Portugal.

The highest point in the Spain is Pico de Teide on Tenerife in the Canary Islands. The mountain rises to 3,718 meters (12,198 feet).

Plants & Animals

With its wide range of terrains, Spain enjoys great biodiversity. Forests and woodlands cover most of the country. Common trees include pine, laurel, beech and cork oak. Typical flowers include orchids, gentians, lavender, thyme and rosemary.

Spain maintains 12 national parks which protect representative species of plants and wildlife.

While hunting has eliminated many species of wildlife, red squirrels, tortoises, deer, ibex, wolves, chamois (a horned, hoofed mountain animal similar to a goat), bears, Iberian lynx, wild boar and a variety of reptiles remain in Spain. Gibraltar is home to the famous Barbary macaques, Europe's only species of wild monkey.

Many species of aquatic and migratory birds, mammals, amphibians and reptiles live in the wetlands of Castile. Native Spanish birds include flamingos, kites, vultures, herons, geese, bustards, storks, eagles and spoonbills. Spain has more than twenty breeding species of birds of prey.

CUSTOMS & COURTESIES

Greetings

From Spain's long and turbulent history, there remains an outward structure of sober formality to Spanish society. In that regard, Spanish people can be very somber and formal when greeting people for the first time. When meeting someone older, it is typically customary to look that person in the eye and extend a hand for a handshake. Common greetings include "Buenos días" ("Good morning") or "Buenos tardes" ("Good afternoon"). However, in Spain people often say "Buenos días" ("Good morning") until about 2:00 pm. After that, "Buenos tardes" ("Good afternoon") is commonly used.

Greeting friends and family is an entirely different matter. A customary greeting among adults is to stand about six inches apart, hold each other's arms and make kissing sounds, or "air kisses" to either side of the face. Men often greet each other with a brief hug around the shoulders with some space between their bodies. The customary phrase of welcome is "Hola," meaning "Hello." Young people use the less formal and more familiar phrase, "Que pasa?" ("What's happening?").

Gestures & Etiquette

Conversations in Spain are often characterized by physical gestures, in which one can see the warmth of Spanish people in their facial expressions and body language. Arms and hands are often in motion along with speech, and a speaker's face can reinforce their point of view as eyes, eyebrows, mouth, and lips all move together. In addition, conversation is not exactly an orderly activity, people interrupt constantly. Also, several people can talk at once. To the outsider, it can seem disorderly, or chaotic, but this kind of conversation is normal among friends and family.

In addition, personal space is not an issue most people think about in Spain. Typically, people stand closer to each other than is customary in other cultures. It is also important for younger people to show respect and deference to their elders. Finally, eye contact is important, especially during greetings and conversations.

Eating/Meals

Spaniards commonly start the day with a small breakfast, referred to as desayuno. Typically, this consists of sweet rolls or toast with jam, and café con leche, which is strong coffee made with frothed milk. A churro, a type of fried pastry similar to a doughnut and often sprinkled with honey or sugar, is another traditional Spanish breakfast food. However, they are also commonly eaten as a snack throughout the day, and are often sold by street vendors. Recently, cold cereal and hot chocolate have become more popular among children as breakfast staples.

Before the main meal Spaniards often eat a smaller and more informal meal, which can commonly feature tapas, a uniquely Spanish custom. Tapas are tiny portions, or appetizers, and cover a wide variety of basic ingredients such as eggs, meat, fish, cheese and vegetables. Common tapas dishes include omelets, battered squid, olives and cheeses, and seafood. Often, tapas are represented as a main meal when Spanish cuisine is prepared internationally.

The main meal is usually eaten sometime between 1:30 pm and 3:30 pm. Called la comida, it is made up of several courses. At typical meal might consist of soup, a main course such as a seafood or chicken dish and salad before concluding with dessert and coffee. Around 4:30 or 5:00 pm, it is common to have a snack called la marienda. A typical snack might just be bread and ham or, popular among children, bread with a piece of chocolate on top.

In Spain, dinner, called la cena, usually consists of a simple dish and a light dessert. It is rarely eaten before 9:00 pm, and sometimes may not start until midnight. There are historical reasons for this custom dating back several centuries. With its warm climate, Spanish businesses and schools often closed from 2:00 pm through 5:00 pm. Workers and students went home for their midday meal and then a nap called the siesta. Businesses reopened around 5:00 pm and did not close until around 8:00 pm.

Visiting

In Spain, it is considered common courtesy to bring a small gift when visiting. A typical gift might be pastries, cakes or chocolate. Adults might choose a bottle of wine. While flowers can also be given, it should be noted that chrysanthemums are associated with death in Spain, and are therefore commonly used in times of grieving, such as a funeral. In addition, it is considered polite for the host or hostess to be referred to by title—"señor" for men and "señora" for married women.

There are also a number of traditional or common manners one should follow when invited for a meal. These include waiting to be seated, or until the host or hostess is seated first; keeping one's hands on the table (it can be considered rude to put your hands in your lap); placing the fork or knife parallel to each other when finished eating; and avoiding leftovers, as good manners in Spain typically require that whatever is placed on the plate is eaten.

LIFESTYLE

Family

For most people in Spain, social life revolves around the family. Many Spanish families have three generations living under one roof, and young people typically do not leave home until they get married. It is also common for college students to attend universities in their hometown and to continue living at home. Spain has few retirement communities or nursing homes, and older people are cared for by their children.

Meals are often considered the center of family life. Meals at home are not rushed, and in addition to an abundance of food, there is an abundance of conversation. It is also common for all generations living under one roof to be included in all social gatherings or visits.

Housing

Spain largely transitioned from a rural to a mostly urban country in the last half of the 20th century. In fact, about 79 percent of the Spanish population now lives in urban areas. Because of this shift, housing has become a critical issue. In the early 21st century, Spain—along with Great Britain—had the least affordable housing market in Europe. As such, home ownership has become too expensive for low-income families or households.

In urban areas, multi-story apartment buildings or complexes are the norm, with most of them built in the latter half of the 20th century. Older apartment buildings are typically built around a courtyard, a feature commonly found in older Spanish homes. However, more recent urban housing is more utilitarian in nature, and contains fewer architectural details. In rural areas, older Spanish homes vary according to the region, and many are also built around a courtyard or enclosed patio.

Food

Spanish cuisine is considered one of the more distinctive in Europe, and Spaniards often take great pride in their food. Staple ingredients of Spanish cuisine include tomatoes, rice, fish and meats, and potatoes. Also, because Spain vies with Italy as the world's largest producer of olive oil, it is a staple of Spanish cooking.

Spanish cuisine has had some distinct historical influences. The influence of the Moors can be seen in the prevalence of such Middle Eastern ingredients as cumin and honey in Spanish dishes. Similarly, the conquest of the Americas by Spanish explorers beginning in the 16th century introduced chocolate to Spanish culture. As such, chocolate is another ingredient often used liberally in Spanish cuisine. Overall, there are four basic regional cuisines that can be found in Spain.

Galicia, on the Atlantic Ocean in northwestern Spain, is known for its seafood dishes, local scallops and veal. Asturias, a coastal region just east of Galicia, is famous for a bean dish called fabada. It is made with white beans, spicy pork sausage and the spice saffron. The Basque region in northern Spain is known for seafood dishes and fish soup. The area around Barcelona, known as Catalonia, is famous for a dish called seafood zarzuela, a fish stew. The area around Valencia is famous for paella, a stew made with saffron flavored rice and meat or fish. Andalusia in southern Spain is famous for gazpacho, a tomato soup served chilled.

Life's Milestones

For centuries, the Catholic Church was central to social and cultural life in Spain. Since the end of Franco's rule, actual church attendance has declined dramatically. However, religious ceremonies are still important functions in the life of Spanish families. Both the baptism of a child and first communion are considered important milestones. After the church ceremony it is customary to stage a reception for invited guests and serve a meal. For communion, boys are typically adorned in suits while girls wear long, white dresses. In addition, family members often purchase new clothes for the occasion.

CULTURAL HISTORY

Art & Architecture

The rich tradition of Spanish art and architecture began in the Middle Ages. This period in European history spans from the collapse of Roman civilization to the beginnings of the Renaissance. During the eighth century CE, the Iberian Peninsula, in which modern-day Spain is located, was largely conquered by the Moors, or Muslim people from North Africa. As the Moors began to gradually inhabit the peninsula, the arts became an important part of Moorish life. This is especially evident in Moorish architecture, which is heavily influenced by traditional Islamic architecture. Many grand mosques and palaces were constructed, most notably the Alhambra, a Moorish citadel overlooking Granada, Spain. Among the contributions from this period are the use of mosaics and the outdoor patio.

Spain was also heavily influenced by Baroque architecture, which came to prominence during the 17th century. Spanish Baroque is particularly evident in Spain's cathedrals and colonial architecture. The style is characterized as appealing more to emotions rather than to intellectualism, with lavish detailing and ornamentation. The Churrigueresque style was a prominent Spanish Baroque style. This style was attributed to architect José Benito de Churriguera, whose main works included churches and cathedrals.

In the 16th and 17th centuries, the Spanish Empire flourished, and Imperial Spain was considered the most powerful country in the world. Enriched by conquests in North and South America, the Spanish royal court commissioned art to celebrate its place in the world. Together, the court and the Spanish Catholic Church, which began a counter-reformation against Protestantism, created the "golden age" of Spanish art. This period is also referred to as the Spanish Renaissance due to the influence of the Italian Renaissance on the uniquely Spanish art styles.

During this period Spanish art flourished. Significant painters from this extended era included Domenikos Theotokopoulos (1541–1614), Diego Velasquez (1599–1660) and Francisco de Zurbaráán (1598–1664). Theotokopoulos, known as El Greco (the Greek) because he was born on the Greek isle of Crete, was renowned for his paintings of saints, often distinguished by the striking use of light on his subject's faces. Velasquez, appointed the court painter for King Phillip IV, used figures in the royal court and people of his native Seville as subjects for his paintings. Zurbarán was known for his religious depictions in his paintings. In this regard, he is considered a Spanish Baroque painter, a style often characterized by the use of color and light, and the depiction of drama. Zurbarán is also known for his portrait and still life paintings.

Spanish painter Francisco Goya (1746–1828) is considered one of the last masters of European painting prior to the 1800s. He worked in a realist style until late in his career. Then he began painting more grotesque figures and scenes of violence. One his most famous works, *The Third of May 1808,* shows Spanish soldiers being executed by the conquering army of Emperor Napoleon of France.

Spanish art flourished once again in the 20th century. Paradoxically, this was a time when Spain was impoverished and in conflict. Pablo Picasso (1881–1973) was perhaps the most famous artist during this century. He gave birth to the revolutionary art style called cubism. In this style of art, the artist reassembles the subject into components with more angular forms. Picasso's painting *Guernica* was a protest about the bombing of a town in the Basque region of Spain during the Spanish Civil war. Two other Spanish masters, Joan Miró (1893–1983) and Salvador Dali (1904–1989), achieved world fame for their paintings in the surrealist style.

Music

The Catholic Church especially dominated Spain's cultural life until the 20th century. One consequence of this is the absence of established concert music until that time. Most classical music in Spain was composed for church services and did not achieve prominence on the world stage. Spanish composers of prominence during the early and late Renaissance periods included Tomás, Luis de Victoria (1548–1611), Cristóbal de Morales (1500–1553), and Francisco Guerrero (1528–1599), all known for their sacred, or religious, compositions.

However, two composers changed the fortunes of Spanish classical music. Both Isaac Albéniz (1860–1909) and Enrique Granados (1867–1916) wrote solo piano music that is performed by pianists all over the world. One of the most frequently played pieces of classical music composed in the 20th century is *Concierto de Aranjuez,* a piece for solo guitar and orchestra by Joaquín Rodrigo (1901–1999).

The most influential Spanish musician of the last century was the classical guitarist Andrés Segovia (1893–1987). The guitar was invented in a town in Andalucia (Andalusia) in the late 18th century, but before Segovia, the instrument was mostly associated with folk music, not classical music. However, Segovia arranged older compositions for classical guitar, and many composers then composed pieces for Segovia. Essentially, Segovia is widely credited with bringing the guitar as a solo instrument to the classical concert state.

Dance & Drama

Flamenco is a form of Spanish folk music and dance that has deep roots in Spain's history. Flamenco originated in Andalusia in southern Spain as the music of the Roma people, commonly called gypsies. Flamenco is often characterized by tragic songs of romance and love sung or danced in dramatic fashion with the accompaniment of a guitar. The dancing typically uses the heel and toe with prominent hand clapping and finger snapping. Flamenco began to be performed in cafés in the 19th century as it spread outward from Andalusia to the rest of Spain. Today, it is often performed in concert halls and looked upon as an important part of Spain's unique cultural tradition.

Drama in Spain has not been as well developed an art form. This is due perhaps to the restraining influence of the Catholic Church throughout much of Spanish history. Lope de Vega (1562–1635) was the one Spanish playwright to achieve lasting fame until the 20th century. Said to have written between 1,500 and 2,200 plays, Vega is considered the first Spanish dramatist to make a living exclusively as a playwright. Other famous early Spanish dramatists include Juan de la Encina (1469–1533). Often regarded as the founder of Spanish drama, Encina is known for his secular drama.

Literature

Much of the knowledge of ancient Greece and Rome that was rediscovered during the Renaissance periods of Europe was preserved in Moorish Spain. Moorish Spain itself was also home to two giants of medieval thought: the Jewish philosopher, Moses Maimonides (1135–1204) and the Muslim philosopher, Averroes (1126–1198), also known as Ibn Rushd. The former, though he settled in Egypt, is known for his code of Jewish law and his influential Jewish teachings. The latter is known for his integration of Greek though with Muslim philosophy.

The re-conquest of Spain from the Moors produced the medieval epic poem *Cantar de Mio Cid*. Considered the oldest epic poem in Spanish history, it retells the true story of El Cid as he defended Spain from the Muslims. Miguel de Cervantes (1547–1616) remains the prominent historical figure of Spanish literature. Cervantes' *Don Quixote* is considered the first novel written in Western Europe. The novel is about the adventures undertaken by a romantic and somewhat confused nobleman named Don Quixote. After reading too many stories about knights, he rides off in search of adventure. The novel records the comic adventures of the idealistic Don Quixote in a world turned more cynical since the Middle Ages.

In the 20th century, as political tensions mounted in Spain, nationalism, socialism and civil strife became themes of Spanish literature. One notable Spanish writer was Federico García Lorca (1898–1936), whose works of drama and poetry were translated into many languages after his death. Lorca was strongly committed to the ideals of the Spanish Republic during the Spanish Civil War (1936–1939). He was executed after being captured by the Nationalist forces of General Francisco Franco during the war.

CULTURE

Arts & Entertainment

The arts play a vital role in contemporary Spanish cultural life. From the 1930s until 1975, Spain was ruled by a dictatorship under General Francisco Franco. During Franco's reign, the government used censorship and political intimidation to curb free expression among Spanish artists. Spain finally established a democracy in the 1970s, allowing artists to freely practice their art in their own homeland. Artists and writers who had lived in exile returned to Spain. With censorship lifted, influential works of art, film and ideas that had dominated art scenes throughout Europe and the rest of the world were freely expressed and integrated into Spanish art and culture.

Contemporary Spanish art is still influenced by this release of creative energy that came with the restoration of democracy in the 1970s. Since that time, the Spanish public, once thought of as conservative and disapproving, has developed a robust appetite for the arts. The Constitution of 1978, in particular, had an important effect on this change, as it gave more power to regional government. In addition, the Spanish ministry of culture provides funding to these regional governments to distribute locally. The result has been a vigorous growth of arts education, contemporary arts museums, festivals and concerts nationwide.

Pedro Almodóvar is often considered the most famous filmmaker in modern Spain. Born into a rural peasant family, his films are more concerned with social relationships and families, and he often focused on exploring comedy in situations that other artists would portray as tragic. Overall, his films deal frankly, and comically, with sexual and family issues. This candor has helped make him one of the most popular and award-winning international filmmakers. Some of Almodóvar's most celebrated films include *Volver*, *All about My Mother*, and *Talk to Her*.

In the realm of literature, Javier Marías is a Spanish writer who has achieved international success. His books have been translated into more than thirty languages. In Spain his books typically achieve bestseller status. Perhaps his popularity in Spain is partly due to his work as a newspaper columnist. Every week, he produces a column of his thoughts and opinions that is widely read.

What is typically considered the greatest form of Spanish drama takes place away from a stage or theater, and in a bullfighting ring. Bullfighting is the dramatic sport for which Spain is most famous. The first corrida (bullfight) honored the coronation of Alfonso VIII in the 12th century. Bullrings are found all over the country. Each year, 30 million people watch 24,000 bulls perish in these rings.

In a highly stylized ritual, the torero (bull-fighter) is usually armed with a small cape and a sword, and faces down a bull. The torero waves the cape to draw the bull close in a series of charges, which fatigues the bull, and give the matador torero a better chance to perform and ultimately, stab the bull. Critics view bullfighting as a violent spectacle, because the event is highly dangerous to both animal and human, and often concludes with the bull's death.

Another uniquely Spanish drama is an annual event called the running of the bulls. Famous in the city of Pamplona, this tradition features a crowd of people attempting to outrun a herd of bulls set loose on the narrow city streets.

Cultural Sites & Landmarks

The Alhambra, located in the city of Granada, is perhaps Spain's most famous cultural site. One of the best representations of Moorish architecture, this palace and fortress was built in the Middle Ages by the Moorish sultans who ruled the area. From the outside the Alhambra looks more like a fortress with a plain redbrick exterior. Inside, there is a series of connected structures built around open courtyards. Beautifully proportioned columns and rounded arches separate the rooms, and intricate carving and ornamentation covers the interior walls and columns.

The city of Barcelona is home to several buildings, and parks designed by famous Spanish architect Antoni Gaudi (1852–1926). Two of Gaudi's most famous works are the Church of the Holy Family, known as La Sagrada Familia, and an apartment building called Casa Batlló. Most apartment buildings are rectangular and feature crisp right angles. However, the façade, or outer wall, of Casa Batlló, contains no straight lines or right angles. Instead, there are wavy, undulating lines, similar to the appearance of rippling water. Gaudi's architectural innovations were designed to surprise the viewer with the unexpected.

Altamira Cave is a unique Spanish historical site located in northern Spain, west of the city of Santander. The site contains Paleolithic art, including paintings of bison and other animals drawn approximately 15,000 years ago. The use of perspective, or depth, in drawing is often thought to have been invented during the Renaissance. Yet, these cave drawings achieve the same effect by using the uneven surfaces of the cave's walls. In fact, the cave art is of such outstanding quality that its authenticity was initially questioned when it was first discovered by an eight-year-old girl and her father in 1879. After their authenticity was firmly established, Pablo Picasso is reputed to have said, "After Altamira, all [art] is decadence!"

One of the most renowned religious landmarks in Spain is the Mesquita (mosque), located in the city of Cordoba in southern Spain. Built during the Middle Ages at the height of Muslim power in Spain, the building is famous for its many columns and the play of light in the building's vast spaces. Also of interest is how it embodies the long history of Cordoba. It was built on the site of an early Christian Visigoth church from the seventh century. Spain then was ruled by people called the Visigoths, who had replaced the rulers of the Roman Empire. After Cordoba was re-conquered by Christian rulers, the Mesquita was turned into the Cathedral for Cordoba.

Libraries & Museums

Madrid's three major museums are all located within walking distance of each other, on the named Paseo del Arte. The three museums, the Prado, the Centro de Arte de Reina Sofía, and the Thyssen-Bornemisza, also form the center of a wealthy district called Paseo del Prado on the eastern side of the city. This area is home to upscale restaurants and the famous Retiro Botanical Gardens, as well as several smaller museums.

The Museo del Prado is considered one of the greatest art museums in the world. It owes its extensive collection to the reach and power of the ancient Spanish kings. Their royal collections, dating back to the 16th century, are housed in the museum. The Prado holds more than 7,000 sculptures, paintings, and other works. It is most famous for its collection of paintings by Botticelli, Caravaggio, and the greatest Spanish masters, including El Greco, Velasquez, and Goya.

The Reina Sofía museum has many more modern and experimental pieces, including the work of Salvador Dali and the films of Luis Buñuel. It also houses some of Picasso's most famous paintings.

Holidays

Official holidays observed in Spain include Labor Day (May 1), National Day (October 12), and Constitution Day (December 6), which honors the approval of the constitution in 1978.

Local fiestas and celebrations are held in towns and regions throughout Spain. The Reconquest Festival, held each January in Granada, celebrates the Christian defeat of the Moors in 1492. In the south, the Festival de Cadiz is held in March. The country's oldest festival, it features parades and costumes.

During the first weekend in July, wild horses are rounded up and branded in the Rapa das Bestas, held in San Lorenzo, Galicia.

Youth Culture

In many ways, Spanish youth culture is very similar to youth culture in other Western nations, especially the U.S. Interest in music, food and fashion trends and styles is high, and Spanish teens are very much adapted to technology, such as cell phones and the Internet. In addition, while football (soccer) is the most popular sport, basketball and tennis also have gained huge followings.

However, marketers have pointed out in recent years that there are some important differences between Spanish and European youth and their American counterparts. Teens from the EU have developed and popularized different styles in dress and music than American youth culture. In fact, European youth are often more influenced by Asian culture than American culture. La Oreja de Van Gogh (Van Gogh's Ear) and La Quinta Estación (The Fifth Season) are two examples of bands popular among Spanish youth. In addition, Spain is further distinguished from the rest of Europe by the difference in family relationships. Most Spanish youth live at home until they get married and many men do no marry until the age of 30, taking the time to establish careers first.

There are also some disturbing trends affecting Spain's youth culture. Spain has a high dropout rate among high school youth. One of the consequences of the dropout rate is a high unemployment rate for young workers who lack necessary job skills.

SOCIETY

Transportation

It is estimated that more than three quarters of all passenger trips in Spain are made by car in the early 21st century. However, many Spanish cities or towns have older sections characterized by narrow streets, which can make driving challenging. Spain's largest metropolitan areas are still connected by rail, or high-speed trains. In addition to taxis and buses, the largest cities, such as Madrid and Barcelona, have metro trains.

Traffic travels on the right in Spain. In addition, wearing a seatbelt is compulsory while cellular phone use while driving is prohibited (unless using a hands-free system).

Transportation Infrastructure

Spain is often recognized for its history of public-private partnerships in the building and maintaining of transportation infrastructure. In fact, six of the world's top ten infrastructure companies (as of 2010) are based in Spain. Much of the growth since the 1960s has been concentrated on roadways. In addition, Madrid has a sophisticated rail system that connects the city to the farthest corners of Spain. The Madrid Metro is the second largest in Western Europe, and is a modern, efficient public transportation system used by tourists and locals alike.

In 2005, the Spanish government announced plans to invest a total of approximately $295 billion (USD) in transportation infrastructure over 15 years, with much of that investment going to railways; 10 percent was slated for maritime infrastructure, such as ports; and 25 percent was slated for highway improvements and developments.

Media & Communications

There are about 150 daily newspapers published in Spain. The Madrid daily, *El País*, is considered the most important paper in the country. Almost all papers are written in Spanish. However, a leading Barcelona paper, *Avui*, is written in Catalan, and there are several smaller papers written in English that serve the substantial expatriate English communities in Spain.

Spain has numerous privately owned television stations all across the country. Prior to democratic rule, however, all stations were controlled by the government. Certain regions, such as Catalonia, the Basque country, Galicia and Valencia, have stations that broadcast programming in the local language. Radio continues to be an important mode of communication, and the telephone system remains state-controlled. In addition, the rate of Internet usage was nearly 72 percent as of 2012.

SOCIAL DEVELOPMENT

Standard of Living:

In 2014, Spain had a Human development Index (HDI) ranking of 27th out of 187 countries.

Water Consumption

Generally, water supply and sanitation in Spain is characterized by good service quality and universal access. However, water usage has become a concern in Spain in the early 21st century. With growing pressure on the country's water resources, it was estimated in 2009 that an additional 22 percent of Spain's water resource capacity, as measured in 2001, would be needed to meet demand by 2015. In 2006, agriculture accounted for approximately 78 percent of water consumption. Additionally, in Southern Spain, where droughts are more common, desalination has become a focus.

Education

Education is compulsory six to 16 years of age. Primary education begins at age six and lasts for six years. After secondary school, students may take one or two years of vocational training or a two-year college-preparatory course that leads to the Bachillerato degree.

Education is free in public schools, which educate about 70 percent of the students in Spain. Most private schools, run by the Catholic Church, also receive subsidies that allow them to offer tuition-free instruction.

Spain has 71 universities, many with long-established histories. The Universidad Compultense de Madrid was founded in the 13th century by King Sancho IV of Castile. The University of Salamanca was founded in 1218 by King Alfonso IX of Leon.

The literacy rate in Spain is 97 percent overall (98 percent for men and 97 percent for women).

Women's Rights

Spain, perhaps more than other Western European nations, has had to overcome particular political and cultural challenges in establishing and protecting women's rights. This is largely because Spain's conservative political history has reinforced the concept of "machismo." Machismo is understood today as an exaggerated sense of masculine pride. In Spanish culture it is the ultimate sexist belief that men are superior to women. Historically, the Catholic Church taught women to serve men. During the Franco regime, a government propaganda agency advised women to:

> "Encourage him to enjoy his hobbies and support him without being too insistent. If you have a hobby, don't bore him by talking about it because women's interests are trivial compared with the interests of men. . . ."

This started to change with the Constitution of 1978, which guaranteed women equal rights. Furthermore, in 1986, Spain legalized abortion. As recently as 2007, Spain passed a gender equity law assuring women equal rights in the workplace. Progress can be seen at almost every level of Spanish society. Women's health and life expectancy has improved, educational opportunities for women have grown dramatically, and there are almost as many as women as men at Spanish universities. Many more women work out of the home than before, and achieve higher levels of employment in both business and government.

The UN produces an annual report that ranks countries according to gender empowerment. In the 2007–08 report, Spain was ranked 13th in the world, one behind the United States. Given Spain's political and cultural heritage, this high ranking shows how much has been achieved in women's rights in Spain in a relatively short time.

However, the rights, equality and safety of women are less secure in Spain than in most other members of the EU and the U.S. While the dictatorship of Franco may be thirty years in the past, there are still organized conservative groups that are strongly opposed to many of the changes brought by democracy, such as women's rights. Domestic violence against women remains a serious issue of concern, and violence and discrimination is even worse among immigrant women in Spain.

Health Care

The Spanish government pays for health care for those who pay social security. The quality of facilities and care varies widely.

Spain has approximately 34 doctors for every 1,000 people, but the distribution of physicians is uneven. Large cities have the best hospitals and the most medical personnel. In other areas, especially the interior, patients may have to wait a long time to see a doctor.

Patients who have private health insurance may choose their own doctors and generally receive better care than public health care patients. Despite these drawbacks, annual per capita health expenditure in Spain has increased in the past 20 years, from $220 to $2,601 (USD).

Life expectancy is 81 years overall; 78 for men and 84 for women (2014 estimate). Spain ranks 27th on the Human Development Index of 187 countries.

GOVERNMENT

Structure

Spain's government is a constitutional monarchy. The king is the hereditary chief of state. The head of government is the president. Normally, the king nominates the president from the majority party (or coalition) in Las Cortes Gnerales (the National Assembly), and the Assembly votes the president into office. The president then chooses a Council of Ministers.

The National Assembly is a bicameral legislature consisting of the Senado (Senate) and the Congreso de los Diputados (Congress of Deputies). The Senate consists of 259 members who serve four-year terms. The 350 Deputies are elected to four-year terms by popular vote. There is also a Council of State that makes recommendations to the government, but cannot make binding recommendations.

The Tribunal Supremo, or Supreme Court, represents the judicial branch of government. The voting age is 18, and suffrage is universal. There are 47 provinces on the peninsula and three island provinces. In addition, there are 17 autonomous communities and two autonomous cities.

Political Parties

Spain has a multi-party system of politics, but generally only two parties are dominant: the Popular Party (PP), which is the country's main center-right party, and the Spanish Socialist Workers Party (PSOE), which is center-left and characterized as progressive. Other major political parties include the Basque Nationalist Party (PNV), the Democratic Union of Catalonia (UDC), and the Galician Nationalist Block (BNG). In the 2004 elections, the PP became the governing party.

Local Government

Spain is divided into seventeen autonomous communities (similar to federated states), whose regional governments administer executive and legislative power. These communities are further divided into 50 provinces and then municipalities, which have their own extensions of governance. On the provincial level, there is a provincial deputation, which is not legislative and composed of a president and provincial deputies that are elected by city councils. Governance of municipalities falls to city councils, made up of a council-elected mayor and popularly elected city councilors.

Judicial System

While Spain stresses autonomy in its political divisions, the country is mostly judicially centralized. Thus, the autonomous communities only have state courts. Each community has a High Court of Justice, while there are provincial courts, or one court of appeal, in each province. Major cases go before the national Supreme Court. Courts known as first instance courts and examining courts are at the provincial level.

Legal aid is considered a public right and available for all cases in Spain.

Taxation

Spain has a national and provincial tax rate, with the rate varying at the provincial level. Taxes are also levied at the municipal level. Each citizen is responsible for income taxes and wealth taxes, the latter payable on capital assets such as property. Indirect taxes in Spain included the value-added tax (VAT), stamp tax, and transfer tax. Spain's standard corporate income tax rate is 35 percent.

Armed Forces

The Spanish Army, Navy, and Air Force make up the Spanish Armed Forces. In 2000, Spain abolished the draft and then struggled with recruiting. In fact, in 2008, an estimated seven percent of the military—estimated at 80,000 members—were foreigners.

Foreign Policy

In 1982, Spain joined the North Atlantic Treaty Organization (NATO). Spain's membership linked the country to the security concerns of the United States and Western Europe. In 1986, Spain joined the European Community, the organization that preceded the European Union (EU), of which Spain remains a prominent member. This inclusion marked Spain's acceptance and integration among the democracies of Western Europe.

For the most part, Spain has been content to follow the leadership of the EU on foreign policy issues. One significant exception is in Spain's dealings with the U.S. For many years, Spain and the U.S. remained close allies. However, when the EU did not favor the U.S.-led invasion of Iraq in 2003, arguing instead for a peaceful diplomatic resolution, most Spanish voters agreed with the EU's position. Nonetheless, José María Aznar, then head of government in Spain, favored American action, and sent Spanish troops to Iraq.

On March 11, 2004, three days before the general election, terrorists carried out an attack on the commuter train system in Madrid, resulting in the deaths of 191 people. While it was initially suspected that the attacks were carried out by Basque separatists, an armed group that demanded independence for the Basque people, it was officially determined that the attacks were directed by an Islamist terrorist cell. This confusion led many Spanish voters to conclude that the government had deliberately misrepresented the facts, and that the attacks were a result of the presence of Spanish troops in the Middle East. As a result, newly elected President Jose Luis Rodriguez Zapatero promptly withdrew Spanish troops from Iraq, a move which strained relations with the U.S. Nonetheless, economic and cultural ties between Spain and the U.S. have remained close.

Spain has also been content to follow the lead of the EU in European affairs. One point of disagreement between the EU leadership and Spain, however, is Cuba. Spain has always maintained close political, economic and cultural ties with Latin America. In fact, Spain has set itself up as the leader on Latin American affairs in the EU. While the EU has sided with the US in strongly criticizing communism in Cuba, Spain, which ruled Cuba for almost four hundred years, has overlooked the island nation's human rights issues and developed closer economic ties with Cuba.

Dependencies

Spanish dependencies include the Islas Chafarinas, the Peñón de Alhucemas, and the Peñón de Vélez de la Gomera, the latter two being rock fortresses, and the autonomous cities of Ceuta and Melilla, all located in North Africa.

Human Rights Profile

International human rights law insists that states respect civil and political rights, and also promote an individual's economic, social and cultural rights. The United Nations Universal Declaration on Human Rights (UDHR) is recognized as the standard for international human rights. Its authors sought the counsel of the world's great thinkers, philosophers, and religious leaders, and were careful to create a document that reflects the core values shared by every world culture. To read this document or view the articles relating to cultural human rights, click here: http://www.udhr.org/UDHR/default.htm.

In general, the Spanish government respects human rights. Millions of Spaniards remember living under a dictatorship, and their memories of the past have made them sensitive to human rights issues. As such, most Spaniards are determined to preserve democracy and the rule of law. However, a small minority continues to favor harsh treatment for people of differing political views, religions, races or sexual orientation that was prevalent under Franco's regime.

Spain has struggled with the Basque separatist movement and the Euskadi Ta Askatasuna (ETA), the armed Basque organization considered a terrorist operation. The organization has used bombing and assassinations as tools in its struggle to achieve independence from Spain. It is a continual challenge for Spain's democratic government to adhere to international laws when dealing with terrorist tactics.

Article 2 of the UDHR guarantees rights and freedoms to people without discrimination. Domestic violence against women has been an ongoing issue in Spain. While Spain has recently

undertaken educational campaign and set up special courts to deal with the issue, more than 60,000 cases are reported annually, with many more suspected as going unreported.

Discrimination against immigrants, especially those from Africa, is also a problem. Article 7 states that all people are equal before the law, and Article 9 states that no individual should be subject to arbitrary arrest or detention. However, there have been numerous cases where immigrants and other ethnicities were denied their rights and were subject to arbitrary detention. In fact, there have been several incidences of violence carried out against immigrants. Work conditions for undocumented workers have also been criticized as precarious and unsanitary. In light of Spain's recent increasing immigration, the country began considering immigration reform in 2009 that would target undocumented workers.

ECONOMY

Overview of the Economy

As a member of the European Union, Spain is required to have an open, modern, industrial economy. Prior to World War II, its economy was mainly agricultural. As of 2014, Spain's gross domestic product (GDP) was estimated at $1.5 trillion (USD). The per capita GDP was estimated at $33,000 (USD). In 2009, Spain's GDP per capital decreased nearly four percent, spelling the end of a growth trend of 16 years. Real growth did not return until 2014.

Madrid's rate of economic growth exceeds that of Spain as a whole. In addition, 73 percent of Spain's foreign investment typically goes to Madrid. The city's unique position in proximity to Africa, North America, and the rest of Europe has made it an important industrial hub.

Industry

Major industrial activities in Spain include the manufacture of processed consumer goods, machine tools, steel, automobiles, and electronics. Most of the country's industry is concentrated near the city of Barcelona, in the region of Catalonia.

Exports, primarily of motor vehicles, food, machinery and consumer goods bring in roughly $150 billion USD annually. Spain's largest single trading partner is France.

Labor

Spain's unemployment rate was almost 24 percent in 2014, an increase from 15 percent in 2008. Madrid's unemployment rate is significantly lower than Spain's. Madrid's workforce is generally highly educated, due in large part to the city's three major colleges, the Complutense, the Universidad Autonoma, and Carlos III University.

Energy/Power/Natural Resources

Among Spain's major natural resources are iron ore, lignite, copper, lead, zinc, coal, mercury, magnesite (magnesium carbonate), gypsum, fluorspar, uranium, potash, tungsten, and hydropower.

Environmental concerns include pollution by offshore oil and gas production, pollution of the Mediterranean Sea by raw sewage, air pollution, deforestation, desertification, and availability of clean water. Overpopulation and erosion have damaged the coast.

Fishing

The fishing industry is a centuries-old industry in Spain, spanning generations of expertise and tradition. As such, the Spanish fishing industry, in its modern form, is considered competitive and carries with it a good global reputation. In fact, the Spanish fishing fleet is considered one of the world's largest. Major catches include yellowfin tuna, sardines, horse mackerel, and pollock.

However, the Spanish fishing industry is facing challenges and struggles in the 21st century, such as an increase in illegal fishing, resulting largely from economic necessity and unemployment, and a domestic decrease in seafood consumption. (Spain, nonetheless, remains one of the largest per-capita consumers of seafood among European Union nations). This has caused the industry to focus more on exporting.

Forestry

Heading into the 21st century, the country was considered the fourth largest country in Europe for forest resources. It is estimated that roughly 35 percent of Spain is forested. Forest administration in the country is decentralized—the 17 autonomous communities oversee forest activities and administration—and deforestation has historically remained a concern. In 2002, the government approved the Spanish Forest Plan, which has a thirty-year time span.

Mining/Metals

Spain has a long history of mining and is home to the rich Iberian Pyrite Belt (IPB), which extends from Portugal to Spain, and is one of the world's largest deposits of sulphide. The Spanish mining industry is experiencing what some would consider a revitalization in the early 21st century, due to better technologies and exploration techniques, as well as the high price of metals. Much of the industry is based on gold and base metals. Coal remains Spain's most plentiful native source of energy. Other significant outputs in the mining industry include iron, pyrites, copper, lead, and zinc.

Agriculture

When Rome ruled Europe, Spain was known as the "Garden of the Empire." Today, arable land accounts for 26 percent of the country's area, and only nine percent of the labor force is engaged in agriculture.

Spain's dry climate limits the types of crops that can be grown successfully. The country is known for its oranges and olives, and is the world's largest producer of olive oil. Spanish farmers also produce barley, wheat, sugar beets, grapes, tomatoes, tangerines, peaches and nectarines, dry onions, chilies and green peppers, corn and potatoes.

Animal Husbandry

Spain's livestock industry is considered to be well developed, and became much improved after EU ascension in 1986. Pork production showed the largest gains between 2009 and 2013.

Spain also has large populations of both sheep and goat, and continues to be a leading exporter of meat.

Tourism

Spain is one of the most popular destinations for European travelers, and more than 48 million tourists visit Spain each year. In 2008 and 2009, Spain experienced an 11 percent decrease in tourism, which was attributed to increased, and inexpensive, competition and poor marketing. However, in recent years the tourism industry has rebounded.

Attractions include the climate, beaches and historical cities such as Ávila, Toledo, and Segovia. Popular attractions in Madrid include the Puerta del Sol ("Gate of the Sun"), the cathedral of San Isidro, and the Museo de Pinturas ("Museum of Paintings"), also known as the Prado.

The Costa del Sol ("Coast of the Sun") in the southern part of the country features many luxury resorts. The Summer Olympic Games were held in Barcelona in 1992.

The government has made efforts to attract even more tourists by improving infrastructure, especially the country's railroad system and highways.

Dan Rosen, Ellen Bailey, Alex K. Rich

DO YOU KNOW?

- The Extremadura section of Madrid is home to the endangered Iberian lynx, as well as more than 200 other species.

Bibliography

Anthony Ham. *Spain*. Oakland, CA: Lonely Planet, 2014

David T. Gies. *The Cambridge Companion to Modern Spanish Culture*. New York: Cambridge University Press, 1999.

Giles Tremlett. *Ghosts of Spain: Travels through Spain and Its Silent Past*. New York: Walker and Co., 2008.

Hamilton M. Stapell. *Remaking Madrid: Culture, Politics, and Identity after Franco*. New York: Palgrave Macmillan, 2010.

Joanna Styles. *Rough Guide to Spain*. London: Rough Guides, 2015.

John A Crow. *Spain: The Root and the Flower: An Interpretation of Spain and the Spanish People*. Berkeley, CA: University of California Press, 2005

John Hooper. *The New Spaniards*. New York: Penguin, 2006.

John F. Moffitt. *The Arts in Spain*. New York: Thames & Hudson, 1999.

Marian Meaney. *Spain - Culture Smart!: the essential guide to customs and etiquette*. London: Kuperard Publishers, 2010.

William D. Phillips Jr. and Carla Rahn Phillips. *A Concise History of Spain*. New York: Cambridge University Press, 2010.

Works Cited

http://elt.britcoun.org.pl/elt/y_euro.htm

http://encarta.msn.com/text_761575057__1/Spain.html

http://encarta.msn.com/text_761575057__1/Spain.html

http://encarta.msn.com/text_761575057__1/Spain.html

http://encarta.msn.com/text_761575057__1/Spain.html

http://encarta.msn.com/text_761575057__1/Spain.html

http://encarta.msn.com/text_761575057__1/Spain.html

http://findarticles.com/p/articles/mi_m2078/is_n3_v36/ai_13929553/pg_1?tag=artBody;col1

http://hdrstats.undp.org/indicators/279.html

http://portal.unesco.org/culture/en/ev.php-URL_ID=26064&URL_DO=DO_TOPIC&URL_SECTION=201.html

http://spanishfood.about.com/od/discoverspanishfood/a/spain_meals.htm

http://www.alhambra.org/eng/index.asp?secc=/alhambra/virtual_visit

http://www.alhambradegranada.org/historia/alhambraHistoria_en.asp

http://www.amnesty.org/en/library/asset/EUR41/006/2005/en/dom-EUR410062005en.pdf

http://www.andalucia.com/cities/cordoba/mosque.htm

http://www.answers.com/topic/spanish-literature-and-language

http://www.answers.com/topic/spanish-literature-and-language

http://www.askoxford.com/languages/culturevulture/spain/cervantes/?view=uk

http://www.askoxford.com/languages/es/culture/

http://www.britannica.com/EBchecked/topic/557573/Spain

http://www.britannica.com/EBchecked/topic/557573/Spain/258827/Internationalization-of-culture

http://www.clubcultura.com/clubcine/clubcineastas/almodovar/eng/homeeng.htm

http://www.csmonitor.com/2003/0626/p01s04-woeu.html

http://www.csmonitor.com/2005/0411/p05s01-woeu.html

http://www.dw-world.de/dw/article/0,2144,3183588,00.html

http://www.dw-world.de/dw/article/0,2144,3183588,00.html

http://www.ediplomat.com/np/cultural_etiquette/ce_es.htm

http://www.escuelai.com/spanish_culture/typically_spanish/customs.html

http://www.escuelai.com/spanish_culture/typically_spanish/customs.html

http://www.eurofound.europa.eu/eiro/2006/02/feature/es0602207f.htm

http://www.euroresidentes.com/Blogs/2005/03/women-in-spain.htm

http://www.eurotopics.net/en/magazin/magazin_aktuell/frauen-2008-3/artikel_villagomez_frauen_spanien/

http://www.expatica.com/es/survival/just_arrived/braving-the-highways-driving-in-spain-17302.html

http://www.fpa.org/topics_info2414/topics_info_show.htm?doc_id=673236

http://www.gaudiallgaudi.com/AA006.htm#Description

http://www.gaudiclub.com/ingles/I_VIDA/batllo.htm

http://www.greatbuildings.com/architects/Antonio_Gaudi.html

http://www.greatbuildings.com/buildings/The_Alhambra.html

http://www.iberianature.com/material/altamira.html

http://www.imagi-nation.com/moonstruck/clsc67.html

http://www.internetworldstats.com/eu/es.htm

http://www.kwintessential.co.uk/resources/global-etiquette/spain-country-profile.html

http://www.mcah.columbia.edu/alhambra/flash/start.html

http://www.nationsencyclopedia.com/World-Leaders-2003/Spain-FOREIGN-POLICY.html

http://www.ndpublishing.com/authors/marias.html

http://www.newyorker.com/archive/2005/11/14/051114crbo_books

http://www.nysun.com/opinion/housing-pain-in-spain/72501/

http://www.oddee.com/item_93915.aspx

http://www.rhrealitycheck.org/blog/2008/01/22/witch-hunt-against-spains-abortion-clinics-leads-to-strike

http://www.sallys-place.com/food/cuisines/spain.htm

http://www.sensesofcinema.com/contents/directors/06/almodovar.html

http://www.spainexpat.com/spain/information/business_etiquette_and_business_culture_in_spain/

http://www.spainexpat.com/spain/information/business_etiquette_and_business_culture_in_spain/

http://www.spainexpat.com/spain/information/business_etiquette_and_business_culture_in_spain/

http://www.spainexpat.com/spain/information/spanish art_culture/

http://www.spain-info.com/Living_in_Spain/Spanish-Public-Transport.htm

http://www.spanish-fiestas.com/art/spanish-artists-el-greco.htm

http://www.spanish-fiestas.com/art/spanish-artists-goya.htm

http://www.spanish-fiestas.com/art/spanish-artists-miro.htm

http://www.spanish-fiestas.com/art/spanish-artists-picasso.htm

http://www.spanish-fiestas.com/art/spanish-artists-velazquez.htm

http://www.spanish-fiestas.com/bullfighting/history.htm

http://www.spanish-fiestas.com/flamenco/

http://www.spanish-fiestas.com/spain-information/population.htm

http://www.spanish-fiestas.com/spanish-festivals/pamplona-bull-running-san-fermin.htm

http://www.spanishprograms.com/learn_spanish/learn_spanish_15.htm

http://www.state.gov/g/drl/rls/hrrpt/2004/41709.htm

http://www.state.gov/g/drl/rls/hrrpt/2007/100586.htm#

http://www.tripadvisor.com/ShowTopic-g187427-i42-k1351702-l8154803-Guide_to_Etiquette_in_Spain-Spain.html

https://www.cia.gov/library/publications/the-world-factbook/geos/sp.html

Several varieties of owls, including the great grey owl, are native to Swedish forests /Stock photo © PABimages

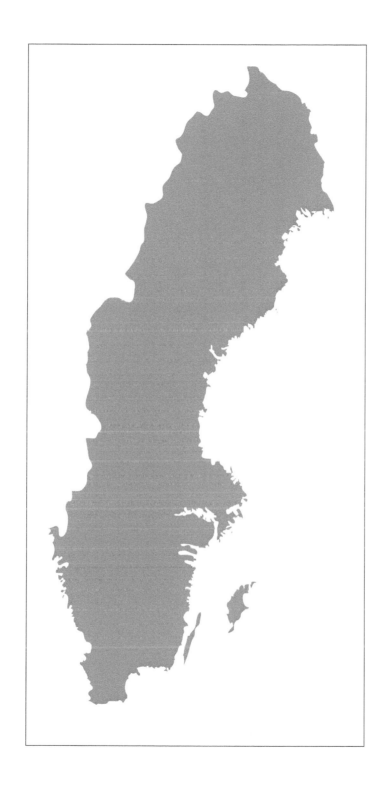

SWEDEN

Introduction

Sweden is one of the five nations that make up the area of northern Europe known as Scandinavia. The country's northern location creates extremes in daylight hours in the summer and winter. In fact, part of Sweden lies within the Arctic Circle.

In addition to its own contributions to world culture, Sweden also actively promotes cultural achievements and efforts benefiting the world at large. Since 1901, due to the legacy of Swedish chemist and armaments manufacturer Alfred Nobel, the Nobel Prize honors laureates from all over the world for their contributions to the sciences, literature, and the cause of peace.

As one of the only European countries to remain politically neutral throughout the 20th century, Sweden has long been a land of peace and prosperity.

GENERAL INFORMATION

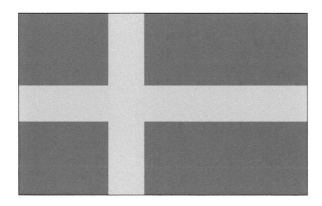

Official Language: Swedish
Population: 9,723,809 (2014 estimate)
Currency: Swedish Krona
Coins: Each Krona is subdivided into 100 öre. Coin comes in denominations of 50 öre, as well as in 1, 5, and 10 Krona.
Land Area: 410,335 square kilometers (410,335 square miles)

Water Area: 39,960 square kilometers (15,428 square miles)
National Motto: För Sverige i tiden ("For Sweden, with the times")
National Anthem: "Du gamla, du fria, du fjäll-höga nord" ("Thou ancient, thou free, thou mountain-crowned north")
Capital: Stockholm
Time Zone: GMT +2
Flag Description: The flag of Sweden features a golden-yellow cross displayed vertically against a blue background. The arms of the cross are situated closer to the hoist (left) side of the flag. The colors blue and yellow are also featured on the Swedish coat of arms.

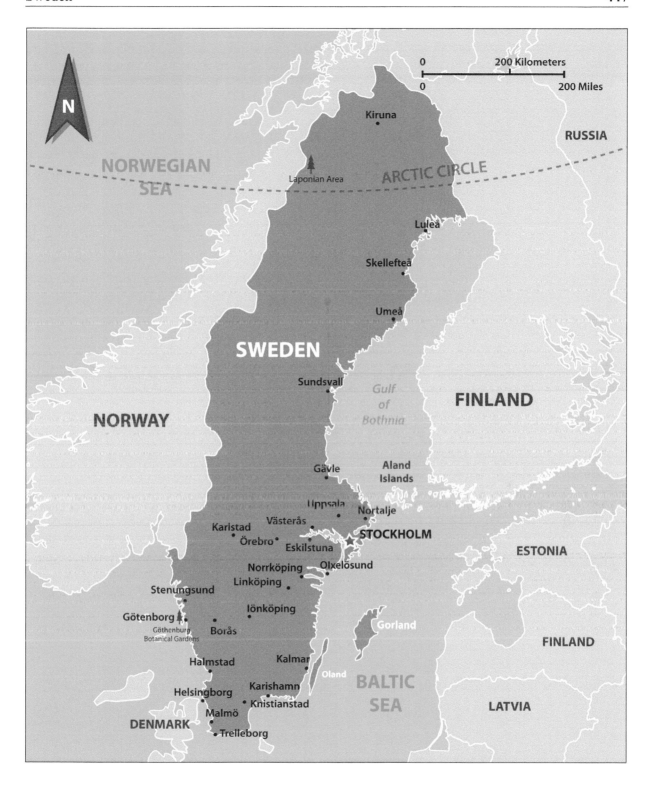

N

NORWEGIAN
SEA

Kiruna

RUSSIA

Laponian Area   ARCTIC CIRCLE

0   200 Kilometers
0   200 Miles

Luleå

Skellefteå

Umeå

SWEDEN

Sundsvall

NORWAY

Gulf
of
Bothnia

FINLAND

Gävle

Åland
Islands

Uppsala
Västerås   Nortalje
Karlstad
Örebro   STOCKHOLM
Eskilstuna
ESTONIA
Norrköping   Oixelösund
Linköping
Stenungsund
Iönköping
Götenborg
Göthenburg   Borås   Gorland
Botanical Gardens   FINLAND

Halmstad   Kalmar

Öland
Karishamn   BALTIC
Helsingborg   SEA   LATVIA
Kristianstad
Malmö
DENMARK   Trelleborg

Principal Urban Areas by Population (2012):

- Stockholm (1,300,000)
- Göteborg (528,237)
- Malmö (269,549)
- Uppsala (135,367)
- Västerås (109,092)
- Örebro (101,614)
- Linköping (101,031)
- Helsingborg (95,886)

Population

In 2014, the population of Sweden was estimated to be 9,723,809. Sweden has one of the highest life expectancies of any nation in the world: 81 years (80 for men and 83 for women). It is said that Swedes benefit from the healthy environment in which they live.

Sweden's population consists of several prominent minority groups, including 50,000 ethnic Swedes of Finnish descent. Other minority groups include people from the former Yugoslavia, Iran, Poland, and the other Scandinavian nations.

Large land area and relatively low population cause Sweden to have a low population density. However, the population distribution is heavily lopsided. The majority of Swedes live around the urban areas in the southern region of the country, called Götaland.

Languages

The official language of the country is Swedish; however, the Sami indigenous ethnic group, of which approximately 20,000 live in Sweden in the early 21st century, speaks Sami languages. Finnish is also spoken by Sweden Finns, who number approximately 170,000.

Native People & Ethnic Groups

Archaeologists believe that Sweden may have been inhabited as early as the Stone Age, 6000 to 4000 BCE. These ancient people were the earliest of the Sami tribes, who have remained in

Sweden ever since. Modern Swedes are descended from the medieval Vikings, with whom they share Germanic physical traits.

It is believed that the Vikings established a trading port on the island of Björkö, located west of Stockholm. Many European artifacts dating back to the ninth and 10th centuries can be traced to Birka, a Viking town on Björkö that for 200 years was one of Europe's busiest trading centers.

Despite being conquered by the Vikings in the ninth century and Russia in the 11th century, the Sami have remained in Sweden. They inhabit the northern area of Norrland, which is called Lapland.

The Sami speak a dialect of Swedish that is closely related to Finnish. Their colorful, patterned clothing is designed to protect against the cold. Ancient Sami were nomadic groups, but today, they live in villages and on family farms in Lapland. Most Sami families raise reindeer as livestock and use them for food, clothing, and farm work. There are over 100,000 Sami living in Scandinavia, 20,000 of which live in Sweden.

Religions

It was estimated in 2014 that 87 percent of the country's population was Lutheran. The remaining 13 percent comprised Roman Catholic, Muslim, Jewish, and Baptist faiths.

Climate

Sweden has a moderate climate and a long winter. Although summer temperatures are favorable, especially in the southern urban areas, some parts of Norrland reach cold extremes during the winter. Sweden's winter temperature average is in the range of –5° to –1° Celsius (22° to 30° Fahrenheit) and the summer average is roughly 14° to 21° Celsius (57° to 70° Fahrenheit).

Rainfall is not remarkably high or low in Sweden. Stockholm averages 55 centimeters annually (22 inches) while Goteborg receives roughly 67 centimeters (26 inches). Norrland and the Mountain Range receive copious amounts of snow during the winter. Typically all of the rivers and lakes in Sweden freeze over in the winter, and some are used as traffic routes for autos once they are frozen thick enough.

ENVIRONMENT & GEOGRAPHY

Topography

The country can be divided into four main geographic regions. These are the Mountain Range in the northwest, the Inner Northland, the Swedish Lowland in the central region, and the South Swedish Highland in the south. The Mountain Range area consists of the Kölen Mountains, which divide Norway and Sweden. Sweden is separated from its other Scandinavian neighbors by the Baltic Sea and the North Atlantic Ocean.

The southern region of the country, called Götaland, is separated into distinct highlands and lowlands. The Skåne region is made up of vast plains and has the best land for farming. It is also a very wealthy area that has many ancient castles and manors.

Småland is a rocky coastal region with many bays and inlets. There are several islands off the Småland shore, including the 137 kilometer (85 mile)-long Öland Island. Götland Island is another large island, known for its beautiful array of wildflowers and natural limestone formations.

The northern area of Norrland comprises three-fifths of the country's area. Much of this region is a vast, uninhabited forest that extends above the Arctic Circle. In the northern parts of Norrland, known as the "Land of the Midnight Sun," there is no sunlight during the winter, and the sun never sets during the summer.

Sweden's highest point is Mount Kebnekaise, in the Kölen Mountains, at 2,111 meters (6,926 feet). Along the Baltic and the Gulf of Bothnia, there are 7,600 kilometers (4,700 miles) of coastline. Major lakes include Vänern, the largest lake, as well as Märlaren and Hjälmaren. Major rivers include the Göta, the Dal, the Angerman, the Ume, and the Luleålv.

The capital city, Stockholm, is located on Sweden's eastern coast. It is a city surrounded by water, and some have called it "Venice of the North." Nearly a third of the city's central area consists of bays and channels separating the more than a dozen small islands and peninsulas upon which Stockholm is built. The coastal city lies on 14 main islands, and there are 24,000 more islands making up a nearby archipelago. This archipelago is casually referred to as Stockholm's "pearl necklace." Stockholm is also renowned for its so-called green zones. While water makes up almost a third of the city's area, parks and open spaces occupy another third.

Plants & Animals

Much of Sweden is covered by forest, lake and river habitats. Combined with its extensive coastline and vast national parks, the nation is home to many varieties of plants and animals. Wild orchids can be found on the island of Gotland. Swedish trees are mostly hardwood or coniferous. Common trees include birch, oak, pine, maple, and ash.

An unwritten law known as Allemansrätt, or Everyman's Right, allows Swedes to pick any vegetables, berries, flowers and any other plants on any Swedish land. The absence of trespassing laws means that families are welcome to wander into each other's fields and collect wildflowers. The same precept applies to swimming, hiking, and other nature-oriented activities.

Moose and deer are a common sight in the forests of central and northern Sweden. Squirrels, rabbits and badgers are also found in the forests. Further north, bears and wolverines roam the forests of Norrland, though these larger mammals are generally few in numbers and are considered endangered. Reindeer are important to the Sami tribes, who use them for carrying sleds and performing other tasks. The arctic lemming is a small migratory rodent native to Sweden.

Several varieties of owls, including the great grey owl, are also native to Swedish forests. Coastal birds include the Caspian tern, gull, and sea eagle. Inland waterfowl thrive in the country's lake habitats. The native whooping swan can be found living among ducks, cranes, and partridges.

Otters and whales are the most common sea mammals. Sweden's coast is heavily fished for cod, mackerel, herring, shellfish, and flounder, while the freshwater areas supply salmon, trout, and pike.

CUSTOMS & COURTESIES

Greetings

The most common salutation or greeting in Sweden is "Hej" ("Hello"). Along with "God mórgon" ("Good morning"), this can be used in formal or informal situations. "God dag," ("Good day") is also common, but is more equivalent to the phrase "How do you do" and often used formally. "God kväll" ("Good evening") is used mainly in formal situations and with elderly people. A more casual and humorous way of greeting friends is to say "Tjänare," ("Your servant"), which derives from the old fashioned phrase, "Jag förbliver Eder ödmjukaste tjänare" ("I remain your most humble servant").

Sweden is a rather reserved society in terms of interpersonal interaction. Nodding one's head is a common way to great a stranger in passing. If introduced in a formal situation, one can reply "Angenämt" ("Delighted"). Handshakes are common ways of greeting in both business and social situations, and should be firm and given while establishing eye contact. Traditionally, it is considered polite to shake hands with everyone in the room upon entry and exit, including children. Young people, however, will typically not shake hands when meeting friends. Close personal contact such as embracing or thumping on the back is not common among acquaintances, especially in public. Additionally, unnecessary touching is usually avoided.

Gestures & Etiquette

Since Sweden is a socialist and highly egalitarian society, emphasis is on equality and moderation, or "lagom" (a word loosely translated as "just the right amount"). Therefore, bragging, expressing emotional extremes, or speaking loudly or raucously are all considered impolite. Rather, one should speak calmly, softly, and truthfully, and exhibit modest behavior. Similarly, expressing competitive feelings or promoting competition is also not encouraged.

Eye contact in Sweden is seen as a mark of honesty and respect, and should be made when shaking hands, offering toasts or speaking to someone. In conversation, it is generally considered rude to interrupt the person speaking. Overall, Swedish culture emphasizes speaking only when one has something important to say. Thus, emphasis is on speaking in an honest and straightforward manner instead of beating around the bush.

The Swedish language does not have a word that corresponds directly to "Please" and it is common to use alternate phrases such as "Kan du" ("Can you?") or "Skulle du kunna" ("Would you be able to?"). Additionally, "Tack" ("Thank you") is used very often in a variety of circumstances. For instance, when leaving a store, it is common for both the customer and the clerk to thank each other as a way of saying goodbye. Similarly, after a meal one is expected to say "Tack för maten" ("Thank you for the food"). After a conversation with a stranger, an appropriate response is "Tack för sällskapet" ("Thank you for the company").

In Sweden, work and private life are distinctly separate. For example, it is considered impolite to discuss work at home, and it is also rare for work friendships to carry over into one's private life. It is also rare for family members to become coworkers. Oftentimes, this can make it difficult for foreigners working in Sweden to adapt to the culture.

Littering in Sweden is highly uncommon, and residents tend to have a great respect for public property.

Eating/Meals

The Swedish typically eat three meals per day. Traditionally, Swedish mealtimes centered on the daily routines and lifestyles of farmers and blue collar workers. They included an early breakfast (morgonmål), an early lunch (frukost) and a heavy dinner in the late afternoon (middag). Today, however, it is becoming increasingly common for most Swedes to eat breakfast when they wake, have lunch at noon, and then dinner in the evening, with lunch being typically no more than a single course. Additionally, having a mid-day snack of an open-faced sandwich (smörgas) or fruit is also common. Also, the famous Swedish smörgåsbord (a meal served buffet-style) is usually served at lunchtime.

Generally, Swedish dining etiquette is rather strict in formal situations. Swedes follow the European, or continental, style of eating: the fork in the left hand and the knife in the right. Elbows should always be off the table, and hands should always be visible and never in one's lap. After eating, the knife and fork should be placed at an angle on the right hand side of the plate.

One particular dining tradition unique to Sweden is the crayfish party, or kräftskiva. Due to restrictions on overfishing established in the 20th century, crayfishing was limited to the summer months, and crayfish parties are usually held in August. (Additionally, crayfish must be caught at night with nets or wire traps, usually using rotten or raw fish as bait). However, the high prices of locally caught crayfish have recently induced many Swedes to buy crayfish imported from the United States or China.

At the kräftskiva, guests wear paper bibs and hats, which traditionally feature designs of the man in the moon. The favored cooking method is to immerse the crayfish live in a pot of boiling water with sugar, salt, and dill. The crayfish are then typically eaten with the fingers, and it is common for all attempts at polite behavior to be disregarded (after all, sucking and slurping the crayfish out of the shell is considered the best way to get the meat). Side dishes at crayfish parties include bread and strong-smelling Västerbotten cheese (named after the province from which it comes). Beer and schnapps (strong Scandinavian alcohol) are also consumed in large quantities, and typically accompanied by snapsvisor, or drinking songs.

Visiting

In Sweden, guests are usually invited for coffee and cake, and less often for dinner. When visiting a Swedish family, it is common to bring a small gift for the hostess, such as flowers, wine, books, music, or chocolate (the latter especially if the family has children). However, flowers should not include white lilies or chrysanthemums, since these are often associated with funerals.

When visiting a particular town or region, knowledge of the region will be appreciated by a host. Visitors should avoid praising towns or regions other than the one they are presently in, since it might be offensive to the host's sense of local pride. Punctuality is appreciated, and guests should avoid arriving early. Additionally, it is important for guests to dress neatly and somewhat conservatively so as not to offend the host. It is also impolite to ask to see any rooms of the house other than the one in which the guest has been received. When invited for a meal, guests should try to finish everything on their plates, since not doing so would be an insult to the host. Lastly, within a day or two after visiting, guests should write or call to thank the host.

LIFESTYLE

Family

Family is highly valued in Sweden. In fact, in 2008, an estimated 74 percent of children under the age of seventeen lived with their parents. In addition, the number of children whose parents have separated has decreased since the turn of the 21st century. As further evidence of the high value of family in Sweden, the government has made it easier for its citizens to balance work and family life. Both men and women receive paid parental leave to care for newborn children, and universal low-cost daycare is provided to ensure that children are taken care of while their parents return to or enter the workforce.

Care of the elderly is also important in Swedish culture. In fact, Sweden spends more of its gross domestic product (GDP) on its elderly citizens than any other country in the world. Most elderly people receive benefits from the municipality in which they live, such as home care by health and service providers or options for special senior living.

Housing

Traditional houses in Sweden were notched or cross-joint log houses (knuttimmerhus), typically made of pine or spruce. This building technique, known as knuttimring, is thought to date as far back as the 11th or 12th century. The spaces between the tightly-notched logs were stuffed with moss or tarred flax, making the houses both sturdy and snug, and roofs were typically made of thatch, turf or wood. Swedish log houses had several rooms, and many had two stories. Often, the exterior was richly decorated with wood carvings.

In the 17th and 18th centuries, painting the outside of buildings red—using a deep red paint called falu rödfärg, which was dyed with a pigment from the Falu Copper Mine in the Dalarna Province—indicated wealth and social status. After the 19th century, Swedish farmers began to paint their farm buildings red as well, since the paint, which was similar to whitewash, protected the buildings from bad weather. Today, red buildings with white trim are seen as traditionally Swedish. Until the mid-19th century, this building style was prevalent in both the countryside and the cities.

In recent decades, particularly since the turn of the 21st century, there has been a significant migratory trend from rural to urban areas in Sweden, which has resulted in an increase of vacant rural homes and more pressure for cities to provide housing. In fact, as of 2005, over half of the population—an estimated 61 percent—resided in municipalities that reported a shortage in housing. In addition, roughly 20 percent of houses in Sweden are owned and operated by public housing companies.

Food

Generally, the cuisine of Sweden is similar to that of other Scandinavian cultures, most notably the native cuisines of Denmark and Norway, and is often based on simple and mild cooking. Traditional Swedish cooking is called husmanskost, and includes local meats, such as fish, pork and poultry, and local produce, such as cabbages, potatoes, turnips and other root vegetables. Since Sweden's cold winters limit the availability of fresh food, salted fish, preserved vegetables such as sauerkraut, and jams are common ingredients in meals. (Lingonberry jam is the most popular and traditional of Swedish jams, and it is often added to lighten the flavor of a heavy winter meal.) Smörgåsar, or open-faced sandwiches, are popular light meals for breakfast or lunch, and may include cheese, ham, hardboiled eggs, tomatoes, cucumber or fish roe (ripe fish eggs).

Probably the most internationally famous Swedish dish is köttbullar, or Swedish meatballs. This dish was believed to have been invented as a way to use up leftover scraps around the kitchen. Traditionally, the meatballs are made from ground beef, pork or veal mixed with cream, mustard and nutmeg. They are a popular dish at any smorgasbord, a Scandinavian-style buffet traditionally consisting of one course of cold fish dishes, one course of cold meat dishes and one course of hot dishes.

Desserts are an important part of Swedish cuisine. One of the most popular desserts is semla, a type of Swedish pastry made from cardamom-flavored wheat buns filled with cream and almond flavoring. Semla were traditionally eaten on Shrove Tuesday, just before Lent (in Christianity, a period of fasting and prayer prior to the observance of Easter), when all eggs, cream, and butter had to be consumed. Since semla require large amounts of all these ingredients, it was the perfect pre-Lent dessert. In fact, semla was the favorite dessert of Sweden's King Adolf Frederick (1710–1771), who died from digestion problems after consuming fourteen servings of it (in addition to a rich meal that featured caviar, sauerkraut and lobster).

Life's Milestones

The observance of Name Day is an important celebration in Swedish culture. The tradition, which began sometime in the 17th century, is celebrated much like birthdays, and typically includes parties and the presentation of gifts and cake. Traditionally, the Church of Sweden encouraged people to honor name days instead of birthdays, which they viewed as pagan (irreligious). Every year, the almanac put out by the Royal Swedish Academy of Sciences includes a calendar of every date and the name it celebrates. The list was revised most recently in 2001, and many dates now have two names, for a total of 651 names in the calendar. (Most days are named after saints or members of Sweden's royal family, but names are also added as they grow in popularity in the country). However, most of the names are still Swedish in origin, which can be unfortunate or considered exclusionary for foreigners. For example, due to the large number of immigrants from the Middle East, Mohammad is one of the most common names in Sweden, but there is no "Mohammad" on the official name day calendar.

Christmas remains the largest holiday in Sweden, with many Swedes returning home for family reunions. In fact, the Swedish version of Santa Claus was modeled on St. Nicholas, the patron saint of school children, further emphasizing the importance Swedish culture has historically placed on its youth.

CULTURAL HISTORY

Art

Sweden was somewhat removed from the rest of Europe throughout its history—it shares a land border with Finland and Norway. As a result, Swedish artistic traditions developed mainly in isolation and drew extensively from folk culture. One of the most prominent traditional arts of Sweden is glassmaking. King Gustav Vasa (1496–1560) founded the first Swedish glassworks in the mid-16th century. Early glassmaking centered on more practical items such as chandeliers, window glass, inkpot, and tableware. With the advent of modern techniques, glassmaking and glassblowing have been highly refined. Today, artistic glass pieces such as vases, figurines and goblets are blown and painted at these glassworks. In fact, the region of Småland, which is home to fifteen famous Swedish glassworks, is known as the "kingdom of crystal," or Glasriket.

Swedish painting of the 19th and 20th centuries is also quite well known. One notable Swedish painter is Carl Larsson (1853–1919). Larsson is famous for his oil and watercolor paintings celebrating Swedish family life, such as *Christmas Eve* (1904–1905). One of his most famous paintings is *Midvinterblot* (Midwinter Sacrifice, 1915), which features a scene from Norse mythology in which a king sacrifices himself for his people. Although Larsson created the painting at the request of the Swedish National Museum (spelled national museum in Swedish) in Stockholm, the museum later rejected it, which engendered much controversy. Larsson viewed this work as one of the most beautiful he had ever painted, and in 1997 the National Museum finally hung the painting where it was originally intended.

Architecture

The oldest surviving architecture of Sweden dates back to the Middle Ages, during which time religious buildings such as monasteries and churches were constructed in the Romanesque style. An example of this is Lund Cathedral, which was constructed in the early 12th century and features tall towers, few windows, and an astronomical clock, which was added in the 15th century. Another prominent style during this time was Gothic architecture; many churches were constructed in this style, which is distinctive for its red brick, such as 15th-century St. Petri Church, located in the city of Malmo. An example of Renaissance architecture is the Gripsholm Castle, which was constructed between the 16th and 18th centuries and is located near Stockholm. Baroque architecture is evident in the interior of Tyska Kyrkan, a 17th-century church in Stockholm. It features an atrium, tall altar, and large windows. The National Romantic Style, a merging of Nordic culture and the Arts and Crafts and Art Nouveau movements, was prominent in the 19th and 20th centuries. The Stockholm Court House and Stockholm City Hall, constructed in the early 20th century, were built in the National Romantic Style.

Drama

Cinema gained a foothold in Sweden as early as 1897, with King Oscar II (1829–1907) becoming the first person to be filmed in Sweden. During the silent film era, Swedish cinema received international acclaim, which eventually led prominent Swedish directors such as Victor Sjöström (1879–1960), considered the father of Swedish film, to relocate to Hollywood.

During World War II, cinema served as one of Sweden's central psychological defenses against the war. Films during this period became more serious and artistic, and often embraced nationalist or escapist themes. After the war, Swedish films were widely praised in international film festivals.

The 1970s and 1980s saw many women enter the film industry for the first time in roles other than actress, including directors such as Mai Zetterling (1925–1994), Gunnel Lindblom (1931–) and Marianne Ahrne (1940–). Swedish director Ingmar Bergman (1918–2007), who directed 62 films and 170 plays, became famous worldwide for his explorations of despair, death, hope, and insanity in his films. Nominated for an Academy Award nine times, Bergman remains the most influential voice of Swedish cinema.

Music

Swedish folk music coalesced, or blended together, in the early 19th century. Central instruments in the tradition are the fiddle, which arrived in Sweden in the 18th century, and the nyckelharpa. The latter is also called the "Swedish key fiddle" because it resembles a fiddle with keys, and is an instrument unique to Sweden. Players of Swedish folk music are generally known as spelmän. In 1910, the first National Gathering of Folk Musicians was held in Stockholm.

Although folk music was initially performed individually at local or family gatherings, in the 1940s, folk music groups known as spelmänslag became popular. The 1960s saw a folk music revival, and the genre became influenced by new styles such as jazz, as well as new instruments such as the saxophone, guitar and mandola,

creating a new hybrid of folk ensemble music. Other traditional instruments such as the hurdy-gurdy, a fiddle with a wheel or crank, and the Swedish bagpipe, or säckpipa, were also revived.

Every year since 1933, as many as 10 Swedish folk musicians are honored with the title riksspelmän, or National Folk Musician, after performing in front of a folk music jury. During the summer months, so-called "fiddler's meets" are typically held throughout the country.

Swedish film and music have been especially successful on a global scale. In 2005 alone, Swedish exports of music totaled $19 billion (USD). The first Swedish band to become popular outside the country was The Spotnicks, an instrumental rock group that has released 42s albums—selling more than 18 million records—since 1961. Perhaps the best-known Swedish band is ABBA, which made its international debut in England in 1974. As Sweden's largest musical export, ABBA has sold more than 350 million records worldwide. Even though the group disbanded in 1982, their music continues to be influential several decades later, even spawning a Broadway musical and film adaptation.

In the 1960s and 1970s, Swedish music experienced a movement known as "progg." Progg, which stands for progressive, was largely a reaction against capitalism and commercialization, and developed into an umbrella movement encompassing different musical styles, such as reggae, rock and folk. The movement also included diverse musical groups, from solo artists to record labels started by the two communist parties of Sweden. Liberal themes are central to the progg movement, and include eating organic food, living in the countryside and not importing clothing made by sweatshop laborers. Some more extreme groups within the movement embraced communism or anarchism, as well.

Among the indigenous Sami population in northern Sweden, a traditional musical form known as the yoik (or joik) has also experienced a resurgence in popularity. Rather than serve as an art form, the yoik is intended to be a method of memory sharing, community building and self-expression. For example, a yoik is conceived of as being part of that person or thing—a transformation of the essence of the person or thing into a musical form—rather than just a song. Among the northern Sami, yoiks are composed for a person at their birth. They are traditionally chanted a cappella, and may be accompanied by a drum, though in recent years other instruments have been introduced.

In the past, yoiking played a central role in traditional Sami shamanism, which caused the practice to be denounced by Christian missionaries as a form of witchcraft. For many years, yoiking was threatened with extinction and was primarily practiced in secret. After World War II, and particularly during the 1960s and 1970s, renewed interested in traditional culture spurred a revival of the yoik tradition. Sami artists such as Nils-Aslak Valkeapää (1943–2001) were central to raising awareness of, and pride in, the yoik tradition among both the Sami and outside communities. Today, popular Sami yoik artists include Wimme Saari (1959–), Mari Boine (1956–) and Ánde Somby (1958–). The rise in the popularity of the yoik has helped promote awareness and respect of Sami culture.

Dance

Swedish folk music is intended primarily as an accompaniment for dancing, with the triple-time polska being the most common dance and music tradition. Although the polska has existed in various forms for hundreds of years, it nearly disappeared from Swedish culture during the intense industrialization that occurred at the turn of the 20th century. Fortunately, through unearthing early films of dances and conducting oral interviews with elderly Swedes, researchers during the mid-20th century were able to collect enough information about the polska to preserve the tradition.

Literature

The earliest known literary work in Sweden is the Rök Runestone, a giant rock slab carved with the longest known runic inscription in stone, and which dates back to 800 CE. The stone is thought to have been written by a Norse king in honor of his son, a war hero. Following the introduction of

the printing press—as well as the standardization of the language that resulted when the Bible was translated into Swedish in 1541—Swedish literature developed rapidly. In 1766, the first Swedish Freedom of the Press Act was composed, which allowed for much greater literary freedom.

Many notable authors hail from Sweden. The famous botanist Carl Linnaeus (1707–1778), who invented the modern system of taxonomy, was one of the first Swedish authors to write for the general public. Selma Lagerlöf (1858–1940), a Swedish author famous for her fanciful children's book, *The Wonderful Adventure of Nils* (1906–07), won a Nobel Prize in Literature in 1909. One of the most influential Swedish authors is August Strindberg (1849–1912), a playwright who is known as one of the founders of modern theater. Strindberg was famous for writing naturalistic plays, such as *Miss Julie* (1888), which focuses on the complicated relationship between love, lust, hatred and social mores. He is also considered a pioneer of expressionism, a 20th-century literary movement which emphasized emotional state over reality.

Perhaps the most famous and read of all Swedish authors is Astrid Lindgren (1907–2002), whose children's books have been translated into more than eighty languages. These include *Pippi Longstocking* (1945), whose title character Pippi, a rebellious girl who does what she likes instead of what she is told, originally shocked many adults. This publication of *Pippi Longstocking* marks a shift in children's literature from books that emphasized morality to books that were true to children's feelings and experiences. Other noted Swedish authors have had success with the crime genre, including Stieg Larsson (1954–2004) and his "Millennium trilogy" (*The Girl with the Dragon Tattoo,* etc.).

CULTURE

Arts & Entertainment

Architecture is considered one of Sweden's most important art forms. The simplified, relaxed furniture design and textile styles used in Swedish homes have been highly influential in the Western World.

Twenty-first century Swedish artists include Benny Ekman (1955–), a painter, and Arne Isacsson (1917–2010), a watercolorist who founded the Gerlesborg School of Fine Arts and whose work is featured in the National Museum of Sweden (Nationalmuseum). The work of Palle Torsson (1970), a contemporary artist, is often interactive; he works in video, video games, and computer games.

Folk music and dance are also artistically important. The north-central city of Dalarna hosts many summer folk festivals, which include traditional costumes, dancing, and outdoor entertainment.

In the 20th century, director Ingmar Bergman and playwright August Strindberg emerged from Sweden as important figures in film and drama. Sweden has also produced many internationally famous film actresses, including Greta Garbo, Ann-Margaret, Liv Ullman, Bibi Andersson, and Ingrid Bergman.

Before World War II, Swedish pop culture was primarily influenced by Germany. After the war, Swedish contemporary artists largely took their inspiration from the United Kingdom and the United States, and began to experience global success. One reason for the international success of Swedish artists—particularly musicians—may be that Sweden subsidizes musical education for its youth, encouraging musical talent to grow from a young age.

Nordic (cross-country) skiing is the most popular sport, both professionally and recreationally. An annual 89-kilometer (55-mile) Nordic skiing race is held in Dalarna. This competition, called the Vasa Race, is a large national event in which hundreds of Swedes participate. Other popular sports include soccer, ice hockey, sailing, and tennis. International tennis star Björn Borg is one of Sweden's most popular athletes.

Cultural Sites & Landmarks
In 1991, Sweden was honored with its first World Heritage Site, the Royal Domain of Drottningholm, which includes the private residence of the Swedish royal family. These sights are recognized by the United Nations Educational, Scientific and Cultural Organization (UNESCO) for their natural or cultural significance to humanity. Since 1991, Sweden has added an additional thirteen World Heritage Sites, encompassing both the cultural and geographical importance of this Scandinavian nation.

In northern Sweden, the part of Swedish Lapland (the northernmost province) known as Laponia became a World Heritage Site in 1996. Encompassing 9,400 kilometers (about 5,841 miles) of magnificent landscape, Laponia is located entirely within the Arctic Circle. It is the largest region in the world in which an indigenous people, the Saami, preserve their ancestral way of life by following animal migrations. The Sami, a nomadic culture, base their livelihood on herding reindeer between Lapland's forests and its glacial mountains, and have occupied the region for nearly 7,000 years. (They are considered Europe's only indigenous people.) UNESCO has praised Laponia as a site of ecological and geological beauty, as well as of historic significance and the largely unchanged Saami culture.

In 1994, the rock carvings of Tanum, located at the historic site at Tanumshede, were listed as a World Heritage Site. These prehistoric petroglyphs (rock carvings), which date back to the Nordic Bronze Age (in Sweden circa 1800–600 BCE), depict humans, oxen, snakes, birds, boats, wagons, hunting weapons and farming tools, among other subjects. Most notably, they provide a detailed and consistent glimpse into the culture of the people who inhabited the western region of Sweden during that period. However, many of the petroglyphs have been painted red to make them more visible to tourists.

Other World Heritage Sites in Sweden include the Engelsberg Ironworks, built in 1681; the Agricultural Landscape of Southern Öland, a largely limestone plane important for its cultural history and biodiversity; the Church Village of Gammelstad, Luleå, recognized as a well-preserved example of traditional church towns in the Scandinavian peninsula; the Naval Port of Karlskrona, recognized as an example of a planned naval city in 17th-century Europe; and Skogskyrkogården, a cemetery in Stockholm recognized for its blending of natural and architectural elements.

A major architectural landmark in Sweden is Vadstena Castle (Vadstena slot), built by King Gustav Vasa. Although intended as a fortress to protect Stockholm from invaders from the south, the building was turned into a castle by King Johan III (1537–1592), Vasa's son. Various royal families inhabited the castle throughout the centuries. Today, the castle holds concerts and other cultural events, such as kraftivaler, or crayfishing festivals. It also features a museum showcasing artifacts from the 17th century.

Other places of cultural significance include the Fish Church (Feskekôrka) and the Gothenburg Botanical Gardens, both located in Gothenburg. Built in 1874, the Fish Church was designed by the city architect, Victor von Gegerfelt (1817–1915), to resemble a Gothic cathedral, although its purpose was to be a market for fish. In fact, it still operates as a fish market today. The Gothenburg Botanical Gardens is one of the most famous botanical gardens in Europe. With an area of 174 hectares (430 acres), the gardens include 16,000 different species, many brought back from the travels of botanist and explorer Carl Skottsberg (1880–1963), one of the garden's creators. Planned in 1910, the garden emphasizes both horticulture and Swedish community life.

Libraries & Museums

Stockholm is home to a number of major museums. These include the Nordic Museum, famous for its exhibits on Renaissance and post-Renaissance Swedish culture; the Museum of National Antiquities, which features thousands of precious objects including gold jewelry from the Viking era; Skansen, the world's oldest open-air museum, which has on exhibit more than 100 authentic old houses from all regions of Sweden; and the Vasa Museum, dedicated to the world's oldest restored warship, salvaged 333 years after she sank in Stockholm Harbor as she set out on her maiden voyage in 1628. Göteborg Stadsmuseum (Gothenburg City Museum) focuses on Swedish history; its collections include remnants of a Viking warship as well as regional artifacts and religious objects.

The National Library of Sweden (Kungliga biblioteket), also called the Royal Library, is located in Stockholm and began amassing its collection in 1661. That same year, the Legal Deposits Act mandated that a copy of every work printed in Sweden be sent to the library. It has more than 15 million items in its collection, in addition to over five million hours worth of audio and/or visual recordings. Its collections on foreign and historical works include a papyrus scroll from 300 CE and 16th-century science books.

Holidays

Secular holidays observed in Sweden include Nationaldagen (National Day), celebrated on June 6. In late June, Swedes celebrate Midsommardagen, or Midsummer Day, with many festivities including outdoor music, dancing, and food.

On December 13, Swedes celebrate Saint Lucia Day, also known as the Festival of Light. On this day, the young girls in a Swedish family wear white gowns and garland wreaths in their hair, and wake up the rest of the family by singing to them and then serving breakfast.

Youth Culture

Swedish youth culture has been profoundly influenced by the influx of immigrants to Sweden since the end of World War II. One of the most obvious influences is the creation of a pidgin form of Swedish known as "Rinkeby Swedish." This hybrid language was named after a heavily multiethnic suburb in Stockholm called Rinkeby, one of the prominent areas in which it is spoken. Mixing words from Turkish, Serbo-Croatian, Arabic, English and Spanish, Rinkeby Swedish is the chosen form of expression for a growing street culture in Sweden. The trend is fueled primarily by immigrant or first-generation youth who feel segregated from mainstream Swedish society. Recently, several books and magazines have been published in Rinkeby Swedish, and it is widely featured in Swedish hip hop music as well.

In terms of entertainment, video gaming and online role-playing are very popular (perhaps due in part to Sweden's long, dark winter). In fact, the now defunct role-playing virtual world Second Life was so popular that, in 2007, Sweden became the first country to open a virtual embassy in the game. In the summer, outdoor activities such as hiking and skiing are particularly popular among youth.

SOCIETY

Transportation
Public transport is well-established in Sweden. Göteborg (Gothenburg), the second largest municipality in Sweden, is home to the most extensive tram network in Europe. Sweden's capital, Stockholm, has light rail, bus, metro, and taxi services. Since Stockholm is built on a series of islands, ferry service is also available to any of the islands in the archipelago. Ferry service is available from Finland, the Baltic States, Poland, Germany, Denmark, England and Norway, as well.

Although travel by car is common outside of the larger cities, rail service is also convenient. The Inland Railway Line (Inlandsbanan AB/IBAB), which connects central Sweden with the northern part of the country—and is primarily used for timber transport and tourism—has 13,000 kilometers (approximately 8,077 miles) of track. This makes it the twentieth longest rail line in the world. There is also a high speed railway operated by the Swedish State Railways (SJ). Traffic in Sweden moves on the right-hand side of the road.

Transportation Infrastructure
There were 59 national roads (riksvag) in Sweden. National roads are numbered one through 100, with lower-number roads located in the southern portion of the country and higher-number roads in the north. There are approximately 83,000 kilometers (51,000 miles) of county roads in the country, which are numbered from 100 and up.

Major airports in Sweden include the Stockholm-Arlanda International Airport, which is the largest in the country and the third largest in Scandinavia, as well as Gothenburg International Airport and Malmo-Sturup International Airport.

Media & Communications
Sweden has a self-regulating press overseen by the Swedish Press Council and the Press Ombudsman. The three major media conglomerates are the Norwegian-owned Schibsted, which, along with the Swedish Trade Union Confederation, controls the most widely-circulated newspaper, *Aftonbladet*; Bonnier AB, which owns *Dagens Nyheter* and *Expressen*, the second- and third-most widely-circulated papers; and Stenbeck, which owns seventeen TV channels. Swedish newspapers, particularly second-tier provincial papers, have been subsidized by the state since the 1960s, in the view that multiple media sources are a key component of a democracy. Subsidizing newspapers is a controversial practice, however, as it sometimes seen as contravening freedom of the press. In 2006, it was reported that, on average, an estimated 87 percent of Swedes read a daily newspaper, either in paper format or online. Additionally, as of 2009, an estimated 8.3 million citizens were classified as Internet users.

A unique feature of Swedish media policy is not to publish the names and personal details of suspected criminals until they have been convicted. Police investigators fear that to do so could hamper the collection of unbiased evidence before a trial. Violations of this policy, as when *Expressen* published the name of a suspected serial rapist after his arrest in March 2006, have been severely criticized.

SOCIAL DEVELOPMENT

Standard of Living
Sweden ranked 12th out of 187 countries on the United Nations 2014 Human Development Index, which measures quality of life indicators.

Water Consumption

The majority of the water supply in Sweden comes from surface water; the country has an estimated 100,000 lakes. Access to water and sanitation services is very high. In the early 21st century, 95 percent of the country's wastewater goes through intensive treatment processes, both chemical and biological, and over half of the wastewater undergoes a nitrogen-removal process. Thanks to an ambitious and ongoing program of environmental conservation and restoration efforts dating to the 1970s, the waters surrounding Stockholm are so clean that it is safe to swim and fish virtually anywhere in the city.

Education

Children in Sweden begin their education at age six, when they attend compulsory comprehensive school. Once students reach the ninth grade, they are allowed to choose their own course of study from nine distinct subject fields.

Roughly 90 percent of Swedish students continue their education through upper secondary school, and most go on to study at one of Sweden's six national universities, in Umeå, Stockholm, Lund, Linköping, Göteborg, and Uppsala. The literacy rate among Swedes is virtually 100 percent, and the average amount of time spent in school is sixteen years: 15 years for men and 17 years for women.

In 2009, the World Economic Forum published the Gender Gap Report, which ranks countries according to gender equality in areas such as politics, health, and education. Sweden ranked high across all areas, earning the rank of fourth of the 134 countries analyzed.

Women's Rights

Women in Sweden achieved suffrage in 1921. Since then, Sweden has been considered a pioneering and progressive nation in terms of the legal protection of women. In 1965, Sweden was the first country in the world to outlaw rape in marriage, and since 1975, Sweden has had free, legal abortions for women up until the 18th week of pregnancy. Additionally, in 1999, Sweden made the purchasing of sexual services illegal. Unlike many other countries, which often criminalize sex workers by emphasizing the illegality of selling sexual services, Sweden focuses on the illegal actions of the clients of sex workers instead.

Sweden was also among the first countries to ratify the 1979 UN Convention on the Elimination of All Forms of Discrimination against Women (CEDAW). Chapter two of the Instrument of Government (the Swedish Constitution) prohibits discrimination on the basis of gender in any form, such as employment and pay, except when enacted by legislation for the purposes of achieving equality and gender balance, or in cases such as compulsory military service.

Sweden has the world's highest level of representation of women in government. In 2003, 45 percent of the Swedish parliament (the Riksdag) were women, as were 10 of the 22 government ministers. Women also account for 41 percent of elected officials at the county and local levels. In 2005, 25 percent of private companies and 31 percent of public companies were headed by women. However, even taking into account differences in type and level of employment, women's monthly salaries are still only 92 percent of the salary of their male counterparts. However, the UN Women's Rights Committee has expressed concern about the low numbers of women in high-ranking posts in Sweden, most significantly in academia. For example, as of February 2008, only 17 percent of professorships in Sweden were held by women. The committee was also critical of the pervasiveness of gender stereotypes in the Swedish media.

Violence against women has been an issue in Sweden. In 2006, around 25,500 cases of violence perpetrated by men against women were reported, but the Swedish National Council for Crime Prevention expects the actual number of cases to be much higher. In fact, according to a 2001 study, nearly half of all Swedish women over age 15 reported having been subject to some form of violence in their lives. In 2007, the Swedish government set out 800 million Swedish krona ($118 million USD) for a four-year plan to combat violence against women, a move that has been applauded by the UN Women's Rights Committee. This plan included addressing honor-related violence against women, which Swedish authorities estimate affected 1,500 to 2,500 Swedish women in 2007, particularly among the Muslim immigrant population.

Swedish family law has taken great pains to ensure equal rights of men and women with regard to the family. Swedes receive a Parental Allowance for the first 480 days after a child is born or adopted, which can be up to $874 Swedish krona ($110 USD) per day. Additionally, each parent has 60 days of paid maternal or paternal leave, and fathers may have 10 extra days' leave to spend with a newborn child. Over two-thirds of Swedish fathers take parental leave, as opposed to one-third of European fathers.

Health Care

Sweden's health care and social welfare systems provide for citizens from birth to death. Young children receive day care services before they begin school, and parents are granted extensive maternity and paternity leave from work. Limits on health care costs make the system affordable to people with health problems, although most Swedes are accommodated by free medical services.

Pensions are set for retired citizens, who are given 65 percent of the income they made during their 15 highest-paid years of work. Widows, children who have lost one parent, and orphans are all granted pensions as well. Unemployment compensation is available to citizens at a rate of 80 percent of their former pay until they find another job.

GOVERNMENT

Structure

Despite the fact that the Kingdom of Sweden is a parliamentary monarchy, political power rests with the people. There is a royal family, but the king is a figurehead who acts as a moral leader and a representative of the nation rather than a political chief. The prime minister actually controls the government.

Sweden has a constitution that outlines its laws and the rights of the Swedes. There are three constitutional documents: the Instrument of Government, which explains the societal laws and constructs; the Act of Succession, which outlines the succession of the royal throne; and the Freedom of the Press Act, which guarantees freedom of speech and expression to all Swedes.

Sweden's parliament is called the Riksdag. Its 349 members are elected every four years from a variety of political parties. The age of suffrage is 18, and voter participation is exceptionally high at above 80 percent.

Political Parties

Political parties include the Swedish Social Democratic Party (S), which gained 113 seats in the 2014 election. The party, founded in 1889, supports progressive taxation and social welfare. The Moderate Party (M), founded in 1904, is a liberal conservative party; in 2014, the party won 84 seats in parliament. The Moderate Party advocates social welfare, as well as military funding, free markets, and tax reform. The pro-environmental Green Party (MP) won 25 seats in parliament in 2014. The Centre Party (C), founded in 1919, won 22 seats in parliament in 2014; the party has an agrarian-minded social liberal ideology. The Liberal People's Party (FP) won 19 seats in 2014. The party advocates a mixed economy and women's equality, and in 2003, supported the U.S.-led invasion of Iraq. The Christian Democrats Party (KD), founded in 1964, won 16 seats in the 2014 election. The party supports tax reduction, improved elder care, and corporate deregulation.

Other political parties include the Left Party (V) and the Pirate Party (PP), which supports patent and copyright reform, as well government transparency and privacy rights.

Local Government

There are 29 counties in Sweden, which are subdivided into 290 municipalities. Every four years, assemblies comprising an odd number of members (ranging from 31 to 101) are elected; they, in turn, appoint a chairman (or kommunal-råd) and an executive committee. Municipal governments provide health care, education, elder care, sanitation services, and urban planning.

Judicial System

The judicial system of Sweden has two main branches. The General Courts hear civil and criminal cases; the highest general court is the Supreme Court of Sweden, under which are the courts of appeal and district courts. The General Administrative Courts hear administrative cases, with the highest court being the Supreme Administrative Court of Sweden, under which fall administrative courts of appeal and administrative courts. Jury trials are only held in cases related to freedom of expression issues (i.e., censorship).

Taxation

Sweden has one of the highest tax rates in the world. The progressive income tax rate falls between 31 and 57 percent, while the corporate tax rate is 26.3 percent (2009). Sweden also levies a value-added tax (VAT) of 25 percent and a capital gains tax of 30 percent.

Armed Forces

The Swedish Armed Forces comprise an army, navy, air force, and the Swedish Home Guard, a local defense unit.

Foreign Policy

Historically, Sweden's foreign policy has centered on nonalignment in peacetime and neutrality during war. This policy was questioned in the aftermath of World War II, when Sweden received 7,500 Jewish refugees from Denmark, but also sold iron-ore to Germany and provided rail transportation to the German army. During the Cold War, Sweden maintained its policy of neutrality due to its distrust of both the U.S. and the Soviet Union, though in private the Swedish government was very friendly to the U.S.

In 2002, Sweden altered its security policy to include the possibility of cooperating with peace-building missions and peacekeeping military alliances. Sweden's foreign policy now emphasizes cooperation in issues of international development, nuclear nonproliferation, arms control, democracy and sustainable development, as well as aid to vulnerable countries, particularly in Africa. According to Sweden's 2008 Foreign Policy statement, Sweden believes firmly in multilateralism as a means of addressing global problems. At the time of the statement's release, Swedish troops were preparing to leave for Chad as part of a European Union (EU) peacekeeping force to help stabilize the situation in neighboring Sudan. Sweden also favors humanitarian intervention and aid, and has devoted significant assistance to the Darfur region of Sudan. Sweden also has placed a high priority on intervention and aid in Afghanistan, and opened an embassy in Kabul in 2008.

Sweden is an outspoken and involved member of numerous international organizations, such as the UN, the World Bank, the World Trade Organization (WTO), the International Labor Organization (ILO), the World Health Organization (WHO), and the NATO-affiliated Partnerships for Peace. Sweden has worked with NATO on peacekeeping and security missions in Kosovo, Afghanistan, and Bosnia and Herzegovina.

After much debate, in 1994 Sweden voted with a 52.3 percent majority to enter the EU, primarily for economic reasons. To satisfy concerns that belonging to the EU might upset its policy of neutrality, Sweden maintained a caveat stating that it would not be obliged to participate in EU defense alliances. Sweden hosted its first presidency of the EU in 2001 (the EU maintains a rotating presidency, which changes between EU member states every six months). Sweden is also a member of the Nordic Council, whose other members include Norway, Denmark, Finland, Iceland and the autonomous territories of Greenland, the Faroe Islands, and the Åland Islands. The purpose of the Nordic Council is to foster cooperation on issues of mutual concern to members, such as the environment, development, trade, culture and education.

The friendship between Sweden and the United States is particularly strong, due in part to the fact that 14 million Americans are of Swedish descent. In June 2007, Sweden and the U.S. signed a biofuels cooperation agreement, which focuses on renewable energy for vehicle technology.

Human Rights Profile

International human rights law insists that states respect civil and political rights, and also promote an individual's economic, social and cultural rights. The United Nations Universal Declaration on Human Rights (UDHR) is recognized as the standard for international human rights. Its authors sought the counsel of the world's great thinkers, philosophers, and religious leaders, and were careful to create a document that reflects the core values shared by every world culture. (To read this document or view the articles relating to cultural human rights, go to: http://www.udhr.org/UDHR/default.htm.)

Swedish law prohibits discrimination based on race, religion, gender, disability, language or social status. Although the Swedish Ombudsman against Ethnic Discrimination and other government bodies work to enforce this law, discrimination—particularly against immigrants, the Roma people (also known as Gypsies) and homosexuals—is still an issue. In addition, discrimination against the indigenous Sami people of northern Scandinavia is also present. In the past, relations between the Swedish government and the Sami were very tense, with assimilation being the government's main strategy. (Sami people were looked down on for what was seen as a primitive lifestyle).

However, in the past several decades, respect for Sami culture has grown, and in 1998, the Swedish government formally apologized to the Sami for wrongs committed against them. Furthermore, in 1999, the Swedish government officially recognized Sami as a minority language. Despite these positive steps, Sweden still has not ratified the ILO's Convention 169 regarding the treatment and rights of indigenous peoples. There are also ongoing tensions between the Sami and local Swedish farmers over reindeer grazing rights.

In reference to Article 16 of the UDHR, Sweden is largely considered of the most supportive countries in the world in terms of family law and family protection for both male-female and same-sex partnerships. Sweden has recognized "registered partnerships" for same-sex couples since 1995, which provides most of the same rights and has most of the same legal effects as marriage. In 2009, marriage between same-sex couples became legal.

In reference to Article 18—which concerns freedom of religion—due to an influx of immigrants, Islam is now the second largest religion in Sweden after Christianity. Freedom of religion is protected in the Swedish constitution, and Swedish courts have upheld the right of female Muslim students and public employees to wear headscarves at work and in school.

In reference to Article 19 of the UDHR, Sweden has outlawed hate speech, which consists of expressing contempt for a person or group on the basis of race, color, national origin, ethnic origin, religious belief or sexual orientation. People who engage in hate speech, such as the National Socialist Front (NSF), a neo-Nazi political party, are not allowed to display provocative writing or symbols such as swastikas. In 2007, 721 cases of hate speech were reported to the Swedish National Council for Crime Prevention.

Human rights are a significant part of Sweden's foreign policy. According to the government of Sweden, the country works to promote human rights abroad though cooperation with the human rights initiatives of the EU and the UN. Human rights issues that receive particular focus are asylum and immigration, trade and labor relations, human trafficking, the death penalty and the relationship between security and development.

Migration

Sweden is one of the most open countries in the world to asylum seekers from the Middle East, particularly from Iraq. Sweden has admitted more than 80,000 asylum seekers from Iraq since 1984, admitting 18,500 refugees in 2006 alone. However, the minister of migration announced that 2009 would be a "Year of Return" during which some Iraqi asylum seekers would be returned to northern (Kurdish-controlled) Iraq.

ECONOMY

Overview of the Economy
Engineering is the largest sector of Sweden's economy. The majority of Sweden's labor force is employed in service industries. In 2014, Sweden's gross domestic product (GDP) was an estimated $559 billion (USD). The per capita GDP was approximately $44,700 (USD).

Industry
Industrial centers in Sweden include Småland, home of numerous glassworks factories; and Göteborg, site of the largest port in Scandinavia and the tenth-largest port in Europe, as well as the Volvo automobile factory. There are many more factories in Malmö, the capital of the Skåne region. Industrial production includes textiles, food processing, timber, ironworks and shipbuilding.

Sweden's primary trading partners are members of the European Union, the United States, and Norway. Swedish exports include motor vehicles, iron products, televisions and paper. These generate a great deal of revenue because Sweden's imported goods are less valuable than the exports.

Labor
In 2014, the labor force of Sweden was 5.12 million, and the unemployment rate was 7.9 percent. Seventy percent of the labor force works in the services industry, while one percent works in agriculture and 28 percent works in the industrial sector.

Energy/Power/Natural Resources
One of Sweden's most abundant natural resources is copper. The copper mines in the city of Falun once provided two-thirds of the world's copper. Cottages all over Sweden are painted red because the paint contains copper, which helps guard against harsh winter weather. Other important natural resources include crystal, iron, and hydroelectric and nuclear power.

Fishing
In 2003, an estimated 4,000 workers were employed in the fishing industry. Approximately 280,000 tons of fish were caught that year, with common catches including herring and cod from the Baltic Sea. Nearly 1,319 tons of freshwater fish were harvested from the country's many lakes in 2004, including pike, perch, eel, and vendace.

Forestry
The Swedish forestry industry represents a very important part of the country's economy. Sweden is the second largest exporter of paper, wood pulp, and timber in the world (2008). Between 10 and 12 percent of the labor force is employed in the forestry industry. Approximately 12 percent of Sweden's total exports are wood products. Seventy percent of the timber harvested is exported, and 85 percent of its pulp and paper is also exported.

Mining/Metals
The mining industry has been a vital part of Sweden for centuries, and its infrastructure is well developed in the early 21st century. Sweden produces an annual 45 million tons of metal ores and is the largest producer of iron ore in the European Union (EU). Other commonly mined metals include copper, gold, lead, silver, and zinc. There are many prominent mines in the northern region of the country.

Agriculture
Despite low population density, abundant vacant plains and forests, and rich natural resources, agriculture is not a substantial factor in Sweden's economy. Agriculture accounts for only 1.5 percent of the nation's GDP, and employs only two percent of the labor force.

There are many hills, peat bogs and clay deposits in the lowlands of Sweden. The southern towns are arranged with the farms and the towns blocked off systematically.

Grains, potatoes, and other field crops are grown, but Sweden's main agricultural activity is animal husbandry.

Animal Husbandry

The most common farm-raised animals are cows, pigs, and sheep. In 2009, it was estimated that there were 1.7 million cattle, of which approximately 450,000 were used for dairy production. Approximately 60 percent of poultry consumed in Sweden is bred domestically.

Tourism

Tourism in Sweden is focused on the natural beauty of the country's landscape. There are popular downhill ski resorts in Åre and Vemdalen. Many tourists visit the northern part of Sweden to take advantage of the cross-country ski tracks there.

Another popular attraction in northern Sweden is the village of Jukkasjärvi, near the town of Kiruna. Every winter, the village is the site of the ICEHOTEL, a hotel constructed entirely of ice.

Tourists can also arrange a home stay with a Sami family. The families are generally pleased to host visitors, as this is a fundamental part of Sami income. Visitors may also enjoy riding in sleighs pulled by reindeer.

Stockholm, famous for its parkland and open space, is another popular destination for tourists visiting Sweden. The Skansen open-air museum is located on the Djurgärden peninsula. Drottningholm Palace, on an island in Lake Mälaren, is open to tourists. The island has been home to the royal family since the 16th century, and is a UNESCO World Heritage Site.

Evelyn Atkinson, Richard Means,
Beverly Ballaro

DO YOU KNOW?

- Swedish businessman Alfred Nobel instituted the Nobel Prize in the late 19th century. Nobel also invented dynamite in 1866.

- In 1844, Swedish chemist Gustav Pasch invented the safety match.

- The system for classifying organisms into kingdom, phylum, class, order, family, genus and species was devised by Swedish scientist Carolus Linnaeus.

- The first national parks in Europe were established in Sweden.

- An image of St. Erik, patron saint of Sweden and special protector of Stockholm, has adorned the city's coat of arms since 1376. Legend has it that Erik, a beloved Swedish king beheaded by the Danes in 1160, miraculously cured the blind and the seriously ill who made pilgrimages to the healing waters of a spring that flowed near Erik's gravesite.

Bibliography

Becky Ohlsen. *Sweden.* Oakland, CA: Lonely Planet, 2012

Charotte Rosen Svensson. *Culture Shock! Sweden.* Tarrytown, NY: Marshall Cavendish, 2012

Ingemar Algulin. *A History of Swedish Literature.* The Swedish Institute. Sweden: 1989.

James Proctor and Neil Roland. *Rough Guide to Sweden.* London: Rough Guides, 2012

John Bauer, Polly Lawson, and Holger Lundburgh. *Swedish Folk Tales.* Edinburgh: Floris Books, 2004

Judith Pierce Rosenberg. *A Swedish Kitchen: Recipes and Reminiscences.* New York: Hippocrene Cookbook Library, 2004

Michael Booth. *The Almost Nearly Perfect People: Behind the Myth of Scandinavian Utopia.* London: Picador, 2015

Marie Demker, et al. *Culture, Health, and Religion at the Millennium: Sweden Unparadised.* New York: Palgrave Macmillan, 2014

Neil Kent. *A Concise History of Sweden.* New York: Cambridge University Press, 2008

Vilhelm Moberg and Paul Britten Austin. *A History of the Swedish People, Volumes I & II.* Minneapolis: University of Minnesota Press, 2005

Works Cited

Jens Allwood. "Are There Swedish Patterns of Communication?" *Gothanberg University Institution for Linguistics.* http://www.ling.gu.se/~jens/publications/docs076-100/087.pdf.

Henrik Bachner. "Anti-Jewish stereotypes in Swedish public discourse." *Engage Journal,* Issue 5. www.engageonline.org.uk/journal/index.php?journal_id=16&article_id=62.

Kathryn Burke. "The Sami Yoik." Sami Culture. http://www.utexas.edu/courses/sami/diehtu/giella/music/yoiksunna.htm.

Charlotte Celsing. "Are Swedes Losing Their Religion?" The Official Gateway to Sweden. http://www.sweden.se/templates/cs/Article 15193.aspx.

Una Cunningham-Andersson. *Growing Up with Two Languages.* New York: Routledge, 1999.

Anne-Marie Ericsson et al. *The Brilliance of Swedish Glass, 1918–1939: An Alliance of Art and Industry.* New Haven: Yale University Press, 1997.

Leif Furhammer. "Film in Sweden." *The Gateway to Sweden.* www.sweden.se/templates/cs/FactSheet 15600.aspx.

Marie-Noelle Godin. *Urban Youth Language in Multicultural Sweden.* http://lettuce.tapor.uvic.ca/cocoon/journals/scancan/article.pdf?id=godin_1_16.

Fredrik Haeffner. "Traditions: Lent." www.rootsweb.ancestry.com/~swegw/Fact/Cult/facCulTrad02.htm.

Jonas Hato. "Swedish Customs." www.nada.kth.se/~jsh/resor/svenskaseder.html.

Marta E. Hethmon, "Name Days." http://skandland.com/namedaysalphacover.htm.

Hans Högman. "The History of Swedish X-joint Log Houses." www.hhogman.se/loghouses.htm

David Kaminsky. *Hidden Traditions: Conceptualizing Swedish Folk Music in the Twenty-First Century.* Harvard University: 2005.

Gaby Katz. "Video games are becoming "the new TV" in Sweden." *Network Europe.* http://networkeurope.radio.cz/feature/video-games-are-becoming-the-new-tv-in-sweden.

Tiina Meri. "Pippi Longstocking: Swedish rebel and feminist role model." *The Swedish Institute.* www.sweden.se/templates/cs/Article____11230.aspx.

Tobias Petterson. *The Encyclopedia of Swedish Progressive Music 1967 - 1979: From Psychedelic Experiments to Political Propaganda.* Premium Forlag AB. Sweden: 2007.

William P. Reaves, "The Heroic Saga on the Rökstone." *The Runestone Journal 1.* Asatru Folk Assembly. 2007.

Karl Ritter. "Sami struggle for ancestral lands in Sweden." *Galdu: Resource Center for Indigenous Peoples.* www.galdu.org/web/index.php?odas=117&giella1=eng.

Lena Katarina Swanberg and Carl Jan Granqvist. "Swedish Culinary Classics." *The Official Gateway to Sweden.* www.sweden.se/templates/cs/CommonPage____12925.aspx.

Urban Sikeborg. "Greetings & Goodbyes." *Stockholm School of Economics.* www2.hhs.se/isa/swedish/chap2.htm.

Ánde Somby. "Joik and the theory of knowledge." *University of Tromsø.* www.uit.no/ssweb/dok/Somby/Ande/95.htm.

Po Tildhom. "Celebrating the Swedish way – traditions and festivities." *The Swedish Institute.* www.sweden.se.

Po Tidholm. 2004. "The crayfish party." *The Official Gateway to Sweden.* http://www.sweden.se/templates/cs/CommonPage____11371.aspx.

"About the Nordic Council." *Norden: Official Cooperation in the Nordic Region.* www.norden.org.

"An Indigenous Song Celebrates Nature in Sweden." *The UN Works for Cultural Diversity, UNESCO.* http://www.un.org/works/OLD/culture/sweden_story.html.

"Astrid Lindgren's Works." *The Astrid Lindgren Archive.* www.astridlindgren.se/eng/index_1024.htm

"Cultural Etiquette: Sweden." *eDiplomat: Global Portal for Diplomats.* www.ediplomat.com/np/cultural_etiquette/ce_se.htm.

"Elderly Care." *The Swedish Institute.* www.sweden.se.

"Excerpt from the Statement of Government Policy." *Prime Minister Fredrik Reinfeldt at the Riksdag.* http://www.sweden.gov.se/sb/d/3103.

"The Fate of the Danish Jews." Holocaust Education. *The Danish Center for Holocaust and Genocide Studies.* www.holocaust-education.dk/holocaust/danmarkogholocaust.asp.

"Foreign Policy." Background Note: Sweden. *U.S. Department of State.* http://www.state.gov/r/pa/ei/bgn/2880.htm.

"Gender equality in Sweden." *The Official Gateway to Sweden.* http://www.sweden.se/templates/cs/FactSheet____17932.aspx.

"Goteborgs Botaniska Tradgord [Gothenburg's Botanical Garden]." www.gotbot.se/engelska/english_start.html.

"Human Rights in Swedish Foreign Policy." *Ministry of Foreign Affairs, Sweden.* http://www.regeringen.se/content/1/c6/04/10/01/032fd549.pdf.

"Ingmar Bergman Face to Face". http://www.ingmarbergmanfoundation.com/

"Instructions for the Office of the Press Ombudsman." *Po-Pon.* www.po.se/Article.jsp?article=2291&avd=english.

"Laponia World Heritage." www.laponia.nu.

"Laponian Area." *UNESCO World Heritage*. http://whc. unesco.orghttp://whc.unesco.org.

"NATO's Relations with Sweden." *North Atlantic Treaty Organization*. http://www.nato.int/issues/nato-sweden/practice.html.

"Ombudsman calls time on Sami discrimination." *The Local*. http://www.thelocal.se/12872/20080706.

"Peace-building and state-building." Foreign Policy Statement. *Ministry of Foreign Affairs, Sweden*. http://www.regeringen.se/sb/d/10275/a/97814.

"Population in the country, counties and municipalities by sex and age 31/12/2007." *Statistics Sweden*. www.scb.se.

"Scandinavian Cooking." http://scandinaviancooking.com.

"Scandinavian Food Culture." www.scandinavianfoodculture.com.

Scandinavian Society for Prehistoric Art. www.rockartscandinavia.se.

"Second Life: the Second House of Sweden." *The Official Gateway to Sweden*. http://www.sweden.se/templates/cs/CommonPage____18195.aspx.

"Sweden: Country Reports on Human Rights Practices – 2006." *U.S. Department of State*. http://www.state.gov/g/drl/rls/hrrpt/2006/78841.htm.

"Sweden: Country Reports on Human Rights Practices." *The U.S. Department of State*. http://www.state.gov/g/drl/rls/hrrpt/2007/100587.htm.

"Sweden reviewed by the UN's women's rights committee." *The Swedish Government's Human Rights Website*. www.manskligarattigheter.gov.se/extra/pod/?id=71&module_instance=2&action=pod_show&navid=71.

"Sweden's support for parents with children is comprehensive and effective but expensive." Directorate for Employment, Labour and Social Affairs, *Organization for Economic Cooperation and Development*. www.oecd.org.

"Sweden to set up embassy in Second Life." *The Local*. http://www.thelocal.se/6219/20070126/.

"Sweden's welfare programmes hinder Iraqi integration." *The Local: Sweden's News in English*. http://www.thelocal.se/13060/20080715.

"Swedish Art - Tradition and Renewal." *Smorgasbord: The Shortcut to Sweden*. www.sverigeturism.se/smorgasbord/smorgasbord/culture/lifestyle/art.html.

"Swedish Film History in Brief." *Swedish Cinema*. http://utenti.lycos.it/filmproj/experiences5.html.

"Swedish mass media." *The Official Gateway to Sweden*. www.sweden.se/templates/cs/FactSheet____15670.aspx.

"Swedish Pop." *The Official Gateway to Sweden*. http://www.sweden.se/templates/cs/FactSheet_18700.aspx

"Registration of Partnership Act." *HomO: the Office of the Obudsman against Discrimination on the Grounds of Sexual Orientation*. 17 November 1994. http://www.homo.se/o.o.i.s/1630.

"Rock Carvings in Tanum." *UNESCO World Heritage*. http://whc.unesco.org/en/list/557.

"U.S. Expands Energy Cooperation with Sweden." *U.S. Department of Energy*. http://www.energy.gov/news/5185.htm.

"Vadstena Slot." *Vadstena Odeshog*. www.tidernaslandskap.se.

"A Warm Welcome to Carl Larsson-Garden." *The Official Website of Carl Larssen*. www.carllarsson.se/enstart.aspx.

"Welcome to Sapmi – the Samiland." *Sami Information Center*. www.eng.samer.se/servlet/GetDoc?meta_id=1001.

"What is a Nyckelharpa?" *The American Nyckelharpa Association*. www.nyckelharpa.org.

"What is a Swedish Municipality?" *Örebro*. 10 December 2007. http://www.orebro.se/doldasidor/welcometoorebro/whatisaswedishmunicipality.4.37c0d5e810d685ee730800021961.htmlhttp://www.orebro.se/doldasidor/welcometoorebro/whatisaswedishmunicipality.4.37c0d5e810d685ee730800021961.html

"Women's Rights." The Swedish Government's Human Rights Website. www.manskligarattigheter.gov.se/extra/pod/?id=39&module_instance=2&action=pod_show&navid=39www.manskligarattigheter.gov.se/extra/pod/?id=39&module_instance=2&action=pod_show&navid=39.

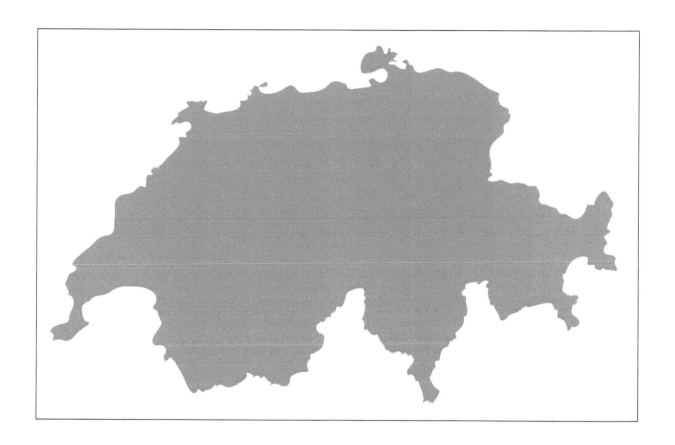

SWITZERLAND

Introduction

Switzerland is located in Central Europe, in the heart of the Alps mountain range. Officially known by its Latin name of Confoederatio Helvetica (The Swiss Confederation, in English), Switzerland is one of the world's oldest democracies. Switzerland is known for its strict neutrality in international affairs; it is also a strong supporter of international cooperation. The country officially joined the United Nations in 2002.

Switzerland is a global center for banking and other financial services, as well as high-quality manufactured goods, pharmaceuticals, and tourism. Switzerland attracts many tourists to its alpine scenery, quaint villages, and sophisticated cities such as Bern, Zurich, and Geneva.

GENERAL INFORMATION

Official Language: German, French, Italian, Rhaeto-Romanic
Population: 8,061,516 (2014 estimate)
Currency: Swiss franc
Coins: Swiss coins come in denominations of 5, 10, and 20 rappen (a rappen is equal to one hundredth of a franc), and 0.5, 1, 2, and 5 francs. While older coins of varying denominations are still in circulation, these are the only coins now minted.
Land Area: 41,277 square kilometers (15,937 square miles)
Water Area: 1,280 square kilometers (494 square miles)
National Motto: "Unus pro omnibus, omnes pro uno" ("One for all, all for one")
National Anthem: "Schweizerpsalm" ("Swiss Psalm")
Capital: Bern
Time Zone: Central European Time, GMT +1
Flag Description: The flag of Switzerland is a red flag with a large, centered white cross. It is a square-shaped flag, one of only two officially used in the world (the other is the flag of the Vatican City).

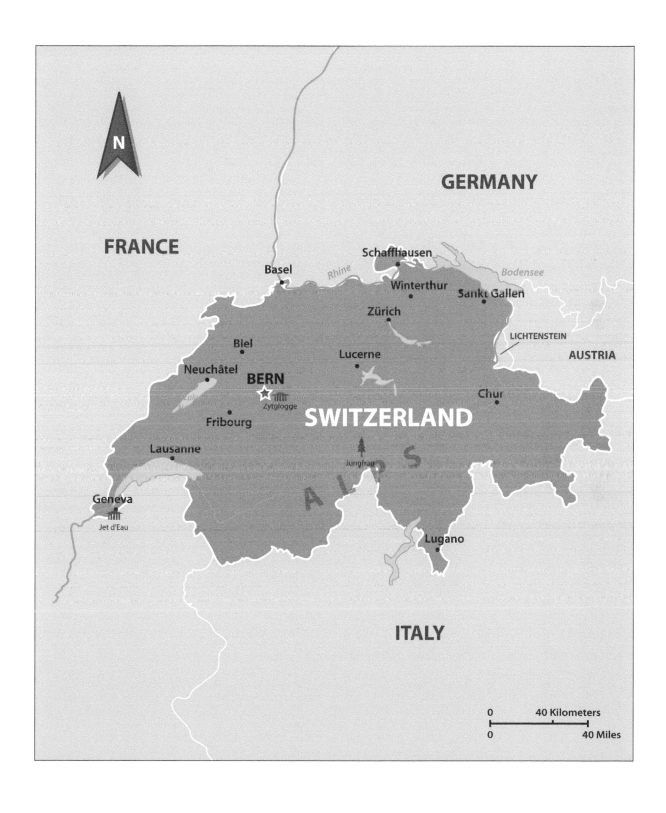

Principal Cities by Population (2012):

- Zürich (380,723)
- Geneva (190,544)
- Basel (167,297)
- Lausanne (129,944)
- Bern (122,925)
- Winterthur (102,654)
- St. Gallen (73,637)
- Lucerne (59,241) (2009 estimate)
- Lugano (59,922)
- Biel/Bienne (50,013) (2009 estimate)

Population

Located in the middle of Europe, Switzerland is a mixture of many European peoples and languages. About 20 percent of the population is foreign—an estimated 1.4 million—including many guest workers. An estimated 90 percent of the foreign population hails from other European nations and Geneva's foreign population numbers 40 percent.

Many communities are small (under 10,000 inhabitants) due to the mountainous geography, though many large cities do exist. The largest is Zurich, the country's commercial center, with a population of around 380,723. Bern, the national capital, is the fourth-largest, with a population of 122,925. Other large cities are Geneva (190,544), Basel (167,297), and Lausanne (129,944). About two-thirds of the Swiss population resides in urban areas—73.8 percent as of 2014—with about a third residing in the metropolitan areas of Zurich, Geneva, Basel, Bern, and Lausanne.

Languages

Swiss culture is highly regional, focusing on the language zones of the country's four official languages. German speakers predominate, making up around 64 percent of the population; they live largely in the central and northern parts of the country. (Seventeen of Switzerland's 26 cantons, or administrative divisions, speak German.) Swiss German (Schwyzerdütsch), as a spoken language, differs markedly from the "High

German" (Hochdeutsch) used in Germany, though the written forms are similar.

French-speakers make up about 20 percent of the population, and live mostly in western Switzerland. Italians comprise around 6.5 percent of the population, and live mostly in the south. Rhaeto-Romansch is spoken by a small minority (around 1 percent of the population), who live mostly in the canton of Graubünden (or Grisons), in southern Switzerland. According to Swissworld.org, the combined foreign languages spoken amongst the country's foreign-born population outnumber both Italian and Rhaeto-Romansch, with Serbians and Croatians the largest of that group at the turn of the 21st century.

Native People & Ethnic Groups

During the Stone and Bronze Ages, many peoples settled in what is now Switzerland. The Celts arrived around 1500 BCE. The dominant tribe was the Helvetii or Helvetians, from whom Switzerland takes its formal name of "Helvetic Confederation." The Raetians, another Celtic tribe, settled in the eastern lands now inhabited by Rhaeto-Romansch speakers.

The Romans arrived in the first century BCE, and developed the region extensively; the cities of Zurich, Geneva, and Basel were once Roman settlements. As Rome declined in the third and fourth centuries, Germanic tribes including the Alemanni and Burgundians settled Switzerland. The modern Swiss-German language is based on "Alemannic" dialects.

Religions

Roman Catholicism and Protestantism are the predominant religious groups in Switzerland. Catholics slightly outnumber Protestants 42 percent to 33 percent. There is a small Islamic minority that accounts for about 4 percent of the population.

Climate

Switzerland's climate is largely continental, experiencing cold winters and warm summers.

A Mediterranean climate prevails in the southern Ticino region, where palm trees grow. The Alpine region has snow and ice throughout the year, including over 3,000 square kilometers (1,158 square miles) of glaciers.

ENVIRONMENT & GEOGRAPHY

Topography

Switzerland is located in Central Europe, in the heart of the Alps mountain range. Its many mountain passes have made Switzerland an important stopover for travelers throughout history. The Jura Mountains to the northwest extend into France. The country's highest mountain is the Dufourspitze, at 15,203 feet (4,634 meters). It is part of the Monte Rose massif, located near the Italian border.

Switzerland's capital, Bern, sits on very uneven terrain, with height variations of several meters between the lowest and highest parts of the city. Glacier formed the hilly landscape around Bern, as well as the sprawling peninsula to which the city was originally confined.

Several large rivers flow through the country, including the Rhine and Rhone, whose headwaters begin there. The largest lakes are Lac Léman, also known as Lake Geneva, on the French border, Lake Constance (known in German as the Bodensee) on the German-Austrian border, and Lake Maggiore near the Italian border.

Plants & Animals

In addition to its forests, Switzerland is noted for the wide variety of wildflowers that grow in the mountains. Among the most common varieties are edelweiss, columbine, and gentian.

Switzerland has few large carnivores; bears and wolves are now mostly extinct, due to the spread of human habitation. Smaller mammals such as deer and fox are still plentiful, especially in the mountainous regions. Alpine species include the mountain goat species known as the ibex, and the horned antelope known as the chamois.

CUSTOMS & COURTESIES

Greetings

With four official languages— German, French, Italian, and Romansh—and a multitude of represented ethnic groups, greetings in Switzerland can be complicated. Furthermore, the French and Italian spoken in Switzerland are of a Swiss variety: Swiss French and Swiss Italian. These two hybrids differ slightly from their original, non-Swiss forms. Additionally, there are two kinds of German: High German, which is both written and spoken, and Swiss German, which is only spoken. To a lesser extent, Switzerland also features Romansh, relatively confined to the southeast of Switzerland and in danger of extinction, and Latin, used for the country's official designation, Confoederatio Helvetica (CH). Helvetica comes from the Helvetii tribe, which settled in what is now Switzerland in around 1500 BCE.

With such diversity, the Swiss are quick to point out that there is no Swiss norm. This is relatively true when comparing one region with another. For example, well acquainted friends in the French and Italian regions may kiss on the cheek three times when greeting each other, while in other regions the common gesture of greeting is the traditional handshake. Overall, there is a certain level of formality in Swiss culture. First names, though given in an initial meeting, are generally not used in an opening conversation. This practice is especially true of older Swiss; younger Swiss tend to be less formal.

Gestures & Etiquette

A common gesture of greeting among the Swiss is the traditional shaking of hands, while some Swiss in certain regions extend this gesture by kissing on the cheek. When taking leave, the Swiss will generally be precise in wishing favor or fortune, such as in "Have a nice afternoon" or "Have a good weekend." Departures typically may end with handshakes or kisses, again depending on how well the people know each other and what region they are in. In general, the Swiss are not given to expressive hand and arm gestures.

One particular aspect of Swiss etiquette is refraining from discussions about personal financial matters. This social custom may derive from the fact that Switzerland has one of the highest collective per capita incomes in the world—nearly 65,000 Swiss francs ($60,000 USD) according to the 2007 International Monetary Fund (IMF) ranking. There is even a Swiss law forbidding workers from discussing their salaries with each other. Generally, the only time money is openly discussed is as a national issue.

Eating/Meals
The Swiss typically have three meals a day, with a coffee or tea break common in the morning and afternoon. A popular breakfast food is muesli, a cereal of rolled oats developed by a Swiss physician around 1900. Traditional bread with jam and butter is also common at breakfast. A country influenced by the three major cultures that surround it—German, Italian, and French—produces staples that are intrinsically Swiss. These are the "peasant" foods of porridge, potatoes, stew, and perhaps most importantly, cheese. Nearly half of all Swiss milk is made into cheese.

When gathering for a meal, Swiss courtesy dictates that no one eat until the host does. This custom may also extend to the oldest individuals present at a meal. Before the meal, toasts are commonly given—often by the host. These toasts are known as "En guete" in Swiss German. The Swiss typically eat in a continental style, with the fork in the left hand and the knife in the right. Commonly, hands, but never elbows, remain on the table. When a meal is finished, it is often customary for utensils to be placed on the plate, side by side.

Visiting
Visits to Swiss homes are generally pre-arranged as opposed to being spontaneous social calls. If bringing a gift, the Swiss generally tend to favor small, inexpensive tokens such as chocolate, flowers or wine. Bringing a small gift for any children of the host is also looked upon favorably. In a nation known for its clocks and watches

(there are over 200 watchmakers, from the affordable Swatch to the high-end Patek Philippe), punctuality is appreciated.

While the Swiss are famously industrious—working on average forty-two hours a week—the typical four-week-long vacations, evenings, weekends, and many holidays allow ample time for socializing. As the Swiss are an active, athletic nation, quite often families will spend their off-hours hiking, mountaineering, and skiing.

LIFESTYLE

Family
Family and background are essential elements of the Swiss identity. For example, a Swiss passport lists not one's hometown, but one's ancestral home. Children ensure each family's future, and most Swiss families have two children. Since 1972, however, birth rates have dropped so low that the Swiss are no longer numerically replacing themselves. In addition, most women are over 27 years old when they have their first child. Although roughly one-third of marriages end in divorce, most of these divorces are postponed until after the children move out.

Up until the first half of the 20th century, young people remained home until they were married. Today, many Swiss choose to live together before marriage. However, single-parent families—usually led by mothers—have increased significantly in the last few decades. On average, women who do marry do so at the age of 27, with 29 for men.

Housing
While often synonymous or symbolic of Swiss housing, the chalet—a cottage with sloping roofs, ample eaves, and flower boxes in the windows—is only common in rural areas.

In the more densely populated and urban areas, the average Swiss family lives in a four-room rented apartment. Each apartment typically contains two children's rooms, a room for the parents, and one communal living space for living and dining. Often, a balcony can be attached, and the kitchen is in a corridor. Most flats often have storage, either in the attic and basement, with separate areas specifically for bicycles and cars. Laundry facilities are commonly shared among the families in each building.

Until the Second World War, more than 60 percent of Swiss lived in farmhouses. Today, that number has decreased dramatically, and most Swiss now live in cities and towns. Over 70 percent of Swiss live in rental units, giving Switzerland the lowest rate of property ownership in the developed world.

Food

Swiss cuisine has many influences, particularly the cultures of Germany, France and Italy. Nonetheless, the Swiss boast many unique and traditional staples and specialties, many of which are associated with pork and cheese, the latter being an internationally renowned Swiss product and export. The secret of Swiss cheese is in the milk, said to be unlike any other, largely due to the particular Alpine herbs and grasses the cows consume.

One meal each day, usually lunch, will typically include either sausage (wurst), veal (kalbsfleisch), or smoked meat (bündnerfleisch). A vegetable will also be served. A favorite vegetable dish, especially in the mountains, is rösti. The base is hash browns (fried grated potatoes) often covered with melted cheese, onions, bacon and fried eggs. Other popular main courses include cheese or meat pies, pork cutlets, quiches (a baked dish commonly made with eggs and cream), cheese fondue, and typical Italian staples such as pasta.

Naturally, cheese takes center stage in cheese fondue. Diners affix bread cubes to the ends of long forks, then dip them into a heated wine and cheese mixture. In some areas, custom demands that a lost bread cube lead to a round of Kirschwasser, or Kirsch (a type of brandy) for the table. Beef fondue (beef bourguignon) takes more preparation. Meat is skewered onto long forks and cooked in frying oil. As in cheese fondue, the pot has a heat source right on the table. Unlike cheese fondue, though, the cooked meat is then dipped into prepared sauces. Such dips may include a mayonnaise-based curry sauce, a mustard sauce, and one made of an onion and horseradish blend.

Switzerland is also known for its chocolates, and Swiss chocolatiers attribute the success of their chocolate to the choice of cocoa bean. A very dark and not too sweet bean makes for strong but not bitter chocolate. Chocolate was first brought to Europe from Central America in 1528. By the mid-1800s, the Swiss had popularized the treat, creating the first chocolate bar. It was also in Switzerland that milk was first added to chocolate. In yet another first, Switzerland is the home of the first chocolate factory built to manufacture chocolate bars. The United States now makes more chocolate, but Swiss chocolate is considered the world's finest. On average, a Swiss person eats 11.3 kilograms (25 pounds) of chocolate per year, more than anyone else in the world.

Life's Milestones

Switzerland is overwhelmingly Christian, with Catholics making up 42 percent of the population and Protestants 35 percent. As such, the major milestones in Swiss life are marked with religious ceremonies, and include rites associated with birth (baptism), marriage (traditional wedding ceremony) and death (funerals). For the most part, these occasions are marked with a church service, and weddings and funerals are traditionally followed by large meals.

CULTURAL HISTORY

Art

Switzerland is home to a unique and diverse culture. The country has no written language of its own, and over 80 percent of citizens speak either French or German, with a small percentage speaking either Italian or Romansh, a Romance language with Latin roots. As such, Switzerland's twenty-six cantons—or federal states—each boast unique traditional customs and cultural ties.

Sculpting wood is a centuries-old tradition in Switzerland. After creating a clay or wax model, carvers draw an outline of the desired shape on a block of wood. After cutting that shape with a band saw, the hand-carving begins. Big chisels give way to smaller chisels, the smallest of which are used to fashion details such as hair and eyes. Popular items range from figurines, bears and music boxes, to everyday items such as walking sticks and milking stools. Embroidery is another popular traditional folk art in Switzerland. Colorful and intricate needlework designs are common on traditional Swiss clothing, including hats, scarves and other accessories.

Ice sculpting is a traditional Swiss art still practiced today. Examples of this cold-climate art form can be seen at the ice museum located high in the Alps.

The visual arts in Switzerland did not fully emerge until modern times, particularly the 20th century. Prior to that, European art movements such as the Renaissance exerted little influence (save for architecture) on Swiss artists. Prominent Swiss painters prior to the 20th century include Arnold Böcklin (1827–1901), known for his landscapes and symbolist paintings; Albert Anker (1831–1910), who painted portraitures and often depicted rural Swiss life; and Ferdinand Hodler (1853–1918), whose works developed from landscapes and portraits into elements of symbolism and expressionism.

In 1916, two years into World War I, Zürich's Café Voltaire became the birthplace of the cultural movement known as Dada or Dadaism, which lasted roughly from 1916–1923. The philosophy behind Dada was to essentially question what made art, art. Largely a reflection of antiwar sentiment, Dadaism also universally rejected established forms of art and culture. Basically, the value of everything was questioned, often in a nihilistic sense (nihilism is the belief that nothing has value). Dadaists were known for taking ordinary objects, such as a bicycle wheel, and transforming them into art. After the movement's end, artists still worked in the Dada tradition. For example, Swiss artist Jean Tinguely (1925–1991) created sculptures in the Dada tradition that actually self-destructed.

More importantly, Dada is viewed by art historians as the spark that lit the more lasting art movement of surrealism. Surrealism is similar to abstract art and is often characterized as an expression of the subconscious. One of the best-known surrealist artists was Swiss sculptor Alberto Giacometti (1901–1966). His bronze figures—often knobby, tall and thin—are instantly recognizable. Abstract painter Paul Klee (1879–1940) is another famous Swiss surrealist. His works, much like Giacometti's, are still acclaimed worldwide.

Architecture

Architectural traditions in Switzerland date back to the 12th century, when the Romanesque style was prevalent in the construction of fortresses and cathedrals. This would later evolve into the Gothic style, particularly evident in the cathedrals of Zürich, Switzerland's cultural center. Later, the baroque style, which began in the 17th century, was used to build many of Switzerland's grand churches and abbeys. Because of Switzerland's neutrality, its many historic medieval castles and churches were, unlike those in other European countries, largely spared during the aerial bombing campaigns of World War II.

Switzerland is also home to progressive architectural innovations that challenge old notions of space and design. Swiss-born architect and city planner Le Corbusier (1887–1965) is considered one of the greatest architects of the 20th century. A renowned philosopher of architecture in addition to being a designer, Le Corbusier had strong ideas about creating space. His modular system of building design held that structures should be created in proportion to the human body. Further, he said that these buildings should be pure in form and materials, without unnecessary ornamentation. Ironically, only two of his buildings were ever built in Switzerland—a home for his parents on Lake Geneva and an apartment block in Geneva.

Switzerland's capital city, Bern, is most renowned for its medieval style; rebuilt after a devastating 1405 fire, the city—originally constructed of timber logged from surrounding forests—reemerged sculpted in locally mined gray-green sandstone. It has undergone remarkably little structural change over the centuries that followed.

Music

Though not known for its musical history in comparison to other European nations, Switzerland nonetheless has its own unique musical traditions. While little is known about the exact origins of Swiss folk music, it undoubtedly has its roots in the alpine and agrarian cultures of Switzerland, as well as the religious music popular in early Europe. As such, Swiss folk music is largely associated with yodeling and the alphorn.

Yodeling is a form of singing where high and low notes are cycled through rapidly. Yodeling was originally used as a way for distant herders to communicate with each other.

A musical instrument that figures prominently in Swiss folk music is the alphorn or alpenhorn. It is a very long wooden horn that resembles an over-extended tobacco pipe. Alphorns can be up to 4 meters (12 feet) in length, and were first used in Swiss folk music in the 18th century. Other popular folk instruments include the Schwyzerörgeli, a type of compact accordion named after the Swiss canton in which it was developed; the hammered dulcimer, a stringed musical instrument; and the violin. Switzerland also made important contributions to classical music, notably through Swiss composers Arthur Honegger (1892–1955) and Othmar Schoeck (1886–1957).

Literature

Swiss literature developed distinct branches due to the prevalence of three major European languages—French, Italian and German. Perhaps the most famous literary work associated with Swiss literature is *Heidi* (1880), the tale of a young girl in the Alps written by Swiss author Johanna Spyri (1827–1901). Another famous literary work associated with Swiss literature is *Swiss Family Robinson* (1812), written by Johann David Wyss (1743–1818). Both works were originally written in German.

Another famous Swiss writer was Jean-Jacques Rousseau (1712–1778). In addition to being credited with the first modern autobiography, Rousseau was known for his writings on political philosophy and his contributions as a music composer. In fact, Rousseau's anti-monarchist writings were believed to be influential to the French Revolution of the late 18th century. Other famous Swiss writers include Gottfried Keller (1819–1890), who advocated against writing in a Swiss national language; and poet Carl Spitteler (1845–1924), who was awarded the Nobel Prize in Literature in 1919.

CULTURE

Arts & Entertainment

Swiss culture is part of the European mainstream, and has produced many leading authors, composers, and artists. There are many important arts events, such as the music festivals at Lucerne and Montreux, held each year.

The performing arts are becoming increasingly popular in Switzerland, with roughly 200 small theatres throughout the country. The nation's most famous theatrical export is the gymnastic pantomime troupe known as Mummenschanz. Additionally, contemporary Swiss cinema, spurred on by a 1963 federal law encouraging the Swiss to explore their world via film, is growing. In fact, the 1991 film *Journey of Hope*, about a Kurdish family trying to move to Switzerland, won the Oscar for Best Foreign Film that year.

The practice of proclaiming everyday objects as art, known as Dadism, continues in contemporary Swiss culture with assemblage or object art, created with found objects. Swiss artist Daniel Spoerri (1930–) is credited with having revitalized this idea of reclaiming the everyday—even the thrown-away—as art. He is particularly known for his "snare pictures," which are random still life arrangements, often on tabletops. These may include half-eaten meals along with the plates, cutlery and glasses used while dining affixed to tables, then hung on walls.

The Zürich-born artistic duo of Peter Fischli (b. 1952–) and David Weiss (b. 1946–), often shortened to Fischli/Weiss, also feature found objects in their films, photographs and sculptures. Partners in art since 1979, their work is not only considered thought-provoking, but decidedly humorous. In one photograph, carved hot dogs are transformed into cars, while burnt cigarette butts are configured into people. In their 1981 film *The Least Resistance*, the two artists, one dressed as a rat and the other a panda, explore the art world of 1980s Los Angeles. Their work also includes photographs of some of Switzerland's great natural icons, such as the Matterhorn, an image they felt was being taken over by commercial and nationalist interests.

While Switzerland is famous for its many historic and well-preserved cathedrals and castles, the country's increasing secularism has led architects to focus more on the family home, rather than a communal building such as a church, as the center of spiritual life. Architect Mario Botta (1943-) has received international acclaim for his treatment of the house as a sculptural element set in its landscape. Similarly, Jacques Herzog and Pierre de Meuron, founders of the Basel-based architecture firm Herzog and de Meuron Architekten, are held in high esteem worldwide for their close attention to the use of materials. Often at the cutting-edge of modern design, Herzog and de Meuron have won numerous prestigious awards, including the coveted Pritzker Prize in 2001. Their designs range from the austere simplicity of the Tate Modern Museum in London, England, to the fantastically complex "Bird Nest" stadium of the 2008 Beijing Summer Olympics in China.

Beyond the world of arts, the Swiss greatly enjoy sports, particularly alpine sports such as skiing and mountaineering. Marksmanship events are highly popular, in part because of the country's tradition of citizen-soldiers.

Switzerland has produced some unique sports of its own: the wrestling style known as schwingen, and the ballgame known as hornussen.

Cultural Sites & Landmarks

Switzerland is home to numerous cultural sites and landmarks, many of which reflect the country's diverse cultural blend of German, Italian and French influences. In particular, Switzerland boasts nine sites designated as World Heritage Sites by the United Nations Educational, Scientific and Cultural Organization (UNESCO), an agency of the United Nations (UN) that promotes international culture. One such site is the medieval Old City of Bern, Switzerland's capital and fourth largest city. The layout of the old city dates back to the 12th century.

Other manmade sites protected by UNESCO include the Abbey of St. Gall, which dates back to the seventh century; the Benedictine Convent of Saint John, an ancient monastery; and the Three Castles of Bellinzona, a grouping of ancient fortifications located in the town of Bellinzona.

While not a World Heritage Site, one of the best-known Swiss castles is the oval-shaped Château de Chillon on Lake Geneva. The 13th-century picturesque fortress features numerous courtyards, halls and dungeons. The castle has been the subject of artistic works throughout history, notably by poet Lord Byron (1788–1824), authors Alexandre Dumas (1802–1870) and Mary Shelley (1797–1851), and painters William Turner (1508–1568) and Gustave Courbet (1819–1877). The castle reportedly has been host to more visitors than any other historical building in all of Switzerland.

Switzerland's capital is also home to two other enduring cultural symbols: the bear and the Zytglogge landmark. Bern is named for the bears that live in the city's bear pits, where they have resided since 1480. The Zytglogge is a 13th-century clock tower that features an hourly performance of several clock faces and emerging figurines, including a crowing rooster, bears, jesters and knights.

Albert Einstein made Bern home in the early 1900s when he lived in the city and worked as a patent clerk. It is believed that Einstein developed his world-changing theory of relativity in Bern. His home, on a busy shopping street, is now a small museum.

Further south and situated on the Swiss peninsula that dips into France, Geneva is very much a global city. It is a university city, and more than 200 international organizations have offices there, including the European headquarters of the UN. A popular tourist attraction in Geneva is the Jet d'Eau, a fountain on Lake Geneva that shoots water to a height of 140-meters (460-feet). It is Europe's tallest fountain. Not far from the Jet d'Eau, in the Jardin Anglais sits the Flower Clock, a working clock whose face is a bed of planted seasonal flowers.

If Switzerland is the world's bank then Zürich is the vault. A plaque dating from the Roman Empire attests to the city's early and successful management of money. By the 14th century, Zürich's workers had amassed tremendous wealth, and the workers' guilds were able to replace nobility as the movers and shakers of the national congress.

South of Zürich, in the medieval town of Einsiedeln, is a statue of the Black Madonna dating to the 15th century. Years of candles, oil lamps and incense turned the once-white statue's face and hands black. An Austrian craftsman cleaned the statue, but the locals so disliked the new white Madonna that in 1803, they settled the matter by painting it black.

Switzerland's biggest landmarks, both literally and figuratively, are the Alps mountain range. The Matterhorn is the peak perhaps most identified with Switzerland. It towers above the small town of Zermatt at a staggering 4,478 meters (14,691 feet) high. North of the Matterhorn three legendary Alpine mountains dominate the landscape—Eiger (ogre), Mönch (monk), and Jungfrau (maiden). Swiss legend holds that the monk protects the maiden from the ogre. UNESCO designated the mountains a World Heritage Site in 2001.

In addition to the Alps, Switzerland is home to several other World Heritage Sites. These include the Sardona Tectonic Area, a major fault

in the Swiss Alps; the Vineyard Terraces wine region in the district of Lavaux; and the natural area of Monte San Giorgio, a wooded mountain which contains fossil records of marine life dating back 230 million years.

Libraries & Museums

Bern features a number of prominent museums. These include the Bern Historical Museum, a Museum of Natural History, and a Museum of Fine Arts, which exhibits the work of some of the most important 20th-century artists. The Paul Klee Center holds the largest collection of Paul Klee paintings in the world, around 4,000 works, nearly half of his creations. The Swiss Alpine Museum offers visitors insights into unique cultural and natural aspects of the alpine world. The Einstein Museum is located in what was once Albert Einstein's home in Bern.

Basel, a commercial center in Switzerland, also has a large number of museums, including one devoted to cartoon characters and another to paper.

Holidays

Switzerland celebrates the major Christian holidays, such as Christmas and Easter, as well as Christian festivals such as Fastnacht (Carnival), which celebrates the arrival of Lent. Switzerland's national holiday is August 1, commemorating the establishment of the Confederation in 1291.

Youth Culture

Swiss children are encouraged to participate in group and recreational activities at an early age. These pastimes are often sports, including football (soccer), schlagball (a variation on softball) and gymnastics. In fact, a national poll conducted in 1999 revealed that 63 percent of those aged between 18 and 39 regarded leisure or recreational pursuits as "very important."

Generally, Swiss youth culture is similar to that of the United States, with many of the same trends and varying tastes. Swiss youth are on par with their Western counterparts in terms of adapting and using technology, particularly mobile communication technology and the Internet. Lastly, the most popular name for boys in 2007 was Luca, while Sara(h) topped the charts for girls.

SOCIETY

Transportation

A popular form of transportation in Switzerland is the rail system, which has a reputation for efficiency and elegance. The national train lines account for about half of all trains; private lines, which usually have the more scenic routes, cover the rest. The Rhaetian Railway (RhB) operates the largest network of railways in the country. In fact, RhB-operated routes through the Albula/Bernina landscapes were designated as a World Heritage Site by UNESCO in 2008. In addition, the Alpine town of Brienz still operates a steam-powered train.

In Switzerland, traffic drives on the right side of the road, and the use of seat belts, both front and rear, is legally required.

Transportation Infrastructure

Switzerland is generally seen as having a comprehensive and robust transportation infrastructure. One important aspect of transportation in Switzerland is its transalpine network, particularly the crossing of the Alps. This network consists of numerous railway tunnels, including the Gotthard Base Tunnel (GBT), which will become the longest road or railway tunnel in the when it is completed in 2017. In 2007, the rail network in Switzerland spanned 5,107 kilometers (3,173 miles).

Switzerland also has a vast network of well-maintained private and public roads, including the autobahn network of high-speed roads. At the beginning of the 21st century, the Swiss autobahn was nearly 1,650 kilometers (1,025 miles) long. Motorists travel these highways, keeping to the right side of the road, and passing on the left.

Major cities feature intercity or metro trains, and bus travel is prominent in both urban and rural areas. In addition, Switzerland has

sixty-five airports, more than forty of which have paved runways.

According to the 2009 Travel and Tourism Competitiveness Report, which measures the best environments for investing in and developing travel and tourism industry, Switzerland ranks No. 1 overall (out of 133 countries).

Media & Communications

Switzerland has more than 200 regional newspapers (none are national) and most newspapers and magazines are written in German. Widely read newspapers include *Neue Zürcher Zeitung* (NZZ), published in Zürich in the German language, and *Le Temps*, published in Geneva in the French language. Television and radio programs are largely broadcast in French, German and Italian. Major TV networks include Schweizer Fernsehen (SF), Télévision Suisse Romande (TSR) and Televisione Svizzera Italiana (TSI).

When it comes to news, High German is the dominant language, and sports are most often broadcast in Swiss German. While there is no separate Romansh TV channel, Romansh cultural programs are available on other Swiss channels, and there is a Romansh radio station. The number of Internet users rose from 0.7 million in 1998 to over 6.1 million in 2009; it is estimated that more than three-quarters of Swiss homes have computers.

SOCIAL DEVELOPMENT

Standard of Living

Switzerland has an extremely high standard of living, with a well-educated populace and high life expectancy. Average life expectancy is 82 years; 80 for men and 84 for women (2014 estimate). In 2014, the country ranked third on the United Nations' Human Development Index.

Water Consumption

Due to its proximity to the Alps, Switzerland is considered a water-rich nation. The Swiss Alps, in fact, serve as the source of an estimated 6 percent of freshwater reserves in Europe, and is called the "water tower of Europe." Switzerland is also known for the quality of its drinking water; according to Swissworld.org, which is administered by the Federal Department of Foreign Affairs, the county's drinking water is equal in quality to bottled mineral water.

Groundwater is the source for over 80 percent of drinking water in Switzerland. According to the Swiss Agency for the Environment, Forests and Landscape, as of 2010, water consumption in the country is about 160 liters (42 gallons) per household, per inhabitant.

Education

The Swiss are highly educated; the country's literacy rate is around 99 percent. Education is handled largely at the local level, through organizations such as the Swiss Conference of Cantonal Education Directors (Schweizerische Konferenz der kantonalen Erziehungsdirektoren). There is no federal education agency, though the government docs operate a few institutions of higher education.

At age six or seven, children are eligible for free and mandatory public education, and 95 percent of Swiss children attend their local, publicly-funded school. At age sixteen or seventeen, students may continue academic training or opt for vocational studies. One third of Swiss students go on to study at the university level.

Schools vary widely from canton to canton. Some cantons require that their students attend forty hours a week. Although school curriculums and sessions vary, one constant is taken very seriously throughout Switzerland: attendance. Swiss schools have among the lowest student absentee rate in the world.

In the mid-19th century, Switzerland became one of the first countries to adopt the kindergarten model of early education. Primary school lasts until about age fifteen. There are two main types of secondary education: gymnasium is a school which focuses on academic studies and prepares students for university, while other students take vocational courses and apprenticeships, to prepare for a career.

Post-secondary education is largely under the control of the cantons, which are similar to states in the U.S. Public universities are operated by the cantonal governments. Several Swiss universities date from the Renaissance; those at Basel and Geneva were founded in the 15th century. Most, however, were founded in the 19th century, including the universities of Bern, Lausanne, and Zurich. The federal government operates two technical institutes (Eidgenössischen Technischen Hochschulen).

Women's Rights

Women earned the right to vote in Swiss national elections in 1971. In one of Switzerland's 26 cantons, the right to vote on local matters wasn't granted for another twenty years. However, once women had federal suffrage, they rose quickly through the political ranks, twice reaching the presidency by 2008. (Swiss presidents, selected from a seven-member executive council, serve one-year terms.) In recent years, one quarter of all cantonal legislators have been women.

A 1981 amendment to the Federal Constitution established equal rights and wages for women and men, with less than optimum results. According to a 2004 government study, women's gross salaries were on average 21 percent lower than men's. This discrepancy is in part due to the lower-paying nature of the work that many women do: in sales, as teachers, and as serving staff. An underlying cause for any continuing imbalance between men and women's salaries is usually identified as the consequence of women's role in childrearing. A 1990 survey showed that 50 percent of older men and 33 percent of older women thought that a woman's place was exclusively in the home. However, such attitudes are changing.

Although Swiss men maintain a life-long obligation to national military service, women are not required to serve. However, the Women's Military Corps is a volunteer group with equal status to men. Unlike their male counterparts who are required to keep and maintain a rifle, Women's Military Corps members don't generally carry arms. They may have a pistol if they so choose. Originally founded in 1939 as the Women's Auxiliary Corps, the Corps welcomed 20,000 Swiss women who signed up to assist during World War II. Swiss women are also eligible to volunteer for the Red Cross, which is headquartered in Geneva.

Abuse against girls and women is a problem in Switzerland. In a 1996 survey conducted by a British medical journal, nearly 20 percent of 1,200 randomly-selected ninth-grade girls reported having been sexually abused at least once. A 2003 survey revealed that 25 percent of women aged twenty to sixty had been the victim of domestic abuse at least once. According to a survey that same year, 70 percent of physical violence cases go unreported to the police. Ninety-four percent of sexual abuse cases are believed not reported.

Health Care

Public health in Switzerland is handled entirely by the cantons. Most hospitals and health-care facilities are public, but dozens of private institutions exist as well. All Swiss citizens must have health insurance, though this is often publicly subsidized. Switzerland has an extensive social-welfare system which provides medical care for the poor, disabled, and elderly.

GOVERNMENT

Structure

The Swiss Confederation was established in the late 13th century when the cantons of Uri, Schwyz, and Unterwalden signed a mutual aid pact to maintain peace and protect their independence from aggression by the Holy Roman Empire.

In 1499, the Confederation achieved full independence from Austria. In 1515, the government adopted its long-standing policy of strict neutrality after severe defeats by the French and Venetians.

Switzerland was also sharply divided between Catholics and Protestants during the 16th century Reformation and the religious wars which followed. Ultimately, the government's modern federal system was established in 1848, following a short civil war (the 1847 Sonderbundskrieg) between Catholics and Protestants. The constitution was revised in 1874, 1891 and 1999.

Because of its neutrality, Switzerland has generally refused to join international alliances, though it participates in many other international groups. It does not belong to the European Union (EU), and it did not become a full member of the United Nations until 2002.

Swiss federalism is modeled partly on that of the United States, with its three branches of government (legislative, executive, and judicial) and the doctrine that all powers not specifically given to the federal government are retained by the cantons. Switzerland is famous for its direct democracy, making frequent use of the initiative and the referendum. Despite Switzerland's long democratic tradition, women's suffrage came late, granting women the right to vote in federal elections in 1971.

The legislative branch is the most powerful of the three. It is composed of a two-house parliament known as the Federal Assembly, consisting of the 46-member Council of States (Ständerat) and the 200-member National Council (Nationalrat). Unlike many other national legislatures, the two houses are equal in power.

Switzerland's unusual executive branch consists of the seven-member Federal Council (Bundesrat), which serves as a joint head of state. The members are elected by and responsible to the Federal Assembly. Although all Federal Council members share power equally, each year one member is elected to serve as Chancellor of the Confederation; this official represents Switzerland internationally and has other administrative and ceremonial functions. The council members also serve as heads of the various government departments.

The Federal Supreme Court comprises the judiciary. This court is composed of two courts: the Federal Court (Bundesgericht), which handles constitutional issues as well as appeals from the cantonal courts; and the Federal Insurance Court, which handles social security issues. The Federal Criminal Court (Bundesstrafgericht), located in Bellinzona, Canton Tessin, was established in 2004.

Political Parties

The main political parties in Switzerland are the Christian Democratic People's Party (CVP), the Social Democratic Party (SPS), the Free Democratic Party (FDP), and the Swiss People's Party (SVP). The CVP party, formed in 1912, is a center-right party; the SPS party, formed in 1881, is considered Switzerland's most leftist party; the FDP party, known as the Radical Free Democratic Party, is characterized as center-right/liberal; and the SVP, formed in 1971, is a nationalist right party. The Conservative Democratic Party of Switzerland (PBD) is a newer party, an offshoot of the SVP, formed in 2008. Minority parties include the Greens (Die Grünen), who, as of 2010, are represented in the Swiss Council of States with two seats.

From the late 1950s until 2003, these four parties had an informal agreement for allocating seats on the Federal Council, based on their strength in the National Assembly. Known as the "magic formula," it allocated seven cabinet seats in the Federal Council among these four parties. As of 2010, the council consisted of one CVP representative, two FDP representatives, two Social Democratic representatives, one SVP representative, and one representative from the Conservative Democratic Party of Switzerland. The council now includes the splinter PBD party within the "magic formula."

Local Government

Switzerland is a confederation (German: Eidgenossenschaft) of 26 "cantons," or member localities, which are considered sovereign states and which retain a high level of autonomy. The cantons are divided into districts (Bezirke). These handle the local educational system and courts. The districts are divided into municipalities (Gemeinden), which administer local services, schools, mass transit, and taxation. A larger municipality (one with more than 10,000 people) is called a town (Stadt), while a smaller one is known as a village (Dorf).

Judicial System

The Judiciary system in Switzerland consists of the Swiss Federal Tribunal, or Supreme Court, the Swiss Federal Criminal Court, the trial court of first instance, and the Swiss Federal Administrative Court. Each canton also operates cantonal courts, organized into civil, criminal or administrative courts of first instance or courts of appeals.

Taxation

Switzerland does not have a centralized tax system, and some taxes are levied concurrently at the federal, cantonal, and municipal level. The personal income tax, levied at all three levels, has a progressive rate, and does not exceed 40 percent. Other taxes include the annual wealth tax and inheritance taxes, levied at the cantonal level, stamp duties and social security tax, levied by the federation, a value-added tax (VAT), and capital gains tax on real estate transactions. Generally, taxation in Switzerland is much lower than neighboring European nations, and its 20 percent marginal tax rate on average income workers is among the lowest in the world.

Armed Forces

The Swiss Armed Forces consists of the Swiss Land Forces and the Swiss Air Force. With an official policy of neutrality, the primary mission of the Swiss armed forces is to support civil affairs and international peace initiatives, and for national security. All male citizens are required by law to perform military service in Switzerland; military service for women is voluntary.

Foreign Policy

Switzerland is famous for its international policy of neutrality. The last time the Swiss were engaged in warfare was during a brief civil war in 1847, a conflict that itself came after over 30 years of peace. In 1848, the Swiss constitution, modeled on that of the United States, was written. Switzerland's neutrality was codified in this document. In addition, Switzerland is not a member of the European Union (EU), and one of the last remaining countries to not have membership. The Swiss maintain numerous bilateral contracts with the EU, but have not accepted the EU currency of the euro, instead maintaining the Swiss franc. Switzerland was accepted as a full member of the UN in 2002, an initiative narrowly approved by voters. Switzerland is not a member of the North Atlantic Treaty Organization (NATO), in accordance with its policy of avoiding alliances.

Financially, neutrality has historically been a smart move for the Swiss. This was particularly true in the 20th century, when Switzerland's agricultural resources allowed it to become the region's primary supplier of food during wartime. Additionally, the stability of neutrality has made Switzerland an attractive place for investors, evident in the international success and reputation of Swiss banks. Swiss banks are particularly known for their secrecy, an aspect which has often figured into the country's foreign relations. Ever since World War II, Swiss bank accounts have had numbers, but no names associated to them. Such a system appeals to those who wish to keep their financial assets unknown, but has drawn international criticism as well. The practice largely began in order to hide financial assets from the Nazi regime in Germany.

Swiss insularity is also evidenced by the policies relating to gaining Swiss citizenship. The process can only begin when a person has lived in the country for twelve years. However, applicants between the ages of ten and twenty require only six years of residency.

Human Rights Profile

International human rights law insists that states respect civil and political rights, and also promote an individual's economic, social and cultural rights. The United Nations Universal Declaration on Human Rights (UDHR) is recognized as the standard for international human rights. Its authors sought the counsel of the world's great thinkers, philosophers, and religious leaders, and were careful to create a document that reflects the core values shared by every world culture. (To read this document or view the articles relating to cultural human rights, go to: http://www.udhr.org/UDHR/default.htm).

Twenty percent of the people living in Switzerland are foreign, including nationals from Europe, the U.S., Asia, Africa, and the Middle East. Anti-foreign sentiment within Switzerland has been on the rise over the last few decades. By the 1970s, when unemployment threatened, quotas on the number of foreign workers allowed entry were established.

Such quotas and the political sentiment they invoke would appear to be in violation of Article 2 of the UDHR, prohibiting the denial of rights based on factors including language or national origin. In July 2008, the right-wing Swiss People's Party gained well over the 100,000 signatures needed to force a nationwide vote to ban the building of Muslim minarets.

In the 1990s, Jewish groups forced major Swiss banks to admit that millions of dollars of money belonging to Holocaust victims and survivors sat in sheltered accounts. In 1998, two of Switzerland's largest banks—UBS and Credit Suisse—paid out 1.4 billion Swiss francs ($1.25 billion USD) in restitution to the victims and their families.

According to the U.S. State Department's 2005 Human Rights Country Report on Switzerland, child abuse is a national issue. A study published in January of that year estimated that the number of children under thirty months old who had either been slapped, hit with an object, or had their hair pulled by their parents was nearly 50,000.

Nonetheless, Switzerland has a reputation for tolerance and progressive thinking. It is the home of more than 200 international organizations, including the League of Nations, the World Council of Churches (WCC), the Boy Scouts, the Young Men's Christian Association (YMCA) and the European headquarters of the UN. It is also the birthplace of the International Committee of the Red Cross (ICRC).

ECONOMY

Overview of the Economy

Switzerland's economy is based largely on services and manufacturing. The service sector dominates, accounting for more than 50 percent of the economy and focusing on banking and financial services, international commerce, and tourism. Financial services alone account for around 10 percent of the gross domestic product (GDP). Swiss banks have become famous because of their stability and discretion.

In 2014, the gross domestic product (GDP) was estimated at $444.7 billion USD. Switzerland has one of the highest income per capita in the developed world, estimated at $55,200 (USD).

Industry

Swiss manufacturing has a worldwide reputation for high quality, particularly for fine items such as clocks and watches, as well as for industrial parts. The chemical and pharmaceutical industries are also large.

The northern part of the canton of Bern is a world center for the manufacture of precision timepieces. The expertise generated by this industry has found many cross-applications. The capital has become a center of research innovation in medical and information technology, the automotive and engineering industries, and the manufacture of precision instruments and nanotechnology tools.

The Swiss chocolate industry has its origin in the capital as well. The first chocolate shop in Switzerland opened in Bern in 1792. Rodolphe Lindt founded his chocolate factory in Bern in 1879. Jean Tobler opened a chocolate shop in Bern in 1867, and in 1899 founded his own factory in the capital. Lindt and Tobler's companies today represent key global players in the multi-billion-dollar chocolate industry.

The EU is a major trading partner, and Switzerland belongs to international organizations such as the European Free Trade Association.

Labor

Switzerland has one of the highest income rates per capita in the developed world, estimated at $43,196 (USD). As of early 2014, the unemployment rate in Switzerland was 3.2 percent.

Energy/Power/Natural Resources

Switzerland has extensive forests, covering about one-quarter of the country. These are a mix of deciduous species such as beech and oak, as well as coniferous species such as fir and pine. Despite the presence of so many mountains, there are only a few mineral resources. The country's lakes and rivers are major sources of hydroelectric power.

Fishing

Commercial fishing is a relatively minor industry in Switzerland. According to the Federal Office for the Environment, there were only 310 professional fishermen in 2010. Lake Geneva, Europe's second largest lake, was once an important fishing ground. Common species of fish in Switzerland include pike, trout, char, and perch.

Forestry

Switzerland has extensive forests, covering an estimated 31 percent of the country in the early 21st century. These are a mix of deciduous species such as beech and oak, as well as coniferous species such as fir and pine.

Mining/Metals

Despite the presence of so many mountains in Switzerland, mineral resources are sparse.

Agriculture

Switzerland's agricultural sector is very small, mostly due to the country's limited supply of arable land. Dairy and beef farming are the main activities. Food crops include sugar beets, fruit, potatoes, and barley.

Most farms are small and run by their owners. The federal government closely controls agriculture in order to ensure that Switzerland always has a sufficient food supply, but since the 1990s, has increased the role of the free-market system.

Animal Husbandry

Dairy and beef farming are Switzerland's main agricultural activities. Other common livestock include pigs, goats, and sheep.

Tourism

The tourist industry comprises a major portion of the Swiss economy, employing several hundred thousand people. In 2008, there were an estimated 270,487 hotels and health establishments (in terms of supplying beds). In 2011, tourism was valued at more than $18 billion (USD).

Tourists come to Switzerland to enjoy winter sports and mountaineering, the rustic charm of alpine villages, and to take part in the cosmopolitan cultural life of cities such as Geneva, Bern, and Zurich.

Hope L. Killcoyne, Eric Badertscher, Beverly Ballaro

DO YOU KNOW?

- The Swiss Guards that defend the Pope in Vatican City are vestiges of the Swiss mercenaries who served in European armies centuries ago.

- The wildflower edelweiss is an unofficial national symbol of Switzerland.

- In 1999, Switzerland celebrated the 150th anniversary of the establishment of the modern federal state.

- Wilhelm (William) Tell, the legendary Swiss hero, reportedly fought in the 14th century to gain Swiss independence from the Holy Roman Empire. Many modern historians, however, doubt that Tell ever existed.

Bibliography

Bewes, Diccon. *Swiss Watching: Inside the Land of Milk and Honey.* Boston: Nicholas Brealey, 2012.

Birmingham, David. *Switzerland: A Village History.* Athens, OH: Swallow Press, 2004.

Church, Clive H. and Randolph C. Head. *A Concise History of Switzerland.* New York: Cambridge University Press, 2013.

Maycock, Kendall. *Culture Smart! Switzerland.* London: Kuperard, 2006.

Simonis, Damien, Nicola Williams and Sarah Johnstone. *Switzerland.* 5th ed. Oakland: Lonely Planet, 2006.

Teller, Matthew. *Rough Guide to Switzerland.* London: Rough Guides, 2010.

Weiner, Eric. *The Geography of Bliss.* 2008. New York: Hachette Book Group USA, Inc., 2008.

Williams, Nicola. *Switzerland.* Oakland, CA: Lonely Planet, 2012.

Works Cited

"Alps of France and Switzerland." Rick Steves' Europe. Rick Steves. *Oregon Public Broadcasting,* Edmonds, WA. 2005.

"Bread and Chocolate." Dir. Franco Brusati. Perf. Nino Manfredi, Johnny Dorelli, Anna Karina. DVD. *Hen's Tooth Video*, 1974.

"Country Reports on Human Rights Practices." Bureau of Democracy, Human Rights, and Labor. *U.S. Department of State* http://www.state.gov/g/drl/rls/hrrpt/2005/61678.htm

"Facts and Figures on Violence Against Women." Say No to Violence Against Women. *UNIFEM, United Nations Development Fund for Women.* http://www.unifem.org/campaigns/vaw/facts_figures.php?page=3

"Finfacts: Ireland's Business and Financial Portal." From World Bank Development Indicators 2007 Feb 2008: International Comparison Program.

"First same-sex union registered in Switzerland." *Swissinfo.ch.* 2 Jan 2007. http://www.swissinfo.ch/eng/swissinfo.html?siteSect=105&sid=7396788

"Germany, Switzerland and Austria." Passport to Europe. Samantha Brown. *Travel Channel*, Chatsworth, CA. 2007.

"Mercer's Quality of Living Survey Highlights." Mercer LLC. Mercer LLC. http://www.mercer.com/qualityofliving

David Cay Johnston. David Cay. "Jews Remember Forced Labor Camps in Wartime Swiss Refuge." The *New*

York Times 15 Jan 1998. http://query.nytimes.com/gst/fullpage.html?res=9E0CE2D91E39F936A25752C0A96E958260

Diener, Roger, Jacques Herzog, Marcel Meili, Pierre de Meuron, and Christian Schmid. "Switzerland, an Urban Portrait: Materials (Book 3)." *Basel: Birkhäuser - Publishers for Architecture*, 2006.

Felicity Rash. "Greeting Rituals in Switzerland." *Languagechat.com* http://www.languagehat.com/archives/001737.php

Guy Raz and Sylvia Poggioli. National Public Radio, Washington, DC. 10 Jul 2008 http://www.npr.org/templates/story/story.php?storyId=92421149

Helen Fairbairn, Helen and Gareth McCormack, Sandra Bardwell, Grant Dixon and Clem Lindenmayer. "Walking in the Alps." 1st. *Oakland: Lonely Planet*, 2004.

Helena Bachmann, Helena. "Bye-Bye, Black Sheep." *Time Magazine* 21 Sep 2007 http://www.time.com/time/world/article/0,8599,1664269,00.html

http://topics.nytimes.com/top/news/international/countriesandterritories/switzerland/index.html

http://www.bfs.admin.ch/bfs/portal/de/index/news/publikationen.html?publicationID=2848

http://www.finfacts.ie/biz10/globalworldincomepercapita.htmlglobalworldincomepercapita.htm

http://www.geneve-tourisme.ch/?rubrique=0000000168&lang=_eng *Geneva Tourism*.

http://www.swissinfo.ch/eng/front/index.html?siteSect=100 Swiss News, Worldwide

http://www.swissworld.org/en/people/ Swissworld.org, Your Gateway to Switzerland

Ian Traynor. Ian. "Islamophobia: Swiss far right seeks vote on minarets ban ," *The Guardian 9* Jul 2008. Guardian.co.uk.

Louis René Beres, Louis René. "Invited Remarks to Swiss Task Force on World War II." The Jewish Press. Swiss Ambassador Thomas Borer. *The Jewish Press*. Bern. 23 Jun 1998. http://www.jewishpress.com/displaycontent_new. cfm?contentid=33815&contentname=Invited percent20 Remarkspercent20topercent20Swisspercent20 Taskpercent20Forcepercent20onpercent20Worldpercent 20Warpercent20IIpercent20percent20Deliver& sectionid= 20&mode=a&recnum=0

"Peter Fischli and David Weiss." Press Packet. *Matthew Marks Gallery*. http://www.matthewmarks.com/press/115.pdf

Paul Karr, Paul and Martha Coombs. "Hostels - Austria and Switzerland." 2nd. Guilford, CT: *The Globe Pequot Press*, 2002.

Peter Popham. "William Tell: Celebrating a Republican Icon," *The Independent* 17 Nov 2007. ndependent.co.uk. http://www.independent.co.uk/news/world/europe/william-tell-celebrating-a-republican-icon-400705.html

"Proposed Swiss immigration laws show 'rise of new racism and xenophobia.'" Mail Online 07 Sep 2007. UK Daily Mail, *Associated Newspapers Ltd.* http://www.dailymail.co.uk/news/article-480493/Proposed-Swiss-immigration-laws-rise-new-racism-xenophobia.html

R. Veenhoven. *World Database of Happiness*, Erasmus University Rotterdam. http://worlddatabaseofhappiness.eur.nl

Roger Diener, Roger, Jacques Herzog, Marcel Meili, Pierre de Meuron, and Christian Schmid. "Switzerland, Anan Urban Portrait: Introduction (Book 1)." *Basel: Birkhäuser - Publishers for Architecture,* 2006.

Roger Diener, Roger, Jacques Herzog, Marcel Meili, Pierre de Meuron, and Christian Schmid. "Switzerland, an Urban Portrait: Borders, Communes – A Brief History of the Territory (Book 2)." *Basel: Birkhäuser - Publishers for Architecture*, 2006.

"Seeds of Ethnic Cleansing Sprout in Europe." *Talk of the Nation*. World.

"Statistical Data on Switzerland." *Swiss Confederation.* http://www.bfs.admin.ch/bfs/portal/en/index/themen/die_schweiz_in_ueberblick/ts.Document 107701.pdf

Statistik des jährlichen Bevölkerungsstandes (ESPOP) Definitive Ergebnisse.

"Swiss Etiquette Tips." *Vayama* (travel web site), Swiss Etiquette Tips. http://www.vayama.com/switzerland-etiquette

"Switzerland." *CIA - The World Factbook*. Central Intelligence Agency. https://www.cia.gov/library/publications/the-world-factbook/geos/sz.html

Thanh-Huyen Ballmer-Cao, Thanh-Huyen, Pietro Bellasi, Michael J. Enright, Shuhei Hosokawa, Claude Imbert, Natalja Ivanova, Sohan P. Modak, Michael Rutschky, Darcy Ribeiro, Ali Salem, Carol Thatcher, and Daniel Vernet. "Switzerland Through through the Eyes of Others." *Zürich: Der Alltag/Scalo*, 1992.

x.html World news News about Switzerland, including breaking news and archival articles published in The *New York Times*.

Italian artist, sculptor and architect Gianlorenzo Bernini (1598-1680) designed St. Peter's Square, pictured above, as a gathering place for the faithful, a purpose it still fulfills today. /Stock photo © Nikada

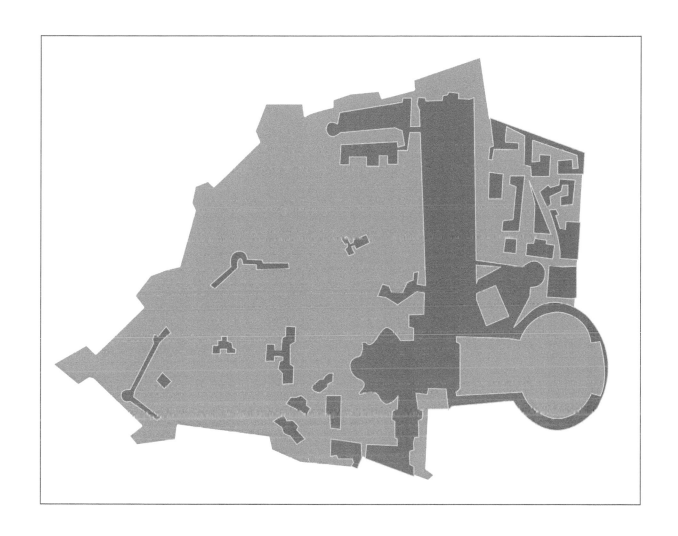

VATICAN CITY

Introduction

Vatican City now stands as the world's smallest independent nation and the physical headquarters of the Holy See (Holy Seat). The Holy See carries the responsibility of the spiritual leadership of Roman Catholicism, as well as being a state with diplomatic responsibilities on the international stage. This is distinct from Vatican City's more mundane and local political function, which is to oversee and conduct the Catholic Church's properties in Rome. The pope is the head of all these entities, both spiritual and temporal.

Vatican City was officially established as a nation in 1929, by means of an historic treaty between the Archdiocese of Rome and the Italian government. The Italian government agreed to guarantee the ability of the Church and the pope to control the city-state, and to protect the safety of the pope and the people of the now tax-exempt Vatican City. In return, the Catholic Church gave up any claim to control or ownership of any territory in Italy outside the walls of Vatican City, save for thirteen buildings. These buildings are considered part of Vatican territory.

GENERAL INFORMATION

Official Language: Latin (affairs of state)
Population: 824 (2014)
Currency: Euro, Vatican lire
Coins: Vatican City euro coins come in denominations of .01, .02, .05, .10, .20, .50, 1, and 2.
Land Area: 0.44 square kilometers (0.17 square miles)
National Anthem: "Inno e Marcia Pontificale" ("Hymn and Pontifical March")
Capital: Vatican City
Time Zone: GMT +2
Flag Description: The flag of Vatican City comprises two equally sized vertical bands of yellow (hoist side) and white. In the center of the white band are the crossed keys of St. Peter, over which the three-tiered papal tiara rests.

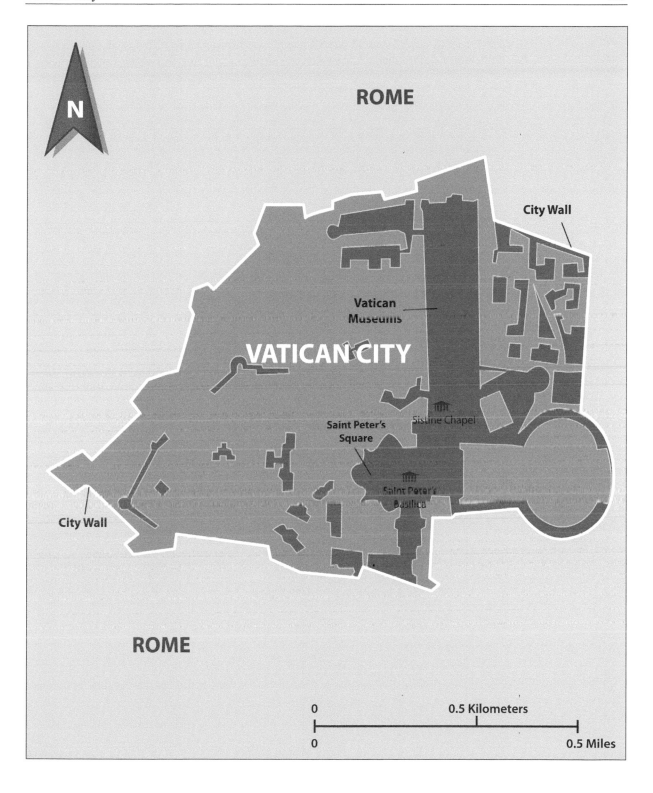

Population

Vatican City is the smallest nation in the world, in terms of both area and population. As of 2014, it had a population of 824. Most of the residents are clergy and hold posts in the Holy See (the Catholic Church's governing body) or are employed in the Swiss Guard. Other Vatican City residents include those in the diplomatic service, those employed in services such as the post office and fire department, and Catholic nuns of various nationalities. Just over half of the residents hold citizenship, while the rest hold temporary citizenship that lasts only as long as their jobs with the Vatican do. In addition, about half of Vatican City's citizens reside in different countries due to their occupations as diplomatic personnel. The dominant ethnicities among residents are Italian and Swiss, and many of the people who live there hold Vatican City passports as well as the passports issued by their home countries.

Languages

Latin (or Ecclesiastical Latin) is considered the official language of the city-state, though Italian is also considered a primary language. French and various other languages are also spoken.

Native People & Ethnic Groups

Very few of the people who reside in Vatican City were actually born there, and the majority of residents and citizens have traveled there for their jobs. Exceptions to this are children born to Swiss Guards—comprised of Swiss nationals as well as Vatican City citizens—as well as children born to laypeople whose jobs have been handed down within their own families for generations. Over history, the land that now comprises Vatican City has been held by different peoples. However, for most of its history until the reign of Pope John XXIII (1881–1963) and the Second Vatican Council, the makeup of Vatican City was predominantly Italian.

Religions

The majority, if not all, of the citizens of Vatican City are Roman Catholic.

Climate

Vatican City enjoys a typically Mediterranean climate, with temperatures averaging above 24° Celsius (75° Fahrenheit) in the hot and dry summers and 7° Celsius (45° Fahrenheit) in the usually mild winters. Between November and April, the average monthly rainfall is between three and five inches. The months between May and October each average less than two inches of rain.

ENVIRONMENT & GEOGRAPHY

Topography

Vatican City is a roughly triangular area of land within the city of Rome, Italy, on the west bank of the Tiber River and west of the Castel Sant'Angelo (Mausoleum of Hadrian). It sits on one of the famous seven hills that are a feature of Rome's topography. Two miles of medieval and Renaissance walls surround the roughly 44 hectares (108 acres) of geographical area that comprises Vatican City. The city-state also counts as part of its territory thirteen buildings in Rome, including churches, palaces, and other buildings, such as the famous papal summer residence of Castel Gondolfo.

CUSTOMS & COURTESIES

Greetings

When greeting the Pope, refer to him as Your Holiness or Holy Father. A person meeting the pope may genuflect (bend one knee to the ground), and, if the person is Catholic, he or she may kiss the Pope's ring, which signifies the papacy. The act of kissing the Pope's ring relays both affection and respect.

Gestures & Etiquette

Both when the pope enters and leaves a room, those in it generally stand. When he enters a room, it is common for him to be met with applause. The venue and occasion will characterize the type of applause, which can range from polite and quiet to enthusiastic and loud.

If one is invited to an audience with the pope, one should dress formally and conservatively. Men are advised to wear jackets and ties, while women are encouraged to wear dresses or suits. If addressed by the pope, one should introduce him or herself. Those interacting with the pope are reminded to speak clearly and avoid whispering, and are also encouraged to share something about themselves with him.

Access to sites in Vatican City such as the Sistine Chapel, Saint Peter's Basilica, the Vatican Museum, and the Vatican gardens is contingent upon appropriate attire. Male and female visitors to Saint Peter's Basilica may be denied admittance if they are wearing shorts, short skirts, or tank tops.

CULTURAL HISTORY

Art

The period of artistic renewal known as the Renaissance, which spanned from the 14th to the 17th century, culminated in Italy during the High Renaissance (1450–1527) due to papal patronage. Considered one of the most explosive artistic periods in history, it spawned "old masters" such as Michelangelo and Raphael, as well as Leonardo da Vinci (1452–1519) and Sandro Botticelli (1445–1510), among others. Many of these artists had studios and a number of pupils studying their techniques and producing near-comparable works of their own.

The buildings that comprised the Vatican were rebuilt and beautified during this period, resulting in prolific and ornate architecture and artwork in what would later become Vatican City. Pope Sixtus IV (1414–1484) commissioned what would become the Sistine Chapel, and also added to the already rich Vatican Library. Pope Julius II (c. 1443–1513) instituted the army known as the Swiss Guard that still guards the pope and Vatican City. He also began the

magnificent Vatican gardens, and commissioned Michelangelo (1475–1564) to decorate the Sistine Chapel.

Architecture

St. Peter's Basilica was first built in 320 CE, and then rebuilt after centuries of disrepair from earthquake damage and neglect. Pope Nicholas V (1397–1455) commissioned the reconstruction in 1450, during the Renaissance. The project spanned 176 years, three popes, and owed much of its distinction to Michelangelo Buonarotti. The artist would not live to see the completion of this particular masterpiece, but many of his ideas and masterpieces, including the basilica's towering dome and the marble sculpture known as the *Pietà*, stand as tribute to him. In 1650, Italian artist, sculptor and architect Gianlorenzo Bernini (1598–1680) added the gold, marble, and mosaic decoration inside the basilica, as well as the massive gilded canopy above the altar.

St. Peter's Square surrounds the Basilica. Bernini designed the space to provide a gathering place for the faithful, a purpose it still fulfills today. At the time of its construction, it could easily accommodate the entire population of Rome. The square is actually oval in shape and modeled on ancient Greek and Roman gathering places. It holds up to 200,000 people.

Music

Many of the masterpieces of medieval and Renaissance music were first heard in the chapels and churches of the Vatican. The plainsong vocals known as Gregorian chant predate the Renaissance and are named for Pope Gregory I (c. 540–604), whose rule began in the year 590. Later, famous Italian Renaissance composers whose works were first used in Vatican religious observances, and which are still heard in both churches and concert halls around the world, include Gregorio Allegri (1582–1652), Tomás Luis de Victoria (c. 1548–1611), and Giovanni Palestrina (c. 1525–1594). These composers were among the first to introduce polyphony (multiple harmonic lines) to music.

CULTURE

Cultural Sites & Landmarks

Vatican City is home to an extensive collection of artwork, and the papacy has historically commissioned works by the best artists of the day. This has made Vatican City a living museum, with more famous art and architectural treasures per square inch than any other place in the world. For this reason, Vatican City is the only entire nation to have been declared a World Heritage Site by the United Nations Educational, Scientific, and Cultural Organization (UNESCO).

St. Peter's Basilica is the largest church in the world. It is situated over what many Christians believe is the site of the grave of St. Peter, considered the most prominent of the 12 apostles of Jesus. Its exterior and interior owe their beauty, design, and symmetry to the artists Michelangelo Buonarotti and Gianlorenzo Bernini.

St. Peter's Square surrounds the basilica. It's most recognizable feature is perhaps the enormous colonnade that encloses the space with 144 identical columns. The square is also known for the tall obelisk at its center, brought to Rome from Egypt in the year 37 CE by the Roman Emperor Caligula (12–41 CE), and installed in front of St. Peter's Basilica by Pope Sixtus V in 1585. Every Sunday at noon, the pope appears at a window of the Apostolic Palace that overlooks the square and administers his blessing to the people congregated there.

Pope Sixtus V is also responsible for Vatican City's other famous site, the Sistine Chapel. The name of the chapel derives from the name Sixtus. The chapel is part of the Vatican's Apostolic Palace, the pope's official residence.

The Sistine Chapel was constructed using the dimensions cited in the Bible for the measurements of Solomon's Temple, known as the First Temple. However, the features for which the Sistine Chapel is best known—the magnificent painted ceiling and frescoes – were commissioned years later by Sixtus' nephew, Pope Julius II. Michelangelo, who at first refused the task, started work on the chapel in the spring of 1508. Besides the massive scale of the undertaking—the ceiling of the Sistine Chapel is 131 feet long and 43 feet wide—the job was physically grueling, as Michelangelo's writings at the time attest. The artist had to paint from the scaffolding below the ceiling, bending backward or lying on his back with paint and plaster dripping onto his face. His first effort left him unsatisfied with the result. He had the ceiling plastered over and began again.

Michelangelo was the sole artist of the masterpiece seen in the chapel today: lively paintings that depict biblical accounts from the Book of Genesis: the Creation of the Earth, the story of Adam and Eve and their expulsion from the Garden of Eden, and the story of Noah's Ark. Michelangelo's frescoes created perspective and a three-dimensional illusion that was unprecedented for its time. The work took about three years to complete.

Although the Sistine Chapel is one of the world's top tourist attractions, it is also used for official Vatican functions. It is the site where the College of Cardinals gathers to elect a new pope. In 1980, Vatican officials decided to have the ceilings and walls of the Sistine Chapel cleaned, drawing anxious protests and ire worldwide. However, after twelve years of careful work, the chapel's colors, muted by 450 years of candle wax and soot, were restored to their original brilliance. A new air filtration system now protects the artwork.

The Vatican Gardens, which cover about half the area of the territory of Vatican City, are only accessible to the public for special tours. Beside beautifully manicured grounds, it has areas for growing produce that is used in the pope's kitchen and sold in the Vatican supermarket, as well as an observatory. It is also where the heliport is located. Before the Lateran Treaty, when successive popes were protesting against the

Italian government by refusing to vacate or leave the Vatican, the gardens were the only source of outdoor recreation in the city-state. In certain areas of the garden, some of the original ninth-century walls are still standing.

Libraries & Museums

The Vatican museums are housed primarily in the Apostolic Palace, also known as Vatican Palace. The museums contain fourteen major collections and dozens of smaller ones, including sacred and profane art (art related to non-religious subjects) from around the world, as well as antiquities, rare books, coins, jewels, and antique armor. Rivaling the famed Louvre Museum in Paris, the Vatican Museum complex is one of the largest in the world, with most of its holdings in storage. The reason for the opulence and sheer volume of these treasures is the fact that a number of popes were voracious art collectors. Many of these works were acquired as tribute or spoil during wars with foreign countries, while many were commissioned. The commissioned works had the partial purpose of educating the people, as most could not read and had to learn the stories of the Bible using pictures. In addition, acquisition of pre-Christian art from ancient Greece and elsewhere was meant to contrast the temporary nature of those civilizations against the perceived everlasting quality of Roman Catholicism. Because of this, the popes were among the first rulers to make their art collections available to be viewed by the public.

Among the most famous treasures to be viewed in the Vatican Museums is the ancient marble statue *Apollo Belvedere*. The statue was celebrated for its aesthetic perfection after it was rediscovered in the 15th century during the Renaissance. Other well-known works include a series of frescoes by the Renaissance painter Raphael (1483–1520), a contemporary of Michelangelo's. Known as the *Stanze*, these frescoes are located in the Stanze di Raffaello ("Raphael's Rooms"), which comprises four rooms, as well as the public part of the building's papal apartments. These frescoes depict biblical scenes, but also imagined scenes from antiquity, such as the monumental *The School of Athens* in which ancient philosophers such as Plato and Aristotle are shown conversing with disciples.

The Library of the Vatican contains one of the oldest and largest collections of historical texts. The library has been in existence since the early days of the church but saw significant growth in time periods such as the Renaissance and during the 17th century. One of the most famous works in the Vatican Library is the Codex Vaticanus Graecus 1209, which is the oldest known nearly complete manuscript of the Bible. By the 21st century, the library held over 75,000 manuscripts and over 1 million printed books.

The Vatican Secret Archives, so named because they were meant for use by the pope and his most trustworthy clergy, is a collection of church archives that was separated from the Vatican Library in the 17th century. In 1883, Pope Leo XIII allowed qualified researchers and scholars to access portions of the archives. In 2003, Pope John Paul II made more sections of the archives public. In the early 21st century, an annual 1,500 scholars gain access to the archives. One of the most famous works in the archives is the eighth-century papal book *Liber Diurnus Romanorum Pontificum*.

SOCIETY

Transportation

Vatican City's small size renders the need for any highways or a mass transit system as unnecessary. Everything within the city-state's limits is within walking distance. The speed limit in Vatican City is 30 kph (19 mph), and drivers use the right side of the road. As of 2007, there were roughly 1,000 cars within the city-state.

Transportation Infrastructure

Vatican City has a railway station that connects it with the greater transit system of Rome, though most of the trains that come into the station in Vatican City transport cargo rather than passengers. There is also a heliport for use by the pope, papal officials, and visiting heads of state. There is no airport and Vatican City is served by Rome's various facilities, including Leonardo Da Vinci Airport and the smaller Ciampino Airport.

Media & Communications

Since the Holy See must communicate with an estimated 1 billion Catholics worldwide, as well as with the city of Rome and the city-state's numerous diplomatic missions, its media infrastructure is well developed. The Vatican Radio station was set up in 1931 by the Italian inventor Guglielmo Marconi (1874–1937), who developed wireless telegraphy, or radio. While Marconi's original radio tower can still be seen in the Vatican Gardens, transmission now takes place via the world's largest rotating antenna, located in an unpopulated area outside of Rome. Vatican Radio broadcasts over short, medium wave, and FM frequencies, as well as over the Internet. Broadcasts are made all over the world in thirty-five different languages. The Vatican also has its own television station, Centro Televisivo Vaticano, which covers Vatican news and broadcasts both taped and live around the world.

Established in 1861, the newspaper of the Holy See is called *L'Osservatore Romano* (*The Rome Observer*). The newspaper is published daily in Italian, with a weekly edition in English as well as French, Portuguese, Spanish, and German. It covers the activities and schedule of the pope and prints his speeches. The newspaper also contains extensive editorial commentary on the issues facing the world. It is important to note that all the above media in Vatican City are under the purview of the Holy See, rather than Vatican City itself.

GOVERNMENT

Structure

To understand the structure of the government of Vatican City, it is important to make the distinction between the city-state, the physical location, and the Holy See, the entity that directs the Catholic Church worldwide. The head of both Vatican City and the Holy See is the pope. Elected by the College of Cardinals, he is considered a monarch with absolute legislative, judicial, and executive powers over both the Holy See and Vatican City. Separate staffs administer the services of the city-state (including telecommunications, health services, and other such services) and the activities of the Holy See.

The national government concerns itself with the day-to-day internal functions of the physical territory and its relationship with the city of Rome. Executive authority is delegated to the governorate of Vatican City. The governorate consists of officials appointed by the pope for five-year terms. The various offices associated with the governorate focus on matters concerning the state's territory, including matters of security, finances, and transportation. The governorate also oversees a security and police force. However, actions of the governorate are generally subject to approval by the pope's secretariat of state.

On the other hand, Vatican City as the Holy See focuses on matters relating to Catholicism worldwide, the official activities of its leader, and the pope, as well as with diplomatic relationships with other countries. The body that advises the pope and executes governing policies is called the Roman Curia. It is made up of numerous committees called discateries. These are each charged with a different focus; for example, one is concerned with religious practices within the Catholic Church, another with rules concerning marriage and family life, and another with media and communications. The Roman Curia is comprised of some 2,500 people, among whom the most powerful are ordained priests, cardinals, and bishops.

Armed Forces

Established in 1506, the Papal Swiss Guard is the smallest and oldest army in the world. To be eligible for service, men must be Catholic, Swiss, single, at least 19 years of age and at least 5'9" tall. They are allowed to marry once they are 25 years old. Their uniforms were designed during the Renaissance by Michelangelo and are still the same design today. According to most accounts, the Papal Swiss Guard is the world's most photographed armed force.

Foreign Policy

While Vatican City, as a physical locale, essentially only has relations with Italy and the city of Rome, foreign policy and diplomacy are among the top daily concerns of the Holy See. It is the Holy See that has the power to conclude treaties and to send and receive diplomats to and from other countries. (In common discussion involving foreign policy, the Holy See is usually referred to as "the Vatican," much in the same way that the American government or administration is referenced as "the White House"). While other religious groups may sometimes be able to exert influence in the local politics of countries in which they are active, only the Vatican is recognized as a sovereign state on the international stage.

The Vatican uses diplomacy to exert its influence around the world in accordance with the pope's articulation of the teachings of the Catholic Church. Some of the most important foreign policy objectives the Vatican promotes are peace, human rights, justice, and the protection of the environment. In addition, since the edicts and teachings of the Vatican carry weight with 1.1 billion Catholics around the world (a group larger than many countries), world leaders often meet with the pope on matters concerning their own foreign relations, an act of diplomacy that carries a significant influence. For example, many people partially credit the strong support of human rights communicated by John Paul II (1920–2005) with the collapse of totalitarian communist governments in Europe. The Vatican will also serve a mediating role during international disputes, as with the ongoing conflicts in the Middle East. The Holy See also sponsors humanitarian organizations and efforts around the world to aid in the reduction of poverty, illiteracy, and human injustices. Since his election in 2013, Pope Francis has made human rights a central focus of the Vatican.

The Vatican's ambassadors are called nuncios. As of 2009, there were 214 Vatican nunciatures (embassies) in countries around the world. The nuncios stationed in these countries deal with the local Catholic cardinals and bishops there, as well as with local governments. Nuncios are all ordained Catholic priests, and all have trained for four years at an academy in Rome before being sent to a post as an assistant to a sitting nuncio. There are many ranks within the diplomatic corps of the Vatican, and it may take as many at twenty years for an academy graduate to achieve the post of nuncio.

Human Rights Profile

International human rights law insists that states respect civil and political rights, and also promote an individual's economic, social and cultural rights. The United Nations Universal Declaration on Human Rights (UDHR) is recognized as the standard for international human rights. Its authors sought the counsel of the world's great thinkers, philosophers, and religious leaders, and were careful to create a document that reflects the core values shared by every world culture. (To read this document or view the articles relating to cultural human rights, go to: http://www.udhr.org/UDHR/default.htm).

While the Vatican is concerned with human rights around the world, some of the observable practices in Vatican City itself would seem to conflict with some provisions of the UDHR, due to the adherence to Catholic religious rules. For example, Article 2 of the UDHR states that women are entitled to equal rights and freedoms. Since the Catholic Church does not ordain women, many of the more powerful posts in government are closed to women; all of the holders of these posts must be ordained priests, and only cardinals under the age of eighty are allowed to vote. Article 18 guarantees freedom of religion, but most, if not all, of the people who work in Vatican City are required to be Catholic. Article 16 guarantees the right of men and women to marry regardless of religion; marriages in Vatican

City must be between two Catholics, and neither may be divorced. However, due to the special circumstances inherent in the city-state, many provisions of the UDHR would not seem to apply, and no serious protests about these questions have ever been lodged.

ECONOMY

Industry

The primary industry in Vatican City, apart from the administration of the activities of the papacy and the Vatican, is tourism. Everything that happens in the city is paid for by contributions from Catholics worldwide, known as Peter's Pence. The economy is supplemented by museum admissions and other revenue generated by tourism, including the sale of postage stamps from the Vatican Post office. In 2014, the total revenue of Vatican City was $308 million (USD).

Vatican City's attractions also generate jobs. The approximately 3,000 people who come to work each day in Vatican City include gardeners, sanitation workers, carpenters, and others, many of whom have inherited these highly sought-after jobs from relatives over several generations.

There is a small amount of industry in the production of mosaics for export, postage stamps, and of official uniforms such as those of the Swiss Guard. The Holy See also engages in worldwide financial investment activity. There is no agricultural activity in Vatican City apart from the tiny farm in the Vatican Gardens. Vatican City also has its own coins (it does not issue paper money), but since 1999 has adopted the euro as its currency along with the European Union (EU). Before that, its currency was linked to the Italian lire.

Tourism

Tourism is Vatican City's most important industry. Visitors to Vatican City flock to sites such as St. Peter's Square and St. Peter's Basilica, the Vatican Palace and Museum, and the Sistine Chapel. Approximately 18 million people visit the Vatican each year. Approximately 20,000 visitors may be accommodated in the Vatican complex of museums and chapels. Many come to see the pope deliver his blessing to the crowd in the St. Peter's Square at noon every Sunday. Tens of thousands, and even sometimes hundreds of thousands, fill the square during religious holidays such as Easter and Christmas. A popular stop is the Vatican Post Office, which issues its own stamps and a unique postmark. The stamps are popular with tourists and stamp collectors alike.

Lisa Rothstein

DO YOU KNOW?

- The Vatican Post Office is one of the most efficient in the world. Its mail typically arrives at its destination much faster than mail sent from any post office in Rome. While only just over 800 people live in Vatican City, over six million pieces of mail, mostly postcards, are sent from the Vatican Post Office every year.

- The Vatican Bank's automated teller machines (ATMs) have an option for instructions in Latin.

Bibliography

Bart McDowell. *Inside The Vatican*. National Geographic Society, 2006.

Brigitte Hintzen-Bohlen. *Rome and the Vatican City: Art and Architecture*. Cologne: Könemann, 2001.

Orazio Petrosillo. *Vatican City*. Vatican City: Edizioni Musei Vaticani, 2005.

John L. Allen Jr. *All The Pope's Men: The Inside Story of How the Vatican Really Thinks*. New York: Doubleday, 2004.

John Thavis. *The Vatican Diaries: A Behind-the-Scenes Look at the Power, Personalities, and Politics at the Heart of the Catholic Church*. New York: Penguin Books, 2013.

Works Cited

"Vatican City." The Columbia Encyclopedia, Sixth Edition. *Encyclopedia.com.* <http://www.cncyclopedia.com>

"Vatican City." Britannica Concise Encyclopedia. *Encyclopedia.com.* <http://www.encyclopedia.com>

http://www.vaticanstate.va/EN/homepage.htm

http://vatican.usembassy.gov/english/

http://www.stpetersbasilica.org/

http://www.vatican.va/

http://www.britannica.com/EBchecked/topic/623972/Vatican-City

http://whc.unesco.org/en/list/286

http://travel.nytimes.com/2007/02/18/travel/18journeys.html

https://www.cia.gov/library/publications/the-world-factbook/geos/vt.html

http://eudocs.lib.byu.edu/index.php/History_of_Vatican_City:_Primary_Documents

http://news.bbc.co.uk/2/hi/europe/country_profiles/1066140.stm

View of Conway Castle built by King Edward I as one of the fortifications during the conquest of Wales in the 13th Century. /Stock photo © starekase

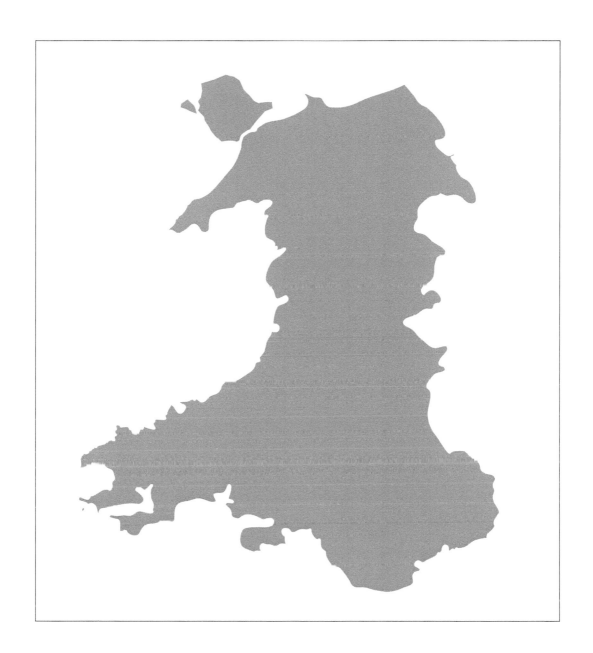

WALES

Introduction

Wales is a European country, located on the western side of the island of Great Britain. Wales is one of the four nations composing the United Kingdom of Great Britain, also referred to as the United Kingdom, and is not an independent member of the European Union. Officially, the country is a principality, though the Welsh people generally ignore this title since the Prince of Wales has no active role in the nation's political affairs. Wales is known for the complexity of its language, its mountainous countryside, and for its contributions to Western art, literature, and music.

GENERAL INFORMATION

Official Language: Welsh, English
Population: 3,063,456 (2011 census)
Currency: Pound Sterling (GBP)
Coins: The pound sterling is available in 1, 2, 5, 10, 20 and 25 pence denominations. A 1 and 2 pound coin is also available.
Land Area: 20,779 square kilometers (8,022 square miles)
National Motto: "Cymru am byth" (Welsh, "Wales Forever")
National Anthem: "Hen Wlad fy Nhadau" (Welsh, "Land of My Fathers")
Capital: Cardiff
Time Zone: GMT
Flag Description: The flag of Wales comprises a white horizontal band on top of a green horizontal band. Over both bands is an image of a large, red dragon.

Population

The population of Wales, as of 2014, is estimated to be just over 3.1 million, with the vast majority being white European. Ethnically, Welsh people tend to have fair skin and hair. According to the 2013 statistics, roughly two-thirds of Wales' population is heavily distributed in the southern, industrialized half of the country, near Swansea and the capital of Cardiff. Between 1991 and 2013, the population of Wales increased by 7.3 percent. In 2011, the median age was 41 in Wales.

Languages

The Welsh language is one of the oldest and most difficult in Western Europe, yet, in 2013, it is still used by over 19 percent of the population of Wales. It is spoken more in rural areas, but is used in business in the cities as well. The dialect comes from ancient Celtic, and because of its unique alphabet, it is different from languages such as Irish, to which it is often compared.

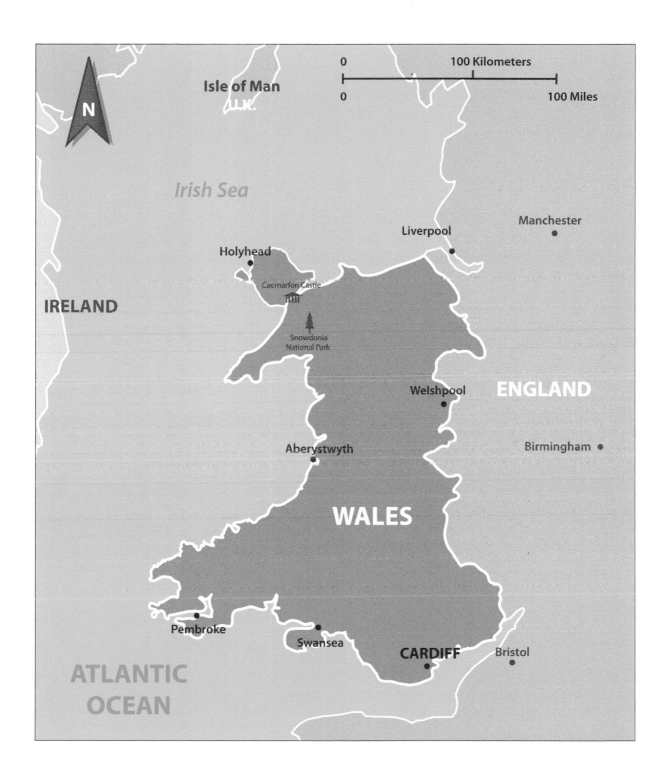

Isle of Man
U.K.

Irish Sea

Manchester

Liverpool

Holyhead

Caernarfon Castle

IRELAND

Snowdonia
National Park

Welshpool

ENGLAND

Aberystwyth

Birmingham

WALES

Pembroke

Swansea

CARDIFF

Bristol

ATLANTIC
OCEAN

0   100 Kilometers

0   100 Miles

N

Principal Cities by Population (year data collected):

- Cardiff (351,710) (2013)
- Swansea (240,332) (2013)
- Newport (146,558) (2013)
- Rhondda (62,545) (2011)
- Wrexham (61,603) (2011)
- Barry (54,673) (2011)
- Neath (50,658) (2011)
- Cwmbran (46,915) (2011)
- Bridgend (46,757) (2011)
- Llanelli (43,878) (2011)

In Welsh, "y" and "w" are vowels, while many letters in the English alphabet are not even used. Double consonants are considered part of the Welsh alphabet as well. There are many regional accents in Wales, but unlike England, the quality of a person's accent is not a basis for judging one's economic status. Rather, the different Welsh accents indicate which area of the country one inhabits.

Native People & Ethnic Groups

The Celts, Normans, Vikings, Romans, English and Anglo-Saxons are the groups that are typically considered the original inhabitants of the British Isles, the earliest being the Celts. Most Welsh people trace their European heritage to these groups. There is very little ethnic diversity in Wales, and therefore the native population is essentially the same as the current population.

According to the 2011 census, slightly more than 93 percent of Wales citizens identify as being White British, while 0.6 percent identify as White Irish, and an addition 1.8 percent identify as being some other white ethnicity. Approximately 4.4 percent of the population, around 135,000 people, identify as non-white. Of those 135,000, roughly 70,000 identified as Asian (including those of Indian and Pakistani descent), 31,000 identified as being of mixed ethnicities, 18,000 identified as being Black, and

13,000 identified as Chinese. As of 2011, the largest population of non-white ethnicities lived in the capital of Cardiff.

Religions

As with England and Northern Ireland, Wales is a Protestant country. The Church of England was the official church of Wales for centuries while Wales was under England's rule, but eventually the Welsh broke away and declared their own rights of worship. According to the 2011 census, roughly 58 percent of the country identified as Christian, and less than 1.5 percent of the population (approximately 45,000) identified as Muslim. Other religions in Wales with less than 0.5 percent of the population as adherents include Hinduism, Buddhism, and Judaism. Over 32 percent of the population answered the census question regarding religion, as having "no religion."

Climate

Wales has the cool, rainy climate that is typical of the British Isles. Temperatures are comfortable but rarely very warm. The average summer temperature is about 15.6° Celsius (60° Fahrenheit), and the average winter temperature is about 5.6° Celsius (42° Fahrenheit).

For more than half of the year, the sky over Wales is overcast, and there is often dense fog when it is not raining. The average annual rainfall is extremely high in the north, which usually receives about 254 centimeters (100 inches). In the south, the average is lower but still quite high at 76 centimeters (30 inches).

ENVIRONMENT & GEOGRAPHY

Topography

Wales has a surprisingly long coastline (988 kilometers, or 614 miles) in relation to its area. Most major cities are situated along the coast, which faces Cardigan Bay, as well as the Irish Sea to the west and Bristol Channel to the south.

The primarily rural eastern regions form the border between Wales and England. The northern part of Wales is the Snowdonia region, which contains the country's highest point atop Mount Snowdon, which measures 1,085 meters (3,561 feet) at its peak. The Cambrian Mountain chain runs south from Snowdon through the center of the country.

There are many bodies of water in Wales, most of which are formed in the valleys of the Cambrian Mountains. Major rivers include the Dee, the Wye and the Severn River, which is one of the longest in Great Britain. The major lakes in Wales are the Bala Lake in the north and the Llangorse Lake in the south. The Isle of Anglesey is located in the northeast. The Menai Strait separates it from mainland Wales.

Plants & Animals

Deforestation and unregulated animal activity have depleted much of the forest habitat of Wales. Forests are generally full of hardwood trees such as hawthorn and oak, in addition to a vast amount of evergreens. The national flower is the daffodil, which grows throughout the countryside.

Wales has five regions designated as "Areas of Outstanding Natural Beauty." These are the Gower Peninsula in the southwest, the Lleyn Peninsula on the north of Cardigan Bay, the Clywdian Hills Range in the northeast, the Wye Valley in the southeast, and the Isle of Anglesea. Several small islands off of the coast of Wales are mostly covered in moss and small vegetation, and are used as nature reserves.

Many species of fish inhabit the rivers, lakes, and coastal waters of Wales, including the gwiniad, a native salmon. This encourages a large population of seabirds. Bardsey Island, Ramsey Island and Grassholm Island are the homes of thousands of seabirds such as the Manx shearwater, the gannet, and the chough. Native land birds are equally unique, and include the merlin, the dipper, and the red kite, in addition to many species of smaller European birds.

A great number of Wales' native animals live wildly in the central countryside. The pine marten, polecat and numerous rodent species are among the smaller animals, while goats, ponies, and coastal ringed seals are among the largest.

CUSTOMS & COURTESIES

Greetings

Greetings in Wales are similar to those used in other cultures, and vary widely. Often, they are influenced by a number of factors, including age, degree of a friendship, the social situation, and language. The handshake is the most common greeting amongst the Welsh, and is considered customary when being introduced for the first time. Business associates and social acquaintances usually accompany a firm handshake with the verbal English greeting, "How d'you do?" or "Pleased to meet you." Handshakes are usually not used when friends meet. Common greetings among friends include "How are you?", "Hello," and "Hi." It is not uncommon for good friends who have not seen each other in some time to kiss each other once lightly on the cheek.

Roughly 20 percent of the population in Wales speaks the Welsh language. Greetings among Welsh-speaking people are similar to those of the English-speaking population. Casual verbal greetings in Welsh range from "Bore da," which is "Good morning," and "Dydd da," which means "Good day." The phrase "Sut mae?" is a common informal greeting that means "How are you?"

Gestures & Etiquette

Most Welsh typically do not use large, expressive hand or body gestures to accompany their speech. When in public, or when among new acquaintances, the Welsh are not openly demonstrative when they speak, and they usually keep a small distance, typically a few feet, between themselves and the person to whom they are speaking. Generally, the Welsh are friendly and very social, but may at times seem indifferent and often formal, especially with those whom they do not know well. The Welsh and their British neighbors value their privacy and they expect visitors to respect that. Kissing and placing hands on others is usually reserved for family members or very close friends.

Overall, most Welsh adhere to a standard protocol in social settings. Although not as stringent in Wales, it is still considered proper etiquette to introduce a younger person to an older person. Also, class distinction is often a factor. Usually, a person of lower status is introduced to a person of higher status. Loud, boisterous public displays that might be normal in other countries are generally considered inappropriate in Wales. Staring and whispering are also considered impolite. In addition, etiquette adhered to in business settings is typically formal, and usually follows an established protocol, especially in older, more established companies.

Eating/Meals

Most Welsh eat a breakfast consisting of toast, cereal, and tea or coffee. For the midday meal, which is usually called "dinner," meat or fish and vegetables are considered standard fare. The main meal is eaten later in the day, and can be called "supper," "tea," or "dinner." On Sundays, the main meal is traditionally served in the middle of the day and consists of a main course of meat accompanied by vegetables. In addition, most meals are eaten family-style, with everyone at the table serving themselves from large central bowls and platters.

Standard cutlery—forks, knives and spoons—are the common eating utensils. The Welsh use their cutlery in the continental style. Right-handed diners hold a knife in their right hand and the fork in their left, with the tines pointed down. It is considered improper table manners to use a fork with the tines turned up when holding a knife in the other hand.

Visiting

The Welsh are very social, and they enjoy conversing with friends and neighbors, often calling unannounced. Although it is more common for invited visitors to arrive 10 to 20 minutes after the stated time in other parts of the United Kingdom, the Welsh expect their visitors to be punctual. It is a common courtesy to bring a small gift to the hosts. Gifts can include chocolates, wine, champagne and even books. During

most visits, it is considered improper to ask for a tour of the host's home.

LIFESTYLE

Family

Family life in Wales varies according to region. However, families throughout Wales have traditionally been very close, with great value placed on kinship. In rural and farming communities, adult sons often remain at home to help work their parents' farms until they marry and start a family, often very close to where they grew up. Even today, it is common for many rural Welsh to live their entire lives within thirty miles of where they were born. With the decline of the agricultural industry, however, many rural communities have seen a developing trend of urban migration among younger people due to better job prospects in larger cities.

Family life in urban Wales shares characteristics with that of neighboring England. The nuclear family is the common family group, consisting of two parents and their children, typically two. Similar to families living in rural locations, Urban Welsh families spend a great deal of free time together, especially on holidays and for special occasions. Special occasions include Christmas, Easter, milestone occasions such as weddings and birthdays, and St. David's Day, which celebrates the patron saint of Wales.

Wales has also experienced an increasing number of women and mothers entering the workforce. In fact, in 2015, about 67 percent of women aged 16 to 59 maintain some form of employment. This is largely a result of declining manufacturing jobs and the shift to more service-focused employment. This shift, along with the increase in single-parent households, has impacted traditional family life.

Housing

Traditional stone cottages and family farmhouses are abundant in rural Wales. The long-house, which is a single-story home with rooms for a family on one side and an area for livestock at the other, is another type of traditional Welsh home, commonly found in rural settings. Many long-houses have been refurbished with added modern amenities for single family habitation or commercial purposes.

The traditional mining and industrialized urban areas of southern and northeast Wales are home to four-fifths of the Welsh population. Rows of terraced housing were built in the 19th century along the steep, narrow valleys to accommodate workers and their families. These terraced housing developments were built with local brick, often red in color, or stone walls, and were topped with slate tiles. For many people, the terraced housing of Wales is one of the most vivid images of the country.

Although older homes and the terraced housing built before 1929 are still heavily in use, almost a quarter of all Welsh homes are less than thirty years old. Economic policies implemented in the 1980s enabled many Welsh to become homeowners, including the terraced housing units in which they lived. In the early 21st century, nearly three-quarters of the Welsh population own the homes in which they live, the highest ownership rate in the UK. In 2014, a housing act was implemented, to improve the quality of available housing, and to increase the number of Welsh who will own their own homes.

Food

Welsh cuisine has traditionally been very functional and simple, and was largely influenced by the country's agriculture. Meat, oats, vegetables, and dairy products are all important to most traditional Welsh recipes. Famous or traditional Welsh dishes include cawl, a vegetable stew made with lamb, cabbage, bacon, potatoes, and swede, a root vegetable. Other distinctive dishes include Welsh cakes, which are traditionally baked on a flat baking stone; and varieties of meat pie, which is meat wrapped in pastry and is a staple food throughout the UK.

Welsh rarebit is another specialty. This consists of toast coated with a mixture of milk, eggs, cheese, and beer. The name of the dish was supposedly coined as an insult directed at poorer or unsophisticated Welsh people who could not afford rabbit. Perhaps one of the most uniquely Welsh dishes is laver bread. Laver bread is eaten at breakfast and is made of boiled seaweed mixed with oatmeal and served with bacon and toast. Cockles, or mussels, are popular throughout Wales, and are commonly prepared steamed.

Contemporary Welsh chefs and diners are rediscovering the quality of locally grown and raised products. More Welsh restaurants are using local suppliers, and there has been a dramatic rise in the number of farmer's markets and shops. Welsh lamb, Welsh black beef, local cheeses, and traditional breads and cakes can be found in many eating establishments. Gastropubs have become one of the leading proponents of Welsh cuisine and locally produced specialties. Gastropubs combine the relaxed atmosphere of the traditional pub with high-quality cuisine. Gastropubs have sprouted up throughout Wales, and throughout Europe, from urbanized areas to rural locations.

Life's Milestones

As citizens of Great Britain for more than four hundred years, the Welsh share many of the same common milestones with their English, Scottish and Irish neighbors. Wales is a predominantly Christian culture; therefore, many celebrations are religious in nature. Celebrations or religious traditions that are commonly observed or practiced include baptisms or christenings, first communion, confirmation, and wedding ceremonies.

It is common for many Welsh to incorporate national symbols in their wedding ceremonies. As such, ceremony invitations and wedding cakes are typically decorated with daffodils, leeks, and the Welsh dragon, a red dragon that features prominently on the national flag. All three are considered common representations or national emblems of Wales. Although not as common as it used to be, traditional Welsh love spoons still play a role in many Welsh weddings. In contemporary Welsh society, love spoons can be presented as wedding favors to guests, and are also given as wedding anniversary, birthday, Christmas, and baby gifts.

CULTURAL HISTORY

Art

Welsh culture has its roots in the ancient Celtic cultures of the British Isles. In fact, the Welsh language is the oldest language spoken in Britain, dating back at least 2,500 years. Yet, Welsh culture is distinguished from other ancient cultures of the region by more than just its language.

Traditional Welsh crafts that have become part of the country's historical culture include wooden spoon carving and quilting. The tradition of spoon carving dates back to at least the 17th century when suitors would carve intricate spoons, called love spoons, as a token of affection. Many of these are on display at the Welsh Fold Museum, with one dating back to 1667. Quilting became a popular craft in Welsh culture in the 18th century, and it remained an important profession in Wales until the early 20th century. Many of these quilts are on display in museums throughout Wales.

Painters have long been attracted to the scenic Welsh landscapes. The influential English painter J.M.W. Turner (1775–1851) visited Wales in the late 18th century to find inspiration in the Wye Valley and the Valle Crucis Abbey, among other landscapes and historic sites. Perhaps the most famous early Welsh painter was landscape artist Richard Wilson (1714–1782), who focused on capturing the varying atmosphere and light of the Welsh countryside. Another famous landscape painter of Wilson's era was Thomas Jones (1742–1803), who was, in fact, a pupil of Wilson. Jones painted both Welsh and Italian landscapes during his lifetime.

Augustus John (1878–1961) was a famous Welsh portraiture artist also renowned for his bold post-impressionist canvases. Ceri Richards (1903–1971) became one of the most influential Welsh artists of the 20th century, and Peter Prendergast (1946–2007) was known as the leading Welsh landscape painter during his lifetime. Although the Welsh country landscapes are still popular with visual artists, contemporary Welsh artists, such as Prendergast and Kevin Sinnott (b. 1947-), also focus on the urban areas of South and Northeast Wales in their work.

Film

Since the 1920s, film directors have been pulled to the picturesque landscapes of Wales, but very few contained both Welsh actors and locales. In fact, one film largely associated with the history of Welsh cinema, *How Green Was My Valley* (1941)—adapted from Welsh writer Richard Llewellyn's novel of the same name—was filmed entirely in Hollywood and featured only one Welsh actor. For that matter, Karl Francis's *Above Us the Earth* (1977) is often considered the first true Welsh film, using amateur actors and authentic locations. Since then, Welsh cinema has begun to receive the recognition it lacked earlier when its filmmaking was largely neglected or unknown.

Several contemporary Welsh-language films have garnered international acclaim. Paul Turner's documentary *Hedd Wyn* was nominated for an Academy Award for Best Foreign Language Film in 1994. In 1999, *Solomon a Gaenor*, directed by Paul Morrison, was nominated in the same category. Realistic portraits of contemporary Welsh society were the focus of *Eldra,* the winner of the Spirit of Moondance award at the 2003 Sundance Film Festival, and *Human Traffic* (1999), a popular film that chronicled the Cardiff club culture.

Music

Wales is often referred to as the "land of song," or "gwlad y gan," due to the country's rich musical heritage. In particular, Welsh music is known for its distinct choral and folk traditions, and the use of instruments such as the Welsh triple harp, or crwth, a stringed instrument, and the pibgorn, a wind instrument traditionally made from an animal's horn. One popular Welsh folk tradition is Penillion, the often improvised singing of folk songs accompanied by a harp. Penillion was popular until the 18th century, but a folk revival has begun to bring back this culturally significant music. In addition, Welsh choirs, particularly male choirs, have long been associated with the music of Wales. Choirs have remained popular and respected for the complexity of their harmonies.

Joseph Parry (1841–1903) was a famous Welsh composer who penned numerous hymn tunes. His most famous choral work, *Myfanwy*, was popularized by Welsh male voice choirs. Other famous Welsh composers include Morfudd Llwyn-Owen (1891–1918) and James James (1833–1902), who composed the national anthem of Wales, *Hen Wlad Fy Nhadau*, which means "Land of my Fathers." It was also common for Welsh composers, musicians and poets to adapt a bardic name, or pseudonym, in the traditional Welsh language. This custom is most associated with the Eisteddfod tradition, which was a competitive gathering of musicians and poets that dates back to the 12th century. These traditional festivals, which still occur today, also featured folk dancing, which has a long history in Wales. Revival efforts, including the 1949 establishment of the Welsh Folk Dance Society, have ensured that traditional folk dancing remains a living part of Welsh culture.

Literature

Welsh literature dates to the sixth century CE, making it one of the oldest continuous literary traditions in Europe. Aneirin, Taliesin, and Geoffrey of Monmouth, who collected the legends of King Arthur, are among the famous early Welsh poets. By the 18th century, English had surpassed Welsh as the literary language of choice. Many modern Welsh writers have examined the working and social lives of the Welsh people, both rural and urban. Richard Llewellyn's (1906–1983) *How Green Was My Valley* (1939) and the works of Kate Roberts (1891–1985), including the novel *Feet in Chains* (1936) and the short story collection *Tea in Heather* (1959), are significant for their exploration of the Welsh spirit.

In the 20th century, Welsh poet Dylan Thomas (1914–1953) quickly established himself as the "roaring boy" of Welsh literature. Thomas was as famous for his turbulent personal life, including his alcoholism, as he was for his writing. The author of many famous poems, including "Fern Hill" and "Do Not Go Gentle Into that Good Night," Thomas is widely read and taught in schools around the world. Thomas also explored the idiosyncrasies of Welsh life in his works for radio, namely "A Child's Christmas in Wales" (1954) and "Under Milk Wood" (1954). Significant contemporary Welsh poets include Robert Minhinnick, Gillian Clarke, and John Barnie.

CULTURE

Arts & Entertainment

Although a part of England since 1536, the Welsh people have maintained and nurtured their own cultural identity, largely through artistic expression. An influx of immigrants and non-Welsh-speaking citizens has also created a vibrant and culturally diverse contemporary arts scene. With the 1997 approval of the Welsh Assembly Government (WAG), which enabled the Welsh government to enact legislation, Wales has begun to strengthen this unique cultural identity.

Funded by the government, the Arts Council of Wales (ACW) works to develop the arts in Wales, as well as advise the government on arts-related issues. Under the ACW umbrella are the Wales Tourist Board, the Welsh Development Agency (WDA), the Sports Council, the Arts Council, and the National Library of Wales (Llyfrgell Genedlaethol Cymru). In addition, the Artes Mundi (Arts of the World) award was established in Wales in 2003 to recognize influential artists throughout the world. It is considered the largest art prize in world.

Perhaps nothing showcases and reinvigorates Welsh art and culture quite like the annual Royal National Eisteddfod, held annually in August, and the various eisteddfodau ("gathering" or "session") held throughout Wales each year.

Traditionally, these festivals were competitive gatherings in which musicians and artists would perform under their bardic names. Today, in the same spirit of performance, eisteddfodau bring together artists, poets, musicians and actors who compete in various artistic events.

The eisteddfod tradition lost its importance following the sixteenth-century Act of Union, or Laws in Wales Acts 1535–1542. This series of parliamentary laws systematically annexed Wales to England. It was not until the late eighteenth century when the gatherings were once again accepted and embraced. Eisteddfodau have become significant not only for celebrating Welsh cultural traditions, but also for providing venues for up-and-coming performers and visual artists. The Royal National Eisteddfod attracts more than 150,000 attendees each year. All events are in the Welsh language, and translations are provided for the more popular events.

The International Musical Eisteddfod takes place each July in Llangolen. Unlike the Royal National Eisteddfod, which is a celebration of Welsh culture, the International Musical Eisteddfod welcomes performers from around the world. Performers from more than fifty countries take the stage to compete each day, and well-known artists perform concerts in the evenings. This week-long festival provides an opportunity for Welsh performers and fans to share their musical heritage with others from around the world.

Performing since 1946, the Welsh National Opera has gained international acclaim and has become Europe's busiest touring opera company. The 1990s saw an explosion in the popularity of Welsh pop and rock musicians and groups. Dubbed "Cool Cymru," by the media, this short-lived wave of Welsh-inspired rock music was propelled by the new sense of Welsh nationalism and helped launched the careers of such bands as Stereophonics, Catatonia, and the bilingual band Super Furry Animals, whose 2000 release *Mwng* became the biggest selling Welsh-language album of all time

The failure of a devolution referendum (the handing off of political power to a lower level government) in 1979 may have been a political defeat for Welsh nationalists, but it sparked a creative outflow of Welsh-language literature. Much of the poetry and prose created was politically charged, and it motivated many young Welsh writers. Iwan Llwyd, Steve Eaves, Gerwyn Williams and other poets brought Welsh-language poetry out of the classroom and lecture halls and into pubs and nightclubs. Poetry readings thus became a vital form of protest and political engagement in contemporary Wales, as well as a popular way to promote the Welsh language.

In addition, contemporary Welsh-language writers are finding new audiences around the world. Welsh Literature Abroad is an organization that actively pursues the translation of Welsh literature into other languages. As globalization in all aspects of Welsh life races forward, and with a new and stronger sense of cultural identity, many Welsh-language writers are exploring global issues from a Welsh perspective.

Cultural Sites & Landmarks

Wales has a wealth of cultural sites, natural landmarks and three national parks, as well as six designated United Nations Educational, Scientific and Cultural Organization (UNESCO) World Heritage Sites. Snowdonia National Park (Cenedlaethol Eryri), established in 1951, was the country's first national park. The park features 60 kilometers (37 miles) of coastline. Snowdon Mountain (Yr Wyddfa), which rises to a height of 1,085 meters (3,560 feet) and is the highest point in England and Wales, is also found there.

Pembrokeshire Coast National Park and Brecon Beacons National Park offer contrasting opportunities and landscapes. The Pembrokeshire Coast National Park straddles the rugged Welsh coastline for 416 kilometers (258 miles). Many fortifications from the Iron Age (1000–400 BCE in Europe) dot the park, including Castell Henllys, a partially reconstructed hillfort that was occupied from around 600 BCE to the first century CE. This archeological site is often used to train young archaeologists.

Brecon Beacons National Park occupies about 1,344 square kilometers (519 square miles) in south central Wales. Within the park are the Brecon Beacon Mountains. Horseback riding, fishing, hiking and caving are the park's chief attractions. The area covering the western region of the park is known as Fforest Fawr. Because of its geological heritage and diversity, it was designated a UNESCO Global Geopark in 2006.

Located near Brecon Beacons National Park is the Blaenavon Industrial Landscape. Designated a UNESCO World Heritage Site in 2000, the landscape lies in the heart of the once-flourishing mining region of Wales. The site chronicles the region's history as an important producer of iron and coal in the 19th century. Within the complex are Blaenavon Ironworks, the Big Pit National Mining Museum, and the Pontypool & Blaenavon Railway, among other historically significant sites. Similarly, in 2009, the Pontcysyllte Aqueduct & Canal was designated a World Heritage Site, with the aqueduct being the highest navigable canal in the world.

The fortified complexes of Caernarfon and Conwy, along with Beaumaris and Harlech castles, are located in the former principality of Gwynedd. The structures were granted World Heritage Site designation as the Castles and Town Walls of King Edward in Gwynedd in 1986. The structures were built during the reign of Edward I (1272–1307), and feature the architectural designs of James of Saint George (c. 1230–1309), Edward's chief architect. The most striking features of the Caernarfon are its eleven towers and massive walls that protect the interior. Edward's son, the future King Edward II, was born in Caernarfon in 1284, and since 1911, the castle has been the site of the ceremonial confirmation of the Prince of Wales—the title given to the heir of the United Kingdom's (UK) reigning monarch—most recently in 1969, with the confirmation of Prince Charles.

Libraries & Museums

The National Library of Wales is located in Aberystwyth and was established in 1907. Several libraries are also run through the University of Wales. National museums in Wales include the National Waterfront Museum, the National Coal Museum, the National Slate Museum, the National Wool Museum, the National Roman Legion Museum, St. Fagan's National History Museum, and the National Museum (Cardiff). In 2014, these museums attracted a total of over 1.6 million visitors.

Holidays

Being a Protestant nation, Wales celebrates the same Christian holidays as the rest of Great Britain. However, there are certain events, called festivals, which are specific to Wales. A festival called the Eisteddfod has been celebrated for centuries. The day is arranged as a competition between poets and musicians, who perform for large crowds. A group of people called the Gorsedd of Bards is chosen to award the competitors with prizes for their artistic contributions to the festival.

The patron saint of Wales is Saint David. His day is celebrated on March 1, and although there are no substantial religious guidelines for the observation of Saint David, many Welsh people honor him by wearing leeks on their heads or in their caps. Leeks are a symbol of Welsh heritage, as the rose is to English heritage. The tradition of wearing of leeks on one's head comes from superstition and folklore regarding the celebration of Saint David.

Youth Culture

As in other Western cultures, the youth culture in Wales in the early 21st century is largely a product of the digital age. Most young people are extremely proficient at communicating with each other through electronic media, such as cell phones and instant messaging. An Internet-savvy group, Welsh children between the ages of 10 and 15 access the Internet at least once a week, more than any other age group.

The number of Welsh-language speakers has decreased dramatically since 1891, when just over half the population could speak Welsh. This decline persisted until the early 1990s, when the number began to increase. This is largely attributed to a resurgence in national pride and the Welsh Language Act, which placed Welsh on par with English. The Welsh language is now taught in all public schools, and as of 2011, about 40 percent of children between the ages of five and 15 could speak, write, and read Welsh, the highest percentage of any age group in Wales. Of this group, just over 16 percent identified Welsh as their primary language, in the 2011 census. Overall, less than 27 percent of the people had any Welsh language skills.

SOCIETY

Transportation

Drivers use the left-hand side of the road in the United Kingdom, which includes Wales; the driver's side of vehicles, which features the steering wheel and the gas and brake pedals, is on the left side, as well. In Wales, public transportation is mainly by bus, and is primarily limited to the industrialized southern coastal area and the populated northeast. The hilly terrain and low populations in the interior have made a country-wide, interconnected public transportation system financially unfeasible. A fairly well-developed network of paved roads throughout the country makes travel by automobile a primary mode of transportation.

Built to haul the products of the quarries and mines in Wales, narrow-gauge railroads became a major method of transportation in the 19th century. In 1865 the Ffestiniog railroad became the first steam-driven railroad in the world to provide passenger and freight services. Sections of many 18th-century narrow gauge railroads are still in operation today, primarily as tourist attractions.

Transportation Infrastructure

The main train lines run along the north and south coasts of Wales and link the major cities with London and other cities in England. Holyhead and Fishguard, ports on the west coast, and Swansea in the south, link Wales with ports in Ireland. Major airports in Wales include

Cardiff Airport, which was used by approximately 1 million people in 2012 (a drop of over 30 percent in the previous three years), as well as the Hawarden Airport, Swansea Airport, and Anglesey Airport.

Media & Communications

Radio and television service in Wales has been dominated by the British Broadcasting Corporation (BBC). Until the 1980s, radio and television broadcasts were mostly in English. BBC Wales, however, does operate with a considerable amount of autonomy, and continues to be a powerful influence in the Welsh cultural revival. The BBC broadcasts television programming on two channels, BBC-1 Wales and BBC-2 Wales. HTV Wales (Harlech Television) and ITV are two independently owned stations that also broadcast in Wales.

S4C (Sianel Pedwar Cymru, or Channel 4 Wales) was launched in 1982. This primarily Welsh-language television channel has had tremendous success and is considered the driving force in the reemergence of the Welsh language. S4C has produced Welsh-language instruction programming, soap operas and documentaries. However, S4C has been the most commercially successful in the realm of children's animation. S4C's creation "Super Ted" was the first ever British animation series to be broadcast by Disney, and several other series have been picked up by international broadcasters.

The national newspaper in Wales is *The Western Mail*. The *Liverpool Daily Post* also has a strong presence in the northeast. As of 2013, daily circulation figures were about 23,000 for the *Western Mail* and 27,000 for the *Daily Post.* Fewer Welsh are reading newspapers and only about 15 percent of Welsh readers buy newspapers produced in Wales. Although smaller regionally-authored newspapers remain popular, there has been a shift to online reading, with the Daily Post site increasing readers by over nine percent in 2013.

As of 2013, about 73 percent of all households in Wales had access to the Internet, which has become a powerful force in promoting the

Welsh-language and in strengthening Welsh national identity. Of those with Internet access, about 45 percent had broadband connections. According to statistics from a 2012 report, the number of Wi-Fi hotspots tripled in the previous two years. Wales has a similar number of Wi-Fi hotspots per million people as the rest of the UK, as well as the United States, Japan, and Germany. In early 2015, it was announced that Wales would experiment with increasing rural Wi-Fi hotspots, by making the collars on sheep act as hotspots.

SOCIAL DEVELOPMENT

Standard of Living
As part of the United Kingdom, Wales ranked fourteenth, in 2014, in the Human Development Index, out of 187 total countries.

Water Consumption
In a 2015 report, per capita use of water in England and Wales was approximately 150 liters. Access to water in Wales is considered to be universal, and the water service industry, which was privatized in the 1990s, is overseen by the Water Services Regulation Authority (OFWAT), which regulates price. It is also overseen by the Environment Agency, which addresses environmental issues surrounding the water supply, and the Drinking Water Inspectorate, which assesses water quality. Roughly two-thirds of water in the United Kingdom comes from surface water such as rivers, while one-third comes from groundwater reserves.

Education
The importance of regional language is stressed in schools, which require that all students learn Welsh. In many areas, families can choose between schools which use Welsh as the basic medium of instruction or an English medium school. The education system in Wales, where children between the ages of five and 16 must attend school, is identical to that of England. The University of Wales has many campuses specializing in different subjects. The literacy rate in

Wales and the rest of Great Britain is exceptionally high at 99 percent.

In 2015, of the approximately 128,000 students enrolled in Welsh higher education, roughly 54 percent of students enrolled in post-secondary institutions were female and 46 percent were male.

Women's Rights
In Wales, women's rights are generally protected by legislation enacted by the Parliament. This legislation is designed to prevent gender discrimination and expand opportunities for women in Wales and throughout the UK. The Sex Discrimination Act 1975 made it illegal in Wales to discriminate on the basis of gender in employment, vocational training and education. The act also provides protection for women in the sale of goods and services, the renting or selling of property, and in the arena of public functions. Statistics released by the Welsh government in 2007 report that gender discrimination is the eighth-ranked form of social discrimination.

The decline in wages and the shift from heavy industry and manufacturing to more service-oriented jobs in Wales has thrust more Welsh women into the workforce than ever before, although this began to decline in the second decade of the 21st century. As of 2015, just under 67 percent of women of working age were employed. The Equal Pay Act 1970 made it unlawful for employers to discriminate between men and women in terms of pay and conditions where they are doing the same or similar work. At the time the act was passed, women earned about 37 percent less than men. Although the gap has closed, women are still earning less than men. A recent report indicates that women, in 2013, are now earning about 16.5 percent less than the male workers. In addition, more of the lower paying jobs have a higher percentage of women filling them.

As of the 2012–2013 academic year, 57 percent of students attaining a first degree from a university in Wales were female. However, women are still finding it difficult to turn their educations into high-profile, career launching positions that fully utilize their skills and education. Roughly 84 percent of female jobs in Wales were in the service industries including about 75 percent in the education, social care, and health sectors. The traditional patriarchal Welsh society is also quite prevalent in the boardroom, with men having over 65 percent of the senior management positions. Welsh women are still finding it difficult to rise in the corporate structure. For example, about 25 percent of major companies in Wales have no woman board members. However, there has been an increase in the number of female directorships, and this trend is on the rise.

Welsh women over the age of 30 have had the right to vote and run for a seat in Parliament since 1918. Seven years later, women under the age of 30 were given the same right. In the early years of the 21st century, women comprise more than half of the Welsh population. In 2003, Wales became the first country in the world to elect as many women as men to a national legislative body. Although that number has decreased since then, the Welsh National Assembly women still comprise 42 percent of the Assembly, following elections in 2011. This ranks tops among the four countries in the UK, and second among countries within the EU. Only Sweden, at 43.6 percent, has more female representation. Interestingly, the percentage of women elected to local authorities is considerably lower. In 2014, of the 1,257 local authorities, only nine percent have a woman as the leader, with 27 percent of the council members being women.

Health Care

Wales is generally a very healthy nation with high life expectancies; 77 years for men, 82 years for women (2014 estimate). Statistically, Welsh people who have worked in mines have the most severe health problems, including black lung and bronchitis. Cancer and heart disease are the major causes of illness and death.

All Welsh citizens received free medical care through the National Health System (NHS). Drugs and prescriptions are provided at a fee, however.

GOVERNMENT

Structure

The prime minister and parliament of Great Britain directly govern Wales with the same constitution. Wales is therefore considered a part of the constitutional monarchy, despite its technical status as a principality. The United Kingdom has a bicameral parliament consisting of a House of Lords and a House of Commons, which are both overseen by the prime minister.

Wales is divided into 11 county boroughs, which contain nine counties and two major cities, Cardiff and Swansea. Politically, this makes Wales much smaller than its partners in the United Kingdom.

Since the population of Wales represents only 5 percent of the entire population of the United Kingdom, Welsh voters may elect only forty of the 659 members of the House of Commons. Therefore, a smaller government was established to address matters within Wales. The National Assembly for Wales, consisting of 60 members, regulates certain internal affairs and oversees programs and services within the country. However, the parliament of Great Britain remains the only legislative body that has the power to make laws that affect Wales.

The voting age in Wales is 18, the same as the rest of the United Kingdom. Welsh voters elect the members of the National Assembly, which has representatives from a number of political parties.

Political Parties

As of 2015, there are four major political parties in Wales. The Welsh Labor Party, established in 1947, is a social democratic that holds thirty of the 60 seats in the Welsh Assembly. The party also holds 25 of the 40 seats in the UK Parliament and one of the four Welsh seats in the European Parliament.

Established in 1925, the pro-independent social democratic party Plaid Cymru ("Party of Wales") holds, as of 2015, 11 seats in the Welsh Assembly, three out of 40 seats in the UK

Parliament and one out of four in the European Parliament.

The Welsh Conservative and Unionist Party, established in 1921, is conservative in its ideology and holds, as of 2015, 14 seats in the Welsh Assembly, 11 Welsh seats in the UK Parliament, and one Welsh seat in the European Parliament.

The Welsh Liberal Democrats hold five seats in the Welsh Assembly and one seat in the UK Parliament. A fifth party trying to gain influence is the UK Independence Party. As of 2015, the fourth Welsh seat in the European Parliament is held by the UK Independence Party, which advocates Wales becoming an independent member of the European Union, instead of falling under the United Kingdom's membership.

Local Government

Wales is divided into 22 unitary authority areas, each of which provides education, roads services, and social assistance to its citizens. These principal areas are often referred to in Wales as being "counties," but these areas actually comprise nine counties, 10 county boroughs, and three cities. Each principal area or county is further subdivided into "communities" that are represented by elected bodies known as community councils.

Judicial System

The criminal and civil courts of England and Wales are known collectively as Her Majesty's Courts of Justice of England and Wales. Senior courts of England and Wales include the Court of Appeal, High Court, and Crown Court. Other courts include Youth Courts, Magistrates' Courts, Family Proceedings Courts, County Courts, and Tribunals.

Taxation

Citizens of Wales are subject to many of the same taxes as the rest of the United Kingdom, including income taxes, inheritance taxes, sales taxes, business taxes, council taxes, and capital gains taxes.

Armed Forces

Wales is part of the constitutional monarchy of the United Kingdom, with which it shares its armed forces, known officially as Her Majesty's Armed Forces. The armed forces are made up of an army, navy, air force, and Special Forces.

Foreign Policy

Wales is a constituent unit of the UK (the heir of the UK's reigning monarch is bestowed the title Prince of Wales). Therefore, the National Assembly of Wales does not have the authority to implement foreign policy and many domestic agendas. The parliament of Great Britain is the only legislative body that has the power to implement foreign relations policies.

However, the WAG does maintain its own European Union (EU) office in Brussels, Belgium, to help promote and protect Welsh economic interests. Also, the European and External Affairs Division (EEAD) of the Welsh government reaches out to other countries and regions within countries to promote Wales and Welsh interests. This division has four main activities: public diplomacy issues and international relationships; promotional activities; overseas events; and inward visits. To promote its economic interests abroad, the WAG established International Business Wales (IBW). This body actively seeks out relationships between Welsh companies and trading partners throughout the world, and also tries to encourage foreign investment in Wales.

Historically, Wales has maintained a relationship with Argentina when Welsh settlements were established in that country in the 19th century. A large percentage of Welsh-Argentineans live in the Welsh-speaking province of Chubut, in southern Argentina. Wales maintained little contact with Chubut throughout the majority of the 20th century. In 2000, however, the Welsh government funded an initiative to support Welsh culture in southern Argentina.

Human Rights Profile

International human rights law insists that states respect civil and political rights, and also promote an individual's economic, social and cultural rights. The United Nations (UN) Universal Declaration of Human Rights (UDHR) is recognized as the standard for international human rights. Its authors sought the counsel of the world's great thinkers, philosophers, and religious leaders, and were careful to create a document that reflects the core values shared by every world culture. (To read this document or view the articles relating to cultural human rights, go to: http://www.udhr.org/UDHR/default.htm.)

Generally, Wales's human rights profile is a positive one. The UK Parliament's Human Rights Act of 1998 enacted broad, sweeping guidelines that are in line with Article 2 of the Universal Declaration of Human Rights. The act also further supports citizens in the UK against human rights abuses that are outlined in the European Convention on Human Rights. In addition, the Equality and Human Rights Commission of the WAG was created in 2007 to further protect the basic human rights of those living in Wales.

The rights of marriage outlined in Article 16 of the UDHR are protected in Wales. Currently, a government-recognized marriage in Wales is between a man and a woman. In addition, Parliament enacted the Civil Partnership Act of 2004, granting same-sex partnerships the same rights granted to those in civil marriages.

Religious freedoms, as outlined in Article 18, are fully protected in Wales. However, the increase in the number of immigrants moving to Wales, particularly from India, Pakistan, and Bangladesh, has led to an increase in claims of religious discrimination. For example, some citizens have been denied the right to wear certain articles of clothing that are symbols of their faith. Discrimination is primarily in the private sector—schools, businesses, local governments and the Welsh Assembly have provided guidelines to help eliminate religious discrimination. Until early 2008, Christianity and the Church of England, primarily in England and Wales, was given special protection in Great Britain under the English Blasphemy Law. The law made it illegal to publicly slander God, Christianity, or the Church of England. Although rarely cited,

debate raged about the law's usefulness and whether it violated the Human Rights Declaration. The Criminal Justice and Immigration Act 2008 repealed the law.

Article 27 of the UDHR protects the universal right to freely participate in the cultural life of the community. The Welsh Language Act 1993, an act of the UK Parliament, required all organizations that provide services to the public in Wales to treat the Welsh language on an equal basis with English. The act protected the civil rights of some by allowing them to speak Welsh in courts of law. The act also created the Welsh Language Board (Bwrdd yr Iaith Gymraeg) to oversee the implementation of the act. In 2006 the Welsh Language Board approved the Welsh Language Scheme. The scheme is a plan to promote a bilingual Wales so that all citizens can fully participate in the social and cultural life of Wales, regardless of language.

ECONOMY

Overview of the Economy
In 2013, the gross domestic product (GDP) of Wales was $50.2 billion (USD), and its per capita income in 2014 was $17,326 (USD).

Industry
As a fully developed nation, Wales has many technological and industrial advantages. The service industry is the most important sector of the Welsh economy. The majority of the working class is employed in service jobs, which range from teaching to banking to trade.

Manufacturing is another large part of the industrial economy. Steel products are the most commonly manufactured, including automobile parts, tin and aluminum. The per capita gross domestic product (GDP) was estimated at $17,326 in 2014.

Labor
In November, 2014, the unemployment rate in Wales was seven percent, comprising roughly 103,000 unemployed people and giving Wales

the highest unemployment rate in the United Kingdom. The current job market is reliant upon the industrial sector, which is centered in factories in the urban coastal areas. The government is concerned for the future of rural agriculture, as more people move to the cities and away from the farmland of central Wales.

Energy/Power/Natural Resources

Great Britain has a wealth of natural resources, many of which are found in Wales. Coal mining has been a significant part of Welsh industrial history.

In addition to coal, petroleum deposits and natural gas, and metals such as tin, gold, zinc, and iron ore can be found in the rocky earth. There are mines throughout Wales devoted to exploiting these resources. Other important natural resources include lime, salt, clay, and slate.

Fishing

The fishing industry in Wales is the smallest of all the countries in the United Kingdom and employs approximately 1,000 full-time employees and 400 part time workers. In 2009, the European Fisheries Fund granted $1.4 billion (USD) to help develop and grow the fisheries sector. The Welsh government has pledged to double finfish and shellfish production by 2020.

Forestry

Deforestation and unregulated animal activity have depleted much of the forest habitat of Wales.

Mining/Metals

Coal mining has been a significant part of Welsh industrial history. In addition to coal, metals such as tin, gold, zinc, and iron ore can be found in the rocky earth. There are mines throughout Wales devoted to exploiting these resources.

Agriculture

Although certain staple grains are farmed in Wales, including barley and oats, livestock is much more significant in Welsh agriculture.

The problem of deforestation is one that may seriously affect agriculture in Wales. As forests are depleted and urban development grows, farmlands may become planting grounds for new conifers that will not sustain Welsh plant and animal life. If these changes occur, Wales could become even more economically reliant on its industrial sector.

Animal Husbandry

Although certain staple crops are farmed in Wales, livestock is much more significant than the country's crop-growing capabilities. Dairy cattle and beef are raised in the southern regions. As of mid-2014, there were approximately 9.75 million sheep in Wales, and mutton and wool are therefore abundant. Dairy cattle and beef are raised in the southern regions.

Tourism

In 2013, approximately 10 percent of the population of Wales was employed by the tourism industry, which contributed approximately $8 billion (USD) to the country's economy. There are a number of points of interest for visitors to southern Wales, including the quarry from which England's famous Stonehenge monoliths came. Tourism draws an important amount of Wales' revenue, with many people visiting castles and nature conservatories.

Wales has approximately 400 castles—more than 100 are still standing—as well as remains of Roman forts, and the country boasts numerous museums. Other attractions include the historic railways that operated as part of the mining industry. Welsh mines have now been abandoned, but are still visited by tourists.

Michael Carpenter, Richard Means

DO YOU KNOW?

- Wales is home to the town of Llanfairpwllgwyngyllgogerychwyrndrobwllllantysiliogogogoch, which has the longest name of any place in the entire world.
- Some famous celebrities from Wales include pop singer Tom Jones, actor Anthony Hopkins, and actress Catherine Zeta-Jones.

Bibliography

Bobby Freeman. *Traditional Foods from Wales.* New York: Hippocrene Books, Inc.,

Dafydd Johnston. *The Literature of Wales.* Cardiff: University of Wales Press, 1996.

Darren Longley, Tim Burford, and James Stewart. *The Rough Guide to Wales.* 8th ed. London: Rough Guides, 2015.

Filmer Cath Davies. *The Eisteddfod.* Cardiff: University of Wales Press, 2008.1997.

Geraint H. Jenkins. *A Concise History of Wales (Cambridge Concise Histories).* Cambridge: Cambridge University Press, 2007.

Jan Morris. *The Matter of Wales: Epic Views of a Small Country.* New York: Oxford University Press USA, 1985.

Jon Gowen. *The Story of Wales.* Reprint ed. London: BBC Books, 2013.

Julie Brake and Christine Jones. *Teach Yourself World Cultures: Wales.* New York: McGraw-Hill, 2004.

Trefor Owen. *The Customs and Traditions of Wales.* Cardiff: University of Wales Press, 1991.

Works Cited

"'Bangle' Girl Case Heard in Court." *BBC News,* June 17, 2008. http://news.bbc.co.uk/1/hi/wales/7458139.stm

"2007 Economic Activity Report." Carmarthenshire County Council website. http://www.carmarthenshire.gov.uk/attached_files/ Melita/2007 data/Economic Activity 2007.doc

"A Brief Analysis of the Labour Market by Main Equality Strands." *National Assembly for Wales Statistical Article.* http://new.wales.gov.uk/.../40382313/statistics/ compendia/comp2008/sdcatalogue08/sdcatalogue08equale.pdf?lang=en

"A Brief History of the Welsh Language." *Llanegwad City website.* http://www.llanegwad-carmarthen.co.uk/welshwords.htm

"Brecon Beacons." *Encyclopedia Britannica Online.* http://www.britannica.com/eb/article-9016323

"Caernarfon." *Encyclopedia Britannica Online.* http://www.britannica.com/eb/article-9018519/Caernarfon

UK Ministry of Justice. "Criminal Justice and Immigration Act of 2008." *UK Ministry of Justice.* http://www.justice.gov.uk/publications/criminal-justice-bill.htm

"Diversity in the Boardroom." UK Government Equalities Office website. http://www.equalities.gov.uk/boardroom_diversity/index.htm

"J.M.W. Turner." *Encyclopedia Britannica Online.*

"Living in Wales Survey." *Institute for Social & Economic Research website.* http://liwsurvey.essex.ac.uk/reports/2002LIW_RR.htm

"Narrow Gauge Railways." *The Transport Trust website.* http://www.transporttrust.com/10042.html

"Statistical First Release, 2006–07." *UK Higher Education Statistical Agency.* http://www.hesa.ac.uk/index.php/content/view/1100/161/

"UK: Language, Culture, Customs and Etiquette." *Kwintessential* website. http://www.kwintessential.co.uk/resources/global-etiquette/UK.html

"United Kingdom." *eDiplomat website.* http://www.ediplomat.com/np/cultural_etiquette/ce_gb.htm

"Wales Its Peoples—Working Lives." *UK National Statistics website.* http://www.statistics.gov.uk/CCI/nugget.asp?ID=452

"Wales Narrows Broadband Gap." *UK Office of Communications report May 24, 2007.* http://www.ofcom.org.uk/media/news/2007/05/walescmr.pdf

"Wales." *Encyclopedia Britannica Online.* http://www.britannica.com/eb/article-9110755

"Wales: Customs of Wales Sidebar. *MSN Encarta website.* http://encarta.msn.com/sidebar_631522279/customs_of_wales.html

"Wales: Society and Culture."

"Wedding Customs around the World." *Which Wedding website.* http://www.whichwedding.co.uk/types/customs.htm

"Welsh and the Law." *Welsh Language Board.* http://www.byig-wlb.org.uk/English/welshlanguage/Pages/WelshandtheLaw.aspx

"Welsh Rabbit; Welsh rarebit." *Bartleby.com website.* http://www.bartleby.com/68/69/6469.html

"Welsh." *High Beam Encyclopedia Online.* http://www.encyclopedia.com/doc/1G2-3435900514.html

"Women Win Half Welsh Seats." The Guardian News. http://www.guardian.co.uk/politics/2003/may/03/uk.wales1

"Women's Representation in Politics." UK Government Equalities Office website. http://www.equalities.gov.uk/public_life/parliament.htm

Allison Griffiths, Allison. "Wales." *The Museum of Broadcast Communications website*. http://www. museum.tv/archives/etv/W/htmlW/wales/wales.htm

Artes Mundi website. http://artesmundi.org/aboutUs.php

BBC News Channel. "Wales: Society and Culture." http://www.bbc.co.uk/wales/culture/sites/aboutwales/pages/culture.shtml

Betsan Powys, Betsan. "Western Mail Selling Fewer Copies." *BBC News*, August 31, 2006. http://news.bbc.co.uk/1/hi/wales/5302250.stm

Blaenavon. *World Heritage Site website*. http://www.world-heritage-blaenavon.org.uk/visit/places-of-interest/attractions.htm

Brecon Beacons National Park website. http://www.breconbeacons.org/content/visit-us/feature-stories/welcome-to-the-brecon-beacons-national-park

David Atkinson, David, and Neil Wilson. "Wales." London: *Lonely Planet, 2007*.

Gwyneth Lewis, Gwyneth. "Welsh Words." *Welsh Literature Abroad website*. http://www.welshlitabroad.org/features.cfm?lan=e&switch=dsp&feature_id=55&featuretype=3

http://www.britannica.com/EBchecked/topic/610274/J-M-W-Turner

http://www.celticlands.com/page2.html

http://www.pcnpa.org.uk/website/default.asp?SID=228&SkinID=4

http://www.welsh-lovespoons.co.uk/

Llangollen International Musical Eisteddfod website. http://www.eisteddfod-ryngwladol.co.uk/about-the-eisteddfod/

Paine, Neil. "Business Etiquette in the UK." *Buzzle.com website*. http://www.buzzle.com/articles/business-etiquette-in-the-uk.html

Pembrokeshire Coast National Park Authority website.

Richard Means, Richard. Wales. *EBSCO Student Research Center: Country Studies*. http://web.ebscohost.com/src/detail?vid=4&hid=12&sid=7f2b4391–274b-4598-b6fb-a33470e6233f@SRCSM1&bdata=JnNpdGU9c3JjLWxpdmU - db=ulh&AN=16492913

Snowdon Mountain Railway website. http://www.snowdonrailway.co.uk/

Snowdonia National Park website. http://www.snowdonia-npa.gov.uk/page/index.php?nav1=learning&nav2=11&nav3=1&lang=eng&view=graphic&contrast=1

UK Government Equalities Office website. http://www.equalities.gov.uk/legislation/discrimination_act.htm

UNESCO World Heritage website. http://whc.unesco.org/en/list/374

Welsh Assembly Government website. http://new.wales.gov.uk/topics/international/international affairs/?lang=en

Welsh National Opera website. http://www.wno.org.uk/about.history.html

Worrall, Simon. "Wales: Finding Its Voice." National Geographic, June 2002, 62–83.

Appendix One:
World Governments

Commonwealth

Guiding Premise

A commonwealth is an organization or alliance of nations connected for the purposes of satisfying a common interest. The participating states may retain their own governments, some of which are often considerably different from one another. Although commonwealth members tend to retain their own sovereign government institutions, they collaborate with other members to create mutually agreeable policies that meet their collective interests. Some nations join commonwealths to enhance their visibility and political power on the international stage. Others join commonwealths for security or economic reasons. Commonwealth members frequently engage in trade agreements, security pacts, and other programs. Some commonwealths are regional, while others are global.

Typical Structure

A commonwealth's structure depends largely on the nature of the organization and the interests it serves. Some commonwealths are relatively informal in nature, with members meeting on a periodic basis and participating voluntarily. This informality does not undermine the effectiveness of the organization, however—members still enjoy a closer relationship than that which exists among unaffiliated states. Commonwealths typically have a president, secretary general, or, in the case of the Commonwealth of Nations (a commonwealth that developed out of the British Empire), a monarch acting as the leader of the organization. Members appoint delegates to serve at summits, committee meetings, and other commonwealth events and programs.

Other commonwealths are more formal in structure and procedures. They operate based on mission statements with very specific goals and member participation requirements. These organizations have legislative bodies that meet regularly. There are even joint security operations involving members. The African Union, for example, operates according to a constitution and collectively addresses issues facing the entire African continent, such as HIV/AIDS, regional security, environmental protection, and economic cooperation.

One of the best-known commonwealths in modern history was the Soviet Union. This collective of communist states was similar to other commonwealths, but the members of the Soviet Union, although they retained their own sovereign government institutions, largely deferred to the organization's central leadership in Moscow, which in turn deferred to the Communist Party leadership. After the collapse of the Soviet Union, a dozen former Soviet states, including Russia, reconnected as the Commonwealth of Independent States. This organization features a central council in Minsk, Belarus. This council consists of the heads of state and heads of government for each member nation, along with their cabinet ministers for defense and foreign affairs.

Commonwealth structures and agendas vary. Some focus on trade and economic development, as well as using their respective members' collective power to address human rights, global climate change, and other issues. Others are focused on regional stability and mutual defense, including prevention of nuclear weapons proliferation. The diversity of issues for which commonwealths are formed contributes to the frequency of member meetings as well as the actions carried out by the organization.

Role of the Citizen

Most commonwealths are voluntary in nature, which means that the member states must choose to join with the approval of their respective governments. A nation with a democratic government, therefore, would need the sanction of its popularly elected legislative and executive bodies in order to proceed. Thus, the role of the private citizen with regard to a commonwealth is indirect—the people may have the power to vote for or against a legislative or executive candidate based on his or her position concerning membership in a commonwealth.

Some members of commonwealths, however, do not feature a democratic government, or their respective governmental infrastructures are not yet in place. Rwanda, for instance, is a developing nation whose 2009 decision to join the Commonwealth of Nations likely came from the political leadership with very little input from its citizens, as Rwandans have very limited political freedom.

While citizens may not directly influence the actions of a commonwealth, they may work closely with its representatives. Many volunteer nonprofit organizations—having direct experience with, for example, HIV/AIDS, certain minority groups, or environmental issues—work in partnership with the various branches of a commonwealth's central council. In fact, such organizations are frequently called upon in this regard to implement the policies of a commonwealth, receiving financial and logistical support when working in impoverished and/or war-torn regions. Those working for such organizations may therefore prove invaluable to the effectiveness of a commonwealth's programs.

Michael Auerbach
Marblehead, Massachusetts

Examples

African Union
Commonwealth of Independent States
Commonwealth of Nations
Northern Mariana Islands (and the United States)
Puerto Rico (and the United States)

Bibliography

"About Commonwealth of Independent States." *Commonwealth of Independent States*. CIS, n.d. Web. 17 Jan. 2013.

"AU in a Nutshell." *African Union*. African Union Commission, n.d. Web. 17 Jan. 2013.

"The Commonwealth." *Commonwealth of Nations*. Nexus Strategic Partnerships Limited, 2013. Web. 17 Jan. 2013.

Communist

Guiding Premise

Communism is a political and economic system that seeks to eliminate private property and spread the benefits of labor equally throughout the populace. Communism is generally considered an outgrowth of socialism, a political and economic philosophy that advocates "socialized" or centralized ownership of the economy and the means of production.

Communism developed largely from the theories of Karl Marx (1818–83), who believed that a revolution led by the working class must occur before the state could achieve the even distribution of wealth and property and eliminate the class-based socioeconomic system of capitalist society. Marx believed that a truly equitable society required centralized control of credit, transportation, education, communication, agriculture, and industry, along with eliminating the rights of individuals to inherit or to own land.

Russia (formerly the Soviet Union) and China are the two largest countries to have been led by communist governments during the twentieth and twenty-first centuries. In both cases, the attempt to bring about a communist government came by way of violent revolutions in which members of the former government and ruling party were executed. Under Russian leader Vladimir Lenin (1870–1924) and Chinese leader Mao Zedong (1893–1976), strict dictatorships were instituted, curtailing individual rights in favor of state control. Lenin sought to expand communism into developing nations to counter the global spread of capitalism. Mao, in his form of communism, considered ongoing revolution within China a necessary aspect of communism. Both gave their names to their respective versions of communism, but neither Leninism nor Maoism managed to achieve the idealized utopia envisioned by Marx and other communist philosophers.

The primary difference between modern socialism and communism is that communist groups believe that a social revolution is necessary to create the idealized state without class structure, where socialists believe that the inequities of class structure can be addressed and eliminated through gradual change.

Typical Structure

Most modern communist governments define themselves as "socialist," though a national communist party exerts control over all branches of government. The designation of a "communist state" is primarily an external definition for a situation in which a communist party controls the government.

Among the examples of modern socialist states operating under the communist model are the People's Republic of China, the Republic of Cuba, and the Socialist Republic of Vietnam. However, each of these governments in fact operates through a mixed system of socialist and capitalist economic policies, allowing private ownership in some situations and sharply enforcing state control in others.

Typically, a communist state is led by the national communist party, a political group with voluntary membership and members in all sectors of the populace. While many individuals may join the communist party, the leadership of the party is generally selected by a smaller number of respected or venerated leaders from within the party. These leaders select a ruling committee that develops the political initiatives of the party, which are thereafter distributed throughout the government.

In China, the Communist Party elects both a chairperson, who serves as executive of the party, and a politburo, a standing committee that makes executive decisions on behalf of the party. In Cuba, the Communist Party selects individuals who sit for election to the National Assembly of People's Power, which then serves directly as the state's sole legislative body.

In the cases of China, Cuba, and Vietnam, the committees and leaders chosen by the communist party then participate directly in electing leaders to serve in the state judiciary. In addition, the central committees typically appoint individuals to serve as heads of the military and to lower-level, provincial, or municipal government positions. In China, the populace elects individuals to local, regional, and provincial councils that in turn elect representatives to sit on a legislative body known as the National People's Congress (NPC), though the NPC is generally considered a largely ceremonial institution without any substantial power to enact independent legislation.

In effect, most modern communist states are controlled by the leadership of the national communist party, though this leadership is achieved by direct and indirect control of lesser legislative, executive, and judicial bodies. In some cases, ceremonial and symbolic offices created under the communist party can evolve to take a larger role in state politics. In China, for instance, the NPC has come to play a more important role in developing legislation in the twenty-first century.

Role of the Citizen

In modern communist societies, citizens have little voice in selecting the leadership of the government. In many communist states, popular elections are held at local and national levels, but candidates are chosen by communist party leadership and citizens are not given the option to vote for representatives of opposing political parties.

In most cases, the state adopts policies that give the appearance of popular control over the government, while in actuality, governmental policies are influenced by a small number of leaders chosen from within the upper echelons of the party. Popularly elected leaders who oppose party policy are generally removed from office.

All existing communist states have been criticized for human rights violations in terms of curtailing the freedoms available to citizens and of enacting dictatorial and authoritarian policies. Cuba, Vietnam, and China, for instance, all have laws preventing citizens from opposing party policy or supporting a political movement that opposes the communist party. Communist governments have also been accused of using propaganda and misinformation to control the opinion of the populace regarding party leadership and therefore reducing the potential for popular resistance to communist policies.

Micah Issitt
Philadelphia, Pennsylvania

Examples

China
Cuba
Laos
North Korea
Vietnam

Bibliography

Caramani, Daniele. *Comparative Politics*. New York: Oxford UP, 2008. Print.

Priestland, David. *The Red Flag: A History of Communism*. New York: Grove, 2009. Print.

Service, Robert. *Comrades! A History of World Communism*. Cambridge: Harvard UP, 2007. Print.

Confederation/Confederacy

Guiding Premise

A confederation or confederacy is a loose alliance between political units, such as states or cantons, within a broader federal government. Confederations allow a central, federal government to create laws and regulations of broad national interest, but the sovereign units are granted the ultimate authority to carry out those laws and to create, implement, and enforce their own laws as well. Confederate governments are built on the notion that a single, central government should not have ultimate authority over sovereign states and populations. Some confederate governments were born due to the rise of European monarchies and empires that threatened to govern states from afar. Others were created out of respect for the diverse ideologies, cultures, and ideals of their respective regions. Confederations and confederacies may be hybrids, giving comparatively more power to a federal government while retaining respect for the sovereignty of their members. True confederate governments are rare in the twenty-first century.

Typical Structure

Confederate governments are typically characterized by the presence of both a central government and a set of regional, similarly organized, and sovereign (independent) governments. For example, a confederate government might have as its central government structure a system that features executive, legislative, and judicial branches. Each region that serves as members of the confederation would have in place a similar system, enabling the efficient flow of lawmaking and government services.

In some confederations, the executive branch of the central government is headed by a president or prime minister, who serves as the government's chief administrative officer, overseeing the military and other government operations. Meanwhile, at the regional level, another chief executive, such as a governor, is charged with the administration of that government's operations.

Legislative branches are also similarly designed. Confederations use parliaments or congresses that, in most cases, have two distinct chambers. One chamber consists of legislators who each represent an entire state, canton, or region. The other chamber consists of legislators representing certain populations of voters within that region. Legislatures at the regional level not only have the power to create and enforce their own laws, but also have the power to refuse to enact or enforce any laws handed down by the national government.

A confederation's judiciary is charged with ensuring that federal and regional laws are applied uniformly and within the limits of the confederation's constitutional framework. Central and regional governments both have such judicial institutions, with the latter addressing those legal matters administered in the state or canton and the former addressing legal issues of interest to the entire country.

Political parties also typically play a role in a confederate government. Political leadership is achieved by a party's majority status in either the executive or the legislative branches. Parties also play a role in forging a compromise on certain matters at both the regional and national levels. Some confederations take the diversity of political parties and their ideologies seriously enough to create coalition governments that can help avoid political stalemates.

Role of the Citizen

The political role of the citizen within a confederate political system depends largely on the constitution of the country. In some confederacies, for example, the people directly elect their legislative and executive leaders by popular vote. Some legislators are elected to open terms—they may technically be reelected, but this election is merely a formality, as they are allowed to stay in office until they decide to leave or they die—while others may be subject to term limits or other reelection rules. Popularly elected legislators and executives in turn draft, file, and pass new laws and regulations that ideally are favorable to the voters. Some confederate systems give popularly elected legislators the ability to elect a party leader to serve as prime minister or president.

Confederations are designed to empower the regional government and avoid the dominance of a distant national government. In this manner, citizens of a confederate government, in some cases, may enjoy the ability to put forth new legislative initiatives. Although the lawmaking process is expected to be administered by the legislators and executives, in such cases the people are allowed and even encouraged to connect and interact with their political representatives to ensure that the government remains open and accessible.

Michael Auerbach
Marblehead, Massachusetts

Examples
European Union
Switzerland
United States under the Articles of Confederation (1781–89)

Bibliography
"Government Type." *The World Factbook.* Central Intelligence Agency, n.d. Web. 17 Jan. 2013.
"Swiss Politics." *SwissWorld.org.* Federal Department of Foreign Affairs Presence Switzerland, n.d. Web. 17 Jan. 2013.

Constitutional Monarchy

Guiding Premise

A constitutional monarchy is a form of government in which the head of state is a monarch (a king or queen) with limited powers. The monarch has official duties, but those responsibilities are defined in the nation's constitution and not by the monarch. Meanwhile, the power to create and rescind laws is given to a legislative body. Constitutional monarchies retain the ceremony and traditions associated with nations that have long operated under a king or queen. However, the constitution prevents the monarch from becoming a tyrant. Additionally, the monarchy, which is typically a lifetime position, preserves a sense of stability and continuity in the government, as the legislative body undergoes periodic change associated with the election cycle.

Typical Structure

The structure of a constitutional monarchy varies from nation to nation. In some countries, the monarchy is predominantly ceremonial. In such cases, the monarch provides a largely symbolic role, reminding the people of their heritage and giving them comfort in times of difficulty. Such is the case in Japan, for example; the emperor of that country was stripped of any significant power after World War II but was allowed to continue his legacy in the interest of ensuring that the Japanese people would remain peaceful. Today, that nation still holds its monarchical family in the highest regard, but the government is controlled by the Diet (the legislature), with the prime minister serving in the executive role.

In other countries, the sovereign plays a more significant role. In the United Kingdom, the king or queen does have some power, including the powers to appoint the prime minister, to open or dissolve Parliament, to approve bills that have been passed by Parliament, and to declare war and make peace. However, the monarch largely defers to the government on these acts. In Bahrain, the king (or, until 2002, emir or

hereditary ruler) was far more involved in government in the late twentieth and early twenty-first centuries than many other constitutional monarchs. In 1975, the emir of Bahrain dissolved the parliament, supposedly to run the government more effectively. His son would later implement a number of significant constitutional reforms that made the government more democratic in nature.

The key to the structure of this type of political system is the constitution. As is the case in the United States (a federal republic), a constitutional monarchy is carefully defined by the government's founding document. In Canada, for example, the king or queen of England is still recognized as the head of state, but that country's constitution gives the monarch no power other than ceremonial responsibilities. India, South Africa, and many other members of the Commonwealth of Nations (the English monarch's sphere of influence, spanning most of the former British colonies) have, since gaining their independence, created constitutions that grant no power to the English monarch; instead, they give all powers to their respective government institutions and, in some cases, recognize their own monarchs.

A defining feature of a constitutional monarchy is the fact that the monarch gives full respect to the limitations set forth by the constitution (and rarely seeks to alter such a document in his or her favor). Even in the United Kingdom itself—which does not have a written constitution, but rather a series of foundational documents—the king or queen does not step beyond the bounds set by customary rules. One interesting exception is in Bahrain, where Hamad bin Isa Al-Khalifa assumed the throne in 1999 and immediately implemented a series of reforms to the constitution in order to give greater definition to that country's democratic institutions, including resuming parliamentary elections in 2001. During the 2011 Arab Spring uprisings, Bahraini protesters called for further democratic reforms to be enacted, and tensions between the ruler and his opposition continue.

Role of the Citizen

In the past, monarchies ruled nations with absolute power; the only power the people had was the ability to unify and overthrow the ruling sovereign. Although the notion of an absolute monarchy has largely disappeared from the modern political landscape, many nations have retained their respective kings, queens, emperors, and other monarchs for the sake of ceremony and cultural heritage. In the modern constitutional monarchy, the people are empowered by their nation's foundational documents, which not only define the rights of the people but the limitations of their governments and sovereign as well. The people, through their legislators and through the democratic voting process, can modify their constitutions to expand or shrink the political involvement of the monarchy.

For example, the individual members of the Commonwealth of Nations, including Canada and Australia, have different constitutional parameters for the king or queen of England. In England, the monarch holds a number of powers, while in Canada, he or she is merely a ceremonial head of state (with all government power centered in the capital of Ottawa). In fact, in 1999, Australia held a referendum (a general vote) on whether to abolish its constitutional monarchy altogether and replace it with a presidential republic. In that case, the people voted to retain the monarchy, but the proposal was only narrowly defeated. These examples demonstrate the tremendous power the citizens of a constitutional monarchy may possess through the legislative process and the vote under the constitution.

Michael Auerbach
Marblehead, Massachusetts

Examples

Bahrain
Cambodia
Denmark
Japan
Lesotho
Malaysia
Morocco
Netherlands
Norway
Spain
Sweden
Thailand
United Kingdom

Bibliography

Bowman, John. "Constitutional Monarchies." *CBC News*. CBC, 4 Oct. 2002. Web. 17 Jan. 2013.
"The Role of the Monarchy." *Royal.gov.uk*. Royal Household, n.d. Web. 17 Jan. 2013.

Constitutional Republic

Guiding Premise

A constitutional republic is a governmental system in which citizens are involved in electing or appointing leaders who serve according to rules formulated in an official state constitution. In essence, the constitutional republic combines the political structure of a republic or republican governmental system with constitutional principles.

A republic is a government in which the head of state is empowered to hold office through law, not inheritance (as in a monarchy). A constitutional republic is a type of republic based on a constitution, a written body of fundamental precedents and principles from which the laws of the nation are developed.

Most constitutional republics in the modern world use a universal suffrage system, in which all citizens of the nation are empowered to vote for or against individuals who attempt to achieve public office. Universal suffrage is not required for a nation to qualify as a constitutional republic, and some nations may only allow certain categories of citizens to vote for elected leaders.

A constitutional republic differs from other forms of democratic systems in the roles assigned to both the leaders and the citizenry. In a pure democratic system, the government is formed by pure majority rule, and this system therefore ignores the opinions of any minority group. A republic, by contrast, is a form of government in which the government's role is limited by a written constitution aimed at promoting the welfare of all individuals, whether members of the majority or a minority.

Typical Structure

To qualify as a constitutional republic, a nation must choose a head of state (most often a president) through elections, according to constitutional law. In some nations, an elected president may serve alongside an appointed or elected individual who serves as leader of the legislature, such as a prime minister, often called the "head of government." When the president also serves as head of government, the republic is said to operate under a presidential system.

Typically, the executive branch consists of the head of state and the executive offices, which are responsible for enforcing the laws and overseeing relations with other nations. The legislative branch makes laws and has overlapping duties with the executive office in terms of economic and military developments. The judicial branch, consisting of the courts, interprets the law and the constitution and enforces adherence to the law.

In a constitutional republic, the constitution describes the powers allotted to each branch of government and the means by which the governmental bodies are to be established. The constitution also describes the ways in which governmental branches interact in creating, interpreting, and enforcing laws. For instance, in the United States, the executive and legislative branches both have roles in determining the budget for the nation, and neither body is free to make budgetary legislation without the approval of the other branch.

Role of the Citizen

In a constitutional republic, the citizens have the power to control the evolution of the nation through the choice of representatives who serve on the government. These representatives can, generally through complicated means, create or abolish laws and even change the constitution itself through reinterpretations of constitutional principles or direct amendments.

Citizens in a republic are empowered, but generally not required, to play a role in electing leaders. In the United States, both state governments and the federal government function according to a republican system, and citizens are therefore allowed to take part in the election of leaders to both local and national offices. In addition, constitutional systems generally allow individuals to join political interest groups to further common political goals.

In a constitutional democratic republic such as Guatemala and Honduras, the president, who serves as chief of state and head of government, is elected directly by popular vote. In the United States, a constitutional federal republic, the president is elected by the Electoral College, whose members are selected according to the popular vote within each district. The Electoral College is intended to provide more weight to smaller states, thereby balancing the disproportionate voting power of states with larger populations. In all constitutional republics, the citizens elect leaders either directly or indirectly through other representatives chosen by popular vote. Therefore, the power to control the government is granted to the citizens of the constitutional republic.

Micah Issitt
Philadelphia, Pennsylvania

Examples
Guatemala
Honduras
Iceland
Paraguay
Peru
United States
Uruguay

Bibliography
Baylis, John, Steve Smith, and Patricia Owens. *The Globalization of World Politics: An Introduction to International Relations*. New York: Oxford UP, 2010. Print.
Caramani, Daniele. *Comparative Politics*. New York: Oxford UP, 2008. Print.
Garner, Robert, Peter Ferdinand, and Stephanie Lawson. *Introduction to Politics*. 2nd ed. Oxford. Oxford UP, 2009. Print.
Hague, Rod, and Martin Harrop. *Comparative Government and Politics: An Introduction*. New York: Palgrave, 2007. Print.

Democracy

Guiding Premise

Democracy is a political system based on majority rule, in which all citizens are guaranteed participatory rights to influence the evolution of government. There are many different types of democracy, based on the degree to which citizens participate in the formation and operation of the government. In a direct democratic system, citizens vote directly on proposed changes to law and public policy. In a representative democracy, individuals vote to elect representatives who then serve to create and negotiate public policy.

The democratic system of government first developed in Ancient Greece and has existed in many forms throughout history. While democratic systems always involve some type of majority rule component, most modern democracies have systems in place designed to equalize representation for minority groups or to promote the development of governmental policies that prevent oppression of minorities by members of the majority.

In modern democracies, one of the central principles is the idea that citizens must be allowed to participate in free elections to select leaders who serve in the government. In addition, voters in democratic systems elect political leaders for a limited period of time, thus ensuring that the leadership of the political system can change along with the changing views of the populace. Political theorists have defined democracy as a system in which the people are sovereign and the political power flows upward from the people to their elected leaders.

Typical Structure

In a typical democracy, the government is usually divided into executive, legislative, and judicial branches. Citizens participate in electing individuals to serve in one or more of these branches, and elected leaders appoint additional leaders to serve in other political offices. The democratic system, therefore, involves a combination of elected and appointed leadership.

Democratic systems may follow a presidential model, as in the United States, where citizens elect a president to serve as both head of state and head of government. In a presidential model, citizens may also participate in elections to fill other governmental bodies, including the legislature and judicial branch. In a parliamentary democracy, citizens elect individuals to a parliament, whose members in turn form a committee to appoint a leader, often called the prime minister, who serves as head of government.

In most democratic systems, the executive and legislative branches cooperate in the formation of laws, while the judicial branch enforces and interprets the laws produced by the government. Most democratic systems have developed a system of checks and balances designed to prevent any single branch of government from exerting a dominant influence over the development of governmental policy. These checks and balances may be instituted in a variety of ways, including the ability to block governmental initiatives and the ability to appoint members to various governmental agencies.

Democratic governments generally operate on the principle of political parties, which are organizations formed to influence political development. Candidates for office have the option of joining a political party, which can provide funding and other campaign assistance. In some democratic systems—called dominant party or one-party dominant systems—there is effectively a single political party. Dominant party systems allow for competition in democratic elections, but existing power structures often prevent opposing parties from competing successfully. In multiparty democratic systems, there are two or more political parties with the ability to compete for office, and citizens are able to choose among political parties during elections. Some countries only allow political parties to be active at the national level, while other countries allow political parties to play a role in local and regional elections.

Role of the Citizen

The citizens in a democratic society are seen as the ultimate source of political authority. Members of the government, by contrast, are seen as servants of the people, and are selected and elected to serve the people's interests. Democratic systems developed to protect and enhance the freedom of the people; however, for the system to function properly, citizens must engage in a number of civic duties.

In democratic nations, voting is a right that comes with citizenship. Though some democracies—Australia, for example—require citizens to vote by law, compulsory participation in elections is not common in democratic societies. Citizens are nonetheless encouraged to fulfill their voting rights and to stay informed regarding political issues. In addition, individuals are responsible for contributing to the well-being of society as a whole, usually through a system of taxation whereby part of an individual's earnings is used to pay for governmental services.

In many cases, complex governmental and legal issues must be simplified to ease understanding among the citizenry. This goal is partially met by having citizens elect leaders who must then explain to their constituents how they are shaping legislation and other government initiatives to reflect constituents' wants and needs. In the United States, citizens may participate in the election of local leaders within individual cities or counties, and also in the election of leaders who serve in the national legislature and executive offices.

Citizens in democratic societies are also empowered with the right to join political interest groups and political parties in an effort to further a broader political agenda. However, democratic societies oppose making group membership a requirement and have laws forbidding forcing an individual to join any group. Freedom of choice, especially with regard to political affiliation and preference, is one of the cornerstones of all democratic systems.

Micah Issitt
Philadelphia, Pennsylvania

Examples

Denmark
Sweden
Spain
Japan
Australia
Costa Rica
Uruguay
United States

Bibliography

Barington, Lowell. *Comparative Politics*: *Structures and Choices*. Boston: Wadsworth, 2012. Print.

Caramani, Daniele. *Comparative Politics*. New York: Oxford UP, 2008. Print.

Przeworski, Adam. *Democracy and the Limits of Self Government*, New York: Cambridge UP, 2010. Print.

Dictatorship/Military Dictatorship

Guiding Premise

Dictatorships and military dictatorships are political systems in which absolute power is held by an individual or military organization. Dictatorships are led by a single individual, under whom all political control is consolidated. Military dictatorships are similar in purpose, but place the system under the control of a military organization comprised of a single senior officer, or small group of officers. Often, dictatorships and military dictatorships are imposed as the result of a coup d'état in which the regime in question directly removes the incumbent regime, or after a power vacuum creates chaos in the nation. In both situations, the consolidation of absolute power is designed to establish a state of strict law and order.

Typical Structure

Dictatorships and military dictatorships vary in structure and nature. Some come about through the overthrow of other regimes, while others are installed through the democratic process, and then become a dictatorship as democratic rights are withdrawn. Still others are installed following a complete breakdown of government, often with the promise of establishing order.

Many examples of dictatorships can be found in the twentieth century, including Nazi Germany, Joseph Stalin's Soviet Union, and China under Mao Tse-tung. A number of dictatorships existed in Africa, such as the regimes of Idi Amin in Uganda, Charles Taylor in Liberia, and Mu'ammar Gadhafi in Libya. Dictatorships such as these consolidated power in the hands of an individual leader. A dictator serves as the sole decision-maker in the government, frequently using the military, secret police, or other security agencies to enforce the leader's will. Dictators also have control over state institutions like legislatures. A legislature may have the ability to develop and pass laws, but if its actions run counter to the dictator's will, the latter can—and

frequently does—dissolve the body, replacing its members with those more loyal to the dictator's agenda.

Military dictatorships consolidate power not in the hands of a civilian but in an individual or small group of military officers—the latter of which are often called "juntas." Because military dictatorships are frequently installed following a period of civil war and/or a coup d'état, the primary focus of the dictatorship is to achieve strict order through the application of military force. Military dictatorships are often installed with the promise of an eventual return to civilian and/or democratic control once the nation has regained stability. In the case of North Korea, one-party communist rule turned into a communist military dictatorship as its leader, Kim Il-Sung, assumed control of the military and brought its leadership into the government.

In the late twentieth and early twenty-first centuries, dictatorships and military dictatorships are most commonly found in developing nations, where poverty rates are high and regional stability is tenuous at best. Many are former European colonies, where charismatic leaders who boast of their national heritage have stepped in to replace colonial governments. National resources are typically directed toward military and security organizations in an attempt to ensure security and internal stability, keeping the regime in power and containing rivals. Human rights records in such political systems are typically heavily criticized by the international community.

Role of the Citizen

Dictatorships and military dictatorships are frequently installed because of the absence of viable democratic governments. There is often a disconnect, therefore, between the people and their leaders in a dictatorship. Of course, many dictatorships are identified as such by external entities and not by their own people. For example, the government of Zimbabwe is technically identified as a parliamentary democracy, with Robert Mugabe—who has been the elected leader of the country since 1980—as its president. However, the international community has long complained that Mugabe "won" his positions through political corruption, including alleged ballot stuffing. In 2008, Mugabe lost his first reelection campaign, but demanded a recount. While the recount continued, his supporters attacked opposition voters, utilizing violence and intimidation until his opponent, Morgan Tsvangirai, withdrew his candidacy, and Mugabe was restored as president.

By definition, citizens do not have a role in changing the course of a dictatorship's agenda. The people are usually called upon to join the military in support of the regime, or cast their vote consistently in favor of the ruling regime. Freedom of speech, the press, and assembly are virtually nonexistent, as those who speak out against the ruling regime are commonly jailed, tortured, or killed.

Michael Auerbach
Marblehead, Massachusetts

Examples

Belarus (dictatorship)
Fiji (military dictatorship)
North Korea (military dictatorship)
Zimbabwe (dictatorship)

Bibliography

Clayton, Jonathan. "China Aims to Bring Peace through Deals with Dictators and Warlords." *Times* [London]. Times Newspapers, 31 Jan. 2007. Web. 6 Feb. 2013.
"Robert Mugabe—Biography." *Biography.com.* A+E Television Networks, 2013. Web. 6 Feb. 2013.

Ecclesiastical

Guiding Premise

An ecclesiastical government is one in which the laws of the state are guided by and derived from religious law. Ecclesiastical governments can take a variety of forms and can be based on many different types of religious traditions. In some traditions, a deity or group of deities are considered to take a direct role in the formation of government, while other traditions utilize religious laws or principles indirectly to craft laws used to manage the state.

In many cultures, religious laws and tenets play a major role in determining the formation of national laws. Historically, the moral and ethical principles derived from Judeo-Christian tradition inspired many laws in Europe and North America. Few modern governments operate according to an ecclesiastical system, but Vatican City, which is commonly classified as a city-state, utilizes a modernized version of the ecclesiastical government model. All states utilizing an ecclesiastical or semi-ecclesiastical system have adopted a single state religion that is officially recognized by the government.

In some predominantly Islamic nations, including the Sudan, Oman, Iran, and Nigeria, Islamic law, known as sharia, is the basis for most national laws, and government leaders often must obtain approval by the leaders of the religious community before being allowed to serve in office. Most modern ecclesiastical or semi-ecclesiastical governments have adopted a mixed theocratic republic system in which individuals approved by religious authorities are elected by citizens to hold public office.

Typical Structure

In an ecclesiastical government, the church or recognized religious authority is the source of all state law. In a theocracy, which is one of the most common types of ecclesiastical governments, a deity or group of deities occupies a symbolic position as head of state, while representatives are chosen to lead the government based on their approval by the prevailing religious authority. In other types of ecclesiastical governments, the chief of state may be the leading figure in the church, such as in Vatican City, where the Catholic Pope is also considered the chief of state.

There are no modern nations that operate on a purely ecclesiastical system, though some Islamic countries, like Iran, have adopted a semi-ecclesiastical form of republican government. In Iran, the popularly elected Assembly of Experts—comprised of Islamic scholars called mujtahids—appoints an individual to serve as supreme leader of the nation for life, and this individual has veto power over all other governmental offices. Iranian religious leaders also approve other individuals to run as candidates for positions in the state legislature. In many cases, the citizens will elect an individual to serve as head of government, though this individual must conform to religious laws.

In an ecclesiastical government, those eligible to serve in the state legislature are generally members of the church hierarchy or have been approved for office by church leaders. In Tibet, which functioned as an ecclesiastical government until the Chinese takeover of 1951, executive and legislative duties were consolidated under a few religious leaders, called lamas, and influential citizens who maintained the country under a theocratic system. Most modern nations separate governmental functions between distinct but interrelated executive, legislative, and judicial branches.

Many modern semi-ecclesiastical nations have adopted a set of state principles in the form of a constitution to guide the operation of government and the establishment of laws. In mixed constitutional/theocratic systems, the constitution may be used to legitimize religious authority by codifying a set of laws and procedures that have been developed from religious scripture.

In addition, the existence of a constitution facilitates the process of altering laws and governmental procedures as religious authorities reinterpret religious scriptures and texts.

Role of the Citizen

Citizens in modern ecclesiastical and semi-ecclesiastical governments play a role in formulating the government though national and local elections. In some cases, religious authorities may approve more than one candidate for a certain position and citizens are then able to exercise legitimate choice in the electoral process. In other cases, popular support for one or more candidates may influence religious authorities when it comes time to nominate or appoint an individual to office.

In ecclesiastical governments, the freedoms and rights afforded to citizens may depend on their religious affiliation. Christians living in a Christian ecclesiastical government, for instance, may be allowed to run for and hold government office, while representatives of other religions may be denied this right. In addition, ecclesiastical governments may not recognize religious rights and rituals of other traditions and may not offer protection for those practicing religions other than the official state religion.

Though religious authority dominates politics and legislative development, popular influence is still an important part of the ecclesiastical system. Popular support for or against certain laws may convince the government to alter official policies. In addition, the populace may join local and regional religious bodies that can significantly affect national political developments. As local and regional religious groups grow in numbers and influence, they may promote candidates to political office, thereby helping to influence the evolution of government.

Micah Issitt
Philadelphia, Pennsylvania

Examples

Afghanistan
Iran
Nigeria
Oman
Vatican City

Bibliography

Barrington, Lowell. *Comparative Politics: Structures and Choices.* Boston: Wadsworth, 2012. Print.
Hallaq, Wael B. *An Introduction to Islamic Law.* New York: Cambridge UP, 2009. Print.
Hirschl, Ran. *Constitutional Theocracy.* Cambridge, MA: Harvard UP, 2010. Print.

Failed State

Guiding Premise

A failed state is a political unit that at one point had a stable government that provided basic services and security to its citizens, but then entered a period marked by devastating conflict, extreme poverty, overwhelming political corruption, and/or unlivable environmental conditions. Often, a group takes hold of a failed state's government through military means, staving off rivals to fill in a power vacuum. The nominal leadership of a failed state frequently uses its power to combat rival factions, implement extreme religious law, or protect and advance illicit activities (such as drug production or piracy). Failed states frequently retain their external borders, but within those borders are regions that may be dominated by a particular faction, effectively carving the state into disparate subunits, with some areas even attaining relative stability and security—a kind of de facto independence.

Typical Structure

Failed states vary in appearance based on a number of factors. One such factor is the type of government that existed prior to the state's collapse. For example, a failed state might have originally existed as a parliamentary democracy, with an active legislature and executive system that developed a functioning legal code and administered to the needs of the people. However, that state may not have adequately addressed the needs of certain groups, fostering a violent backlash and hastening the country's destabilization. An ineffectual legislature might have been dissolved by the executive (a prime minister or president), and in the absence of leadership, the government as a whole ceased to operate effectively.

Another major factor is demographics. Many states are comprised of two or more distinct ethnic, social, or religious groups. When the ruling party fails to effectively govern and/or serve the interests of a certain segment of the population, it may be ousted or simply ignored by the marginalized faction within the state. If the government falls, it creates a power vacuum that rival groups compete to fill. If one faction gains power, it must remain in a constant state of vigilance against its rivals, focusing more on keeping enemies in check than on rebuilding crippled government infrastructure. Some also seek to create theocracies based on extreme interpretations of a particular religious doctrine. Frequently, these regimes are themselves ousted by rivals within a few years, leaving no lasting government and keeping the state in chaos.

Failed states are also characterized by extreme poverty and a lack of modern technology. Potable water, electricity, food, and medicine are scarce among average citizens. In some cases, these conditions are worsened by natural events. Haiti, for example, was a failed state for many years before the devastating 2010 earthquake that razed the capitol city of Port au Prince, deepening the country's poverty and instability. Afghanistan and Ethiopia—with their harsh, arid climates—are also examples of failed states whose physical environments and lack of resources exacerbated an already extreme state of impoverishment.

Most failed states' conditions are also worsened by the presence of foreigners. Because their governments are either unable or unwilling to repel terrorists, for example, failed states frequently become havens for international terrorism. Somalia, Afghanistan, and Iraq are all examples of states that failed, enabling terrorist organizations to set up camp within their borders. As such groups pose a threat to other nations, those nations often send troops and weapons into the failed states to engage the terrorists. In recent years, NATO, the United Nations, and the African Union have all entered failed states to both combat terrorists and help rebuild government.

Role of the Citizen

Citizens of a failed state have very little say in the direction of their country. In most cases, when a faction assumes control over the government, it installs strict controls that limit the rights of citizens, particularly such rights as freedom of speech, freedom of assembly, and freedom of religion. Some regimes allow for "democratic" elections, but a continued lack of infrastructure and widespread corruption often negates the legitimacy of these elections.

Citizens of failed states are often called upon by the ruling regime (or a regional faction) to serve in its militia, helping it combat other factions within the state. In fact, many militias within failed states are comprised of people who were forced to join (under penalty of death) at a young age. Those who do not join militias are often drawn into criminal activity such as piracy and the drug trade.

Some citizens are able to make a difference by joining interest groups. Many citizens are able to achieve a limited amount of success sharing information about women's rights, HIV/AIDS and other issues. In some situations, these groups are able to gain international assistance from organizations that were unable to work with the failed government.

Michael Auerbach
Marblehead, Massachusetts

Examples

Chad
Democratic Republic of the Congo
Somalia
Sudan
Zimbabwe

Bibliography

"Failed States: Fixing a Broken World." *Economist*, 29 Jan. 2009. Web. 6 Feb. 2012.

"Failed States." Global Policy Forum, 2013. Web. 6 Feb. 2012.

"Somalia Tops Failed States Index for Fifth Year." *CNN.com*. Turner Broadcasting System, 18 June 2012. Web. 6 Feb. 2012.

Thürer, Daniel. (1999). "The 'Failed State' and International Law." *International Review of the Red Cross*. International Committee of the Red Cross, 31 Dec. 1999. Web. 6 Feb. 2012.

Federal Republic

Guiding Premise

A federal republic is a political system that features a central government as well as a set of regional subunits such as states or provinces. Federal republics are designed to limit the power of the central government, paring its focus to only matters of national interest. Typically, a greater degree of power is granted to the regional governments, which retain the ability to create their own laws of local relevance. The degree to which the federal and regional governments each enjoy authority varies from nation to nation, based on the country's interpretation of this republican form of government. By distributing authority to these separate but connected government institutions, federal republics give the greatest power to the people themselves, who typically vote directly for both their regional and national political representation.

Typical Structure

A federal republic's structure varies from nation to nation. However, most federal republics feature two distinct governing entities. The first is a central, federal government, usually based in the nation's capital city. The federal government's task is to address issues of national importance. These issues include defense and foreign relations, but also encompass matters of domestic interest that must be addressed in uniform fashion, such as social assistance programs, infrastructure, and certain taxes.

A federal republic is comprised of executive, legislative, and judicial branches. The executive is typically a president or prime minister—the former selected by popular vote, the latter selected by members of the legislature—and is charged with the administration of the federal government's programs and regulations. The legislature—such as the US Congress, the Austrian Parliament, or the German Bundestag—is charged with developing laws and managing government spending. The judiciary is charged

with ensuring that federal and state laws are enforced and that they are consistent with the country's constitution.

The federal government is limited in terms of its ability to assert authority over the regions. Instead, federal republics grant a degree of sovereignty to the different states, provinces, or regions that comprise the entire nation. These regions have their own governments, similar in structure and procedure to those of the federal government. They too have executives, legislatures, and judiciaries whose foci are limited to the regional government's respective jurisdictions.

The federal and regional segments of a republic are not completely independent of one another, however. Although the systems are intended to distribute power evenly, federal and regional governments are closely linked. This connectivity ensures the efficient collection of taxes, the regional distribution of federal funds, and a rapid response to issues of national importance. A federal republic's greatest strength, therefore, is the series of connections it maintains between the federal, regional, and local governments it contains.

Role of the Citizen

A federal republic is distinguished by the limitations of power it places on the national government. The primary goal of such a design was to place the power of government in the hands of the people. One of the ways the citizens' power is demonstrated is by participating in the electoral process. In a federal republic, the people elect their legislators. In some republics, the legislators in turn elect a prime minister, while in others, the people directly elect a president. The electoral process is an important way for citizens to influence the course of their government, both at the regional and federal levels. They do so by placing people who truly represent their diverse interests in the federal government.

The citizen is also empowered by participating in government as opposed to being subjected to it. In addition to taking part in the electoral process, the people are free to join and become active in a political party. A political party serves as a proxy for its members, representing their viewpoint and interests on a local and national level. In federal republics like Germany, a wide range of political parties are active in the legislature, advancing the political agendas of those they represent.

Michael Auerbach
Marblehead, Massachusetts

Examples

Austria
Brazil
Germany
India
Mexico
Nigeria
United States

Bibliography

"The Federal Principle." *Republik Österreich Parlament.* Republik Österreich Parlament, 8 Oct. 2010. Web. 6 Feb. 2013.

"The Federal Republic of Germany." *Deutscher Bundestag.* German Bundestag, 2013. Web. 6 Feb. 2013.

Collin, Nicholas. "An Essay on the Means of Promoting Federal Sentiments in the United States." *Friends of the Constitution: Writings of the "Other" Federalists, 1787–1788.* Ed. Colleen A. Sheehan and Gary L. McDowell. Online Library of Liberty, 2013. Web. 6 Feb. 2013.

Federation

Guiding Premise

A federation is a nation formed from the unification of smaller political entities. Federations feature federal governments that oversee nationwide issues. However, they also grant a degree of autonomy to the regional, state, or other local governments within the system. Federations are often formed because a collective of diverse regions find a common interest in unification. While the federal government is installed to address those needs, regions with their own distinct ethnic, socioeconomic, or political characteristics remain intact. This "separate but united" structure allows federations to avoid conflict and instability among their regions.

Typical Structure

The primary goal of a federation is to unify a country's political subunits within a national framework. The federal government, therefore, features institutions comprised of representatives from the states or regions. The representatives are typically elected by the residents of these regions, and some federal systems give the power to elect certain national leaders to these representatives. The regions themselves can vary considerably in size. The Russian Federation, for example, includes forty-six geographically large provinces as well as two more-concentrated cities as part of its eighty-three constituent federation members.

There are two institutions in which individuals from the constituent parts of a federation serve. The first institution is the legislature. Legislatures vary in appearance from nation to nation. For example, the US Congress is comprised of two chambers—the House of Representatives and the Senate—whose directly elected members act on behalf of their respective states. The German Parliament, on the other hand, consists of the directly elected Bundestag— which is tasked with electing the German federal chancellor, among other things—and the

state-appointed Bundesrat, which works on behalf of the country's sixteen states.

The second institution is the executive. Here, the affairs of the nation are administered by a president or similar leader. Again, the structure and powers of a federal government's executive institutions varies from nation to nation according to their constitutional framework. Federal executive institutions are charged with management of state affairs, including oversight of the military, foreign relations, health care, and education. Similarly diverse is the power of the executive in relation to the legislative branch. Some prime ministers, for example, enjoy considerably greater power than the president. In fact, some presidents share power with other leaders, or councils thereof within the executive branch, serving as the diplomatic face of the nation but not playing a major role in lawmaking. In India, for example, the president is the chief executive of the federal government, but shares power with the prime minister and the Council of Ministers, headed by the prime minister.

In order to promote continuity between the federal government and the states, regions, or other political subunits in the federation, those subunits typically feature governments that largely mirror that of the central government. Some of these regional governments are modified according to their respective constitutions. For example, whereas the bicameral US Congress consists of the Senate and House of Representatives, Nebraska's state legislature only has one chamber. Such distinctive characteristics of state/regional governments reflect the geographic and cultural interests of the region in question. It also underscores the degree of autonomy given to such states under a federation government system.

Role of the Citizen

Federations vary in terms of both structure and distribution of power within government institutions. However, federal systems are typically democratic in nature, relying heavily on the participation of the electorate for installing representatives in those institutions. At the regional level, the people vote for their respective legislators and executives either directly or through political parties. The executive in turn appoints cabinet officials, while the legislators select a chamber leader. In US state governments, for example, such a leader might be a Senate president or speaker of the House of Representatives.

The people also play an important role in federal government. As residents of a given state or region, registered voters—again, through either a direct vote or through political parties—choose their legislators and national executives. In federations that utilize a parliamentary system, however, prime ministers are typically selected by the legislators and/or their political parties and not through a direct, national vote. Many constitutions limit the length of political leaders' respective terms of service and/or the number of times they may seek reelection, fostering an environment in which the democratic voting process is a frequent occurrence.

Michael Auerbach
Marblehead, Massachusetts

Examples

Australia
Germany
India
Mexico
Russia
United States

Bibliography

"Federal System of India." *Maps of India*. MapsOfIndia. com, 22 Sep. 2011. Web. 7 Feb. 2013.

"Political System." *Facts about Germany*. Frankfurter Societäts-Medien, 2011. Web. 7 Feb. 2013.

"Russia." *CIA World Factbook*. Central Intelligence Agency, 5 Feb. 2013. Web. 7 Feb. 2013.

Monarchy

Guiding Premise

A monarchy is a political system based on the sovereignty of a single individual who holds actual or symbolic authority over all governmental functions. The monarchy is one of the oldest forms of government in human history and was the most common type of government until the nineteenth century. In a monarchy, authority is inherited, usually through primogeniture, or inheritance by the eldest son.

In an absolute monarchy, the monarch holds authority over the government and functions as both head of state and head of government. In a constitutional monarchy, the role of the monarch is codified in the state constitution, and the powers afforded to the monarch are limited by constitutional law. Constitutional monarchies generally blend the inherited authority of the monarchy with popular control in the form of democratic elections. The monarch may continue to hold significant power over some aspects of government or may be relegated to a largely ceremonial or symbolic role.

In most ancient monarchies, the monarch was generally believed to have been chosen for his or her role by divine authority, and many monarchs in history have claimed to represent the will of a god or gods in their ascendancy to the position. In constitutional monarchies, the monarch may be seen as representing spiritual authority or may represent a link to the country's national heritage.

Typical Structure

In an absolute monarchy, a single monarch is empowered to head the government, including the formulation of all laws and leadership of the nation's armed forces. Oman is one example of a type of absolute monarchy called a sultanate, in which a family of leaders, called "sultans," inherits authority and leads the nation under an authoritarian system. Power in the Omani sultanate remains within the royal family. In the event of the sultan's death or incapacitation, the Royal Family Council selects a successor by consensus from within the family line. Beneath the sultan is a council of ministers, appointed by the sultan, to create and disseminate official government policy. The sultan's council serves alongside an elected body of leaders who enforce and represent Islamic law and work with the sultan's ministers to create national laws.

In Japan, which is a constitutional monarchy, the Japanese emperor serves as the chief of state and symbolic representative of Japan's culture and history. The emperor officiates national ceremonies, meets with world leaders for diplomatic purposes, and symbolically appoints leaders to certain governmental posts. Governmental authority in Japan rests with the Diet, a legislative body of elected officials who serve limited terms of office and are elected through popular vote. A prime minister is also chosen to lead the Diet, and the prime minister is considered the official head of government.

The Kingdom of Norway is another example of a constitutional monarchy wherein the monarch serves a role that has been codified in the state constitution. The king of Norway is designated as the country's chief of state, serving as head of the nation's executive branch. Unlike Japan, where the monarch's role is largely symbolic, the monarch of Norway has considerable authority under the constitution, including the ability to veto and approve all laws and the power to declare war. Norway utilizes a parliamentary system, with a prime minister, chosen from individuals elected to the state parliament, serving as head of government. Though the monarch has authority over the executive functions of government, the legislature and prime minister are permitted the ability to override monarchical decisions with sufficient support, thereby providing a system of control to prevent the monarch from exerting a dominant influence over the government.

Role of the Citizen

The role of the citizen in a monarchy varies depending on whether the government is a constitutional or absolute monarchy. In an absolute monarchy, citizens have only those rights given to them by the monarch, and the monarch has the power to extend and retract freedoms and rights at will. In ancient monarchies, citizens accepted the authoritarian role of the monarch, because it was widely believed that the monarch's powers were derived from divine authority. In addition, in many absolute monarchies, the monarch has the power to arrest, detain, and imprison individuals without due process, thereby providing a strong disincentive for citizens to oppose the monarchy.

In a constitutional monarchy, citizens are generally given greater freedom to participate in the development of governmental policies. In Japan, Belgium, and Spain, for instance, citizens elect governmental leaders, and the elected legislature largely controls the creation and enforcement of laws. In some countries, like the Kingdom of Norway, the monarch may exert significant authority, but this authority is balanced by that of the legislature, which represents the sovereignty of the citizens and is chosen to promote and protect the interests of the public.

The absolute monarchies of medieval Europe, Asia, and Africa held power for centuries, but many eventually collapsed due to popular uprisings as citizens demanded representation within the government. The development of constitutional monarchies may be seen as a balanced system in which the citizens retain significant control over the development of their government while the history and traditions of the nation are represented by the continuation of the monarch's lineage. In the United Kingdom, the governments of Great Britain and Northern Ireland are entirely controlled by elected individuals, but the continuation of the monarchy is seen by many as an important link to the nation's historic identity.

Micah Issitt
Philadelphia, Pennsylvania

Examples

Belgium
Bhutan
Japan
Norway
Oman
United Kingdom

Bibliography

Barrington, Lowell. *Comparative Politics: Structures and Choices*. Boston: Wadsworth, 2012. Print.
Dresch, Paul, and James Piscatori, eds. *Monarchies and Nations: Globalisation and Identity in the Arab States of the Gulf*. London: Tauris, 2005. Print.
Kesselman, Mark, et al. *European Politics in Transition*. New York: Houghton, 2009. Print.

Parliamentary Monarchy

Guiding Premise

A parliamentary monarchy is a political system in which leadership of the government is shared between a monarchy, such as a king or queen, and the members of a democratically elected legislative body. In such governments, the monarch's role as head of state is limited by the country's constitution or other founding document, preventing the monarch from assuming too much control over the nation. As head of state, the monarch may provide input during the lawmaking process and other operations of government. Furthermore, the monarch, whose role is generally lifelong, acts as a stabilizing element for the government, while the legislative body is subject to the periodic changes that occur with each election cycle.

Typical Structure

Parliamentary monarchies vary in structure and distribution of power from nation to nation, based on the parameters established by each respective country's constitution or other founding document. In general, however, parliamentary monarchies feature a king, queen, or other sovereign who acts as head of state. In that capacity, the monarch's responsibilities may be little more than ceremonial in nature, allowing him or her to offer input during the lawmaking process, to approve the installation of government officials, and to act as the country's international representative. However, these responsibilities may be subject to the approval of the country's legislative body. For example, the king of Spain approves laws and regulations that have already been passed by the legislative branch; formally appoints the prime minister; and approves other ministers appointed by the prime minister. Yet, the king's responsibilities in those capacities are subject to the approval of the Cortes Generales, Spain's parliament.

In general, parliamentary monarchies help a country preserve its cultural heritage through their respective royal families, but grant the majority of government management and lawmaking responsibilities to the country's legislative branch and its various administrative ministries, such as education and defense. In most parliamentary monarchies, the ministers of government are appointed by the legislative body and usually by the prime minister. Although government ministries have the authority to carry out the country's laws and programs, they are also subject to criticism and removal by the legislative body if they fail to perform to expectations.

The legislative body itself consists of members elected through a democratic, constitutionally defined process. Term length, term limit, and the manner by which legislators may be elected are usually outlined in the country's founding documents. For example, in the Dutch parliament, members of the House of Representatives are elected every four years through a direct vote, while the members of the Senate are elected by provincial government councils every four years. By contrast, three-quarters of the members of Thailand's House of Representatives are elected in single-seat constituencies (smaller districts), while the remaining members are elected in larger, proportional representation districts; all members of the House are elected for four-year terms. A bare majority of Thailand's senators are elected by direct vote, with the remainder appointed by other members of the government.

Role of the Citizen

While the kings and queens of parliamentary monarchies are the nominal heads of state, these political systems are designed to be democratic governments. As such, they rely heavily on the input and involvement of the citizens. Participating in legislative elections is one of the most direct ways in which the citizen is empowered. Because the governments of such systems are subject to legislative oversight, the people—through their respective votes for members of parliament—have influence over their government.

Political parties and organizations such as local and municipal councils also play an important role in parliamentary monarchies. Citizens' participation in those organizations can help shape parliamentary agendas and build links between government and the public. In Norway, for example, nearly 70 percent of citizens are involved in at least one such organization, and consequently Norway's Storting (parliament) has a number of committees that are tied to those organizations at the regional and local levels. Thus, through voting and active political involvement at the local level, the citizens of a parliamentary monarchy help direct the political course of their nation.

Michael Auerbach
Marblehead, Massachusetts

Examples
Netherlands
Norway
Spain
Sweden
Thailand
United Kingdom

Bibliography
"Form of Government." *Norway.org*. Norway–The Official Site in the United States, n.d. Web. 17 Jan. 2013.
"Issues: Parliament." *Governmentl.nl*. Government of the Netherlands, n.d. Web. 17 Jan. 2013.
"King, Prime Minister, and Council of Ministers." *Country Studies: Spain*. Lib. of Congress, 2012. Web. 17 Jan. 2013.
"Thailand." *International Foundation for Electoral Systems*. IFES, 2013. Web. 17 Jan. 2013.

Parliamentary Republic

Guiding Premise

A parliamentary republic is a system wherein both executive and legislative powers are centralized in the legislature. In such a system, voters elect their national representatives to the parliamentary body, which in turn appoints the executive. In such an environment, legislation is passed more quickly than in a presidential system, which requires a consensus between the executive and legislature. It also enables the legislature to remove the executive in the event the latter does not perform to the satisfaction of the people. Parliamentary republics can also prevent the consolidation of power in a single leader, as even a prime minister must defer some authority to fellow legislative leaders.

Typical Structure

Parliamentary republics vary in structure from nation to nation, according to the respective country's constitution or other governing document. In general, such a system entails the merger of the legislature and head of state such as a president or other executive. The state may retain the executive, however. However, the executive's role may be largely ceremonial, as is the case in Greece, where the president has very little political authority. This "outsider" status has in fact enabled the Greek president to act as a diplomatic intermediary among sparring parliamentary leaders.

While many countries with such a system operate with an executive—who may or may not be directly elected, and who typically has limited powers—the bulk of a parliamentary republic's political authority rests with the legislature. The national government is comprised of democratically elected legislators and their appointees. The length of these representatives' respective terms, as well as the manner by which the legislators are elected, depend on the frameworks established by each individual nation. Some parliamentary republics utilize a constitution for this

purpose, while others use a set of common laws or other legal precepts. In South Africa, members of the parliament's two chambers, the National Assembly and the National Council of Provinces, are elected differently. The former's members are elected directly by the citizens in each province, while the latter's members are installed by the provincial legislatures.

Once elected to parliament, legislators are often charged with more than just lawmaking. In many cases, members of parliament oversee the administration of state affairs as well. Legislative bodies in parliamentary republics are responsible for nominating an executive—typically a prime minister—to manage the government's various administrative responsibilities. Should the executive not adequately perform its duties, parliament has the power to remove the executive from office. In Ireland, for example, the Dail Eireann (the House of Representatives) is charged with forming the country's executive branch by nominating the Taoiseach (prime minister) and approving the prime minister's cabinet selections.

Role of the Citizen

A parliamentary republic is a democratic political system that relies on the involvement of an active electorate. This civic engagement includes a direct or indirect vote for representatives to parliament. While the people do not vote for an executive as well, by way of their vote for parliament, the citizenry indirectly influences the selection of the chief executive and the policies he or she follows. In many countries, the people also indirectly influence the national government by their votes in provincial government. As noted earlier, some countries' parliaments include chambers whose members are appointed by provincial leaders.

Citizens may also influence the political system through involvement in political parties. Such organizations help shape the platforms of parliamentary majorities as well as selecting candidates for prime minister and other government positions. The significance of political parties varies from nation to nation, but such organizations require the input and involvement of citizens.

Michael Auerbach
Marblehead, Massachusetts

Examples
Austria
Greece
Iceland
Ireland
Poland
South Africa

Bibliography

"About the Oireachtas." *Oireachtas.ie*. Houses of the Oireachtas, n.d. Web. 7 Feb. 2013.

"Our Parliament." *Parliament.gov*. Parliament of the Republic of South Africa, n.d. Web. 7 Feb. 2013.

Tagaris, Karolina, and Ingrid Melander. "Greek President Makes Last Push to Avert Elections." *Reuters*. Thomson Reuters, 12 May 2012. Web. 7 Feb. 2013.

Presidential

Guiding Premise

A presidential system is a type of democratic government in which the populace elects a single leader—a president—to serve as both head of state and the head of government. The presidential system developed from the monarchic governments of medieval and early modern Europe, in which a royal monarch, holder of an inherited office, served as both head of state and government. In the presidential system, the president does not inherit the office, but is chosen by either direct or indirect popular vote.

Presidential systems differ from parliamentary systems in that the president is both the chief executive and head of state, whereas in a parliamentary system another individual, usually called the "prime minister," serves as head of government and leader of the legislature. The presidential system evolved out of an effort to create an executive office that balances the influence of the legislature and the judiciary. The United States is the most prominent example of a democratic presidential system.

Some governments have adopted a semi-presidential system, which blends elements of the presidential system with the parliamentary system, and generally features a president who serves only as head of state. In constitutional governments, like the United States, Mexico, and Honduras, the role of the president is described in the nation's constitution, which also provides for the president's powers in relation to the other branches of government.

Typical Structure

In most modern presidential governments, power to create and enforce laws and international agreements is divided among three branches: the executive, legislative, and judicial. The executive office consists of the president and a number of presidential advisers—often called the cabinet—who typically serve at the president's discretion and are not elected to office. The terms of office for the president are codified in the state constitution and, in most cases, the president may serve a limited number of terms before he or she becomes ineligible for reelection.

The president serves as head of state and is therefore charged with negotiating and administering international treaties and agreements. In addition, the president serves as head of government and is therefore charged with overseeing the function of the government as a whole. The president is also empowered, in most presidential governments, with the ability to deploy the nation's armed forces. In some governments, including the United States, the approval of the legislature is needed for the country to officially declare war.

The legislative branch of the government proposes new laws, in the form of bills, but must cooperate with the executive office to pass these bills into law. The legislature and the executive branch also cooperate in determining the government budget. Unlike prime ministers under the parliamentary system, the president is not considered a member of the legislature and therefore acts independently as the chief executive, though a variety of governmental functions require action from both branches of government. A unique feature of the presidential system is that the election of the president is separate from the election of the legislature.

In presidential systems, members of the legislature are often less likely to vote according to the goals of their political party and may support legislation that is not supported by their chosen political party. In parliamentary systems, like the government of Great Britain, legislators are more likely to vote according to party policy. Presidential systems are also often marked by a relatively small number of political parties, which often allows one party to achieve a majority in the legislature. If this majority coincides with the election of a president from the same party, that party's platform or agenda becomes dominant until the next election cycle.

The judicial branch in a presidential system serves to enforce the laws among the populace. In most modern presidential democracies, the president appoints judges to federal posts, though in some governments, the legislature appoints judges. In some cases, the president may need the approval of the legislature to make judicial appointments.

Role of the Citizen

In a democratic presidential system, citizens are empowered with the ability to vote for president and therefore have ultimate control over who serves as head of government and head of state. Some presidential governments elect individuals to the presidency based on the result of a popular vote, while other governments use an indirect system, in which citizens vote for a party or for individuals who then serve as their representatives in electing the president. The United States utilizes an indirect system called the Electoral College.

Citizens in presidential systems are also typically allowed, though not required, to join political parties in an effort to promote a political agenda. Some governmental systems that are modeled on the presidential system allow the president to exert a dominant influence over the legislature and other branches of the government. In some cases, this can lead to a presidential dictatorship, in which the president may curtail the political rights of citizens. In most presidential systems, however, the roles and powers of the legislative and executive branches are balanced to protect the rights of the people to influence their government.

In a presidential system, citizens are permitted to vote for a president representing one political party, while simultaneously voting for legislators from other political parties. In this way, the presidential system allows citizens to determine the degree to which any single political party is permitted to have influence on political development.

Micah Issitt
Philadelphia, Pennsylvania

Examples

Benin
Costa Rica
Dominican Republic
Guatemala
Honduras
Mexico
United States
Venezuela

Bibliography

Barington, Lowell. *Comparative Politics: Structures and Choices.* Boston: Wadsworth, 2012. Print.

Caramani, Daniele. *Comparative Politics.* New York: Oxford UP, 2008. Print.

Garner, Robert, Peter Ferdinand, and Stephanic Lawson. *Introduction to Politics.* 2nd ed. Oxford: Oxford UP, 2009. Print.

Republic

Guiding Premise

A republic is a type of government based on the idea of popular or public sovereignty. The word "republic" is derived from Latin terms meaning "matters" and "the public." In essence, a republic is a government in which leaders are chosen by the public rather than by inheritance or by force. The republic or republican governmental system emerged in response to absolute monarchy, in which hereditary leaders retained all the power. In contrast, the republican system is intended to create a government that is responsive to the people's will.

Most modern republics operate based on a democratic system in which citizens elect leaders by popular vote. The United States and Mexico are examples of countries that use a democratic republican system to appoint leaders to office. However, universal suffrage (voting for all) is not required for a government to qualify as a republic, and it is possible for a country to have a republican government in which only certain categories of citizens, such as the wealthy, are allowed to vote in elections.

In addition to popular vote, most modern republics are further classified as constitutional republics, because the laws and rules for appointing leaders have been codified in a set of principles and guidelines known as a "constitution." When combined with universal suffrage and constitutional law, the republican system is intended to form a government that is based on the will of the majority while protecting the rights of minority groups.

Typical Structure

Republican governments are typically led by an elected head of state, generally a president. In cases where the president also serves as the head of government, the government is called a "presidential republic." In some republics, the head of state serves alongside an appointed or elected head of government, usually a prime minister.

This mixed form of government blends elements of the republic system with the parliamentary system found in countries such as the United Kingdom or India.

The president is part of the executive branch of government, which represents the country internationally and heads efforts to make and amend international agreements and treaties. The laws of a nation are typically created by the legislative branch, which may also be composed of elected leaders. Typically, the legislative and executive branches must cooperate on key initiatives, such as determining the national budget.

In addition to legislative and executive functions, most republics have a judiciary charged with enforcing and interpreting laws. The judicial branch may be composed of elected leaders, but in many cases, judicial officers are appointed by the president and/or the legislature. In the United States (a federal republic), the president, who leads the executive branch, appoints members to the federal judiciary, but these choices must be approved by the legislature before they take effect.

The duties and powers allotted to each branch of the republican government are interconnected with those of the other branches in a system of checks and balances. For instance, in Mexico (a federal republic), the legislature is empowered to create new tax guidelines for the public, but before legislative tax bills become law, they must first achieve majority support within the two branches of the Mexican legislature and receive the approval of the president. By creating a system of separate but balanced powers, the republican system seeks to prevent any one branch from exerting a dominant influence over the government.

Role of the Citizen

The role of the citizen in a republic depends largely on the type of republican system that the country has adopted. In democratic republics, popular elections and constitutional law give the public significant influence over governmental development and establish the people as the primary source of political power. Citizens in democratic republics are empowered to join political groups and to influence the development of laws and policies through the election of public leaders.

In many republican nations, a powerful political party or other political group can dominate the government, preventing competition from opposing political groups and curtailing the public's role in selecting and approving leaders. For instance, in the late twentieth century, a dominant political party maintained control of the Gambian presidency and legislature for more than thirty years, thereby significantly limiting the role of the citizenry in influencing the development of government policy.

In general, the republican system was intended to reverse the power structure typical of the monarchy system, in which inherited leaders possess all of the political power. In the republican system, leaders are chosen to represent the people's interests with terms of office created in such a way that new leaders must be chosen at regular intervals, thereby preventing a single leader or political entity from dominating the populace. In practice, popular power in a republic depends on preventing a political monopoly from becoming powerful enough to alter the laws of the country to suit the needs of a certain group rather than the whole.

Micah Issitt
Philadelphia, Pennsylvania

Examples
Algeria
Argentina
Armenia
France
Gambia
Mexico
San Marino
South Sudan
Tanzania
United States

Bibliography
Caramani, Daniele. *Comparative Politics*. New York: Oxford UP, 2008. Print.
Przeworski, Adam. *Democracy and the Limits of Self-Government*. New York: Cambridge UP, 2010. Print.

Socialist

Guiding Premise

Socialism is a political and economic system that seeks to elevate the common good of the citizenry by allowing the government to own all property and means of production. In the most basic model, citizens cooperatively elect members to government, and the government then acts on behalf of the people to manage the state's property, industry, production, and services.

In a socialist system, communal or government ownership of property and industry is intended to eliminate the formation of economic classes and to ensure an even distribution of wealth. Most modern socialists also believe that basic services, including medical and legal care, should be provided at the same level to all citizens and not depend on the individual citizen's ability to pay for better services. The origins of socialism can be traced to theorists such as Thomas More (1478–1535), who believed that private wealth and ownership led to the formation of a wealthy elite class that protected its own wealth while oppressing members of lower classes.

There are many different forms of socialist philosophy, some of which focus on economic systems, while others extend socialist ideas to other aspects of society. Communism may be considered a form of socialism, based on the idea that a working-class revolution is needed to initiate the ideal socialist society.

Typical Structure

Socialism exists in many forms around the world, and many governments use a socialist model for the distribution of key services, most often medical and legal aid. A socialist state is a government whose constitution explicitly gives the government powers to facilitate the creation of a socialist society.

The idealized model of the socialist state is one in which the populace elects leaders to head the government, and the government then oversees the distribution of wealth and goods among the populace, enforces the laws, and provides for the well-being of citizens. Many modern socialist governments follow a communist model, in which a national communist political party has ultimate control over governmental legislation and appointments.

There are many different models of socialist states, integrating elements of democratic or parliamentary systems. In these cases, democratic elections may be held to elect the head of state and the body of legislators. The primary difference between a socialist democracy and a capitalist democracy can be found in the state's role in the ownership of key industries. Most modern noncommunist socialist states provide state regulation and control over key industries but allow some free-market competition as well.

In a socialist system, government officials appoint leaders to oversee various industries and to regulate prices based on public welfare. For instance, if the government retains sole ownership over agricultural production, the government must appoint individuals to manage and oversee that industry, organize agricultural labor, and oversee the distribution of food products among the populace. Some countries, such as Sweden, have adopted a mixed model in which socialist industry management is blended with free-market competition.

Role of the Citizen

All citizens in a socialist system are considered workers, and thus all exist in the same economic class. While some citizens may receive higher pay than others—those who work in supervisory roles, for instance—limited ownership of private property and standardized access to services places all individuals on a level field with regard to basic welfare and economic prosperity.

The degree to which personal liberties are curtailed within a socialist system depends upon the type of socialist philosophy adopted and the degree to which corruption and authoritarianism play a role in government. In most modern communist governments, for instance, individuals are often prohibited from engaging in any activity seen as contrary to the overall goals of the state or to the policies of the dominant political party. While regulations of this kind are common in communist societies, social control over citizens is not necessary for a government to follow a socialist model.

Under democratic socialism, individuals are also expected to play a role in the formation of their government by electing leaders to serve in key positions. In Sri Lanka, for instance, citizens elect members to serve in the parliament and a president to serve as head of the executive branch. In Portugal, citizens vote in multiparty elections to elect a president who serves as head of state, and the president appoints a prime minister to serve as head of government. In both Portugal and Sri Lanka, the government is constitutionally bound to promote a socialist society, though both governments allow private ownership and control of certain industries.

Citizens in a socialist society are also expected to provide for one another by contributing to labor and by forfeiting some ownership rights to provide for the greater good. In the Kingdom of Sweden, a mixed parliamentary system, all citizens pay a higher tax rate to contribute to funds that provide for national health care, child care, education, and worker support systems. Citizens who have no children and require only minimal health care benefits pay the same tax rate as those who have greater need for the nation's socialized benefits.

Micah Issitt
Philadelphia, Pennsylvania

Examples
China
Cuba
Portugal
Sri Lanka
Venezuela
Zambia

Bibliography
Caramani, Daniele. *Comparative Politics*. New York: Oxford UP, 2008. Print.
Heilbroner, Robert. "Socialism." *Library of Economics and Liberty*. Liberty Fund, 2008. Web. 17 Jan. 2013.
Howard, Michael Wayne. *Socialism*. Amherst, NY: Humanity, 2001. Print.

Sultanate/Emirate

Guiding Premise

A sultanate or emirate form of government is a political system in which a hereditary ruler—a monarch, chieftain, or military leader—acts as the head of state. Emirates and sultanates are most commonly found in Islamic nations in the Middle East, although others are found in Southeast Asia as well. Sultans and emirs frequently assume titles such as president or prime minister in addition to their royal designations, meshing the traditional ideal of a monarch with the administrative capacities of a constitutional political system.

Typical Structure

A sultanate or emirate combines the administrative duties of the executive with the powers of a monarch. The emir or sultan acts as the head of government, appointing all cabinet ministers and officials. In Brunei, a sultanate, the government was established according to the constitution (set up after the country declared autonomy from Britain in 1959). The sultan did assemble a legislative council in order to facilitate the lawmaking process, but this council has consistently remained subject to the authority of the sultan and not to a democratic process. In 2004, there was some movement toward the election of at least some of the members of this council. In the meantime, the sultan maintains a ministerial system by appointment and also serves as the nation's chief religious leader.

In some cases, an emirate or sultanate appears similar to a federal system. In the United Arab Emirates (UAE), for example, the nation consists of not one but seven emirates. This system came into being after the seven small regions achieved independence from Great Britain. Each emirate developed its own government system under the leadership of an emir. However, in 1971, the individual emirates agreed to join as a federation, drafting a constitution that identified the areas of common interest to the entire group of emirates. Like Brunei, the UAE's initial government structure focused on the authority of the emirs and the various councils and ministries formed at the UAE's capital of Abu Dhabi. However, beginning in the early twenty-first century, the UAE's legislative body, the Federal National Council, has been elected by electoral colleges from the seven emirates, thus further engaging various local areas and reflecting their interests.

Sultanates and emirates are at times part of a larger nation, with the sultans or emirs answering to the authority of another government. This is the case in Malaysia, where the country is governed by a constitutional monarchy. However, most of Malaysia's western political units are governed by sultans, who act as regional governors and, in many cases, religious leaders, but remain subject to the king's authority in Malaysia's capital of Kuala Lumpur.

Role of the Citizen

Sultanates and emirates are traditionally non-democratic governments. Like those of other monarchs, the seats of emirs and sultans are hereditary. Any votes for these leaders to serve as prime minister or other head of government are cast by ministers selected by the emirs and sultans. Political parties may exist in these countries as well, but these parties are strictly managed by the sultan or emir; opposition parties are virtually nonexistent in such systems, and some emirates have no political parties at all.

As shown in the UAE and Malaysia, however, there are signs that the traditional sultanate or emirate is increasingly willing to engage their respective citizens. For example, the UAE, between 2006 and 2013, launched a series of reforms designed to strengthen the role of local governments and relations with the people they serve. Malaysia may allow sultans to continue their regional controls, but at the same time, the country continues to evolve its federal system, facilitating multiparty democratic elections for its national legislature.

Michael Auerbach
Marblehead, Massachusetts

Examples

Brunei
Kuwait
Malaysia
Qatar
United Arab Emirates

Bibliography

"Brunei." *The World Factbook*. Central Intelligence Agency, 2 Jan. 2013. Web. 17 Jan. 2013.

"Malaysia." *The World Factbook*. Central Intelligence Agency, 7 Jan. 2013. Web. 17 Jan. 2013.

"Political System." *UAE Interact*. UAE National Media Council, n.d. Web. 17 Jan. 2013.

Prime Minister's Office, Brunei Darussalam. Prime Minister's Office, Brunei Darussalam, 2013. Web. 17 Jan. 2013.

Theocratic Republic

Guiding Premise

A theocratic republic is a type of government blending popular and religious influence to determine the laws and governmental principles. A republic is a governmental system based on the concept of popular rule and takes its name from the Latin words for "public matter." The defining characteristic of a republic is that civic leaders hold elected, rather than inherited, offices. A theocracy is a governmental system in which a supreme deity is considered the ultimate authority guiding civil matters.

No modern nations can be classified as pure theocratic republics, but some nations, such as Iran, maintain a political system largely dominated by religious law. The Buddhist nation of Tibet operated under a theocratic system until it was taken over by Communist China in the early 1950s.

In general, a theocratic republic forms in a nation or other governmental system dominated by a single religious group. The laws of the government are formed in reference to a set of religious laws, either taken directly from sacred texts or formulated by religious scholars and authority figures. Most theocratic governments depend on a body of religious scholars who interpret religious scripture, advise all branches of government, and oversee the electoral process.

Typical Structure

In a typical republic, the government is divided into executive, legislative, and judicial branches, and citizens vote to elect leaders to one or more of the branches of government. In most modern republics, voters elect a head of state, usually a president, to lead the executive branch. In many republics, voters also elect individuals to serve as legislators. Members of the judiciary may be elected by voters or may be appointed to office by other elected leaders. In nontheocratic republics, the citizens are considered the ultimate source of authority in the government.

In a theocratic republic, however, one or more deities are considered to represent the ultimate governmental authority. In some cases, the government may designate a deity as the ultimate head of state. Typically, any individual serving as the functional head of state is believed to have been chosen by that deity, and candidates for the position must be approved by the prevailing religious authority.

In some cases, the religious authority supports popular elections to fill certain governmental posts. In Iran, for instance, citizens vote to elect members to the national parliament and a single individual to serve as president. The Iranian government is ultimately led by a supreme leader, who is appointed to office by the Assembly of Experts, the leaders of the country's Islamic community. Though the populace chooses the president and leaders to serve in the legislature, the supreme leader of Iran can overrule decisions made in any other branch of the government.

In a theocratic republic, the power to propose new laws may be given to the legislature, which works on legislation in conjunction with the executive branch. However, all laws must conform to religious law, and any legislation produced within the government is likely to be abolished if it is deemed by the religious authorities to violate religious principles. In addition, religious leaders typically decide which candidates are qualified to run for specific offices, thereby ensuring that the citizens will not elect individuals who are likely to oppose religious doctrine.

In addition, many modern nations that operate on a partially theocratic system may adopt a set of governmental principles in the form of a constitution, blended with religious law. This mixed constitutional theocratic system has been adopted by an increasing number of Islamic nations, including Iraq, Afghanistan, Mauritania, and some parts of Nigeria.

Role of the Citizen

Citizens in a theocratic republic are expected to play a role in forming the government through elections, but they are constrained in their choices by the prevailing religious authority. Citizens are also guaranteed certain freedoms, typically codified in a constitution, that have been formulated with reference to religious law. All citizens must adhere to religious laws, regardless of their personal religious beliefs or membership within any existing religious group.

In many Middle Eastern and African nations that operate on the basis of an Islamic theocracy, citizens elect leaders from groups of candidates chosen by the prevailing religious authority. While the choices presented to the citizens are more limited than in a democratic, multiparty republic, the citizens nevertheless play a role in determining the evolution of the government through their voting choices.

The freedoms and rights afforded to citizens in a theocratic republic may depend, in part, on the individual's religious affiliation. For instance, Muslims living in Islamic theocracies may be permitted to hold political office or to aspire to other influential political positions, while members of minority religious groups may find their rights and freedoms limited. Religious minorities living in Islamic republics may not be permitted to run for certain offices, such as president, and must follow laws that adhere to Islamic principles but may violate their own religious principles. Depending on the country and the adherents' religion, the practice of their faith may itself be considered criminal.

Micah Issitt
Philadelphia, Pennsylvania

Examples

Afghanistan
Iran
Iraq
Pakistan
Mauritania
Nigeria

Bibliography
Cooper, William W., and Piyu Yue. *Challenges of the Muslim World: Present, Future and Past*. Boston: Elsevier, 2008. Print.
Hirschl, Ran. *Constitutional Theocracy*. Cambridge: Harvard UP, 2010. Print.

Totalitarian

Guiding Premise

A totalitarian government is one in which a single political party maintains absolute control over the state and is responsible for creating all legislation without popular referendum. In general, totalitarianism is considered a type of authoritarian government where the laws and principles used to govern the country are based on the authority of the leading political group or dictator. Citizens under totalitarian regimes have limited freedoms and are subject to social controls dictated by the state.

The concept of totalitarianism evolved in fascist Italy in the 1920s, and was first used to describe the Italian government under dictator Benito Mussolini. The term became popular among critics of the authoritarian governments of Fascist Italy and Nazi Germany in the 1930s. Supporters of the totalitarian philosophy believed that a strong central government, with absolute control over all aspects of society, could achieve progress by avoiding political debate and power struggles between interest groups.

In theory, totalitarian regimes—like that of Nazi Germany and modern North Korea—can more effectively mobilize resources and direct a nation toward a set of overarching goals. Adolf Hitler was able to achieve vast increases in military power during a short period of time by controlling all procedural steps involved in promoting military development. In practice, however, pure totalitarianism has never been achieved, as citizens and political groups generally find ways to subvert complete government control.

Totalitarianism differs from authoritarianism in that a totalitarian government is based on the idea that the highest leader takes total control in order to create a flourishing society for the benefit of the people. By contrast, authoritarian regimes are based on the authority of a single, charismatic individual who develops policies designed to maintain personal power, rather than promote public interest.

Typical Structure

In a fully realized totalitarian system, a single leader or group of leaders controls all governmental functions, appointing individuals to serve in various posts to facilitate the development of legislation and oversee the enforcement of laws. In Nazi Germany, for instance, Adolf Hitler created a small group of executives to oversee the operation of the government. Governmental authority was then further disseminated through a complex network of departments, called ministries, with leaders appointed directly by Hitler.

Some totalitarian nations may adopt a state constitution in an effort to create the appearance of democratic popular control. In North Korea, the country officially operates under a multiparty democratic system, with citizens guaranteed the right to elect leaders to both the executive and legislative branches of government. In practice, the Workers' Party of North Korea is the only viable political party, as it actively controls competing parties and suppresses any attempt to mount political opposition. Under Supreme Leader Kim Il-sung, the Workers' Party amended the constitution to allow Kim to serve as the sole executive leader for life, without the possibility of being removed from office by any governmental action.

In some cases, totalitarian regimes may favor a presidential system, with the dictator serving officially as president, while other totalitarian governments may adopt a parliamentary system, with a prime minister as head of government. Though a single dictator generally heads the nation with widespread powers over a variety of governmental functions, a cabinet or group of high-ranking ministers may also play a prominent role in disseminating power throughout the various branches of government.

Role of the Citizen

Citizens in totalitarian regimes are often subject to strict social controls exerted by the leading political party. In many cases, totalitarian governments restrict the freedom of the press, expression, and speech in an effort to limit opposition to the government. In addition, totalitarian governments may use the threat of police or military action to prevent protest movements against the leading party. Totalitarian governments maintain absolute control over the courts and any security agency, and the legal/judicial system therefore exists only as an extension of the leading political party.

Totalitarian governments like North Korea also attempt to restrict citizens' access to information considered subversive. For instance, North Korean citizens are not allowed to freely utilize the Internet or any other informational source, but are instead only allowed access to government-approved websites and publications. In many cases, the attempt to control access to information creates a black market for publications and other forms of information banned by government policy.

In some cases, government propaganda and restricted access to information creates a situation in which citizens actively support the ruling regime. Citizens may honestly believe that the social and political restrictions imposed by the ruling party are necessary for the advancement of society. In other cases, citizens may accept governmental control to avoid reprisal from the military and police forces. Most totalitarian regimes have established severe penalties, including imprisonment, corporal punishment, and death, for criticizing the government or refusing to adhere to government policy.

Micah Issitt
Philadelphia, Pennsylvania

Examples

Fascist Italy (1922–1943)
Nazi Germany (1933–1945)
North Korea
Stalinist Russia (1924–1953)

Bibliography

Barrington, Lowell. *Comparative Politics: Structures and Choices*. Boston: Wadsworth, 2012. Print.

Gleason, Abbot. *Totalitarianism: The Inner History of the Cold War*. New York: Oxford UP, 1995. Print.

McEachern, Patrick. *Inside the Red Box: North Korea's Post-Totalitarian Regime*. New York: Columbia UP, 2010. Print.

Treaty System

Guiding Premise

A treaty system is a framework within which participating governments agree to collect and share scientific information gathered in a certain geographic region, or otherwise establish mutually agreeable standards for the use of that region. The participants establish rules and parameters by which researchers may establish research facilities and travel throughout the region, ensuring that there are no conflicts, that the environment is protected, and that the region is not used for illicit purposes. This system is particularly useful when the region in question is undeveloped and unpopulated, but could serve a number of strategic and scientific purposes.

Typical Structure

A treaty system of government is an agreement between certain governments that share a common interest in the use of a certain region to which no state or country has yet laid internationally recognized claim. Participating parties negotiate treaty systems that, upon agreement, form a framework by which the system will operate. Should the involved parties be United Nations member states, the treaty is then submitted to the UN Secretariat for registration and publication.

The agreement's founding ideals generally characterize the framework of a treaty. For example, the most prominent treaty system in operation today is the Antarctic Treaty System, which currently includes fifty nations whose scientists are studying Antarctica. This system, which entered into force in 1961, focuses on several topics, including environmental protection, tourism, scientific operations, and the peaceful use of that region. Within these topics, the treaty system enables participants to meet, cooperate, and share data on a wide range of subjects. Such cooperative activities include regional meetings, seminars, and large-scale conferences.

A treaty system is not a political institution in the same manner as state governments. Rather, it is an agreement administered by delegates from the involved entities. Scientists seeking to perform their research in Antarctica, for example, must apply through the scientific and/or government institutions of their respective nations. In the case of the United States, scientists may apply for grants from the National Science Foundation. These institutions then examine the study in question for its relevance to the treaty's ideals.

Central to the treaty system is the organization's governing body. In the case of the Antarctic Treaty, that body is the Antarctic Treaty Secretariat, which is based in Buenos Aires, Argentina. The Secretariat oversees all activities taking place under the treaty, welcomes new members, and addresses any conflicts or issues between participants. It also reviews any activities to ensure that they are in line with the parameters of the treaty. A treaty system is not a sovereign organization, however. Each participating government retains autonomy, facilitating its own scientific expeditions, sending delegates to the treaty system's main governing body, and reviewing the treaty to ensure that it coincides with its national interests.

Role of the Citizen

Although treaty systems are not sovereign government institutions, private citizens can and frequently do play an important role in their function and success. For example, the Antarctic Treaty System frequently conducts large-scale planning conferences, to which each participating government sends delegates. These teams are comprised of qualified scientists who are nominated and supported by their peers during the government's review process. In the United States, for example, the State Department oversees American participation in the Antarctic

Treaty System's events and programs, including delegate appointments.

Another area in which citizens are involved in a treaty system is in the ratification process. Every nation's government—usually through its legislative branch—must formally approve any treaty before the country can honor the agreement. This ratification is necessary for new treaties as well as treaties that must be reapproved every few years. Citizens, through their elected officials, may voice their support or disapproval of a new or updated treaty.

While participating governments administer treaty systems and their secretariats, those who conduct research or otherwise take part in activities in the region in question are not usually government employees. In Antarctica, for example, university professors, engineers, and other private professionals—supported by a combination of private and government funding—operate research stations.

Michael Auerbach
Marblehead, Massachusetts

Example

Antarctic Treaty System

Bibliography

"Antarctic." *Ocean and Polar Affairs.* US Department of State, 22 Mar. 2007. Web. 8 Feb. 2013.

"About Us." *Antarctic Treaty System.* Secretariat of the Antarctic Treaty, n.d. Web. 8 Feb. 2013.

"United Nations Treaty Series." *United Nations Treaty Collection.* United Nations, 2013. Web. 8 Feb. 2013.

"Educational Opportunities and Resources." *United States Antarctic Program.* National Science Foundation, 2013. Web. 8 Feb. 2013.

Appendix Two:
World Religions

African Religious Traditions

General Description

The religious traditions of Africa can be studied both religiously and ethnographically. Animism, or the belief that everything has a soul, is practiced in most tribal societies, including the Dogon (people of the cliffs), an ethnic group living primarily in Mali's central plateau region and in Burkina Faso. Many traditional faiths have extensive mythologies, rites, and histories, such as the Yoruba religion practiced by the Yoruba, an ethnic group of West Africa. In South Africa, the traditional religion of the Zulu people is based on a creator god, ancestor worship, and the existence of sorcerers and witches. Lastly, the Ethiopian or Abyssinian Church (formally the Ethiopian Orthodox Union Church) is a branch of Christianity unique to the east African nations of Ethiopia and Eritrea.

Number of Adherents Worldwide

Some 63 million Africans adhere to traditional religions such as animism. One of the largest groups practicing animism is the Dogon, who number about six hundred thousand. However, it is impossible to know how many practice traditional religion. In fact, many people practice animism alongside other religions, particularly Islam. Other religions have spread their adherence and influence through the African diaspora. In Africa, the Yoruba number between thirty-five and forty million and are located primarily in Benin, Togo and southwest Nigeria. The Zulu, the largest ethnic group in South Africa, total over eleven million. Like Islam, Christianity has affected the number of people who still hold traditional beliefs, making accurate predictions virtually impossible. The Ethiopian or Abyssinian Church has over thirty-nine million adherents in Ethiopia alone.

Basic Tenets

Animism holds that many spiritual beings have the power to help or hurt humans. The traditional faith is thus more concerned with appropriate rituals rather than worship of a deity, and focuses on day-to-day practicalities such as food, water supplies, and disease. Ancestors, particularly those most recently dead, are invoked for their aid. Those who practice animism believe in life after death; some adherents may attempt to contact the spirits of the dead. Animists acknowledge the existence of tribal gods. (However, African people traditionally do not make images of God, who is thought of as Spirit.)

The Dogon divide into two caste-like groups: the inneomo (pure) and innepuru (impure). The hogon leads the inneomo, who may not sacrifice animals and whose leaders are forbidden to hunt. The inneomo also cannot prepare or bury the dead. While the innepuru can do all of the above tasks, they cannot take part in the rituals for agricultural fertility. Selected young males called the olubaru lead the innepuru. The status of "pure" or "impure" is inherited. The Dogon have many gods. The chief god is called Amma, a creator god who is responsible for creating other gods and the earth.

The Dogon have a three-part concept of death. First the soul is sent to the realm of the dead to join the ancestors. Rites are then performed to remove any ritual polluting. Finally, when several members of the village have died, a rite known as dama occurs. In the ritual, a sacrifice is made to the Great Mask (which depicts a large wooden serpent and which is never actually worn) and dancers perform on the housetops where someone has died to scare off any lingering souls. Often, figures of Nommo (a worshipped ancestral spirit) are put near funeral pottery on the family shrine.

The Yoruba believe in predestination. Before birth, the ori (soul) kneels before Olorun, the wisest and most powerful deity, and selects a destiny. Rituals may assist the person in achieving his or her destiny, but it cannot be altered. The Yoruba, therefore, acknowledge a need for ritual and sacrifice, properly done according to the oracles.

Among the Yoruba, the shaman is known as the babalawo. He or she is able to communicate with ancestors, spirits and deities. Training for this work, which may include responsibility as a doctor, often requires three years. The shaman is consulted before major life decisions. During these consultations, the shaman dictates the right rituals and sacrifices, and to which gods they are to be offered for maximum benefit. In addition, the Yoruba poetry covers right conduct. Good character is at the heart of Yoruba ethics.

The Yoruba are polytheistic. The major god is Olorun, the sky god, considered all-powerful and holy, and a father to 401 children, also gods. He gave the task of creating human beings to the deity Obatala (though Olorun breathed life into them). Olorun also determines the destiny of each person. Onlie, the Great Mother Goddess, is in some ways the opposite of Olorun. Olorun is the one who judges a soul following death. For example, if the soul is accounted worthy, it will be reincarnated, while the unworthy go to the place of punishment. Ogun, the god of hunters, iron, and war, is another important god. He is also the patron of blacksmiths. The Yoruba have some 1,700 gods, collectively known as the Orisa.

The Yoruba believe in an afterlife. There are two heavens: one is a hot, dry place with pot-sherds, reserved for those who have done evil, while the other is a pleasant heaven for persons who have led a good life. There the ori (soul) may choose to "turn to be a child" on the earth once more.

In the Zulu tradition, the king was responsible for rainmaking and magic for the benefit of the nation. Rainmakers were also known as "shepherds of heaven." They performed rites during times of famine, drought or war, as well as during planting season, invoking royal ancestors for aid. Storms were considered a manifestation of God.

The Zulu are also polytheistic. They refer to a wise creator god who lives in heaven. This Supreme Being has complete control of everything in the universe, and is known as Unkulunkulu, the Great Oldest One. The Queen of heaven is a virgin who taught women useful arts; light surrounds her, and her glory is seen in rain, mist, and rainbows.

The Ethiopian Church incorporates not only Orthodox Christian beliefs, but also aspects of Judaism. The adherents distinguish between clean and unclean meats, practice circumcision, and observe the seventh-day Sabbath. The Ethiopian (or Abyssinian) Church is monotheistic and believes in the Christian God.

Sacred Text

Traditional religions such as animism generally have no written sacred texts. Instead, creation stories and other tales are passed down orally. The Yoruba do have some sacred poetry, in 256 chapters, known as odus. The text covers both right action in worship and ethical conduct. The Ethiopian Church has scriptures written in the ancient Ge'ez language, which is no longer used, except in church liturgy.

Major Figures

A spiritual leader, or hogon, oversees each district among the Dogon. There is a supreme hogon for the entire country. Among the Yoruba, the king, or oba, rules each town. He is also considered sacred and is responsible for performing rituals. Isaiah Shembe is a prophet or messiah among the Zulu. He founded the Nazareth Baptist Church (also called the amaNazaretha Church or Shembe Church), an independent Zulu Christian denomination. His son, Johannes Shembe, took the title Shembe II. In the Ethiopian Church, now fully independent, the head of the church is the Patriarch. Saint Frumentius, the first bishop of Axum in northern Ethiopia, is credited with beginning the Christian tradition during the fourth century. King Lalibela, noted for authorizing construction of monolithic churches carved underground, was a major figure in the twelfth century.

Major Holy Sites

Every spot in nature is sacred in animistic thinking. There is no division between sacred and profane—all of life is sacred, and Earth is Mother. Sky and mountains are often regarded as sacred space.

For the Yoruba of West Africa, Osogbo in Nigeria is a forest shrine. The main goddess is Oshun, goddess of the river. Until she arrived, the work done by male gods was not succeeding. People seeking to be protected from illness and women wishing to become pregnant seek Osun's help. Ilé-Ifè, an ancient Yoruba city in Nigeria, is another important site, and considered the spiritual hub of the Yoruba. According to the Yoruba creation myth, Olorun, god of the sky, set down Odudua, the founder of the Yoruba, in Ilé-Ifè. Shrines within the city include one to Ogun. The shrine is made of stones and wooden stumps.

Mount Nhlangakazi (Holy Mountain) is considered sacred to the Zulu Nazareth Baptist Church (amaNazaretha). There Isaiah Shembe built a High Place to serve as his headquarters. It is a twice-yearly site of pilgrimage for amaNazarites.

Sacred sites of the Ethiopian Church include the Church of St. Mary of Zion in Axum, considered the most sacred Ethiopian shrine. According to legend, the church stands adjacent to a guarded chapel which purportedly houses the Ark of the Covenant, a powerful biblical relic. The Ethiopian Church also considers sacred the eleven monolithic (rock-hewn) churches, still places of pilgrimage and devotion, that were recognized as a collective World Heritage Site by the United Nations Educational, Scientific and Cultural Organization.

Major Rites & Celebrations

Most African religions involve some sacrifice to appease or please the gods. Among the Yoruba, for example, dogs, which are helpful in both hunting and war, are sacrificed to Ogun. In many tribes, including the Yoruba, rites of passage for youth exist. The typical pattern is three-fold: removal from the tribe, instruction, and return to the tribe ready to assume adult responsibilities. In this initiation, the person may be marked bodily through scarification or circumcision. The Yoruba also have a yearly festival re-enacting

the story of Obatala and Oduduwa (generally perceived as the ancestor of the Yorubas). A second festival, which resembles a passion play, re-enacts the conflict between the grandsons of these two legendary figures. A third festival celebrates the heroine Moremi, who led the Yoruba to victory over the enemy Igbo, an ethnicity from southeastern Nigeria, and who ultimately reconciled the two tribes.

Yoruba death rites include a masked dancer who comes to the family following a death, assuring them of the ancestor's ongoing care for the family. If the person was important in the village, a mask will be carved and named for them. In yearly festivals, the deceased individual will then appear with other ancestors.

Masks are also used in a Dogon funeral ritual, the dama ceremony, which is led by the Awa, a secret society comprised of all adult Dogon males of the innepuru group. During ceremonial times, the hogon relinquishes control and the Awa control the community. At the end of the mourning period the dama ceremony begins when the Awa leave the village and return with both the front and back of their heads masked. Through rituals and dances, they lead the spirit of the deceased to the next world. Control of the village reverts to the hogon at that point. The Wagem rites govern contact with the ancestors. Following the dama ceremony, the eldest male descendant, called the ginna bana, adds a vessel to the family shrine in the name of the deceased. The spirit of the ancestor is persuaded to return to the descendents through magic and sacrificial offerings, creating a link from the living to the first ancestors.

Ethiopian Christians observe and mark most typical Christian rites, though some occur on different dates because of the difference in the Ethiopian and Western calendars. For example, Christmas in Ethiopia is celebrated on January 7.

ORIGINS

History & Geography

The Dogon live along the Bandiagara Cliffs, a rocky and mountainous region. (The Cliffs of Bandiagara, also called the Bandiagara Escarpment, were recognized as a UNESCO World Heritage Site due to the cultural landscape, including the ancient traditions of the Dogon and their architecture.) This area is south of the Sahara in a region called the Sahel, another region prone to drought (though not a desert). The population of the villages in the region is typically a thousand people or less. The cliffs of the Bandiagara have kept the Dogon separate from other people.

Myths of origin regarding the Dogon differ. One suggestion is that the Dogon came from Egypt, and then lived in Libya before entering the the region of what is now Burkina Faso, Mauritania, or Guinea. Near the close of the fifteenth century, they arrived in Mali.

Among the Yoruba, multiple myths regarding their origin exist. One traces their beginnings to Uruk in Mesopotamia or to Babylon, the site of present-day Iraq. Another story has the Yoruba in West Africa by 10,000 BCE.

After the death of the Zulu messiah Isaiah Shembe in 1935, his son Johannes became the leader of the Nazareth Baptist Church. He lacked the charisma of his father, but did hold the church together. His brother, Amos, became regent in 1976 when Johannes died. Johannes's son Londa split the church in 1979 when Amos refused to give up power. Tangled in South African politics, Londa was killed in 1989.

The Ethiopian Orthodox Church is the nation's official church. A legend states that Menelik, supposed to have been the son of the Queen of Sheba and King Solomon, founded the royal line. When Jesuits arrived in the seventeenth century, they failed to change the church, and the nation closed to missionary efforts for several hundred years. By retaining independence theologically and not being conquered politically, Ethiopia is sometimes considered a model for the new religious movements in Africa.

Founder or Major Prophet

The origins of most African traditional religions or faiths are accounted for through the actions of deities in creation stories rather than a particular founder. One exception, however, is Isaiah Shembe, who founded the Nazareth Baptist Church, also known as the Shembe Church or amaNazarite Church, in 1910 after receiving a number of revelations during a thunderstorm. Shembe was an itinerant Zulu preacher and healer. Through his influence and leadership, amaNazarites follow more Old Testament regulations than most Christians, including celebrating the Sabbath on Saturday rather than Sunday. They also refer to God as Jehovah, the Hebrew name for God. Shembe was regarded as the new Jesus Christ for his people, adapting Christianity to Zulu practice. He adopted the title Nkosi, which means king or chief.

The Ethiopian Orthodox church was founded, according to legend, by preaching from one of two New Testament figures—the disciple Matthew or the unnamed eunuch mentioned in Acts 8. According to historical evidence, the church began when Frumentius arrived at the royal court. Athanasius of Alexandria later consecrated Frumentius as patriarch of the church, linking it to the Christian church in Egypt.

Creation Stories

The Dogon believe that Amma, the sky god, was also the creator of the universe. Amma created two sets of twins, male and female. One of the males rebelled. To restore order, Amma sacrificed the other male, Nommo, strangling and scattering him to the four directions, then restoring him to life after five days. Nommo then became ruler of the universe and the children of his spirits became the Dogon. Thus the world continually moves between chaos and order, and the task of the Dogon is to keep the world in balance through rituals. In a five-year cycle, the aspects of this creation myth are re-enacted at altars throughout the Dogon land.

According to the Yoruba, after one botched attempt at creating the world, Olorun sent his son Obatala to create earth upon the waters. Obatala tossed some soil on the water and released a five-toed hen to spread it out. Next, Olorun told Obatala to make people from clay. Obatala grew bored with the work and drank too much wine. Thereafter, the people he made were misshapen or defective (handicapped). In anger, Olorun relieved him of the job and gave it to Odudua to complete. It was Odudua who made the Yoruba and founded a kingdom at Ilé-Ifè.

The word *Zulu* means "heaven or sky." The Zulu people believe they originated in heaven. They also believe in phansi, the place where spirits live and which is below the earth's surface.

Holy Places

Osun-Osogbo is a forest shrine in Nigeria dedicated to the Yoruba river goddess, Osun. It may be the last such sacred grove remaining among the Yoruba. Shrines, art, sculpture, and sanctuaries are part of the grove, which became a UNESCO World Heritage site in 2005.

Ilé-Ifè, regarded as the equivalent of Eden, is thought to be the site where the first Yoruba was placed. It was probably named for Ifa, the god associated with divination. The palace (Afin) of the spiritual head of the Yoruba, the oni, is located there. The oni has the responsibility to care for the staff of Oranmiyan, a Benin king. The staff, which is eighteen feet tall, is made of granite and shaped like an elephant's tusk.

Axum, the seat of the Ethiopian Christian Church, is a sacred site. The eleven rock-hewn churches of King Lalibela, especially that of Saint George, are a pilgrimage site. According to tradition, angels helped to carve the churches. More than 50,000 pilgrims come to the town of Lalibela at Christmas. After the Muslims captured Jerusalem in 1187, King Lalibela proclaimed his city the "New Jerusalem" because Christians could no longer go on pilgrimage to the Holy Land.

AFRICAN RELIGIONS IN DEPTH

Sacred Symbols

Because all of life is infused with religious meaning, any object or location may be considered or become sacred in traditional African religions. Masks, in particular, have special meaning and may be worn during ceremonies. The mask often represents a god, whose power is passed to the one wearing the mask.

Sacred Practices & Gestures

The Yoruba practice divination in a form that is originally Arabic. There are sixteen basic figures—combined, they deliver a prophecy that the diviner is not to interpret. Instead, he or she recites verses from a classic source. Images may be made to prevent or cure illness. For example, the Yoruba have a smallpox spirit god that can be prayed to for healing. Daily prayer, both morning and evening, is part of life for most Yoruba.

In the amaNazarite Church, which Zulu Isaiah Shembe founded, singing is a key part of the faith. Shembe himself was a gifted composer of hymns. This sacred music was combined with dancing, during which the Zulu wear their traditional dress.

Rites, Celebrations & Services

The Dogon have three major cults. The Awa are associated with dances, featuring ornately carved masks, at funerals and on the anniversaries of deaths. The cult of the Earth god, Lebe, concerns itself with the agricultural cycles and fertility of the land; the hogon of the village guards the soil's purity and presides at ceremonies related to farming. The third cult, the Binu, is involved with communication with spirits, ancestor worship, and sacrifices. Binu shrines are in many locations. The Binu priest makes sacrifices of porridge made from millet and blood at planting time and also when the help of an ancestor is needed. Each clan within the Dogon community has a totem animal spirit—an ancestor spirit wishing to communicate with descendents may do so by taking the form of the animal.

The Dogon also have a celebration every fifty years at the appearing of the star Sirius B between two mountains. (Sirius is often the brightest star in the nighttime sky.) Young males leaving for three months prior to the sigui, as it is called, for a time of seclusion and speaking in private language. This celebration is rooted in the Dogon belief that amphibious creatures, the Nommo, visited their land about three thousand years ago.

The Yoruba offer Esu, the trickster god, palm wine and animal sacrifices. Because he is a trickster, he is considered a cheater, and being on his good side is important. The priests in Yoruba traditional religion are responsible for installing tribal chiefs and kings.

Among the Zulu, families determine the lobola, or bride price. They believe that a groom will respect his wife more if he must pay for her. Further gifts are then exchanged, and the bride's family traditionally gives the groom a goat or sheep to signify their acceptance of him. The groom's family provides meat for the wedding feast, slaughtering a cow on the morning of the wedding. The families assemble in a circle and the men, in costume, dance. The bride gives presents, usually mats or blankets, to members of her new family, who dance or sing their thanks. The final gift, to the groom, is a blanket, which is tossed over his head. Friends of the bride playfully beat him, demonstrating how they will respond if he mistreats his new wife. After the two families eat together, the couple is considered one.

In the traditional Zulu religion, ancestors three generations back are regarded as not yet settled in the afterlife. To help them settle, offerings of goats or other animals are made and rituals to help them settle into the community of ancestors are performed.

Christmas is a major celebration in Ethiopian Christianity. Priests rattle an instrument derived from biblical times, called the sistra, and chant to begin the mass. The festivities include drumming and a dance known as King David's dance.

Judy A. Johnson, MTS

Bibliography

A, Oladosu Olusegun. "Ethics and Judgement: A Panacea for Human Transformation in Yoruba Multireligious Society." *Asia Journal of Theology* 26.1 (2012): 88–104. Print.

Barnes, Trevor. *The Kingfisher Book of Religions*. New York: Kingfisher, 1999. Print.

Dawson, Allan Charles, ed. *Shrines in Africa: history, politics, and society*. Calgary: U of Calgary P, 2009. Print.

Doumbia, Adama, and Naomi Doumbia. *The Way of the Elders: West African Spirituality*. St. Paul: Llewellyn, 2004. Print.

Douny, Laurence. "The Role of Earth Shrines in the Socio-Symbolic Construction of the Dogon Territory: Towards a Philosophy of Containment." *Anthropology & Medicine* 18.2 (2011): 167–79. Print.

Friedenthal, Lora, and Dorothy Kavanaugh. *Religions of Africa*. Philadelphia: Mason Crest, 2007. Print.

Hayes, Stephen. "Orthodox Ecclesiology in Africa: A Study of the 'Ethiopian' Churches of South Africa." *International Journal for the Study of the Christian Church* 8.4 (2008): 337–54. Print.

Lugira, Aloysius M. *African Religion*. New York: Facts on File, 2004. Print.

Mbiti, John S. *African Religions and Philosophy*. 2nd ed. Oxford: Heinemann, 1991. Print.

Monteiro-Ferreira, Ana Maria. "Reevaluating Zulu Religion." *Journal of Black Studies* 35.3 (2005): 347–63. Print.

Peel, J. D. Y. "Yoruba Religion as a Global Phenomenon." *Journal of African History* 5.1 (2010): 107–8. Print.

Ray, Benjamin C. *African Religions*. 2nd ed. Upper Saddle River: Prentice, 2000. Print.

Thomas, Douglas E. *African Traditional Religion in the Modern World*. Jefferson: McFarland, 2005. Print.

Bahá'í Faith

General Description

The Bahá'í faith is the youngest of the world's religions. It began in the mid-nineteenth century, offering scholars the opportunity to observe a religion in the making. While some of the acts of religious founders such as Buddha or Jesus cannot be substantiated, the modern founders of Bahá'í were more contemporary figures.

Number of Adherents Worldwide

An estimated 5 to 7 million people follow the Bahá'í faith. Although strong in Middle Eastern nations such as Iran, where the faith originated, Bahá'í has reached people in many countries, particularly the United States and Canada.

Basic Tenets

The Bahá'í faith has three major doctrines. The first doctrine is that there is one transcendent God, and all religions worship that God, regardless of the name given to the deity. Adherents believe that religious figures such as Jesus Christ, the Buddha, and the Prophet Muhammad were different revelations of God unique to their time and place. The second doctrine is that there is only one religion, though each world faith is valid and was founded by a ""manifestation of God" who is part of a divine plan for educating humanity. The third doctrine is a belief in the unity of all humankind. In light of this underlying unity, those of the Bahá'í faith work for social justice. They believe that seeking consensus among various groups diffuses typical power struggles and to this end, they employ a method called consultation, which is a nonadversarial decision-making process.

The Bahá'í believe that the human soul is immortal, and that after death the soul moves nearer or farther away from God. The idea of an afterlife comprised of a literal "heaven" or "hell" is not part of the faith.

Sacred Text

The Most Holy Book, or the Tablets, written by Baha'u'llah, form the basis of Bahá'í teachings. Though not considered binding, scriptures from other faiths are regarded as "Divine Revelation."

Major Figures

The Bab (The Gate of God) Siyyad 'Ali Mohammad (1819–50), founder of the Bábí movement that broke from Islam, spoke of a coming new messenger of God. Mirza Hoseyn 'Ali Nuri (1817–92), who realized that he was that prophet, was given the title Baha'u'llah (Glory of God). From a member of Persia's landed gentry, he was part of the ruling class, and is considered the founder of the Bahá'í faith. His son, 'Abdu'l-Bahá (Servant of the Glory of God), who lived from 1844 until 1921, became the leader of the group after his father's death in 1892. The oldest son of his eldest daughter, Shogi Effendi Rabbani (1899–1957), oversaw a rapid expansion, visiting Egypt, America, and nations in Europe. Tahirih (the Pure One) was a woman poet who challenged stereotypes by appearing unveiled at meetings.

Major Holy Sites

The Bahá'í World Center is located near Haifa, Israel. The burial shrine of the Bab, a pilgrimage site, is there. The Shrine of Baha'u'llah near Acre, Israel, is another pilgrimage site. The American headquarters are in Wilmette, Illinois. Carmel in Israel is regarded as the world center of the faith.

Major Rites & Celebrations

Each year, the Bahá'í celebrate Ridvan Festival, a twelve-day feast from sunset on April 20 to sunset on May 2. The festival marks Baha'u'llah's declaration of prophethood, as prophesized by the Bab, at a Baghdad garden. (Ridvan means Paradise.) The holy days within that feast are the first (Baha'u'llah's garden arrival), ninth (the arrival of his family), and twelfth (his departure from Ridvan Garden)—on these days, the Bahá'í do not work. During this feast, people attend social events and meet for devotions. Baha'u'llah referred to it as the King of Festivals and Most Great Festival. The Bahá'í celebrate several other events, including World Religion Day and Race Unity Day, both founded by Bahá'í, as well as days connected with significant events in the life of the founder. Elections to the Spiritual Assemblies, and the national and local administrations; international elections are held every five years.

ORIGINS

History & Geography

Siyyad 'Ali Muhammad was born into a merchant family of Shiraz in 1819. Both his parents were descendents of the Prophet Muhammad, Islam's central figure. Like the Prophet, the man who became the Bab lost his father at an early age and was raised by an uncle. A devout child, he entered his uncle's business by age fifteen. After visiting Muslim holy cities, he returned to Shiraz, where he married a distant relative named Khadijih.

While on pilgrimage in 1844 to the black stone of Ka'bah, a sacred site in Islam, the Bab stood with his hand on that holy object and declared that he was the prophet for whom they had been waiting. The Sunni did not give credence to these claims. The Bab went to Persia, where the Shia sect was the majority. However, because Muhammad had been regarded as the "Seal of the Prophets," and the one who spoke the final revelation, Shia clergy viewed his claims as threatening, As such, nothing further would be revealed until the Day of Judgment. The authority of the clergy was in danger from this new movement.

The Bab was placed under house arrest, and then confined to a fortress on the Russian frontier. That move to a more remote area only increased the number of converts, as did a subsequent move to another Kurdish fortress. He

was eventually taken to Tabriz in Iran and tried before the Muslim clergy in 1848. Condemned, he was caned on the soles of his feet and treated by a British doctor who was impressed by him.

Despite his treatment and the persecution of his followers—many of the Bab's eighteen disciples, termed the "Letters of the Living," were persistently tortured and executed—the Bab refused to articulate a doctrine of jihad. The Babis could defend themselves, but were forbidden to use holy war as a means of religious conquest. In three major confrontations sparked by the Shia clergy, Babis were defeated. The Bab was sentenced as a heretic and shot by a firing squad in 1850. Lacking leadership and grief-stricken, in 1852 two young Babis fired on the shah in 1852, unleashing greater persecutions and cruelty against those of the Bahá'í faith.

A follower of the Bab, Mirza Hoseyn 'Ali Nuri, announced in 1863 that he was the one who was to come (the twelfth imam of Islam), the "Glory of God," or Baha'u'llah. Considered the founder of the Bahá'í Faith, he was a tireless writer who anointed his son, 'Abdu'l-Bahá, as the next leader. Despite deprivations and imprisonments, Baha'u'llah lived to be seventy-five years old, relinquishing control of the organization to 'Abdu'l-Bahá before the time of his death.

'Abdu'l-Bahá, whom his father had called "the Master," expanded the faith to the nations of Europe and North America. In 1893, at the Parliament of Religions at the Chicago World's Fair, the faith was first mentioned in the United States. Within a few years, communities of faith were established in Chicago and Wisconsin. In 1911, 'Abdu'l-Bahá began a twenty-eight month tour of Europe and North America to promote the Bahá'í faith. Administratively, he established the spiritual assemblies that were the forerunner of the Houses of Justice that his father had envisioned.

During World War I, 'Abdu'l-Bahá engaged in humanitarian work among the Palestinians in the Holy Land, where he lived. In recognition of his efforts, he was granted knighthood by the British government. Thousands of people, including many political and religious dignitaries, attended his funeral in 1921.

'Abdu'l-Bahá conferred the role of Guardian, or sole interpreter of Bahá'í teaching, to his eldest grandson, Shoghi Effendi Rabbani. To him, all questions regarding the faith were to be addressed. Shoghi Effendi Rabbani was a descendent of Baha'u'llah through both parents. He headed the Bahá'í faith from 1921 to 1963, achieving four major projects: he oversaw the physical development of the World Centre and expanded the administrative order; he carried out the plan his father had set in motion; and he provided for the translating and interpreting of Bahá'í teachings, as the writings of both the Bab and those of Baha'u'llah and 'Abdu'l-Bahá have been translated and published in more than eight hundred languages.

Beginning in 1937, Shoghi Effendi Rabbani began a series of specific plans with goals tied to deadlines. In 1953, during the second seven-year plan, the house of worship in Wilmette, Illinois, was completed and dedicated.

Although the beliefs originated in Shi'ite Islam, the Bahá'í Faith has been declared a new religion without connections to Islam. To followers of Islam, it is a heretical sect. During the reign of the Ayatollah Khomeini, a time when Iran was especially noted as intolerant of diverse views, the Bahá'í faced widespread persecution.

Founder or Major Prophet

Mirza Husayn Ali Nuri, known as Baha'u'llah, was born into privilege in 1817 in what was then Persia, now present-day Iran. At twenty-two, he declined a government post offered at his father's death. Although a member of a politically prestigious family, he did not follow the career path of several generations of his ancestors. Instead, he managed the family estates and devoted himself to charities, earning the title "Father of the Poor."

At twenty-seven, he followed the Babis's movement within Shia Islam, corresponding with the Bab and traveling to further the faith. He also provided financial support. In 1848, he organized and helped to direct a conference that explained the Bab's teaching. At the conference, he gave symbolic names to the eighty-one followers who had attended, based on the spiritual qualities he had observed.

Although he managed to escape death during the persecutions before and after the Bab's death, a fact largely attributed to his upbringing, Baha'u'llah was imprisoned several times. During a four-month stay in an underground dungeon in Tehran, he realized from a dream that he was the one of whom the Bab had prophesied. After being released, he was banished from Persia and had his property confiscated by the shah. He went to Baghdad, refusing the offer of refuge that had come from Russia. Over the following three years a small band of followers joined him, including members of his family. When his younger brother attempted to take over the leadership of the Babis, Baha'u'llah spent two years in a self-imposed exile in the Kurdistan wilderness. In 1856, with the community near anarchy as a result of his brother's failure of leadership, Baha'u'llah returned to the community and restored its position over the next seven years.

Concerned by the growing popularity of the new faith, the shah demanded that the Babis move further away from Persia. They went to Constantinople where, in 1863, Baha'u'llah revealed to the whole group that he was "He Whom God Will Make Manifest." From there the Bahá'í were sent to Adrianople in Turkey, and at last, in 1868, to the town of Acre in the Holy Land. Baha'u'llah was imprisoned in Acre and survived severe prison conditions. In 1877, he moved from prison to a country estate, then to a mansion. He died in 1892 after a fever.

Philosophical Basis

The thinking of Shia Muslims contributed to the development of Bahá'í. The writings incorporate language and concepts from the Qur'an (Islam's holy book). Like Muslims, the Bahá'í believe that God is one. God sends messengers, the Manifestations of God, to instruct people and benefit society. These have included Jesus Christ, the Buddha, the Prophet Muhammad, Krishna, and the Bab. Bahá'í also goes further than Islam in accepting all religions—not just Judaism, Christianity, and Islam—as being part of a divinely inspired plan.

Shia Muslims believe that Muhammad's descendents should lead the faithful community. The leaders, known as imams, were considered infallible. The Sunni Muslims believed that following the way (sunna) of Muhammad was sufficient qualification for leadership. Sunni dynasties regarded the imams as a threat and executed them, starting with two of Muhammad's grandsons, who became Shia martyrs.

In Persia, a state with a long tradition of divinely appointed rulers, the Shia sect was strong. When the Safavids, a Shia dynasty, came to power in the sixteenth century, the custom of the imamate was victorious. One tradition states that in 873, the last appointed imam, who was still a child, went into hiding to avoid being killed. For the following sixty-nine years, this twelfth imam communicated through his deputies to the faithful. Each of the deputies was called bab, or gate, because they led to the "Hidden Imam." Four babs existed through 941, and the last one died without naming the next bab. The Hidden Imam is thought to emerge at the end of time to bring in a worldwide reign of justice. From this tradition came the expectation of a Mahdi (Guided One) to lead the people.

During the early nineteenth century, many followers of both the Christian and Islamic faiths expected their respective messiahs to return. Shia teachers believed that the return of the Mahdi imam was near. In 1843, one teacher, Siyyid Kázim, noted that the Hidden Imam had disappeared one thousand lunar years earlier. He urged the faithful to look for the Mahdi imam.

The following year in Shiraz, Siyyad 'Ali Mohammad announced that he was the Mahdi. (*Siyyad* is a term meaning descended from Muhammad.) He referred to himself as the Bab, though he expanded the term's meaning. Eighteen men, impressed with his ability to expound the Qur'an, believed him. They became the Letters of the Living, and were sent throughout Persia (present-day Iran) to announce the dawning of the Day of God.

In 1853, Mirza Husayn Ali Nuri experienced a revelation that he was "He Whom God Shall Make Manifest," the one of whom the Bab prophesied. Accepted as such, he began writing the words that became the Bahá'í scriptures. Much of what is known of the early days of the faith comes from a Cambridge academic, Edward Granville Browne, who first visited Baha'u'llah in the 1890. Browne wrote of his meeting, introducing this faith to the West.

The emphasis of the Bahá'í faith is on personal development and the breaking down of barriers between people. Service to humanity is important and encouraged. Marriage, with a belief in the equality of both men and women, is also encouraged. Consent of both sets of parents is required prior to marrying.

Holy Places

The shrine of the Bab near Haifa and that of Baha'u'llah near Acre, in Israel, are the two most revered sites for those of the Bahá'í faith. In 2008, the United Nations Educational, Scientific, and Cultural Organization (UNESCO) recognized both as World Heritage Sites. They are the first such sites from a modern religious tradition to be added to the list of sites. Both sites are appreciated for the formal gardens surrounding them that blend design elements from different cultures. For the Bahá'í, Baha'u'llah's shrine is the focus of prayer, comparable to the significance given to the Ka'bah in Mecca for Muslims or to the Western Wall for Jews.

As of 2013, there are seven Bahá'í temples in the world; an eighth temple is under construction in Chile. All temples are built with a center dome and nine sides, symbolizing both diversity and world unity. The North American temple is located in Wilmette, Illinois. There, daily prayer services take place as well as a Sunday service.

THE BAHÁ'Í FAITH IN DEPTH

Governance

Elected members of lay councils at international, national, and local levels administer the work of the faith. The Universal House of Justice in Haifa, Israel, is the location of the international nine-member body. Elections for all of these lay councils are by secret ballot, and do not include nominating, candidates, or campaigns. Those twenty-one and older are permitted to vote. The councils make decisions according to a process of collective decision-making called consultation. They strive to serve as a model for governing a united global society.

Personal Conduct

In addition to private prayer and acts of social justice, those of the Bahá'í faith are encouraged to have a profession, craft, or trade. They are also asked to shun and refrain from slander and partisan politics. Homosexuality and sexual activity outside marriage are forbidden, as is gambling.

The Bahá'í faith does not have professional clergy, nor does it engage in missionary work. However, Bahá'í may share their faith with others and may move to another country as a "pioneer." Pioneers are unlike traditional missionaries, and are expected to support themselves through a career and as a member of the community.

Avenues of Service

Those of the Bahá'í Faith place a high value on service to humanity, considering it an act of worship. This can be done through caring for one's own family or through one's choice of vocation. Within the local community, people may teach classes for children, mentor youth groups, host devotional programs, or teach adult study circles. Many are engaged in economic or social development programs as well. Although not mandated, a year or two of service is often undertaken following high school or during college.

United Nations Involvement

Beginning in 1947, just one year after the United Nations (UN) first met, the Bahá'í Faith was represented at that body. In 1948, the Bahá'í International Community was accredited by the UN as an international nongovernmental organization (NGO). In 1970, the faith received special consultative status with the UN Economic and Social Council (ECOSOC). Following World War I, a Bahá'í office opened in Geneva, Switzerland, where the League of Nations was headquartered. Thus the Bahá'í Faith has a long tradition of supporting global institutions.

Money Matters

The International Bahá'í Fund exists to develop and support the growth of the faith, and the Universal House of Justice oversees the distribution of the money. Contributions are also used to maintain the Bahá'í World Center. No money is accepted from non-Bahá'í sources. National and local funds, administered by National or Local Spiritual Assemblies, are used in supporting service projects, publishing endeavors, schools, and Bahá'í centers. For the Bahá'í, the size of the donation is less important than regular contributions and the spirit of sacrifice behind them.

Food Restrictions

Bahá'í between fifteen and seventy years of age **fast** nineteen days a year, abstaining from food and drink from sunrise to sunset. Fasting occurs the first day of each month of the Bahá'í calendar, which divides the year into nineteen months of nineteen days each. The Bahá'í faithful do not drink alcohol or use narcotics, because these will deaden the mind with repeated use.

Rites, Celebrations & Services

Daily prayer and meditation is recommended in the Bahá'í faith. During services there are mediations and prayers, along with the reading of Bahá'í scriptures and other world faith traditions. There is no set ritual, no offerings, and no sermons. Unaccompanied by musical instruments, choirs also sing. Light refreshments may be served afterwards.

Bahá'í place great stress on marriage, the only state in which sex is permitted. Referred to as "a fortress for well-being and salvation," a monogamous, heterosexual marriage is the ideal. To express the oneness of humanity, interracial marriages are encouraged. After obtaining the consent of their parents, the couple takes the following vow: "We will all, verily, abide by the will of God." The remainder of the service may be individually crafted and may also include dance, music, feasting, and ceremony. Should a couple choose to end a marriage, they must first complete a year of living apart while trying to reconcile differences. Divorce is discouraged, but permitted after that initial year.

Judy A. Johnson, MTS

Bibliography

Albertson, Lorelei. *All about Bahá'í Faith.* University Pub., 2012. E-book.

Bowers, Kenneth E. *God Speaks Again: an Introduction to the Bahá'í Faith.* Wilmette: Bahá'í, 2004. Print.

Buck, Christopher. "The Interracial 'Bahá'í Movement' and the Black Intelligentsia: The Case of W. E. B. Du Bois." *Journal of Religious History* 36.4 (2012): 542–62. Print.

Cederquist, Druzelle. *The Story of Baha'u'llah.* Wilmette: Bahá'í, 2005. Print.

Echevarria, L. *Life Stories of Bahá'í Women in Canada: Constructing Religious Identity in the Twentieth Century.* Lang, 2011. E-book.

Garlington, William. *The Bahá'í Faith in America.* Lanham: Rowman, 2008. Print.

Hartz, Paula R. *Bahá'í Faith.* New York: Facts on File, 2006. Print.

Hatcher, William S. and J. Douglas Martin. *The Bahá'í Faith: The Emerging Global Religion.* Wilmette: Bahá'í, 2002. Print.

Karlberg, Michael. "Constructive Resilience: The Bahá'í Response to Oppression." *Peace & Change* 35.2 (2010): 222–57. Print.

Lee, Anthony A. *The Bahá'í Faith in Africa: Establishing a New Religious Movement, 1952–1962.* Brill NV, E-book.

Momen, Moojan. "Bahá'í Religious History." *Journal of Religious History* 36.4 (2012): 463–70. Print.

Momen, Moojan. *The Bahá'í Faith: A Beginner's Guide.* Oxford: Oneworld, 2007. Print.

Smith, Peter. *The Bahá'í Faith.* Cambridge: Cambridge UP, 2008. Print.

Wilkinson, Philip. *Religions.* New York: DK, 2008. Print.

Buddhism

General Description

Buddhism has three main branches: Theravada (Way of the Elders), also referred to as Hinayana (Lesser Vehicle); Mahayana (Greater Vehicle); and Vajrayana (Diamond Vehicle), also referred to as Tantric Buddhism. Vajrayana is sometimes thought of as an extension of Mahayana Buddhism. These can be further divided into many sects and schools, many of which are geographically based. In Buddhism, these different divisions or schools are regarded as alternative paths to enlightenment (Wilkinson 2008).

Number of Adherents Worldwide

An estimated 474 million people around the world are Buddhists. Of the major sects, Theravada Buddhism is the oldest, developed in the sixth century BCE. Its adherents include those of the Theravada Forest Tradition. From Mahayana Buddhism, which developed in the third to second centuries BCE, came several offshoots based on location. In what is now China, Pure Land Buddhism and Tibetan Buddhism developed in the seventh century. In Japan, Zen Buddhism developed in the twelfth century, Nichiren Buddhism developed a century later, and Soka Gakkai was founded in 1937. In California during the 1970s, the Serene Reflection Meditation began as a subset of Sōtō Zen. In Buddhism, these different divisions or schools are regarded as alternative paths to enlightenment.

Basic Tenets

Buddhists hold to the Three Universal Truths: impermanence, the lack of self, and suffering. These truths encompass the ideas that everything is impermanent and changing and that life is not satisfying because of its impermanence and the temporary nature of all things, including contentment. Buddhism also teaches the Four Noble Truths: All life is suffering (Dukkha). Desire and attachment cause suffering (Samudaya). Ceasing to desire or crave conceptual attachment

ends suffering and leads to release (Nirodha). This release comes through following the Noble Eightfold Path—right understanding (or view), right intention, right speech, right conduct, right occupation, right effort, right mindfulness, and right concentration (Magga).

Although Buddhists do not believe in an afterlife as such, the soul undergoes a cycle of death and rebirth. Following the Noble Eightfold Path leads to the accumulation of good karma, allowing one to be reborn at a higher level. Karma is the Buddhist belief in cause-effect relationships; actions taken in one life have consequences in the next. Ultimately, many refer to the cessation or elimination of suffering as the primary goal of Buddhism.

Buddhists do not believe in gods. Salvation is to be found in following the teachings of Buddha, which are called the Dharma (law or truth). Buddhism does have saint-like bodhisattvas (enlightened beings) who reject ultimate enlightenment (Nirvana) for themselves to aid others.

Sacred Text

Buddhism has nothing comparable to the Qur'an (Islam's holy book) or the Bible. For Theravada Buddhists, an important text is the Pāli Canon, the collection of Buddha's teachings. Mahayana Buddhists recorded their version of these as sutras, many of them in verse. The Lotus Sutra is among the most important. The Buddhist scriptures are written in two languages of ancient India, Pali and Sanskrit, depending on the tradition in which they were developed. Some of these words, such as karma, have been transliterated into English and gained common usage.

Major Figures

Siddhartha Gautama (ca. 563 to 483 BCE) is the founder of Buddhism and regarded as the Buddha or Supreme Buddha. He is the most highly regarded historical figure in Buddhism.

He had two principle disciples: Sariputta and Mahamoggallana (or Maudgalyayana). In contemporary Buddhism, the fourteenth Dalai Lama, Tenzin Gyatso, is a significant person. Both he and Aung San Suu Kyi, a Buddhist of Myanmar who was held as a political prisoner for her stand against the oppressive regime of that nation, have been awarded the Nobel Peace Prize.

Major Holy Sites

Buddhist holy sites are located in several places in Asia. All of those directly related to the life of Siddhartha Gautama are located in the northern part of India near Nepal. Lumbini Grove is noted as the birthplace of the Buddha. He received enlightenment at Bodh Gaya and first began to teach in Sarnath. Kusinara is the city where he died.

In other Asian nations, some holy sites were once dedicated to other religions. Angkor Wat in Cambodia, for example, was constructed for the Hindu god Vishnu in the twelfth century CE. It became a Buddhist temple three hundred years later. It was once the largest religious monument in the world and still attracts visitors. In Java's central highlands sits Borobudur, the world's largest Buddhist shrine. The name means "Temple of Countless Buddhas." Its five terraces represent what must be overcome to reach enlightenment: worldly desires, evil intent, malicious joy, laziness, and doubt. It was built in the eighth and ninth centuries CE, only to fall into neglect at about the turn of the millennium; it was rediscovered in 1815. The complex has three miles of carvings illustrating the life and teachings of the Buddha. In Sri Lanka, the Temple of the Tooth, which houses what is believed to be one of the Buddha's teeth, is a popular pilgrimage site.

Some of the holy sites incorporate gifts of nature. China has four sacred Buddhist mountains, symbolizing the four corners of the universe. These mountains—Wǔtái Shān, Éméi Shān, Jiǔhuá Shān, and Pǔtuó Shān—are believed to be the homes of bodhisattvas. In central India outside Fardapur, there are twenty-nine caves carved into the granite, most of them with frescoes based on the Buddha's life. Ajanta, as

the site is known, was created between 200 BCE and the fifth century CE. Five of the caves house temples.

The Buddha's birthday, his day of death, and the day of his enlightenment are all celebrated, either as one day or several. Different traditions and countries have their own additional celebrations, including Sri Lanka's Festival of the Tooth. Buddhists have a lunar calendar, and four days of each month are regarded as holy days.

ORIGINS

History & Geography

Buddhism began in what is now southern Nepal and northern India with the enlightenment of the Buddha. Following his death, members of the sangha, or community, spread the teachings across northern India. The First Buddhist Council took place in 486 BCE at Rajagaha. This council settled the Buddhist canon, the Tipitaka. In 386 BCE, a little more than a century after the Buddha died, a second Buddhist Council was held at Vesali. It was at this meeting that the two major schools of Buddhist thought—Theravada and Mahayana—began to differ.

Emperor Asoka, who ruled most of the Indian subcontinent from around 268 to 232 BCE, converted to Buddhism. He sent missionaries across India and into central parts of Asia. He also set up pillars with Buddhist messages in his own efforts to establish "true dharma" in the kingdom, although he did not create a state church. His desire for his subjects to live contently in this life led to promoting trade, maintaining canals and reservoirs, and the founding a system of medical care for both humans and animals. Asoka's son Mahinda went to southern Indian and to Sri Lanka with the message of Buddhism.

Asoka's empire fell shortly after his death. Under the following dynasties, evidence suggests Buddhists in India experienced persecution. The religion continued to grow, however, and during the first centuries CE, monasteries and monuments were constructed with support from local rulers. Some additional support came from women within the royal courts. Monastic centers also grew in number. By the fourth century CE, Buddhism had become one of the chief religious traditions in India.

During the Gupta dynasty, which lasted from about 320 to 600 CE, Buddhists and Hindus began enriching each other's traditions. Some Hindus felt that the Buddha was an incarnation of Vishnu, a Hindu god. Some Buddhists showed respect for Hindu deities.

Also during this era, Mahavihara, the concept of the "Great Monastery," came to be. These institutions served as universities for the study and development of Buddhist thinking. Some of them also included cultural and scientific study in the curriculum.

Traders and missionaries took the ideas of Buddhism to China. By the first century CE, Buddhism was established in that country. The religion died out or was absorbed into Hinduism in India. By the seventh century, a visiting Chinese monk found that Huns had invaded India from Central Asia and destroyed many Buddhist monasteries. The religion revived and flourished in the northeast part of India for several centuries.

Muslim invaders reached India in the twelfth and thirteenth centuries. They sacked the monasteries, some of which had grown very wealthy. Some even paid workers to care for both the land they owned and the monks, while some had indentured slaves. Because Buddhism had become monastic rather than a religion of the laity, there was no groundswell for renewal following the Muslim invasion.

Prominent in eastern and Southeast Asia, Buddhism is the national religion in some countries. For example, in Thailand, everyone learns about Buddhism in school. Buddhism did not begin to reach Western culture until the nineteenth century, when the Lotus Sutra was translated into German. The first Buddhist temple in the United States was built in 1853 in San Francisco's Chinatown.

Chinese Communists took control of Tibet in 1950. Nine years later, the fourteenth Dalai Lama left for India, fearing persecution. The Dalai Lama is considered a living teacher (lama) who is to instruct others. (The term *dalai* means "great as the ocean.") In 1989, he received the Nobel Peace Prize.

Buddhism experienced a revival in India during the twentieth century. Although some of this new beginning was due in part to Tibetan immigrants seeking safety, a mass conversion in 1956 was the major factor. The year was chosen to honor the 2,500th anniversary of the Buddha's death year. Buddhism was chosen as an alternative to the strict caste structure of Hinduism, and hundreds of thousands of people of the Dalit caste, once known as untouchables, converted in a ceremony held in Nagpur.

Founder or Major Prophet

Siddhartha Gautama, who became known as the "Enlightened One," or Buddha, was a prince in what is now southern Nepal, but was then northern India during the sixth century BCE. The name Siddhartha means "he who achieves his aim." He was a member of the Sakya tribe of Nepal, belonging to the warrior caste. Many legends have grown around his birth and early childhood. One states that he was born in a grove in the woods, emerging from his mother's side able to walk and completely clean.

During Siddhartha's childhood, a Brahmin, or wise man, prophesied that he would grow to be a prince or a religious teacher who would help others overcome suffering. Because the life of a sage involved itinerant begging, the king did not want this life for his child. He kept Siddhartha in the palace and provided him with all the luxuries of his position, including a wife, Yashodhara. They had a son, Rahula.

Escaping from the palace at about the age of thirty, Gautama first encountered suffering in the form of an old man with a walking stick. The following day, he saw a man who was ill. On the third day, he witnessed a funeral procession. Finally he met a monk, who had nothing, but who radiated happiness. He determined to leave his privileged life, an act called the Great Renunciation. Because hair was a sign of vanity in his time, he shaved his head. He looked for enlightenment via an ascetic life of little food or sleep. He followed this path for six years, nearly starving to death. Eventually, he determined on a Middle Way, a path neither luxurious as he had known in the palace, nor ascetic as he had attempted.

After three days and nights of meditating under a tree at Bodh Gaya, Siddhartha achieved his goal of enlightenment, or Nirvana. He escaped fear of suffering and death.

The Buddha began his preaching career, which spanned some forty years, following his enlightenment. He gave his first sermon in northeast India at Sarnath in a deer park. The first five followers became the first community, or sangha. Buddha died around age eighty, in 483 BCE after he had eaten poisoned food. After warning his followers not to eat the food, he meditated until he died.

Buddhists believe in many enlightened ones. Siddhartha is in one tradition regarded as the fourth buddha, while other traditions hold him to have been the seventh or twenty-fifth buddha.

His disciples, who took the ideas throughout India, repeated his teachings. When the later Buddhists determined to write down the teachings of the Buddha, they met to discuss the ideas and agreed that a second meeting should occur in a century. At the third council, which was held at Pataliputta, divisions occurred. The two major divisions—Theravada and Mahayana—differ over the texts to be used and the interpretation of the teachings. Theravada can be translated as "the Teachings of the Elders," while Mahayana means "Great Vehicle."

Theravada Buddhists believe that only monks can achieve enlightenment through the teachings of another buddha, or enlightened being. Thus they try to spend some part of their lives in a monastery. Buddhists in the Mahayana tradition, on the other hand, feel that all people can achieve enlightenment, without being in a monastery. Mahayanans also regard some as bodhisattvas, people who have achieved the enlightened state but renounce Nirvana to help others achieve it.

Philosophical Basis

During Siddhartha's lifetime, Hinduism was the predominant religion in India. Many people, especially in northern India, were dissatisfied with the rituals and sacrifices of that religion. In addition, as many small kingdoms expanded and the unity of the tribes began to break down, many people were in religious turmoil and doubt. A number of sects within Hinduism developed.

The Hindu belief in the cycle of death and rebirth led some people to despair because they could not escape from suffering in their lives. Siddhartha was trying to resolve the suffering he saw in the world, but many of his ideas came from the Brahmin sect of Hinduism, although he reinterpreted them. Reincarnation, dharma, and reverence for cows are three of the ideas that carried over into Buddhism.

In northeast India at Bodh Gaya, he rested under a bodhi tree, sometimes called a bo tree. He meditated there until he achieved Nirvana, or complete enlightenment, derived from the freedom of fear that attached to suffering and death. As a result of his being enlightened, he was known as Buddha, a Sanskrit word meaning "awakened one." Wanting to help others, he began teaching his Four Noble Truths, along with the Noble Eightfold Path that would lead people to freedom from desire and suffering. He encouraged his followers to take Triple Refuge in the Three Precious Jewels: the Buddha, the teachings, and the sangha, or monastic community. Although at first Buddha was uncertain about including women in a sangha, his mother-in-law begged for the privilege.

Greed, hatred, and ignorance were three traits that Buddha felt people needed to conquer. All three create craving, the root of suffering. Greed and ignorance lead to a desire for things that are not needed, while hatred leads to a craving to destroy the hated object or person.

To the Four Noble Truths and Eightfold Path, early devotees of Buddhism added the Five Moral Precepts. These are to avoid taking drugs and alcohol, engaging in sexual misconduct, harming others, stealing, and lying.

The precepts of the Buddha were not written down for centuries. The first text did not appear for more than 350 years after the precepts were first spoken. One collection from Sri Lanka written in Pāli during the first century BCE is known as Three Baskets, or Tipitaka. The three baskets include Buddha's teaching (the Basket of Discourse), commentary on the sayings (the Basket of Special Doctrine), and the rules for monks to follow (the Basket of Discipline). The name Three Baskets refers to the fact that the sayings were first written on leaves from a palm tree that were then collected in baskets.

Holy Places

Buddhists make pilgrimages to places that relate to important events in Siddhartha's life. While Lumbini Grove, the place of Siddhartha's birth, is a prominent pilgrimage site, the primary site for pilgrimage is Bodh Gaya, the location where Buddha received enlightenment. Other pilgrimage sites include Sarnath, the deer park located in what is now Varanasi (Benares) where the Buddha first began to teach, and Kusinara, the city where he died. All of these are in the northern part of India near Nepal.

Other sites in Asia that honor various bodhisattvas have also become pilgrimage destinations. Mountains are often chosen; there are four in China, each with monasteries and temples built on them. In Japan, the Shikoku pilgrimage covers more than 700 miles and involves visits to eighty-eight temples along the route.

BUDDHISM IN DEPTH

Sacred Symbols

Many stylized statue poses of the Buddha exist, each with a different significance. One, in which the Buddha has both hands raised, palms facing outward, commemorates the calming of an elephant about to attack the Buddha. If only the right hand is raised, the hand symbolizes friendship and being unafraid. The teaching gesture is that of a hand with the thumb and first finger touching.

In Tibetan Buddhism, the teachings of Buddha regarding the cycle of rebirth are symbolized in the six-spoke wheel of life. One may be reborn into any of the six realms of life: hell, hungry spirits, warlike demons called Asuras, animals, humans, or gods. Another version of the wheel has eight spokes rather than six, to represent the Noble Eightfold Path. Still another wheel has twelve spokes, signifying both the Four Noble Truths and the Noble Eightfold Path.

Tibetan Buddhists have prayer beads similar to a rosary, with 108 beads representing the number of desires to be overcome prior to reaching enlightenment. The worshipper repeats the Triple Refuge—Buddha, dharma, and sangha—or a mantra.

The prayer wheel is another device that Tibetan Buddhists use. Inside the wheel is a roll of paper on which the sacred mantra—Hail to the jewel in the lotus—is written many times. The lotus is a symbol of growing spiritually; it grows in muddied waters, but with the stems and flowers, it reaches toward the sun. By turning the wheel and spinning the mantra, the practitioner spreads blessings. Bells may be rung to wake the hearer out of ignorance.

In Tantric Buddhism, the mandala, or circle, serves as a map of the entire cosmos. Mandalas may be made of colored grains of sand, carved or painted. They are used to help in meditation and are thought to have a spiritual energy.

Buddhism recognizes Eight Auspicious Symbols, including the banner, conch shell, fish, knot, lotus, treasure vase, umbrella, and wheel. Each has a particular significance. A conch shell, for example, is often blown to call worshippers to meetings. Because its sound travels far, it signifies the voice of Buddha traveling throughout the world. Fish are fertility symbols because they have thousands of offspring. In Buddhist imagery, they are often in facing pairs and fashioned of gold. The lotus represents spiritual growth, rooted in muddy water but flowering toward the sun. The umbrella symbolizes protection, because servants once used them to protect royalty from both sun and rain.

Sacred Practices & Gestures

Two major practices characterize Buddhism: gift-giving and showing respect to images and relics of the Buddha. The first is the transaction between laity and monks in which laypersons present sacrificial offerings to the monks, who in return share their higher state of spiritual being with the laity. Although Buddhist monks are permitted to own very little, they each have a begging bowl, which is often filled with rice.

Buddhists venerate statues of the Buddha, bodhisattvas, and saints; they also show respect to his relics, housed in stupas. When in the presence of a statue of the Buddha, worshippers have a series of movements they repeat three times, thus dedicating their movements to the Triple Refuge. It begins with a dedicated body: placing hands together with the palms cupped slightly and fingers touching, the devotee raises the hands to the forehead. The second step symbolizes right speech by lowering the hands to just below the mouth. In the third movement, the hands are lowered to the front of the chest, indicating that heart—and by extension, mind—are also dedicated to the Triple Refuge. The final movement is prostration. The devotee first gets on all fours, then lowers either the entire body to the floor or lowers the head, so that there are five points of contact with the floor.

Statues of the Buddha give a clue to the gestures held important to his followers. The gesture of turning the hand towards the ground indicates that one is observing Earth. Devotees assume a lotus position, with legs crossed, when in meditation.

Allowing the left hand to rest in the lap and the right hand to point down to Earth is a gesture used in meditation. Another common gesture is to touch thumb and fingertips together while the palms of both hands face up, thus forming a flat triangular shape. The triangle signifies the Three Jewels of Buddhism.

Food Restrictions

Buddhism does not require one to be a vegetarian. Many followers do not eat meat, however, because to do so involves killing other creatures. Both monks and laypersons may choose not to eat after noontime during the holy days of each month.

Rites, Celebrations, & Services

Ancient Buddhism recognized four holy days each month, known as *uposatha*. These days included the full moon and new moon days of each lunar month, as well as the eighth day after each of these moons appeared. Both monks and members of the laity have special religious duties during these four days. A special service takes place in which flowers are offered to images of the Buddha, precepts are repeated, and a sermon is preached. On these four days, an additional three precepts may be undertaken along with the five regularly observed. The three extra duties are to refrain from sleeping on a luxurious bed, eating any food after noon, and adorning the body or going to entertainments.

In Theravada nations, three major life events of the Buddha—birth, enlightenment, and entering nirvana—are celebrated on Vesak, or Buddha Day. In temples, statues of Buddha as a child are ceremonially cleaned. Worshippers may offer incense and flowers. To symbolize the Buddha's enlightenment, lights may be illuminated in trees and temples. Because it is a day of special kindness, some people in Thailand refrain from farm work that could harm living creatures. They may also seek special merit by freeing captive animals.

Other Buddhist nations that follow Mahayana Buddhism commemorate these events on three different days. In Japan, Hana Matsuri is the celebration of Buddha's birth. On that day, people create paper flower gardens to recall the gardens of Lumbini, Siddhartha's birthplace. Worshippers also pour perfumed tea over statues of Buddha; this is because, according to tradition, the gods provided scented water for Siddhartha's first bath.

Poson is celebrated in Sri Lanka to honor the coming of Buddhism during the reign of Emperor Asoka. Other holy persons are also celebrated in the countries where they had the greatest influence. In Tibet, for instance, the arrival of

Padmasambhava, who brought Buddhism to that nation, is observed.

Buddhists also integrate their own special celebrations into regular harvest festivals and New Year activities. These festivities may include a performance of an event in the life of any buddha or bodhisattva. For example, troupes of actors in Tibet specialize in enacting Buddhist legends. The festival of the Sacred Tooth is held in Kandy, Sri Lanka. According to one legend, a tooth of Buddha has been recovered, and it is paraded through the streets on this day. The tooth has been placed in a miniature stupa, or sealed mound, which is carried on an elephant's back.

Protection rituals have been common in Buddhism from earliest days. They may be public rituals meant to avoid a collective danger, such as those held in Sri Lanka and other Southeast Asia nations. Or they may be designed for private use. The role of these rituals is greater in Mahayana tradition, especially in Tibet. Mantras are chanted for this reason.

Customs surrounding death and burial differ between traditions and nations. A common factor, however, is the belief that the thoughts of a person at death are significant. This period may be extended for three days following death, due to a belief in consciousness for that amount of time after death. To prepare the mind of the dying, another person may read sacred texts aloud.

Judy A. Johnson, MTS

Bibliography

Armstrong, Karen. *Buddha*. New York: Penguin, 2001. Print.

Barnes, Trevor. *The Kingfisher Book of Religions*. New York: Kingfisher, 1999. Print.

Chodron, Thubten. *Buddhism for Beginners*. Ithaca: Snow Lion, 2001. Print.

Eckel, Malcolm David. *Buddhism*. Oxford: Oxford UP, 2002. Print.

Epstein, Ron. "Application of Buddhist Teachings in Modern Life." *Religion East & West* Oct. 2012: 52–61. Print.

Harding, John S. *Studying Buddhism in Practice*. Routledge, 2012. E-book. Studying Religions in Practice.

Harvey, Peter. *An Introduction to Buddhism: Teachings, History and Practices*. 2nd ed. Cambridge UP, 2013. E-book.

Heirman, Ann. "Buddhist Nuns: Between Past and Present." *International Review for the History of Religions* 58.5/6 (2011): 603–31. Print.

Langley, Myrtle. *Religion*. New York: Knopf, 1996. Print.

Low, Kim Cheng Patrick. "Three Treasures of Buddhism & Leadership Insights." *Culture & Religion Review Journal* 2012.3 (2012): 66–72. Print.

Low, Patrick Kim Cheng. "Leading Change, the Buddhist Perspective." *Culture & Religion Review Journal* 2012.1 (2012): 127–45. Print.

McMahan, David L. *Buddhism in the Modern World*. Routledge, 2012. E-book.

Meredith, Susan. *The Usborne Book of World Religions*. London: Usborne, 1995. Print.

Morgan, Diane. *Essential Buddhism: A Comprehensive Guide to Belief and Practice*. Praeger, 2010. E-book.

Wilkinson, Philip. *Buddhism*. New York: DK, 2003. Print.

Wilkinson, Philip. *Religions*. New York: DK, 2008. Print.

Christianity

General Description

Christianity is one of the world's major religions. It is based on the life and teachings of Jesus of Nazareth, called the Christ, or anointed one. It is believed that there are over thirty thousand denominations or sects of Christianity worldwide. Generally, most of these sects fall under the denominational families of Catholicism, Protestant, and Orthodox. (Anglican and Oriental Orthodox are sometimes added as separate branches.) Most denominations have developed since the seventeenth-century Protestant Reformation.

Number of Adherents Worldwide

Over 2.3 billion people around the world claim allegiance to Christianity in one of its many forms. The three major divisions are Roman Catholicism, Eastern Orthodox, and Protestant. Within each group are multiple denominations. Roman Catholics number more than 1.1 billion followers, while the Eastern Orthodox Church has between 260 and 278 million adherents. An estimated 800 million adherents follow one of the various Protestant denominations, including Anglican, Baptist, Lutheran, Presbyterian, and Methodist. Approximately 1 percent of Christians, or 28 million adherents, do not belong to one of the three major divisions

There are a number of other groups, such as the Amish, with an estimated 249,000 members, and the Quakers, numbering approximately 377,000. Both of these churches—along with Mennonites, who number 1.7 million—are in the peace tradition (their members are conscientious objectors). Pentecostals have 600 million adherents worldwide. Other groups that are not always considered Christian by more conservative groups include Jehovah's Witnesses (7.6 million) and Mormons (13 million) (Wilkinson, p. 104-121).

Basic Tenets

The summaries of the Christian faith are found in the Apostles Creed and Nicene Creed.

In addition, some churches have developed their own confessions of faith, such as Lutheranism's Augsburg Confession. Christianity is a monotheistic tradition, although most Christians believe in the Trinity, defined as one God in three separate but equal persons—Father, Son, and Holy Spirit. More modern, gender-neutral versions of the Trinitarian formula may refer to Creator, Redeemer, and Sanctifier. Many believe in the doctrine of original sin, which means that the disobedience of Adam and Eve in the Garden of Eden has been passed down through all people; because of this sin, humankind is in need of redemption. Jesus Christ was born, lived a sinless life, and then was crucified and resurrected as a substitute for humankind. Those who accept this sacrifice for sin will receive eternal life in a place of bliss after death. Many Christians believe that a Second Coming of Jesus will inaugurate a millennial kingdom and a final judgment (in which people will be judged according to their deeds and their eternal souls consigned to heaven or hell), as well as a resurrected physical body.

Sacred Text

The Bible is the sacred text of Christianity, which places more stress on the New Testament. The canon of the twenty-six books of the New Testament was finally determined in the latter half of the fourth century CE.

Major Figures

Christianity is based on the life and teachings of Jesus of Nazareth. His mother, Mary, is especially revered in Roman Catholicism and the Eastern Orthodox tradition, where she is known as Theotokos (God-bearer). Jesus spread his teachings through the twelve apostles, or disciples, who he himself chose and named. Paul (Saint Paul or Paul the Apostle), who became the first missionary to the Gentiles—and whose writings comprise a bulk of the New Testament—is a key figure for the theological treatises embedded in his letters to early churches. His conversion occurred after Jesus' crucifixion. All of these figures are biblically represented.

Under the Emperor Constantine, Christianity went from a persecuted religion to the state religion. Constantine also convened the Council of Nicea in 325 CE, which expressed the formula defining Jesus as fully God and fully human. Saint Augustine (354–430) was a key thinker of the early church who became the Bishop of Hippo in North Africa. He outlined the principles of just war and expressed the ideas of original sin. He also suggested what later became the Catholic doctrine of purgatory.

In the sixth century, Saint Benedict inscribed a rule for monks that became a basis for monastic life. Martin Luther, the monk who stood against the excesses of the Roman Catholic Church, ignited the seventeenth-century Protestant Reformation. He proclaimed that salvation came by grace alone, not through works. In the twentieth century, Pope John XXIII convened the Vatican II Council, or Second Vatican Council, which made sweeping changes to the liturgy and daily practice for Roman Catholics.

Major Holy Sites

The key events in the life of Jesus Christ occurred in the region of Palestine. Bethlehem is honored as the site of Jesus's birth; Jerusalem is especially revered as the site of Jesus's crucifixion. The capital of the empire, Rome, also became the center of Christianity until the Emperor Constantine shifted the focus to Constantinople. Rome today is the seat of the Vatican, an independent city-state that houses the government of the Roman Catholic Church. Canterbury, the site of the martyrdom of Saint Thomas Becket and seat of the archbishop of the Anglican Communion, is a pilgrimage site for Anglicans. There are also many pilgrimage sites, such as Compostela and Lourdes, for other branches of Christianity. In Ethiopia, Lalibela is the site of eleven churches carved from stone during the twelfth century. The site serves as a profound testimony to the vibrancy of the Christian faith in Africa.

Major Rites & Celebrations

The first rite of the church is baptism, a water-related ritual that is traditionally administered to infants or adults alike through some variant of sprinkling or immersion. Marriage is another rite of the church. Confession is a major part of life for Roman Catholics, although the idea is also present in other branches of Christianity.

The celebration of the Eucharist, or Holy Communion, is a key part of weekly worship for the liturgical churches such as those in the Roman Catholic or Anglican traditions. Nearly all Christians worship weekly on Sunday; services include readings of scripture, a sermon, singing of hymns, and may include Eucharist. Christians honor the birth of Jesus at Christmas and his death and resurrection at Easter. Easter is often considered the most significant liturgical feast, particularly in Orthodox branches.

Many Christians follow a calendar of liturgical seasons. Of these seasons, perhaps the best known is Lent, which is immediately preceded by Shrove Tuesday, also known as Mardi Gras. Lent is traditionally a time of fasting and self-examination in preparation for the Easter feast. Historically, Christians gave up rich foods. The day before Lent was a time for pancakes—to use up the butter and eggs—from which the term Mardi Gras (Fat Tuesday) derives. Lent begins with Ash Wednesday, when Christians are marked with the sign of the cross on their foreheads using ashes, a reminder that they are dust and will return to dust.

ORIGINS

History & Geography

Christianity was shaped in the desert and mountainous landscapes of Palestine, known as the Holy Land. Jesus was driven into the wilderness following his baptism, where he remained for forty days of fasting and temptation. The Gospels record that he often went to the mountains for solitude and prayer. The geography of the deserts and mountains also shaped early Christian spirituality, as men and women went into solitude to pray, eventually founding small communities of the so-called desert fathers and mothers.

Christianity at first was regarded as a sect within Judaism, though it differentiated itself early in the first century CE by breaking with the code of laws that defined Judaism, including the need for circumcision and ritual purity. Early Christianity then grew through the missionary work of the apostles, particularly Paul the Apostle, who traveled throughout the Mediterranean world and beyond the Roman Empire to preach the gospel (good news) of Jesus. (This is often called the Apostolic Age.)

Persecution under various Roman emperors only served to strengthen the emerging religion. In the early fourth century, the Emperor Constantine (ca. 272-337) made Christianity the official religion of the Roman Empire. He also convened the Council of Nicea in 325 CE to quell the religious controversies threatening the Pax Romana (Roman Peace), a time of stability and peace throughout the empire in the first and second centuries.

In 1054 the Great Schism, which involved differences over theology and practice, split the church into Eastern Orthodox and Roman Catholic branches. As Islam grew stronger, the Roman Catholic nations of Europe entered a period of Crusades—there were six Crusades in approximately 175 years, from 1095-1271—that attempted to take the Holy Land out of Muslim control.

A number of theologians became unhappy with the excesses of the Roman church and papal authority during the fifteenth and sixteenth centuries. The Protestant Reformation, originally an attempt to purify the church, was led by several men, most notably Martin Luther (1483-1546), whose ninety-five theses against the Catholic Church sparked the Reformation movement. Other leaders of the Protestant Reformation include John Knox (ca. 1510-1572), attributed as the founder of the Presbyterian denomination, John Calvin (1509-1564), a principle early developer of Calvinism, and Ulrich Zwingli (1484-1531), who initially spurred the Reformation in Switzerland. This period of turmoil resulted in the founding of a number of church denominations: Lutherans, Presbyterians, and Anglicans. These groups were later joined by the Methodists and the Religious Society of Friends (Quakers).

During the sixteenth and seventeenth centuries, the Roman Catholic Church attempted to stem this wave of protest and schism with the Counter-Reformation. Concurrently, the Inquisition, an effort to root out heresy and control the rebellion, took place. There were various inquisitions, including the Spanish Inquisition, which was led by Ferdinand II of Aragon and Isabella I of Castile in mid-fifteenth century and sought to "guard" the orthodoxy of Catholicism in Spain. There was also the Portuguese Inquisition, which began in 1536 in Portugal under King John III, and the Roman Inquisition, which took place in the late fifteenth century in Rome under the Holy See.

During the modern age, some groups became concerned with the perceived conflicts between history (revealed through recent archaeological findings) and the sciences (as described by Charles Darwin and Sigmund Freud) and the literal interpretation of some biblical texts. Fundamentalist Christianity began at an 1895 meeting in Niagara Falls, New York, with an attempt to define the basics (fundamentals) of Christianity. These were given as the inerrant nature of the Bible, the divine nature of Jesus, his literal virgin birth, his substitutionary death and literal physical resurrection, and his soon return. Liberal Christians, on the other hand, focused more on what became known as the Social Gospel, an attempt to relieve human misery.

Controversies in the twenty-first century throughout Christendom focused on issues such as abortion, homosexuality, the ordination of women and gays, and the authority of the scriptures. An additional feature is the growth of Christianity in the Southern Hemisphere. In Africa, for example, the number of Christians grew from 10 million in 1900 to over 506 million a century later. Initially the result of empire-building and colonialism, the conversions in these nations have resulted in a unique blend of native religions and Christianity. Latin America has won renown for its liberation theology, which was first articulated in 1968 as God's call for justice and God's preference for the poor, demonstrated in the ministry and teachings of Jesus Christ. Africa, Asia, and South America are regions that are considered more morally and theologically conservative. Some suggest that by 2050, non-Latino white persons will comprise only 20 percent of Christians.

Founder or Major Prophet

Jesus of Nazareth was born into a peasant family. The date of his birth, determined by accounts in the Gospels of Matthew and Luke, could be as early as 4 or 5 BCE or as late as 6 CE. Mary, his mother, was regarded as a virgin; thus, Jesus' birth was a miracle, engendered by the Holy Spirit. His earthly father, Joseph, was a carpenter.

At about age thirty, Jesus began an itinerant ministry of preaching and healing following his baptism in the Jordan River by his cousin, John the Baptist. He selected twelve followers, known as apostles (sent-ones), and a larger circle of disciples (followers). Within a short time, Jesus' ministry and popularity attracted the negative attention of both the Jewish and Roman rulers. He offended the Jewish leaders with his emphasis on personal relationship with God rather than obedience to rules, as well as his claim to be coequal with God the Father.

For a period of one to three years (Gospel accounts vary in the chronology), Jesus taught and worked miracles, as recorded in the first four books of the New Testament, the Gospels of Matthew, Mark, Luke, and John. On what has become known as Palm Sunday, he rode triumphantly into Jerusalem on the back of a donkey while crowds threw palm branches at his feet. Knowing that his end was near, at a final meal with his disciples, known now to Christians as the Last Supper, Jesus gave final instructions to his followers.

He was subsequently captured, having been betrayed by Judas Iscariot, one of his own twelve apostles. A trial before the Jewish legislative body, the Sanhedrin, led to his being condemned for blasphemy. However, under Roman law, the Jews did not have the power to put anyone to death. A later trial under the Roman governor, Pontius Pilate, resulted in Jesus being crucified, although Pilate tried to prevent this action, declaring Jesus innocent.

According to Christian doctrine, following the crucifixion, Jesus rose from the dead three days later. He appeared before many over a span of forty days and instructed the remaining eleven apostles to continue spreading his teachings. He then ascended into heaven. Ultimately, his followers believed that he was the Messiah, the savior who was to come to the Jewish people and deliver them. Rather than offering political salvation, however, Jesus offered spiritual liberty.

Philosophical Basis

Jesus was a Jew who observed the rituals and festivals of his religion. The Gospels reveal that he attended synagogue worship and went to Jerusalem for celebrations such as Passover. His teachings both grew out of and challenged the religion of his birth.

The Jews of Jesus' time, ruled by the Roman Empire, hoped for a return to political power. This power would be concentrated in a Messiah, whose coming had been prophesied centuries before. There were frequent insurrections in Judea, led in Jesus' time by a group called the Zealots. Indeed, it is believed that one of the twelve apostles was part of this movement. Jesus, with his message of a kingdom of heaven, was viewed as perhaps the one who would usher in a return to political ascendancy.

When challenged to name the greatest commandment, Jesus answered that it was to love God with all the heart, soul, mind, and strength. He added that the second was to love one's neighbor as one's self, saying that these two commands summarized all the laws that the Jewish religion outlined.

Jewish society was concerned with ritual purity and with following the law. Jesus repeatedly flouted those laws by eating with prostitutes and tax collectors, by touching those deemed unclean, such as lepers, and by including

Gentiles in his mission. Women were part of his ministry, with some of them providing for him and his disciples from their own purses, others offering him a home and a meal, and still others among those listening to him teach.

Jesus's most famous sermon is called the Sermon on the Mount. In it, he offers blessings on those on the outskirts of power, such as the poor, the meek, and those who hunger and thirst for righteousness. While not abolishing the law that the Jews followed, he pointed out its inadequacies and the folly of parading one's faith publicly. Embedded in the sermon is what has become known as the Lord's Prayer, the repetition of which is often part of regular Sunday worship. Much of Jesus' teaching was offered in the form of parables, or short stories involving vignettes of everyday life: a woman adding yeast to dough or a farmer planting seeds. Many of these parables were attempts to explain the kingdom of heaven, a quality of life that was both present and to come.

Holy Places

The Christian church has many pilgrimage sites, some of them dating back to the Middle Ages. Saint James is thought to have been buried in Compostela, Spain, which was a destination for those who could not make the trip to the Holy Land. Lourdes, France, is one of the spots associated with healing miracles. Celtic Christians revere places such as the small Scottish isle of Iona, an early Christian mission. Assisi, Italy, is a destination for those who are attracted to Saint Francis (1181-1226), founder of the Franciscans. The Chartres Cathedral in France is another pilgrimage destination from the medieval period.

Jerusalem, Rome, and Canterbury are considered holy for their associations with the early church and Catholicism, as well as with Anglicanism. Within the Old City of Jerusalem is the Church of the Holy Sepulchre, an important pilgrimage site believed to house the burial place of Jesus. Another important pilgrimage site is the Church of the Nativity in Bethlehem. It is built on a cave believed to be the birthplace of

Jesus, and is one of the oldest operating churches in existence.

CHRISTIANITY IN DEPTH

Sacred Symbols

The central symbol of Christianity is the cross, of which there are many variant designs. Some of them, such as Celtic crosses, are related to regions of the world. Others, such as the Crusader's cross, honor historic events. The dove is the symbol for the Holy Spirit, which descended in that shape on the gathered disciples at Pentecost after Jesus's ascension.

Various symbols represent Jesus. Candles allude to his reference to himself as the Light of the World, while the lamb stands for his being the perfect sacrifice, the Lamb of God. The fish symbol that is associated with Christianity has a number of meanings, both historic and symbolic. A fish shape stands for the Greek letters beginning the words Jesus Christ, Son of God, Savior; these letters form the word *ichthus*, the Greek word for "fish." Fish also featured prominently in the scriptures, and the early apostles were known as "fishers of man." The crucifixion symbol is also a popular Catholic Christian symbol.

All of these symbols may be expressed in stained glass. Used in medieval times, stained glass often depicted stories from the Bible as an aid to those who were illiterate.

Sacred Practices & Gestures

Roman Catholics honor seven sacraments, defined as outward signs of inward grace. These include the Eucharist, baptism, confirmation, marriage, ordination of priests, anointing the sick or dying with oil, and penance. The Eastern Orthodox Church refers to these seven as mysteries rather than sacraments.

Priests in the Roman Catholic Church must remain unmarried. In the Eastern Orthodox, Anglican, and Protestant denominations, they may marry. Both Roman Catholic and Eastern Orthodox refuse to ordain women to the priesthood.

The Orthodox Church practices a rite known as chrismation, anointing a child with oil following its baptism. The "oil of gladness," as it is known, is placed on the infant's head, eyes, ears, and mouth. This is similar to the practice of confirmation in some other denominations. Many Christian denominations practice anointing the sick or dying with oil, as well as using the oil to seal those who have been baptized.

Many Christians, especially Roman Catholics, use a rosary, or prayer beads, when praying. Orthodox believers may have icons, such as small paintings of God, saints or biblical events, as part of their worship. There may be a font of water that has been blessed as one enters some churches, which the worshippers use to make the sign of the cross, touching fingers to their forehead, heart, right chest, and left chest. Some Christians make the sign of the cross on the forehead, mouth, and heart to signify their desire for God to be in their minds, on their lips, and in their hearts.

Christians may genuflect, or kneel, as they enter or leave a pew in church. In some churches, particularly the Catholic and Orthodox, incense is burned during the service as a sweet smell to God.

In some traditions, praying to or for the dead is encouraged. The rationale for this is known as the communion of saints—the recognition that those who are gone are still a part of the community of faith.

Catholic, Orthodox, and some branches of other churches have monastic orders for both men and women. Monks and nuns may live in a cloister or be engaged in work in the wider world. They generally commit to a rule of life and to the work of prayer. Even those Christians who are not part of religious orders sometimes go on retreats, seeking quiet and perhaps some spiritual guidance from those associated with the monastery or convent.

Food Restrictions

Historically, Christians fasted during Lent as preparation for the Easter celebration. Prior to the Second Vatican Council in 1962,

Roman Catholics did not eat meat on Fridays. Conservative Christians in the Evangelical tradition tend to eliminate the use of alcohol, tobacco, and drugs.

Rites, Celebrations & Services

For churches in the liturgical tradition, the weekly celebration of the Eucharist is paramount. While many churches celebrate this ritual feast with wine and a wafer, many Protestant churches prefer to use grape juice and crackers or bread.

Church services vary widely. Quakers sit silently waiting for a word from God, while in many African American churches, hymns are sung for perhaps an hour before the lengthy sermon is delivered. Some churches have a prescribed order of worship that varies little from week to week. Most services, however, include prayer, a sermon, and singing, with or without musical accompaniment.

A church's architecture often gives clues as to the type of worship one will experience. A church with the pulpit in the center at the front generally is a Protestant church with an emphasis on the Word of God being preached. If the center of the front area is an altar, the worship's focus will be on the Eucharist.

Christmas and Easter are the two major Christian celebrations. In liturgical churches, Christmas is preceded by Advent, a time of preparation and quiet to ready the heart for the coming of Christ. Christmas has twelve days, from the birth date of December 25 to the Epiphany on January 6. Epiphany (to show) is the celebration of the arrival of the Magi (wise men) from the East who came to worship the young Jesus after having seen his star. Their arrival is believed to have been foretold by the Old Testament prophet Isaiah, who said "And the Gentiles shall come to thy light, and kings to the brightness of thy rising" (Isaiah 60:3). Epiphany is the revealing of the Messiah to the Gentiles.

In the early church, Easter was preceded by a solemn period of fasting and examination, especially for candidates for baptism and penitent sinners wishing to be reconciled. In Western churches, Lent begins with Ash Wednesday, which is six and half weeks prior to Easter. By excluding Sundays from the fast, Lent thus gives a forty-day fast, imitating that of Jesus in the wilderness. Historically forbidden foods during the fast included eggs, butter, meat, and fish. In the Eastern Church, dairy products, oil, and wine are also forbidden.

The week before Easter is known as Holy Week. It may include extra services such as Maundy Thursday, a time to remember Jesus's new commandment (*maundy* is etymologically related to *mandate*) to love one another. In some Catholic areas, the crucifixion is reenacted in a Passion play (depicting the passion—trial, suffering, and death—of Christ). Some churches will have an Easter vigil the Saturday night before or a sunrise service on Easter morning.

Judy A. Johnson, MTS

Bibliography

Bakker, Janel Kragt. "The Sister Church Phenomenon: A Case Study of the Restructuring of American Christianity against the Backdrop of Globalization." *International Bulletin of Missionary Research* 36.3 (2012): 129–34. Print.

Bandak, Andreas and Jonas Adelin Jørgensen. "Foregrounds and Backgrounds—Ventures in the Anthropology of Christianity." *Ethos: Journal of Anthropology* 77.4 (2012): 447–58. Print.

Barnes, Trevor. *The Kingfisher Book of Religions*. New York: Kingfisher, 1999. Print.

Chandler, Daniel Ross. "Christianity in Cross-Cultural Perspective: A Review of Recent Literature." *Asia Journal of Theology* 26.2 (2012): 44–57. Print.

Daughrity, Dyron B. "Christianity Is Moving from North to South—So What about the East?" *International Bulletin of Missionary Research* 35.1 (2011): 18–22. Print.

Kaatz, Kevin. *Voices of Early Christianity: Documents from the Origins of Christianity*. Santa Barbara: Greenwood, 2013. E-book.

Langley, Myrtle. *Religion*. New York: Alfred A. Knopf, 1996.

Lewis, Clive Staples. *Mere Christianity*. New York: Harper, 2001. Print.

McGrath, Alistair. *Christianity: An Introduction*. Hoboken, New Jersey: Wiley, 2006. Print.

Meredith, Susan. *The Usborne Book of World Religions*. London: Usborne, 1995. Print.

Ripley, Jennifer S. "Integration of Psychology and Christianity: 2022." *Journal of Psychology & Theology* 40.2 (2012): 150–54. Print.

Stefon, Matt. *Christianity: History, Belief, and Practice*. New York: Britannica Educational, 2012. E-book.

Wilkinson, Philip. *Christianity*. New York: DK, 2003. Print.

Wilkinson, Philip. *Religions*. New York: DK, 2008. Print.

Zoba, Wendy Murray. *The Beliefnet Guide to Evangelical Christianity*. New York: Three Leaves, 2005. Print.

East Asian Religions

General Description

East Asian religious and philosophical traditions include, among others, Confucianism, Taoism, and Shintoism. Confucianism is a philosophy introduced by the Chinese philosopher Confucius (Kongzi; 551–479 BCE) in the sixth century BCE, during the Zhou dynasty. Taoism, which centers on Tao, or "the way," is a religious and philosophical tradition that originated in China about two thousand years ago. Shinto, "the way of the spirits," is a Japanese tradition of devotion to spirits and rituals.

Number of Adherents Worldwide

Between 5 and 6 million people, the majority of them in China, practice Confucianism, once the state religion of China. About 20 million people identify as Taoists. Most of the Taoist practitioners are in China as well. In Japan, approximately 107 million people practice Shintoism, though many practitioners also practice Buddhism. Sects of Shinto include Tenrikyo (heavenly truth), founded in 1838, with nearly 2 million devotees. Shukyo Mahikari (divine light) is another, smaller sect founded in the 1960s. Like other sects, it is a blend of different religious traditions (Wilkinson 332–34).

Basic Tenets

Confucianism is a philosophy of life and does concerns itself not with theology but with life conduct. Chief among the aspects of life that must be tended are five key relationships, with particular focus on honoring ancestors and showing filial piety. Confucianism does not take a stand on the existence of God, though the founder, Confucius, referred to "heaven." Except for this reference, Confucianism does not address the question of life after death.

Taoists believe that Tao (the way or the flow) is in everything. Taoism teaches that qi, or life energy, needs to be balanced between yin and yang, which are the female and male principles

of life, respectively. With its doctrine of the evil of violence, Taoism borders on pacifism, and it also preaches simplicity and naturalness. Taoists believe in five elements—wood, earth, air, fire and water—that need to be in harmony. The five elements lie at the heart of Chinese medicine, particularly acupuncture. In Taoism, it is believed that the soul returns to a state of nonbeing after death.

Shinto emphasizes nature and harmony, with a focus on lived experience rather than doctrine. Shinto, which means "the way of the gods," is a polytheistic religion; Amaterasu, the sun goddess, is the chief god. At one point in Japan's history, the emperor was believed to be a descendant of Amaterasu and therefore divine. In Tenrikyo Shinto, God is manifested most often as Oyakami, meaning "God the parent."

Shinto teaches that some souls can become kami, a spirit, following death. Each traditional home has a god-shelf, which honors family members believed to have become kami. An older family member tends to the god-shelf, placing a bit of food and some sake (rice wine) on the shelf. To do their work, kami must be nourished. The Tenrikyo sect includes concepts from Pure Land Buddhism, such as an afterlife and the idea of salvation.

Sacred Texts

Five classic texts are sacred to the Confucians. These include the I Ching, or Book of Changes; the Book of Odes; the Book of History; the Book of Rites; and the Annals of Spring and Autumn. The Analects, a collection of Confucius's sayings, is another revered classic. The Tao Te Ching (The Way of Power) is the most sacred book of the Taoists. Those who practice Shinto hold sacred two works: the Kojiki (Record of Ancient Matters) and the Nihon-gi (Chronicles of Japan). Both texts, which contain legends and creation myths, were written during the eighth century.

Major Figures

Confucius, who lived during the sixth century, was the first great philosopher of China. Mengzi (Meng-tzu; 371–289 BCE), known in the West as Mencius, developed Confucius's teachings about the higher power guiding human life. Another ancient Chinese philosopher, Laozi(or Lao-tzu), is the founder of Taoism. He is believed to have been a contemporary of Confucius's in the central region of China. Modern scholars are not certain he ever existed, though one account includes the story of Confucius visiting Laozi. Chuang Tzu wrote of Laozi and his ideas during the fourth and third centuries BCE. Shinto's major figures include Ō no Yasumaro (d. 723), the compiler of the Kokiji who acted under the orders of Empress Gemmei and consulted a bard known to have an infallible memory; the scholar Motoori Norinaga (1730–1800), whose work led to a revived interest in ancient Shinto texts; and Nakayama Miki (1798–1887), the farmer's wife who founded Tenrikyo.

Major Holy Sites

Most Confucian sacred places are located within private homes, where an ancestral shrine and an altar to gods and spirits are maintained. In China's Shandong Province is Qufu, the site of Confucius's family mansion, temple, and cemetery. The temple was built in 478 BCE, only a year after Confucius's death, and has been maintained and enlarged. In addition to its status as a holy site, the United Nations Educational, Scientific, and Cultural Organization (UNESCO) has placed it on their World Heritage List.

Taoists regard mountains as a way to communicate with Earth's primeval powers and with those who are immortal. Five of the nine sacred mountains in China are associated with Taoism: Hengshan in both the north and the south, Songshan in the south, Taishan in the east, and Huashan in the west. The holiest of the five is Taishan, which symbolizes stability, prevents natural disasters, and ensures fertility.

Shintoism has a high regard for natural beauty. As such, Shinto shrines are everywhere, particularly in mountains or near waterfalls.

Mountains in particular are regarded as homes of the gods. Mount Fuji is the holiest Shinto mountain, and climbing it to reach the shrine on its peak is an act of worship. More than forty thousand shrines are dedicated to Inari, the rice god.

Shinto was formalized during the Yamato period (the name for ancient Japan), and because the emperor of the imperial dynasty was from the Yamato area and was considered divine, the whole region is revered. At Ise, located near the coast in Mie Prefecture, southeast of Nara, the shrine has been rebuilt every twenty years for at least fourteen centuries. This rebuilding ensures that Toyouke-Ōmikami (the harvest goddess) and Amaterasu (the sun goddess) are renewed in vigor, which in turn invigorates both the rice crop and the imperial line. Those who have died in war are revered as kami in Japan. In Tokyo, a shrine called Yasukuni is dedicated to them. However, there is controversy surrounding the place because of its association with Japan's extreme nationalism prior to World War II.

Sacred Texts

Five classic texts are sacred to the Confucians. These include the I Ching, or Book of Changes; the Book of Odes; the Book of History; the Book of Rites; and the Annals of Spring and Autumn. The Analects, a collection of Confucius's sayings, is another revered classic. The Tao te Ching (The Way of Power) is the most sacred book of the Taoists. Those who practice Shinto hold sacred two works: the Kojiki (Record of Ancient Matters) and the Nihon-gi (Chronicles of Japan). Both texts, which contain legends and creation myths, were written during the eighth century.

Major Figures

Confucius, who lived during the sixth century, was the first great philosopher of China. Mengzi (Meng-tzu; 371–289 BCE), known in the West as Mencius, developed Confucius's teachings about the higher power guiding human life. Another ancient Chinese philosopher, Laozi,(or Lao-tzu) is the founder of Taoism. He is believed to have been a contemporary of Confucius in the central region of China. Modern scholars are not certain he ever existed, though one account includes the story of Confucius visiting Laozi. Chuang Tzu wrote of Laozi and his ideas during the fourth and third centuries BCE. Shinto's major figures include Ō no Yasumaro, the compiler of the Kokiji who acted under the orders of Empress Gemmei and consulted a bard known to have an infallible memory; the scholar Motoori Norinaga (1730–1800), whose work led to a revived interest in ancient Shinto texts; and Nakayama Miki (1798–1887), the farmer's wife who founded Tenrikyo.

Major Holy Sites

Most Confucian sacred places are located within private homes, where an ancestral shrine and an altar to gods and spirits are maintained. In China's Shandong Province is Qufu, the site of Confucius's family mansion, temple and cemetery. The temple was built in 478 BCE, only a year after Confucius's death, and has been maintained and enlarged. In addition to being a holy site, the United Nations Educational, Scientific, and Cultural Organization (UNESCO) has placed it on their World Heritage List.

Taoists consider mountains as a way to communicate with Earth's primeval powers and with those who are immortal. Five of the nine sacred mountains in China are associated with Taoism. They are Hengshan in both the north and south, Songshan in the south, Taishan in the east, and Huashan in the west. The holiest of the five is Taishan, which symbolizes stability, prevents natural disasters, and ensures fertility.

Shintoism has a high regard for natural beauty. As such, Shinto shrines are everywhere, particularly in mountains or near waterfalls. Mountains in particular are regarded as homes of the gods. Mount Fuji is the holiest Shinto mountain, and climbing it to reach the shrine on its peak is an act of worship. More than forty thousand shrines are dedicated to Inari, the rice god.

Shinto was formalized during the Yamato period (the name for ancient Japan), and because the emperor of the imperial dynasty is from the Yamato area, and was considered divine, the whole region is revered. At Ise, located near

the coast in the Mie prefecture southeast of Nara, the shrine has been rebuilt every twenty years for at least fourteen centuries. This rebuilding ensures that Toyouke-Ōmikami (the harvest goddess) and Amaterasu (the sun goddess) are renewed in vigor, which in turn invigorates both the rice crop and the imperial line. Those who have died in war are revered as kami in Japan. In Tokyo, a shrine called Yasukuni is dedicated to them. However, there is controversy surrounding the place because of its association with Japan's extreme nationalism prior to World War II.

Major Rites & Celebrations

Confucian celebrations have to do with honoring people rather than gods. At Confucian temples, the philosopher's birthday is celebrated each September. In Taiwan, this day is called "Teacher's Day." Sacrifices, music and dance are part of the event.

Taoism has a jiao (offering) festival near the winter solstice. It celebrates the renewal of the yang force at this turning of the year. During the festival priests, who have been ritually purified, wear lavish clothing. The festival includes music and dancing, along with large effigies of the gods which are designed to frighten away the evil spirits. Yang's renewal is also the focus of New Year celebrations, which is a time for settling debts and cleaning house. Decorations in the yang warm colors of gold, orange and red abound.

Many of the Shinto festivals overlap with Buddhist ones. There are many local festivals and rituals, and each community has an annual festival at the shrine dedicated to the kami of the region. Japanese New Year, which is celebrated for three days, is a major feast. Since the sixteenth century, the Gion Festival has taken place in Kyoto, Japan. Decorated floats are part of the celebration of the shrine.

ORIGINS

History & Geography

During the Zhou dynasty (1050–256 BCE) in China, the idea of heaven as a force that controlled events came to the fore. Zhou rulers believed that they ruled as a result of the "Mandate of Heaven," viewing themselves as morally superior to those of the previous dynasty, the Shang dynasty (1600-1046 BCE). They linked virtue and power as the root of the state.

By the sixth century the Zhou rulers had lost much of their authority. Many schools of thought developed to restore harmony, and were collectively known as the "Hundred Schools." Confucius set forth his ideas within this historical context. He traveled China for thirteen years, urging rulers to put his ideas into practice and failing to achieve his goals. He returned home to teach for the rest of his life and his ideas were not adopted until the Han dynasty (206 BCE–220 CE). During the Han period, a university for the nation was established, as well as the bureaucratic civil service that continued until the twentieth century. When the Chinese Empire fell in 1911, the Confucian way became less important.

Confucianism had influenced not only early Chinese culture, but also the cultures of Japan, Korea, and Vietnam. The latter two nations also adopted the bureaucratic system. In Japan, Confucianism reached its height during the Tokugawa age (1600–1868 CE). Confucian scholars continue to interpret the philosophy for the modern period. Some regard the ideas of Confucius as key to the recent economic booms in the so-called "tiger" economies of East Asia (Hong Kong, Singapore, South Korea, Taiwan, and Thailand). Confucianism continues to be a major influence on East Asian nations and culture.

Taoism's power (te) manifests itself as a philosophy, a way of life, and a religion. Philosophically, Taoism is a sort of self-help regimen, concerned with expending power efficiently by avoiding conflicts and friction, rather than fighting against the flow of life. In China, it is known as School Taoism. As a way of life, Taoism is concerned with increasing the amount of qi available through what is eaten and through meditation, yoga, and tai chi (an ancient Chinese martial art form). Acupuncture and the use of medicinal herbs are outgrowths of this way of life. Church Taoism, influenced by Buddhism and Tao Chiao (religious Taoism), developed during the second century. This church looked for ways to use power for societal and individual benefit.

By the time of the Han dynasty (206–220 CE), Laozi had been elevated to the status of divine. Taoism found favor at court during the Tang dynasty (618–917 CE), during which the state underwrote temples. By adapting and encouraging people to study the writings of all three major faiths in China, Taoism remained relevant into the early twentieth century. During the 1960s and 1970s, Taoist books were burned and their temples were destroyed in the name of the Cultural Revolution (the Great Proletarian Cultural Revolution). Taoism remains popular and vital in Taiwan.

Shinto is an ancient religion, and some of its characteristics appeared during the Yayoi culture (ca. 300 BCE–300 CE). The focus was on local geographic features and the ancestry of local clan leaders. At first, women were permitted to be priests, but that equality was lost due to the influence of Confucian paternalism. The religion declined, but was revived in 1871 following the Meiji Restoration of the emperor. Shoguns (warlords) had ruled Japan for more than 250 years, and Shinto was the state religion until 1945. It was associated with the emperor cult and contributed to Japan's militarism. After the nation's defeat in World War II, the 1947 constitution forbade government involvement in any religion. In contemporary Shinto, women are permitted to become priests and girls, in some places, are allowed to carry the portable shrines during festivals.

Founder or Major Prophet

Confucius, or Kongzi ("Master Kong"), was a teacher whose early life may have included service in the government. He began traveling throughout the country around age fifty, attempting and failing to interest rulers in his ideas for creating a harmonious state. He returned to his home state after thirteen years, teaching a group of disciples who spread his ideas posthumously.

According to legend, Taoism's founder, Laozi, lived during the sixth century. Laozi may be translated as "Grand Old Master," and may be simply a term of endearment. He maintained the archives and lived simply in a western state of China. Weary of people who were uninterested in natural goodness and perhaps wanting greater solitude in his advanced years, he determined to leave China, heading for Tibet on a water buffalo. At the border, a gatekeeper wanted to persuade him to stay, but could not do so. He asked Laozi to leave behind his teachings. For three days Laozi transcribed his teachings, producing the five-thousand-word Tao Te Ching. He then rode off and was never heard of again. Unlike most founders of religions, he neither preached nor promoted his beliefs. Still, he was held with such regard that some emperors claimed descent from him.

No one is certain of the origin of Shinto, which did not have a founder or major prophet. Shinto—derived from two Chinese words, *shen* (spirit) and *dao* (way)—has been influenced by other religions, notably Confucianism and Buddhism.

Philosophical Basis

Confucianism sought to bring harmony to the state and society as a whole. This harmony was to be rooted in the Five Constant Relationships: between parents and children; husbands and wives; older and younger siblings; older and younger friends; and rulers and subjects. Each of these societal relationships existed to demonstrate mutual respect, service, honor, and love, resulting in a healthy society. The fact that three of the five relationships exist within the family highlights the importance of honoring family. Ritual maintains the li, or rightness, of everything, and is a way to guarantee that a person performed the correct action in any situation in life.

Taoism teaches that two basic components—yin and yang—are in all things, including health, the state, and relationships. Yin is the feminine principle, associated with soft, cold, dark, and moist things. Yang is the masculine principle,

and is associated with hard, warm, light, and dry things. By keeping these two aspects of life balanced, harmony will be achieved. Another concept is that of wu-wei, action that is in harmony with nature, while qi is the life force in all beings. The Tao is always in harmony with the universe. Conflict is to be avoided, and soldiers are to go as if attending a funeral, solemnly and with compassion. Taoism also teaches the virtues of humility and selflessness.

Shinto is rooted in reverence for ancestors and for the spirits known as kami, which may be good or evil. By correctly worshipping the kami, Shintoists believe that they are assisting in purifying the world and aiding in its functioning.

Holy Places

Confucianism does not always distinguish between sacred and profane space. So much of nature is considered a holy place, as is each home's private shrine. In addition, some Confucian temples have decayed while others have been restored. Temples do not have statues or images. Instead, the names of Confucius and his noted followers are written on tablets. Like the emperor's palace, temples have the most important halls placed on the north-south axis of the building. Temples are also internally symmetrical, as might be expected of a system that honors order. In Beijing, the Temple of Heaven, just south of the emperor's palace, was one of the holiest places in imperial China.

Taoism's holy places are often in nature, particularly mountains. The holiest of the five sacred mountains in China is Taishan, located in the east. Taoism also reveres grottoes, which are caves thought to be illuminated by the light of heaven.

In the Shinto religion, nature is often the focus of holy sites. Mount Fuji is the most sacred mountain. Near Kyoto the largest shrine of Inari, the rice god, is located. The Grand Shrines at Ise are dedicated to two divinities, and for more than one thousand years, pilgrims have come to it. The Inner Shrine (Naiku) is dedicated to Amaterasu, the sun goddess, and is Shinto's most holy location. The Outer Shrine (Geku) is dedicated to

Toyouke, the goddess of the harvest. Every twenty years, Ise is torn down and rebuilt, thus renewing the gods. Shinto shrines all have torii, the sacred gateway. The most famous of these is built in the sea near the island of Miyajima. Those going to the shrine on this island go by boat through the torii.

EAST ASIAN RELIGIONS IN DEPTH

Sacred Symbols

Water is regarded as the source of life in Confucianism. The water symbol has thus become an unofficial symbol of Confucianism, represented by the Japanese ideogram or character for water, the Mizu, which somewhat resembles a stick figure with an extra leg. Other sacred symbols include the ancestor tablets in shrines of private homes, which are symbolic of the presence of the ancestor to whom offerings are made in hopes of aid.

While not a sacred symbol as the term is generally used, the black and white symbol of yin and yang is a common Taoist emblem. Peaches are also of a symbolic nature in Taoism, and often appear in Asian art. They are based on the four peaches that grew every three thousand years and which the mother of the fairies gave to the Han emperor Wu Ti (140–87 BCE). They are often symbolic of the Immortals.

The Shinto stylized sun, which appears on the Japanese flag, is associated with Amaterasu, the sun goddess. The torii, the gateway forming an entrance to sacred space, is another symbol associated with Shinto.

Sacred Practices & Gestures

Confucian rulers traditionally offered sacrifices honoring Confucius at the spring and autumnal equinoxes. Most of the Confucian practices take place at home shrines honoring the ancestors.

Taoists believe that one can reach Tao (the way) through physical movements, chanting, or meditation. Because mountains, caves, and springs are often regarded as sacred sites, pilgrimages are important to Taoists. At a Taoist

funeral, a paper fairy crane is part of the procession. After the funeral, the crane, which symbolizes a heavenly messenger, is burned. The soul of the deceased person is then thought to ride to heaven on the back of the crane.

Many Shinto shrines exist throughout Japan. Most of them have a sacred arch, known as a torii. At the shrine's entrance, worshippers rinse their mouths and wash their hands to be purified before entering the prayer hall. Before praying, a worshipper will clap twice and ring a bell to let the kami know they are there. Only priests may enter the inner hall, which is where the kami live. During a festival, however, the image of the kami is placed in a portable shrine and carried in a procession through town, so that all may receive a blessing.

Rites, Celebrations & Services

Early Confucianism had no priests, and bureaucrats performed any rituals that were necessary. When the Chinese Empire fell in 1911, imperial ceremonies ended as well. Rituals have become less important in modern times. In contemporary times the most important rite is marriage, the beginning of a new family for creating harmony. There is a correct protocol for each aspect of marriage, from the proposal and engagement to exchanging vows. During the ceremony, the groom takes the bride to his family's ancestor tablets to "introduce" her to them and receive a blessing. The couple bows to the ancestors during the ceremony.

After a death occurs, mourners wear coarse material and bring gifts of incense and money to help defray the costs. Added to the coffin holding are food offerings and significant possessions. A willow branch symbolizing the deceased's soul is carried with the coffin to the place of burial. After the burial, family members take the willow branch to their home altar and perform a ritual to add the deceased to the souls at the family's shrine.

Confucians and Taoists celebrate many of the same Chinese festivals, some of which originated before either Confucianism or Taoism began and reflect aspects of both traditions. While some festivals are not necessarily Taoist, they may be led by Taoist priests. During the Lantern Festival, which occurs on the first full moon of the New Year, offerings are made to the gods. Many of the festivals are tied to calendar events. Qingming (Clear and Bright) celebrates the coming of spring and is a time to remember the dead. During this time, families often go to the family gravesite for a picnic. The Double Fifth is the midsummer festival that occurs on the fifth day of the fifth month, and coincides with the peak of yang power. To protect themselves from too much of the male force, people don garments of the five colors—black, blue, red, white, and yellow—and with the five "poisons"—centipede, lizard, scorpion, snake, and toad—in the pattern of their clothes and on amulets. The gates of hell open at the Feast of the Hungry Ghosts. Priests have ceremonies that encourage the escaped evil spirits to repent or return to hell.

Marriage is an important rite in China, and thus in Taoism as well. Astrologers look at horoscopes to ensure that the bride and groom are well matched and to find the best day for the ceremony. The groom's family is always placed at the east (yang) and the bride's family to the west (yin) to bring harmony. When a person dies, the mourners again sit in the correct locations, while the head of the deceased points south. White is the color of mourning and of yin. At the home of the deceased, white cloths cover the family altar. Mourners may ease the soul's journey with symbolic artifacts or money. They may also go after the funeral to underground chambers beneath the temples to offer a sacrifice on behalf of the dead.

In the Shinto religion, rites exist for many life events. For example, pregnant women ask at a shrine for their children to be born safely, and the mother or grandmother brings a child who is thirty-two or thirty-three-days-old to a shrine for the first visit and blessing. A special festival also exists for children aged three, five or seven, who go to the shrine for purifying. In addition, a bride and groom are purified before the wedding, usually conducted by Shinto priests. Shinto priests may also offer blessings for a new car or building. The New Year and the Spring Festival are among the most important festivals, and shrine virgins, known as miko girls, may dance to celebrate life's renewal. Other festivals include the Feast of the Puppets, Boys' Day, the Water Kami Festival, the Star Feast, the Festival of the Dead, and the autumnal equinox.

Judy A. Johnson, MTS

Bibliography

Barnes, Trevor. *The Kingfisher Book of Religions*. New York: Kingfisher, 1999. Print.

Bell, Daniel A. "Reconciling Socialism and Confucianism? Reviving Tradition in China." *Dissent* 57.1 (2010): 91–99. Print.

Chang, Chung-yuan. *Creativity and Taoism: A Study of Chinese Philosophy, Art and Poetry*. London: Kingsley, 2011. E-book.

Coogan, Michael D., ed. *Eastern Religions*. New York: Oxford UP, 2005. Print.

Eliade, Mircea, and Ioan P. Couliano. *The Eliade Guide to World Religions*. New York: Harper, 1991. Print.

Lao Tzu. *Tao Te Ching*. Trans. Stephen Mitchell. New York: Harper, 1999. Print.

Li, Yingzhang. *Lao-tzu's Treatise on the Response of the Tao*. Trans. Eva Wong. New Haven: Yale UP, 2011. Print.

Littlejohn, Ronnie. *Confucianism: An Introduction*. New York: Tauris, 2011. E-book.

Littleton, C. Scott. *Shinto*. Oxford: Oxford UP, 2002. Print.

Mcvay, Kera. *All about Shinto*. Delhi: University, 2012. Ebook.

Merton, Thomas. *The Way of Chuang Tzu*. New York: New Directions, 1965. Print.

Oldstone-Moore, Jennifer. *Confucianism*. Oxford: Oxford UP, 2002. Print.

Poceski, Mario. *Chinese Religions: The EBook*. Providence, UT: Journal of Buddhist Ethics Online Books, 2009. E-book.

Van Norden, Bryan W. *Introduction to Classical Chinese Philosophy*. Indianapolis: Hackett, 2011. Print.

Wilkinson, Philip. *Religions*. New York: DK, 2008. Print.

Hinduism

General Description

Hinduism; modern Hinduism is comprised of the devotional sects of Vaishnavism, Shaivism, and Shaktism (though Smartism is sometimes listed as the fourth division). Hinduism is often used as umbrella term, since many point to Hinduism as a family of different religions.

Number of Adherents Worldwide

Between 13.8 and 15 percent of the world's population, or about one billion people, are adherents of Hinduism, making it the world's third largest religion after Christianity and Islam. The predominant sect is the Vaishnavite sect (Wilkinson, p. 333).

Basic Tenets

Hinduism is a way of life rather than a body of beliefs. Hindus believe in karma, the cosmic law of cause and effect that determines one's state in the next life. Additional beliefs include dharma, one's religious duty.

Hinduism has no true belief in an afterlife. Rather, it teaches a belief in reincarnation, known as samsara, and in moksha, the end of the cycle of rebirths. Different sects have different paths to moksha.

Hinduism is considered a polytheist religion. However, it is also accurate to say that Hinduism professes a belief in one God or Supreme Truth that is beyond comprehension (an absolute reality, called Brahman) and which manifests itself in many forms and names. These include Brahma, the creator; Vishnu, the protector; and Shiva, the re-creator or destroyer. Many sects are defined by their belief in multiple gods, but also by their worship of one ultimate manifestation. For example, Shaivism and Vaishnavism are based upon the recognition of Shiva and Vishnu, respectively, as the manifestation. In comparison, Shaktism recognizes the Divine Mother (Shakti) as the Supreme Being, while followers of Smartism worship a particular deity of their own choosing.

Major Deities

The Hindu trinity (Trimurti) is comprised of Brahma, the impersonal and absolute creator; Vishnu, the great preserver; and Shiva, the destroyer and re-creator. The goddesses corresponding to each god are Sarasvati, Lakshimi, and Parvati. Thousands of other gods (devas) and goddesses (devis) are worshipped, including Ganesha, Surya, and Kali. Each is believed to represent another aspect of the Supreme Being.

Sacred Texts

Hindus revere ancient texts such as the four Vedas, the 108 Upanishads, and others. No single text has the binding authority of the Qur'an (Islam's holy book) or Bible. Hindu literature is also defined by Sruti (revealed truth), which is heard, and Smriti (realized truth), which is remembered. The former is canonical, while the latter can be changing. For example, the Vedas and the Upanishads constitute Sruti texts, while epics, history, and law books constitute the latter. The Bhagavad Gita (The Song of God) is also considered a sacred scripture of Hinduism, and consists of a philosophical dialogue.

Major Figures

Major figures include: Shankara (788–820 CE), who defined the unity of the soul (atman) and absolute reality (Brahman); Ramanuja (1077–1157 CE), who emphasized bhakti, or love of God; Madhva (1199–1278 CE), scholar and writer, a proponent of dualism; Ramprahsad Sen (1718–1775 CE), composer of Hindu songs of devotion, poet, and mystic who influenced goddess worship in the; Raja Rammohun Roy (1772–1833 CE), abolished the custom of suttee, in which widows were burned on the funeral pyres of their dead husbands, and decried polygamy, rigid caste systems, and dowries; Rabindranath Tagore (1861–1941 CE), first Asian to win the Nobel Prize in Literature; Dr. Babasaheb R. Ambedkar (1891–1956 CE), writer of India's constitution and leader of a mass conversion to Buddhism; Mohandas K. Gandhi (1869–1948 CE), the "great soul" who left a legacy of effective use of nonviolence.

Major Holy Sites

The major holy sites of Hinduism are located within India. They include the Ganges River, in whose waters pilgrims come to bathe away their sins, as well as thousands of tirthas (places of pilgrimage), many of which are associated with particular deities. For example, the Char Dham pilgrimage centers, of which there are four—Badrinath (north), Puri (east), Dwarka (west) and Rameshwaram (south)—are considered the holy abodes or sacred temples of Vishnu. There are also seven ancient holy cities in India, including Ayodhya, believed to be the birthplace of Rama; Varanasi (Benares), known as the City of Light; Dwarka; Ujjian; Kanchipuram; Mathura; and Hardwar.

Major Rites & Celebrations

Diwali, the Festival of Lights, is a five-day festival that is considered a national holiday in India. Holi, the Festival of Colors, is the spring festival. Krishna Janmashtmi is Krishna's birthday. Shivaratri is Shiva's main festival. Navaratri, also known as the Durga festival or Dasserah, celebrates one of the stories of the gods and the victory of good over evil. Ganesh Chaturthi is the elephant-headed god Ganesha's birthday. Rathayatra, celebrated at Puri, India, is a festival for Jagannath, another word for Vishnu.

ORIGINS

History & Geography

Hinduism, which many people consider to be the oldest world religion, is unique in that it has no recorded origin or founder. Generally, it developed in the Indus Valley civilization several thousand years before the Common Era. The faith blends the Vedic traditions of the Indus Valley civilization and the invading nomadic tribes of the Aryans (prehistoric Indo-Europeans). Most of what is known of the Indus Valley civilization comes from archaeological excavations at Mohenjo-Daro (Mound of the Dead) and Harappa. (Because Harappa was a chief city of the period, the Indus Valley civilization is also referred to as the Harappan civilization.) The Vedas, a collection of ancient hymns, provides information about the Aryan culture.

The ancient Persian word *hind* means Indian, and for centuries, to be Indian was to be Hindu. Even now, about 80 percent of India's people consider themselves Hindu. The root word alludes to flowing, as a river flows. It is also etymologically related to the Indus River. At first, the term Hindu was used as an ethnic or cultural term, and travelers from Persia and Greece in the sixteenth century referred to those in the Indus Valley by that name. British writers coined the term *Hinduism* during the early part of the nineteenth century to describe the culture of India. The Hindus themselves often use the term Sanatana Dharma, meaning eternal law.

The Rigveda, a collection of hymns to various gods and goddesses written around 1500 BCE, is the first literary source for understanding Hinduism's history. The Vedas were chanted aloud for centuries before being written down around 1400 CE. The Rigveda is one of four major collections of Vedas, or wisdom: Rigveda, Yajurveda, Samaveda, and Atharvaveda. Together these four are called Samhitas.

Additionally, Hinduism relies on three other Vedic works: the Aranyakas, the Brahamans, and the Upanishads. The Upanishads is a philosophical work, possibly written down between 800 and 450 BCE, that attempts to answer life's big questions. Written in the form of a dialogue between a teacher (guru) and student (chela), the text's name means "to sit near," which describes the relationship between the two. Along with the Samhitas, these four are called Sruti (heard), a reference to their nature as revealed truth. The words in these texts cannot be altered.

Remaining works are called Smriti, meaning "remembered," to indicate that they were composed by human writers. The longer of the Smriti epics is the Mahabharata, the Great Story of the Bharatas. Written between 300 and 100 BCE, the epic is a classic tale of two rival, related families, including teaching as well as story. It is considered the longest single poem in existence, with about 200,000 lines. (A film made of it lasts for twelve hours.)

The Bhagavad Gita, or Song of the Lord, is the sixth section of the Mahabharata, but is often read as a stand-alone narrative of battle and acceptance of one's dharma. The Ramayana is the second, shorter epic of the Mahabharata, with about fifty thousand lines. Rama was the seventh incarnation, or avatar, of Vishnu. The narrative relates the abduction of his wife, Sita, and her rescue, accomplished with the help of the monkey god, Hanuman. Some have regarded the Mahabharata as an encyclopedia, and the Bhagavad Gita as the Bible within it.

Although many of the practices in the Vedas have been modified or discontinued, sections of it are memorized and repeated. Some of the hymns are recited at traditional ceremonies for the dead and at weddings.

Hinduism has affected American life and culture for many years. For example, the nineteenth-century transcendental writers Margaret Fuller and Ralph Waldo Emerson were both influenced by Hindu and Buddhist literature, while musician George Harrison, a member of the Beatles, adopted Hinduism and explored his new faith through his music, both with and without the Beatles. In 1965, the International Society for Krishna Consciousness (ISKCON), or the Hare Krishna movement, came to the Western world. In addition, many people have been drawn to yoga, which is associated with Hinduism's meditative practices.

Founder or Major Prophet

Hinduism has no founder or major prophet. It is a religion that has developed over many centuries and from many sources, many of which are unknown in their origins.

Philosophical Basis

Hinduism recognizes multiple ways to achieve salvation and escape the endless cycle of rebirth. The way of devotion is the most popular.

Through worship of a single deity, the worshipper hopes to attain union with the divine. A second path is the way of knowledge, involving the use of meditation and reason. The third way is via action, or correctly performing religious observances in hope of receiving a blessing from the gods by accomplishing these duties.

Hinduism is considered the world's oldest religion, but Hindus maintain that it is also a way of living, not just a religion. There is great diversity as well as great tolerance in Hinduism. While Hinduism does not have a set of dogmatic formulations, it does blend the elements of devotion, doctrine, practice, society, and story as separate strands in a braid.

During the second century BCE, a sage named Patanjali outlined four life stages, and the fulfilled responsibilities inherent in each one placed one in harmony with dharma, or right conduct. Although these life stages are no longer observed strictly, their ideas still carry weight. Traditionally, these codes applied to men, and only to those in the Brahman caste; members of the warrior and merchant classes could follow them, but were not obligated. The Shudra and Dalit castes, along with women, were not part of the system. Historically, women were thought of as protected by fathers in their childhood, by husbands in their youth and adulthood, and by sons in old age. Only recently have women in India been educated beyond the skills of domestic responsibility and child rearing.

The earliest life stage is the student stage, or brahmacharya, a word that means "to conduct oneself in accord with Brahman." From ages twelve to twenty-four, young men were expected to undertake learning with a guru, or guide. During these twelve years of studying the Veda they were also expected to remain celibate.

The second stage, grihastha, is that of householder. A Hindu man married the bride that his parents had chosen, sired children, and created a livelihood on which the other three stages depended.

Vanaprastha is the third stage, involving retirement to solitude. Historically, this involved leaving the house and entering a forest dwelling.

A man's wife had the option to go with him or to remain. This stage also involved giving counsel to others and further study.

At the final stage of life, sannyasis, the Hindu renounces material goods, including a home of any sort. He may live in a forest or join an ashram, or community. He renounces even making a fire, and lives on fruit and roots that can be foraged. Many contemporary Hindus do not move to this stage, but remain at vanaprastha.

Yoga is another Hindu practice, more than three millennia old, which Patanjali codified. The four forms of yoga corresponded to the Hindu avenues of salvation. Hatha yoga is the posture yoga seeking union with god through action. Jnana yoga is the path to god through knowledge. Bhakti yoga is the way of love to god. Karma yoga is the method of finding god through work. By uniting the self, the practitioner unites with God. Yoga is related etymologically to the English word *yoke*—it attempts to yoke the individual with Brahman. All forms of yoga include meditation and the acceptance of other moral disciplines, such as self-discipline, truthfulness, nonviolence, and contentment.

Aryan society was stratified, and at the top of the social scale were the priests. This system was the basis for the caste system that had long dominated Hinduism. Caste, which was determined by birth, affected a person's occupation, diet, neighborhood, and marriage partner. Vedic hymns allude to four varnas, or occupations: Brahmins (priests), Kshatriyas (warriors), Vaishyas (merchants and common people), and Shudras (servants). A fifth class, the Untouchables, later known as Dalit (oppressed), referred to those who were regarded as a polluting force because they handled waste and dead bodies. The belief was that society would function properly if each group carried out its duties. These varnas later became wrongly blended with castes, or jatis, which were smaller groups also concerned with a person's place in society.

The practice of Hinduism concerns itself with ritual purity; even household chores can be done in a ritualistic way. Some traditions demand ritual purity before one can worship. Brahmin priests, for example, may not accept water or food from non-Brahmins. Refusal to do so is not viewed as classism, but an attempt to please the gods in maintaining ritual purity.

Mohandas Gandhi was one of those who refused to use the term *Untouchable*, using the term *harijan*(children of God), instead. Dr. Babasaheb R. Ambedkar, who wrote India's constitution, was a member of this class. Ambedkar and many of his supporters became Buddhists in an attempt to dispel the power of caste. In 1947, following India's independence from Britain, the caste system was officially banned, though it has continued to influence Indian society.

Ahimsa, or dynamic harmlessness, is another deeply rooted principle of Hinduism. It involves six pillars: refraining from eating all animal products; revering all of life; having integrity in thoughts, words, and deeds; exercising self-control; serving creation, nature, and humanity; and advancing truth and understanding.

Holy Places

In Hinduism, all water is considered holy, symbolizing the flow of life. For a Hindu, the Ganges River is perhaps the most holy of all bodies of water. It was named for the goddess of purification, Ganga. The waters of the Ganges are said to flow through Shiva's hair and have the ability to cleanse sin. Devout Hindus make pilgrimages to bathe in the Ganges. They may also visit fords in the rivers to symbolize the journey from one life to another.

Pilgrimages are also made to sites associated with the life of a god. For example, Lord Rama was said to have been born in Ayodhya, one of the seven holy cities in India. Other holy sites are Dwarka, Ujjian, Kanchipuram, Mathura, Hardwar, and Varanasi, the City of Light.

After leaving his mountain home, Lord Shiva was thought to have lived in Varanasi, or Benares, considered the holiest city. Before the sixth century, it became a center of education for Hindus. It has four miles of palaces and temples along the river. One of the many pilgrimage circuits covers thirty-five miles, lasts for five days, and includes prayer at 108 different shrines. Because of the river's sacred nature, Hindus come to bathe from its many stone steps, called ghats, and to drink the water. It is also the place where Hindus desire to be at their death or to have their ashes scattered. Because Varanasi is regarded as a place of crossing between earth and heaven, dying there is thought to free one from the cycle of rebirth.

The thirty-four Ellora Caves at Maharashtra, India, are known for their sculptures. Built between 600 and 1000 CE, they were cut into a tufa rock hillside on a curve shaped like a horseshoe, so that the caves go deeply into the rock face. Although the one-mile site includes temples for Buddhist, Jain, and Hindu faiths, the major figure of the caves is Shiva, and the largest temple is dedicated to Shiva.

Lastly, Hindu temples, or mandirs, are regarded as the gods' earthly homes. The buildings themselves are therefore holy, and Hindus remove their shoes before entering.

HINDUISM IN DEPTH

Sacred Symbols

The wheel of life represents samsara, the cycle of life, death and rebirth. Karma is what keeps the wheel spinning. Another circle is the hoop of flames in which Shiva, also known as the Lord of the Dance, or Natraja, is shown dancing creation into being. The flames signify the universe's energy and Shiva's power of both destruction and creation. Shiva balances on his right foot, which rests on a defeated demon that stands for ignorance.

The lotus is the symbol of creation, fertility, and purity. This flower is associated with Vishnu because as he slept, a lotus flower bloomed from his navel. From this lotus Brahma came forth to create the world. Yoga practitioners commonly assume the lotus position for meditation.

Murtis are the statues of gods that are found in both temples and private homes. They are often washed with milk and water, anointed with oil, dressed, and offered gifts of food or flowers. Incense may also be burned to make the air around the murti sweet and pure.

One of Krishna's symbols is the conch shell, a symbol of a demon he defeated. A conch shell is blown at temples to announce the beginning of the worship service. It is a visual reminder for followers of Krishna to overcome ignorance and evil in their lives.

For many years, the Hindus used the swastika as a holy symbol. (*Swastika* is a Sanskrit word for good fortune and well-being.) The four arms meet at a central point, demonstrating that the universe comes from one source. Each arm of the symbol represents a path to God and is bent to show that all paths are difficult. It is used at a time of new beginnings, such as at a wedding, where it is traditionally painted on a coconut using a red paste called kum kum. The symbol appears as a vertical gash across the horizontal layers on the southern face of Mount Kailas, one of the Himalayas's highest peaks, thought to have been the home of Shiva. The mountain is also near the source of the Ganges and the Indus Rivers. The use of the swastika as a symbol for Nazi Germany is abhorrent to Hindus.

Some Hindus use a mala, or rosary, of 108 wooden beads when they pray. As they worship, they repeat the names of God.

Sacred Practices & Gestures

Many homes have private altars or shrines to favorite gods. Statues or pictures of these deities are offered incense, flowers and food, as well as prayers. This daily devotion, known as puja, is generally the responsibility of women, many of whom are devoted to goddesses such as Kali or Sita. A rich family may devote an entire room of their house to the shrine.

Om, or Aum, a sacred syllable recorded first in the Upanishads, is made up of three Sanskrit letters. Writing the letter involves a symbol resembling the Arabic number three. Thus, it is a visual reminder of the Trimurti, the three major Hindu gods. The word is repeated at the beginning of all mantras or prayers.

Each day the Gayatri, which is perhaps the world's oldest recorded prayer, is chanted during the fire ritual. The prayer expresses gratitude to the sun for its shining and invokes blessings of prosperity on all. The ritual, typically done at large consecrated fire pits, may be done using burning candles instead.

Holy Hindu men are known as sadhus. They lead ascetic lives, wandering, begging, and living in caves in the mountains. Regarded as having greater spiritual power and wisdom, they are often consulted for advice.

Food Restrictions

Many Hindus are vegetarians because they embrace ahimsa (reverence for and protection of all life) and oppose killing. In fact, Hindus comprise about 70 percent of the world's vegetarians. They are generally lacto-vegetarians, meaning that they include dairy products in their diets. However, Hindus residing in the cold climate of Nepal and Tibet consume meat to increase their caloric intake.

Whether a culture practices vegetarianism or not, cows are thought to be sacred because Krishna acted as a cowherd as a young god. Thus cows are never eaten. Pigs are also forbidden, as are red foods, such as tomatoes or red lentils. In addition, garlic and onions are also not permitted. Alcohol is strictly forbidden.

Purity rituals before eating include cleaning the area where the food is to be eaten and reciting mantras or praying while sprinkling water around the food. Other rituals include Annaprasana, which celebrates a child's eating of solid food— traditionally rice—for the first time. In addition, at funerals departed souls are offered food, which Hindus believe will strengthen the soul for the journey to the ancestors' world.

Serving food to those in need also generates good karma. Food is offered during religious ceremonies and may later be shared with visiting devotees of the god.

To show their devotion to Shiva, many Hindus fast on Mondays. There is also a regular fast, known as agiaras, which occurs on the eleventh day of each two-week period. On that day, only one meal is eaten. During the month of Shravan, which many consider a holy month, people may eat only one meal, generally following sunset.

Rites, Celebrations & Services

Many Hindu celebrations are connected to the annual cycle of nature and can last for many days. In addition, celebrations that honor the gods are common. Shiva, one of the three major gods, is honored at Shivaratri in February or March. In August or September, Lord Krishna is honored at Krishnajanmashtmi. Prayer and fasting are part of this holiday.

During the spring equinox and just prior to the Hindu New Year, Holi is celebrated. It is a time to resolve disputes and forgive or pay debts. During this festival, people often have bonfires and throw objects that represent past impurity or disease into the fire.

Another festival occurs in July or August, marking the beginning of the agricultural year in northern India. Raksha Bandhan (the bond of protection) is a festival which celebrates sibling relationships. During the festivities, Hindus bind a bauble with silk thread to the wrists of family members and friends.

To reenact Rama's defeat of the demon Ravana, as narrated in the Ramayana, people make and burn effigies. This festival is called Navaratri in western India, also known as the Durgapuja in Bengal, and Dasserah in northern India. It occurs in September or October each year as a festival celebrating the victory of good over evil. September is also time to celebrate the elephant-headed god Ganesha's birthday at the festival of Ganesh Chaturthi.

Diwali, a five-day festival honoring Lakshmi (the goddess of good fortune and wealth), occurs in October or November. This Festival of Lights is the time when people light oil lamps and set off fireworks to help Rama find his way home after exile. Homes are cleaned in hopes that Lakshmi will come in the night to bless it. People may use colored rice flour to make patterns on their doorstep. Competitions for designs of these patterns, which are meant to welcome God to the house, frequently take place.

Jagannath, or Vishnu, is celebrated during the festival Rathayatra. A large image of Jagannath rides in a chariot pulled through the city of Puri.

The temple for Hindus is the home of the god. Only Brahmin priests may supervise worship there. The inner sanctuary of the building is called the garbhagriha, or womb-house; there the god resides. Worshippers must be ritually pure before the worship starts. The priest recites the mantras and reads sacred texts. Small lamps are lit, and everyone shares specially prepared and blessed food after the service ends.

Judy A. Johnson, MTS

Bibliography

Barnes, Trevor. *The Kingfisher Book of Religions.* New York: Kingfisher, 1999. Print.

Harley, Gail M. *Hindu and Sikh Faiths in America.* New York: Facts on File, 2003. Print.

Iyengar, B. K. S. and Noelle Perez-Christiaens. *Sparks of Divinity: The Teachings of B. K. S. Iyengar from 1959 to 1975.* Berkeley: Rodmell, 2012. E-book.

"The Joys of Hinduism." *Hinduism Today* Oct./Dec. 2006: 40–53. Print.

Langley, Myrtle. *Religion.* New York: Knopf, 1996. Print.

Meredith, Susan. *The Usborne Book of World Religions.* London: Usborne, 1995. Print.

Rajan, Rajewswari. "The Politics of Hindu 'Tolerance.'" *Boundary 2* 38.3 (2011): 67–86. Print.

Raman, Varadaraja V. "Hinduism and Science: Some Reflections." *Journal of Religion & Science* 47.3 (2012): 549–74. Print.

Renard, John. *Responses to 101 Questions on Hinduism.* Mahwah: Paulist, 1999. Print.

Siddhartha. "Open-Source Hinduism." *Religion & the Arts* 12.1–3 (2008): 34–41. Print.

Shouler, Kenneth and Susai Anthony. *The Everything Hinduism Book.* Avon: Adams, 2009. Print.

Soherwordi, Syed Hussain Shaheed. "'Hinduism'—A Western Construction or an Influence?" *South Asian Studies* 26.1 (2011): 203–14. Print.

Theodor, Ithamar. *Exploring the Bhagavad Gita: Philosophy, Structure, and Meaning.* Farnham and Burlington: Ashgate, 2010. E-book.

Whaling, Frank. *Understanding Hinduism.* Edinburgh: Dunedin, 2010. E-book.

Wilkinson, Philip. *Religions.* New York: DK, 2008. Print.

Islam

General Description

The word *Islam* derives from a word meaning "submission," particularly submission to the will of Allah. Muslims, those who practice Islam, fall into two major groups, Sunni and Shia (or Shi'i,) based on political rather than theological differences. Sunni Muslims follow the four Rightly Guided Caliphs, or Rashidun and believe that caliphs should be elected. Shia Muslims believe that the Prophet's nearest male relative, Ali ibn Abi Talib, should have ruled following Muhammad's death, and venerate the imams (prayer leaders) who are directly descended from Ali and the Prophet's daughter Fatima.

Number of Adherents Worldwide

Approximately 1.6 billion people, or 23 percent of the world's population, are Muslims. Of that total, between 87 and 90 percent of all Muslims are Sunni Muslims and between 10 and 13 percent of all Muslims are Shia. Followers of the Sufi sect, noted for its experiential, ecstatic focus, may be either Sunni or Shia.

Basic Tenets

Islam is a monotheistic faith; Muslims worship only one God, Allah. They also believe in an afterlife and that people are consigned to heaven or hell following the last judgment.

The Islamic faith rests on Five Pillars. The first pillar, Shahadah is the declaration of faith in the original Arabic, translated as: "I bear witness that there is no god but God and Muhammad is his Messenger." The second pillar, Salah, are prayers adherents say while facing Mecca five times daily at regular hours and also at the main service held each Friday at a mosque. Zakat, "the giving of a tax," is the third pillar and entails giving an income-based percentage of one's wealth to help the poor without attracting notice. The fourth pillar is fasting, or Sawm, during Ramadan, the ninth month of the Islamic calendar. Certain groups of people are excused from the fast, however. The final pillar is the Hajj, the pilgrimage to Mecca required of every able-bodied Muslim at least once in his or her lifetime.

Sacred Text

The Qur'an (Koran), meaning "recitation," is the holy book of Islam.

Major Figures

Muhammad, regarded as the Prophet to the Arabs—as Moses was to the Jews—is considered the exemplar of what it means to be a Muslim. His successors—Abu Bakr, Umar, Uthman, and Ali—were known as the four Rightly Guided Caliphs.

Major Holy Sites

Islam recognizes three major holy sites: Mecca, home of the Prophet; Medina, the city to which Muslims relocated when forced from Mecca due to persecution; and the Dome of the Rock in Jerusalem, believed to be the oldest Islamic building in existence. Muslims believe that in 621 CE Muhammad ascended to heaven (called the Night Journey) from a sacred stone upon which the Dome was constructed. Once in heaven, God instructed Muhammad concerning the need to pray at regular times daily...

There are also several mosques which are considered primary holy sites. These include the al-Aqsa Mosque in the Old City of Jerusalem, believed by many to be the third holiest site in Islam. The mosque, along with the Dome of the Rock, is located on Judaism's holiest site, the Temple Mount, where the Temple of Jerusalem is believed to have stood. Muslims also revere the Mosque of the Prophet (Al-Masjid al-Nabawi) in Medina, considered the resting place of the Prophet Muhammad and the second largest mosque in the world; and the Mosque of the Haram (Masjid al-Haram or the Sacred or Grand Mosque) in Mecca, thought to be the largest mosque in the world and site of the Ka'bah, "the sacred house," also known as "the Noble Cube," Islam's holiest structure.

Major Rites & Celebrations

Two major celebrations mark the Islamic calendar. 'Id al-Adha, the feast of sacrifice—including animal sacrifice—held communally at the close of the Hajj (annual pilgrimage), commemorates the account of God providing a ram instead of the son Abraham had been asked to sacrifice. The second festival, 'Id al-Fitr, denotes the end of Ramadan and is a time of feasting and gift giving.

ORIGINS

History & Geography

In 610 CE, a forty-year-old businessman from Mecca named Muhammad ibn Abdullah, from the powerful Arab tribe Quraysh, went to Mount Hira to meditate, as he regularly did for the month of Ramadan. During that month, an entire group of men, the hanif, retreated to caves. The pagan worship practiced in the region, as well as the cruelty and lack of care for the poor, distressed Muhammad. As the tribe to which he belonged had become wealthy through trade, it had begun disregarding traditions prescribed by the nomadic code.

The archangel Jibra'il (Gabriel) appeared in Muhammad's cave and commanded him to read the words of God contained in the scroll that the angel showed him. Like most people of his time, Muhammad was illiterate, but repeated the words Jibra'il said. Some followers of Islam believe that this cave at Jebel Nur, in what is now Saudi Arabia, is where Adam, the first human Allah created, lived.

A frightened Muhammad told only his wife, Khadija, about his experience. For two years, Muhammad received further revelations, sharing them only with family and close friends. Like other prophets, he was reluctant about his calling, fearing that he was—or would be accused of being—possessed by evil spirits or insane. At one point, he tried to commit suicide, but was stopped by the voice of Jibra'il affirming his status as God's messenger.

Muhammad recalled the words spoken to him, which were eventually written down. The Qur'an is noted for being a book of beautiful language, and Muhammad's message reached many. The Prophet thus broke the old pattern of allegiance to tribe and forged a new community based on shared practice.

Muhammad considered himself one who was to warn the others of a coming judgment. His call for social justice and denunciation of the wealthy disturbed the powerful Arab tribe members in Mecca. These men stood to lose the status and income derived from the annual festival to the Ka'bah. The Prophet and his followers were persecuted and were the subject of boycotts and death threats. In 622 CE, Muslim families began a migration (hijrah) to Yathrib, later known as Medina. Two years earlier, the city had sent envoys seeking Muhammad's leadership for their own troubled society. The hijrah marks the beginning of the Islamic calendar.

The persecutions eventually led to outright tribal warfare, linking Islam with political prowess through the victories of the faithful. The Muslims moved from being an oppressed minority to being a political force. In 630 CE, Muhammad and ten thousand of his followers marched to Mecca, taking the city without bloodshed. He destroyed the pagan idols that were housed and worshipped at the Ka'bah, instead associating the hajj with the story of Abraham sending his concubine Hagar and their son Ishmael (Ismail in Arabic) out into the wilderness. With this victory, Muhammad ended centuries of intertribal warfare.

Muhammad died in 632, without designating a successor. Some of the Muslims believed that his nearest male relative should rule, following the custom of the tribes. Ali ibn Abi Talib, although a pious Muslim, was still young. Therefore, Abu Bakr, the Prophet's father-in-law, took the title khalifah, or caliph, which means successor or deputy. Within two years Abu Bakr had stabilized Islam. He was followed by three additional men whom Muhammad had known. Collectively, the four are known as the Four Rightly Guided Caliphs, or the Rashidun. Their rule extended from 632 until 661. Each of the final three met a violent death.

Umar, the second caliph, increased the number of raids on adjacent lands during his ten-year rule, which began in 634. This not only increased wealth, but also gave Umar the authority he needed, since Arabs objected to the idea of a monarchy. Umar was known as the commander of the faithful. Under his leadership, the Islamic community marched into present-day Iraq, Syria, and Egypt and achieved victory over the Persians in 637.

Muslims elected Uthman ibn Affan as the third caliph after Umar was stabbed by a Persian prisoner of war. He extended Muslim conquests into North Africa as well as into Iran, Afghanistan, and parts of India. A group of soldiers mutinied in 656, assassinating Uthman.

Ali, Muhammad's son-in-law, was elected caliph of a greatly enlarged empire. Conflict developed between Ali and the ruler in Damascus whom Uthman had appointed governor of Syria. The fact that the governor came from a rival tribe led to further tensions. Increasingly, Damascus rather than Medina was viewed as the key Muslim locale. Ali was murdered in 661 during the internal struggles.

Within a century after Muhammad's death, Muslims had created an empire that stretched from Spain across Asia to India and facilitated the spread of Islam. The conquerors followed a policy of relative, though not perfect, tolerance toward adherents of other religions. Christians and Jews received special status as fellow "People of the Book," though they were still required to pay a special poll tax in exchange for military protection. Pagans, however, were required to convert to Islam or face death. Later, Hindus, Zoroastrians, and other peoples were also permitted to pay the tax rather than submit to conversion. Following the twelfth century, Sufi mystics made further converts in Central Asia, India, sub-Saharan Africa, and Turkey. Muslim traders also were responsible for the growth of Islam, particularly in China, Indonesia, and Malaya.

The Muslim empire continued to grow until it weakened in the fourteenth century, when it was replaced as a major world power by European states. The age of Muslim domination ended with the 1683 failure of the Ottoman Empire to capture Vienna, Austria.

Although lacking in political power until recent years, a majority of nations in Indonesia, the Middle East, and East and North Africa are predominately Islamic. The rise of Islamic fundamentalists who interpret the Qur'an literally and seek victory through acts of terrorism began in the late twentieth century. Such extremists do not represent the majority of the Muslim community, however.

Like Judaism and Christianity, Islam has been influenced by its development in a desert climate. Arabia, a region three times the size of France, is a land of steppe and desert whose unwelcoming climate kept it from being mapped with any precision until the 1950s. Because Yemen received monsoon rains, it could sustain agriculture and became a center for civilization as early as the second millennium BCE. In the seventh century CE, nomads roamed the area, guarding precious wells and oases. Raiding caravans and other tribes were common ways to obtain necessities.

Mecca was a pagan center of worship, but it was located not far from a Christian kingdom, Ethiopia, across the Red Sea. Further north, followers of both Judaism and Christianity had influenced members of Arab tribes. Jewish tribes inhabited Yathrib, the city later known as Medina. Neither Judaism nor Christianity was especially kind to those they considered pagans. According to an Arabian tradition, in 570 the Ethiopians attacked Yemen and attempted an attack on Mecca. Mecca was caught between two enemy empires—Christian Byzantine and Zoroastrian Persia—that fought a lengthy war during Muhammad's lifetime.

The contemporary clashes between Jews and Muslims are in part a result of the dispersion of Muslims who had lived in Palestine for centuries. More Jews began moving into the area under the British Mandate; in 1948, the state of Israel was proclaimed. Historically, Jews had been respected as a People of the Book.

Founder or Major Prophet

Muslims hold Allah to be the founder of their religion and Abraham to have been the first Muslim. Muhammad is God's prophet to the Arabs. The instructions that God gave Muhammad through the archangel Jibra'il and through direct revelation are the basis for the Islamic religion. These revelations were given over a period of twenty-one years. Because Muhammad and most of the Muslims were illiterate, the teachings were read publicly in chapters, or suras.

Muhammad did not believe he was founding a new religion. Rather, he was considered God's final Prophet, as Moses and Jesus had been prophets. His task was to call people to repent and to return to the straight path of God's law, called Sharia. God finally was sending a direct revelation to the Arab peoples, who had sometimes been taunted by the other civilizations as being left out of God's plan.

Muhammad, who had been orphaned by age six, was raised by an uncle. He became a successful businessman of an important tribe and married Khadija, for whom he worked. His integrity was such that he was known as al-Amin, the trusted one. He and Khadija had six children; four daughters survived. After Khadija's death, Muhammad married several women, as was the custom for a great chief. Several of the marriages were political in nature.

Muhammad is regarded as the living Qur'an. He is sometimes referred to as the perfect man, one who is an example of how a Muslim should live. He was ahead of his time in his attitudes toward women, listening to their counsel and granting them rights not enjoyed by women in other societies, including the right to inherit property and to divorce. (It should be noted that the Qur'an does not require the seclusion or veiling of all women.)

Islam has no religious leaders, especially those comparable to other religions. Each mosque has an imam to preach and preside over prayer at the Friday services. Although granted a moral authority, the imam is not a religious leader with a role comparable to that of rabbis or priests.

Philosophical Basis

Prior to Muhammad's receiving the Qur'an, the polytheistic tribes believed in Allah, "the god." Allah was far away and not part of worship rituals, although he had created the world and sustained it. He had three daughters who were goddesses.

Islam began pragmatically—the old tribal ways were not working—as a call for social justice, rooted in Muhammad's dissatisfaction with the increasing emphasis on accumulating wealth and an accompanying neglect of those in need. The struggle (jihad) to live according to God's desire for humans was to take place within the community, or the ummah. This effort was more important than dogmatic statements or beliefs about God. When the community prospered, this was a sign of God's blessing.

In addition, the revelation of the Qur'an gave Arab nations an official religion. The Persians around them had Zoroastrianism, the Romans and Byzantines had Christianity, and the Jews of the Diaspora had Judaism. With the establishment of Islam, Arabs finally could believe that they were part of God's plan for the world.

Four principles direct Islam's practice and doctrine. These include the Qur'an; the traditions, or sunnah; consensus, or ijma'; and individual thought, or ijtihad. The term sunnah, "well-trodden path," had been used by Arabs before Islam to refer to their tribal law.

A fifth important source for Islam is the Hadith, or report, a collection of the Prophet's words and actions, intended to serve as an example. Sunni Muslims refer to six collections made in the ninth century, while Shia Muslims have a separate Hadith of four collections.

Holy Places

Mecca was located just west of the Incense Road, a major trade route from southern Arabia to Palestine and Syria. Mecca was the Prophet's home and the site where he received his revelations. It is also the city where Islam's holiest structure, the Ka'bah, "the sacred house," was located. The Ka'bah was regarded as having been built by Abraham and his son Ishmael. This forty-three-foot gray stone cube was a center for pagan idols in the time of Muhammad. In 628 the Prophet removed 360 pagan idols—one for each day of the Arabic lunar year—from inside the Ka'bah.

When the followers of Muhammad experienced persecution for their beliefs, they fled to the city of Medina, formerly called Yathrib. When his uncle Abu Talib died, Muhammad lost the protection from persecution that his uncle had provided. He left for Ta'if in the mountains, but it was also a center for pagan cults, and he was driven out. After a group of men from Yathrib promised him protection, Muhammad sent seventy of his followers to the city, built around an oasis about 215 miles north. This migration, called the hijra, occurred in 622, the first year of the Muslim calendar. From this point on, Islam became an organized religion rather than a persecuted and minority cult. The Prophet was buried in Medina in 632, and his mosque in that city is deeply revered.

Islam's third holiest site is the Dome of the Rock in Jerusalem. Muslims believe that the Prophet Muhammad ascended to heaven in 621 from the rock located at the center of this mosque. During this so-called night journey, Allah gave him instructions about prayer. In the shrine at the Dome of the Rock is a strand of hair that Muslims believe was Muhammad's.

Shia Muslims also revere the place in present-day Iraq where Ali's son, Husayn, was martyred. They regard the burial place of Imam Ali ar-Rida in Meshed, Iran, as a site of pilgrimage as well.

ISLAM IN DEPTH

Sacred Symbols

Muslims revere the Black Stone, a possible meteorite that is considered a link to heaven. It is set inside the Ka'bah shrine's eastern corner. The Ka'bah is kept covered by the kiswa, a black velvet cloth decorated with embroidered calligraphy in gold. At the hajj, Muslims walk around it counterclockwise seven times as they recite prayers to Allah.

Muslim nations have long used the crescent moon and a star on their flags. The crescent moon, which the Ottomans first adopted as a symbol during the fifteenth century, is often placed on the dome of a mosque, pointing toward Mecca. For Muhammad, the waxing and waning of the moon signified the unchanging and eternal purpose of God. Upon seeing a new moon, the Prophet confessed his faith in God. Muslims rely on a lunar calendar and the Qur'an states that God created the stars to guide people to their destinations.

Islam forbids the making of graven images of animals or people, although not all Islamic cultures follow this rule strictly. The decorative arts of Islam have placed great emphasis on architecture and calligraphy to beautify mosques and other buildings. In addition, calligraphy, floral motifs, and geometric forms decorate some editions of the Qur'an's pages, much as Christian monks once decorated hand-copied scrolls of the Bible. These elaborate designs can also be seen on some prayer rugs, and are characteristic of Islamic art in general.

Sacred Practices & Gestures

When Muslims pray, they must do so facing Mecca, a decision Muhammad made in January 624 CE. Prior to that time, Jerusalem—a holy city for both Jews and Christians—had been the geographic focus. Prayer involves a series of movements that embody submission to Allah.

Muslims sometimes use a strand of prayer beads, known as subhah, to pray the names of God. The beads can be made of bone, precious stones, or wood. Strings may have twenty-five, thirty-three or 100 beads.

Food Restrictions

Those who are physically able to do so fast from both food and drink during the daylight hours of the month Ramadan. Although fasting is not required of the sick, the aged, menstruating or pregnant women, or children, some children attempt to fast, imitating their parents' devotion. Those who cannot fast are encouraged to do so the following Ramadan. This fast is intended to concentrate the mind on Allah. Muslims recite from the Qur'an during the month.

All meat must be prepared in a particular way so that it is halal, or permitted. While slaughtering the animal, the person must mention the name of Allah. Blood, considered unclean, must be allowed to drain. Because pigs were fed garbage, their meat was considered unclean. Thus Muslims eat no pork, even though in modern times, pigs are often raised on grain.

In three different revelations, Muslims are also forbidden to consume fermented beverages. Losing self-control because of drunkenness violates the Islamic desire for self-mastery.

Rites, Celebrations, and Services

The **mosque** is the spiritual center of the Muslim community. From the minaret (a tower outside the mosque), the call to worship occurs five times daily—at dawn, just past noon, at midafternoon, at sunset, and in the evening. In earliest times, a muezzin, the official responsible for this duty, gave the cry. In many modern countries, the call now comes over a speaker system. Also located outside are fountains to provide the necessary water for ritual washing before prayer. Muslims wash their face, hands, forearms, and feet, as well as remove their shoes before beginning their prayers. In the absence of water, ritual cleansing may occur using sand or a stone.

Praying involves a series of movements known as rak'ah. From a standing position, the worshipper recites the opening sura of the Qur'an, as well as a second sura. After bowing to demonstrate respect, the person again stands, then prostrates himself or herself to signal humility. Next, the person assumes a sitting posture in silent prayer before again prostrating. The last movement is a greeting of "Peace be with you and the mercy of Allah." The worshipper looks both left and right before saying these words, which are intended for all persons, present and not.

Although Muslims stop to pray during each day when the call is given, Friday is the time for communal prayer and worship at the mosque. The prayer hall is the largest space within the mosque. At one end is a niche known as the mihrab, indicating the direction of Mecca, toward which Muslims face when they pray. At first, Muhammad instructed his followers to pray facing Jerusalem, as the Jewish people did. This early orientation was also a way to renounce the pagan associations of Mecca. Some mosques serve as community centers, with additional rooms for study.

The hajj, an important annual celebration, was a custom before the founding of Islam. Pagan worship centered in Mecca at the Ka'bah, where devotees circled the cube and kissed the Black Stone that was embedded in it. All warfare was forbidden during the hajj, as was argument, speaking crossly, or killing even an insect.

Muslims celebrate the lives of saints and their death anniversaries, a time when the saints are thought to reach the height of their spiritual life. Mawlid an-Nabi refers to "the birth of the Prophet." Although it is cultural and not rooted in the Qur'an, in some Muslim countries this is a public holiday on which people recite the Burdah, a poem that praises Muhammad. Muslims also celebrate the night that the Prophet ascended to heaven, Lailat ul-Miraj. The Night of Power is held to be the night on which Allah decides the destiny of people individually and the world at large.

Like Jews, Muslims practice circumcision, a ceremony known as khitan. Unlike Jews, however, Muslims do not remove the foreskin when the male is a baby. This is often done when a boy is about seven, and must be done before the boy reaches the age of twelve.

Healthy adult Muslims fast between sunrise and sunset during the month of Ramadan. This commemorates the first of Muhammad's revelations. In some Muslim countries, cannons are fired before the beginning of the month, as well as at the beginning and end of each day of the month. Some Muslims read a portion of the Qur'an each day during the month.

Judy A. Johnson, MTS

Bibliography

Al-Saud, Laith, Scott W. Hibbard, and Aminah Beverly. *An Introduction to Islam in the 21st Century*. Wiley, 2013. E-book.

Armstrong, Lyall. "The Rise of Islam: Traditional and Revisionist Theories." *Theological Review* 33.2 (2012): 87–106. Print.

Armstrong, Karen. *Islam: A Short History*. New York: Mod. Lib., 2000. Print.

Aslan, Reza. *No god but God: The Origins, Evolution, and Future of Islam*. New York: Random, 2005. Print.

Badawi, Emran El-. "'For All Times and Places': A Humanistic Reception of the Qur'an." *English Language Notes* 50.2 (2012): 99–112. Print.

Barnes, Trevor. *The Kingfisher Book of Religions*. New York: Kingfisher, 1999. Print.

Ben Jelloun, Tahar. *Islam Explained*. Trans. Franklin Philip. New York: New, 2002. Print.

Esposito, John L. *Islam: the Straight Path*. New York: Oxford UP, 1988. Print.

Glady, Pearl. *Criticism of Islam*.Library, 2012. E-book.

Holland, Tom. "Where Mystery Meets History." *History Today* 62.5 (2012): 19–24. Print.

Langley, Myrtle. *Religion*. New York: Knopf, 1996. Print.

Lunde, Paul. *Islam: Faith, Culture, History*. London: DK, 2002. Print.

Nasr, Seyyed Hossein. *Islam: Religion, History, and Civilization*. New York: Harper, 2002. Print.

Pasha, Mustapha Kamal. "Islam and the Postsecular." *Review of International Studies* 38.5 (2012): 1041–56. Print.

Sayers, Destini and Simone Peebles. *Essence of Islam and Sufism*. College, 2012. E-book.

Schirmacher, Christine. "They Are Not All Martyrs: Islam on the Topics of Dying, Death, and Salvation in the Afterlife." *Evangelical Review of Theology* 36.3 (2012): 250–65. Print.

Wilkinson, Philip. *Islam*. New York: DK, 2002. Print.

Wilkinson, Philip. *Religions*. New York: DK, 2008. Print.

Jainism

General Description

Jainism is one of the major religions of India. The name of the religion itself is believed to be based on the Sanskrit word *ji*, which means "to conquer or triumph," or *jina*, which means "victor or conqueror." The earliest name of the group was Nirgrantha, meaning bondless, but it applied to monks and nuns only. There are two sects: the Svetambaras (the white clad), which are the more numerous and wear white clothing, and the Digambaras (the sky clad), the most stringent group; their holy men or monks do not wear clothing at all.

Number of Adherents Worldwide

Jainism has about five million adherents, most of them in India (in some estimates, the religion represents approximately 1 percent of India's population). Because the religion is demanding in nature, few beyond the Indian subcontinent have embraced it. Jainism has spread to Africa, the United States, and nations in the Commonwealth (nations once under British rule) by virtue of Indian migration to these countries.

Basic Tenets

The principle of nonviolence (ahimsa) is a defining feature of Jainism. This results in a pacifist religion that influenced Mohandas Gandhi's ideas on nonviolent resistance. Jains believe that because all living creatures have souls, harming any of those creatures is wrong. They therefore follow a strict vegetarian diet, and often wear masks so as to not inhale living organisms. The most important aspect of Jainism is perhaps the five abstinences: ahimsa, satya (truthfulness), asteya (refrain from stealing), brahmacarya (chaste living), and aparigraha (refrain from greed).

A religion without priests, Jainism emphasizes the importance of the adherents' actions. Like Buddhists and Hindus, Jainists believe in karma and reincarnation. Unlike the Buddhist and Hindu idea of karma, Jainists regard karma as tiny particles that cling to the soul as mud clings to shoes, gradually weighing down the soul. Good deeds wash away these particles. Jainists also believe in moksha, the possibility of being freed from the cycle of death and rebirth. Like many Indian religions, Jainism does not believe in an afterlife, but in a cycle of death and rebirth. Once freed from this cycle, the soul will remain in infinite bliss.

While Jains do not necessarily believe in and worship God or gods, they believe in divine beings. Those who have achieved moksha are often regarded by Jains in the same manner in which other religions regard deities. These include the twenty-four Tirthankaras (ford makers) or jinas (victors), those who have escaped the cycle of death and rebirth, and the Siddhas, the liberated souls without physical form. The idea of a judging, ruling, or creator God is not present in Jainism.

Jainists believe that happiness is not found in material possessions and seek to have few of them. They also stress the importance of environmentalism. Jainists follow the Three Jewels: Right Belief, Right Knowledge, and Right Conduct. To be completely achieved, these three must be practiced together. Jainists also agree to six daily obligations (avashyaka), which include confession, praising the twenty-four Tirthankaras (the spiritual leaders), and calm meditation.

Sacred Text

The words of Mahavira were passed down orally, but lost over a few centuries. During a famine in the mid-fourth century BCE, many monks died. The texts were finally written down, although the Jain sects do not agree as to whether they are Mahavira's actual words. There are forty-five sacred texts (Agamas), which make up the Agam Sutras, Jainism's canonical literature. They were probably written down no earlier than 300 BCE. Two of the primary texts are the Akaranga

Sutra, which outlines the rule of conduct for Jain monks, and the Kalpa Sutra, which contains biographies of the last two Tirthankara. The Digambaras, who believe that the Agamas were lost around 350 BCE, have two main texts and four compendia written between 100 and 800 CE by various scholars.

Major Figures

Jainism has no single founder. However, Mahavira (Great Hero) is one of the Tirthankaras or jinas (pathfinders). He is considered the most recent spiritual teacher in a line of twenty-four. Modern-day Jainism derives from Mahavira, and his words are the foundation of Jain scriptures. He was a contemporary of Siddhartha Gautama, who was revered as the Buddha. Both Mahavira and Rishabha (or Adinatha), the first of the twenty-four Tirthankaras, are attributed as the founder of Jainism, though each Tirthankara maintains founding attributes.

Major Holy Sites

The Jain temple at Ranakpur is located in the village of Rajasthan. Carved from amber stone with marble interiors, the temple was constructed in the fifteenth century CE. It is dedicated to the first Tirthankara. The temple has twenty-nine large halls and each of the temple's 1,444 columns has a unique design with carvings.

Sravanabegola in Karnataka state is the site of Gomateshwara, Lord Bahubali's fifty-seven-foot statue. It was constructed in 981 CE from a single chunk of gneiss. Bahubali is considered the son of the first Tirthankara. The Digambara sect believes him to have been the first human to be free from the world.

Other pilgrimage sites include the Palitana temples in Gujarat and the Dilwara temples in Rajasthan. Sometimes regarded as the most sacred of the many Jain temples, the Palitana temples include 863 marble-engraved temples. The Jain temples at Dilwara were constructed of marble during the eleventh and thirteenth centuries CE. These five temples are often considered the most beautiful Jain temples in existence.

Major Rites & Celebrations

Every twelve years, the festival of Mahamastakabhisheka (anointing of the head) occurs at a statue of one of Jain's holy men, Bahubali, the second son of the first Tirthankara. The statue is anointed with milk, curd, and ghee, a clarified butter. Nearly a million people attend this rite. Jainists also observe Diwali, the Hindu festival of lights, as it symbolizes Mahavira's enlightenment.

The solemn festival of Paryusana marks the end of the Jain year for the Svetambaras (also spelled Shvetambaras). During this eight-day festival, all Jains are asked to live as an ascetic (monk or nun) would for one day. Das Laxana, a ten-day festival similar to that of Paryusana, immediately follows for the Digambara sect. During these special religious holidays, worshippers are involved in praying, meditating, fasting, forgiveness, and acts of penance. These holy days are celebrated during August and September, which is monsoon season in India. During the monsoons, monks prefer to remain in one place so as to avoid killing the smallest insects that appear during the rainy season. The Kalpa Sutra, one of the Jain scriptures, is read in the morning during Paryusana.

The feast of Kartaki Purnima follows the four months of the rainy season. It is held in the first month (Kartik) according to one calendar, and marked by a pilgrimage to the Palitana temples. Doing so with a pure heart is said to remove all sins of both the present and past life. Those who do so are thought to receive the final salvation in the third or fifth birth.

ORIGINS

History & Geography

In the eastern basin of the Ganges River during the seventh century BCE, a teacher named Parshvanatha (or Parshva) gathered a community founded on abandoning earthly concerns. He is considered to be the twenty-third Tirthankara (ford-maker), the one who makes a path for salvation. During the following century, Vardhamana, called Mahavira (Great Hero), who was considered the twenty-fourth and final spiritual teacher of the age, formulated most Jain doctrine and practice. By the time of Mahavira's death, Jains numbered around 36,000 nuns and 14,000 monks.

A division occurred within Jainism during the fourth century CE. The most extreme ascetics, the Digambaras (the sky-clad), argued that even clothing showed too great an attachment to the world, and that laundering them in the river risked harming creatures. This argument applied only to men, as the Digambaras denied that a soul could be freed from a woman's body. The other group, the Svetambaras (the white-clad), believed that purity resided in the mind.

In 453 or 456 CE, a council of the Svetambara sect at Saurashtra in western India codified the canon still used. The split between the Digambaras, who did not take part in the meeting, and Svetambaras thus became permanent. Despite the split, Jainism's greatest flowering occurred during the early medieval age. After that time, Hindu sects devoted to the Hindu gods of Vishnu and Shiva flourished under the Gupta Empire (often referred to as India's golden age), slowing the spread of Jainism. Followers migrated to western and central India and the community became stronger.

The Digambaras were involved in politics through several medieval dynasties, and some Jain monks served as spiritual advisers. Royalty and high-ranking officials contributed to the building and maintenance of temples. Both branches of Jainism contributed a substantial literature. In the late medieval age, Jain monks ceased to live as ascetic wanders. They chose instead to don orange robes and to live at temples and other holy places.

The Muslims invaded India in the twelfth century. The Jains lost power and fractured over the next centuries into subgroups, some of which repudiated the worship of images. The poet and Digambara layman Banarsidas (1586-1643) played a significant role in a reform movement during the early 1600s. These reforms focused on the mystical side of Jainism, such as spiritual exploration of the inner self (meditation),

and denounced the formalized temple ritual. The movement, known as the Adhyatma movement, resulted in the Digambara Terapanth, a small Digambara sect.

The Jainists were well positioned in society following the departure of the British from India. Having long been associated with the artisan and merchant classes, they found new opportunities. As traditional Indian studies grew, spurred by Western interest, proponents of Jainism began to found publications and places of study (In fact, Jain libraries are believed to be the oldest in India.) The first Jain temple outside India was consecrated in Britain during the 1960s after Jains had gone there in the wake of political turmoil.

The Jains follow their typical profession as merchants. They publish English-language periodicals to spread their ideas on vegetarianism, environmentalism, and nonviolence (ahimsa). The ideas of ahimsa were formative for Mohandas Gandhi, born a Hindu. Gandhi used nonviolence as a wedge against the British Empire in India. Eventually, the British granted independence to India in 1947.

Virchand Gandhi (1864–1901) is believed to be the first Jain to arrive in America when he came over in 1893. He attended the first Parliament of World Religions, held in Chicago. Today North America has more than ninety Jain temples and centers. Jains in the West often follow professions such as banking and business to avoid destroying animal or plant life.

Founder or Major Prophet

Mahavira was born in India's Ganges Basin region. By tradition, he was born around 599 BCE, although some scholars think he may have lived a century later. His story bears a resemblance to that of the Buddha, with whom he was believed to have been a contemporary. His family was also of the Kshatriya (warrior) caste, and his father was a ruler of his clan. One tradition states that Mahavira's mother was of the Brahman (priestly) caste, although another places her in the Kshatriya.

Because he was not the eldest son, Mahavira was not in line for leadership of the clan.

He married a woman of his own caste and they had a daughter. Mahavira chose the life of a monk, with one garment. Later, he gave up wearing even that. He became a wandering ascetic around age thirty, with some legends stating that he tore out his hair before leaving home. He sought shelter in burial grounds and cremation sites, as well as at the base of trees. During the rainy season, however, he lived in towns and villages.

He followed a path of preaching and self-denial, after which he was enlightened (kevala). He spent the next thirty years teaching. Eleven disciples, all of whom were of the Brahman caste, gathered around him. At the end of his life, Mahavira committed Santhara, or ritual suicide through fasting.

Philosophical Basis

Like Buddhists and the Brahmin priests, the Jains believe in human incarnations of God, known as avatars. These avatars appear at the end of a time of decline to reinstate proper thinking and acting. Such a person was Mahavira. At the time of Mahavira's birth, India was experiencing great societal upheaval. Members of the warrior caste opposed the priestly caste, which exercised authority based on its supposed greater moral purity. Many people also opposed the slaughter of animals for the Vedic sacrifices.

Jainists share some beliefs with both Hinduism and Buddhism. The Hindu hero Rama, for example, is co-opted as a nonviolent Jain, while the deity Krishna is considered a cousin of Arishtanemi, the twenty-second Tirthankara. Like Buddhism, Jainism uses a wheel with twelve spokes; however, Jainism uses the wheel to explain time. The first half of the circle is the ascending stage, in which human happiness, prosperity, and life span increase. The latter half of the circle is the descending stage, involving a decrease of life span, prosperity, and happiness. The wheel of time is always in motion.

For Jainists, the universe is without beginning or ending, and contains layers of both heaven and hell. These layers include space beyond, which

is without time, matter, or soul. The cosmos is depicted in art as a large human. The cloud layers surrounding the upper world are called universe space. Above them is the base, Nigoda, where lowest life forms live. The netherworld contains seven hells, each with a different stage of punishment and misery. The middle world contains the earth and remainder of the universe—mankind is located near the waist. There are thirty heavens in the upper world, where heavenly beings reside. In the supreme abode at the apex of the universe, liberated souls (siddha) live.

Jainism teaches that there are six universal entities. Only consciousness or soul is a living substance, while the remaining five are nonliving. They include matter, medium of rest, medium of motion, time, and space. Jainism also does not believe in a God who can create, destroy, or protect. Worshipping goddesses and gods to achieve personal gain or material benefit is deemed useless.

Mahavira outlined five basic principles (often referred to as abstinences) for Jainist life, based on the teachings of the previous Tirthankara. They are detachment (aparigraha); the conduct of soul, primarily in sexual morality (brahmacharya); abstinence from stealing (asteya); abstinence from lying (satya); and nonviolence in every realm of the person (ahimsa).

Like other Indian religions, Jainism perceives life as four stages. The life of a student is brahmacharya-ashrama; the stage of family life is gruhasth-ashrama; in vanaprasth-ashrama, the Jainist concentrates on both family and aiding others through social services; and the final stage is sanyast-ashrama, a time of renouncing the world and becoming a monk.

Like many religions, Jainism has a bias toward males and toward the rigorous life of monks and nuns. A layperson cannot work off bad karma, but merely keeps new bad karma from accruing. By following a path of asceticism, however, monks and nuns can destroy karma. Even members of the laity follow eight rules of behavior and take twelve vows. Physical austerity is a key concept in Jainism, as a saint's highest ideal is to starve to death.

Holy Places

There are four major Jain pilgrimage sites: the Dilwara temples near Rajasthan; the Palitana temples; the Ranakpur temple; and Shravan Begola, the site of the statue of Lord Bahubali. In addition, Jains may make pilgrimages to the caves of Khandagiri and Udayagiri, which were cells for Jain monks carved from rock. The spaces carved are too short for a man to stand upright. They were essentially designed for prayer and meditation. Udayagiri has eighteen caves and Khandagiri has fifteen. The caves are decorated with elaborate carvings.

JAINISM IN DEPTH

Sacred Symbols

The open palm (Jain Hand) with a centered wheel, sometimes with the word *ahimsa* written on it, is a prominent Jain symbol. Seen as an icon of peace, the open palm symbol can be interpreted as a call to stop violence, and also means "assurance." It appears on the walls of Jain temples and in their publications. Jainism also employs a simple swastika symbol, considered to be the holiest symbol. It represents the four forms of worldly existence, and three dots above the swastika represent the Three Jewels. The Jain emblem, adopted in 1975, features both the Jain Hand (the open palm symbol with an inset wheel) and a swastika. This year was regarded as the 2,500th anniversary of Mahavira being enlightened.

Sacred Practices & Gestures

Jains may worship daily in their homes at private shrines. The Five Supreme Beings stand for stages in the path to enlightenment. Rising before daybreak, worshippers invoke these five. In addition, devout Jainists set aside forty-eight minutes daily to meditate.

To demonstrate faithfulness to the five vows that Jains undertake, there are four virtuous qualities that must be cultivated. They are compassion (karuna), respect and joy (pramoda), love and friendship (maitri), and indifference toward and noninvolvement with those who are arrogant (madhyastha). Mahavira stressed that Jains must be friends to all living beings. Compassion goes beyond mere feeling; it involves offering both material and spiritual aid. Pramoda carries with it the idea of rejoicing enthusiastically over the virtues of others. There are contemplations associated with these virtues, and daily practice is suggested to attain mastery.

Some Jainists, both men and women, wear a dot on the forehead. This practice comes from Hinduism. During festivals, Jains may pray, chant, fast, or keep silent. These actions are seen as removing bad karma from the soul and moving the person toward ultimate happiness.

Food Restrictions

Jainists practice a strict vegetarian way of life (called Jain vegetarianism) to avoid harming any creature. They refuse to eat root vegetables, because by uprooting them, the entire plant dies. They prefer to wait for fruit to drop from trees rather than taking it from the branches. Starving to death, when ready, is seen as an ideal.

Rites, Celebrations & Services

Some festivals are held annually and their observances are based on a lunar calendar. Mahavir Jayanti is an example, as it celebrates Mahavira's birthday.

Jains may worship, bathe, and make offerings to images of the Tirthankaras in their home or in a temple. Svetambaras Jains also clothe and decorate the images. Because the Tirthankaras have been liberated, they cannot respond as a deity granting favors might. Although Jainism rejects belief in gods in favor of worshipping Tirthankaras, in actual practice, some Jainists pray to Hindu gods.

When Svetambara monks are initiated, they are given three pieces of clothing, including a small piece of white cloth to place over the mouth. The cloth, called a mukhavastrika, is designed to prevent the monk from accidentally eating insects.

Monks take great vows (mahavratas) at initiation. These include abstaining from lying, stealing, sexual activity, injury to any living thing, and personal possessions. Monks own a broom to sweep in front of where they are going to walk so that no small creatures are injured, along with an alms bowl and a robe. The Digambara monks practice a more stringent lifestyle, eating one meal a day, for which they beg.

Nuns in the Svetambaras are three times more common than are monks, even though they receive less honor, and are required to defer to the monks. In Digambara Jainism, the nuns wear robes and accept that they must be reborn as men before progressing upward.

The observance of Santhara, which is religious fasting until death, is a voluntary fasting undertaken with full knowledge. The ritual is also known as Sallekhana, and is not perceived as suicide by Jains, particularly as the prolonged nature of the ritual provides ample time for reflection. It is believed that at least one hundred people die every year from observing Santhara.

Judy A. Johnson, MTS

Bibliography

Aristarkhova, Irina. "Thou Shall Not Harm All Living Beings: Feminism, Jainism, and Animals." *Hypatia* 27.3 (2012): 636–50. Print.

Aukland, Knut. "Understanding Possession in Jainism: A Study of Oracular Possession in Nakoda." *Modern Asian Studies* 47.1 (2013): 103–34. Print.

Barnes, Trevor. *The Kingfisher Book of Religions*. New York: Kingfisher, 1999. Print.

Langley, Myrtle. *Religion*. New York: Knopf, 1996. Print.

Long, Jeffery. *Jainism: An Introduction*. London: I. B. Tauris, 2009. Print.

Long, Jeffrey. "Jainism: Key Themes." *Religion Compass* 5.9 (2011): 501–10. Print.

Rankin, Aidan. *The Jain Path*. Berkeley: O Books, 2006. Print.

Shah, Bharat S. *An Introduction to Jainism*. Great Neck: Setubandh, 2002. Print.

Titze, Kurt. *Jainism: A Pictorial Guide to the Religion of Non-Violence*. Delhi: Motilal Banarsidass, 2001. Print.

Tobias, Michael. *Life Force: the World of Jainism*. Berkeley:Asian Humanities, 1991. E-book, print.

Wiley, Kristi L. *The A to Z of Jainism*. Lanham: Scarecrow, 2009. Print.

Wiley, Kristi L. *Historical Dictionary of Jainism*. Lanham: Scarecrow, 2004. Print.

Wilkinson, Philip. *Religions*. New York: DK, 2008. Print.

Judaism

General Description

In modern Judaism, the main denominations (referred to as movements) are Orthodox Judaism (including Haredi and Hasidic Judaism); Conservative Judaism; Reform (Liberal) Judaism; Reconstructionist Judaism; and to a lesser extent, Humanistic Judaism. In addition, the Jewry of Ethiopia and Yemen are known for having distinct or alternative traditions. Classical Judaism is often organized by two branches: Ashkenazic (Northern Europe) and Sephardic Jews (Spain, Portugal, and North Africa).

Number of Adherents Worldwide

Judaism has an estimated 15 million adherents worldwide, with roughly 41 percent living in Israel and about 41 percent living in the United States. Ashkenazi Jews represent roughly 75 percent, while Sephardic Jews represent roughly 25 percent, with the remaining 5 percent split among alternative communities. Within the United States, a 2000-01 survey stated that 10 percent of American Jews identified as Orthodox (with that number increasing), 35 percent as Reform, 26 percent as Conservative, leaving the remainder with an alternative or no affiliation. [Source: Wilkinson, 2008]

Orthodox Judaism, which was founded around the thirteenth century BCE, has 3 million followers. Members of Reform Judaism, with roots in nineteenth-century Germany, wanted to live peacefully with non-Jews. Therefore, they left the laws that prevented this vision of peace and downplayed the idea of a Jewish state. Reform Judaism, also known as Progressive or Liberal Judaism, allows women rabbis and does not require its adherents to keep kosher. About 1.1 million Jews are Reform; they live primarily in the United States. When nonkosher food was served at the first graduation ceremony for Hebrew Union College, some felt that the Reform movement had gone too far. Thus the Conservative movement began in 1887. A group of rabbis founded the Jewish Theological Seminary in New York City, wanting to emphasize biblical authority above moral choice, as the Reform tradition stressed. Currently about 900,000 Jews practice this type of Judaism, which is theologically midway between Orthodox and Reform. The Hasidim, an ultra-conservative group, began in present-day Ukraine around 1740. There are 4.5 million Hasidic Jews.

Basic Tenets

Though there is no formal creed (statement of faith or belief), Jews value all life, social justice, education, generous giving, and the importance of living based on the principles and values espoused in the Torah (Jewish holy book). They believe in one all-powerful and creator God, Jehovah or Yaweh, a word derived from the Hebrew letters "YHWH," the unpronounceable name of God. The word is held to be sacred; copyists were required to bathe both before and after writing the word. Jews also believe in a coming Messiah who will initiate a Kingdom of Righteousness. They follow a complex law, composed of 613 commandments or mitzvot. Jews believe that they are God's Chosen People with a unique covenant relationship. They have a responsibility to practice hospitality and to improve the world.

The belief in the afterlife is a part of the Jewish faith. Similar to Christianity, this spiritual world is granted to those who abide by the Jewish faith and live a good life. Righteous Jews are rewarded in the afterlife by being able to discuss the Torah with Moses, who first received the law from God. Furthermore, certain Orthodox sects believe that wicked souls are destroyed or tormented after death.

Sacred Text

The complete Hebrew Bible is called the Tanakh. It includes the prophetic texts, called the Navi'im, the poetic writings, the Ketubim, and the Torah, meaning teaching, law, or guidance. Torah may refer to the entire body of Jewish law or to the first five books of the Hebrew Bible, known as the Pentateuch (it is the Old Testament in the Christian Bible). Also esteemed is the Talmud, made up of the Mishnah, a written collection of oral traditions, and Gemara, a commentary on the Mishnah. The Talmud covers many different subjects, such as law, stories and legends, medicine, and rituals.

Major Figures

The patriarchs are held to be the fathers of the faith. Abraham, the first patriarch, was called to leave his home in the Fertile Crescent for a land God would give him, and promised descendents as numerous as the stars. His son Isaac was followed by Jacob, whom God renamed Israel, and whose twelve sons became the heads of the twelve tribes of Israel. Moses was the man who, along with his brother Aaron, the founder of a priestly line, and their sister Miriam led the chosen people out of slavery in Egypt, where they had gone to escape famine. The Hebrew Bible also details the careers of a group of men and women known as judges, who were really tribal rulers, as well as of the prophets, who called the people to holy lives. Chief among the prophets was Elijah, who confronted wicked kings and performed many miracles. Several kings were key to the biblical narrative, among them David, who killed the giant Goliath, and Solomon, known for his wisdom and for the construction of a beautiful temple.

Major Holy Sites

Most of Judaism's holy sites are within Israel, the Holy Land, including Jerusalem, which was the capital of the United Kingdom of Israel under kings David and Solomon; David captured it from a Canaanite tribe around 1000 BCE. Within the Old City of Jerusalem is the Temple Mount (where the Temple of Jerusalem was built), often considered the religion's holiest site, the Foundation Stone (from which Judaism claims the world was created), and the Western (or Wailing) Wall. Other sites include Mount Sinai in Egypt, the mountain upon which God gave Moses his laws.

Major Rites & Celebrations

The Jewish calendar recognizes several important holidays. Rosh Hashanah, literally "first of the year," is known as the Jewish New Year and inaugurates a season of self-examination and repentance that culminates in Yom Kippur, the Day of Atonement. Each spring, Passover commemorates the deliverance of the Hebrew people from Egypt. Shavuot celebrates the giving of the Torah to Moses, while Sukkot is the harvest festival. Festivals celebrating deliverance from enemies include Purim and Hanukkah. Young adolescents become members of the community at a bar or bat mitzvah, held near the twelfth or thirteenth birthday. The Sabbath, a cessation from work from Friday at sundown until Saturday when the first star appears, gives each week a rhythm.

ORIGINS

History & Geography

Called by God perhaps four thousand years ago, Abraham left from Ur of the Chaldees, or the Fertile Crescent in Mesopotamia in present-day Iraq, to go the eastern Mediterranean, the land of Canaan. Several generations later, the tribe went to Egypt to escape famine. They were later enslaved by a pharaoh, sometimes believed to have been Ramses II (ca. 1279–1213 BCE), who was noted for his many building projects. The Israelites returned to Canaan under Moses several hundred years after their arrival in Egypt. He was given the law, the Ten Commandments, plus the rest of the laws governing all aspects of life, on Mount Sinai about the thirteenth century BCE. This marked the beginning of a special covenant relationship between the new nation, known as Israel, and God.

Following a period of rule by judges, kings governed the nation. Major kings included David, son-in-law to the first king, Saul, and David's son, Solomon. The kingdom split at the beginning of the reign of Solomon's son

Rehoboam, who began ruling about 930 BCE. Rehoboam retained the ten northern tribes, while the two southern tribes followed a military commander rather than the Davidic line.

Rehoboam's kingdom was known as Israel, after the name Jehovah gave to Jacob. Judah was the name of the southern kingdom—one of Jacob's sons was named Judah. Prophets to both nations warned of coming judgment unless the people repented of mistreating the poor and other sins, such as idolatry. Unheeding, Israel was taken into captivity by the Assyrians in 722 BCE. and the Israelites assimilated into the nations around them.

The Babylonians captured Judah in 586 BCE. After Babylon had been captured in turn by Persians, the Jewish people were allowed to return to the land in 538 BCE. There they began reconstructing the temple and the walls of the city. In the second century BCE, Judas Maccabeus led a rebellion against the heavy taxes and oppression of the Greek conquerors, after they had levied high taxes and appointed priests who were not Jewish. Judas Maccabeus founded a new ruling dynasty, the Hasmoneans, which existed briefly before the region came under the control of Rome.

The Jewish people revolted against Roman rule in 70 CE, leading to the destruction of the second temple. The final destruction of Jerusalem occurred in 135 under the Roman Emperor Hadrian. He changed the city's name to Aelia Capitolina and the name of the country to Palaestina. With the cultic center of their religion gone, the religious leaders developed new methods of worship that centered in religious academies and in synagogues.

After Christianity became the official state religion of the Roman Empire in the early fourth century, Jews experienced persecution. They became known for their scholarship, trade, and banking over the next centuries, with periods of brutal persecution in Europe. Christians held Jews responsible for the death of Jesus, based on a passage in the New Testament. The Blood Libel, begun in England in 1144, falsely accused Jews of killing a Christian child to bake unleavened bread for Passover. This rumor persisted for centuries, and was repeated by Martin Luther during the Protestant Reformation. England expelled all Jews in 1290; they were not readmitted until 1656 under Oliver Cromwell, and not given citizenship until 1829. Jews were also held responsible for other catastrophes—namely poisoning wells and rivers to cause the Black Death in 1348—and were often made to wear special clothing, such as pointed hats, or badges with the Star of David or stone tablets on them.

The relationship between Muslims and Jews was more harmonious. During the Muslim Arab dominance, there was a "golden age" in Spain due to the contributions of Jews and Muslims, known as Moors in Spain. This ideal and harmonious period ended in 1492, when both Moors and Jews were expelled from Spain or forced to convert to Christianity.

Jews in Russia suffered as well. An estimated two million Jews fled the country to escape the pogroms (a Russian word meaning devastation) between 1881 and 1917. The twentieth-century Holocaust, in which an estimated six million Jews perished at the hands of Nazi Germany, was but the culmination of these centuries of persecution. The Nazis also destroyed more than six hundred synagogues.

The Holocaust gave impetus to the creation of the independent state of Israel. The Zionist movement, which called for the founding or reestablishment of a Jewish homeland, was started by Austrian Jew Theodor Herzl in the late nineteenth century, and succeeded in 1948. The British government, which had ruled the region under a mandate, left the area, and Israel was thus established. This ended the Diaspora, or dispersion, of the Jewish people that had begun nearly two millennia before when the Romans forced the Jews to leave their homeland.

Arab neighbors, some of whom had been removed forcibly from the land to create the nation of Israel, were displeased with the new political reality. Several wars have been fought, including the War of Independence in 1948, the Six-Day War in 1967, and the Yom Kippur War in 1973. In addition, tension between Israel and its neighboring Arab states is almost constant.

When the Jewish people were dispersed from Israel, two traditions began. The Ashkenazi Jews settled in Germany and central Europe. They spoke a mixture of the Hebrew dialect and German called Yiddish. Sephardic Jews lived in the Mediterranean countries, including Spain; their language, Ladino, mixed Hebrew and old Spanish.

Founder or Major Prophet

Judaism refers to three major patriarchs: Abraham, his son Isaac, and Isaac's son Jacob. Abraham is considered the first Jew and worshipper in Judaism, as the religion began through his covenant with God. As the forefather of the religion, he is often associated as the founder, though the founder technically is God, or Yahweh (YHWH). Additionally, the twelve sons of Jacob, who was also named Israel, became the founders of the twelve tribes of Israel.

Moses is regarded as a major prophet and as the Lawgiver. God revealed to Moses the complete law during the forty days that the Jewish leader spent on Mount Sinai during the wilderness journey from Egypt to Canaan. Thus, many attribute Moses as the founder of Judaism as a religion.

Philosophical Basis

Judaism began with Abraham's dissatisfaction with the polytheistic worship of his culture. Hearing the command of God to go to a land that would be shown to him, Abraham and his household obeyed. Abraham practiced circumcision and hospitality, cornerstones of the Jewish faith to this day. He and his descendents practiced a nomadic life, much like that of contemporary Bedouins. They migrated from one oasis or well to another, seeking pasture and water for the sheep and goats they herded.

The further development of Judaism came under the leadership of Moses. A Jewish child adopted by Pharaoh's daughter, he was raised and educated in the palace. As a man, he identified with the Jewish people, killing one of the Egyptians who was oppressing a Jew. He subsequently fled for his life, becoming a shepherd in the wilderness, where he remained for forty years. Called by God from a bush that burned but was not destroyed, he was commissioned to lead the people out of slavery in Egypt back to the Promised Land. That forty-year pilgrimage in the wilderness and desert of Arabia shaped the new nation.

Holy Places

The city of Jerusalem was first known as Salem. When King David overcame the Jebusites who lived there, the city, already some two thousand years old, became the capital of Israel. It is built on Mount Zion, which is still considered a sacred place. David's son Solomon built the First Temple in Jerusalem, centering the nation's spiritual as well as political life in the city. The Babylonians captured the city in 597 BCE and destroyed the Temple. For the next sixty years, the Jews remained in exile, until Cyrus the Persian conqueror of Babylon allowed them to return. They rebuilt the temple, but it was desecrated by Antiochus IV of Syria in 167 BCE. In 18 BCE, during a period of Roman occupation, Herod the Great began rebuilding and expanding the Temple. The Romans under the general Titus destroyed the Temple in 70 CE, just seven years after its completion.

The city eventually came under the rule of Persia, the Muslim Empire, and the Crusaders before coming under control of Britain. In 1948 an independent state of Israel was created. The following year, Jerusalem was divided between Israel, which made the western part the national capital, and Jordan, which ruled the eastern part of the city. The Western or Wailing Wall, a retaining wall built during Herod's time, is all that remains of the Second Temple. Devout Jews still come to the Wailing Wall to pray, sometimes placing their petitions on paper and folding the paper into the Wall's crevices. The Wall is known as a place where prayers are answered and a reminder of the perseverance of the Jewish people and faith. According to tradition, the Temple will be rebuilt when Messiah comes to inaugurate God's Kingdom.

The Temple Mount, located just outside Jerusalem on a natural acropolis, includes the Dome of the Rock. This shrine houses a rock held sacred by both Judaism and Islam. Jewish tradition states that it is the spot from which the world was created and the spot on which Abraham was asked to sacrifice his son Isaac. Muslims believe that from this rock Muhammad ascended for his night journey to heaven. Much of Jerusalem, including this holy site, has been and continues to be fought over by people of three faiths: Judaism, Islam, and Christianity.

Moses received the law from God on Mount Sinai. It is still regarded as a holy place.

JUDAISM IN DEPTH

Sacred Symbols

Observant Jewish men pray three times daily at home or in a synagogue, a center of worship, from the word meaning "meeting place." They wear a tallis, or a prayer shawl with tassles, during their morning prayer and on Yom Kippur, the Day of Atonement. They may also cover their heads as a sign of respect during prayer, wearing a skullcap known as a kippah or yarmulka. They find their prayers and blessings in a siddur, which literally means "order," because the prayers appear in the order in which they are recited for services. Jewish daily life also includes blessings for many things, including food.

Tefillin or phylacteries are the small black boxes made of leather from kosher animals that Jewish men wear on their foreheads and their left upper arms during prayer. They contain passages from the Torah. Placing the tefillin on the head reminds them to think about the Torah, while placing the box on the arm puts the Torah close to the heart.

The Law of Moses commands the people to remember the words of the law and to teach them to the children. A mezuzah helps to fulfill that command. A small box with some of the words of the law written on a scroll inside, a mezuzah is hung on the doorframes of every door in the house. Most often, the words of the Shema,

the Jewish recitation of faith, are written on the scroll. The Shema is repeated daily. "Hear, O Israel: the Lord your God, the Lord is one. . . . Love the Lord your God with all your heart, and with all your soul, and with all your might."

Jews adopted the Star of David, composed of two intersecting triangles, during the eighteenth century. There are several interpretations of the design. One is that it is the shape of King David's shield. Another idea is that it stands for daleth, the first letter of David's name. A third interpretation is that the six points refer to the days of the work week, and the inner, larger space represented the day of rest, the Sabbath, or Shabot. The Star of David appears on the flag of Israel. The flag itself is white, symbolizing peace and purity, and blue, symbolizing heaven and reminding all of God's activity.

The menorah is a seven-branch candlestick representing the light of the Torah. For Hanukkah, however, an eight-branched menorah is used. The extra candle is the servant candle, and is the one from which all others are lit.

Because the Torah is the crowning glory of life for Jewish people, a crown is sometimes used on coverings for the Torah. The scrolls of Torah are stored in a container, called an ark, which generally is covered with an ornate cloth called a mantle. The ark and mantle are often elaborately decorated with symbols, such as the lion of Judah. Because the Torah scroll, made of parchment from a kosher animal, is sacred and its pages are not to be touched, readers use a pointed stick called a yad. Even today, Torahs are written by hand in specially prepared ink and using a quill from a kosher bird. Scribes are trained for seven years.

A shofar is a ram's horn, blown as a call to repentance on Rosh Hashanah, the Jewish New Year. This holiday is the beginning of a ten-day preparation for the Day of Atonement, which is the most holy day in the Jewish calendar and a time of both fasting and repentance.

Sacred Practices & Gestures

Sacred practices can apply daily, weekly, annually, or over a lifetime's events. Reciting the Shema, the monotheistic creed taken from the

Torah, is a daily event. Keeping the Sabbath occurs weekly. Each year the festivals described above take place. Circumcision and bar or bat mitzvah are once-in-a-lifetime events. Each time someone dies, the mourners recite the Kaddish for seven days following death, and grieve for a year.

Food Restrictions

Kosher foods are those that can be eaten based on Jewish law. Animals that chew the cud and have cloven hooves, such as cows and lamb, and domestic poultry are considered kosher. Shellfish, pork, and birds of prey are forbidden. Keeping kosher also includes the method of preparing and storing the food. This includes animals which are slaughtered in a way to bring the least amount of pain and from which all blood is drained. In addition, dairy and meat products are to be kept separate, requiring separate refrigerators in the homes of the Orthodox.

Rites, Celebrations & Services

Sabbath is the weekly celebration honoring one of the Ten Commandments, which commands the people to honor the Sabbath by doing no work that day. The practice is rooted in the Genesis account that God rested on the seventh day after creating the world in six days. Because the Jewish day begins at sundown, the Sabbath lasts from Friday night to Saturday night. Special candles are lit and special food—included the braided egg bread called challah—for the evening meal is served. This day is filled with feasting, visiting, and worship.

Boys are circumcised at eight days of age. This rite, B'rit Milah, meaning "seal of the covenant," was first given to Abraham as a sign of the covenant. A trained circumciser, or mohel, may be a doctor or rabbi. The boy's name is officially announced at the ceremony. A girl's name is given at a special baby-naming ceremony or in the synagogue on the first Sabbath after she is born.

A boy becomes a "son of the commandment," or bar mitzvah, at age thirteen. At a special ceremony, the young man reads a portion of Torah that he has prepared ahead of time. Most boys also give a speech at the service. Girls become bat mitzvah at age twelve. This ceremony developed in the twentieth century. Not all Orthodox communities will allow this rite. Girls may also read from the Torah and give a sermon in the synagogue, just as boys do.

When a Jewish person dies, mourners begin shiva, a seven-day mourning period. People usually gather at the home of the deceased, where mirrors are covered. In the home, the Kaddish, a collection of prayers that praise God and celebrate life, is recited. Traditionally, family members mourn for a full year, avoiding parties and festive occasions.

The Jewish calendar offers a series of feasts and festivals, beginning with Rosh Hashanah, the Jewish New Year. At this time, Jews recall the creation. They may also eat apples that have been dipped into honey and offer each other wishes for a sweet New Year. The next ten days are a time of reflection on the past year, preparing for Yom Kippur.

This Day of Atonement once included animal sacrifice at the Temple. Now it includes an all-day service at the synagogue and a twenty-five-hour fast. A ram's horn, called a shofar, is blown as a call to awaken to lead a holier life. The shofar reminds Jewish people of the ram that Abraham sacrificed in the place of his son, Isaac.

Passover, or Pesach, is the spring remembrance of God's deliverance of the people from slavery in Egypt. In the night that the Jewish people left Egypt, they were commanded to sacrifice a lamb for each household and sprinkle the blood on the lintels and doorposts. A destroying angel from God would "pass over" the homes with blood sprinkled. During the first two nights of Passover, a special meal is served known as a Seder, meaning order. The foods symbolize different aspects of the story of deliverance, which is told during the meal by the head of the family.

Shavuot has its origins as a harvest festival. This celebration of Moses receiving the Torah on Mount Sinai occurs fifty days after the second day of Passover. To welcome the first fruits of the season, the synagogue may be decorated with fruit and flowers. Traditionally, the Ten Commandments are read aloud in the synagogue.

Purim, which occurs in February or March, celebrates the deliverance of the Jews during their captivity in Persia in the fifth century BCE. The events of that experience are recorded in the Book of Esther in the Hebrew Bible (Tanakh). The book is read aloud during Purim.

Sukkot, the feast celebrating the end of the harvest, occurs in September or October. Jews recall God's provision for them in the wilderness when they left Egypt to return to Canaan. Traditionally, huts are made and decorated with flowers and fruits. The conclusion of Sukkot is marked by a synagogue service known as Simchat Torah, or Rejoicing in the Law. People sing and dance as the Torah scrolls are carried and passed from person to person.

Hanukkah, known as the Festival of Lights, takes place over eight days in December. It celebrates the rededicating of the Temple under the leader Judas Maccabeus, who led the people in recapturing the structure from Syria in 164 BCE. According to the story, the Jews had only enough oil in the Temple lamp to last one day, but the oil miraculously lasted for eight days, after which Judas Maccabeus re-dedicated the Temple. On each day of Hanukkah, one of the eight candles is lit until all are burning. The gift-giving custom associated with Hanukkah is relatively new, and may derive from traditional small gifts of candy or money. The practice may also have been encouraged among those integrated with communities that exchange gifts during the Christmas season.

Judy A. Johnson, MTS

Bibliography

Barnes, Trevor. *The Kingfisher Book of Religions.* New York: Kingfisher, 1999. Print.

"A Buffet to Suit All Tastes." *Economist* 28 Jul. 2012: Spec. section 4–6. Print.

Charing, Douglas. *Judaism.* London: DK, 2003. Print.

Coenen Snyder, Saskia. *Building a Public Judaism: Synagogues and Jewish Identity in Nineteenth-Century Europe.* Cambridge: Harvard UP, 2013. E-book.

Diamant, Anita. *Living a Jewish Life.* New York: Collins, 1996. Print.

Exler, Lisa and Rabbi Jill Jacobs. "A Judaism That Matters." *Journal of Jewish Communal Service* 87.1/2 (2012). 66–76. Print.

Gelernter, David Hillel. *Judaism: A Way of Being.* New Haven: Yale UP, 2009. E-book.

Kessler, Edward. *What Do Jews Believe?* New York: Walker, 2007. Print.

Krieger, Aliza Y. "The Role of Judaism in Family Relationships." *Journal of Multicultural Counseling & Development* 38.3 (2010): 154–65. Print.

Langley, Myrtle. *Religion.* New York: Knopf, 1996. Print.

Madsen, Catherine. "A Heart of Flesh: Beyond 'Creative Liturgy.'" *Cross Currents* 62.1 (2012): 11–20. Print.

Meredith, Susan. *The Usborne Book of World Religions.* London: Usborne, 1995. Print.

Schoen, Robert. *What I Wish My Christian Friends Knew About Judaism.* Chicago: Loyola, 2004. Print.

Stefon, Matt. *Judaism: History, Belief, and Practice.* New York: Britannica Educational, 2012. E-book.

Wertheimer, Jack. "The Perplexities of Conservative Judaism." *Commentary* Sept. 2007: 38–44. Print.

Wilkinson, Philip. *Religions.* New York: DK, 2008. Print.

Sikhism

General Description

The youngest of the world religions, Sikhism has existed for only about five hundred years. Sikhism derives from the Sanskrit word *sishyas*, which means "disciple"; in the Punjabi language, it also means "disciple."

Number of Adherents Worldwide

An estimated 24.5 million people follow the Sikh religion. Most of the devotees live in Asia, particularly in the Punjab region of India (Wilkinson, p. 335).

Basic Tenets

Sikhism is a monotheistic religion. The deity is God, known as Nam, or Name. Other synonyms include the Divine, Ultimate, Ultimate Reality, Infinity, the Formless, Truth, and other attributes of God.

Sikhs adhere to three basic principles. These are hard work (kirt kao), worshipping the Divine Name (nam japo), and sharing what one has (vand cauko). Meditating on the Divine Name is seen as a method of moving toward a life totally devoted to God. In addition, Sikhs believe in karma, or moral cause and effect. They value hospitality to all, regardless of religion, and oppose caste distinctions. Sikhs delineate a series of five stages that move upward to gurmukh, total devotion to God. This service is called Seva. Sahaj, or tranquility, is practiced as a means of being united with God as well as of generating external good will. Sikhs are not in favor of external routines of religion; they may stop in their temple whenever it is convenient during the day.

Sikhism does not include a belief in the afterlife. Instead, the soul is believed to be reincarnated in successive lives and deaths, a belief borrowed from Hinduism. The goal is then to break this karmic cycle, and to merge the human spirit with that of God.

Sacred Text

The Guru Granth Sahib (also referred to as the Aad Guru Granth Sahib, or AGGS), composed of Adi Granth, meaning First Book, is the holy scripture of Sikhism. It is a collection of religious poetry that is meant to be sung. Called shabads, they were composed by the first five gurus, the ninth guru, and thirty-six additional holy men of northern India. Sikhs always show honor to the Guru Granth Sahib by carrying it above the head when in a procession.

A second major text is the Dasam Granth, or Tenth Book, created by followers of Guru Gobind Singh, the tenth guru. Much of it is devoted to retelling the Hindu stories of Krishna and Rama. Those who are allowed to read and care for the Granth Sahib are known as granthi. Granthi may also look after the gurdwara, or temple. In the gurdwara, the book rests on a throne with a wooden base and cushions covered in cloths placed in a prescribed order. If the book is not in use, it is covered with a cloth known as a rumala. When the book is read, a fan called a chauri is fanned over it as a sign of respect, just as followers of the gurus fanned them with chauris. At Amritsar, a city in northwestern India that houses the Golden Temple, the Guru Granth Sahib is carried on a palanquin (a covered, carried bed). If it is carried in the city, a kettle drum is struck and people welcome it by tossing rose petals.

Major Figures

Guru Nanak (1469–1539) is the founder of Sikhism. He was followed by nine other teachers, and collectively they are known as the Ten Gurus. Each of them was chosen by his predecessor and was thought to share the same spirit of that previous guru. Guru Arjan (1581–1606), the fifth guru, oversaw completion of the Golden Temple in Amritsar, India. Guru Gobind Singh (1675–1708) was the tenth and last human guru. He decreed that the True Guru henceforth would be the Granth Sahib, the scripture of the Sikhs. He also founded the Khalsa, originally a military order of male Sikhs willing to die for the faith; the term is now used to refer to all baptized Sikhs.

Major Holy Sites

Amritsar, India, is the holy city of Sikhism. Construction of the city began under Guru Ram Das (1574–1581), the fourth guru, during the 1570s. One legend says that the Muslim ruler, Emperor Akbar, gave the land to the third guru, Guru Amar Das (1552–74). Whether or not that is true, Amar Das did establish the location of Amritsar. He chose a site near a pool believed to hold healing water.

When construction of the Golden Temple began, only a small town existed. One legend says that a Muslim saint from Lahore, India, named Mian Mir laid the foundation stone of the first temple. It has been demolished and rebuilt three times. Although pilgrimage is not required of Sikhs, many come to see the shrines and the Golden Temple. They call it Harmandir Sahib, God's Temple, or Darbar Sahib, the Lord's Court. When the temple was completed during the tenure of the fifth guru, Arjan, he placed the first copy of the Guru Granth Sahib inside.

Every Sikh temple has a free kitchen attached to it, called a langar. After services, all people, regardless of caste or standing within the community, sit on the floor in a straight line and eat a simple vegetarian meal together. As a pilgrimage site, the langar serves 30,000–40,000 people daily, with more coming on Sundays and festival days. About forty volunteers work in the kitchen each day.

Major Rites & Celebrations

In addition to the community feasts at temple langars, Sikhs honor four rites of passage in a person's life: naming, marriage, initiation in Khalsa (pure) through the Amrit ceremony, and death.

There are eight major celebrations and several other minor ones in Sikhism. Half of them commemorate events in the lives of the ten gurus.

The others are Baisakhi, the new year festival; Diwali, the festival of light, which Hindus also celebrate; Hola Mahalla, which Gobind Singh created as an alternative to the Hindu festival of Holi, and which involves military parades; and the installing of the Guru Granth Sahib.

ORIGINS

History & Geography

The founder of Sikhism, Nanak, was born in 1469 CE in the Punjab region of northeast India, where both Hinduism and Islam were practiced. Both of these religions wanted control of the region. Nanak wanted the fighting between followers of these two traditions to end and looked for solutions to the violence.

Nanak blended elements of both religions and also combined the traditional apparel of both faiths to construct his clothing style. The Guru Granth Sahib further explains the division between Sikhs and the Islamic and Muslim faiths:

Nanak would become the first guru of the Sikh religion, known as Guru Nanak Dev. A Muslim musician named Bhai Mardana, considered the first follower, accompanied Nanak in his travels around India and Asia. Guru Nanak often sang, and singing remains an important part of worship for Sikhs. Before his death, Nanak renamed one of his disciples Angad, a word meaning "a part of his own self." He became Guru Angad Dev, the second guru, thus beginning the tradition of designating a successor and passing on the light to that person.

Guru Baba Ram Das, the fourth guru, who lived in the sixteenth century, began constructing Amritsar's Golden Temple. The structure was completed by his successor, Guru Arjan Dev, who also collected poems and songs written by the first four gurus and added his own. He included the work of Kabir and other Hindu and Muslim holy men as well. This became the Adi Granth, which he placed in the Golden Temple.

Guru Arjan was martyred in 1606 by Jehangir, the Muslim emperor. His son Hargobind became the sixth guru and introduced several important practices and changes. He wore two swords, representing both spiritual and worldly authority. Near the Golden Temple he had a building known as Akal Takht, or Throne of the Almighty, erected. In it was a court of justice as well as a group of administrators. Even today, orders and decisions enter the community from Akal Takht. Guru Hargobind was the last of the gurus with a direct link to Amritsar. Because of conflict with the Muslim rulers, he and all subsequent gurus moved from the city.

The tenth guru, Gobind Singh, created the Khalsa, the Community of the Pure, in 1699. The members of the Khalsa were to be known by five distinctive elements, all beginning with the letter *k*. These include kes, the refusal to cut the hair or trim the beard; kangha, the comb used to keep the long hair neatly combed in contrast to the Hindu ascetics who had matted hair; kaccha, shorts that would allow soldiers quick movement; kara, a thin steel bracelet worn to symbolize restraint; and kirpan, a short sword not to be used except in self-defense. Among other duties, members of this elite group were to defend the faith. Until the middle of the nineteenth century, when the British created an empire in India, the Khalsa remained largely undefeated.

In 1708, Guru Gobind Singh announced that he would be the final human guru. All subsequent leadership would come from the Guru Granth Sahib, now considered a living guru, the holy text Arjan had begun compiling more than a century earlier.

Muslim persecution under the Mughals led to the defeat of the Sikhs in 1716. The remaining Sikhs headed for the hills, re-emerging after decline of Mughal power. They were united under Ranjit Singh's kingdom from 1820 to 1839. They then came under the control of the British.

The British annexed the Punjab region, making it part of their Indian empire in 1849, and recruited Sikhs to serve in the army. The Sikhs remained loyal to the British during the Indian Mutiny of 1857–1858. As a result, they were given many privileges and land grants, and with

peace and prosperity, the first Singh Sabha was founded in 1873. This was an educational and religious reform movement.

During the early twentieth century, Sikhism was shaped in its more modern form. A group known as the Tat Khalsa, which was more progressive, became the dominant way of understanding the faith.

In 1897, a group of Sikh musicians within the British Army was invited to attend the Diamond Jubilee of Queen Victoria in England. They also traveled to Canada and were attracted by the nation's prairies, which were perfect for farming. The first group of Sikhs came to Canada soon after. By 1904, more than two hundred Sikhs had settled in British Columbia. Some of them later headed south to Washington, Oregon, and California in the United States. The first Sikh gurdwara in the United States was constructed in Stockton, California, in 1912. Sikhs became farmers, worked in lumber mills, and helped to construct the Western Pacific railroad. Yuba City, California, has one of the world's largest Sikh temples, built in 1968.

Sikh troops fought for Britain in World War I, achieving distinction. Following the war, in 1919, however, the British denied the Sikhs the right to gather for their New Year festival. When the Sikhs disobeyed, the British troops fired without warning on 10,000 Sikhs, 400 of whom were killed. This became known as the first Amritsar Massacre.

The British government in 1925 did give the Sikhs the right to help manage their own shrines. A fragile peace ensued between the British and the Sikhs, who again fought for the British Empire during World War II.

After the war ended, the Sikh hope for an independent state was dashed by the partition of India and Pakistan in 1947. Pakistan was in the Punjab region; thus, 2.5 million Sikhs lived in a Muslim country where they were not welcome. Many of them became part of the mass internal migration that followed Indian independence.

In 1966, a state with a Sikh majority came into existence after Punjab boundaries were redrawn. Strife continued throughout second half of twentieth century, however, as a result of continuing demands for Punjab autonomy. A second massacre at Amritsar occurred in 1984, resulting in the death of 450 Sikhs (though some estimates of the death toll are higher). Indian troops, under orders from Indian Prime Minister Indira Gandhi, fired on militant leaders of Sikhs, who had gone to the Golden Temple for refuge. This attack was considered a desecration of a sacred place, and the prime minister was later assassinated by her Sikh bodyguards in response. Restoration of the Akal Takht, the administrative headquarters, took fifteen years. The Sikh library was also burned, consuming ancient manuscripts.

In 1999, Sikhs celebrated the three-hundredth anniversary of the founding of Khalsa. There has been relative peace in India since that event. In the United States, however, Sikhs became the object of slander and physical attack following the acts of terrorism on September 11, 2001, as some Americans could not differentiate between Arab head coverings and Sikh turbans.

Founder or Major Prophet

Guru Nanak Dev was born into a Hindu family on April 15, 1469. His family belonged to the merchant caste, Khatri. His father worked as an accountant for a Muslim, who was also a local landlord. Nanak was educated in both the Hindu and Islamic traditions. According to legends, his teachers soon realized they had nothing further to teach him. After a direct revelation from Ultimate Reality that he received as a young man, Nanak proclaimed that there was neither Muslim nor Hindu. God had told Nanak "Rejoice in my Name," which became a central doctrine of Sikhism.

Nanak began to preach, leaving his wife and two sons behind. According to tradition, he traveled not only throughout India, but also eventually to Iraq, Saudi Arabia, and Mecca. This tradition and others were collected in a volume known as Janamsakhis. A Muslim servant of the family, Mardana, who also played a three-stringed musical instrument called the rebec, accompanied him, as did a Hindu poet, Bala Sandhu, who had been a friend from childhood

(though the extent of his importance or existence is often considered controversial).

Nanak traveled as an itinerant preacher for a quarter century and then founded a village, Kartarpur, on the bank of Punjab's Ravi River. Before his death he chose his successor, beginning a tradition that was followed until the tenth and final human guru.

Philosophical Basis

When Guru Nanak Dev, the first guru, began preaching in 1499 at about age thirty, he incorporated aspects of both Hinduism and Islam. From Hinduism, he took the ideas of karma and reincarnation. From Islam, he borrowed the Ultimate as the name of God. Some scholars see the influence of the religious reformer and poet Kabir, who lived from 1440 until 1518. Kabir merged the Bhakti (devotional) side of Hinduism with the Islamic Sufis, who were mystics.

Within the Hindu tradition in northern India was a branch called the Sants. The Sants believed that God was both with form and without form, unable to be represented concretely. Most of the Sants were illiterate and poor, but created poems that spoke of the divine being experienced in all things. This idea also rooted itself in Sikhism.

Guru Nanak Dev, who was raised as a Hindu, rejected the caste system in favor of equality of all persons. He also upheld the value of women, rejecting the burning of widows and female infanticide. When eating a communal meal, first begun as a protest against caste, everyone sits in a straight line and shares karah prasad (a pudding), which is provided by those of all castes. However, Sikhs are expected to marry within their caste. In some cases, especially in the United Kingdom, gurdwaras (places of worship) for a particular caste exist.

Holy Places

Amritsar, especially the Golden Temple, which was built in the sixteenth century under the supervision of the fifth guru, Guru Arjan, is the most sacred city.

Ram Das, the fourth guru, first began constructing a pool on the site in 1577. He called it

Amritsar, the pool of nectar. This sacred reflecting pool is a pilgrimage destination. Steps on the southern side of the pool allow visitors to gather water in bottles, to drink it, to bathe in it, or to sprinkle it on themselves.

SIKHISM IN DEPTH

Sacred Symbols

The khanda is the major symbol of Sikhism. It features a two-edged sword, representing justice and freedom, in the center. It is surrounded by a circle, a symbol of both balance and of the unity of God and humankind. A pair of curved swords (kirpans) surrounds the circle. One sword stands for religious concerns, the other for secular concerns. The khanda appears on Sikh flags, which are flown over every temple.

Members of the Khalsa have five symbols. They do not cut their hair, and men do not trim their beards. This symbol, kes, is to indicate a harmony with the ways of nature. To keep the long hair neat, a comb called a kangha is used. The third symbol is the kara, a bracelet usually made of steel to represent continuity and strength. When the Khalsa was first formed, soldiers wore loose-fitting shorts called kaccha. They were worn to symbolize moral restraint and purity. The final symbol is a short sword known as a kirpan, to be used only in self-defense. When bathing in sacred waters, the kirpan is tucked into the turban, which is worn to cover the long hair. The turban, which may be one of many colors, is wound from nearly five yards of cloth.

Sacred Practices & Gestures

Sikhs use Sat Sri Akal (truth is timeless) as a greeting, putting hands together and bowing toward the other person. To show respect, Sikhs keep their heads covered with a turban or veil. Before entering a temple, they remove their shoes. Some Sikhs may choose to wear a bindhi, the dot on the forehead usually associated with Hinduism.

When Guru Gobind Singh initiated the first men into the Khalsa, he put water in a steel bowl and added sugar, stirring the mixture with his sword and reciting verses from the Guru Granth as he did so. He thus created amrit (immortal), a holy water also used in baptism, or the Amrit ceremony. The water represents mental clarity, while sugar stands for sweetness. The sword invokes military courage, and the chanting of verses brings a poetic spirituality.

The Sikh ideal of bringing Ultimate Reality into every aspect of the day is expressed in prayers throughout the day. Daily morning prayer (Bani) consists of five different verses, most of them the work of one of the ten gurus; there are also two sets of evening prayers. Throughout the day, Sikhs repeat the Mul Mantra, "Ikk Oan Kar" (There is one Being). This is the first line of a brief creedal statement about Ultimate Reality.

Food Restrictions

Sikhs are not to eat halal meat, which is the Muslim equivalent of kosher. Both tobacco and alcohol are forbidden. Many Sikhs are vegetarians, although this is not commanded. Members of the Khalsa are not permitted to eat meat slaughtered according to Islamic or Hindu methods, because they believe these means cause pain to the animal.

Rites, Celebrations, & Services

The Sikhs observe four rite of passage rituals, with each emphasizing their distinction from the Hindu traditions. After a new mother is able to get up and bathe, the new baby is given a birth and naming ceremony in the gurdwara. The child is given a name based on the first letter of hymn from the Guru Granth Sahib at random. All males are additionally given the name Singh (lion); all females also receive the name Kaur (princess).

The marriage ceremony (anand karaj) is the second rite of passage. Rather than circle a sacred fire as the Hindus do, the Sikh couple walks four times around a copy of the Guru Granth Sahib, accompanied by singing. The bride often wears red, a traditional color for the Punjabi.

The amrit initiation into the Khalsa is considered the most important rite. It need not take place in a temple, but does require that five

Sikhs who are already Khalsa members conduct the ceremony. Amrit initiation may occur any time after a child is old enough to read the Guru Granth and understand the tenets of the faith. Some people, however, wait until their own children are grown before accepting this rite.

The funeral rite is the fourth and final rite of passage. A section of the Guru Granth is read. The body, dressed in the Five "K's," is cremated soon after death.

Initiation into the Khalsa is now open to both men and women. The earliest gurus opposed the Hindu custom of sati, which required a widow to be burned on her husband's funeral pyre. They were also against the Islamic custom of purdah, which required women to be veiled and covered in public. Women who are menstruating are not excluded from worship, as they are in some religions. Women as well as men can be leaders of the congregation and are permitted to read from the Guru Granth and recite sacred hymns.

The Sikh houses of worship are known as gurdwaras and include a langar, the communal dining area. People remove their shoes and cover their heads before entering. They touch their foreheads to the floor in front of the scripture to show respect. The service itself is in three parts. The first segment is Kirtan, singing hymns (kirtans) accompanied by musical instruments, which can last for several hours. It is followed by a set prayer called the Ardas, which has three parts. The first and final sections cannot be altered. In the first, the virtues of the gurus are extolled. In the last, the divine name is honored. In the center of the Ardas is a list of the Khalsa's troubles and victories, which a prayer leader recites in segments and to which the congregation responds with Vahiguru, considered a word for God. At the end of the service, members eat karah prasad, sacred food made of raw sugar, clarified butter, and coarse wheat flour. They then adjourn for a communal meal, Langar, the third section of worship.

Sikhism does not have a set day for worship similar to the Jewish Sabbath or Christian Sunday worship. However, the first day of the month on the Indian lunar calendar, sangrand,

and the darkest night of the month, masia, are considered special days. Sangrand is a time for praying for the entire month. Masia is often considered an auspicious time for bathing in the holy pool at the temple.

Four of the major festivals that Sikhs observe surround important events in the lives of the gurus. These are known as gurpurabs, or anniversaries. Guru Nanak's birthday, Guru Gobind Singh's birthday, and the martyrdoms of the Gurus Arjan and Tegh Bahadur comprise the four main gurpurabs. Sikhs congregate in the gurudwaras to hear readings of the Guru Granth and lectures by Sikh scholars.

Baisakhi is the Indian New Year, the final day before the harvest begins. On this day in 1699, Guru Gobind Singh formed the first Khalsa, adding even more importance to the day for Sikhs. Each year, a new Sikh flag is placed at all temples.

Diwali, based on a word meaning string of lights, is a Hindu festival. For Sikhs, it is a time to remember the return of the sixth guru, Hargobind, to Amritsar after the emperor had imprisoned him. It is celebrated for three days at the Golden Temple. Sikhs paint and whitewash their houses and decorate them with candles and earthenware lamps.

Hola Mohalla, meaning attack and place of attack, is the Sikh spring festival, which corresponds to the Hindu festival Holi. It is also a three-day celebration and a time for training Sikhs as soldiers. Originally, it involved military exercises and mock battles, as well as competitions in archery, horsemanship, and wrestling. In contemporary times, the festival includes athletic contests, discussion, and singing.

Judy A. Johnson, MTS

Bibliography

Barnes, Trevor. *The Kingfisher Book of Religions*. New York: Kingfisher, 1999. Print.

Dhanjal, Beryl. *Amritsar*. New York: Dillon, 1993. Print.

Dhavan, Purnima. *When Sparrows Became Hawks: The Making of the Sikh Warrior Tradition, 1699–1799*. Oxford: Oxford UP, 2011. Print.

Eraly, Abraham, et. al. *India*. New York: DK, 2008. Print.

Harley, Gail M. *Hindu and Sikh Faiths in America*. New York: Facts on File, 2003. Print.

Jakobsh, Doris R. *Sikhism and Women: History, Texts, and Experience*. Oxford, New York: Oxford UP, 2010. Print.

Jhutti-Johal, Jagbir. *Sikhism Today*. London, New York: Continuum, 2011. Print.

Langley, Myrtle. *Religion*. New York: Knopf, 1996. Print.

Mann, Gurinder Singh. *Sikhism*. Upper Saddle River: Prentice, 2004. Print.

Meredith, Susan. *The Usborne Book of World Religions*. London: Usborne, 1995. Print.

Sidhu, Dawinder S. and Neha Singh Gohil. *Civil Rights in Wartime: The Post-9/11 Sikh Experience*. Ashgate, 2009. E-book.

Singh, Nikky-Guninder Kaur. *Sikhism*. New York: Facts on File, 1993. Print.

Singh, Nikky-Guninder Kaur. *Sikhism: An Introduction*. Tauris, 2011. E-book.

Singh, Surinder. *Introduction to Sikhism and Great Sikhs of the World*. Gurgaon: Shubhi, 2012. Print.

Wilkinson, Philip. *Religions*. New York: DK, 2008. Print.

Index

Aalto, Alvar (1898–1976), 111

Aaltonen, Wäinö (1894–1966), 110

Above Us the Earth, 1977 (film), 506

Accardo, Salvatore, 232

The Adventures of Pinocchio (Collodi), 232

The Adventures of Tintin (comic series), 50

Aeneid (poem), 232

Aeschylus (c. 525–456 BCE), 170

Aftenposten, 360

Aftonbladet, 458

Agricola, Mikael (c. 1510–1557), 112

Ahrne, Marianne (1940–), 454

Albéniz, Isaac (1860–1909), 433

Alberti, Antonio (1390–1449), 393

Albert I (1848–1922), Prince of Monaco, 300

Alexander the Great (356–323 BCE), 173

All about My Mother (film), 434

Allegri, Gregorio (1582–1652), 491

Allegro Vivo Association (2002), 394

Allemansrätt (Everyman's Right), Sweden, 449

Almodóvar, Pedro, 434

Alps mountain range (Switzerland), 477

Alta Fjord (Norway), 358

Altamira Cave (Spain), 435

The Alzheimer Case, 2003 (film), 49

American Battle Monuments Commission (ABMC), 264

American Independence Day (July 4), 71

Ammaniti, Niccolo, 232

Amnesty International (AI), 253

Amsterdam, 308, 310–311, 316–318, 322

Andersen, Hans Christian (1805–1875), 69

Andorra
  agriculture, 18
  animal husbandry, 18
  architecture, 9–10
  armed forces, 16
  arts, 9, 11
  capital, 4
  climate, 6
  coins, 4
  cultural sites and landmarks, 11–12
  currency, 4
  dance, 10
  eating/meals, 7
  economy, 17
  education, 14
  energy/power/natural resources, 18
  entertainment, 11
  ethnic groups, 6
  families, 8
  fishing, 18
  flag description, 4
  food, 8–9
  food festivals, 7
  foreign policies, 16
  forestry, 18
  gestures and etiquette, 7
  government structure, 15
  greetings, 7
  health care, 14
  holidays, 12
  housing, 8
  human rights profile, 17
  industry, 18
  judicial system, 15
  labor, 18
  land area, 4
  languages, 6
  libraries, 12
  life's milestones, 9
  literature, 10–11
  local government, 15
  media and communications, 13
  mining/metals, 18
  museums, 12
  music, 10
  national anthem, 4
  national motto, 4
  native people, 6
  official language, 4
  plants and animals, 6
  political parties, 15
  population, 4, 6
  religions, 6
  standard of living, 13
  taxation, 15–16
  time zone, 4
  topography, 6
  tourism, 18
  transportation, 13
  visiting, 8
  water consumption, 13
  women's rights, 14
  youth culture, 12–13

Andorra la Vella, 4, 6, 9–13, 15

Andorran International Women's Association (AIWA), 14

Andorran Women's Association (AWA), 14

Andromache (play), 170

Anker, Albert (1831–1910), 474

Anne Boleyn (Queen of England), 92

Antigone (play), 170

Antoine I (1661–1731), Prince of Monaco, 298

Antonioni, Michelangelo, 230

Apollinaire, Guillaume (1880–1918), 300

Apollo Belvedere (statue), 493

Apostolic Palace (Vatican Palace), 493

Appel, Karel (1921–2006), 68

Aristophanes (c. 427–387 BCE), 170

Ari Thorgilsson, 187

Arouet, François-Marie (1694–1778), 131

Article 2 of UDHR, 56, 98, 157, 218, 253, 322, 343, 363, 383, 440, 482, 495, 514
Article 3 of UDHR, 76
Article 5 of UDHR, 343, 400
Article 6 of UDHR, 400
Article 7 of UDHR, 440
Article 9 of UDHR, 344, 440
Article 13 of UDHR, 344
Article 14 of UDHR, 344
Article 16 of UDHR, 36–37, 56, 76, 98, 215, 218, 363, 383, 462, 495, 514
Article 18 of UDHR, 37, 56, 98, 158, 178, 218, 322, 343, 363, 383, 462, 495, 514
Article 19 of UDHR, 37, 57, 98, 218, 344, 462
Article 20 of UDHR, 37, 57, 98, 344
Article 21 of UDHR, 76
Article 27 of UDHR, 514
Article 41 of UDHR, 215
Arts Council of Wales (ACW), 507
Asbjørnsen, Peter (1812–1885), 357
Asmunder Sveinsson (1893–1982), 190
Athens, 162, 164–165, 170–175, 178–179
Athens Festival (June to October), 173
The Athens News, 174
Auld Lange Syne (folk song), 413
Austria
    agriculture, 38
    animal husbandry, 38
    architecture, 28–29
    armed forces, 35–36
    arts, 28, 30–31
    capital, 22
    climate, 24
    coins, 22
    cultural sites and landmarks, 31–32
    currency, 22
    dance, 29
    eating/meals, 26
    economy, 37
    education, 34

energy/power/natural resources, 38
entertainment, 30–31
ethnic groups, 24
families, 27
fishing, 38
flag description, 22
food, 27–28
foreign policies, 36
forestry, 38
gestures and etiquette, 26
government structure, 35
greetings, 25
health care, 34–35
holidays, 32
housing, 27
human rights profile, 36–37
industry, 37–38
judicial system, 35
labor, 38
land area, 22
languages, 24
libraries, 32
life's milestones, 28
literature, 30
local government, 35
media and communications, 33
mining/metals, 38
museums, 32
music, 29–30
national anthem, 22
native people, 24
official language, 22
plants and animals, 25
political parties, 35
population, 22, 24
religions, 24
standard of living, 33
taxation, 35
time zone, 22
topography, 25
tourism, 38
transportation, 33
visiting, 26–27
water area, 22
water consumption, 33–34
women's rights, 34
youth culture, 33
Austrian National Library, 32
Avui, 437

Bacchae (play), 170
Bach, Johann Sebastian (1685–1750), 149
Balada da Praia dos Cães (Ballad of Dog's Beach, 1892) (Cardoso Pires), 377
Balzac, Honoré de (1799–1850), 131
Bambi, A Life in the Woods, 1923 (Salten), 30
Bank holidays (Scotland), 415
Barbour, John (c. 1320–1395), 413
Barnie, John, 507
Barral, Louis (1910–1999), 298
Barrie, J.M (1860–1937), 413
Battisti, Luccio, 232
Baudelaire, Charles (1821–1867), 150
Bayern Munich (football club), 151
BBC Radio Foyle, 339
BBC Radio Ulster, 339
BBC Scotland, 416–417
Beaubourg Museum, France, 132
The Beauty Queen of Leenane (play), 211
Beckett, Samuel (1906–1989), 210
Beckmann, Max (1884–1950), 149
Beethoven, Ludwig van (1770–1827), 29, 50, 149
The Beheading of Saint John the Baptist, 1608 (painting), 280
Belfast, 330, 335–341, 344–345
Belfast Agreement (Good Friday Agreement), 341–342, 344
Belfast Castle, 338
Belfast Telegraph, 339
Belgium
    agriculture, 58
    animal husbandry, 58
    architecture, 49
    armed forces, 55
    arts, 48–49, 50–51
    capital, 42
    climate, 44–45
    coins, 42
    cultural sites and landmarks, 51–52

currency, 42
drama, 49
eating/meals, 46
economy, 57
education, 53–54
energy/power/natural
    resources, 57
entertainment, 50–51
ethnic groups, 44
families, 47
fishing, 57–58
flag description, 42
food, 47–48
foreign policies, 55–56
forestry, 58
gestures and etiquette, 46
government structure, 54 55
greetings, 45–46
health care, 54
holidays, 52
housing, 47
human rights profile, 56–57
industry, 57
judicial system, 55
labor, 57
land area, 42
languages, 44
libraries, 52
life's milestones, 48
literature, 50
local government, 55
media and communications, 53
mining/metals, 58
museums, 52
music, 49–50
national anthem, 42
national motto, 42
native people, 44
official language, 42
plants and animals, 45
political parties, 55
population, 42, 44
religions, 44
standard of living, 53
taxation, 55
time zone, 42
topography, 45
tourism, 58
transportation, 52–53
visiting, 46–47
water area, 42

water consumption, 53
women's rights, 54
youth culture, 52
Belgium-Luxembourg Economic
    Union (BLEU), 269
Belgium's Armistice Day
    (November 11), 52
Belgium's Independence Day
    (July 21), 52
Bellando de Castro, Théophile,
    298
Belle Époque (1890–1914), 297
The Benaki Museum, Greece, 173
Benigni, Roberto (1952–), 231
Ben X, 2007 (film), 49
Beowulf (poem), 90
Bergman, Ingmar (1918–2007),
    454, 456
Berio, Luciano, 232
Berlin, 142, 144–147, 149–154,
    156–157, 159
Berlin Wall, 152
Berlioz, Hector (1803–1869), 131
Bern, 468, 470–471, 475–477,
    479, 483–484
Bernhard, Thomas (1931–1989),
    30
Bernini, Gianlorenzo
    (1598–1680), 491–492
Bertelsmann, 135
Biedermeier movement
    (1815–1848), 30
Big House novel, 209
Billy Elliot (film), 91
Bizet, Georges (1838–1875), 131
Björk (1965–), 189–190
Bjørneboe, Jens (1920–1977),
    356
Bjørnson, Bjørn, 356
Bjørnson, Bjørnstjerne
    (1832–1910), 356
Black Sea Economic Cooperation
    (BSEC), 177
Blair, Tony, 95
Blake, William, 90
Blasphemy Law, 514
The Blind (play), 50
Blixen, Karen (1885–1962), 69
The Blue Danube (music), 30
Boccaccio, Giovanni
    (1313–1375), 232

Böcklin, Arnold (1827–1901),
    474
Boléro (orchestral piece), 131
Bondebladet, 360
Borgen, Johan (1902–1977), 356
Borge, Victor (1909–2000), 69
Bosch, Hieronymus (1450–1516),
    314
Botta, Mario (1943–), 476
Botticelli, Sandro (c. 1445–1510),
    229, 491
Boucher, François (1703–1770),
    130
Bournonville, August
    (1805–1879), 69
Bouygues, 135
Bowen, Elizabeth (1899–1973),
    209
Boxing Day (December 26), 93
Branagh, Kenneth, 337
Brandenburg Concertos (music),
    149
Braque, Georges (1882–1963),
    130
Brecht, Bertolt (1898 1956), 150
Breidfjord, Sigurdur
    (1798–1846), 189
Bridget Jones's Diary (film), 91
British Armed Forces, 97
The British Broadcasting
    Corporation (BBC), 94, 214,
    339, 510
British Invasion, 89
The Bruce, 1376 (poem), 413
Brunelleschi, Filippo
    (1377–1446), 229–230
Bullfighting (dramatic sport),
    Spain, 434
Bull, Ole (1810–1880), 356
Bundeswehr (German armed
    forces), 156
Bunting, Edward (1773–1843),
    209
Burke, Augustus Joseph Nicholas
    (1838–1891), 335
Burke, Edmund (1729–1797),
    209
Burke, Kevin, 210
Burns, Robert (1759–1796), 413,
    416
Bush, George W., 217

Byron, Lord (1788–1824), 90, 476

Byzantine period (c. 300–1453 CE), 169

Caballé, Montserrat (1933–), 11

Calvino, Italo (1923–1985), 232

Camões, Luís Vaz de (1524–1580), 376–377

Camus, Albert (1913–1960), 132

Cantar de Mio Cid (poem), 434

Cantata No. 4 (music), 149

The Canterbury Tales (book), 90

Caravaggio, Michelangelo Merisi da (1571–1610), 280

Cardiff, 500, 502, 506, 509–510, 512

Cardoso Pires, José (1925–1998), 377

Carling, Finn (1925–2004), 356

Carmen (opera), 131

The Carnival of the Animals (musical suite), 131

Carroll, Liz, 210

Caruso, Enrico (1873–1921), 231

Casals, Pau (1876–1973), 11

Cash Benefit Act, 1998 (Norway), 361

Cassarino, Giulio (1588–1637), 280

Castle Rackrent, 1800 (Edgeworth), 209

Castorf, Frank, 151

Catalan Countries, 4

Cavafy, Constantine (1863–1933), 172

Celentano, Adriano, 232

Celtes, Conradus (1459–1508), 150

Ceramic arts (San Marino), 393

Cervantes, Miguel de (1547–1616), 434

Charlemagne (742–814), 10, 44, 148

Château de Chillon (castle), 476

Chevalier, Maurice (1888–1972), 131

Child abuse
    Malta, 287
    Switzerland, 482

Children of Nature, 1991 (film), 190

Christiana Theatre (Norway), 356

The Christian Democratic Union (CDU), 156

Christmas Eve (1904–1905) (painting), 453

The Chronicles of Narnia (Lewis), 337

Cicero (106–43 BCE), 231

The Civil Partnership Act of 2004, 98, 514

Clarke, Gillian, 507

Clinton, Bill, 217

CoBrA movement, 68

Cocteau, Jean (1889–1963), 299

Coleridge, Samuel Tyler, 90

Collamarini, Edoardo (1863–1928), 393

Collodi, Carlo (1826–1890), 232

The Communal Council of Monaco, 302–303

Communications. *See* Media and communications

Community of Portuguese Language Countries (Comunidade dos Países de Língua Portuguesa, or CPLP), 370, 383

Comprehensive Education Act (1921), 116

Concierto de Aranjuez (music), 433

Congreve, William (1670–1729), 335

Conscience, Henri "Hendrik" (1812–1883), 50

Constable, John (1776–1837), 88

Constant Nieuwenhuys (1920–2005). *See* Nieuwenhuys, Constant (1920–2005)

Constitution Day (May 17), Norway, 359

The Convent, 1995 (film), 376

Copenhagen, 62, 64–65, 71–77

Copenhagen Jazz Festival, 70

The Copenhagen Post, 72

Corriere della Sera, 235

Cosi fan Tutte (music), 29

Costa, Pedro (1959–), 376

The Council for Equality, 1972 (Finland), 116

Council of Cultural Associations, 1991 (San Marino), 395

The Count of Monte Cristo, 1845 (Dumas), 131

Courbet, Gustave (1819–1877), 476

The Courier, 417

Courtesies. *See* Customs and courtesies

Courts. *See* Judicial system

Cousins, James (1873–1956), 336

Cousteau, Jacques-Yves (1910–1997), 300

Crayfish party (Sweden), 451

Cré na Cille (Ó Cadhain), 210

Croce, Benedetto (1866–1952), 232

Cubism (revolutionary art style), 433

Culliford, Pierre (1928–1992), 50

Dada/Dadaism (cultural movement in Switzerland), 474

Dagbladet, 360

Dagens Nyheter, 458

Dagsavisen, 360

The Daily Mail, 94, 417

Dali, Salvador (1904–1989), 433

Dallapiccola, Luigi, 232

Danish Film Institute (DFI), 69

Dante Alighieri (c. 1265–1321), 232, 394

Das Leben der Anderen (film), 151

David (sculpture), 229

The Day of Unity (October 3), Germany, 152

Debussy, Claude (1862–1918), 131

The Decameron (Boccaccio), 232

The Decayed Gentleman (Conscience), 50

Declaration of the Rights of Man, 136, 138

Degas, Edgar (1834–1917), 130

De Gougesl, Olympe (1748–1793), 136

De Kooning, Willem
  (1904–1997), 314
Delacroix, Eugène (1798–1863),
  130, 132
Denmark
  agriculture, 77
  animal husbandry, 77
  architecture, 68–69
  armed forces, 74
  arts, 67–68, 70
  capital, 62
  climate, 64
  coins, 62
  cultural sites and landmarks,
    70–71
  currency, 62
  dependencies, 75
  drama, 69
  eating/meals, 65–66
  economy, 76
  education, 73
  energy/power/natural
    resources, 76–77
  entertainment, 70
  ethnic groups, 64
  families, 66
  fishing, 77
  flag description, 62
  food, 67
  foreign policies, 74–75
  forestry, 77
  gestures and etiquette, 65
  government structure, 74
  greetings, 65
  health care, 73–74
  holidays, 71
  housing, 66
  human rights profile, 75–76
  industry, 76
  judicial system, 74
  labor, 76
  land area, 62
  languages, 64
  libraries, 71
  life's milestones, 67
  literature, 69–70
  local government, 74
  media and communications, 72
  mining/metals, 77
  museums, 71
  music, 69

national anthem, 62
national motto, 62
native people, 64
official language, 62
plants and animals, 65
political parties, 74
population, 62, 64
religions, 64
standard of living, 73
taxation, 74
time zone, 62
topography, 64–65
tourism, 77
transportation, 72
visiting, 66
water area, 62
water consumption, 73
women's rights, 73
youth culture, 71–72
De Paor, Louis (1961–), 211
Dependencies
  Denmark, 75
  England, 97
  France, 138
  Netherlands, 321
  Norway, 363
  Spain, 440
Der Freishütz (German opera),
  149
Der Spiegel, 154
Der Standard, 33
De Sica, Vittorio (1901–1974),
  230
De Standaard, 53
The Deutsches Museum (German
  Museum), 152
Diari d'Andorra, 13
Diário Notícias, 380
Die Falscher (film), 31
Diepenbrock, Alphons
  (1862–1921), 315
Die Presse, 33
Die Welt, 154
Die Zeit, 154
Divine Comedy (poem), 232, 394
Domestic violence
  Andorra, 14
  Belgium, 56
  France, 136
  Germany, 155
  Greece, 175

Iceland, 194
Liechtenstein, 253
Luxembourg, 267
Malta, 285
Monaco, 302
Netherlands, 319
Northern Ireland, 340
Norway, 361, 363
Portugal, 381
San Marino, 398
Scotland, 418
Spain, 438, 440
Switzerland, 480
Donatello (1386–1466), 229
Don Giovanni (music), 29
Donne, John, 90
Donner, Georg Rafael
  (1693–1741), 28
*Do Not Go Gentle Into that Good
  Night* (poem), 507
Don Quixote (Cervantes), 434
Doric order, 170
Douwes Dekker, Eduard
  (1820–1887), 315
Doyle, Arthur Conan
  (1859–1930), 413
Doyle, Roddy (1958–), 211
Dracula, 1897 (Stoker), 209
Dreyer, Carl Theodor
  (1889–1968), 69
Dublin, 202, 204–205, 207–208,
  211–216, 219
Dufay, Guillaume (c. 1397–1474),
  50
Dumas, Alexandre (1802–1870),
  131, 476
Duncan, Isadora (1877–1927),
  150
Duodji (Sami handicraft),
  354–355
Dürer, Albrecht (1471–1528),
  148
DV (Dagblaðið Vísir), 193

Eaves, Steve, 508
Ebejer, Francis (1925–1993), 282
Eckersberg, Christoffer Wilhelm
  (1783–1853), 68
Eco, Umberto (1932–), 232
Edgeworth, Maria (1767–1849),
  209

Edinburgh (City of Literature), 406, 408, 414–417, 419, 421–422
Edinburgh Castle (Scotland), 414
Eduskunta (Finland), 117
Eiffel, Gustave, 133
Eiffel Tower, Paris, 133
8½ (1963) (film), 230
Einstein, Albert, 476–477
Eisteddfod festival, Wales, 509
Ekman, Benny (1955–), 456
Eldra (film), 506
Electra (play), 170
Eleftherotypia (Free Press), 174
Eliot, T.S. (1888–1965), 210
Elizabethan era (1558–1603), 90
Elizabeth II (Queen of England), 97
El País, 437
El Periodic, 13
Elytis, Odysseus (1911–1996), 172
Emperor Concerto (symphonies), 149
The Emperor's New Clothes (fairy tale), 69
The Employment Rights Act of 1996, 95
Engel, Carl Ludvig (1778–1840), 111
England
  agriculture, 99
  animal husbandry, 99
  architecture, 88–89
  armed forces, 97
  arts, 88–89, 91
  capital, 82
  climate, 84–85
  coins, 82
  cultural sites and landmarks, 91–92
  currency, 82
  dependencies, 97
  eating/meals, 86
  economy, 98
  education, 94–95
  energy/power/natural resources, 99
  entertainment, 91
  ethnic groups, 84
  families, 87

  film, 90–91
  fishing, 99
  flag, 82
  food, 87–88
  foreign policies, 97
  forestry, 99
  gestures and etiquette, 86
  government structure, 96
  greetings, 85–86
  health care, 95
  holidays, 93
  housing, 87
  human rights profile, 97–98
  industry, 98
  judicial system, 96
  labor, 99
  land area, 82
  languages, 84
  libraries, 92–93
  life's milestones, 88
  literature, 90
  local government, 96
  media and communications, 94
  mining/metals, 99
  museums, 92–93
  music, 89–90
  national anthem, 82
  native people, 84
  official language, 82
  plants and animals, 85
  political parties, 96
  population, 82, 84
  religions, 84
  standard of living, 94
  taxation, 96–97
  time zone, 82
  topography, 85
  tourism, 99–100
  transportation, 93–94
  visiting, 86–87
  water consumption, 94
  women's rights, 95
  youth culture, 93
Enright, Anne (1962–), 211
The Equal Pay Act of 1970, 95, 511
Erardi, Stefano (1620–1716), 280
Erasmus, Desiderius (1466–1536), 315
Erotokritos (poem), 171
Erro (1932–), 190

Espoo, Finland, 106
Espoo Jazz Festival, 113
Ethnos (Nation), 174
Etiquette. *See* Gestures and etiquette
Euripides (c. 485–406 BCE), 170
European and External Affairs Division (EEAD), 513
European ballroom dance styles (Norway), 357
European Coal and Steel Community (ECSC), 256
The European Court of Human Rights (ECHR), 157
European Environment Agency (EEA), 196
European Free Trade Association (EFTA), 196
European Security and Defence Policy (EDSP), 237
Evening Herald, 214
Exclusive economic zone (EEZ), France, 126
Expressen, 458

Fashion capital of the world. *See* Paris
Father of Reykjavik. *See* Skuli Magnusson
Faust (play), 150
Federal Assembly (Switzerland), 480
Federal Supreme Court (Switzerland), 480–481
Feet in Chains, 1936 (Roberts), 507
Fellini, Federico, 230
Fenech, Victor, 282
Fern Hill (poem), 507
Festival dei Due Mondi (Festival of Two Worlds), 233
Festival de la Bande Dessinee (comic strip festival), 132
Festival of Avignon, France, 132
Fête de la Musique (festival of music), 134
Fête Nationale (National Day, July 14), France, 134
Fidelio (symphonies), 149
Film
  England, 90–91

France, 131
Wales, 506
Finland
  agriculture, 120
  animal husbandry, 120
  architecture, 110–111
  armed forces, 117
  arts, 110, 112–113
  capital, 104
  climate, 106–107
  coins, 104
  cultural sites and landmarks,
    113–114
  currency, 104
  drama, 111
  eating/meals, 108
  economy, 119
  education, 115–116
  energy/power/natural
    resources, 119
  entertainment, 112–113
  ethnic groups, 106
  families, 109
  fishing, 119–120
  flag description, 104
  food, 109
  foreign policies, 117–118
  forestry, 120
  gestures and etiquette, 108
  government structure, 116
  greetings, 107–108
  health care, 116
  holidays, 114
  housing, 109
  human rights profile, 118–119
  industry, 119
  judicial system, 117
  labor, 119
  land area, 104
  languages, 106
  libraries, 114
  life's milestones, 109–110
  literature, 112
  local government, 117
  media and communications,
    115
  mining/metals, 120
  museums, 114
  music, 111–112
  national anthem, 104
  native people, 106

  official language, 104
  plants and animals, 107
  political parties, 117
  population, 104, 106
  religions, 106
  standard of living, 115
  taxation, 117
  time zone, 104
  topography, 107
  tourism, 120
  transportation, 115
  visiting, 108
  water area, 104
  water consumption, 115
  women's rights, 116
  youth culture, 114
Finlandia, 1899 (symphonic
  poem), 112
Finlandization, 118
Finland's Independence Day
  (December 6), 114
Fischli, Peter (b. 1952–), 476
Fishing
  Andorra, 18
  Austria, 38
  Belgium, 57–58
  Denmark, 77
  England, 99
  Finland, 119–120
  France, 139
  Germany, 159
  Greece, 179
  Iceland, 197–198
  Ireland, 219
  Italy, 239
  Luxembourg, 271
  Malta, 289
  Netherlands, 323
  Northern Ireland, 345
  Norway, 364
  Portugal, 384
  Scotland, 422
  Spain, 441
  Sweden, 463
  Switzerland, 483
  Wales, 515
Flamenco (Spanish folk music
  and dance), 433
Flesch, Colette (1937–), 267
Fontaine, Edmond de la
  (1823–1891), 263

Football. See Soccer
Forestry Commission Scotland,
  422
The Four Seasons (song), 231
Fragonard, Jean-Honoré
  (1732–1806), 130
France
  agriculture, 139
  animal husbandry, 139
  architecture, 130–131
  armed forces, 137
  arts, 130, 132–133
  capital, 124
  climate, 126
  coins, 124
  cultural sites and landmarks,
    133–134
  currency, 124
  dependencies, 138
  eating/meals, 127–128
  economy, 138
  education, 135–136
  energy/power/natural
    resources, 139
  entertainment, 132–133
  ethnic groups, 126
  families, 128
  film, 131
  fishing, 139
  flag description, 124
  food, 129
  foreign policies, 137–138
  forestry, 139
  gestures and etiquette, 127
  government structure, 136–137
  greetings, 127
  health care, 136
  holidays, 134
  housing, 128–129
  human rights profile, 138
  industry, 139
  judicial system, 137
  labor, 139
  land area, 124
  languages, 124, 126
  libraries, 134
  life's milestones, 129
  literature, 131–132
  local government, 137
  media and communications,
    135

mining/metals, 139
museums, 134
music, 131
national anthem, 124
national motto, 124
native people, 126
official language, 124
plants and animals, 127
political parties, 137
population, 124, 126
religions, 126
standard of living, 135
taxation, 137
time zone, 124
topography, 126–127
tourism, 139
transportation, 134–135
visiting, 128
water consumption, 135
women's rights, 136
youth culture, 134
Francesca da Rimini
  (1255–1285), 394
Francis, Karl, 506
Franco, Francisco (1892–1975),
  10
Franzi, Georges (1914–1997), 298
Franz Joseph II (1906–1989),
  Prince of Liechtenstein, 248,
  250
The Free Democratic Party
  (FDP), 156
Freedom Day (April 25),
  Portugal, 378
French Academy (Académie
  française), 126
French Armed Forces, 137
French language
  Belgium, 44
  France, 124, 126
  Greece, 164
  Luxembourg, 258
  Monaco, 294
  Switzerland, 470
  Vatican City, 490
Fréttablaðið (*The Newspaper*),
  193
Fridrik Thor Fridriksson (1954–),
  189–190
Friedrich, Casper David
  (1774–1840), 148

Friel, Brian (1929–), 336–337
From Morning to Midnight
  (Kaiser), 150

Gainsborough, Thomas
  (1727–1788), 88
Gallen-Kallela, Akseli
  (1865–1931), 110
Gallen-Kallela Museum
  (Finland), 114
Galway, James, 337
García Lorca, Federico
  (1898–1936), 434
Garnier, Charles (1825–1898),
  297, 299
Gaskell, Elizabeth, 90
Gaudi, Antoni (1852–1926), 435
Gazette Monaco-Côte d'Azur,
  301
Gazier, Michèle (1946–), 11
Gegerfelt, Victor von
  (1817–1915), 457
Gender Empowerment Measure
  (GEM), Austria, 34
Gender Equality Duty (Scotland),
  418
Gender Inequality Index,
  England, 95
Geography. *See* Environment and
  geography
The German Humanist
  Association, 148
German language
  Austria, 24
  Belgium, 44
  Denmark, 64
  Germany, 144
  Liechtenstein, 246
  Luxembourg, 258
  Switzerland, 470
The German National Library,
  152
Germany
  agriculture, 159
  animal husbandry, 159
  architecture, 148–149
  armed forces, 156
  arts, 148–149, 151
  capital, 142
  climate, 144
  coins, 142

cultural sites and landmarks,
  151–152
currency, 142
dance, 149–150
drama, 149–150
eating/meals, 146
economy, 158
education, 154
energy/power/natural
  resources, 159
entertainment, 151
ethnic groups, 144
families, 146–147
fishing, 159
flag description, 142
food, 147
foreign policies, 156–157
forestry, 159
gestures and etiquette,
  145–146
government structure, 155–156
greetings, 145
health care, 155
holidays, 152
housing, 147
human rights profile, 157–158
industry, 158
judicial system, 156
labor, 159
land area, 142
languages, 144
libraries, 152
life's milestones, 148
literature, 150
local government, 156
media and communications,
  153–154
migration, 157
mining/metals, 159
museums, 152
music, 149
national anthem, 142
native people, 144
official language, 142
plants and animals, 145
political parties, 156
population, 142, 144
religions, 144
sports, 151
standard of living, 154
taxation, 156

time zone, 142
topography, 144–145
tourism, 159
transportation, 153
visiting, 146
water consumption, 154
women's rights, 154–155
youth culture, 152–153
Ghana (għannej), Maltese folk music, 281
Giacometti, Alberto (1901–1966), 474
Giribaldi, Giuseppe (1807 1882), 394
Glasgow (World Centre of Music), 414
Glasgow School of Art (Scotland), 414
Glassmaking (Sweden), 453
Glencoe (Scottish Highlands), 415
Glencoe Massacre (Scotland), 415
Godard, Jean-Luc (1930–), 131
Goethe, Johann Wolfgang von (1749–1832), 150
Goldberg Variations (music), 149
Golden Age of Danish art, 68
Goldsmith, Oliver (1728–1774), 335
Good Bye Lenin! (film), 151
Gottfried von Strassburg, 150
Gotthard Base Tunnel (GBT), Switzerland, 478
The Government of Ireland Act of 1920, 341
Goya, Francisco (1746–1828), 432
Gramsci, Antonio (1891–1937), 232
Granados, Enrique (1867–1916), 433
Grand Duke Jean Museum of Modern Art (MUDAM), 263–264
Grass, Günter (1927–2015), 150
Greece
agriculture, 179
animal husbandry, 179
architecture, 169–170
armed forces, 176
arts, 169, 172

capital, 162
climate, 164–165
coins, 162
cultural sites and landmarks, 172–173
currency, 162
dance, 170–171
drama, 170
eating/meals, 166
economy, 178
education, 175
energy/power/natural resources, 179
entertainment, 172
ethnic groups, 164
families, 167
fishing, 179
flag description, 162
food, 167–168
foreign policies, 176–177
forestry, 179
gestures and etiquette, 166
government structure, 176
greetings, 165–166
health care, 175–176
holidays, 173
housing, 167
human rights profile, 177–178
industry, 178
judicial system, 176
labor, 178–179
land area, 162
languages, 164
libraries, 173
life's milestones, 168–169
literature, 171–172
local government, 176
media and communications, 174
mining/metals, 179
museums, 173
music, 170–171
national anthem, 162
national motto, 162
native people, 164
official language, 162
plants and animals, 165
political parties, 176
population, 162, 164
religions, 164
standard of living, 175

taxation, 176
time zone, 162
topography, 165
tourism, 179
transportation, 174
visiting, 166–167
water area, 162
water consumption, 175
women's rights, 175
youth culture, 173–174
Greek art, periods, 169
Greek Independence Day (March 15), 173
Green Heart of Europe. *See* Luxembourg
Gregorian chant (church music), 491
Lady Gregory, Isabella Augusta (1852–1932), 210, 336
Grenz Echo, 53
Grieg, Edvard (1843–1907), 356, 358
Grieg, Nordahl (1902–1943), 356
Grimm, Jacob, 154
Grimm, Wilhelm, 154
Gripsholm Castle (Sweden), 453
Gropius, Walter (1883–1969), 149
Gross domestic product (GDP)
Andorra, 13, 17
Austria, 37 38
Belgium, 57–58
Denmark, 74, 76–77
England, 98
Finland, 119–120
France, 138–139
Germany, 154, 158 159
Greece, 175, 178–179
Iceland, 197–198
Ireland, 218
Italy, 239–240
Liechtenstein, 250
Luxembourg, 270–271
Malta, 288–289
Monaco, 304
Netherlands, 321–322
Northern Ireland, 345
Norway, 364
Portugal, 384
San Marino, 401
Scotland, 421
Spain, 440

Sweden, 451, 463
Switzerland, 483
Wales, 514
Gross national product (GNP), 75
  Denmark, 75
  Germany, 158
  Monaco, 304
  Netherlands, 322
Grundtvig, Nikolai Frederik
  Severin (1783–1872), 69–70
Guernica (painting), 433
Guido da Montefeltro
  (1223–1298), 394
Gulliver's Travels, 1726 (Swift),
  209
Gustav Vasa (1496–1560), King
  of Sweden, 453, 457
Gutenberg, Johannes (c. 1400–
  1468), 150
Guy Fawkes Day (November 5),
  England, 93

Hachette-Lagardère, 135
Hakala, Pentti (1949–), 113
Hallgrimur Helgason (1959–),
  190
Häme Castle, Finland, 113
Hamlet (Shakespeare), 70
Hammershøi, Vilhelm
  (1864–1916), 68
Hamsun, Knut (1860–1952), 357
Handel, George Frederic
  (1685–1759), 208
Hans-Adam I, 1657–1712
  (Johann Adam Andreas), 247
Hans-Adam II (1945–), 248
Hansard, Glen, 211
Hardy, Thomas, 90
Haydn, Joseph (1732–1809), 29
Heaney, Seamus (1939–2013),
  210, 337
Hedd Wyn (film), 506
Heidi, 1880 (Spyri), 475
Heikkinen, Mikko (1949–), 113
Heine, Heinrich (1797–1856),
  150
Hellenic Air Force, 176
Hellenic Army, 176
Hellenic Navy, 176

Hellenistic period (323 BCE–146
  CE), 169–170
Helsingin Sanomat, 115
Helsinki, 104, 106–107, 110–111,
  113–116, 119–120
Henry, Paul (1876–1958), 335
Hen Wlad Fy Nhadau (national
  anthem of Wales), 507
The Herald, 417
Herbert, George, 90
Hergé, 50
Her Majesty's Armed Forces, 97
Hermans, Willem Frederik
  (1921–1995), 315
Hertz, Heinrich, 154
Hesiod (c. 700 BCE), 171
Het Nieuwsblad, 53
High Renaissance (1450–1527),
  491
Highway system
  England, 93
  France, 135
  Germany, 153
  Luxembourg, 266
  Portugal, 379
  San Marino, 397
  Switzerland, 478
Hiltunen, Eila (1922–2003), 110
Hinduism. *See also* Religions
  England, 84
  Portugal, 371
  Wales, 502
Hodler, Ferdinand (1853–1918),
  474
Hoel, Sigurd (1890–1960), 357
Hoffmann, E.T.A. (1776–1822),
  150
Hogarth, William (1697–1764),
  88
Holbein, Hans (c. 1497–1543),
  148
Holberg, Ludvig (1684–1754), 69
Hölderlin, Friedrich (1770–1843),
  150
Homer, 171
Honegger, Arthur (1892–1955),
  475
Hooft, Pieter Corneliszoon
  (1581–1647), 315

Hopkins, Gerard Manley
  (1844–1899), 210
Horta, Victor (1861–1947), 49
How Green Was My Valley, 1939
  (Llewellyn), 507
How Green Was My Valley, 1941
  (film), 506
Hugo, Victor (1802–1885), 131,
  264
Human Development Index (HDI).
  See also Social development
  Andorra, 13
  Austria, 33
  Belgium, 53
  Denmark, 73
  England, 94
  Finland, 115
  France, 135
  Germany, 154
  Greece, 175
  Iceland, 193, 196
  Ireland, 214
  Italy, 235
  Luxembourg, 266
  Malta, 284
  Netherlands, 318
  Northern Ireland, 340
  Norway, 360
  San Marino, 397
  Scotland, 417
  Spain, 437
  Sweden, 458
  Switzerland, 478
  Wales, 511
Human Rights Act of 1998 (UK),
  98, 514
Human rights profile
  Andorra, 17
  Austria, 36–37
  Belgium, 56–57
  Denmark, 75–76
  England, 97–98
  Finland, 118–119
  France, 138
  Germany, 157–158
  Greece, 177–178
  Iceland, 196–197
  Ireland, 217–218
  Italy, 238–239

Liechtenstein, 253
Luxembourg, 270
Malta, 287–288
Monaco, 303–304
Netherlands, 321–322
Northern Ireland, 343–344
Norway, 363–364
Portugal, 383–384
San Marino, 400–401
Scotland, 420–421
Spain, 440
Sweden, 462
Switzerland, 482–483
Vatican City, 495–496
Wales, 513–514
Human Traffic, 1999 (film), 506
Human trafficking
   Andorra, 14
   Belgium, 56
   Luxembourg, 267, 270
   Portugal, 381
   Sweden, 462
The Hunchback of Notre Dame,
   1831 (Hugo), 131
101 Reykjavik (dark comedy), 190
Hunt, William Holman
   (1827–1910), 89
Hutton, Ulrich von (1488–1523),
   150
Hyde, Douglas (1860 1949),
   210
Hymne Monégasque (Monaco's
   national anthem), 298

Ibsen, Henrik (1828–1906),
   356–357
Iceland
   agriculture, 198
   animal husbandry, 198
   armed forces, 195
   arts, 188, 189–190
   capital, 182
   climate, 184
   coins, 182
   cultural sites and landmarks,
      190–192
   currency, 182
   eating/meals, 186
   economy, 197
   education, 194

energy/power/natural
   resources, 197
entertainment, 189–190
ethnic groups, 184
families, 186–187
fishing, 197–198
flag description, 182
food, 187–188
foreign policies, 195–196
forestry, 198
gestures and etiquette, 186
government structure, 195
greetings, 185–186
health care, 194–195
holidays, 192
housing, 187
human rights profile, 196–197
industry, 197
judicial system, 195
labor, 197
land area, 182
languages, 184
libraries, 192
life's milestones, 188
literature, 189
local government, 195
media and communications,
   193
migration, 197
mining/metals, 198
museums, 192
music, 188–189
national anthem, 182
native people, 184
official language, 182
plants and animals, 185
political parties, 195
population, 182, 184
religions, 184
standard of living, 193–194
taxation, 195
time zone, 182
topography, 185
tourism, 198
transportation, 193
visiting, 186
water area, 182
water consumption, 194
women's rights, 194
youth culture, 192–193

The Icelandic Coast Guard, 195
Ice sculpting (Switzerland), 474
The Iliad (poem), 171
Il Solo Mio (song), 231
I'm Not Scared, 2001 (Ammaniti),
   232
Impressionism, France, 130
Independence Day (September
   21), Malta, 283
Inferno (poem), 394
Informalism movement, Finland,
   110
Ingibjorg Bjarnason (1867–1941),
   194
In-Nazzjon Taghna, 284
The Intelligence of Flowers
   (Maeterlinck), 50
International Business Wales
   (IBW), 513
The International Herald Tribune,
   235
International human rights law,
   196, 287, 303, 321–322
International Monetary Fund
   (IMF), 16
International Musical Eisteddfod,
   508
The Intruder (play), 50
Ionesco, Eugene (1909–1994),
   132
Ireland (Republic of Ireland)
   agriculture, 219
   animal husbandry, 219
   armed forces, 216
   arts, 210–211
   capital, 202
   climate, 204
   coins, 202
   cultural sites and landmarks,
      211–212
   currency, 202
   dance, 209
   eating/meals, 205–206
   economy, 218
   education, 214–215
   energy/power/natural
      resources, 219
   entertainment, 210–211
   ethnic groups, 204
   families, 206–207

fishing, 219
flag description, 202
food, 207–208
foreign policies, 216–217
forestry, 219
gestures and etiquette, 205
government structure, 215–216
greetings, 205
health care, 215
holidays, 213
housing, 207
human rights profile, 217–218
industry, 219
judicial system, 216
labor, 219
land area, 202
languages, 204
libraries, 212–213
life's milestones, 208
literature, 209–210
local government, 216
media and communications, 214
migration, 218
mining/metals, 219
museums, 212–213
music, 208–209
national anthem, 202
native people, 204
official language, 202
plants and animals, 205
political parties, 216
population, 202, 204
religions, 204
standard of living, 214
taxation, 216
time zone, 202
topography, 204–205
tourism, 219
transportation, 213–214
visiting, 206
water area, 202
water consumption, 214
women's rights, 215
youth culture, 213
The Irish Constitution, 215
Irish Defence Forces (Óglaigh na
    hÉireann), 216
Irish Independent, 214
Irish Lace Museum, 334–335
Irish literary revival period, 210

Irish News, 339
Irish Times, 214
Isacsson, Arne (1917–2010), 456
ISAF (International Security
    Assistance Force in
    Afghanistan), 269
Islam. *See also* Religions
    Norway, 350
    Spain, 428
    Sweden, 462
    Switzerland, 470
Istituto Musicale Sammarinese
    (San Marino Musical
    Institute), 394
The Italian Football Federation,
    233
Italian language. *See also*
    Languages; Official language
    Austria, 24
    Germany, 144
    Italy, 224
    Malta, 276
    Monaco, 294
    San Marino, 390
    Switzerland, 470
    Vatican City, 490
Italian neorealism, 230
Italy
    agriculture, 240
    animal husbandry, 240
    architecture, 230
    arts, 229, 232–233
    capital, 222
    climate, 224–225
    coins, 222
    cultural sites and landmarks,
        233–234
    currency, 222
    dance, 231
    drama, 230–231
    eating/meals, 226–227
    economy, 239
    education, 235
    energy/power/natural
        resources, 239
    entertainment, 232–233
    ethnic groups, 224
    families, 227
    fishing, 239
    flag description, 222
    food, 227–228

foreign policies, 237–238
forestry, 239–240
gestures and etiquette, 226
government structure, 236
greetings, 225–226
health care, 236
holidays, 234
housing, 227
human rights profile, 238–239
industry, 239
judicial system, 237
labor, 239
land area, 222
languages, 224
libraries, 234
life's milestones, 228
literature, 231–232
local government, 237
media and communications,
    235
mining/metals, 240
museums, 234
music, 231
national anthem, 222
native people, 224
official language, 222
plants and animals, 225
political parties, 236–237
population, 222, 224
religions, 224
standard of living, 235
taxation, 237
time zone, 222
topography, 225
tourism, 240
transportation, 234–235
visiting, 227
water area, 222
water consumption, 235
women's rights, 236
youth culture, 234
It-Torca, 284
Ivanhoe, 1819 (Scott), 413
Ivers, Eileen, 210

Jacobsen, Arne (1902–1971), 68
James James (1833–1902), 507
Lady Jane Grey (Queen of
    England), 92
Johann II (1840–1929), Prince of
    Liechtenstein, 248

John, Augustus (1878–1961), 506
Johnson, Samuel, 90
Jones, Thomas (1742–1803), 506
Jonsson, Asgrimur (1876–1958), 188
Jonsson, Einar (1874–1954), 188
Jornal de Notícias, 380
Jorn, Asger (1914–1973), 68
Josephine Mutzenbacher, 1906 (Salten), 30
Journal de Monaco, 301
Journey of Hope (film), 475
Joyce, James (1882–1941), 210
Judaism. *See also* Religions
    Norway, 350
    Spain, 428
    Wales, 502
Jugendweihe/Jugendfeier (youth ceremony), Germany, 148
The Jyllands Posten, 72

Kafka, Franz (1883–1924), 30, 150
Kaiser, Georg (1878–1945), 150
Kalevala (epic poem), 111–112
Kant, Immanuel, 154
Karagiozis, Greece, 170
Karahnjukar hydroelectric project (Iceland), 198
Kathimerini (Daily), 174
Kaurismaki, Aki, 111
Kazantzakis (1883–1957), 172
Kekkonen, Urho, 118
Keller, Gottfried (1819–1890), 475
Kelly, Grace (1929–1982), Princess of Monaco, 298
Kelly, Oisin, 337
KFOR (Kosovo Force), 269
The Kiasma (museum in Finland), 110
Kidnapped, 1886 (Stevenson), 413
Kierkegaard, Søren (1813–1855), 69, 356
Kingo, Thomas Hansen (1634–1703), 69
Kirscht, Émile (1913–1994), 262
The Kiss (1907–1908) (painting), 28
Kivi, Aleksis, 111–112
Klee, Paul (1879–1940), 474

Klimt, Gustav (1862–1918), 28
Klint, Karre (1888–1954), 68
Klopp, Nico (1894–1930), 262
Købke, Christen (1810–1848), 68
Koch, Robert, 154
Kongeriget Danmark. *See* Denmark
Kornaros, Vitsenzos (1553–1617), 171
Koun, Karolos (1909–1987), 170
Krag, Vilhelm, 356
Krog, Helge (1889–1962), 356
Kullervo, 1859 (drama), 111
Kullervo, 1892 (symphony), 112
Kurier, 33
Kutter, Joseph (1894–1941), 262
Kvindemuseet (women's museum in Denmark), 73

Laban, Rudolf (1879–1958), 150
La Dolce Vita, 1960 (film), 230
The Lady of the Lake, 1810 (poem), 413
Lagerlöf, Selma (1858–1940), 455
La Giaconda (*Mona Lisa*) (art work), 229
La Libre Belgique, 53
Landmarks. *See* Cultural sites and landmarks
Land of the Midnight Sun (Norrland, Sweden), 449
Landscape in the Silesian Mountains (painting), 148
Lang, Jack (1939–), 132
Larsson, Carl (1853–1919), 453
Larsson, Stieg (1954–2004), 455
La Sortie des usines Lumière (*Workers Leaving the Lumière Factory*) (film), 131
La Stampa, 235
The Last King of Scotland (film), 91
The Last September, 1929 (Bowen), 209
The Last Supper (painting), 229
Lawrence, D.H., 90
Laws in Wales Acts (1535–1542), 508
Laxness, Halldór (1902–1998), 189–190

The Least Resistance (film), 476
Le Brun, Charles (1619–1690), 130
Le Clézio, J.M.G. (1940–), 132
Le Corbusier (1887–1965), 474
Leganda de Santa Devota, or *Santa Devota* (Notari), 297
Lentz, Michel (1820–1893), 263
Leonardo da Vinci (1452–1519), 134, 229, 491
Leone, Sergio (1929–1989), 231
Les Miserables, 1862 (Hugo), 131
Le Soir, 53
Lessing, Doris, 90
Le Temps, 478
Letter to Brezhnev (film), 90
Lëtzebuerger Journal, 266
Lewis, C.S. (1898–1963), 337
Liberty Leading the People, 1830 (painting), 130
Liechtenstein
    agriculture, 251
    area, 244
    arts, 249–250
    capital, 244
    climate, 246
    coins, 244
    cultural sites and landmarks, 249
    currency, 244
    economy, 250
    energy/power/natural resources, 250–251
    entertainment, 249–250
    ethnic groups, 246
    foreign policies, 252–253
    government structure, 252
    history, 247–249
    human rights profile, 253
    industry, 250
    languages, 246
    libraries, 250
    media and communications, 251–252
    museums, 250
    national anthem, 244
    national motto, 244
    native people, 246
    official language, 244
    plants and animals, 247
    population, 244, 246

religions, 246
topography, 246–247
tourism, 251
transportation, 251
Liechtensteiner Vaterland, 251
Liechtensteiner Volksblatt,
251–252
Liewo, 251
Life is Beautiful (film), 231
Lindblom, Gunnel (1931–), 454
Lindgren, Astrid (1907–2002),
455
Lindt, Rodolphe, 483
Linnaeus, Carl (1707–1778), 455
Linna, Väinö (1920–1992), 112
The Lion of Flanders
(Conscience), 50
Lisbon, 368, 370, 373, 375–380,
382–383, 385
Lisbon Metro (Portugal), 379
Literacy. *See* Education
The Little Mermaid (fairy tale), 69
Liverpool Daily Post, 510
Living standard. *See* Standard of
living
Llewellyn, Richard (1906–1983),
506–507
Llwyd, Iwan, 508
Lobo Antunes, António (1942–),
377
Loch Ness Monster (Scotland),
415
London, 82, 84, 90–98, 100
Lönnrot, Elias (1802–1884), 112
Loos, Adolf (1870–1933), 29
Lope de Vega (1562–1635), 433
Lorenzetti, Pietro, 233
L-Orizzont, 284
L'Osservatore Romano (*The
Rome Observer*), 494
Louça de Coimbra (Portuguese
pottery), 375
The Louis Notari Library, 300
Louis XIV (1638–1715), 130
Louvre Museum, France, 134
Ludwig II (1845–1886), 152
Luke, John, 337
Lumière, Auguste (1862–1954),
131
Lumière, Louis (1864–1948),
131

Lundbye, Johan Thomas
(1818–1848), 68
Luther, Martin, 149–150, 154
Luxembourg
agriculture, 271
animal husbandry, 271
architecture, 262
armed forces, 269
arts, 262, 263–264
capital, 256
climate, 258
coins, 256
cultural sites and landmarks,
264
currency, 256
dance, 262
drama, 262
eating/meals, 260
economy, 270
education, 267
energy/power/natural
resources, 271
entertainment, 263–264
ethnic groups, 258
families, 260
fishing, 271
flag description, 256
food, 261
foreign policies, 269
forestry, 271
gestures and etiquette,
259–260
government structure, 268
greetings, 259
health care, 267–268
holidays, 265
housing, 260–261
human rights profile, 270
industry, 270
judicial system, 268–269
labor, 271
land area, 256
languages, 258
libraries, 264–265
life's milestones, 261
literature, 262–263
local government, 268
media and communications,
266
mining/metals, 271
museums, 264–265

national anthem, 256
national motto, 256
native people, 258
official language, 256
plants and animals, 259
political parties, 268
population, 256, 258
religions, 258
standard of living, 266
taxation, 269
time zone, 256
topography, 259
tourism, 271
transportation, 266
visiting, 260
water consumption, 266
women's rights, 267
youth culture, 265
Luxembourg Army, 269
Luxemburger Sitten und Bräuche
(Luxembourg Customs and
Traditions, 1883) (Fontaine),
263
Luxemburger Wort, 266
Lycabettus Festival (May to
September), 173
The Lyric Theatre in Belfast, 336

Machiavelli, Nicolo (1469–1527),
232
Machismo concept (Spain), 437
Macke, Auguste (1887–1914),
149
Mackintosh, Charles Rennie
(1868–1928), 412, 414
Madrid, 426, 428–429, 435–437,
439–442
Madrid Metro (Spain), 436
Madriu-Claror-Perafita valley,
Andorra, 18
Maeterlinck, Maurice
(1862–1949), 50
The Magic Mountain (Mann), 150
Magritte, René (1898–1967), 49
Mahler, Gustav (1860–1911), 30
Mahon, Derek, 337
Mallarmé, Stéphane, 150
Malta
agriculture, 289
animal husbandry, 289
armed forces, 286

arts, 280–282
capital, 274
climate, 276–277
coins, 274
cultural sites and landmarks, 282–283
currency, 274
dance, 281
eating/meals, 278
economy, 288
education, 284–285
energy/power/natural resources, 288
entertainment, 281–282
ethnic groups, 276
families, 278–279
fishing, 289
flag description, 274
food, 279
foreign policies, 286–287
forestry, 289
gestures and etiquette, 278
government structure, 286
greetings, 277
health care, 285
holidays, 283
housing, 279
human rights profile, 287–288
industry, 288
judicial system, 286
labor, 288
land area, 274
languages, 276
libraries, 283
life's milestones, 279–280
local government, 286
media and communications, 284
mining/metals, 289
museums, 283
music, 281
national anthem, 274
native people, 276
official language, 274
plants and animals, 277
political parties, 286
population, 274, 276
religions, 276
standard of living, 284
taxation, 286
time zone, 274

topography, 277
tourism, 289
transportation, 284
visiting, 278
water area, 274
women's rights, 285
youth culture, 283–284
Man Bites Dog, 1992 (film), 49
Mann, Thomas (1875–1955), 150
The Manoel Theater, Valletta, 282
Manueline architecture (Portugal), 375
Marc, Franz (1880–1916), 149
Marconi, Guglielmo (1874–1937), 494
Margrethe II (b. 1940–), Queen of Denmark, 73
Marías, Javier, 434
Marinetti, Filippo Tommaso (1876–1944), 232
The Marriage of Figaro (music), 29
Martin, Violet (1862–1915), 209
Marti Petit, Antoni, 15
Mary Shelley (1797–1851), 476
Mass in B Minor (music), 149
Maupassant, Guy de (1850–1893), 131
Max Havelaar, 1860 (Douwes Dekker), 315
McCabe, Patrick (1955–), 211
McDonagh, Martin (b. 1970–), 211
McKeown, Gerard (1980–), 337
McLaverty, Bernard, 337
Meals. *See* Eating/meals
Medea (play), 170
Mediterraneo (film), 231
Menotti, Gian Carlo, 233
Metals. *See* Mining/metals
The Metamorphosis, 1915 (Kafka), 30
Michelangelo Buonarotti (1475–1564), 229, 491–492
Middleton, Colin (1910–1983), 335, 337
Midsummer's Day, Finland, 114
Midvinterblot (Midwinter Sacrifice, 1915) (painting), 453

Mies Vailla Menneisyyttä (The Man without a Past) (film), 111
Mies van der Rohe, Ludwig (1886–1969), 149
Migration
    Germany, 157
    Iceland, 197
    Ireland, 218
    Netherlands, 322
    Northern Ireland, 344
    Scotland, 421
    Sweden, 462–463
Military. *See* Armed forces
Millais, John Everett (1829–1896), 89
Minhinnick, Robert, 507
Minoan and Mycenaean period (c. 2700–1100 BCE), 169
Minotis, Alexis (1904–1990), 170
Minoves Triquell, Juli (1969–), 10
Miró, Joan (1893–1983), 433
The Miser (Conscience), 50
Miss Julie, 1888 (play), 455
Mitterrand, François (1916–1996), 133–134
Mizzi, Achille, 282
Modiano, Patrick (1945–), 132
Moe, Jørgen (1813–1882), 357
Monaco
    agriculture, 305
    architecture, 297
    armed forces, 303
    arts, 298–299
    capital, 292
    climate, 294
    coins, 292
    cultural sites and landmarks, 299–300
    currency, 292
    eating/meals, 295–296
    economy, 304
    education, 301–302
    energy/power/natural resources, 305
    entertainment, 298–299
    ethnic groups, 294
    families, 296
    flag description, 292
    food, 296–297
    foreign policies, 303

gestures and etiquette, 295
government structure, 302
greetings, 295
health care, 302
holidays, 300
housing, 296
human rights profile,
   303–304
industry, 304–305
judicial system, 303
labor, 305
land area, 292
languages, 294
libraries, 300
life's milestones, 297
literature, 297–298
local government, 302–303
media and communications,
   301
museums, 300
national anthem, 292
national motto, 292
native people, 294
official language, 292
plants and animals, 295
political parties, 302
population, 292, 294
religions, 294
taxation, 303
time zone, 292
topography, 294–295
tourism, 305
transportation, 300–301
visiting, 296
water consumption, 301
women's rights, 302
youth culture, 300
Monaco Actualité, 301
Monaco Hebdo, 301
Monaco's National Day
   (November 19), 296
Mona Lisa (portrait), 134
Mondriaan, Pieter Cornelis
   (1872–1944), 314
Monet, Claude (1840–1926), 130,
   132
Montaigne, Michel de
   (1533–1592), 131
Monte-Carlo International
   Sculpture Festival, 298
Monte Carlo Méditerranée, 301

Monte-Carlo Television Festival,
   298
Montesquieu, Baron de
   (1689–1755), 131
Moonlight Sonata (symphonies),
   149
Moore, Brian (1921–1999), 337
Moore, Henry, 337
Morgunblaðið (*The Morning
   Paper*), 193
Morricone, Ennio (1928–), 231
Morris dance in England, 89
Morrison, Paul, 506
Morrison, Van, 337
Mozart, Wolfgang Amadeus
   (1756–1791), 29
Muldoon, Paul, 337
Mulholland, Caroline, 337
Mument, 284
Munch, Edvard (1863–1944),
   355, 358
Murdoch, Rupert, 94
Musharraf, Pervez, 97
Mussolini, Benito, 230
My Beautiful Launderette (film),
   90
Myfanwy (music), 507

Name Day (Sweden), 452–453
The Name of the Rose (*Il nome
   della rosa,* 1980) (Eco), 232
Napoleon Bonaparte
   (1769–1821), 133, 247
National Assembly for Wales, 512
Nationaldagen (National Day,
   June 6), Sweden, 457
National Day (June 17), Iceland,
   192
National Day (June 23),
   Luxembourg, 265
National Health Service/System
   (NHS), 95, 418, 512
National Insurance Act (Norway),
   364
National Library of Finland, 114
National Library of France
   (Bibliothèque nationale de
   France), 134
National Library of Greece, 173
National Library of Ireland,
   213, 338

National Library of Luxembourg,
   265
National Library of Malta, 283
National Library of Portugal, 378
National Library of San Marino,
   396
National Library of Scotland, 415
National Library of Sweden, 457
National Library of the
   Netherlands, 317
National Library of Wales, 509
National Literature Centre (CNL),
   Luxembourg, 263
National Museum of Ancient Art,
   378
National Museum of Fine Art,
   283
National Museum of Monaco,
   300
National Museum of Rome, 234
National Museum of San Marino,
   396
National museums in Wales, 509
National Museums Scotland, 415
National Theater, 1899 (Norway),
   356
Natural resources. *See* Energy/
   power/natural resources
Nauplia International Music
   Festival (June), 173
Neeson, Liam (1952–), 336–337
Netherlands
   agriculture, 323
   animal husbandry, 324
   armed forces, 321
   arts, 314, 316
   capital, 308
   climate, 310
   coins, 308
   cultural sites and landmarks,
      316–317
   currency, 308
   dance, 315
   dependencies, 321
   eating/meals, 312
   economy, 322
   education, 318–319
   energy/power/natural
      resources, 323
   entertainment, 316
   ethnic groups, 310

families, 313
fishing, 323
flag description, 308
food, 313–314
foreign policies, 321
forestry, 323
gestures and etiquette, 312
government structure, 320
greetings, 311
health care, 319–320
holidays, 317
housing, 313
human rights profile, 321–322
industry, 323
judicial system, 320
labor, 323
land area, 308
languages, 310
libraries, 317
life's milestones, 314
literature, 315–316
local government, 320
media and communications, 318
migration, 322
mining/metals, 323
museums, 317
music, 314–315
national anthem, 308
native people, 310
official language, 308
plants and animals, 311
political parties, 320
population, 308, 310
religions, 310
standard of living, 318
taxation, 320 321
time zone, 308
topography, 310–311
tourism, 324
transportation, 317–318
visiting, 312–313
water area, 308
water consumption, 318
women's rights, 319
youth culture, 317
Neue Kronen-Zeitung, 33
Neue Zürcher Zeitung (NZZ), 478
Neuschwanstein Castle, Germany, 152
News Letter, 339

Nibelungenlied (Song of the Nibelungen) (poem), 150
Nice-Matin, 301
Nicolaï Siadristy's (1937–) microminiature museum, 12
Ni Dhomhnaill, Nuala (1952–), 211
Nielsen, Carl August (1865–1931), 69
Nietzsche, Friedrich (1844–1900), 150
Nieuwenhuys, Constant (1920 2005), 68
Ninth Symphony (symphonies), 149
Nokia, 119
Nono, Luigi, 232
Nooteboom, Cees (1933–), 315
North Atlantic Treaty Organization (NATO), 55, 137, 362, 383
Northern Ireland
  agriculture, 345
  architecture, 335
  armed forces, 342
  arts, 334–335, 337
  capital, 330
  climate, 331
  coins, 328
  cultural sites and landmarks, 337–338
  currency, 328
  dance, 336
  drama, 335–336
  eating/meals, 332–333
  economy, 344
  education, 340
  energy/power/natural resources, 345
  entertainment, 337
  ethnic groups, 330–331
  families, 333
  fishing, 345
  flag description, 330
  food, 333–334
  foreign policies, 342–343
  forestry, 345
  gestures and etiquette, 332
  government structure, 341–342
  greetings, 331–332
  health care, 341

holidays, 338
housing, 333
human rights profile, 343–344
industry, 344–345
judicial system, 342
labor, 345
land area, 328
languages, 330
libraries, 338
life's milestones, 334
literature, 336–337
local government, 342
media and communications, 339–340
migration, 344
mining/metals, 345
museums, 338
music, 336
national anthem, 330
native people, 330–331
official language, 328
plants and animals, 331
political parties, 342
population, 328, 330
religions, 331
standard of living, 340
taxation, 342
time zone, 330
topography, 331
tourism, 345
transportation, 339
visiting, 333
water area, 328
water consumption, 340
women's rights, 340–341
youth culture, 338 339
The Northern Ireland Human Rights Commission, 343–344
Norway
  agriculture, 365
  animal husbandry, 365
  architecture, 355
  armed forces, 362
  arts, 354–355, 357–358
  capital, 348
  climate, 350–351
  coins, 348
  cultural sites and landmarks, 358–359
  currency, 48
  dance, 356–357

dependencies, 363
drama, 355–356
eating/meals, 352–353
economy, 364
education, 360
energy/power/natural
	resources, 364
entertainment, 357–358
ethnic groups, 350
families, 353
fishing, 364
flag description, 348
food, 353–354
foreign policies, 362–363
forestry, 364–365
gestures and etiquette, 352
government structure, 361
greetings, 351–352
health care, 361
holidays, 359
housing, 353
human rights profile, 363–364
industry, 364
judicial system, 362
labor, 364
land area, 348
languages, 350
libraries, 359
life's milestones, 354
literature, 357
local government, 361–362
media and communications,
	360
mining/metals, 365
museums, 359
music, 356
national anthem, 348
national motto, 348
native people, 350
official language, 348
plants and animals, 351
political parties, 361
population, 348, 350
religions, 350
standard of living, 360
taxation, 362
time zone, 348
topography, 351
tourism, 365
transportation, 359–360
visiting, 353

water area, 348
water consumption, 360
women's rights, 360–361
youth culture, 359
Norway's National Insurance
	Scheme, 361
Norwegian Association for
	Women's Rights (NAWR), 360
Norwegian folk music, 356
Norwegian Literature Abroad
	(NORLA), 357
Notari, Louis (1879–1961),
	297–298
Nouvel, Jean (1945–), 130
Nuncios (Vatican's ambassadors),
	495
Nuovo Cinema Paradiso, 1988
	(film), 231

Obama, Barack, 217
O'Brien, Flann (1911–1946), 337
Ó Cadhain, Mairtín (1906–1970),
	210
O'Carolan, Turlough
	(1670–1738), 208
O'Casey, Sean (1880–1964), 336
O'Connor, Frank (1903–1966),
	210
Odigitis, 174
The Odyssey (poem), 171
Oedipus Rex (play), 170
*O Evangelho Segundo Jesus
	Cristo* (*The Gospel According
	to Jesus Christ,* 1991)
	(Saramago), 377
Ó Faoláin, Seán (1900–1991),
	210
O'Flaherty, Liam (1896–1984),
	210
Olavinlinna Castle, Finland,
	113–114, 120
Oliveira, Manoel de (1908–2015),
	376
O'Malley, Mary, 336
O'Malley, Pearse, 336
Operation Althea, 269
Oprechte Haarlemsche Courant,
	318
O Público, 380
O Quinto Império (*The Fifth
	Empire,* 2004) (film), 376

Ó Rathaille, Aodhagán
	(c.1670–c.1726), 210
O Regresso das Caravelas (*The
	Return of the Caravels*) (Lobo
	Antunes), 377
Oresteia trilogy, 170
Orestes (play), 170
Organization for Economic
	Co-operation and Development
	(OECD), 16, 36, 75, 196
Organization for Security and
	Co-operation in Europe
	(OSCE), 16, 36
Ó Ríordáin, Séan (1917–1977),
	210
Ormsby, Frank (1947–), 337
The Orquestra Nacional Clàssica
	d'Andorra (National Classical
	Orchestra of Andorra, or
	ONCA), 11
Orr, James (1770–1816), 336
Oscar II (1829–1907), King of
	Sweden, 454
Oslo, 348, 350, 355–356,
	359–360, 362–363, 365
Os Lusiadas (poem), 377
Ostermeier, Thomas, 151
Our Lady of Meritxell Day
	(September 8), 12
Out of Africa, 1937 (Blixen), 69
Owen, Morfudd Llwyn
	(1891–1918), 507

Paasikivi, J.K., 118
Paasikivi-Kekkonen Line, 118
Pacher, Michael (1440–1498), 28
Pacius, Fredrik (1809–1891), 112
Palácio da Bolsa (Portugal), 378
Palamas, Kostis (1859–1943),
	172
Palestrina, Giovanni
	(c. 1525–1594), 491
Palladio, Andrea, 89
Papal Swiss Guard, 494–495
Paris, 124, 126–127, 129–130,
	132–135, 137, 139
Parry, Joseph (1841–1903), 507
The Parthenon in Athens (438
	BCE), 170
Pasolini, Pier Palo (1922–1975),
	230

The Passion of Joan of Arc (film), 69

Patton, George (1885–1945), 264

Pavarotti, Luciano (1935–2007), 231–232

Paxinou, Katrina (1900–1978), 170

Pedersen, Christiern (c. 1480–1554), 69

Pei, I.M., 265

Pericles (c. 495–429), 172

Personal allowance system, England, 97

Peter Pan, 1911 (Barrie), 413

Peter's Pence (voluntary payment by Roman Catholics), 496

Petrarca, Francesco. *See* Petrarch

Petrarch, 232

Petrie, George (1790–1866), 209

Petrospheres (Scotland), 412

Philip II of Macedonia (382–336 BCE), 173

Piaf, Édith (1915–1963), 131

Piano, Renzo (1937–), 230

Picasso, Pablo (1881–1973), 130, 299, 433, 435

Pierre, Duke of Valentinois (1895–1964), 298

Pietà (sculpture), 491

Pijper, Willem (1894–1947), 315

Pintasilgo, Maria de Lourdes (1930–2004), 381

Pippi Longstocking, 1945 (Lindgren), 455

Pirandello, Luigi (1867–1936), 232

Polfer, Lydie (1952–), 267

Political Prisoner (sculpture), 262

Pollini, Maurizio, 232

Pombaline architecture (Portugal), 375–376

Pope, Alexander, 90

Pope Julius II (c. 1443–1513), 491–492

Pope Sixtus IV (1414–1484), 491

Pope Sixtus V, 492

Pori Jazz Festival, 113

Porta di San Francesco (Gate of San Francesco), 395

Portugal
    agriculture, 384–385

animal husbandry, 385
architecture, 375–376
armed forces, 382
arts, 374–375, 377
capital, 368
climate, 371
coins, 368
cultural sites and landmarks, 377–378
currency, 368
dance, 376
drama, 376
eating/meals, 372
economy, 384
education, 380–381
energy/power/natural resources, 384
entertainment, 377
ethnic groups, 370
families, 373
fishing, 384
flag description, 368
food, 373–374
foreign policies, 382–383
forestry, 384
gestures and etiquette, 372
government structure, 382
greetings, 371–372
health care, 381
holidays, 378
housing, 373
human rights profile, 383–384
industry, 384
judicial system, 382
labor, 384
land area, 368
languages, 370
libraries, 378
life's milestones, 374
literature, 376–377
local government, 382
media and communications, 380
mining/metals, 384
museums, 378
music, 376
national anthem, 368
native people, 370
official language, 368
plants and animals, 371
political parties, 382

population, 368, 370
religions, 371
standard of living, 380
taxation, 382
time zone, 368
topography, 371
tourism, 385
transportation, 379–380
visiting, 372
water area, 368
water consumption, 380
women's rights, 381
youth culture, 379

The Postage Stamp Museum, Lichtenstein, 250

Power. *See* Energy/power/natural resources

Prendergast, Peter (1946–2007), 506

Preti, Mattia (1613–1699), 280

The Prince (Machiavelli), 232

Progg (Swedish musical movement), 454

Prostitution. *See also* Human trafficking
    Austria, 37
    France, 138
    Germany, 155
    Malta, 285
    Netherlands, 319, 324
    Norway, 361
    Portugal, 381
    San Marino, 398

Protestants. *See also* Christianity; Roman Catholicism
    Andorra, 6
    Denmark, 64
    Finland, 106
    Germany, 144
    Ireland, 204
    Italy, 224
    Liechtenstein, 246
    Luxembourg, 258
    Netherlands, 310
    Northern Ireland, 331
    Norway, 350
    Scotland, 408
    Switzerland, 470, 473
    Wales, 502

Provisional Irish Republican Army (IRA), 341

Puccini, Giacomo, 232
Pullinen, Laila (1933–), 110
Purcell, Lewis (David Parkhill), 336

The Queen (film), 91
Queen's Day (April 30), Netherlands, 317

Radio France, 135
Radio France Internationale (RFA), 301
Ràdio i Televisió d'Andorra (RTVA), 13
Radio Monte-Carlo, 301
Radio Teilifís Éireann (RTÉ) network, Ireland, 214
Railroad network/system
    Austria, 31–33
    Denmark, 72
    England, 93
    Finland, 115
    France, 134–135, 139
    Germany, 153
    Greece, 174
    Ireland, 213–214
    Italy, 234–235
    Liechtenstein, 251
    Luxembourg, 266, 271
    Netherlands, 318
    Northern Ireland, 339
    Norway, 360
    Portugal, 379
    San Marino, 397
    Scotland, 416
    Spain, 436, 442
    Sweden, 458
    Switzerland, 478
    Vatican City, 493
    Wales, 510
Rainier III (1923–2005), Prince of Monaco, 298
Rameau, Jean-Philippe (1683–1784), 131
Rape. *See also* Sexual harassment
    Finland, 119
    Greece, 175
    Iceland, 194
    Malta, 285
    Monaco, 302
    Netherlands, 319

Norway, 361
Portugal, 381
San Marino, 398
Raphael (1483–1520), 229
Ravel, Maurice (1875–1937), 131
The Real Charlotte, 1894 (Martin and Somerville), 209
Rea, Stephen, 337
A Red, Red Rose (folk song), 413
Redtenbacher, Ferdinand, 154
Rembrandt Harmenszoon van Rijn (1606–1669), 314
The Rembrandt House Museum in Amsterdam, 317
Remi, Georges Prosper (1907–1983). *See* Hergé
Rénert the Fox, 1872 (Rodange), 263
Renoir, Jean (1894–1979), 131
Renoir, Pierre-Auguste (1841–1919), 132
Republic Day (December 13), Malta, 283
Reykjavík, 182, 184, 186, 189–193, 197–198
The Reykjavík Art Museum, 190, 192
The Reykjavík Grapevine, 193
Reynolds, Joshua (1723–1792), 88
Rhaetian Railway (RhB), 478
Richards, Ceri (1903–1971), 506
Riksdag (Sweden's parliament), 460
Ring, Laurits Andersen (1854–1933), 68
Ring of the Nibelung (German opera), 149
Riska, Kristina (1960–), 113
Riverdance (theatrical show), Ireland, 209, 211
Riviera Reporter, 301
Rizospastis, 174
Roberts, Kate (1891–1985), 507
Robinson, Mary, 215
Rob Roy, 1817 (Scott), 413
Rodange, Michel (1827–1876), 263
Rodin, Auguste (1840–1917), 130
Rodrigo, Joaquín (1901–1999), 433

Roentgen, Wilhelm Conrad, 154
Rök Runestone (Swedish literature), 455
Roma (Rome), 222, 224–225, 227, 229–231, 233–235, 239–240
Roman Catholicism. *See also* Christianity; Protestants
    Andorra, 6
    Austria, 24
    Belgium, 44
    Denmark, 64
    Finland, 106
    Germany, 144
    Icelander, 184
    Ireland, 204
    Italy, 224
    Liechtenstein, 246
    Luxembourg, 258
    Malta, 276
    Monaco, 294
    Netherlands, 310
    Norway, 350
    Portugal, 371
    San Marino, 390
    Scotland, 408
    Spain, 428
    Sweden, 448
    Switzerland, 470
    Vatican City, 490
Roman Curia, 494
Rosetta, 1999 (film), 49
Rossellini, Roberto (1906–1977), 230
Rossetti, Dante Gabriel (1828–1882), 89
Rottmayr, Johann Michael (1656–1730), 28
Rousseau, Jean-Jacques (1712–1778), 475
Royal Academies for Science and the Arts of Belgium (RASAB), 50
Royal Air Force, 342, 420
Royal Danish Air Force (Flyvevåbnet, or FLV), 74
Royal Danish Army (Hæren, or HRN), 74
Royal Danish Navy (Søværnet, or SVN), 74
Royal Danish Theater, 69

Royal Library of Belgium, 52
Royal National Eisteddfod, 508
Royal Netherlands Air Force, 321
Royal Netherlands Army, 321
Royal Netherlands Navy, 321
Royal Scottish Academy of Arts, 412
RTL Group, 266
Rubens, Peter Paul (1577–1640), 48
Rudolf, Germar, 157
Running of the bulls (Spanish drama), 435
Russell, George (1867–1935), 336

Saadi, Suhayl (1961–), 414
Saint Agatha's Day (February 5), San Marino, 396
Saint Brigid's Day (February 1), Ireland, 213
Saint David day (March 1), 509
Saint Lucia Day (Festival of Light, December 13), Sweden, 457
Saint Marinus (Marino), 398
Saint Rainier's Day (November 19), Monaco, 300
Saint Roman's Day (August 9), Monaco, 300
Saint-Saëns, Camille (1835–1921), 131
Sakmann, Bert, 154
Salazar, António de Oliveira (1889–1970), 377
Salten, Felix (1869–1945), 30
Salvadó, Albert (1951–), 11
Salvatores, Gabriele (1950–), 231
Salzburg Festival, Austria, 31
Sammarinese coins (San Marino), 394
Sammy and Rosie Get Laid (film), 90
Sandemose, Aksel (1899–1965), 65
San Marino
    agriculture, 402
    architecture, 393
    armed forces, 399
    arts, 393, 394–395
    capital, 388
    climate, 390

coins, 388
cultural sites and landmarks, 395–396
currency, 388, 393–394
eating/meals, 391
economy, 401
education, 397
energy/power/natural resources, 401
entertainment, 394–395
ethnic groups, 390
families, 392
flag description, 388
food, 392–393
foreign policies, 400
gestures and etiquette, 391
government structure, 398–399
greetings, 390–391
health care, 398
holidays, 396
housing, 392
human rights profile, 400–401
industry, 401
judicial system, 399
labor, 401
land area, 388
languages, 390
libraries, 396
life's milestones, 393
literature, 394
local government, 399
media and communications, 397
museums, 396
national anthem, 388
national motto, 388
native people, 390
official language, 388
plants and animals, 390
political parties, 399
population, 388, 390
religions, 390
standard of living, 397
taxation, 399
time zone, 388
topography, 390
tourism, 402
transportation, 397
visiting, 392
water consumption, 397

women's rights, 397–398
youth culture, 396
San Marino Grand Prix, 395
Saramago, José (1922–2010), 377
Sartre, Jean-Paul (1905–1980), 132
Savonlinna Opera Festival, Finland, 113
Sax, Adolphe (1814–1894), 50
Schiller, Friedrich (1759–1805), 150
Schoeck, Othmar (1886–1957), 475
Scotland
    agriculture, 422
    animal husbandry, 422
    architecture, 412
    armed forces, 420
    arts, 412, 413–414
    capital, 406
    climate, 408
    coins, 406
    cultural sites and landmarks, 414–415
    currency, 406
    dance, 413
    drama, 412
    eating/meals, 410
    economy, 421
    education, 417
    energy/power/natural resources, 422
    entertainment, 413–414
    ethnic groups, 408
    families, 410
    fishing, 422
    flag description, 406
    food, 411
    foreign policies, 420
    forestry, 422
    gestures and etiquette, 409–410
    government structure, 418–419
    greetings, 409
    health care, 418
    holidays, 415–416
    housing, 410–411
    human rights profile, 420–421
    industry, 421
    judicial system, 419
    labor, 421

land area, 406
languages, 408
libraries, 415
life's milestones, 411
literature, 413
local government, 419
media and communications, 416–417
migration, 421
mining/metals, 422
museums, 415
music, 412–413
national anthem, 406
native people, 408
official language, 406
plants and animals, 409
political parties, 419
population, 406, 408
religions, 408
standard of living, 417
taxation, 419
time zone, 406
topography, 408–409
tourism, 422
transportation, 416
visiting, 410
water area, 406
water consumption, 417
women's rights, 418
youth culture, 416
Scotland's National Library, 415
Scots law (Scotland), 419
The Scotsman, 417
Scottish Commission for Human Rights (2006), 421
Scottish Executive's Education Department (SEED), 417
Scottish folk music, 413
Scottish Highland dancing, 413
Scott, Walter (1771–1832), 413
Scott, William, 337
Sean-nos (old-style) dancing, Ireland, 209
Secondat, Charles de. *See* Montesquieu, Baron de (1689–1755)
Seferis, George (1900–1971), 172
Segovia, Andrés (1893–1987), 433
Senckenberg Natural History Museum, 152

Seven Brothers, 1870 (Kivi), 112
Sex Discrimination Act (1975), 511
Sexual harassment
Andorra, 14
Finland, 116
Germany, 155
Italy, 236
Malta, 287
Monaco, 302
Netherlands, 319, 322
Portugal, 381
San Marino, 398
Scotland, 418
Switzerland, 480
Shakespeare, William, 70
Shannon, Sharon, 210
Shaw, George Bernard (1856–1950), 335
Sheridan, Richard (1751–1816), 335
Sibelius, Jean (1865–1957), 110, 112
Sillanpää, Eemil (1888–1964), 112
Sinnott, Kevin (b. 1947–), 506
Sistine Chapel, 491–492
Sjöström, Victor (1879–1960), 454
Skagestad, Tormod (1920–1997), 356
Skottsberg, Carl (1880–1963), 457
Skuli Magnusson, 190
The Smurfs (comic series), 50
Soccer
Austria, 31
Belgium, 51
England, 91
Finland, 113
Germany, 151
Ireland, 211
Italy, 233
Luxembourg, 265
Malta, 282–283
Monaco, 300
Netherlands, 316–317
Northern Ireland, 337
Norway, 358
Portugal, 377, 379
San Marino, 395–396

Scotland, 414, 416
Spain, 436
Sweden, 456
Switzerland, 477
The Social Democratic Party (SDP), Germany, 156
Solomon a Gaenor (film), 506
Somerville, Edith (1858–1949), 209
Sophocles (c. 496–406 BCE), 170
Sorbonne, France, 133
The Sound of Music (music), 25
The Sound of Music, 1965 (film), 31
Spain
agriculture, 441
animal husbandry, 441–442
architecture, 432–433
armed forces, 439
arts, 432–433, 434–435
capital, 426
climate, 428–429
coins, 426
cultural sites and landmarks, 435
currency, 426
dance, 433
dependencies, 440
drama, 433
eating/meals, 430–431
economy, 440
education, 437
energy/power/natural resources, 441
entertainment, 475–476
ethnic groups, 428
families, 431
fishing, 441
flag description, 426
food, 431–432
foreign policy, 439–440
forestry, 441
gestures and etiquette, 430
government structure, 438
greetings, 430
health care, 438
holidays, 436
housing, 431
human rights profile, 440
industry, 440–441
judicial system, 439

labor, 441
land area, 426
languages, 428
libraries, 435–436
life's milestones, 432
literature, 433–434
local government, 438–439
media and communications, 437
mining/metals, 441
museums, 435–436
music, 433
national anthem, 426
national motto, 426
native people, 428
official language, 426
plants and animals, 429–430
political parties, 438
population, 426, 428
religions, 428
standard of living, 437
taxation, 439
time zone, 426
topography, 429
tourism, 442
transportation, 436–437
visiting, 431
water area, 426
water consumption, 437
women's rights, 437–438
youth culture, 436
Spanish Air Force, 439
Spanish Army, 439
Spanish Baroque style, 432
Spanish language. *See also* Languages; Official language
Andorra, 6
Spain, 428
Spitteler, Carl (1845–1924), 475
Spoerri, Daniel (1930–), 475
Spyri, Johanna (1827–1901), 475
Stevenson, Robert Louis (1850–1894), 413
St. Matthew's Passion (music), 149
Stockholm, 446, 448–450, 453–454, 457–459, 464
Stoker, Bram (1847–1912), 209
St. Peter's Basilica, 491–492
St. Peter's Square, 491–492

Strauss, Johann Sebastian (1825–1899), 29–30
Strindberg, August, 456
The Sunday Times, 284
Supreme Court
Andorra, 15
Austria, 35
Belgium, 55
Denmark, 74
England, 96
Finland, 117
France, 137
Greece, 176
Iceland, 195
Ireland, 216
Italy, 236
Luxembourg, 269
Monaco, 303
Netherlands, 320
Norway, 362
Portugal, 382
San Marino, 399
Scotland, 419
Spain, 438–439
Sweden, 461
Switzerland, 480–481
Surrealism, 130
Sweden
agriculture, 463–464
animal husbandry, 464
architecture, 453
armed forces, 461
arts, 453, 455–456
capital, 446
climate, 448
coins, 446
cultural sites and landmarks, 456–457
currency, 446
dance, 455
drama, 454
eating/meals, 450–451
economy, 463
education, 459
energy/power/natural resources, 463
entertainment, 455–456
ethnic groups, 448
families, 451
fishing, 463
flag description, 446

food, 452
foreign policy, 461–462
forestry, 463
gestures and etiquette, 450
government structure, 460
greetings, 450
health care, 460
holidays, 457
housing, 452
human rights profile, 462
industry, 463
judicial system, 461
labor, 463
land area, 446
languages, 448
libraries, 457
life's milestones, 452–453
literature, 455
local government, 460–461
media and communications, 458
migration, 462–463
mining/metals, 463
museums, 457
music, 454–455
national anthem, 446
national motto, 446
native people, 448
official language, 446
plants and animals, 449
political parties, 460
population, 446, 448
religions, 448
standard of living, 458
taxation, 461
time zone, 446
topography, 449
tourism, 464
transportation, 458
visiting, 451
water area, 446
water consumption, 459
women's rights, 459–460
youth culture, 457–458
Swedish Freedom of the Press Act, 455
Swedish National Museum, 453
Swelinck, Jan Pieterszoon (1562–1621), 315
Swift, Jonathan (1667–1745), 90, 209

Swiss Air Force, 481
Swiss Family Robinson, 1812
  (Wyss), 475
Switzerland
  agriculture, 483–484
  animal husbandry, 484
  architecture, 474–475
  armed forces, 481
  arts, 473–474, 475–476
  capital, 468
  climate, 470–471
  coins, 468
  cultural sites and landmarks,
    476–477
  currency, 468
  eating/meals, 472
  economy, 483
  education, 479
  energy/power/natural
    resources, 483
  entertainment, 475–476
  ethnic groups, 470
  families, 472
  fishing, 483
  flag description, 468
  food, 473
  foreign policy, 481–482
  forestry, 483
  gestures and etiquette,
    471–472
  government structure, 480–481
  greetings, 471
  health care, 480
  holidays, 477
  housing, 472–473
  human rights profile, 482–483
  industry, 483
  judicial system, 481
  labor, 483
  land area, 468
  languages, 470
  libraries, 477
  life's milestones, 473
  literature, 475
  local government, 481
  media and communications,
    478
  mining/metals, 483
  museums, 477
  music, 475
  national anthem, 468

national motto, 468
native people, 470
official language, 468
plants and animals, 471
political parties, 481
population, 468, 470
religions, 470
standard of living, 478
taxation, 481
time zone, 468
topography, 471
tourism, 484
transportation, 478
visiting, 472
water area, 468
water consumption, 478–479
women's rights, 479–480
youth culture, 477–478
Switzerland's Confederation,
  1291 (August 1), 477, 480–481
*Symphonie fantastique (Fantasy
  Symphony),* 131
Synge, John Millington
  (1871–1909), 210, 336

Tageblatt, 266
Talk to Her (film), 434
The Tate (Tate Modern Gallery),
  92
Tea in Heather, 1959 (Roberts),
  507
Télé Monte Carlo (TMC), 301
Television. *See* Media and
  communications
Television Malta (TVM), 284
The Terrorism Act of 2006, 98
Theotokas (1906–1966), 172
The Thinker, 1902 (sculpture),
  130
The Third of May 1808 (painting),
  433
Thirty Years' War (1618–1648),
  247
Thomas, Dylan (1914–1953), 507
Thorlaksson, Thorarinn
  (1867–1924), 188
Thornhill, James (1675–1734), 88
Thorvaldsen, Bertel (1770–1844),
  68
Three Metres above the Sky
  (film), 234

The Three Musketeers, 1844
  (Dumas), 131
Tieck, Ludwig (1773–1853), 150
The Times (Scotland), 417
The Times (Malta), 284
The Times of London, 94
Tintoretto (1518–1584), 229
Titian (c. 1488–1576), 229
Tobler, Jean, 483
Tóibín, Colm (1955–), 210
Toldrà, Eduard (1895–1962), 11
Tornatore, Giuseppe (1956–), 231
Trafficking. *See* Human
  trafficking
Translations (play), 337
Treasure Island, 1883
  (Stevenson), 413
The Trial, 1925 (Kafka), 30
Tristan and Isolde (German
  opera), 149
Troger, Paul (1698–1762), 28
Truffaut, François (1932–1984),
  131
The Tube (London Underground),
  94
Tuhlaajapoika (The Prodigal Son)
  (theatrical event), 111
Tulindberg, Erik (1761–1814),
  112
Turkish Republic of Northern
  Cyprus (TRNC), 177
Turku Castle, Finland, 113
Turner, J.M.W. (1775–1851), 88,
  506
Turner, Paul, 506
Turner, William (1508–1568),
  476

Ughi, Uto, 232
The Ugly Duckling (fairy tale), 69
UK Department for Education
  and Skills (DfES), 94
The Ulster Literary Theatre, 336
Ulster Television PLC, 339
Ulysses, 1922 (Joyce), 210
UN Convention on the
  Elimination of All Forms of
  Discrimination against Women
  (CEDAW), 14, 34, 116, 253,
  267, 398, 459
Undset, Sigrid (1882–1949), 357

Unemployment rate
  Andorra, 18
  Austria, 38
  Belgium, 57
  Denmark, 76
  England, 99
  Finland, 114
  France, 139
  Germany, 159
  Greece, 179
  Iceland, 197
  Ireland, 218–219
  Italy, 239
  Luxembourg, 271
  Netherlands, 323
  Northern Ireland, 344–345
  Norway, 364
  Portugal, 384
  San Marino, 401
  Scotland, 421
  Spain, 441
  Sweden, 463
  Switzerland, 483
  Wales, 514–515
UNESCO World Heritage Site
  Andorra, 11, 18
  Austria, 31
  Belgium, 49, 51–52, 58
  Denmark, 69–70, 77
  England, 92
  Finland, 113–114
  France, 133–134
  Germany, 152
  Greece, 172–173
  Iceland, 191
  Ireland, 212
  Luxembourg, 262
  Malta, 282
  Netherlands, 316
  Northern Ireland, 337
  Norway, 358
  Portugal, 377–378
  San Marino, 395
  Scotland, 413–415
  Sweden, 456, 464
  Switzerland, 476–478
  Vatican City, 492
  Wales, 508–509
UN Human Development Index.
  See Human Development
  Index (HDI)

United Nations Educational,
  Scientific and Cultural
  Organization (UNESCO), 11,
  114, 172, 358, 413–414, 456.
  See also UNESCO World
  Heritage Site
The United Nations Universal
  Declaration on Human Rights
  (UDHR)
  Andorra, 17
  Austria, 36
  Belgium, 56
  Denmark, 75–76
  England, 98
  Finland, 118
  France, 138
  Germany, 157
  Greece, 177
  Iceland, 196
  Ireland, 215, 217–218
  Italy, 238
  Liechtenstein, 253
  Luxembourg, 270
  Malta, 287
  Monaco, 303
  Netherlands, 322
  Northern Ireland, 343–344
  Norway, 363
  Portugal, 383
  San Marino, 400
  Scotland, 420
  Spain, 440
  Sweden, 462
  Switzerland, 482
  Vatican City, 495
  Wales, 514
The Unknown Soldier, 1954
  (Linna), 112
UN Security Council (UNSC),
  137
Utzøn, Jørn (1918–2008), 68

Vadstena Castle (Sweden), 457
Vaduz, 244, 246–247, 249–251
Vaduz Castle, Liechtenstein, 249
Valkeapää, Nils-Aslak
  (1943–2001), 455
The Valkyrie (German opera),
  149
Valletta, 274, 276–277, 280–282,
  284, 288

Van de Velde, Henry
  (1863–1957), 49
Van Dyck, Anthony (1599–1641),
  49
Van Dyk, Paul, 153
Van Eyck, Hubert (c. 1366–1426),
  48
Van Eyck, Jan (c. 1385–1441), 48
The Van Gogh Museum in
  Amsterdam, 317
Van Gogh, Vincent (1853–1890),
  314
Vasa Race (skiing race), Sweden,
  456
Vassilikos (1934–), 172
Vatican City
  architecture, 491
  armed forces, 494–495
  arts, 491
  capital, 488
  climate, 490
  coins, 488
  cultural sites and landmarks,
    492–493
  currency, 488
  ethnic groups, 490
  flag description, 488
  foreign policy, 495
  gestures and etiquette,
    490–491
  government structure, 494
  greetings, 490
  human rights profile, 495–496
  industry, 496
  land area, 488
  languages, 490
  libraries, 493
  media and communications,
    494
  museums, 493
  music, 491–492
  national anthem, 488
  native people, 490
  official language, 488
  population, 488, 490
  time zone, 488
  topography, 490
  tourism, 496
  transportation, 493–494
Vatican Museum complex, 493
Vatican Radio station (1931), 494

Vatican Secret Archives, 493

The Venice Commission, 253

Venus de Milo (sculpture), 134

Venus of Willendorf (sculpture), 28

Verdens Gang, 360

Verdi, Guiseppe, 232

Verhaeren, Emile (1855–1916), 50

Vermeer, Jan (1632–1675), 314

Vespasian (9–79 CE), 233

Viagem ao Princípio do Mundo (*Voyage to the Beginning of the World,* 1997) (film), 376

Victorian era (roughly 1837–1901), 90

Victoria, Tomás Luis de (c. 1548–1611), 491

Vienna, 22, 32, 34

Vienna Basin, 25

Vienna Secession (1897–1905), 28–29

Vigeland, Gustav (1869–1943), 355

Viking Age (c. 700–1066 CE), 68

Viladomat, Josep (1899–1989), 11–12

Villaverde, Teresa (1966–), 376

Violence, domestic. *See* Domestic violence

Virgil, 231–232

Vivaldi, Antonio, 231

Volver (film), 434

Vondel, Joost van den (1587–1679), 315

Wagner, Otto (1841–1918), 29

Wagner, Richard (1813–1883), 149, 151

Wales

  agriculture, 515

  animal husbandry, 515

  armed forces, 513

  arts, 506, 507–508

  capital, 500

  climate, 502

  cultural sites and landmarks, 508–509

  currency, 500

  eating/meals, 504

  economy, 514

  education, 511

  energy/power/natural resources, 515

  entertainment, 507–508

  ethnic groups, 502

  families, 504

  film, 506

  fishing, 515

  flag description, 500

  food, 505

  foreign policy, 513

  forestry, 515

  gestures and etiquette, 503–504

  government structure, 512

  greetings, 503

  health care, 512

  holidays, 509

  housing, 504–505

  human rights profile, 513–514

  industry, 514

  judicial system, 513

  labor, 514–515

  land area, 500

  languages, 500, 502

  libraries, 509

  life's milestones, 505–506

  literature, 507

  local government, 513

  media and communications, 510–511

  mining/metals, 515

  museums, 509

  music, 506–507

  national anthem, 500

  national motto, 500

  native people, 502

  official language, 500

  plants and animals, 503

  political parties, 512–513

  population, 500, 502

  religions, 502

  standard of living, 511

  taxation, 513

  time zone, 500

  topography, 502–503

  tourism, 515

  transportation, 510

  visiting, 504

  water consumption, 511

  women's rights, 511–512

  youth culture, 509–510

Wartburg Castle, Germany, 152

Water Services Regulation Authority (OFWAT), 511

Water tower of Europe (Switzerland), 479

Waterways

  Austria, 33, 37

  Denmark, 65, 72

  England, 94

  Finland, 115

  Germany, 145

  Italy, 235

  Liechtenstein, 246

  Netherlands, 318

  Scotland, 409

Weber, Carl Maria von (1786–1826), 149

Weiss, David (b. 1946–), 476

Well-Tempered Clavier (music), 149

Welsh Assembly Government (WAG), 507, 513

Welsh Folk Dance Society, 507

Welsh, Irvine (1958–), 414

Welsh Language Act, 510, 514

Welsh Literature Abroad, 508

Welsh National Opera, 508

Wercollier, Lucien (1908–2002), 262

Wergeland, Henrik, 356

Wertmuller, Lina (1926–), 230

The Western Mail, 510

Whelan, Bill (1950–), 211

Wilde, Oscar (1854–1900), 335

Williams, Gerwyn, 508

Willibrord (658–739), 262

Wilson, Richard (1714–1782), 506

Wilson, Robert MacLiam, 337

Wolkers, Jan Hendrik (1925–2007), 315

Women's rights

  Andorra, 14

  Austria, 34

Belgium, 54
Denmark, 73
England, 95
Finland, 116
France, 136
Germany, 154–155
Greece, 175
Iceland, 194
Ireland, 215
Italy, 236
Luxembourg, 267
Malta, 285
Monaco, 302

Netherlands, 319
Northern Ireland,
    340–341
Norway, 360–361
Portugal, 381
San Marino, 397–398
Scotland, 418
Spain, 437–438
Sweden, 459–460
Switzerland, 479–480
Wales, 511–512
Wordsworth, William, 90
World Bodypainting Festival, 31

World Heritage Site.
    See UNESCO World
    Heritage Site
Wyss, Johann David
    (1743–1818), 475

Yeats, William Butler
    (1865–1939), 210, 336
Yleisradio Oy (YLE) (Finland's
    National Broadcasting
    Company), 115

Zetterling, Mai (1925–1994), 454